DEVELOPMENTAL PSYCHOLOGY TODAY

● ● ● ● ● ● ● ● ● ● ● ● ●

SIXTH EDITION

DEVELOPMENTAL PSYCHOLOGY TODAY

• • • • • • • • • • • • • • •

LOIS HOFFMAN
University of Michigan

SCOTT PARIS
University of Michigan

ELIZABETH HALL

McGRAW-HILL, INC.

New York   St. Louis   San Francisco   Auckland   Bogotá
Caracas   Lisbon   London   Madrid   Mexico City   Milan
Montreal   New Delhi   San Juan
Singapore   Sydney   Tokyo   Toronto

DEVELOPMENTAL PSYCHOLOGY TODAY

1 2 3 4 5 6 7 8 9 0 VNH VNH 9 0 9 8 7 6 5 4 3

ISBN 0-07-029338-4

This book was set in Garamond Book by York Graphic Services, Inc.
The editors were Jane Vaicunas and James R. Belser;
the design was done by Caliber/Phoenix Color Corp.;
the production supervisor was Richard A. Ausburn.
The cover was designed by Wanda Lubelska.
The photo editors were Elyse Rieder and Safra Nimrod.
Von Hoffmann Press, Inc., was printer and binder.

Cover Art

Faith Ringgold. *The Purple Quilt.* 1986. Acrylic on cotton canvas, tie-dyed, printed, and pieced fabrics; 7′7″ × 6′.
Collection Bernice Steinbaum.

Chapter-Opening Photo Credits

Chapter 1   Mimi Cotter/International Stock Photo; Chapter 2   T. Kevin Smyth/The Stock Market; Chapter 3   Petit Format/Nestle/Science Source/Photo Researchers; Chapter 4   B. K. Productions/International Stock Photo; Chapter 5   Lorraine Rorke/The Image Works; Chapter 6   Lawrence Migdale/Stock, Boston; Chapter 7   Doug Mazzapica/Black Star; Chapter 8   Michael Lichter/International Stock Photo; Chapter 9   L. Powers/H. Armstrong Roberts; Chapter 10   Geoff Juckes/The Stock Market; Chapter 11   Peter Tenzer Studio/International Stock Photo; Chapter 12   Bob Rashid/Monkmeyer Press; Chapter 13   Jim Whitmer; Chapter 14   Johnson Wenk/Black Star; Chapter 15   Stacy Pick/Stock, Boston; Chapter 16   Michael McDermott/Black Star; Chapter 17   Frank Siteman/The Picture Cube; Chapter 18   Michael Philip Manheim/Southern Light; Chapter 19   John Eastcott/Yva Momatiuk/The Image Works; and Chapter 20   Kindra Clineff/The Picture Cube.

Library of Congress Cataloging-in-Publication Data

Hoffman, Lois Norma Wladis, (date).
    Developmental psychology today / Lois Hoffman, Scott Paris,
Elizabeth Hall. — 6th ed.
        p.   cm.
    Rev. ed. of: Developmental psychology today / Robert E. Schell.
4th ed. c 1993.
    Includes bibliographical references and index.
    ISBN 0-07-029338-4
    1. Developmental psychology.   I. Paris, Scott G., (date).
II. Hall, Elizabeth, (date).   III. Schell, Robert E.
Developmental psychology today.   IV. Title.
BF713.D48   1994
155—dc20   93-9832

International Edition

ABOUT THE AUTHORS

Courtesy of Joni Stricktaden

LOIS HOFFMAN is professor of psychology at the University of Michigan, where she has served for six years as chair of the developmental psychology department. She received her B.A. from SUNY-Buffalo, her M.S. from Purdue University, and her Ph.D. from the University of Michigan. Since 1967, she has taught the undergraduate course in developmental psychology, alternating since 1980 with Scott Paris. In 1981, she was given an award for outstanding teaching.

Professor Hoffman is perhaps best known for her work on the effects of maternal employment on the child, and she is currently studying the effects of maternal employment on the child and the family in a large midwestern urban sample. She coauthored two books on this topic with F. Ivan Nye, *The Employed Mother in America* (1963) and *the Working Mother* (1974); has published many articles; and has given lectures in Europe, Asia, and South America, as well as throughout the United States. She is also well known for her research on parent-child interaction and the child's social and personality development and on the value of children to parents.

Professor Hoffman's other books include the *Review of Child Development Research*, Volumes 1 and 2 (with M. L. Hoffman), *Women and Achievement* (with M. Mednick and S. Tangri), and *Parenting: Its Causes and Consequences* (with R. Gandelman and R. Shiffman).

She has served as president of the Developmental Psychology Division and the Society for the Psychological Study of Social Issues of the American Psychological Association. In 1989, the American Psychological Association selected her as an Eminent Woman in Psychology. She has served on the editorial boards of *Developmental Psychology,* the *Journal of Applied Developmental Psychology, Women and Work,* the *Review of Child Development Research,* and other professional journals.

SCOTT PARIS is professor of psychology and education at the University of Michigan. Since receiving his B.A. from the University of Michigan and his Ph.D. from Indiana University, Professor Paris has taught at Purdue University and Michigan. He has also been a visiting scholar at Stanford University, UCLA, the University of Auckland (New Zealand), Flinders University (Australia), and the University of Queensland (Australia).

His research in developmental psychology has focused primarily on memory and problem-solving skills in children, while his research on education has investigated children's learning and reading. He has written more than eighty articles and book chapters; is a coauthor of *Psychology,* 3rd ed. (with H. Roediger et al.); and is coeditor of *Learning and Motivation in the*

Classroom (with G. Olson and H. Stevenson). He has served on the editorial boards of *Child Development,* the *Journal of Educational Psychology, Developmental Review, Educational Psychologist,* and *Reading Research Quarterly.* Professor Paris has also created educational materials entitled "Reading and Thinking Strategies" for grades 3 through 8, and he is a coauthor of *Heath Reading,* a K-8 basal reading program.

ELIZABETH HALL is the co-author of several textbooks, including *Child Psychology Today* (2nd ed.), *Sexuality, Psychology Today: An Introduction* (7th ed., published by McGraw-Hill), and *Adult Development and Aging* (2nd ed.). She is also coauthor of *Seasons of Life* (with John Kotre), a book developed to accompany the *Seasons of Life* television series on human development produced by the University of Michigan and WQED, Pittsburgh.

Before she turned to college textbooks, she was editor-in-chief of *Human Nature,* a magazine about the human sciences. She was formerly managing editor of *Psychology Today,* and after she left that post, she continued to interview prominent psychologists for the magazine. Some of those conversations with developmental psychologists have been published as *Growing and Changing: What the Experts Say* (Random House, 1987). She has also written a number of books for children; two of them, *Why We Do What We Do: A Look at Psychology* and *From Pigeons to People: A Look at Behavior Shaping,* received honorable mention in the American Psychological Foundation's National Media Awards.

To our parents,
Gus and Etta, George and Muriel, Ed and Mae;
and to our children,
Amy and Jill, Jeff, Kristin, and Julie, Susan and David

CONTENTS IN BRIEF

CONTENTS

PREFACE

Our goal in the sixth edition of *Developmental Psychology Today* remains the same as it has always been: to give students an up-to-date, comprehensive, research-based introduction to developmental psychology. Since the fifth edition was published, research in developmental psychology has expanded in every direction. Old theories are being interpreted in new ways, and new theories are shedding light on unexplored corners of development. The excitement of new findings has kept pace with the increasing complexity of the field. Organizing and synthesizing the wealth of research, the complicated issues, and the theoretical debates that characterize the field presents an increasing challenge.

To meet the challenge, we have field-tested the book and the support materials. *Developmental Psychology Today* is used in the classroom by both of our academic authors, who together have forty-five years experience in teaching developmental psychology. Lois Hoffman, professor of developmental psychology at the University of Michigan, has taught the course at Rutgers University, Temple University, Arizona State, and the University of Michigan. She is an expert on family interaction and the social context of development, and her work on maternal employment in the family is central to an understanding of its effects. Scott Paris, a professor of psychology and education at the University of Michigan, has taught the course at Purdue and the University of Michigan. He is an expert on children's learning, reading, metacognition, and educational achievement, as well as coauthor of a basal reading series. Classroom experience convinced them that a text can best convey continuity and change in development by presenting childhood development in three parts: the beginnings of life (from conception to the end of the neonatal period), infancy and early childhood (from 1 month through the age of 3), and childhood (age 4 to 12). Elizabeth Hall, a professional writer, has made the book readable and accessible to students, as she has since the second edition.

The New Sixth Edition

Sweeping changes in the field of developmental psychology have led to continued reorganization and rewriting of *Developmental Psychology Today*. Through all six editions, however, we have retained a research-based orientation, and our determination to keep the text interesting and readable remains firm. The accent of this sixth edition is on change. Our guiding theme is that development occurs in the context of a varied and changing society. Instead of assuming that development is the same for every group and every time, we take the position that differences in the way people live alter the experience of every life stage. For that reason, we have enlarged our coverage to emphasize the effect of class, ethnic group, and culture on development. While presenting development within today's society, we note trends that could affect development in the future. Finally, we have increased our emphasis on the child as an active agent in socialization, through his or her influence on the environment and interpretation of it. As in earlier editions, we have continued to integrate theory and research so that coverage is not tied to a single theory or theorist. This approach gives instructors the freedom to emphasize particular theoretical positions as they see fit—through either supplementary lectures, assigned readings, or other means.

New Organization

The sixth edition of *Developmental Psychology Today* places more emphasis on adolescence than did earlier editions. We have expanded our coverage on adolescence to three chapters. This shift reflects the new research focus on young adolescents, which has grown out of the realization that puberty is a major milestone in human development. Because people develop and change throughout the life span, we have continued the fifth edition's emphasis on adulthood. For this edition, however, we have eliminated the final chapter on death, because much of the substantive work on this topic is not truly developmental and because extensive coverage of death seemed to send some students away from the course with negative feelings. Instead, we have incorporated essential portions of that chapter into appropriate sections of our discussion of social development during late adulthood (Chapter 20): coverage of life expectancy and longevity is now part of the discussion of physical changes, and coverage of grieving and the adjustment to widowhood has been added to the section on the sociopsychological aspects of life as a widowed spouse. A brief discussion of developmental issues connected with death provides the conclusion to that chapter. These changes allow us to complete our survey of human development without increasing the length of the book.

Instructors familiar with previous editions will notice other major and minor changes. In Part One (Chapters 1 and 2), we have reorganized Chapter 1. In the process, we increased our emphasis on the interaction between genes and the environment, enriched our coverage of the nature of developmental change, emphasized a critical interpretation of developmental research, and strengthened our discussion of methodology. In Chapter 2, we have expanded our coverage of social cognition, providing specific discussions of Robert Selman's and Lawrence Kohlberg's theories. In line with developmentalists' renewed emphasis on the social context of development, we have expanded coverage of cultural-contextual theories, particularly the theories of Vygotsky and Bronfenbrenner.

In Part Two (Chapters 3 and 4), on the beginnings of life, we have continued this emphasis. In Chapter 3, we have strengthened the discussion of interaction be-

tween heredity and environment and presented recent advances in in-vitro fertilization. Our discussion of teratogens reflects the most recent research and expands coverage of the effects of AIDs, cocaine, and lead. In Chapter 4, we have added a section on the newborn's states and rhythms, integrating the roles of crying, sleeping, and sucking into the infant's life. We have expanded the discussions of perceptual development in early infancy, and we have taken a broader look at early temperament and social interaction, reflecting our theme of development within a social context.

Part Three (Chapters 5 through 8), on infancy and early childhood, has also seen extensive revision. In our exploration of physical development (Chapter 5), we have expanded the section on cortical control, adding a discussion of lateralization. We have also extended the section on play skills in early childhood, incorporating a developmental view of play. Our focus on the interaction of the determinants of development has led to expanded coverage of sociocultural influences on health, including malnutrition, deprivation, and enrichment. The chapter on cognition (Chapter 6) has been enriched with a new section on perceptual development and with new research on mental representation in toddlers which indicates that Piaget underestimated their representational ability. Our discussion of language (Chapter 7) continues to focus on the precursors to language and expands the discussion of required cognitive advances. New research will help students understand the constraints on learning new words and the tendency to overregularize language. The section on theories of language acquisition has been rearranged, expanded with new research, and recast so that students will find it easier to grasp. Our discussion of early social development (Chapter 8) has been revised, expanded, and updated, as the changed section headings indicate. Chapter 8 now includes new theories, a strong focus on class, ethnic, and cultural differences in mothering and attachment, a recognition of limitations in the traditional ways of measuring attachment, new insight into early peer relations, an expanded discussion of sibling influence, and a revised coverage of self-concept, which for the first time incorporates the development of emotions and emotional self-regulation.

Part Four (Chapters 9 through 12), on childhood, pays equal attention to social and cognitive development. In our discussion of the child within the family (Chapter 9), we have added coverage on latchkey children, the effects of birth order, and single parenting and the extended family in ethnic groups. We have rewritten the chapter to incorporate new research that traces the influence of family discord and parental style on the developing child. Chapter 10 describes how influences from beyond the family affect social development. The chapter provides in-depth coverage of class, ethnic, and cultural differences and increases coverage on peer relations, which has recently become the focus of renewed research interest. We have added new sections on friendships across ethnic groups and on the effects of unemployment on developing children, and we have substantially strengthened the discussion of developmental effects of ethnic-group membership. The first cognitive chapter in this part (Chapter 11) covers the shift from preoperational to concrete-operational thought and continues to emphasize what children *can,* rather than *cannot,* do. New sections on categorization and the development of self-regulated learning, as well as the expanded coverage of problem solving, provide a more comprehensive picture of children's thought. The chapter on intelligence (Chapter 12) emphasizes aspects of family and community life that influence academic intelligence. To this end, we have added a discussion of multiple intelligences, explored the connection between social class and IQ scores, and looked at specific aspects of the home environment and community beliefs that affect scores. In order to incorporate this material, we have shortened the discussion of cognition applied to specific subjects while retaining our exploration of motivation and self-regulated learning.

Part Five (Chapters 13 through 15), which traces development in adolescence, has been expanded to reflect recent social change and heightened interest in this phase of the life span. The first chapter (Chapter 13), which covers biological changes and change within the self, has been extensively reorganized. The new discussion of identity formation is sensitive to different paths for different subgroups in society, and the discussion of family life, which focuses on the conflict between the quest for autonomy and the maintenance of family ties, now includes sections on parenting styles, parental divorce, and maternal employment. Other new sections provide coverage of adolescent homosexuality and of the adolescent as worker, paying attention to class and ethnic differences in occupational experience. The new chapter on cognitive development (Chapter 14) looks at the physiological and social changes that underlie adolescent thinking and the adolescent's transition and adjustments to school. The chapter goes beyond the traditional coverage of adolescent thought to examine practical intelligence. The chapter on adolescent problems (Chapter 15) has been retained but rewritten to reflect society in the 1990s, with increased

attention to different patterns among various social classes and ethnic groups.

Coverage of adulthood continues to fill Parts Six (Chapters 16 through 18) and Seven (Chapters 19 and 20). The chapters on social development in young adulthood (Chapter 16) and middle adulthood (Chapter 18), which interweave the experience of adulthood in a changing society with the effects of gender on that experience, also emphasize the new strand of membership in an ethnic group. The chapter on intellectual development in young and middle adulthood (Chapter 17) still emphasizes progressive changes in general thinking and the role of health and life style on intelligence. Chapter 19, however, which explores cognition in later adulthood and focuses on changes in information processing, has been reorganized to reflect new emphases among developmentalists. The chapter includes new theories on the causes of slowed processing, as well as a discussion of cognitive plasticity and training and a section on wisdom. The final chapter, on social development in later adulthood (Chapter 20), emphasizes the influence of ethnic-group membership on the experience of later adulthood, as well as the impact of life style on the nature and pace of aging. As noted earlier, it incorporates material on theories of aging, grief, adjustment to widowhood, and death as a developmental issue.

Selective Coverage

Developmental Psychology Today makes no attempt to survey *all* research in *all* areas of development or to look at *all* the issues and topics that concern developmentalists. Such a goal would be unrealistic. For the sixth edition, we have tried, as before, to present the most important studies in the most important areas and to help students understand what they have read. We analyze the presented material, explain the implications of research, synthesize viewpoints and theories, and discuss their applications. We believe that this approach helps students gain an appreciation for developmental issues that will last long beyond the final exam.

Up-to-Date Research

In order to retain the text's emphasis on development *today,* we have sought out the latest research on issues, methods, and ground-breaking discoveries. In this book, students will encounter new research showing that

A baby's temperament tends to match the expectations of the parents during the prenatal period.

Babies as young as 2 months prefer attractive faces.

Family context and culture influence the way infants show attachment in the Strange Situation.

Human breast milk seems to spur cognitive development in preterm infants.

The nature of family interactions affects the speed with which children move through Kohlberg's stages of moral development.

Having even one friend protects neglected children from the negative effects of peer rejection.

Latchkey children who stay in their own homes after school do as well as children who are supervised by a parent.

High blood pressure may be a major factor in IQ declines among adults.

During the coming decade, age differences in IQ scores will probably shrink.

Authentic Examples from Daily Life

Our policy is to use individuals in the news, specific people from studies, incidents from the experiences of the authors, and experiences reported by various researchers in a way that brings developmental issues to life for the reader. These actual examples are scattered through every chapter and provide chapter-opening vignettes. Social effects on development seem clear when, for example, students watch the morning routine in a two-career family, learn about the way a young girl reacted to her parents' divorce, or observe the after-school routine of a young adolescent whose mother is a single parent. Adolescent suicide is no longer an abstract problem when students meet a 14-year-old who takes his own life. The effects of aging on memory processes take on new meaning when psychologists B. F. Skinner and Donald Hebb describe their own memory problems. And when an African-American couple on the verge of retirement talk about their future, the meaning of generativity becomes clear.

Highlights on Current Issues

Students will find boxed inserts in every chapter of *Developmental Psychology Today*. The boxes are varied, drawing from in-depth coverage of a particular study or reports from the world outside the research laboratory. They may discuss a particular research technique, illuminate a controversial or newsworthy topic from the standpoint of developmental issues, or present

experiences from other cultures. As they read these boxes, students will learn about technology that allows researchers to watch the spread of neural activity across the living infant brain. They will learn about the way culture determines the nature of interaction between mother and baby, the influence of physical attractiveness on development, and the psychological effects of parental battles on toddlers. Students will discover how the context of a study affects research results, how China's one-child policy may influence children's development, when peer collaboration spurs problem solving and when it interferes, why the students who most need help are least likely to ask for it, why students with high grades may not get high SAT scores, how social context influences marital happiness, why there is no connection between IQ and the complex ability to handicap horses, and how stereotypes about old people affect our perceptions of their behavior.

Study Aids

In order to assist the learning process, an outline precedes each chapter, serving as an advance organizer. Each chapter is followed by a summary organized under major chapter headings so that students can review its content. At its first use, each new term is printed in boldface type. Following each chapter is a list of these key terms, which are also defined in the glossary at the end of the book.

A complete teaching and learning package is available with *Developmental Psychology Today,* sixth edition. The package is coauthored by a team of experienced instructors from Texas Christian University: David Cross, Don Dansereau, and Julie Mason. The package includes a Student Study Guide, which has been completely revised and updated and uses concept maps to organize and present review material for students; a Test Bank that contains a mix of factual and conceptual questions for each chapter (also available in computerized formats for IBM and Macintosh computers); and an Instructor's Manual that includes a variety of teaching resources. The McGraw-Hill Overhead Transparencies in Developmental Psychology are also available with this text.

Acknowledgments

We would like to acknowledge three people whose assistance enabled us to keep the book's reports timely and accurate: Dr. Kristin Moore at Child Trends supplied many statistics, Dr. Jerald Bachman at the Institute for Social Research supplied us with fresh data from the Monitoring the Future study, and Dr. Karl Rosengren at the University of Illinois supplied material and advice on the adolescent cognition chapter. We would also like to thank Dr. Joseph Adelson of the University of Michigan, Dr. Marc Bornstein of the National Institute of Child Health and Human Development, and Dr. Esther Thelen of Indiana University, whose materials and guidance continue to make their imprint on this book.

This edition would not have been possible without the strength and support of the team at McGraw-Hill, whose hard work, attention to detail, and enthusiasm kept us going. Our special thanks go to Jane Vaicunas, our editor; James Belser, our editing supervisor; and Susan Gottfried, our copy editor. The book's handsome appearance is the work of Caliber/Phoenix Color Corp.; Safra Nimrod, our photo editor; and Elyse Rieder, our photo researcher.

We are also grateful to the following individuals, whose ideas, comments, and suggestions were of great help to us as we revised this edition: Nancy Acuff, East Tennessee State University; Fredda Blanchard Fields, Louisiana State University; Vaughn Crowl, Hagerstown Junior College; Dorothy Flannagan, University of Texas at San Antonio; Wayne Hall, San Jacinto College; Kathleen Hulbert, University of Massachusetts at Lowell; John S. Klein, Castleton State College; Pamela A. Manners, Troy State University; Richard Metzger, University of Tennessee at Chattanooga; Sarah C. O'Dowd, Community College of Rhode Island; Sallie H. Plymale, Professor Emeritus, Marshall University; Paul Retzlaff, University of Northern Colorado; Cynthia Scheibe, Ithaca College; Bonnie Seegmiller, Hunter College; Kevin Seybold, Grove City College; David Shwalb, Koryo Women's College, Nagoya; and Ronald D. Taylor, Temple University.

Lois Hoffman
Scott Paris
Elizabeth Hall

THE MEANING
OF DEVELOPMENT

As parents contemplate their newborn infant, they are full of pride and plans. The baby's grandparents recall how, thirty years ago, they re-acted in the same way—as did their own parents a quarter of a century before. Thirty years from now, the infant in turn will be a parent gazing down at his or her own child. Around the world, in every culture, the cycle of human development goes ever on. The progression from infant to child to young adult to aging elder is a familiar one, but what does it mean? What are the major forces behind development? What sorts of pro-cesses are responsible for the changes we see? Why do people brought up in the same culture, even living on the same block, turn out so differently? Explaining how babies develop into adults and why their developmental path takes one turning and not another is an important question studied by developmental psychologists. Yet it is understanding the general rules of development and not the precise prediction of any one person's life course that is the developmental psychologist's goal. As you will soon discover, explanations of human development vary. Although each has increased our understanding of the mysterious process of development, none can, by it-self, adequately describe the progression from cradle to grave. ■

CHAPTER

1

CONCEPTS AND METHODS IN DEVELOPMENTAL PSYCHOLOGY

● ● ● ● ● ● ● ● ● ● ● ● ● ● ●

THE NATURE OF HUMAN DEVELOPMENT

The complex study of human development
The stages of life
The nature of developmental change

DETERMINANTS OF DEVELOPMENT

Nature: Biological determinants
Nurture: Environmental determinants

RESEARCH METHODS IN DEVELOPMENTAL PSYCHOLOGY

Observational studies
Interview studies
Experimental studies
Correlational studies
Developmental designs

THE FIELD OF DEVELOPMENTAL PSYCHOLOGY

Careers in developmental psychology
Using developmental psychology

SUMMARY

KEY TERMS

Early in the twentieth century, many psychologists believed that babies came into the world as alike as peas in a pod. Psychologist John Watson (1924/1970) was so convinced of our initial similarity that he said,

> *Give me a dozen healthy infants, well-formed, and my own specified world to bring them up in and I'll guarantee to take any one at random and train him to become any type of specialist I might select—doctor, lawyer, artist, merchant-chief and, yes, even beggar-man and thief, regardless of his talents, penchants, tendencies, abilities, vocations, and race of his ancestors. (p. 104)*

Watson believed that a baby's mind was like a blank tablet and that learning inscribed on it the traits, talents, and peculiarities that would appear in the adult.

This extreme view of the causes of the differences among us has fallen out of favor. Today, most psychologists agree that we become the kind of people we are through the **interaction** of heredity and environment. Our inherited predispositions influence our environment, which influences our inherited predispositions, in a never-ending spiral that produces a unique individual with specific interests, capabilities, limits, and ways of responding to events. This process of age-related change over the life span, which describes the transition from fertilized egg to aged adult, is known as **development.** Understanding that change is the aim of developmental psychologists.

This chapter builds the foundation for the study of human development. We begin by exploring the nature of development and its complexity; then we go on to consider the nature of developmental change and the issue of continuity versus discontinuity. Next we look at the determinants of development and discover that the influences of nature and nurture are inextricably intertwined. We then examine the various methods and designs used by developmental psychologists to study developmental determinants. The chapter closes with a brief history of developmental psychology, its uses, and the various career opportunities it presents.

The Nature of Human Development

A good way to think about development is as a process of change within the individual across the life span. This developmental change has several characteristics: it is continuous, cumulative, directional, differentiated, organized, and holistic.

Development is *continuous,* which means that changes occur over hours, days, weeks, months, and years. For example, a person is not an adolescent one day and a mature adult the next. Continuity means that developmental changes continue throughout life, indicating that childhood experience does not rigidly determine the rest of a person's life. Instead, change and development can occur at every period of life.

Development is *cumulative,* which means that it builds upon what has gone before. How children and adults respond and what they can learn today depends in part on their earlier experiences in related situations. Babies are born without any notion of right or wrong, for example; moral development occurs gradually, emerging from children's experiences in home, school, and playground, from their own emotional reactions to those experiences, and from their growing understanding of others (Boom and Molenaar, 1989; M. Hoffman, 1988).

Development is *directional,* which means that it moves in the direction of greater complexity. Infants grow first into children and then into adults. Lacking any coordination, a baby reaches for a ball with an open hand. As muscles, nerves, and bones mature, the young child becomes increasingly skillful at picking up and throwing the ball. With further maturation of small muscles and practice, the child develops the speed and coordination required for athletic competition.

Development is *differentiated,* which means that it consists of increasingly finer distinctions. Babies who may find it difficult to distinguish among their perceptions, thoughts, feelings, and actions become children who first separate these elements of experience and then make finer distinctions in what they perceive, what they feel, what they think, and what they do (Flavell, 1985).

Development moves in the direction of increasing complexity. As muscles, bones, and nerves mature, the baby's open-handed attempt to reach a toy becomes a skilled grasp. *(Laura Dwight)*

Development is *organized,* which means that skills are increasingly integrated. Infants slowly become able to organize and control their actions. Just as babies learn to coordinate their muscles and perceptual functions, adults learn to organize and control the various tasks related to their work and family lives.

Finally, development is *holistic,* which means that advances never occur in isolation. Each aspect of development, whether physical, cognitive, or social, depends on every other aspect, and all development is the result of interaction. Acquiring language, for example, requires maturation of throat, mouth, and brain; the understanding that words can stand for objects that are not present; and interaction with other people.

Our lives are thus interwoven fabrics of individual change, and each life is a fabric produced in a specific social, cultural, and historical setting, which directs the weaving in special ways.

The Complex Study of Human Development

Human development is so complex that, although developmental psychology has grown out of the general field of psychology, developmentalists also rely on other fields of study to help them understand the processes of development. The complexity of the undertaking becomes clearer when we consider the five overarching goals of developmental psychologists:

To *describe* changes with age and experience in physical growth, thinking, and personality. Such descriptions provide a picture of the general course of development.

To *compare* people from diverse backgrounds, people with different rearing histories, and people with different biological histories. This comparison provides a picture of individual differences.

To *explain* developmental changes and sequences according to principles, rules, theories, and mechanisms.

To *predict* patterns of development. Once development can be predicted, we can devise ways to *control* it, and intervention becomes possible. Intervention permits us to *improve* the lives of infants, children, or adults for whom the course of development has gone astray and perhaps to *prevent* other developmental problems from arising. Individuals then might develop their capabilities to the utmost and lead more fulfilling lives.

To *relate* the findings of developmental psychology to the work of other disciplines. Once this relation is made clear, the field's basic knowledge becomes useful to educators, health-care providers, parents, therapists, social workers, and scientists.

In pursuit of these goals, developmental psychologists draw on the knowledge and resources of allied fields of study. So many strands of influence are involved in development that developmental psychologists need information from biology, sociology, anthropology, and history to help them understand its course. They depend on information about human evolutionary history, embryological development, biological development and maturation, and the various sociocultural contexts in which development occurs—the family, the society, and the historical time.

When studying development, however, psychologists can look only at specific aspects of the process. They isolate small parts of development in order to interpret the process under study with as much precision as possible. In studying the development of intelligence, for example, a researcher could look at memory, at the way people solve problems, at the effects of accumulated knowledge, at the effects of aging, or at the effects of family relationships. This means that studies of development are all simply slices of human development taken at a specific time, using a specific group, covering a specific range of phenomena. From these studies, researchers may generalize their findings, always paying attention to the interaction among the various domains and contexts of development.

The Stages of Life

One influence on development is a person's place in the life span. When we think about the life span, we divide it into the stages of prenatal development, infancy, childhood, adolescence, and adulthood. This division makes sense to us, but our view of the life span is not shared by all contemporary societies or even by our own society in earlier times. Some societies divide life into three periods (such as infancy, childhood, and adulthood) or only two (infancy and adulthood) (Mead, 1928/1968).

The way in which people in a society view the life span depends largely on their social and economic system. During the Middle Ages, for example, infancy lasted for about seven years; then a young person began working alongside adults (Aries, 1962). And Western cultures did not view adolescence as a separate stage of life until industrialization and economic productivity freed most young adolescents from farm and factory labor. More recently, increases in life expectancy have led to a substantial number of people living well into their eighties. So many of these older adults have remained active and vigorous that the period of later adulthood has been divided into the "young-old" and the "old-old," in order to separate healthy older adults from those who are sickly and frail (Neugarten and Hall, 1987).

The use of physical and mental conditions as the dividing line between the young-old and the old-old points up the problem of finding appropriate markers to divide the life span. We are not consistent in choosing

So many older Americans are living healthy, vigorous lives that developmentalists now call them the "young-old." *(Donald Dietz/Stock, Boston)*

our markers and seem unable to decide whether biological, social, or cognitive events give us the best way of sectioning off a person's life. Some biological markers seem to make sense: the moment of birth separates the prenatal period from infancy; puberty separates childhood from adolescence. Social events also make convenient markers of the life span. The assumption of adult roles in work or marriage marks the end of adolescence and the start of adulthood, while the loss of roles—such as retirement from work—is similarly significant. Cognitive events also can be used. Meaningful speech marks the end of infancy and the start of childhood, and mature reasoning separates childhood from adolescence.

Our inconsistency in the selection of life markers highlights one fact about development that evokes general agreement from psychologists. Chronological age is a poor way to divide the life span; and the older people get, the less helpful it is (Neugarten and Neugarten, 1986). During infancy and early childhood, when so many developmental advances depend on biological maturation, chronological age is less misleading than it is during childhood. The age of an adult gives little information beyond the fact that she or he has lived a certain number of years (Neugarten and Hall, 1987).

The biological, chronological, and social markers roughly coincide with major phases in the life span but rarely fall at exactly the same place (See Figure 1.1). In talking about development, however, it seems convenient to use five chronological periods that more or less correspond to our culture's usage.

The **prenatal period** begins at conception and ends at birth. It is the least arbitrary and easiest to define because its beginning and end are clearly marked by biological events. **Infancy** begins at birth and continues until approximately age 2. By the end of the second year, most children have begun to acquire language and symbolic thought. In addition, most adults think of 2-year-olds as children rather than as infants, which corresponds to the developmental shift from nonlinguistic to linguistic communication.

The third phase, **childhood,** begins around age 2 and continues through late childhood, at around age 12. So much development takes place during this phase that we often find it necessary to use additional terms, such as *toddler* (a transitional stage from about 18 months until a child's third birthday) and *preschooler* (from about 3 to 6 years). Puberty is usually accepted as the end of childhood and the beginning of adolescence. **Adolescence,** the fourth stage, is a less definite period than childhood because its end is not defined as well as the end of other phases of development.

Adulthood, the fifth stage, generally begins in the

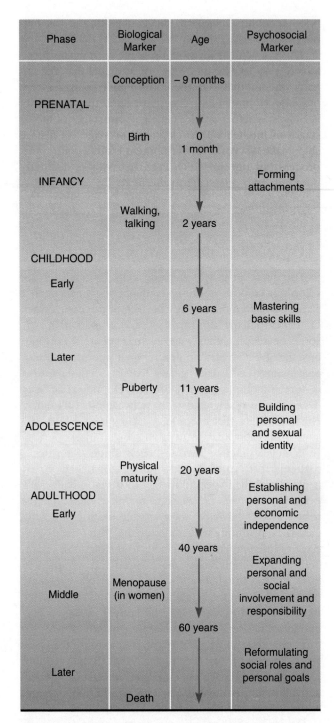

Phase	Biological Marker	Age	Psychosocial Marker
PRENATAL	Conception	– 9 months	
	Birth	0	
INFANCY		1 month	Forming attachments
	Walking, talking	2 years	
CHILDHOOD Early			
		6 years	Mastering basic skills
Later			
	Puberty	11 years	
ADOLESCENCE			Building personal and sexual identity
	Physical maturity	20 years	
ADULTHOOD Early			Establishing personal and economic independence
		40 years	
			Expanding personal and social involvement and responsibility
Middle	Menopause (in women)		
		60 years	
			Reformulating social roles and personal goals
Later			
	Death		

Figure 1.1 Because the phases of human development are based on cultural views of the life span, they vary from one society to another. Each phase of development used in this book is marked by particular biological or psychosocial events.

late teens or early twenties and continues until death. This is clearly the longest phase of development, spanning early adulthood, the middle years, and late adulthood (encompassing both the young-old and the old-old).

This convenient division of the life span makes it relatively easy to discuss behavioral changes that accompany one another. Yet the convenience of stages may make development look simpler or tidier than it actually is. Stages, whether we are talking about stages of life or stages of intellectual development or stages of friendship, make it seem as if development is not a continuous process but one in which each behavior is distinctly different from one stage to the next.

The Nature of Developmental Change

The question of whether our skills and abilities develop in a smooth, continuous manner or go through a series of discontinuous stages is one of the basic issues of development: *continuity versus discontinuity.* Some developmentalists see development as continuous; they believe that we develop in a smooth, continuous manner, as a daisy grows from a seedling into a mature, blooming plant. Other developmentalists see development as stagelike, with each stage sharply different from stages that precede or follow it, as a butterfly goes from caterpillar to pupa to winged insect.

In developmental theories, each **stage** describes a particular pattern of abilities, motives, or behavior that is predicted by a specific theory of development. As a person passes from one stage to the next, the pattern is restructured. Behavior, motives, and abilities become qualitatively different. Children who move from one stage of intellectual development to the next, for example, do not simply know more about the world; they think in radically different ways. Another characteristic of stages is their predictability; the abilities or behavior typical of a particular stage will appear in a given sequence. Children who are learning to talk always go through a stage in which they can put no more than two words together ("two-word stage") before they are able to produce longer sentences. Even though stages generally follow chronological age, level of function, *not* age, is the developmental marker of stage theories.

Developmentalists who see development as smooth and continuous look for a gradual emergence of skills and behavior. They find later development foreshadowed in earlier behavior or abilities. For example, they trace language development back to infancy, where they see social games like peekaboo as specific lessons in nonverbal conversational skills that are crucial to the emergence of language. Instead of seeing children moving from one "stage" of thought to another, they see a faster and more experienced use of a handful of basic mental processes.

Some of the most powerful theories of human development are cast in the form of stages. Sigmund Freud's theory of psychosexual development and Jean Piaget's theory of cognitive development, for example, have had an enormous influence. Yet these strict stage theories are declining in popularity. The reason for this decline is the inability of most stage theories to meet all the characteristics that are demanded by the concept of stages. According to John Flavell (1985), each developmental stage in a strict stage theory is characterized by structures (a cohesive pattern of abilities, motives, or skills), qualitative changes (a clear-cut difference in abilities, motives, or skills compared with those of the preceding stage), abruptness (a simultaneous change in the stage's typical abilities, motives, or skills), and concurrence (all the changes develop at about the same pace).

Few, if any, stage theories can meet all these standards. For one thing, there is little consensus over exactly where one stage ends and another begins. No one can point to the day, the week, or even the month when a child moves from one of Piaget's stages to the next. For another, a close look at any particular stage often reveals some aspect of behavior that is supposed to emerge, full blown, in a later stage. Finally, the transition between stages is usually lengthy, and the various abilities within a stage may develop at staggered intervals and sometimes in a different order (Flavell, 1985).

Although the use of stages in this strict theoretical sense is declining, many developmental psychologists continue to use the concept in a less restrictive manner. This less restrictive usage is still related to theory, but whether it refers to stages of language acquisition or stages of marriage, the stages are not intended to meet strict theoretical standards. Instead, developmental psychologists use this enormously useful concept as a convenient way to describe major phases of life in a particular domain.

Determinants of Development

Another issue in developmental psychology regards the determinants of development, particularly the respective influences of nature (the person's genetic makeup) and nurture (the environment). This issue is often cast as *nature versus nurture.* Because developmental psychologists study change across time, they are especially aware that behavior depends on both nature and nurture. They may disagree, however, about how genes and environment interact, and they may emphasize either nature or nurture in specific areas of development. Some, for example, believe that personality is heavily influenced by a baby's inborn temperament (nature); others believe that experiences while growing up are the primary influence (nurture).

In truth, development is the product of many interacting causes, and any explanation requires an integrated interpretation of the various factors (Tronick, 1992). When we examine hereditary influences, we need to keep reminding ourselves that heredity never operates in isolation from the environment. The way in which biological determinants are expressed depends on determinants in the environment. And conversely, the same environmental influence may work differently, depending on a person's heredity.

Nature: Biological Determinants

Developmental psychologists study two kinds of biological influences on development. The first kind is **species-specific influences,** which are the genetic characteristics that are shared by all members of a species. These are the influences that make us like all other humans. For example, all human newborns need others for nourishment and care, a biological characteristic that makes human babies dependent on their mothers (or some other caregiver) for a relatively long period of time compared with other species. The second kind of biological influence is the genetic characteristics that are specific to each person. These influences contribute to differences among individuals. Only **identical twins** (who develop when a single egg cell, fertilized by a single sperm, splits early in development) have the same combination of genes—and thus develop under identical biological influences. Other relatives share fewer genes. Like other siblings, **fraternal twins** (who are born when two eggs are fertilized during the same menstrual cycle) share, on average, half their genes; grandparents and grandchildren share one-quarter of their genes. These two kinds of biological influences are our endowment from nature, and they allow developmental psychologists to study how nature can contribute to both similarities and differences among us.

Biological determinants begin working on us at the moment of conception and continue their work until we die. Clearly, biological determinants are powerful in some areas of development. Sitting, standing, and walking depend heavily on the biological maturation of mus-

cles, nerves, and brain. Babies also come into the world biologically prepared to form social bonds, to investigate their surroundings, and to acquire language. Our heredity as a species so strongly disposes human infants to develop these abilities that they will appear in any natural human environment (Scarr, 1983). Only extreme deprivation will prevent their development.

Biological determinants operate through genes, microscopic bits of protein in the nucleus of each body cell. (In Chapter 3, we will examine the work of genes in some detail.) It is important to remember that the influence of genes on behavior is indirect and is exerted only through interaction with the environment. What appears at first glance to be primarily a genetic effect, such as similarities in personality, behavior, or intelligence between twins, is often in good part the effect of similar environments. This becomes clear when we look at identical twins who were separated at birth and grew up in different families. When reunited as adults, they achieve similar scores on intelligence tests (Bouchard and McGue, 1981). Because we tend to assume that twins who are reared apart have dissimilar environments, we may conclude that any similarities between them are the result of their common genetic heritage. Yet when we group reunited twins on the basis of environmental similarities, we discover that the more similar the environment, the more similar their intellectual abilities (Bronfenbrenner, 1986). Intelligence test scores are much more similar among those who grow up in the same town that those who grow up in different towns. If the separated twins also attend the same school, their scores are even more alike. When separated twins grow up in separate but similar communities (both twins in an agricultural or a mining community), their scores are quite similar. But when they grow up in extremely different communities (one in an agricultural and one in a mining community), the twins' scores are no more alike than those of first cousins, who share only a quarter of their genes. Such results do *not* show an *absence* of genetic effects on intelligence— even twins who grow up in radically different environments have scores that are more similar than those of unrelated persons. This analysis reminds us that the interaction between nature and nurture determines the course of development.

Nurture: Environmental Determinants

Environmental determinants may be physical or social. The physical environment may be the mother's uterus in the prenatal period or an inner-city neighborhood or an Iowa farm. Social environments encompass

Surviving the crash of an airliner is a dramatic example of an experience that contributes to differences among people. *(Robert Nichols/Black Star)*

other people and social institutions. But environmental determinants may also be examined in another way, as to whether they affect the individual or the group. One kind of environmental determinant consists of that portion of the environment that is ours alone—the idiosyncratic experiences that are not part of the expected life course. These environmental determinants make us like *no* other people, and they may be fortunate or unfortunate aspects of our lives. Among the environmental determinants that contribute to differences among people are a special relationship with an admired teacher, severe injuries from a car accident, admission to a particular college, an unexpected meeting that produces a marriage or a switch in occupations, divorce, loss of a job, a move to another community, or a winning lottery ticket (Bandura, 1982). The list is virtually endless.

The second kind of environmental determinant consists of that portion of the environment that is shared by individuals, such as their culture or the historical time in which they are born. Such environmental determinants help to produce similarities; they make us like some other people. Major historical events can have a profound effect on development, but the nature of that effect may depend on a person's age at the time. Each person belongs to a **cohort**, which is a group of people born at about the same time. Among young people who

lived through the Great Depression of the 1930s, for example, whether the influence was positive or negative depended on the youngster's cohort (G. H. Elder, 1980, 1986). Among families who were hardest hit, whose real income dropped at least one-third, the influence on boys who were adolescents at the time seemed generally positive. These boys, on the average, showed a greater desire to achieve, had a firmer sense of career goals, and derived greater satisfaction in later life than boys who did not suffer economic deprivation. But boys who were preschoolers during the depths of the Great Depression seemed vulnerable to the family instability, emotional conflict, and stress that accompanied deprivation. These boys, on the average, tended to be passive and feel helpless or inadequate. They did worse in school and in their occupations, and their goals were lower than those of boys their age who had not gone through economic hardship and were also lower than those of boys who had been adolescents during economic deprivation.

Boys and girls were separated for analysis in this study because gender provides another strand of influence—girls and boys may experience the same event differently. Influences from the shared social environment are especially clear in the development of gender roles, where family, friends, and society all shape our ideas of masculinity and femininity. Parents treat their sons and daughters differently, giving them different toys, playing with them differently, and encouraging girls to cling and be "mother's helpers" while pushing boys to do things on their own (L. Hoffman, 1991). The outside world helps the process along, as children see stereotypical sex roles portrayed in programs and commercials.

The influence of culture affects development by providing or withholding the opportunities to learn and practice various skills and behavior (Rogoff, Gauvain, and Ellis, 1984). Because we are so immersed in our own culture, these developmental effects may be difficult for us to see. A society may encourage children to be more or less nurturant, more or less aggressive, or more or less competitive. Americans, for example, are generally seen as self-assertive, individualistic, and future-oriented, whereas Japanese are generally seen as tradition-oriented and devoted to the interest and harmony of the group (Bornstein, 1989). These differences are encouraged by the culture's adults. In Japan, adults expect children to be patient, persistent, and accommodating; in the United States, adults expect children to be original, explorative, and self-assertive.

Some developmentalists suppose that the seeds of these differences can be found in the nature of infant-mother interactions. Researchers have found, for example, that American mothers talk to and look at their babies more often than do Japanese mothers (Caudill and Weinstein, 1969; Otaki et al., 1986). They propose that the way the mothers respond to their babies either stimulates activity (in the case of American mothers) or discourages it (in the case of Japanese mothers). Other researchers believe that a biological influence may also be at work and that the mothers are responding to genetic differences in their babies' temperament (D. Freedman, 1979). Such influences are difficult to tease out, because so many other environmental factors —including the physiological and psychological consequences of pregnancy and delivery, feeding routines, the way infants are clothed, the health of the babies, and their state of arousal (alert or drowsy)—affect the results of studies (Bornstein, 1989). The interweaving of so many factors reminds us to be careful about attributing any aspect of development either to nature or to nurture. It also reminds us to consider the effects of culture when comparing racial or ethnic groups within a society. (The interaction of determinants is explored further in the accompanying box, "Pretty Babies and Their Parents.")

Research Methods in Developmental Psychology

Disentangling the multiple influences on development is not easy, but the patient efforts of researchers have given us the information we need to make general observations and claims about the course of human development. Research is important, because without it our knowledge of development would be limited to anecdotes and opinions. Through research, we can discover new facts and test hypotheses about development.

Suppose, for example, that we want to know whether the experience of being abused by a parent affects a child's emotional development. The first step in identifying various determinants and their effects on human development is to formulate a hypothesis about the way a determinant might act. A **hypothesis** is a prediction that we can test by gathering appropriate information. So we might begin our investigation with the hypothesis that being abused affects the way young children respond to another child in distress. The next step is to devise a study in which we can gather the sort of information that would test the hypothesis, and as we will see, a pair of researchers carried out just such a study. From the results of their test, we can draw conclusions about the hypothesis.

The Japanese insistence that children be patient, persistent, and accommodating may derive from the culture's emphasis on tradition and group harmony. *(Michal Heron/ Woodfin Camp & Associates)*

PRETTY BABIES AND THEIR PARENTS—AN INTERACTION BETWEEN GENES AND ENVIRONMENT

Some babies are adorable and others are homely. Homely babies are not abnormal or repellent, but something about the spacing, shape, or size of their features makes them unattractive. Physical appearance is determined by genes, and through its interaction with the social environment, a baby's appearance may affect its future development in unexpected ways.

We expect attractive babies to be better in all ways than unattractive infants. Studies have shown that attractive babies hold this edge regardless of race; whether Caucasian, African-American, or Hispanic, adults shown photos of unfamiliar babies pick the attractive infants as the "best" behaved, the smartest, and the most likeable babies (Stephan and Langlois, 1984). They pick unattractive infants as the most likely to cause their parents trouble.

Physical appearance even affects the way parents treat their babies. Researchers observed mothers of various ethnic and socioeconomic groups with their babies at intervals from birth (Langlois, 1986). The less attractive the baby, the less involved the mother seemed; her attention tended to be directed toward others rather than toward her baby, and she demonstrated less maternal affection. The more attractive the baby, the more the mother cuddled, kissed, smiled at, and cooed at her baby. Mothers of less attractive babies tended to worry more about them and to be disappointed in them. Other researchers have found that fathers react in a similar manner (Parke and Sawin, 1975).

These differences in expectations and behavior may affect babies' development in a predictable manner. Some researchers believe that children behave in the way that their parents, other relatives, and teachers expect them to behave (Langlois, 1986).

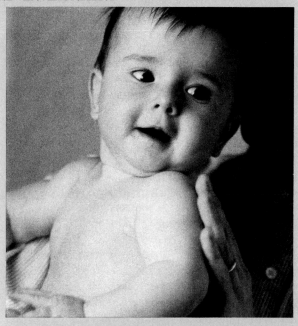

Parents and strangers alike treat attractive babies as if they were smarter, better-behaved, and more likeable than homely infants. *(David Witbeck/The Picture Cube)*

Those who are treated as if they are smart and popular and friendly tend to live up to these expectations, whereas those who are treated as if they are mentally slow, unpopular, and aggressive may also match expectations. The old saying "Your face is your fortune" may be more accurate than we would like to believe.

Hypotheses can be tested using any of several different methods, and the distinctions among them depend on how much *control* we have over various aspects of a study. A researcher may or may not have control over (1) the selection of subjects for study, (2) the experiences the subjects have in the study, and (3) the possible responses they can give to that experience. Each of the methods we might use has advantages and disadvantages, and our choice will depend on our purpose and the circumstances.

A single study, no matter how well executed, cannot answer all our questions. At best, it will support our hypothesis or show that it is wrong, but it cannot really *prove* it. The final test comes when other researchers **replicate,** or repeat, our results. A scientific finding is established when several different researchers, in different places, using the same basic method, replicate the results.

The major methods used by developmental psychologists are observational studies, interview studies, and experimental studies, and each allows a researcher a different degree of control (see Table 1.1). When a study is well controlled, all extraneous factors affect all subjects similarly, allowing researchers to assume that the behavior under study is actually affected by the factors they are studying.

TABLE 1.1   METHODS OF STUDYING DEVELOPMENT

Method	Advantages	Disadvantages
Observational studies	Situation is close to everyday life.	Researcher has no control over selection of participants. Observations may be unreliable. Unknown and uncontrollable factors may influence results.
Interview studies	Situation is close to everyday life. Researcher has some control over selection of participants. Experience and responses of participants may be standardized.	Unknown and uncontrollable factors may influence results. Observations may be unreliable.
Experimental studies	Unwanted factors may be controlled or eliminated. Generally this is the most efficient and least expensive method.	Situation may be far removed from daily life.

Observational Studies

In an **observational study,** a researcher observes people as they go about their daily activities and carefully records their behavior. Observational studies can take place in homes, schools, or offices; on playgrounds and city streets; at parties, parades, or nursing homes. Because people are behaving spontaneously in natural settings, researchers feel fairly confident in generalizing from the results of their observations to other situations.

Observational studies can produce valuable information about the effects of environmental **variables,** or factors, on behavior. In order for observational studies to be successful, however, researchers must establish explicit rules for categorizing and recording what they see, so that two observers watching the situation will produce comparable records. Researchers use various techniques to record behavior. Some use a checklist, marking off listed actions each time they occur. Some use time sampling, observing each subject for a specified number of minutes and recording behavior of interest. Others, who are interested in recording as much natural behavior as possible, videotape activities and then analyze them frame by frame for behavior that might otherwise go unnoticed. There are two kinds of observational studies: naturalistic and field studies.

Naturalistic Studies

In a **naturalistic study,** a researcher simply observes and records what he or she sees, without changing the situation in any way. For example, Mary Main and Carol George (1985) wondered whether young children who had been battered by their parents would be less likely than other youngsters to show concern for a distressed child. Researchers visited two nursery schools for battered children and two nursery schools that served "families under stress," and they recorded the social behavior of selected children at each school. All the children were from disadvantaged homes. When the records were analyzed, Main and George discovered that the abused toddlers not only failed to respond sympathetically to the distress of other children but also became fearful or angry, sometimes threatening a child in distress or even attacking the crying toddler. Toddlers who had never been abused often showed concern or sadness at another child's distress and almost never became angry (see Figure 1.2, p. 16). Although the researchers' hypothesis seemed to be confirmed, the fact that all toddlers at the school for battered children had been abused makes it impossible to determine whether the distressed child's temperament might have elicited unsympathetic responses.

In this observational study of young children, the researcher records specific behavior that later will be analyzed to test her hypothesis. *(David Young-Wolff/Photo Edit)*

DOES METHODOLOGY AFFECT RESULTS?

Some descriptions of interactions between children and parents seem to assume that parents treat all their children in the same manner. But several factors have led researchers to wonder whether this is so. For one thing, the birth of a first child is more likely than subsequent births to disrupt the relationship between the parents. For another, parents may have unrealistic expectations for a first child. The second child is born to parents who have adjusted to the experience of children in the family and who are veterans at the task of parenting (L. Hoffman, 1991).

Two research teams attempted to discover whether mothers treat their first- and second-born children similarly. One team, headed by Joan Lasko (1954), conducted a naturalistic study; the other, headed by Judy Dunn (Dunn and Plomin, 1990; Dunn, Plomin, and Daniels, 1986; Dunn, Plomin, and Nettles, 1985), conducted a field study. The two teams reached opposite conclusions. Lasko found striking differences throughout the first six years of the children's lives, whereas Dunn found that mothers treated their children similarly.

Lasko found that the first-born is advantaged during infancy, getting more attention than subsequent children. But once the second child comes along, the first-born gets less attention than the second-born will receive at the same age. As 3-year-olds, first-borns are hedged in with more restrictions and receive less warmth and affection than second-borns do at the same age. Dunn found that mothers treated first- and second-borns consistently, handling them the same way at the same age. Both were treated similarly as 12-month-olds, as 2-year-olds, and as 3-year-olds.

How could two careful investigators come up with opposite conclusions? The differences in their conclusions were produced by an important difference in the conditions under which the researchers observed their subjects (L. Hoffman, 1991). Lasko, whose study was naturalistic, observed mothers and children together in the home. At home, mothers of more than one preschooler are rarely alone with any of their children. Once a second child is born, the mother has to juggle the responsibilities for two children simultaneously, all the while controlling the behavior of the older child toward the younger sibling. These demands lead to changes in the mother's behavior. Dunn, using a field study, videotaped sev-

Whether researchers find that parents treat their children similarly or differently seems to depend on the conditions under which parent-child interaction is observed. *(Deborah Kahn-Kalas/Stock, Boston)*

eral five-minute segments of the mother and the child interacting by themselves at home, either while they were playing together or while the mother instructed the child in a specified task. Thus, another sibling was never around to change the nature of the mother's interaction.

These studies demonstrate the importance of the context of research, and both give us important information. Yes, mothers do tend to treat siblings similarly when they are alone with each child. But once the second child comes along, mothers rarely have an opportunity to interact with one youngster when the other is not around. Most of the time, therefore, mothers treat siblings differently.

Field Studies

In the study of abused children just described, researchers had to wait for distress to develop naturally. Their results would be more conclusive if they could have set up a situation in a natural setting and then observed children's responses. (The importance of a study's context is discussed in the accompanying box, "Does Methodology Affect Results?") When the investigator introduces some factor into the natural situation that changes it, the research is known as a **field study.** For example, when Laura Adamson and Roger Bakeman (1985) wondered how infants' expression of pleasure during play changed as they grew older, they observed infants playing in their homes. But they set up the situation beforehand, making arrangements with the babies' mothers so that the babies could be observed playing

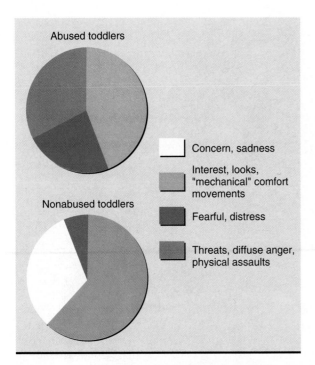

Abused toddlers

Nonabused toddlers

Concern, sadness

Interest, looks, "mechanical" comfort movements

Fearful, distress

Threats, diffuse anger, physical assaults

Figure 1.2 Responses of abused toddlers and disadvantaged toddlers to the distress of other children. The figures indicate the average proportion of responses falling into each category. *(From Main and George, 1985, p. 410)*

alone with specific toys provided by the researchers, playing with their mothers, and playing with another baby. When Adamson and Bakeman examined videotapes of the babies' play, they found that 6-month-old babies showed their pleasure by squealing, smiling broadly, or waving their arms but that 18-month-old babies usually expressed their pleasure vocally. They also found that babies of any age were more likely to show pleasure in social play than in playing by themselves and that babies communicate their pleasure more openly to their mothers than to another baby. Adamson and Bakeman concluded that babies use expressions of pleasure as greetings, as social communication, and as a means of communicating about some object.

Interview Studies

In an **interview study,** the investigator asks questions of the subjects and then analyzes the replies. The same method can be applied in a standardized way to each subject, or the psychologist can vary the approach. The nature of the interview depends on the purpose of the study. Sometimes the interview takes the form of a questionnaire; sometimes a researcher talks separately with each subject; sometimes the researcher spends many hours interviewing each subject in considerable depth. The interviews may be used to establish some aspect of development or to evaluate individuals. This method may provide subjective information on attitudes and feelings, or it may provide objective data—or both.

Researchers have used in-depth interviews, often supplemented by observation and questionnaires, to explore development in children and adults. Jean Piaget (1978), for example, used interviews to study developmental change in the way children thought about problems he asked them to solve. In studying adult development, Daniel Levinson (Levinson et al., 1978) conducted extensive interviews with forty men to explore his theory that men's lives tend to fall into similar patterns. In addition to free-ranging biographical interviews (up to twenty hours with each man), Levinson gave each man a standard psychological test in which the man looked at five pictures and told a story about each one. Then Levinson interviewed the man's wife and, after a lapse of two years, reinterviewed the man himself. From his clinical study, Levinson concluded that he had uncovered a universal pattern of development that characterizes American men today. The pattern may not, however, be universal. Although his subjects came from diverse socioeconomic and religious backgrounds and he included African-American males, the proportion in each group may not have corresponded to the proportion in the society at large. Furthermore, all the men came from the northeastern section of the United States and all were middle-aged, which meant that their descriptions of early adulthood were retrospective. Finally, we have no way of knowing whether the pattern also describes midwestern farmers, northwestern lumberjacks, or Arizona copper miners. Nor do we know whether the pattern is stable and will continue to describe northeastern men in 2000 as it described men in 1975.

Experimental Studies

An **experiment** is the most objective means of testing a hypothesis. It gives the investigator the greatest amount of control over the situation, which can be constructed to eliminate extraneous influences that might be present in a natural setting. In an experiment, researchers examine the effects of selected variables on behavior, controlling and manipulating whatever variable is being studied. Suppose we want to study the effect of aging on memory. We might give young adults and retirees an opportunity to learn word lists and then test the subjects to see how many words each group remembers. The variable that is selected or changed in some way by the investigator is called the **independent variable:** it is independent of whatever subjects do. In our experiment, the independent variable is the word list, which we might vary by changing the number of words in the list, the categories from which the words are drawn, or the amount of study time we allow.

The variable that changes in some way because of the introduction of the independent variable is called the **dependent variable;** it usually is some measure of the subjects' behavior. In our experiment, the dependent variable is the number of words recalled. If we compare the performance of younger and older adults in each condition, we would know something about the effects of aging on memory.

As we follow an actual experiment, we can see how researchers may manipulate the independent variable merely by changing the instructions they give to their subjects. Older children have better memories than young children because they have discovered techniques that help them store information. If we give 12-year-olds a list of words to learn, for example, they repeat the words, several at a time, varying the words on each repetition. This practice is called *active rehearsal.* Seven-year-olds simply repeat the same word over and over. But what if we taught the younger children how to rehearse words the way older children do? Would they remember as many?

Peter Ornstein and his colleagues (1985) tested this hypothesis in an experiment with second- and sixth-graders. Some of the second-graders were given eighteen easy words to learn; the words were printed on index cards, and as the investigators read a word, the children saw it for five seconds. The only instructions they received were to repeat the words aloud. These children represented the **control group** in the experiment. They would be tested on the words, but they would not have the same experimental experience (instruction in active rehearsal) as the other children. The rest of the children made up the **experimental groups**. All of them—both second- and sixth-graders—were given instruction in active rehearsal before they started learning the list. But for half of them the independent variable was manipulated again: they were allowed to see all eighteen words displayed on a board while the words were read aloud. As expected, second-graders in the control group did poorly. Second-graders who got instruction in active rehearsal did somewhat better. But second-graders whose active rehearsal was

supported by viewing all the words throughout the learning period did as well as the sixth-graders. Second-graders apparently need more than instruction in a sophisticated rehearsal technique to equal the performance of older children. Because both groups of sixth-graders remembered about the same number of words, the researchers learned something else from this study. As children develop, the researchers learned, they also gain another skill: the ability to remember the word they are supposed to be rehearsing when the word is not in sight.

Only experiments allow us to study the cause of developmental change directly. In experiments, we assign subjects to the control group or to an experimental group; every person has an equal chance of receiving the treatment. Then, by controlling extraneous variables and manipulating the independent variable, we can discover whether the independent variable caused a particular outcome. At the end of our study, we may conclude that the treatment caused the outcome. Many studies in developmental psychology cannot be done in this manner. Sometimes a controlled experiment would be unethical. Suppose a researcher wanted to know if harsh discipline in the home makes children aggressive. It is neither ethical nor reasonable to ask some parents to treat their children harshly in the interest of developmental research.

This technique points up another problem in developmental research: the nature of the groups being studied. In many developmental studies, the subjects have been assigned to groups on the basis of their past experiences: infants at risk, abused children, children in day care, children with reading problems, single-parent families, juvenile delinquents, unemployed adults, retired workers, or widows. Through circumstance or choice, individuals place themselves in groups, and there is no way to be certain that people in the experimental group do not differ from people in the control group in various ways rather than only on the dimension being investigated.

Correlational Studies

When we have no control over assigning subjects to groups and the study requires that the behavior that interests us be studied in the natural environment, we can carry out a **correlational study**. Such studies can suggest explanations for developmental outcomes, but they do not establish causation. They reveal only that changes between two events are correlated. **Correlation** refers to how closely two factors are related; it

Among older couples, researchers have found a strong correlation between an active sex life and coffee-drinking, but correlation cannot determine which activity is cause and which is effect. *(Herb Snitzer/Stock, Boston)*

describes how changes in one factor are associated with changes in the other. The larger the correlation, the more closely the two factors are related, and the better one factor predicts the other.

Although correlation demonstrates a relationship between factors, it does not establish that either variable *causes* the other. Correlational studies have shown, for example, that older couples who drink coffee have a more active sex life than older couples who do not drink coffee. Before you decide that drinking coffee increases sexual activity and buy your grandparents a pound of coffee, consider other possible interpretations. Perhaps older couples who have an active sex life need coffee to keep them awake during the day. In this case, sexual activity causes coffee drinking. Or perhaps older couples who are healthy and active are more likely to drink coffee *and* engage in sexual activity. In this case, a third factor is causing both coffee drinking and sexual activity. Although correlational studies cannot establish causation, they are extremely valuable because they tell us where to begin looking for explanations.

Developmental Designs

Because development is age-related change, researchers studying developmental issues have to grapple with a problem that is rarely encountered by researchers who investigate other areas of behavior. The problem is to discover whether developmental changes are due to influences that affect most people at the same point in the life span (such as walking, learning to talk, starting school, reaching puberty, or retiring) or whether the changes are due to factors that are not related to development. Sometimes change is due to shifts in the social climate: attitudes, stereotypes, and ideas of acceptable behavior change (Schaie and Hertzog, 1985). Ideas about the nature of infants and children, for example, can have major effects on what we expect of children, on parenting, on the way youngsters are disciplined, and on the experiences that are open to them.

Sometimes change is the result of historical events (such as economic depression, war, television, or computers) that affect all cohorts but affect each cohort somewhat differently. Earlier we saw that growing up during the Great Depression affected boys' development in predictable ways and that preschoolers showed one kind of effect but adolescents showed an entirely different effect. Similarly, cohorts born early in the twentieth century may see computers as little more than an annoyance that makes a nightmare out of attempts to correct mistakes in a credit card statement. But cohorts born toward the end of the century will grow up using computers daily and will find it impossible to think of studying, writing, handling their personal finances, or transacting business without them. Will cohorts who grow up playing computer games show differences from earlier cohorts in memory, reaction time, or psychomotor coordination? No one knows.

When studying development, researchers have used several different designs: cross-sectional, longitudinal, and sequential. Some are less susceptible than others to cohort effects, but each has an important place in the study of development (see Table 1.2).

Cross-Sectional Designs

Most of the information we have on development comes from studies that have used a **cross-sectional design.** In this design, researchers study two or more

Computers are the sort of historical event that affects all members of society but has differing effects on different cohorts. *(Joel Gordon)*

TABLE 1.2   DEVELOPMENTAL DESIGNS

Type	Method	Data Obtained	Advantages	Disadvantages
Cross-sectional design	Observe several cohorts on one occasion.	Age differences in behavior	Is quick and inexpensive	Differences may reflect cohort changes rather than developmental changes
Longitudinal design	Observe one cohort on several occasions.	Changes in behavior with time	Shows developmental trends Shows changes within individuals	Differences may reflect changes in society. Studies are lengthy and expensive. Practice effect and attrition of subjects may affect sample.
Sequential design	Observe several cohorts on several occasions.	Age-related changes in behavior	Reveals effects of age, cohort, and society changes	Studies are lengthy and expensive.

age groups at the same time and compare the results. The comparison may be between different cohorts within the same period of life (6-year-olds and 10-year-olds) or between cohorts in different periods of life (18-year-olds and 60-year-olds). Cross-sectional studies are popular for two reasons: they are relatively inexpensive, and they can be done quickly. Researchers can gather in a few days the sort of information that would require years, even decades, to obtain through other methods. Among the cross-sectional studies already encountered in this chapter is the experimental study on rehearsal techniques. The cross-sectional design can be used with any type of developmental study.

The problem with cross-sectional studies is that there is no way to tell whether differences that appear with age are the result of developmental change or of membership in different cohorts. When cohort effects have a strong influence on the outcome of a study, we may make erroneous assumptions about developmental change. A cross-sectional study of IQ scores through adulthood leads us to assume that IQ scores decline with age, beginning at about the age of 40. But people studied at age 80 in 1990 were born in 1910, and those studied at age 20 were born in 1970. In the time between those cohorts, the cultural and social environment changed in many ways. Those changes may have affected the development and maintenance of intellectual skills. Longer education and mass communication, for example, have exposed more people in each cohort tested to the information and skills in abstract thinking that are required to score well on such tests. What appears to be a dramatic decline in IQ scores over age is in part an effect of the lower test scores for older groups throughout their lives. Age does affect test scores, but many people are well into their seventies before the first measurable age-related decline appears (Schaie, 1990b). When we examine intellectual development in late adulthood, we will return to the issue of cohort effects.

Cross-sectional studies have another limitation: they do not show the pattern of changes within the individual. Each person is tested only once, so we have information only about group differences. Studies show that most children begin putting two words together just before their second birthday, but each child develops at his or her own pace, and no one can predict when a specific child will begin producing sentences. Cross-sectional studies show that personality tends to remain stable across adulthood, yet some individuals show major changes in their personality.

Longitudinal Designs

Individual change can be detected in a **longitudinal design,** in which people from the same cohort are followed over weeks, months, years, or decades. The same people can be compared with themselves at ages 8 and 20. Cohort differences do not affect the results of longitudinal studies, and changes within the individual become clear. Studying development in this way is an expensive and lengthy way to proceed: a research project may take many years to complete.

Several longitudinal studies have been providing valuable information about development. In the Intergenerational Studies, for example, researchers have been following three groups of Californians for more than sixty years (Eichorn et al., 1981). Subjects in two of the three groups have been studied since their births, in 1928 and 1929; those in the third group have been studied since 1931, when they were fifth- and sixth-graders. From information collected on these individuals, we have learned a great deal about intellectual and social development, including factors that affect changes in IQ, political attitudes, personality, emotional stability, sex roles, careers, and marriage. This study also has given us a detailed picture of the effect of two historical events—the Great Depression of the 1930s and World War II—on development (G. H. Elder, 1974, 1986).

Not all longitudinal studies go on for decades. Earlier we discussed Adamson and Bakeman's (1985) study of infant pleasure in play. This was a longitudinal study in which babies were observed every three months over a twelve-month period.

Longitudinal studies escape the errors that cohort differences can cause, but they have their own problems. They may confuse development with changes in the social climate of society. Take the matter of drug and alcohol use. Suppose a longitudinal study found that subjects when tested in 1990 were less favorable to the use of drugs and alcohol than when they were tested twenty years earlier. Is this change the result of aging? Not necessarily. From 1970 to 1990, society changed from regarding drug use as "normal" or "glamorous" to seeing it as dangerous. During the late 1970s, 76 percent of a representative sample of young adults (age 18 to 25) said they used alcohol and 37 percent said they used illicit drugs (Kolata, 1991). By 1990, the proportions had dropped to 63 percent for alcohol and 15 percent for illicit drugs. Thus, historical change affects private behavior.

Another problem that limits the conclusions we can

draw from longitudinal studies has to do with the subjects themselves. When people are tested repeatedly over many years, they may become familiar with the type of tests that are administered. If this happens, their scores show a *practice effect,* so comparisons with earlier scores may not be completely valid. And in lengthy longitudinal studies, the people in poorest health begin to die and others move away or refuse to take part in further testing. Survivors tend to be healthier, be more intelligent, and have larger incomes and higher-ranking occupations than the subjects who are lost (Schaie and Hertzog, 1982). This produces an unrepresentative sample with higher-than-average scores and may lead us to underestimate the debilitating effects of age.

Sequential Designs

What can researchers do to escape the weaknesses of cross-sectional and longitudinal designs? Some investigators have suggested combining both designs in a single study, which they call a **sequential design** (P. Baltes, Reese, and Nesselroade, 1977).

A sequential study directed by Warner Schaie (1983) led to the realization that IQ scores do not decline drastically with age. This project, known as the Seattle Longitudinal Study, began in 1956 with a cross-sectional group of 500 men and women between the ages of 21 and 70. The group was tested again in 1963, 1970, and 1977. On each occasion, another cross-sectional group was added to the study, also to be tested at subsequent points. In addition, researchers tested two different cross-sectional groups toward the close of the study: one in 1974 and the other in 1975. Testing these last two groups allowed the researchers to discover whether the performance of the longitudinal group had been affected by repeated testing.

Schaie concluded from his research that the "most efficient design" combines cross-sectional and longitudinal testing in a systematic manner (Schaie and Hertzog, 1982). First, two or more cohorts are tested in a cross-sectional study. After several years, the same cohorts are retested, providing longitudinal data. At the same time, a new cross-sectional study repeats the earlier study on new groups from the original cohorts and on a group from a new cohort (see Figure 1.3).

Like longitudinal designs, sequential designs are expensive and time-consuming. Which design a researcher chooses depends on the kind of information the researcher is seeking. Cross-sectional and longitudinal studies provide valuable information, as long as investigators are sensitive to the factors that might be affecting their results.

Using a variety of designs and methods increases the confidence that researchers have in their findings. As noted earlier, replicating a study increases confidence in its results; when research results are verified by researchers using a different method or design, psychologists' confidence in their results also is bolstered. In fact, the more ways in which a finding can be verified, the more confident they are. When the various designs and methods yield the same general findings, we can put some confidence in the developmental change that has been described and the conclusions of the researchers.

The Field of Developmental Psychology

Developmental psychology began in biography. During the seventeenth and eighteenth centuries, a number of parents wrote detailed accounts of their babies' first few years. Some of these baby biographies were sentimental, but others, such as the account written by Charles Darwin (1809–1882) about his son Doddy's development, were careful descriptions of growth and development. Other scientific baby biographers were influenced by Darwin, whose theory led to a scientific interest in childhood (Kessen, 1965). The child became the prototype for the species, and scientists began to draw parallels between the child and our earliest ancestors.

These ideas influenced G. Stanley Hall (1844–1924), who developed the first scientifically based picture of child development and established child and adolescent development as a field of study (White, 1992). Hall introduced European psychological theories and methods to the United States and applied them to development. Hall and his students were responsible for early research in the areas of mental testing, early childhood education, adolescence, life-span developmental psychology, evolutionary influences on development, and child study (Cairns, 1983).

During the first two decades of the twentieth century, there were virtually no developmental psychologists. Most scientific research in child development was done by general psychologists. A few years after the first child-development research center was set up in Iowa in 1917, developmental research was spurred by grants from charitable foundations, made in the hope that stud-

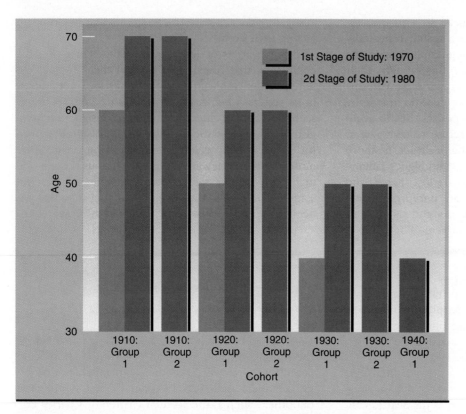

Figure 1.3 Schaie's "most efficient" sequential design combines cross-sectional and longitudinal studies in a systematic way. In this study of intelligence across the last half of life, the first stage of the study is cross-sectional, comparing three groups of people, age 40 to 60. Ten years later, (1) the same people are retested, providing longitudinal data, (2) new groups of people from the original cohorts are tested, providing new cross-sectional data, and (3) a group from a new cohort (born in 1940) is tested to make the cross-sectional data comparable. What might we conclude if the results from the first and second cross-sectional studies are not the same?

ies would discover ways to prevent social ills (Smuts, 1985). Over the next twenty years, research in child development expanded rapidly, but little attention was paid to adult development (Birren and Birren, 1990). Although medical research into aging was under way, and researchers in Germany had been studying adulthood since the 1930s, not until after World War II was any major research center devoted to the study of aging.

During the second half of the twentieth century, developmental psychologists became interested in the entire life span and in aspects of adult development that were not related to aging. By 1975, developmentalists were expanding their study of development within the family. Instead of seeing the family as a household unit at one point in time, they began considering it as a process that extended throughout the lives of its members. Interest grew in the historical aspects of the family, and researchers began looking at the influence of cohorts and historical time on development (Hareven, 1985).

Careers in Developmental Psychology

As the field has grown, developmental psychologists have come to work in a wide variety of situations. They may conduct research; teach in colleges; or work in schools, clinics, businesses, or foundations. Some specialize in disseminating information about development to the public.

Researchers in developmental psychology usually are on university faculties, although they may carry out their research in schools, hospitals, or the community. They generally specialize in studying a particular age group and focus on a particular area of research. One researcher may specialize in perception in young babies, for example; another may focus on the effects of heredity on development, another on the effects of the family on the competence of preschool children, another on the development of memory in school-age children, and yet another on the effects of various environments on the competence of older adults. Some developmental psychologists do not work with people at all, but do their research with animals, hoping to find parallels to human development in the development of monkeys, kittens, or other species. The accompanying list of developmental journals gives an idea of the vast amount of research done today (see Table 1.3). Because development is influenced at various levels, developmental psychologists often conduct their research in collaboration with physicians, nutritionists, endocrinologists, physiologists, sociologists, psychiatrists, or anthropologists.

Developmental psychologists also serve as consultants to business and industry. They might develop children's television programs, for example, or advise companies on the design of toys or consult with schools, textbook publishers, and government agencies. They might work for foundations, where they would be concerned with research, training, and services related to the foundation's various programs connected with a developmental area such as birth defects.

Using Developmental Psychology

Information about human development is used in many ways. General information comes from basic research, in which potential practical applications of the knowledge gained are not a primary consideration of the investigator. A researcher might, for example, be concerned with whether babies can perceive color. Whether a young baby sees the world in shades of gray or in color is a fascinating question, but the information has no immediate use. At other times, developmentalists use research to advance practical goals. In the field of infancy, for example, researchers have developed ways of coaching parents of premature infants, in the hope of preventing destructive interaction patterns between parent and child (T. Field, 1983). Premarital training programs have been devised to train couples in communicating and problem solving, in the hope of making marriages less vulnerable to divorce (Ridley et al., 1981). A program that teaches coping skills to residents of nursing homes has resulted in healthier, happier older adults whose success in managing daily events has

TABLE 1.3   DEVELOPMENTAL JOURNALS

Adolescence
Aging and Human Development
Behavior Genetics
Child Development
Child Development Abstracts and Bibliography
Children's Environments Quarterly
Child Study Journal
Cognitive Development
Developmental Neuropsychiatry
Developmental Psychobiology
Developmental Psychology
Developmental Review
Experimental Aging Research
Generations
The Genetic Epistemologist
The Gerontologist
Human Development
Industrial Gerontology
Infant Behavior and Development
Infant Mental Health Journal
*International Journal of Aging and Human
   Development*
International Journal of Behavioral Development
International Journal of Child Abuse
Journal of Abnormal Child Psychology
Journal of Adolescence
Journal of Adolescent Research
Journal of Aging and Social Policy
Journal of Applied Developmental Psychology
Journal of Autism and Developmental Disorders
Journal of Child Language
Journal of Child Psychology and Psychiatry
Journal of Clinical Child Psychology
Journal of Cross-Cultural Psychology
Journal of Early Adolescence
Journal of Experimental Child Psychology
Journal of Family History
Journal of Genetic Psychology
Journal of Geriatric Psychiatry
Journal of Gerontology
Journal of Marriage and the Family
Journal of Pediatric Psychology
Journal of Research on Adolescence
Journal of Women & Aging
Journal of Youth and Adolescence
Language Acquisition
*Merrill-Palmer Quarterly of Behavior and
   Development*
*Monographs of the Society for Research in Child
   Development*
Psychology and Aging
Sage Family Studies Abstracts
Youth and Society

given them a sense of control over their lives (Rodin and Hall, 1987).

The practical application of information about development is not restricted to professionals. Each of us can use information about development to improve our own lives. What we learn about the typical course of development can help us cope with situations that might otherwise seem overwhelming. We find that our problems of choosing a career, selecting a mate, parenting, or coming to terms with aging are not unique, and we begin to see what a wide range of options we can choose among. As we understand the variables that influence human development, we gain insight into our own situation. This insight further widens our choices and opens the way to personal growth.

Studying developmental psychology often provides a new way of looking at development. A major message of psychology is that human behavior has its antecedents and its consequences, that there is a regularity and a degree of lawfulness in development. After reading this book, you should be able to discover why certain types of behavior occur and how conditions may influence later behavior. You will begin to understand, for example, how temperament, family background, and experiences with peers can interact to produce a person who frequently helps others.

Our investigation of human development will be both chronological and topical. After tracing the course of prenatal development and discovering the newborn's capabilities, we will move through infancy, childhood, adolescence, and adulthood. Within each broad chronological period, we will look separately at cognitive and social development. But before we begin our exploration of the life span, we need to understand the various frameworks that have been used to explain development. These theories make up the content of the next chapter.

SUMMARY

THE NATURE OF HUMAN DEVELOPMENT

Development, the process of age-related change over the life span, is the result of the **interaction** of heredity and environment. Development is continuous, cumulative, directional, differentiated, organized, and holistic. In studying development, psychologists have five goals: description, comparison, explanation, prediction, and the relation of their findings to the work of other disciplines. Societies may use biological, cognitive, or social markers to divide the life span. In the United States, the divisions are the **prenatal period, infancy, childhood, adolescence,** and **adulthood.** Developmentalists disagree about whether development is stagelike (and therefore discontinuous) or continuous (and therefore quantitative instead of qualitative). In its strict usage, a developmental **stage** is structured, it displays qualitative change, it appears abruptly, and the distinguishing abilities and behavior develop concurrently.

DETERMINANTS OF DEVELOPMENT

Developmentalists agree that behavior depends on the interaction between nature and nurture, but they may disagree about the nature of the interaction in specific areas of development. Biological determinants (nature) may be **species-specific influences,** affecting all members of a species, or the result of a person's individual genetic heritage. Only **identical twins** have precisely the same genetic heritage; **fraternal twins** share the same proportion of genes as other siblings. Environmental determinants (nurture) may be physical or social. They may also be individual, consisting of idiosyncratic experiences, or they may be general, consisting of the shared environment. The effects of historical events on development depend on a person's **cohort,** since the nature of an event's influence varies, depending on a person's age at the time of the event.

RESEARCH METHODS IN DEVELOPMENTAL PSYCHOLOGY

In studying development, researchers form a **hypothesis** about the way a determinant might act and then test it by gathering information about the effect of environmental **variables** on behavior. The results of a study are supported when other researchers **replicate** the findings. **Observational studies** may be **naturalistic studies,** in which researchers observe without changing the situation, or **field studies,** in which they introduce some factor into the natural situation. **Interview studies** may consist of questionnaires, brief interviews, or in-depth interviews, supplemented by observation and questionnaires. An **experiment** is the most objective means of testing a hypothesis, because it allows researchers to control the presence, absence, or intensities of different variables. In an experiment, researchers change the **independent variable** and observe its effect on the **dependent variable** (some measure of the subjects' behavior). The behavior of individuals in the **experimental group** is compared with that of individuals in the **control group,** who are not exposed to the experimental condition. When researchers have no control over assigning individuals to groups, they rely on **correlational studies,** in which **correlations** suggest explanations but do not establish causation.

Because development occurs over time, researchers are also concerned as to whether observed change is the result of development, of historical events, or of changes in society's attitudes and beliefs. **Cross-sectional designs,** in which researchers study more than one age group at a single time, may be flawed by cohort effects. **Longitudinal designs,** in which researchers follow a single age group for a period of time, may be affected by changes in society. **Sequential designs,** which combine longitudinal and cross-sectional studies, are least likely to be affected by the factors that confound other research designs.

THE FIELD OF DEVELOPMENTAL PSYCHOLOGY

Developmental psychologists work in a variety of settings, conducting research, teaching, counseling individuals who need special assistance, and serving as consultants to schools, business, and industry. Most researchers specialize in a particular age group and a particular area of development. Researchers may conduct basic developmental research, in which the potential value of their findings is not a primary consideration, or applied research, in which the purpose is to advance practical goals. Underlying the study of development are the convictions that behavior has antecedents and that development is regular and lawful.

KEY TERMS

adolescence	experiment	longitudinal design
adulthood	experimental group	naturalistic study
childhood	field study	observational study
cohort	fraternal twins	prenatal period
control group	hypothesis	replicate
correlation	identical twins	sequential design
correlational study	independent variable	species-specific influences
cross-sectional design	infancy	stage
dependent variable	interaction	variable
development	interview study	

THEORIES OF DEVELOPMENT

● ● ● ● ● ● ● ● ● ● ● ● ● ●

BIOLOGICAL THEORIES

Maturational theories
Ethological theories

PSYCHODYNAMIC THEORIES

Freud's psychosexual theory
Erikson's psychosocial theory

LEARNING THEORIES

Conditioning theories
Cognitive social-learning theories

COGNITIVE THEORIES

Piaget's cognitive-developmental
theory
Theories of social cognition
Information-processing theories

CULTURAL-CONTEXTUAL THEORIES

Vygotsky's socio-historical theory
Bronfenbrenner's ecological theory

UNDERSTANDING HUMAN
DEVELOPMENT

SUMMARY

KEY TERMS

The advice given American parents who seek help in rearing their children has varied dramatically over the past sixty years. During the 1920s, pamphlets published by the U.S. Children's Bureau urged parents to curb their babies' sensuous impulses. Parents were to stamp out thumb-sucking by sewing mittens over the ends of nightgown sleeves or by pinning the tiny sleeves to the crib sheet. And they were to eliminate masturbation by tying little feet to bars on opposite sides of the crib, so babies could not get pleasurable sensations by rubbing their thighs together. Ten years later, concern had shifted to another area of child rearing. Parents were told that they must not permit their babies to run the household. If infants were dry, full, and not being stuck by a pin, said the experts, let them cry it out; otherwise, parents would be ruled by their babies' whims. Government experts who advised parents during the 1940s were not horrified by thumb-sucking and masturbation, but they were still uncomfortable with these activities. Now the advice was to distract the baby with a toy whenever a thumb wandered into the mouth or a little hand strayed to the genitals. At last, however, parents were permitted to pick up a crying child (Wolfenstein, 1955).

During the 1950s, experts no longer talked about stifling babies' impulses and attempts at tyranny. Instead, the basic message was "enjoy your baby." Parents were told that development follows a biological plan, one that is deflected only by severe deprivation. Babies would regulate themselves, and parents need only be warm and loving and alert to their babies' needs.

Today the message is slightly different. Parents are still urged to be warm and loving and sensitive to their babies' needs, but they are advised to provide stimulation as well. Now that research has established the baby's great ability to learn, experts talk about infant capabilities and how parents can develop social and intellectual skills by talking to their babies and playing games with them. Over the past few decades, most of the restrictions and fears that alarmed our grandparents have been banished from the nursery. How did they get there in the first place? And why do experts say one

Today's parents are advised to provide intellectual stimulation to their infants and young children. *(Michal Heron/Woodfin Camp & Associates)*

thing to one generation of parents and something quite different to the next?

The answer to both questions is the same: over the years, theories of development change, and the advice of experts generally reflects whichever theory of development happens to be most influential at the time (Young, 1990). A **theory** is a network of logically related statements that generates testable hypotheses and explains some aspects of experience.

How important are theories? Without theories, we would have only a collection of facts without any kind of interpretation. The logical statements of theories indicate which facts are most important for interpreting development and show how our facts about development fit together. Because every theory is built on certain assumptions, theories act like a lens, filtering out certain facts and arranging the others in a particular pattern (R. Thomas, 1979). The lens both helps to organize the facts and influences their interpretation.

Theories are important for another reason: they guide research. A good theory leads to hypotheses about development. As we saw in Chapter 1, before we can design a study that will tell us something about development, we must have a hypothesis to test—a prediction concerning the relation among the facts we observe. Thus, theories are also important because they enable us to predict the outcome of situations—in life as well as in the laboratory. As we consider the major developmental theories, try to see how each theory filters out some facts and focuses on others.

In this chapter, we explore the major developmental theories, noting the perspective of each. In biological theories of development, the evolutionary history of the species and the maturation of the individual are the dominant factors in development. Psychodynamic theories spring from Sigmund Freud's insights into human motivation and sexual development. Learning theorists focus on the role of environmental experiences. Cognitive theorists, by contrast, focus on the activities of the learner and the processes of thought. Cultural-contextual theories look at the interaction between the individual and the environment, stressing the way that development is altered by historical and cultural influences. The chapter closes by explaining why the different perspectives are difficult to compare and showing how each addresses important developmental issues.

Biological Theories

Biological theories lean to the nature side of the nature-nurture question, although they recognize the necessary interactions that must occur between the developing person and the environment. All biological theories have been heavily influenced by the ideas of Charles Darwin, which led many developmentalists to look at behavior from an evolutionary perspective. Some biological theories emphasize the maturation of the individual, and others focus on the way biologically based behavior increases the child's chances of surviving.

Maturational Theories

Developmentalists who propose **maturational theories** believe that development is directed from within, unfolding according to a biological timetable. The major advocate of the biological approach to development was Arnold Gesell. Gesell believed that capabilities appeared when children reached the appropriate stage of maturity. No matter how many opportunities a child had to learn some skill, until muscles, nerves, brain, and bones were ready, all attempts to teach the child would be futile. Some children walked, talked, and developed self-control early, and some were much slower, but each capability appeared when the child was ready to acquire it.

This belief was accompanied by a faith in self-regulation. Gesell believed that children indicate when they are ready for some developmental step. A newborn baby knows when she is hungry, an older infant knows when she is ready to talk, and so on. If parents follow their babies' signals, instead of trying to impose their own expectations, family life runs more smoothly. As you can see, this advice is similar to the message from government experts during the 1950s—that you should stop worrying and enjoy your baby.

Like many developmentalists, Gesell believed that development went through a series of stages, with periods of smooth, coordinated behavior sandwiched between transitional periods of unstable behavior, when a child first acquired new ways of doing things and then consolidated them. This process was common to all aspects of development—physical coordination, temperament, personality, and intellectual skills.

Although most psychologists agree that maturation plays an important role in early development, they believe that Gesell's position does not give enough importance to learning, and that its reliance on maturation leaves little room for the study of developmental processes (Thelen and Adolph, 1992). Some contemporary psychologists are influenced by Gesell's views, but many believe that optimal development requires an environment that is more than simply adequate: it must be directive, supportive, didactic, and challenging.

Ethological Theories

A group of dedicated naturalists who sought to observe development in its natural settings have brought

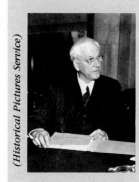
the ideas of Charles Darwin and the methods of behavioral biology into the field of developmental psychology. They have developed **ethological theories,** which translate biological evolutionary concepts into behavioral terms in order to study human development. Konrad Lorenz and Niko Tinbergen, who worked primarily with animals, pioneered this way of studying behavior. Together with Karl von Frisch, they received the Nobel prize for their research in 1973.

When seen from the ethological viewpoint, human behavior is best understood by the way it enables babies, children, and adults to survive and flourish in an environment similar to the one in which our species evolved. When psychiatrist John Bowlby (1969) examined the bond between infant and mother, for example, he concluded that it was part of a behavioral system that had evolved to protect the developing organism. Because human infants are helpless for so long, their survival depends on protection by mature members of the species. The attachment of babies to their caregivers promotes survival by generally keeping the pair in close proximity. Although attachment is expressed in varying ways in different cultures, some variety of bond between infant and caregiver has been present in every society studied.

If babies develop attachments to keep them near adults, what sort of evolved response guarantees that the adult caregiver will care for a baby's needs? Ethologists believe that the baby's smile, the baby's cuteness, and the baby's cry act as **releasing stimuli,** which are events that regularly evoke certain behavior in members of a species. Darwin (1872/1955) first pointed out that the baby's smile evokes feelings of joy in the caregiver, a "released" response that tends to keep the caregiver nearby. Lorenz (1942–1943) has noted that in most species, adult animals respond to very young animals with caregiving—yet they rarely respond this way to other adults. In fact, most people respond to cuteness in babies and baby animals by wanting to pick them up and cuddle them. Young animals are cute because they have relatively large heads, particularly foreheads, and foreshortened facial features. This combination of features apparently acts as a releasing stimulus, improving the chances of adequate infant care and survival. Finally, the baby's cry also serves as a releaser (Hinde, 1983). Cries may not release joy or an urge to cuddle, but they are extremely effective in bringing an adult to the infant's side.

Ethologists also have noted remarkable similarity in the social behavior of human beings and their nearest primate relatives. This resemblance has led them to see the structure of children's play groups as formed by evolved behavior. These groups invariably have **dominance hierarchies,** in which members are ranked in terms of dominance and submission. These hierarchies are so similar to those that characterize monkey and ape troops that they may have the same evolutionary source (Rajecki and Flanery, 1981). Children climb the domi-

Ethologists regard the infant's cry as a releasing stimulus that brings aid and comfort from adults. *(David Grossman/Photo Researchers)*

nance ladder by means of physical attack, threats, or struggles over objects.

Ethological theories suggest that human development is best understood by looking at behavior as partially the product of our evolutionary history. This approach has been most useful when it is applied to infancy, although developmentalists have also begun to look at older age groups. The research method developed by ethologists, which involves careful observation in natural settings, has been adopted by investigators in many areas of developmental psychology.

Psychodynamic Theories

Most psychodynamic theories discuss human development in terms of various confrontations between the growing individual and the demands of the social world. They emphasize how the individual must accommodate to society while gratifying basic human drives. Most also emphasize that the child gradually develops a sense of self, an identity against which to judge his or her own behavior.

As a group, psychodynamic theorists have centered their attention on personality development. Their concern has been to understand and explain the development of both rational and irrational feelings and behavior. To some extent, all psychodynamic theorists have tried to account for human development by looking at early sexual and emotional experiences that may influence later behavior.

Freud's Psychosexual Theory

As Sigmund Freud (1905/1955) saw it, from earliest infancy human beings are motivated by irrational urges toward pleasure. These urges are an expression of the **libido,** which is the "life force" or "psychic energy" that motivates human behavior. The young child's instincts inevitably conflict with social demands, forcing the youngster to alter his or her behavior in socially acceptable ways. Out of this continual conflict, rational behavior gradually develops. In Freud's view, intelligence or adaptation is much less important than a sensuality that has become socialized.

Freud proposed the existence of three conflicting aspects of human personality: the id, the ego, and the superego. In the **id** reside all the **unconscious** impulses; the person is unaware of these forces. The newborn baby is pure id. The **ego,** which begins to develop when a baby is about 6 months old, guides a person's realistic coping behavior. It uses memory, reason, and judgment in its task, which is to mediate the eternal conflicts between what one wants to do (the province of the id) and what one must or must not do (the province of the superego). The **superego** is the conscience, which develops in early childhood as a child internalizes parental values and standards of conduct.

Freud's **psychosexual theory** of development is a stage theory that ties psychological development to the resolutions of the conflicts that characterize each stage of life (see Table 2.1). The five stages of the theory are the *oral stage* (birth to 18 months), the *anal stage* (18 months to 3 years), the *phallic stage* (3 to 6 years), *latency* (6 to 11 years), and the *genital stage* (from puberty onward). In each of the major stages, the pleasures of the libido are focused on a different area of the body.

Because Freud saw personality as determined by the conflicts of infancy and early childhood, his writings stress development during the first three stages of life. If these stages are excessively gratifying or if the drive is unsatisfied, the growing child becomes **fixated** at that stage, which means that the concerns of that stage dominate the adult personality. Among individuals who be-

SIGMUND FREUD
(1856–1939)

(Edmund Engelman)

Sigmund Freud's theories reflect his training in the biological sciences and his clinical experience. He specialized in physiology, received his M.D. degree in Vienna in 1881, and began lecturing and doing research in neuropathology. A grant enabled him to go to Paris and study under the famous neurologist Jean Martin Charcot, who was using hypnosis to treat hysteria.

Freud became interested in personality when he realized that many of his patients' physical symptoms were caused by mental or emotional factors. This led to his development of free association and dream interpretation as therapeutic methods. He found that his adult neurotic patients had repressed their memories of early childhood emotional experiences, which generally involved sex, aggression, or jealousy. Because these experiences were so unpleasant, Freud proposed that they became lost to awareness; that is, they were pushed into an unreachable area of the mind, the unconscious.

In his theory of psychosexual development, he interpreted what he learned from treating his patients in the light of embryology and physics. He proposed that the emergence of psychosexual stages was primarily determined by maturation and that mental life followed the law of the conservation of energy, which states that energy cannot be created or destroyed, only transformed. People's mental and emotional lives, he believed, show a comparable transformation of psychic energy from one stage to the next. This energy motivates people's thinking, their perceptions, and their memories, and it remains constant even though it becomes associated with different regions of the body during development.

come orally fixated, oral concerns such as smoking or overeating will be present throughout life. Fixation at the anal stage produces excessive orderliness or excessive sloppiness, or some mixture of the two.

Freud saw the third, or phallic, stage of development as most important. During this period, a boy develops a close relationship to his mother, wanting to have her to himself. He wishes to marry her and do away with his father, whom he sees as a rival. Although he loves his father and needs his protection, the boy fears that his powerful father will punish him with castration for his lustful and murderous impulses. The boy resolves his conflicts by repressing his desires and identifying with his father. In the process, the boy takes on the male gender role and internalizes his parents' moral standards, thereby developing a superego. From this point, if he deviates from his internalized moral standards, he will suffer guilt. Freud called this period the "Oedipal period" after the prince of Greek myth who inadvertently murdered his father and married his mother. Although Freud developed a parallel description of a girl's development during the phallic stage, he was never satisfied with his account of female development, and few developmentalists find it acceptable.

In Freud's view of development, the latency period is a lull between the important phallic and genital stages, a time when the libido is quiescent and not much hap-

pens. Other developmentalists see latency as an important period during which children develop skills and a sense of competence, but these aspects of development were not of concern to Freud. The genital stage marks the attainment of adult sexuality, but because of his focus on the early stages of development, Freud paid little attention to its significance.

Few developmental psychologists now see development in terms of Freud's theory. For one thing, Freud constructed his theory from his observations of psychiatric patients. Such a sample is so unlike the normal population that it is likely to produce a distorted picture of development. Despite the limitations of his sample, some of Freud's insights into personality are still widely accepted. Many developmentalists accept the following proposals: (1) Early experiences influence later personality even when the events are not remembered; (2) early experiences that are recalled by children may be distorted because children do not understand much of what happens to them during their early years and they may confuse dreams with reality; (3) many human motivations are unconscious; (4) people cope with anxiety with common strategies known as **defense mechanisms.** Among the common defense mechanisms are *repression,* in which we push unbearable thoughts into the unconscious; *rationalization,* in which we manufacture an acceptable reason for doing something we

TABLE 2.1   FREUD'S PSYCHOSEXUAL DEVELOPMENTAL STAGES

Age*	Psychosexual Stage	Focus of Pleasurable Feelings	Characteristic Behavior	Unfavorable Outcome (Fixation)
Birth to 18 months	Oral	Mouth, lips	Seeks oral stimulation Sucks although not hungry	Alcoholism, smoking, nailbiting Immature, demanding personality
18 months to 3 years	Anal	Rectum	Enjoys expelling and retaining feces	Highly rigid conformism Compulsive neatness, miserliness Hostile, defiant personality
3 to 6 years	Phallic	Genitals	Fondles genitals Falls in love with parent of other sex	Sexual problems (impotence, frigidity) Homosexuality Inability to handle competition
6 to 11 years	Latency	—	—	—
From puberty onward	Genital	Genitals	Engages in mature sexual relationships	—

*Ages approximate.

want to do (or did) but know we shouldn't; and *projection,* in which we see an unacceptable aspect of ourselves (such as hostility) in others but not in ourselves.

Erikson's Psychosocial Theory

Erik Erikson (1982) heavily modified Freud's psychoanalytic theory, turning it into an elaborate stage theory that describes emotional development across the life span. In Erikson's **psychosocial theory,** personality develops through a progressive resolution of conflicts between needs and social demands. At each of eight stages, conflicts must be resolved, at least partially, before progress can be made on the next set of problems (see Table 2.2). The goal is not to eliminate the defeated quality (such as mistrust or despair) from the personality but to shift the balance so that the healthy quality (such as trust or integrity) becomes dominant

(Erikson and Hall, 1987). At any stage, a failure to resolve the conflict can result in psychological disorders that affect the rest of the life span.

Stages of Childhood
Babies need to develop a sense of *trust,* which grows out of constant, reliable care from a person who is ready and able to provide it—almost always a mother. Once babies have developed basic trust, they can learn to tolerate frustrations and delay immediate gratifications. Babies whose needs are not consistently met may develop a sense of *mistrust* and react to frustration with anxiety and upset.

As toddlers begin to walk and to exercise some self-direction, they run into social restraints. During this second stage, they increasingly demand to determine their own behavior. Their task is to develop *autonomy* (a sense of self-control and self-determination) while

TABLE 2.2   ERIKSON'S PSYCHOSOCIAL STAGES*

Age†	Psychosocial Stage	Psychosocial Conflict	Favorable Outcome	Unfavorable Outcome
Birth to 18 months	Infancy	Basic trust vs. mistrust	Hope Ability to tolerate frustration, delay gratification	Suspicion; withdrawal
18 months to 3 years	Early childhood	Autonomy vs. shame, doubt	Will Self-control; self-esteem	Compulsion; impulsivity
3 to 6 years	Play age	Initiative vs. guilt	Purpose Enjoyment of accomplishments	Inhibition
6 to 11 years	School age	Industry vs. inferiority	Competence	Inadequacy; inferiority
Puberty to early twenties	Adolescence	Identity vs. role confusion	Fidelity	Diffidence, defiance; socially unacceptable identity
Early twenties to 40	Young adulthood	Intimacy vs. isolation	Love	Exclusivity; avoidance of commitment
40 to 60 years	Middle adulthood	Generativity vs. stagnation	Care Concern for future generations, for society	Rejection of others; self-indulgence
From 60 years onward	Old age	Integrity vs. despair	Wisdom	Disdain; disgust

*Erikson's first four stages correspond to Freud's psychosexual stages, but Erikson has subdivided Freud's fifth stage into four stages.
†Ages approximate. Erikson (Erikson and Hall, 1987) recently suggested that the period of generativity may last much longer today, now that adults remain healthy and active until an advanced age.

avoiding the *shame* that may fester when they are made to feel incompetent. Because they have little judgment about their actual capabilities, they need to be gently protected from excesses while granted autonomy in those matters that they can handle.

Children in the preschool years are in the third stage of development and are ready to develop *initiative* while avoiding the *guilt* that the development of conscience makes possible. As Erikson sees it, initiative adds to autonomy the quality of undertaking, planning, and attacking a task for the sake of being active and on the move. Harsh parental responses to a child's sexual overtures and other initiatives during this period (which corresponds to Freud's phallic stage) can lead to an overdeveloped, harsh conscience that may always plague the person with guilt.

About the time children go to school, they enter the fourth stage of development, in which their task is to develop *industry* while avoiding feelings of *inferiority*. Industry, which is essentially the realization that they will gain recognition by producing things, fosters the desire to learn the technical skills that characterize

(Olive R. Pierce/Black Star)

ERIK ERIKSON
(1902–   )

Erik Erikson was born in Germany of Danish parents. After graduating from art school, he went to Florence, Italy, intending to become an art teacher. In Vienna, where he had gone to teach children of American families, he met Freud and other analysts and soon entered psychoanalytic training.

When Hitler came to power in Germany, Erikson emigrated to the United States. He held a series of positions in child-guidance clinics and major universities while maintaining a private practice. During an appointment at Harvard University, Erikson devel-

oped an interest in anthropology and studied the Sioux and Yurok Indians. During a subsequent appointment at the University of California, he studied 10- to 12-year-olds, using a technique in which the way children played with toys revealed their unconscious thoughts and feelings.

Erikson is one of the few people to describe emotional development across the life span. He suggested that Freud's psychosexual theory was incomplete and proposed additional stages to cover middle and late adulthood. His own psychosocial theory is important for several reasons. Unlike Freud, he believes that neuroses are not necessarily the result of problems in infancy and early childhood. He emphasizes the healthy personality instead of the disturbed individual. He includes society and history as well as the family among forces affecting emotional development.

adults and prepares children to take on adult roles. If children are not praised for their accomplishments, they may instead develop a sense of inadequacy and inferiority.

Stages of Adolescence and Adulthood

In the fifth stage, adolescents question all their previous resolutions to problems of trust, autonomy, initiative, and industry. Rapid body growth and genital maturation create a "physiological revolution" within them as they stand on the brink of adulthood. They are searching for a sense of *identity,* a continuity and sameness within themselves, while avoiding the *role confusion* that can develop in young people who do not learn who they are as people, as sexual beings, as adult workers, as potential parents. If the search for identity fails, they will be unable to commit themselves to any goal.

Young adults emerging from the search for identity are ready to develop *intimacy,* which describes relationships with others in which they are strong enough to make sacrifices for another's welfare without losing themselves in another's identity. At this point, true sexual love can emerge. The potential problem during the young adult stage is *isolation* from others, a failure to commit oneself to loving relationships because of competition or fear.

The stage of middle adulthood focuses on the struggle for *generativity,* which refers to the adult's concern with establishing and guiding the next generation. Merely producing children does not give a person a sense of generativity; adults must see that rearing children contributes to humankind and the larger society. Those who are childless can express generativity through productivity in their work and creativity in their lives. The possible dangers of this period are self-absorption and *stagnation,* a feeling that you are going nowhere, doing nothing important.

The task that dominates the final stage of the life cycle is to develop *ego integrity,* which allows people to see meaning in their lives and believe that they did the best they could under the circumstances. The person with integrity accepts death as the end of a meaningful lifetime. The potential problem of late adulthood is regret and *despair* over wasted chances and unfortunate choices. A despairing person fears death and wishes desperately for another chance.

Although Erikson's theory is complex and vague, researchers have been able to derive hypotheses from it. Longitudinal studies of men through middle adulthood have generally supported the theory, whether the men are Harvard graduates or live in the inner city (Vaillant and Milofsky, 1980). Erikson's theory may, however, describe development across the life span only in indi-

According to Erikson, adults who volunteer for community service are showing generativity, the ego strength that develops during middle age. *(Joel Gordon)*

vidualistic, economically favored societies. Researchers suggest that the model may describe both sexes only in societies that give women the same options that are open to men (Vaillant and Milofsky, 1980).

Learning Theories

The theorists we have just considered, whether maturational or psychodynamic, see development as originating primarily within the person. Developmentalists who take a learning approach see the major influence as coming from the environment. Although they agree that biological factors set limits on the sort of behavior that develops, learning theorists lean toward the nurture side of the nature-nurture question. They believe that experience or learning is responsible for most of what babies become and that learning may begin before the

child leaves the uterus. Because learning theorists reject the notion that development comes primarily from within, they see it as a continuous process—one without stages.

Conditioning Theories

When psychologists explain development by **conditioning theories,** they interpret developmental changes in terms of learning to associate one event with another, through either classical or operant conditioning. These psychologists, whose work is heavily influenced by the theories of behaviorists John B. Watson and B. F. Skinner, believe that conditioning can explain all learning, from how children acquire language to what makes people attend a ballet, cherish free speech, or go to war.

Watson explained learning in terms of classical conditioning. In **classical conditioning,** we learn to associate two events that happen at about the same time. In this form of conditioning, there are no rewards, only a temporal association. Studies of classical conditioning grew out of the work of Ivan Pavlov (1927) in Russia. Pavlov demonstrated that some kinds of behavior, which he called reflexes, were responses to external stimuli. Some reflexes are natural responses to specific stimuli; Pavlov called them **unconditioned reflexes.** We blink an eye, for example, when a puff of air strikes the eyeball, and we salivate when food is placed in the mouth. Other reflexes, which Pavlov called **conditioned reflexes,** are learned by associating a neutral stimulus, such as a bell or light, with an unconditioned stimulus, such as a puff of air or the taste of food.

We learn these conditioned reflexes through the process of classical conditioning, which works in a predictable way. If the conditioned stimulus occurs repeatedly just before the unconditioned stimulus, we come to respond to the conditioned stimulus much as we originally responded to the unconditioned stimulus. If a bright light suddenly shines in your eyes, you will squeeze your eyelids shut. This is a reflexive movement; even a newborn baby behaves this way. Suppose that someone sounds a buzzer and then shines a spotlight in your eyes. After this happens several times, you will squeeze your lids shut each time you hear the buzzer, even though the light never comes on.

Emotions are particularly susceptible to classical conditioning. Parents have noticed this process at work in their children; they commonly observe that by the time their baby is 1 year old, he or she begins to cry at the sight of a nurse who has always been present when the baby got a painful injection.

In **operant conditioning,** we are still learning to connect two events, but one of the events is our behavior. (We "operate" on the environment.) Operant conditioning is also known as *instrumental conditioning,* because our actions are "instrumental" in producing whatever pleasant or unpleasant consequences follow. In this basic kind of learning, which was described and studied by Skinner (1938), any action that is followed by some pleasant consequence or any action that ends some unpleasant situation is strengthened, or "reinforced."

Reinforcement can take many forms. *Positive reinforcement* brings us a pleasant consequence; it includes concrete rewards (such as money, toys, or candy) and intangible rewards (such as affection, praise, attention, or the satisfaction that comes with the completion of a difficult task). Suppose, for example, that a boy sees an adult leave a package behind on a counter. If he receives a reward (a quarter or warm praise) when he runs after the adult and returns the package, the boy will be likely to respond that way again. *Negative reinforcement* removes something unpleasant from our immediate situation. It includes relief from pain, the ending of arguments or cries, or the removal of some barrier that stands between us and what we want. If a baby stops crying when the father picks it up, for example, then the father will be likely to pick up the baby the next time he hears his child crying. Responses that are not reinforced decrease in frequency or may even be eliminated, a process known as **extinction.** If the boy who returned the package gets no reward, he will be less likely to be so helpful in the future; if the baby keeps wailing, the father will be less likely to rush to the crib the next time the baby cries.

When our actions are punished, our tendency to repeat them is weakened. **Punishment** includes any unpleasant consequence, from a spanking or a scolding to the removal of something pleasant, such as the loss of privileges when a teenager is grounded or the loss of money when a speeding motorist is fined.

If we had to experience every situation for conditioning to operate, we would learn very slowly. Yet we learn rapidly, in part because both classical conditioning and operant conditioning generalize to other situations—even when the generalization may be inappropriate. The baby who fears the nurse who gives injections, for example, may come to fear all people in white uniforms or all rooms that look like an examining room. The young child who learns to call mother "Mommy" may also call the caregiver at the day-care center "Mommy."

Few of today's developmentalists use Skinnerian theory to guide their research, but principles derived from Skinner's work explain some behavior that baffles parents. A mother may wonder, for example, why her child seems so dependent on her assistance. A basic Skinnerian principle is that organisms who are reinforced intermittently learn slowly but that once the behavior is learned, it is extremely difficult to extinguish. Now listen to a typical exchange between mother and child:

> *Child: I can't do it. Help me.*
> *Mother: Yes you can, if you try.*
> *Child: Please help me.*
> *Mother: No, do it yourself.*
> *Child: Pleeeeze help me.*
> *Mother: Oh, all right. I will this
>   time.*

The mother thinks that she is discouraging dependency,

but instead she has reinforced dependency by teaching her child that repeated demands for help are eventually rewarded.

Cognitive Social-Learning Theories

Some psychologists considered the radical behavioral approach too narrow and inflexible. They believed that not all learning can be explained as a result of classical and operant conditioning. In its place they developed cognitive social-learning theories, which grew out of earlier conditioning theories but which stress that (1) people learn much of their behavior by watching others and (2) people's expectations, beliefs, self-perceptions, and intentions are important influences on their behavior.

Cognitive social-learning theories have evolved over the past half-century. The earliest researchers described them as simply **social-learning theories,** which gave the process of **imitation** a key role in human development. These researchers noted the increasing resemblance of the child's behavior to that of adult models and focused on the child's imitation of his or her parents. Neal Miller and John Dollard (1941) proposed that nurturance from parents becomes the motivating force for a child's imitations. Because the parents' behavior is reinforcing, the child begins imitating whatever the parent does to reward himself or herself. Other social-learning theorists suggested that the parents' power and status also lead the child to imitate them (Kagan, 1958). The child envies the parents' status and copies them in the hope of gaining some of their power.

Imitation was not the only concern of early social-learning theorists. Dollard and Miller (1950) also looked for similarities between their work and that of psychodynamic theorists. They tried to translate Freudian concepts into the language of social-learning theory, seeing "reinforcement" where Freud saw "pleasure." Dollard and Miller more or less accepted Freud's stages of psychosexual development, but they did not accept his view that specific body sites were the focus of subsequent stages. Instead, they traced personality to the child's typical experiences, the stimuli encountered, the responses made, and the habits that developed. Personality disturbances were the result not of "fixation" but of responses learned by children in situations of conflict between their drives and social pressures.

Social-learning theorists soon broadened their view of imitation, noting that children can learn new responses merely from watching another person (Bandura and Walters, 1963). If children see this model rewarded for some behavior, they are as likely to imitate the behavior as they would be if they had been rewarded themselves.

Children tend to copy a model's complete pattern of behavior, instead of slowly learning bits of a pattern in response to reinforcement. When watching a model, children can learn entirely new behavior, although they might not immediately show it. A 10-year-old girl might, for example, watch a television program in which one child helps another who is in trouble. Although there is no observable change in the watching girl, she may go out of her way a week or two later to offer assistance when she sees a child in need of aid.

Over the years, social-learning theorists have shifted their emphasis in a radical direction, one that takes into account the influence of **cognition,** which encompasses all the processes we use to gain knowledge of the world. Cognitive processes are important because they help determine what events we observe, what meaning we give to them, whether they will leave lasting effects, whether they have power to motivate us, and how we organize for future use the information conveyed by these events. Thus, the stimuli provided by events serve as information that help us decide what we will do. Albert Bandura (1986, 1989b) has been one of the theorists responsible for this new direction; his restated version of social-learning theory is known as **cognitive social-learning theory** because it assumes that thoughts, expectations, beliefs, self-perceptions, goals, and intentions join environmental influences in determining behavior.

Our behavior modifies our expectations, beliefs, and competencies; what is more, it alters the environment. This means, says Bandura (1989b), that people are neither driven by inner forces (as psychodynamic theories imply) nor automatically shaped and controlled by the environment (as conditioning theories imply). At certain times and in certain contexts, one of the three forces may be strongest, but no single force acts in isolation. As children grow, changes occur in the environmental influences that affect them and in their cognitive skills that process these influences (Perry, 1989).

Although cognitive social-learning theorists give human thought and knowledge central importance in explaining development, other cognitive theorists are less interested in learning than in the processes of thought and how cognitive levels affect development.

Cognitive Theories

Cognitive theorists are primarily interested in the development and functioning of the mind. When they turn their attention to some other aspect of development, such as aggression, they explain it in cognitive terms. As we shall see, the approaches and assumptions of various cognitive theorists differ dramatically. During the 1960s and 1970s, the cognitive-developmental theory of Jean Piaget dominated the field. Nearly all research was aimed at extending or refuting his theory. Today, however, researchers tend to use concepts and methods derived from theories of social cognition or information processing (R. Siegler, 1991).

Piaget's Cognitive-Developmental Theory

Piaget produced a stage theory of development in which the child actively constructs his or her knowledge of the world. As the child develops, the mind undergoes a series of reorganizations. With each reorganization, the child moves into a higher level of psychological functioning. These stages are determined by human evolutionary history; children are born with a set of specifically human systems (called *sensorimotor systems*) that allow them to interact with the environment and incorporate experience and stimulation.

Piaget's theory gives meaningful continuity to the development of human understanding. In it, cognition is a spontaneous biological process, and the function and characteristics of thought are like those of digestion and respiration—taking in, modifying, and using whatever elements were needed. Piaget called his approach **genetic epistemology.** Epistemology is the study of knowledge—how we know what we know. The term *genetic* here refers to growth and development. Piaget's theory covers the development of intelligence (ways of knowing) over the life span.

For Piaget, all knowledge comes from action. From birth, babies actively engage and use the environment, and they construct their own understanding of it. For example, babies act on objects around them—feel, turn, bang, and mouth them—and grow in their knowledge of those objects through structuring their own experiences. The baby's knowledge grows neither from the objects themselves nor from the baby but from the in-

---

JEAN PIAGET
(1896–1980)

(Yues de Braine/Black Star)

Jean Piaget was born and reared in Switzerland. As a boy he was a keen observer of animal behavior and, when he was only 15, published a paper on shells in a scientific journal. He came by his interest in knowledge and knowing (epistemology) as a result of studying philosophy and logic. Whereas most American psychologists have been influenced by the evolutionary theories of Charles Darwin, Piaget was influenced by the creative evolution of Henri Bergson, who saw a divine agency instead of chance as the force behind evolution.

After receiving his doctorate in biological science at the University of Lausanne in 1918, Piaget became interested in psychology. In order to pursue his interest in abnormal psychology, he went to Paris and, while studying at the Sorbonne, secured a position in Alfred Binet's laboratory. During his work there, he began to pay more attention to children's wrong answers than to their right ones, realizing that the wrong answers provided invaluable clues to the nature of their thought.

Piaget's interest in children's mental processes shifted and deepened when he began observing his own children from birth. As he kept detailed records of their behavior, he worked at tracing the origins of children's thought to their behavior as babies. Later, he became interested in the thought of adolescents. Piaget's primary method was to present problems in a standardized way to children of different ages. He then asked each child to explain his or her answers and probed these explanations with a series of carefully phrased questions.

Soon after completing his work in Paris, Piaget accepted an appointment as director of research at the Jean Jacques Rousseau Institute in Geneva. He lived in Geneva until his death, conducting research and writing on cognitive development as professor of experimental psychology and genetic epistemology at the University of Geneva.

teraction of the two and the consequent links between actions and objects.

Schemes

In Piaget's view, a child's understanding of the world arises from the coordination of actions and the interrelationships of objects. The infant is a **constructivist,** who constructs reality from the relationships of actions and objects, not simply from actions alone or from the perceptual quality of objects. Infants can, for example, shake a rattle and throw it; they can apply those same actions to a small stuffed bear. When the rattle is shaken, it makes a noise; when it is thrown, it lands with a sharp clatter. But the tiny bear is noiseless when shaken and makes only a soft thud when thrown. Yet the bear can be squeezed, whereas the rattle resists the pressure of the baby's fingers. From such ordinary and simple actions on objects, infants come to know the effects of their actions and the properties of objects. They learn to coordinate their actions—they cannot simultaneously throw and roll an orange, but they can finger it first and then throw or roll it. Grasping, throwing, and rolling are examples of what Piaget called **schemes:** patterns of action that are involved in the acquisition and structuring of knowledge. Action schemes are the infant's form of thought, and in babies they are like concepts without words.

Older children and adults still think in action schemes when they drive a car, type a term paper, or play a piano. But they also have developed internalized action schemes, which are mental operations. Mental operations allow them to manipulate objects mentally, classifying them and understanding their relationships.

Assimilation and Accommodation

According to Piaget, children's thinking develops through two simultaneous processes: assimilation and accommodation. **Assimilation** refers to the incorporation of new knowledge into existing schemes. **Accommodation** refers to the modification of the child's existing schemes to incorporate new knowledge that does not fit them. The processes of assimilation and accommodation always work together in complementary fashion. To assimilate is to use what one already knows how to do; to accommodate is to acquire a new way of doing something. Both processes function throughout the life span.

At any given time, a developing person can change his or her cognitive structures only in a limited fashion. There always must be some continuity. The balance, or

In Piaget's view, to obtain the toy this baby first tries a familiar grasping scheme (assimilation) and then alters it with new knowledge (accommodation) to get the toy through the bars. *(George S. Zimbel/ Monkmeyer Press)*

equilibrium, between assimilation and accommodation is a process of continual readjustment over the life span. **Equilibration** is the most general developmental principal in Piaget's theory; it states that the organism always tends toward biological and psychological balance and that development is a progressive approximation to an ideal state of equilibrium that it never fully achieves. A child's equilibrium at any one stage may be upset by external events, such as new information he or she cannot readily assimilate, or by internal processes that bring the child to a new "readiness" to accommodate. In both cases, the child's previous temporary equilibrium is upset, and development advances to a new, higher stage of organization.

Stages

The organization of behavior is qualitatively different at each stage of Piaget's theory. The two essential points are that (1) stages emerge in a constant order of succession and (2) neither heredity nor environment can by itself explain the progressive development of mental structures.

Piaget proposed four major stages of intellectual development: a sensorimotor stage, a preoperational stage, a concrete-operational stage, and a formal-operational stage (see Table 2.3). The *sensorimotor stage,* which begins at birth and extends through the first two years of life, roughly corresponds to infancy. The *preoperational stage* corresponds to the preschool years. It begins around the age of 2, when children start to record experiences symbolically. This advance indicates the dawn of representational thought, when children can think about objects and people that are not present. The *concrete-operational stage* emerges at about the age of 7, after children in Western cultures have begun formal education. Children now think logically, but only about concrete objects. This allows them to understand logical operations in which they can mentally reverse actions. They can, for example, understand that a flattened ball of clay can be reshaped into its original spherical shape and can think about it as round without actually squeezing it back into a ball. By 11 or 12, young adolescents begin to develop a formal logic and are able to think in terms of propositions ("If . . . then" statements). At this time, they enter the *formal-operational stage,* which Piaget regarded as the culmination of cognitive development. The ages given for each stage are, of course, approximate. For example, although the concrete-operational stage begins at about age 7, many 5- and 6-year-olds already have entered it. Piaget (1972) noted, however, that cultural and subcultural environments affect the speed with which children progress through the stages.

As developmentalists have begun to stress the effect of context, individual differences, and education on children's abilities, Piaget's theory has become less influential than it once was. Its premises are derived from contrived tasks that depend on a child's linguistic abili-

TABLE 2.3 STAGES IN PIAGET'S COGNITIVE-DEVELOPMENTAL THEORY

Age*	Stage	Major Characteristic
Infancy (birth to 2 years)	Sensorimotor	Thought confined to action schemes
Preschool (2 to 7 years)	Preoperational	Representational thought Thought intuitive, not logical
Childhood (7 to 11 years)	Concrete operational	Systematic, logical thought but only in regard to concrete objects
Adolescence and adulthood (from 11 years onward)	Formal operational	Abstract, logical thought

*Ages approximate.

ties and generally neglect educational and socioemotional factors in development. In addition, the theory often underestimates children's abilities (P. Harris, 1983). Yet Piaget's insistence on the active role played by the child in learning about the world remains valid, and his work continues to be influential.

Theories of Social Cognition

As a cognitive-developmental theorist, Piaget sought to explain the development of knowledge. His influence was so extensive, however, that his work affected theories of personality and social development. Many prevalent views of social development include the following Piagetian ideas: (1) the active role of the person in his or her development and (2) the importance of cognition in social development and the development of personality. The way children interpret events in their lives depends on their level of cognitive development. Young children, for example, often interpret the departure of the father at the time of divorce as a response to their own behavior. In one study of divorce (Wallerstein and Blakeslee, 1989), a little boy in one family thought that his father left because the boy's dog was too noisy; a little girl in another family thought her father left because she had failed to deliver a note from one parent to the other. Older children would not interpret the father's departure in this way. Theories influenced by Piaget tend to focus on the development of **social cognition,** the understanding of thoughts, emotions, and behavior—whether our own or those of other people.

Selman's Theory of Peer Relations

Traces of Piaget's cognitive-developmental views can be seen in Robert Selman's stage theory, which charts the development of children's relations with their peers. Selman and his colleagues (Yeates and Selman, 1989) propose that children move through four stages of social competence in peer relations, which reflect an increasing capability to differentiate the perspective of others and to integrate their own perspective with those of another. Most preschoolers are mired in the *impulsive stage*; they cannot distinguish between actions and feelings and do not understand that others may interpret the same behavior differently than they do. To these children, conflict with another person is resolved by the impulsive use of force (fighting, grabbing, or hitting) or by a protective withdrawal (whining, fleeing, hiding). Sometime between the ages of 4 and 9, children begin moving into the *unilateral stage.* Children know that others may have different views of

the same action, but they cannot simultaneously consider their own perspective and that of another. They resolve conflicts by acting unilaterally, either attempting to control the other person (commanding, bullying) or submitting passively to the other person's power (obeying, giving in). The *reciprocal stage* may begin as early as age 6 or as late as age 12. Children in this stage can mentally step outside their own perspective and take the other's view of their own thoughts and actions; they can appreciate both viewpoints but not in relation to each other. They resolve conflicts by making trades, exchanges, or deals, either persuading the other person to go along with their wishes or agreeing to wait until the other person's wishes are met. The final stage, known as the *collaborative stage,* begins sometime between the ages of 9 and 15. Children can see themselves and others as both actor and object, and they are able to coordinate their perspectives with those of another. They resolve conflicts by working with the other person to adjust both parties' wishes in a way that meets mutual goals.

Kohlberg's Theory of Moral Development

Another theorist whose work reflects the influence of Piaget is Lawrence Kohlberg (1969). Kohlberg believed that emotional development parallels cognitive development and that social and emotional development also passes through a series of qualitatively different stages, in which the child restructures the concept of the self in its relationship to concepts of others. In his view, the child's stage of cognitive development determines the child's level of social cognition and thus how the child interprets environmental events and what he or she learns from experiences. Kohlberg is best known for his theory of moral development, which expands Piaget's early work on the development of moral reasoning and judgment.

Kohlberg (1969) proposed that moral reasoning passes through a series of six stages (see Table 2.4). Each succeeding stage builds on the preceding stage, reorganizing the child's earlier understanding into a more complex and balanced view of morality. Children advance through the stages in unvarying progression. They must understand the reasoning typical of one stage before they can begin to understand the greater complexities of the next. Each stage indicates increased skill in taking another person's role, and in each stage children look at moral issues in a new and different way. The proposed six stages form three basic developmen-

TABLE 2.4   **KOHLBERG'S STAGES OF MORAL DEVELOPMENT***

Moral Reasoning	Stage	Dominant Motive
PREMORAL LEVEL		
Values reflect external pressure.	Stage 1	Avoid punishment.
	Stage 2	Serve your own needs and interests.
CONVENTIONAL LEVEL		
Values reflect importance of others' expectations and the need to maintain social order.	Stage 3	Be a good person in the eyes of self and others.
	Stage 4	Avoid breakdowns in the social system.
PRINCIPLED LEVEL		
Values reflect shared principles and standards.	Stage 5	Meet obligation to social contract.
	Stage 6	Adhere to universal moral principles.

*In 1980, Kohlberg and his associates (Colby et al., 1980) revised the stages, merging Stage 6 into Stage 5, although other researchers (Rest, 1983) have retained the six-stage structure.

tal levels of moral reasoning, distinguished by what defines right or moral action.

In Kohlberg's longitudinal study of boys (Colby et al., 1983), premoral reasoning declined after the age of 10, and the use of Stage 3 reasoning began declining in adolescence. Principled reasoning did not appear until the boys reached young adulthood—and it developed in only 10 percent of them. Socioeconomic level and formal education proved to be important factors in movement through the stages, and only college graduates ever reached the principled level.

Because no females were included in Kohlberg's research, some researchers have charged that the theory has a built-in male bias. According to Carol Gilligan (1982), Kohlberg's theory equates moral development with the acceptance of justice, so moral problems arise from competing rights. But women are socialized to equate goodness with helping others and tend to see moral problems as the result of conflicting responsibilities. To them, says Gilligan, the morality of rights and noninterference seems to justify indifference and lack of concern. Women base their moral reasoning on issues of compassion, responsibility, and obligation, which places them at a lower stage on the Kohlberg scale than men. In recent years, however, the scoring system for

Kohlberg's scale has been modified to avoid this problem.

Other criticisms of Kohlberg's theory have focused on its neglect of the fact that moral reasoning depends more on context than the stages suggest, that the theory is culturally biased and expresses the values of a constitutional democracy, and that principled reasoning requires a level of education that places it beyond most of the world's population (Saltzstein, 1983; Simpson, 1974). Studies in peasant or tribal communities, for example, have replicated advancement through lower stages but have found no one who advanced to Stage 4 or beyond (Rest, 1983). Such results do not indicate an absence of advanced moral judgment in these societies but suggest that Kohlberg's theory does not capture moral development across societies.

Information-Processing Theories

Not all cognitive theories are characterized by stages. Cognitive theorists who take an information-processing approach see human beings as manipulators of symbols. People are believed to process information about the world much as another symbol manipulator, the computer does: both take information from the outside world, register the information in symbolic form (a process called *encoding*), combine it with other information, store it, retrieve it, and send it back into the world in a decoded form (see Figure 2.1). Using the precise language developed for computer science, researchers have tried to analyze the way people represent and manipulate information (R. Siegler, 1991).

Unlike Piaget, most adherents of **information-processing theory** see no major change in the structure of the mind as children grow. They believe that thought and behavior are built upon a series of separate processes that manipulate and transform encoded representations (Kuhn, 1988). These processes include recognition, visual scanning of the environment, the analysis of perceptual events into features, learning, and the integration of the senses. With experience, basic capacities increase, and these processes become faster and more efficient.

Each of the processes develops in much the same way. As children develop, mental operations that were once conscious become automatic. Once this *automatization* occurs, children become able to hold and ma-

nipulate more information at one time, which leads to an apparent increase in the basic capacity of the system (Case, 1985). When children read, for example, they must decode the words on the paper and understand what they have decoded. But beginning readers may have to devote so much attention and effort to decoding the words (translating the letters *d-o-g* into the sound "dawg") that there is little space left for comprehending what they have decoded. And even if they understand the word, they may forget it before they can go on to the next word.

Children also develop more efficient methods of storing information and getting it back out again, and they begin to understand how to direct the manipulation of information within the system (Paris and Lindauer, 1982). As these developments take place, children build up a rich network of concepts and a broad knowledge about how things are done (Flavell, 1985). Their knowledge keeps increasing. Indeed, some theorists believe that children's increased knowledge base may underlie many of the apparent changes in the system's basic capacities and control processes. For in-

Figure 2.1 Information from the environment (sights, sounds, touches, tastes, odors) strikes the sensory receptors, which transmit it to the sensory register in the brain. After brief processing, the information enters short-term memory, where it can be encoded, elaborated, and rehearsed. These processes facilitate permanent storage in long-term memory. Unless information in short-term memory is actively processed, it may be lost. When people plan, talk, or act, information is retrieved from long-term memory.

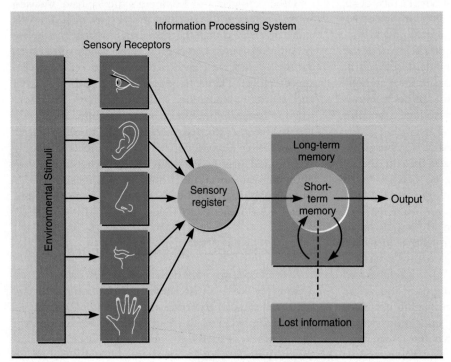

stance, Michelene Chi and Randi Koeske (1983) studied a 4-year-old boy whose knowledge of dinosaurs surpassed that of most adults. The child not only knew the names of forty-six different kinds of dinosaurs but also had an organized store of information about his twenty favorites. He could describe each of them, tell you its nickname, what sort of habitat it lived in, what it ate, how it moved about, and how it defended itself.

Today, many studies of development use an information-processing approach. Although information-processing views were once confined to issues in cognitive development, some researchers have used this framework in the study of personality and social development. In fact, Selman's cognitive-developmental theory of peer relations attempts to integrate information-processing views by specifying information-processing steps (strategy choices) that typify each stage. Other studies that have drawn on information-processing

When children develop an intense interest in a subject, they may amass such a store of knowledge that they are more expert in that area than the average adult. *(Craig Hammell/The Stock Market)*

views indicate, for example, that aggressive boys encode the intentions of other children far less accurately than nonaggressive boys do and that they often encode hostile intent where none exists (Dodge et al., 1986).

Cultural-Contextual Theories

In recent years, an increasing number of developmental psychologists have become convinced that human development should be studied within the contexts in which it naturally occurs. "Contexts" include not simply a person's physical surroundings but also the settings constructed by the people present, what they are doing, and when and where they are doing it (Laboratory of Comparative Human Cognition, 1983). Cultural-contextual theories assume that historical time and culture both have profound effects on many aspects of development. The structure of a society and its institutions set limits on the range of behavior and adaptation of its members. At the same time, the patterns of development that prevail at a given time in any society affect further development and change the context in which younger cohorts develop (R. Campbell and O'Rand, 1988). Two important cultural-contextual theories of development are Vygotsky's socio-historical theory and Bronfenbrenner's ecological theory.

Vygotsky's Socio-historical Theory

In the view of Lev Vygotsky (1978), human development cannot be understood without considering how historical-social changes affect behavior and its development. Knowledge is seen as social, created by society and transmitted to the individual. Major cultural changes (such as those brought about by the introduction of the printing press, cars, computers, and television) may alter how we perceive the world, categorize it, think, and organize our inner consciousness.

Vygotsky generated his socio-historical theory in the Soviet Union, where he lived in a political climate that required him to create a theory of human behavior that was Marxist, dialectical, and socialist. For Vygotsky and many Soviets, all psychological theories were necessarily social, developmental, and contextual. Vygotsky's **socio-historical theory,** then, sees development in terms of activity and social interaction. The child's social context channels development so that cognitive development becomes a process of acquiring culture (Cole, 1985). Thought develops from experience in

LEV SEMANOVICH VYGOTSKY
(1896–1934)

Russian Lev S. Vygotsky was a contemporary of Piaget. In 1917 he graduated from Moscow University, and until 1923 he taught both literature and psychology in Gomel. In 1924 Soviet psychology officially adopted "reactology"— an approach to psychology that depended on behavioral reactions in a Marxist framework (Cole and Scribner, 1978). Shortly afterward, Vygotsky returned to Moscow to work at the Institute of Psychology. His views did not coincide with the major European approaches to psychology, which were either introspective or behavioristic (as was reactology). Nor did Vygotsky find the Gestalt psychologists' attempts to study behavior and experience as wholes a very satisfactory solution.

Vygotsky believed that the study of psychology was the study of changing processes, for as people respond to a situation, they alter it. One of his complaints about Piaget's theory was that the Swiss psychologist did not give enough weight to the influence of the environment on the developing child.

Vygotsky believed that the internalization of social and cultural activities was the key to human development and that internalization distinguished human beings from animals.

Vygotsky's research and writings focus on thought, language, memory, and play. At the end of his life, he worked on problems of education. But Vygotsky was also trained as a physician and advocated the combination of neurology and physiology with experimental studies of thought processes. Just before his death from tuberculosis in 1934, he had been asked to head the department of psychology in the All-Union Institute of Experimental Medicine.

Vygotsky died at 38, but his influence on Soviet psychology continued through his students, who held major positions throughout the Soviet Union. For years after his death, Vygotsky had no influence in North America. Then, in 1962, *Thought and Language* was translated, and his ideas entered the American psychological community. With each passing year, his theories have received more attention. In 1978, his essays, *Mind in Society,* were translated and published, and toward the end of the 1980s, the six-volume edition of his collected works began to appear in English.

---

socially structured activity, as the child internalizes the processes and practices provided by society and its members (Rogoff, Gauvain, and Ellis, 1984). Thus, the key to understanding mental processes can be found in the settings in which children function (Wertsch and Tulviste, 1992).

Researchers have discovered, for example, that social contexts influence the way people use cognitive skills. When researchers asked Brazilian street children to solve arithmetic problems, they found that problems the children solved easily in one context baffled them in another (Carraher, Carraher, and Schliemann, 1985). These 9- to 15-year-olds had little formal schooling, but they worked as street vendors, selling popcorn, coconuts, corn on the cob, and the like. Asked to solve a problem set in the context of their street transactions ("How much do a coconut and a corn on the cob cost?"), the children came up with the right answer 98 percent of the time. If the transaction was similar, but the items were not goods sold by the children ("A banana costs 85 cruzeiros and a lemon costs 63 cruzeiros. How much do the two cost together?"), their answers were right 74 percent of the time. But if the same problem was stripped of any natural context ("How much is

85 and 63?"), they solved it only 37 percent of the time. Similarly, when researchers observed new members of Weight Watchers as they prepared meals in their own kitchens, they found that dieters were consistently able to solve math problems concerning the size of food portions that they could not solve on formal arithmetic tests (Lave, 1990).

Developmental advances come as children, in the process of internalizing what they have practiced in social interactions, reconstruct and transform the process or activity. As children reconstruct a process, they move through a series of spiral stages, passing through the same point at each new reconstruction, but on a higher level. With each new level, they gain more and more control over their behavior.

Vygotsky's view of the social-interactional process at work in development led him to stress the importance of what he called the **zone of proximal development (ZPD).** The zone of proximal development is the area in which children, with the help of an adult or more capable child, can solve problems that they could never solve by themselves. When working within this zone, the experienced person must have some understanding of the child's requirements and must function as a sup-

Older children who work as street vendors in Brazil can solve arithmetic problems in the context of their transactions that baffle them when presented in a different context. *(Albano Guatti/The Stock Market)*

port system—almost as a vicarious form of consciousness for the child (Bruner, 1985). By enhancing learning and motivation, this support enables the child to internalize knowledge and thereby achieve conscious control over a new function or conceptual system. Vygotsky maintained that learning in the ZPD is the only "good learning," because it "pulls" development. When Vygotsky talked about the zone of proximal development, he was, of course, using a metaphor to describe the critical role played by social influences on cognitive development (Paris and Cross, 1988).

Bronfenbrenner's Ecological Theory

Urie Bronfenbrenner (1979) developed his ecological theory of development in response to the concern that most developmental studies isolated children from their natural settings and therefore missed the interaction between children and environments. Researchers, he said, seemed oblivious to the fact that events and conditions outside the laboratory could have a profound effect on behavior. Instead, developmental psychology had become "the science of strange behavior of children in strange situations with strange adults for the briefest possible periods of time" (p. 19). He urged researchers to turn away from "development-out-of context" and to begin studying children where they lived: in their homes, their neighborhoods, and their schools.

In his **ecological theory,** Bronfenbrenner proposed that development was a joint function of the person and all levels of the environment. He saw the ecological environment as a system of four nested structures that ranged from the immediate face-to-face setting to the remote setting of the larger culture. The innermost structure, the **microsystem,** is the immediate setting surrounding the person. The microsystem includes the family, the day-care center, the church, the school, the playground. Each microsystem includes the people present as well as the physical and symbolic features of the setting that invite, permit, or inhibit activity (Bronfenbrenner, 1989a). Recognizing that the experiences a child has at school or on the playground affect what a child does at home—and vice versa—Bronfenbrenner proposed that the interrelations between microsystems make up a **mesosystem.**

The mesosystem links settings that include the child; the third structure, the **exosystem,** links settings that include the child with those that affect the child but do not include him or her. What happens at work, for example, often affects the way a parent responds at home. If Mother has just been promoted, she will respond to her child in a different manner from the way she responds after she has had a run-in with her boss. For the child, the exosystem consists of the home and the mother's workplace. What happens during neighborhood play similarly affects the way a child responds at home. So for the parent, the exosystem is the home and the neighborhood peer group.

The developmental processes that occur within a microsystem are in good part defined and limited by the beliefs and practices of society, and so the final and largest structure affecting development is the **macrosystem,** which is society's blueprint for a particular culture or subculture. Macrosystems consist of social classes, ethnic or religious groups, and particular regions or communities that share similar belief systems, values, social and economic hazards, or life styles. Macrosystems change in response to historical events, and new macrosystems may emerge. Over the past few decades, for example, the macrosystem of single parenthood has developed in the United States, as has the macrosystem of the two-wage-earner family (Bronfenbrenner, 1989b).

Understanding Human Development

Faced with such an array of developmental theories, we may simply become bewildered. A few common themes are clear. Human growth and development, all theorists agree, is regular; behavior is at least potentially predictable. With the exception of conditioning theorists, who see the individual as passive and merely reacting to environmental changes, all theorists see the individual as at least reasonably active. Yet when we set the theories side by side, there are obstacles that make comparisons difficult.

One obstacle is the differing focus of various theories. Psychodynamic theorists are interested in explaining personality development; they pay little attention to the development of thought. With some cognitive theorists, the pattern is reversed. This difference in focus can lead to confusion because of differences in language.

When describing the same process, theorists use different terms—terms that reflect the world view of their own particular theory. Take the relationship between baby and caregiver, called *attachment*. Psychodynamic theorists regard attachment as an outgrowth of the caregiver's satisfying the infant's need to suck—the dominant feature of the oral period. Learning theorists see attachment as the result of conditioning: the primary caregiver both satisfies the infant's basic needs and provides interesting and satisfying stimulation. Ethological theorists view attachment as an evolved response that increases the likelihood of the infant's—and therefore the species'—survival. These descriptions suggest different explanations, but they simply focus on different aspects of the process.

So how do we evaluate the theories that we have explored in this chapter? Because each theory is based on different assumptions, we cannot say that one is superior to another. We can say, however, that one theory may do a better job than another in explaining a particular aspect of development. As Neil Salkind (1985) suggests, we can also look at the way each one addresses the important issues in development (see Table 2.5).

One issue that differentiates theories has to do with

the *nature of development:* What does the theory regard as the major force that influences development? The way a theory answers this question locates it on the nature-nurture issue. All theories regard both as important but stress one side or the other. As we have seen, biologically based theories of development focus on heredity, whereas learning theorists see environment as primary. The other theories tend to be more strongly interactional, although cognitive-developmental theorists lean slightly toward nature, and cultural-contextual theorists lean toward nurture.

Another issue is the *process that guides development:* What underlying process is seen as primarily responsible for changes in development? This question asks how development occurs, while the first question asked what is responsible. On this issue, theories align themselves as they did on the first question. Biological theorists see maturation as the underlying process that guides development, while learning theorists point to learning. Again, other theorists are less extreme, viewing both processes as important. However, both psychodynamic and cognitive-developmental theorists believe that maturation is essential for the emergence of various stages. Information-processing theorists regard experience and the development of a knowledge base as essential, whereas cultural-contextual theorists believe that development is based in social interaction.

Theories also vary on the *shape of development:* Is development smooth and continuous, or do changes occur abruptly, as a child moves from one stage to another? As we saw in Chapter 1, distinguishing clear stages in development is extremely difficult. Among the theories we have explored, maturational, psychodynamic, cognitive-developmental, and social-cognition theories see development as stagelike.

Finally, theories must be able to explain *individual differences:* How does the theory explain differences that appear among individuals? All theorists agree that individual differences develop as heredity interacts with experience. Biological theorists would remind us that we are all born with individual predispositions, and learning theorists would look at our histories of reinforcement. Psychodynamic theorists would stress the importance of experiences within the family during the first five or six years of life. Cultural-contextual theorists would emphasize the effects of the various settings that affect our lives, as well as the effects of historical and idiosyncratic events.

Each of the theories we have explored contributes something to our understanding of development, and as you read this book, you will notice that different sec-

TABLE 2.5

DEVELOPMENTAL THEORIES*

	Nature of Development	Guiding Process	Individual	Shape of Development	Focus
Biological theories	Nature	Maturation	Active	Stage	Observable changes in structure and behavior
Psychodynamic theories	Nature and nurture	Maturation	Active	Stage	Internal changes in personality structure
Conditioning theories	Nurture	Learning	Passive	Continuous	Observable changes in behavior
Cognitive social-learning theories	Nurture	Learning	Moderately active	Continuous	Observable changes in behavior
Cognitive-developmental theories	Nature and nurture	Maturation	Active	Stage	Internal changes in mental structure
Information-processing theories	Nurture	Learning	Active	Continuous	Observable changes in behavior
Cultural-contextual theories	Nature and nurture	Maturation and learning	Interactive	Spiral	Relationship between individual and society

Each theory addresses development in its own way. The lens through which the theory interprets development is ground by the way the theory regards the nature of development (what development occurs), the process of development (how it occurs), the role of the individual, and the shape of development and by which aspect of development the theory takes as its major concern.

tions stress different theories. Work that implements cognitive theories is discussed most extensively in the chapters on language and intellectual development. Ethological theories are drawn on primarily when infant social development is discussed. Psychodynamic theories appear most often in discussions of personality. Because learning theorists regard all behavior as learned, their theories appear throughout the book. Cultural-contextual theories appear in almost every chapter, and they are especially strong among researchers who study adult development.

As we go on to the next chapter, our focus changes from general principles to the development of the individual. The rest of the book traces the way a person develops, from the union of two cells at conception to the ending of a long life.

BIOLOGICAL THEORIES

No matter what approach developmentalists take, they work from **theories,** or sets of logically related statements that provide an interpretation of development. Biological theories emphasize the role of nature in development. Arnold Gesell was the major advocate of **maturational theory,** which sees development as directed from within in accordance with a biological timetable. **Ethological theories** view behavior in terms of the way it enables babies, children, and adults to survive and flourish in an environment similar to the one in which humans evolved. Some adaptive behavior appears in response to **releasing stimuli,** which evoke similar responses from most members of the species, and the **dominance hierarchies** of human children and primate groups are similar.

PSYCHODYNAMIC THEORIES

Psychodynamic theories view development as arising out of confrontations between the individual and the demands of society. In Freud's **psychosexual theory,** development passes through five stages, each typified by a particular conflict. If an early stage is not handled successfully, the individual becomes **fixated** at that stage. The **libido** (psychic energy) is the basis of human motivation. Within each person, the **unconscious** forces of the **id** are tempered by the **ego** (which guides realistic behavior) and the **superego** (conscience). In Erikson's **psychosocial theory,** development passes through eight stages, each typified by a conflict between inner needs and social demands. A failure to resolve the conflicts of a stage can result in psychological disorder.

LEARNING THEORIES

Learning theories see the environment as the major force in development. **Conditioning theories** explain development in terms of two kinds of learning: **classical conditioning** and **operant conditioning.** In classical conditioning, **unconditioned reflexes** become associated with neutral stimuli; in the process, they are transformed into **conditioned reflexes.** In operant conditioning, the association is between some event and the person's behavior. Actions are **reinforced** by their consequences; actions that are not reinforced are **extinguished. Punishment** weakens the tendency to repeat behavior. **Social-learning theory** expands on conditioning theories by giving **imitation** a key role in

the development of behavior. In Bandura's **cognitive social-learning theory,** behavior, internal forces, and environmental influences interact to influence behavior, and **cognition** has a major role in the determination of behavior.

COGNITIVE THEORIES

Jean Piaget's cognitive-developmental theory is a stage theory in which the mind undergoes a series of evolutionarily determined reorganizations. This development takes the child through a series of four cognitive stages: sensorimotor, preoperational, concrete operational, and formal operational. Piaget described his approach as **genetic epistemology,** and he believed that the infant was a **constructivist** whose knowledge came from action. Understanding depends on **schemes** (at first action patterns, then mental operations) with which the child **assimilates** and **accommodates** new knowledge. Development follows the principle of **equilibration,** always tending toward balance between internal schemes and the outside world.

Theories of **social cognition** have been influenced by Piaget. In Selman's stage theory of peer relations, children move through four stages of social competence, which reflect an increasing capability to differentiate and integrate the perspectives of self and others. In Kohlberg's theory of moral development, individuals move through three levels (six stages) of moral judgment, with each new stage requiring a reorganization of understanding into a more complex and balanced view of morality.

According to **information-processing theories,** people process information much as a computer does, with thought and behavior built on a small set of processes that are present early in life. Experience leads to automatization, the development of efficient strategies, and an ever-increasing store of knowledge, all of which result in faster, more efficient processing.

CULTURAL-CONTEXTUAL THEORIES

In cultural-contextual theories, development is heavily influenced by the context in which it occurs. According to Vygotsky's **socio-historical theory,** knowledge is social, created by society and transmitted to the individual, who internalizes the processes and practices provided by others. Historical and social changes heavily influence development. Learning in the **zone of proxi-**

mal development, where more capable individuals can enhance the child's learning and motivation, can speed the internalization of knowledge and increase the child's conscious control over cognitive function. According to Bronfenbrenner's **ecological theory,** development is a joint function of the person and all levels of the environment. Environmental levels move from **microsystem** (immediate setting) to **mesosystem** (interrelations between microsystems) to **exosystem** (interrelation between an individual's microsystem and a microsystem that affects the individual but does not include him or her) to **macrosystem** (subculture or culture).

UNDERSTANDING HUMAN DEVELOPMENT

Each group of theories tends to focus on a different aspect of the developmental process. In evaluating theories, it is important to consider how a theory views the nature of development, the process that guides development, and the shape of development, as well as how the theory explains individual differences.

KEY TERMS

accommodation	exosystem	psychosocial theory
assimilation	extinction	punishment
classical conditioning	fixated	reinforcement
cognition	genetic epistemology	releasing stimulus
cognitive social-learning theory	id	scheme
conditioned reflex	imitation	social cognition
conditioning theories	information-processing theory	social-learning theory
constructivist	libido	socio-historical theory
defense mechanism	macrosystem	superego
dominance hierarchy	maturational theories	theory
ecological theory	mesosystem	unconditioned reflex
ego	microsystem	unconscious
equilibration	operant conditioning	zone of proximal development
ethological theories	psychosexual theory	(ZPD)

PART

TWO

● ● ● ● ● ● ● ● ● ● ●

THE BEGINNING OF LIFE

No matter how sophisticated we are, the miracle of birth can reduce us to an awestruck silence. In only thirty-eight weeks, an undifferentiated cluster of cells becomes an individual capable of unassisted life. During those weeks within the uterus, the developing organism is utterly dependent on the mother's body. The moment of birth ruptures this close relationship, forcing infants to rely on their own mouths for sustenance, their own lungs for air, and their own eyes and ears for information about the world. Despite their obvious helplessness, newborns come into the world prepared to gather the information they need to make sense of their new environment. Their heredity, determined at the moment of conception, has provided them with the evolved capabilities of their species as well as the unique constellation of genes that makes them individuals. In Chapters 3 and 4, we see how development within the uterus prepares the newborn for an independent life, and we follow the progress of the first four weeks.

CHAPTER

3

••••••••••••

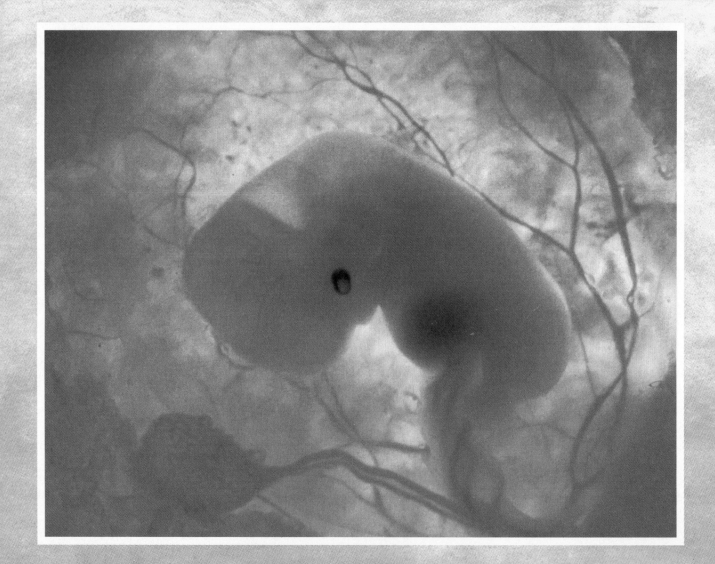

PRENATAL DEVELOPMENT

● ● ● ● ● ● ● ● ● ● ● ● ●

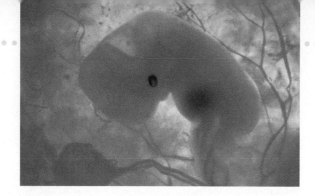

Development begins when a cell from the father and a cell from the mother unite deep within the mother's body. At that instant, the inheritance of a new individual is established. The newly fertilized cell, or **zygote,** which is no larger than a period on this page, contains all the instructions for a unique physical appearance and a disposition toward certain personality characteristics and mental abilities. But this genetic composition can express itself only in an environmental context; the two together determine how a person looks and behaves. Their interaction is at the heart of one of the oldest debates in psychology: how much influence inheritance or environment has in producing any given trait. The debate continues in part because even when a characteristic is inherited, life experiences affect the way the trait develops.

Although expectant parents may come to feel that the **prenatal period** lasts forever, only thirty-eight weeks after the two tiny cells come together a human being emerges. In no other comparable segment of life will such swift and intricate growth and development occur. The structures and functions that emerge during this brief period form the basis of the individual's body and behavior for the rest of life.

In this chapter, we follow the development of the fertilized egg into a healthy, normal baby who is ready for life outside the mother's womb. Before we watch the unfolding of individual development, we examine the workings of heredity and the transmission of specific traits from parent to child. Some of the growing fetus's behavior and capabilities will become apparent, and some problems that can arise in the course of development will be spelled out. As we look at the link between the mother and her unborn child, we will discover the importance of the mother's health, habits, and emotions during the prenatal period. The chapter closes with a consideration of the changing nature of premature infants as technology makes survival a possibility for the exceedingly immature fetus.

How Life Begins

The development of each person begins at the moment of conception, when the sperm cell, or **spermatozoon,** from the father unites with the egg, or **ovum,** of the mother. The ovum is the largest cell in the human body; it sometimes can be seen without a microscope. Ova mature in the female's ovaries, which normally release one egg during each **menstrual cycle** of around twenty-eight days. The freed egg, which probably can be fertilized for less than twenty-four hours, travels down the **Fallopian tube** toward the uterus.

When we look at the obstacles that stand in the way of conception, it is a wonder that sperm and egg ever get together. First, the vaginal tract is so acidic that millions of sperm die before they can begin their journey. Second, except around the time of ovulation, the small opening in the **cervix,** or lower part of the uterus, is so

Development begins when the head of the spermatozoon penetrates the wall of the ovum. *(D.W Fawcett/Science Source/ Photo Researchers)*

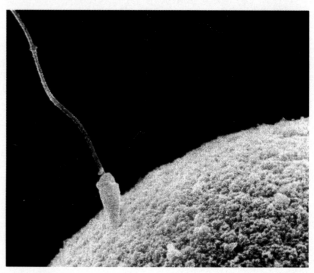

densely covered with mucus that sperm cannot penetrate it. Third, of the sperm that enter the uterus, only a few will find the correct Fallopian tube, for only one contains an egg. Fourth, the egg must be able to enter the Fallopian tube, which is sometimes blocked by adhesions or scars from pelvic infection. Fifth, the egg must travel down the Fallopian tube fast enough to meet the sperm while both short-lived cells are still capable of fertilization. Sixth, once the sperm finds the egg, it must penetrate several layers of protective material. So many circumstances must be met before conception takes place that about one couple in ten is unable to conceive. Yet some couples conceive after a single act of sexual intercourse.

Combating Infertility

Couples who cannot conceive a child and so are considered **infertile** as a couple can still have a child who carries the genes from one or both. For many years, **artificial insemination,** in which sperm is inserted into the prospective mother's uterus, has been an option. The sperm may be collected from the mother's husband, or, if he cannot provide it, it may come from an anonymous donor.

Since 1979, **in-vitro fertilization,** in which sperm and ova are mingled in a glass dish, has made it possible for other infertile couples to conceive. After the mother takes drugs to stimulate the simultaneous ripening of several ova, physicians remove the ova directly from her ovaries, using a hollow needle that sucks out the eggs. After fertilization with her husband's sperm, one or more zygotes are transferred to the mother's uterus, and she receives hormone injections so that her uterus will accept and nourish them. Either the ova or the sperm—or both—can come from donors. In fact, if the wife is unable to provide a receptive uterus, another woman may serve as an incubator for the couple's child. Babies conceived through this process are as healthy as babies conceived in the traditional manner (Morin et al., 1989).

Chromosomes and Genes

Parents transmit traits and dispositions to their children through **genes,** which are microscopic bits of a complex chemical called **deoxyribonucleic acid (DNA).** Each of the approximately 100,000 pairs of genes in a human cell provides a unit of information for the blueprint of heredity—the genetic code. This code specifies the structure of every body cell; it guides the development of bones and eyes, brain and fingernails, and disposes the offspring toward certain behavioral patterns. Within each cell, genes coalesce into beadlike strings called **chromosomes;** a given gene always occurs at the same place on the same chromosome.

The Production of Sex Cells

Most cells of the human body contain twenty-three pairs of chromosomes, direct copies of the original twenty-three pairs with which each person begins life. There is one major exception to this rule: the **gametes,** or ova and spermatozoa, which are also known as *sex cells.* Gametes can break the rule because they form by a special kind of cell division, called **meiosis.** During meiosis, a normal cell containing twenty-three pairs of chromosomes divides and divides again to produce four cells, each containing twenty-three unpaired chromosomes. We can think of the process as a stately dance, which the chromosomes begin by lining up in pairs within the cell's nucleus. The members of each chromosome pair divide and gravitate to opposite sides of the cell, which then splits into two cells, each containing twenty-three *single* chromosomes rather than twenty-three *pairs.* These cells then duplicate themselves, producing four gametes, each having twenty-three *single* chromosomes. At conception, when a sperm unites with an egg, the result is a single sex cell having twenty-three pairs of chromosomes. Figure 3.1 illustrates meiosis but shows only two of the twenty-three chromosome pairs involved.

With the exception of identical twins, each conception produces a unique individual with a genetic combination unlike that of anyone else in the world. Just over half of the 200,000 genes come from the mother and the rest from the father. The uniqueness of each combination is ensured by a process known as *crossing over.* During a crossover, after the chromosomes have lined up, each pair exchanges corresponding sections before it splits, mingling maternal and paternal genes in a single chromosome (Scarr and Kidd, 1983).

The Transmission of Genes

Children often resemble their parents in certain physical characteristics, but not always. A mother and father both may have brown hair, for example, but one of their three children may be blond. How are physical characteristics passed from parent to child?

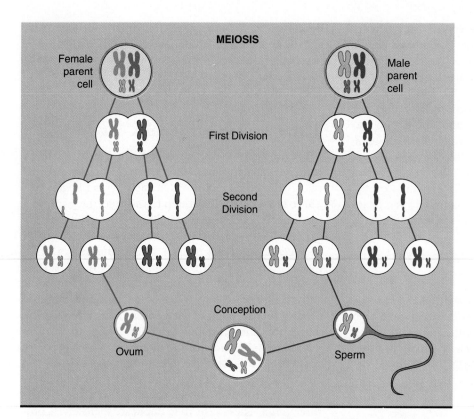

MEIOSIS

Female parent cell

Male parent cell

First Division

Second Division

Conception

Ovum

Sperm

Figure 3.1 The production of sex cells. Sex cells divide in a pattern of cell division called *meiosis* to produce gametes (ova and sperm) that have only half the number of chromosomes of the parent cells. As the cells undergo meiosis, first the members of each chromosome pair split up (first division), and then the single chromosomes themselves split in half (second division). In a subsequent step, the single chromosomes regenerate their missing halves (next line in diagram). At conception, the union of gametes produces a zygote that has the full number of chromosomes, half from the mother and half from the father.

The Mechanics of Genetic Transmission

Although hair color is a common and obvious characteristic, its transmission is complicated. Genetic transmission is easier to understand if we examine a characteristic that depends on a single pair of genes. A dramatic example of single-gene transmission occurs in **phenylketonuria (PKU),** an inherited inability to metabolize phenylalanine (a component of milk and other foods). During normal metabolism, phenylalanine is converted into tyrosine, an amino acid that is essential in the production of chemicals that regulate brain function. In the baby with PKU, phenylpyruvic acid and other metabolic compounds in the blood climb to dangerous levels. These compounds damage the developing nervous system. If the metabolic abnormality is left untreated, the child will be mentally retarded within two or three years.

Each person has two genes related to the metabolism of phenylalanine, one on each chromosome of the same pair. Let P symbolize the gene corresponding to normal metabolic activity and p represent the gene for PKU. When a gene can have several forms, the related genes (in this case, P and p) are called **alleles.** Suppose the mother's and father's cells each carry the Pp combination of alleles. When the parent cells divide to form gametes, half of the father's sperm cells and half of the mother's ova will carry the gene for PKU (p), and half will carry a gene for normal metabolic ability (P). When sperm and egg meet, one of four possible combinations will result: PP, pP, Pp (which is the same as pP), or pp (Figure 3.2).

Which of the children will have PKU and which will have normal metabolism? Any baby born with PP will be normal, and any baby born with pp will have PKU. These offspring are **homozygous** for PKU, which

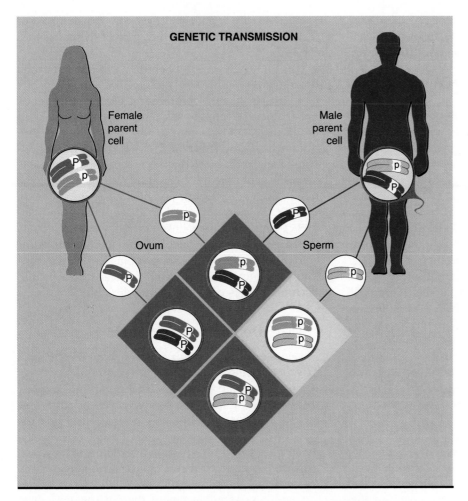

GENETIC TRANSMISSION

Female parent cell

Male parent cell

Ovum

Sperm

Figure 3.2 Transmission of alleles in the inheritance of PKU. The chromosomes in this pair carry alleles *P* and *p*. Both parents have both forms of the gene, and therefore they produce gametes with chromosomes bearing either the *P* or the *p* genes in equal numbers. Depending on which gametes happen to unite in conception, the new cell may have the alleles *PP*, *Pp*, *pP*, or *pp*. Because *p* is a recessive gene, only babies with *pp* will have PKU.

means that their cells have matching genes for this characteristic. But what about babies who are **heterozygous** for PKU, meaning that their cells have different alleles for the same trait. Are these *Pp* babies normal, or do they have PKU?

The answer depends on which gene is **dominant** and which is **recessive.** A dominant gene is one whose trait appears in the individual even when that gene is paired with a different gene for the trait. The paired gene whose trait fails to appear is recessive. In the case of PKU, the normal gene is dominant over the recessive PKU gene. Therefore, *Pp* babies have normal metabolism, although they can transmit the PKU gene to their offspring.

This difference between the genes a person carries and the traits that appear illustrates the difference between **genotype** and **phenotype.** The genotype is the specific combination of alleles in a person's genetic makeup (in this case, *PP*, *Pp*, or *pp*), and the phenotype is the nature of the trait as it appears in the person (in this case, normal or PKU). The genotypes *PP* and *Pp* both produce the normal phenotype because *P* is dominant over *p*.

Yet genetic combinations are not the only factor responsible for differences between a person's genetic makeup (genotype) and what that person actually looks like and how he or she behaves (phenotype). Experiences always affect the development of a person's phenotype. When a baby with *pp* genes is placed at birth on a phenylalanine-free diet, for example, he or she develops more or less normally. In addition, **modifier genes** may affect the way genetic traits are expressed. In the case of PKU, modifier genes on other chromosomes affect the severity of the disease.

Only a few human traits, mainly diseases, are the result of single-gene transmission. One "normal" trait that is controlled by a single gene is freckling. The gene for freckles is dominant, so that people without freckles have two recessive "nonfreckling" genes (*ff*), whereas people with freckles may have two (*FF*) or only one (*Ff*) freckling gene. For a variety of reasons, genetic transmission is rarely this simple. First, dominance is not always all or none. Some single-gene traits may be **codominant,** so neither allele can dominate the other. In such cases, the person who carries both alleles shows a combination of the traits. Type AB blood is an example of codominant genes. There are three alleles for the major blood types: *A*, *B*, and *O*; and each person carries two of these alleles. *A* and *B* are both dominant over *O*, so a person with *AO* or *BO* genes has the same blood type as people with *AA* (Type A) or *BB* (Type B) genes; only people with two recessive *O* alleles have Type O. But people with *A* and *B* alleles have Type AB, because both alleles are expressed.

Second, the vast majority of human traits are **polygenic,** which means that several genes are required to produce the trait. Sometimes all the genes have an equal and cumulative effect; in other cases, some genes in the combination have more influence than others on the phenotype. In addition, many polygenic traits, such as height, skin color, and resistance to disease, show continuous variation. That is, the trait appears in varying degrees; height, for example, can range from extremely short to extremely tall.

The more scientists study the process of human genetic transmission, the more complex it seems. Most behavioral traits are probably influenced by many genes, each having only a small effect (Plomin, 1990). Indeed, researchers have been unable to identify the individual genes involved in most polygenic traits.

The Importance of X and Y

One pair of chromosomes is different from all the rest. This pair, called the sex chromosomes, is unique because its members do not have matching alleles. All normal ova carry the female chromosome (X), but normal sperm may carry either the female chromosome (X) or the male chromosome (Y). When ovum and sperm join, the zygote will be either female (XX) or male (XY), depending on which type of sperm fertilizes the egg.

The influence of the sex chromosomes goes beyond determining whether the zygote will develop into a boy or a girl. The large X chromosome carries many genes, but the small Y chromosome carries only a few. This means that a boy gets more genes from his mother than from his father, a situation that sometimes has serious consequences. Because there is no corresponding allele for many genes on the X chromosome, the male zygote has no protection against potentially harmful recessive genes carried by the mother (Ehrman and Probber, 1983). One of these sex-linked conditions is hemophilia (a disease in which the blood does not clot); another is color blindness; a third is a form of muscular dystrophy. These conditions are rare in girls, appearing only if both X chromosomes carry the related gene.

How Do Genes Affect Behavior?

Genes exert their influence throughout the life span. At various points in development, genes "turn on," becoming active in producing substances within the body that create new structures, regulate their functions, or maintain their states. Genes, for example, may alter the way the nervous system functions, change the sensitivity of sensory systems, alter the threshold level at which cells can be activated by hormones, or modify the timing of developmental events.

Genes always interact with the environment, even during the prenatal period. The effects of the same environment differ from one person to the next because the genetic makeup of each person has a **reaction range—** a unique range of possible responses to the environments that he or she may encounter. In other words, there are some limits on how any person can respond to good or bad environmental conditions. Take the case of height. Good nutrition from birth will make all of us taller than poor nutrition will, but in both kinds of environments some will be taller than others, as Figure 3.3 indicates. Genes do not specify a particular pattern of height. They specify a pattern of growth that varies with nutrition and other environmental factors. The final height any of us achieves depends on both genetic and environmental factors.

The interaction between good nutrition and genes in determining height is easy to grasp, but the way genes and environment might interact to affect behavior is more difficult to discern. Sandra Scarr (1982; Scarr and McCartney, 1983) has suggested three ways in which

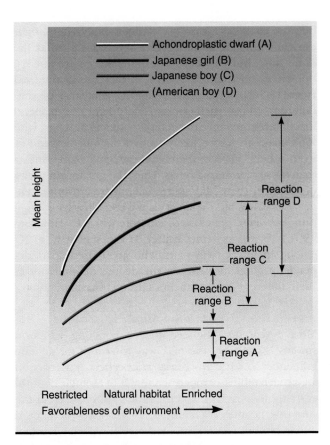

Figure 3.3 When the heights of adolescents with four different genetic makeups are compared, it becomes clear that environment and genes combine to produce development. The Japanese boy (genetic makeup C) who grew up in an optimum environment would be taller than the American boy (genetic makeup D) who grew up in a severely restricted environment. But if both environments were natural, severely restricted, or optimum, the American boy would be taller. Under no circumstances could the dwarf (genetic makeup A) be as tall as any of the other three. *(From Gottesman, 1974, p. 60)*

this interaction might occur. First, the home may provide a passive genetic influence. Children not only share their parents' genes but also live in an environment selected by their parents, where the available experiences are partly determined by the parents' own genes. A child whose parents are both artists will grow up surrounded by art, will experiment with paints and clay at an early age, and will have artists as role models at home. This kind of influence is strongest in childhood, when the home is the dominant environmental influence. Second, a child's genetically influenced appearance and behavior evoke particular responses from others. These responses to the child's attractiveness (or lack of it), physical skills and strength (or lack of them),

and temperament will in turn affect the way the child behaves. This kind of influence, although modified by the environment, seems equally important throughout life. Finally, a child actively seeks out some kinds of experience and ignores others. Because the child cannot pay attention to everything that goes on, he or she selects experiences that are pleasant, interesting, or challenging. And things that are boring, too easy, or too hard will be avoided. This influence probably gets increasingly stronger as a person grows older and personally determines more of the environment.

Studying Genetic Influences on Behavior

Researchers have developed several techniques for discovering how genes contribute to the development of individual differences. Some investigators breed other animals and apply principles derived from that research to human genetics. Others study families, on the assumption that the more closely people are related and the more similar a trait, the more likely it is that genetic factors have influenced its development. Only in the case of some abnormal physical traits, such as PKU, have researchers been able to discover just how genes affect development.

Most physical and behavioral traits are polygenic. Appearance is obviously influenced by genetic differences, because genetically related people resemble each other more than unrelated people do, whether they grow up together or not. Family resemblances, such as ears that stick out or lie close to the head, are common. Among European royal families, where there was a good deal of inbreeding, genetic traits often became pronounced. The Hapsburg royal family, for example, was noted for the "Hapsburg jaw," a long, protruding chin that was so exaggerated in Charles II of Spain that he could not chew (Durant and Durant, 1963).

Some physiological measures, such as heart rate and blood pressure, show a genetic influence (Claridge and Mangan, 1983), and so do some complicated behavioral disorders. Researchers have found, for example, that genes are involved in schizophrenia, although the disorder does not appear unless the person's environment fosters its development (Plomin, 1990).

Assessing Genetic Similarity

Chromosomal analysis is unlikely to be of much use in the study of normal behavioral traits, because these traits all seem to be polygenic. So instead of analyzing chromosomes, researchers use mathematical techniques to assess the degree of similarity they find through different types of studies.

Both major types of family studies, twin studies and studies of adopted children, rely on correlation, and as we saw in Chapter 1, correlation demonstrates a relationship between two factors but does not establish that either factor *causes* the other. Cognitive abilities, especially as measured by IQ scores, have been studied in this manner.

The correlation between the IQ scores of unrelated children reared apart is generally close to 0.00. As relatedness between two people increases, the correlation between their IQ scores also increases. Note that in Table 3.1 the correlation for unrelated children reared together is +0.38. Because these children have no common genes, the figure primarily reflects the effect of the environment on IQ. The correlation for siblings (brothers and sisters) is about the same as the correlation for fraternal twins. This is to be expected, because on the average both siblings and fraternal twins share half their genes. But identical twins have identical genetic makeups, and their IQs show much higher correlations whether the twins are reared together or apart.

On the basis of such evidence, can we say that genetic makeup is the primary determinant of a person's IQ? Not at all. As relatedness between individuals increases, so does the similarity of their environments. Brothers and sisters share some environmental influences, but because they are born at different times and because each has a variety of unique experiences, their environments are not identical. Twins are born at the same time, but this does not eliminate environmental influences on their IQ scores. In the case of fraternal twins, their appearances and temperaments may be very different, and so their parents and others may respond in a different manner to each twin. Identical twins, who look alike, are more likely to evoke similar responses from others, making their environments more similar than those of fraternal twins. Thus, the greater similarity of identical twins' IQ scores cannot be attributed entirely to genes but depends on the complicated interaction between genes and environment (L. Hoffman, 1991). As we saw in Chapter 1, the similarity of IQ among identical twin pairs who are reared apart depends in good measure on the degree of similarity in their different environments (Bronfenbrenner, 1986).

Adoption Studies

Most researchers believe that conducting adoption studies is probably the best way to search for genetic influences on IQ. In Texas, researchers studied 300 adoptive families, comparing the IQs of biological mothers, adoptive parents, and the biological children in the adoptive families (Willerman, 1979). They compared children whose biological mothers had IQs of 95 or less with children whose biological mothers had IQs of 120 or more (see Table 3.2). No children of low-IQ mothers had IQs of 120 or more, and no children of high-IQ mothers had IQs of 95 or less. Children in both groups responded to good environments, but children of the mothers with high IQs responded the most, indicating that their reaction range for these skills was probably higher.

As this study seems to demonstrate, intellectual skills have a reaction range. No matter how stimulating the environment, few people become Albert Einsteins or Leonardo da Vincis. And unless the environment is extremely deprived, most people do not become mentally retarded. Each of us has a range of at least 25 IQ points in which our IQ score tends to fall, depending on rearing conditions (Scarr, 1981). A good environment allows these skills to develop toward the upper end of that range. Sandra Scarr and Richard Weinberg (1983) tested this idea by studying more than 100 poor African-American children who were adopted as babies by middle-class white families, in which most of the parents were college graduates. The average IQ score of these children was above the national average of both African-American and white children, indicating the profound effect of environment on IQ.

TABLE 3.1	CORRELATIONS OF INTELLIGENCE TEST SCORES
Unrelated children reared apart	+0.00
Unrelated children reared together	+0.38
Siblings reared together	+0.54
Fraternal twins reared together	+0.53
Identical twins reared apart	+0.74
Identical twins reared together	+0.86

Source: All data except those for unrelated children reared apart are from Rowe and Plomin, 1978. (Note that these data are from American studies and do not include data from studies by Sir Cyril Burt.)

TABLE 3.2   IQ OF ADOPTEES AS A FUNCTION OF BIOLOGICAL MOTHER'S IQ

IQ of Biological Mother	Adoptees' IQ ≥ 120	Adoptees' IQ ≤ 95	Adoptees' Average IQ
Low IQ (89.4) (*n* = 27)	0%	15%	102.6
High IQ (121.6) (*n* = 34)	44%	0%	114.8

Source: Willerman, 1979.

Environment affects development by providing certain stimuli and certain opportunities for people to develop particular characteristics. Genes affect development by producing different responses to given environments. Individual differences among people apparently are caused by genetic differences in their reaction ranges *and* by specific differences in their environments. Later in the chapter we will explore some of the issues and complexities involved in genetic transmission.

Prenatal Growth

As soon as sperm and egg unite, development begins and progresses at a rapid rate. The course of prenatal development falls into roughly three periods. During the first two weeks after conception, called the **germinal period,** the zygote is primarily engaged in cell division. During the **embryonic period,** which covers the next six weeks, the organism (now called an **embryo**) begins to take shape, and its various organ systems begin to form. The **fetal period** lasts from approximately eight weeks after conception to birth, and during this time the developing organism is called a **fetus.** The total **gestation period** usually lasts about 266 days (thirty-eight weeks) from conception or 280 days (forty weeks or nine calendar months) from the beginning of the mother's last normal menstruation. Because most women do not know exactly when they conceived, physicians usually go by **menstrual age;** however, **gestational age** is a more accurate measure of fetal development.

The Germinal Period

Almost immediately after fertilization, the zygote begins the process of cell division that will eventually produce a human body made up of billions of cells. Although an adult's body cells are highly differentiated according to their location and function (for example, nerve cells are quite different in form and function from muscle cells), the cells at this point in development are all identical.

The zygote takes about three days to move through the Fallopian tube into the uterus, where it floats freely

A zygote during the first few days after conception; at this stage all its cells are identical. *(Petit Format/Nestle/Science Source/Photo Researchers)*

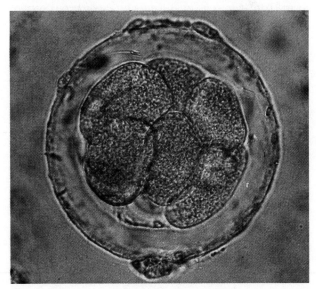

for another four or five days before implanting itself in the nutrient-rich uterine wall (see Figure 3.4). By the end of the first two weeks, the cells have multiplied greatly in number and have begun to differentiate themselves according to genetic instructions. An outer membrane **(chorion)** and an inner membrane **(amnion)** form a sac that surrounds and protects the developing organism. By now, the microscope can distinguish the **placenta,** a supple structure of tissue and blood formed jointly by fetus and mother. From it develops the bluish-red **umbilical cord,** through which oxygen and nourishment pass from maternal to fetal blood vessels and through which fetal wastes are removed. A membrane separates the two circulatory systems and provides the fetus with some protection. Large particles in the mother's blood, such as bacteria, cannot pass through the barrier, but minute particles, such as many viruses and chemical molecules, can slip through. As we will see, the permeability of this barrier has significant implications for the developing fetus.

If all the zygote's cells are identical, how does a cell know whether it is destined to be part of the nervous system, the skeleton, the heart, the lungs, or the liver? Researchers believe they have identified a substance that is responsible. This substance (called *activin*) is generated in only a few cells located in a specific region of the zygote. As activin spreads from this region through the zygote, cells receiving the highest concentration become the endoderm, which forms the digestive and respiratory systems; those with a medium concentration become the mesoderm, which forms muscle, bones, blood, heart, and kidneys; and those with the weakest concentration become the endoderm, which forms skin, hair, sensory organs, and the nervous system (Cherfas, 1990). Activin's power has been demonstrated; when it is added to cells from the endoderm, they become mesoderm cells. Other researchers have discovered that embryonic organ development may be a two-step process, with each organ beginning to form under general instructions but requiring the action of a specific gene to complete its formation (Schnabel and Schnabel, 1990).

As the germinal period ends, the two-week-old organism is firmly anchored to the lining of the uterus, which maternal hormones have prepared for the developing egg. Life is on its way, although the mother does not yet know she is pregnant.

The Embryonic Period

Within four weeks after conception, the organism is already about one-fifth of an inch long, 10,000 times larger than the original fertilized egg. Its two-chambered heart beats, moving blood back and forth, although it cannot yet pump blood in a continuous circuit through the tubelike body (Grobstein, 1988). The beginnings of a brain, kidneys, a liver, and a digestive tract have appeared. Indentations at the top will eventually become jaws, eyes, and ears.

The two principles that guide development during the embryonic period, when organs, limbs, and physiological systems form, are the same principles that will guide later growth and development in the fetus, infant, and child. The first principle, called **proximodistal development,** refers to the fact that development generally progresses from the center of the body toward the periphery. During the embryonic period, organs along the central axis of the body develop first; the extremities develop later. Thus, in the early weeks the organism is literally all head and heart. The embryo also follows the principle of **cephalocaudal development:** growth generally progresses from head to foot. So the embryonic head develops first, and only later does the lower part of the body begin to enlarge and to assume its newborn proportion and size. This development follows a pattern of staggered starts, so different organs begin to form at different points in the embryonic period.

By the end of the embryonic period, the organism is

A 5-week-old embryo; at this stage organs are forming. *(Petit Format/Nestle/Science Source/Photo Researchers)*

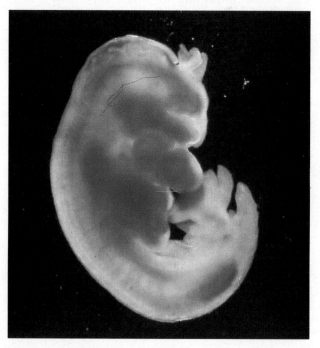

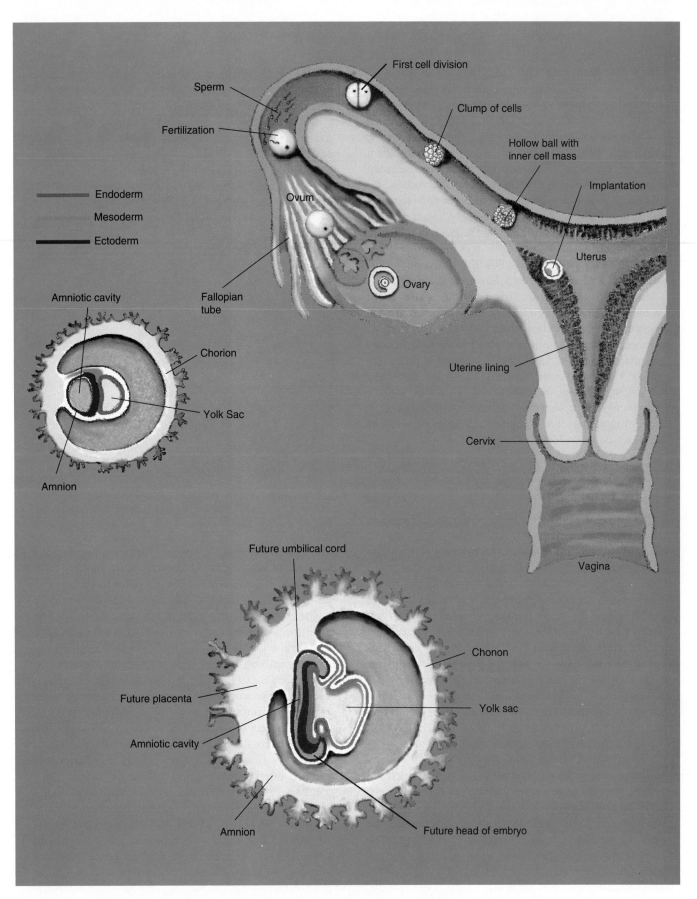

Figure 3.4 The early development of the human zygote. Fertilization occurs at the upper end of the Fallopian tube. By the time the fertilized ovum reaches the uterus, it has already divided many times. Within seven or eight days, it is securely implanted in the uterine wall, where the process of prenatal development continues.

almost an inch long but does not yet look human (Grobstein, 1988). What appear to be the gill slits of fish are really rudimentary forms of structures in the neck and lower face. What seems to be a primitive tail eventually becomes the tip of the spine; the tail reaches its maximum length at about six weeks and then slowly recedes. The head is clearly distinct from the rounded, skin-covered body and accounts for about half of the embryo's total size. The eyes have come forward from the sides of the head, and eyelids have begun to form. Eyes, nose, lips, tongue, and even the buds of teeth can be distinguished. The knobs that will be arms and legs grow; in a matter of weeks, they will differentiate into hands and feet and then into fingers and toes.

As early as the sixth week a few neurons form in the spinal cord, providing circuits needed for reflex arcs. As the period ends, the heart beats sturdily, the stomach produces minute quantities of digestive juices, the liver manufactures blood cells, and the kidneys purify the blood. Testes and ovaries have formed, and the endocrine system has begun to produce hormones. But the embryo has a long way to go. All its organ systems are in a primitive form, and it will be several months before they can be considered fully functional.

The Fetal Period

About eight weeks after conception, when the major organs have taken shape, the fetal period begins. Development shifts from the formation of rudimentary organs to organizing their structure and establishing their function. Now bone cells first appear. By twelve weeks, the fetus has begun to stretch out a little from its C-shaped posture, and the head is more erect. The limbs are nicely molded, and folds for fingernails and toenails are present. If the fetus is in the right position, a close look could determine its sex. The lips have become separate from the jaws, the nasal passages have formed, the brain has attained its general structure, and the eyes are organized but sightless. The bone marrow has begun to produce blood. Yet the fetus is only about 3 inches long and weighs little more than an ounce.

By sixteen weeks the fetus is between 6 and 7 inches long and weighs about 4 ounces. The head, which has been enormous in relation to the rest of the body, now takes up only one-fourth of the mass. The lower part of the body has grown, and the fetus looks like a miniature baby. Its face looks human, bones can be distinguished throughout the body, and the sense organs approximate their final appearance.

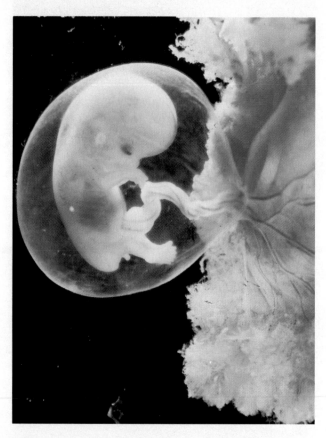

A 12-week-old fetus, with umbilical cord and placenta attached. (© *Lennart Nilsson, A Child Is Born, Dell Publishing*)

Although most of the basic systems are present, the fetus could not survive if it were born at this point. There are no connections between neurons in the cerebral cortex (Grobstein, 1988), and functions necessary for life outside the uterus have not yet developed. The fetus floats in a watery world and receives its oxygen through the placenta, so it cannot yet handle the problem of breathing air. Before it can breathe successfully, it must be able to produce the liquid **surfactin,** which coats the air sacs of the lungs and permits them to transmit oxygen from the air to the blood. The first production of surfactin comes at about twenty-three weeks, but at first the fetus is unable to keep surfactin levels high enough to avoid **respiratory distress syndrome,** which is often fatal.

Babies born between twenty-four and twenty-eight weeks are viable, but their viability is statistically improbable (Grobstein, 1988). Babies born this young *can* survive, but few do. Only 20 percent of those born at twenty-four weeks and weighing less than 1 pound 11 ounces (750 grams) survive. Those who live must have

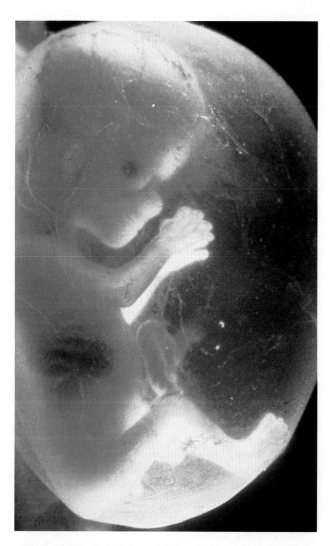

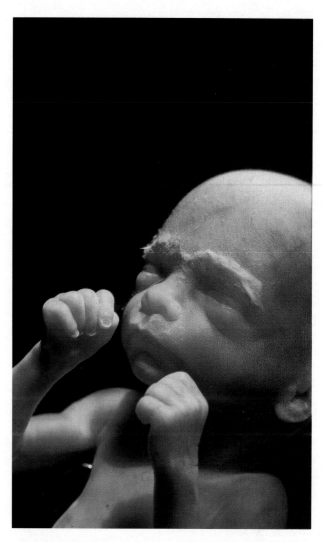

A 16-week-old fetus, which looks like a miniature baby but is still unable to survive outside the uterus. *(Petit Format/ Nestle/Science Source/Photo Researchers)*

A 25-week-old fetus, which has a slim chance of survival, but only with prolonged, intensive care. *(© Lennart Nilsson, A Child Is Born, Dell Publishing Company)*

prolonged intensive care, and the vast majority have serious problems with lung disease, hemorrhaging within the brain, and eye disorders (Meisels and Plunkett, 1988). The longer that birth is postponed, the more likely it is that the fetus will survive. The majority of fetuses born after thirty weeks survive, and those born after thirty-six weeks are considered to be of normal term, although unusual circumstances may still make special care necessary for the first few days or weeks of life. The technical viability of the fetus after twenty-four weeks raises the question of fetal rights (see the accompanying box, "The Question of Fetal Rights").

A fetus that remains in the uterus much after term also may need special care. About 3 fetuses in 100 re-main in the uterus forty-two weeks or more. As the placenta ages, less and less oxygen and nourishment reach the fetus, so it begins to lose weight and waste away. At birth, an older fetus may need immediate oxygen and nourishment.

During the final weeks of prenatal development, when the fetus could survive on its own, its organs step up their activity. Its heart rate becomes quite rapid. Fat forms over the entire body, smoothing out the wrinkled skin and rounding out contours. The fetus usually gains about ½ pound a week during the last eight or nine weeks in the uterus. At birth, the average full-term baby is about 20 inches long and weighs a little more than 7 pounds.

Prenatal Development

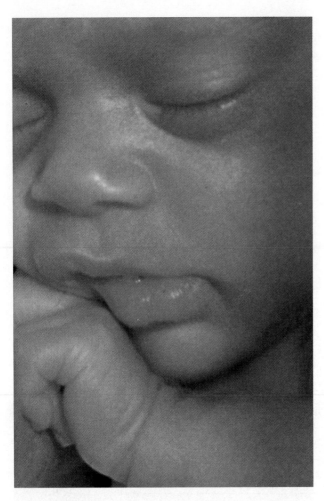

A 30-week-old fetus, which would probably survive but would need special care. *(Petit Format/Nestle/Science Source/ Photo Researchers)*

Prenatal Behavioral Development

How early in life can the fetus move spontaneously? How soon does it respond to a stimulus? And what kinds of responses does it make? Although most mothers say that they feel fetal movement at about sixteen weeks (an event known as *quickening*), by that time the fetus has already been able to move its muscles for approximately eight weeks. By twelve weeks, the fetus can kick its legs, turn its feet, close its fingers, bend its wrists, turn its head, squint, frown, open and close its mouth, and respond to touch, although these early movements seem purely reflexive (Grobstein, 1988).

By twenty-three weeks, the fetus often moves spontaneously. It sleeps and wakes as a newborn does and even has a favorite position for its naps. At twenty-four weeks, it can cry, open and close its eyes, and look up, down, and sideways. It has developed a grasp reflex and soon will be strong enough to support its weight with one hand. As mothers are uncomfortably aware, during the final eight or nine weeks, the fetus is quite active, often delivering unexpectedly sharp kicks or elbow jabs. These spontaneous actions, which are limited by the increasingly snug fit of the uterus, seem to be embedded in a regular pattern of movement, for the older fetus moves its arms and legs about once each minute, in a cycle similar to that found in newborns (Robertson et al., 1982). Researchers are not sure just how early this pattern develops but have shown that it is not related to other fetal rhythms, such as breathing. As we will see in Chapter 4, most newborn behavior is rhythmic, and some of the rhythms have social meaning.

Behavioral development before birth corresponds to the development of the nervous system and muscles. As early as seven and one-half weeks, the embryo responds reflexively by moving its upper trunk and neck when its mouth is stroked with a fine hair. By nine weeks, the fetus bends its fingers when the palm of its hand is touched and either curls or straightens its toes in response to a touch on the sole of the foot. By eleven weeks, the fetus can swallow. As development progresses, the fetus's response changes from a diffuse, general movement of the whole body to a movement limited to the muscles in the stimulated area. Now, for example, a touch on the mouth evokes only movements of the mouth muscles. Within the last few months before birth, the fetus behaves essentially as does a newborn, grasping, sucking, and kicking.

At about this time, the fetus also hears sounds and responds to them. Researchers have established the existence of this capacity by using **ultrasound** to watch fetal movements. In this technique, sound is passed through the mother's abdominal wall and bounced off the fetus, and the echoes are transformed into thousands of dots that appear on a screen. These pictures are called **sonograms.** When researchers make a loud noise next to the mother's abdomen, just over a fetal ear, the fetus moves abruptly. It squeezes its eyelids shut, averts its head, waves its arms, and extends its leg. After observing more than 900 fetuses in this way, researchers (Birnholz and Benacerraf, 1983) discovered that a fetus who does *not* respond to sounds probably has major developmental problems (see Table 3.3). Every fetus that did not react to sounds was later found to be deaf, structurally deformed, or dangerously ill.

A fetus may remember sound patterns if they are repeated frequently. The possibility that a fetus may be capable of this sort of rudimentary learning emerged when researchers asked pregnant women to read the same children's story, *The Cat in the Hat,* aloud twice each day during the last few months of pregnancy. Three days after the babies were born, Anthony DeCasper and Melanie Spence (1986) played a recording of a woman reading both the familiar story and a new story, but the new one was written in a different meter. The babies could regulate the sound by sucking on a pacifier; their sucks kept the sound on. Babies seemed to recognize the familiar story and prefer it, sucking more consistently to hear the familiar tale, whether both stories were read by their mother or another woman.

The Birth Process

As the time for birth approaches, the fetus generally lies head down in the uterus. The uterus at this time resembles a large sack that opens into the vagina through the cervix. Exactly what event triggers the birth process? Researchers are not certain, but many believe that the fetus plays a major role in determining its onset.

Labor and Delivery

When the birth process begins, the upper portion of the uterus contracts at regular and progressively shorter intervals while the lower part of the uterus thins out, and the cervix dilates to permit the fetus to pass

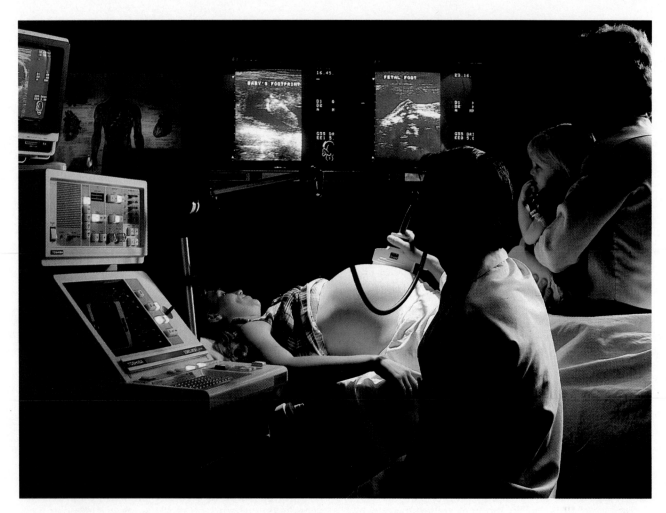

By using ultrasound, physicians can detect some abnormalities and determine whether a woman is carrying more than one fetus. *(Alexander Tsiaras/Stock, Boston)*

through the birth canal. Later, the mother's abdominal muscles also contract in a bearing-down motion. Unless drugs deaden her sensations, she usually pushes hard to get the baby out. The entire process is called **labor,** and it may be completed in less than three hours or drag on for more than a day. For first-born infants, the average labor lasts from thirteen to fifteen hours. It is markedly shorter for later-born children.

The first stage of labor lasts until the cervix is completely dilated. It usually begins with faint contractions that grow stronger and more frequent. In the second stage of labor, the fetus passes head first through the birth canal and is born, a process that lasts approximately eighty minutes for first-born children (see Figure 3.5). After birth, the attendant cleans the baby's

nose and mouth with a suction apparatus to prevent substances from entering the lungs and to make breathing easier. Then the umbilical cord is tied and cut. In the final stage of labor, uterine contractions expel the **afterbirth**—the placenta, its membranes, and the rest of the umbilical cord. This process lasts approximately five to twenty minutes, and the afterbirth is immediately examined by the attendant to determine whether it is complete and normal.

Not all deliveries proceed in this normal fashion. In fact, among the mothers in various studies, only 45 percent had no complications of any kind. Most complications are mild or moderate, but in some instances complications are severe (Grossman, Eichler, and Winickoff, 1980). In a breech delivery, for example, the baby's but-

TABLE 3.3   FETAL HEARING

Gestational Age (Weeks)	AUDITORY RESPONSE			
	No Response	Inconsistent	Blink*	Total
12–15.9	17	0	0	17
16–19.9	26	0	0	26
20–23.9	32	0	0	32
24–24.9	14	7	0	21
25–25.9	9	14	1	24
26–26.9	5	20	3	28
27–27.9	2	12	9	23
28–28.9	0	3	17	20
29–32	0	0	36	36

*Among this group of fetuses, the characteristic startled blink first appeared at twenty-five weeks, and by twenty-nine weeks all fetuses reacted to the sound.

Source: Birnholz and Benacerraf, 1983.

tocks appear first in the birth canal, then the legs, and finally the head. In a transverse presentation, the baby lies crosswise in the uterus, and a shoulder, arm, or hand first enters the vagina. Both kinds of deliveries can be dangerous because the baby may experience anoxia, or even suffocate, before the head emerges. In **anoxia,** the air supply is cut off temporarily. Its effects may be fleeting, long-lasting, or permanent, depending on how long the baby cannot get air, whether the baby is also affected by anesthetics, and the baby's general health.

Because of this danger, physicians have become increasingly likely to deliver babies lying in a breech or transverse position by Caesarean section, in which the baby is removed through an incision in the mother's abdomen. This surgical procedure is also used when the mother's pelvis is too small to permit her baby to pass through; when the mother suffers from diabetes, high blood pressure, or some other ailment; when the mother has active herpes; or when the fetus seems in danger, perhaps from a prolonged delivery.

Methods of Childbirth

Over the past few decades, American methods of childbirth have undergone dramatic change. At one time, all labors were considered difficult and painful. In most American hospitals, drugs were routinely given, and episiotomies (surgical incisions to enlarge the vaginal opening) and forceps were used to speed the birth process. Such practices were considered the best ways to care for mothers and babies. But a growing number of parents and medical personnel began to question these procedures (Hahn and Paige, 1980), and their dissatisfaction seemed to be supported by evidence from other cultures.

Anthropologists reported that childbirth practices varied dramatically around the world. In cultures that regarded birth as something to be hidden, women often had prolonged and difficult labors. But in cultures that regarded birth as an open, easy process, women generally had short, uncomplicated labors (Mead and Newton, 1967).

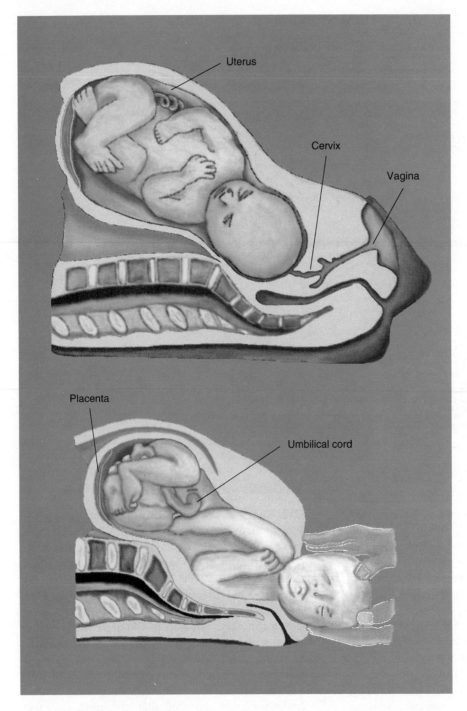

Figure 3.5 Models indicating the position of the fetus during passage through the birth canal. (Redrawn with permission, from *Birth Atlas,* Maternity Center Association, New York)

Grantly Dick-Read (1944), a British physician who had noticed that some of his patients found childbirth a relatively peaceful, painless experience, believed fear generated a tension that produced pain in most women. His urging of what he called "natural childbirth" met with some success, and his techniques, combined with the Lamaze method, brought about changes in the way many obstetricians handle childbirth.

In the Lamaze method, women learned to substitute new responses for learned responses of pain and, by concentrating on breathing, tried to inhibit painful sensations (Chabon, 1966). Another feature of this method was a "coach," who stayed with the mother during labor to provide psychological encouragement. Since the Lamaze method was invented, additional methods of natural childbirth have been devised. In all of them, parents learn about the birth process, a coach stays with the mother, and the mother is urged to take as little medication as possible and to participate actively in the birth.

Whether or not parents choose natural childbirth, they will find that childbirth procedures in many hospitals have changed since midcentury. In most hospitals, the husband may accompany his wife into the delivery room, where he can offer her emotional support and participate in the birth process. In addition, in many hospitals, some of the routine customs, from automatic medication to episiotomy, that tend to make birth an abnormal and unpleasant procedure, have been eliminated for normal deliveries. The medical profession has come to realize that all family members benefit from sharing the experience of childbirth. Today, professionals urge a more homelike hospital atmosphere, the presence of the father, a bed that allows the mother to give birth in a near-sitting position, an opportunity for mother, father, and infant to be together after delivery,

Many couples choose natural childbirth, in which the mother remains awake and the father can participate in the birth. *(Ken Biggs/International Stock Photo)*

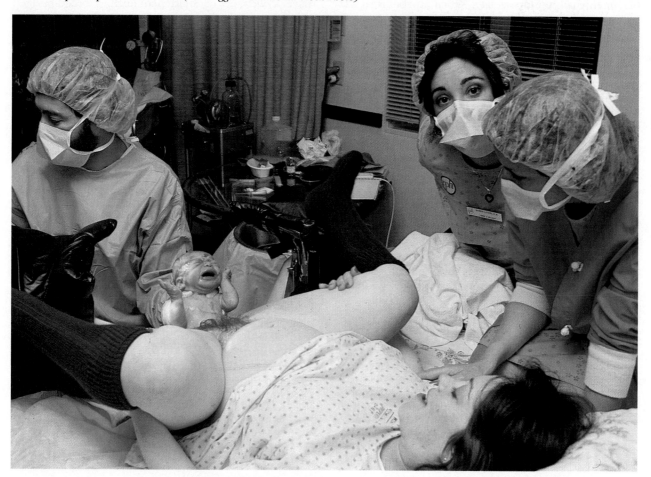

and the encouragement of breast feeding (Interprofessional Task Force, 1978).

Fetal Abnormalities and Birth Complications

Most pregnancies follow a normal course of development, and most babies are normal. On occasion, however, a genetic abnormality affects the developing fetus. Sometimes the process of meiosis goes wrong. At other times, a change takes place in the chemical structure of a single gene, producing a new allele that carries different genetic information—information that can be transmitted to a person's children. Such **mutations** may be spontaneous, or they may be caused by radiation or exposure to environmental chemicals. Most zygotes with chromosomal or genetic abnormalities do not survive; when they die, the mother usually assumes that her menstrual period was late. When an abnormal zygote lives, the defect usually is minor, although some defects require medical or surgical intervention, and a few are so serious that they threaten the life of the baby. By using the techniques described in the accompanying box, "Detecting Complications," physicians can discover many serious abnormalities before birth.

Chromosomal Abnormalities

When a cell divides to form a gamete, a pair of chromosomes may fail to separate, so one of the gametes has one chromosome too many and the other has one too few. When the sex chromosome is involved, the fertilized egg may carry either a single female chromosome (XO), an extra female chromosome (XXY), or an extra male chromosome (XYY). The X chromosome is necessary for development, so a zygote with only a male chromosome (OY) never survives.

Zygotes with the XO pattern develop into girls with **Turner's syndrome,** a condition that affects about 1 birth in every 2500. These girls are especially short, have a webbed or shortened neck, a broad-bridged

---

DETECTING COMPLICATIONS

Some years ago, fetal abnormalities or potentially fatal diseases went undetected until a child was born. Today, several prenatal diagnostic procedures can answer questions about fetal development.

Gross abnormalities in fetal development now can be discovered early in pregnancy by the use of ultrasound. Sonograms can show visible abnormalities, resolve confusion over the age of the fetus, and uncover the presence of more than one fetus or such conditions as placenta previa (in which the placenta blocks the birth canal and normal deliveries sometimes lead to fatal anoxia).

Ultrasound often is used as a guide for performing other diagnostic procedures. In **amniocentesis,** the physician inserts a hollow needle through the mother's abdomen and draws out a sample of amniotic fluid. The fluid contains cells shed by the fetus, which reveal such abnormalities as Down's syndrome and Turner's syndrome. The chemical composition of amniotic fluid can provide clues to other diseases, such as Tay-Sachs (a genetically transmitted disease in which the absence of a fat-metabolizing enzyme leads to death before the age of 7). The fluid also reveals whether the fetus can produce enough surfactin to avoid respiratory distress when it is born. In addition, tests can detect the blood group and sex of the fetus. The procedure cannot be done until between the fourteenth and sixteenth week after conception, and it carries a slight risk of spontaneous abortion (Tabor et al., 1986).

As early as the eighth week of pregnancy, physicians can insert a hollow tube through the vagina and remove cells from the fingerlike projections of the chorion. This procedure, known as **chorionic villi sampling,** detects the same range of conditions as amniocentesis, and the information is available early enough for an abortion by uterine aspiration. The risk to the embryo posed by this sampling technique is somewhat higher than that with amniocentesis (Brozan, 1985).

A simple test, together with amniocentesis, can uncover neural tube defects, another serious condition. The procedure begins by testing the maternal blood for alpha-fetoprotein (AFP), a substance produced in excessive amounts by a fetus with a neural tube defect. Positive results indicate a 1-in-25 chance that the fetus is defective, and amniocentesis will indicate whether the high APF levels are the result of a neural tube defect, the presence of twins, or an incorrect estimate of fetal age.

Neural tube defects, in which the tube that forms the brain and spinal column fails to close, can be disabling or fatal. The defect occurs in 1.2 births in every 1000; it is found in all population groups. No one knows why it happens in one pregnancy and not another (Leonard, 1981). When the tube fails to

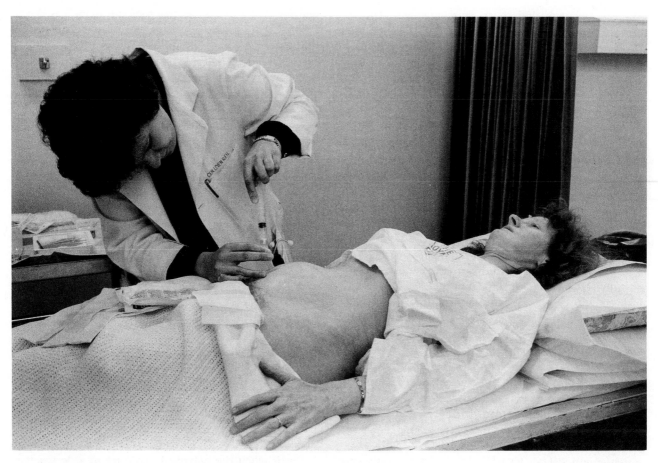

In amniocentesis, cells from a sample of amniotic fluid are cultured and examined for genetically transmitted conditions. *(Nancy Durrell McKenna/Photo Researchers)*

close at the top, babies are born without a brain or with an incomplete one. If they are alive at birth, they die within a few days. When the tube fails to close along the spinal column, the babies have a condition known as **spina bifida:** a bundle of nerves protrudes through an opening in the spinal column. These babies generally live, although many are paralyzed below the waist or are retarded. In some, fluid does not drain properly from the skull, so they also have **hydrocephaly,** an accumulation of fluid within the skull that presses on the brain.

Most often, prenatal diagnostic techniques remove parents' anxiety over possible defects. Even if both parents carry the recessive Tay-Sachs gene, for example, the chances are still 3 in 4 that their baby will be normal. If the test indicates an abnormal fetus, parents can discuss the situation with a genetic counselor, who can tell them how extensive the defect may be and what sort of care their child will require.

On the basis of that information, parents make their own decision. Among couples interviewed by Michael Gold (1981), for example, the results of prenatal screening for neural tube defects varied widely. All mothers had shown high AFP levels at their initial screening. Like most couples, Steve and Julie found that their fetus was normal; they became parents of a healthy boy. Anne and Joe discovered their fetus had spina bifida and chose abortion. Within a year, Anne was pregnant again. This time the fetus showed no abnormality. Five months later, they were parents of a normal, healthy girl. Pat and Tony found that their fetus was seriously deformed but could not bring themselves to consider abortion. Their baby was born with only part of a brain and died almost immediately. Many parents who discover their fetus is defective follow Pat and Tony's example and decide not to terminate the pregnancy. When the defective baby is born, there is no shock, and they find it easier to form emotional bonds with their baby and to adapt to his or her condition than if they had not been initially prepared.

nose, low-set ears, and short, chubby fingers. Unless they are given female hormones, they do not develop secondary sex characteristics. Although most seem to have normal verbal skills, their spatial skills are significantly below normal (Rovet and Netley, 1982).

About 1 in 400 babies is born with an XXY pattern, a condition known as **Klinefelter's syndrome.** Some of these boys develop normally, but unless they are given male sex hormones, the majority never develop secondary sex characteristics. The boys are generally passive, dependent, and mentally slow (R. Rubin, Reinisch, and Haskett, 1981). Zygotes that have inherited an XYY pattern develop into apparently normal boys and men. Only a microscopic examination of their cells reveals the unusual chromosome pattern. As men, they are often impulsive and antisocial, although they do not seem to be especially violent toward other people (R. Rubin, Reinisch, and Haskett, 1981).

If the zygote has an extra chromosome 21 (three instead of two), the egg develops into a baby who suffers from **Down's syndrome** (formerly called *mongolism*). Boys and girls with this condition frequently have congenital heart disease and other problems. Most children with Down's syndrome are mentally retarded, although the extent of retardation varies. Many do not live past young adulthood, and virtually all of those who live past the age of 40 develop brain lesions identical with lesions found in patients with Alzheimer's disease (Joachim and Selkoe, 1989).

Although Down's syndrome generally is caused by an extra chromosome, sometimes it develops when extra material from chromosome 21 becomes attached to another chromosome. This tendency is extremely rare, and it is inherited. Most cases of Down's syndrome arise when an error in cell division produces an offspring with an entire extra chromosome 21, a genetic makeup unlike that of either parent. Up to 30 percent of the cases of Down's syndrome are caused by faulty cell division in the sperm; the rest are caused by faulty cell division in the ovum (Gunderson and Sackett, 1982).

The likelihood of producing a Down's syndrome child because of an error in cell division increases as parents age. The risk of producing a child with Down's syndrome is only about 1 in 2000 for mothers at the age of 20, but 1 in 1000 at age 30, and 1 in 500 at age 35. By the age of 40, the ratio rises to about 1 in 100, and by age 45, it is 1 in 45 (Omenn, 1983). However, prenatal tests can tell women whether they are carrying a Down's syndrome fetus (see the box, "Detecting Complications").

Women who postpone pregnancy until they are past the age of 40 often worry that they run an increased risk of producing a baby with other serious defects. Recent studies are reassuring. They indicate that if the mother is in good general health, is of normal weight, and does not smoke, her risk of having a baby with abnormalities other than Down's syndrome may be no higher than the risk for women in their twenties (Kopp and Kaler, 1989). Other studies indicate that nonsmoking women older than 35 who have good prenatal care run only a slightly higher risk of having a low-birthweight baby but are no more likely than younger women to have a pre-term baby or a baby who dies in infancy (Berkowitz et al., 1990). Older first-time mothers are, however, at increased risk for complications during pregnancy, and they are more likely to have a Caesarean birth than younger women.

Environmental Hazards

Although the environment within the uterus protects the fetus from many harmful influences, some agents that can alter or kill the developing organism are able to cross the placental barrier (see Table 3.4). It seems ironic that most of these agents, which are called **teratogens,** reach the fetus through the same connections with the mother that bring life-sustaining nutrients and oxygen. Teratogens include diseases, drugs, smoking, and environmental pollutants.

Even when the extent of exposure to a destructive agent is known, however, there is no way to predict the extent of its influence on the developing fetus. Timing is apparently the crucial factor in determining whether an environmental influence will produce an abnormality. As noted earlier, different organ systems generate and develop on a staggered schedule. Because organs are most vulnerable during their period of most rapid growth, different teratogens can have the same effect at a given point in fetal development and the same teratogen can have different effects depending on the age of the fetus at the time of exposure (see Figure 3.6). Thus, if a destructive agent is introduced at the time an organ is forming, that organ may never develop properly. Yet the same agent may have less serious effects—or no effect at all—on organs that are already formed or on those that are not yet ready to make their appearances. A general rule is that younger fetuses run much higher risks than older fetuses. Exposure is especially dangerous during the embryonic period, when the mother does not know she is pregnant and is unaware that teratogens are at their insidious work.

Timing is not the only factor that determines the ex-

TABLE 3.4 SOME SUBSTANCES THAT MAY HARM THE FETUS*

ANESTHETIC GASES	**THERAPEUTIC DRUGS**
ANTIBIOTICS	**Acne drug (Accutane)**
Quinine, Quinidine	**Anticonvulsive drugs**
Streptomycin	**(Dilantin)**
Sulfonamides	**Antidiabetic drugs:**
Tetracyclines	**Chlorpropamide**
ENVIRONMENTAL POLLUTANTS	**Tolbutamide**
Cadmium	**Antihistamines**
Carbon disulfide	**Antitumor drugs**
Chlordane	**Appetite depressants**
Lead	**that work on the**
Mercury	**central nervous**
Polychorinated biphenyls	**system (Didrex)**
(PCBs)	**Aspirin**
Vinyl chloride	**Barbiturates**
HORMONAL AGENTS	**Drugs for heart**
Androgens	**disease or high**
Diethylstilbestrol (DES)	**blood pressure:**
Insulin	**Thiazides**
Oral contraceptives	**Reserpine**
RECREATIONAL DRUGS	**TRANQUILIZERS**
Alcohol	**Valium**
Caffeine	**Librium**
Cigarettes	**Meprobamate**
Cocaine	**Phenothiazines**
Heroin	**Thalidomide**
Marijuana	**VITAMINS (excessive**
Methadone	**doses)**
	A, B$_6$, D, K

This sampling from a growing list of harmful substances reinforces the wisdom of the obstetrician's advice to take as little medication during pregnancy as possible.

tent of damage. The amount of exposure, the genetic susceptibility of the fetus, and the mother's physical condition can reduce or exaggerate the likelihood of malformation (E. Johnson and Kochlar, 1983).

Gross physical damage usually is apparent at birth or during early infancy. But some teratogens produce **sleeper effects:** their influence is not apparent until later in the course of development. Either the damage is masked by some compensatory mechanism, or behavior that is affected by the damage emerges only later (S. Jacobson et al., 1985). Damage to the central nervous system that affects the ability to talk, for example, goes unnoticed until a child is at least 2 years old; damage that affects the ability to concentrate or to master school skills goes unnoticed until even later.

Disease

If a woman contracts rubella, commonly known as German measles, early in pregnancy, her child may be born blind, deaf, brain-damaged, or with heart disease. Fortunately, serious damage seems restricted to the first three months of the prenatal period, and the later the mother catches rubella, the less likely it is that her baby will be affected. Chicken pox is another of the common viral diseases that increase the risk of malformation or mental retardation, whereas mumps and rubeola (commonly known as red measles) increase the likelihood of miscarriage.

Sexually transmitted diseases in the mother also can have unfortunate consequences for the fetus. The organisms that cause *syphilis* pass through the placental barrier, transmitting the disease to the fetus. If a pregnant woman is in the early stages of syphilis, and if she receives treatment, her baby is likely to be born without ill effects. But if she remains untreated or if she is in a more severe stage of the disease, her baby may be born with congenital syphilis. When the mother is seriously infected, her baby may suffer a wide variety of debilitating and severe abnormalities.

As the fetus moves down the birth canal, it can come into contact with gonococcus, the bacterium that produces *gonorrhea.* A number of years ago, many babies became blind when their eyes were infected by gonococci during the birth process. Because many women have gonorrhea without showing any symptoms, it has become common practice to place drops of silver nitrate or antibiotics in the eyes of all newborn babies. The practice has almost wiped out this kind of blindness. *Chlamydia,* another bacterium, today is more common than gonorrhea. Like gonorrhea, it may be a silent, symptomless infection that lurks in the vagina and enters the baby during labor. About 100,000 babies each year develop eye infections, middle-ear infections, gastroenteritis, or pneumonia from chlamydia infections. Although antibiotic ointments can prevent the eye infections, they seem unable to keep pneumonia from developing (E. Larson, 1987; Schaefer et al., 1985).

The prospects are less hopeful for a *genital herpes* infection, which represents a real danger for a fetus that picks up the virus while moving down the birth canal. Because the incubation period for this virus is from four to twenty-one days, infected babies may not show any symptoms (which include skin eruptions, hepatitis, pneumonia, clots within blood vessels, and neurological impairment) until after they go home from the hospital (E. Larson, 1987). Up to half of the babies born to mothers with a primary active genital herpes infection con-

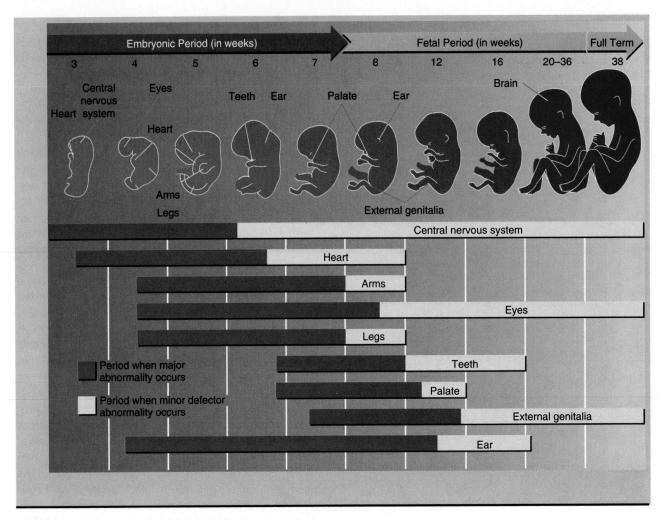

Figure 3.6 Sensitivity to teratogens is greatest during the embryonic period when organs are forming (dark band), and exposure may produce major structural abnormalities. Once organs have formed (light band) exposure to teratogens may produce abnormalities in function, stunt growth, or have no effect at all. With most teratogens, exposure becomes progressively less destructive as the fetus matures. (*From K. L. Moore, 1974, p. 96*)

tract the disease, and many do not survive it (Remington and Kleine, 1990).

Another sometimes sexually transmitted disease that can pass through the placental barrier is **acquired immune deficiency syndrome (AIDS).** In most cases, the mother (or her partner) contracts the disease when injecting street drugs with a contaminated needle, but whatever the source of the mother's infection, the danger to the baby is the same. Symptoms resulting from the collapse of the baby's immune system usually appear within the first year: recurrent bacterial infections, failure to thrive, severe neurological impairments, and delayed development. Up to 70 percent of affected infants have neurological problems, which include ab-

normally small heads and brain degeneration (Nyhan, 1990).

Drugs

A golden rule of obstetric practice has been to advise women to take as little medication during pregnancy as possible. Even aspirin has become suspect. Some authorities believe that it can lengthen pregnancy and lead to bleeding in the newborn infant, whereas other researchers have found poor balance and impaired fine motor skills in 4-year-olds whose mothers took aspirin several times a week during pregnancy (Barr et al., 1990).

One of the more spectacular examples of drug effects

appeared in the 1960s, when women who took the drug thalidomide early in pregnancy (while fetal limbs were forming) gave birth to babies without arms or legs. These infants' hands and feet grew from their bodies like flippers. Accutane, a drug often prescribed today for severe acne, causes fetal death or serious malformations of the face, skull, brain, heart, and thymus gland (Sun, 1988).

Sometimes drugs given to keep a mother from miscarrying can affect the developing fetus. Diethylstilbestrol (DES), for example, a synthetic hormone that was widely prescribed from the 1940s until 1975, has been associated with a rare form of vaginal and cervical cancer in women whose mothers received the drug, with the highest damage among those exposed to large doses during the embryonic period. When these exposed women later became pregnant themselves, they were much more likely than other women to miscarry, to have abnormal pregnancies that required surgical termination, and to give birth before term (Sandberg et al., 1981). Adolescent boys whose mothers received the drug tend to have low sperm counts.

The proportion of babies born to mothers who abuse drugs during pregnancy has been growing steadily. In New York City, for example, the incidence of drug-exposed newborns more than tripled from 1981 to 1987 (Habel, Kaye, and Lee, 1990). The newborn infant of a heroin or methadone user often must go through withdrawal, because both drugs pass through the placental barrier. These babies have tremors, diarrhea, high temperatures, and convulsions. They are irritable, sleep poorly, and cry a great deal. When they are older, they often are restless, find it difficult to sit still, and have short attention spans.

The damage done by cocaine is now becoming apparent. The widespread availability of crack (free-base cocaine that can be smoked) has turned cocaine addiction among newborns and cocaine-related developmental complications into major problems in some large urban hospital nurseries. Newborns whose growth has been stunted by cocaine react slowly and sluggishly, but once provoked into crying, they scream inconsolably. Exposed newborns of normal birthweight respond quickly with fierce cries (Lester, 1990). Cocaine use during pregnancy appears to increase fetal death rates; exposure may also produce heart defects, deformed genital or urinary tracts, strokes, serious respiratory problems, or seizures. Although physicians report a number of long-range neurological problems, the problem of widespread cocaine exposure is so new that few controlled studies exist. Two studies, however, indicate

that its effect on motor performance and vision may linger for at least six months (Roland and Volpe, 1989).

In the United States, 1 in 750 newborns shows the effects of **fetal alcohol syndrome,** a condition that is many times more prevalent among Eskimos and Native Americans than among any other ethnic group (Kopp and Kaler, 1989). These babies, who are born to alcoholic mothers, are extremely light and have a conical-shaped head with characteristic facial features; most are mentally retarded. Occasionally, these babies have cleft palates, heart murmurs, hernias, damaged kidneys, and eye, neural tube, or skeletal defects. Studies indicate that heavy alcohol consumption is especially risky before a woman realizes that she is pregnant: human embryos run the greatest danger of gross brain malformation during the third week of development (Sulik, Johnston, and Webb, 1981).

Social drinking may also harm the fetus. Heavy social drinkers have about three times as many stillbirths as light drinkers, and their babies are light, have abnormal heart rates, receive low scores on standard tests of their physical condition, suck weakly, and perform poorly on tests of newborn behavior. Mothers who averaged three drinks a day during pregnancy had children whose IQs at age 4 were about 5 points less than IQs of children with similar backgrounds whose mothers averaged one drink or less. These children's motor skills and balance were also significantly poorer than those of children whose mothers did not drink during pregnancy (Barr et al., 1990; Streissguth et al., 1989). Among mothers who drank less, children's language and cognitive development was below normal at age 3, but within another year the effects were no longer significant (Fried and Watkinson, 1990). Yet pregnant women who restrict their alcohol intake to weekend parties should be wary. When the blood alcohol level rises sharply, as it does when several drinks are consumed, the umbilical cord appears to collapse, perhaps cutting off the supply of oxygen to the fetal brain (Mukherjee and Hodgen, 1982). Even so, not all children born to alcoholic mothers show fetal alcohol syndrome, and some show no obvious symptoms of prenatal exposure (Kopp and Kaler, 1989).

Smoking

Cigarette smoking has been associated with a wide variety of effects on the fetus, in part because both nicotine and increased carbon monoxide in the mother's blood deprive the fetus of oxygen. Nicotine also crosses the placental barrier, speeding the fetus's heart and depressing its respiratory rate. Smokers are more likely to miscarry or have babies who die early in infancy, and they are twice as likely as nonsmokers to have low-birth-weight babies. Babies of smokers also have a significantly higher rate of cleft palates and harelips. As newborns, the babies of women who smoked just under one package of cigarettes a day tend to be slow to cry or to respond to sounds (S. Jacobson et al., 1984).

The long-term effects of smoking during pregnancy are uncertain. Some studies have found poorer language development and lower cognitive scores among 4-year-olds whose mothers smoked (Fried and Watkinson, 1990), whereas others have found no lingering effects (Streissguth et al., 1989). Since women who smoke also tend to drink alcohol and to be primarily young and poorly educated, the long-term effects found in some studies may be confounded by these factors (Streissguth et al., 1989). Low scores on tests of language and memory persist among youngsters with prenatal exposure to marijuana, however, even after researchers adjust for such confounding variables (Fried and Watkinson, 1990).

Environmental Pollutants

Chemicals in the air that expectant mothers breathe and in the food that they eat may pass through the placental barrier. Mercury, lead, and polychlorinated biphenyls (PCBs—synthetic hydrocarbons) are among the best-known environmental pollutants. They accumulate in the body, and from time to time, areas of high contamination provide dramatic proof of their insidious effects on the growing fetus. During the 1970s, for example, Japanese mothers who regularly ate mercury-contaminated fish gave birth to infants with severely damaged nervous systems (Takeuchi, 1972). The babies who survived had abnormal motor development, found it difficult to chew or swallow, and were profoundly retarded.

Lead is another pollutant with long-term effects. In a longitudinal study, 2-year-olds whose umbilical cords had shown lead contamination at birth got lower-than-normal scores on the Bayley Scales of Infant Development (Bellinger et al., 1987). The higher the lead content at birth, the lower the score, and differences in performance between groups with high and low levels of contamination at birth widened over time.

PCBs are a third type of pollutant. Researchers discovered that women who ate PCB-contaminated fish from Lake Michigan gave birth to babies who were lower in birthweight and had smaller head circumferences and shorter gestation periods than babies born to women who lived in the same area but did not eat fish. By the time these infants were 7 months old, a sleeper

effect appeared. Although their behavior as newborns seemed normal, these infants now showed memory problems: they found it difficult to recognize objects they had just seen (S. Jacobson et al., 1985). Memory problems, as well as slowed visual processing, were still apparent at 4 years (J. Jacobson et al., 1992).

As with other teratogens, the amount of pollutant that reaches the fetus and the time of exposure are important. In addition, any genetic predisposition or temporary condition that might sensitize the fetus to the pollutant's harmful effects can either heighten or diminish the damage.

Emotional Stress

Because stress alters a pregnant woman's hormone production, it also alters the environment of her fetus. There is little doubt that these real physiological changes have momentary effects on the fetus, because they divert blood flow away from the fetus and cut back on its oxygen supply (Stechler and Halton, 1982). The question is whether oxygen deprivation and the chemical changes that accompany stress have lasting effects. Although some studies have shown that highly anxious mothers tend to have difficult deliveries and that their infants score poorly on newborn assessment scales, other research indicates little connection between stress and the outcome of pregnancy (Istvan, 1986).

When lingering effects do appear, they may be heightened by postnatal stress on the mother. A mother who is emotionally upset during her pregnancy is likely to be upset after her baby is born. Prenatal hormones may make a baby irritable and more difficult to care for, but continued stress on the mother may make her unhappy, tense, and inconsistent in her behavior. As a result, she may be less responsive to her baby—whether to infant distress or social overtures (Rutter, 1990).

Anesthetics

In recent years, American women have been asking for fewer pain-relieving drugs during the birth process. Their reluctance to take unnecessary drugs is probably wise, because many of the drugs given for pain cross the placental barrier and have a depressant effect on the fetus. The effects of these drugs may linger for days or even months, depending on the drug, the dosage, and the time of administration. In most studies, babies whose mothers were given drugs performed poorly on standard tests of infant behavior compared with babies whose mothers received no drugs. Among the baby's basic functions that are affected by pain-relieving drugs given to the mother are visual attention, sucking, weight gain, smiling, movement, and responses to various stimuli (Stechler and Halton, 1982).

Prematurity

Any condition that interferes with fetal development can result in a baby's being born before **term,** which refers to a gestational age of thirty-six to forty weeks from conception. All such babies were once called "premature" and given special medical care. This definition was inadequate, because a baby born at term sometimes is seriously underweight and needs intensive medical care. Today, physicians are concerned about two kinds of babies: (1) any newborn (pre- or full-term) who weighs less than 5½ pounds (2500 grams) and (2) any newborn who is **small for gestational age (SGA).** Babies in the latter group weigh less than 90 percent of other babies of the same gestational age. Babies in the former group (weighing less than 2500 grams) account for only 7 percent of all U.S. newborns, yet up to 65

percent of all neonatal deaths occur in this group (Meisels and Plunkett, 1988).

Out of every 1000 babies born alive during 1990 in the United States, 9.1 died during their first year (Hilts, 1991). This rate is twice as high as the infant mortality rate in Japan. In fact, twenty-two countries have lower infant mortality rates than the United States. Excess U.S. deaths are found primarily among minority groups. Among African-Americans, for example, the rate is 17.6, whereas it is only 8.5 among whites. Researchers believe that the excessive death rate in some minority groups is the result of poverty, teenage pregnancies, and lack of prenatal care—all conditions associated with low birthweights.

Babies who need the most medical attention are those who once would never have survived. They have a gestational age of less than thirty weeks (no matter what their weight), or they weigh less than 1250 grams (no matter what their age). These **very low birthweight** babies are so neurologically immature that re-

The life-support system of a preterm infant. *(David Hurn/Magnum)*

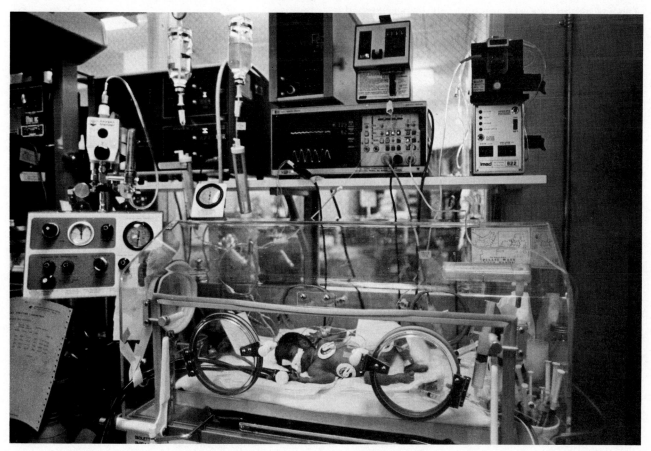

searchers describe them as almost a different species, "looking more like each other than like their siblings, parents, or full-term infants" (L. Newman, 1981). They need prolonged hospital care, with continual monitoring of their blood pressure, temperature, respiration, and heart rate; feedings of water and milk through a tube directly into the stomach; and careful control of their oxygen supply (too little and they develop cerebral palsy; too much and they become blind). Between one-third and one-half of these high-risk babies have severe handicaps, and even with the best of care, 20 percent of those who survive the neonatal period die in infancy (Meisels and Plunkett, 1988).

The prospect of normal development in preterm infants has markedly increased from the 1960s. Indeed, the effects of prematurity may gradually dissipate for those considered at low risk. Little is known about the long-term consequences for very low birthweight infants, because almost no research exists (Meisels and Plunkett, 1988). In virtually the only published study of babies weighing less than 1000 grams at birth, 75 percent died (Kitchen et al., 1987). But among the 25 percent who reached the age of 5, most showed no effects of their early precarious status and only 19 percent had major handicaps.

What is the best predictor of a very low birthweight baby's future? Although medical or physiological problems of high-risk infants may produce a degree of disability in any environment, babies who grow up in advantaged homes often do well and show no lasting effects. But babies with similar problems who grow up in disadvantaged homes often have learning disabilities or some neurological effect. Poverty does not doom a preterm baby; the quality of parent-child interaction, preschool experiences, and the level of family stress also play an important role in preventing or promoting the development of preterm babies (Meisels and Plunkett, 1988).

In spite of all the possible complications of the prenatal period, most babies come into the world as normal individuals. As a baby emerges from the dark of the womb, the most intimate human relationship ends. Within the uterus, the child is completely dependent on the mother for the automatic satisfaction of every need. At birth, the baby starts life as a separate individual. In the next chapter, we look at the beginnings of independent life—the world of the newborn child.

SUMMARY

HOW LIFE BEGINS

The **prenatal period** begins when the father's **spermatozoon** unites with the mother's **ovum** to form a **zygote.** Conception occurs within the **Fallopian tube,** as the ovum released during the **menstrual cycle** travels toward the uterus. **Infertile** couples can conceive through **artificial insemination** or **in-vitro fertilization.** Each **gamete,** or sex cell, was formed by **meiosis,** which produces cells containing twenty-three single **chromosomes.** Chromosomes are composed of **genes,** tiny bits of **deoxyribonucleic acid (DNA),** which transmits traits and predispositions to the offspring.

THE TRANSMISSION OF GENES

The complex processes of genetic combination determine the offspring's **genotype,** the unique set of genes carried by the child. The **phenotype,** or physical expression of those genes, often is different from the genotype. This difference is in part due to the fact that, for

some single-gene traits, the **dominant** gene masks the **recessive** gene. For example, the inherited metabolic difficulty **phenylketonuria (PKU)** appears when two recessive **alleles** (genes) for the trait are paired; in this case the offspring is **homozygous** for PKU. When only one PKU allele is present, the offspring is **heterozygous** and the phenotype is normal. Some single-gene traits are **codominant,** and **modifier genes** may affect the expression of a trait. The majority of traits are **polygenic.**

Genes always interact with the environment, and any genotype has a **reaction range** in which it may be expressed. This interaction can affect behavior through passive genetic influence (experience provided by parents), through the responses a child's appearance and behavior evoke from others, and through the child's actively seeking out some experiences and ignoring others. Researchers use animal breeding experiments and family studies (including twin studies and adoption studies) to study genetic influences on development.

PRENATAL GROWTH

During a 266-day **gestation period,** the organism rapidly progresses from a zygote primarily engaged in cell division **(germinal period),** to an **embryo** in which organ systems are forming **(embryonic period),** to a **fetus** in which organs are structured and functions are established **(fetal period).** During the germinal period, the **placenta** and **umbilical cord** develop; they nourish the organism and carry away its wastes. Prenatal growth is **proximodistal** (from the center of the body to the periphery) and **cephalocaudal** (from head to toe). After all systems have formed, the fetus still cannot survive on its own, in part because it cannot produce enough **surfactin** to protect it from **respiratory distress.** Babies born between twenty-four and twenty-eight weeks can survive, but few do.

PRENATAL BEHAVIORAL DEVELOPMENT

The fetus begins to move reflexively at about eight weeks and seems to move spontaneously at about twenty-three weeks. Behavioral development corresponds to the development of muscles and the nervous system. The ability of the older fetus to hear has been established through **ultrasound,** which uses the echoes of sound bounced off the fetus to produce **sonograms.** The older fetus may also be capable of remembering sound patterns.

THE BIRTH PROCESS

During **labor,** uterine contractions push the infant, and then the **afterbirth,** through the **cervix** and down the birth canal. Babies sometimes are delivered by Caesarean section, especially if they are in danger of **anoxia.**

The popularity of natural childbirth has allowed the father to participate and made the entire process more normal and less threatening for many couples.

FETAL ABNORMALITIES AND BIRTH COMPLICATIONS

When genetic **mutations** occur during meiosis, the zygote generally dies. Sometimes meiosis produces chromosomal abnormalities: the fetus may have a single female chromosome **(Turner's syndrome),** two female chromosomes and one male chromosome **(Klinefelter's syndrome),** one female and two male chromosomes, or an extra chromosome 21 **(Down's syndrome).** Many abnormalities, including **spina bifida,** can be detected before birth by **amniocentesis** or **chorionic villi sampling.**

Teratogens, agents that can reach the fetus by crossing the placental barrier, include diseases (such as rubella, syphilis, or **AIDS**), drugs, smoking, emotional stress, and environmental pollutants. Alcohol can produce **fetal alcohol syndrome.** The effect of teratogens depends on the timing of the exposure, the dosage, and the genetic susceptibility of the fetus, and **sleeper effects** may not appear for months or years.

Babies who are born before **term** need extra attention after birth if they weigh less than 2500 grams or are **small for gestational age (SGA).** Most extensive care is required by **very low birthweight** babies who have a gestational age of less than thirty weeks or who weigh less than 1250 grams. Low-birthweight babies who do best grow up in advantaged homes; the quality of parent-child interaction, preschool experiences, and the level of family stress are also important.

KEY TERMS

acquired immune deficiency syndrome (AIDS)

afterbirth

allele

amniocentesis

amnion

anoxia

artificial insemination

cephalocaudal development

cervix

chorion

chorionic villi sampling

chromosomes

codominant

deoxyribonucleic acid (DNA)

dominant

Down's syndrome

embryo

embryonic period

Fallopian tube

fetal alcohol syndrome

fetal period

fetus

gametes

genes

genotype

germinal period

gestational age

gestation period

heterozygous

homozygous

hydrocephaly

infertile

in-vitro fertilization

Klinefelter's syndrome

labor

meiosis

menstrual age

menstrual cycle

modifier genes

mutation

ovum

phenotype

phenylketonuria (PKU)

placenta

polygenic

prenatal period

proximodistal development

reaction range

recessive

respiratory distress syndrome

sleeper effect

small for gestational age (SGA)

sonogram

spermatozoon

spina bifida

surfactin

teratogen

term

Turner's syndrome

ultrasound

umbilical cord

very low birthweight

zygote

• • • • • • • • • • • • • •

THE NEWBORN'S WORLD

· · · · · · · · · · · · ·

THE NEWBORN'S WORLD

• • • • • • • • • • • • • •

The newborn infant is suddenly thrust from a warm, dark, watery world into a cold, gaseous universe filled with light. The transition must be a shock. A century ago, American psychologist William James (1890/1950) supposed the new world must appear terribly chaotic to the naive baby, "assailed by eyes, ears, nose, skin, and entrails at once, [who] feels it all as one great blooming, buzzing confusion." This new sensory world may not be as confusing as James assumed, for babies enter the world possessing a variety of capacities and skills that help them reduce the confusion and begin to sort out their surroundings. Newborns may be strangers in a strange land, but they are prepared strangers, equipped with the tools they need to make sense of their new world.

The baby's vital organs are formed and functional, but the newborn baby is a curious mixture of competence and incapacity. Unlike the eyes of a newborn kitten or puppy, a human baby's eyes are open. Babies can see and hear and smell and taste and feel; they can cry and eat and move their limbs. They possess a set of reflexes that help them to cope with their strange new world and sample its character. They are prepared to learn and very quickly begin searching their surroundings for information. Yet babies are helpless. Unlike the newborn calf, who stands within the hour and staggers over to its mother to nurse, the human baby must be carried to the mother and the nipple placed near the tiny mouth before the baby's ability to nurse is of any use.

In this chapter, we explore the capabilities and limitations of newborn babies, beginning with the natural biological rhythms that keep many of the basic body functions in balance. After a look at the baby's reflexes and their possible significance, we consider early perceptual capabilities and try to establish just what a newborn can taste, smell, hear, and see. Our examination of the newborn's temperament will show how successful psychologists have been in their attempts to find the rudiments of personality in the first weeks of life. Finally, we look at the baby's social world, discovering that the way newborn infants look and listen or the way they quiet when upset may provide the roots for their individual social development.

The Neonate

At the moment of birth, a transition in development occurs. The fetus becomes a **neonate,** a word derived from Greek and Latin roots meaning "newborn." The baby is called a neonate until the end of his or her first month of life outside the womb, when the period of early infancy begins.

Immediately after birth, the neonate is examined so that attendants can determine whether further medical help is needed. Most physicians rely on the baby's **Apgar score** on a test devised by physician Virginia Apgar to assess the newborn's appearance (skin color), heart rate, reflex irritability, muscle tone, and respiratory effort (Apgar et al., 1958). Each of these five characteristics is rated 0, 1, or 2 (2 being best), and these scores are added to constitute the baby's total Apgar score, which may vary from 0 to 10 (see Table 4.1). At one minute after delivery, most normal newborns achieve a score of 8 to 10. Those whose scores are still 4 or less after five minutes require immediate medical care.

Another widely used method is the Dubowitz scoring system, which gives a fairly accurate estimate of the newborn's gestational age (Dubowitz, Dubowitz, and Goldberg, 1970). A baby's score on ten neurological signs (such as limb reflexes and hand flexion) and eleven characteristics of appearance (such as skin texture, genitals, and ears) can be determined in less than five minutes (Self and Horowitz, 1979). The highest possible score (70) indicates a baby that is past term. The Dubowitz system has become increasingly popular because it separates the preterm baby from the very small full-term baby. It also indicates which babies are most at risk for developmental problems (Eyler et al., 1991).

Most babies are highly alert just after they are born. They generally are responsive in the delivery room

TABLE 4.1   THE APGAR SCALE

Sign	SCORE		
	0	**1**	**2**
Heart rate	None	Less than 100 beats/min	100 or more beats/min
Respiratory effort	None	Shallow, irregular	Normal crying and breathing
Reflex irritability	No response	Weak response	Vigorous response to stimulation
Muscle tone	Limp	Weak, no resistance	Limbs resistant to applied force Spontaneous flexing
Skin color*	Blue, yellowish	Body pink, limbs blue	Entire body pink

The skin color measure, which reflects circulation and checks for jaundice, was devised for Caucasian infants and is difficult (but not impossible) to evaluate in infants from some ethnic groups.

Source: Adapted from Apgar et al., 1958.

when parents hold and get acquainted with their new daughter or son. Later, when newborns finally fall asleep for the first time in the world of air, their sleep is usually deep. Even a loud sound may fail to elicit any obvious response. During this sleep, the body is beginning to function on its own. Within the womb, the placenta linked the fetus's circulatory, digestive, temperature-regulation, and excretory systems with those of the mother. Now the baby's own physiological equipment must take over these necessary functions.

Preterm babies are less proficient at assuming these functions than are full-term babies. Even when healthy preterm babies are tested two weeks after their expected date of birth (from five to twenty-two weeks after actual birth), they have not yet caught up with full-term babies of the same gestational age in their ability to regulate autonomic states, motor performance, or attention (Duffy, Als, and McAnulty, 1990). Much of this slowness is probably due to minor, but unavoidable, complications that accompany most preterm births. The rest may be due to sensorimotor stimulation that immature systems are not prepared to handle. The preterm nursery is a place of constant loud noises (as loud as inside a city bus), high levels of illumination, painful medical experiences, and a minimum of rewarding social interaction (Meisels and Plunkett, 1988). As the

accompanying box, "A Boost for Preterm Babies," indicates, researchers have devised various programs to assist the preterm baby's adaptation to the world.

Infant States and Rhythms

The neonate's major task is to integrate the action of bodily systems. Much of the newborn's behavior already is organized, but until babies learn to control these interacting systems, they may be unable to sleep properly or attend to things in their environment. Their motor activity will be ineffective, and they will spend much of their time crying, which wastes precious energy (Brazelton, 1990).

Many of the baby's basic functions have detectable rhythms that repeat in cycles ranging from seconds to hours. Breathing and sucking cycles, which are measured in seconds, are essential to the maintenance of life. Spontaneous limb movements, which occur every minute or so, may be linked to the same timing mechanism that bolsters breathing during sleep by causing the neonate to sigh regularly (Robertson, 1982). Some daily rhythms, such as the rise and fall of temperature, appear shortly after birth; others, such as rhythmical swaying,

A BOOST FOR PRETERM BABIES

Life in the preterm nursery is highly stressful, especially for low-birthweight neonates. These babies work desperately hard to adjust their bodies for survival outside the uterus. Their effort shows in their high heart rates. The hearts of preterm babies beat about thirty times more each minute than the hearts of full-term neonates. Preterm babies seem to require more active sleep; their sleep is restless; and they are less responsive to stimuli (Rose, 1983).

Because the immaturity of preterm systems seems aggravated by the noisy, brightly lighted nursery, researchers arranged an alternative nursery (Fajardo et al., 1990). Noise and light levels during the day were lowered, and night activity and light were cut to a minimum. The babies responded with fewer changes in arousal each hour, spending more time in each state, whether sleep, drowsiness, alertness, fussiness, or crying, before moving to another. The less disruptive atmosphere apparently supported the neonates' ability to regulate their level of consciousness.

Another way to alleviate the stress of the preterm nursery is the use of pacifiers, which are known to soothe newborns. Preterm babies who were fed by tube sucked a pacifier before and during each tube feeding. These babies were ready for bottle feeding several days earlier than babies in a control group, they went home from the hospital four days sooner, and they had fewer complications (G. Anderson, Burroughs, and Measel, 1983). The soothing pacifier reduced crying. Since crying allows blood to bypass the lungs, the pacifier apparently helped to maintain a better supply of oxygen in the babies' bloodstream.

Other researchers used a program of mild tactile stimulation to increase preterm infants' chances of normal development (Scafidi et al., 1990). These researchers regularly stroked each tiny baby's head, shoulders, back, arms, hands, legs, and feet. They also gently flexed and then extended the infant's arms and legs. To reduce light in the nursery, they covered the cribs with blankets. The babies gained weight more rapidly than babies in a control group, although both groups ate the same amount of formula. Apparently, mild stimulation improved the efficiency of their metabolism. The stimulated babies also performed better on a standard test of newborn behavior. They did so well that they were able to leave the hospital five days before the other babies.

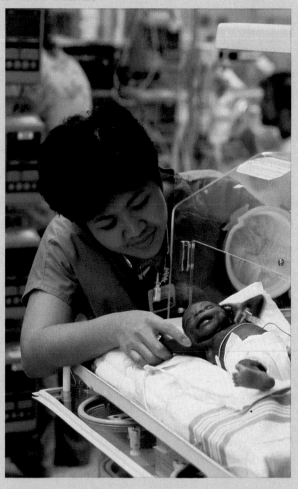

Regular tactile stimulation in the hospital nursery speeds the preterm infant's adjustment to the world. *(Ted Horowitz/The Stock Market)*

None of these programs is complicated, but small interventions early in a preterm baby's life may help compensate for immaturity and thus be as effective as much more complicated interventions at a later age.

---

rocking, and kicking, emerge during the first year as neuromuscular pathways develop (Thelen, 1979).

Babies pass through six **states** of consciousness, which reflect responses to the internal environment as well as responses to the world. As these states change,

babies move through deep sleep, active sleep, drowsiness, alertness, fussiness, and crying (see Table 4.2). With each change, babies become more or less attentive and receptive to the environment. Sometimes it is difficult to decide just what state a baby is in. For example, a

TABLE 4.2   INFANT STATES OF CONSCIOUSNESS*

State	Description
Deep sleep	Little movement; deep, regular breathing
Active sleep	Facial and body movement; shallow, irregular, fast breathing; rapid eye movements often present
Drowsy	Slow movements; if eyes are open, baby appears dazed; shallow, fast breathing
Alert	Eyes open, bright; baby quiet and inactive
Fussy	Generalized movement; facial grimaces; brief cries (about 1/10 sec)
Crying	Intense movements; continuous crying

Most researchers rely on these six states when assessing infants' arousal. Some researchers, however, make finer distinctions among the states.

Source: Adapted from Brazelton, 1973.

nursing infant whose eyes are closed and who seems unresponsive to touch may keep feeding. Is the baby asleep, drowsy, or going from one state to another?

Neonates are quietly alert for only short periods. Unless they are feeding, most newborns become either drowsy or fussy after five or ten minutes. This brief attentiveness probably is useful in cutting down the amount of potentially overwhelming stimulation that surrounds them. But the same brevity also has implications for learning: because newborns can pick up information only in small bits, they are unlikely to remember much of what they see or hear. Within a few months, the situation changes dramatically: 3-month-olds remain alert for about ninety minutes at a time (Olson and Sherman, 1983).

During the first week, babies experience all states of consciousness but begin to show stable patterns that reflect individual differences (Colombo, Moss, and Horowitz, 1989). The majority of newborns spend up to 75 percent of their time in one of the sleep states, and they cry infrequently. At 2 weeks, these babies tend to be especially cuddly and to be more adept than others at coordinating their hand-to-mouth movements. A smaller group of newborns spend much more time awake—alert, fussy, or crying. At 2 weeks, these babies are more alert and pay more attention to sounds and sights, perhaps because they receive more stimulation from caregivers. A few neonates show an unstable profile of states. Berry Brazelton (1990) proposes that an infant's profile reflects individual capacities for organiz-

ing systems to interact with the environment, and he speculates that an unstable profile from day to day may reflect a heightened ability to change and to adapt to the environment.

Distress and Crying

The ability of neonates to regulate their state reveals how much control they have over their internal systems. One immediate test of this efficiency is the stress on their temperature control system. Within the watery uterus, temperature hovers around 98.6 degrees Fahrenheit, but the air in the delivery room is usually colder by 20 to 30 degrees. The baby's temperature control system thus begins its work under considerable stress. Most babies prove equal to the task. Within fifteen minutes, they are constricting their surface blood vessels and shunting blood away from the surface of the body, where it would cool.

Babies' ability to control body temperature will not be at peak efficiency until they are between 4 and 9 weeks old (Rovee-Collier and Gekoski, 1979). In the meantime, neonates rely on other techniques to meet the stress of cold (Woodson, 1983). They reduce their body surface by drawing up their arms and legs and curling their bodies, thus shrinking heat loss. They become restless and cry, a response that helps them in two ways: the muscular activity required generates heat, and the close contact that results when a caregiver picks them up provides additional warmth from the caregiver's body.

Babies who are small for gestational age (SGA) are less adept at controlling their autonomic systems, perhaps because their central and autonomic nervous systems are hypersensitive to stimulation (Brazelton, 1990). They have little ability to console themselves (which would regulate their state) and are not easily soothed by caregivers. They cry relentlessly, and their cry is high-pitched and piercing. The quality of a newborn's cry reflects the condition of the central nervous system and is related to later development (Lester, 1983). Unusual, high-pitched cries, for example, signal brain damage or some other insult to the central nervous system. "Crack babies" have such ominous cries (see Chapter 3), and in a recent study, researchers found that babies born to Jamaican mothers who smoked marijuana during pregnancy cried in short, turbulent, high-pitched shrieks with a lower-pitched resonance indicating additional respiratory problems (Lester and Dreher, 1989). As we will see in a later section, the characteristics of an infant's cry can affect the relationship with caregivers.

Sleep Patterns

Newborn infants sleep a great deal—about sixteen or seventeen out of each twenty-four hours. Unfortunately for most parents, they rarely sleep much more than four hours without waking. The typical newborn begins life by staying awake and alert for a couple of hours and then immediately goes into the regular four-hour sleep/wake cycle (Emde, Swedberg, and Suzuki, 1975). During each cycle the baby is awake for only about half an hour. From the first week, the baby sleeps a little more at night and stays awake slightly longer during the day. Throughout the first five weeks the amount of daytime wakefulness steadily increases (Thoman and Whitney, 1989). By 16 weeks the baby may sleep as long as six hours at a stretch, and daytime sleep becomes naps. By the last half of the first year, the typical infant sleeps through the night without waking. Each baby's sleep schedule is highly personal, however, as parents of 10-month-olds who still wake up at 2 A.M. ruefully report. Why do neonates sleep so much? Sleep conserves energy, and the sleeping infant has more calories left over to fuel growth. In addition, during sleep the infant is protected against possible overload from the multitude of stimuli that bombard infants during their waking hours.

From the beginning, newborns' sleep is coordinated with a shorter, hourly rest/activity cycle in which the quality of sleep varies in a rhythmic fashion. During sleep, babies go from active to quiet sleep in rhythmic cycles, similar to the longer cycles seen in adults. However, newborns go directly into active sleep; not until they are several months old will they begin each cycle with a period of quiet sleep as adults do (Berg and Berg, 1979). At birth, about half of each hour-long sleep cycle is spent in active sleep, but the proportion of active sleep begins to drop almost immediately during the night, when sleep is more concentrated (Thoman and Whitney, 1989). Within three months, the baby spends twice as much time in quiet sleep, and older preschoolers spend four-fifths of sleep time in quiet sleep, which is the adult average.

Among adults, active sleep and quiet sleep are distinguished primarily by whether rapid eye movement (REM) occurs. Although not all of the newborn's active sleep is marked by rapid eye movement, much of it is. Adults wakened during active sleep usually report that they have been dreaming. It is unlikely that newborn babies in active sleep experience anything resembling an adult dream. For one thing, their experiences are limited, and whatever "dreams" they might have are probably no more than random patterns of light and sound (McCall, 1979). For another thing, the active sleep of neonates is physiologically different from that of dreaming adults, and the distinctive brain-wave patterns that characterize active sleep do not appear until babies are 3 or 4 months old (A. Parmelee and Sigman, 1983).

What is the function of active sleep in neonates and young infants? Some researchers suggest that it simply indicates neural immaturity in higher brain levels that are involved in quiet sleep. Others believe that periodic neural activity, from either external or internal sources, is necessary for brain development. Because neonates sleep so much and have little opportunity to respond to events in the world around them, they provide their own neurological self-stimulation—stimulation at a level they can handle. Preterm babies spend even more time in active sleep than full-term infants do. Babies born as early as twenty-five weeks spend all their time in some sort of active sleep. Perhaps such activity is necessary before birth if neurological development is to proceed normally.

Sucking Patterns and Comfort

The neonate's sleep/wake cycle is closely tied to the need for nourishment. The typical neonate sleeps, wakes up hungry, eats, remains quietly alert for a short time, becomes drowsy, and then falls back to sleep.

How smoothly this cycle meshes with the world depends on the society into which the child is born. Among the !Kung San, a much-studied band of hunter-gatherers who live a nomadic life in Africa's Kalahari Desert under conditions that may be like those of our early ancestors, breast milk is always available (Konner and Worthman, 1980). The baby rides next to the mother's body by day and sleeps with her at night. During the day, the baby sucks for only about six minutes at a time but does this about three times each hour. At night, the breast is always available, and so the baby sucks each time it wakes up. Contrast this sucking experience with that of a bottle-fed newborn in the United States, who may eat about every three hours. Breast-fed neonates may eat somewhat more often, but few are given the

access enjoyed by the !Kung San infant. The striking difference suggests that adapting to life outside the uterus is more complicated for a bottle-fed baby than for a baby of the !Kung San.

Sucking Patterns

At the first feeding, the neonate may suck raggedly, but within a few days he or she sucks, swallows, and breathes in smooth coordination. The fact that a newborn can swallow almost three times faster than an adult and can suck at the same time he or she takes in air aids in the accomplishment of this feat. Adults who sucked in a liquid and breathed at the same time probably would choke. Babies can manage simultaneous sucking and breathing because they can extract milk from the nipple by pressing it against the roof of the mouth instead of by drawing in milk as you would when using a

Although neonates in the U.S. lack the free access to the breast customary among hunter-gatherer cultures, newborns who are allowed to nurse on demand may find their adjustment to the world outside the uterus eased. *(Joel Gordon)*

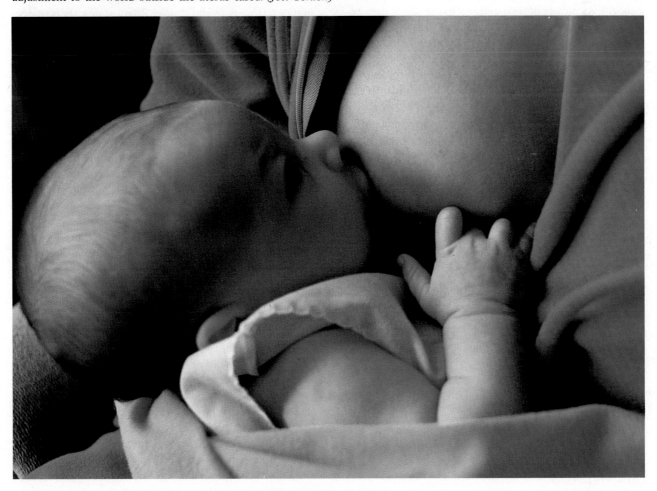

straw. Babies quickly adapt their sucking to the consistency and flow of liquid by changing their bite pressures or by lowering their jaws to create a vacuum (suction).

The young baby sucks rhythmically, in bursts separated by pauses. On the average, the baby puts together approximately five to twenty-four sucks in a single burst, sucking at a rate of approximately one to two and one-half times each second, and then takes a brief rest. Hunger, age, health, and level of arousal all influence the baby's pattern of sucking, but each baby sucks in his or her own characteristic pattern.

Comfort

Sucking is much more than a way of satisfying hunger. It also serves as pleasant oral stimulation, satisfies the baby's taste, exercises mouth and throat muscles, supplies social contact, and provides a potent source of comfort to a baby in distress. Research with 2-week-old babies whose heels were pricked in a routine test for PKU has demonstrated the soothing power of sucking (R. Campos, 1989). Neonates who sucked a pacifier after the painful puncture quieted much faster than babies who were swaddled with strips of cotton cloth and flannel blankets (see Figure 4.1). (Other research has shown that swaddling comforts babies, and many cultures use it for that purpose [Lipton, Steinschneider, and Richmond, 1965].) Sucking apparently soothes by reducing the baby's heart rate and shifting the infant into an alert state. Babies in the PKU test experiment who sucked a pacifier, for example, later spent almost three times as long in an alert state as did babies who were swaddled (R. Campos, 1989).

Nonnutritive sucking is considered contact comfort, a calming system that operates in newborns, and it generally lasts as long as the contact is provided. When the pacifier is taken away, or the baby is put down, crying tends to rebound. Sucking is similar, in this sense, to cuddling by a caregiver. A second calming system, which provides more lasting comfort, is activated by milk or sugar solutions. When babies get sweetened water through a nipple, the brain responds by producing endorphins, natural opiatelike chemicals that ease pain and distress (Blass and Smith, 1992). Researchers have found that crying newborns who get sugar solutions through a nipple remain calm after the nipple is removed, whereas crying newborns who get water begin crying again when the nipple is taken away (B. Smith, Fillion, and Blass, 1990). Other studies indicate that babies who are given a sugar solution *before* a PKU heelprick cry less than other babies during the procedure and stop crying much sooner afterward (Blass, 1990).

Crying, sleeping, and sucking apparently work together to preserve and change infant states, thereby regulating periods of calm and attentiveness. When sucking, the average baby is soothed, becoming calm and alert. Head movements cease, so objects on either side no longer distract the sucking infant. The baby seems to pay serious attention to the world, focusing intently on objects that are straight ahead and probably processing sights more efficiently than he or she does when not sucking (Crook, 1979). It appears that the neonate is learning most during the feeding period, when she or he is most likely to be interacting with a parent.

Figure 4.1 Babies who sucked a pacifier after a heelprick cried much less during each fifteen-second scoring interval than babies who were swaddled. *(From R. Campos, 1989, p. 788)*

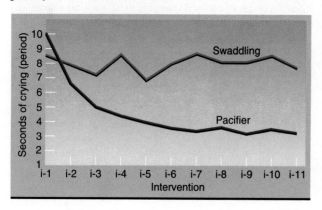

Reflexes

The possible chaos of the newborn's world is further reduced by some responses that he or she does not have to learn. A neonate comes equipped with more than a dozen **reflexes,** which are unlearned responses to specific stimuli—responses that are not affected by motivation and that are common to all members of the species (see Table 4.3). Some of these reflexes are adaptive. They may help the baby to avoid danger: babies close their eyes to bright light and twist their bodies or move their limbs away from sources of pain. Some reflexes may help the baby to feed: babies reflexively root, suck, and swallow. Other reflexes appear to be vestiges of the past, left over from our prehuman ancestors whose infants had to be good grabbers to survive. Still others are

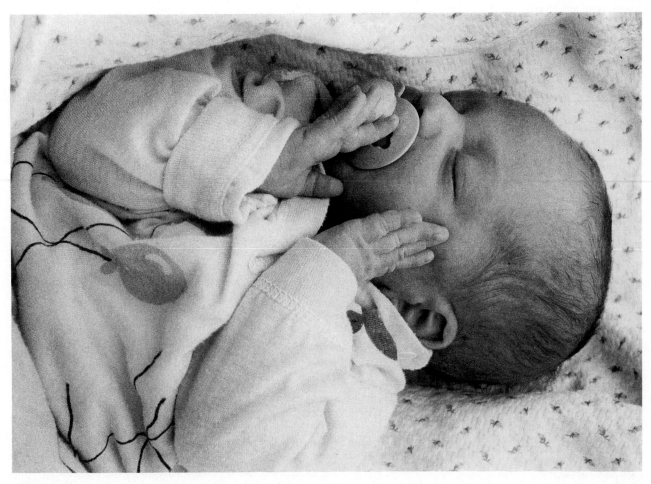

Sucking is such a powerful souce of comfort that a pacifier often quiets a distressed neonate. *(Frank Siteman/Stock, Boston)*

simple manifestations of neurological circuitry in the baby that later will be suppressed or integrated into more mature patterns of behavior. Some reflexes, such as the eyeblink or cough, are permanent, but most disappear within a few weeks or months, as the brain matures. When these immature reflexes persist, they may be a sign of abnormal neurological development.

The Rooting Reflex

All babies have a **rooting reflex**—a tendency to turn the head and mouth in the direction of any object that gently stimulates the corner of the mouth. This reflex has obvious adaptive significance because it helps the baby place the nipple in the mouth, where the swallowing and sucking reflexes come into play. If you stroke the corner of a newborn's mouth with your index finger, moving sideways from the mouth toward

the cheek, the baby may move tongue, mouth, or even the whole head toward the stimulated side. At first, this reflex appears even when you stroke the cheek a long way from the mouth. As the baby gets older, the reflex appears only when stimulation is at the mouth, and only the baby's mouth responds. Both the rooting and sucking reflexes are present before the baby is born, and the rooting reflex disappears when the baby is 3 or 4 months old. Babies learn to suck their thumbs while rooting: if one of their hands happens to brush a cheek, the reflex is triggered and the thumb winds up inside the mouth, where the sucking reflex takes over.

Grasping and the Moro Reflex

Babies are born with a strong **grasping reflex.** If you place a week-old baby on his or her back and insert your finger in the baby's hand, the infant grasps it firmly.

TABLE 4.3 NEONATAL REFLEXES

Reflex	Description
PERMANENT REFLEXES	
Eyeblink	Eyes close to strong light or approaching object.
Breathing	Lungs take in oxygen and expel carbon dioxide.
Knee jerk	Leg extends or kicks when tendon below kneecap is struck.
Pupillary	Pupil changes in size, widening under dim light and constricting in bright light.
Coughing	Air is expelled from throat to clear mucus or foreign object.
Sneezing	Air is expelled from nose to clear foreign object.
Swallowing	Contents of mouth are sent to stomach; reflex protects against choking.
TEMPORARY REFLEXES	
Babinski	Toes spread out and foot twists inward when side of foot is stroked. Gone by 12 months.
Grasping	Fingers curl around and cling to any object that touches palm. Gone by 4 months.
Moro	Arms thrust out and then seem to embrace as fingers curl when support for neck and head is removed. Gone by 7 months.
Placing	Foot lifts and is placed on any surface whose edge touches top of foot. Gone by 4 months.
Rooting	Head and mouth turn in the direction of object that stimulates mouth. Gone by 4 months.
Stepping	Walking movements are made when baby is held upright and lowered until feet touch surface. Gone by 4 months.
Sucking	Rhythmic sucking occurs in response to insertion of object in mouth. Replaced by voluntary sucking by 2 months.
Swimming	Active arm and leg motion, combined with breathholding, occurs in response to immersion in water. Gone by 6 months.
Tonic neck	Head turns to side, arm and leg on that side extend, and opposite arm and leg draw up when baby is placed on back. Gone by 4 months.

Sometimes a grasping newborn can literally hang by one hand. The grasping reflex gets stronger during the first month and then begins to decline in strength, disappearing when the infant is about 3 or 4 months old.

The **Moro reflex** appears when a baby suddenly loses support for both neck and head. It consists of thrusting out the arms in an embracelike gesture and curling the hands as if to grasp something. The Moro reflex is easy to see. Simply hold a baby with one hand under the head and the other in the small of the back, and then rapidly lower your hands, especially the hand holding the head, and bring them to an abrupt halt. The Moro reflex is strongest after the first week, when the baby is alert, with open or barely closed eyes. It, too, decreases as the baby gets older. The Moro is difficult to elicit after the baby is 3 months old, and it is almost always gone by 5 or 6 months.

Many scientists believe that the grasping and Moro reflexes are once-adaptive responses left over from our prehuman history (Prechtl, 1982). Although they are no longer useful to human babies, the reflexes are still vital among monkeys, whose infants ride on their backs or cling to their stomachs. An infant monkey who loses support and automatically reaches out will grasp its mother's fur or skin and remain safe; one who does not will fall to the ground.

Walking Movements

A baby only a week or two old may look as if he or she is trying to walk. If you hold the baby under the arms while gently lowering him or her to a surface until both feet touch it and the knees bend, the baby will respond with a reflexive **stepping** motion. If you slowly bounce the baby lightly up and down, the baby may straighten out both legs at the knee and hip as if to

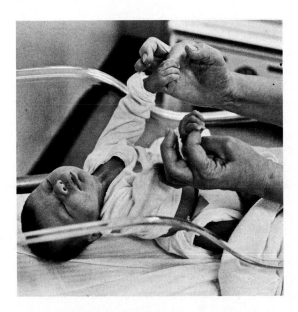

(a) The grasping reflex. *(William MacDonald)*

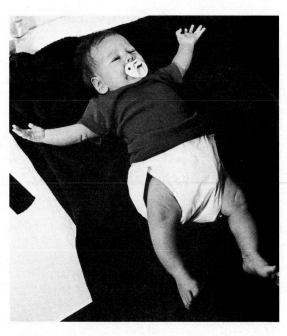

(b) The Moro reflex. *(Lawrence Frank)*

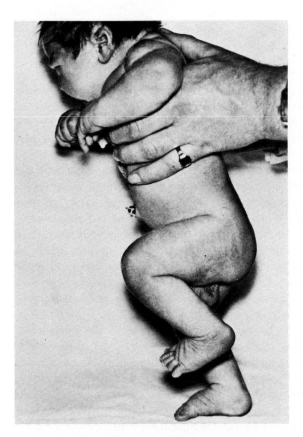

(c) The stepping reflex. *(A.K. Tunstill)*

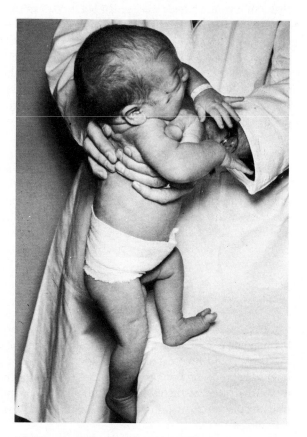

(d) The placing reflex. *(A.K. Tunstill)*

stand. Then if moved forward, the baby may try stepping motions, as if walking.

Newborns also show a second walking motion, called a **placing reflex.** This reflex is simply the baby's propensity to lift his or her feet onto a surface. If held up and moved toward a table until the top part of the foot touches the edge, the baby is likely to lift up a foot and place it on the table. Both the stepping and placing responses disappear between the third and fourth months after birth.

Neither behavior has much practical utility, because 1- or 2-week-old babies have neither the strength nor the balance to walk or step. The reflexes appear to indicate a certain inborn neurological organization that forms the basis for later standing and walking. Early walking movements seem to be under the control of primitive areas of the brain, but researchers cannot agree on why they disappear. The traditional view has been that as the baby's higher brain centers mature, they take over control from the lower brain centers and suppress these reflexes. But Philip Zelazo (1983) has argued that the disappearance of walking movements is due primarily to the baby's failure to use them. He notes that when young babies were given practice in stepping for several weeks, they lost the response more slowly and walked about a month sooner than other babies. However, Esther Thelen and her associates (Thelen, Fisher, and Ridley-Johnson, 1984) maintain that babies stop stepping because their legs gain fat and other tissue so rapidly that their muscles simply aren't strong enough to lift their heavy legs against gravity. When these researchers weighted the legs of 4-week-old babies, stepping movements dropped by nearly one-third; and when they placed the babies in water (where gravity is less of a burden), stepping movements nearly doubled. All three explanations may be involved. Although the movements disappear, they reappear as voluntary acts from a baby who is ready to walk.

Early Perceptual Development

Some years ago, many people believed that the newborn baby's senses were not functional. They assumed that the baby could not see, smell, or taste and could feel only pain, cold, and hunger. Since that time research has established that neonates' senses, although not as precise as those of adults, do inform them about their surroundings.

Some of the neonate's sensory systems are further developed than others. The newborn's senses of touch, taste, and smell, for example, are more acute than the sense of hearing. The baby's sight—although functional—is probably the least highly developed (Gottlieb, 1983). This staggered development of sensory systems probably minimizes the chaotic jumble of sensation a newborn might otherwise have to deal with. If the baby "concentrates" on one sense at a time, he or she does not have to solve the problems involved in adjusting to all varieties of sensory stimuli at once (Turkewitz and Kenny, 1982).

Researchers believe that knowing about the newborn's sensory capabilities is valuable. If we know what newborn babies can see, hear, smell, taste, and feel, we can discover which events in the environment might influence them. And if we can establish normal sensory levels, we may be able to detect—and help—babies whose sensory systems are not developing normally. Deafness, for example, often is not discovered until a child is 3 years old (Meadow, 1978). Detection of deafness early in infancy would keep babies with severe hearing loss from being treated as if they were mentally retarded.

Tasting

Babies' sensitivity to taste is much more highly developed than was believed only a few years ago. When drops of various concentrated solutions are placed on their tongues, newborn babies respond with facial expressions much like those of adults. Jacob Steiner (1979) tested 175 full-term babies before they had their first feeding and found that an extremely sweet liquid brought forth smiles, followed by eager licking and sucking. When they tasted a sour solution, most babies pursed their lips, wrinkled their noses, and blinked their eyes. When a bitter fluid was dripped into their mouths, they stuck out their tongues and spat. Some even tried to vomit. Yet when Steiner placed distilled water on their tongues, the babies simply swallowed, showing no expression at all. A group of twenty preterm newborns, given plain water and a sour solution, responded just as the full-term infants had done.

Newborns also seem sensitive to the intensity of taste. If they are given stronger solutions, their expressions intensify—a sign that they can tell the difference between sweet and very sweet and between bitter and very bitter (Ganchrow, Steiner, and Daher, 1983). Their sucking also changes when a solution becomes sweeter: they suck more slowly, and their heart rates increase. These results appear contradictory, because we might

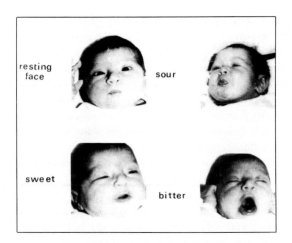

Newborns respond to strong tastes much as adults do. When tested within a few hours of birth, they stick out their tongues, spit, or even vomit when a bitter liquid is dripped onto the tongue. *(From Steiner, 1979)*

expect a baby to suck more vigorously when given something that tastes especially good. In an attempt to resolve this paradox, Charles Crook and Lewis Lipsitt (1976), who conducted the experiment, suggest that babies are simply enjoying the taste. They slow down to savor the sweet taste, and pleasurable excitement causes their hearts to speed up.

Smelling

Newborns definitely react to strong odors. Babies less than 12 hours old reacted in a recognizable manner to synthetic odors of various foods (Steiner, 1979). When a cotton swab saturated with the odor of rotten eggs or concentrated shrimp was waved beneath their noses, the infants responded as babies in Steiner's previous experiment had responded to bitter tastes. To the aromas of butter, bananas, vanilla, chocolate, strawberry, and honey, the babies responded with expressions of enjoyment and satisfaction.

The keenness of the newborn's sense of smell has been demonstrated by the ability of breast-fed babies to recognize their own mother's odor. Two-week-old babies showed that they recognized their mother's odor by their reaction to gauze pads that had been taped overnight to each mother's armpit (Cernoch and Porter, 1985). Researchers placed the mother's pad on one side of the baby's head, next to the cheek, and on the other side they placed a similar pad from another lactating woman. (Neither woman had used a deodorant.) Because many babies prefer one side or the other, care

was taken to alternate the pads' placement. The babies preferred their own mother's pad (as measured by the amount of time they turned their heads toward each pad). Bottle-fed babies showed no preference for the pad from their own mother's armpit, and neither breast- nor bottle-fed babies could distinguish between a pad from their father's armpit and a pad from the armpit of an unfamiliar man. Researchers believe that breast-fed babies recognize their own mother's odor because they have a greater physical intimacy with their mothers than do bottle-fed infants. When babies nurse at the breast, their noses are next to their mothers' bare skin at each feeding. A bottle-fed baby generally is held by a clothed person (and not always the mother), so the baby does not get the same exposure to the mother's scent as does the breast-fed baby.

There may be something about the odor of milk that attracts babies, whether they are fed by breast or bottle. Following research that established the ability of breast-fed babies to recognize their own mother's breast pad, Jennifer Makin and Richard Porter (1989) tested bottle-fed newborns, using techniques like those in the previous experiment. They discovered that 2-week-old girls spent more time turned toward a pad that had been worn over the breast of a lactating woman than toward a pad that had been worn by a woman who had not given birth recently. Since none of these newborns had any experience breast feeding, the researchers concluded that there is an inborn preference for the breast odors of lactating females, which may increase the baby's tendency to nurse.

Hearing

Discovering just what newborns can hear and what they seem to listen to can add to our understanding of the baby's perceptual world. As we saw in Chapter 3, the fetus apparently can hear and respond to sounds by the age of twenty-eight weeks (Birnholz and Benaceraff, 1983). Discovering just what babies hear and listen to is complicated by the fact that there is no unique physiological response to hearing. Researchers have used several techniques to discover what sounds babies can hear and whether they can distinguish among them: head-turning, startling, heart rate, respiration, brain waves, and sucking patterns (Aslin, Pisoni, and Jusczyk, 1983). When researchers chart brain waves, they record the baby's brain-wave responses to repeated presentations of the same stimulus and then average the activity. When researchers use sucking patterns, they give babies a nipple that is attached to electronic recording equipment, which monitors the rate and intensity of sucking. The babies get nothing through the nipple, but sucking vigorously triggers a recorded sound or keeps a sound playing. When the sound no longer interests them, their sucking slows. If babies who have been listening to one sound respond to a new sound with forceful sucking, researchers assume that the babies have noticed the difference between the two sounds.

What Do Newborns Hear?

For the first few days of life, the middle-ear passages are filled with amniotic fluid, and so the sounds reaching a neonate may be somewhat dampened. Yet all normal newborns can hear, and some can hear very well. Most newborns turn their heads in the direction of a shaking rattle, but instead of turning immediately, they take about two and one-half seconds to respond (Muir and Field, 1979). Preterm babies are even more sluggish in their response; they wait about twelve seconds before turning their heads toward the sound (Aslin, Pisoni, and Jusczyk, 1983).

Human beings distinguish most sounds on the basis of their pitch and their intensity. Pitch is determined by the frequency of sound waves, which are measured in hertz (Hz). Generally, the higher a sound's pitch, the louder it must be before we can hear it, and this is as true for neonates as for adults (L. Werner and Gillenwater, 1990). Newborns' ears are not as sensitive as the average adult's; at any frequency a sound heard by an adult must be 10 to 20 decibels louder before a newborn can detect it (Aslin, Pisoni, and Jusczyk, 1983). (An increase of 10 decibels nearly doubles the perceived loudness of a sound.) The shrillest sounds of the typical human voice are 1100 Hz; at 1000 Hz, neonates can detect sounds at 25 decibels (L. Werner and Gillenwater, 1990). Since leaves rustling in a breeze are about 20 decibels, it would seem that the hearing of neonates is more than adequate for their needs. Some researchers believe that it is easy to underestimate the sensitivity of young infants (Trehub et al., 1991). Babies vary widely in their overt reactions to sounds, and some babies are relatively inscrutable and show little reaction even to sounds that they can hear.

What Do Newborns Listen To?

Babies seem to prefer some sounds to others, but their preferences probably change, depending on their state. Adults seem to realize this, for the way they talk to an alert baby or one they are trying to rouse differs sharply from the way they talk to a crying baby. When talking to a newborn, parents change the intonation, tempo, and rhythm of their speech; automatically, they fall into a pattern known as "motherese." The pitch of their voices becomes higher; their intonation rises and falls in an exaggerated fashion; they say only a few words at a time and make lengthy pauses; they often repeat words or phrases (Fernald and Simon, 1984). But when a mother is trying to comfort a crying baby, her voice falls to a lower pitch than that of her normal speaking voice, and her intonation remains fairly steady.

Newborns seem to prefer the exaggerated speech to normal speech. Awake and alert neonates were swaddled in blankets and placed in an infant seat facing a screen that covered a black-and-white checkerboard (R. Cooper and Aslin, 1990). When the baby looked toward the screen, a researcher lifted the screen to expose the display and a woman's taped voice spoke the same sentences in either exaggerated or normal speech. Babies only a few days old looked significantly longer at the display when the voice used exaggerated speech, indicating a preference for this infant-directed speech. Other research has shown that babies this young prefer their own mother's voice to the voice of another woman (DeCasper and Fifer, 1980); that they prefer their own language to a foreign language (but that they cannot tell the difference between two foreign languages) (Mehler et al., 1988); that they prefer a story their mothers read aloud daily before they were born (DeCasper and Spence, 1986); and that they prefer a melody that was sung near their mothers before they were born (Panneton, 1985). The preference for human speech may be an innate predisposition, but prenatal experience also affects early preferences. The attraction that exaggerated speech holds for newborns indicates that adults can influence a baby's attention by the *way* in which they speak to the infant.

Seeing

Just what can neonates see, and which aspects of the world do they notice? Apparently, they can see a lot, but what they see is blurry—almost as if you were to smear Vaseline on a pair of glasses and then inspect your surroundings. As the visual cortex and the pathways between it and the eyes mature, vision rapidly improves. By the end of the neonatal period, the infant's sight is clearer and better organized—although it will be several months before she or he can see as well as an adult.

What Do Newborns See?

The clarity of vision is based on the eye's ability to change focus and how sharply it can resolve objects once they are in focus. The ability to focus is known as **visual accommodation,** and you can demonstrate it by holding one finger a few inches from your nose and another at arm's length and then quickly alternating the focus from one to the other. The newborn can accommodate, but not very well, tending to overaccommodate for distant objects and to underaccommodate for objects nearby (Banks and Salapatek, 1983). This tendency probably does not bother the baby, because objects seem somewhat blurry even when they are in focus. A baby's natural focus, and thus the clearest vision, is set for about 9 inches—which is the typical distance between a baby cradled in the caregiver's arm and the caregiver's face. When the newborn's **acuity,** which is the ability to resolve detail, is translated into terms of the standard eye chart, a week-old baby sees objects at 20 feet about as clearly as the average adult does at 600 feet. Taken together, these factors sharply reduce the amount of *distinctive* visual stimulation that gets through and probably minimize the baby's "blooming, buzzing confusion."

Both accommodation and acuity improve rapidly with experience and with the maturation of the visual system. Accommodation is already better at 10 days than at birth; by 3 months, the baby's accommodation errors are small; and by 5 months, he or she can accommodate to objects that are only a few inches from the eye. Acuity also improves rapidly; by 6 months, a baby can detect (and investigate) specks of lint on the carpet that may escape a parent's notice, although distance vision is probably no better than 20/100 (Banks and Salapatek, 1983).

Each eye sees a slightly different image, and by a visual mechanism called **convergence,** the two images come together until only a single object appears. The newborn probably sees mostly misaligned images, much like those you can produce by pressing gently at the side of one eye. This poor convergence tells us that neonates cannot use cues from both eyes to sense depth in the world. The mechanisms that enable them to detect depth in this manner start emerging when they are about 2 months old, but research indicates that it will be several more months before they are consistently using both eyes to perceive a three-dimensional world (Banks and Salapatek, 1983). Depth also can be perceived from cues to one eye, known as *monocular cues,* but young babies can use such cues only if they involve movement. The ability to use stationary monocular cues is even slower to develop than cues that require the use of both eyes. Experience plays an important role in the emergence of depth perception, and

babies probably notice depth cues before they translate them into the experience of depth.

What Do Newborns Notice?

Babies seem organized to acquire information through their eyes. When they are awake, they keep moving their eyes, looking about them even in the dark. Marshall Haith (1980) proposes that a baby is born prepared to seek visual stimulation and that the search has an overriding purpose: to keep cells in the visual cortex firing at a high level. This activity is necessary for maintaining established neural pathways and for developing new ones. The search has an additional benefit: it brings the baby in contact with whatever useful information might be available in the visual field.

Once newborns locate a potentially interesting sight, they generally do not scan the entire shape but concentrate on a side or a corner, where black-white contrast is highest and thus where sensory information is richest (Bornstein, 1988). As a result, a neonate probably does not perceive entire forms, just their specific features—an angle, an edge. The neonate's concentrated scanning probably means that the very young baby may miss the most interesting and informative part of a stimulus. When a 3-week-old baby looks at your face, he or she is likely to look at the edge, where your hair stands out against the background, or at the edge of your cheek or chin, instead of at your eyes or mouth.

Within a few months, babies perceive depth and form, and they find faces increasingly fascinating. Their interest shifts from the edge of a face to its internal features—especially the eyes. Born with functioning sensory systems, babies are genetically predisposed (1) to respond in ways that help them to survive and (2) to learn certain events easily. This **preparedness** enables them to make rudimentary connections between events, and these simple connections provide the basis for all later behavior, including the baby's social relationships.

Personality and Social Relations

The parent-child relationship begins in the delivery room. Once they have assured themselves that their baby is complete and normal, parents start looking for the first signs of personality in their child. It is difficult to talk about the personality of a newborn. When we think of personality, we have in mind the way verbal, cognitive, and emotional behavior is displayed in a social context. A neonate cannot express personality in this way, but the seeds of the developing personality may be apparent in the baby's **temperament,** which consists of early, observable differences in the intensity and duration of babies' arousal and emotionality (J. Campos, Campos, and Barrett, 1989). Many researchers believe that infant emotionality and the infant's response to stimulation, which is referred to as **reactivity,** provide the most productive framework for understanding temperament and early social interaction.

Temperament

Any parent who has had more than one child is aware that babies are different from the first day of life. Some babies are irritable and fussy; others are easygoing and easy to soothe. Some babies seem interested in the world around them; others seem to pay it little attention. Although medication during delivery may affect early responses, wide differences are also apparent among babies whose birth was unmedicated and uneventful (Bornstein, Gaughran, and Homel, 1986).

Researchers used to believe that a newborn's temperament was determined primarily by his or her geno-

type, but a recent study of newborn twins suggests that much of the difference among newborns can be traced to differences in the prenatal environment and the birth experience (Riese, 1990). In the first few weeks after birth, environmental influences appear to be so strong that they obscure any genetic influences on temperament.

Efforts to establish infant temperament have been difficult, in part because of the way in which temperament traditionally has been rated. In most cases, mothers rate their own babies, and a mother's interpretation of her baby's behavior often reflects the mother's personal characteristics as much as it does those of the infant (Vaughn et al., 1987). Researchers have also found that parents' *expectations* of their babies' temperament, measured *before the baby's birth,* correlate with their ratings of the babies at age 6 months (Zeanah and Anders, 1987), and one study indicates that the ratings change only modestly over the babies' first fourteen months (Mebert, 1989). Whether because of environmental influence or parents' expectations, the temperament of adopted babies resembles the personalities of their adopted parents more closely than the personalities of their biological parents (Loehlin, Willerman, and Horn, 1988; Plomin and Defries, 1985).

Individual differences in temperament are apparent at birth; some neonates are fussy, some rarely cry, some are highly sensitive to sights and sounds, some pay little attention to them. *(Craig Sillitoe/Black Star)*

Differences in Temperament

Nevertheless, researchers have documented some differences among newborns. One aspect of emotional reactivity that seems to show clear differences is *irritability.* Some babies cry a great deal during the first few days (up to one-third of the time) and may even cry or fret after a feeding (Korner et al., 1981). Their mood changes often, they have fits of irritability, and they are upset by events that do not bother other babies. They are hard to soothe, and their parents often consider them "difficult" babies. This aspect of temperament seems relatively stable. Highly irritable neonates are still irritable at 12 months (Worobey and Bajda, 1989), and at 2 years they are easily upset, relatively inattentive to objects and events, and less responsive to people outside the family (Riese, 1987). Irritability is not always a disadvantage. Among young Masai babies in Kenya, where food was scarce, difficult babies were more likely than "easy" babies to survive (deVries and Sameroff, 1984). Their demanding cries apparently ensured that they got enough food, whereas babies who did not complain sometimes died of malnutrition or disease.

Neonates who fall at the two extremes of emotional *reactivity* show stable responses to frustration over the first year or so. In a longitudinal study (N. Fox, 1989; Stifter and Fox, 1990), highly reactive newborns who cried strenuously when a pacifier was removed from their mouths became 5-month-olds who cried when their arms were held in restraint and who were difficult to soothe. At 14 months, they were highly sociable toddlers who were not especially frightened by novel situations. Passive newborns who did not cry when the pacifier was taken away still did not cry at 5 months when their arms were restrained, and when they became distressed, they soothed easily. At 14 months, they were unsociable toddlers who tended to be wary of novel situations. By the time the infants were 5 months old, this difference in emotional reactivity could be measured in terms of differences in heart rate variability, but the link between autonomic functioning and behavior was not apparent in neonates.

Another prominent difference among newborns is *activity level.* Some babies are restless and active, waving their arms or legs about; others seem placid and move more slowly. During the first few days, this difference shows more strongly in the energy with which babies move, not necessarily the frequency of their movements (Korner et al., 1981). Later this quality may affect how often or how vigorously an infant reaches for, mouths, and bangs objects or attempts to stand and crawl (Bornstein, Gaughran, and Homel, 1986).

Temperament and Interaction

Personality is, of course, much more complex than simple categories of temperament imply. A child's personality is a developing and evolving set of tendencies to behave in various ways. The way these tendencies evolve is affected by parent-child interaction. Over months and years, early aspects of temperament may remain stable, be modulated, or even disappear.

Parents often interpret the smallest behavior as revealing their newborn's personality, and their interpretations are influenced by their expectations, their life circumstances, and their psychological functioning (Lamb and Bornstein, 1986). By the time a baby is 2 weeks old, the mother may develop a style of relating to the baby and an opinion of his or her personality (Osofsky and Connors, 1979). A baby's characteristics affect the parents' attitudes toward the baby, and they may also affect the parents' feeling about themselves. Parents who had been looking forward to cuddling and kissing their newborn and who find themselves with a baby who either stiffens or remains impassive when cuddled may falsely infer that their baby dislikes them

or that they are somehow inadequate. The negative attitudes they form could color the way they customarily interact with their child. As the accompanying box, "Baby Blues and Social Interaction," suggests, a mother's emotional state affects her interactions with her newborn.

According to Alexander Thomas and Stella Chess (1977), the key to personality development is the **goodness of fit** between infant temperament and parents' style. When a baby's temperament and the parents' style mesh comfortably, development generally is healthy. But when they clash, as when an impatient parent has a difficult baby, problems may lie ahead. Parents who are upset by a difficult child's impulsiveness and who react to a 12-month-old's forays with repeated prohibitions and handslaps may wind up with a 2-year-old who is always in trouble, whereas parents who keep tempting objects out of a difficult baby's way may have no more than average trouble with their 2-year-old (Lee and Bates, 1985).

Rearranging the environment so that an unpleasant characteristic does not manifest itself is probably a common parental response (J. Campos et al., 1983). Parents of one highly active toddler who climbed on every available surface simply installed a set of pegs on the wall and hung the kitchen chairs out of reach between meals. Parents of a highly irritable baby learned to arrange their shopping excursions so that they got home before the baby's patience wore out or the next feeding was due. Such adjustments to temperamental characteristics indicate why parents often treat one child differently from another.

An infant's temperament has other practical implications besides provoking different treatment from his or her parents (Lamb and Bornstein, 1986). As babies get older, their temperament becomes more consistent, which makes their behavior more predictable. We might say that temperament serves as a form of social communication. Perhaps most important, the baby's temperament may lead parents to respond and rearrange the environment in ways that directly form personality and encourage the development of specific characteristics. If parents believe that their baby is inquisitive, they may go out of their way to make experiences available to the child. If they believe that their baby is shy, they may protect the child from interactions with outsiders. Such parental perceptions are potent, whether they are accurate or not, and they are another example of the way genes and environment interact, as the child's temperament evokes certain responses from parents.

BABY BLUES AND SOCIAL INTERACTION

Becoming a new parent requires enormous changes in the lives of everyone concerned. Some women find the changes of pregnancy and motherhood especially stressful, in part, perhaps, because of the shifts in hormone levels that accompany the birth. As many as 15 percent of new mothers develop **postpartum depression,** an emotional letdown (generally called "baby blues") that may follow the birth of a baby. Women with postpartum depression are depressed and anxious and tend to feel that they have little control over their own lives. Research has established that the depressed mother's mood affects her interaction with her baby. She tends to express anger, sadness, or irritation with her baby and either to be highly intrusive in her interactions or to seem disinterested in her child (J. Cohn et al., 1990; T. Field et al., 1990). She also spends much less time playing with her baby than do mothers who are not depressed.

Depressed mothers seem to differ from other mothers in their views of child rearing. In one study (T. Field et al., 1985), depressed women tended to favor strictness with children and punitive disciplinary methods. They also saw themselves and their babies as more emotional than nondepressed mothers did.

A mother's unhappy atmosphere seems contagious, and her behavior—or lack of it—may influence her baby's reactivity, emotionality, temperament, and sociability. Babies of depressed mothers cry much more and play much less than other babies (see the accompanying Figure). They behave this way even when they are with people who are not depressed (T. Field et al., 1990). Babies whose depressed mothers work outside the home fare better than babies whose depressed mothers stay home all day. These infants behave more like the babies of nondepressed mothers (J. Cohn et al., 1990). Re-

Babies of mothers with postpartum depression cry more and play less than other babies.
(Joel Gordon)

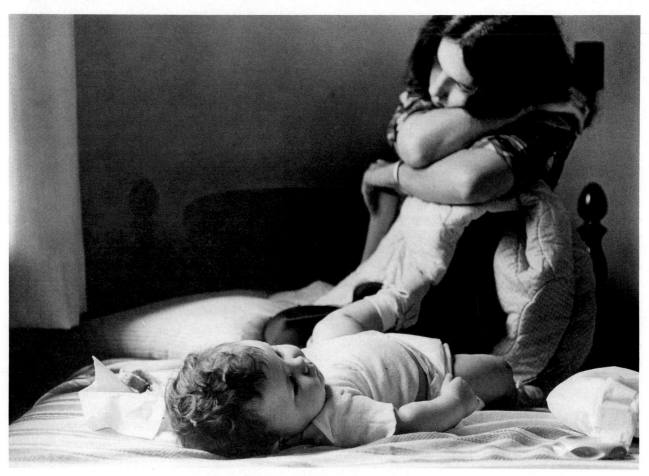

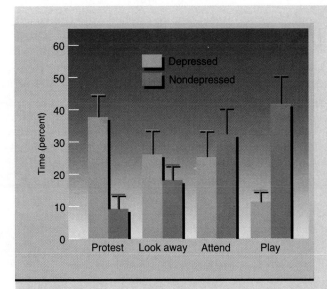

Babies of depressed mothers spend significantly more time protesting and significantly less time playing than do babies whose mothers are not depressed. *(From T. Field et al., 1990, p. 10)*

searchers are not certain why this is so, but suggest three possibilities (J. Cohn et al., 1990). First, depressed mothers may get social support at their workplace that helps them cope with their depression. Second, depressed mothers who work have learned to mask their feelings, so babies are less likely to pick up their sadness. Third, alternative caregiving shields the mother from the baby's daily demands, diminishes the baby's exposure to a depressed adult, and makes the mother more interesting to the baby.

Infants are resilient, and if their mothers come out of their depression within about three months—as most do—so do the babies (T. Field et al., 1990). But when mothers are still depressed six months after giving birth, the babies often have insecure relations with their parents and do poorly on tests of development.

Social Relations

Social relations in the newborn are primitive by adult standards, yet babies and their parents carry on intricate sorts of nonverbal communication from the first days. Much of it takes place while the baby is feeding, when the neonate gets his or her first lesson in taking turns.

Taking Turns

The design of the human body ensures that the nursing neonate and mother are placed in a situation that facilitates communication. When a mother breast-feeds her newborn baby, the infant's face is about 9 inches from hers—the distance at which the baby's eyes are naturally in focus. The feeding situation may contain the seeds of turn-taking, a skill that is essential to language and social development. Mothers, whether breast- or bottle-feeding, seem to assume that the baby is drowsy or has lost interest when sucking stops, and so they either jiggle the nipple in the baby's mouth or stroke the baby about the mouth. The baby does not resume sucking until the mother stops jiggling (Kaye, 1982). It appears that the infant's normal sucking routine of bursts and pauses fits naturally into the turn-taking of human dialogue: the mother accommodates her behavior to her child's natural feeding rhythm, and the pattern

forms a basis for developing early social communication.

Social relations outside the feeding situation also evolve into a turn-taking arrangement. Parents try to catch their baby's gaze, smile, tap or blow on the skin, and jiggle their baby. The baby responds by returning the gaze or by smiling reflexively—at first reacting to touch and later to vocalizations. By the third week, the smile is accompanied by brightened eyes and a near grin, especially if the parent nods the head while talking to the baby. Toward the end of the neonatal period, the baby begins smiling in response to vigorous physical stimulation—games of pat-a-cake, for example, in which the parent bounces the baby's hands (T. Field, 1981).

From the very beginning, parents imitate their newborn's sounds and facial expressions. As noted earlier, they speak to their baby in a high-pitched voice; they also interpret their newborn's smiles, noises, and changes in expression as if they were thoughtful answers to their own questions. Parents then act as interpreters, expressing the baby's reply in words, taking both parts of the dialogue. Smiles are considered an indication that the baby understands them. Cries, fretting, or frowns may be seen as signs that the baby either doesn't understand or is trying to figure out what the parent has said (H. Papousek and Papousek, 1984).

Social interaction is possible only when a baby is alert, and as we have seen, the newborn's alertness is confined to brief periods. By analyzing films and videotapes, Hanus Papousek and Mechthild Papousek (1984) have discovered that parents tend to adjust their behavior to the baby's signals. If the baby stops responding or seems drowsy, they stop the play and often ask the baby what is wrong. At the same time, they test the baby's muscle tone, either gently pushing the chin down to open the baby's mouth or opening the baby's hand and stretching the fingers. These tests allow parents to tailor their behavior to the baby's state, and afterward they either increase the level of stimulation or end the interaction.

Individual differences among babies affect early social relations in several ways. Babies who return a parent's gaze steadily or who smile early encourage their parents' attempts to establish a social relationship. Babies who rarely have periods of quiet alertness but seem to spend all their time either sleeping or crying can frustrate the parents' attempts to communicate (Osofsky and Connors, 1979).

Social Aspects of Crying

Perhaps the most obvious method by which the neonate communicates with others is crying. Generally speaking, a neonate cries as a signal of distress, as if to say, "Help me!" Even newborns cry in different ways, depending on the level of their distress. Women who have never had children are almost as adept as mothers of young infants at deciding whether the taped cry of an infant is from a baby in moderate distress (hunger, wet diaper) or one in severe distress (pain) (Gustafson and Harris, 1990).

Fathers respond to an infant's wail just as mothers do. There is no detectable difference in the physiological reaction of mothers and fathers to the crying of an unfamiliar baby: in each, blood pressure rises and skin conductance increases (Frodi et al., 1978). This physiological arousal is accompanied by feelings of annoyance, irritation, and distress. The higher the pitch of the cry, the more aversive its sound (Bisping et al., 1990). When a parent answers a baby's cry for help, he or she is also trying to stop the unpleasant sound.

Yet the response of a mother to her own baby's cry differs from her response to the cry of an unfamiliar baby. When a mother hears her own baby wailing with anger or pain, her heart slows down and then speeds up, as if she were getting ready to take care of the baby's needs. But when she hears the cry of an unfamiliar baby, her heart slows down—and stays that way (Wiesenfeld

and Malatesta, 1982). The researchers who conducted the study that produced these findings suggest that mothers respond to their own babies empathically, but their response to other babies indicates that they probably have no intention of aiding the baby and feel no obligation to do so.

Parents interpret a baby's cries in the context of the parent-child relationship, using such cues as the length of time since the last feeding, the infant's idiosyncrasies, and such behavioral cues as mouthing, thrashing, stiffening, and the way the baby responds to the parent's at-

Mothers interpret their babies' cries within the context of the parent-child relationship, using behavioral cues, the infant's temperament, time since the last feeding, and other factors to decide how to intervene. *(Mimi Forsyth/ Monkmeyer)*

tempts at comfort (Gustafson and Harris, 1990). What they know about the baby's health also affects their reactions; for example, when parents believe a newborn is "sick," the cries seem less unpleasant (Bisping et al., 1990). Over the next few months, as throat and mouth mature and the baby gains experience, the nature of the cry changes, making the baby's signals more specific and easier to decipher (Fogel and Thelen, 1987). "Difficult" babies have their own special cry; they tend to pause longer between wails than other babies do, and their pauses seem to communicate the urgency of their demands (Lounsbury and Bates, 1982). Some mothers interpret these difficult cries as "spoiled," so the quality of the cry may affect the nature of the relationship between mother and child.

The nature of the early mother-infant relationship may also affect the amount of crying that babies do. In one study (Thoman, Acebo, and Becker, 1983), researchers noted how mothers allocated the time they spent with their infants (feeding, bathing, changing,

holding, touching, and so on). Mothers who were inconsistent in the way they allocated their time had babies who cried often, and the crying was concentrated into periods when the mothers were holding or touching their babies. The researchers believe that wide fluctuations in the way a mother spends time with her baby indicate an unstable relationship and that the baby's cries are a way of letting the mother know that their relationship is in trouble.

Babies come into the world prepared to regulate their bodily systems and adapt to their new environment. Their reactions to the world help them to survive and to learn about the people and things around them. Their initial inability to hold up their end of any social relationship is disguised by their caregivers, who treat them as if they had intentions and intelligence. Sheltered within the family, newborns meet the common tasks and challenges of development, each in his or her own way.

SUMMARY

THE NEONATE
Babies are called **neonates** during the first month after birth. Physicians rely on **Apgar scores** to determine a neonate's condition and on Dubowitz scores when they need to determine gestational age.

INFANT STATES AND RHYTHMS
The neonate's basic functions have detectable rhythms, ranging from seconds to hours. Babies pass through six **states** of consciousness (deep sleep, active sleep, drowsiness, alertness, fussiness, and crying), and only when they are quietly alert are they likely to learn from their environment. Body temperature becomes regulated soon after birth, a task that is difficult for high-risk SGA babies. The pitch and quality of a neonate's cry reflect the condition of the central nervous system. Neonates sleep about sixteen hours each day, and most of their extra sleeptime is spent in active sleep. Neonates suck rhythmically, in bursts separated by pauses. Researchers have detected two calming systems in newborns: one depends on contact comfort and soothes temporarily, and the other leads to endorphin production and soothes for longer periods.

REFLEXES
From birth, the newborn is equipped with a set of **reflexes** that are elicited by specific stimuli. These include the **rooting reflex,** the **grasping reflex,** the **Moro reflex,** and the **stepping** and **placing reflexes.** Most disappear within a few months, although some reflexes, such as coughing and blinking, are permanent.

EARLY PERCEPTUAL DEVELOPMENT
The newborn's sensory systems appear to develop in sequence, with sight being the least highly developed. Neonates react to tastes and smells much as adults do. Researchers study hearing by monitoring head turns, startle response, heart rate, respiration, brain waves, and sucking patterns. Newborns' hearing is less sensitive than the average adult's; sounds heard by an adult must be somewhat louder before a neonate can detect them. Neonates prefer some sounds to others, and they are especially attracted by the exaggerated speech used by adults with infants.

Newborns' **acuity** and **visual accommodation** are poor, so only a limited amount of distinct visual stimulation gets through; however, both improve rapidly. Until a baby is 2 or 3 months old, **convergence** is also poor. Depth perception begins to emerge at about 2 months. Newborns actively select visual stimulation, gathering information from the environment. **Preparedness** enables newborns to make rudimentary connections between events.

PERSONALITY AND SOCIAL RELATIONS

Newborns differ in temperament, but the subjectivity of most ratings has made reliable measurements of individual differences difficult to establish. Newborns show clear differences in irritability, reactivity, and activity level. These temperamental predispositions influence the tone of the baby's social relationships, which may in turn affect later personality development. **Goodness of fit** between newborn and parental personalities may determine whether development progresses satisfactorily.

Early social relations often evolve into turn-taking, a skill necessary for language and social development. Parents imitate their newborn's sounds and facial expressions, interpreting the infant's sounds, smiles, and body movements as intelligent replies to the parents' words. Both the quality of a baby's cry and the mother's emotional state may affect the nature of the parent-infant relationship.

KEY TERMS

acuity	neonate	rooting reflex
Apgar score	placing reflex	state
convergence	postpartum depression	stepping reflex
goodness of fit	preparedness	temperament
grasping reflex	reactivity	visual accommodation
Moro reflex	reflex	

THREE

• • • • • • • • • • • •

THE FIRST FOUR YEARS

In the course of their first four years, dependent babies become independent, inquisitive children. As their bodies grow, their nervous systems mature, and their experiences deepen, an enormous change takes place. From sensory beings who are sorting out the world, they become youngsters who not only perceive it in detail and act effectively on it but also remember the past and plot future actions. By the time children approach their fourth birthday, the chubby hands that clumsily shook rattles have become coordinated instruments that throw balls, build sand castles and block towers, and paint glowing pictures. Three-year-olds are competent talkers, whose early cooing and babbling has become an impressive command of language that they use to get things done. They are highly social beings, who make friends with other children and enjoy playing with them. The early attachment to mother has become a comfortable partnership that is preparing children to leave the tight world of the family circle and venture into the ever-expanding world of childhood. ■

••••••••••••••••

FUNDAMENTALS OF PHYSICAL GROWTH

• • • • • • • • • • • • • •

The first time an infant (usually about 10 or 12 months old) tries to eat with a spoon not much food reaches the mouth. A baby girl may suck the spoon, pass it from hand to hand, bang it on the highchair tray, rub it through her hair, or drop it on the floor. But among all this activity, the baby engages in two repetitive actions: she repeatedly sticks the spoon in the dish and pulls it out again, and she puts the spoon in her mouth and takes it out. When she removes the spoon from the dish, it is usually empty, just as it is when she puts it into her mouth, but the infant clearly has the intention to eat and some idea about the purpose of a spoon. If she did not, she would never master the art of feeding herself with a spoon, which is one of the first tool-using skills to develop.

When researchers (Connolly and Dalgleish, 1989) regularly observed infants and toddlers as they developed the ability to feed themselves, they noted that the process moved from separate, unconnected actions at 11 months to an organized action sequence at 23 months. The sequence included strategies for correcting errors. Over the months, the rigid grasp of the spoon became flexible, the side-to-side scoop that often came up empty became a dip that captured food, the hand steadied so that food no longer fell off the spoon before reaching the mouth, the same hand increasingly held the spoon, and the other hand braced the dish. As toddlers mastered the strategies of skilled spoon use, their motions became highly coordinated: smoother, faster, and more efficient.

This progression is typical of other motor skills, and tool use is only one aspect of physical development that we will investigate in this chapter. After exploring the genetically guided physical growth of infancy, we follow the course of brain development and the lateralization of various skills. Our outline of motor development shows that the mastery of various skills is much more than a matter of cortical maturation and that each separate skill is a developing system. After an examination of the connection between nutrition and health, we move on to the interaction between maturation and experience. We find a consistent link between growth and socioeconomic level and discover that deprivation and enrichment can delay or hasten the development of motor skills.

The Process of Physical Development

Physical development results from interaction between the child and the environment. During the process, children *grow* (they become larger), they *develop* (their body structures and functions become increasingly complex), and they *mature* (their size, organic structure, and body build progress toward their adult physiological state). These aspects of development are so intertwined that they are rarely separated for study.

The growth of infants and toddlers continues to follow the cephalocaudal and proximodistal patterns begun in the embryonic period (see Chapter 3). Growth continues to progress from head to foot. Although the brain still has a lot of growing to do, the dimensions of a newborn's head are closer to its adult size than is any other part of the body. Throughout childhood the largest increase in height takes place in the growth of the legs. As the child develops, the head contributes proportionately less to body length, shrinking from one-quarter of the total length at birth to one-twelfth at maturity (Bayley, 1956) (see Figure 5.1).

Physical development during infancy and childhood seems as orderly and lawful as the development of the fertilized egg into the newborn infant. This regular progression results from the canalization of growth. **Canalization** is the process in which growth is channeled along a predictable path when genes are expressed within a normally occurring human environment (Gottlieb, 1991). This species-typical growth is extremely difficult to deflect from its genetically influenced course. As we saw in Chapter 3, however, the normal path of development reflects each individual's reaction range, so environmental enrichment or deprivation also

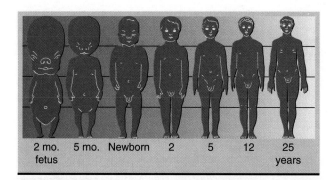

Figure 5.1 Changes in body proportions with growth. As growth progresses, the head becomes smaller in proportion to the rest of the body, the trunk remains approximately the same, and the legs occupy an increasing proportion of the body's length. *(From C. Jackson, 1929, p. 118)*

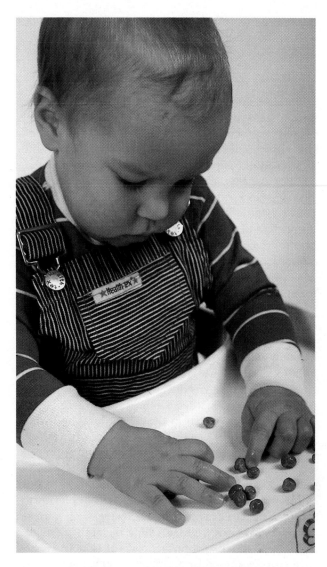

Motor control progresses in a proximodistal pattern; precise control over the fingers comes only after the development of shoulder, arm, and hand control. *(Ray Ellis/ Photo Researchers)*

influences the extent of development and the speed with which it occurs. Thus, despite its predictability, physical development is the result of dynamic interactions and reciprocal causality between genes and experience. This principle suggests that just as genes affect the context of physical development, so contexts at every level (cells, tissues, nutrition, hormones, family, culture) influence the structure and function of genes (Lerner, 1991).

Cephalocaudal and proximodistal patterns of growth also characterize the development of motor control. As body structures and functions become increasingly complex, the baby achieves progressively greater control over movements. Babies gain control over the muscles of the head and neck, then the arms and abdomen, and finally the legs. They learn to control the movements of their shoulders before they can direct their arms or fingers. They use their hands as a unit before they can control the finer movements of their fingers.

A third growth principle, differentiation and integration, also describes the progression of physical development. Motor abilities become increasingly distinct and specific, so the infant who made gross swipes with the whole hand at an attractive object becomes a child who delicately picks up the object with the fingertips. This is possible because as the child is able to make finer distinctions in muscle control, he or she also learns to coordinate and integrate separate skills into a single, practiced motion.

In the process of acquiring control over their bodies, babies master a series of basic skills (Gentile et al., 1975). First comes the establishment of *body stability,* which is essential to the mastery of all other motor skills. Babies cannot sit, stand, walk, manipulate objects,

or investigate the world effectively unless they can keep their balance. *Locomotion,* or the ability to move their bodies through the environment, provides a second basis for motor skills. Crawling, walking, and running depend on the successful coordination of joints and muscles into patterns of action. *Limb manipulation,* the ability to reach, grasp, and investigate with the fingers, presents a third basis for motor skills. All these elements must be mastered within a constantly changing environment, which keeps altering the nature of each task. Walking up stairs, for example, requires muscles and joints to respond in different ways than does walking on a sandy beach.

Norms

Because development is canalized, children master various skills in a similar and predictable manner. This became apparent during the first half of this century, when psychologists systematically observed many children, analyzing the sequence in which physical characteristics and motor, language, and social skills emerge (Bayley, 1956; P. Cattell, 1940; Gesell, 1925; Griffiths, 1954). These investigators discovered that the sequence, as well as the appearance, of various skills is highly predictable. The studies produced **norms,** or typical patterns, that describe the approximate ages at which important attributes and skills appear. Norms are based on simple mathematical calculations that reflect average growth tendencies. They do not explain growth or development; they merely describe it, indicating what is most likely to appear in the development of children within a particular society at a particular time in history, as will become clear in a later section when we examine the effects of culture, deprivation, and enrichment on physical development.

Norms can be useful in describing how most children develop. They can help us assess the effects of environmental changes on behavior (such as the effects of separating infants from their mothers), and they can be useful in studying cultural or subcultural variations. Norms have also been helpful in studies of prematurity and of atypical development. The baby whose size or motor development lags far behind the norm alerts the pediatrician to look for further signs of trouble. Norms have also been used to examine the effects of institutionalization on the growth of infants and children, of gender differences in growth, and of birth order on a child's development.

Yet the value of norms as a diagnostic tool for an individual child is limited. In every aspect of development, normal children vary widely on each side of a norm. Parents who are unaware of the large normal range for the onset of various motor skills may become unnecessarily alarmed when they see young infants who have been walking for several months while their own, older baby still cannot stand. Some children never creep or crawl but go directly from sitting to taking their first steps. The normal range for the onset of walking is large, from as early as 8 months to as late as 20, although the average U.S. baby walks at about 13 months and 90 percent are walking by 15 months

Norms give us the approximate age at which most infants begin to walk, but the age at which a particular infant will take his or her first steps is impossible to predict. *(Elizabeth Crews)*

(Hopkins and Westra, 1990; Frankenburg, 1978). Figure 5.2 shows the norms for some of the early motor milestones.

In many aspects of growth, norms differ for girls and boys. Girls and boys grow at different rates, and the difference begins before birth. By the time the fetuses are halfway through the prenatal period, girls' skeletal development is three weeks ahead of boys', and by the time the babies are born, girls have outstripped boys by four to six weeks in skeletal maturity, although not in size (Tanner, 1978). Some organ systems are more developed at birth in girls, and this may help explain why more girls than boys survive.

During the first few months, boys grow faster than girls, but from the age of 7 months until they are 4 years old, girls surpass boys. Then both sexes grow at the same rate until puberty. According to an old rule, children reach half their adult height by the end of the second year. This rule is helpful only when parents want to

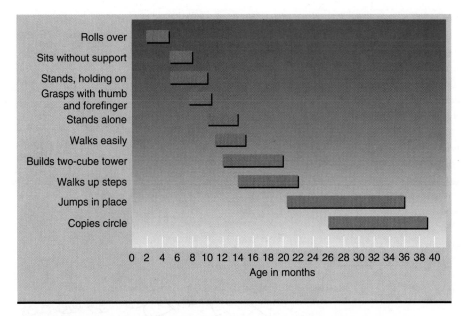

Figure 5.2 Each band in this figure shows the typical spread in development, from the age at which 25 percent of children are able to perform the motor skill to the age at which 90 percent of the children can do so. *(Data from Frankenburg, 1978)*

predict the height of boys. Because girls mature earlier than boys, they reach the halfway mark sooner: at about 18 months.

Individual Growth Patterns

The first thing an observer notices about a group of infants is how different each appears. Marked structural differences have existed among them since soon after conception. Newborn infants differ in such physical variables as height (length), weight, muscularity, hairiness, dental development, and a host of other measurable characteristics. As children grow, individual physical differences persist. Some differences, such as height and weight, become more pronounced; others, such as hairiness, become less noticeable.

The rate of growth differs nearly as much as structure does. Healthy children may grow much more slowly or quickly than the mythical average child described by norms. Maturation rates seem to be related to body build, which is largely dictated by heredity. A child who is broadly built, large, and strong is likely to grow rapidly, but a small, lightly muscled child is likely to grow more slowly (Bayley, 1956).

Because norms do not provide an adequate yardstick for measuring individual growth, researchers have discovered ways to assess the individual child's growth progress. The rate at which teeth erupt is one fairly accurate measure. Another is skeletal age; the degree of calcification, the shape, and the position of bones reveal how far a child has progressed toward physiological maturity. Because skeletal age is assessed by x-raying the wrist and hand, this measurement is taken only when some medical problem is suspected.

Several hormones have important roles in the regulation of growth, but the **growth hormone (GH)** itself is one of the most important, because it seems to have a general growth-promoting effect throughout the body. It promotes muscle cell division and stimulates long-bone growth. Growth hormone is secreted primarily at night, but physical or emotional stress can lead to its production during the day (Bogin, 1988). GH also stimulates the production of **somatomedins,** a second growth factor, which promote cell division in muscles and in cartilage cells at the ends of bones.

Children whose bodies produce no GH at all become midgets unless they are given Protopin, a synthetic form of GH produced through genetic engineering. Like human GH, Protopin stimulates rapid growth. One youngster whose body lacked GH took the new drug and grew 5 inches the first year. By the age of 11, he was 52 inches tall. His eventual height was expected to fall within the normal range (Abramson, 1985). Not all dwarfism is caused by an absence of GH; sometimes it results when children's bodies produce adequate GH but low levels of somatomedins (Bogin, 1988).

Although individual growth patterns are generally stable, severe dietary deficiencies, disease, or stress can disrupt them and temporarily slow growth, perhaps by interfering with GH and somatomedin levels and balance (Bogin, 1988). If the condition responsible for retarded growth is eliminated, the child usually goes through a period of **catch-up growth,** during which growth accelerates to compensate for the slowdown, as shown in Figure 5.3. Researchers are not certain whether this compensatory growth is the result of increases in somatomedin levels or of heightened sensitivity of cells throughout the body. In any case, each child's growth curve seems to be genetically determined and self-stabilizing.

Brain Development

Within two years, the baby's brain will triple in size, reaching about 75 to 80 percent of its adult weight and dimensions. Perhaps because of its extensive, rapid growth, the baby's central nervous system is more adaptable than it will be later in life. If an infant is born with a malformed major brain tract, the nervous system may be capable of correcting for it, perhaps by developing the function in a different area. When an infant's brain is damaged, the recovery may be so complete that the baby shows no apparent aftereffects. If, for example, the part of the brain that controls language function should be injured, the baby still may develop normal language function. Although the recovery seems complete, extensive testing can detect damage that is not apparent in most situations (Goldman-Rakic et al., 1983). Psychologists interested in the relation between brain development and behavior have studied electrical activity, the gradual assumption of control by the brain's cortex, and differences in function between the brain's hemispheres.

Electrical Activity

When newborn babies are awake or asleep, the electrical activity of their brains shows characteristic wave patterns. At this age, a baby's electroencephalogram (EEG) tracings show no alpha waves (a wave pattern that appears in adults when their eyes are closed and they are not actively processing information). A slowed form of alpha rhythm appears at about 4 months; over

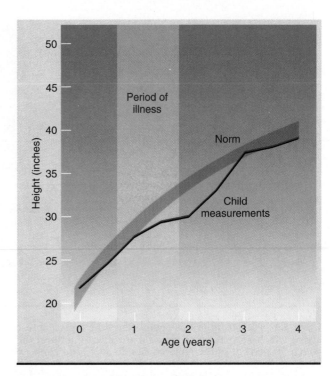

Figure 5.3 The effect on growth in a young child whose food intake was greatly reduced for approximately one year is apparent. When the illness ended and food intake rose to normal levels, catch-up growth was completed in approximately two years. *(Adapted from Prader, Tanner, and Von Harnack, 1963)*

the years, it gradually increases in frequency, assuming adult form when the child is about 16 years old. Because of this regular development, alpha frequency sometimes is used as a measure of brain maturation (A. Parmelee and Sigman, 1983). Other brain-wave patterns also show regular maturational changes in speed as well as form. At birth, the brain's electrical response to sights or sounds comes slowly. At about 3 months, the response is faster, and by the age of 4 years, the child's brain responds as quickly as the adult's (A. Parmelee and Sigman, 1983).

Cortical Control

At birth, the baby's **cortex** (the mantle of cells covering the two cerebral hemispheres) is exceedingly immature, an indication that much neonatal behavior may be reflexive or controlled by lower parts of the brain. The areas of the brain that control particular sensory and motor functions develop at different rates. Once a specific area in the cortex develops, the corresponding function can appear in the baby's develop-

WINDOW ON THE INFANT BRAIN

Techniques that allow researchers to watch the brain at work have confirmed developmentalists' speculations about the gradual development of cortical function in babies. **Positron emission tomography (PET)** is based on the biochemistry of the nervous system. When neurons function, they use glucose for energy, and the more active they are, the more glucose they require. If radioactive glucose is injected into the body, the presence of glucose in the neurons can be translated into maps of brain activity made by recording the decay of radioactive glucose. These maps, called *PET scans,* have given researchers a window into the living brain.

PET scans of nine nearly normal infants and four severely retarded infants and toddlers allowed Harry Chugani and Michael Phelps (1986) to trace the development of cortical function in babies. The "normal" infants were developing normally, although they had suffered from some sort of neurological seizures as newborns.

PET scans made on these infants between the ages of 5 days and 18 months clearly show the gradual spread of function through the developing brain. As the accompanying figure shows, there were vast areas of silence in the newborn's frontal cortex, a pattern that is consistent with a mostly subcortical control of behavior. The most active areas of the brain were the primary motor and sensory areas, the brainstem (which controls such automatic activities as breathing and circulation), parts of the cerebellum (which is involved in movement), and the thalamus. At 11 weeks, activity spread through the cortex and the basal ganglia (which integrate information from various parts of the brain), while energy use increased in primary motor and sensory areas. By 7½ months, the pattern of activity in these babies' brains resembled that seen in adults.

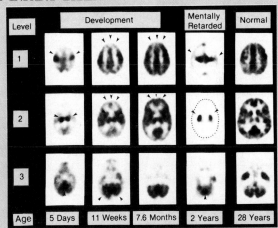

These PET scans show developmental changes in brain function while the babies were awake and had their eyes open. The PET scans show brain activity at three levels, with level 1 corresponding to the top of the brain (cortex). Dark areas indicate functioning neurons. Note the widespread white areas in the PET scans of the severely retarded 2-year-olds, indicating a lack of neural functioning in those areas. *(From Chugani and Phelps, 1986, p. 84)*

This pattern did not appear in the PET scans of severely retarded 2-year-olds; instead, their brain function resembled that of "normal" newborns. These retarded toddlers, who had suffered severe anoxia at birth, showed little cortical activity. They also had retained many of the neonatal reflexes that disappear in normal infants.

---

ment. When the area of the motor cortex that controls signals to the hands and arms develops, for example, infants learn to use their hands skillfully. The accompanying box, "Window on the Infant Brain," shows how various areas of the cortex come "on line" over the first eight months.

The relationship between cortical maturity and behavior is not so straightforward as it might seem, however. Development in the sensory receptors and other parts of the brain and spinal cord also may be related to the appearance of new behavior (A. Parmelee and Sigman, 1983). In addition, neurons that seem to be structurally mature may not be able either to generate nerve impulses or to manufacture chemicals that transmit nerve impulses from one cell to another (Goldman-

Rakic et al., 1983). Finally, the development of many motor skills may depend as much on the growth of joints and muscles as on neural development (Thelen, Kelso, and Fogel, 1987).

Normal brain development depends on experience. Stimulation from the environment spurs the development of connections between cells, thus canalizing brain development (Gottlieb, 1991) (see Figure 5.4). During infancy, there is such a rampant overgrowth of synapses that the 2-year-old has more connections between neurons than an adult (Goldman-Rakic, 1987). Overgrowth ensures that connections needed to deal with essential environmental information are in place by the time infants encounter necessary experiences (Greenough, Black, and Wallace, 1987). Then the cir-

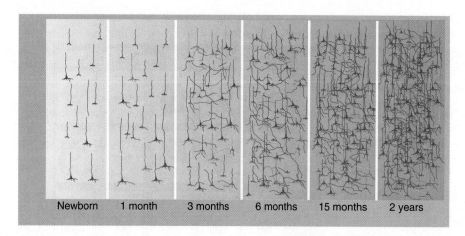

Figure 5.4 At birth, neurons are immature and connections between them are sparse. In response to environmental stimulation, connections develop rapidly, so that the 2-year-old has more neural connections than the adult. *(From Conel, 1939–1959)*

cuits actually used when moving, seeing, hearing, and the like, can be organized into networks. Connections that go unused at the anticipated time wither and die. Researchers have speculated that adult competence may depend on eliminating some of these connections.

Researchers have found evidence of this growth and dieback in the brains of monkeys. If a monkey's eye is sutured shut during a short period after birth, most of its connections to the visual cortex are lost (LeVay, Wiesel, and Hubel, 1980). Neurons from the free eye take over connections that would normally have gone to the shuttered eye; when the sutures are removed, the monkey's sight in that eye is seriously impaired.

Whenever children have to learn something that is not part of the universal human experience, the stimulation apparently generates new connections between neurons (Greenough, Black, and Wallace, 1987). This process not only enables children to take advantage of unique experiences but may also allow them to rebuild connections that are "erased" if, like the monkey, they fail to encounter "expected" stimulation because of severe environmental deprivation. In the case of the monkey with impaired vision, if the good eye is sutured shut and the barely functioning eye left open, neurons from the impaired eye begin seeking new connections and vision greatly improves (LeVay, Wiesel, and Hubel, 1980).

Lateralization

The two halves of the human brain have different functions. Each hemisphere receives sensation from and controls voluntary muscles on the opposite side of the body. In most right-handed people, language is processed in the left hemisphere. Melodies and nonspeech sounds apparently are processed in the right hemisphere, which also seems to perceive and analyze visual patterns. Most tasks, however, draw on both hemispheres, with the left hemisphere specialized to process discrete items in a temporal arrangement, and the right hemisphere specialized for processing unified patterns (Witelson, 1987). The situation and the individual's way of approaching the task seem to determine which hemisphere will be more heavily involved. When a person is reading technical material, for example, the left hemisphere is active; when he or she is reading folktales, activity in the left hemisphere does not change, but the right hemisphere also becomes active (R. Ornstein et al., 1979). Most people process music in the right hemisphere, but trained musicians (who analyze the structure of music) also use the left hemisphere (Kinsbourne and Hiscock, 1983).

Developmental psychologists have tried to establish the course of **lateralization,** which refers to the way that various functions are established in one hemisphere or the other. Developmentalists used to believe that lateralization is a gradual process that is not complete until adolescence, but an increasing number of researchers are convinced that the hemispheres already are specialized for basic functions at birth (Kinsbourne and Hiscock, 1983). Studies using brain waves indicate that the left hemisphere of newborns processes speech sounds much faster than the right, and that among 2-year-olds (the youngest age tested), children rely primarily on the right hemisphere to process spatial relationships. The gradual assumption of tasks by each hemisphere is apparently related to the development of new skills (Witelson, 1987). As each new skill appears, it is handled by the side of the brain that is most efficient in the appropriate style of processing.

The Development of Motor Skills

Within a year, the baby who could not even turn over learns to sit, stand, crawl, and manipulate objects and may even begin to walk. Soon the baby becomes a child who runs, climbs, and is a skilled user of tools. As Esther Thelen (1989) has pointed out, all motor skills follow the same five general developmental principles: (1) Because movement results from the interaction of many subsystems (perceptions, motivation, plans, physiological status, emotions) with the mechanical system of muscles, bones, and joints, motor development can be understood only in terms of *the developing system.* (2) The *task,* not preexisting genetic instructions, determines how these components are assembled. Tasks involving motor skills depend on context, and babies (as well as adults) draw on whichever available components best fit the task at hand. (3) Developmental processes are *nonlinear.* As small changes occur in one or more available components, the baby reorganizes the

system. When this happens, the skill may show an uneven spiral development. That is, instead of steadily increasing in smoothness and accuracy, the skill goes through a period in which it again becomes clumsy or even disappears. (4) Action and perception form an *inseparable loop.* Babies are built to seek and receive information from the surrounding context, and they modify their actions to fit their perceptions. (5) *Variability* is an important aspect of development. Babies vary in the way they attack specific tasks, in part because they may draw on different components. In learning to eat with a spoon, for example, babies grasp the spoon differently, and some flex their elbows to lift the spoon to their mouths, but others rotate their wrists (Connolly and Dalgleish, 1989) (see Figure 5.5). The best way to see these principles in action is to trace the development of single skills, such as learning to grasp objects and learning to walk. Try to discern these general principles in the following descriptions.

Limb Manipulation: Using the Hand

Limb manipulation is one of the major bases for motor skills. Skilled hand use can be considered a sort of manual intelligence, and some researchers (Bruner, 1970) believe that it reveals a good deal about the nature of thought and problem solving. Unlike the hands of most primates, the human hand is a despecialized organ—it can do almost anything. This lack of speciali-

Figure 5.5 When learning to eat with a spoon, the majority of babies use grip A (transverse palmar—radial), and the pattern remains equally popular among toddlers. Grip B (transverse digital—radial) gradually becomes more popular, with users increasing from less than 10 percent at 12 months to more than 20 percent at 23 months. Preference for grip C (transverse palmar—ulnar) drops from 14 percent among 12-month-olds to less than 1 percent at 23 months. Grip D (clenched transverse digital—radial) becomes increasingly popular until about 18 months and then declines in popularity, with about 10 percent of 23-month-olds using it. Even at 23 months, no babies use grip E, which is the adult way of holding a spoon. *(From Connolly and Dalgleish, 1989, p. 898)*

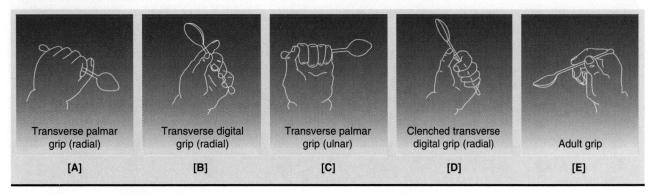

Transverse palmar grip (radial)	Transverse digital grip (radial)	Transverse palmar grip (ulnar)	Clenched transverse digital grip (radial)	Adult grip
[A]	**[B]**	**[C]**	**[D]**	**[E]**

zation means that the joints and tendons in our fingers, wrists, elbows, shoulders, and trunk can operate independently. It takes years before the child can combine and coordinate them to express full manual intelligence.

Reaching and Grasping

Almost from birth, babies follow moving objects with their eyes. Their ability to reach out and grasp the objects they see develops in a characteristic pattern, seeming to disappear and reappear, as the various components of the grasp rearrange themselves in different ways. In a series of studies, Claes von Hofsten (1982, 1983, 1984) dangled a brightly colored yarn ball in front of babies. The ball was connected by a rod to an electric motor, which slowly moved the ball in a horizontal path from one side of the infant to the other. As the newborn reached rapidly toward the object, his or her hand opened, and as the hand neared the object, the motion slowed. But the baby rarely managed to touch the ball of yarn with these swipes. This early motion is neither functional nor goal-oriented. The baby is not attempting to grab and manipulate the object. The reach simply indicates that the baby is paying attention to the object. In these early weeks, the arm and hand act as information-gathering feelers, which infants point toward an object that has attracted their gaze.

When babies are about 2 months old, they reach with a fist instead of an open hand. Hofsten suggests that the

At 5 months, babies reach for objects with an open hand, using the eyes to direct the hand's slow, but not yet skilled, movement. *(Laura Dwight)*

baby's arm and shoulder are controlled by the brain-stem, but the coordination of hand and fingers is guided by the cortex. At 2 months, the cortical system is not yet coordinated with the system that controls gross motor movements. The apparent backsliding in ability indicates that the prestructured motor pattern has broken down so that its constituents can be reassembled in a more mature manner.

By the end of the fourth month, most of the baby's reaches are again open-handed. Now the reach is slower, and the baby often succeeds in grasping—or at least touching—the object. The hand moves toward and with the object at the same time, with the eyes guiding the hand. The baby must be able to see both the hand and the object in order to reach the fascinating ball of yarn. The precision of aim and its timing indicate a delicately tuned system of sensorimotor functioning, which allows the baby to monitor and correct the reach (Mathew and Cook, 1990).

The final stage in reaching appears at about 9 months. Once again, the reach is rapid, but now it is highly accurate and direct. Catching hold of some interesting object no longer requires a baby's complete attention. Babies may or may not watch the reaching hand, because the motion has become so skilled and practiced that visual control is not necessary when the path between hand and object is obvious (Bushnell, 1985).

One of the baby's purposes in reaching and grasping is the exploration of interesting objects. Grasping is only the first step in exploring an object, and even 6-month-olds adapt their exploratory actions to the characteristics of the object (Palmer, 1989). Although everything goes into their mouths at some time, babies squeeze soft toys, mouth plastic toys, and scoot toys with wheels. They wave bells in the air, and the way they use toys with a table depends on whether its surface is hard (and makes a satisfactory noise) or soft. By 12 months, babies rely less on their mouths to explore, and their increased control over their hands and fingers produces increasingly subtle and economical actions. As we saw in the chapter opening, they are beginning to use tools, although they are not yet able to organize separate actions into a smooth sequence (Connolly and Dalgleish, 1989).

Handedness

Handedness develops slowly. Although most toddlers tend to use one hand more often than the other, many children do not settle on the consistent use of one hand until they are about 5 years old (Goodall, 1980). When lying on their backs, most newborns (65 percent) turn their heads to the right; a few (15 percent) prefer lying with their heads turned to the left; and the rest show no preference for either side. This preference, which is still apparent at 2 months, predicts which hand the baby is likely to use in reaching for objects at 4 months (Michel, 1981). However, the preference for the right-handed reach declines during this period. In Hofsten's (1984) study, the percentage of right-handed reaches declined from 72 percent at 1 week to 55 percent at 4 months.

By 4 months, most infants hold a toy longer when it is placed in the right hand than when it is placed in the left. Between 6 and 9 months, many babies tend to rely on the right hand when they reach for an object directly in front of them. But the use of the right hand is not yet stable in all conditions. When manipulating an object, however, 7- to 9-month-olds in one study were consistent in using the right hand (Michel, Harkins, and Ovrut, 1986).

Some children begin relying exclusively on one hand much earlier than others. The timing of this preference interacts with gender in an unusual way. In a longitudinal study of children between the ages of 18 and 42 months (Gottfried and Bathurst, 1983), girls who developed a consistent hand preference (whether right or left) scored significantly higher on tests of intellectual development than girls who did not. No relation between hand preference and test performance appeared for boys. Researchers have concluded that young girls who do not develop a hand preference process language in both hemispheres but that the connection between hand preferences and lateralization for language does not hold for young boys (Kee et al., 1987). In another study (Tan, 1985), 4-year-old boys (but not girls) who had failed to develop a consistent hand preference were poorly coordinated. Despite the widespread belief that left-handers tend to be more awkward than right-handers, right- and left-handers were equally well coordinated.

Locomotion: From Crawling to Walking

Locomotion is another of the major underpinnings of motor skills. Before infants can crawl or walk, various components of the abilities must mature and become coordinated (Goldfield, 1989; Thelen, Kelso, and Fogel, 1987). During the first two months, a baby's legs gain a good deal of fat but not much muscle. As we saw in

Chapter 4, the chubby legs become too heavy for babies to move unless they have some relief from gravity (Thelen, Fisher, and Ridley-Johnson, 1984). Although reflexive stepping movements disappear when babies are held upright, babies continue this pattern of motor activity while lying on their backs (Thelen, 1985). All the joints (hip, knee, ankle) work in unison, producing the same rhythmic kicks. Although the movements are different from those used in mature walking, there are enough parallels between them to suggest that this pattern, which is probably generated in the spinal cord, forms the basis for later walking. Between 2 and 5 months, the stereotypical kick breaks down. The action of each joint becomes individualized, only to be reorganized into more mature motor patterns. This temporary disorganization paves the way for the development of voluntary control so that the baby will be able to turn over, crawl, stand up, walk, and climb.

During these same months, babies slowly gain body stability (the third major underpinning of motor skills).

Their proportions change: their legs lengthen, their shoulders widen, and their center of gravity shifts downward. But before they can crawl, they must also gain the muscular strength in their arms that is required to lift the head, chest, and abdomen, and then they must integrate the developing systems of head orientation, reaching, and kicking. At first, they can reach effectively for objects, coordinating hand and eye, but they cannot use their arms for support and they kick without pushing against the ground. During the next stage, they support their weight on both hands, but they simply rock back and forth, without moving forward. They begin to crawl when they need only one hand to support their weight and when they begin to show consistency in the hand they use to reach for objects. As they shift from a seated to a crawling position, they generally land on the unpreferred hand and then begin to crawl by reaching out with the preferred hand (Goldfield, 1989).

As babies gain control over their posture, they get ready to stand up and walk. Around the time of their

Crawling is a complicated procedure that depends on the development of muscular strength and the integration of the baby's systems for reaching, kicking, and head orientation. *(Elizabeth Crews/Stock, Boston)*

first birthday, most infants take their first steps. But this walking lacks the characteristics of adult walking. Youngsters land on their toes or flat on their feet, instead of striking the ground with their heels, as adults do (Forssberg, 1985). The adult walking pattern develops gradually toward the end of the second year, probably in response to (1) changes in organization and control in the spinal cord and brain or (2) improvements in posture and strength—or both.

The consequences of walking for both child and parent are incalculable. The infant's world widens, and new possibilities open. When youngsters master the art of moving around with comparative ease, systematic changes occur in the way they explore their surroundings. They are likely to feel more competent. Now they can approach other people (fostering social interaction) or leave them (fostering autonomy) (Kopp, 1979). As we saw in Chapter 2, Erik Erikson (1963) views the

This 7-month-old boy is not ready to walk. When his father holds him upright, the baby does not step but keeps his feet fixed as if they were glued to the floor. *(Rae Russel)*

establishment of autonomy as the toddler's major developmental task.

Walking changes children's lives in other ways. Suddenly, they find their actions interrupted as never before. Their explorations of interesting objects that once lasted until they grew weary or bored are abruptly terminated by parents who move them bodily away, distract them from their fascinating forays, begin to shout "No!" and perhaps even slap an infant hand. Parents treat children who can walk differently from infants, seeing them less as "babies" and more as individuals. This shift in perspective leads parents to expect their child to adapt to family routines and rules. Walking also exposes the child to accident, and so leads to even more parental intervention.

Play Skills

As the months pass, youngsters become confident walkers. With the basic underpinnings of motor skills developed, they turn to testing and refining new skills—running, jumping, climbing, and manipulating objects. Jumping first appears at age 2, for example, and the patterns of coordination that are established in early childhood are virtually identical to those found in adults (J. Clark, Phillips, and Petersen, 1989). Early hopping, however, changes from an ungainly hop made with a stiff body, the nonhopping leg held motionless, and a flat-footed landing to a graceful hop made with reduced stiffness, the nonhopping leg swinging, and a landing on the ball of the foot (Getchell and Roberton, 1989).

Coordination, which includes the child's accuracy of movement, poise, smoothness, rhythm, and ease, is the basis of almost all play skills. It provides a fairly good index for determining a child's ability and agility at physical play. A child acquires coordination more slowly than strength or speed, because coordination requires the interplay of sensory and motor skills that often depend on the maturation of small muscles and on practice.

The nature of children's play depends on their cognitive level and social experience. The simplest, least mature form of play is functional. The child engaged in **functional play** makes simple, repetitive movements with or without an object. It appears early, when babies bang the side of the crib or shake a rattle purely for the pleasure that they derive from the motion. Functional play declines sharply with age, from 53 percent of the 2-year-old's activity to 14 percent among 6- and 7-year-olds (K. Rubin, Fein, and Vandenberg, 1983). As children emerge from toddlerhood, too much functional

The ability to walk gives toddlers a feeling of competence and enables them to work on other skills such as climbing, running, or jumping. *(Brenda L. Lewison/The Stock Market)*

play may be a signal that preschoolers lack social competence and are rejected by their peers (K. Rubin and Maioni, 1975).

A growing proportion of toddlers' and preschoolers' playtime is devoted to **constructive play,** in which they manipulate objects to construct or create something. Toddlers, for example, may stack blocks into a tower or put together a jigsaw puzzle. Because constructive play requires children to manipulate objects, to fit them together, or to solve some sort of problem, it helps children learn *how* to solve problems.

By the time they are 3 years old, most children are deep into **pretend play,** which incorporates their increasing ability to symbolize and imagine. Pretend play seems to enhance social and cognitive skills. Highly imaginative youngsters tend to score higher on various cognitive tests; they are also more cooperative, friendlier, less aggressive, and more empathic than children who rarely pretend (K. Rubin, Fein, and Vandenberg, 1983). They are also likely to be happy children—if smiles, laughter, and similar indications of mood are used as a measure of happiness (J. Singer and Singer, 1979).

Among 3-year-olds, boys are much more likely than girls to engage in **rough-and-tumble play,** a variety of play that combines characteristic patterns of motor activity. Such play appears in children as young as 18 months, and Nicholas Blurton-Jones (1976) believes that those who do not begin it early may never engage in it. In a typical bout of rough-and-tumble play, one child chases another, and the chase is followed by scuffling, wrestling, and laughter. Because children in all cultures studied give the same signals (facial expression, laughter, using only the open hand instead of the fist) to indicate a lack of hostility, rough-and-tumble play may have had an important role in the evolution of human beings.

Similar gender differences in rough-and-tumble play appear among rhesus monkeys (Blurton-Jones, 1976), but socialization apparently plays a major role in its development. Socialization may explain why young girls seem to perceive a physical threat in the same action that young boys interpret as an invitation to roughhouse. In a group of preschoolers studied by Janet DiPietro (1981), girls showed just as much vigorous activity on the trampoline as boys. But rough-and-tumble play developed primarily among boys, with the scuffle beginning as one boy tried to take a toy from another. The boy in possession of the toy seemed to think that the grab was a bid to play. When someone tried to take a toy from a girl, she interpreted the action not as an invitation to play but as a bid for dominance.

The effects of rough-and-tumble play appear to be positive. Researchers have suggested that it encourages youngsters to form and consolidate friendships (P. K. Smith, 1977) and provides a safe way to practice controlled aggression (Suomi, 1977). As we will see in Chapter 10, rough-and-tumble play does not end when children get older.

Nutrition and Health

The internal mechanisms that regulate growth appear to be affected by hormonal and chemical factors. Nutrition seems to affect the composition of these chemicals; malnourished infants and fasting adults both have low somatomedin levels, which may allow the body to use dietary protein to maintain and repair body tissues at the expense of growth (Bogin, 1988). Because nutrition is a major determinant of normal physical growth, dietary deficiencies often are responsible for abnormal growth patterns.

Research has established the value of breast feeding in providing babies with protection against disease through antibodies produced by the mother (E. Pollitt, Garza, and Leibel, 1984). A recent study suggests that babies' diets may also affect cognitive development. The 300 children studied had all been preterm infants who were fed by tube, but on intelligence tests administered when the children were 8 years old, those who had received breast milk or a mixture of breast milk and formula achieved scores that were more than 10 points higher than the scores of children who had received only formula (Lucas et al., 1992). After corrections for mother's socioeconomic status, the scores of children who had received breast milk were still more than 8 points higher than the scores of children who had received formula. Researchers speculate that human breast milk may contain some yet-to-be identified substance that affects mental development. Whether or not this is true, it is clear that malnutrition and obesity have important effects on development.

Malnutrition

General malnutrition, in which children simply do not get enough to eat, is marked by a lack of calories as well as a lack of protein, vitamins, and minerals. As the number of calories available to a young child drops dangerously near the level required for maintenance and growth, the child becomes listless and ceases to play or to explore the environment. When calorie intake drops below the minimum level, growth ceases.

The effects of temporary malnutrition were established when researchers studied children who were subjected to severe wartime malnutrition in Europe and Asia after each of the world wars (Acheson, 1960; Wolff, 1935). Among these children, when the episode of malnutrition was neither too severe nor too long, the effects of acute malnourishment were usually overcome through catch-up growth. Once these children returned to a normal diet, they caught up with their peers by adolescence. Among Japanese children, recovery in height and weight was most rapid in large cities (where diets improved first) and slowest in rural mountain villages (where improvements in diet occurred last) (Kimura, 1984).

Short periods of malnutrition can be overcome, but children who are chronically undernourished may suffer permanent effects. In many developing countries, where infants not only are malnourished but also suffer from infectious diseases, growth begins to falter at six months. By the time these children are two years old, they are smaller than 95 percent of 2-year-olds in technological societies (Gorman and Pollitt, 1992). Severe malnutrition in infancy can also disrupt brain development, affecting connections between neurons and the development of chemicals that transmit signals through the brain (A. Parmelee and Sigman, 1983). Among a group of malnourished Guatemalan infants, for example, height and weight were good predictors of performance on mental and motor tests (Lasky et al., 1981).

Children with a history of severe, chronic malnutrition tend to receive lower scores on IQ tests and tests of specific cognitive abilities than other children in the same community, and their school achievement lags behind. Among youngsters in rural Kenya, for example, malnourishment from birth was associated with poor performance on mental tests and with distractibility and difficulty in concentrating in the classroom (Sigman et al., 1989). The disparity continues even after the children receive an adequate diet. But as Ernesto Pollitt and his associates (E. Pollitt, Garza, and Leibel, 1984) point out, when testing malnourished youngsters, it is difficult to separate social factors from the physiological effects of malnutrition. In addition, the sluggishness of the malnourished child may lead to lowered motivation when the youngster takes tests.

Deficiencies of specific nutrients also can disrupt development. Severe, prolonged protein deficiency, for example, can lead to a serious, often fatal, disease called **kwashiorkor.** This ailment is prevalent among infants whose diet consists primarily of breast milk after they are a year old or who are fed a low-protein substitute for breast milk (such as cassava or arrowroot) (Jelliffe and Jelliffe, 1979; Waterlow, 1973). Such infants are profoundly apathetic; they have scaly skin, diarrhea, swollen limbs and abdomens, and liver degeneration. If the disease goes untreated for more than four months, they may be severely retarded (Cravioto and Delicardie, 1970). Given adequate protein, infants with kwashiorkor grow rapidly, but they never catch up with infants of their own age.

Few American youngsters suffer from kwashiorkor, but chronic undernutrition has been a continuing problem in the United States, where approximately 25 percent of children live in poverty. In one study, 10 percent of the poor children in Massachusetts were chronically malnourished (O'Discoll and Neuman, 1983). Children who get enough calories may still have deficiencies of specific nutrients. Among infants and preschoolers in the United States, the most common nutritional problem is a lack of iron (E. Pollitt, Garza, and Leibel, 1984). When infants do not get enough iron, they lag behind other babies on tests of motor and mental development. The link seems fairly well established, because when these infants are given iron supplements, they catch up with other babies (Oski et al., 1983). Iron is believed to affect brain chemistry, but perhaps the supplements simply improve general health and well-being so that a child is no longer listless and becomes motivated (E. Pollitt, Garza, and Leibel, 1984).

An intervention program with pregnant Guatemalan women highlighted the long-term effects of early malnutrition (Super, Herrera, and Mora, 1990). Families in the program received supplementary food during the last trimester of pregnancy and for three years after the birth of the baby. At age 6, three years after the program had ended, more than half of the chronically malnourished children in control families were stunted in growth. Among families who had received supplementary food and counseling, fewer than one-fifth of the children were stunted. The timing and duration of supplemental food seem to be important. In the United States, researchers followed the families of poor women who were enrolled in the Special Supplemental Food Program for Women, Infants, and Children (WIC) during the last trimester of pregnancy. At the age of four, the babies who had had the benefit of extra nutrition during the fetal period received higher scores on mental tests than did their older siblings who were already into their second year when the family started receiving supplements (E. Pollitt, Garza, and Leibel, 1984). Public health programs apparently can have significant effects on physical and mental development.

Obesity

A major nutritional problem that is the result of interactions between genes and environment is **obesity,** a condition in which body weight is at least 20 percent more than the norm for height. Study after study has shown that adopted children's relative weight is more like the weight of their biological parents than of their adoptive parents (Biron, Mongeau, and Bertrand, 1977; Kolata, 1986). In a longitudinal study, William Kessen and Judith Rodin compared children of normal-weight parents with children of overweight parents (Rodin and Hall, 1987). When these children were newborns, three factors predicted whether they would be obese as preschoolers: obesity in the parents; a heightened responsiveness to sweet tastes at birth; and a heightened responsiveness to environmental stimuli at birth. Many obese children and adults show a similar heightened responsiveness to all environmental cues. Not only does food appeal more to them, but when they see it or smell it, their insulin levels rise dramatically (Rodin, 1983). High insulin levels make people eat more and speed the conversion of food to fat.

Fat babies are not necessarily fat children. After reviewing various studies, Alex Roche (1981) found almost no correlation between obesity in infancy and obesity at age 16. But when obesity persists throughout the preschool period, a child is likely to carry excess weight into young adulthood (Wicks-Nelson and Israel, 1984). Several environmental factors have been implicated in later obesity. Parents may inadvertently encourage their preschoolers to overeat. Some become alarmed when their 3-year-olds seem to stop eating, so they press food on children who burn fewer calories now that their growth has slowed. Other parents are so afraid that their child will become fat that they put rigid restraints on the youngster's food consumption. Dependent on parental guidance, the child never develops any internal psychological controls over eating (Rodin and Hall, 1987). Another factor that seems to affect weight is the speed with which children eat. Overweight preschoolers chew each bite of food less than preschoolers of normal weight, which allows them to take more bites of food (and thus more calories) during a meal (Drabman et al., 1979). This difference appears as early as 18 months—the youngest age studied.

More and more American children are becoming obese; since 1960, obesity among school-age children has increased 54 percent. Some researchers believe that television bears a good part of the responsibility for this increase. Studies have found that television viewing and obesity are correlated; for every increase of one hour in television viewing, there is a 2 percent increase in obesity among children (Dietz and Gortmaker, 1985). Children eat more while they watch TV, TV ads encourage them to eat more, and their inactivity while watching TV reduces their energy needs, so they gain weight. No matter what factors are linked with obesity, the basic problem remains the same: obesity is the result of consuming more calories than the body can use.

Maturation and Experience

The interaction of genes and experience becomes obvious when we examine the influence of social class on growth. Experience is equally important in the development of canalized motor skills, because certain basic human experiences are required for their appearance. When children grow up in an environment that is both socially and physically impoverished, their development may lag severely. Conversely, when children grow up in an environment that pushes the development of motor skills, they may develop certain skills early.

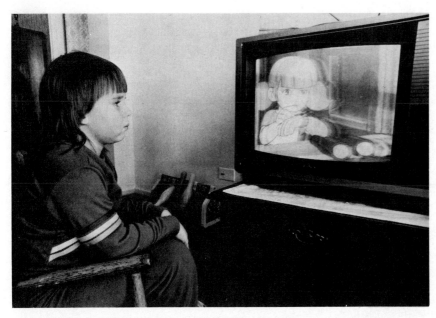

Some researchers have connected the recent increase in obesity among American children with a heavy diet of television. *(Annette Pelaez/Woodfin Camp & Associates)*

Socioeconomic Factors

Many children in lower socioeconomic classes show normal growth patterns. Yet setbacks to growth are concentrated among low-income groups. When all English children born during a single week in 1958 were followed through the preschool years, growth differences between those with fathers in highly skilled occupations and those with fathers in less skilled occupations became steadily larger (Tanner, 1978). Studies conducted in Europe, Asia, Africa, and North and South America (including the United States) support these findings (Bogin, 1988; Meredith, 1984). In each country, children in upper socioeconomic groups were taller, were heavier, and had larger head circumferences, wider pelvises, and thicker upper arms than their peers in lower socioeconomic groups.

Researchers explain the relationship between socioeconomic status and human growth as the result of four factors: nutrition, health care, physical labor required from children, and psychological stimulation from parents, schools, and peers (Bielicki and Welon, 1982). We have already described the effect of malnutrition on growth. Chronic undernourishment also makes children vulnerable to infection, and children in low-income families may have to devote nutrients that would normally have gone to growth to overcoming disease. Many have diseases of the eyes, skin, and respiratory and intes-

tinal tracts. The effect on health is clear at birth; families living in poverty areas have an infant mortality rate that is 30 percent higher than that of families in other areas (Bronfenbrenner, Moen, and Garbarino, 1984). As the accompanying box, "Sudden Infant Death Syndrome," indicates, low socioeconomic status is one of the risk factors involved in this major cause of death. In addition, small-for-gestational-age (SGA) and very low birthweight babies who grow up in disadvantaged homes frequently have learning disabilities or neurological defects that SGA babies in middle-class homes escape (see Chapter 3).

Low-income children are also less likely than other children to have a regular source of medical care (J. Butler, Starfield, and Stenmark, 1984). This lack of medical care means that lower-class children may have no preventive medical attention, and their nagging ailments, including badly decayed teeth, may persist for years. Concerning the third factor, in some societies, children in low-income families may have to work in the fields or the factories, laboring for long hours while other children are in school. The role of psychological stimulation in growth appeared in the intervention study with Guatemalan infants (Super, Herrera, and Mora, 1990). Babies whose families received supplementary food were larger than babies whose families received no supplements. But babies whose mothers were also instructed in ways to provide social and cog-

SUDDEN INFANT DEATH SYNDROME

On a cold winter night, parents put their 3-month-old son in his crib for the night. The baby has a runny nose but otherwise seems healthy. Early the next morning, they discover that their child has died in his sleep. The baby is the victim of **sudden infant death syndrome (SIDS),** more commonly called "crib death." SIDS rarely claims babies less than a month old, but 90 percent of the deaths occur before babies are 6 months old. Victims of SIDS come from every country, every race, and every socioeconomic level, although deaths are more frequent among babies whose medical histories and family backgrounds include certain risk factors (see the accompanying table).

Researchers have searched diligently for the cause of SIDS, which kills 2 out of every 1000 babies born in the United States and accounts for more than 8000 deaths each year (Burns and Lipsitt, 1991). Among American babies older than 1 month, it is the major cause of death. Most researchers believe that normal, healthy babies are not at risk, because the syndrome is apparently caused by some abnormality in the maturation of the brainstem, which regulates breathing and heart rate (C. Hunt, 1991). Babies who fall victim to SIDS have such impaired arousal and gasping responses that they may die in situations that would not threaten the survival of a baby with normal responses.

Barbara Burns and Lewis Lipsitt (1991) believe that the slight head colds found in about half the SIDS victims may implicate a learning problem. Babies are born with unconditioned, defensive reflexes that help them clear their air passages. If these reflexes are weak or do not work properly during the neonatal period, babies may not learn to clear obstructions by the time the reflexes drop away. Because babies at risk for SIDS are weaker, are visually less alert, and engage their environment less than other infants, they may have fewer opportunities to learn the voluntary responses that might later save their lives. This tendency may be especially true among bottle-fed infants, because they do not get any practice in learning to breathe when the nose is partially obstructed, as breast-fed babies do.

A final strand in the web of factors leading to SIDS may be modern child-care practices. Anthropologist James McKenna (1983) notes that our hunting-and-gathering ancestors carried their infants with them wherever they went by day and slept with them at night. Being continually carried about provides the jiggling, rocking, bouncing stimulation that some researchers believe may be essential for motor, cognitive, and social development (Thoman, Korner, and Beason-Williams, 1977).

American sleeping practices also deprive babies of rhythmic stimulation that babies receive in Japan and other societies in which babies customarily sleep with their mothers (Valsiner, 1989). McKenna believes that babies who sleep in cribs by themselves may be at increased risk for SIDS. He proposes that the smell, touch, and movement of parents' bodies provide stimulation that helps regulate infant breathing in babies with weak voluntary responses to obstructed respiration. The regular rise and fall of the parent's chest and the sound of the parent's breathing may "remind" such infants to breathe. This proposal has been supported by lower SIDS rates in cultures that encourage parents and infants to sleep together (Davies, 1985), as well as by a study in which preterm infants with weak, ragged respiratory patterns stabilized their breathing after mechanically breathing teddy bears were placed in their cribs (Thoman and Graham, 1987).

CHARACTERISTICS OF BABIES AT RISK FOR SIDS*

Baby:
  Male
  African-American
  1 to 6 months old
  Birthweight of 5½ pounds or less
  Low Apgar score (7 or less)
  Signs of jaundice at birth
  Severe respiratory problems at birth
  Abnormal Moro reflex at birth
  Abnormal cries
  Mild upper respiratory infection
  Not vaccinated for polio, diphtheria, whooping cough, or tetanus
  Bottle-fed

Family:
  Low socioeconomic status

Mother:
  Is an adolescent
  Failed to complete high school
  Smokes
  Was anemic at time of birth
  Had complications during pregnancy
  Had little or no pre- or postnatal medical care

Each of these factors increases an infant's risk of developing SIDS. For example, 70 percent of SIDS victims' mothers smoke, as compared with 40 percent of other mothers. None of the factors has been shown to cause the syndrome, but all are correlated with it.

Source: Information from Burns and Lipsitt, 1991; McKenna, 1983.

nitive stimulation showed the greatest growth, and their advantage over other children widened over the years.

Deprivation

Environmental supports are also necessary for the mastery of motor skills. In 1990, when Eastern European countries opened their borders, people in the United States were shocked at the reports that came out of Rumanian institutions for abandoned children. Some preschoolers who had been in these unstimulating institutions since birth could neither walk nor talk. Psychologists are familiar with such effects. More than a quarter of a century ago, Wayne Dennis and his associates (Dennis, 1960; Dennis and Najarian, 1957; Dennis and Sayegh, 1965) studied children in such institutions. They found that when youngsters are ignored by adults and surrounded by an unstimulating environment, the children show retarded motor development from the time they are 2 months old.

But when these children receive the necessary environmental inputs, development tends to reassert itself. In the Creche, a Lebanese foundling home, infants spent most of their first year lying on their backs in cribs. Some of these infants were more than a year old but could not sit up. Then researchers propped the babies into a sitting position and allowed them to spend an hour each day playing with such simple, attractive objects as fresh flowers, pieces of colored sponge, and colored plastic disks strung on a chain (Dennis and Sayegh,

Retarded motor skills are common among children in institutions like this Rumanian orphans' home, where children are ignored by adults and surrounded by an unstimulating environment. *(Anthony Suau/Black Star)*

1965). This seemingly small amount of stimulation caused the babies' developmental age to jump dramatically.

If babies are denied certain experiences, a particular motor skill will appear late in their development—even though they otherwise develop normally. Among the Ache of eastern Paraguay, for example, babies are not allowed to crawl or move away from their mothers. The Ache are nomadic people who change campsites so frequently that they do not make covered shelters or clear away vegetation. The surrounding jungle is too dangerous for babies to explore. Until children are 3 years old, they spend from 80 to 100 percent of their time in physical contact with their mothers, for whom child rearing is the primary job. Denied most experience in crawling or exploring, Ache children do not walk until they are nearly 2 years old (Kaplan and Dove, 1987). Similarly, on the Yucatán Peninsula of Mexico, babies are swad-

dled so that they cannot move their arms or legs. As they grow older and the swaddling is removed, they are carried much of the time and rarely placed on the ground to play. At night they sleep in hammocks, which restrict movement. At 11 months, these babies are far behind American babies in their mastery of motor skills (Solomons, 1978). But motor development is not stopped, only retarded. Once they are allowed greater freedom of movement, their motor skills develop rapidly.

Enrichment

Cultures can also foster the early development of motor skills. Among the Kipsigis in western Kenya, babies sit, stand, and walk about a month sooner than most American babies do. Kipsigi mothers deliberately teach their babies to sit, stand, and walk, and the teaching

As the grandmother watches, this Kenyan mother begins the "kitwalse" walking exercise, in which she swings the baby's legs so that they just touch the support of her own legs. By stimulating the stepping reflex, this regular exercise seems to speed the development of walking. *(Charles M. Super/Department of Human Development, Pennsylvania State University)*

methods are relatively standardized (Super, 1976). From the earliest months, Kipsigi babies sit about 60 percent of the time—at first in their mothers' laps, later in a shallow hole that protects the back. Mothers play with their young babies by holding them under the arms and bouncing them on their laps. The baby responds with the stepping response, which does not disappear among Kipsigi infants. (In Chapter 3, we saw that American newborns who get practice in the stepping response lose the response slowly and begin walking early [Zelazo, 1983].) When Kipsigi babies are about 7 months old, their mothers begin training them to walk. The mother holds the infant under the arms or by the hands and, with the baby's feet on the ground, slowly moves the infant forward.

Jamaican babies get similar training in sitting and walking. From shortly after birth, Jamaican mothers regularly massage and stretch their babies' limbs, and from about the second month they encourage the babies to make stepping movements. Babies who receive this treatment every day sit about a month earlier than American babies, and they walk at 10 months—about 3 months before American babies do (Hopkins and Westra, 1990). Neither Kipsigi nor Jamaican mothers train their babies to crawl, and the babies do not crawl early.

In the United States, many middle-class parents strive to stimulate motor development. Some enroll their 3-month-old babies in exercise classes at Gymboree or Playorena franchise outlets. Others buy kiddie exercise kits that include instructional videocassettes, plastic barbells, a baby balance beam, and a clutch ball to encourage eye-hand coordination (Kantrowitz and Joseph, 1986).

Do regular, intensive workouts accelerate motor development? Babies who would otherwise spend their days lying alone in a barren crib probably profit a great deal from such exercise, but such babies are not enrolled in the classes. No one yet has shown that the extra stimulation provided by exercise classes greatly accelerates the development of children's motor skills. Although practice in motor skills appears to speed up their acquisition, early gains are likely to be washed out before many months pass.

When a new motor skill emerges, there are wide differences among babies in their control of the skill. But once the skill becomes part of babies' general behavior, differences between babies shrink markedly (Kopp, 1979). Whether children live in a culture that teaches babies to walk at 10 months or 22 months, by the time they are 3 years old, all youngsters act pretty much alike. Motor skills can be accelerated significantly, but the difference is neither large nor permanent. Kipsigi and Jamaican babies walk early, but the age at which they walk falls within the normal range of development for human infants. We can say with some confidence that a history of regular workouts in an infant exercise class is unlikely to put a baby on the road to the Olympics.

As our examination of physical development implies, the maturation of brain and the development of body stability, locomotion, and limb manipulation widen the infant's world and make possible the kind of experiences that enhance cognitive development. In the next chapter, we change our focus, tracing the emergence of cognitive skills across infancy and toddlerhood.

SUMMARY

THE PROCESS OF PHYSICAL DEVELOPMENT

Physical growth and motor development follow the proximodistal, cephalocaudal patterns found in the fetus; motor skills become differentiated and integrated. Physical development is predictable because of the **canalization** of growth; genetic programming is so strong that human development is self-stabilizing and will appear in any normal human environment. Motor control involves the mastery of three basic abilities: body stability, locomotion, and limb manipulation. All

must be mastered within a constantly changing environment.

Norms are typical patterns that describe the approximate ages at which important attributes and skills appear. Normal children vary widely on each side of a norm, and maturation rates seem related to body build. Norms provide global reference points for development, and they indicate that girls and boys differ in the rate and timing of growth. **Growth hormone (GH)** and **somatomedins** regulate growth. When growth is disrupted by severe malnutrition, stress, or illness, later

catch-up growth generally returns the child to his or her normal pattern.

BRAIN DEVELOPMENT

The immature brain is more plastic than the adult brain. The development of motor control is correlated with development in specific areas of the **cortex,** although new behavior also depends on development in sensory receptors and the spinal cord and on the growth of joints and muscles. Normal brain development depends on experience, and during infancy so many neural connections develop that the 2-year-old's brain has more connections than the adult's brain. Many researchers believe that the brain's hemispheres are specialized for basic functions at birth; as each new skill appears, it is handled by the appropriate side of the brain, so **lateralization** seems to be a gradual process.

THE DEVELOPMENT OF MOTOR SKILLS

All motor skills follow the same general principles: motor development occurs in terms of the developing system; the task assembles behavior; motor development is nonlinear; action and perception form an inseparable loop; motor development shows high variability. Babies' skill at reaching out and grasping an object develops through, first, an open-handed swoop that signifies attention; second, a closed-fisted reach that indicates a breakdown in the reflexive motor pattern; third, an open-handed, visually directed grasp; and fourth, a highly accurate, skilled grasp that no longer requires full attention. Handedness is established slowly, with periods when hand preference seems to disappear. Although about half of children consistently use the same hand by 18 months, some children do not settle on one hand until they are 5 years old.

Crawling and walking depend on the maturation and coordination of various components. Head orientation, reaching, and kicking are major components of crawling. The newborn's stepping response, which is probably generated in the spinal cord, seems to form the basis for later walking.

Functional play is the earliest form of play to develop, and is soon followed by **constructive play. Pretend play** is well established by the age of 3. **Rough-and-tumble play** is more common among boys, and may appear around the age of 18 months.

NUTRITION AND HEALTH

Severe malnutrition in infancy can disrupt brain development, and long-term, severe, chronic malnutrition generally leads to low scores on cognitive tests. **Kwashiorkor,** which is caused by prolonged protein deficiency, leads to slowed growth, severe mental retardation, or even death. **Obesity** is becoming more common among American children. Genes, a heightened responsiveness to stimulation, eating habits, and lack of exercise all seem involved in its development.

MATURATION AND EXPERIENCE

In all countries, children in upper socioeconomic classes grow more rapidly and are healthier than children in lower socioeconomic classes, perhaps because of differences in nutrition, health care, amount of physical labor required from children, and psychological stimulation from parents, schools, and peers. An unstimulating physical and social environment leads to retarded motor development from the age of 2 months. When cultures deny certain experiences, specific motor skills may be delayed in infants; when cultures give instruction in specific motor skills, they appear early in the course of development.

KEY TERMS

canalization	growth hormone (GH)	positron emission tomography (PET)
catch-up growth	kwashiorkor	pretend play
constructive play	lateralization	rough-and-tumble play
cortex	norms	somatomedins
functional play	obesity	sudden infant death syndrome (SIDS)

CHAPTER

6

• • • • • • • • • • • • •

COGNITION: FROM SENSING
TO KNOWING

CHAPTER

6

COGNITION: FROM SENSING TO KNOWING

● ● ● ● ● ● ● ● ● ● ● ● ● ●

When Elizabeth Hall's son David was 15 months old, he discovered his mother's pen, which was lying open on the coffee table. When his mother came to check on her quiet son, she found ink on his mouth, on his hands, and on his clothes. She took away the pen, put it on a high shelf, and, when David protested, picked him up for a moment. As soon as she put him down, he toddled over to the shelf, stretched out his arm, opened and closed his fingers, and said "Day-boo"—his word for himself—to indicate that he wanted the pen. Although he could not see the pen, he knew that it was lying on the shelf. David was not always so persistent. When he was 8 months old, he forgot about forbidden playthings when his mother distracted him. But as he grew older, his memory developed, and he had a mental image of the forbidden toy. Since the day of his entry into this exciting, often puzzling world, David had taken some important steps on the journey called cognitive development, and he still had many challenging adventures ahead of him.

● ● ● ● ● ●

In this chapter, we follow the development of the child's mind during infancy and toddlerhood. Perception underlies cognition, and so we begin with perceptual development, noting that babies find some things more interesting than others, and try to determine what factors attract their attention. Next we look at basic learning processes, discovering what they tell us about the minds of infants and toddlers. We examine cognitive growth in infancy, tracing the baby's separation of self from the world. As we watch the development of memory, we find that the process is selective and that context may determine how much a baby or toddler remembers. Finally, we explore the implications of mental representation, as revealed in the child's understanding of the object concept, egocentrism, and search strategies.

Perceptual Development

Infants rely on their eyes, ears, mouths, noses, and skin to extract information about the sights and sounds, the pains and pressures, the tastes and smells of their world. In these investigations, babies' senses work as a team. Babies learn to coordinate sight with sound and sight with touch, and, of course, they learn to coordinate eye and hand, as we saw in Chapter 5. Although all senses are developing and becoming integrated, we will focus on the senses of vision, touch, and their coordination. What we know about perceptual ability in infancy comes from careful monitoring of behavior during experiments, because babies cannot talk at all and toddlers do not talk very well.

Visual Tracking and Scanning

As human beings of any age look at the world, their eyes continually move: they track moving objects, and their gaze shifts from one feature of an object to another. Newborns have trouble following moving objects; their tracking is jerky. By 2 months, their pursuit is smooth, but only if the object is moving slowly (Kremenitzer et al., 1979). Even after their motor control improves, babies can track objects in a smooth, coordinated manner only if they can program their eye movements to coincide with the future location of the object. In order to do this, they must have some expectation of the path the object is following. Between the ages of 6 and 15 weeks, babies produce an increasing proportion of anticipatory eye movements, indicating that they have built up expectations concerning the way objects and people move (Haith and McCarty, 1990).

Scanning probably plays an important role in the process of learning about the world, and the way babies scan objects in their field of vision changes during the early months. Newborns search for the edges of objects with broad, jerky sweeps of the visual field, and as we saw in Chapter 4, once they find an edge they concentrate on it. At 1 month, babies still scan only edges and corners; once their gaze encounters an edge, they seem unable to shift their eyes. If one object in a target is enclosed within another, for example, they do not look at the inside shape. Their eyes stop when they find the edge of the outer shape (Fantz and Miranda, 1975; Salapatek, 1975). By 2 months, babies scan more extensively, with their eye movements covering wider areas of the target. They cross the outside shape and examine the enclosed shape. This change may indicate that they are now processing the entire object, instead of merely a part of it (Banks and Salapatek, 1983).

One- to three-year-olds are much more efficient scanners than babies, but their scanning is still unsystematic and their gaze tends to wander from one place to another. As we will see in Chapter 11, children do not scan rapidly and efficiently until after they start school.

Attending to Complexity and Novelty

Babies prefer some patterns and colors to others, but they prefer any pattern to a plain stimulus—no matter how colorful it is. In a classic experiment, Robert Fantz (1961) showed infants ranging in age from 2 to 6 months a set of six flat disks. Three of the disks were patterned; the other three had no patterns but were brightly colored. At all ages, babies looked longer at the patterned disks than at the brightly colored but unpatterned disks (see Figure 6.1). Babies may pay more attention to pattern than to color because pattern is more informative.

As babies grow older, the qualities of a stimulus that *attract* their attention do not change. Bold patterns, large objects, motion, sudden changes in illumination, and loud sounds will attract a baby's attention at any age (Olson and Sherman, 1983). But attracting attention and holding it are two different processes. A baby's attention may be momentarily grabbed by a blinking light or the crash of a dropped plate, but when nothing else happens, attention wanders to some other object in the

Figure 6.1 When babies were shown disks of various colors and designs, they preferred patterns to color or brightness, as shown by the percentages of time they looked at each disk. *(Adapted from Fantz, 1961)*

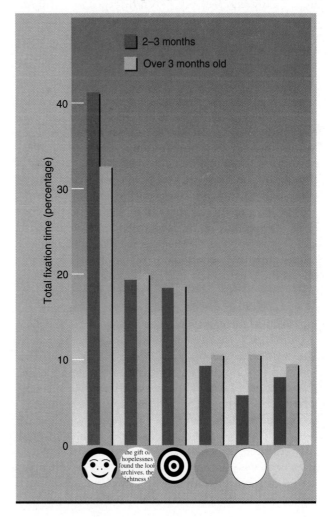

environment. As babies learn more about the world, the characteristics that *hold* their attention change (L. Cohen, 1972). They prefer increasingly complex sights, such as objects with more angles or more elements. For example, a design with 128 small squares scattered over it holds a 4-month-old's attention much longer than a design of the same size with 2 large squares. Yet both designs are equally fascinating to newborns (Fantz, Fagan, and Miranda, 1975).

After babies are about 3 months old, their previous experience seems to play an increasing role in determining what holds their attention. Babies seem to watch an object as long as they can glean new information from it. In one study (M. Hunter, Ames, and Koopman, 1983), researchers placed several toys in front of 8- and 12-month-olds. Most babies played with toys that were new to them. But if their play session was stopped before they had finished exploring a new toy, the babies went back to it at the next play session instead of picking up a toy they had never seen before. As we will see in later sections, the length of time that babies watch an object is used by many researchers as a measure of learning and memory during infancy.

Attending to Faces

The human face is one of the most important patterns in the baby's visual field, and babies explore faces in the way that they explore other visual stimuli. Like newborns, 1-month-olds tend to inspect details along the edge of the face, such as the chin or the ear—where contour is obvious and contrast is highest. Two-month-olds gaze instead at features within the face, such as the nose, the mouth, or the eye (Maurer and Salapatek, 1976) (see Figure 6.2). The eyes seem to hold a special interest for the 2-month-old baby. In one study (Hainline, 1978), eyes drew the attention of 2-month-olds under all conditions—whether the face remained still, moved slightly from side to side, or talked. Not even the mouth movements involved in speech draw a baby's attention away from the eyes (Haith, Bergman, and Moore, 1977).

Using looking time as a measure of preference, researchers found that by the age of 2 weeks, babies preferred faces to nonfacial patterns (Fagan, 1979). (The accompanying box, "Does Looking Time Indicate Preference?" explores the limitations of this technique.) But later research suggests that it is not the face itself that attracts newborns but the size and contrast of the pattern it presents (Kleiner, 1990) (see Figure 6.3). Babies are about 12 weeks old before the "faceness" of

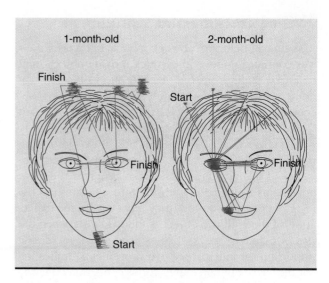

Figure 6.2 The lines represent the visual scanning of a real head by a representative 1-month-old and 2-month-old. *(Adapted from Maurer and Salapatek, 1976)*

Babies are fascinated by the human face, but researchers do not know whether the preference is innate or learned. *(Larry Lawfer/The Picture Cube)*

an object becomes more important than its intensity. Researchers showed babies two patterns with identical size and contrast; adults perceive one of these patterns (stimulus A) as facelike but not the other (stimulus B). Six-week-olds found stimulus B just as attractive as stimulus A, but stimulus A captured the attention of 12-week-olds (Dannemiller and Stephens, 1988). Researchers cannot agree on whether babies come to prefer faces because changes in their scanning patterns allow them to learn about faces or whether babies have an innate preference for faces. If they do have an innate preference, there would have to be some inborn "template" that corresponds to face-size stimuli containing three high-contrast areas or "blobs" arranged in the triangular formation of eyes and mouth (Morton, Johnson, and Maurer, 1990).

By 5 months, babies have made enormous strides that reflect their developing cognitive abilities. They can tell one photographed face from another; they can distinguish between photos of a woman and a baby or a woman and a man; by 7 months, they can distinguish between two dissimilar men (Fagan, 1979). They can also distinguish between expressions of sorrow and anger, and they do not like an angry face. Five-month-olds keep gazing at the photograph of a sorrowful face but look away when shown an angry face (Schwartz, Izard, and Ansul, 1985). All these tasks with photographs are much more difficult than recognizing actual familiar people, because photos have fewer cues. In their homes, where voices, odors, and the movements of animated faces provide additional cues, babies have been recognizing their mothers and fathers since the infants were about 2 months old.

One aspect of babies' preference does not seem to change after the age of 2 months (the youngest babies tested). All babies like attractive faces. In a series of studies, Judith Langlois and her colleagues (Langlois, Roggman, and Rieser-Danner, 1990; Langlois et al., 1987, 1991) discovered that babies prefer to look at faces that adults find attractive, whether the faces are those of women or men, children or infants, African-Americans or whites. The attractiveness of the baby's mother has no relation to this preference. By the time babies are 12 months old, attractiveness affects the way they interact with adults. Babies display more positive emotions toward, play more with, and are less likely to withdraw from attractive than unattractive adults. Researchers believe that this preference is related to the fact that at all ages and among all races and cultures, attractive faces have symmetrical features. Either the preference for symmetrical, "typical" faces is inborn or babies learn cultural preferences with very little exposure to faces.

Depth Perception

Unless babies have some idea of depth, they cannot locate objects in their world. From the beginning, babies behave as if they are aware that as objects come closer, the objects loom larger; that as they move their heads or bodies, objects that are close to them seem to move more rapidly than do distant objects; and that when one object moves in front of another, the closer object covers part of the farther object. For the first few months, these are the only indications babies have that their world has depth, and all these indications are

Figure 6.3 Researchers cannot decide whether a preference for stimuli that resemble the human face is present from birth. Stimulus C has the stimulus quality of the lattice (stimulus B), and stimulus D has the stimulus quality of the face (stimulus A). Adults interpret C as a face and D as a design. Although newborn infants prefer A (face) over B (design), they prefer D (design) over C (face). *(From Morton, Johnson, and Maurer, 1990, p. 101; stimuli from Kleiner, 1987, pp. 54–55)*

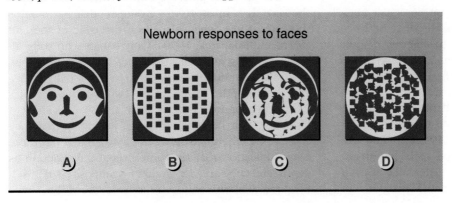

DOES LOOKING TIME INDICATE PREFERENCE?

For some years, researchers have used *looking time* as a sign that babies prefer one stimulus over another. When two stimuli are placed before them, most babies look longer at a novel stimulus than at a familiar stimulus, presumably because they find the novel stimulus more interesting. But Charles Nelson and Paul Collins (1991) point out that looking time is not simply a matter of interest; the baby's attention also depends on the ability to initiate, control, and end a gaze. What is needed, they say, is a way to explore the neutral and cognitive events that underlie this display of attention and memory.

In a recent experiment, Nelson and Collins (1991) looked for an involuntary sign of perception and attention produced by the nervous system. They used **event-related potentials (ERPs),** which are momentary changes in babies' brain waves when they look at a stimulus. Researchers derive ERPs by recording brain-wave responses to a stimulus; then they use a computer to average the activity. The activity presumably reflects the firing of the neurons involved in processing the stimulus.

When Nelson and Collins looked at the responses of 6-month-old babies to pictures of faces, they discovered that the babies' brains responded differently to highly familiar faces (those that had appeared in 60 percent of earlier familiarization trials), somewhat familiar faces (those that had appeared in 20 percent of the earlier trials), and novel faces (those that had not been seen before). Approximately half a second after any faces appeared on the screen, the tracings showed a sharp dip, known as a *negative peak*. When babies looked at novel faces, the negative peak continued. When the faces were somewhat familiar, the negative peak was followed by a sharp rise, known as a *positive peak*. When the faces were highly familiar, the tracings quickly returned to the earlier, relatively smooth, level.

The babies' responses display what appear to be two separate processes in perception. One process (the continued negative peak) may reflect *novelty detection*, which indicates that the stimulus has grabbed the baby's attention. It may be related to the initial encoding of a stimulus that is new to the baby—either because it is novel or because the baby has completely forgotten it. The second process (the positive peak) may reflect *attention holding*, which indicates that the baby is updating short-term memory after recognizing a stimulus that has been partially encoded. That is, the stimulus is not so familiar that it bores the baby; there is still more to be learned from it.

If the researchers had relied on looking time instead of brain waves in this experiment, all they could have said about the study was that the babies seemed to prefer the novel faces to either the highly familiar or the somewhat familiar faces. The babies gazed no longer at somewhat familiar faces than at highly familiar ones. Yet brain waves showed that the babies were processing these two kinds of stimuli differently.

---

based on monocular cues that involve movement (R. Siegler, 1991). As we saw in Chapter 4, most stationary monocular cues used by adults (such as the relative size of objects) give babies no awareness of depth, perhaps because they lack the information needed to interpret these cues. Babies first use stationary monocular cues when they are about 7 months old (Arterberry, Yonas, and Bensen, 1989).

Depth perception that depends on binocular cues, which require the brain to note the disparity between the images from each eye, begins to emerge in some babies at about 3 months. By 6 months, most babies show clear evidence that they use these cues (R. Fox et al., 1980).

How soon can babies use visual depth cues as warnings about such dangers as falling off tables or chairs? Eleanor Gibson and Richard Walk (1960) studied this sort of depth perception by placing 8- to 12-month-old infants on the edge of a "visual cliff." The cliff consisted of a patterned platform covered with Plexiglas and lighted so that it seemed to have a shallow side and a deep side. Most babies refused to crawl over the deep side of the cliff, even to reach their mothers (see the accompanying photograph). The youngest baby in this study was 8 months old, and so it was not clear whether the refusal to venture over the edge of the cliff was due to the maturation of visual perception or whether experience in crawling played a central role. Later research showed that most babies younger than 7 months showed no fear when placed on the edge of the cliff (Scarr and Salapatek, 1970). Only babies who were already crawling avoided the edge.

Perhaps experience is necessary for the baby to discover that depth signals danger. Two-month-old babies can distinguish between the deep and shallow sides of the cliff. Their hearts slow down, indicating that they sense some difference between the two sides, but there is no indication that they interpret the distinction as depth, and they are not afraid (J. Campos, 1976). Neither are 6-month-olds who cannot crawl but have

Most infants who can crawl will not venture out on the glass surface over the "deep" side of the visual cliff. Not even the sight of mother holding an attractive toy can persuade a baby to cross what appears to be a sudden drop. *(Steve McCarroll)*

objects within their grasp, an act that provides more than the pleasure of sucking; it also gives them information about the form, texture, hardness, and taste of the object. When babies are not sucking objects, they may run their fingers over the surfaces and through crevices. If objects are squeezable, they are squeezed; if crushable, crushed; and if throwable, thrown.

During the first year, babies seem to find their mouths more satisfactory than their hands in gathering information. Three-month-olds seem to recognize objects by mouthing them, because they suck more on a novel object than on one that is familiar to them (T. Allen, 1982). In fact, when they hold an object with both hands, they do so in order to transport it to their mouths. At about 4 months, hands become more than servants of the mouth. Now babies grasp an object in one hand while running the fingers of the other hand over it. Fingering quickly becomes informative, but provides less information than mouthing. Five-month-olds explore objects by mouthing, then looking at them. Mouthing peaks at 7 months, then begins to decline, its critical role in information gathering dropping from 61 percent of the time spent exploring a new object to 35 percent at 11 months (Ruff et al., 1992).

During these early months, babies are learning to coordinate their senses. This integration and transfer of information among the senses is known as **cross-modal perception.** Most events or objects provide multiple kinds of stimulation, and infants soon discover that one kind of stimulation (a sound) signals that stimulation of other kinds is nearby. They learn that it pays to look at the source of a sound because they may see some interesting sight. During the last half of the first year, babies learn to transfer information between touch and sight. Peter Bryant (1974) showed babies between the ages of 6 and 12 months a pair of objects that were identical except for a small square notch in the end of one. Each baby looked at both objects but did not touch them. Then, with the baby unable to see the objects, one of them was placed in his or her hand. While the baby held it, it bleeped. When 8-month-old babies later looked again at the objects, two thirds of them reached for the object they had just held. Twelve-month-olds do not need to see the object first. When they are allowed to explore a novel object by touch, but not allowed to see it, they can later recognize the object when they see it for the first time (Rose, Gottfried, and Bridger, 1978). As babies mouth, touch, grasp, and reach for the world, they develop cross-modal perception, integrating haptic information with the information that comes in through their eyes and ears.

learned to use a walker. These babies presumably can use both eyes to discriminate depth, yet when placed on the cliff, they charge fearlessly over the deep side (J. Campos et al., 1978). By 9 months, when babies are placed on the deep side, their hearts speed up, a sign that suggests they are afraid (J. Campos, 1976).

Haptic Perception

In their exploration of the world, babies also learn a great deal through **haptic perception,** which is perception based on the sense of touch. They try to suck

In the early months, babies glean more information about the world from their mouths than from their hands. Mouthing an object provides information about its form, texture, solidity, and taste. *(Linda Rogers/Woodfin Camp & Associates)*

Basic Learning Processes

Using their developing perceptual skills, children progress from the limited and poorly organized store of knowledge and intellectual skills they possess at birth to the concept-rich, well-ordered store of knowledge that most adults use so well. Born into an unfamiliar world, babies immediately begin gathering information about this strange environment. Gradually, they learn to recognize specific objects—mother, the juice bottle, a rattle. They learn where objects are located—the cookie jar in the kitchen, the television in the family room, their crib in the bedroom. Infants and toddlers also learn many skills—how to roll a ball, how to manipulate a spoon, how to climb up on a chair, how to ride a tricycle.

How rapidly youngsters learn all these things depends on the way they perceive a stimulus, how they represent that information, and whether they register it so that it can be retrieved. In this section we focus on four basic processes: habituation, operant conditioning, contingency awareness, and imitation.

Habituation

Most studies of young infants' cognitive abilities rely on **habituation,** which refers to an apparent lack of interest in a stimulus after a lengthy exposure to it. Thus, habituation is roughly analogous to boredom, and it implies that the baby has learned and remembered something about the stimulus. Habituation provides an efficient way of studying learning in young infants because babies will look at any new object or listen to any new sound. Thus, habituation gives us a window through which we can infer the cognitive processes of infancy. Using this simple form of learning, researchers have tested babies' ability to detect various stimuli, to tell the differences among them, to classify them into groups, and to develop concepts (Bornstein and Benasich, 1986).

In a typical habituation experiment, researchers showed alert babies a color slide of a person's face (Colombo et al., 1987). The slide was displayed to the baby until he or she looked away for at least one second. Then it was presented again and again (at least five times) until the amount of time the baby spent gazing at the stimulus on two consecutive trials dropped to half or less than half of the average time spent during the two longest trials. When this happened, the baby had habituated; the stimulus no longer seemed very interesting (see Figure 6.4).

Babies habituate to some stimuli faster and more efficiently than they do to others. They habituate faster to conspicuous stimuli than to less conspicuous, complex stimuli; faster to happy faces than to other expressions; and faster to three-dimensional objects than to photographs or drawings (Bornstein, 1985). Babies also habituate more quickly as they get older: newborns habituate only under special conditions, 3-month-olds habituate relatively slowly, and 7-month-olds habituate rapidly. This increase in efficiency is due in part to the maturation of the cortex, which gradually takes over control from lower parts of the brain, and in part to the baby's increasing knowledge of the world, which makes a greater array of objects familiar and hence less interesting.

There are wide individual differences in the speed and efficiency with which babies habituate. Those who habituate quickly (often with only a single trial) and show a rapid recovery of interest when they see a novel sight or hear a novel sound are acquiring information about a stimulus rapidly. This pattern of habituation and recovery is associated with accelerated intellectual functioning in early childhood. Babies who show this pattern have higher-than-average language scores as toddlers and preschoolers (Bornstein and Sigman, 1986; Tamis-LeMonda and Bornstein, 1989). Other longitudinal studies have shown a similar connection between a preference for novel stimuli at 7 months and intelligence test scores of 6-year-olds (Rose, Feldman, and Wallace, 1992).

Habituation is an extremely simple form of learning, but development depends on it (Dannefer and Perlmutter, 1990). Habituation allows human beings to cope with the environment, freeing their attention from having to deal with unimportant, routine events. This "boredom" with the familiar makes it possible to notice and act upon new situations.

Conditioning

A central feature of learning is the ability to associate one event with another, and so many researchers use operant conditioning to study cognitive development in infants (see Chapter 2). Although some responses condition more easily than others, by arranging for babies to get a reward only for specific actions, researchers have successfully conditioned babies to suck, smile, cry, turn their heads, look, or kick (Lancioni, 1980). The rewards that have proved effective are quite varied. One of them is the privilege of seeing a sharply focused picture. Ilze Kalnins and Jerome Bruner (1973) placed 5- to 12-week-old babies where they could see a blurred color movie of Eskimo life. When the babies began sucking on a pacifier, the picture became sharp. As long as the babies sucked at the rate of 0.75 suck per second, the picture remained clear. But when sucking lagged, the picture blurred. The babies soon learned to increase their rate of sucking. Yet when the control was reversed, so that sucking blurred the picture, the babies were not able to inhibit their sucking even though they averted their gaze from the blurred screen (see Figure 6.5).

This difference in response probably occurs because sucking is a response that enhances survival, so the baby is prepared to suck (see Chapter 4). Asking babies to stop sucking a nipple is asking them to respond in a way that goes against their biological preparation. Researchers have discovered that babies condition rapidly when asked to use any response that helps them to survive—such as head-turning or sucking. Babies are born pre-

Figure 6.4 One baby's response in a habituation study. After seven sixty-second exposures to the standard (familiar) stimulus, the baby habituated. When the baby was then shown a novel (unfamiliar) stimulus on the ninth presentation, the infant immediately looked at it with renewed interest. *(After S. Friedman, unpublished paper, 1972)*

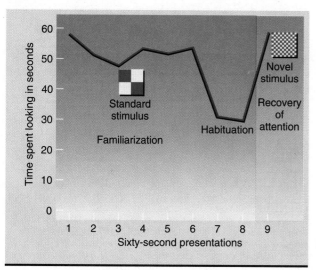

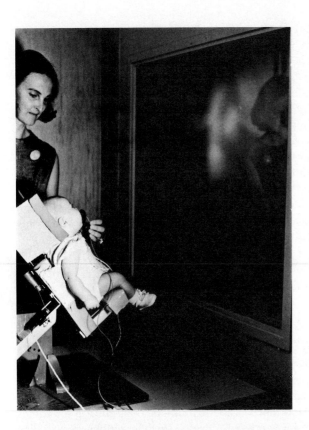

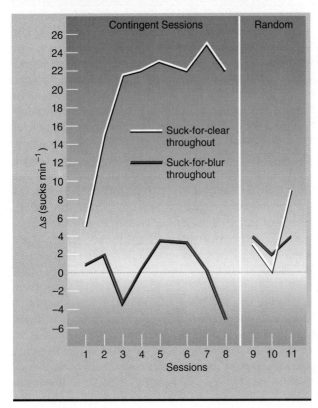

Figure 6.5 When young infants could clear a blurred movie by sucking on a nipple, they quickly learned to keep the picture sharp (contingent). But when their sucking no longer had an effect on the picture (random), it quickly dropped back to normal levels ("O"). Babies whose sucking blurred the picture could not learn to keep it clear; instead, they averted their gaze. *(Halftones courtesy Dr. Ilze Kalnins; graph from Kalnins and Bruner, 1973, p. 310)*

pared to make such responses, and they often encounter situations that demand them. Asking babies to kick vigorously in order to get a sweet drink is less likely to be successful, because such situations do not resemble anything a baby is likely to encounter.

Another important factor in conditioning is the baby's level of arousal, or state. As we saw in Chapter 4, a baby's state changes rapidly, especially in the early months, and with it, the baby's ability to detect sights and sounds. A sound may have to be louder and a design brighter, clearer, or larger for a baby to detect them as he or she moves from active alertness to quiet alertness to drowsiness (T. Field, 1981). A baby who is hungry responds differently from one who has just eaten or another who is midway in the feeding cycle.

From the results of conditioning experiments, we might suppose that rewarding babies and toddlers is an easy way to rear children. Handing out cookies and praise when children act appropriately would seem to guarantee well-behaved children. Unfortunately, rewards do not always strengthen children's responses. In a lengthy series of experiments, Mark Lepper (1983) has shown that when 3-year-olds are rewarded for some activity they normally enjoy, they become *less* likely to engage in that activity in the future. For example, 3-year-olds who enjoyed playing with colored markers were offered "Good Player Awards" (a colored card with a large gold star and a red ribbon) if they used the markers to draw pictures for the researcher. The children eagerly agreed, drew their pictures, and accepted their awards. Other youngsters either were praised (no tangible reward) for drawing the pictures or were given Good Player Awards although they had not expected them. A week later, the children were observed at play. Children who had been praised and those who had received an unexpected award were using the colored markers as frequently as they had used them before (see Figure 6.6). But children who had received an expected award paid little attention to the markers—they spent about half as much time with the pens as they had before they got the awards (Lepper, Greene, and Nisbett, 1973).

Why did the rewards backfire? Mark Twain (1876/1936) explained the process in *Tom Sawyer:* "Work consists of whatever a body is *obliged* to do. . . . Play consists of whatever a body is not obliged to do." When children engage in some activity spontaneously, they see the activity as fun: they are intrinsically motivated. But when children undertake the same activity to get a reward, their spontaneous enjoyment fades. It is Lepper's (1983) contention that in such cases, children

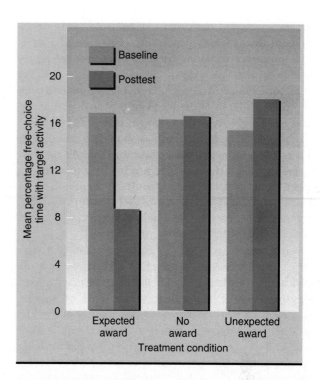

Figure 6.6 After preschoolers received expected rewards for engaging in one of their favorite playtime activities, they seemed to lose interest in it. Preschoolers whose rewards were not expected and those who got no reward at all continued to enjoy the activity. *(Adapted from Lepper, Greene, and Nisbett, 1973)*

perceive that they are being controlled by others, and their intrinsic interest in the activity is undermined. Along with the promised rewards go surveillance by adults (to make certain the task is completed), the expectation of being evaluated, and the pressure to complete the task by a certain time. Play suddenly becomes work. However, once children are old enough to compare their performance with that of others, rewards that depend on successful performance (an award for the best picture or a place on the Honor Roll) are unlikely to destroy intrinsic interest. They give the child no reason to consider why he or she undertook the activity; instead, they serve as information about the child's competence.

Contingency Awareness

When babies become aware that one event generally follows another, they have developed **contingency awareness,** which is the ability to understand that, under certain conditions, their actions have predictable consequences. The realization that their actions can affect their world fosters a sense of control over the environment that is highly rewarding. This sense of control is so important to young babies that they soon master responses that provide it. Two-month-olds quickly learn, for example, to control a mobile suspended over the crib with kicks of the leg (Linde, Morrongiello, and Rovee-Collier, 1985). If a ribbon tied around one ankle is attached to the mobile, babies soon discover that by kicking that foot, they can make the mobile bounce. When they learn this, they are not working to receive a sweet drink or to please an adult. By experimenting, they learn that kicking is an effective way to get the mobile to do their bidding. Their activity is intrinsically motivated, and they are controlling it.

Some years ago, John Watson and Craig Ramey (1972) explored the importance of control and the unpleasant consequences of helplessness. They placed a pressure-sensitive pillow beneath the heads of 8-week-old babies. When the infants turned their heads to the side, a switch inside the pillow tripped, and a color mobile above their heads began to move. Before long, the infants were turning their heads to operate the display. From their coos and delighted smiles, it was clear that the infants were pleased. A second group of infants lay beneath the same display, but they had no control over its movements. Instead, the mobile's motions were started and stopped by a timer. These babies soon lost interest in the mobile and rarely smiled. Later, when the pressure-sensitive pillow was placed beneath their heads, the babies made no attempt to control the display. Apparently, they had learned that they were helpless to control the environment.

Infants seem to have an urge to understand the environment and to manage it. They seek out tasks that promote learning and increase their competence. When they succeed in mastering some task, most infants show joy—or at least satisfaction (Dweck and Elliott, 1983). Experiences with their parents and other caregivers can foster this sense of control. Babies' cries generally bring comfort; their smiles and coos evoke enjoyable social stimulation. One conclusion we might draw from research is that it is unwise to ignore crying babies in the belief that picking them up will spoil them. Babies who are consistently left to "cry it out" may learn that their actions have little effect on the environment.

Imitation

Babies and toddlers learn a great deal from the successes and failures of their own efforts. But they also learn from watching others. As we saw in Chapter 2,

observational learning, in which youngsters learn how to do something by watching a model, is basic to a child's development. If babies and toddlers were forced to discover everything for themselves, the process of learning how to do things and when—or when not—to do them would make many normal cognitive advances difficult, if not impossible. Before children can learn by observation, they must be able to imitate another person, and so developmentalists have tried to establish just how early babies can imitate people around them. Attempts to fix that age have led to a great deal of controversy.

For decades, psychologists have agreed that babies of 8 weeks or so will imitate an adult who has first imitated a habitual response of the baby's, but this has been regarded as "pseudoimitation," as we will see in the description of Piaget's theories. Not until the latter part of the first year were infants supposed to be able to imitate actions they could neither see nor hear themselves perform, such as opening and closing their eyes or mimicking facial expressions.

Then, in 1977, Andrew Meltzoff and Keith Moore reported that babies who were 2, 3, or 6 weeks old would stick out their tongues, protrude their lips, open their mouths, and open and close their fists in mimicry of an adult's action. Later Meltzoff and Moore (1983) tested forty newborns who were less than 3 days old. These babies seemed to be born imitators: they often opened their mouths or stuck out their tongues when the experimenters modeled the action for them. In a more recent experiment (Meltzoff and Moore, 1989), another group of 3-day-olds imitated a researchers' tongue protrusion and head movements. Despite the success of Meltzoff and Moore and some other investigators, most experiments involving infants ranging in age from 1 hour to 6 weeks have failed to replicate these findings (Anisfeld, 1991). Some researchers contend that this failure, together with methodological flaws in the experiments, places claims of early imitation in jeopardy (Poulson, Nunes, and Warren, 1989).

The controversy over early imitation is important, because if Meltzoff and Moore's findings are generally replicated, views of early cognitive development may change. Imitating adult facial expressions or gestures would require babies to engage in some sort of cross-modal, integrated representation, in which newborns match what they have seen to sensory information from their own mouths, lips, tongues, and fingers. Most theories of cognitive development deny that very young infants can form representations of human movement patterns, yet Meltzoff and Moore (1989) contend that neonates do something very close to that.

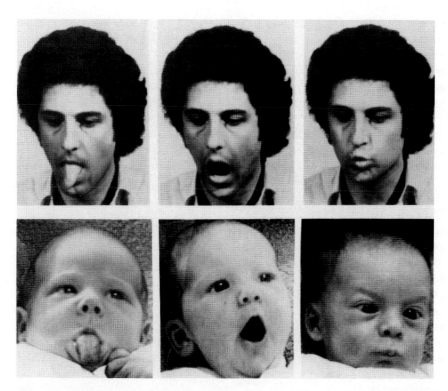

Neonates seem to imitate the facial contortions of adults; researchers cannot agree whether this is an example of cross-modal perception or a simpler, less cognitive response. *(From: A. N. Meltzoff and M. K. Moore, Science, 1977, 198, 75–78.)*

Explanations of young babies' responses to adult facial contortions have taken three forms: a rebound of spontaneous movements; a release of the sucking reflex; and an innate mechanism that promotes baby-caregiver interaction. Moshe Anisfeld (1991), who has reviewed the research, believes that tongue protrusions are the *rebound of spontaneous movement.* He reports that only tongue protrusion appeared in a majority of conditions (twelve out of twenty-three experiments) and that success seemed connected to the length of time the experimenter demonstrated the protrusion. In almost every failure, the researcher had protruded a tongue for 40 seconds or less. That, says Anisfeld, may explain why neonates who watch researchers for at least 60 seconds seem to imitate them. Anisfeld argues that young babies "spontaneously" stick out their tongues about twice each minute and that when they pay attention to the researcher, the competing effort "dams up" the response. When the demonstration ends and the demand on their attention is over, babies protrude their tongues at a higher-than-usual rate, making it appear as if they were imitating the researcher.

Others believe that tongue protrusion is a *release of the sucking reflex.* Whenever anything moves toward a baby's mouth, the baby perceives it as "suckable" and sticks out the tongue as a part of the response. Research has shown that 6-week-old babies stick out their tongues if a small white ball or a black felt-tipped pen is moved toward their mouths, held there for a few seconds, and then moved away (S. Jacobson, 1979). Finally, some researchers have suggested that tongue protrusion is part of an *innate survival response* that directs the baby's attention to the adult's face (Bjorklund, 1987). When the young baby reflexively matches adult facial gestures, the behavior helps maintain social interaction between baby and caregiver, thus keeping the caregiver nearby. The response declines when babies can "intentionally" direct their gaze or smile. Several researchers (Abravanel and Sigafoos, 1984; Heimann, Nelson, and Schaller, 1989; Vintner, 1986) have found that young babies seem to stick out their tongues reflexively but that the response declines and disappears once babies are about 2 months old.

Toward the end of the first year, babies can imitate behavior that is entirely new to them. Now they no longer have to stumble accidentally onto some new action but can learn it by watching others. However, they can imitate an action only immediately after they have seen it performed. During the second year, their ability to imitate what they see and hear advances markedly. They become able to defer their imitations. They can imitate on Wednesday the actions they saw their parents perform on Monday or Tuesday.

The glimmerings of **deferred imitation** appear soon after a child's first birthday, but at first, the ability to imitate is limited. In one study, 12-month-olds imitated simple actions, such as placing a crown on a doll's head, after a ten-minute delay (Abravanel and Gingold, 1985). But almost none could imitate a simple, repetitive action (such as stacking three blocks in the correct order) or a task that required two different actions in a given order (such as using a drumstick to push a doll out of a clear plastic tube). A majority of 18-month-olds were successful on such tasks.

Among older toddlers, the quality of imitation changes (Kuczynski, Zahn-Waxler, and Radke-Yarrow, 1987). More and more of their imitations are deferred, and most of their immediate imitations are displays of emotion (such as laughing, clapping, cheering, and sighing) or contrived, clearly unfelt, emotional actions. Two-year-olds pretend to cry, fake a laugh, and pretend to be hurt after a sibling's accident. The majority of deferred imitations involve doing household tasks, engaging in self-care (such as toothbrushing), caring for a doll, or copying parental disciplinary actions. Thus, imitation becomes an important means of socialization.

Sensorimotor Thought

Knowing that a 12-month-old can recognize a toy that has been touched but not seen tells us almost nothing about what the toy means to the baby, just as knowing that a young baby can tell the difference between two and three dots tells us nothing about what number means to the baby (see the accompanying box, "Can Babies Count?"). As infants move from being reflexive, self-centered creatures to being symbol-using individuals who act purposefully on their surroundings, they gradually come to understand the world. The story of this change details the appearance and gradual development of thought. Because Piaget's (1951, 1952, 1954) picture of this transformation is so comprehensive, it provides us with a useful way to look at cognition in infancy.

The baby's own activity spurs cognitive development, and the baby's principal tools are assimilation and accommodation, which were discussed in Chapter 2.

This little girl's play with a toy telephone and a date book is an example of deferred imitation and demonstrates the ability to represent information symbolically. *(Laura Dwight)*

When 3-month-old babies are offered their first chance to drink from a cup, for example, they first try to assimilate the cup to their current mouth-using skills, sucking at the cup's edge as they suck at a nipple. When this does not work, babies modify, or accommodate, those mouth-using skills so that they are as effective with the hard rim of the cup as they were with the soft nipple. As babies grow, they continue to use old responses on new objects and then modify those old responses, thus learning to adapt to a widening world.

Piaget developed his account of the **sensorimotor stage,** which covers development in the first two years, by carefully observing youngsters, including his three

Babies seem to come into the world possessing basic number skills. That statement may sound farfetched, but some developmental psychologists are convinced that it is so (R. Gelman, 1982b; Keil, 1981). Toddlers spontaneously count the objects in their world, although 2-year-olds may count only as far as 2 and may use invented number words. But long before their second birthday, babies are aware of number.

Studies with newborns in a Baltimore hospital indicate that babies only a day or so old seem to know the difference between two objects and three objects (Antell and Keating, 1983). These babies looked at patterns of dots until they habituated. Each card had the same number of dots on it, but the dots were arranged differently. When they had habituated to a card containing three dots, the babies showed new interest in a two-dot card; and when they had habituated to two dots, they found three dots interesting. But when the numbers increased, the task was beyond them. None of the babies could tell the difference between four dots and six dots.

The babies' responses were apparently no fluke. Similar tests with 4- to 7-month-old babies produced the same results: babies detected the difference between two- and three-dot displays but could not handle four- and six-dot patterns (Starkey and Cooper, 1980). Six- to nine-month-olds also responded differ-

ently to slides in which the number of common household objects changed from two to three or back again (Starkey, Spelke, and Gelman, 1980). In this study, babies who habituated to a slide with three objects (such as a scraper, a memo pad, and a comb) showed no interest in another three-object slide, even though it portrayed different objects arranged differently. But a two-object slide immediately attracted their attention. In fact, six-month-olds can detect differences even when the objects are moving slowly across the screen (van Loosbroek and Smitsman, 1990).

What does this mean? Young babies apparently detect equivalences, yet they surely cannot reason meaningfully about quantities, and there is no indication that they consciously represent number. John Flavell (1985) speculates that babies are born with some sort of inborn neurological process that handles nonverbal counting—a counting scheme of some sort that is similar to a sucking or grasping scheme. Other researchers (Antell and Keating, 1983; van Loosbroek and Smitsman, 1990) suggest that babies can perceive number because they recognize small numerical quantities as perceptual features of objects. Number, like other features, is perceived in regular ways as an important characteristic of the world.

---

children—Jacqueline, Lucienne, and Laurent. Frequently, he intervened in their activities to study their reactions. He concluded that thought during the sensorimotor stage progresses through six substages in which babies' behavior reflects the contents of their minds (see Table 6.1). Each of these substages represents a clear advance in cognitive development.

Substage 1: Reflex Acts

The first substage covers the neonatal period. During the first month, babies' responses to sights and sounds, smells and tastes, pressure and touch are not purposeful investigations of the world. Instead, they are reflexive responses babies possessed when they entered the world. Much of their behavior is a response to internal stimulation, and many of their actions seem rigidly programmed. As noted in Chapter 4, if you brush a baby's mouth or cheek with your finger, for example, the baby will suck reflexively. Yet these seemingly inflexible actions can be affected by experience. As Piaget (1954) observed:

Laurent, as early as the second day, seems to seek with his lips the breast which has escaped him. . . . From the third day he gropes more systematically to find it. . . . He searches in the same way for his thumb, which brushed his mouth or came out of it. . . . Thus it seems that the contact of the lips with the nipple and the thumb gives rise to a pursuit of those objects, once they have disappeared, a pursuit connected with reflex activity in the first case and with a nascent or acquired habit in the second case. (p. 8)

Habits are acquired through experiences; they are learned. Using operant conditioning, Arnold Sameroff (1968) showed how newborns learn to modify their reflexive sucking. One group of infants could get milk only by squeezing the nipple between the tongue and palate; the other group could get milk only by lowering the bottom jaw to create a partial vacuum in the mouth. Both groups of infants quickly adjusted their style of sucking, with the first group steadily squeezing the nip-

TABLE 6.1   PIAGET'S SUBSTAGES OF SENSORIMOTOR THOUGHT

Age*	Substage	Action Scheme	Behavioral Characteristics
0 to 1 month	Substage 1	Reflex acts	Rigid, stereotyped reflexive actions Reflexive imitations No object concept: behaves as if hidden object no longer existed
1 to 4 months	Substage 2	Primary circular reactions	Sensorimotor schemes based on reflexes Pseudoimitation: imitates immediate imitations of his or her own actions No object concept: behaves as if hidden object no longer existed
4 to 8 months	Substage 3	Secondary circular reactions	Sensorimotor schemes based on learning True imitation of actions baby already performs, but only if sees self performing the act First glimmerings of object concept: searches only if sees object begin to move away
8 to 12 months	Substage 4	Coordination of secondary schemes	Intentional acts toward goals Observational learning through immediate imitation of simple actions Searches for hidden object but makes A-not-B error
12 to 18 months	Substage 5	Tertiary circular reactions	Solution of problems through overt trial and error Immediate imitation of acts; perhaps some deferred imitation of very simple, single actions Searches for toy in last hiding place, but only if sees researcher move it
18 to 24 months	Substage 6	Symbolic thought	Solution of problems through mental trial and error Representation of objects by mental symbols Deferred imitation of more complicated actions Object concept developed: searches in all possible places

*Ages approximate.

ple and the second group just as steadily obtaining milk through suction.

Substage 2: Primary Circular Reactions

During the second substage, when babies are from 1 to 4 months old, they incorporate experience in their reflexive schemes and begin to coordinate their senses. Through accommodation, the schemes become acquired adaptations, which are the first true sensorimotor schemes (see Chapter 2). For example, infants use their eyes to direct their grasp and turn their heads toward the source of a sound. In Chapter 4, we saw that newborns show similar coordination but that the response seems to be reflexive and disappears after the first month.

The hallmark of this stage is what Piaget called the **primary circular reaction.** This term refers to any action that the baby repeats because of the pleasurable stimulation it provides. For example, when babies lie on their backs, unconfined by clothing, they often flail their arms and kick their legs rhythmically. Some developmentalists interpret these rhythmic movements as responses by an infant who is too immature to produce a goal-directed response (Thelen, 1981). Thumb-sucking is another typical primary circular reaction, and like most of these reactions, it centers on the baby's own body. Such sucking, grasping, looking, or vocalizing is different from the reflexive actions of the first substage because it is initiated by the baby instead of being a response to internal stimulation. At this substage, however, babies cannot distinguish their actions from the world and the objects in it.

Sometimes babies imitate the actions of adults, but Piaget regarded such primary circular reactions as "pseudoimitation," because at this stage babies can imitate only one of their own customary responses—and only if someone else mimics that response immediately after they make it. For example, Piaget (1951) describes how, at 10 weeks, Lucienne imitated him after he had observed her nodding her head:

She was upright in her mother's arms opposite me. I began to nod my head up and down. While she was watching, Lucienne kept quite still except for slight movements in order to watch what I was doing. As soon as I stopped, she distinctly reproduced the up and down movement. I then moved my head from left to right and vice versa. Lucienne moved her head slightly as she

watched, and as soon as I stopped, reproduced the sideways movement. Her mother, who was holding her, clearly felt the difference in the movements of the spine and muscles. (p. 12)

Substage 3: Secondary Circular Reactions

Babies in this substage, who are about 4 to 8 months old, are busy with actions they have learned. Their sensorimotor coordination has improved, and their new skill at grabbing attractive objects gives them many opportunities for such activity. Now babies' action schemes have become what Piaget calls **secondary circular reactions.** They serve to prolong events that interest the baby. In this advance, babies repeat learned responses as opposed to the unlearned behavior that appears in primary circular reactions. Laurent's behavior at 4 months, while passing a stick from hand to hand, is typical:

The stick then happens to strike a toy hanging from the bassinet hood. Laurent, immediately interested by this unexpected result, keeps the stick raised in the same position, then brings it noticeably nearer to the toy. He strikes it a second time. Then he draws the stick back but moving it as little as possible as though trying to conserve the favorable position, then he brings it nearer to the toy, and so on, more and more rapidly. (Piaget, 1952, p. 176)

According to Piaget, infants in the third substage are capable of "true imitation." They can imitate actions that they see others make—but only if the action is one they already perform and only if they can see themselves perform it. They are also tireless explorers of objects. They look at objects, handle them, mouth them, rotate them, transfer them from one hand to another, and bang them against any available surface. These early explorations seem to be a quest for information; after babies have completed their initial investigation, they seem to lose interest and begin throwing, pushing, or dropping the object (Ruff, 1984).

Perceptions and actions are still so intertwined at this age that babies find it hard to separate them. The infant apparently has no mental image of objects as separate things; instead, he or she represents an object through motor responses. The meaning of the object is intertwined with the actions the baby has connected with it. When babies catch sight of a familiar object, they indicate their recognition by going through a mild version of whatever secondary circular reaction they use with it. Piaget (1952) describes Lucienne as "opening or closing her hands or shaking her legs, but very briefly and without effort," when she glimpses a doll she had often manipulated by kicking or striking it as it hung from the bassinet hood (p. 187).

Substage 4: Coordination of Secondary Schemes

In the latter part of the first year (8 to 12 months), slowly but surely, intentional, goal-directed behavior emerges. Instead of simply prolonging interesting events, babies intentionally use their schemes to reach a goal. They have become active problem solvers who use objects as tools, remove obstacles, circumvent barriers, and are undeterred by detours. Piaget (1952) describes Laurent's determined efforts toward a goal:

I present a box of matches above my hand, but behind it, so that he cannot reach it without setting the obstacle aside. But Laurent, after trying to take no notice of it, suddenly tries to hit my hand as though to remove or lower it; I let him do it to me and he grasps the box.—I recommence to bar his passage, but using as a screen a sufficiently supple cushion to keep the impress of the child's gestures. Laurent tries to reach the box, and, bothered by the obstacle, he at once strikes it, definitely lowering it until the way is clear. (p. 217)

On this occasion, Laurent combined two schemes, grasping (which he temporarily set aside) and striking, to reach the coveted matchbox.

Babies' capabilities are expanding rapidly during this period, because for the first time they can imitate behavior they have never performed. As noted earlier, this advance means that observational learning is possible. Games like peekaboo take on new excitement, because the baby now can be an active participant instead of a fascinated observer. Babies are ready to play, "Where's your nose?" or "Where's your belly button?" because now they can connect a series of sounds with the responses they have seen their parents make—pointing to the appropriate part of their bodies.

Substage 5: Tertiary Circular Reactions

Babies in this stage of sensorimotor thought (12 to 18 months) often behave like little scientists. Faced with a problem, they now set about solving it through the process of trial and error. They cannot predict the results of a new action but must first try it out. They often become so caught up in their experimentation that they may vary their schemes simply to see what will happen, as if they are working away at understanding the world. Piaget (1952) describes Laurent's experiments with gravity:

Once children reach Substage 5 of the sensorimotor period, they solve the problem of building a block tower through a trial-and-error method of experimentation. *(Charles Gupton/Stock, Boston)*

Laurent is lying on his back. . . . He grasps in succession a celluloid swan, a box, etc., stretches out his arms, and lets them fall. Sometimes he stretches out his arm vertically, sometimes he holds it obliquely, in front of or behind his eyes, etc. When the object falls in a new position (for example on his pillow), he lets it fall two or three times more on the same place, as though to study the spatial relation; then he modifies the situation. (pp. 268–269)

With this advance, the infant's schemes become **tertiary circular reactions.** They differ from secondary circular reactions in that they are intentional adaptations to specific situations. The baby who once explored objects by taking them apart now tries to put them back together, stacking blocks or nesting cups. When a toy is out of reach, the baby will pull on the tablecloth beneath it—a procedure that brings the toy within grasp. Piaget (1968a) describes the infant's behavior now as "intelligent"; but it is an action-oriented intelligence, one based on perceptions and movements rather than on words and concepts.

Substage 6: Beginning of Symbolic Thought

The final stage of sensorimotor thought (18 to 24 months) is really a transitional period between the sensorimotor and preoperational stages. Babies now can represent objects by means of symbols, an advance known as **symbolic representation,** which allows them to think about their own actions and events involving others. In the baby's daily life, two important changes show up. First, because babies can visualize their own actions, they can solve problems in their heads, working out a solution with mental combinations and then applying it. They no longer must go through a lengthy trial-and-error test. Piaget (1952) describes Jacqueline's mental solution of a problem:

Jacqueline . . . arrives at a closed door— with a blade of grass in each hand. She stretches out her right hand toward the knob but sees that she cannot turn it without letting go of the grass. She puts the grass on the floor, opens the door, picks up the grass again, and enters. But when she wants to leave the room things become complicated. She puts the grass on the floor and grasps the doorknob. But then she perceives that in pulling the door toward her she will simultane-

ously chase away the grass which she placed between the door and the threshold. She therefore picks it up in order to put it outside the door's zone of movement. (p. 339)

The second change is in babies' ability to defer their imitations. Jacqueline, for example, watched with amazement as another toddler threw a horrendous temper tantrum, screaming, stamping his feet, and trying to push his way out of his playpen. Placed in her own playpen the next day, Jacqueline screamed and shoved and stamped her foot lightly several times in succession (Piaget, 1951). Clearly, the little girl had stored some mental representation of the little boy's actions.

Along with the ability to form mental images comes the capacity for pretend play. Because toddlers can mentally represent objects, they can pretend that a box is a cup or that a cup is a hairbrush. This ability is a striking advance over play during the fifth substage, when youngsters might pretend to drink tea from a cup that they could see and hold. Within another year, they will be engrossed in full-blown dramatic play, as we saw in Chapter 5.

Babies may enter the various substages earlier or later than the ages suggested by Piaget. The opportunities or restrictions in the environment affect the speed with which infants move through the stages.

Memory in Infants and Toddlers

The course of cognitive development described by Piaget depends on babies' ability to remember people, objects, and events in their lives. Memory is not an isolated skill but is basic to children's cognitive and social life; thus, an understanding of changes in the cognitive processes involved in memory can provide valuable insights into changes in cognitive functioning (Kail, 1990). As we trace the development of memory, we will see that from the time they are about 6 months old, children are actively constructing knowledge on the basis of their experiences and continually modifying their memories. They can demonstrate that they remember some object or person through either recognition or recall.

Recognizing Familiar Objects

The simplest form of memory, known as **recognition,** requires that infants perceive an object as something that they have perceived in the past. It takes place in the presence of the original object and so requires little retrieval effort. Habituation studies have shown that newborns can remember a stimulus for five to ten seconds and can detect a difference between that memory and another stimulus. As babies grow, it takes them less time to register sights in memory, and so when they are allowed to look at a pattern or some other stimulus for a specified length of time, they show gradual improvements with age in their ability to recognize objects. But when they are allowed to look at an object until they lose interest, even 2-month-old babies seem to remember sights as well as older babies do. This finding suggests that although there are age differences among babies in the speed of encoding visual information, once it is processed, retention probably does not differ (J. Werner and Perlmutter, 1979).

Forgetting seems to be both a selective and a gradual process, with first one and then another aspect of a stimulus fading from memory. By measuring the length of time babies looked at various forms of an arrow design, researchers discovered such a pattern of forgetting among 5-month-olds (Strauss and Cohen, 1980). A few seconds after babies looked at a large black arrow, they remembered its size, color, and shape and the direction in which it was pointed. Fifteen minutes later, they remembered only its shape and color. The next day, they remembered only that they had seen an arrow.

Carolyn Rovee-Collier (1984) believes that babies selectively process events and are likely to remember some response that has had an effect on their world. For that reason, she has focused on babies' recognition of a mobile that they have controlled with foot kicks. Rovee-Collier and her associates (Greco et al., 1986) have discovered that with equal amounts of training, 2-month-olds forget the mobile within two to three days, 3-month-olds forget within nine to thirteen days, and 6-month-olds forget sometime between fourteen to twenty days. If the training is rearranged, however, so that 2-month-olds get to operate the mobile six minutes at a time in three sessions spread over a week, they can recognize the mobile after a lapse of fourteen days (Linde, Morrongiello, and Rovee-Collier, 1985) (see Figure 6.7).

Why should breaking the training into three short sessions improve a baby's recognition memory? The researchers believe that when babies have three opportunities with a mobile, they probably notice different features at each session. Two weeks later, in the test session, there are more cues to remind them of the original situation. When 2-month-olds seem to have forgotten how to operate the mobile after two weeks, the memory still may be stored although it is inaccessible. Seventeen days after 2-month-olds learned to work a mobile, they watched a researcher operate it—but were not allowed to operate it themselves. The next day, as soon as the ribbon was tied to an ankle, the babies began operating the mobile (Davis and Rovee-Collier, 1983). Such a reestablishment of memory following a brief encounter is known as **reinstatement** of memory (Kail, 1990).

Among 2- and 3-month-olds, memories can be effectively reinstated about two weeks after they have been forgotten, but 6-month-olds can be reminded successfully for only about a week after they have forgotten (Boller et al., 1990). Memory processing is similar in 3- and 6-month-olds, although 6-month-olds are much faster at both encoding and retrieving memories. So why should reminders fail with the older babies? Kimberly Boller and her colleagues (1990) believe that the answer lies in the great behavioral transition that occurs at about 6 months. Younger babies remain in infant seats or playpens, but 6-month-olds have begun to move about the environment—either by creeping, crawling, or scooting around in a walker, which allows them to actively explore their world. In the process, they encounter so much new and often conflicting information and have become so adept at reconstructing and modifying their memories that unused memories may become permanently lost.

Throughout the rest of infancy and toddlerhood, recognition memory becomes more enduring. Preschoolers can recognize pictures of realistic objects as accurately as adults can, although adults are much better at recognizing abstract pictures (K. Nelson and Kosslyn, 1976). Before children can recognize complex stimuli with the proficiency of adults, they must become skilled at scanning and registering information, and they must acquire the broad store of knowledge on which some types of recognition depend (A. Brown et al., 1983; Perlmutter, 1984).

Recalling the Past

Recall is more complex than recognition, because it takes place in the absence of the object or information to be remembered and thus requires retrieval from long-term memory. Because the object is missing, researchers must find some indirect way to assess recall in infants who cannot talk. They may note a baby's surprise when an expected object is missing, or they may note a baby's actions, such as searching for a hidden object or

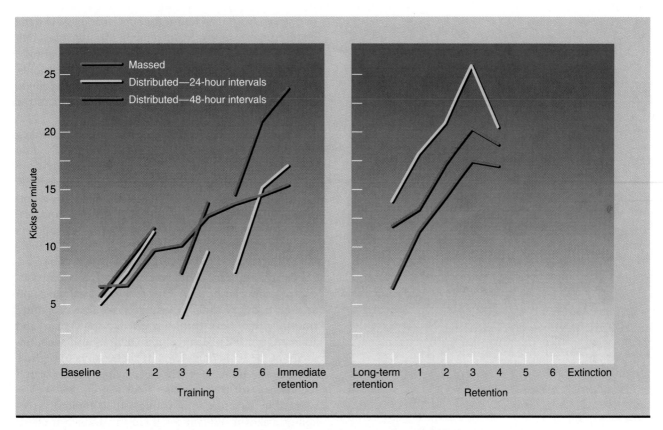

Figure 6.7 After a two-week delay, babies whose training in the control of a mobile had been distributed over several sessions showed clear evidence that they remembered their formal training. Babies with the same amount of training massed in a single session had to relearn that their kicks controlled the mobile. *(From Linde, Morrongiello, and Rovee-Collier, 1985, p. 609)*

acting out familiar routines. By the time they are about 7 months old, babies begin to show some evidence of recall in their daily lives. When parents of 7- to 11-month-old babies were asked to record any incidents of recall, they reported many such instances (Ashmead and Perlmutter, 1980). Most babies remembered where household items, such as baby lotion, belonged and showed surprise when an item was not in its correct place. They searched for people or objects and remembered the routine of such games as peekaboo. The natural surroundings of home helped these babies to remember common routines and objects. The assistance of parents was also an important factor, for parents generally structure infants' attempts to remember and often provide memory cues during social interactions (Paris, Newman, and Jacobs, 1985).

Most families have familiar routines: pets must be fed, baths taken, teeth brushed, prayers said at night. By the time they are a year old, babies can remember these old,

established routines on their own, although they sometimes need slight prompting (Wellman and Somerville, 1980). Although daily repetition makes it easier to remember a routine, repeated experience is not necessary for toddlers. When tested in the laboratory, 16-month-olds repeated simple sequences of three events after seeing them performed once (Bauer and Mandler, 1989). Some sequences resembled familiar routines (bathing a teddy bear, cleaning the table with a spray cleaner), and some were novel (hitting a board to make a toy frog jump, making a picture with chalk and stickers). Two weeks later, on a return visit, 16-month-olds recalled the familiar routines but not the novel routines. Twenty-month-olds recalled both kinds of sequences, but they could not manage sequences involving four events. At both ages, toddlers found it easier to recall sequences that included causal events. Such studies indicate that toddlers incorporate temporal and causal information in their memory for events.

When infants pull their pajamas from the drawer at bedtime, they are demonstrating recall, an ability that seems to emerge at about 7 months. *(Peter Vandermark/ Stock, Boston)*

The important role played by parents in the toddler's expanding memory skills became clear when researchers observed mothers looking at picture books with their 17- to 22-month-old children (Ninio, 1983). The mothers were sensitive to their children's level of knowledge: they simply provided labels when children showed that they did not know the word for a pictured object, but they asked questions ("Where is the puppy?" "What's that?") when children showed that they understood the word. By requiring youngsters to generate stored information, parents apparently promote children's ability to regulate their own memory (Price, 1984).

By the time they are 3 years old, most toddlers sing advertising jingles and chant nursery rhymes, and their recall of parental promises is almost perfect. Researchers (Somerville, Wellman, and Cultice, 1983) have studied this sort of intentional memory in 2- to 4-year-olds. Parents asked children to remind them to do something in the future, such as take the laundry out of the dryer or buy candy for the child at the supermarket. When the children were supposed to remind parents about dull tasks, 4-year-olds were much better than 2-year-olds. But when the task interested the child, 2-year-olds' memory was equally good: they remembered to remind their parents about promised treats 80 percent of the time.

Despite their dazzling performance when reminding parents about promised candy, 2- and 3-year-olds often do poorly on formal tests of memory. When shown a group of nine toys, for example, most 3-year-olds remember only two of them. What accounts for the difference between their poor showing in the psychological lab and their extensive recall at home? When toddlers take part in a memory experiment, they are in an unfamiliar setting, and they face situations that require sophisticated language skills, speedy response, focused attention, cooperation with strangers, and the application of their memory skills to strange tasks that bear little similarity to their daily experience (Wellman and Somerville, 1982). Many young children also seem unaware of the techniques used by their elders to register information in memory. They use inappropriate search techniques to retrieve the information, and—even when they have the information—their limited verbal ability makes it difficult for them to produce it (Perlmutter, 1980).

By the time children are 3, however, some have learned to use rehearsal as an aid to recall (Weissberg and Paris, 1986). When 3-year-olds were asked to memorize a list of six words, nearly half of them audibly repeated the words to themselves. After a delay of sixty to ninety seconds, the children recalled from 2.5 to 3 words from the list. These children recalled more words when memorizing a list than they did when memorization was part of a game. The researchers speculated that nursery school experience, wide exposure to television, and parents' behavior may have increased young children's familiarity with remembering as a goal itself.

Mental Representation by Infants and Toddlers

Once children emerge from the sensorimotor period, their skill at representing information symbolically grows by leaps and bounds. Mental representations provide the basis for their understanding of the world, and as children develop, their representations tend to become more elaborate and more highly differentiated.

The Object Concept

Two-year-olds believe that a hairbrush remains the same, even though it may appear on the bathroom shelf on one day and on the bedroom dresser the next. They also believe that the hairbrush continues to exist, even though it is tucked away in a drawer or closed up in a cupboard. These ideas about identity *(object identity)* and permanence *(object permanence)* make up the **object concept.** The object concept is not present at birth but is slowly built up as a result of the infant's sensory, perceptual, and motor interactions with the environment. Piaget (1952, 1954), who studied the object concept by hiding objects and observing his children's reactions to their sudden disappearance, maintained that the construction is not complete until toward the end of the second year. By this time, youngsters have reached the last stage of the sensorimotor period.

Out of Sight, Out of Existence

During the first few months, babies react to the disappearance of objects in a peculiar manner. When an object being watched by a baby of less than 4 months disappears from sight, the baby either keeps gazing at the spot where it was last visible or acts as if the object had never been in view. The baby in Substages 1 and 2 does not search for the object but behaves as though it no longer existed. Indeed, Piaget concluded that this is exactly the baby's attitude: when a toy vanishes, it has ceased to exist; when the toy reappears, it has been re-created.

During the next four months or so, the baby in Substage 3 often searches for an object that disappears from view. If a cup falls from the highchair tray, the 6-month-old may lean toward the floor to see where it went. But this visual search occurs only when the baby sees the object starting to move away. At this point in the development of the object concept, an object seems to exist for babies only as long as they can continue looking at it. If you hide a toy under a transparent cup, most babies will move the cup to get the toy; but if you hide the

This 6-month-old (top) has not yet developed a concept of object permanence. She looks intently at a toy elephant that is in front of her (left), but when the toy is blocked from view (right), she seems to have forgotten its existence. This older infant (bottom) knows that objects continue to exist after they disappear. When the object in front of this baby (left) is shielded from view by a towel (middle), the baby searches for it and crawls under the towel to find the object. *(George Zimbel/Monkmeyer)*

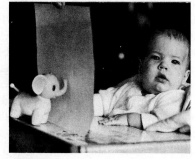

same toy under a cup babies cannot see through, they make no attempt to retrieve it (Bower and Wishart, 1972).

The Beginnings of Object Permanence

In observations of his own children, Piaget (1952, 1954) found that during the last four months of their first year, they searched for objects that they saw him place behind a screen. Yet their search was strictly limited. For instance, Piaget moved a toy behind a screen while one of his children was watching. The child retrieved it. Piaget hid the toy again, and the child again recovered the toy. Then the game changed. With his child watching, Piaget hid the toy behind a screen located in a different place (place B). Surprising as it may seem, the child insisted on searching for the toy in the original location (place A). Psychologists call this the A-not-B error, referring to the baby's persistent searches at place A. Piaget concluded that the error demonstrated a baby's failure to dissociate the objects of the world from the baby's own actions on them. Babies were not actually searching but were repeating an action that had earlier "re-created" the toy (Wellman, Cross, and Bartsch, 1987).

Babies in Substage 5 are not deceived when a toy is hidden in a new place. Even if the toy is moved several times, they immediately search at the final location. But they are fooled when the toy is moved and they do not see the researcher moving it. When the object concept is fully developed, as it is during Substage 6, toddlers search for a toy in all the hiding places. According to Paul Harris (1983), this thoroughness indicates two advances in mental representation. The youngsters have developed, first, the ability to represent the toy despite its invisibility and, second, the ability to represent the place where the toy might be. Other researchers (Bertenthal and Fischer, 1983) have suggested that complete search indicates a cognitive advance that is also a social advance: youngsters now understand that a person can surreptitiously move an object from one place to another.

Egocentrism

If Piaget is correct about the A-not-B error, the error may be due in part to the Substage 4 baby's **egocentrism,** which among infants is the inability to differentiate the self from the world. At the age of 9 months, for example, babies use their own bodies as the frame of reference for spatial relations. Babies reach toward the same spot because that is where they have seen the toy

in relation to their own bodies. In laboratory studies, 9-month-old babies do seem to locate objects in reference to themselves (Acredolo and Evans, 1980). However, if given some striking marker—such as blinking lights and garish stripes—they switch from relying on an egocentric viewpoint to using the landmark. Tested at home, babies show less evidence of egocentrism. A crawling 9-month-old appears to use familiar surroundings as landmarks, doing as well on tests as 16-month-olds do in the laboratory (Acredolo, 1979).

After reviewing the research, Henry Wellman and his colleagues (Wellman, Cross, and Bartsch, 1987) concluded that egocentrism is not responsible for the A-not-B error. They believe that 9-month-olds have developed object permanence and that the error develops because babies now have competing search strategies that govern their search for a toy. If the baby uses the "direct-finding approach," he or she searches (successfully) at the place where the object vanished (place B). When babies are allowed to search immediately (within a second) after the toy is hidden in a second place, this is what babies do. But if there is a delay, the baby has a chance to reflect on the object's location. Now he or she uses the "inferred-location approach," in which the baby infers the object's hidden position from information about the object's movements in time and space. This leads to a search at place A. Paul Harris (1987) agrees that the A-not-B error is not the result of egocentrism. But Harris believes that during a delay, the baby's memory of place B fades, causing the baby to rely on the landmarks for place A, which were encoded in long-term memory by earlier successful searches at that location. Researchers have found that as babies get older, the permissible delay between the hiding of the toy at place B and the baby's successful search lengthens— from one second at 7 months to as much as ten seconds among 12-month-olds (Diamond, 1985).

Even after toddlers grasp the object concept, said Piaget, they are still egocentric in other ways. They appear to think that another person sees things the way they see them and experiences the same behavior and the same thoughts and feelings about things as they do. Yet research indicates that although 2-year-olds are egocentric, they are not so egocentric as Piaget believed. When toddlers are asked to show a picture to another person, 18-month-olds hold it flat—to share the picture with the other person. Two-year-olds turn the picture around so that its back is to them. What is more, if the other person covers his or her eyes with a hand, some 18-month-olds and all 2-year-olds will uncover the person's eyes before they show the picture (Flavell, 1985).

In another study (Flavell, Shipstead, and Croft,

1978), 2½-year-olds could hide a Snoopy doll behind a tabletop screen so that the experimenter could not see Snoopy from where she sat (see Figure 6.8). The youngsters apparently could distinguish what they saw from what another person might see, could think about what the other person saw, and could both produce and recognize some physical situations in which another person could not see some object that they could see.

From such studies, John Flavell (1985) has concluded that toddlers' and young children's understanding of other people's perceptions goes through two stages as it develops. At Level 1, children recognize that another person may not always see the same object that they see. Children know *whether* another person does or does not see the object but are unaware that the person's perception may differ from their own. At Level 2, children understand that even though they and another person see the same object, the two may have different perceptions if they view it from different places. Children are beginning to understand *how* another person perceives an object. Apparently, egocentrism is not absolute but declines gradually during early childhood.

Search Strategies

When infants search for a hidden toy, they engage in an extremely important task, because they are demonstrating their ability to solve problems. By tracing the

development of search strategies, we can follow the growth of these essential skills (Wellman and Somerville, 1982).

During the first year, babies recognize the need to search only if they watch as an object is hidden. They are aware that there is something to search for, but their strategies seem inconsistent, and they are easily distracted. As we have seen, when babies are in their own homes, they locate objects by using landmarks much earlier than they do in the psychology lab.

Toddlers have no trouble finding an object that they have seen being hidden. When tested in their homes, 18-month-olds proved expert at the task. In one study (DeLoache, 1980), mothers hid a stuffed Big Bird toy while the toddlers watched; then the mothers set a kitchen timer, telling the youngsters they could go find the toy when the bell rang. In nearly 70 percent of the cases, the toddlers jumped up and got the coveted toy as soon as the bell sounded, indicating that they remembered the promise and the location of the toy. Children this age can also use distinctive cues. For example, 18-month-olds find it easier to remember which box holds a small toy when the correct box differs radically in size or color from the other boxes (Daehler and Greco, 1985).

While waiting to search for a toy they have seen hidden, 18- to 24-month-olds use rudimentary memory strategies to remember a hiding place (DeLoache, Cassidy, and Brown, 1985). Although they have attractive toys to play with while they wait, the youngsters talk about the toy or its hiding place, look toward the hiding place, point at it, or move toward it. These strategies are more common in the psychology lab than at home, apparently because the strange surroundings of the lab make children either less secure generally or less confident about their ability to find the toy. This uncertainty apparently leads them to keep monitoring the situation.

When a researcher surreptitiously changes a toy's hiding place, older toddlers (25 to 30 months) seem to use their general knowledge to find out where the toy might be (DeLoache and Brown, 1984). When Big Bird was spirited away from beneath a couch cushion, one 30-month-old searched under the couch and beside it for the toy. And when another toddler discovered that a toy was missing from a desk drawer, he said, "Did Mickey Mouse fall out?" and then searched behind the desk.

Toddlers will often search for an object they have not seen being hidden. They will search for a misplaced toy, but even their persistent searches are not comprehensive. When there are three possible locations for the toy, for example, 16-month-olds make an exhaustive

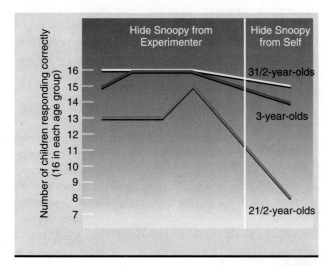

Figure 6.8 When young children were asked on four occasions to hide a Snoopy doll so that the experimenter could not see it, even 2½-year-olds did well; but when asked to hide Snoopy from themselves, the youngest children's performance dropped sharply. *(Adapted from Flavell, Shipstead, and Croft, 1978, p. 1209)*

search about 75 percent of the time. Two-year-olds look in all possible places on every trial (Sophian and Wellman, 1983).

When there are many possible locations for an item, 2-year-olds become much less efficient searchers. In one study, youngsters looked through eight trash cans to find Oscar the Grouch (Wellman et al., 1984). When the lids on the cans remained open (providing a cue that the can had been searched), 2-year-olds looked in every can on most of their trials. But when the lids closed automatically, their performance deteriorated badly. In contrast, 3-year-olds were fairly proficient searchers, whether the lids remained open or closed. Also, 2-year-olds were more likely than 3-year-olds to look in the same can more than once. Two-year-olds seem to look in likely places as they catch sight of them, whereas older youngsters plan their simple search strategies in advance.

About the age of 3, children make another important advance: they can form and coordinate two internal representations of a single meaningful object. Judy DeLoache (1989) studied the development of this ability by using the scale model of a room. After seeing a miniature Snoopy Dog hidden in the scale model, children tried to find the large Snoopy Dog in the room itself. Researchers told the youngsters about the correspondence between the scale model and the room, and 3-year-olds were able to use the information. They inferred that if "Baby Snoopy" was inside a cupboard in the model, then "Daddy Snoopy" would be inside the cupboard in the room. Although 2½-year-olds could not do this, they could use line drawings or photographs in a similar fashion to find hidden objects. DeLoache believes that toddlers have trouble seeing the scale model both as a real, manipulable object and as a representation of something else. Once they can do so, they are freed from situational constraints that keep them from ignoring what they know about an object in order to use it in a different way. For example, 2½-year-olds can pretend that a block is a comb, because a block has ambiguous functions. But when asked to comb their hair with a tennis ball, they are likely to refuse, saying, "I can't. It's a ball" (DeLoache, 1989; J. Elder and Pederson, 1978). Three-year-olds have no trouble with this request, and as a result, they can use symbols—whether scale models or maps—as tools (R. Siegler, 1991).

In this chapter, we have watched the action-oriented infant slowly become the symbol-using child who can recall the past, who may stop to think before acting, and whose flexible mind can infer something about the real world from drawings and scale models. Babies accomplish this feat by becoming active explorers. As tireless investigators of their surroundings, they use old responses on new objects and then modify these responses, assimilating and accommodating their skills as they learn to adapt to a widening world. In the next chapter, we will see how the same process turns them into competent communicators who can express their ideas, needs, and demands in words.

SUMMARY

PERCEPTUAL DEVELOPMENT

As babies grow older, the qualities of a stimulus that *attract* their attention do not change, but the qualities that *hold* it do. With age, babies prefer increasingly complex sights and watch objects as long as they can gain information from them. Babies prefer faces to nonfacial patterns, but whether the preference is due to the stimulus quality of the face or its "faceness" is uncertain. **Event-related potentials (ERPs)** indicate that the nature of information processing within the brain differs, depending on the familiarity of a stimulus. Binocular depth perception develops by 6 months, but some experience in crawling may be necessary before babies can use visual depth cues as warnings of danger. **Haptic perception** is an important source of information about the world, and babies can learn enough to habituate to an unseen object simply by fingering it. Babies older than 6 months display **cross-modal perception,** in which they integrate information picked up by the various senses.

BASIC LEARNING PROCESSES

Studies using **habituation** allow researchers to infer the infant's cognitive processes. Much of babies' learning is the result of operant conditioning, as they come to associate an action with its consequences. Yet rewards for activities that are normally enjoyed seem to undermine intrinsic motivation in toddlers and reduce time spent in the rewarded activity. The development of **contingency awareness** appears to spur learning in babies.

In some studies, newborns have imitated the facial expressions of adults. This imitation is the result of either (1) cross-modal, integrated representation; (2) a rebound of spontaneous movement; (3) a release of the sucking reflex; or (4) an innate survival response that directs attention to the adult face. Toward the end of the first year, babies can imitate novel behavior; this advance makes **observational learning** possible. During the second year, **deferred imitation** appears, so imitation no longer must come immediately after the youngster observes the novel behavior.

SENSORIMOTOR THOUGHT

The **sensorimotor stage,** Piaget's first period of cognitive development, is divided into six substages, each representing an advance in cognitive development. The first substage covers the neonatal period, when babies' responses are primarily reflexive. During Substage 2, babies produce **primary circular reactions,** in which they repeat unlearned actions because of the pleasurable stimulation that accompanies them. Babies in Substage 3 produce **secondary circular reactions,** in which they repeat learned responses. During Substage 4, babies can perform intentional acts to reach some goal. Substage 5 brings out **tertiary circular reactions,** which are intentional adaptations to specific situations and which the baby uses to solve problems through trial and error. Finally, in Substage 6, **symbolic representation** becomes possible. Babies can now represent objects by means of symbols and defer their imitations—advances that allow them to solve problems mentally and use language.

MEMORY IN INFANTS AND TODDLERS

Recognition is present from birth, although babies seem to begin forgetting almost immediately, through a selective, gradual process. Memory improves with age, and the improvement seems primarily based on quicker registration of stimuli in memory. Infants of any age seem most likely to remember those responses that have had an effect on their world. Brief encounters with apparently forgotten objects can lead to **reinstatement** of memory. Instances of **recall** begin appearing at about 7 months, and parental assistance plays an important part in helping babies to remember. Intentional memory improves steadily among toddlers, but they do poorly on formal tests of memory. Most toddlers are unaware of strategies that will help them register information in memory, but widespread experience with television and nursery school may be changing this situation.

MENTAL REPRESENTATION BY INFANTS AND TODDLERS

The **object concept** (in the form of object identity and object permanence) develops slowly and usually is not complete until the second half of the second year. It begins to form during Substage 3, when babies search for objects that they see disappearing, but not until Substage 6 do babies search in all hiding places for a vanished toy. Now they can represent the invisible toy as well as the place where it might be hidden. Piaget believed that babies and young children are characterized by **egocentrism.** Babies, he said, cannot distinguish between self and world, and toddlers believe that another person sees things exactly as they see them and experiences the same thoughts and feelings as they do. Research indicates that babies are less egocentric at home than in the lab and that the A-not-B failure may be the result of competing search strategies or elusive memories—or both. Toddlers develop increasingly effective search strategies; by the time they are 3 years old, they are efficient searchers. They use cues, simple memory strategies, and their store of general knowledge, and they plan their search sequences in advance. They can also represent an object in two ways and use symbols as tools.

KEY TERMS

contingency awareness	haptic perception	reinstatement
cross-modal perception	object concept	secondary circular reaction
deferred imitation	observational learning	sensorimotor stage
egocentrism	primary circular reaction	symbolic representation
event-related potential (ERP)	recall	tertiary circular reaction
habituation	recognition	

CHAPTER

7

COGNITION: THE EMERGENCE OF LANGUAGE

• • • • • • • • • • • • • • •

When he was 2½, young Scott Paris watched with fascination as his grandfather chopped at a small log with a hatchet. Each time the sharp blade bit into the wood, chips flew through the air. Finally, the toddler could restrain himself no longer. When his grandfather paused between strokes, the child's words came tumbling out: "I want to hatch wood, too." Clearly, Scott did not expect to sit on the log like a mother hen until it gave birth to twigs. Instead, he coined a word to extend his vocabulary so that he could talk about something important to him—a chance to wield the hatchet. Scott was learning the regular features of language. He understood the meaning of words and the way they are put together to convey ideas. His conversion of a noun (hatchet) into a verb (hatch) shows that he even grasped one of the processes used in English to form new words.

Scott still had a long way to go. When his grandfather refused to hand over the hatchet, saying, "Sorry, Scott. Not this time," the little boy asked, "Why I can't have it?" He did not understand the rule for wh- *questions; he did not place the auxiliary verb (can't) in front of the subject (I). Yet in less than three years, Scott had accomplished an amazing feat. At birth he could not say a word; now he knew hundreds of words and used them to get things done in the world. How did he master this complicated system of symbols? What did he have to do? What did he have to know?*

● ● ● ● ● ●

Before children go off to kindergarten, they have mastered their native language. They can turn their thoughts and intentions into patterns of sounds that others can understand, and they can decipher the sound patterns produced by others. To reach this level of skill, children must understand the sounds, meaning, and structure of their native tongue. And if their mastery is to be of much value to them, children also must become skilled at using it to reach their goals.

In this chapter, we discuss the way children master their native language. Before we trace the child's journey, we consider what capabilities children must develop before language acquisition becomes possible. We take up the first attempts at speech, looking at what children say with their first words and what they mean. Next we follow children's grasp of syntax, tracing the gradual growth of their sentences in length and complexity. Finally, we investigate the various theories that attempt to explain how children acquire language.

Getting Ready to Talk

Long before they say their first words, babies are deep into the task of acquiring language. Before a baby can say "Dada," substantial progress occurs in four areas of development. First, physical maturation is important;

language development is impossible until a child reaches a certain age. Second, perceiving and producing the sounds of speech are essential; unless babies can separate speech from the other noises in the world, language acquisition will not occur. Third, social interaction plays a vital role; without the society of other human beings, a child will not learn to speak. Fourth, cognitive advances obviously are essential; until babies have developed a certain understanding of the world, they cannot talk.

Maturational Readiness

Why does it take so long for most infants to talk? Why do most youngsters say their first words near their first birthdays? Whether they live in a mansion or a tent, on a farm in Kansas, the streets of Calcutta, the steppes of Russia, or a Pacific atoll, children begin to talk at about the same age. In fact, it is almost impossible to keep them from talking. Normal children who have regular contact with older speakers invariably learn to talk. If experience has such a small effect, then we might expect that physiological maturation plays an important part in the emergence of language.

Young babies could not speak even if they knew what they wanted to say. Speech occurs when air from the lungs passes over the vibrating vocal cords in the larynx. The position of the tongue, teeth, and lips determines the shape of the vocal cavity and, therefore, the sounds that escape the lips. At birth, the baby has little control over the flow of air through the larynx, the tongue fills the toothless mouth, and the vocal cords are positioned so high that only minute changes in the shape of the vocal tract are possible (Sachs, 1985). This arrangement means that for many months babies cannot produce the sounds of speech; the newborn's vocal tract is shaped more like that of an adult chimpanzee than of an adult human (Stark, 1986).

As the baby's head and neck grow and the cheeks lose fat, the oral cavity becomes larger. The tongue no longer takes up the available mouth space, and the vocal cords have a wider range of possible positions. At about 6 months, teeth begin to erupt. While the mouth and throat are growing, the baby is also gaining command over the body. Soon he or she will be able to control the muscles of the lips and tongue, the flow of air through the larynx, and the position of the vocal cords. These changes make it possible for the older baby to produce the wide range of sounds necessary for speech.

The control of speech sounds is not simply the result of increases in the baby's size and strength. As we saw in Chapter 5, maturation of the cortex is closely linked with control over various parts of the body. In the sensorimotor cortex, where an extremely large area is devoted to control of the lips, tongue, and jaw, connections among neurons are multiplying and becoming stronger. Similar events are taking place in specialized areas of the brain's left hemisphere, where the production and reception of language sounds are processed. This growth of connections goes on throughout the first two years (Goldman-Rakic, 1987), which is precisely the period during which the foundations of language are developing.

Speech Perception and Production

Before they can acquire language, babies must separate speech from the other noises in the environment. Indeed, they seem born prepared to do just that, and their perception of speech sounds races far ahead of their ability to produce them.

Perceiving Speech

Newborns not only distinguish between human and nonhuman sounds but also seem to recognize voices that are important to them. Newborns will alter their sucking pattern in order to hear their own mother's voice (DeCasper and Fifer, 1980). Very soon, differences in adult stress and intonation affect a baby's emotional state and behavior. Long before babies understand the words they hear, they respond to cues in the rate, volume, and melody of adult speech. From these cues, babies sense when an adult is playful or angry, whether the adult is attempting to initiate or end the interaction, and so on (M. Papousek et al., 1990).

Just as significant for language development as the response to intonation is evidence that a tiny baby can make fine distinctions between speech sounds. By the time babies are a month old, they can tell the difference between most language sounds (Aslin, Pisoni, and Jusczyk, 1983). Using habituation techniques, researchers have found that 6-week-old infants (the youngest age tested) distinguish between "bad" and "bag," a situation in which only the final sound differs (Jusczyk, 1977). Babies come into the world with precisely those perceptual discriminations that are necessary if they are to acquire human language.

If the language spoken around a baby does not discriminate between two sounds, the baby eventually will be unable to detect the difference between them. In a longitudinal study, Janet Werker and Richard Tees (1984) traced the gradual loss of this ability. When they

Although this baby cannot understand any words, she detects her father's mood by the stress and intonation of his voice. *(George Malave/Stock, Boston)*

were 6 to 8 months old, infants from an English-speaking culture easily distinguished between the contrasting *t*'s (the *t* in "tar" and the *t* in "star") that change the meaning of words in Hindi but not in English. But by the time the babies were 10 to 12 months old, they could no longer tell the difference between the sounds. Over the same period, these babies also lost the ability to distinguish between two sounds that change the meaning of words in Salish (a northwestern Native American language) but not in English. Heredity had prepared the babies to distinguish these sounds, but experience had closed the door to their use. Apparently, experience and the heredity of the species both play a role in the decoding of speech sounds.

From Crying to Babbling

Although babies can discriminate early among the sounds they hear, most are at least a year old before they can produce sounds that can be identified as words. It is much easier to perceive differences between sounds than to acquire motor control over the various muscles and organs involved in producing speech. In their production of prelinguistic sounds, ba-

bies go through five overlapping stages (see Table 7.1), with some progressing through these stages more rapidly or more slowly than the average baby (Sachs, 1985; Stark, 1986).

Stage I: Reflexive Crying and Vegetative Sounds (0 to 8 weeks). A baby's first sounds are cries. Although they may serve as communication, during the first few months cries are simply reflexive signs of distress. After about 3 weeks, vocalizations gradually change in frequency and variety. Some sounds are only vegetative noises—burps, coughs, and sneezes that help keep the airway open. During this stage, the baby's physical immaturity sharply restricts the variety of possible sounds.

Stage II: Cooing and Laughter (8 to 20 weeks). Sounds of joy, called **cooing**, now appear, usually during social interaction while babies watch a parent's smiling face or listen to singing or talking. These pleasurable sounds, which also are heard after babies eat and while they look at or handle objects, are made in the back of

TABLE 7.1   PRELINGUISTIC LANGUAGE DEVELOPMENT

Age	Stage	Characteristics
0 to 8 weeks	Stage 1: Reflexive crying and vegetative sounds	Cries of distress; burps, coughs, sneezes
8 to 20 weeks	Stage 2: Cooing and laughter	Pleasurable sounds
16 to 30 weeks	Stage 3: Vocal play	Single, distinctive syllables
25 to 50 weeks	Stage 4: Reduplicated babbling	Strings of alternating vowels and consonants
9 to 18 months	Stage 5: Nonreduplicated babbling and expressive jargon	Stress and intonational pattern, often with contour of adult speech

Source: Information from Sachs, 1985.

the mouth. Babies cry less now, perhaps because they have additional ways of expressing themselves. They also burst into peals of sustained laughter when something delights them.

Stage III: Vocal Play (16 to 30 weeks). This is a transitional stage between cooing and true babbling. As the size and shape of the oral cavity changes and maturation progresses in the brain, the baby's noises change from a gurgling "coo" or "goo" to single, distinctive syllables, such as "da" or "ba." The baby produces these sounds, which Piaget would call secondary circular reactions, while exploring and mapping the possibilities of the vocal tract. During this period, babies seem to use their cries to communicate; when they begin to cry, they often look directly at their caregivers (Gustafson and Green, 1991).

Stage IV: Reduplicated Babbling (25 to 50 weeks). Babies now begin to babble, producing strings of alternating vowels and consonants, such as "bababababa." These sound sequences give the impression that the baby is uttering a string of syllables. Such repetitions indicate greatly improved control over the muscles that govern speech. This control, together with babies' coordination of their speech with the perception of sound, is probably the primary function of babbling. Toward the end of this period, babies may combine their cries with gestures, such as pointing or reaching for the caregiver (Gustafson and Green, 1991).

After they are about 8 weeks old, babies may burst into peals of delighted laughter during play. *(M. Siluk/The Image Works)*

Stage V: Nonreduplicated Babbling and Expressive Jargon (9 to 18 months). As babies near the end of the first year, babbling changes again. The strings of syllables may alternate consonants and take on a variety of stress and intonational patterns. The rising and falling pitch of this **expressive jargon** begins to sound like adult speech. Infants often produce long, complex sequences of meaningless sounds with the pitch contour of adult sentences. These sequences often appear in situations where language is appropriate, as when a child "talks" on a toy phone or "reads" a picture book. The period of expressive jargon often overlaps with the production of the child's first real words.

Social Precursors to Language

If children are to be competent speakers, they must be able to get things done with words. In fact, we can consider words as a form of "meaningful social behavior" (Bruner, 1976). The view of language as a social act, in which the speaker is trying to accomplish something, is known as **pragmatics.** This approach leads researchers to look at the context in which language is used and the functions it serves. They find that language seems to emerge from social interactions between baby and caregiver. Because they acquire language in social situations, children seem to grasp its pragmatic aspects early. Long before babies can talk, they influence others by touching, pointing, and gazing. These acts can be considered prelinguistic **speech acts,** because the communication is intended to help the baby achieve some goal (Bruner, 1983).

From a baby's first days, parents speak to their child in special ways, a form of speech that is often called **motherese.** As we saw in Chapter 4, even newborns seem to prefer this exaggerated form of infant-directed language to normal speech (R. Cooper and Aslin, 1990). Speech directed toward young babies seems to have little formal structure, for it consists largely of interjections, naming, and playful sounds that are often imitations of the baby's own gurglings and coos. Parents also draw out syllables, giving motherese the characteristics of a pleasant melody (M. Papousek, Papousek, and Bornstein, 1985). The adult seems to be both conveying affection and capturing the baby's attention for the task at hand. By 4 months, babies are sensitive to emotional messages embedded in the melodic contours of motherese, which are relatively stable across languages. The pitch contours for soothing or arousing a baby, indicating approval or disapproval, beginning or closing a communication, or encouraging imitation, for example, are

similar in Mandarin Chinese and English (M. Papousek, Papousek, and Symmes, 1991). Researchers have found that when babies hear affectionate motherese, they look intently at the slide of a human face, but that babies tend to look away when the stimulus is accompanied by a disapproving voice, such as that used by a parent to prevent a baby from carrying out some dangerous movement (M. Papousek et al., 1990).

Motherese appears in societies around the world; its presence has been documented in at least fifteen cultures, and it is used by both parents, by childless adults, and by children (Ferguson, 1977; J. Jacobson et al., 1983; M. Papousek et al., 1990). For this reason, some researchers have begun to call it either "infant-directed" or "child-directed" speech.

Toward the end of the first year, motherese changes in quality. It moves closer to adult speech, but parents continue to speak more slowly, using simple sentences and inserting pauses into their words. They use very short sentences, replace difficult consonants with easy ones, substitute nouns for pronouns, and repeat phrases or whole sentences. Parents use pitch in a way that highlights important words and helps infants pick out words from the stream of speech (Fernald and Mazzie, 1991). Researchers have found, for example, that infants are sensitive to clause boundaries in infant-directed speech but not in speech that is directed to adults (Kemler-Nelson et al., 1989).

Adults also talk to children primarily about the here and now. They comment on what they are doing or on what the infant is doing or is about to do. They limit their vocabularies, and they select words that are most useful for the infant, words that relate to what babies are interested in. The adult is not trying to teach the child language; instead, the adult is trying to maintain interaction with the child (Shatz, 1984).

The content and intonation of motherese are childish, but the dialogue pattern is strictly adult (Bruner, 1981). How important is motherese? Researchers are uncertain whether this special speech is necessary to ensure normal language development. Heavy doses of motherese early in life seem to speed the acquisition of a baby's first few words. In a longitudinal study, Marc Bornstein and Margaret Ruddy (1984) found that mothers who encouraged their 4-month-old babies to pay attention to objects and events around them (by using motherese and gestures) fostered the babies' early language acquisition. At 12 months, these babies had larger vocabularies than babies whose mothers gave them little encouragement. Among another group of youngsters, those who were highly responsive to motherese at

3 months tended to perform especially well on tests of linguistic functioning at 12 years (Roe, McClure, and Roe, 1982). Although some researchers believe that motherese is unlikely to help a child learn language rules and structure (Gleitman and Wanner, 1982), others have found that the structure of mothers' speech to their 26-month-olds predicts aspects of their children's later language growth (Hoff-Ginsberg, 1986). A number of developmentalists go even further, suggesting that without some minimal exposure to motherese, infants might never become competent speakers (Moerk, 1989).

Other aspects of child-caregiver interaction seem to be as important as motherese in stimulating linguistic development. As we saw in Chapter 4, parents encourage their newborns to "take their turn" in conversation. These dialogues, in which the caregiver at first supplies both sides of the conversation, teach young babies about the nature of human conversation.

Carrying on a conversation requires infants to master a number of language conventions: they must learn to take turns, speaking at the proper time and not interrupting their partners; they must learn to make eye contact and to indicate that they are paying attention. Turntaking and other nonverbal conversational skills grow out of early games, such as peekaboo, in which the baby and adult share experiences and exchange roles in ritualized ways.

Cognitive Precursors to Language

The basis for the child's ability to understand and speak a language is an understanding of the world. Until a number of cognitive advances occur, a child cannot use words meaningfully.

Object Permanence

Before children can talk, they must have some notion that there is an enduring world of objects and people. A child who cannot remember the existence of vanished objects cannot attach labels to objects with any consistency and so cannot speak about them. As children develop the notion of object permanence, the nature of their early vocabulary shows a characteristic change. Most children begin to communicate with words at about the time they enter Substage 5 of the sensorimotor period (see Chapter 6). At this time, they understand that an object can be moved from one hiding place to another but are fooled if the experimenter secretly changes the object's location. In Substage 6, they are not tricked by such surreptitious moves. When re-

searchers followed a group of 12-month-olds for a year, they found that most youngsters in Substage 5 were using words that indicated *visible* movements of objects, such as "hi," "bye," "move," "stuck," "uh-oh," and "thank you" (Tomasello and Farrar, 1984). Not until they reached Substage 6 did they use words that indicated *invisible* movements (including the disappearance or reappearance of objects). Now they were saying "allgone," "more," "find," and "another."

Development of Concepts

Concepts give us ways of organizing the world so that we have to store less information in order to think about it. Each concept can be viewed as a set of features that are associated with one another so that they form a unit in memory (E. Clark, 1983). Concepts can refer to individuals (Miss Piggy) or to groups that share certain properties (Muppet, bird), situations (walking), or states (asleep, alive). When talking about the group described by a concept, we generally call it a *category*.

When children learn a word, they actually are learning the concept or category to which the word refers. In most cases, children first learn the concept and then figure out what word it refers to (Macnamara, 1972). Before babies know any words, they begin noting what features appear together in members of a concept. Researchers have discovered that by the age of 10 months, most babies are sorting the world in this manner, but that the ability seems to be beyond the capabilities of 7-month-olds (Younger and Cohen, 1983). In one study that tested concept formation, Barbara Younger (1990) showed drawings of twelve different hypothetical animals to 10- and 13-month-olds. Although the animals differed from one another, all animals with ears had feathered tails and all animals with antlers had furry tails (see Figure 7.1). After habituating to these two groups of animals, the babies looked at new drawings. They seemed bored by a new animal within each of the old groups, but when an animal's appearance violated their expectations (antlers with a feathered tail or ears with a furry tail), the babies seemed surprised and stared much longer at the drawing. Apparently, these babies had extracted the correlation among features and generalized it to a new situation.

Whether these early perceptual groupings are true categories has not been established, but youngsters who sort objects into separate groups may be demonstrating genuine categorization. This advance usually comes at about 18 months. Given four plastic Raggedy Andy dolls and four plastic cars, for example, an 18-month-old (but not a 12-month-old) spontaneously organizes them into

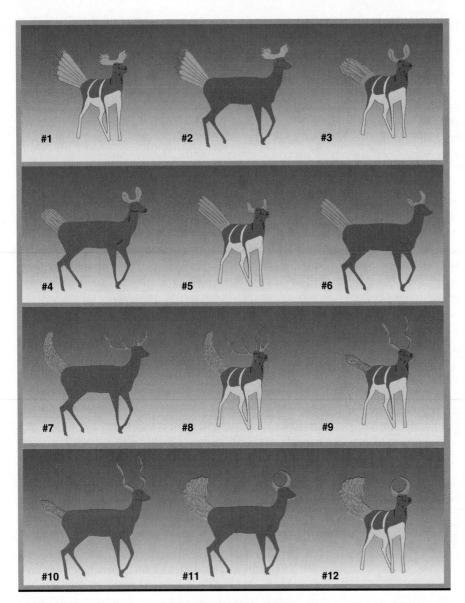

Figure 7.1 The appearance of correlated features (ears and feathered tails, antlers and furry tails) in this group of twelve hypothetical animals varies from one animal to the next. Other properties vary independently of correlated features. When shown new hypothetical animals with the same correlated features along with an animal whose features violated the correlation (e.g., antlers with feathered tail), 10- to 13-month-olds were most interested in the new combination. *(From Younger, 1990, p. 614)*

groups, putting the four dolls in one place and the four cars in another. The tendency to classify objects in this way is closely linked to two other cognitive advances: the attainment of Substage 6 object permanence and the "naming explosion," which refers to toddlers' intense interest in naming objects and the concurrent rise in the number of words that they use (Gopnik and Meltzoff, 1987).

Imitation
When babies form concepts, they are representing objects or events mentally. Once babies begin to imitate

events after they have occurred, they clearly are storing internal images of sights and sounds. As we saw in Chapter 6, deferred imitation first appears in Substage 6 of the sensorimotor period. Children who imitate the way Mommy stirs with a wooden spoon or the way an older sibling rocks a doll show that they have developed the memory abilities required for the acquisition of language. Before they can speak, children also must be able to imitate the sound patterns of language that they hear about them.

Symbolic Play

An infant's first words emerge at about the same time as the infant begins to use symbolic gestures and to engage in pretend play. A baby girl who pushes a building block along the floor, pretending that it is a car, or runs her fingers through her hair, pretending that she is combing it, has demonstrated symbolic play. In this early pretend play, children carry out familiar activities away from their customary settings, but the play is not social. Pretend play allows children to separate meaning from action (Vygotsky, 1978). When a little girl stamps the ground and pretends that she is riding a horse, for example, she has detached the meaning of her action from a real action (an actual horseback ride).

At first, pretend play is solitary, but among 3-year-olds it blossoms into dramatic play with other children. Most young players understand the nature of the fantasy game: a Play-Dough hamburger is never eaten, and the child who plays "Daddy" is aware of his own identity and may step out of the role to give directions ("Now you say that I'm supposed to go to work"). This ability

Symbolic play requires the same cognitive competence as language: the ability to translate experience into symbols and then combine them according to rules. *(Arlene Collins/Monkmeyer)*

indicates a giant step in cognitive development: young-sters realize that they can play a role and be themselves at the same time. The ability to switch back and forth from self to role emerges gradually. In a longitudinal study, pretend play of this complexity appeared in 25 percent of children before they were 3 years old and in 56 percent before they reached their fourth birthday (Howes and Matheson, 1992).

Children engaged in symbolic play are translating their experience into symbols and then combining them according to specific rules (playing house, driving a car, combing hair, and so on). This is exactly what children must do in order to use language, an indication that the same rules underlie the development of play and the development of language (Ungerer and Sigman, 1984). Researchers have found that such play is closely related to both the child's use of words and his or her comprehension of others' speech (Bates et al., 1982). At the same time that children begin connecting two or more symbolic gestures in play (pouring pretend tea, drinking it, then wiping their mouths), they are begin-ning to combine two or more words in a single utter-ance.

Intention

Until babies are about 9 months old, none of their sig-nals indicates true intent; instead, they seem to be built-in reactions to a particular internal state (Bates, 1979). About the age of 9 or 10 months, babies undergo a great change in their behavior. Now if they want a toy that is out of reach, they look at a nearby adult, then at the toy, then back at the adult. If there is no response, they may fuss loudly to attract attention. Quickly, the grasp to-ward the elusive toy becomes an intentional signal, per-haps a repetitive opening and shutting of the hand, and the fussing sound becomes short, regular noises, such as "uh, uh" or "eeeee." These first signals change in vol-ume and insistence, depending on whether the adult responds. This is a great moment, says Elizabeth Bates (1979), in the dawn of language. It shows the child's intent to communicate as well as the realization that there are mutually agreed-upon signals, such as point-ing, that can be used for mutually agreed-upon pur-poses. Earlier, the infant may have wanted to communi-cate but lacked any shared notion of conventional ways to express intention.

The way is now open for the baby's first words. This next advance, which comes at about 12 months, re-quires another realization by the baby—that an arbi-trary symbol (a word) can refer to a particular object. This understanding indicates that the baby has grasped

another aspect of language: **semantics,** which refers to the arbitrary meaning conveyed by language forms.

Once children have developed intent, their early communications are far more successful than we would expect from their tentative grasp of symbols. These communications succeed in part because adults are good at guessing children's intentions. Youngsters give clues to their intentions in intonation and gesture. Tod-dlers, whose language comprehension is far ahead of their spoken vocabulary, use a variety of gestures as sub-stitutes for words, and as their spoken vocabulary in-creases, the gestures drop away (Bates et al., 1989). Even when there are no clues from gestures, it is gener-ally possible to figure out what young children are try-

Waving "bye-bye" is a nonverbal way to communicate meaning, and this 1-year-old is learning to accompany her gestures with appropriate words. *(Michael Newman/Photo Edit)*

ing to say, because their communicative needs are always embedded in an ongoing context of activity.

The process works both ways. Children assess a communication in terms of its context, often figuring out what a parent wants even if they don't understand all the words they hear. When the context is ambiguous, they assume that language demands action, and so they do whatever seems appropriate (Shatz, 1983). Because a toddler's actions often match whatever the parent has requested or ordered, parents often overestimate their child's linguistic knowledge.

Early Utterances

When an infant shifts from babbling to saying words, something very important has happened. Instead of simply playing with sound, the baby is planning and controlling speech (de Villiers and de Villiers, 1979). As a result, the infant's utterances shrink in length. One word has to do the work of many, because babies' limited cognitive processing ability does not permit them to plan and produce a longer utterance before they run out of working memory.

After a slow start, when each new word is a remarkable feat of memory, the toddler enters Substage 6 and the naming explosion occurs. From this time, toddlers and preschoolers acquire new words at a prodigious rate, with some researchers estimating that between the ages of 2 and 6, children learn an average of six words per day (Templin, 1957). Although six words per day may be the average rate of vocabulary growth, individual differences are extremely wide. These differences seem to correlate with the amount of speech directed to the toddler by parents. At first, however, girls pick up words faster than boys do, even when both genders have the same exposure to child-directed speech. Gender differences start to narrow at 20 months and disappear by the third birthday (Huttenlocher et al., 1991).

First Words

First words tend to be either a single syllable ("ma") or a duplicated syllable ("mama"), consisting of a consonant followed by a vowel. The sounds are those that are easiest for the baby to say, so no matter what a child's native language, the first words generally contain consonants that are produced at the front of the mouth, such as *b, p, d,* or *m.* The first syllable may occur when infants release their lips while vocalizing, producing such sounds as "ma" or "ba." The very first words may not be recognizable as such; babies often copy animal sounds, pick up some sound from the environment, or invent words, applying one of their own sounds (such as "uh" or "deh") in a consistent manner (de Villiers and de Villiers, 1978). Two weeks before she produced her first conventional word, for example, 11-month-old Sarah began to say "di" to mean "Look at that" (Stoel-Gammon and Cooper, 1984). Sarah produced only this one invented word, but some babies use many, and the words cover a variety of situations. A few seem to indicate emotion, as did "dididi," which one little girl spoke loudly to indicate disapproval and softly to indicate satisfaction (see Table 7.2).

The first conventional words come quickly, but individual differences are wide. In a study of three children's early linguistic development (Stoel-Gammon and Cooper, 1984), Daniel had a fifty-word vocabulary within four months, Sarah took five and one-half months to reach that point, and Will required six and one-half months.

Children simplify their early words. They may drop an initial consonant ("addy" for *daddy,* "poon" for *spoon* or a final consonant ("du" for *duck,* "ba" for *ball*). If an adult word has two syllables, children often make the second syllable a duplicate of the first ("baba" for *button.*). Or they may use duplication to stretch out a one-syllable word ("coat-coat," "go-go"). Individual vocabularies vary widely, both in the consonants used and in the form of words. Apparently, each child uses words whose sounds or syllables they can produce easily, while avoiding words with sounds or syllable types they cannot articulate (Stoel-Gammon and Cooper, 1984).

From the content of their early vocabulary, we can tell quite a bit about the way in which infants and toddlers perceive and arrange their world. One of their first few words is likely to be "baby," which they generally use to refer to themselves. Many of the first words refer to the appearance or disappearance of some person ("Daddy!"), animal ("doggie"), or thing ("ball") or describe situations, usually the outcomes of actions ("up," "broken," "stuck," "off") and the transient states of objects ("dirty," "wet"). Most children are about two years old before they talk about the permanent state of objects ("red" or "little") (E. Clark, 1983).

What Do First Words Mean?

During the one-word stage, which generally lasts until toddlers are about 18 months old, their one-word

TABLE 7.2   THE FIRST SEVEN "WORDS" IN ONE CHILD'S LINGUISTIC DEVELOPMENT

Utterance	Age in Months	Meanings
uh?	8	Interjection. Also singles out person or thing; "addressed" to persons, distant objects, and "escaped" toys.
dididi	9	Disapproval (loud). Comfort (soft).
mama	10	Refers vaguely to food. Also means "tastes good" and "hungry."
nenene	10	Scolding.
tt!	10	Used to call squirrels.
piti	10	Always used with a gesture and always whispered. Seems to mean "interest (-ed), (-ing)."
deh	10	Interjection. Also singles out person or thing. Used with the same gesture as above.

Source: Adapted from McNeill, 1970, p. 22; based on material from Leopold, 1949, p. 6.

utterances have to do the work of an entire sentence. Because youngsters mean more than they can say with a single word, their one-word statements are called **holophrases.** The child may have an entire proposition in mind but can convey only one part of it at a time.

Most simple utterances can be understood only in context, as we saw in the discussion of intent. When a parent sees the toy on the floor or the empty cup of milk, the meaning of the child's "gone" is clear. The context of a situation goes far beyond the arrangement of objects and people in the environment. It includes beliefs, assumptions, actions, prior remarks, knowledge, and intentions (Ochs, 1979). When it is mealtime, whether a small boy says "up" or "chair," his mother knows that the toddler wants the tray removed so that he can climb into the highchair. Children's gestures—pointing, waving, stamping their feet, jerking or nodding their heads—often provide clues to meaning.

Intonation is an especially strong clue to a child's intent. Its ability to clarify meaning was evident in a classic study that used tapes of a toddler saying "door" in several situations (Menyuk and Bernholtz, 1969). When the researchers played the tapes for listeners, there was general agreement about whether the child's use of "door" was a declaration, a question, or an emphatic statement (see Figure 7.2). When the word was spoken with a falling pitch (frequency contour), listeners judged the utterance as referring to a door ("That's a door"). When the same word was uttered with a rising intonation, listeners interpreted it as a question ("Is that a door?" or "Are you going to open the door?"). When the intonation rose sharply and then fell, the word was heard as an emphatic assertion or demand ("Open the door!" "Close the door!"). Thus, a single word can convey a number of meanings, depending on how a child says it.

Overextending Words

After children have learned a word, they may extend its meaning to cover objects or actions that resemble the original labeled item in some way; this process is called **overextension.** When an infant extends a word, usually it is possible to find some perceived similarity of form or function among the objects and events it includes. Most overextensions are based on appearance, with up to 90 percent of such overextensions based on shape (E. Clark, 1983). One child, for example, extended "baw" from a word originally meaning "ball" to one referring to apples, grapes, eggs, squash, the clapper of a bell, and anything round. Some overextensions are based on movement, size, taste, texture, or sound.

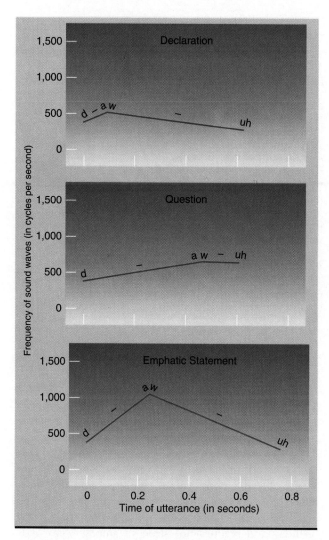

Figure 7.2 Three intonation patterns for "door" as spoken by an infant at the one-word stage. *(Adapted from P. Menyuk, 1971, p. 62)*

If this child has no label for the concept "horse," he may temporarily overextend another label "bow-wow" that refers to a somewhat similar concept. *(Charles Harbutt)*

Do children's overextensions signify a confusion in the meaning of words? Sometimes they may. As noted earlier, in most cases children have concepts before they have words for them, but the child's concept may be very different from that of the adult. If the child's concept of "bow-wow" is a four-legged animal, then the child's overextension is just what it seems to be. Yet children often know that their overextensions are "wrong." Many youngsters who refer to all animals as "bow-wow," when asked to point to the "bow-wow," always pick a dog from a group of animals. They never point to a cat or a sheep (Gruendel, 1977). In such cases, the child knows that a cat is not a "bow-wow" but has no special word for cat.

Sometimes children's extensions may reveal greater sensitivity than we give youngsters credit for. The child may be trying to draw attention to a perceived similarity, as when a youngster calls a grapefruit a moon (roundness). If the child's grasp of language were firmer, she or he might say, "It's like a moon" or "It's round."

Learning New Words

Children pick up words in the context of some specific situation, and a word's initial meaning depends on the way the child represents the linguistic context (the grammatical structure of the utterance) and the nonlinguistic context (the physical situation) (Carey, 1982). (See the accompanying box, "Sorting Out the World.") A toddler who has an older brother may at first believe, for example, that the meanings of "boy" and "brother"

SORTING OUT THE WORLD

Children in the midst of the naming explosion are fascinated by the names of things, but not every word is the label of an object. Some words label actions, and others highlight contrasts within a single category. Preschoolers are alert to grammatical clues that tell them to look for such contrasts. Preschoolers have worked out the conceptual relation between nouns and adjectives and clearly understand the use of adjectives to pick out contrasts. Researchers confirmed this understanding by showing 4-year-olds four pictures (two identical caps, a spotted cap, and a geometric figure) (Gelman and Markman, 1985). When asked to point to "the fep," the children pointed to the figure. But if they were asked to point to "the fep one," they chose the spotted cap.

Young children know that nouns distinguish superordinate categories (such as animals, vehicles, plants). In another study, researchers used a hand puppet who could not speak English and had "his own special words for things" to explore the word-learning biases of 2-year-olds (Waxman and Kosowski, 1990). Once again, children were sensitive to the linguistic structure in which they heard new words. The experimenter pointed to pictures of animals, foods, and plants and then labeled them. She pointed to the picture of a bunny, for example, and said "See this? This is a 'fopin.'" Later she asked the children to find "another fopin." Children generally chose animals such as skunks and squirrels as fopins, instead of items usually associated with rabbits, such as carrots and Easter eggs. By the age of 2, children can recognize the relations that link members of a superordinate category (for example, animals), even though its members (for example, a horse and a mouse) bear little resemblance to one another.

Two-year-olds did not understand the role of adjectives. Asked about "the fopish one," they were uncertain as to whether they were to pick another animal or items associated with the target animal. But 3- and 4-year-olds did make the distinction. When asked to find "another one that is fopish," they chose items associated with the target animal. These experiments demonstrate the existence of implicit biases that lead young children to prefer some possible meanings of words over others.

are identical. The question is how toddlers decide, on first hearing a word, just what that word means.

Constraints on learning new words

Some researchers believe that the naming explosion is possible because children follow two "rules" that lead them to prefer some possible meanings over others, thus helping them sort out the world and avoid linguistic confusion (Markman, 1989; R. Siegler, 1991). According to the first rule, the child has a tendency to *prefer categories* when decoding the meaning of a new word. That is, when a young child hears a new word in the presence of some unfamiliar object, the child assumes that the word refers to the entire class of objects to which the new "thing" belongs and not to any of the thing's parts or properties or to any relation that involves the thing. Suppose the teacher brings a hamster into the nursery school. When the teacher says, "This is a hamster," the child assumes that "hamster" refers to the category of hamsters, not to the hamster's whiskers, legs, tail, or eyes and not to the pellets the hamster is eating or the cage that surrounds it. This rule is operating by the time children are 2, and if they did not follow it, figuring out exactly what each word means would pose enormous problems (Waxman and Kosowksi, 1990).

According to the second rule, the child assumes that *words usually refer to one thing*. Young children assume that labels are mutually exclusive and thus that each concept or category has only one label. This bias seems absent among young toddlers, who are most likely to overextend words. Studies indicate that the bias begins to develop a few months after the second birthday and reaches full strength among 3-year-olds (Merriman and Bowman, 1989). The principle of mutual exclusivity not only affects children's decisions about the meaning of new words and helps them correct overextensions but also may lead them to reject a new label for some concept that already has a name. A child who can label a cow as "cow," for example, may reject the broader term *animal*. By the time children are 4, however, they can suspend this bias when they have compelling evidence that the new label and the old one have overlapping meanings (Au and Glusman, 1990). Bilingual preschoolers have no trouble learning two labels for each category (one in each language), although they adhere to the bias *within* each language.

Creativity and Invented Expressions

Children often coin new words for objects, situations, or events, like the child who made up the word "sassy" to refer to a butterfly (Mervis et al., in press). These new words are different from the invented quasi-words that children used as 12-month-olds. Now their new words follow word-formation patterns of English (E. Clark, 1983). Youngsters add suffixes; one 5-year-old came up with "hateable" to describe the food in a hospital. They convert nouns to verbs; a toddler who hits an object with a stick may say, "I sticked it." And they create compound words. One youngster called a psychologist who worked with rats a "ratman," and another called someone who smiled a lot a "smileperson."

Linguistic creativity does not depend on the child's ability to hear people talk. Children who cannot hear spoken language invent their own silent speech. In a study of ten deaf children whose parents did not know sign language, researchers found that the youngsters had invented signs that referred to people, animals, toys, clothing, and vehicles (Goldin-Meadow and Morford, 1985). The children strung their signs together to form "sentences" that followed grammatical rules, and their silent utterances noted the existence of items, commented on them, and asked for actions involving the objects (Goldin-Meadow, 1991).

Deaf youngsters also use signs metaphorically, in the same way that hearing children use words. In various studies (for example, J. Hudson and Nelson, 1984), children as young as 20 months deliberately used language metaphorically. For example, one toddler (who knew the correct name for puppets and for paper bags) put a bag over his head and said "puppet." By the time children are coining words and using other words metaphorically, they have traveled a long way on the road of language acquisition. Figure 7.3, which charts the highlights of language development in the first two years, shows just how far they have come.

Putting Words Together

Toward the end of the one-word period, toddlers make a sequence of separate one-word utterances that seem to relate to a larger meaning. Yet they speak each word separately, with its own falling intonation. One 18-month-old girl, for example, looked at researcher Ronald Scollan (1979), held her foot threateningly above his tape recorder, and said, "Tape. Step." Within two months, she was combining two words in a smooth utterance, saying such things as "Wash clothes" with no pause between the words.

The two-word stage is significant because it marks a striking advance in children's ability to code their understanding in linguistic terms and to project their ideas into the world of human interaction. It begins when children can process two words at a time without running out of space in working memory.

Semantic Relations in Two-Word Sentences

Despite this limit on the length of their sentences, children are able to express a wide variety of ideas. They do this by combining their two words in a series of patterns that are based on semantic relations. From the study of Adam, Eve, and Sarah, Roger Brown (1970) discovered that all the children's two-word statements could be described by four patterns in which the youngsters referred to some object or event and seven patterns that depended on the relations between the two words in the utterance (see Table 7.3). These relations, such as actor, possessor, and location, reflect the situational meanings of words. Formal categories, such as nouns and verbs, subjects and objects, are absent from children's speech at this early age. Because they rely on semantic relations in forming their speech patterns, children often treat words from the same adult speech category (verbs such as *want* and *tickle*) differently. As Michael Maratsos (1983) has concluded, the structure of children's two-word utterances does not seem to follow the general rules of English **syntax,** that is, the rules for combining words into sentences.

In fact, trying to analyze two-word utterances by formal grammatical rules that govern the distribution of word classes like nouns and verbs is futile. Such an analysis would treat the sentence "Baby chair" as having the same meaning no matter how it was used (Bloom, 1970). But an 18-month-old boy may say "Baby chair" and mean "Baby is sitting in her highchair," or he may say "Baby chair" and mean "That is baby's highchair." In both cases, he is using only nouns, yet in the first he is indicating the baby's location and in the second, her possession of the chair.

Telegraphic Speech

The utterances of children who run around saying "Baby chair" or "Daddy shoe" resemble the statements of a telegram, stripped to their barest essentials. So it is not surprising that psychologists call two-word utterances **telegraphic speech.** At this stage, the words children choose are content words, full of information. All the little "functional" words (articles, prepositions, conjunctions) that would enable listeners to distinguish

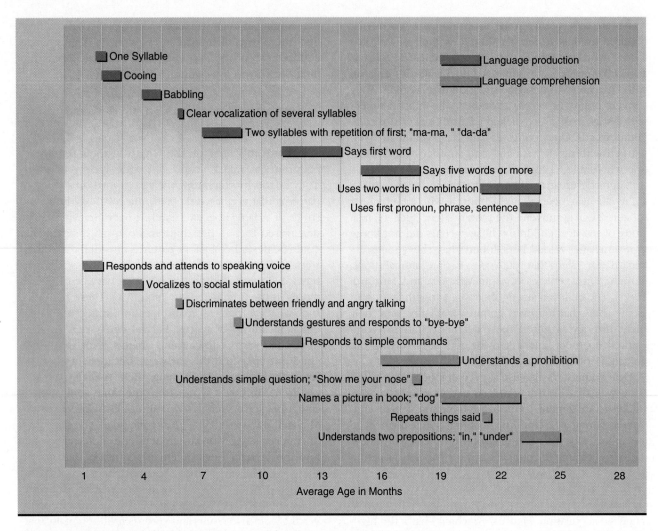

One Syllable
Cooing
Babbling
Clear vocalization of several syllables
Two syllables with repetition of first; "ma-ma, " "da-da"
Says first word
Says five words or more
Uses two words in combination
Uses first pronoun, phrase, sentence

Language production
Language comprehension

Responds and attends to speaking voice
Vocalizes to social stimulation
Discriminates between friendly and angry talking
Understands gestures and responds to "bye-bye"
Responds to simple commands
Understands a prohibition
Understands simple question; "Show me your nose"
Names a picture in book; "dog"
Repeats things said
Understands two prepositions; "in," "under"

1   4   7   10   13   16   19   22   25   28
Average Age in Months

Figure 7.3 Highlights of language development during the first two years of life. The ages shown are approximate, and the length of the bars reflects the age range that researchers have reported for the appearance of a particular linguistic advance. *(Adapted from Bayley, 1969; Lenneberg, 1967; McCarthy, 1954)*

between the two uses of "Baby chair" are absent. How, then, do children make their meaning clear?

They rely on two grammatical devices that are basic tools of human language: intonation and word order. As they did in the one-word stage, they use intonation to distinguish a statement from a question. Now they also use another intonational device: *stress*. This vocal emphasis easily distinguishes the two possible meanings of "Baby chair." If the little boy wanted to indicate possession, he would emphasize the first word, saying "*Baby* chair" ("That is baby's chair"). By emphasizing the second word, saying "Baby *chair*," he could convey location ("Baby is in the chair") or destination ("Put baby in

the chair"). The context of the utterance would indicate which he meant.

Instead of using their two-word limit in any order to produce a random collection of words, children combine their words in patterns that generally fit comfortably into the word order of English sentences (R. Brown, 1973). The typical English sentence follows a subject-verb-object word order, and many of children's early sequences conform to this order, which listeners find easy to follow. Such sequences include agent + action, agent + patient (recipient of action), and action + patient. Toddlers produce such sentences as "Daddy throw," "Daddy ball," and "Throw ball," and

TABLE 7.3   SEMANTIC PATTERNS IN TWO-WORD UTTERANCES*

REFERENCES		RELATIONS	
Meaning	**Example**	**Meaning**	**Example**
Identification (demonstrative + object)	That (it, there) + cat	Attributive (attribute + object)	Big + train, red + book
Notice (greeting + name)	Hi + mommy	Possessive (possessor + object)	Adam + checker
Recurrence	More ('nother) + milk	Locative 1 (object + location)	Sweater + chair
Nonexistence	Allgone (no more) + rattle	Locative 2 (action + location or goal)	Go + store
		Agent + action	Adam + put
		Agent + patient (recipient of action)	Mommy + sock
		Action + patient	Put + book

*These eleven patterns show the range of meanings expressed in two-word sentences.

Adapted from R. Brown, 1970; Maratsos, 1983.

they do not say "Throw Daddy" or "Ball throw." Yet children in this stage have not developed a general concept of word order, and each of their patterns follows its own separate rule. Once youngsters leave the two-word stage, the patterns come together and children grasp the general rules governing word order (Maratsos, 1983).

Although toddlers may not use a general rule in producing sentences, they seem to use one in interpreting the speech of others. When asked to act out simple sentences (such as "The cat kissed the dog"), in which word order is the only cue to meaning, children in the two-word stage correctly portray the sentence, making the cat—not the dog—the one who does the kissing (de Villiers and de Villiers, 1978).

The Tendency to Overregularize

Once children have figured out a rule, they may try to make the language more systematic than it actually is. In English, **overregularization** shows clearly when children use the past tense of verbs. The regular way to form the past tense for English verbs is to add -ed: walk,

walked. Yet many common verbs form their past tenses in an irregular manner: go, went; break, broke. Children often learn a number of the irregular past forms as separate words and produce correct sentences: "It broke"; "Daddy went out"; "I fell." After using these correct past-tense forms for many months, they discover the rule for forming regular past tenses. The irregular forms now may disappear from their speech, to be replaced by overregularized forms. The child of 3 or 4 may say, "It breaked"; "Daddy goed out"; "I falled."

As children get older, a curious pattern of redundant usage sometimes develops. Five- and six-year-olds may drop forms like "eated," "goed," and "maked" and in their place use a doubled past form, like "ated," "wented," and "maded" (Kuczaj, 1978). By the time children are 7, they will have nothing to do with the redundant form; most have ceased to overregularize the verb in any way.

What looks like regression in the younger children is actually a sign of progress in their analysis of language. Clearly, children have not heard the overregularized forms from their parents; instead, they construct the

By the age of 2½, children have left telegraphic speech behind them and, like this boy, have mastered enough language to advise grandpa on the construction of a toy.
(Elizabeth Crews/The Image Works)

forms to conform with the regularities they have noticed in the speech of others. And so a change from "went" to "goed" indicates that children have, on their own, discovered a regular pattern in English.

When children overregularize their speech, they often seem impervious to gentle efforts at correction, as the following conversation reported by Jean Berko Gleason (1967) shows:

> *Child: My teacher holded the baby*
> *rabbits and we patted them.*
> *Mother: Did you say your teacher*
> *held the baby rabbits?*
> *Child: Yes.*
> *Mother: What did you say she did?*
> *Child: She holded the baby rabbits*
> *and we patted them.*
> *Mother: Did you say she held them*
> *tightly?*
> *Child: No, she holded them loosely.*

Although his mother substituted the correct form of the verb twice in this short dialogue, the little boy persisted in repeating "holded" for *held*. In this case, regularity was more powerful than the child's immediate imitation of adult forms.

After analyzing longitudinal records of children's speech accumulated by various researchers, Gary Marcus and his colleagues (1992) reported that children are often inconsistent in their overregularizations and that they vary widely in levels of overregularization. Children are most likely to overregularize verbs that infrequently appear in their parents' speech and less likely to overregularize verbs that fall into families with their own rules (sting, stung; swing, swung; string, strung). The researchers propose that overregularization occurs when children forget the correct form and fall back on the language rule they have discovered for marking the past.

Thus, children may shift back and forth between correct and overregularized forms. Once children consistently say "held" instead of "holded," they may continue to say "goed" or "maked," because they eliminate over-regularization errors slowly. Children learn, one at a time, that only a single past-tense form exists for each irregular verb (Kuczaj, 1978).

Children also overregularize when forming plurals. English has some irregular plural forms, many of them common words: *feet, mice, men, children.* These irregular forms, like irregular-verb past-tense forms, must be learned as separate vocabulary items. Researchers have found that the child who has been correctly using irregular plural forms *(feet, men, mice)* may, for a time, overgeneralize the newly discovered rules of formation and say "foots," "mans," "mouses"—another example of the regularization that appears in the child's use of verbs. A child may even learn the irregular form but apply the plural rule anyway, saying the redundant "feets," "mens," "mices." Children also show their grasp of the plural rule by producing back formations, dropping the final *s* in a noun that requires it (Mervis and Johnson, 1991). They may say "plier" for *pliers,* "clipper" for *clippers,* or "pant" for *pants.*

Understanding Complex Constructions

Children's ability to understand and produce complex sentences develops slowly. At first they are unable to handle several language rules at once. As they acquire new constructions, they rely on their knowledge of the world and the immediate context to help them in the task. The gestures and actions of others often serve as clues to the meaning of their words. And because others generally talk about the immediate situation, children tend to apply whatever they have heard to some nearby object or event. This practice sometimes betrays them. For example, children assume that people talk about things in the order that they occur. So when a parent says, "Eat your pie after you eat your broccoli," children are likely to believe that they have been told to eat the dessert first. We can see children's gradual grasp of various constructions by looking at their acquisition of questions.

Children discover a great deal by asking questions that begin with *who, what, where, why, how,* and *how come.* Questions are more difficult than statements because the child must use two rules to produce the correct form. They not only must begin with the question word, but in all but one of these forms, they also must place the auxiliary verb immediately after their *wh-* word. (The exception is *how come,* in which the child

Because children begin asking about the world before they know the general rules for forming questions, they are likely to produce such queries as "Why Cathy is crying?" at the sight of a friend in distress. *(Rohn Engh/The Image Works)*

simply attaches the question words to the beginning of the statement: "How come Lauren is laughing?") If children are to use the *wh-* rules correctly, they must say, "Why is David crying?" or "When will Santa Claus come?" In most cases, this requires them to separate the auxiliary verb and the main verb by placing the noun between them—a violation of standard English word order.

Stanley Kuczaj and Nancy Brannick (1979) have traced the child's gradual grasp of these rules. In learning to ask questions, children begin by placing the *wh-* tag at the beginning of the sentence. Using this single rule produces correct *how come* questions, but fails with the others. Children say such things as "What he can ride in?" or "Who the girl will kiss?" This kind of construction is not surprising because youngsters hear it in their parents' speech—embedded in other sentences. For example, adults say, "Have you found out where you can catch the bus?" and "Did I tell you what he was singing?"

After using the incorrect form for a time, children realize that some adjustment is necessary, and they correctly place the auxiliary verb after the *wh-* tag—but only with *what* and *where.* Their *who, when, why,* and *how* questions are still incorrect. Apparently, children do not learn the second general rule all at once but begin by learning some of its specific applications (Kuczaj and Brannick, 1979). Once they understand the rule, however, they generalize it to all *wh-* questions, so their formerly correct *how come* questions now are wrong.

They produce such overregularizations as "How come can the dog sleep on the couch?" Just as with the acquisition of past tenses and plurals, children's language goes through a stage when it gets worse before it gets better.

Children do not proceed directly toward adult grammar. Instead, they construct and discard a variety of provisional grammars as they go along (Slobin, 1986). As a result of these changing strategies, sentences that are correctly interpreted at one age may be misinterpreted later. The rapidity with which children acquire language, developing and discarding rules as they go, indicates that human beings are born prepared to learn language but that extensive experience is needed for its acquisition. Exactly how children acquire a command of their native language is still a matter of debate. (The box, "Talking about Thinking," explores the role of cognitive development in the child's use of language.)

Explanations of Language Acquisition

From thousands of studies, we can piece together a convincing description of the child's dawning grasp of language. We know *what* happens, but no one yet has been able to provide a satisfactory explanation of *how* children acquire language. An adequate explanation must take into account the maturational, cognitive, and social

TALKING ABOUT THINKING

When children begin to contemplate their own knowledge and beliefs, they have taken a giant step in cognitive development. When they understand that others also carry out such contemplation, they have made another advance. Yet researchers have found it difficult to assess this aspect of the young child's development (Miscione et al., 1978). Although children begin using mental verbs, such as *think, know,* and *remember,* when they are about 2½ years old, these words often are conventional ways of holding the floor while a person decides what to say next ("you know") or of softening the edge of a request ("I think I'd like a cookie").

Marilyn Shatz, Henry Wellman, and Sharon Silber (1983) carried out two studies in which they monitored young children's speech and noted the context whenever a child used a verb that referred to mental processes. In the first study, they collected samples of a little boy's speech, taping Abe's conversation twice a day from the time he was 28 months old until he was 4 years old. In the second study, they regularly taped the conversations of thirty 2-year-olds over a six-month period.

The analysis showed that early in the third year of life, children begin using mental verbs but that at first the words do not refer to mental states or to mental processing. Until children are at least 30 months old, they use the terms to aid social interaction, as when they preface a remark with "Know what?" or tag a remark with "you know." Or they say "I don't know," which the researchers regarded as usually indicating a negative attitude. Children probably pick up these expressions long before they understand their derivation.

Once children begin referring to mental states, the verbs proliferate in their conversation (see the accompanying graph). Three-year-olds say such things as "I was testing you; I was *pretending* 'cept you didn't *know* that"; "The people *thought* Dracula was mean, but he was nice"; and "I *thought* there wasn't any socks, but when I looked I saw them." Shortly after children use words to refer to their own minds, children also use them to refer to the thoughts of others. Some researchers (for example, Shatz, 1983) contend that children cannot take part in a mature conversation until they understand that others also have beliefs, thoughts, and goals. According to Shatz and her colleagues, this important advance seems to occur near the child's third birthday.

One child's use of mental verbs. *(Information from Shatz, Wellman, and Silber, 1983)*

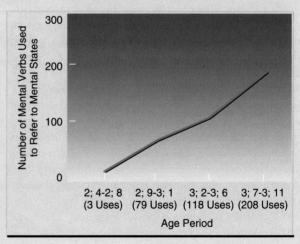

precursors of language; it must explain the diversity of children's first words, how children figure out the rules of syntax, and how early acquisition leads to the adult's mature command of language. For years, developmentalists veered between two explanations of language: the behavioristic and the biological. The first, said psychologist George Miller, was impossible; the second was miraculous (see Bruner, 1983). A third explanation, which stresses social and cognitive interaction, has tried to fill the gap between the impossible and the miraculous, but success remains elusive.

Behavioristic Theories

Behaviorists, among them B. F. Skinner (1957) and Sidney Bijou and Donald Baer (1965), see language as simply vocal behavior that is reinforced by the action of another person. Reinforcement occurs in many ways. Because mothers generally talk to babies while they care for them, using words to express affection, a mother's speech becomes reinforcing. Babies also can rein-

force themselves by listening to their own vocalizations. As they mature and gain control over their speech apparatus, babies begin to direct the sounds they produce, and the more closely their babbling resembles their mothers' speech, the more reinforcing their vocalizations become. When babies babble, their mothers often reward them with attention, thereby providing additional reinforcement.

When babies begin to label the objects in their world, their parents reinforce them with attention or approval. The reinforcement is for the sound itself, but the child soon responds to the sight of the object (ball, sock, doll) with the label. Other words are learned because the child receives tangible rewards for producing them, as when the words "cookie" or "bottle" are followed by the objects they represent.

How do children acquire rules for combining words? They learn patterns of words (such as "the boy's X," "on the X," or "hit the X") into which they can insert new items. These patterns, called **grammatical frames,** function in sentences just as sounds function in words.

According to behaviorists, reinforcement is a powerful tool in language acquisition; for labeling the "light," this 13-month-old will probably be reinforced by her parent's attention and approval. *(Laura Dwight)*

Children build sentences out of grammatical frames, a process that allows them to produce sentences that are different from the sentences they hear. Gradually, children accumulate a patchwork of thousands of separately acquired frames, patterns, responses, and rules. On this base, they develop language by making small generalizations, inferences, and analogies (Whitehurst, 1982).

Social-learning theorists would add that imitation plays a major role in the acquisition of speech and that both comprehension and speech are based on observational learning (Bandura, 1977). Parents (and others) serve as models for children, who imitate the speech they hear. They imitate grammatical frames as well as vocabulary, substituting their own words in frames they have heard others use. As noted in Chapter 2, imitation does not have to be immediate. A child can learn by observing and imitating the forms of adult speech when a later occasion warrants it. When a small girl says, "I seed two mouses," says Albert Bandura, she is modeling structures she has heard in the speech of others—but modeling them "too well." Indeed, some social-learning theorists have summed up children's acquisition of language as "delayed selective imitation" (Whitehurst and Vasta, 1975).

Critics make three basic arguments against behaviorist views of language acquisition. First, the process of reinforcement is too slow to explain the rapidity with which children acquire language. Second, there is little evidence that parents reinforce their children for producing passable syntax. Although parents often correct gross errors in a child's choice of words or pronunciation, they usually are more interested in the truth of an utterance than in its syntax (R. Brown, 1973). If there is no relation between children's syntax and patterns of reinforcement, it seems unlikely that their language is simply reinforced behavior, as behaviorists maintain. Third, children play an active and creative role in language acquisition, as their invention of new words indicates, but reinforcement is a passive process.

Biological Theories

Given the problems with the "impossible" theory of language acquisition, what about the "miraculous" theory? In biological approaches, language development is primarily a matter of maturation because, according to linguist Noam Chomsky (1975, 1979), the structure of language is laid down in our genes. He calls this innate capacity a **language acquisition device (LAD)** and believes that it allows children to speak just as wings allow birds to fly. All human languages, despite their surface differences, share an underlying deep structure, which he calls a *universal grammar*. This grammar consists of principles, conditions, and rules for producing sound, meaning, and structure. The grammatical categories of subject, predicate, object, and verb are part of this universal grammar.

Because biological constraints characterize the grammar children will construct, they take the bits and pieces of language they hear, analyze them, and fit them to the universal grammar. Only in this way, says Chomsky, can we explain how children in a given community—each hearing entirely different and mostly fragmentary language—come up with the same rich, complex language system. In this view, language is partly predetermined, in the same way that genes determine the pattern of sexual maturation, and—given experience—children inevitably acquire language.

If Chomsky is correct, then children do not use the same cognitive mechanisms to learn language that are used to acquire other cognitive skills, such as mathematics or logic (R. Siegler, 1991). Some evidence supports the position that language is special (Maratsos, 1989). Children everywhere and in every level of society acquire language at about the same time. The desire to learn language is so deeply embedded in human beings that language acquisition is self-motivating. Language processing (for both speech and sign language) is localized in particular areas of the brain's left hemisphere, and damage to various regions of the left hemisphere affect language in different ways.

This localization of language has led to the assumption that brain maturation is deeply involved in language acquisition. According to Eric Lenneberg (1967), language can be acquired only during a sensitive period in human development. The period begins when children are about 2 years old and lasts until they reach sexual maturity. At that time, the ability to learn a language declines, and by the late teens it is difficult—or even impossible—to acquire a first language. The end of the sensitive period, said Lenneberg (1973), coincides with the maturation of the brain; the mature brain has lost its plasticity and can no longer make the adjustments that the acquisition of language requires.

Some researchers believe that the case of Genie, a California girl who grew up in almost total isolation, indicates that a weakened version of Lenneberg's claim may be true (Curtiss, 1977). Genie was discovered when she was nearly 14, and her social experiences had been limited to spoon feeding by her almost blind mother. No one spoke to her, and whenever she made a noise, her father beat her. When Genie was found, she was severely disturbed and had no language. Although she slowly learned to understand the language of others, the syntax of her own language was impaired. After several years, Genie still lacked many basic linguistic structures, such as passive sentences and *wh-* questions. Yet some aspects of Genie's development fail to support biological theories. Her speech is rule-governed and productive, and she can speak of people and objects that are not present. Genie's sharply restricted childhood, however, also affected her cognitive development. Her store of the concepts and world knowledge on which children build their language was so limited that this restriction, together with her emotional disturbance, may explain her problems with language.

Social-Cognitive Interaction Theories

The interaction approach to language acquisition agrees with the biological contention that maturation is vital and that until children reach a certain cognitive level, they cannot acquire language. It also agrees with the behaviorist contention that social interaction is the place to look for the emergence of language. But interaction theorists maintain that innate mechanisms cannot, by themselves, explain the child's grasp of language. The basis for linguistic competence goes beyond conditioning and observational learning to include nonlinguistic aspects of human interaction: turn-taking, mutual gazing, joint attention, context, assumptions, and cultural conventions. The forms of language are acquired so that children can carry out communicative functions (Bates, 1979). Children are motivated to learn language not because they have some innate language propensity but because they can do useful and wondrous things with it: get attractive items they want, receive assistance with tasks, and acquire the information needed to predict and control events (Bandura, 1986).

Investigators with these interactionist views see general cognitive development and pragmatics as the keys to language development in a child. They point out that until children reach a certain stage of cognitive development, language is impossible. Children must be able to perceive speech elements, recognize and remember sequential structures, abstract rules from various instances of speech, and select the appropriate words and rules to form utterances (Bandura, 1986). Interactionists also maintain that the nonlinguistic aspects of babies' social interactions build the prespeech bases of language (Bruner, 1983; Moerk, 1989). Instead of unfolding from preprogrammed language behavior, language is the product of the child's active interaction with an environment provided by other human beings. As Jean Berko Gleason and Sandra Weintraub (1978) point out, cognitive development can result from interaction with the physical world, but children cannot acquire language merely through simple exposure to it as passive listeners.

Children communicate before they use language, and they understand other people and the world before they have words to express themselves. Indeed, without a store of nonlinguistic knowledge, children would have no basis from which to guess about meanings of words or to figure out the rules for arranging them. Figuring out the rules may require quiet, unemotional reflection. In a longitudinal study (Bloom and Capatides, 1987), the age at which toddlers entered the naming explosion was related to the amount of time the children spent in a quiet, alert, attentive state. Two-year-olds who frequently expressed their emotions (even though most of those emotions were happiness or joy) lagged behind others in language development.

Finally, the quality of children's social interaction may affect the acquisition of language. Earlier, we saw that language development was accelerated in babies whose mothers called their attention to objects in the world. Other research indicates that abused toddlers lag behind other youngsters in vocabulary, knowledge of syntax, and functional communication (Coster et al., 1989).

Will we ever have a satisfactory explanation of language development? Michael Maratsos (1983) believes that our knowledge of language acquisition is in a transitional state. He suggests that some of our most important findings either do not fit any of the current theories or do not seem relevant to them. His advice seems to be to check back again in a few years. In the meantime, some variety of the interactionist approach may be the most promising (Bohannon and Warren-Leubecker, 1985; Moerk, 1989). Because interactionist theories borrow freely from other major approaches, they give us the broadest available view of language acquisition.

SUMMARY

GETTING READY TO TALK

During the first year, the baby's vocal tract changes in shape and structure, and areas of the cortex involved with language mature. From birth, babies can detect slight distinctions between sounds that are critical to the perception of speech, and within a few months they respond to changes in intonation and stress. Babies go through five overlapping stages in their production of prelinguistic sounds. **Cooing** first appears at about 8 weeks. Around 9 months, when babies enter the fifth stage, they use **expressive jargon.**

Very early, babies grasp the **pragmatic** aspect of language. During interactions with their parents, babies learn to produce **speech acts** and to follow many of the conventions of language use, including turn-taking. Without some exposure to **motherese,** infants might never become competent speakers. Among the cognitive precursors to language are object permanence, the development of concepts, delayed imitation, symbolic play, and the development of intent. The cognitive precursors culminate in the baby's awareness of **semantics.**

EARLY UTTERANCES

At first, infants speak in **holophrases,** and these simple utterances can be understood only in context. **Overextension** is fairly common among young children. In learning new words, children follow two general rules: (1) prefer categories, and (2) a word usually refers to one thing. Children often coin new words to fill gaps in their vocabulary.

PUTTING WORDS TOGETHER

Two-word utterances are called **telegraphic speech.** Children in the two-word stage combine their two words in patterns that are based on semantic relations; these utterances do not follow the general rules of English **syntax.** Children in this stage have begun to use stress to express meaning.

As children acquire language rules, their language is marked by **overregularization.** Asking questions follows a gradual course. First, children simply place the *wh-* tag at the beginning of a sentence. Then they begin using the auxiliary verb after the tag, learning to do so through specific instances.

EXPLANATIONS OF LANGUAGE ACQUISITION

Behavioristic theories assert that language is simply vocal behavior reinforced by the action of others. Rules are acquired as children learn word patterns, known as **grammatical frames.** Social-learning theorists add observational learning and imitation to the behavioristic account.

Biological theories of language acquisition, such as the theory proposed by Noam Chomsky, assert that language development is largely a matter of brain maturation and that biological constraints characterize the universal grammar that underlie all languages. Chomsky calls the innate language capacity a **language acquisition device (LAD).**

Social-cognitive interaction theorists agree that maturation is important but assert that nonlinguistic aspects of human interaction are equally important and that language is acquired for its pragmatic function. None of these theories yet provides a satisfactory explanation of language development, but some sort of interaction theory gives the broadest available view.

KEY TERMS

cooing	motherese	semantics
expressive jargon	overextension	speech act
grammatical frames	overregularization	syntax
holophrase	pragmatics	telegraphic speech
language acquisition device (LAD)		

8

. . . .

SOCIAL DEVELOPMENT: BECOMING A PERSON

SOCIAL DEVELOPMENT: BECOMING A PERSON

• • • • • • • • • • • • • • •

Thirteen-month-old Christine Nowicki and her 3-year-old sister, Kate, wake up each morning at six and eat breakfast with their orthodontist father in the kitchen. Later their mother comes in, picks up Christine, and holds her while she talks with Kate about the coming day. When the housekeeper arrives, mother leaves for her own dental practice. In the Nowicki family, father takes care of morning child-care duties, and mother takes over in the evening (Shreve, 1984).

● ● ● ● ● ●

Only 20 years ago, the Nowicki family would have been considered an oddity. Even then, however, about one-third of all married mothers of children younger than 3 years old worked. The employed mother has become such a fixture in American society that today almost 57 percent of married mothers of *infants* are in the labor force—more than double the rate of 24 percent that prevailed in 1970. Today, the unusual mother is not the one who goes out to work but the one who stays home with her children (L. Hoffman, 1989). The American family has moved so far from its traditional image that our old views of infancy and early childhood may need radical change.

This chapter examines the beginnings of social development in infants and toddlers. We start by tracing the development of the baby's first social bond with primary caregivers and discover that this attachment can take different forms. After considering the effects of caregiver deprivation, we investigate class, ethnic, and cultural differences in child care and the question of substitute care. Next we turn to the baby's developing sociability, examining the emergence of self-concept and how it affects empathy and the control of emotions. Then we consider the way that early social interactions encourage independence in boys and dependence in girls. Finally, we watch the baby become a social toddler and note the influence of peers and siblings on this development. Throughout the chapter, we examine ways in which the important lessons of the child's first few years lay the groundwork for later development.

The Development of Attachment

Human babies are born prepared by millions of years of primate evolution to respond to the sights and sounds of people and to behave in ways that elicit responses from them. Developmentalists who take an ethological view, among them John Bowlby (1969) and Mary Ainsworth (Ainsworth et al., 1978), have argued that the baby's inborn tendencies, such as crying or fussing when distressed, keep adults nearby and so help the baby to survive. Adults, in turn, have been prepared by evolution to respond to the baby's signals, providing care and giving the infant opportunities for social interaction.

These tendencies seem to be the foundation of complex systems of social behavior that begin in the family. In most cultures, mothers and infants are involved for a time in a close symbiotic relationship in which the child is almost an extension of the mother's being. For this reason, many investigators have concentrated on the development of **attachment,** the special bond between infant and caregiver, usually the mother.

Our understanding of the development and consequences of attachment is heavily indebted to research with animals, and such research has dispelled some early assumptions about the nature of the bond. For many years, psychoanalysts and learning theorists assumed that babies develop close bonds with their caregivers because the caregiver satisfies the baby's physical needs. J. P. Scott (1962) noted that this assumption leads us to an unromantic conclusion: infants love us only because we feed them. Research with monkeys has demonstrated, however, that there is more to attachment than being fed. In a series of studies by Harry F. Harlow and Margaret Harlow (1966, 1969), infant monkeys grew up in cages with two surrogate mothers. One mother substitute was covered with soft terry cloth; the other, equipped with a feeding mechanism, was made of hard wire mesh. If feeding were the major factor in attachment, the infant monkeys would have become attached to the wire mother, which fed them. But the monkeys spent much more time clinging to the cloth mother, which gave them no nourishment at all.

The monkeys seemed genuinely attached to the cloth mother. When monkeys raised with these artificial mothers were put in a strange place or when frightening objects were placed near them, they ran to the security of the cloth, not the wire, mother. Clinging to the cloth mother seemed to calm their fears. Eventually, the monkeys used the cloth mother as a base for exploring the world, leaving to investigate strange objects but often returning to cling to their soft, snuggly mother, as monkeys raised with real mothers do. The wire mothers were never used in this way.

Baby monkeys may have become attached to the terry-cloth mother because contact is important to the formation of attachment in monkeys. At birth, young monkeys must cling to their mothers if they are to survive. When the mother travels or flees from danger, she uses her arms and hands, and the baby rides with her by clinging to her body. A soft terry-cloth mother encourages such clinging, but a cold, hard wire mother does not. The difference between these mothers has lasting effects. After a year's separation, a monkey will run to embrace its terry-cloth mother, holding on passionately to the soft form. But after a similar separation from its wire mother, a monkey shows no affection at all when they are reunited.

Contact comfort may be as important to humans as it is to other primates, but we have no way of being certain. The survival of human babies does not depend on clinging to a mother who is bounding from tree to tree. Despite the species difference, however, the Harlows' research has cast valuable light on the importance of attachment in development. But monkeys need more than a soft, cuddly form to develop properly. In later research, the Harlows showed that even the monkeys reared by a cloth mother were not good mothers to their own babies (Arling and Harlow, 1967). They would not mate and, when artificially inseminated, would not care for their offspring.

The Stages of Attachment

Attachment in people and in monkeys follows a similar pattern (see Table 8.1), but the response of the human baby to his or her mother develops more slowly than the monkey's attachment to its mother. In human beings, the bond takes many months to appear, involves

TABLE 8.1   STAGES OF ATTACHMENT

Age	Stage	Description
Birth to 2 months	I	**Indiscriminate social responsiveness** (accepts comfort from anyone)
2 to 7 months	II	**Discriminate social responsiveness** (prefers familiar figures but does not protest when parents leave)
7 to 30 months Around 8 months Around 10 months	III	**Specific attachment** **A. Separation distress** (is distressed when separated from caregiver; attempts to follow) **B. Stranger wariness or anxiety** (has aversion to unfamiliar person who seeks proximity)
From 30 months onward	IV	**Goal-directed partnership** (is no longer distressed at caregiver's departure; can work toward shared goals)

a complex intermeshing of behavior between infant and caregiver, and assumes widely different forms.

Attachment in human babies refers to the early emotional relationship between the baby and the caregiver (usually one or both parents). Babies show this bond by reacting in characteristic ways. They smile and greet the caregiver joyously; when the caregiver leaves, they often cry. A crucial aspect of behavior that signifies attachment is that it is directed toward some people and not toward others.

A baby's earliest responses to people are indiscriminate and do not reflect attachment. This impartial, indiscriminate stage of responsiveness lasts for about the first two months of life. During this time, the baby's cries bring milk, dry diapers, an end to physical discomfort; they also bring the pleasures of close human contact. But the baby accepts such aid and comfort from anyone. Toward the end of this period, the baby becomes a social being, smiling and cooing. Because these coos and social smiles are directed toward anyone, it appears that their onset is primarily controlled by maturation.

During the next stage of attachment, which lasts from 2 months until about 7 months, babies begin to discriminate among the people around them (see Figure 8.1). At 5 months, they may smile at familiar faces as often as they did before, but the smiling at strangers that was so prevalent at about 2 or 3 months drops

Figure 8.1   During the first few months, most infants prefer not to be separated from the person they are with, regardless of who that person is. Such *indiscriminate attachments* begin to decline at about the same time that an infant starts to show preferences for specific persons, usually the primary caregiver. *(Adapted from Schaffer and Emerson, 1964)*

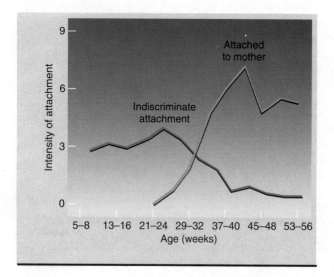

off and even disappears. Gradually, the baby comes to recognize those people who consistently relieve his or her distress. At the sight of their faces, the baby feels an upsurge of positive emotion and responds socially, with bright-eyed smiles, coos, and arm-waving. Although at this stage babies may respond in special ways to specific people, they probably have not developed a true attachment to a caregiver. If parents leave a 5-month-old baby with a sitter, for example, the baby is unlikely to protest.

By the time they are 8 months old, most babies have developed the intense bond that signifies true attachment. This third stage generally begins at about 7 months and lasts until the infant is 2 or 2½ years old. Before true attachment can emerge, the baby must realize not only that the same people react to his or her needs in the same predictable ways but also that people continue to exist after they disappear from view. Most babies are aware of their mothers as objects that continue to exist when out of sight slightly before the babies show a similar awareness of the continued existence of physical objects (S. Bell, 1970). Although person permanence may not always appear before object permanence (Levitt, Antonucci, and Clark, 1984), it seems likely that the baby pays particular attention to the location of the human caregiver. After all, the activities of this very important "object" are closely associated with the satisfaction of the baby's needs.

Some time after their second birthday, toddlers stop showing visible distress each time their mothers leave. They have entered the fourth, and enduring, stage of attachment, which begins around 2½ years of age. In this mature attachment, the original relationship becomes a partnership as the child comes to understand the caregiver's feelings and motives. The emotional bond remains strong, and the child still wants to be near the parent, but give-and-take has entered the relationship. The child now can use words and hugs and other devices in an attempt to influence the parent's plans. But when parents leave, the child continues to feel secure, as long as he or she knows where the parents have gone and when they are likely to return.

In their studies of attachment, researchers have focused on the third stage, when infants are distressed at a caregiver's absence. This unhappiness generally shows itself in separation distress and stranger wariness.

Separation Distress

When a mother leaves her 10-month-old baby in an unfamiliar place, the baby is likely to cry and stop playing. When the mother leaves, the baby may reach for her and, if able, may crawl in pursuit of her. Such a reaction to an attachment figure is called **separation distress.** Although the adaptive function of attachment is to keep the infant alive, the bond also provides the baby with emotional security. Because an attachment figure is a secure base for the baby, the figure's presence prevents or reduces any fear the baby may experience when confronted with an unusual situation.

Separation distress appears to be a universal phenomenon, although it may emerge at slightly different ages in various cultures. Babies in Uganda, for example, begin to protest as early as 6 months when separated from their mothers (Ainsworth, 1967), but most Guatemalan babies do not object until they are 9 months old (Lester et al., 1974). In all cultures that have been studied, separation distress is apparent by 8 or 9 months and remains high until about 18 months, when it begins to decline (Kagan, 1984).

When they find themselves in a strange situation, most 9- to 12-month-old babies become concerned if their primary caregivers are not nearby. In a strange place, a baby's first action is to establish contact with his or her caregiver. After a time, the baby ventures out on short forays to explore the strange environment but always returns to the caregiver between expeditions (Lamb et al., 1985). Most of us are familiar with this concern on the part of older infants and toddlers. When a mother brings her toddler on a first visit to a friend's home, for example, the young child may cling to (or even hide behind) the parent. Only after the child becomes accustomed to the new setting is she or he likely to let go of mother's leg. Young monkeys behave similarly; whether reared normally or with a cloth surrogate mother, they venture forth only gradually from the physical security of their mothers.

Yet an attachment figure does more than act as a secure haven. The presence of the attachment figure allows babies to maintain their emotional bonds, learn about the world by observing the caregiver's actions, and exchange information they discover on their expeditions (Hay, 1980). When placed in a novel situation, infants who follow the separation-and-return pattern show no apparent distress. In one study (Rheingold and Eckerman, 1970), infants seemed to share joy and excitement with their attachment figures. Babies apparently use attachment figures both to reduce their fear and to share in the pleasure of life, and the same general pattern of behavior seems to serve both purposes.

Wariness of Strangers

The baby's wariness of strangers usually develops a month or two after specific attachments emerge. **Stran-**

ger wariness appears to be a natural reaction that complements attachment and helps the baby avoid situations, people, or objects that might endanger life. Babies' reactions to strangers appear to pass through four phases. At first, there seems to be no difference in babies' emotional responses to strangers and familiar persons. Later, babies respond positively to strangers, although not as positively as they do to people they know. Then they go through a period of reacting uneasily to strangers; if an attachment figure is present, they look back and forth between the stranger and the caregiver. At this time, babies merely become sober and stare at the stranger. The final phase, in which some babies respond to strangers with fear and withdrawal, looking away, frowning, whimpering, or even crying, does not appear until babies are about 8 months old. This reaction is particularly intense when the baby's attachment figure is absent (Sroufe, Waters, and Matas, 1974).

When a stranger approaches, the caregiver's reaction (expression, tone of voice, and gestures) may either reassure the baby or increase wariness. For example, when mothers of 9-month-old infants frowned at an approaching stranger and said "hello" in an abrupt and unfriendly tone, the babies reacted warily. Their hearts speeded up, their smiles disappeared, and some of them were visibly distressed. But when the mothers smiled at both baby and stranger and said "hello" in a cheerful, friendly tone, the babies relaxed. Their hearts slowed, many of them smiled, and fewer showed any signs of distress (Boccia and Campos, 1983).

The way a stranger approaches also influences babies' reactions. Most babies become fearful if a stranger arrives and immediately reaches for them, touches them, or picks them up. When babies are given time to evaluate the stranger, however, many show little distress. As Mary Anne Trause (1977) found, if a stranger pauses before walking up to a year-old baby, the baby may smile, but if the stranger walks over rapidly, the infant probably will frown, turn away, or even burst into tears.

A stranger's sex, appearance, and manner affect the baby's reaction, but so do the surroundings. In lab experiments, where strangers act out a rigid script, babies show more wariness or fear than they do when the stranger interacts naturally with them. Babies are much less likely to show wariness in their own homes. In a longitudinal study (Tracy, Lamb, and Ainsworth, 1976), researchers observed babies in their own homes from the time they were 3 weeks old until they were more than a year old. Once the babies began to crawl, they tended to follow their mothers from place to place and to play comfortably in the presence of strangers. Al-

Young babies' positive response to strangers gives way to wariness as the attachment bond develops. *(The Photo Works)*

though no baby at any age ever followed a stranger, few cried or showed other distress at a stranger's approach. The psychologist's laboratory is a strange and perhaps frightening place to a baby. Its strangeness may explain why babies explore and vocalize less in the lab than they do at home.

The Security of Attachment

Babies become attached to their mothers, their fathers, their siblings, and their substitute caregivers, but the nature of the bond is not always the same. For at least thirty years, researchers have been studying characteristics of caregiver, baby, and culture that might affect the

way attachment develops. Some infants seem to derive more security from an attachment figure than others do, an observation that has led researchers to study the quality of the attachment relationship.

Security in the Strange Situation

The most popular means of assessment has been the **Strange Situation** design, an experimental setting devised by Mary Ainsworth and her associates (Ainsworth et al., 1978) (see Table 8.2). This design assumes that evidence of attachment appears when babies are under stress, and so the experiment places them in a series of eight increasingly stressful episodes that evoke separation distress or stranger wariness.

Studies using the Strange Situation have discerned three major kinds of attachment: secure, avoidant, and resistant (Ainsworth et al., 1978). Infants with a **secure attachment** seem comfortable in a strange place as long as their mothers are nearby. At first they react pleasantly to a stranger's approach, but they are clearly distressed when their mothers leave. When their mothers return, these babies actively seek them out, and the contact quickly ends the distress. About two-thirds of babies react in this way. The rest, who are less securely attached, fall into two roughly equal groups. Infants in the first group, who have an **avoidant attachment,** seem almost oblivious to their mothers' presence. They explore without checking back; they show no distress when their mothers leave; and when their mothers return, the babies do not seek contact with them. They seem almost too independent. Infants in the second group, who have a **resistant attachment** (also called an *ambivalent attachment*), seem distressed throughout the procedure. Although their mothers are present, the strange room and the stranger both disturb them, and they stay close to their mothers' sides. They are extremely upset when their mothers leave, but when their mothers return they either continue to cry and fuss, become passive, or show ambivalence. They may alternate between seeking contact (perhaps holding out their arms to their mothers) and angrily squirming to get away when picked up. A few babies do not seem to fit any of these categories. When placed in the Strange Situation, they show dazed or confused behavior during reunions. These babies have thus been described as having a **disorganized attachment** (Main, Kaplan, and Cassidy, 1985). Which type of attachment bond develops appears to depend on an interaction among the caregiver's style of relating to the baby, the baby's temperament, and cultural expectations and practices.

TABLE 8.2   THE STRANGE SITUATION

Episode	Persons Present	Duration	Action
1	Mother, baby, observer	30 sec	Observer introduces mother and baby to experimental room, then leaves.
2	Mother, baby	3 min	Mother sits quietly while baby explores.
3	Stranger, mother, baby	3 min	Stranger enters, is silent for 1 min, talks with mother for 1 min, then approaches baby. After third minute, mother leaves.
4*	Stranger, baby	3 min	First separation episode.
5†	Mother, baby	3 min	First reunion episode. After baby is settled, mother leaves.
6*	Baby alone	3 min	Second separation episode.
7*	Stranger, baby	3 min	Stranger enters.
8	Mother, baby	3 min	Second reunion episode. Stranger leaves quietly after mother enters.

*If the baby is unduly distressed when left alone or with a stranger (Episodes 4, 6, and 7), the episode is cut short.
†If the baby requires more time to calm down and begin playing, Episode 5 is prolonged.

Source: Adapted from Ainsworth et al., 1978.

Factors That Affect Attachment

What is it about a *caregiver's style of interaction* that affects the quality of a baby's attachment? Ainsworth believed that a mother's sensitivity to her infant's needs was vital to the development of a secure attachment, and research continues to support this finding (D. Pederson et al., 1990). Among babies of poor, unmarried mothers, those who developed secure attachments tended to have mothers who were cooperative with them and sensitive to their needs (Egeland and Farber, 1984). After reviewing a number of longitudinal studies, Michael Lamb and his colleagues (1985) concluded that securely attached babies generally had mothers who were warm, responsive, not intrusive, and not abusive. Insecurely attached babies generally had mothers who lacked some or all of these qualities.

In trying to link these maternal qualities with the attachment bond, we might note that warm mothers show affection freely, often touch their infants tenderly, smile a good deal, and talk to them. Responsive mothers are dependable about answering their babies' cries of distress and pleas for attention—and they are quick to

do so. Sensitive mothers are accurate at reading their babies' signals, whether calls for assistance or signs of fatigue, fear, or a desire to play. Nonintrusive mothers are likely to cooperate with their babies' efforts to accomplish a new goal—even when the goal of a 1-year-old is to spoon in the oatmeal all by herself. And, of course, nonabusive mothers do not abuse their infants—either physically or psychologically. Among a group of infants who had been abused or neglected, only 29 percent of the 12-month-olds and 23 percent of the 18-month-olds were securely attached to their mothers (Schneider-Rosen et al., 1985). All the maternal qualities that are linked with secure attachment are likely to make a baby feel trusting, less fearful, and more secure.

When Swedish researchers looked at mothers of insecurely attached babies, they discovered that resistant babies tended to have intrusive mothers who seemed inconsistent in their interactions, perhaps because their actions were geared more to their own needs than to the needs of their babies (Bohlin et al., 1989). Perhaps resistant babies have learned that they cannot predict what their mothers will do. At times, the mother is re-

Babies with secure attachments tend to have caregivers who are warm, responsive, not intrusive, and not abusive. *(David Young Wolff/Photo Edit)*

sponsive and warm; at other times, she is unresponsive and rebuffs them. Consequently, they aren't certain whether they can depend on her for comfort. Avoidant babies tended to have mothers who were slow to respond to their social overtures and who provided little satisfying physical contact. Perhaps avoidant babies have learned that their mothers dispense coldness instead of a warm welcome.

Some researchers believe that *the baby's temperament* is as important as the mother's style of interaction in its effect on the security of attachment (H. Goldsmith and Alansky, 1987). Most avoidant babies in the Swedish study, for example, tended to be highly active, intense infants. Other researchers have found that babies who later developed resistant attachments often were less alert and active as newborns and seemed to develop

more slowly, both physically and mentally, than other babies (Egeland and Farber, 1984). They were less sociable than other babies and may have been more difficult to care for.

A baby's temperament is not, however, *directly related* to attachment. Temperament, as rated by parents, shows no relationship to the security of the attachment bond (R. Thompson, 1986). The effect of temperament on attachment seems to depend on the goodness of fit between the baby's temperament and the mother's personality and behavior. Some babies, for example, are especially prone to distress. When placed in the Strange Situation, they burst into tears. If these babies have rigid mothers who value control and are unwilling to take risks, they tend to develop insecure attachments. Yet babies who are just as prone to distress tend to develop secure attachments if their mothers are flexible women who are somewhat impulsive (Mangelsdorf et al., 1990).

Until recently, many researchers assumed that the Strange Situation was a fairly accurate means of assessing any baby's attachment bond. But research indicates that a *culture's child-rearing practices* affect the way babies react during the Strange Situation. In Japan, mothers encourage their babies to be dependent and rarely leave them with a sitter. Because they are never left alone with strangers, babies in traditional Japanese families find the Strange Situation highly stressful (Takahashi, 1990). They become so upset that a large proportion react as resistant babies do, but almost none show avoidant attachments (Miyake, Chen, and Campos, 1985).

In Germany, mothers try to promote independence and obedience in their children. They are less likely than American mothers to pick up a crying infant and, once babies begin to crawl, are more likely to discourage them from staying nearby. It is not surprising, then, that in the Strange Situation about half of the German babies react as avoidant babies do (Grossmann et al., 1985). Later in the chapter, we will see how changes in child-rearing practices may affect the response of American babies in the Strange Situation.

Attachment and Later Personality

If secure attachment to a mother has important effects on a baby's social development, we might expect to find its effects persisting past infancy. Some investigators have found such a connection and believe that babies with secure attachments are likely to become competent, independent children. In one study (Matas,

Because Japanese mothers tend to foster dependency in their children, most Japanese infants find the Strange Situation highly stressful. *(Mark S. Wexler/Woodfin Camp & Associates)*

Arend, and Sroufe, 1978), toddlers with a history of secure attachment attacked a series of increasingly difficult problems with an enthusiasm rarely shown by toddlers who earlier had been rated as having insecure attachments. Similar results appeared among a group of 3-year-olds who played a game in their homes with a stranger (Lutkenhaus, Grossmann, and Grossmann, 1985). The game was a race to build a tower by stacking wooden rings on a peg. Securely attached youngsters (as rated at 12 months) began the game without hesitation and increased their effort when they fell behind. Insecurely attached youngsters were hesitant to start and tended to slow down or give up when they fell behind.

The links between secure attachment and later competence have been traced even further. Among a group of 4-year-olds, those with secure attachments during infancy were self-reliant children who sought their teachers' assistance only when a task was clearly beyond their capabilities (Sroufe, Fox, and Pancake, 1983). Four-year-olds with a history of insecure attachment behaved quite differently. They seemed to need frequent contact, approval, and attention from their nursery school teachers and clung to them closely. By the age of 10, those with secure histories tended to be self-confident, independent, and competent, whereas those who had been insecurely attached tended to be dependent and were more likely to be socially isolated (Sroufe and Jacobvitz, 1989).

Such behavior is not necessarily *caused* by insecure early attachments, but it is predicted by the nature of the early relationship (Sroufe, Fox, and Pancake, 1983). Behavior reflects the nature of the child's continuing relationship with caregivers. Unless the nature of the relationship changes, it continues to affect the child's development through the daily behavior of the mother and the child's interactions with her. In the study of 2-year-olds who worked a series of problems, for example, mothers of securely attached infants offered hints when their children reached a difficult problem (Matas, Arend, and Sroufe, 1978). Their hints were subtle enough to allow the children to feel that they had solved the problem themselves. In contrast, most mothers of insecurely attached infants allowed their children to become frustrated before they offered help, and then the mothers often solved the problem themselves.

Attachment to Fathers

In traditional two-parent families, most fathers spent little time with their young babies. So for a long while, fathers were regarded as relatively unimportant in their children's early development. As fewer families meet the definition of the traditional family, in which the father is the sole wage earner and the mother stays in the home, more fathers are taking part in child care. When researchers began to look at fathers and babies, they found that infants become attached to both parents at about the same time, although the nature of the attachment to each parent may be somewhat different (Parke, 1981).

The quality of babies' attachment to their fathers may vary, just as it does with mothers. Although the security of an infant's attachment tends to be similar with each parent (N. Fox, Kimmerly, and Schafer, 1991), some infants are securely attached to one parent and insecurely attached to the other. When this occurs, the secure attachment is as likely to be with the father as with the mother (Main and Weston, 1981). Among a group of 20-month-olds, most of those who were securely attached to their fathers had fathers who were sensitive to the toddler's needs, were not aggravated by the child, and were unruffled by their lack of knowledge about child rearing (Easterbrooks and Goldberg, 1984).

A father's attachment to his baby can be just as deep as that of a mother. Fathers make nurturant, competent caregivers, and they can become intensely involved with their babies. Even so, fathers' daily interactions with their babies differ sharply from the nature of the babies' interactions with their mothers (Parke and Tinsley, 1988). Perhaps because mothers are usually responsible for most child care, mothers generally pick up their babies to care for them. When fathers pick them up, it is usually to play. Mothers' play with their babies is highly verbal and includes such traditional games as peekaboo and pat-a-cake; fathers engage in rough-and-tumble play, regardless of the infant's sex (Radin, 1986). Yet fathers do distinguish between sons and daughters: they tumble boys more than girls, laugh more with them, and are more likely to feed and diaper a son than a daughter. Once babies reach their first birthdays, fathers spend more time with them.

An increasing, but still limited, number of fathers have assumed the responsibility of infant care. This shift in society has led researchers to wonder whether fathers who play the traditional maternal role behave differently from other fathers. Researchers have discovered that fathers who are primary caregivers are just as sensitive to their babies' needs as are mothers but that

Although fathers are warm, nurturant caregivers, their style of interaction with their babies differs from that of most mothers. *(Rhoda Sidney/Stock, Boston)*

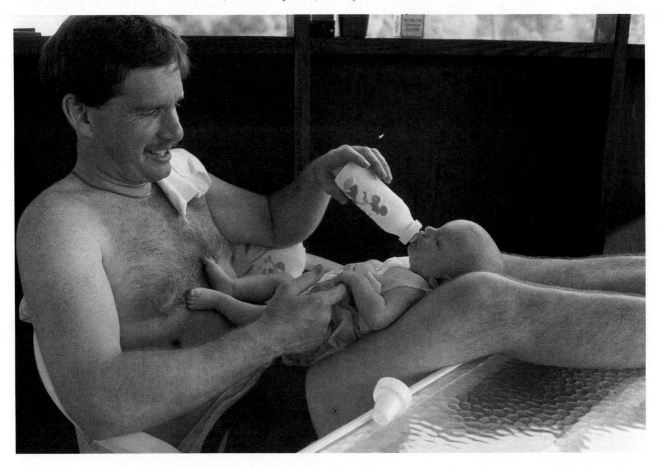

fathers seem to bring the fast-paced, exciting nature of playtime to the daily tasks of bathing, diapering, and feeding (Yogman, 1982).

As babies pass their first birthday, they begin to respond differently to fathers and mothers. This change is probably a response to differences in the way fathers and mothers behave with them. Behavior also shifts, depending on the situation. When observed in their homes, girls may prefer either parent and boys generally prefer their fathers. But when a situation becomes stressful, a preference for the primary caregiver appears—as attachment theory would predict. Both boys and girls go to their mothers for security and comfort (Lamb, 1981).

Infant Characteristics

Infants also affect the caregiving relationship and so influence the course of socialization. As we saw in Chapter 1, attractive babies get more parental attention and affection than do unattractive babies. Perhaps this means that parents are likely to show heightened sensitivity to the needs of an attractive infant—at least as compared with the same parents' responses to an unattractive baby.

A baby's fussiness also may affect the relationship with either parent. Parents of babies who often fuss tend to wait longer before picking up the child than do parents of babies who rarely fuss (Dunn, 1977). This tendency may develop because parents of fussy babies interpret their signals of distress as being simply bids for attention. Or if the baby does not quiet easily, the parents may decide that because responding has little effect, they might as well ignore the cries until they become intolerable.

The increased crying, together with the slowed responding, means that the baby may be slow to discover that parents can be depended on to ease infant distress (R. Thompson, 1986). Seeing no connection between his or her distress and maternal soothing, the fussy baby may perceive mother as less reliable than does a placid baby. The placid baby cries so rarely that connecting distress with maternal response is a relatively easy task. Placid babies may find relationships with parents more tranquil. Because they soothe immediately, their response tends to reinforce their parents' attention and makes the parents feel more secure as caregivers.

Later, the baby's relative speed of development may affect relationships with parents. The baby who walks early, say at 9 or 10 months, but does not learn to respond to commands until 14 or 15 months is likely to require more parental patience, provoke more irritation, need more physical restraint, and generally get into more trouble than the child who walks later. The baby who walks late, however, may provoke parental anxiety and concern in other ways. Alarmed at their child's slowness, parents may frequently pull the baby upright or even drag him or her along in attempts to speed development.

As we saw in Chapter 4, the way that any infant characteristic affects relationships with parents depends on the goodness of fit between infant and parent. When the infant's and parents' styles are alike or complementary, the relationship tends to develop smoothly. When they are not, a baby who might have been "easy" with one mother becomes "difficult" with another.

Caregiving Deprivation

The emotional bond between baby and parent has dominated our story of infant and toddler development. As we have seen, the individualized care of a parent for a child seems to encourage healthy emotional and cognitive development. Basic to this relationship are reciprocal interaction (the baby does something, the caregiver responds, the baby responds in turn), warmth and affection, and the caregiver's sensitivity to the baby's signals.

Babies in Institutions

What happens if a baby has no primary caregiver? Is development severely affected? Early studies of children reared in institutions revealed devastating effects on their social and intellectual development. As toddlers, such children often could not speak, walk, or even feed themselves (Spitz, 1949). It is now clear that the environment of the institution was responsible for some of these harmful effects, which recently have been repeated in Rumanian institutions, as we saw in Chapter 5.

A general lack of environmental stimulation radically slowed the children's cognitive development. Their world was limited to what they could see from their cribs. They had no rattles, no stuffed animals, no mobiles; they simply stared at bare walls. The babies in Lebanese institutions, described in Chapter 5, made rapid gains in cognitive and physical development when introduced to interesting objects for only a few minutes each day.

The babies' social deficits came from the lack of "mothering," not from the lack of a mother or father. Babies were fed, bathed, and changed on schedule; they ate from a bottle propped on a pillow. No one played with them. They received little cognitive or social stimulation. Their desires were ignored, and their cries were unanswered. This experience gave them a feeling of ineffectiveness, and their response was to give up and fall silent. Unable to depend on anyone, they probably failed to develop basic trust.

The severe effects found in Lebanon and Rumania do not appear when institutions have a stimulating environment (which encourages cognitive development) and a staff large enough to enable a child to have one or more warm social relationships (which encourage social development). In one Greek institution—the Mitera Babies' Center in Athens—babies get consistent mothering by a limited number of caregivers. In most cases, one nurse takes responsibility for primary care. Infants in this orphanage become attached to their primary caregiver at about the same time as other infants develop attachments to their parents (Dontas et al., 1985).

Can development proceed in a relatively normal manner when youngsters do not become attached to an adult caregiver? Research with monkeys suggests that a peer relationship can provide some of the security a child gets from the caregiver. Monkeys raised without mothers or mother surrogates but with other baby monkeys for company are more normal in their behavior than are monkeys raised with a surrogate mother but without peer contact (Suomi and Harlow, 1975). Similarly, a young institutionalized child has a better chance to develop normally if he or she forms a warm relationship with another child. But when children in institutions do not become attached to a caregiver or an older child within the institution during their first two years, their social development suffers. As 8-year-olds, they tend to cling to caregivers, to demand attention, and to show shallow, indiscriminate friendliness (MacDonald, 1985). They are often restless, disobedient, and unpopular with other children.

Separation

Sometimes babies or toddlers are separated from their parents, usually because of long or repeated hospitalizations, or they are permanently separated from their first caregivers, as when a youngster is adopted from a foster home. What effect does this have on social development? Separation before children are 6 months old seems to have little effect, but once the attachment process has begun, some children become distressed. They seem especially vulnerable from about 6 months until they are about 2 years old—the period when infants are susceptible to separation distress.

This vulnerability may have led to the apparent depression John Bowlby (1973, 1980) observed in older infants and toddlers who had been temporarily separated from their parents and placed in hospitals or other institutions. They became withdrawn and inactive, made no demands on the environment, cried intermittently, and seemed to feel increasing hopelessness and sadness. Later, they began to interact in a pleasant but shallow manner with institutional caregivers. When their parents visited, they responded in an aloof and detached way.

Such separations need not have a permanent effect on children. Brief separations, such as hospital stays of a week or less, seem to have no lasting effect (Rutter, 1979). Lengthier separations sometimes leave their mark. Among children between the ages of 6 months and 3 years who were hospitalized for lengthy, recurrent periods, the effects were still apparent in adolescence (MacDonald, 1985).

Babies who are adopted from the Mitera Babies' Center (described earlier) face the same adjustment as babies adopted from foster homes. But the institution provides a two-week transition period during which the adoptive parents spend their days with the baby in the institutional setting, giving the baby a chance to adapt to the new caregivers. By the end of the period, most babies have already begun to transfer their primary attachments (Dontas et al., 1985). Similarly, 18-month-olds in New York and New Jersey who had been adopted by the age of 10 months showed no difference in attachment from infants the same age who lived with their biological parents (L. Singer et al., 1985).

Reversing the Effects

Good environments often can make up for early deprivation. The earlier the change is made, however, the better the chances of reversing the effects. A child who is placed in a good environment at age 3 has three years of deprivation to overcome; but a child who is placed in a good environment at age 10 must overcome ten years of deprivation.

Children *can* develop attachments after the first two years, but whether they can overcome all the effects of early deprivation is uncertain. Among a group of 8-year-olds who had been adopted between the ages of 4 and 6, most had formed warm relationships with their adoptive parents, but they still showed the indiscriminate affection, the restlessness, and the unpopularity with their peers that were typical of 8-year-olds who remained in institutions (Tizard and Hodges, 1978).

Yet some children seem to surmount devastating early experiences. When a group of refugee children were brought to the United States and placed in adoptive homes, most seemed to overcome the ill effects of their early deprivation (Rathbun et al., 1965). When they came to this country, these thirty-eight youngsters (most of whom were Korean or Greek) ranged in age from 5 months to 10 years. Six years later, when the children were between the ages of 6 and 16, a team of researchers studied them. On the average, these children (who had to learn a new language and adopt a new culture) were socially competent, were physically healthy, and had above-average IQs. Only two were rated by psychologists as clinically disturbed and in need of professional help (Clarke and Clarke, 1977). Such studies hold out hope for the many Rumanian children who were adopted from orphanages in 1990 by Americans.

Just how completely the effects of early deprivation can be reversed depends in good part on the age of the child, the child's temperament and genetic susceptibility to adverse environmental influence, the severity of the early deprivation, and the quality of the new environment—both materially and emotionally (MacDonald, 1985; Rutter, 1979). Improvements are likely to occur in most cases, but complete reversal is less likely.

The Effects of Class and Culture

No matter where they live, young children become attached to their caregivers, but the nature of the parent-child relationship varies widely across classes and cultures. Differences in this basic relationship may leave different marks on the growing child.

Socioeconomic Differences

Social class has a powerful influence on a child's development, because it affects values, life style, child-rearing practices, and even parents' views of their children's competence. These effects grow out of the fact that social class tends to determine a person's educational level, power, and opportunities. Most researchers use the father's occupation as the determinant of social class, although in the United States today, the occupation of the major wage earner might be a better standard. "Middle class" generally refers to white-collar workers, and "working class" or "lower class" to blue-collar, semiskilled workers. Many studies, however, confine their lower-class sample to unskilled, often unemployed, workers (L. Hoffman, 1984). When education is the index of social class, those with some college

are considered middle class and those with none, working class. Sometimes researchers divide their sample into four groups: at least four years of college, some college, high-school completion, less than four years of high school.

Working-class parents spend less time caring for each child than do middle-class parents, and they have more children to care for (L. Hoffman, 1984). Poverty increases the amount of environmental stress on parents, and this may explain the finding that poor mothers tend to be less responsive to their children's social and emotional needs (McLoyd, Ceballo, and Mangelsdorf, 1993).

Early research showed that social class affected mothers' attitudes toward their babies and the way they interacted with them (Kagan and Tulkin, 1971). A middle-class mother was more likely than a working-class mother to imitate her baby's sounds, to engage in long bouts of social interaction, to reward her baby with words, and to encourage her baby to walk. About two-thirds of the working-class mothers used food to soothe their babies, but less than one-third of the middle-class mothers solved problems with food. Engaging in extensive verbal interactions is connected with higher social class in the United States, but it may reflect educational levels. Among low-income families in Mexico City, the more schooling a mother had, the more she talked to her baby. The researchers suggest that schooling gives mothers verbal skills that foster mother-infant relationships based on verbal communication (Richman, Miller, and LeVine, 1992). Even so, the practice varies widely across cultures as does the kind of speech mothers use. Middle-class mothers in Buenos Aires and New York City, for example, are more likely to speak to 13-month-olds in full sentences that impart information than are middle-class mothers in Tokyo, who favor emotionally laden remarks, such as endearments, greetings, and recitations (Bornstein et al., 1992).

Ethnic Differences

Until recently, most studies of infancy in minority families tended to confuse socioeconomic level with ethnicity and to attribute any differences that appeared to deficits in the ethnic minority (Garcia-Coll, 1990). Now, however, many researchers believe that rather than reflecting deficiencies, differences in child-rearing practices among ethnic groups reflect techniques designed to foster the skills and competencies required for economic, political, and social roles filled by the group's adults (Ogbu, 1981).

Puerto-Rican parents place a high value on children who are "well brought up." When asked to rate the behavior of 18-month-olds, Puerto-Rican mothers who had resided in the United States for nearly ten years valued evidence of obedience, courtesy, and respectful attention, whereas Anglo mothers (whether middle- or working-class) valued evidence that toddlers felt secure (Harwood, 1992).

Mexican-American and African-American parents may see early control of body functions as a step toward responsibility and autonomy. In one study, they urged their infants toward weaning, walking, and toilet training earlier than did Anglo-American parents of the same socioeconomic status (Bartz and Levine, 1978). When asked directly about their child-rearing goals, Mexican-American parents tended to be less authoritarian, less achievement-oriented, and more protective and to place less emphasis on individual responsibility than African-American and Anglo-American parents of the same socioeconomic status (Durrett, O'Bryant, and Pennebaker, 1975).

Research indicates that Mexican-American mothers tend to talk less to their babies than do other mothers but to cuddle them more (Garcia-Coll, 1990). Among other Hispanic groups, maternal practices differ. In a study of lower-class Cuban, Puerto Rican, South American, and African-American mothers, Cuban mothers talked the most and played the most teaching games with their 3- to 4-month-old babies (T. Field and Widmayer, 1981). Among the other groups, talking diminished and social game playing increased from Puerto Rican to South American to African-American groups, with African-American mothers talking the least and playing the most social games. The researchers suggested that Cuban mothers talk so much to their babies because the Cuban mother's predominant goal is to educate her child.

Some psychologists have suggested that differences among minority groups in the way they "teach" their babies may not reflect ethnicity or class but instead are related to education. Mexican-American mothers tend to teach their toddlers by modeling an action, whereas Anglo-American mothers tend to ask questions of their toddlers and lavish praise on them. But when a researcher controlled for parents' educational level, the differences in teaching style disappeared (Laosa, 1980).

Navajo mothers tend to be relatively inactive in play with their babies and rarely initiate a bout of play. When compared with African-American and Anglo-American mothers, Navajo mothers tended to be silent and passive with their babies (Fajardo and Freedman, 1981). The Navajo mothers seemed to express social interaction by the silent exchange of gazes with their babies.

Within most minority groups, the extended family is often deeply involved in the child's socialization. Minority babies are accustomed to a variety of caregivers; grandparents, godparents, siblings, aunts, uncles, and cousins engage in extensive and frequent interactions with the baby (Garcia-Coll, 1990). Members of the extended family often share the same residence, which means that studies focusing on the mother-child relationship may miss important aspects of the baby's life.

Cultural Differences

Some aspects of mothering are similar across all cultures as they are dictated by membership in the same species and by the baby's need to survive. But other aspects reflect the values and ecology of a particular culture and the necessity of preparing the child for adulthood in that culture, as indicated by the accompanying box, "Mothering in the Context of the Culture." These differences affect development in various ways.

Research with Ugandan infants, whose mothers generally interact more extensively with their babies than Western mothers do, supports the notion that experiences with the caregiver speed the development of attachment (Ainsworth, 1967). These babies formed specific attachments somewhat earlier than did a group of babies in Scotland (Schaffer and Emerson, 1964).

Close human contact is also a prominent feature of early life among the !Kung San, whom we met in Chapter 4. !Kung San babies spend most of their first year or so either on their mothers' laps or in a sling on their mothers' hips. As we saw, the babies have continual access to the breast and nurse frequently. When they cry, their mothers respond immediately, and the babies' whims are gratified. Even so, their social world is wider than that of most babies in Western societies. Unless U.S. babies are in day care, about 98 percent of their interactions are with their mothers. Among the !Kung San, about half of a baby's interactions are with other people—even though the mother is present (Bakeman et al., 1990). Perhaps this explains why !Kung San preschoolers show considerable independence, interacting less with their mothers and more with other children than English children of the same age (Konner, 1977).

!Kung San babies become interested in objects when they are between 4 and 6 months olds, just as U.S. babies do. But !Kung San adults pay little attention to a baby's exploration of objects, unlike adults in the United States, who notice it, encourage it, comment on it, and join in the exploration. !Kung San adults save their encouragement for the exchange of objects, be-

Navajo mothers rarely talk to their babies and tend to interact by exchanging silent gazes. *(Rick Browne/Stock, Boston)*

cause in their society such exchange (known as *hxaro*) is embedded in a complex formal system. Thus, among the !Kung San, a universal aspect of development (object exploration) is channeled into a path that is relevant to the culture. Researchers suggest that this difference in child rearing may lead to adults who place a greater value on the exchange (and sharing) of objects than on their manufacture and possession (Bakeman et al., 1990).

Wide variations also exist in the child-rearing practices of industrialized societies. More than thirty years ago, Urie Bronfenbrenner (1970) noted that babies in the Soviet Union got much more hugging, kissing, and cuddling than American babies did but that they were also held more tightly and allowed little freedom of movement. Soviet mothers seemed so solicitous and protective that they curtailed the babies' mobility and

initiative. As we have seen, Japanese and German mothers encourage different characteristics in their babies.

Multiple Caregiving

In today's world, multiple caregiving is a frequent form of infant care, even among babies who are not in institutions. In noninstitutional surroundings, multiple caregiving seems to produce no ill effects on children. After reviewing the research, Alison Clarke-Stewart and Greta Fein (1983) concluded that when the main attachment figure shares caregiving with other people, as when mothers work or when the baby is part of an extended family, children thrive as long as the other caregivers provide stable relationships.

Research indicates that caregiving arrangements reflect the social and ecological context of a culture.

MOTHERING IN THE CONTEXT OF THE CULTURE

Research in a variety of cultures indicates that although the demands of mothering are universal, the cultural situation and the way mothers define the task of infant care vary in dramatic ways and the differences among cultures widen throughout the baby's first year. In a unique study, Amy Richman and her associates (1988) compared mother-infant pairs in five societies: a Gusii community in rural Kenya, a Mayan town in Yucatán, a central Italian town, a Swedish city, and a suburb of a large American city. They found cultural differences in the amount of time mothers spent in holding their babies, looking at them, talking to them, and feeding them.

Gusii mothers focus on soothing their babies and keeping them quiet but look at them infrequently and rarely talk to them. Babies are held most of the time, even after they begin to walk. For Gusii mothers, holding is a matter of survival. A crawling baby can creep into a cooking fire. The immediate physical soothing also keeps the babies contented and reduces the drain on the busy mother's energy. Gusii mothers, who have the heaviest workload in the cultures studied, may not even look at their babies while they are breast feeding them. Their failure to look at their babies or to talk to them may be related to the cultural practices of averting the gaze in conversation and of showing emotional restraint in parent-child interactions.

Mayan mothers also concentrate on soothing and quieting their babies but may put them in hammocks to sleep during the day. Mayan mothers share work with other women in their compound, and so they are free to give the baby more of their attention. Living in a society that lacks the emotional restraints of the Gusii, Mayan mothers look at their babies more, although they do not often talk to them.

In a suburb of Boston, babies spend much of their waking time in infant seats, swings, highchairs, or playpens rather than in their mothers' arms. In line with the cultural emphasis on independence, mothers hold their babies even less as the babies begin to sit and crawl. The cultural difference in holding and soothing leads to a difference in crying, with Boston babies crying about twice as much as Gusii and Mayan babies. Boston mothers often interact visually and verbally with their babies and frequently use words to soothe them from a distance.

Italian mothers stress visual and verbal interaction, looking at their babies and talking to them even more than Boston mothers do. Although they hold their babies no more than Boston mothers do, the babies are not allowed to crawl about on the tile floors, because mothers are worried about hygiene and protection from the cold. Swedish mothers talk even more to their babies than Italian mothers do, but they look at their babies infrequently.

American and European mothers focus on visual and verbal interaction, an approach which may be related to the urban-industrial nature of their societies, the low levels of fertility and infant mortality, and the high educational levels of the mothers. Gusii and Mayan mothers, who live in agrarian societies with high levels of fertility and infant mortality and low levels of education, focus on physical nurturance and the safety of their babies. In each group, the mothers' behavior seems adapted to the environment.

Among the Efe hunter-gatherers of Zaire, for example, infants are accustomed from birth to intense social contact with up to five different individuals per hour (Tronick, Morelli, and Ivey, 1992). They are rarely alone with their mothers, and during the first two years of life spend at least 50 percent of their time with someone other than the mother. By the age of three, 70 percent of their time is spent with others, mostly other children. The researchers suggest that this changing pattern of multiple, simultaneous relationships may foster security, social skills, and self-regulation, while enhancing self-confidence.

Children reared in Israeli kibbutzim show normal social and emotional development. In the early kibbutzim, infants were reared communally in residential nurseries and saw their parents for only a few hours each day or on weekends. In most kibbutzim today, babies join their families at four o'clock each afternoon and stay with them until the next morning. In all kibbutzim, the caregiver, or *metapelet,* takes care of the infant's daily needs and training; the parents primarily provide emotional gratification. Research has shown that kibbutzim babies become attached to their mothers, their fathers, and the metapelet, although they develop somewhat different relationships with each one (Sagi et al., 1985). Such studies suggest that parents may be absent for significant amounts of time without radically influencing attachment patterns, as long as someone who cares is present.

With the enormous rise in employment among mothers of young children (see Table 8.3), multiple caregiving has become typical of American families. The U.S. Census Bureau has documented the immense change that has overtaken the American family: during the

TABLE 8.3 PERCENTAGE OF MOTHERS IN THE LABOR FORCE

Age of Child	TWO-PARENT FAMILIES					MOTHER-HEADED FAMILIES		
	1970	1975	1980	1985	1992	1975	1985	1992
0 to 1 year	24.0	30.8	39.0	49.4	56.7	38.5	38.0	44.3
2 years	30.5	37.1	48.1	54.0	60.9	49.1	55.7	51.3
3 years	34.5	41.2	51.5	55.1	63.5	53.5	54.8	58.7

Source: Child Trends, Inc. Calculated from unpublished data, Bureau of Labor Statistics, 1989, 1992.

1960s, less then 40 percent of women were back at work within five *years* after the birth of their first child; by the early 1980s, 40 percent were back at work within five *months* (O'Connell, 1989). Among women who were college graduates, had their first child after the age of 30, and had worked full-time before the baby's birth, 75 percent were back at work within a year.

Mothers' involvement in the labor force means that a considerable proportion of infants and toddlers are in substitute care. Sometimes parents share child care by working different shifts. Sometimes a relative or a sitter comes into the home, or the child is taken to a day-care home. And sometimes a child is placed in day care. For infants, placement in day care is less likely than one of the other arrangements. In a national study of employed mothers, 20 percent of those with children younger than 3 years placed them in day care. Another 22 percent took their children to a day-care home; 32 percent relied on relatives; and only 3 percent had sitters come to their own homes (Willer et al., 1991).

With 56.7 percent of all married mothers with babies less than 1 year old in the work force, together with 44.3 percent of the single mothers, the attachment bond between babies and their employed mothers has become the focus of research (see Table 8.3). Most—but not all—studies show no significant rise in the proportion of insecure attachments among the babies of working mothers (Barglow, Vaughn, and Molitor, 1987; Chase-Lansdale and Owen, 1987; L. Hoffman, 1989). But because these studies use the Strange Situation to assess the security of the attachment relationship, they may not provide an accurate measure of the baby's emotional bond. As we have seen, the experimental setting is meant to place the baby under a level of stress that evokes attachment behavior, but for infants who are accustomed to multiple caregiving, the situation may

not seem truly "strange" or stressful (Clarke-Stewart, 1989; L. Hoffman, 1989). Earlier we saw a relationship between the quality of attachment and later social-emotional competence. In one study (Vaughn, Deane, and Waters, 1985), however, the Strange Situation predicted later social-emotional competence for children whose mothers were full-time homemakers but did *not* predict social-emotional competence for children whose mothers had been employed while they were infants. There is, therefore, some question as to whether the Strange Situation is the best means of assessing attachment in children with day-care experience. When researchers use other measures to assess security, self-confidence, and emotional adjustment, infants in day care seem no more anxious, insecure, or emotionally disturbed than other infants (Clarke-Stewart, 1989).

Mothers who are away from their young children during working hours seem to make up for their absence after work and on weekends (Easterbrooks and Goldberg, 1985). Employed mothers do spend less time on child care, but some studies indicate that they spend as much time in direct, intensive interaction with their children as do mothers who are home all day (L. Hoffman, 1989).

Researchers have investigated the effects of day care on the social and cognitive development of infants. Adequate day care apparently accelerates the intellectual development of infants and toddlers, especially those in the lower class. Yet the early advantage fades; once home-reared children enter preschool or kindergarten, they quickly catch up with—but do not surpass—children who spent their early years in day care (Clarke-Stewart, 1989). When the quality of day care is poor, however, as when there are large groups of infants and toddlers but few caregivers, early day-care experience may place youngsters at a cognitive disadvantage.

In the social realm, children with early day-care ex-

Like Mission Specialist Anna Fischer, the first mother to make a space flight, mothers who work outside the home make up for their absence with direct, intensive interaction at other times. *(AP/Wide World Photos)*

perience tend to be more aggressive and less compliant with adults than home-reared children are. Yet these "aggressive, noncompliant" youngsters do as well as or *better* than home-reared children on such measures of development as sociability, social competence, language, persistence, achievement, self-confidence, and problem solving (Clarke-Stewart, 1989). In one study (Siegal and Storey, 1985), preschoolers with a history of day-care experience believed that moral transgressions (like hitting or stealing) were worse than social transgressions (like not putting toys away), but preschoolers who had never been in day care thought that social transgressions were just as naughty as moral transgressions. Alison Clarke-Stewart (1989), who reviewed the research, suggests that day care teaches toddlers to think for themselves and that they interact more with peers in both positive and negative ways.

Despite these general findings, there is no way to predict exactly what effect the daily separation will have on a particular child. Among the factors that inter-

act with the mother's daily absence are the attitudes of the parents toward the mother's employment, the number of hours the mother is employed, the amount of social support available to the mother, her satisfaction with day care, and the sex of the child (L. Hoffman, 1989).

The Development of Sociability

As infants grow, their significant relationships broaden beyond the important attachment to parents. Within the first two years of life, the rudimentary development of personality that we call *sociability* first appears. But all infants and toddlers are not equally sociable; they regard other people with varying degrees of positive expectations, warmth, and trust. Although their temperament has some effect on youngsters' sociability, their early experiences play an extremely important role in the way they approach others.

Day care may foster preschoolers' tendency to think for themselves and to act independently. *(David Butow/Black Star)*

Early Experience and Sociability

The results of studies showing the importance of the emotional bond between infants and their caregivers are in harmony with Erik Erikson's (1963) theory of personality development. The child's first task is to resolve the conflict between trust and mistrust in situations involving others. Babies who have developed secure attachments show evidence of basic trust, which reflects the history of their interactions with the social world. Their experiences with their parents have led them to expect that parents can be counted on. As they generalize these expectations to other people, their basic trust colors their future social interactions. Gradually, a rudimentary sense of personal identity emerges. Infants realize that their memories, images, and anticipated sensations are firmly linked with familiar and predictable things and people. This comfortable certainty about the world and their place in it allows babies to venture into new realms of experience.

Self-Concept

As babies begin to distinguish themselves from the world, they develop a sense of the self as an active, independent agent who can cause his or her own movements in space. This realization, which depends on cognitive development, seems to emerge at about the time a baby is 12 to 15 months old. Once the concept of self as agent has developed, the baby can develop a sense of self as an object—a "thing" that has unique features and can be recognized (Harter, 1983). This blossoming self-awareness in turn influences the baby's interest in others and how he or she relates to them.

The Emergence of Self-Concept

In most toddlers, self-concept appears to develop in three gradual, somewhat overlapping stages: self-recognition, self-description, and emotional responses associated with self-evaluation (Stipek, Gralinski, and Kopp, 1990). The stage of *self-recognition,* which first demonstrates the sense of self as object, emerges gradually during the second year. A typical test of self-recognition is whether the toddler clearly recognizes himself or herself in a mirror. Toddlers without a sense of self as object treat the reflection as another youngster. In a test of self-recognition, researchers placed babies and toddlers before a mirror after first surreptitiously daubing rouge on their noses (M. Lewis and Brooks-Gunn, 1979). No babies under a year seemed to recognize that the smudged nose in the mirror belonged to them; among babies who were between 15 and 18 months old, 25 percent immediately touched their noses; and among 24-month-olds, 75 percent grabbed for their noses as soon as they looked in the mirror. Self-recognition is related to development of the object concept, which, as we saw in Chapter 7, occurs gradually in a process that extends well into the second year. Most babies do not understand that the nose in the mirror is their own until they also understand that objects continue to exist when out of sight (Bertenthal and Fischer, 1978). Apparently, the concept of object permanence is basic to babies' sense of their own continuing identities.

Social experience also influences the development of self-recognition. Insecurely attached infants recognize themselves in the mirror some months before securely attached infants do. In one study (M. Lewis, Brooks-Gunn, and Jaskir, 1985), most of the insecurely attached infants who recognized themselves had developed avoidant attachments and showed heightened attention to the environment. Perhaps they developed self-concepts early because they relied less on their caregivers for security and more on themselves than securely attached infants do.

Self-description, the second aspect of self-concept to develop, emerges when toddlers recognize themselves first as entities with distinguishing characteristics and then as entities that can be evaluated (Stipek, Gralinski, and Kopp, 1990). They may describe themselves in terms of their physical characteristics ("curly hair," "little," "boy,") or may use evaluative terms ("I'm a good girl," "sticky hands"). This aspect of self is associated with an increased capacity for symbolic representation and the development of language. Many youngsters demonstrate self-description by 24 months, and most demonstrate it by 29 months.

Emotional responses to their own transgressions, the final aspect of the toddler's self-concept, emerge when toddlers begin hiding evidence of wrongdoing, are upset by disapproval, inhibit "naughty" behavior when watched, or call attention to their own misbehavior (Stipek, Gralinski, and Kopp, 1990). This aspect of

self-concept may represent the early stirrings of conscience, although it is probably associated with parents' reactions and not with feelings of guilt (Emde et al., 1987).

Self-Concept and Empathy

Infants' increasing sense of self may play an essential role in the development of **empathy,** an understanding of another person's emotional state (Eisenberg et al., 1989). Until children conceive of themselves as a separate self, they are unlikely to be able to put themselves in another's place.

Babies less than a year old, who cannot distinguish between themselves and another person in distress, try to comfort themselves as well as the distressed person, perhaps by sucking their thumbs at the sight of a sobbing toddler. Throughout the second year, youngsters assume that the distressed person feels exactly as they do and will respond to the same sort of comfort. If a toddler's friend becomes distressed, for example, the youngster will come to the friend's aid by fetching his or her own mother—even when the distressed toddler's mother is present. Finally, some time after their second birthday, toddlers begin to understand that other people may respond differently to a distressing situation. At last, they have a rudimentary ability to put themselves in the other person's place (M. Hoffman, 1988).

The development of empathy may be influenced by genes as well as by family environment. Researchers have found that, among toddler girls, identical twins are closer than fraternal twins in the amount of empathy they display (Zahn-Waxler, Robinson, and Emde, 1991). But environment is equally important. The degree of a toddler's distress and whether he or she tries to help are heavily influenced by whether the toddler's parents are sensitive to the toddler's needs and tend to help others (Zahn-Waxler et al., 1992). The strength of parental models may explain why the effect of genes diminishes during the second year among twin girls and disappears among twin boys.

Whether or not children develop empathy for others may affect the course of their social relations. Three-year-olds who understand the plight of their playmates in distress and who go to their aid are generally liked by their peers. But those who do not help or who do not seem to understand when their playmates are in distress tend to be disliked (Denham et al., 1990). As we will see in the next section, being able to control their own emotions may be as important an advance as understanding the emotions of others.

Preschoolers have developed empathy and often come to the aid of a distressed peer. *(Lora E. Askinazi/The Picture Cube)*

Emotions: Their Expression and Control

Some researchers believe that babies can feel most of the basic emotions (interest, joy, surprise, sadness, anger, and fear) within the first few months of life, whereas others believe that early emotions are limited to distress and nondistress and that the various emotions emerge gradually after the baby is 2 or 3 months old (Malatesta et al., 1989). Emotional experience certainly changes as the infant's perceptual and cognitive capacities develop, as goals change, and as the infant learns to modulate emotions and their expression. The course of emotional development during the first two years appears to be strongly affected by the emotional reactions of primary caregivers. As indicated in the accompanying box, "When Mommy and Daddy Fight," the display of parental emotions, even when they are not in response to the child, has clear effects on toddlers.

We can see how infants learn to handle their emotions by following the development of control over distress. Even the youngest infant is sometimes uncomfortable, and learning to tolerate, endure, or modulate this distress is a major developmental task (Demos, 1986). Babies react to early distress by turning their heads, putting their hands to their mouths, or sucking a thumb or pacifier. As we saw in Chapter 4, sucking is a great source of comfort for newborns.

When babies are 2 or 3 months old, their vision and motor skills have advanced far enough for them to handle low levels of discomfort by distracting themselves. They may visually explore the world around them or inspect their hands. During social interactions, they begin to gain control over their level of emotional arousal, looking away, for example, to lower arousal. Over the next few months, babies become aware of their distress and the fact that either they or their caregivers can ease their discomfort. They learn new ways of self-comfort: they may rock themselves, rub their genitals, or chew on their fingers and thumbs. They may stop crying and turn their heads at the sound of a caregiver's footsteps approaching the crib (Kopp, 1989). By 5 months, a cry has become an intentional call for comfort, and during the rest of the first year, infants become increasingly adept at communicating their distress.

As self-awareness develops, many toddlers handle distress by seeking out a **transitional object,** which is a specific "security" blanket, soft doll, or stuffed animal. The use of a transitional object for comfort indicates intent on the part of toddlers, as well as the understanding that the object can help the youngsters to manage their own distress (Kopp, 1989). Although the use of transitional objects begins to decline toward the end of the second year, many preschoolers continue to reach for them when upset. Toddlers also often understand the cause of their distress and make plans to relieve it, sometimes by asking others to assist them.

Competence and Autonomy

As their competence grows, babies find increasing satisfaction in exploring the social world. Although they show distress at being left by their parents, they do not seem distressed when they decide to move away from their attachment figures and explore their surroundings—although they do look back from time to time to see that the parent is still there. The nature of toddlers' explorations indicates that during the second year of

A mother who was recovering from flu was overwhelmed by her messy, dirty house. The children's toys covered the floor, dirty dishes littered the kitchen, and food had been left out of the refrigerator to spoil. Enraged at the shambles and at her husband, she yelled, "I don't care if this house stays messed up forever. I am not picking up another damn thing." Through her anger, she heard the squeaky voice of her 20-month-old daughter say, again and again, "Mommy, shut up. Mommy, shut up. Mommy, shut up" (Cummings, Zahn-Waxler, and Radke-Yarrow, 1981, p. 1276).

This incident was reported by a mother who took part in a study of infants' reactions to other people's emotional displays. By the time babies in this study were a year old, they became extremely upset by angry exchanges between their parents. Infants between 12 and 20 months showed their agitation in several ways. Some seemed angry themselves, hitting or pushing one or both parents. Some became distressed, crying, looking concerned, or hiding their heads under a blanket to shut out the sounds. Some ignored the event, staring ahead without expression. And some hugged and kissed their parents in an attempt to distract or reconcile them—this response was most common in families where parents often quarreled. According to the mothers' reports, the more frequently the parents fought, the more distressed the children were over each incident.

Wondering if youngsters' social and emotional functioning was altered by exposure to such quarrels, Mark Cummings, Ronald Iannotti, and Caroline Zahn-Waxler (1985) set out to study the effects of adult conflict on 2-year-olds. Because family quarrels are not accessible to researchers, they staged quarrels between adults. In a laboratory room, juice was served to the toddlers and coffee to the mothers; then, while the toddlers played, the adults switched from friendly interaction to a bitter quarrel over washing dishes.

When the adults began to argue, 42.5 percent of the toddlers showed distress. They either froze in place, tried to shut out the quarrel by covering their faces or ears, ran to their mothers for comfort, looked anxious, cried, asked to leave ("Go home now"), scolded the quarrelers ("Bad ladies"), or tried to end the quarrel ("Stop!"). A month later the same youngsters came back to the laboratory, and another quarrel erupted in front of them. This time, 61.8 percent of the youngsters showed distress.

Among the toddlers who witnessed both quarrels, the background anger spilled over into their play. After the fight had subsided on their second visit, the incidence of aggressive acts among the watching youngsters increased sharply. This reaction was especially noticeable among boys and among toddlers of either sex who previously had been rated as aggressive. Girls tended to become distressed, anxious, or withdrawn.

Small children clearly are affected by the quarrels of others, and it would seem that the effect is magnified among youngsters whose parents fight frequently. The researchers note that public concern over the influence of televised aggression overlooks an influence that may be even more powerful—and one that cannot be turned off.

---

life, a youngster's need for physical contact declines. The decline apparently is spurred by the child's desire to be competent, to find out about the world of people and objects, and to bask in the attention and smiles of new people. Novelty, complexity, and change draw toddlers away from the comfortable familiarity of attachment figures. From their explorations, they bring back new knowledge and abilities that they may incorporate into increasingly complex, interesting interactions with the important people in their lives.

Toward the end of the second year, children make their first concentrated push toward **autonomy,** which is the feeling of self-control and self-determination. Parents suddenly realize that their sunny, independent toddler has become stubborn and disagreeable. The child has entered the period of social development sometimes called "the terrible twos," and family life often seems difficult. No matter what parents suggest, no matter what they ask, the toddler's consistent response is "no!"

This "negativistic crisis" develops as a child becomes aware of the distinction between self and others and between the child's own will and the will of others. Until now, youngsters have depended on their caregivers for the satisfaction of their needs. As toddlers become more aware of their competence and their effects on the world, they strive for autonomy. They want to do things for themselves. The toddler who invariably says "no" is trying to discover the limits of his or her capabilities and initiative. Parents frequently note that the clash of wills seems to have no practical point; the child is concerned not with an issue but with a principle. What often looks like deliberate defiance is a test of social relationships and responses as a youngster tries to discover what effects she or he can have on others. As we trace the course of development, it will become clear that this developing sense of competence and autonomy will be important throughout life.

Boy or Girl

Before infants learn whether they are girls or boys, they must discover what a girl or boy is. The voyage to this discovery begins before they are aware they have embarked on it, for girls and boys are treated differently right from the start. Babies are wrapped in pink or blue blankets in the hospital nursery and surrounded with sex-typed clothes and toys at home. Their gender may even affect the way they are fed, for one study showed that middle-class mothers were more likely to breast-feed a daughter than a son (M. Lewis, 1971).

Gender affects interactions with babies in subtle ways. In one study, Caroline Smith and Barbara Lloyd (1978) found that switching the gender label of a 6-month-old baby changed the ways that mothers interacted with the unfamiliar infant. Told that the baby was a boy, they encouraged "him" to crawl, walk, and behave vigorously. Told that the baby was a girl, they never encouraged motor activity and never offered "her" a hammer as a plaything. Similar differences appeared when Hannah Frisch (1977) changed the gender label on a 14-month-old baby. Even a commitment to feminism did not wipe out the differences. Adults who were sympathetic to feminism often urged a "girl" to ride a tricycle but never encouraged a "boy" to play with a baby doll.

These adults were playing with an unfamiliar baby. Perhaps they were simply acting on the only available information: the baby's age and gender. How do they regard their own infants? From the first, parents perceive gender differences in their newborns. Although girl babies are hardier than boy babies, as we saw in Chapter 3, parents see their newborn daughters as softer, more vulnerable, and less alert than their newborn sons, and fathers see their sons as stronger and hardier than their daughters (Huston, 1983). When parents see baby girls as soft, dainty, and fragile, they are likely to treat them gently; when they see baby boys as strong and tough, they are likely to treat them more roughly. Fathers seem to be especially conscious of gender differences. As noted earlier, they tumble their sons about more, play more roughly with them, and use toys less with them than they do with their daughters.

Clear differences in parental behavior turned up in a study by Beverly Fagot (1978), who observed families with an only child who was just under 2 years old. She discovered that parents often responded differently to the same activity, depending on the child's gender. Girls were not encouraged when they played with blocks, and only girls tended to be discouraged when they manipulated objects. As a result, boys explored the physical world freely, but girls were often criticized for doing so. Girls were encouraged to be helpers and to ask for assistance when they tried to do things. The parents were unaware that they were training their daughters to be dependent and their sons to be independent.

Mothers also teach their young sons to stand up for themselves in arguments with their peers but insist that their daughter retreat. Researchers observed pairs of preschoolers at play in their homes and discovered that when youngsters fight over the possession of a toy, the mother's reaction depends on the gender of her child (Ross et al., 1990). Mothers tended to encourage their 3-year-old sons to hang on to a toy—even if the son had taken it away from a playmate—but they tended to support the other child when their 3-year-old daughters were involved—even if the other child had grabbed the object from the daughter. Daughters were admonished to consider the viewpoints of others; sons were not.

Long before girls and boys are 3 years old, they are paying close attention to gender differences in behavior. At about 18 months they begin to learn gender labels, and many 2-year-olds apply them to others, generally relying on hair and clothes as cues. Although most 2-year-olds are not sure of their own gender, those who can identify the gender of children and adults in photographs tend to spend most of their time playing with children of their own sex. Those who cannot identify gender in pictures spend about half their time playing with children of the other sex (Fagot, 1985). Researchers have found that the ability to identify gender in photographs as well as the ability to categorize items as appropriate for girls or boys develops early when mothers encourage gender-typical play and have traditional attitudes toward gender roles (Fagot, Leinbach, and O'Boyle, 1992). Apparently, a stress placed on gender in the home encourages children to see the world in gender-related terms.

Peers and Siblings

The influence of parents can be strengthened or moderated by the influence of other children. Because peers are at approximately the same stage of development as the child whereas siblings are either older or younger, peers and siblings have somewhat different roles. When playing with peers, children interact with equals, an experience youngsters can get from no one else.

Peers

Not many years ago, infants had little experience outside the home, but the dramatic increase in employment among mothers of young children has led to interaction with peers at a much earlier age. Babies are clearly interested in one another, even if they lack the social skills that make sustained interaction possible (Hartup, 1983). When 6-month-old babies meet for the first time, for example, each tugs at the other's hair, pokes at eyes, and handles the other's toys. Yet the interaction goes smoothly, for neither baby frowns, fusses, resists, or withdraws from the situation (Hay, Nash, and Pedersen, 1983).

Babies are more sociable at home than in the strange surroundings of the psychological laboratory, and they are also more sociable with acquaintances than with young strangers. At 9 months, familiarity leads to an increase in interactions between infants and a greater complexity in their play (Becker, 1977).

After the first year, toddlers become increasingly adept at socializing with unfamiliar peers. They rely primarily on nonverbal methods to develop new relationships (Eckerman, Davis, and Didow, 1989). Imitation is their primary all-purpose tactic, and it increases dramatically between 16 and 28 months. If one toddler throws a ball, the other throws a beanbag; if one jumps off a box, the other jumps off but may fall dramatically to the ground. Sometimes they combine imitation with complementary acts: they play peekaboo, exchange objects or mild blows, or play follow-the-leader. To a lesser degree, they act in a complementary fashion—behaving in a way that is related to the peer's action but expands it so that both can play. Words have a minor role in toddler play. At 32 months, no more than one-third of their interactions are accompanied or introduced by words.

More important than meeting new peers is getting along with the ones you know. Friction is frequent between toddlers, although the amount seems to vary widely. When researchers observed 21-month-olds playing in pairs, they recorded 2.3 squabbles in each fifteen-minute play period. Yet some toddlers never disagreed, and others fought almost once every minute (Hay and Ross, 1982).

In another study, Carollee Howes (1988) followed children in day care over a three-year period, beginning when some of them were only 12 months old. She discovered that children's ability to develop and maintain friendships was related to social competence. Among the youngest toddlers, social competence consisted of the ability to assume complementary and reciprocal roles during peer play. For 2-year-olds, social competence was marked by the ability to communicate meaning during pretend play. By the age of 3, social competence consisted of the ability to think evaluatively about the peer group, so children were aware of the personal characteristics of various peer-group members. Familiarity plays an important part in toddler friendships; youngsters who moved during the course of the study showed a drop in social competence. For the most part, however, individual differences in social competence endured, and socially withdrawn toddlers tended to be either rejected by their peers or ignored by them one year later.

Siblings

Siblings play an important role in one another's lives. Whether children have older or younger siblings, many siblings, or none at all influences personality development. From interactions with their siblings, children develop expectations about the way other people will behave.

When a first-born toddler acquires a baby brother or sister, the world suddenly changes. The toddler is no longer the center of the universe and has to stand by as parental attention and concern is focused on the new baby. Unlike other people in the toddler's world, the baby is not at all concerned with the toddler's needs. In a study of English toddlers, nearly every child was disturbed and unhappy at the birth of a baby brother or sister (Dunn, 1983; Dunn and Kendrick, 1982). Most misbehaved, demanded attention, and were jealous when their fathers played with the baby. Yet these toddlers were also interested in the baby and showed affection. Many tried to entertain the baby, were concerned when the infant cried, and tried to help out with infant care. One mother described her toddler son's concern for his baby sister:

He hates anything to happen to her . . . hates to hear her cry. He moves small toys in case she puts them in her mouth and covers stickle bricks [prickly toy bricks that interlock] with a cloth. (Dunn and Kendrick, 1982, p. 97)

In this study, the toddlers' new status also made many of them more independent; they began dressing themselves, feeding themselves, going to the toilet alone, and playing more by themselves. Others, however, temporarily regressed; they insisted that their mothers dress them, take them to the toilet, or feed them. When this sort of behavior appeared, it usually lingered throughout the first year after the baby's birth.

Older brothers and sisters often act as models and teachers for their young siblings. Studies have shown that toddlers carefully watch their preschool brothers or sisters, often taking over their abandoned toys and imitating their actions. The preschool siblings in turn talk to the toddlers and offer them toys (Lamb, 1978). In fact, young siblings often have similar interests, enjoy the same things, and seem to understand one another.

Familiarity gives siblings ample opportunity to annoy each other. At first, hostility comes from the older child, but by the time the second-born child is 18 months old, he or she is able to retaliate. In one study, all younger siblings at times were physically aggressive, and all knew exactly how to tease or annoy an older brother or sister (Dunn and Munn, 1985). They destroyed the older child's possessions, took away favorite toys, or deliberately provoked the older sibling.

The relationship between young siblings seems to be highly ambivalent. Conflict between siblings appears in every study, but so does affection. A mother described her 8-month-old daughter's reactions to her toddler brother:

She thinks he's marvelous. Hero-worships him. If he plays with her foot, she kills herself laughing. She doesn't cry till he goes out of the room. (Dunn and Kendrick, 1982, p. 83)

In many families, the infant sibling becomes attached to the older brother or sister and often goes to him or her for comfort.

Despite the ambivalence of early sibling relationships, the presence of a sibling may help a youngster to develop empathy. Four aspects of sibling interaction may be linked to increased empathy and decreased selfishness in children. First, sharing the same parents and the same family events places children in situations where they experience the same emotion. Sharing joys and disappointments may encourage the development of empathy. Second, when mothers intervene in sibling clashes over toys or treats, they usually encourage sharing and sensitivity to the other child's wants, needs, and feelings. Thus, the child with siblings has more opportunities than an only child to learn about prosocial behavior. Third, watching a parent reward a sibling for helpfulness—or punish the child for selfishness or cruelty—provides an opportunity for observational learning about the consequences of prosocial and antisocial behavior. Fourth, siblings' common environment, close familiarity with each other's worlds, dependence on each other, and continual interaction may make it easier for a child to develop the ability to take the other's role.

The development of empathy may be speeded by parents who refer to the newborn as a person with feelings and needs and who encourage their toddler to help care for the new baby. Parents who follow this pattern may promote positive sibling relationships (Howe and Ross, 1990). A mother's frequent interaction with the new baby also favors good relationships between siblings. Thus, maternal style influences relationships between siblings, and the encouragement of perspective taking seems to foster friendly relationships (Dunn and Kendrick, 1982; Howe and Ross, 1990). As we will see in the next chapter, siblings continue to play an important role throughout a child's development.

SUMMARY

THE DEVELOPMENT OF ATTACHMENT

Studies of monkeys and human infants have shown the complex nature of **attachment.** In human babies, the relationship takes months to develop; it goes through four major stages: indiscriminate social responsiveness (birth to 2 months), discriminate social responsiveness (2 to 7 months), specific attachment (7 to 30 months), and goal-directed partnership (from 30 months). Once infants develop a specific attachment, they are likely to show **separation distress** when the caregiver leaves and **stranger wariness** when an unfamiliar person is present.

THE SECURITY OF ATTACHMENT

The **Strange Situation** experiment detects variations in the quality of the attachment bond. About two-thirds of babies develop a **secure attachment;** most of the rest develop insecure bonds—either **avoidant attachment** or **resistant attachment**—with a few developing a **disorganized attachment.** Factors that affect attachment include the caregiver's style of interaction, the baby's temperament, and the culture's child-rearing practices. Babies with secure attachments tend to become competent, independent toddlers. Babies also become attached to their fathers, whose interactions are generally more boisterous and playful than those of mothers. The baby's appearance and reactions also influence the tone of the parent-child relationship.

Babies can be reared successfully in institutions—as long as they develop one or more warm, responsive relationships with caregivers. The failure to develop such a relationship may permanently impair social development. Although children can develop attachments after the age of 2, they may not be able to overcome all the effects of early deprivation.

THE EFFECTS OF CLASS AND CULTURE

Through its effects on parents' values, life style, and child-rearing practices, social class affects the way parents interact with their children. Differences in child-rearing practices among various ethnic groups generally develop in an attempt to prepare youngsters for their adult social roles. The nature of parent-child relationships may also vary across cultures. Most research has failed to find significant differences in security of attachment between babies of employed mothers and babies of full-time homemakers. However, the Strange Situation may not accurately measure the emotional bond in babies of employed mothers. Day care seems to speed cognitive and social development, although the cognitive boost may be temporary.

THE DEVELOPMENT OF SOCIABILITY

Babies with secure attachments show evidence of basic trust. Early personality and sociability are largely a product of interaction with parents. At about 15 months,

babies develop a sense of themselves as an active, independent agent; afterward they develop a sense of themselves as an object with unique features. This aspect of self-concept appears to go through three stages of development: self-recognition, self-description, and self-evaluation. Self-concept is essential to the development of **empathy.** Some researchers believe that babies feel most of the major emotions during the first few months of life, but other researchers believe that early emotions are limited to distress and nondistress. Over the first year, infants become increasingly able to handle low levels of distress and realize that their caregivers can help alleviate their distress. Many toddlers use a **transitional object** to relieve distress. As their need for physical contact declines, toddlers begin to develop **autonomy.**

Parents treat boys and girls differently from birth, and these differences in treatment encourage independence in boys and dependence in girls. Babies engage in social interaction with their peers toward the end of the first year, and early experience with peers seems to speed the development of sociability. The ability to develop and maintain friendships is related to social competence, and individual differences in social competence tend to endure through the early years. Siblings influence one another's social development, and most relationships are ambivalent. Sibling interactions may foster the development of empathy. Both the quality of sibling relationships and the development of empathy are affected by the way parents relate to their children.

KEY TERMS

attachment
autonomy
avoidant attachment
disorganized attachment

empathy
resistant attachment
secure attachment
separation distress

stranger wariness
Strange Situation
transitional object

FOUR

• • • • • • • • • • • • •

THE INDUSTRIOUS CHILD

Between the ages of 4 and 11, children undergo profound changes in every aspect of development. At 4, they are still in what Erikson calls the "play age," when they are full of surplus energy and take intense enjoyment in the exercise of mind and muscle. Their growing bodies, widening experiences, and rapidly developing understanding soon propel them from the narrow world of the nursery into the wider world of the schoolchild. Now children turn from initiative to industry as their growing independence from the family opens them to new influences from peers, school, and community. Through this maze of influence, children move, selecting here, rejecting there, but always acting on the environment and influencing others as much as others influence them. During the school years, children seem eager and ready to learn various cultural skills. A tremendous surge in cognitive capabilities allows them to develop new and more realistic ways of understanding the world, operating in it competently, and perceiving the logical and causal relationships within it. All these developmental changes grow out of the continuous interaction of child and society. ▪

SOCIAL DEVELOPMENT: GROWING UP IN THE FAMILY

• • • • • • • • • • • • • • • •

PARENTS AS SOCIALIZERS
Parents as loving caregivers
Parents as identification figures
Parents as active socialization agents
Parents as providers of experience
Parents as builders of self-concept

DISCIPLINE
Disciplinary styles
The context of discipline

INFLUENCES ON GENDER ROLES
Social change and gender roles
How parents influence gender roles
Searching for sex differences

SIBLINGS
Birth order

MATERNAL EMPLOYMENT

ALTERNATIVE FAMILY ARRANGEMENTS
Divorce
The single parent
The blended family

PHYSICAL CHILD ABUSE
The abusing parent
The abused child
The context of abuse

THE FAMILY AS A SYSTEM

SUMMARY

KEY TERMS

Nine-year-old Samantha Drake gets up every morning at six-thirty and goes into her mother's room. For half an hour, she lies in her mother's bed and watches her mother get ready to go to her job as a senior data analyst. Samantha's parents were divorced several years ago, and her mother·has custody. Her father has remarried; every other weekend Samantha visits him and her stepmother. At first the divorce was difficult for Samantha; she blamed herself for her parents' broken marriage. She cried every night. For a long time, Samantha thought her parents would get back together, but eventually she realized that they never would. She says she's happy now, living with her mother, her dog, her cat, and her hamsters in a suburb of Houston, Texas. She makes straight A's at school, and her open, friendly manner indicates that she has indeed come to terms with her parents' divorce. Time, the school counselor, and a therapist she saw for a while after her father remarried have helped her adjust. Samantha's position is not unusual; many of her friends have stepparents, and parents of two other friends are getting divorces (D. Gelman, 1985).

● ● ● ● ● ●

How does the experience of living in a one-parent family affect the way that Samantha—and other children like her—masters the developmental tasks of childhood? With nearly 24 percent of American families with children headed by a single parent, this is an important question, and many psychologists are trying to answer it. Their findings will help us understand how the socialization process contributes to the development of personality. **Socialization** is the process of absorbing the attitudes, values, and customs of a society. It describes the ways in which pressures from parents, peers, teachers, other adults, and the media encourage acceptable behavior in children and discourage undesirable behavior. As a result of these pressures, children learn to behave in culturally approved ways, paying at least lip service to the dominant values, ideals, and motivations of the groups that include them.

The family is perhaps the major influence in the socialization process. By the time children are 4 years old, they are moving into a wider world of peers, school, and community. Yet the family is still the most powerful force in the child's development—and will remain so throughout middle childhood. In this chapter, we focus first on parents in their many roles as agents of socialization; then we look closely at different styles of discipline and their possible effects on the child's social development. After considering parents' role in the socialization of gender roles, we consider the evidence for gender differences. Next we examine siblings' roles in the socialization process. Once more we pick up the issue of maternal employment—this time concentrating on the school-age child. We consider the effects of divorce on children and the differences between growing up in a one-parent family and doing so in a two-parent family.

This topic leads us to explore the special aspects of living with stepparents. Finally, we discuss how considering the family as a system of interacting relationships helps us understand the dynamics of family life.

Parents as Socializers

Parents contribute to the socialization process in at least five ways: by assuming the role of love providers and caregivers; by serving as identification figures; by acting as active, often deliberate, socialization agents; by providing the bulk of the child's experiences; and by participating in the development of the child's self-concept. Various theorists have stressed different aspects of the parents' roles, but each aspect probably plays some part in the child's acceptance of cultural attitudes and values. Yet children are not passive blobs of clay, to be molded by the strong fingers of parental instruction and example. As we saw in Chapters 4 and 8, the process is interactive, with the child's temperament and capabilities influencing the methods used by parents and their effectiveness. Instead of considering parents as doing things *to* their children or *for* their children, we will look at each aspect of parental socialization as being something that parents do *with* their children (L. Hoffman, 1991; Lamb, 1988).

Parents as Loving Caregivers

During the child's first year, the parents' primary responsibilities are to meet their baby's needs and provide him or her with love. This role of caregiver and love provider continues throughout childhood, but its dominance of the relationship fades as other functions become more powerful. This aspect of the parent-child relationship has three important influences on the child. First, we saw in Chapter 8, the dependability of a loving caregiver helps the baby meet the major developmental task of infancy—developing basic trust (Erikson, 1963). Second, this loving relationship may provide the toddler with the capacity to form emotional relationships (Bowlby, 1951). Finally, in carrying out the role of loving caregiver, parents prime the child for future socialization. Children are readily influenced by someone they love who also loves them—especially if they must depend on that person for the satisfaction of their needs. So the relationship enhances the parents' effectiveness as agents of socialization.

Parents as Identification Figures

The notion of parents as identification figures comes from the psychoanalytic view of development. During the process of **identification,** children internalize their parents' values and standards. This process occurs during the phallic period, when youngsters try so hard to become like the same-sex parent that they take that parent's beliefs as their own. Cognitive social-learning theorists (Bandura, 1986, 1989) contend that it is simpler to regard the parent as a model, whom the child copies, than as an identification figure in the Freudian sense. In this view, children imitate models who are warm, powerful, and competent—as most parents seem to their children. Instead of seeing themselves as similar to the parent and trying to react as they think the parent would, they simply imitate the parent's actions and statements. Whether children identify with parents or simply imitate them, the process occurs without the parents' awareness or intention.

Parents as Active Socialization Agents

Sometimes parents intend their actions to have a socializing effect—as when they discipline or instruct a youngster in the right and wrong ways of doing things. At other times, parents' actions are socializing the child even though the parents seem oblivious to the effects of their actions.

Dispensers of Rewards and Punishments

When parents reward or punish a child, they are applying a powerful socialization technique. In the view of cognitive social-learning theorists, children do not blindly repeat rewarded behavior or automatically avoid behavior that is punished. Instead, they use reward and punishment as information when organizing and planning their actions. Rewards and punishments come continually, not just when the parent is disciplining the child. A 5-year-old carries his plate into the kitchen after dinner, and his mother smiles and pats him on the arm. Another 5-year-old reaches for a piece of bread and spills her glass of milk; her mother frowns and says, "Not again!" As we saw in Chapter 2, subtle approval reinforces a child's action, but a frown or the withdrawal of attention punishes it.

Teachers of Skills and Values

Parents often pass along explicit instructions that they hope will guide the child's future conduct. These in-

This father in a hunting culture serves as a model for his son, who watches intently at the exercise of a skill that is vital to the family livelihood. *(N. R. Farbman/Life Magazine, Time Warner Inc.)*

structions may take the form of specific skills (throwing a baseball, making cookies, weeding the garden), or they may be moral guidelines, which parents either believe in themselves or want their children to believe in. These instructions generally are issued in the context of some activity. A child who comes home crying after a fight with a peer may be told, "If he hits you, hit him back." A child who catches a small fish may be told, "Throw the fish back now so it will live." In such situations, children learn about courtesy ("Tell the lady, 'Thank you'"), gender roles ("Dolls are for girls"), prejudice ("She's not the kind of person you should play with—she lives in the projects"), politics ("The Republicans are just out to help the rich get richer"), property ("That doesn't belong to you; give it back to Jimmy"), and other aspects of getting along with other people. Children tend to accept these rules, and unless subsequent experiences convince them otherwise, they con-

tinue to regard them as truth. Many such guidelines are never challenged and remain part of a person's basic beliefs throughout life.

Disciplinarians

Parents become disciplinarians when children break a rule or do something their parents disapprove of. The effect of this discipline or socialization depends on the act itself (which misdemeanor is punished) and the form that the discipline takes. Parents may simply assert their superior power—by yelling, shouting, threatening, or hitting the child. They may withdraw their love for a time. Or they may give the child some reason for behaving acceptably. Parents often use a combination of these forms, but the effect of any discipline depends on which form is dominant (M. Hoffman, 1988). As we shall see in the section on discipline, parents' actions and the context in which they occur frequently lead to unanticipated results.

Parents as Providers of Experience

Parents control so much of the child's world that they determine the sort of experiences their child will have. This aspect of parental socialization actually sets the ground rules for the child's socialization, because from what children see and experience, they draw conclusions about the nature of the world and the people in it. These conclusions form the basis of social cognition, which, as we saw in Chapter 2, refers to the children's understanding of themselves, other people, and society.

At home, children learn what men and women are like. From the behavior of their parents, they learn whether one sex is more capable than the other, has a larger say in the running of the household, or is more affectionate. Parents teach children how to approach other people and what to expect from them, as well as what aspects of the world children should fear.

Children learn about the nature of the world by watching their parents interact with siblings. In the case of punishment, for instance, observational learning sometimes inscribes a deeper lesson in children than they would derive from suffering the consequences themselves: seeing a sibling spanked may lead the child to exaggerate the pain of a spanking.

Finally, children learn about the nature of the world from the environment provided by the parents. The environment provides certain experiences and withholds others. Parents may take their children to museums or ball games or always leave them at home. They may encourage children to play on their own outdoors, with freedom to experiment and investigate, or insist that children stay inside unless a supervising adult is present.

Parents as Builders of Self-Concept

Parents help socialize a child by affecting the development of self-concept. The way they treat the child and the way they perceive the child contribute to the way the child thinks about herself or himself. If parents overprotect a child, for example, the child often may feel in need of protection although he or she actually needs no outside assistance. An overprotected boy may, for example, be unprepared to negotiate difficulties with peers or to take responsibility for his own academic performance. Similarly, a little girl who is treated as if she were fragile, cute, and incompetent may come to see herself in those terms.

Parents attribute qualities to their children and treat their children as though they possessed those qualities. Sometimes they even label the child ("You're stupid"; "You're daring"; "You're a clown"). The children accept the labels and build them into their self-concept. Then they behave as if the parents' attributions were correct. For example, the tallest boy in a short family may be treated as "the tall one" and carry himself as though he were tall. If he is actually short for his age, his peers eventually may correct his misconception, but for a time he may reap the benefits of being tall by acting tall.

Discipline

Before children can crawl or walk, parents have little reason to discipline them. Once children can move around by themselves, however, parents must step in to preserve the child's safety and their own sanity. During the preschool years, the majority of mother-child interaction is devoted to discipline. Mothers of 4-year-olds spend about 60 percent of their interaction time trying to interfere with their child's activities (M. Hoffman, 1983).

If parents' disciplinary efforts are successful, their children develop **self-regulation,** the ability to control their own behavior so that it is appropriate to the prevailing situation (Maccoby and Martin, 1983). Self-regulation encompasses more than refraining from some forbidden act or postponing some pleasure; it also enables children to achieve various aims and goals they have chosen. Because parental discipline may affect the development of children's morality, cognition, and personality, researchers have devoted a good deal of attention to it.

Disciplinary Styles

When a creeping baby reaches out and begins to jerk on a lamp cord, a parent's aim is to get the infant to stop what he or she is doing. So the parent uses the only disciplinary style that is effective with infants: power assertion. In **power-assertive discipline,** the force of the discipline resides in the parent's overwhelming power. The parent may pick up the baby and remove him or her bodily from the source of temptation. The parent may shout "No!" and pull the baby's hand away or even slap the baby's hand. With older children who are developing the capacity to regulate their own behavior, parents may use other power-assertive techniques, such as threats, commands, spankings, and the withdrawal of privileges. But whatever the specific action, power-assertive techniques are based primarily on the child's fear of punishment (M. Hoffman, 1988).

A second disciplinary style relies on the withdrawal of love. In **love withdrawal,** the power of the discipline lies in children's fear that they will lose the emotional support, affection, and approval of the parent. This technique involves nonphysical expressions of the parent's anger or disapproval. When using this style of discipline, parents may withdraw physically (turning their backs on the child), refuse to speak or listen to the child, tell the child that they dislike him or her, or threaten to leave the child.

In a third style, **inductive discipline,** the power of the discipline lies in appeals to the child's reason, pride, or desire to be grown up and to the child's concern for others. Parents use reason and explanations to make the child realize the harmful consequences of the forbidden action—either to the child or to other people. These explanations often encourage youngsters to take the role of another (see Table 9.1).

Love withdrawal and power assertion are both effective in the immediate situation. They get children to stop whatever they are doing and pay attention. When used heavily, however, they may be counterproductive. The prospect of being abandoned or of losing a parent's love may be so frightening that the reason for the parent's withdrawal becomes lost on the child. Children whose parents depend on love withdrawal may learn to repress all their emotions. They may show little aggression or overt anger, but they also may show little excitement or joy in happy situations.

Any form of power assertion stops a child's activity, but the consistent use of physical punishment seems least effective in the long run (M. Hoffman, 1988). The child may learn to behave only to avoid punishment and may fail to internalize moral standards. In addition, the parent who hits a child is modeling physical aggression. The parent demonstrates that when you disapprove of someone's behavior, it is okay to hit that person (Bandura, 1986). Heavy reliance on power assertion, combined with the parent's failure to give reasons or tendency to give reasons when the child is too upset to pay attention, can lead to the development of an externalized conscience. The child with an **externalized conscience** obeys and acts in morally accepted ways solely to avoid punishment. This connection led Gene Brody and David Shaffer (1982) to conclude that parents who rely primarily on power assertion tend to have self-centered children whose aim in resolving moral problems is avoiding punishment. They behave so that they will not get caught.

Induction appears to be the most effective disciplinary technique in establishing self-regulation. Children whose parents regularly use this technique are most likely to internalize their parents' standards and to abide by the rules even when parents or other adults are not around. They are also more likely to feel empathy with others and to feel guilty when they act in a way that

TABLE 9.1   DISCIPLINARY STYLES

Style	Techniques	Basis
Power assertion	Physical punishment Threats Commands Withdrawal of privileges	Fear of punishment
Love withdrawal	Physical withdrawal Refusal to speak or listen to child Verbal expression of parent's dislike for child Threats to leave	Loss of parent's support, affection, and approval
Induction	Reason Explanations	Appeal to child's reason, pride, empathy

The Industrious Child

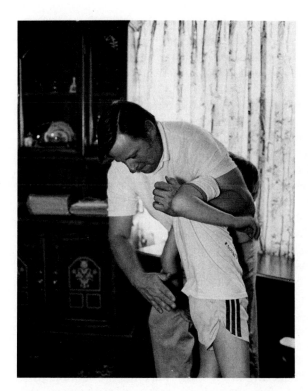

The assertion of physical power secures immediate compliance, but parents who rely primarily on power-assertive discipline may find that their children simply learn to behave so that they do not get caught. *(Tom Ballard/E.K.M.-Nepenthe)*

harms others or when they break a rule. When this happens, they have developed an *internalized* conscience.

Induction seems to have three effects that foster internalized moral standards (M. Hoffman, 1988). First, induction can help the child to understand that he or she has caused another's distress. Second, induction provides a gradually increasing store of emotionally linked information about consequences and moral values, which helps the child identify situations in which some particular action is appropriate. Third, induction creates the perception that moral standards and guilt feelings come from within the child, instead of being imposed from without.

Inductive discipline seems related to the development of **prosocial behavior,** which is any action that promotes or benefits another person. Examples include being generous, coming to the aid of another person, and cooperation. Researchers have found that children who were rated by their peers as generous and helpful had parents who consistently pointed out the consequences of the children's actions on other people (G. Brody and Shaffer, 1982). Such techniques seem ef-

fective. When 9- and 10-year-olds working at an unsupervised task were told that stopping their work in order to play would increase another person's labors, they worked longer and harder than children in other groups—whether the others were simply told not to play or were told that loafing would increase their own labors (Kuczynski, 1983). Prosocial behavior may reflect the development of empathy, which, as we saw in Chapter 8, seems related to parents' own displays of prosocial behavior.

Discipline styles also seem to affect peer relations. In one study (C. Hart, Ladd, and Burleson, 1990), 6- and 9-year-olds whose mothers relied on power assertion tended to be less popular, perhaps because the children themselves endorsed unfriendly, assertive ways to settle peer conflicts. Among older elementary school children, those whose parents used inductive discipline tended to be regarded by their classmates as considerate of other children (M. Hoffman and Saltzstein, 1967). The children who were accustomed to inductive discipline also were more likely than other children to accept the responsibility for their transgressions, to judge an act as being right or wrong independent of rewards or punishment, and to connect transgressions with guilt.

Nearly as important as the parent's style of discipline is its *consistency.* When parents ignore a child's misbehavior one week and punish the same act the next week, the child becomes confused. Patterns of parenting may interact with inconsistent discipline to produce highly aggressive children. An aggressive child often comes from a home with undemanding, unresponsive parents who use power assertion but apply it inconsistently (W. Becker, 1964). Yet even parents who customarily use inductive discipline may begin with love withdrawal or power assertion (M. Hoffman, 1988). Once they have halted the child's misbehavior, they proceed to explain why the child's behavior is harmful or inappropriate.

The Context of Discipline

The way a parent disciplines a child depends on the sort of relationship that has been established between them. That relationship is influenced by many factors: the child's temperament, the parent's perception of the child (see Chapter 4), and the degree of love and concern communicated by the parent. What parents believe about acceptable behavior in children, about the capabilities of children, and about the responsibilities of a parent affects their child-rearing practices. No two sets of parents approach the responsibility of child rearing in exactly the same way, and no two children in a family establish exactly the same relationship with their parents. Because a child's development is affected by so many different factors, it is impossible to single out those parental practices that lead to competent children and then to prescribe them—like daily doses of vitamins.

Yet certain parental characteristics tend to be associated with certain qualities in children—although just how strongly the child's own personality affects these parental characteristics is uncertain. The connection between parents' styles and children's personalities appeared in a longitudinal study by Diana Baumrind (1967, 1986). Baumrind views the parent-child relationship in terms of how much parents demand of a child (including how heavily they exercise their control) and how responsive they are to the child's interests and needs (see Table 9.2). Demanding parents exert firm control over their children; undemanding parents let their children do as they please. Responsive parents tend to be accepting and to place their child's needs first; unresponsive parents tend to reject their children and to see their own needs as primary (Maccoby and Martin, 1983).

In the course of her study, Baumrind gathered information on parents from interviews, standardized tests, and observations at home. She watched the children in nursery school and talked to teachers and parents. When the children were 8 or 9 years old, she studied them again to see whether the characteristics she had found in nursery school endured. Baumrind found four major patterns of parenting: authoritarian, permissive, authoritative, and rejecting-neglecting.

Authoritarian parents are unresponsive and demanding; they see obedience as a virtue. When the child's actions or beliefs conflict with the parents' view of proper conduct, the child is punished with forceful power assertion. Respect for authority, work, and the preservation of order are important. Parents expect the child to accept without question their word on matters of right and wrong.

Permissive parents are responsive and undemanding. They avoid outright physical control, rely on reason alone, and consult with the child about matters of policy. Permissive parents are nonpunitive, accepting, and affirmative; they demand little from their children in the way of household responsibilities or orderly behavior. The children regulate their own activities and are not pushed to obey standards set up by others.

Authoritative parents are responsive and demanding. They believe that control is necessary, but they use reason as well as power assertion to achieve it. When directing their children's activities, authoritative parents use a rational, issue-oriented method and encourage a verbal give-and-take that the authoritarian parent does not tolerate. The aim is the child's responsible conformity to group standards without the loss of his or her independence.

Rejecting-neglecting parents are unresponsive and undemanding. Such parents seem indifferent to their children; their aim seems to be to spend as little time with their children and to exert as little effort as possible. Rejecting-neglecting parents pay little attention to any aspect of the parental role that inconveniences them, and so their children do not have to meet standards concerning aggression or homework (Maccoby and Martin, 1983).

How did each of these regimes affect children's lives? As 4-year-olds, children of either permissive or authoritarian parents turned out similarly. Girls tended to set low goals for themselves and to withdraw in the face of frustration. Boys tended to be hostile. Baumrind specu-

TABLE 9.2   PARENTAL STYLES

	Responsive	Unresponsive
Demanding, Controlling	**Authoritative parents** Disciplinary style: primarily inductive, some power assertion	**Authoritarian parents** Disciplinary style: primarily power assertion
Undemanding, Low in Control	**Permissive parents** Disciplinary style: inductive	**Rejecting-neglecting parents** Disciplinary style: sporadic power assertion

Source: Adapted from Maccoby and Martin, 1983, p. 39.

Authoritative parents, who are warm and encourage their children's individuality but exert firm control buttressed by reason, seem to produce the most competent children. *(Joel Gordon)*

social assertiveness or social responsibility, but they tended to be low in cognitive competence. At the age of 9, daughters of *permissive* parents tended to be high in social responsibility but low in social assertiveness. Sons did not differ from other boys. Both daughters and sons tended to be low in cognitive competence. Compared with other youngsters, children of *rejecting-neglecting* parents tended to be low in all areas of development: social responsibility, social assertiveness, and cognitive competence (see Table 9.3).

Overall, children of *authoritative* parents seemed the most competent. As preschoolers, daughters tended to be independent and socially responsible. Sons were also socially responsible but no more independent than average. According to Baumrind, these youngsters develop responsibility because their parents impose clearly communicated, realistic demands on them. At the age of 9, sons and daughters of authoritative parents continued to do well. They tended to show high social assertiveness, social responsibility, and cognitive competence. Firm but reasonable parental control, combined with some degree of choice by the children, also appeared to encourage self-confidence and high self-esteem (Maccoby and Martin, 1983).

Although the children studied by Baumrind were all middle-class, researchers have found similar links between parental styles and school performance in large groups of older children from various backgrounds (Dornbusch and Gray, 1988; Dornbusch et al., 1987). The relation holds among boys and girls, no matter what their parents' education, social class, or ethnic background and regardless of whether the children live with both parents or with one parent. In *severely* disadvantaged families, however, one study indicates that authoritarian parenting seems to produce children who are more emotionally resilient than does authoritative parenting (Baldwin, Baldwin, and Cole, 1990). Thus, in the United States today, unless families are severely disadvantaged, parental styles seems to affect all children in a similar manner. Future research is needed, however, to ascertain whether dangerous or unstable social environments might make authoritarian parenting advantageous.

lates that the preschool children of permissive or authoritarian parents tend to be dependent, because both kinds of parents tend to shield their children from stress, inhibiting the development of assertiveness and the ability to tolerate frustration. Other studies indicate that 4-year-olds whose parents are rejecting-neglecting tend to be demanding youngsters who are less compliant and more aggressive than the offspring of parents who are involved with their children (Maccoby and Martin, 1983).

Over the years, some effects of parental style moderated (Baumrind, 1986). By the time they were 9-year-olds, daughters of *authoritarian* parents seemed to be high in social assertiveness (they participated comfortably in social interaction, sometimes taking the lead in group activities) but only average in social responsibility (they were about as generous, and helpful, friendly, and cooperative as their peers). They tended to be high in cognitive competence (they enjoyed intellectual challenge and showed originality in thought). Sons of authoritarian parents did not differ from other boys in

Influences on Gender Roles

As children grow, all the factors that encourage gender-typed behavior in infants and toddlers continue to push girls and boys into separate roles. Gradually, through the socialization process that begins in the family and is

TABLE 9.3   OUTCOME OF PARENTAL STYLES*

Area of Development	High	Low
Social responsibility	Authoritative boys Authoritative girls Permissive girls	Rejecting-neglecting girls Rejecting-neglecting boys
Social assertiveness	Authoritative boys Authoritative girls Authoritarian girls	Rejecting-neglecting boys Rejecting-neglecting girls Permissive girls
Cognitive competence	Authoritative boys Authoritative girls Authoritarian girls	Authoritarian boys Permissive boys Permissive girls Rejecting-neglecting boys Rejecting-neglecting girls

*Parental styles seem consistently related to social and cognitive outcomes in older children. When a parental style does not appear in the table, the children tend to be average on that dimension.

Source: Information from Baumrind, 1986.

perpetuated by peers, school, and the mass media, children acquire **gender roles,** which are patterns of behavior that society considers appropriate and desirable for each gender. These prescribed gender roles become magnified and transformed into **gender-role stereotypes,** which are simplified, fixed conceptions about the behavior and traits typical—or even possible—in each sex. Such exaggerated stereotypes probably make the acquisition of gender roles easier for children. In order to understand gender roles and their stereotypes, we first need to examine the emergence of another aspect of this developmental process—gender identity (see Table 9.4).

Besides learning an appropriate gender role, children must develop the sense that they themselves are either male or female (Money and Ehrhardt, 1972). This inner sense, known as **gender identity,** develops by the time they are 3 years old. Most 3-year-olds, says Sandra Bem

TABLE 9.4   ASPECTS OF BEING MALE OR FEMALE

Gender role	Outward behavior considered appropriate or desirable for males or females
Gender-role stereotype	Simplified, exaggerated conception of gender role and characteristics of males or females
Gender identity	Private sense of being male or female
Gender constancy	Concept that gender is permanent and that the child's own gender will never change
Gender schema	Informal theory about maleness and femaleness that children apply to all information that comes their way

(1983), not only know whether they are boys or girls but are also beginning to categorize the world by gender. They know whether toys, clothing, tools, games, and occupations are suitable for girls or boys, and they select and interpret new information through the filter of their naive theories about each gender, called **gender schemas.** This filter may lead them to ignore information that doesn't fit their theories (mother replacing a worn-out electrical switch) or distort their perceptions to fit the theories (recalling a male nurse from a television show as female) (Huston, 1985). Their schemas also include what the child hopes to be and what she or he is determined to avoid becoming (Markus and Nurius, 1986). Parents' emotional reactions (either positive or negative) to their children's gender-typed activities may affect the speed with which gender schemas develop (Fagot and Leinbach, 1989). Once children apply their gender schemas to themselves, they begin forming feminine or masculine self-concepts, or gender identities.

The process is gradual, and the preschoolers' ele-

mentary knowledge of their own gender is only the first step. Children's understanding of gender is not complete until they acquire **gender constancy.** With the acquisition of that concept, the child understands that boys always become men and girls always become women and that maleness and femaleness cannot be changed. More important, the child realizes that no one can wave a magic wand and change his or her own gender. The speed with which children develop this concept may be affected by their knowledge about the genital differences between the sexes. Although only 40 percent of 3- to 5-year-olds in one study (Bem, 1989) showed gender constancy, 74 percent of those who knew that genitals determine gender had acquired gender constancy. Girls tended to acquire gender constancy earlier than boys, perhaps because 3-year-old girls knew as much about genitalia as 5-year-old boys. In fact, all the 3-year-olds with gender constancy were girls.

Social Change and Gender Roles

Much of the difference in the way parents and other social agents treat children reflects differing expectations about boys' and girls' adult roles (L. Hoffman, 1977). When the baby-boom generation was being born, girls were expected to spend most of their adult years as mothers and boys were expected to be the sole breadwinners for their future families. In 1947, less than 30 percent of the female population was in the labor force—and nearly nine out of ten employed women were either single, widowed, or divorced. Only 20 percent of the married men had economic assistance from working wives (U.S. Bureau of the Census, 1982).

Children's toys reflected this world. As in other societies around the world, toys allowed children to play at adult social roles without any of the physical, emotional, or economic consequences that accompany mistakes made when engaging in the real thing (L. Hoffman, 1977). Dishes, dolls, brooms, and toy sewing machines let little girls practice the skills of child care, cooking, and homemaking—the roles their mothers filled. Trucks, tools, building equipment, and doctor's kits let little boys practice the skills of driving, construction, and doctoring—the roles their fathers filled. (Little girls got *nurse's* kits.) When girls grow up to occupy a nurturant role, socialization patterns encourage them to become empathic and attuned to the emotions of others. When boys grow up to run social institutions and fend for the family, socialization patterns encourage

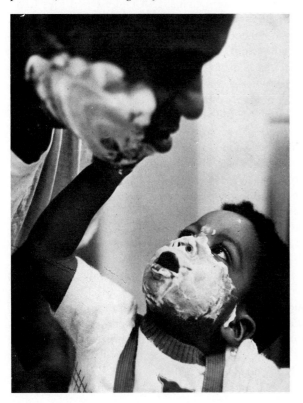

This little boy is developing his own notions of what it is to be male; imitating his father's actions contributes to the process. *(Burk Uzzle/Magnum)*

Most toys for children reflect society's view of gender-appropriate socialization, although the toys may not prepare children for recent broadening of gender roles. *(George Goodwin/Monkmeyer)*

them to become independent achievers and may even discourage the development of empathy.

In the United States today, homemaking is not a full-time job, and motherhood occupies a much smaller proportion of a woman's life than it did fifty years ago. Because women live longer today and have fewer children, they spend more years involved in occupational pursuits than in mothering. As we saw in Chapter 8, employment outside the home has become the norm for today's woman. Women's move into the marketplace has been accompanied by men's increased participation in child care and household tasks. As Lois Hoffman (1977; Eccles and Hoffman, 1984) has pointed out, traditional gender-role training no longer prepares girls to fit their new adult roles—or boys to be nurturant caregivers. Yet a girl still learns that society has defined her spouse-and-parent role as primary and her vocational role as secondary; the reverse is true for boys. In U.S. society, there seems to be a lag between social changes in adult gender roles and society's perception of appropriate gender-role socialization.

Will the convergence of adult roles eventually be followed by changes in the socialization of children? Although some parents make conscious efforts to produce independent daughters with broad vocational interests and to raise nurturant, empathic sons, they have not entirely shaken off the socialization styles of their own parents. Traditional gender differences still appear in their children (Huston, 1983). In the future, the way boys and girls are treated may become more similar, and this could lead to diminished differences in gender roles.

How Parents Influence Gender Roles

The differences in the way parents treat their infant and toddler sons and daughters continue in the way they socialize older children. Often, parents teach expected gender roles directly. They may tell their sons that "boys don't cry" or their daughters that "girls don't get in fistfights." They also are likely to teach skills in a gender-specific manner. Girls may learn to vacuum the floors, do the laundry, or fix a meal when mother stays late at the office. Boys are more likely to learn how to repair a broken stair, fix a bicycle tire, or mow the lawn. (When a *boy's* mother is late, she brings home a pizza for dinner.)

Indirectly, parents encourage the adoption of gender roles by the experiences they provide the child. Parents choose most of their children's toys, and most toys for girls encourage compliance, but boys' toys encourage independence and originality. Gender-typed toys have other influences on children. Playing with blocks, building materials, tools, and model kits encourages manipulation, develops skills connected with mathematics and spatial relationships, and provides boys with information about the physical world. Playing house with Barbie dolls encourages girls to develop verbal skills (Eccles and Hoffman, 1984).

Parents' perceptions of their children lead them to expect more competence and independence from boys than from girls. When youngsters have a task to complete, parents are more likely to let a son figure out his own mistakes but to step in and help a daughter as soon as she gets in trouble (Huston, 1983). Parents also give boys more freedom. Boys are allowed to investigate wider areas of the community without asking their parents' permission (Saegert and Hart, 1976). Such differences in socialization may affect personality and self-concept along gender-related lines. Girls tend to continue checking frequently with their mothers, to be less assertive and more dependent, and to miss many chances to develop a sense of competence, and they may pick up their parents' fears about moving around freely in the world (Huston, 1983).

Parental patterns of reward and punishment also influence children's adoption of gender roles. Boys are more likely to be punished for violating gender roles, a practice that may make them more responsive than girls to gender-typed labels. It's okay to be a tomboy, but sissies are frowned on. Parents do not seem to mind if their daughter climbs trees, rejects ribbons and skirts, and becomes a rabid fan of the Denver Broncos, but they are uneasy when their son shows an interest in dolls or asks to take ballet lessons. Fathers show much more concern than mothers about appropriate gender-role behavior, perhaps because they hold more traditional views of gender roles than mothers do (L. Hoffman and Nye, 1974). When Judith Langlois and Chris Downs (1980) observed parents interacting with their 3- to 5-year-old children, the difference in mothers' and fathers' behavior became clear. Mothers showed no inclination to push their children into traditional gender roles, but fathers interfered actively to stop inappropriate play. If a son played with housekeeping toys or a daughter played with an army set, fathers talked negatively, ridiculed the play, or suggested that the child play with another toy. They balanced this punishment with rewards for playing with gender-appropriate toys.

Parents' beliefs about gender roles and their consequent behavior have strong effects, particularly on older children (Eccles et al., 1993). In one study (Meyer, 1980), although there was no relationship between the gender-role attitudes and future role aspirations of 6- to 8-year-old girls and their mothers, the attitudes and aspirations of 10- to 12-year-old girls tend to correspond with those of their mothers. According to Beverly Fagot (1982), children's ability to distinguish between cultural stereotypes and their parents' specific beliefs and attitudes about gender roles develops gradually.

Traditional gender roles may be strengthened when children identify with the parent of the same sex and model their behavior on that parent's example (Eccles and Hoffman, 1984). In many families, the mother's education and occupation fall below those of the father. Unless daughters get extra encouragement, they are unlikely to aim as high as their brothers or look for a job that falls outside the typical woman's sphere of work (teaching, nursing, librarianship, clerical jobs). Even in homes where the parents' educations and occupations are roughly equal, the major responsibility for household tasks and child care is likely to fall on the mother, while the father usually takes charge of the yard and keeps the family automobiles running (Hochschild, 1989). These conditions suggest that in the United States today, identification may strongly affect children's expectations and limit daughters' aspirations.

Searching for Sex Differences

With boys and girls getting such different treatment from parents, it comes as no surprise to find that girls and boys differ in interests and behavior. Some researchers also have found differences in personality and cognitive capabilities. Boys tend to be more physically aggressive, more physically active, and more competitive than girls. They also seem to have superior visual-spatial ability and mathematical skills (but not arithmetic skills). Girls seem to have superior verbal skills as well as a greater need for emotional connections with other people. They are more empathic and nurturant than boys, less confident about their abilities, and more likely to seek help and reassurance from others, and they tend to avoid risks. When they fail, they are quicker than boys to take responsibility for their shortcomings (L. Hoffman, 1977; Huston, 1983).

In all these areas, the abilities and behavior of boys and girls overlap. The findings describe only the average behavior of a group. Some girls are more aggressive than the average boy, some boys more empathic than the average girl (see, for example, Boldizar, Perry, and Perry, 1989). In most cases, the average differences, although statistically significant, are not very large.

Yet there are problems with studies in nearly every one of these areas. Many experiments designed to test gender differences center on situations that are likely to produce stereotypical responses (Ruble, 1988). For example, 10-year-old girls may be assertive when playing a game with other girls but hesitant about asserting themselves in a situation that includes boys. Other factors that can evoke different responses from boys and girls are the sex of the experimenter, the children's familiarity with the situation, and their interest in the topic of the experiment. In the accompanying box, "The Eye of the Beholder," we can see that a researcher's familiarity with children also may affect his or her perceptions.

Some researchers believe that a few gender differences have a biological basis. Before birth, hormones affect brain development and determine whether the mature individual will produce hormones continually (as males do) or on a cyclical basis (as females do). They also may lead to sex differences in brain organization. As a result, boys and girls may differ in perceptual and cognitive skills. After reviewing the research, Diane McGuinness (1985) concluded that girls' superior performance in reading rests on sharper hearing (they find it easier to distinguish the sounds of language) and faster integration of verbal and visual stimuli. Boys, she

THE EYE OF THE BEHOLDER

Our perception of another's behavior often depends on the label we attach to that person. Do labels also affect our views of gender differences in behavior? When adults watch a crying baby, they assume that they are hearing cries of anger when told the baby is a boy and cries of fear when told the baby is a girl (Condry and Condry, 1976). John Condry and David Ross (1985) wondered if the same effect was responsible for the belief that boys are more aggressive than girls. In other words, they suspected that people would be more likely to perceive aggression among boisterous boys than among sweet girls who were playing just as roughly. So they videotaped a pair of preschoolers playing together in the snow. The play was ambiguous, but it could be interpreted as an attack by one child on the other. Because the youngsters were dressed in snowsuits, viewers could not detect their sex.

The researchers played the tape for men and women enrolled in a child-development class and then asked them to rate the children's behavior. The results disproved the researchers' hypothesis. When viewers believed that both children were boys, they thought the play was least aggressive and most affectionate, and they evaluated the fighting children most favorably. In all the rest of the conditions (fighting girls, a boy attacking a girl, or a girl attacking a boy),

viewers said that the play was highly aggressive. The sex of the observer made no difference: women were as likely as men to attribute the most aggression to girls. When Condry and Ross analyzed their data more carefully, they discovered that observers who had no experience with children tended to see no difference in aggression, whether they thought they were watching girls or boys. But observers who had experience with children consistently saw the boys as less aggressive.

How can we explain these results? Condry and Ross concluded that experience with young children destroys the belief that all kids are alike. Such experience convinces young adults that boys are more aggressive than girls, and so they *discount* what they see. When two boys are wrestling in the snow, experienced observers say, "Boys will be boys." Expecting boys to fight, they judge the activity in terms of their gender schema for boys. Or perhaps they interpret the ambiguous scuffle as a bout of rough-and-tumble play. When they see two girls fighting, the activity so violates their expectations that they overestimate the level of aggression. The results of their experiment have led Condry and Ross to wonder if most observational research (because it is conducted by experienced viewers) *underestimates* gender differences in children's aggression.

---

says, may have genetically superior spatial ability, which makes mathematics easier for them. Other researchers are convinced that any differences are the result of socialization. After a similar review of research, Anne Fausto-Sterling (1985) concluded that none of the studies has successfully demonstrated a biological basis for sex differences in cognition. For example, there are no sex differences in spatial ability among Eskimos, who live in a large, almost featureless environment where the ability to detect minute detail is linked to survival.

The sex difference most often traced to a biological base is aggression. Researchers have suggested that prenatal sex hormones predispose boys toward aggression. In a study of children whose mothers had taken male hormones during pregnancy (Reinisch, 1981), the boys had a much stronger tendency to be physically aggressive than their brothers who had not been exposed to the additional prenatal hormones (see Figure 9.1). The girls were also more aggressive than their unexposed sisters. (In this study, children told researchers how they would react in situations that involved conflict

with other youngsters, but no one actually observed the children in conflict.)

The great overlap between the behavior of boys and girls indicates that any biological push toward different skills or traits must be small. Because behavior can be expressed only within an environment, the cultural influence is also important. Socialization can heighten sex differences or diminish them, depending on whether a culture considers a particular ability or behavior an asset.

Siblings

During childhood, siblings are "always there." This enforced proximity makes the sibling relationship a source of companionship and conflict. Its ambivalent nature may provide children with unique learning experiences (Furman and Buhrmester, 1985). The quality of those experiences depends on a host of factors: the child's

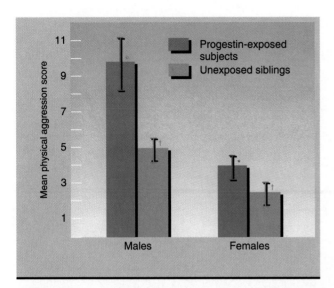

Figure 9.1 When asked how they would solve disputes with other youngsters, children who had been exposed to prenatal male hormones had a stronger tendency to choose physical aggression than their siblings of the same sex. Asterisk (*) indicates significant difference between progestin-exposed and -unexposed subjects ($p < .01$); dagger (†) indicates significant difference between unexposed males and unexposed females ($p < .02$). *(From Reinisch, 1981, p. 1172)*

position in the family birth order, the spacing between siblings, the sex of the sibling, and the number of children in the family. In Chapter 8, we saw how the birth of a sibling radically changes a first-born toddler's life, destroying the toddler's position as center of the universe but allowing the youngster to dominate the baby brother or sister.

Among sibling pairs in a longitudinal study, the older child's domination of the sibling relationship continued after both children started school (Abramovitch et al., 1986). As time passed, sibling pairs of the same sex tended to become more harmonious, but mixed-sex pairs teased, threatened, and competed more. Yet the thread of hostility that ran through these relationships was not major; most of the time, siblings played together and provided each other with affection, praise, approval, and comfort.

The level of sibling aggression may depend in part on the nature of relationships between parents and child. In one longitudinal study (Volling and Belsky, 1992), conflict and aggression between 6-year-olds and their preschool siblings were predicted by the older child's insecure attachment at age one and by intrusive and overcontrolling mothering at age three. Sharing, help,

and comfort between siblings were predicted by positive, facilitative fathering of the older child at age three.

As children grow older, relationships between siblings become less intense and less one-sided. By the time the younger sibling is 12 years old, the older sibling has given up much of the dominance and nurturance that once marked the relationship (Buhrmester and Furman, 1990). Such a development reflects the greater competence and independence of the younger sibling, who no longer requires so much supervision and direction.

Birth Order

Most studies of sibling interaction have focused on infants and preschoolers. With older children, researchers have simply considered such factors as the child's **ordinal position** (his or her place in the birth order), the spacing between siblings, and family size, looking for correlations between these variables and personality traits or cognitive abilities. The patterns that have been found describe group averages; they do not predict the outcome of individuals.

First-Borns

The clearest contrasts appear between first-borns and other siblings. Not only are first-borns treated differently by parents than are later-borns (see Chapter 1), but they also experience life differently. The first-born creates a major upheaval in the family, forcing parents to put the needs of their infant ahead of the marital relationship and their own needs (W. Miller and Newman, 1978). The first-born also has the misfortune of being reared by inexperienced parents (L. Hoffman, 1991). At every stage in the first-born's life, the parents are charting new territory. By the time the second-born reaches each stage, the parents are experienced; their expectations are no longer unrealistically high, and their standards are likely to be less strict.

Being an older sibling is nothing like *having* an older sibling (L. Hoffman, 1991). As infants, first-borns get more of their parents' attention than any subsequent child gets (Lasko, 1954). The family photograph album testifies to this heightened attention; the first-born's infancy and toddlerhood are pictured in great detail, but snapshots of later siblings are few and far between. For a time, first-borns have their parents all to themselves. Fathers talk to their first-born sons more than to any other child and touch them more; mothers smile and vocalize more to first-born daughters (L. Hoffman, 1991; Parke and Sawin, 1975). But no other child suffers

Older siblings often dominate and tease their younger brothers and sisters, but they also provide comfort and affection. *(Bob Krist/Black Star)*

the same loss of attention at the birth of another sibling (see Chapter 8). The dethroned first-born is thus more likely than later-borns to feel sibling rivalry—and to be kept by parents from expressing it (Dunn, 1983).

All these factors contribute to the finding that, emotionally and socially, the first-born tends to be less poised and self-confident than later-borns, to be more anxious in stressful situations (Lahey et al., 1980), and to have more trouble establishing social relations. Often first-borns are less popular with peers than are later-borns (N. Miller and Maruyama, 1976). Perhaps first-borns carry patterns of sibling relationships into interaction with peers. Within the family, first-borns are supposed to be the experts, to assume responsibility for younger siblings, and to interfere on their behalf. Peers may resent this sort of behavior. First-borns also tend to rely on their parents as models of good behavior, a tendency that makes them "good" boys and girls in the eyes of their peers. Later-borns, who imitate older siblings as

well as parents, seem less constrained by adult rules and examples.

Intellectually, however, the first-born excels. First-borns tend to have higher IQs than later-borns and to be higher achievers. The large amounts of early attention and the high parental expectations seem to pay off, as well as the fact that family conversations are pitched at the intellectual level of the first-born (L. Hoffman, 1991). When parents have something to say to their children, they tend to direct their comments to the oldest child.

Such findings may help to explain why, as family size increases, children's intellectual development seems to suffer: the more older siblings a child has, the lower his or her intellectual level (Heer, 1985; Zajonc, 1983). The closer siblings are in age, the more detrimental the effects become. According to **confluence theory,** as families get larger, the level of the family's intellectual environment drops because the presence of younger children lowers its quality (Zajonc, 1983). First-borns interact primarily with adults, but fourth- or fifth-borns interact mostly with other children. First-borns also tend to play teacher to their siblings, an experience that stimulates the older child's intellectual development. According to **resource theory,** however, parental attention and resources are the key to intellectual differences. The size of the family and spacing between siblings affect the amount of time and material resources that parents can give children (L. Hoffman, 1983). Parents have only so much attention to spread among their offspring, and each subsequent child receives less attention and a smaller share of material resources that foster intellectual development. Because of the connection with material resources, the effect of family size on IQ is strongest among low-income families. In low-income families, the IQ drop appears when the number of children rises from two to three, but in high-income families, the drop is not obvious until the fifth child arrives.

The Only Child

In some ways, the only child is like the first-born. Only children have no older sibling to break paths for them in social development, and they get all their parents' attention. Unlike the first-born, the only child is never dethroned, has no opportunity to act as teacher and model for younger siblings, and is deprived of interaction with siblings. How do only children turn out? They are higher in IQ and academic achievement than later-borns but not higher than first-borns (Pollit, 1982; Zajonc, 1983). Even when researchers look only at two-parent families, boys without siblings score about the same as first-born boys, but the scores of girls without siblings are lower than those of first-born girls (Rosenberg and Falk, 1989). Perhaps the difference, which appears only in verbal IQ, comes from the tendency of first-born girls to act as teacher and "substitute mother" for younger siblings.

The personalities of only children are also different from those of first-borns. Only children seem to escape the first-born's higher anxiety levels, and their self-esteem is as high as that of later-borns (Claudy, Farrell, and Dayton, 1979). But the lack of sibling interaction may slow the development of empathy, as we saw in Chapter 8, and may also be connected to a lower social involvement. There are also positive aspects to being an only child. Only children tend to be independent, tend to make their own decisions without considering the group, and are less likely to be "joiners" (Falbo, 1984; Pollit, 1982). The accompanying box, "Country in a Quandary," explores these tendencies among only children in China.

Maternal Employment

Among school-age children, it is the child of the mother who is *not* employed who lives in a statistically "abnormal" family (see Figure 9.2). In most cases, having an employed mother seems to benefit the school-age child (Moorehouse and Sanders, in press). Compared with children in two-parent families whose mothers are at home, the children of employed mothers probably see more of their fathers, because the fathers are less likely to have a second job and thus have more time for the family. The fathers may also help out more at home, giving children an opportunity to see a male in a nontraditional role.

Children of employed mothers also have to help out at home; they are more likely to have household responsibilities than children of full-time homemakers. Such responsibilities, when they are not unreasonable, often contribute to a child's sense of self-esteem (L. Hoffman, 1984, 1989; Medrich, Roizen, and Rubin, 1982). Discipline in lower-income homes is more consistent when the mother is employed. In these families and in one-parent families, employed mothers tend to have structured rules for their children and to enforce the rules consistently (L. Hoffman, 1979, 1984).

Daughters seem to reap special benefits from having a mother in the work force. They tend to be independent, high achievers with high self-esteem. Why should maternal employment have this effect? Mothers serve as role models, preparing their daughters for the sort of roles they will occupy as adults. Daughters of working mothers admire their mothers more than do daughters of full-time homemakers. Accompanying this admiration is higher esteem for the female role and a strong belief in women's competence (Baruch, 1972; Vogel et al., 1970). The fathers are also more likely to approve of competence in women and to encourage it. High-achieving women often report that they had a close relationship with a warm, encouraging father, and the father's approval and participation in child care may have provided this sort of support (L. Hoffman, 1980).

Sons derive some benefit from having employed mothers. They seem better adjusted and hold less traditional views of both sexes; they see women as more competent and men as warmer than do sons of full-time homemakers (Vogel et al., 1970). However, the blurring

COUNTRY IN A QUANDARY: THE ONLY CHILD IN CHINA

Alarmed by population growth that threatened social and economic development plans, the government of China put its weight behind family planning. Since 1979, official government policy has limited families to a single child. The effects of the policy have appeared: about 90 percent of young couples in urban areas and 60 percent of young couples in rural areas have only one child (Tseng et al., 1988).

Cooperation is essential to the success of a socialist society; the individual who acts primarily in his or her own self-interest is unlikely to adapt comfortably to modern Chinese life. Should the Chinese government begin to worry about the possible effects of its family-planning program? That depends on whether you ask the parents and teachers of only children or their peers.

When teachers and mothers in Beijing and Jilin province (a district in northeastern China) rated the personality of elementary school children, teachers gave only children higher ratings on personality than they gave children with siblings. There was no difference in the ratings produced by the children's mothers (Falbo, 1988). In the city of Nanjing and the rural areas around it, parents rated 3- to 6-year-old boys the same whether they were only children or had siblings. But parents rated only girls as more depressed, moody, and temperamental than girls with siblings (Tseng et al., 1988). The effect was strongest in rural areas, where only girls were seen as hot-tempered and aggressive by their parents. The girls' behavior may reflect parents' attitudes toward their daughters. If parents can have only one child, and they live in a rural area, where boys are highly preferred, the birth of a girl is often unwelcome.

The picture changed when kindergartners and 9- to 10-year-old primary school students in the Beijing area rated their classmates (Jiao, Ji, and Jing, 1986). In their classmates' judgment, only children were significantly more likely than children with siblings to act according to their own interest and to refuse to share things with their peers. Only children also were less persistent at tasks, were less cooperative, and were held in lower regard by their peers. Of the fifteen children who were rated as most cooperative

Chinese parents are under pressure to adhere to the government's "one-child" family policy; researchers wonder how the policy's success will affect future generations of Chinese. *(Owen Franken/Stock, Boston)*

by their classmates, one was an only child. Of the fifteen children who were rated as the best liked, a leader, and the child you would ask for advice and help, two were only children. Of the fifteen children who were rated as selfish, eleven were only children.

When researchers looked at family backgrounds, they found that neither parents' occupation nor family structure affected the results. Do children reveal sides of their personalities to their peers that escape the notice of parents? Two other studies seem to support the peer ratings (Tao and Chiu, 1985; Shanghai Preschool Education Study Group, 1980). As we saw in Chapter 8, parents tend to let their expectations color their view of their babies' temperament. Suppose the differences that appeared among the 10-year-old Chinese children are real and that they persist to adulthood. What will happen to Chinese society? Is the strength of these results due to some aspect of Chinese culture, or if the United States moves toward the one-child family, will its citizens become less cooperative and more self-interested? No one yet knows the answers to these questions.

---

of traditional gender roles is not as pronounced among sons of blue-collar fathers, and they sometimes admire their fathers less than do sons of mothers who are full-time homemakers. Since many wives with blue-collar husbands enter the work force primarily because of pinched finances, this view may reflect a perception by both father and son that the father has failed in his job of family provider. Blue-collar sons, as well as daughters,

do better in school when their mothers are employed. This higher academic achievement also characterizes sons and daughters of employed mothers in poor families—whether African-American or white (L. Hoffman, 1980; Vandell and Ramanan, 1992).

In the middle class, sons may not fare so well academically. Some research finds that sons of middle-class employed mothers tend to get lower scores on achieve-

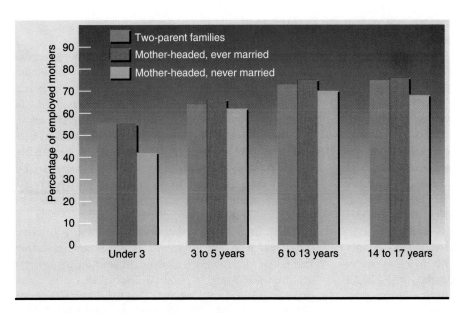

Figure 9.2 Employed mothers. In contemporary American society, the typical mother is part of the labor force. More mothers are employed outside the home than are home with their children. *(From U.S. Bureau of Labor Statistics, 1990)*

ment tests in mathematics and language than sons of full-time homemakers (Desai, Chase-Lansdale, and Michael, 1989; D. Gold and Andres, 1978). Researchers have tried to understand this effect, and some have suggested that it might be the result of heavy socialization by today's full-time homemaker. Close, extended contact with the full-time, middle-class mother may induce boys to conform to adult standards—and thus to perform well in school. This notion is supported by a study that looked at the effect of full-time mothering during

Most children whose mothers work outside the home are expected to help with household chores, a responsibility that tends to increase a child's self-esteem. *(Michal Heron/Woodfin Camp & Associates)*

the preschool years (T. Moore, 1975). Sons who had experienced early full-time mothering tended to be inhibited and conforming at school age, but their school performance was better than that of sons whose mothers had been employed. Perhaps these boys are responding somewhat as girls do to heavily traditional gender-role socialization: with low levels of independence and good grades.

When primary caregivers are employed outside the home, there may be no one to supervise children after school. More than 2 million girls and boys are **latchkey children,** who come home to an empty house and take responsibility for their own after-school care. Contrary to most people's assumptions, these youngsters tend to be white, middle-class children who live in rural or suburban areas, and they are as likely to live in a two-parent family as with a single parent (Galambos and Maggs, 1991a). Research indicates that latchkey children who stay in their own homes each afternoon do just as well as children who are supervised by their own parents or other adults or who go to after-school programs (Galambos and Maggs, 1991a; Rodman, Pratto, and Nelson, 1985; Steinberg, 1986). Among third-graders in the Dallas suburbs, for example, there was no difference in academic grades, conduct, standardized test scores, peer ratings, teacher ratings, or children's feelings about themselves between youngsters who were alone in their homes and those in their mothers' care (Vandell and Corasanati, 1988). In Chapter 13, we will see how young adolescents fare when given latchkey status.

Alternative Family Arrangements

Few couples today stay together "for the sake of the children," and an increasing number of mothers never marry. At least half, and perhaps as many as three-fourths, of the children born in the 1980s will have their lives disrupted by their parents' divorce or separation (Hernandez, 1988). As already noted, 24 percent of all children younger than 18 are living in single-parent families (U.S. Bureau of the Census, 1992), and in nearly 85 percent of the cases, the custodial parent was the mother. Children may spend only a few years in a single-parent family. Because most divorced people remarry within five years, researchers estimate that about 35 percent of today's children will spend part of their lives in a stepfamily (Glick, 1984). Currently, one child in ten lives in a family with a stepparent (Hernandez, 1988).

Divorce

When parents separate, the father usually moves out of the house and life changes in unpleasant, unsettling ways. There is a loss of routine; regular events, such as meals and bedtimes, no longer arrive on schedule. The division of labor within the home changes. The family and the house seem disorganized (Hetherington, Cox, and Cox, 1982). There are specific losses; planned activities and family vacations are canceled. Money may become scarce. The family may have to move (often to a poorer neighborhood), losing friends, neighbors, and perhaps a familiar school in the process.

There is a loss of emotional security; youngsters often watch in bewilderment as the secure nest they had taken for granted is shaken. Most of us assume that children are aware of parental discord that precedes a divorce, but research suggests that the divorce is often a shock to the child (Wallerstein and Blakeslee, 1989). Parents often conceal their difficulties from children; in families where parents argue, children tend to accept the arguments as part of family life. The parents' emotional distress after the break so changes their behavior that children may feel as if they were living with strangers (Hetherington and Camara, 1984). Their parents' moods may swing unpredictably from euphoria to depression, and the custodial parent, usually the mother, may be depressed, angry, impatient, and erratic in dispensing discipline for most of the first year.

The child's response to these disruptions depends on many things, including temperament and past experience, but the effect of the child's age and gender seem particularly important. The loss of routines is most disturbing for young children. Familiar, predictable routines give children a sense of security; such minor changes as the time and nature of meals can upset young children. Young children find their new situation difficult to understand. Often they think that the divorce is their fault—that something they did drove their parents apart—and they feel guilty. (Even older children may feel this way.) Young children also misinterpret a parent's moods and frequently feel that the parent's anger or sadness is their own fault. These feelings are understandable, because children's egocentrism leads them to interpret the event from their own point of view. They may even fear that their own relationship to the parent could dissolve just as the marriage did. ("If Mommy doesn't love Daddy anymore, maybe someday she won't love me either.")

Children may be angry at one or both of the parents.

They tend to focus on their own losses, and their resentment may be expressed in aggressiveness, a refusal to comply with the parent's wishes, whining, nagging, dependence, and withdrawal of affection (Hetherington and Camara, 1984). Older children also may be embarrassed about the divorce, especially if one of the parents has a new sexual partner or begins dating. Yet older children understand the situation better than young children do, and are less likely to distort it.

During the first year after the divorce, conflict may develop between the custodial mother and her young son. Mothers in one longitudinal study who attempted to exert control over their sons generally resorted to authoritarian measures during this transitional period (Hetherington, Cox, and Cox, 1982). The mothers made ineffective and inconsistent attempts to exert discipline, and the boys would respond with increased aggressiveness and noncompliance. This made the mothers feel anxious and incompetent, and when they stepped up power-assertive attempts at discipline, their sons became even more aggressive and noncompliant. The pattern of escalating power assertion, on the one hand, and aggression and noncompliance, on the other, affected the boys' behavior at school, where they became increasingly aggressive throughout the first year after the divorce. Although their aggression then began to wane, six years after the divorce these boys were still perceived as more aggressive by their peers.

Eventually, children come to terms with their new situation. Within two years, most children have fewer problems than those who live in a home filled with marital discord. Indeed, the best predictor of childhood behavior problems is not divorce but marital discord (Gottman and Katz, 1989). Girls seem to adjust better to the divorce than boys; they are doing as well at the two-year mark as girls in intact families where there is little conflict (Hetherington and Camara, 1984). Why do boys seem more vulnerable than girls to the stress that accompanies divorce? Boys seem more vulnerable to any kind of family stress, including marital discord and unemployment. The detrimental effect of divorce on boys may be as much the stress of living with discord *before* the breakup as the stress of adjusting to a broken family. The personality of children who took part in a longitudinal study was assessed when they were 3, 4, and 7 years old (Block, Block, and Gjerde, 1986). Contact with the families continued, and some of the families later divorced. When researchers looked at their data, they found that boys in these families (now adolescents) had shown the aggression and lack of impulse control connected with divorce as early as eleven years before their parents separated.

Other observations provide additional clues to boys' greater vulnerability (L. Hoffman, 1986). First, boys are more likely to lose the parent of the same sex, because the father usually leaves the household. Second, as we have seen, boys are more likely than girls to respond aggressively or defiantly to the mother's disciplinary attempts, which often escalate unpleasantly. Third, parents see boys as less vulnerable than girls, which may lead parents to protect boys less. This perception may account for the fact that parents are more likely to quarrel in front of their sons (Hetherington, Cox, and Cox, 1982). Finally, peers and teachers view boys in divorced families more negatively and give them less support during stressful periods than they give girls (Hetherington and Camara, 1984). Taken together, these factors suggest that boys are exposed to more stress than girls.

When divorce has lingering consequences on children, the culprit once again may be discord. Several studies have found that conflict between the marriage partners often does not end with the breakup of the marriage but increases (Forehand, Long, and Brody, 1988). Ex-mates fight over finances, visitation, child rearing, and intimate relations with others. Children whose divorced parents have pleasant relationships tend to have fewer problems than those whose parents are in conflict. As we shall see in the next section, how well children do after divorce also may depend on which parent they live with.

The Single Parent

When researchers study single-parent families, they generally look for problems and so, in their search, may miss possible benefits. After an interview study with children and parents, Robert Weiss (1979b) concluded that life with a single parent also has its positive aspects. He discovered that in families with school-age and adolescent children, the experience can lead to greater responsibility, self-sufficiency, and maturity. In these families, each child is expected to do his or her share to keep the household running—and most do. These children have more power than children in an intact family, and most develop a peerlike relationship with the custodial parent. As a 17-year-old who had lived in a one-parent family for six years told Weiss:

In the long run—I feel sort of like I shouldn't say it—but a lot of kids are better off if their parents do get divorced, because you grow up a lot quicker. (Weiss, 1979b, p. 111)

Yet some children find more problems than growth in the single-parent family. When they are given early control over their own behavior, as many are, the likelihood of problem behavior increases. Whether the single parent is divorced, widowed, or separated or has never married, the results are the same at every socioeconomic level. Children who live in single-parent families are more likely to commit deviant acts than those in two-parent families. They are more likely to run away from home, cut classes, have behavior problems in school, or get in trouble with the law. This is true whether the custodial parent is a full-time homemaker or works part time or full time outside the home. Researchers believe that the key to the disparity is the high degree of permissive parenting in single-parent families (Dornbusch and Gray, 1988).

Another problem is the lack of role models for heterosexual relationships. Whether the family is headed by a mother or a father, youngsters miss the chance to see successful interaction between men and women (Lamb and Bronson, 1980). Other effects depend on the child's sex and the sex of the parent. Boys are more likely to have problems when mothers are the custodial parent, girls when fathers have custody. On the basis of these findings, some developmentalists suggest that boys may do better when living with their fathers, girls with their mothers (Santrock, Warshak, and Elliott, 1982). They stress that boys who grow up in a mother-headed family and girls who grow up in a father-headed family lack a role model as well as a person whose childhood experiences equip them to deal with the specific problems of growing up male or female. However, other factors may be involved.

Life without Father

Consistent differences appear between children who have fathers and those who do not, but factors other than the absence of the male parent may be responsible. Economics is surely important: 60 percent of the children in families headed by single mothers (whether divorced, widowed, or never married) are living below the poverty level (Dornbusch and Gray, 1988). As the relative number of female-headed families has increased, their economic position has decreased, a fact of life that has led economists to talk about the "feminization" of poverty.

Emotional stress is another factor. Many single mothers are under acute stress, and it affects their behavior with their children (Weinraub and Wolf, 1987). Some of the stress is financial. Most single mothers have to struggle to provide their children with necessities. Counselors who work with children of single parents speak of 9- and 10-year-olds who worry about the light bill or the rent (D. Gelman, 1985). Some of the stress is role overload. The single mother has to deal with all the tasks, responsibilities, and demands that would ordinarily be shared by two (Weiss, 1979b). Some of the stress may come from social isolation. The single mother may be so hemmed in by responsibilities and poverty that she becomes a lonely captive in a child-centered world.

These factors probably interact with the absence of the male parent to produce the effects on children's development that researchers consistently find. The absence of the father may be felt either as the lack of masculine influence or as the absence of another adult who would have enriched the child's environment. Researchers have found that the level of cognitive and social stimulation in single-parent homes is lower than that in two-parent households, perhaps because children in single-parent homes get less adult attention (MacKinnon, Brody, and Stoneman, 1982; Medrich, Roizen, and Rubin, 1982).

Neither boys nor girls in mother-headed households do as well in school as children from two-parent families. Their scores on achievement and IQ tests are lower, their grades are lower, they are more likely to repeat a grade, and they tend to leave school earlier. Boys' intellectual development and academic performance suffer much more than those of girls, and in divorced families, the deepest effects appear if the boys are younger than 5 at the time the father leaves (Radin, 1981). This poor school performance is more a matter of economics and parenting style than of father absence. When researchers control for socioeconomic level, children in single-parent families sometimes do as well on IQ tests and achievement tests as children in two-parent families (Dornbusch and Gray, 1988).

Some studies find that boys without fathers have trouble developing self-control. They tend to be more aggressive and may run the risk of becoming juvenile delinquents (Guidubaldi, Perry, and Cleminshaw, 1983). This is probably due to the climate and tone of the home and the kind of supervision the boy receives. In mother-headed families, boys are much more likely than girls to be treated permissively by mothers, and as we have seen, the lack of authoritative parenting may be responsible for the rise in behavior problems (Dornbusch and Gray, 1988).

The development of gender roles has received the most attention in studies of single-parent families. Earlier in the chapter, we saw that fathers seem to be a dominant influence on the acquisition of gender roles. What happens when the father is missing? In the case of boys, his early loss appears to weaken or slow the acquisition of a male gender role—but does not prevent it (Biller, 1981). Boys tend to prefer feminine activities and shun activities involving competition and physical contact; they receive less masculine scores on gender-role tests. Yet when mothers reinforce their sons for gender-typed behavior, encourage their independence, and have positive attitudes toward the missing father, boys tend to develop stronger masculine attributes (Huston, 1983). In divorced families, when the father leaves after the boy starts school, any effects on gender-role development are much less pronounced.

Evidence that the father's absence affects a girl's gender-role development is scant. Although most studies indicate that girls are affected less than boys, the effects of the father's early departure may not show until girls reach adolescence. In a study of working-class girls, Mavis Hetherington (1972) found that high school girls who had lost their fathers before they were 5 years old seemed uncertain about their actions around men. When taking part in an interview, they were either painfully shy (if their fathers had died) or excessively seductive (if their parents had divorced). But in a study of college women, those who had lost their fathers before they were 5 did not show the same inappropriate responses to men (Hainline and Feig, 1978).

Life without Mother

Since 1970, the number of single-father families in the United States has tripled (U.S. Bureau of the Census, 1992). Single fathers tend to be older, better educated, and less likely to be living with a relative than single mothers (Dornbusch and Gray, 1988). They also have, on the average, at least twice the income of single mothers. Most fathers find that the role of single father requires a major shift in life style and reshapes the bond between them and their children. The result may be a closer relationship with their children than existed before the divorce (Keshet and Rosenthal, 1978b). Like single mothers, single fathers tend to be more permissive than their counterparts in two-parent families (Dornbusch and Gray, 1988).

In a group of single-father families, the boys were more mature and sociable than boys who lived in single-mother families (Santrock, Warshak, and Elliott, 1982). Among these same families, girls' social development was slow; the girls were less sociable, less independent,

An increasing number of fathers are heading single-parent homes, learning to juggle both parental roles—as single mothers always have done. *(Mark Antman/The Image Works)*

and more demanding than girls in single-mother families.

Puberty may be an especially difficult time for girls in father-headed families. Fathers ordinarily expect mothers to discuss menstruation and sexual matters with daughters, and the responsibility of doing so themselves makes single fathers uncomfortable. This may leave girls without any individual adult counsel and guidance in the area of sexuality.

Today's single fathers are an unusual group, because their assumption of child-rearing responsibilities requires them to reject traditional gender roles. Their high involvement with their children, in which they perform the duties that traditionally fall to the mother, may lead their sons and daughters to develop more flexible views of masculinity (Lamb, Pleck, and Levine, 1986).

Sometimes divorced parents share physical custody of children, with the youngsters dividing their time more or less equally between the two homes. This practice does not seem to have negative effects. In a longitudinal study of middle-class divorced families, the social and emotional development of children who shuttled from one home to the other was no different from that of children whose mothers had sole custody (Kline et al., 1989).

Single Parenting in Ethnic Groups

Among various ethnic groups, the role of the single parent may differ in important ways. For one thing, the proportion of single parents is much greater among ethnic minorities than among non-Hispanic white groups. In 1988, only 19 percent of Anglo children lived with a single parent, compared with 30 percent of Hispanic children and 54 percent of African-American children (U.S. Bureau of the Census, 1990). Among Native Americans, the rate of single-parent families is higher than that among Hispanic groups but lower than the rate among African-American groups. Minority children are also more likely to be poor than white children. In 1985, 45 percent of white children but 67 percent of African-American children and 72 percent of Hispanic children in one-parent families were below the poverty level (Laosa, 1988). Yet most studies of single parents focus on white, often middle-class, groups.

Explanations for ethnic differences in the rate of single-parent families include (1) a history of slavery among African-Americans, who were not permitted to marry while slaves; (2) poverty, which often leads to family disorganization; and (3) cultural traditions, which lead to a difference in the structure of the family

(Laosa, 1988). These interpretations overlook demographic factors that may be at least as powerful as the popular explanations. Since World War II, there has been a dramatic increase in the rate of unemployment among African-American men, which reduced the pool of attractive potential marriage partners. This chronic unemployment, coupled with increases in wages of employed African-American women (as a proportion of white wages) may have made African-American women less dependent on men, less likely to marry, and less tolerant of unsatisfactory relationships (Walker, 1988). Whatever the explanation, ethnic minorities rely more heavily on the extended family than do non-Hispanic whites.

Most research on the extended family has focused on African-American families, perhaps because 31 percent of African-American children live in extended families—some with both of their parents, others with only one parent (Tolson and Wilson, 1990). Unlike the nuclear family, which begins with the marriage of a couple, new extended families tend to evolve gradually from old extended families (Wilson, 1986). Additional members may be added to the extended family as a single adult marries, an adolescent mother gives birth, or an unrelated child is absorbed into the group.

The extended family in part reflects the African-based family that was organized around adult siblings of the same sex, their spouses, and their children (Sudarkasa, 1981). But it may also be an adaptable form for impoverished groups. Today the form is strongest among low-income African-Americans, who find that by living together and sharing resources, they can alleviate the pain of poverty (Markides, Liang, and Jackson, 1990). Some researchers contend that the extended family persists because of high rates of poverty, unemployment, extramarital births, and marital dissolutions (Wilson, 1989).

Living in an extended family is an advantage for children in single-parent families, because the presence of an additional adult reduces the level of stress on the single parent. Extended-family members relieve the single mother of household tasks and child care, provide emotional support, and give the mother opportunities for interaction with adults (Wilson, 1989). Perhaps as a result of lessened responsibilities and stress, parental styles in extended families are similar to the pattern found in two-parent families (Dornbusch and Gray, 1988). Mothers exercise greater control over their children, children have less autonomy, and the incidence of deviant acts decreases. In one study, the presence of an additional adult led family members, whether adults or children, to perceive a greater family emphasis on moral and religious values (Tolson and Wilson, 1990).

The Blended Family

The **blended family,** which is formed when a custodial parent marries, may solve some problems for children, but it also puts them under additional stress. Many children dream about reuniting their parents, and the new marriage abruptly ends those fantasies. Accepting the stepparent may even make the child feel disloyal to the noncustodial parent.

Adjustment to the blended family seems most difficult for children between the ages of 9 and 15. The new parent appears "like a main character in a play who arrives in the middle of the second act," and children may be frightened at the prospect (Wallerstein and Blakeslee, 1989). The entry of this new parental figure may dethrone the child from the peerlike relationship she or he has developed with the custodial parent.

In nine out of ten blended families, the new parent is a stepfather. His success in assuming the parental role and how well the family functions depend in good part on the way in which he handles discipline. He is unlikely to be successful if he either abdicates authority, giving the mother little support in child rearing, or becomes extremely involved, restrictive, and authoritarian. But when the stepfather is authoritative and warm and when his involvement is welcomed by the mother, the children do better than those in divorced, single-parent families or in intact families filled with marital discord (Hetherington, Cox, and Cox, 1982). The presence of a stepfather seems to be good for young boys, who often develop warm attachments to their new father and find a role model in him. Girls seem to have more difficulty than boys in establishing a warm relationship with a stepfather (Clingempeel, Brand, and Ievoli, 1984).

When a custodial father remarries and the new parent is a stepmother, boys have more problems than girls. They are less socially competent than boys in single-father families or girls in families with stepmothers (Santrock, Warshak, and Elliott, 1982). In a study of stepmother families with 9- to 12-year-old children (Clingempeel and Segal, 1986), girls who felt that their stepmothers loved them had higher self-concepts, were less withdrawn and fearful, were less aggressive, and were more socially competent than girls who felt unloved.

Time helps smooth family friction. It seems to take stepfathers about two years to develop warm relationships with their stepchildren and to establish themselves in a disciplinary role (P. Stern, 1978). And the age of the child at the time parents divorce affects the process. Among the girls and boys in a study that continued for ten years after the divorce (Wallerstein and Blakeslee, 1989), almost all of those who had been 8 or younger at the time of the divorce said that their stepfathers had enhanced their lives. Two-thirds said they could love their fathers and stepfathers at the same time. But among those who were 9 or older when their parents divorced, almost all felt their lives had *not* been enhanced by their stepfathers, and more than half still resented the stepparent.

Relationships in blended families often are complicated by children from each parent's former marriage. In such cases, families with stepfathers are not as happy as other blended families, even if the stepfather does not have custody of his own children (Clingempeel, 1981). When the stepfather brings his own children into the new family, family functioning suffers. Each parent becomes dissatisfied with the way the other parent handles his or her responsibilities, and all family members believe that each parent gives preferential treatment to his or her own children (Hetherington and Camara, 1984).

Over the long term, children who live in blended families tend to drop out of school three times as often as children from intact families at the same socioeconomic level (Zimiles and Lee, 1991). But a curious pattern develops. Girls are more likely to drop out of school when they live with a stepfather, but boys are more likely to drop out when they live with a stepmother. Perhaps children feel that their close relationship with the parent of their own sex is threatened by the appearance of a stepparent. Similarly, the appearance of a stepparent of the same sex may have a stabilizing effect.

Physical Child Abuse

Although parents without partners are somewhat more likely than parents in two-parent families to abuse their children, child abuse is found in every kind of family. A woman in a two-parent family who had repeatedly beaten her school-age son spoke about her own experience on the television program *60 Minutes:*

He'd come to the table like any typical kid, and he'd spill his milk. Well, I'd take him and hit

*him about ten or fifteen times, but I wouldn't re-
member if I'd hit him ten times or five times except, you know, he'd have great big welts on him.
. . . I have hit him hard enough to break my hand.
(O'Brien, Schneider, and Traviesas, 1980, pp. 234–
235)*

Although few parents batter their children, the incidence of child abuse seems alarmingly high: during
1984, there were 1,727,000 reported cases of child
abuse or neglect in the United States (Cicchetti and
Carlson, 1989).

The number of actual cases may be higher or lower
than this figure, because there is no widely accepted set
of definitions for the problem. Definitions range from
narrow (intentional, severe physical abuse) to broad
(denial of normal experiences that produce feelings of
being loved, wanted, secure, and worthy) (Zigler and
Hall, 1989). Our discussion is limited to physical **child
abuse,** consisting of physical injury of a child because
of intentional acts or failures to act on the part of his or
her caregiver; the acts or omissions must violate the
community's standards concerning the treatment of
children (Parke and Collmer, 1975).

Why do parents abuse their children? Researchers
have no simple answer. The beating of a child seems to
be the result of many interacting factors: characteristics
of the parent, characteristics of the child, patterns of
family interaction, socioeconomic stress, family isolation, and cultural acceptance of violence (Cicchetti and
Carlson, 1989). All these factors correlate with child
abuse, but no single factor—or combination of factors—
clearly distinguishes the abusing from the nonabusing
family (see Table 9.5).

TABLE 9.5   **FACTORS DETERMINING CHILD ABUSE***

Ontogenetic Level[†]	Microsystem Level	Exosystem Level	Macrosystem Level
RISK FACTORS			
History of abuse Low self-esteem Low IQ Poor interpersonal skills	Marital discord Children with behavior problems Premature or unhealthy children Single parent Poverty	Unemployment Isolation; poor social supports Poor peer relations as a child	Cultural acceptance of corporal punishment View of children as possessions Economic depression
COMPENSATORY FACTORS			
High IQ Awareness of past abuse History of a positive relationship with one parent Special talents Physical attractiveness Good interpersonal skills	Healthy children Supportive spouse Economic security/ savings in the bank	Good social supports Few stressful events Strong, supportive religious affiliation Positive school experiences and peer relations as a child Therapeutic interventions	Culture that promotes a sense of shared responsibility in caring for the community's children Culture opposed to violence Economic prosperity

*In this comprehensive ecological model of abuse, the factors that have been associated with abuse are organized
according to ecological levels. Risk factors increase the likelihood of child abuse; compensatory factors decrease it.
[†] Ontogenetic level refers to developmental factors within the parent.*

Source: Adapted from Kaufman and Zigler, 1989, p. 139.

The Abusing Parent

After more than a quarter-century of investigation, researchers cannot predict which parents will abuse their child. Comparisons of child abusers and nonabusers have turned up few personality differences between the parent who scolds the milk-spilling child and the one who hits—and keeps on hitting. Seymour Feshbach (1980) believes that differences in attitudes and values are more important than personality differences in contributing to child abuse. He points out that most abusing parents have unrealistic expectations of children; they tend to believe that their children are capable of adult-like behavior and see any misdeeds as intentional defiance. When such parents also suffer from low self-esteem, they may react to the "deliberate" misbehavior of a child with anger; anger increases the likelihood that the parent will strike out at the child. Remorse and guilt after the incident further lower the parent's self-esteem, and the parent becomes even more vulnerable to the angry response.

The notion of a **generational cycle of abuse** also has been popular. In this view, child abusers are likely to have had a childhood marked by physical or emotional abuse or neglect. As children, they learned from their own parents that aggression is an appropriate way to discipline children. Transmission of the cycle is most likely if the abuse is part of discipline for an actual wrongdoing, if it is made to seem necessary, and if the mother is the abusing parent (Hertzberger, 1983; Simons et al., 1991). Being abused in childhood does make a person more likely to abuse his or her own children: from 25 to 35 percent of abused children grow up to abuse their own children (Kaufman and Zigler, 1989). But the vast majority of parents who were abused do not maltreat their children, and many abusers were never abused themselves. A history of child abuse is only a single strand in the tangled web that leads to child abuse.

The Abused Child

The characteristics of the child also seem to contribute to the likelihood of abuse. Something about the child's appearance or temperament may somehow distance the parent from the child and increase the chances that the parent will be abusive. Just being male puts a child at greater risk of being seriously injured (Straus, Gelles, and Steinmetz, 1980). Boys may become targets for their parents' frustrations, either because they are perceived as especially sturdy, because the culture permits more violence in connection with males, or because boys are more demanding and difficult to care for than girls. Among monkeys, the gender disparity is even greater; abused monkey babies are four times more likely to be males (Suomi and Ripp, 1983).

Any characteristic that makes a youngster different from other children (such as prematurity or a physical or mental handicap) places the child at increased risk throughout childhood (Zigler, 1980). Yet most "different" children are not abused, and not all abused children are "different." Finally, during family interactions, a child may learn to behave in ways that evoke abuse from parents. In fact, the experience of being battered may change the child's behavior in ways that make future abuse more likely.

Researchers have found that, early in life, abused children differ from children who have never been abused. The emotional reactions of abused infants are dampened, as if they had learned that being too happy, interested, sad, or afraid was risky (Gaensbauer, 1982). In observational studies, abused toddlers are more aggressive than other children (George and Main, 1979). At day-care centers they may assault, threaten, or harass the caregiver. They also avoid the friendly advances of children and adults, a reaction that might help to maintain abuse at home. As we saw in Chapter 1, abused toddlers seem to lack empathy (Main and George, 1985). Instead of responding sympathetically to the distress of other children, they become fearful or angry and may even attack a crying child.

Older abused children often seem excessively compliant, passive, and obedient. They seem stoical and accept whatever happens. Yet some abused children are more like the toddlers—they are negative and aggressive. Among school-age children at summer day camps, abused children were low in self-esteem, aggressive, withdrawn, and much less likely to be helpful and cooperative than campers who had not been abused (Kaufman and Cicchetti, 1989). After studying abused children, Ruth and Henry Kempe (1978) concluded that these youngsters never developed a basic sense of trust, which is the major developmental task of infancy. Thus, abused children find it hard to trust adults, make only superficial friendships, and discard new friends at the slightest hint of rejection.

The Context of Abuse

Although child abuse is found in every socioeconomic class, in every ethnic group, in the country and the suburbs as well as in the city, it is more likely to occur when parents have few social supports. When incomes and educational levels are low, when the neighborhood is unstable, when the mother is the sole parent, and when day care is not available, the incidence of child abuse increases (Garbarino and Crouter, 1978). Apparently, the combination of economic stress, the constant burden of child care, lack of support from friends, and ignorance of where help might be obtained can set up a situation in which a child's crying, whining, or aggressiveness can provoke vicious, even deadly, blows from an overwhelmed parent. Thus, the severest injuries occur within the poorest families (McLoyd, Ceballo, and Mangelsdorf, 1993).

Researchers have found that more than 60 percent of abusive incidents develop out of some disciplinary action taken by the parents (Zigler and Hall, 1989). Abusing parents are either unable to control their anger, unable to gauge their own strength, or unaware of a child's physical vulnerabilities. They may not know, for example, that shaking a child vigorously can cause brain damage. In a study of lower-middle-class and working-class children between 4 and 11 years old, abusive and nonabusive parents both used physical punishment, but abusive parents applied it more frequently and used harsher methods (Trickett and Kuczynski, 1986). Two major differences appeared in the behavior of abusive parents. First, they used punishment indiscriminately, no matter what the transgression. Nonabusive parents tailored their methods to the offense. Sometimes they merely told the child to stop whatever he or she was doing. Nonabusive parents also used reasoning along with punishment when a child was aggressive, destructive, or dishonest. They relied on reason alone when the child violated some family rule (coming home late, leaving clothes on the floor, going somewhere without permission). Second, abusive parents tended to become angry when their children were dishonest, aggressive, or destructive or when they broke family rules; nonabusive parents became depressed, anxious, or doubtful. Nonabusive parents were also more successful in their disciplinary actions; nonabused children were less likely to defy their parents or to become angry when their parents intervened than abused children were. Two factors may help explain why abused children were less compliant and more aggressive. First, abusive parents failed to use reasoning, and as we saw earlier, reasoning helps a child internalize rules and regulations. Second, heavy or frightening discipline often obscures the message parents are trying to convey.

The Family as a System

By looking separately at various aspects of the child's socialization, we may get an oversimplified view of social development. Influence within the family does not run in one direction; while children are being socialized by others, they are also active socializing agents (R. Bell and Harper, 1977). The child influences the parents, younger and older siblings, grandparents, and other relatives. The child also may act in ways that affect the family structure and important family events. When we explore the effects of a specific relationship, it is easy to forget that every relationship occurs within a context of interacting influences. This means that the family environment is dynamic and transactional in nature; it is always changing, and behavior can be understood only in terms of its interaction with this environment (L. Hoffman, 1991). It also means, as we have seen, that the environment is somewhat different for each child.

The family is a social system with interrelated parts. Over the years, the system's structure changes as members are added, reach new developmental stages, or depart (R. Hill and Mattessich, 1979). Each member of the family system has a changing series of roles, depending on that person's age, gender, and relationship to other family members. A baby boy, for example, fills the roles of infant, son to his mother, and son to his father. When the boy is 3 years old and a baby sister joins the family, his roles as son remain, but he now assumes the roles of preschooler and older sibling. The relationships between the boy and his parents (and thus the way all three respond to—and affect—one another) will change as a result of the new family structure.

In this view, the child is an interdependent, contributing member of the system, part of the process that controls his or her behavior (Minuchin, 1985). The child's own characteristics contribute to this process. It is too simple to say, for example, that an overprotective mother creates a fearful and anxious child. Instead, the mother and child are caught up in a looping pattern: the mother responds to the child's fears with concerned behavior, which may make the child more fearful; this makes the mother more concerned, and the pattern continues to spiral.

Because mother and child interact within the larger family system, their relationship is affected by the relationship of child to father, the relationship between the parents, the mother's relationship with other children in the family, and the child's relationships with other siblings. The marital relationship is especially important. With small infants, even the wife's competence at feeding the baby is affected by the husband. When the husband esteems her maternal role, she is more competent at the task than when there is marital tension and conflict (F. Pederson, 1975).

The family system exists in a larger social system, which influences the child, the other family members, and the family itself, as we saw in the discussion of child abuse (Kaufman and Zigler, 1989). Other influences on the child, on other family members, and on the family system include the social milieu within which the family operates, the schools, the child's peer group, and television. In the next chapter, we explore these influences.

SUMMARY

PARENTS AS SOCIALIZERS

Personality grows out of the process of **socialization,** in which the child absorbs the attitudes, values, and customs of society. Parents contribute to the interactive socialization process through their roles as love provider and caregiver, **identification** figure, and active socialization agent. They also provide the bulk of the child's experiences and affect the child's developing self-concept. By controlling most of children's experiences, parents contribute to the development of social cognition.

DISCIPLINE

If parents' disciplinary efforts are successful, children develop **self-regulation,** the ability to control their behavior so that it is appropriate to the situation. Discipline may be **power assertive;** it may take the form of **love withdrawal;** or it may be **inductive.** Although both power assertion and love withdrawal are effective in the immediate situation, inductive discipline appears to be most successful in developing self-regulation. Power assertion fosters the development of an **externalized conscience,** but inductive discipline fosters an internalized conscience and **prosocial behavior.** Major parental styles are **authoritarian** (demanding but unresponsive parents), **permissive** (undemanding but responsive parents), **authoritative** (demanding and responsive parents), and **rejecting-neglecting** (undemanding and unresponsive parents). Children seem to fare best when their parents are authoritative.

INFLUENCES ON GENDER ROLES

Children acquire masculine or feminine behavior and qualities through a lengthy process that has five aspects: **gender roles, gender-role stereotypes, gender identity, gender constancy,** and **gender schemas.** Parents influence their children's adoption of gender roles, using all the techniques they employ in other forms of socialization, but fathers seem to be the most concerned with this aspect of child rearing. Boys and girls differ in personality: boys tend to be more aggressive, more active, and more competitive; girls tend to be more empathic, more nurturant, more likely to seek assistance, and less confident. They differ in cognitive capability; boys excel in visual-spatial ability and mathematics; girls excel in verbal skills. Some researchers believe that these differences have a biological basis, but all agree that they are heavily influenced by socialization practices.

SIBLINGS

Siblings tend to get along more harmoniously when they are the same sex, with relationships becoming less intense and less one-sided as children pass through childhood. **Ordinal position,** spacing, and family size seem to affect development, with first-borns tending to have higher IQs and be higher achievers but to be less poised and self-confident, more anxious under stress, and less popular than later-borns. The more older brothers and sisters a child has, and the more closely the siblings are spaced, the lower a child's intellectual development. Family size and spacing may have this influence because they affect the intellectual level of the family environment (**confluence theory**) or because they affect the amount of time and material resources children receive from parents (**resource theory**). Only children tend to be higher in IQ and achievement than later-borns; their self-esteem is as high, and they tend to be independent individuals who make their own decisions but may also be slow to develop empathy.

MATERNAL EMPLOYMENT

Most children's mothers are employed outside the home, and most children seem to profit from this arrangement. Daughters of employed mothers tend to be independent high achievers with high self-esteem. Sons tend to be better adjusted than boys whose mothers are not employed outside the home. Among working-class boys, maternal employment seems to improve academic performance but may diminish the father in the boy's eyes. Among middle-class boys, maternal employment may lower academic performance. **Latchkey children** do as well as other children when they stay in their homes after school.

ALTERNATIVE FAMILY ARRANGEMENTS

When parents divorce, children's routines are upset, their emotional security suffers, and they become angry at one or both parents. Girls generally adjust better than boys; within two years girls are doing as well as children in intact families. Behavior and school problems increase among children in one-parent families, apparently because of economic disparities and a high level of permissive parenting. The absence of a father has the largest effect on boys, who may take longer to acquire the male gender role than boys in two-parent families. The absence of a mother has a deeper effect on girls, who tend to be less sociable, less independent, and more demanding than girls in two-parent families. Single parenting may be somewhat different in ethnic minority groups, because of higher poverty rates and greater reliance on the extended family.

In **blended families,** some problems of the single-parent family are lessened, but others may arise. Stepparents usually find the situation easier when (1) they have no children of their own, (2) the stepchildren were 8 or younger at the time of the divorce, and (3) they and the stepchildren are the same sex. Boys are more likely to accept a stepfather, girls to accept a stepmother.

PHYSICAL CHILD ABUSE

Child abuse has no single cause; it seems to result from the interaction of the parent's characteristics, the child's characteristics, family interaction patterns, socioeconomic stress, family isolation, and the cultural acceptance of violence. Although being abused in childhood may make a person more likely to abuse his or her own children, evidence for the **generational cycle of abuse** is not as strong as once was believed. Being abused affects the way a child interacts with other children and adults and may lead the child to behave in ways that encourage further abuse.

THE FAMILY AS A SYSTEM

The family is a changing social system with interrelated parts. The child is a contributing member of the system who fills a series of roles that change as the child develops. While the child is being socialized by parents and siblings, the child in turn is socializing them, and each family interaction takes place within a context of interacting influences.

KEY TERMS

authoritarian parents	gender role	ordinal position
authoritative parents	gender-role stereotype	permissive parents
blended family	gender schema	power-assertive discipline
child abuse	generational cycle of abuse	prosocial behavior
confluence theory	identification	rejecting-neglecting parents
externalized conscience	inductive discipline	resource theory
gender constancy	latchkey children	self-regulation
gender identity	love withdrawal	socialization

10

SOCIAL DEVELOPMENT:
EXPANDING SOCIAL
INTERACTION

CHAPTER

10

● ● ● ● ● ● ● ● ● ● ●

SOCIAL DEVELOPMENT: EXPANDING SOCIAL INTERACTION

• • • • • • • • • • • • • •

PEERS AS SOCIALIZERS

How peers socialize children
Social skills and popularity
Structure of the peer group
Conformity

PEERS AS FRIENDS

The importance of friendship
How friendships end
Friendships in a multicultural society

SCHOOLS AND SOCIALIZATION

Teachers as socializers
Can teachers instill learned
   helplessness?
Teachers, schools, and gender roles

SOCIALIZATION BY TELEVISION

Aggression
Prosocial behavior
Television and gender roles

THE EFFECT OF SOCIAL CLASS

Effects at home and school
Effects of unemployment

ETHNIC INFLUENCES ON SOCIALIZATION

CULTURAL INFLUENCES ON SOCIALIZATION

SUMMARY

KEY TERMS

When children's author Scott O'Dell was a boy, he often played along the California seashore. One morning Scott watched the other boys run to the edge of a pier and jump into the swirling water below. One by one, they bobbed to the top and swam away. Scott took a hesitant step forward and then stopped and stared. His friends began calling to him, "Come on!" "Jump!" Scott could only dog-paddle; the 10 feet between him and the water seemed like a hundred. "What's the matter, sissy," yelled another boy, "are you scared?" The demands of his friends were stronger than his fear. Scott shut his eyes and jumped into the deep water.

● ● ● ● ● ●

The influence of children's peer groups can be extremely important in shaping their development. Within the peer group, children may find emotional security; norms for their behavior; instruction in cognitive, motor, and social skills; and stimulating company. In learning to get along with peers, children also learn to adjust to life (Parker and Asher, 1987).

The peer group is only one of the forces outside the home that may moderate or reinforce family influence or affect the values and attitudes parents bring to child rearing. And so in this chapter, we turn to the influences of the wider world. In the United States today, the peer group, schools, and television are three major influences on children's development. We begin by considering specific ways in which peers exert their influence. After exploring the connection between social skills and popularity, we take up the structure of the peer group and the ways in which peer pressure can alter children's behavior. Peers are friends as well as socializers, and we trace the course of friendship and the qualities children look for in friends. Next we explore an agency that is designed to serve a socializing function: the school. There, we find, socialization may proceed in an unintended as well as a deliberate fashion. From among the other socializing influences in the child's world, we have chosen to examine television, because it occupies the largest portion of the child's waking hours.

Finally, we turn to influences that are at the level that Uri Bronfenbrenner (1989a) would call *macrosystems:* social class, ethnic group, and culture (see Chapter 2). By considering these influences, we can understand how socialization differs for various subgroups within the United States and how the fact that a child is reared in the United States rather than in New Guinea, Japan, or Finland affects socialization patterns.

Peers as Socializers

The influence of peers on the socialization process begins earlier today than it did a generation ago, when few mothers of infants and small children worked outside the home. At any age peer influence is different from family influence in several respects. First, children must earn their membership in the peer group. At home, family membership is their birthright. No matter how gross their misbehavior, they cannot lose their relationships with parents and siblings. Even if their parents are abusive, the relationship is not totally severed. When children enter the peer group, however, they run the risk of rejection. No one has to accept them.

Second, the peer group gives children (unless they are twins) their first chance at interaction with equals.

Within the family, each member has different responsibilities and different powers. Older family members (whether siblings or parents) dominate younger members, but they also hold back their power in some way. When parents play a game with a child, for example, they restrain their efforts, either allowing the child to win or making sure that the child's loss is not humiliating. Similarly, in arguments they do not insult the child; when punishing the child, they restrain the force of their spanks or slaps. In other ways, however, parents exert their power: they make the family's rules and enforce the discipline. When the child enters the peer group, she or he finds both open competition and a chance to help make social rules.

Finally, the peer group gives children their first opportunity to compare themselves with others their own age. In **social comparison,** children can assess how well their own performance compares with that of other children. When their performance exceeds that of

When children play with their peers, they have their first opportunity to relate to their equals. Competition is open, and each child gets a chance to make the group's rules. *(Alan Carey/The Image Works)*

peers, they are likely to feel pride and enhanced self-esteem. When their performance does not measure up, they are likely to become dejected, and their self-esteem suffers. Through social comparison, children also can readjust any clearly erroneous self-concepts that developed within the family. The short boy who was treated as "the tall one" in a short family soon may discover that he is not tall.

How Peers Socialize Children

By interacting with peers, children learn many essential social skills. They learn how to dominate or protect someone, how to assume responsibility, how to reciprocate favors, how to appreciate another's viewpoint, and how to assess their physical, social, and intellectual skills (Asher and Parker, 1991). These lessons are learned by such processes as reinforcement, modeling, and social comparison.

Peer Reinforcement

When peers show that they approve of a child's actions, the child becomes more likely to act that way again in the future. Reinforcement can take the form of praising the child, joining in the child's activity, imitating the child's actions, showing concern for the child, or simply watching the child attentively. Popular children tend to dispense praise and approval generously. In addition to providing such direct reinforcement, they are lavish with indirect reinforcement (attention and conversation) and approach other youngsters in a friendly manner. As a result, they receive a good deal of reinforcement in return (J. Masters and Furman, 1981).

Reinforcement works somewhat differently in encouraging aggression. When an attacked child becomes passive, cries, or assumes a defensive posture, the young attacker is reinforced and often mounts another foray against the same victim. But when an attacked child fights back, the punishment changes the offender's behavior. The attacker usually finds a new victim or behaves differently toward the former victim, or both. Victims who launch successful counterattacks sometimes become aggressive themselves. Apparently, the success of their own aggression is reinforcing; it teaches former victims that aggression can be useful (Hartup, 1983).

Peers use punishment to pressure children into gender roles. In observational studies, 5-year-olds often make direct attempts to change the behavior of a boy who begins playing with a doll or a girl who begins hammering (Lamb, Easterbrooks, and Holden, 1980). They criticize the activity, ask the youngster to stop playing with the toy, complain loudly, or physically intervene in the play. Regardless of the kind of punishment they receive, children usually stop cross-gender play at once.

Peer Modeling

When some action is modeled by peers, the effect on the watching child's behavior is often as powerful as that of direct reinforcement or punishment. By observing another child, children may learn how to do something they either could not do (such as working a computer) or would not have thought of (such as walking a fence rail). They may learn what happens when one acts in a certain way (destroying property can get children into trouble) or how to behave in a strange situation (attending the first meeting of a scout troop).

Immediate imitation of a peer model declines sharply as children reach school years, and the practice is rare among 9- to 11-year-olds. This decline in immediate imitation does not indicate that the practice is waning. Older children may tend to save their imitations for a later occasion and so avoid being called a "copycat."

Modeling by peers influences all sorts of behavior. In various studies, it has increased or decreased generosity and aggression, led children to wait longer for rewards, helped them overcome their fear of dogs, increased sociability, and made them bold enough to break out of gender-role stereotypes (Hartup, 1983). In Chapter 9, we saw that boys' behavior is more strongly gender-typed than girls'. It is not surprising, then, that girls are more likely than boys to follow the lead of a model who carries out some activity that is clearly associated with the other gender.

Because adults and peers both can serve as models, we might wonder which model a child is likely to follow when their behavior conflicts. The answer seems to depend on the situation and the sort of behavior that is modeled. When it comes to learning new ways to express aggression, for example, children are more likely to imitate other children than adults (Bandura, 1986). Yet they are unlikely to copy, or even to choose as associates, peers whose standards are incompatible with those of their own family.

Social Comparison

Although children compare themselves to others at an early age ("I'm bigger than you are"), most children do not begin to judge their skill or achievements by comparing their own behavior to that of others until they are at least 7 years old (R. Butler, 1990). For example, after children carried out a task, Diane Ruble and her associates (Ruble, Parsons, and Ross, 1976; Ruble et al., 1980) told the youngsters how well other children had done on the same task. Six-year-olds were not bothered when they failed and paid little attention to information about others' performance when judging their own relative success. But 8-year-olds were distressed at failure and paid close attention to information about the way they measured up to their peers. When children first begin comparing their own performance to that of others, they generally use social comparison to justify their own performance, simply searching for inadequacies in the performance of others (R. Butler, 1990).

The interest that developmentalists have taken in social comparison derives from its possible influence on **self-efficacy,** which is the individual's judgment of his or her own competence in a particular situation (Bandura, 1986). Because we tend to avoid activities that we believe are beyond us, and to seek out those that we are good at, children's competence judgments influence whether the youngsters will take part in some activity, how long they will work at it, and how long they will keep trying when they meet obstacles. Thus, the child's decision that she or he cannot run well, throw a ball accurately, make friends, or do arithmetic problems is likely to lead to deteriorating performance on future occasions involving these skills.

Social Skills and Popularity

Children must earn their place in the peer group, and their social skills play a major role in determining their acceptance or rejection by others. Socially competent children, who are usually welcomed into the group, are skilled at initiating new relationships and maintaining old ones and at resolving conflicts (Hartup, 1983). Yet popularity is not solely a matter of social competence. Children's expectations, their behavior, and the responses of others form an interlacing web, so it is difficult to say which comes first. In addition, factors outside a child's control may affect the responses of others. As noted in Chapter 1, physical attractiveness affects a child's popularity. African-American, Anglo, and Hispanic children believe that attractive peers are smarter, friendlier, more likable, and more willing to share than are unattractive peers (Langlois and Stephan, 1977).

Once a child has earned popularity or been denied it, peers interpret the child's behavior in line with that reputation. Among a group of second- and fifth-graders, popular children were given the benefit of the doubt (Hymel, 1986). When they did something unpleasant, the other children attributed their behavior to some sit-

From the time that children are about 8 years old, they begin comparing their own performance with that of peers. How well they feel they measure up may affect their feelings of competence. *(Lawrence Frank)*

uational factor ("He didn't do it to be mean; it was just a joke"). If an unpopular child committed a similar act, the other children tended to hold the child accountable and to blame the youngster's disposition or hostile intent ("That's the kind of person she is"). This pattern of interpretation makes life easier for popular children and more difficult for the unpopular.

Initiating and Maintaining Relationships

When socially competent children try to enter a group of playing children, they are alert to any social cue (such as facial expressions) and respond in a pleasant and agreeable manner (Dodge et al., 1986). They comply with the playing children's wishes, provide requested information, and match their nonverbal behavior to that of the playing children. They avoid disrupting play that is in progress and are usually welcomed into the group. Because peers judge children by their behav-

ior as they first attempt to play, socially competent children tend to be popular playmates.

When unpopular children try to enter a group, they use techniques that seem to doom them to failure. They wait longer than popular children before making their move, and the attempt seems to lack any awareness of the group's frame of reference. Unpopular children ask irrelevant questions, talk about themselves, disagree with the other children, and present their opinions and feelings in a way that disrupts the flow of group play. It is no wonder that the group generally gives them the cold shoulder. Yet the unpopular child's tactics may be a face-saving operation that emerges only after an initial negative response by the group (Puttalaz and Wasserman, 1990). Unfortunately, the concern for saving face ensures the continuance of the child's unpopularity.

Children who get along well with their peers are friendly and generous with approval, as we have seen. In both white and African-American groups, these popular children are also cooperative, show leadership, and rarely start fights, disrupt group play, or ask others for help (Coie, Dodge, and Kupersmidt, 1990). They are usually the children who remind others of the rules and establish group norms. In one study of 9- to 11-year-olds (Nakamura and Finck, 1980), socially competent children were better than unpopular children at understanding the feelings and motives of other youngsters and at anticipating problems and figuring out solutions.

Managing Aggression and Resolving Conflicts

Among monkeys, aggression is incorporated into social play. Within the peer group, young monkeys learn how to keep their boisterous scuffles playful; they threaten one another, wrestle, and bite without causing actual harm to their opponents (Suomi and Harlow, 1978). Human children seem to use rough-and-tumble play in much the same way, and it appears to teach them how to control their aggressive responses. Such play is not serious, and usually no one gets angry (see the accompanying box, "Does Rough-and-Tumble Play Turn Mean?").

It takes a long time for children to learn how to express aggression appropriately and how to control it. Preschoolers quarrel frequently, usually over toys. Among 6- to 8-year-olds, the number of squabbles declines, but the fighting may turn hostile (Parke and Slaby, 1983). At about this time, children also begin to give up blows in favor of words, and verbal aggression (threats, taunts, and insults) becomes prevalent.

Gradually, through the socialization processes described earlier, most children learn when aggression is acceptable and when it is not. Children who start fights for no apparent reason are disliked by their peers, but children who stand up for themselves and refuse to be abused or dominated—even if this requires physical aggression—tend to be popular (Coie, Dodge, and Kupersmidt, 1990). Most children eventually learn other methods of resolving their conflicts. Through a

DOES ROUGH-AND-TUMBLE PLAY TURN MEAN?

Rough-and-tumble does not disappear when children outgrow the nursery. On any playground, older boys can be seen scuffling and tumbling about, while girls tend to engage in a milder variety of chase and flee, in which there is little physical contact. Some researchers have suggested that as boys near puberty, their rough-and-tumble games often become hostile encounters (Neill, 1976). Instead of being fun and games, rough-and-tumble turns into serious struggles for dominance.

In an attempt to trace the evolution of rough-and-tumble play, Anne Humphreys and Peter Smith (1987) combined naturalistic observation with a study in which children rated their classmates on liking (like/in-between/don't like) and strength (strong/in-between/weak). Six weeks of observation indicated that the incidence of rough-and-tumble play remained steady across childhood; whether children were 7 or 11 years old, 10 percent of their playground time was spent in some form of rough-and-tumble play.

During the next twelve weeks, Humphreys and Smith concentrated on ten children in each class who spent the most time in rough-and-tumble play. No evidence of hostility appeared, perhaps because at every age, the play occurred between children who liked one another. Play began in response to an invitation, not a challenge. Younger girls were as likely to invite rough-and-tumble play from boys as

from girls, but no boy ever approached a girl in this way. Less than 4 percent of the bouts led to injury, and in most cases the injured child was comforted by the play partner. Less than 1 percent of the bouts became aggressive, and partners usually stayed together after the rough-and-tumble ended. Research by A. D. Pellegrini (1988) indicates that the outcome of rough-and-tumble is related to the partners' popularity. Among the 5- to 10-year-olds he studied, rough-and-tumble play among popular children tended to turn into some game with rules: tag, jump rope, ball games, or follow-the-leader. The escalation of rough-and-tumble play into aggression was confined to rejected children.

Among 7- and 9-year-olds in Humphreys and Smith's (1987) study, there was no indication that the invitation to rough-and-tumble play was part of a struggle for dominance. The chosen partner might be stronger, weaker, or equal in strength to the initiator. At these ages, rough-and-tumble play seemed purely social. Among 11-year-olds, however, children consistently chose partners who were slightly weaker than themselves. By now the friendly nature of rough-and-tumble had become tinged with either the quest for dominance or the desire to practice fighting skills. Humphreys and Smith suggest that the aggressiveness reported by other researchers may simply reflect the increased roughness that 11-year-olds put into their games.

The Industrious Child

series of studies with preschoolers, kindergartners, and first-graders, Kenneth Rubin and Linda Krasnor (1986) discovered that socially competent children have the most strategies for solving problems and are able to adapt them in order to achieve their goals. Children who cannot get along with their peers tend to have trouble thinking about the problem; they seem to try out the first response that comes to mind—usually an assertive or aggressive strategy. If their attempt fails, instead of trying a different approach, they persist with the original strategy.

When social conflicts end in aggression, the situation usually means that one child has attributed hostile intentions to the other child. An important difference between aggressive and nonaggressive children may be the way in which they interpret the intentions of others. Kenneth Dodge and Daniel Somberg (1987) discovered that in some situations, aggressive and nonaggressive boys interpret the actions of others similarly: when they are relaxed and when the other boys' intentions are clear. In such situations, most boys respond benignly to clearly accidental damage and aggressively to damage that is clearly intentional. When another boy's behavior is ambiguous, aggressive boys are more likely to interpret the damage as intentional, but nonaggressive boys tend to give the other child the benefit of the doubt. If an aggressive boy feels threatened, however, his ability to interpret another child's intentions deteriorates, and his tendency to attribute damage to hostile intentions climbs sharply (see Figure 10.1). This tendency to assume the worst may help explain why highly aggressive children often are rejected by their peers.

The Isolated Child

When children are asked to name their friends, about 10 percent of the members in any group are not named at all. These children are social isolates. Some of them are actively disliked by the others; they are **rejected children**. The rest are **neglected children;** they are not disliked, but they are not chosen by their classmates, who seem simply to ignore them (Asher, 1990). By observing children during their first encounter in a new group, researchers can trace the development of a child's social status. Kenneth Dodge (1983) observed second-grade boys who were brought together each day in summer play groups, and he found that children who became social isolates tried to enter new groups as often as other children did. But because they lacked social skills, their encounters tended to be short and unproductive, and they roamed through the group, trying first one child and then another. Eventually they

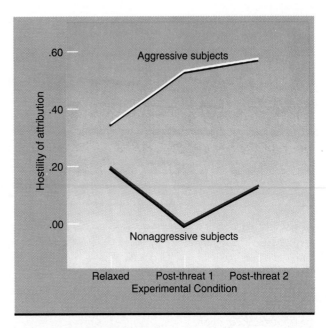

Figure 10.1 When in a relaxed situation, aggressive boys may be somewhat more likely to attribute hostile intentions to the ambiguous acts of others than are nonaggressive boys, although the difference is not significant. But when they feel threatened, aggressive boys' tendency to assume the worst of others is heightened. *(From Dodge and Somberg, 1987, p. 218)*

quit striving for acceptance and began playing alone. Aggressive and antisocial boys were rejected by the group, probably because they insulted, threatened, and hit the others and disrupted the other boys' games. Boys who were neglected by the group tended to be shy and less attractive than other boys.

Most neglected children tend to be somewhat less cooperative, disruptive, or aggressive than the average child and somewhat shyer (Coie, Dodge, and Kupersmidt, 1990). Because their shyness leads them to spend a good deal of time by themselves, some may have been overlooked by their classmates. Their isolation is reflected by the fact that their classmates find it difficult to describe them, and they find it equally difficult to describe their classmates (Rogosch and Newcomb, 1989). Yet neglected children are neither lonely nor depressed, and they often slip back into the group—especially if they move to another situation. In a study of children transferring from elementary to middle school, 80 percent of the neglected children were accepted by their peers at the new school (A. Newcomb and Bukowski, 1984). Neglected children are no more likely than the average child to have social or emotional ties (Coie, Dodge, and Kupersmidt, 1990). Their lack of social competence has been traced to the home. Researchers have found that rejected preschoolers are less likely than other youngsters to have had opportunities to interact in a positive manner with parents or with peers and that their parents often use physical punishment and feel that aggression is an appropriate way to solve problems (Pettit, Dodge, and Brown, 1988).

Youngsters who are rejected by their peers have problems in the classroom as well as on the playground. Kindergarten children who are rejected by their classmates develop unfavorable attitudes toward school, avoid school whenever they can, and do poorly in the classroom (Ladd, 1990). If poor peer relations persist, as they do among about half of rejected children, the consequences may be serious. Rejected children are about three times more likely than other children to drop out of school (Asher and Parker, 1991). Rejected children who are also aggressive—as many of them are—run a high risk of becoming involved in crime. The accompanying box, "Can We Spot Future Delinquents," reports on a study that traces connections between the way kindergarten children behave in school and later delinquency.

The emotional consequences of peer rejection also may be lasting. Rejected children may face an adult life marked by extreme loneliness, anxiety, depression, or feelings of alienation, and some researchers believe that childhood rejection may lead to adult psychopathology (Asher and Parker, 1991). As yet, however, there are no well-designed studies that reveal the links between peer rejection and psychiatric disorders (Parker and Asher, 1987).

Children do not have to be popular to profit from the society of their peers. Average children are about as socially competent as popular children and feel as good about themselves (Asher and Parker, 1991). In the hope of providing rejected children with the competence that will gain them acceptance, researchers have developed various programs to teach these skills. In some cases, the results of the programs seem lasting.

Structure of the Peer Group

When children interact regularly, they develop a structured group with its own standards and code of conduct. When half a dozen unacquainted boys come together, for example, the group structure is apparent—and stable—within forty-five minutes (Pettit et al., 1990). Young children are group members without knowing it. According to Willard Hartup (1983), pre-

Children who are excluded from the peer group often lack social competence, perhaps because they have had few opportunities for positive social interaction. *(Bob Daemmrich/The Image Works)*

problems, but rejected children may develop serious problems in later life.

Rejected children are usually unhappy, lonely children, and many of them say they would like help in learning how to get along better with their classmates (Asher, 1990). The other children regard them as "nasty," "mean," "immature," and "spoiled brats" (Rogosch and Newcomb, 1989). Their behavior matches the descriptions: rejected children start fights, disrupt the group, and often ask for help in school, but they are uncooperative and are low in leadership quali-

CAN WE SPOT FUTURE DELINQUENTS?

From the very beginning, some children have trouble getting along with their peers and teachers. Developmentalists have wondered whether aggression and antisocial behavior among young children warn of future trouble with society or whether these children are simply slower than others in learning self-regulation. In Philadelphia, George Spivack, Janet Marcus, and Marshall Swift (1986) studied about 500 inner-city youngsters who were enrolled in kindergarten. Periodically over the next fifteen years, they checked back on them, hoping to discover whether later delinquency was foreshadowed by specific early-warning signals in the early school years. By the close of the study, 37 percent of the boys and 15 percent of the girls had had at least one brush with the police.

What sort of behavior in primary school was associated with later delinquency? Among both boys and girls, future delinquents tended to tease and torment their classmates, interfering with their work. They often had to be reprimanded by teachers for making noise and disturbing other children. They were impatient and impulsive youngsters who started work too quickly and worked sloppily and fast. They were unwilling to go back over what they had done. They were defiant in the classroom, were disrespectful to teachers, resisted instructions, and broke classroom rules. Somewhat less important was their tendency to interrupt the class with irrelevant comments and blurt their thoughts without thinking.

The children in this study were not rated on how well they were liked or accepted by their peers, but children who show these signs are likely to have problems with adults and may be rejected by their peers. Although these youngsters may enter school without hostile intent, their behavior seems designed to provoke their teachers into anger and their peers into annoyance. As angry interchanges and rebuffs snowball, suggest the researchers, the disruptive behavior intensifies. By adolescence, the youngster has acquired an antisocial label and is treated as such.

Although these early signs of difficulty were consistently associated with trouble in high school and difficulty with the police, not all young children who behaved in this disruptive manner later got into trouble. Other factors, such as absences, grades, and the responses of peers, teachers, and family to the child undoubtedly played a part in determining which children would be involved in serious misconduct. The path toward such behavior may begin at home. Spivack and his associates speculate that their research may even have picked up children who started out as "difficult" infants (see Chapter 4). Such children, unless they have unusually firm, patient, consistent, and tolerant parents, may come into school showing this high-risk pattern of behavior. As we saw in Chapter 4, it may be the mismatch of child's and parent's temperaments that predicts later psychological problems.

The behavior signs that turned up in this study cannot tell us which children *will* get into trouble; many children with the high-risk profile did *not* have later trouble with the law. The signs tell us which children may need some sort of preventive intervention to forestall later difficulties. Other research with similar children has had promising results (Spivack and Shure, 1982). When such youngsters were taught to slow down and think before they acted and to develop an awareness of others' needs, beliefs, and attitudes, they became less disruptive and impulsive.

---

schoolers and kindergartners have little sense of belonging to a group. Even 7- and 8-year-olds see the group as a series of unilateral relations. Older children discern a little more cohesion; 9- to 12-year-olds view the group as made up of interlocking pairs. Not until adolescence do children see the peer group as a community of like-minded people.

A lack of group awareness does not prevent preschoolers from developing **dominance hierarchies,** rankings that reflect the relative social power of group members. These hierarchies are so similar to those found among macaques and chimpanzees that some developmentalists believe that the rankings evolved among our early prehuman ancestors (Rajecki and Flanery, 1981). Children climb the dominance ladder by means of physical attacks, threats, or struggles over objects. Even in preschool play groups, children show by their actions that they know who wields power in the group; the roles of leaders and followers are firmly established. Yet if asked who is the "toughest" or the "strongest," preschoolers often claim the title for themselves (Strayer, Chapeski, and Strayer, 1978). Gradually, children become aware of the rankings. By kindergarten, 62 percent agree on dominance ratings, and by second grade, 72 percent are in accord (Edelman and Omark, 1973). The most aggressive child is not usually the most dominant. In play groups, the most belligerently aggressive child may often submit in favor of another child who—although less aggressive—is on the top rung of the group's dominance ladder (Strayer,

The child at the top of the dominance hierarchy is usually popular, good at games, and knows how to organize the group's activities. *(Spencer Grant/Photo Researchers)*

grade leaders were popular among group members, but among third-graders, dominant boys were no more popular than other group members. Perhaps because of their high levels of aggression, the younger groups were less organized and the dominance hierarchy was less stable than in the older groups. At any age, however, boys' groups are more concerned with dominance, their activities are more hierarchically organized, and the dominance hierarchy is more stable than in groups of girls (Maccoby, 1988).

Power is not the only force that keeps the peer group functioning. Friendships, coalitions, and subgroups are just as important as dominance (Hinde, 1983). These interactions, which include children's prosocial behavior, take place outside the dominance hierarchy. Children's sharing and assistance to one another make up a network of reciprocity that reflects bonds of friendship within the group (Strayer, 1984).

Conformity

No matter what status children hold in a group, its norms exert a great deal of influence on their behavior. Some of these norms reflect the standards of the larger culture, and some are restricted to the group. A norm generated by the group can be as trivial as leaving the laces on your sneakers untied or wearing a single earring.

Conformity to peer pressure may go beyond adhering to the group code and can involve changing one's perceptions or attitudes if they conflict with those of peers. This sort of conformity seems to depend on the child's understanding of social rules, his or her motives, and the nature of the peer group (Hartup, 1983). For example, a child with low self-esteem who feels the need for the group's approval is more likely to conform in an ambiguous situation than a child whose self-esteem is high (Aboud, 1981).

Conformity emerges when children are about 5 years old. Before that time, they are apparently too egocentric to be concerned about peer approval or pressure. When the group's judgment is clearly erroneous, conformity is highest among 5-year-olds and declines steadily with age. Many 5-year-olds can look at two checkers spread out on a table and seem convinced that there are three if several peers unanimously agree that they see three. When the difference between the child's judgment and that of the group is slight, however, conformity steadily increases until children are about 11 years old and then declines throughout adolescence (Allen and Newtson, 1972).

1984). By enabling children to anticipate and avoid aggressive encounters, the dominance hierarchy helps keep the group functioning smoothly.

As children get older, brute force becomes less important, and social power goes to the competent—those who can help the group reach its goals. In early childhood, power depends on keeping possessions and knowing how to use them. In middle childhood, it depends on being good at games and knowing how to organize them (Hartup, 1983). This progression was clear among 20 groups of first- and third-grade boys (Pettit et al., 1990). Leaders of first-grade groups used persuasion and aggression to climb the dominance ladder, but leaders of third-grade groups were more likely to exert leadership qualities, directing the group's activities in a positive fashion. The often aggressive first-

The solidarity of the group increases its power over the individual members. In studies designed to explore the influence of group membership, Muzafer and Carolyn Sherif and their associates (1953; Sherif et al., 1961) discovered that competition between groups increased the cohesiveness of each group and produced considerable friction between the groups. The boys in these groups were attending a summer camp, where they played, hiked, swam, and shared cabins only with members of their own group. Competition in tugs-of-war, baseball, and football turned the groups against each other. The boys in one group looked down on members of the other group, and the situation eventually exploded into open warfare. The hostility further solidified each group and increased its influence over the behavior of its members. Boys who were not hostile participated in intensely aggressive acts for the sake of the group. In this instance, the structured group overpowered the children's internalized standards and led them to engage in behavior that they would normally avoid.

This sort of influence is what parents have in mind when they worry about the influence of the peer group on the child. Will their 10-year-old who refuses to tie his shoelaces because of group norms also vandalize a schoolroom or try drugs because "all the kids do it"? Thomas Berndt (1979) asked children about situations in which peer pressure and parental standards conflict. He discovered that antisocial conformity increased sharply from the third to the ninth grade. The older the child, the more likely she or he was to cheat, steal, soap windows on Halloween, trespass, or destroy property at the urging of peers. During high school, however, conformity to antisocial peer pressure declined. As Figure 10.2 indicates, however, at no time was peer pressure ever *stronger* than parental influence, although among ninth-graders both were equally strong.

Peers as Friends

Peers are friends as well as group members, and the meaning of friendship changes over childhood. To a preschooler, a friend is somebody you play with, and affection has little to do with the relationship (Selman, 1981). As children grow older, doing things together continues to be extremely important, but affection and support soon enter the relationship. When asked, "How do you know that someone is your best friend?" a fourth-grader replied:

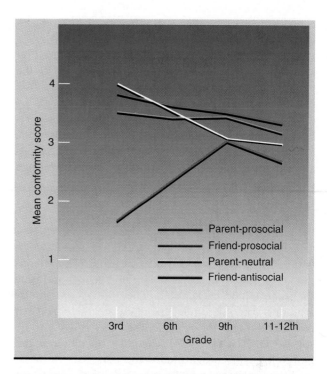

Figure 10.2 Antisocial peer pressure on children follows a characteristic course, rising sharply from third to ninth grade and then declining during the high school years as adolescents begin to accept conventional standards. *(From Berndt, 1979 p. 613)*

I sleep over at his house sometimes. When he's playing ball with his friends he'll let me play. When I slept over, he let me get in front of him in 4-squares [a playground game]. He likes me. (Berndt, 1986)

Asked the same question, a sixth-grader said:

If you tell each other things that you don't like about each other. If you get in a fight with someone else, they'd stick up for you. If you can tell them your phone number and they don't give you crank calls. If they don't act mean to you when other kids are around. (Berndt, 1986)

After reviewing the research, Carolyn Shantz (1983) summed up such changes by concluding that friendships slowly change over childhood in three major ways:

1. Friendships change from a purely behavioral relationship to an emotional relationship. Young children play together and give each other things; adoles-

cents care for each other, share their thoughts and feelings, and comfort each other.

▬▬▬ 2. Friendships change from a self-centered relationship to a mutual relationship. Friends satisfy the young child's needs and wants; adolescent friends satisfy each other's needs and wants.

▬▬▬ 3. Friendships change from a smooth, brief relationship to a sometimes bumpy, enduring relationship. Young children's friendships rupture at the first disagreement; adolescents' friendships persist through stormy quarrels.

The Importance of Friendship

When choosing a friend, most children are drawn to youngsters who resemble them in some way. Friends usually are the same age and the same gender and have the same ethnic background. They often have similar attitudes, interests, and personality characteristics. If one friend is shy, for example, the other is likely to be shy as well (Hartup, 1983). The older the children, the more closely friends' attitudes and personalities mesh.

When compared with friendless children, youngsters with friends usually are more generous and helpful and have higher moral standards (McGuire and Weisz, 1982). Janice Nelson and Frances Aboud (1985) suggest that friendship may contribute to prosocial behavior and morality. In a study with third- and fourth-grade children, these researchers found that when children settled conflicts with friends, they did it in a manner that might promote more mature judgment. With friends, children explained their position more fully and criticized their friends' position more than they did with acquaintances. Apparently, friends feel secure enough with one another to risk retaliation or hurt feelings that may accompany criticism. Children are also more likely to shift their own position after a disagreement with a friend than after one with an acquaintance, an indication that they consider the friend's arguments more carefully.

Friendships serve at least seven important functions for the growing child (Asher and Parker, 1991): (1) They foster the growth of emotional competence, helping children develop skills for managing their emotions and interpreting their own emotional experiences. (2) They support a child's ego and validate the child's self, helping children maintain a competent, attractive, and worthwhile self-image. (3) They provide emotional security, giving children the confidence to enter new or potentially threatening situations. (4) They provide intimacy and affection. (5) They provide guidance and assistance in time of trouble, sometimes in the form of tangible aid (time, energy, material resources) and sometimes in the form of constructive criticism or counsel. (6) Through their loyalty and availability, friends give children a sense that they have a reliable ally. (7) They provide companionship and intellectual stimulation. The many benefits of friendship may explain why children who are not accepted by their classmates but who have a friend in other classes or in their neighborhood have some protection against the negative effects of peer rejection (Parker and Asher, 1987).

Children who are referred to child-guidance clinics are twice as likely as other children to have trouble forming and maintaining friendships (Hartup, 1989). Perhaps children without friends are so socially disadvantaged that they develop behavior disorders, or perhaps children with social and emotional disorders cannot maintain friendships. Researchers are uncertain as to which is cause and which is effect.

How Friendships End

Children's friendships frequently break up. When Thomas Berndt and Sally Hoyle (1985) interviewed first- and fourth-grade children about their friends in the fall and again in the spring, they discovered that friendships over the year were much more stable among fourth-graders. First-grade boys kept many of their friends from kindergarten who were now in the other first-grade classrooms, but during the year, first-grade girls tended to end friendships with old friends who were not in their classroom. The researchers speculate that because boys tend to play in large groups and girls tend to interact in pairs or small groups, it was easier for the boys to maintain their friendships with friends in other classrooms. Perhaps for the same reason, girls in both grades tended to limit the size of their friendship group, making fewer new friends during the year than boys did.

What leads to the rupture of children's friendships? In a study of kindergartners, third-graders, and sixth-graders, aggressiveness was a common cause for ending a friendship at all ages (Berndt, 1986). The notion that a friend should be loyal, intimate, and trustworthy first emerged among the third-graders, but only a few of them felt that way. The rest agreed with the kindergartners, who saw no reason to break off a friendship simply because a friend was disloyal or gossiped about personal information the child had disclosed. Sixth-graders, however, tended to break off friendships when the friend spread rumors about them or failed to support them against other people. Among these older children, faithfulness was more important to girls: about half the girls but one-fifth of the boys had broken off a friendship when the friend was unfaithful (perhaps failing to invite them to a party or ignoring them in favor of other people). Studies consistently show that girls' friendships are more intimate and more exclusive than those of boys; perhaps the intensity of girls' friendships leads them to worry more about being betrayed by a friend.

Friendships in a Multicultural Society

Getting children to accept youngsters from other ethnic groups has proved easier than promoting close friendships that cross group boundaries. When children are asked to name their best friends, African-Americans usually choose African-Americans and whites choose whites—even in schools that have been integrated for some time (Hartup, 1983). In a longitudinal study, Louise Singleton and Steven Asher (1979; Asher, Singleton, and Taylor, 1982) found that third-graders who had been in integrated classrooms since kindergarten enjoyed playing with children of the other race, although they showed a slight preference for their own race. That preference was not as strong as gender preference: boys rated boys of another race higher than girls of either race; girls showed the same pattern, preferring girls of the other race to boys. White children's preference for their own race did not change substantially over the years, but by sixth grade the African-American children were not as comfortable playing and working with whites as they had been earlier. Singleton and Asher suggest that by the age of 11 or 12, African-American children have become much more aware of their minority status and so make ingroup-outgroup distinctions with the emphasis on race.

Best friendships between African-American and white children in this study declined over the years (Singleton and Asher, 1979; Asher, Singleton and Taylor, 1982). Among third-graders, 24 percent of the white children and 37 percent of the African-American children chose a child of the other race as best friend. By the time these children reached the tenth grade, only 8 percent of white adolescents and 4 percent of African-American adolescents had a best friend from the other race.

Among the students of an interracial junior high school in the Midwest, accepting classmates of another race seemed no problem (DuBois and Hirsch, 1990). At this school, approximately 25 percent of the students were African-American and 75 percent were white.

Most primary school children who attended integrated schools enjoy playing with children of other ethnic groups, although only a minority are "best friends." *(Joel Gordon)*

Most students said they had a school friend of the other race, with both closeness and after-school contact increasing among students who lived in neighborhoods with a substantial number of other-race children. Although children of both races were equally likely to report having a school friend of the other race, African-Americans were almost twice as likely as whites to report having a close friend of the other race whom they saw outside of school. This is, of course, an inevitable outcome of the disproportionate number of white students in the school and community.

Aspects of the school environment may influence cross-racial acceptance and friendship. In one study (Rosenfeld et al., 1981), researchers found that four factors determined whether white children were likely to accept African-American children into their peer group: (1) when there was a large percentage of minority children in the classroom, (2) when few of the minority students were hostile toward whites, (3) when the social class and achievement levels of white and minority students were relatively equal, (4) when the white students had high self-esteem themselves.

Most studies of cross-ethnic friendships focus on relationships between African-American and white children. Recently, however, researchers looked at an ethnically diverse California school in which enrollment echoes the national census balance for Anglo, Hispanic, African-American, and Asian-American groups (Howes and Wu, 1990). Among these children, acceptance increased with school experience: third-graders were more likely than kindergartners to play with members of other ethnic groups and less likely to have conflicts with them. Minority-group members were more likely to have cross-group friendships than were Anglo children, although the differences narrowed between kindergarten and third grade as more Anglo children developed cross-group friendships. Children's individual popularity did not affect their incidence of cross-group friendships, and there were no differences among ethnic groups in the likelihood of conflicts with members of another group.

Schools and Socialization

Children spend a major part of childhood in the society of the school, and the school socializes them in many of the same ways that families and peer groups do. As members of that small society, they are supposed to acquire basic academic skills, but the school's influence extends far beyond the curriculum. During their six hours of daily schooling, children are carrying out tasks, relating to other people, and living within the confines of rules that differ in many ways from those of the family system. At school, the rules are impersonal; the relationships between the child and other people are relatively brief; the adults who run the society may hold different— if not conflicting—views from the child's parents; and the child's performance is periodically and publicly compared with that of others (Hess and Holloway, 1984). These experiences interact with the influence of family, peers, religion, and media to affect children's feelings of competence and the way they regard themselves and others.

Teachers as Socializers

In passing along the content of the academic curriculum, teachers instruct, try to motivate, and evaluate the children in their classroom. In turn, the children are supposed to adopt the role of **receptive learner:** to be task-oriented, to be responsible, and to maintain an acceptable level of academic achievement. Teachers also pass along a "hidden curriculum" that stems from the need to manage children so that the classroom remains orderly and under control. When teachers are successful, their students take the role of pupil. **Pupils** are obedient, respect authority, cheerfully share their materials and the teacher's time, and control their impulses and wishes for immediate gratification. How quickly they learn these roles has a profound effect on children's school experience (Hess and Holloway, 1984; Kedar-Voivodas, 1983).

Teachers find it easy to teach students who fit either the receptive-learner or the pupil role. When student teachers rated children, they preferred such children and expected those who adopted the role of receptive learner to get the highest grades (Feshbach, 1969). When teachers were asked about children who have an independent and exploring attitude, are willing to challenge authority, and insist on explanations, their replies suggested that youngsters who adopt this role of **active learner** may find that their quest for knowledge is complicated by adult antagonism.

We might dismiss this study on the grounds that student teachers are unsure of themselves and threatened by bright children who are not satisfied with pat answers. Yet research consistently shows that experienced teachers respond in similar ways to children's characteristics (Minuchin and Shapiro, 1983). They like children who conform to school routines, are high achievers, and make few demands. Their ideal students are apparently high-achieving "pupils." Observations of classroom interaction reveal that teachers pay little attention to children who are silent or withdrawn and they rarely talk to such youngsters. They may actively reject children who continually demand inappropriate attention.

Children's success in school seems to be affected by teachers' perceptions of their ability. Whether a child does well in school may depend in part on whether the teacher expects the youngster to succeed. Twenty-five years ago, Robert Rosenthal and Lenore Jacobson (1968) demonstrated the effect of teachers' expectations on children's school performance in what they called the "self-fulfilling prophecy." A **self-fulfilling prophecy** is an expectation about behavior that produces a situation in which the expectation is confirmed. Rosenthal and Jacobson picked elementary school students at random and told their teachers that these students would make great cognitive strides during the school year, becoming, in effect, "intellectual bloomers." (To back up their claims, the researchers said that the children had achieved unusually high scores on special tests.) Later in the year, the teachers rated these students as more interested in school, more curious, and happier than other students. Among younger students, the predictions came true—the researcher-selected bloomers in the first grade gained an average of 15 IQ points more than other children. Among fifth- and sixth-graders, the predictions had little effect, perhaps because the school records of these students contradicted the predictions (see Figure 10.3).

Why should teachers' expectations have such an effect on young children's school performance? Probably because the teachers' expectations led them to treat the children identified as bloomers in ways that made them likely to fulfill the prophecy made by the researchers (Brophy, 1983; H. Cooper, 1979). When teachers perceive students as high achievers, the teachers give them more opportunities to participate in class and more time to respond. If the children come up with the right answers, they get more praise than low achievers; if they

are wrong, they are criticized for not trying. The teacher assumes that low achievers probably do not know the answers and so calls on them less often. Research indicates that low achievers are criticized not for lack of effort but for messy papers or some other extraneous flaw. Although teachers probably are not aware that they treat high and low achievers differently, the children sense it. In one study (Weinstein et al., 1987), even first-graders were aware of the difference, but they did not seem to apply it to themselves. By fifth grade, however, children's expectations of success mirrored those of the teacher.

All teachers are not the same, of course, and researchers have identified how differences in teachers' characteristics can influence children's attitudes toward learning and their sense of autonomy (Eccles et al., 1993). In a study of fourth- to sixth-grade classrooms (Deci, Neziek, and Sheinman, 1981), teachers who ran their classes with strict control tended to have students who were extrinsically motivated. The children worked primarily for grades, showed little curiosity, and disliked challenges. They also had little confidence in their abil-

Figure 10.3 Elementary school teachers were led to believe that certain of their pupils were "late bloomers" who would show great academic gains during the year. Of these randomly selected students, those in the lower grades showed the largest IQ gains. In the upper grades, the "late bloomer" predictions had little effect, perhaps because the teachers already had strong expectations based on pupils' performance in earlier grades. *(After Rosenthal, 1966. From Bootzin et al., 1982, p. 35)*

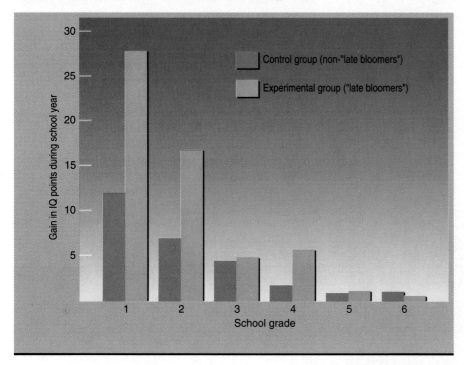

ity. Teachers who encouraged children to take part of the responsibility for their work and to consider all aspects of a situation tended to have students who were intrinsically motivated. These children worked primarily to master a skill or concept, showed curiosity, and preferred challenges. They also had confidence in their ability. A series of teachers with similar attitudes could have a lasting effect on a child's sense of autonomy and self-worth.

Can Teachers Instill Learned Helplessness?

Some children have learned to approach academic tasks with little expectation of success; their main goal is to avoid the teacher's negative appraisal of their work. Carole Dweck and Elaine Elliot (1983) have found that these children fall into two groups. Most of those in the first group are accustomed to poor grades, and they approach tests or other achievement situations in a state of high anxiety. Unable to devise strategies for solving problems, they try to figure out the teacher and look for clues in his or her behavior. The performance of these highly anxious children degenerates rapidly when they are placed under time pressure. In one study of fifth- and sixth-graders (K. Hill and Eaton, 1977), anxious children's performance crumbled when there was not enough time to complete an arithmetic test. Compared with children who felt little anxiety, they took twice as long to work each problem, made three times as many mistakes, and cheated twice as often. When they had all the time they needed, they performed as well as other children.

In the second group of children with low expectations of success, the youngsters have average or better IQs and often have a history of good test scores in various school subjects. These children are the victims of **learned helplessness** (Seligman, 1975). Because they have consistently been placed in situations where their efforts have no effect, they expect that their attempts to solve problems or to master new tasks are doomed to failure. Because they believe that they cannot succeed, they do not try very hard. They may refuse to try even when they could easily succeed.

Their pessimistic view of their own ability may lead "helpless" children to give up on difficult material. By altering the introductory sections in a simple booklet on psychology, Barbara Licht and Carol Dweck (1984) caused the performance of helpless children to plunge. When the beginning sections were written in a confusing style, helpless children did poorly on the entire booklet, even on material that was clearly written. Yet children who had confidence in their own ability apparently saw their initial difficulty as due to a lack of effort and responded by trying harder (see Table 10.1). These mastery-oriented children learned and understood the material. The difference in performance was not due to helpless children's lack of ability, because when all the material was clearly written, helpless children did as well as mastery-oriented children. When their first encounter proved difficult, children who had learned to be helpless quit trying, and their scores on a review booklet showed little improvement.

Once learned helplessness develops, it tends to persist. In a longitudinal study (Fincham, Hokoda, and Sanders, 1989), third-graders with learned helplessness maintained their self-defeating behavior as fifth-graders, and their helplessness was reflected in their achieve-

TABLE 10.1   CHILDREN'S ATTRIBUTIONS AND MASTERY OF NEW MATERIAL

Attributional Style	LEARNING CONDITION	
	No Confusion (%)	Confusion (%)
Material mastered on first attempt:		
Helpless	30	5
Mastery-oriented	34	24
Material mastered on final attempt:		
Helpless	77	35
Mastery-oriented	68	72

Source: Licht and Dweck, 1984, p. 633.

ment scores. Research by Dweck and her colleagues (Dweck et al., 1978) suggests that teachers' responses to children's academic failures are more likely to promote learned helplessness in girls than in boys. While observing in the classroom, Dweck noted that when boys failed at a task, teachers generally attributed the failure to lack of effort, to not following instructions, or to messiness of the work. Because none of these criticisms has anything to do with ability, boys might believe that they have failed because they haven't worked hard enough. When girls failed, teachers ascribed their failure to errors in the work and often accompanied their criticism with praise for the girl's effort. Such criticism, Dweck concluded, might lead girls to decide that they were incapable of success.

Teachers, Schools, and Gender Roles

Teachers' treatment of boys and girls differs in more than just separate styles of criticism. Some of the differences may be important in explaining why, after years of outscoring boys on math tests, girls begin to fall behind when they reach the seventh grade. After reviewing the research, Jacquelynne Eccles and Lois Hoffman (1984) concluded that boys and girls have different experiences in the classroom. Teachers interact more with boys than with girls in math and science classes, and they expect boys to do better than girls. These differences are most extreme among bright students. When a boy and a girl both show superior math ability, teachers praise the boy more than they praise the girl. In addition, girls with superior math ability often escape the teacher's notice, but boys with similar ability are identified. As a result, few girls are encouraged to consider math, science, or other nontraditional majors in college.

When Eccles (1985a) asked nearly 700 fifth- to twelfth-grade children about their attitudes toward mathematics, she found strong acceptance of the notion that math is for boys. Girls and boys agreed that math is more useful for boys than for girls. Boys liked math better than girls did, thought they were better at it, said that they didn't have to work as hard at it, and expected to get better grades in future math courses. As girls got older, they liked math even less and were more likely to take only the minimum number of high school courses in it. Yet girls and boys performed equally well in their math courses.

The organization of the classroom may push children into other aspects of traditional gender roles. Classroom tasks are doled out according to stereotype: girls are class secretaries, and boys are team captains; boys help girls with math assignments, girls help boys with English assignments. In order to motivate and control the boys, teachers often pit one sex against the other in academic competition (Thorne, 1986).

Until recently, girls had few opportunities to participate in organized sports. As a result, they missed the lessons in social skills that athletic participation can provide (Eccles and Hoffman, 1984). For years, only boys got these lessons in competitiveness, confidence, teamwork, persistence in the face of difficult odds, and leadership. Athletic competitions teach children how to lose. Girls are still less likely to go out for sports than boys and thus may have less opportunity to develop these skills and competencies.

The structure of the school may mold students' expectations along the lines of traditional gender roles (Minuchin and Shapiro, 1983). Female teachers are clustered in the early grades, and male teachers in high school. In junior and senior high school, men teach math, science, and shop; women teach languages and literature. At all educational levels, men hold most of the administrative positions, and women hold most of the clerical positions. In the typical primary school, a group of female teachers and clerks is bossed by a male principal. This lesson about the gender-related distribution of power in the adult world is not lost on children.

Socialization by Television

Children watch television for entertainment and sometimes for instruction, but what they get from the "tube" is continual socialization into the attitudes, values, and behavior they see before them. Children in the United States spend more time watching television than in any other activity except sleep (Carpenter, Huston, and Spera, 1991). The heaviest viewing goes on among children from lower socioeconomic classes and among minority children at all socioeconomic levels (Huston, Watkins, and Kunkel, 1989). Forty years ago, the child growing up in Moccasin, Montana, was limited in her or his knowledge of the world by geography and personal experience. That sort of geographic and cultural isolation has ended. Today youngsters in remote villages watch people in every corner of the globe. Before their eyes passes a parade of war, murder, mayhem, divorce, adultery, birth, death, poverty, and riches. Educational opportunities also present themselves: underwater explorations, science specials, symphony orchestras, operas, and public television programs specially designed to teach skills and concepts. Research consistently shows that preschool children learn letter and number skills by watching such programs as *Sesame Street* and that they enter kindergarten with improved vocabularies and prereading skills (Rice et al., 1990).

Television affects every aspect of socialization, but, as Table 10.2 indicates, young children's exposure to adult programming is largely determined by their parents (St. Peters et al., 1991). As children move through the primary grades, however, the amount of coviewing begins to decline, which means that older children tend to choose their own television fare. Reflecting the concerns of parents, educators, and developmentalists, most research into television's effects has focused on aggression, although some investigators have looked at prosocial behavior and gender-role stereotyping.

Aggression

The average adolescent has seen more than 18,000 murders on television. The situation may be worsening. Although the level of televised violence has remained fairly steady over the last twenty-five years, its quality has changed. According to Sally Smith (1985), TV vio-

lence has become more intense and realistic; violent acts often are connected with humor, the line between heroes and villains has blurred, and more violent acts are committed by people with psychological problems. Programs that look for "hard copy" and "unsolved mysteries" often present "real" serial killers, kidnappings, and police shoot-outs. Further concern has been aroused by the widespread broadcasting of rock videos, which are often filled with images of menace and cruelty. In these videos, violence against people and property is ripped out of any justifying context—and it has no consequences. How does this stepped-up, decontextualized violence affect children? Does it teach them new forms of violence? Does it reduce their inhibitions against antisocial behavior?

Two government commissions have analyzed hundreds of studies exploring the effects of TV violence on children, but researchers still argue over the effects of watching violent programs (Freedman, 1984). Without any doubt, a correlation exists between aggressive behavior and the habitual viewing of violent programs, but this link does not tell us that watching the programs causes aggression. It is just as probable that aggressive children are drawn to violent television programs. To

TABLE 10.2   **WEEKLY TELEVISION VIEWING***

Program Type	WITH PARENT(S)		WITHOUT PARENT(S)	
	Hours	Percent	Hours	Percent
Child informative	.87	22	2.8	78
Child entertainment	1.32	25	3.8	75
News and information	.98	81	.14	19
Sports	.56	80	.08	20
Comedy	2.18	60	1.26	40
Drama	1.50	77	.33	23
Action adventure	1.08	70	.41	30
Variety/game	.68	73	.22	27

*In a longitudinal study, children between the ages of 3 and 7 tended to watch adult-oriented programs with their parents and child-oriented programs by themselves. Parents chose the programs watched together, indicating that socialization by television is largely determined by family context.
Source: Information from St. Peters et al., 1991.

tease out the connection, investigators have conducted controlled experiments, but this research is also fraught with problems.

Controlled experiments have shown conclusively that watching violent programs increases later aggression in the laboratory (Freedman, 1984). Clearly, televised violence has some impact on its viewers. Yet several problems with these experiments keep us from applying them with confidence to everyday situations. First, in the lab, children respond with fake aggression. Hitting a plastic Bobo doll is not the same as hitting a person. Second, in these experiments, children have the tacit approval of an adult experimenter. If an adult indicates that it's okay to hit something, the child has no reason to inhibit aggression and can freely join in the "fun." Third, the effects of a single exposure to aggressive stimuli cannot tell us much about the effects of the continual exposure to violence offered by television. Daily exposure to such fare may produce more profound changes in a child's behavior. Finally, experiments detect only the immediate effects of violent television. They tell us only what the child does in the first twenty minutes or so after he or she sees the program. We cannot rule out the possibility that the effects disappear within an hour or so or that a delayed reaction may occur.

Even so, the results of research on TV violence are disquieting. A continual bombardment of TV violence

seems to dull children to its horrors; when they see a violent act, they tend to react with indifference. Third-graders who watched a violent detective program and then were asked to supervise younger children were significantly slower than children in a control group to intervene or to call for adult assistance when a fight broke out (Drabman and Thomas, 1976). There is reason to believe that this slowness to respond is linked to a diminished emotional response by children. When children watch violence, they sweat slightly, and skin resistance to electrical conduction decreases. But witnessing televised violence appears to take the edge off this reaction. Compared with children who had just watched a volleyball game, children who had just finished watching a violent police drama reacted less to an ostensibly real fight on a TV monitor (M. Thomas et al., 1977).

Young children often fail to distinguish between fantasy and reality. Four-year-olds respond to violent cartoons as aggressively (hitting, punching, and kicking a Bobo doll) as they do to films of human violence (Bandura, Ross, and Ross, 1966). Once they can consistently distinguish between fantasy and reality, they are more likely to be influenced by realistic violence. Seymour Feshbach (1972) showed children a film that included scenes of a violent riot. When the watching children believed that the riot was part of a newsreel, they showed much more subsequent aggression than chil-

Heavy viewing of television violence probably desensitizes children and increases violence, but so many factors are involved that researchers have found it difficult to establish television's long-term effects. *(Mark Antman/The Image Works)*

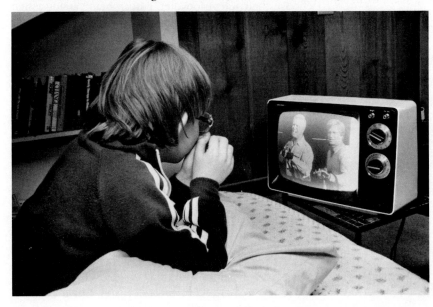

dren who believed that the riot had been staged for a motion picture. Other researchers have found that the younger the child, the more likely he or she is to respond to a televised violent event as if it had no motivation and no consequences (Parke and Slaby, 1983). In one study, kindergartners and second-graders tended to forget the reason for a violent act and its consequences when commercials separated the consequences from the act (W. Collins, Berndt, and Hess, 1974). But they had no trouble remembering the violence. Young children, then, do not learn from the later punishment of a villain that aggression is punished. The insertion of commercials did not disrupt the memory of fifth-graders. They recalled motivation and consequences and used them in judging the act.

Although correlational studies cannot establish whether televised aggression *causes* children to behave aggressively, longitudinal studies indicate that heavy TV viewing probably has some influence on later aggression (Eron et al., 1987). In one study, the amount of television violence that boys watched in the third grade was correlated with their aggression at age 19 (Eron et al., 1972; see Figure 10.4). This relationship was stronger than the link between their preference for violent television at both ages or the link between their third-grade aggressiveness and their preference for violent TV at that time.

Similar trends appeared in a later cross-cultural study. The same investigators followed three waves of

American and Finnish first- and third-graders over a three-year period (Huesmann, Lagerspetz, and Eron, 1984). In both countries, heavy watchers of TV violence at the beginning of the study were likely to be highly aggressive children at the study's close. In an earlier study, the connection appeared only among boys (Eron et al., 1972). This time, American girls' viewing of TV violence also was linked with future aggression, a finding that led the investigators to suggest that recent changes in the socialization of American girls (with its emphasis on assertiveness and physical activity) were responsible. No relationship was found among Finnish girls. Yet television violence alone did not make these children aggressive; instead, it appeared to interact with other factors. The researchers discovered that besides absorbing heavy doses of television violence, the most aggressive children in their study believed that the shows accurately portrayed life, identified strongly with the aggressive characters they watched, performed poorly at school, were unpopular with peers, often fantasized about aggression, and came from low-status homes, where the parents had little education and the mother was aggressive.

Many developmentalists are convinced that heavy doses of violent television have a negative effect on children. They believe that violent TV probably does increase aggressiveness, desensitize children to the horrors of violence, and persuade them that a Rambo-like use of aggression is an acceptable way to solve human problems. Yet the chances of demonstrating that a steady diet of violent TV in childhood is a major cause of adult aggression are slim. Children and their families choose their television diet; researchers cannot assign children randomly to various viewing groups. Thus, correlational research may never provide a clear demonstration of the effects of television on aggression.

Prosocial Behavior

If links exist between television and children's aggressiveness, it stands to reason that similar links should appear between television and prosocial behavior. Yet in one study (Dorr, 1979), kindergarten children often forgot the prosocial themes and behavior in the programs they watched; violent scenes and striking characters were more likely to stick in their memory. With increasing age, children remembered more prosocial aspects of the programs, perhaps because of their increased social understanding.

There seems little doubt that children can learn helpful, generous behavior from television, but it is more difficult to show that they act on this knowledge. Aletha

Figure 10.4   When 211 boys who were studied as 8- and 9-year-olds were restudied after a lapse of ten years, their preference for violent television programs correlated positively with the amount of aggression they displayed as 18- or 19-year-olds. Although correlation does not indicate causation, the relative strength of this correlation is impressive. *(Adapted from Eron et al., 1972)*

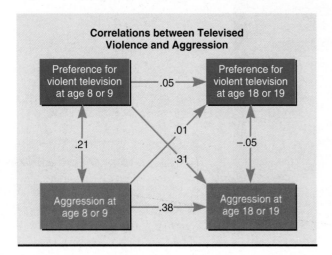

Correlations between Televised Violence and Aggression

Preference for violent television at age 8 or 9 → .05 → Preference for violent television at age 18 or 19

.21

.01

.31

−.05

Aggression at age 8 or 9 → .38 → Aggression at age 18 or 19

Stein and Lynette Friedrich (1975) showed four episodes of *Mr. Roger's Neighborhood* to kindergarten children. These programs focused on (1) understanding others' feelings of jealousy, fear, and anger, and (2) such prosocial actions as expressing sympathy, helping, and sharing. Children who watched the programs learned their prosocial messages. They knew more about each of the themes than did a group of children who watched neutral films. But when placed with a child who needed assistance, most of the *Mr. Roger's* viewers were no more helpful than those who watched the neutral films. There was, however, some good news in the study. If watching prosocial films was combined with an opportunity to role-play the parts with hand puppets, children did provide more assistance. The role-playing experience apparently made it easier for children to understand the feelings and needs of people in distress.

Since this research was completed, other studies have demonstrated similar effects, although none of the increases in prosocial behavior has been dramatic. Marian Radke-Yarrow and her associates (1983) believe that the weak effect of prosocial television may be due to the relative coverage of various emotions in the medium. These researchers point out that children continually see people in danger or need on the nightly news; they observe people and organizations responding to that distress. But these incidents are islands surrounded by commercials and by programs that evoke emotions that are incompatible with concern for others.

Television and Gender Roles

Although gender roles are changing on television, most shows still purvey stereotypical views of male and female roles and personality. Children accept what they see. They say that they get their information about possible occupations from television and that they believe the information is accurate (Greenberg, 1982). In the majority of programs, men and women are portrayed in stereotypical occupations (M. Harris and Vorhees, 1981; Zuckerman and Zuckerman, 1985). Television heroines tend to unmask villains by luck or accident. In children's programs, men are aggressive, constructive, and helpful; their activities bring them tangible rewards. But women tend to be deferential, passive, and ignored; if they are too active, they are punished. Despite the competent, assertive leading roles that have been developed for women, old programs never die; they simply become reruns. This practice may bear on findings that prime-time viewing has no relation to children's stereotypical views of gender roles, but heavy TV viewing after school and on Saturday mornings does show such correlations (Greer, 1980).

Saturday morning remains a male preserve; all the heroes are boys or men. In 1991, the only Saturday morning show featuring a girl, ABC's *Little Rosey,* was canceled because "only girls were watching the show" (Carter, 1991). Network executives admit that children's programs are dominated by male characters, but they say that this is because boys make up a majority of the Saturday morning audience. Even on prime-time shows like *Doogie Howser M.D.* or *The Wonder Years,* young principal characters are almost always male. Network programmers have tried to make up for this male dominance by instructing writers to include a few "female attributes" in their male characters—by having males admire the beauty of nature or hug another character, for example.

When prime-time programs allow their characters to shatter stereotypes, children respond. When positive, nonstereotyped characters are included in major roles, children tend to have more flexible views of gender roles and to accept men and women in nontraditional occupations (Wroblewski and Huston, 1988). Most research has found that girls are more receptive to these changes than boys; they accept nontraditional occupational roles not only for others but for themselves as well. Indeed, *LA Law* has been credited with increasing the number of young women who apply to law school, although it is impossible to say whether the program actually has caused the change or whether the program content and the increase in female applicants are both responses to a change in society. Boys may also be affected. In one study (Rosenwasser, Lingenfelter, and Harrington, 1989), second-grade boys who regularly watched *The Cosby Show* tended to have more flexible views of gender roles than other boys, perhaps because the show combines a strong, positive, but sensitive, male role model with an assertive, nontraditional, yet feminine, female model.

The average child watches more than 20,000 television commercials each year, and few commercials shatter gender-role stereotypes (M. Macklin and Kolbe, 1984). After analyzing 300 commercials, researchers reported that the difference between female and male gender roles in these commercials was far greater than it is in society (Mamay and Simpson, 1981). Some ads now feature female bank managers or traveling sales representatives, but the women in most ads are mothers, housewives, or sex objects who defer to men's needs, wishes, and preferences. It is the commanding male who confronts women shoppers with twelve-hour cold caplets, corrects their choice of detergent, and de-

Boys who watch *The Cosby Show* tend to have more flexible views of gender roles than other boys. *(1988 National Broadcasting Co., Inc.)*

livers the smooth, authoritative, voice-over commentary in most commercials.

Television can reinforce stereotypes or try to break them down. Despite the changes that have appeared in programs like *Who's the Boss?* and *Mr. Mom,* most of today's television portrays a highly stereotyped and distorted world, one that values being male, youthful, and white and denigrates being female, old, dark-skinned, or foreign (Huston, Watkins, and Kunkel, 1989). Given the effects of *The Cosby Show,* if the proportion of nonstereotypical characters grows, we may discover that television viewers have *less* stereotypical attitudes than nonviewers.

The Effect of Social Class

Whether a child's father drives a delivery truck or delivers babies affects many aspects of development. Because social class, which is traditionally determined by the

father's occupation, affects belief systems, values, and life styles, it makes up one of the macrosystems that affect development. Social class helps determine children's physical environment, the neighborhood they live in, their playmates, their access to health care, the composition of their diet, their parents' child-rearing practices, the authority structure of their family, its stability, the number of siblings they have, and the sort of education they get. It is no wonder that researchers try to control the influence of social class when they study various other factors that affect development (L. Hoffman, 1984). Here we single out two aspects of social-class influence: child-rearing practices and the relationship between school and family.

Effects at Home and School

Parents in different classes treat their children differently. Working-class and poor parents tend to rely on power-assertive discipline, whereas middle-class parents are more likely to use inductive discipline (Hess et al., 1968; McLoyd, Ceballo, and Mangelsdorf, 1993). As we saw in Chapter 9, heavy doses of power-assertive discipline are associated with children's low self-esteem, aggressiveness, slowed cognitive development, and adherence to moral behavior simply to avoid punishment. The pressure of the parents' absolute power may erode the child's sense of self-efficacy. She or he also misses out on the verbal enrichment that accompanies inductive discipline and promotes verbal fluency. Inductive discipline also rewards the middle-class child for skillful reasoning (because explaining your intentions can ward off punishment) and teaches him or her that the world is largely orderly and rational. Perhaps these differences reflect in part the work experiences of adults in each class. Working-class parents are themselves more likely to be given orders by their bosses, but middle-class parents are more likely to be given explanations (L. Hoffman, 1984). In addition, Melvin Kohn (1979) has noted that working-class parents tend to base their punishments on the consequences of their child's behavior but middle-class parents more heavily weigh the child's intent.

These differences may also reflect class differences in home conditions. Life in working-class and poor families often involves more stress than life in the middle class, and a parent under stress may find it difficult to give reasons and weigh intent. It is also easier to forgive a child's unintentional destruction of a VCR when there is plenty of money to buy a new one. Such class differences in child-rearing techniques may have additional significance for children's development: the working-class child may be encouraged to conform and the middle-class child encouraged to be autonomous.

Social class affects the quality of a child's experience in school. Because schools are based on middle-class values, the middle-class child usually makes a smooth transition to the classroom. His or her speech, manners, and dress conform to the teacher's expectations. Because middle-class parents generally work at occupations that require extended schooling, the middle-class child is likely to find the school setting meaningful (L. Hoffman, 1984). In contrast, the child from a low-income family may feel like a stranger in a strange land, primed for hostility by the maternal admonishment "Keep out of trouble" (Hess and Shipman, 1968). He or she may have to learn new ways of behaving and new speech conventions. The school's goals may seem alien and its curriculum irrelevant. The middle-class child's way is also smoothed by the ease with which his or her parents move in the school setting. Middle-class parents usually attend parent conferences, Parent-Teacher Or-

ganization meetings, and school functions. Parents from working-class families, especially those with low incomes, may avoid contact with the school (L. Hoffman, 1984).

Parents' expectations have been associated with children's achievement in school, and there are consistent class differences in how well parents expect their children to do, both in the classroom and in problem-solving situations (Seginer, 1983). Asked to predict their 4-year-olds' performance on several tasks, for example, middle-class parents consistently expected their children to do at least as well as the average child, but working-class parents expected their children to do less well (Marcus and Corsini, 1978). Low expectations by parents may lead not only to poor school performance but to lowered self-efficacy as well.

The mismatch between the schools and children from low-income working-class families has led to concerted attempts to involve parents from these families in the schools. After reviewing a number of such programs, Robert Hess and Susan Holloway (1984) found that when the school can involve low-income parents, their children's school attendance increases, the children are less disruptive in class and less aggressive on the playground, their classroom work improves, and they are more likely to complete their homework.

Effects of Unemployment

When the major breadwinner loses his or her job, life within the family changes in predictable ways, often affecting the course of development. This relationship became clear when researchers studied data collected as part of a major lifelong longitudinal study of people whose childhood coincided with the Great Depression of the 1930s (G. Elder, Liker, and Cross, 1984). Studies of economic stress on families at the close of the 1980s confirmed this early research (Conger et al., 1992). Although unemployment affects all levels of society, working-class families generally suffer the most. Those with low seniority, who tend to have young families, are often the first to be fired. Thus, depression's uneven burden widens the gap between social classes (Flanagan, 1990).

Most of the effects of job loss on children are indirect, for they are the result of changed behavior and disposition on the part of the unemployed worker (McLoyd, 1989). When two-parent families suffer major financial reverses, the father becomes depressed, anxious, less nurturant, irritable, and tense. He tends to lose his temper easily, and discipline becomes arbitrary and

Parental unemployment affects children primarily through its influence on their parents' behavior and disposition. *(M. Siluk/The Image Works)*

income pushed her husband into taking an additional night job. Stress permeated the family, finally causing it to explode:

> *At Christmastime I saw my husband shake my son violently, yelling at him. He adores that child. I've never seen him so angry. I knocked my husband to the floor, trying to strangle him in front of the Christmas tree. My son [a preschooler] stood at a safe distance on the stairs and said, "Guys, guys . . . it's Christmas!" We broke my grandmother's coffee table in the struggle. We are not violent people. (Doe, 1991)*

Children whose fathers are unemployed for a lengthy period may develop socioemotional problems: they tend to be more depressed, lonely, and distrustful than other children, and they are more likely to feel excluded by their peers, to have low self-esteem, and to be less competent in coping with stress (McLoyd, 1989). They may become more susceptible to negative peer pressure and get in trouble in school and with the law. The risk increases if the parents feel extreme economic strain, if the child does not feel accepted by the parents, or if the parents' marriage is in trouble (Galambos and Silbereisen, 1987; Perrucci and Targ, in press; Rockwell and Elder, 1982).

Because parents serve as models of achievement for their children, prolonged parental unemployment may lead to lowered educational and occupational aspirations on the part of the children—especially among girls (Flanagan, 1990). Financial pressures may seem to preclude college and push children into the job market early. Thus, the effects of unemployment can shadow children for the rest of their lives.

When studying the effects of unemployment, researchers have focused on two-parent families. Employed single mothers already have higher rates of anxiety, depression, and illness than employed married mothers or childless women. Thus, it seems likely that unemployed mothers would also treat their children harshly (McLoyd, 1989).

primarily power-assertive. Because he is at home more, his contact with the children increases, clashes are frequent, and the children are more often exposed to harsh discipline. Several factors serve to intensify or moderate the effects of these changes in the father. Research indicates that, among boys, temperament is important; young boys who were difficult toddlers suffer most. Among girls, appearance is important; unattractive daughters suffer most. The effects are moderated by a warm, supportive relationship with the mother (G. Elder, Caspi, and Nguyen, 1986). Yet economic stress may make the mother less patient and nurturant with the children, so neither parent is responsive to the child's needs (Flanagan, 1990).

The effects of unemployment are not confined to the working class, and the unemployed partner need not be the father. A mother who lost her middle-class job as a magazine consultant in August said that the loss of her

Ethnic Influences on Socialization

Another macrosystem that influences socialization is the ethnic group to which the child belongs. **Ethnic groups** are distinguished by race, religion, or national identity and have their own attitudes, traditions, values, and beliefs, as well as expectations about gender roles, child rearing, and the family (Perlmutter and Hall, 1992). Italian-Americans, for example, generally have close, interdependent relationships that span generations (C. Johnson, 1983). Italian-Americans, like most European ethnic groups, may belong to arithmetical minorities, but they are generally considered part of society's dominant core. Many researchers reserve the term **minority** for groups that suffer discrimination or subordination because of their physical or cultural characteristics (Markides, Liang, and Jackson, 1990).

Because of their exclusion from the dominant society, the experience of some minority groups deserves extra attention (see Table 10.3). Establishing ethnic differences can be difficult. As we saw in Chapter 8, what at first appear to be ethnic differences often turn out to be socioeconomic effects produced by the concentration of American minorities among low-income families (Garcia-Coll, 1990). Even when ethnic groups are compared within social classes, socioeconomic effects are present because members of minority groups, particularly African-Americans and Hispanics, often fall in the most economically deprived segment of the class. Fur-

ther complicating the picture is the existence of subcultural differences within each ethnic group, due either to different cultural heritages or to socioeconomic differences with the group. This is particularly true of Hispanic and Asian groups.

As we saw in Chapter 9, most minority groups rely on the extended family as a system that helps them solve problems, handle stress, and allocate resources. Minority parents stress interdependence and teach children to think in terms of their responsibilities to parents, siblings, and other close relatives. Some researchers (Harrison et al., 1990) suggest that this focus on the family leads minority children to think, feel, and act in ways that foster cooperation instead of competition. They point out that an emphasis on cooperation, sharing, obligation to the family, and reciprocity conflicts sharply with the white, middle-class stress on competition, autonomy, and self-reliance.

The context of family life may have an important influence on the way African-American parents rear their children. Among poor families in Virginia, mothers who were married, older, and more-educated tended to use authoritative child-rearing methods. Younger, less-

TABLE 10.3   ETHNIC MINORITY GROUPS

Ethnic Group	Size (Millions)	Subgroups	Geographic Concentration
African-American	28.2	African-Caribbean; recent immigrants from Africa	South, Northeast
Native-American: American Indian	1.5	Largest tribes: Cherokee, Navajo, Sioux, Chippewa	Northwest, West
Alaskan Native	.064	Aleut, Eskimo	Northwest
Asian-Pacific American	10.0	Chinese, Japanese, Korean, Vietnamese, Cambodian, Thai, Samoan, Filipino, Laotian, Lao-Hmong, Burmese, Guamanian	West, Northeast
Hispanic	18.8	Mexican, Puerto Rican, Cuban, Central and South American	Southwest, Midwest, Northeast, Florida, California

Source: Harrison et al., 1990, p. 350.

educated, single mothers—especially those who had little involvement with the church—tended to place a heavy emphasis on obedience and thus rely on an authoritarian approach (Kelley, Power, and Wimbush, 1992).

Because of their minority status, African-American parents at all socioeconomic levels are acutely aware of the racism that their children will encounter. Researchers have found that African-American mothers generally believe that developing their children's self-esteem and self-confidence will help prepare them for coping with racism and discrimination (Peters, 1981; M. Spencer and Markstrom-Adams, 1990). Boys may have a special need for strong self-esteem because many researchers see them as especially vulnerable to racism. This may explain the results of one study, in which African-American parents taught their daughters about race in a more egalitarian manner than the way they taught their sons, who generally heard about racial matters in a problack, antiwhite context (Branch and Newcombe, 1986). Better-educated older mothers and parents who live in mixed-race neighborhoods are most likely to see race as a primary element in the socialization of their children, and never-married parents the least likely to provide such instruction (Thornton et al., 1990). African-American children thus are socialized to live in two worlds—in the world of the African-American community, where they must be accepted if they are to have friends, and in the world of the white community, where they must be accepted if they are to do well in the dominant society (Peters, 1981).

The problem may be especially acute in the inner city. As John Ogbu (1985, 1987) points out, parents generally rear their children in ways that develop the competencies and behavior they will need to survive as adults. Ogbu believes that applying middle-class, white child-rearing practices in the inner city would produce children who would be incompetent in the inner-city world yet would be prevented by racial policies from obtaining desirable jobs in the white, middle-class world. Although African-American parents in the inner city may teach their children that education is necessary for conventional jobs, they pass along other knowledge as well. In order to get along, inner-city children must learn to become self-reliant and resourceful, to manipulate situations, to be mistrustful of people in authority, and to fight back or ward off attacks. Like the middle class, residents of the inner city want money, power, social credit, and self-esteem, but, according to Ogbu, most do not see education as a way to get these things. African-American history on this continent has con-

vinced them that only massive changes in political power and economic opportunity would allow them to improve their lot. Thus, inner-city children may see individual adult competence and success exemplified by hustlers, pimps, streetmen, reformers, entertainers, and sports figures. As long as good jobs in the conventional world are unavailable, the street economy will remain attractive, and school success will be elusive.

Children of other minority groups may also find that the values of the larger society conflict with those of their own group. Among Native American groups, tribal spirituality, which revolves around various ceremonies, is fundamental to group identity. Yet participating in required ceremonies means that Native American children must take time off from schools operated by the larger culture. As they grow up, Native American children must choose between tribal and Anglo values, and if they do not take up traditional Native American ways, they may be rejected by the tribe (M. Spencer and Markston-Adams, 1990).

Asian-American families make up a highly varied group. Among first-generation Chinese parents, the twin goals of family emphasis and adapting to the United States affect child-rearing practices (C-Y. Lin and Fu, 1990). Chinese parents tend to control their children more closely than do parents in the larger culture. They also are less emotionally expressive and emphasize emotional restraint. Although Chinese parents stress obligations to and dependence on the family, they also stress a personal independence that enables children to succeed in society. This success allows children to fulfill their obligations to the family and to avoid shaming the family with the disgrace of failure. Finally, Chinese parents place enormous emphasis on academic achievement, which they see as a way to succeed and to overcome discrimination.

There is some indication that Hispanic families tend to be bicultural. That is, within the family they interact in traditional ways that stress family obligations and interdependence, but when they venture outside the family, their interactions are often indistinguishable from those of the majority culture (Harrison et al., 1990). Even so, Hispanic children's orientation to the group carries over into school situations. In one study (Rotheram-Borus and Phinney, 1990), Mexican-American children showed higher levels of sharing, were more group-oriented, and were more likely to rely on authority figures when solving problems than African-American children.

No matter what minority children's ethnicity, their socialization stresses interdependence and a positive view of the ethnic group. And in each ethnic group, parents have developed adaptive strategies in response to their situation within the larger society (Harrison et al., 1990).

Cultural Influences on Socialization

Our focus thus far has been on the way children develop in the United States. How typical of the world's children are the patterns of socialization we have described? Child-rearing patterns in any society reflect the values that are needed for an adult to function successfully in that macrosystem. In a hunting society, for example, parents—and other adults—encourage their sons to show courage, strength, dexterity, and timing. These are the qualities that make an effective hunter; they are vital both to successful life as a man and to the survival of society. When parents encourage these traits in their young sons, they are not deliberately trying to produce good hunters. Instead, they are encouraging qualities they believe are intrinsically desirable—good for all men in any society. This conviction comes from living in a society in which the most successful men are brave, strong, and dexterous and have swift reaction times (L. Hoffman, 1984).

Most parents in the United States are not especially concerned if their son's reaction time is somewhat slow, but they try to make certain that their children are independent, skillful in social interactions, and competitive and that they have a strong sense of self-efficacy. Parents see these qualities as intrinsically desirable; actually, they are simply the qualities that lead to success in middle-class American society. If these same parents lived in a herding society, they would do everything they could to stamp out independence in their children, for they would regard it as a negative trait. Unfortunate innovations in herding techniques can threaten a family's food supply for many months.

Agriculture requires cooperation within the family, and so independence in also discouraged in agrarian societies. Rural parents tend to value obedience because it ensures that the children will fulfill the parental need for labor in the fields and for economic support in the future when the parents are too old to work. As Figure 10.5 indicates, parents in predominantly rural societies overwhelmingly endorse obedience as a quality they would "most like to see" in their children, but few would like their children to be independent and self-reliant (L. Hoffman, 1988).

Some child-rearing practices are based on cultural beliefs about the nature of children or the nature of the world. Among the Kwoma of New Guinea and the

Figure 10.5 Parents who lived in predominantly rural societies tended to say that the most important quality for a school-age child was obedience, whereas those who lived in predominantly industrial societies were more likely to favor independence and self-reliance. (Other values cited were popularity, school achievement, and being a good person.) *(Information from Hoffman, 1988)*

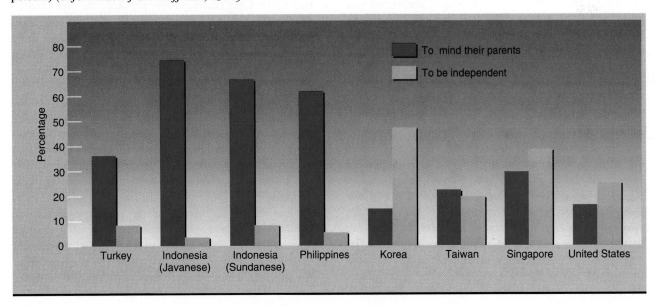

Parents in rural societies, where innovative actions can jeopardize food supplies, tend to value obedience in their children and to discourage independence. *(Peter Carmichael/The Stock Market)*

Zinacantecans of Mexico, for example, the belief that children are in danger from supernatural forces leads parents to keep their babies close by, calm, and quiet—lest they call attention to themselves (Super and Harkness, 1982). This cultural stifling of emotional expression stands in sharp contrast to American practice, in which parents encourage emotional expression in the belief that inhibited emotions can cause lasting psychological harm.

Even disciplinary techniques vary from one country to the next. Although Japan and the United States are both complex industrial societies that place a premium on educational achievement, Japanese and Americans discipline their preschoolers differently. In one study (Conroy et al., 1980), Japanese mothers, who believe that preschoolers should be indulged but should also be receptive to the suggestions of adults, relied on appeals to feelings and consequences when faced with an un-

ruly child. They reminded the child of how misbehavior makes the mother feel or how the child would feel if someone treated him or her that way, and they pointed out the consequences of the behavior to the child or others. American mothers are more likely to use power assertion or to remind the child of the rules governing the situation ("The puzzle belongs to Chris"). When American mothers of preschoolers are compared with German mothers, however, it is the German mothers who are more likely to use power assertion as a disciplinary strategy (Parke, Grossmann, and Tinsley, 1981).

Cultural differences also exist in the influence and function of the peer group. In many societies, a baby graduates from maternal care into a group composed of children of all ages. Older children look after younger ones, and the child is absorbed into the play group. But in industrialized societies, children are segregated by age, isolated from children older or younger than themselves. This isolation, which removes older, skilled children from the play group, drastically changes the context of the child's world.

The peer group can be a force for stabilization or for social change. In Israel, where self-confidence, independence, and new ways of doing things are important, children are expected to be adventurous and full of mischief. There the peer group often has more influence than parents, and Israeli children proudly say that they will break adult rules at the suggestion of the peer groups (Shouval et al., 1975).

In the former Soviet Union, instead of being a force for youthful ideas, the peer group was used to transmit the government's social values to children. The Soviet government deliberately used the peer group in this way in order to bring adult values in harmony with the needs of the system. Rewards or punishments were administered to the group (for example, the classroom), so one child's misbehavior put his or her social unit in jeopardy. Children soon learned to subordinate themselves to the group (Bronfenbrenner, 1970).

Research from other cultures reminds us that most studies of development reported in this book reflect Western conceptions of the individual. Western emphasis on competition, school achievement, and autonomy determines the research questions we ask as well as the way we interpret the results.

SUMMARY

PEERS AS SOCIALIZERS

Peer influence differs from family influence because children must earn a place in the peer group, because in the group they interact with equals, and because the group gives them an opportunity for **social comparison,** in which they can assess their own performance against that of other children. Peers socialize one another through reinforcement, modeling, and social comparison, which affect a child's **self-efficacy.**

Many factors determine a child's acceptance by the peer group, including some, such as physical attractiveness, that are outside the child's control. Popular children tend to be friendly, socially competent, and good at understanding others and solving problems. As children reach school age, they quarrel less often, but their arguments are more often hostile than were their preschool squabbles over toys. Unlike other children, aggressive youngsters tend to interpret ambiguous actions as intentionally hostile. **Neglected children** are no more likely than other children to have social or emotional problems, but **rejected children** often develop such problems and may drop out of school.

The peer group has structure, standards, and a code of conduct. Peer groups develop **dominance hierarchies** that reflect the relative social power of group members. Friendships, coalitions, and subgroups are outside the dominance hierarchy but are just as important to group functioning. Conformity to group norms emerges when children are about 5 years old, increases throughout childhood, and begins to decline in adolescence.

PEERS AS FRIENDS

During childhood, friendships change from purely behavioral, self-centered, smooth, brief relations to emotional, mutual, bumpy, enduring relationships. Friendships foster social and emotional development. At any age, aggressiveness will end a friendship; only among older children do friendships break up because of disloyalty. Children who attend multiracial schools generally accept one another, but close friendships across racial lines are less common.

SCHOOLS AND SOCIALIZATION

Teachers prefer conforming high-achieving children who make few demands; thus, they value **receptive learners** and **pupils** more than **active learners.** Whether a teacher expects a child to do well or not affects the way the teacher treats the child—and may create a **self-fulfilling prophecy.** Some children with little expectation of success in school are highly anxious; others suffer from **learned helplessness,** which may be promoted by the way teachers respond to students' failures. The school experience also enforces traditional gender roles and stereotypical views of boys' and girls' capabilities.

SOCIALIZATION BY TELEVISION

Watching violent TV programs increases the likelihood of immediate violence in controlled experiments, but such studies cannot be applied to everyday life. The habitual viewing of violent TV programs is associated with later aggressive behavior, but there is no simple cause-and-effect relationship. Many other aspects of socialization interact in the development of aggression. Children can learn prosocial behavior from television, but influences on behavior seem weak. Television strengthens stereotypical views of gender roles unless programs have positive, nonstereotyped characters in major roles.

THE EFFECT OF SOCIAL CLASS

Social class affects child rearing. Working-class parents tend to use power-assertive discipline and encourage conformity in their children, whereas middle-class parents tend to use inductive discipline and encourage autonomy. Low-income children are at a disadvantage in school, which is based on middle-class values. Economic depressions tend to heighten class differences, because unemployment falls more heavily on the working class. The indirect effects of job loss on children tend to operate through changes in the behavior and disposition of unemployed parents.

ETHNIC INFLUENCES ON SOCIALIZATION

Expectations about gender roles, child rearing, and the family may differ across **ethnic groups.** Some apparently ethnic influences on socialization are actually socioeconomic effects. Most **minority** groups rely heavily on the extended family, and minority parents tend to stress interdependence and cooperation, teaching their children to think in terms of their responsibilities to the family and its members. The prevalence of racism leads African-American parents to make an extra effort to develop their children's self-esteem and self-confidence. The unavailability of good jobs in the conventional world may keep inner-city African-American children from striving for school success and lead them to adopt role models from successful members of the street economy. Children of other minority groups may find that the values of the larger society conflict with the values of their own group.

CULTURAL INFLUENCES ON SOCIALIZATION

A society's child-rearing patterns encourage the values that are required for successful functioning in that society. Some child-rearing patterns are based on cultural beliefs about the nature of the child or the nature of the world. Cultures also vary in the role they allot to the peer group, which may act as a force for stabilization or a force for social change.

KEY TERMS

active learner	minority	rejected children
dominance hierarchy	neglected children	self-efficacy
ethnic group	pupil	self-fulfilling prophecy
learned helplessness	receptive learner	social comparison

COGNITION: THINKING AND REASONING

COGNITION: THINKING
AND REASONING

• • • • • • • • • • • • • • • •

More and more children are on speaking terms with computers. Six-year-old Alex, who often plays tic-tac-toe with friends, is frustrated when he plays with Merlin, because the computer never makes mistakes (as his friends do) and never eases up to let him win (as most adults do). After losing steadily to Merlin, Alex bursts out, "He cheats. It's not fair." Children's notions about the capacity of computers to cheat undergo a progression that parallels their cognitive development. Five- and six-year-olds believe that cheating requires the possession of body parts. This belief convinces many that computers can't cheat because they don't have hands or eyes. Others are not so sure; they suggest that the computer does have eyes. "Tiny eyes. You just can't see them." Eight-year-olds believe that the ability to cheat is not tied to human anatomy (hands or eyes) and requires only the ability to act: computers cheat "from the inside." Some maintain that a computer can't cheat because "it can't press by itself." For them, computers clearly lack autonomy. As they begin to understand psychological states, most 10-year-olds become convinced that computers cannot cheat, because they regard cheating as the result of deliberate intent. But those with computer experience contend that you can program a computer to cheat, perhaps by writing the program so that it moves twice in a row. In the course of a clinical study with nearly 100 children between the ages of 4 and 14, Sherry Turkle (1984) collected these increasingly sophisticated views, which reflect the changes in children's thinking that are the subject of this chapter.

In this chapter, we pick up our discussion of cognition while children are still "childish." They have not yet undergone the great intellectual revolution of childhood that turns youngsters into flexible, capable thinkers. After exploring the major themes of that revolution, we look at its consequences and examine the new conceptual knowledge and logical thought of the concrete-operational child. Then we turn to advances in information processing that make logical thought possible: changes in attention, memory, and problem solving and

children's increasing knowledge about thought itself. Finally, we trace the development of social cognition. We watch as children gradually come to understand what others know, think, and intend, and we explore the development of their reasoning about moral issues.

An Intellectual Revolution

Young children's words and actions often are amusing, and fond parents frequently relate charming stories about the exploits of their preschool children. These tales reflect the thought of preschoolers, which Piaget found so different from the thought of the schoolchild that he called it **preoperational thought.** He described this thought as intuitive, inflexible, and contradictory and as focused on individual events. The preschool child, he maintained, is not yet capable of mental **operations,** which are flexible, rigorous, and logical thought processes.

Our view of young children's thought was radically changed by Piaget's research. His recognition that children do not see the world as adults do led to new ways of looking at cognitive development. Although preschool children are probably more capable thinkers than Piaget believed, he asked the right questions about their thought, and his view of the way the child's mind gradually develops has been extremely useful.

The thought of preschool children differs from the more systematic thought of the schoolchild in major ways. The changes in children's thinking between the ages of 4 and 10 are so great that they seem to reflect an intellectual revolution. Although we cannot point to a specific day or week—or even year—when this intellectual revolution occurs, we can describe the major changes that distinguish the thinking of 10-year-olds from that of 4-year-olds: the waning power of appearances, the decentering of attention, the reversibility of thought, the self-regulation of learning, and the use of language to facilitate thought.

Appearances Become Less Powerful

Appearances seem to overwhelm preschoolers. They seem to believe that irrelevant changes in the appearance of objects or people change their identity (Flavell, Green, and Flavell, 1986). Nearly twenty-five years ago, Rheta DeVries (1969) convincingly demonstrated the way that appearance overpowers the young child's understanding of reality. While she screened the head of a black cat from sight, she placed over it a realistic mask resembling a fierce dog. When confronted with the masked cat, 3- and 4-year-olds were sure that the cat had become a dog. But 5- and 6-year-olds were not influenced by the mask. They had developed the concept of **identity,** which is the understanding that objects and people remain the same even if irrelevant properties are changed. These children maintained that a cat was a cat, no matter how it looked.

The problems preschoolers have in distinguishing appearance from reality have since been explored by other researchers, who have begun to tease out the circumstances in which appearances overwhelm young children and those in which they can distinguish between appearance and reality. In general, 3-year-olds—and even some 2-year-olds—know when something is

Because most preschoolers lack the concept of identity, they are fooled by appearances and believe that this Teenage Mutant Ninja Turtle is what he seems to be. *(The Photo Works/Monkmeyer)*

clearly real and when it is not. They know, for example, that a toy fire engine is not a real fire engine, that a picture of a cupcake is not a real cupcake, and that when they play house, their friend who pretends to be the daddy is not really a daddy (Woolley and Wellman, 1990). They can even understand when an apparently edible substance is not really good to eat (Siegal and Share, 1990). If you show them a piece of moldy bread and then cover the mold with peanut butter, they can ignore the bread's new appearance and focus on reality: they insist that the bread is not fit to eat. But the same children are baffled by illusions, in which appearance conflicts with reality (Flavell, Green, and Flavell, 1986, 1989).

Suppose you show a 3-year-old a glass of milk that is behind a green filter, which makes the milk look green. You remove the glass and hand it to the child, who sees that it is clearly a glass of white milk. If you then put the glass back behind the filter and ask the child the color of the milk, the 3-year-old says that the milk not only looks green but actually *is* green. Three-year-olds seem overwhelmed by appearance: objects are the way they look. Now give that same 3-year-old a gray sponge that looks exactly like a hunk of granite, allowing the youngster to handle it, heft it, and squeeze it. The child will tell you that the object not only *is* a sponge but that it *looks like* a sponge (and not like a rock), even though it would fool a stonemason who had not touched it. That is, when asked about an object, 3-year-olds insist that it *looks like* what it actually is. Even when Flavell's group trained 3-year-olds in the difference between "real" and "looks like," the children continued to make the same kinds of errors in both kinds of situations (see Table 11.1).

Three-year-olds seem unable to understand that an object can seem different from the way it actually is, because, says Flavell (Flavell, Green, and Flavell, 1989), they cannot represent a single object in two ways (its identity and its appearance). Such seemingly contradictory encoding is "unthinkable" to them, perhaps because they do not yet understand the subjective nature of representations and the fact that they vary within and between people. Faced with a sponge that looks like a rock, they form a single representation of the object and stick with it. They give the same answer whether they are asked about the object's identity (sponge) or its appearance (rock).

Because of this problem with representations, young children are also deceived by irrelevant changes in objects. If you show a 4-year-old a ball of clay and then

TABLE 11.1 WHEN APPEARANCES OVERWHELM REALITY*

	Both Objects Look the Same	The Objects Look Different
Both Objects Are the Same	Identity (Appearance = reality) Cell A	Irrelevant transformation (Milk behind filter is not really green.) Cell B
The Objects Are Different	Illusions (Rocks are not sponges.) Cell C	Different objects Appearance = reality Cell D

*Three-year-olds have trouble only with objects in the two discordant cells (B and C),
in which an object's appearance and its identity are different.*

smash it into a flat pancake, the child will be convinced that there is less clay in the pancake than there was in the ball. Older children are not easily fooled. They can infer reality even when objects or events are distorted, hidden, or camouflaged.

Attention Becomes Decentered

When observing a scene or solving a problem, young children usually concentrate on a single prominent feature of the stimulus. This captive attention, called **centration,** excludes all other aspects of the stimulus. When youngsters are asked to judge which glass holds the most cola, for example, they center on the height of the liquid in the glass and pay no attention to its width. To a 4-year-old, a tall, narrow glass always holds more cola than a short, squat glass. The dominant aspect of a stimulus probably captures the child's attention so effectively because she or he **encodes,** or registers, only that aspect of the stimulus in memory. This rudimentary encoding limits the ways in which a child can think about an object or a situation. As children get older, their attention becomes decentered. They can pay attention to more than one aspect of a stimulus or problem. They can think about it more comprehensively, considering the width as well as the height of a glass before judging how much cola it contains.

Thinking Becomes Reversible

Young children's thinking generally is confined to the immediate state of an object or situation. They seem unable to consider its previous or future states, and they do not seem to think about the sort of action that might

transform an object from one state into another. When a 4-year-old watches cola being poured from a squat glass into a tall, narrow glass, for example, he or she does not seem to realize that pouring the cola back into the squat glass would restore the level of liquid to its original level. Piaget said that the young child's thinking lacked **reversibility,** which is the understanding that irrelevant changes in appearance tend to compensate for one another and that the action can be reversed. Similarly, although most preschoolers can solve very simple problems in addition or subtraction, their understanding that subtraction reverses the effects of addition is still implicit and they can apply it only with very small numbers ($4 + 2 - 2$) and only when there are no conflicting visual cues (R. Gelman and Baillargeon, 1983).

Ten-year-olds understand that pouring cola back into a squat glass restores the original situation. They can also apply the operation of reversibility to new situations. When a fifth-grade class visited a large airport, they discovered that if they walked backward at just the right speed on the moving sidewalk, they stayed in the same place. They learned that compensation between actions can exactly cancel each action and so preserve an invariant relationship. The laughing 10-year-olds who blocked the sidewalk could figure out how to compensate for the walkway's movement because their thought was reversible.

Learning Becomes Self-Regulated and Strategic

Ask a 4-year-old to carry out some simple task, such as setting the table, and chances are that the job will not be completed. The forks and spoons may be put in place, but unless an adult monitors the project, reminding the youngster of each step, the child is likely to abandon the task or omit major items. Most young children seem to be creatures of impulse. They find it difficult to develop a plan (first put a knife, fork, and spoon at each place; next get the napkins; and so on), initiate it, and then carry it out.

This inability to plan and regulate their own behavior interferes with young children's ability to learn, to solve problems, and to communicate effectively. In most instances, their difficulty is not caused by a lack of necessary mental equipment but by a failure to grasp the need to plan a course of action and to understand the strategies that make learning or problem solving easier. Even when they develop a helpful strategy, they confine it to isolated situations and do not apply it in other places where it would be appropriate (A. Brown et al., 1983). When children are acquiring various strategies, most seem to go through a stage of **production deficiency,** during which they are capable of executing the strategy but do not use it spontaneously (Flavell, 1985). As children get older, their use of these strategies becomes automatic.

Language Becomes Instrumental for Thinking

Language plays a critical role in the intellectual revolution of childhood. Increasingly, language helps guide thinking. Infants and toddlers can form simple concepts without language (see Chapter 7), but unless they are able to assign names to concepts, children may find it impossible to combine elementary concepts into complex conceptual structures. Language not only speeds the acquisition of new concepts but allows children to reason more rapidly and effectively as well. The ways in which language affects cognition are especially clear in the cases of memory and of children's growing ability to control their actions.

Language and Memory
A dawning awareness of the way language facilitates memory is responsible for part of the improvement that appears in memory during childhood. In a classic study, John Flavell, David Beach, and Jack Chinsky (1966) demonstrated how the spontaneous use of language helps children solve simple memory problems. The researchers showed children pictures of familiar objects, pointing to some they wished the children to remember. Fifteen seconds later, they asked the children to

point to the same pictures in the same order. The 5-year-olds remembered fewer pictures than the 8-year-olds, apparently because most of the 8-year-olds repeated the names of the pictures they had to remember. Almost none of the 5-year-olds did this—a situation indicating that children do not automatically use their command of language when it would be helpful. The failure to rehearse the names verbally is an example of a production deficiency. When researchers instructed other nonrehearsers to whisper the names of objects they were to remember, they recalled as many objects as children who spontaneously repeated the names to themselves (Keeney, Cannizzo, and Flavell, 1967). Yet when allowed to memorize items in any way they liked, most of the young children whose recall had improved so strikingly when they rehearsed stopped using the strategy.

Language and Self-Control
Language also seems vital to the development of self-control, an advance that is basic to children's socialization (see Chapter 9). Harriet and Walter Mischel (1983) used simple treats to discover how children learn to control themselves when sorely tempted. When youngsters are told that they can have one marshmallow immediately or two marshmallows if they are willing to wait, most say that they will wait. But 4-year-olds usually overestimate their self-control. They want to look at the marshmallows while they wait. Because the 4-year-old's attention is centered, this strategy makes the reward so tempting that after a few minutes most give up and take the single marshmallow. Six-year-olds know that covering the reward makes waiting bearable. They also have discovered how to use language to control their behavior while waiting for the covered reward. They sing or keep telling themselves, "If you wait, you get two marshmallows; if you don't, you get only one." Eight-year-olds can control themselves even when the marshmallows are not covered. Their attention is decentered, and they have learned to use language to turn their thoughts away from the delicious sweet taste of the reward. They tell themselves to think about the marshmallows' abstract qualities (cottony or cloudlike), a strategy that makes waiting easier. Again, researchers have found a production deficiency: preschoolers who are instructed to think about the marshmallows as clouds or cotton balls can delay their gratification for nearly fifteen minutes. But without instructions, they are likely to think about the chewy, sweet, soft taste and wait no longer than five minutes.

Conceptual Development

As the profound intellectual revolution of childhood is completed, the charming but illogical thought of the preoperational child gives way to the **concrete-operational thought** of the schoolchild. This change, said Piaget (Piaget and Inhelder, 1969), is a decisive turning point, because children are now capable of logical thought. Although they can apply logic only to concrete objects, their thought has become flexible. This flexibility allows them to manipulate their mental representations as easily as they manipulate objects (R. Siegler, 1991), as we will see in the areas of conservation, causal reasoning, categories, and knowledge of number. The logical thought of the school years does not suddenly spring out of nowhere. It is based on concepts that developed in earlier years. As infants, children learned that objects continue to exist when out of sight. As preschoolers, they learned that people and animals and objects can change their appearance without losing their identity. Without these basic concepts of object permanence and identity, children could not grasp such principles as conservation.

Conservation

Children who understand **conservation** know that irrelevant changes in the external appearance of an object have no effect on the object's quantity—its weight, length, mass, or volume. In the best-known test of conservation, children watch an experimenter fill two glasses of the same size and shape to an equal level with colored water. The children are asked whether the two glasses contain the same amount of water. When the children assert that the amounts are the same, the researcher (with the children watching) pours the water from one of the glasses into a tall, narrow glass, so the levels of colored water in the two glasses differ. A nonconserver, when asked whether each glass now contains the same amount of water, will point to the tall glass and say, "No! This one has more water in it because it is higher." Nonconservers have not completed the intellectual revolution. Unable to reverse the action mentally, they focus on the present state of the liquid. Their attention centers on the dominant dimension (the liquid's height), and they mistake appearance for reality (Flavell, 1985).

When 7-year-old Larry watches the transformation, he is not fooled. He points out that although the tall glass is higher, it is also narrower. His thought is reversible, and he can prove to himself that the amount of

water has remained the same by imagining the liquid in its previous state. Larry clearly understands the conservation of quantity. Since Larry understands the conservation of liquid quantities, he also understands the conservation of number, which is easier to grasp. If you place two identical rows of checkers in front of him and then spread out one row so that it appears longer than the other, he will tell you that each row still has the same number of checkers. Larry is as convinced of this fact as he is of his knowledge that $2 + 2 = 4$. Once children grasp the conservation of number or liquids, they adamantly insist that nothing the researcher can do will convince them that they are wrong (S. Miller, 1986).

Children understand the conservation of number before they understand the conservation of liquid or solid quantities (such as balls of clay). Why is the conservation of number so much easier for children to grasp? Probably, says Robert Siegler (1991), because children have more cues to guide them when judging discrete quantities (like checkers) than when judging continuous quantities (like water). Faced with two rows of coins, a child can count them or line up the rows in one-to-one correspondence. When children have to judge glasses of water or balls of clay, their only cue is the manipulations done by the experimenter.

As Piaget discovered (Piaget and Inhelder, 1969), children's understanding of conservation is not complete once they understand the conservation of quantity. The other aspects of conservation emerge slowly, and it is several years before children understand the concept completely. First, children understand the conservation of quantity (with number leading the way) and the conservation of continuous length (see Figure 11.1). Then, at about the age of 9 or 10, they grasp the notion that weight is also conserved. Finally, at about 10 or 11, they understand the conservation of volume; they discover that the amount of water displaced by an object is not affected if its shape is changed (Piaget and Inhelder, 1941). Other researchers have confirmed Piaget's basic findings about the general sequence of these acquisitions with children around the world, in places as varied as Hong Kong, Iran, Aden, and Nigeria and among aborigines in Australia (Dasen, 1973; Goodnow, 1962; Mohseni, 1966; Uzgiris, 1964). The speed with which various concepts develop, however, depends on whether the culture values them. Spatial concepts tend to develop early among nomadic, hunting cultures, for example, whereas the conservation of liquids develops early in sedentary, agricultural societies that value precise measurements (Bullinger and Chatillon, 1983).

Conservation is an extremely complex cognitive skill

In this conservation experiment, a child looks at two rows of seven evenly spaced checkers. After she agrees that both rows have the same number, the researcher bunches together the checkers in one row. At this point, children who do not understand conservation say that the undisturbed row contains more checkers. *(William MacDonald)*

that reflects the development of specific cognitive processes and the child's growing store of experiences. As John Flavell (1985) has pointed out, decentration, more exhaustive encoding, reversibility, and the development of cognitive strategies are essential to the child's ability to think about quantity, length, weight, and volume. An increase in **cognitive capacity,** or the amount of information a child can keep in mind at one time, is also critical. When young children try to solve problems, most of the space they have for processing information is used up by such basic tasks as encoding or retrieving information (Case, 1985). As they get older, they process information rapidly and often automatically. When less space is needed for basic processes, more is avail-

able to hold and manipulate information. This increase enables children to consider more than one dimension or think about the transformation involved.

Many of Piaget's experiments have been replicated by other developmental psychologists, and their results support many of his findings. An increasing number of researchers, however, have found that young children seem to understand more about some aspects of conservation than the experiments reveal (R. Siegler, 1991). When the context of the experiment is changed so that children pour the water themselves, more of them solve the problem correctly. As Margaret Donaldson (1979) has pointed out, the conditions of Piaget's experiments push children toward the wrong answer. When the ex-

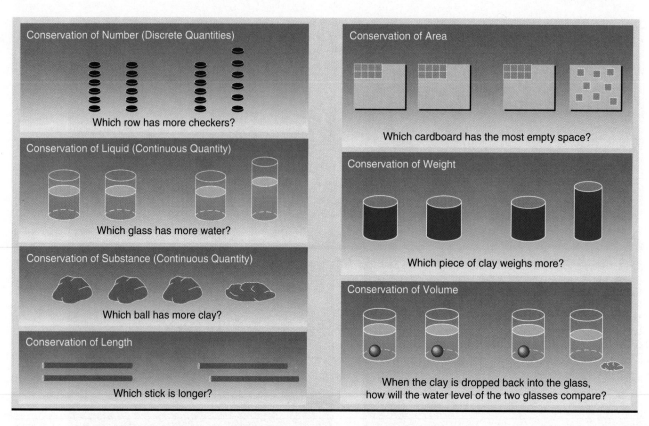

Conservation of Number (Discrete Quantities)

Which row has more checkers?

Conservation of Liquid (Continuous Quantity)

Which glass has more water?

Conservation of Substance (Continuous Quantity)

Which ball has more clay?

Conservation of Length

Which stick is longer?

Conservation of Area

Which cardboard has the most empty space?

Conservation of Weight

Which piece of clay weighs more?

Conservation of Volume

When the clay is dropped back into the glass,
how will the water level of the two glasses compare?

Figure 11.1 In each of these problems, the researcher calls attention to the original situation (the left pair of diagrams) and asks the child whether the two displays are equal. Then, with the child watching, the researcher transforms the items (the right pair of diagrams) and once more asks if the displays are equal. If the child says that they are the same (either because the researcher's manipulations did not affect the display or because the transformation can be reversed), the child has demonstrated a grasp of conservation.

perimenter pours the water, she or he generally says, "Now watch what I do." This indicates to the child that the action is important and will affect whatever follows.

In Piaget's view, however, not even the most skillful teacher can teach a preoperational child that pouring water into a tall, narrow glass does not increase the water's quantity or that twisting a necklace into a curve does not shorten it. Yet a number of investigators have been able to teach 3- and 4-year-olds to pass conservation tests. With training and practice, Rochel Gelman (1982a) has taught preschoolers to solve number conservation problems when there are as many as ten checkers in a row. In her study, the children learned to ignore perceptual cues and rely instead on one-to-one correspondence, mentally lining up the rows of checkers. In Piaget's view, these children may be passing the test, but they are not displaying conservation. He would say that recounting the checkers or using

one-to-one correspondence neither requires concrete operations nor reflects an understanding of the transformation that has occurred.

Do young children actually know more about conservation than Piaget's tests indicate? Perhaps young children who pass conservation tests are simply maintaining their belief in the objects' identity, says Kurt Acredolo (1982). He believes that children probably recognize the identity rule (saying "You just spread the checkers") before they understand compensation. Their thought is not yet reversible, and they do not understand that the change in the less dominant dimension can compensate for change in the dominant dimension.

This explanation squares with the results of a study by Dorothy Field (1981) in which 4-year-olds were given training in conservation. Five months after the training ended, most of the children who had learned about reversibility and compensation no longer could solve conservation problems, but those who had learned to recognize the identity of the altered substances could. The successful children's grasp of conservation seemed to rely on an understanding of identity, which may be the way most children develop their comprehension.

Causal Reasoning

One day when Piaget and his daughter were out walking, 4-year-old Lucienne looked up at the sun and said, "Oh, it's walking like us. Yes, it has little paws and we can't see them." Then she discovered the sun was following them. "It's doing that for fun, to play a joke on us." Asked whether the sun knew that Piaget and Lucienne were there, she said, "Of course it does; it can see us!" (Piaget, 1951, p. 252).

Piaget studied preschoolers' thoughts about the causes, purposes, and activities of such things as dreams, night and day, clouds, the sun and moon, mountains and rivers. He asked the children why boats float and how steam engines operate. From their replies to his open-ended questions, he concluded that young children sought single, final, humanlike causes for things that are difficult to explain. This search seemed driven by three concepts: finalism, artificialism, and animism. **Finalism** is the belief that nothing happens by accident. Even the most trivial occurrence has a simple and direct cause. Four-year-olds say that a river flows because "it wants to" and that clouds move "in order to hide the sun." **Artificialism,** which rests on the child's inability to separate physical causes from nonphysical causes, is the belief that everything in the world has been built—either by humans or by God. The child's God bears little resemblance to the adult's concept of a creator; instead, children see God as a giant or magician who builds things in the way that people do. At various time, Piaget's children told him that lakes were filled by watering cans, that the sky was cut out and painted, and that a house on a riverbank was built before the river "because it's much harder to make streams and rivers and lakes" (Piaget, 1951, p. 249).

When researchers attempted to replicate Piaget's experiments (S. Gelman and Kremer, 1991), they discovered that today's 4-year-olds were able to identify a range of natural causes and provided them spontaneously. The children knew, for example, that people made cups and TVs, and they attributed oceans and flowers to naturalistic or divine sources. But when asked open-ended questions about the details of these processes, they fell back on the artificialistic answers that Piaget reported.

Animism is the belief that inanimate objects have thoughts, feelings, and life itself. As children develop, they tend to ascribe these qualities to objects in different categories. Three-year-olds may believe that any object that can affect people in any way is alive. A gun is alive because it shoots. Soon children limit life to things that normally move, even though people may move them. A bicycle is alive, but a gun is not. About the time children start school, they limit life to things that move by themselves, such as a battery-powered robot. Finally, children limit life to plants and animals. There is some indication, however, that young children's thought is not as animistic as Piaget assumed. Researchers found that 3-year-olds may attribute life to inanimate objects—but only when they lack the knowledge they need for an informed decision (Bullock, 1985). Five-year-olds are almost as accurate as adults in judging the animacy of objects (see Table 11.2)

When Piaget probed children's knowledge of causality, he tended to ask about areas of nature in which children had little experience, such as why the wind

Because battery-powered robots can move, 5-year-olds may believe that they are alive. *(Steven Baratz/The Picture Cube)*

TABLE 11.2   CHILDREN'S CORRECT JUDGMENTS ABOUT THE ANIMACY OF OBJECTS

Age Group	OBJECT			
	Block (%)*	Toy Worm (%)*	Person (%)*	Rabbit (%)*
3-year-olds	69.2	53.8	84.6	69.2
4-year-olds	93.3	86.6	93.3	100
5-year-olds	93.7	100	100	100

*Underlined proportions are significantly greater than chance (less than 1 chance in 1000).

Source: Adapted from Bullock, 1985, p. 222.

blew or what caused rain to fall. But if asked about the causes of simple actions, preschoolers demonstrate a much better grasp of physical causality than the children Piaget questioned. One aspect of causality is that cause always precedes effects. As we saw in Chapter 7, toddlers learn much better when new sequences of events involve causation than when the sequences are arbitrary (Bauer and Mandler, 1989). Preschoolers are even more sensitive to causal relations. In one study (Bullock and Gelman, 1979), 3- to 5-year-olds watched a ball roll down a runway and disappear into a box. A few seconds later a jumping jack popped up from a hole in the box; then another ball rolled down the runway and into the box. When asked which ball made the jack jump, the children chose the first ball. Even when the first ball rolled down a runway that was physically separated from the box and the second ball rolled down the runway into the box, the children chose the ball that preceded the jack's jump.

Three-year-olds have amassed a fund of causal knowledge: they know that knives cut, water makes things wet, and dropped objects break. But they cannot look at an altered object (a broken cup) and any further transformation in its condition (a wet, broken cup) and infer that the cause of the final state was water and not a hammer. Instead of taking into account the difference between initial and final states, they seem overwhelmed by the cup's broken condition in its initial state and, relying on their store of causal knowledge, insist that a hammer was responsible for the broken cup's becoming wet. By the time they are 4 years old, however, they focus on the change in states and make genuine causal inferences (Das Gupta and Bryant, 1989).

Striking as these results are, they do not indicate that

4-year-olds completely understand the basis of physical causality. Four-year-olds can connect causes that occur just before events, but when there is a delay of five seconds between cause and effect, they cannot make the inference. By the time they are 8 years old, children understand that effects need not be immediate (R. Siegler, 1991). It takes many years before children develop a complete understanding of causality; in fact, many adults do not understand some of the basic physical principles involved.

Classes, Collections, and Categories

From the beginning, children apparently try to explain what they see and what happens to them. Because of these attempts, say some researchers (Keil, 1989), young children divide their experiences into fundamental categories and assume that the categories are related in a hierarchy. Animals and plants are both living things, for example. The youngest children make only sweeping distinctions (between objects and events, between animals and plants), but as they grow older, children become aware of more subtle distinctions (intentional and nonintentional events, animals that think and animals that do not think). From their knowledge about these categories, they draw inferences about the nature of the world.

Yet the toddler who spontaneously groups similar objects (see Chapter 7) has only a glimmer of the way in which human beings organize the world. Piaget claimed that young children's early arrangements are the result of a sorting process that lacks any general plan and that often shifts in midstream—changing, for instance, from grouping by color (all the red objects) to grouping by shape (all the triangles)—before the task is completed (Inhelder and Piaget, 1964). He agreed that 5-year-olds use consistent rules to classify objects, but he maintained that they could neither classify objects in terms of multiple attributes (color and shape) nor understand the relations between classes. In his view, children did not have "true concepts" until they were about 7 years old and could think logically.

The Structure of Categories

Preschoolers do best when sorting objects at the level of **basic categories,** because members of these categories are most like one another and most different from members of other categories. Members of basic categories (bird, flower, table) tend to have similar shapes and similar parts (birds have beaks, wings, claws). Parts are especially informative, because they are both elements of appearance and elements of function. Preschoolers find it more difficult to sort objects at the level of **superordinate categories** (animal, plant, furniture), because members of these categories are highly generalized, look least like one another, and are usually based on function. In most cases, a child cannot infer function from an object's appearance; he or she must have prior experience with the object. Researchers have found, for example, that preschoolers can group superordinate categories only if the members share parts (Tversky, 1989). That is, they can group *bear, cow,* and *deer* together as "the same kind of thing," but not *cat, fish,* and *snake.*

Yet even 3-year-olds understand that basic-category membership reflects something deeper than superficial appearance. This became apparent when Susan Gelman and Ellen Markman (1986) showed preschoolers pictures of dinosaurs (brontosaurus and triceratops) and a rhinoceros and told them that a brontosaurus was cold-blooded and a rhinoceros warm-blooded. The youngsters relied on category membership instead of appearance for drawing inductive references, correctly inferring that the triceratops (which was labeled "dinosaur" but which resembled a rhinoceros) was cold-blooded. In another study (S. Gelman and Markman, 1987), the same researchers discovered that it was not even necessary to label the categories. Preschoolers who looked at unnamed pictures drew inferences from a green leaf insect to a black beetle but were unlikely to draw inferences from the green leaf insect to a green leaf. Later research (S. Gelman and Coley, 1990) indicates that when objects are labeled by category, children as young

as 2½ will make inferences based on membership instead of on appearance, but if the category label is not supplied, they go back to relying on appearance.

Children's understanding of categories develops gradually as their store of knowledge increases. As their information about the world increases, the boundaries of their categories broaden. Until a child learns about papayas, for example, they will not be part of the fruit category. Category development in Chinese children, however, seems less dependent on cultural familiarity than it is in English-speaking children, because the Chinese language links nearly half of its nouns with their category (Lin, Schwanenflugel, and Wisenbaker, 1990). English does this with only a few nouns, such as *bluebird.*

Children's comprehension of category structures is fostered by the way parents refer to objects. When parents teach their children about basic categories, they simply point to the object and label it ("That's a dog"). But when they teach about superordinate categories, they give extra information. They often identify an object by providing both the basic and the superordinate labels ("That's a dog; it's an animal"), or they refer to a group (dog, cat, and lamb) by using a plural label ("Here are some animals)." Studies indicate that children as young as 3 years notice these subtle distinctions and use them to decide on the hierarchical level of new category terms (Callanan, 1989).

Although preschoolers seem to understand the nature of superordinate categories and have no trouble grouping typical category members, they are apparently unable to group members that differ radically in appearance. Among first-graders, only those who had demonstrated concrete-operational thought successfully placed atypical objects into their functional categories (Ricco, 1989). Those who also understand conservation knew, for example, that a mirror was furniture and that a balloon was a toy. Their classmates who were still at the preoperational level were overwhelmed by appearances and rejected atypical category members in favor of perceptually similar members of a different category. They grouped a table with a box kite, for example, placing the mirror to one side; and they rejected the balloon, grouping a yo-yo with a clock. Apparently, until children have attained operational thought, they cannot suppress perceptual dissimilarities in favor of the underlying abstract functional properties. That means that they fail to draw the sort of inductive inferences based on category membership that they demonstrate when dealing with basic categories (Ricco, 1989).

Class Inclusion

Piaget explained such failures by saying that until children attained concrete-operational thought, they could not think about objects as simultaneously belonging to two different classes: an object could not be both a carrot *and* a vegetable or a truck *and* a vehicle. (This inability to represent an object in two ways is, as noted earlier, basic to the young child's problem with illusions.) Piaget demonstrated this representational dilemma by testing children's ability to understand **class inclusion,** an aspect of deductive reasoning based on the knowledge that a superordinate class (vegetables) is always larger than any of its basic classes (carrots, peas). Piaget showed children a bouquet of many primroses and few daisies and asked the youngsters whether there were more flowers or more primroses. Preschoolers invariably said, "More primroses." Because youngsters could not think of an entire class and its subclass at the same time, they could not compare them. Instead, they compared the two subclasses, correctly reporting that there were more primroses (than daisies).

Although preschoolers fail on such class-inclusion tasks, they can pass the test when researchers use collective nouns instead of class nouns to compare class with subclass. When Ellen Markman (1981) asked children, "Who would have a bigger party, someone who invited the boys or someone who invited the children?" most kindergartners incorrectly said "boys." But when she asked, "Who would have a bigger party, someone who invited the boys or someone who invited the class?" the kindergartners correctly said "class." Why should changing a single word turn an insoluble problem into an easy one? Markman points out that members of a collection are related in some way; members of a class are not. A boy is a child, but he is *part of* a school class. This part-whole relationship, which is missing from categories, gives collections an internal structure and a psychological integrity. That makes the class-inclusion problem much easier to think about. Even young children can keep the whole collection in mind while thinking about its parts.

Until concrete-operational thought is firmly established, however, children do not understand the logical basis of the typical class-inclusion question. Until they are about 9 years old, they solve the problem by counting the items in the basic group they were asked about (primroses), counting the number in the entire superordinate group (flowers), and choosing the larger number for their answer (R. Siegler, 1991). Not until they are 10 do they rely on reason and answer the question on its logical basis.

Number Knowledge and Number Skill

Children's knowledge of number builds on the baby's ability to recognize the difference between small numbers of objects. As we saw in Chapter 6, young babies seem to know the difference between two objects and three objects (Antell and Keating, 1983). No one suggests that young babies count the number of objects in a display; instead, they simply detect the differences between the patterns. Adults seem to use the same process when dealing with groups of five or less, and 5-year-olds apparently use it with groups no larger than three (Chi and Klahr, 1975).

By the time they are 2 years old, however, most children have begun to count—even though many of them can count only as far as two (R. Gelman and Gallistel, 1978). They count, even if they do not know their language's words for numbers. They may use letters to count, or they may invent their own words. They may borrow number words but invent their own sequence. Young children use their number words consistently. If they count, "one, two, six," "six" always stands for three. Before they are 3, children point at or touch objects they are counting, saying their number words aloud. When they are a little older, they count to themselves and announce only the total. But if a 5-year-old is asked to count many objects, he or she counts them aloud.

Counting and reasoning about numbers are separate understandings, but counting can provide the basis for mathematical reasoning by giving a child a way to represent number (R. Gelman and Gallistel, 1978). Some researchers question whether young children actually understand **cardinality,** that is, numerical size. They wonder if preschoolers recognize that the last word in their counting sequence actually represents the quantity in the set they have counted (Fuson, 1988). Perhaps all that they have learned is that the correct answer to the question "How many?" is the last number in the counting sequence. The evidence is mixed. In one study (J. Becker, 1989), 4-year-olds used number words as large as *six* to decide whether sets of dolls and cups were in one-to-one correspondence, that is, to determine whether each doll had a cup. Yet in another study (Frye et al., 1989), 4-year-olds who counted plastic chips generally answered the "how many" question correctly, but they performed poorly when the experimenter said, "Give me [*x*] chips" (*x* being one less than the quanitity counted).

Perhaps counting and the understanding of number are not as closely tied together as some researchers have supposed. Catherine Sophian (1988) suggests that the mixed performance of young children may indicate that it takes time for children to generalize the relation between various numerical procedures such as counting and one-to-one correspondence. As we saw in the section on conservation, young children can solve simple conservation problems by using one-to-one correspondence. They also seem to understand mathematical magnitude: when comparing numbers, they know that greater numbers indicate more (six is bigger than three) (R. Siegler, 1991). They may, however, fail to apply knowledge they have demonstrated in one area (mathematical magnitude) to problems in another (addition).

The rapidity with which children discover the connection between various skills may reflect the contexts in which they encounter number. Most children regularly engage in number activities within the home, and the complexity of their exposure to number grows out of mother-child interaction. Mothers adjust number activities to reflect their assessment of the child's ability, and the child adjusts his or her goals to the mother's efforts. Whether children are from the middle or the working class, their use of counting words, their ability to read numerals, and their counting accuracy are the same. But middle-class children have a clearer understanding of cardinality and of simple arithmetic, apparently because their mothers have higher expectations and goals for them and structure number activities at a more complex level (Saxe, Guberman, and Gearhart, 1987).

The strides in children's ability to think logically, whether we look at conservation, causal reasoning, categorization, or numerical skills, indicate a change in both the quality and quantity of thought. Studies of the way children process information examine the processes that underlie these cognitive advances.

Advances in Information Processing

Throughout childhood, processing skills function with increasing speed and efficiency, allowing youngsters to handle complex information that would only have confused them in earlier years. This increased competence is apparent whether we look at aspects of attention, memory, problem solving, or metacognition.

Attention

Children's concepts of the world depend on which of its aspects get their attention. As their thought processes become increasingly sophisticated, they look at objects more systematically and attend to their most important aspects. Once they enter school, where they learn to read and to think about events and problems that are removed from daily life, they must use these skills in a different way. When children learn to read, for example, they must discriminate among letter forms, pay close attention to the shapes of letters and to their sequence, but ignore the shading of the print and the size of the letters. Once the letters have been discriminated, children must use them in combination to gain immediate access to meaning—as immediately as the sight of a medium-size, four-footed animal with a wagging tail calls forth the concept *dog* (E. Gibson, 1974).

Scanning

The way that children look at things and the things they notice reflect their interests, their expectations about the world, and their strategies for acquiring information (Day, 1975). When preschoolers look at a picture, for example, their attention first is caught by the center of interest, and they scan downward from that point. They glance randomly from point to point in a display, and they tend to stop scanning before they have all the information they need. In one study (Vurpillot and Ball, 1979), children looked at simple drawings of houses and tried to decide whether the houses were the same or different. When they differed, the changes always appeared in one of the windows, where curtains, blinds,

Once children enter school, they find they must deploy their attention in new ways, such as discriminating one letter from another. *(Elizabeth Crews/Stock, Boston)*

a bird cage, or a window box might have been added. Five-year-olds scanned unsystematically, and they failed to inspect every window. Nine-year-olds, who had learned what aspects of the environment it pays to notice, compared each pair of windows in turn and examined every window in the drawing.

Like these 9-year-olds, older children tend to scan exhaustively and systematically, beginning from the top of a picture, page, or pattern. Most also have learned to scan without being distracted by irrelevant information, as younger children are. Older children's scanning techniques are also efficient; once they have the information they need for a task, they stop scanning. As children grow older, they also scan more rapidly. Their speed increases because they are processing visual information more rapidly, because they are integrating information across glances, or because each fixation of their eyes picks up information from a wider field (Day, 1975).

Selective Attention

Young children may be inefficient scanners because they lack conscious control over their attention. When they begin a task, their attention is easily captured by the prominence of some stimulus, as we saw in the discussion of centration. The result is a playful, rapid, and impulsive response to aspects of the world around them. As children get older, their attention becomes systematic and goal-oriented, with the relevance and informativeness of stimuli becoming increasingly important (Wright and Vliestra, 1975). They gain increasing control over their attention and become able to direct it toward the information they need and to ignore information that is irrelevant to the task (Flavell, 1985).

The skills involved in controlling attention seem to develop at different rates; as children gain control over the various skills, they find it easier to adapt to the requirements of specific situations. Developmental changes in adaptability appeared when researchers tested the effects of various factors on visual attention (Enns and Akhtar, 1989). Preschoolers, kindergartners, second-graders, and college students identified target symbols ($+$, $\times$, $\bigcirc$, $\square$) that appeared in the center of a computer screen, sometimes by themselves and sometimes flanked by other symbols that served as distracters. The results indicated that much of the improvement in selective attention is the result of increased skill in the earliest stages of processing. Preschoolers find it difficult to focus their attention voluntarily on a specific location and are easily distracted by the presence of other stimuli. They, as well as kindergartners, also pay a high price in terms of speed and accuracy when preparing to block the perception of distracting stimuli. By second grade, such preparation, known as *attentional set*, is less likely to slow children's performance.

Eventually, children learn to adapt their attention to their goals, using attentional set in a way that speeds processing. By preparing themselves to gather particular kinds of information, they use appropriate strategies as soon as the task begins. In one study (Pick and Frankel, 1973), researchers asked children to match animal pictures—sometimes by size, sometimes by color, and sometimes by shape. It made no difference whether second-graders knew ahead of time which matching standard would be used; their performance was no faster or more accurate when they had advance knowledge. But sixth-graders matched faster and more accurately when told the standard beforehand than when they received the information after the matching had begun. This growing ability to use appropriate strategies was reflected earlier in the discussion of scanning. Flavell (1985) likens the person with planned, adaptive control of attention to the orchestra conductor who calls forth first one instrument, then another, then a combination, depending on the effect demanded by the score.

Memory

Memory improves throughout childhood. In Chapter 6, we met the infant who recognized a mobile and remembered how to control it and the toddler who could remind a parent of a promised treat. In this chapter, we follow children as they become skillful rememberers. What *is* memory, anyway? And why do children get better at it as they grow older? Memory is not a single process, a passive storehouse of our experiences, or an isolated intellectual skill. When we speak of **memory,** we are talking about a collection of cognitive processes—the same processes involved in perceiving, thinking, and learning (Kail, 1990). When these processes are applied to the storage and retrieval of information, we find it convenient to refer to them as *memory.*

As noted in Chapter 2, memory may be short-term or long-term (see Figure 2.1), and long-term memory may be demonstrated by either recognition or recall. Short-term memory and recognition memory show little improvement after the age of 4 or 5; most of the advance comes in long-term recall memory and is due to greater efficiency in processes connected with recall. Three major factors are responsible for the dramatic improvement as children get older. First, they become skilled at integrating new information with what they already know about the world. Second, they acquire and use increasingly efficient methods of storing and retrieving information in long-term memory. Finally, they develop an awareness of the factors that influence their ability to remember.

The Role of Knowledge

If you listened to a lecture about new ways of programming a computer, you might be baffled by the specialized terminology and be unable to remember much of what you heard. But a computer programmer who heard the same lecture would find it interesting, be able to talk about the ideas presented, and apply them to her work the next day. You were unable to comprehend and retain the material because you lack the rich network of computer-related concepts that the programmer drew on with ease as she listened to the lecture, integrating what she heard with her knowledge about computers.

When you sat down to hear the lecture, you placed yourself in a position much like that of 4- or 5-year-olds as they go about their daily business. A good deal of what they encounter bears little or no relation to their relatively small store of knowledge about the world. When they come upon new information, they may not have any related concepts to connect it with in memory, so the material is difficult to store and/or retrieve (Flavell, 1985). Whether they are trying to learn new facts, new techniques, or new ideas, young children remember best information that they can associate with things they already know about or can do.

Their limited store of knowledge becomes a hindrance even on simple tasks like learning word lists. When youngsters are asked to memorize lists of words, they get progressively better with age. Yet when the lists are varied so that each age group gets a list of words that are meaningful to them, younger children recall as many words as older children do (C. Richman, Nida, and Pittman, 1976). In Chapter 2, we met the 4-year-old with the enormous store of dinosaur knowledge (Chi and Koeske, 1983). He knew much more than the average adult about the habits of the stegosaurus and the triceratops. In fact, when adults are uninformed about a topic, knowledgeable children can best them in learning new, related material. In one study, Michelene Chi (1978) pitted children who were expert chess players against graduate students and research assistants who were mediocre players. Chi arranged chess pieces on boards as if a game were in progress, removed them, and then asked each subject to replace the pieces. The children's memories were far superior to the adult's for the chess positions. Yet when Chi tested both groups by asking them to remember a list of ten numbers, the adults did much better than the children. The difference in performance reminds us that when children acquire expertise in a specific content area (whether chess or dinosaurs), they may function at a higher cognitive level within that area while still functioning at the expected level in other areas (Flavell, 1992).

Background knowledge helps us to remember because of the constructive nature of memory. Instead of storing isolated items and retrieving exact copies of what we have stored, we interpret the information we encounter, make inferences about it, and construct a representation of what we have seen or heard. When we remember something, we reconstruct our memory, produce a logical interpretation of the original information, and perhaps flesh it out with guesses and pertinent knowledge we have picked up since we stored the representation (Flavell, 1985; Paris and Lindauer, 1977).

The Role of Strategies

Strategies are voluntary, conscious techniques that we use in order to remember specific information. Strategies can be obvious: a child may drape her scarf and mittens on the doorknob in the evening so that she won't forget to take them the next day, or she may write a note ("mittens!") and stick it under a magnet on the refrigerator door—just as her parents do. Even kindergartners are aware of such external strategies, although they may forget to use them. Children begin to use strategies as they come to understand that unless they take some deliberate action, they will be unable to recall important information when they need it. As we have seen, youngsters are able to use strategies long before they adopt them on their own. Their first use of strategies may occur in situations that encourage their use or under conditions that give children more time to study the material (Kail, 1990). Much of the improvement in memory that appears during childhood is the result of children's increased use of strategies. But not all memory tasks require the use of strategies for efficient performance, and on those that do not, preschoolers do almost as well as adults (A. Brown et al., 1983).

Encoding Strategies. One of the earliest internal strategies discovered by children is **rehearsal,** which involves repeating material that is to be remembered. A child may rehearse silently or aloud. As we saw earlier, children who repeated the names of pictures they were required to remember did a better job of recalling them than children who did not repeat the names. Until recently, developmentalists believed that preschoolers do not use rehearsal as a memory aid, but many of today's preschoolers have begun to use the technique—at least in some situations. Perhaps watching programs like *Sesame Street* teaches young children that the strategy is helpful.

When children first begin rehearsing, they use the technique inefficiently, and their improvement on memory tasks is slight. But as they become more skilled, the content of their rehearsal changes (P. Ornstein and Naus, 1978). Instead of repeating a single word, or perhaps two, over and over, they begin repeating a series of words, varying them with each repetition. This technique, which makes memory more efficient, is found only among older children. It indicates some sort of plan for the task and helps the child organize recall.

Clustering, or grouping items to be remembered around some common element, is one of the most effective aids to memory. Children who use such **organization** (for example, grouping all the animals, all the toys, and all the furniture to be recalled in a word list) remember many more words than children who do not. Five-year-olds do not deliberately use this strategy. Yet when asked to recall material by category, they remember items they did not recall spontaneously. Many 8-year-olds who do not sort items by category before learning them are aware that such organization makes recall easier (Corsale and Ornstein, 1980). Most children are 9 or 10 years old before they consistently reorganize material that they are trying to learn (Paris and Lindauer, 1982).

Retrieval Strategies. Rehearsal and organization are encoding strategies; children use these techniques at the time they learn material in order to help them recall later. Other strategies are retrieval strategies, which are used at the time children try to remember. External cues are one kind of retrieval strategy—the strategically placed mittens, notes, shopping lists, or landmarks. Simple retrieval cues can sharply increase the efficiency of children's memory. When researchers prompt children by giving them associated names as cues, the children remember many additional words from a memorized list (J. Hall et al., 1979). The effectiveness of cues increases with age. When second-graders are given a picture that serves as a category label, for example, they recall only one word and then move on to another cate-

gory (Kobasigawa, 1977). Fifth-graders try to remember as many words from each category as they can before moving on. Such results suggest that second-graders do not use cues in the conscious, systematic manner employed by fifth-graders. A cue is effective with second-graders only if it is directly linked to the desired information, but fifth-graders have learned to search their memory exhaustively, so a cue that triggers associated information often leads them to the target (B. Ackerman, 1988).

Internal cues, which are generated by the person trying to remember the information, also can be helpful aids to memory. One internal strategy is to focus attention; another is to maintain effort and persist in attempts to remember, even when doing so becomes difficult. Organized searches, such as going through the alphabet when trying to remember someone's name, develop much later, although—once again—6- and 7-year-olds can use this technique if told to do so (Flavell, 1985).

Reading music is a skill that requires attention and the application of memory strategies; when the child begins to play a carefully rehearsed piece, the notes on the sheet music serve as retrieval cues. *(Leonard Speier)*

The Role of Metamemory

Whether children deliberately use memory strategies may depend on how well they understand the way memory works. This understanding, known as **metamemory,** includes an awareness that situations call for remembering, a knowledge of factors that make memory tasks easier or more difficult, and an understanding of the usefulness of various memory skills. Between the ages of 5 and 12, children make giant strides in their awareness of the demands of memory, their acquisition of strategies, and their spontaneous use of them (Paris and Lindauer, 1982).

Although many 4-year-olds know that noise makes it hard to remember and that it is easier to remember a few items than to remember a lot of them, most do not seem to realize what remembering actually entails. In one study (Wellman and Johnson, 1979), 4-year-olds said that a boy who found his coat hanging in a closet had "remembered" where it was—whether or not the boy had seen the coat being placed there. Until children are about 9 years old, most of them do not understand that remembering is a form of knowing that is based on past experience (Kail, 1990).

Kindergartners and first-graders know that events that happened a long time ago are hard to recall, that telephone numbers are quickly forgotten, and that once something is learned, it is easier to relearn the same material than to learn something new (Kreutzer, Leonard, and Flavell, 1975). When asked how to remember something, these children usually suggest using external memory aids, such as other people, tape recordings, written notes, or a string on the finger. Most of them, however, do not seem to understand how external aids work. Although they know that the cue should be associated in some way with whatever they want to remember and that they must see the cue in order to remember it, they do not realize that they must see the cue *before* it is time to do the task (Beal, 1985; Schneider and Sodian, 1988). Yet they do seem to know that a cue placed in a drawer is not very helpful because they are unlikely to open the drawer and find it.

Long before children begin using internal memory strategies, they are able to use them when told to do so. But as we saw earlier, they then discard the strategies and go back to their old methods. Why the delay in adopting memory strategies? Many younger children do not know that they need to do anything special to remember. Kindergartners and first-graders often overestimate their ability to remember objects, assuming that they will have no trouble recalling anything they wish

to remember (Beal, 1985). They also seem unaware that some memory tasks are more difficult than others. About half of them believe that recall is no more difficult than recognition and that recalling something verbatim is as easy as paraphrasing it (Kail, 1990). In contrast, third- and fifth-graders understand that remembering related items is easier than remembering completely dissimilar things and that telling a story in your own words is easier than repeating the story verbatim (Flavell, 1985; Myers and Paris, 1978).

Researchers have assumed that as children begin to understand the way memory operates, they begin acquiring the strategies that make it more efficient (Weed, Ryan, and Day, 1990). Simply knowing that a strategy is effective is not enough, however; children apparently do not adopt a strategy unless they have developed an appropriate theory as to *why* the strategy works (Paris, Newman, and McVey, 1982). This became clear when 4- to 6-year-olds were encouraged to label a group of pictures they were to remember (Fabricius and Cavalier, 1989). Children who said that the strategy was effective but could not explain its success failed to use the strategy on a subsequent trial. But children who had developed mental explanations, saying that labeling helped them keep thinking about the pictures after they said the names, quickly adopted the new strategy (see Figure 11.2). Studies have shown that when a teacher introduces memory strategies, explains how they work and why they are important, children will use them (Moely et al., 1992). Thus, when children understand the value of strategies, they seem ready to adopt them—a fact indicating that the simultaneous advance in metamemory and the use of memory skills is no coincidence.

Problem Solving

The toddler who solves the problem of reaching the cookie jar by pushing a chair over to the kitchen counter becomes the preschooler who applies strategies and mental rules. As children's knowledge accumulates and their memories improve, they can tackle more difficult problems with success. Each time they encounter a new problem, they relate new information to old information and apply it to the task at hand. Their success depends on five important factors: task analysis, rule acquisition, planning, the context of the problem, and collaboration.

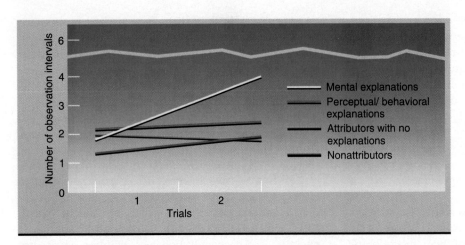

Figure 11.2 Only children who gave mental explanations for the usefulness of labeling increased their use of the strategy on the second trial. They said that labeling worked because it kept them thinking about the pictures. Those with perceptual/behavioral explanations said that labeling worked because it allowed other activities to occur (they had "more time to see the pictures," or because at recall they only had to say the labels to remember). Attributors with no explanation said that labeling worked but they didn't know why. Nonattributors gave labeling no credit for aiding recall. (*From Fabricius and Cavalier, 1989, p. 304*)

Task Analysis

Before children can solve a problem, they must define it, understand its particular demands, and choose an appropriate goal. This process is known as **task analysis,** and when it is done properly, a child's actions will be adapted to the task at hand. When schoolchildren explored a funhouse constructed by researchers, the importance of choosing goals became apparent. Mary Gauvain and Barbara Rogoff (1986) divided a 12-foot square into rooms, using blankets, sheets, wooden screens, and blinds (see Figure 11.3). Each room was decorated to match its name on the map, and as in all funhouses, there were some dead-end rooms. Before the children explored the structure, they were given a goal by the researchers. Half the children were supposed to learn the general layout of the funhouse; the rest were supposed to learn the most direct route through it.

After their explorations, children in both groups remembered equally well how to get through the funhouse. When it came to recalling the general plan, however, those whose problem was to learn the layout remembered much more information and had a better memory for the relation between the rooms. The children's goal had affected their explorations. Children learning the direct route apparently focused their attention on that aspect of the funhouse and paid no attention to information they did not expect to need. They learned landmarks and strung them together in a route but did not integrate the route into any sort of mental

map. In learning either the route or the general layout, goal was much more important than age: 6-year-olds did as well at the task as 9-year-olds.

Rule Acquisition

Children need to acquire rules for solving problems; without them, they lack the means to accomplish their actions. When tackling an unfamiliar problem, they rely on some standard rule that has served them successfully in the past. Because children apply the same rules consistently to a variety of problems, their thinking is similar in many situations. As children grow older, they develop increasingly sophisticated rules that allow them to solve a wider range of problems. Robert Siegler (1981; 1991) traced this development by placing various weights on a balance scale and asking children between the ages of 3 and 12 which arm would go down if the lever were released. Three-year-olds seemed to be operating without any rule, but many 4-year-olds and virtually all 5-year-olds had worked out a simple rule that allowed them to solve the problem when they had to account for weight only. These children, who were at the preoperational stage, focused on a single aspect of the problem. Eight-year-olds, who had moved into the concrete-operational stage, operated by a more complicated rule that took distance as well as weight into account. Their rule allowed them to solve problems unless there was a conflict between the two dimensions. At any age, only a few children used the most sophisti-

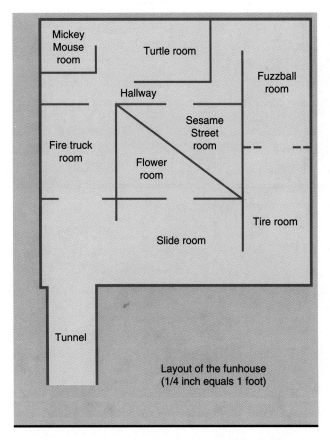

Figure 11.3 By assigning children a goal before they explored this funhouse, researchers were able to see how the children's purpose focused their attention. (*From Gauvain and Rogoff, 1986, p. 73*)

cated rule that would allow them to solve problems when the conflict of weight and distance required arithmetical computation. Siegler discovered that when he taught 5-year-olds to encode the distance of the weights from the fulcrum, they began to use the second rule and performed as well as 8-year-olds, even though their thought was still preoperational. But 8- and 12-year-olds could not use the most sophisticated rule unless they were given external memory aids as well as instruction.

Planning

An important part of problem solving is planning the solution, an activity that is necessary when children face a complex, novel situation for which they have no automatic solution (R. Siegler, 1991). Planning has benefits; it saves us from mistakes that waste both time and effort. But planning is also costly, because it absorbs processing resources that could otherwise be used in carrying out the solution. Studies indicate that children as young as 4 plan ahead and that they adapt their plans to the

situation, but they are less flexible than older children (W. Gardner and Rogoff, 1990). When researchers stressed speed in the solution of mazes, 8- and 9-year-olds tended to improvise somewhat more than did 4- to 6-year-olds. And when researchers stressed accuracy, the older children planned farther ahead than did the younger children, who may already have been operating so close to the limit of their processing capacities that further planning would cost them dearly.

Context

The context of a problem also determines whether children can solve it. If the context in which a problem is presented changes, children may apply different aspects of their knowledge to it. As we saw in Chapter 2, Brazilian street children could solve arithmetic problems that were phrased in the context of their street sales of popcorn, coconuts, and corn on the cob. When the problems involved unfamiliar items, the street children's performance suffered slightly, and when the problems were taken out of context, the children often could not solve them (Carraher, Carraher, and Schliemann, 1985).

Children's cognitive development takes place in a series of social contexts provided by the culture in which they live. These contexts either arrange for the child to have certain problem-solving experiences or withhold them (Laboratory of Comparative Human Cognition, 1983). A child whose major experience with addition takes place in a classroom, where out-of-context problems are worked at a desk, would probably find it difficult to handle the transactions the Brazilian children managed with ease. And children whose culture provides them with a way of visualizing arithmetical problems may tend to excel in mental calculations, as indicated in the accompanying box, "Cultural Support for Cognitive Skills."

Collaboration

Finally, collaboration may make it easier to solve problems. A partner can increase a child's motivation, provide the child with new information, define the problem in a way that makes a solution possible, or start a discussion that leads to a workable solution (Azmitia and Perlmutter, 1989). Piaget (1968b) believed that social interaction was ineffective until children were ready to make the transition into the operational stage, because only then did they become capable of collaborating with another and considering alternative strategies. Vygotsky (1978), however, believed that all skills originate in interaction, and so he contended that even the youngest child's learning was fostered by interacting with adults or more competent peers.

These children have developed sophisticated rules for solving problems; when solving balance-scale problems, they can allow for distance from the fulcrum as well as for weight. *(Bruce Roberts/Rapho/Photo Researchers)*

After a series of studies, Margarita Azmitia and Marion Perlmutter (1989) concluded that the effects of social interaction depend on both the child's skill relative to the problem and the level of the partner's skill relative to the child. They believe that peer partners are ineffective for very young children, because they distract each other from the task. At this age, only parents and older siblings may enhance problem solving. Among preschoolers, social interaction with peers is unlikely to lead to increased competence, but it may increase motivation, either by heightening the child's interest in the task or by increasing the child's feelings of competence (see the accompanying box, "Learning Turtle Talk"). Among young schoolchildren who have enough knowledge to recognize the value of another approach, peer partners may help children solve problems (although not always in the most efficient manner) by suggesting new strategies. As children become more competent, expert partners provide input that leads the child to think or act in ways that lead to efficient prob-

lem solving. Finally, among children who are already proficient problem-solvers, expert partners may provide new information that helps children realize the significance of a strategy and generalize it to future situations.

At any level, the value of interaction depends on its nature. Children who collaborated on a balance-scale problem, for example, profited most when they focused on solutions and strategies, sharing their ideas about the logic of the task (Tudge and Rogoff, 1989). Children in pairs that focused on the partners' respective roles or their behavior and those in pairs in which one partner dominated the other derived little benefit from the experience. Similarly, when children attempted to find the most efficient routes in a supermarket for picking up items on a grocery list, those who shared responsibility for decision making as well as for planning were more efficient later at carrying out the task by themselves than those who shared only the planning (Gauvain and Rogoff, 1989).

When you have to balance your checkbook, you probably whip out your hand-held calculator and punch in the numbers. But no matter how much you use the handy gadget, it will not improve your ability to do mental arithmetic. In many Asian classrooms, children learn to use an abacus, a form of calculator that has been used for thousands of years. The abacus is so popular that children take lessons after school to improve their skill, and nationwide abacus contests bring fame to the most proficient (Stigler, 1984). Instead of acting as a crutch, however, the abacus improves the arithmetic skills of its users.

This became apparent when James Stigler (1984) tested 11-year-old Taiwanese experts with a series of addition problems. As he had expected, the youngsters were fast and accurate with their mechanical calculators. Their fingers flew over the abacus, clicking the beads up and down. What he had not expected to find was that they were just as accurate and even faster when they solved the problems in their heads. Some of the problems were extremely difficult to solve without pencil and paper (23,987 + 47,310 + 98,216 + 52,148 + 11,635), yet they presented little problem for the students.

Why should concentrated use of an abacus improve a child's arithmetic skills? Consider the way you calculate on one of these machines. Each column in the accompanying diagram of the abacus represents a power of ten in arithmetic notation: the first column on the right is for ones, the next column inward is for tens, the next is for hundreds, and so on. The single bead above the divider in each column stands for 5, and each of the beads below stands for 1. When the beads in a column are moved away from the center divider, the value of the column is zero. To represent 1, you move a lower bead in the ones column against the divider; to represent 5, you move

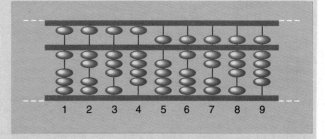

This abacus shows the number 123,456,789. The number reads from left to right, with the counter above the bar standing for 5 in each column. (*From Stigler, 1984*)

the upper bead against the divider. Thus, to represent 652, you would move the upper bead and the first lower bead in the hundreds column against the divider, as well as the upper bead in the tens column and the first two lower beads in the ones column.

All the numbers are represented in a physical way before your eyes. Stigler believes that the Taiwanese children form a mental image of the abacus and, when adding in their heads, imagine that they are carrying out the same motions they would use when solving the problem on an actual abacus. He supports this hypothesis by noting that the children's mental mistakes—although infrequent—almost always consisted of an error of 5 or the omission of an entire column. Other researchers have found that abacus experts have no problem recalling a list of numbers while trying to follow spoken words, but their memory for numbers drops sharply when they try to carry out a simultaneous task involving visual imagery (Hatano and Osawa, 1983).

Metacognition

A 7-year-old busy at homework complains bitterly to a parent because the sound of the television newscast makes it difficult for him to keep his attention focused on the task. A 9-year-old refuses to play a game of Chutes and Ladders because "it's a boring baby game." A 12-year-old decides to reread a paragraph in a textbook because she realizes that she has missed the author's point. All these children are demonstrating **metacognition,** or knowledge about cognition and the ways in which people control cognitive activity. Metamemory is one aspect of metacognition; we could also talk about meta-attention, metareasoning, meta-problem solving, metalanguage, metacommunication, and metacreativ-

ity—although people rarely do. Metacognition has two major aspects. The first is *self-appraisal:* children's personal reflections about their own knowledge and ability—what they know, how they think, and when or why to apply knowledge or strategies. The second is *self-management:* the evaluation, planning, and regulation of thinking skills, which might be called "metacogition in action" (Paris and Winograd, 1990).

Self-Appraisal

Cognitive self-appraisal grows out of children's theories about the mind. These theories begin taking shape when children, at around 3 years of age, understand the basic distinction between the mind and the world, un-

LEARNING TURTLE TALK: WHEN DO PEERS HELP?

Turtles are abstract objects on a computer screen that guide the cursor; in LOGO, children must type complete commands (for example, FORWARD 15) to control the turtle's movements, but in EZLOGO, a single keystroke moves the turtle one step in the desired direction. Marion Perlmutter and her associates (1989) used these computer programs with 150 children between the ages of 4 and 11 in the hope of discovering the effect of collaboration on children's problem solving.

Working with a peer at the computer affected motivation and learning, but the direction of the influence depended on the children's age, the complexity of the task, and the children's familiarity with it. At every age, children who worked in pairs enjoyed their experience more than children who worked alone, so having a partner increased motivation.

Partners affected the way children approached the computer. Seven- to eleven-year-olds who worked alone were more deeply immersed in the task and spent more time running the program than those who worked in pairs. Those who worked in pairs were more involved in peer interaction and spent time setting goals, delegating responsibilities, and determining strategies. Whether the task was easy or complex, children who worked in pairs learned more than children who worked alone. This advantage was apparently related to the competence of the older children, who came to the computers with more experience in following directions and working with letters and numbers.

The experience of preschool children depended on the complexity of the task. On any task, the benefits of a partner increased with age. When working with an extremely simple program, preschool pairs helped each other, and their assistance was often accurate and effective. On more difficult programs, the quantity and quality of assistance dropped off after several sessions, and the children worked in parallel. Among the preschoolers, 5-year-olds received more benefits from a partner than did 4-year-olds, for whom a partner seemed to disrupt the effectiveness of their problem solving. Four-year-olds who worked alone did as well as those with partners on simple tasks; on all other tasks, the solitary 4-year-olds did better than those who worked in pairs. Five-year-olds who worked in pairs on simple tasks learned more

As long as the task is not too complex, children who work in pairs learn more from their computer experience than children who work alone. *(Rogers/ Monkmeyer)*

than those who worked alone. When the tasks were moderately complex, the solitary children and pairs did equally well, but when the task was difficult, partners became a hindrance and the pairs learned less than the children who worked alone.

Perlmutter and her associates concluded that although the benefits of a partner increase with age, those benefits are derived from the partner's increased competence and familiarity with the activities involved.

---

derstand the nature of beliefs and desires, and realize that the contents of the mind represent the world (Wellman, 1990). Children's knowledge about all aspects of cognition keeps developing into late adolescence and even into adulthood (A. Brown et al., 1983). This progression became apparent when researchers questioned a group of schoolchildren about attention (P. Miller and Bigi, 1979). First-graders believed that noise level was the primary factor that affected the deployment of attention, but fifth-graders knew that motivation, mental effort, and resistance to temptation were also important.

Self-appraisal is not a cold, deliberate process but one that is closely tied to emotion and motivation (Paris and Cross, 1983). Children's expectations of success, their perceptions of the cognitive demands of a task, and their attributions for success and failure are examples of emotionally charged metacognition. As the discussion of learned helplessness indicated (see Chapter 10), children who attribute their school failures to lack of ability often quit trying. Motivation also depends on children's perceptions of their own self-efficacy, which encompasses their confidence in their cognitive skills ("I can do it") and their motivation ("I ought to do it") (Bandura, 1989a). As we saw in Chapter 10, self-efficacy determines how much effort children will expend at a task and how long they will work at it. These beliefs can produce pride and satisfaction or guilt, shame, and anger (Paris and Winograd, 1990).

Children's self-appraisal affects their performance at problem solving or in the classroom. Children in grades 3 and 5, for example, who understand their own reading abilities, the goals of reading, and appropriate reading strategies are more successful readers than children who are confused about the nature of the reading process (Cross and Paris, 1988). Similarly, fourth- and fifth-graders with high levels of metacognitive knowledge outperform other children in solving problems that require logical thought (Swanson, 1990).

When children first begin school, metacognitive beliefs concerning the factors that affect performance and success seem to have little impact on a child's behavior. What second-graders believe about the role of effort, ability, powerful others, or luck has no relation to their intelligence test scores or their performance on memory tests (Chapman, Skinner, and Baltes, 1990). But as children move through school, these beliefs become increasingly important. Among fourth-graders, the beliefs that they try hard (or do not try), that they are smart (or lack ability), that their teachers are helpful (or are of no help), and that they are lucky (or are unlucky) are correlated with intelligence test scores. By sixth grade, the beliefs correlate with performance on memory tests as well. Perhaps second-graders lack enough information about their past performance in school for their beliefs to affect their current performance. Or perhaps their convictions have always affected the amount of effort they expend, but the effect on cognitive skills requires time to appear.

Self-Management

Children's increasing proficiency as thinkers, problem solvers, rememberers, and readers reflect changes in the self-management of cognitive skills (Paris and Lindauer, 1982). The first aspect of self-management is the *evaluation* of current knowledge and performance. Because children often fail to take their own "mental temperature," they may not realize when they do not understand. When beginning to prepare for a spelling test, for example, 7-year-olds often are unaware of whether they already know their spelling words or whether they need to study them (Flavell, Friedrichs, and Hoyt, 1970). Young children frequently have inflated notions about their own cognitive skills. As we saw earlier, they overestimate their ability to remember. Nor do they know why some of their attempts at intellectual tasks succeed and why others fail (Paris and Lindauer, 1982). By the time they are 10 or 12 years old, they will have some idea about whether they failed because they lacked the ability, lacked the appropriate information, or just didn't try hard enough.

The second aspect of self-management is *planning* the actions that will allow the child to reach specific goals. Preschoolers sometimes show evidence of metacognitive planning, but most children do not regularly plan their thinking until they are 8 or 9 years old. When taking a second memory test on a list of words, first-graders often chose to study the words they had recalled correctly on the first test, but third-graders tend to study the words they had missed (Masur, McIntyre, and Flavell, 1973). Some primary school children do not plan because they are unaware of the strategies they can use to improve their performance or because they lack the knowledge to apply the strategies properly.

The final aspect of self-management is *self-regulation* or performance: children learn to check and adjust their cognitive activity. First- and second-graders tend to apply rules blindly. When learning to read, they do not check their understanding of what they have read; when doing arithmetic problems, they do not check their answers against their knowledge (Paris and Winograd, 1990). They may defend incorrect answers in the face of clearly contradictory evidence.

As children learn more about cognition, they become more expert at managing their cognitive processes. This progress is the result not simply of age but of experience, expertise, and social contexts that make discovery of these skills probable (A. Brown et al., 1983).

Social Cognition

The advances in thought and information processing that we have traced through childhood are not limited to understanding the physical world and carrying out the kinds of tasks children encounter at school. They also influence social cognition, which, as we saw in Chapter 2, involves the way children reason about themselves and others in social situations. Many years ago, Piaget (1932/1965) spent hours watching children play marbles and found that as the youngsters developed, their understanding of the rules changed. Children between the ages of 6 and 10 regarded the rules for marbles as imposed from the outside by authorities. No one could change them, and even to think about doing so was naughty. Among 12-year-olds, the understanding of the rules changed. Although they still respected the rules, they were ready to change them if everyone agreed. The development of flexible and realistic rules among older children may have been affected by the cooperative nature of their interaction with peers as well as by their improved reasoning skills.

As children's thinking develops, their notions of what other people see, feel, like, and understand change. Social cognition encompasses more than children's understanding of their interactions with others. It includes the way they think about right and wrong, good and evil, politics and society. In this section we examine children's deepening understanding of what others see and know, the requirements of adequate communication, what others are like, and how to make moral judgments.

Understanding What Others See and Know

Children gradually come to understand what another person sees. Two- and three-year-olds' knowledge of other people's visual perception is still limited. These youngsters are not totally egocentric, but they are still at Level 1 in Flavell's (1985) view of perceptual development (see Chapter 6). That is, they recognize that another person does not always see the same objects they see, but all they understand is whether the object is visible to the other person. Four- and five-year-olds have entered Level 2: they are beginning to understand that even though the other person can see objects in the child's field of vision, the objects may appear differently to the other person. Yet these preschoolers have a long way to go before they understand exactly *how* visual perspectives differ.

Of all social-cognitive tasks, understanding another person's visual experience is the most cognitive and the least social. It depends more on the development of the child's spatial representations than on the child's understanding of others (Newcombe, 1989). In most tests of this skill, children look at a group of photographs and choose the one that shows how the three-dimensional scene in front of them would appear to a person viewing it from another angle. Young children find this task difficult, if not impossible. But the technique places preschoolers at a great disadvantage, because they often have trouble matching a two-dimensional picture to the three-dimensional display that is before them (Yaniv and Shatz, 1990).

How well children understand what others see apparently depends on the mental rule they use when encoding the scene. When researchers placed Ernie and Bert dolls in various positions on a square table and asked children to place Ernie's plastic duck "so that Ernie can see his duck just as Bert sees his duck," it became apparent that children at Level 1 follow an extremely simple rule (Yaniv and Shatz, 1990). They imagine a line drawn between the observer and the object. If a barrier lies between the observer and the object, the object is invisible to the observer. This rule reduces the load on information processing but keeps children from considering how the observer's view might differ from their own.

As children enter Level 2, they develop more sophisticated versions of their line-of-sight rule. They realize that parts of an object that are visible to them may be hidden to the observer. They pay attention to the parts and features of the object that are in the observer's line of sight. However, they still cannot tell how a three-dimensional scene appears to another person, because they do not attend to the configuration of cues. That is, if they are looking at a coffee mug, they do not note whether the mug's handle is to the right or the left. By the time children are 5, they are beginning to note such configurations and are successful when the scene involves a single object (Yaniv and Shatz, 1990). When the scene is complicated, however, children younger than 9 or 10 often make mistakes, because until then they encode each object in the scene separately, paying no attention to the way the objects are related in the scene's internal structure (Newcombe, 1989).

Communication

Children's progress in understanding what others know is reflected in the way they communicate. At every age, they adapt their messages to the needs of their listener, although at first their understanding of those needs is rudimentary. When communicating with others, most 4- and 5-year-olds seem to know if they have necessary information that their listener lacks. But few of them understand exactly what information is necessary for the other person to identify an object that the child is describing (R. Roberts and Patterson, 1983). The majority of 6-year-olds understand which information is critical. Children who pass a test of visual perspective taking have no trouble providing needed information to another person; this indicates that understanding what others know progresses through the same levels as understanding what others see. Yet even 8-year-olds have trouble adapting their messages when the situation is complicated, the objects that must be described have many attributes, and the child has to figure out the rules (Flavell et al., 1968/1975).

As they become more experienced and skillful in understanding others, the way children judge the adequacy of communication changes. When others are talking to them, 5- and 6-year-olds rarely complain or ask for clarification when they are given misleading messages. But when a message is ambiguous, incomplete, or contradictory, they usually blame themselves for any misunderstanding. They may say, for example, that they are unsure about how to interpret the message but judge that it was adequate (Beal and Belgrad, 1990). Placed in the same situation, 7- and 8-year-olds reject the message. Their understanding has become so sophisticated that they not only know when messages are ambiguous but they can deliberately mislead others by producing an ambiguous message (Sodian, 1989).

Why do young children often fail to signal their misunderstanding when they know they do not understand a message? Preschoolers apparently lack the planning and monitoring skills needed to handle such a task. Even when they have been told what to do (ask questions) and when to do it (when unsure of the speaker's message), they find it difficult to carry out the plan. Among kindergartners, failure to ask for clarification may be another example of production deficiency, because they can follow a plan provided by someone else. Fourth-graders speak up whether or not a plan has been provided, indicating their ability to manage their cognitive skills.

Role-Taking

Without the ability to take another's role, children would find it difficult to understand what others were like. Earlier we explored the emotional basis of role-taking—the development of empathy. As we saw in Chapter 8, the rudimentary understanding that others may *feel* different in a distressing situation starts to emerge some time after a child's second birthday (M. Hoffman, 1988). But gradually children become aware that other people do more than perceive and feel. They

develop a cognitive component to role-taking: the understanding that others' thoughts, motives, or intentions may differ from their own.

This understanding may develop earlier than developmentalists once believed. Early research indicated that children younger than 8 years had little understanding of the beliefs and desires of others (Shantz, 1983). Yet 3-year-olds regularly explain the actions of others in such terms: "Because she's hungry"; "Because he wants a balloon to hold"; "She thinks it's under there" (Bartsch and Wellman, 1989). Preschoolers apparently are aware of internal psychological states and their role in motivating behavior. Researchers have suggested that early studies underestimated children's perceptions of others because the research design may have inhibited young children's expression of psychological attributes (D. Hart and Damon, 1986). Although preschoolers seem to conceive of their friends as having behavioral characteristics that are frequent and enduring across time (Eder, 1989), they do not yet appreciate stable personality traits (Wellman, 1990). Instead, they tend to describe their friends in terms of general memories ("He usually plays with friends") but not in terms of traits ("He's friendly"). By the time they are 7 or 8, children have organized these general memories in terms of traits and abilities.

Children begin to understand intention before they have developed the notion of traits. As we saw in the discussion of causal reasoning, preschoolers seem to assume that all acts are intentional; there are no accidents in their world. Yet there is some glimmer of the difference between intent and mistakes. When researchers studied children's judgment of simple actions, even 3-year-olds knew that neither they nor other people meant to commit slips of the tongue in tongue twisters or intentionally make mistakes when trying to rub their stomachs and tap their heads at the same time (Shultz, 1980). Yet when asked to judge a series of actions in stories or films, 4-year-olds say that the character intended even accidental events (knocking a box of cookies into the garbage can) to happen (M. Smith, 1978). Five-year-olds have made great strides. In this same study, they distinguished not only between voluntary (walking across a room) and involuntary (sneezing) actions but also between intentional and unintentional consequences of voluntary acts (knocking over a cereal box when you are trying to pick it up). Their distinctions were the same as those adults would make.

This progression in the ability to infer another's intentions is reflected in children's increasing ability to take the role of another. By asking children about the feelings, thoughts, and intentions of characters in a series of stories, Robert Selman (1976, 1980) charted the development of role-taking ability. The stories revolved around dilemmas of childhood, as when a little girl who had been forbidden to climb trees discovers that she can rescue a friend's cat from a tree only by climbing after it. Selman, whose views have been influenced by Piaget's theory of cognitive development, believes that children move through five stages of role-taking (see Table 11.3). These stages are related to children's ability to understand differences between their own perspective (such as visual experience) and that of another. Some researchers believe that children's ability to decenter from their own exclusive view and to take the role of another is related to developments in children's moral judgments.

Morality

When Piaget (1932/1965) questioned Swiss children about the rules that governed their marble games, he was studying their moral judgment. He believed that the rule system of children's games embodied their understanding of right and wrong. Earlier we saw how the socialization process contributes to the development of

internalized moral standards (see Chapter 9). Now we follow Piaget's lead and explore the development of children's ability to reason about moral issues and how children justify their moral judgments.

Piaget's Theory

Piaget believed that young children's view of morality was limited by egocentrism and their deep respect for adults. Their loss of egocentrism and their experiences with their peers led not only to a realization that rules could be changed but also to a move from one stage of morality to another.

Young children were governed by the **morality of constraint** (often called *moral realism*), in which virtuous conduct is based on obedience to authority. Transgressions are inevitably punished, perhaps by accidents or some other misfortune—a concept known as **imminent justice.** In one of his studies, Piaget (1932/1965) told children about a boy who stole some apples and then fell through a rotten bridge into the river. Six- and seven-year-olds felt that the boy had been justly punished. Asked if the boy would have fallen into the water if he had not stolen, a 7-year-old gave a typical answer: "No . . . Because he would not have done

TABLE 11.3   STAGES OF SOCIAL ROLE-TAKING

Age	Stage	Description
About 3 to 6 years	*Stage 0:* Egocentric viewpoint	Children do not realize that other people's thoughts, feelings, intentions, and motivation may differ from their own
About 6 to 8 years	*Stage 1:* Social-informational role-taking	Children know that others have their own views but believe that those views differ from theirs because they are based on different information. Children cannot judge their own actions from another's viewpoint.
About 8 to 10 years	*Stage 2:* Self-reflective role-taking	Children know that others' views are based on their own purposes or set of values. They can anticipate another person's judgment of their own actions. Yet they still cannot consider their own view and that of another at the same time.
About 10 to 12 years	*Stage 3:* Mutual role-taking	Children know that both they and another person can simultaneously consider their own view and that of the other. They can step outside an interaction with another person and see how a third party would interpret it.
About 12 to 15 years and older	*Stage 4:* Social and conventional role-taking	Children are aware of the shared point of view of the social system (social conventions). They realize that mutual awareness of views does not always lead to complete understanding.

Source: Adapted from R. Selman, 1976, p. 309.

Piaget developed his theory of moral development by watching children play marbles and noting changes in their respect for the game's system of rules. *(Donald Dietz/Stock, Boston)*

wrong" (Piaget, 1932/1965, p. 254). In the second stage, known as the **morality of cooperation** (often called *morality of reciprocity*), morality is based on what is expected, fair, or just. Transgressions are not always punished, but a fair punishment should not be arbitrary. The culprit should receive a similar injury (one blow for each blow struck) or should make some sort of restitution.

Piaget realized that these moralities could exist side by side, that a child might apply the morality of constraint to one action and the morality of cooperation to another. As children grew older, they increasingly judged moral situations in terms of the morality of cooperation.

Kohlberg's View of Moral Reasoning

The theory of moral development proposed by Lawrence Kohlberg (1969; Colby et al., 1983) builds on Piaget's analysis. Kohlberg developed his theory, which we examined in Chapter 2, by asking boys between the ages of 10 and 16 to respond to a series of moral dilemmas, in which human needs or welfare conflicted with the commands of authority or obedience to the law. For example, the boys had to decide whether a physician should supply a dying, pain-ridden cancer patient with a large dose of painkiller that would surely kill her.

None of the decisions reached by the boys affected the way Kohlberg designed the stages in his theory; he was interested in the moral reasoning that justified the decisions. A person at any stage may decide either way in a given situation. What distinguishes the stages is the type of concerns that are indicated for self, authority, and society (see Chapter 2, Table 2.4).

Each move to a new stage of understanding follows a cognitive conflict that arises when people encounter levels of moral reasoning that are somewhat more advanced than their own. The conflict leads to a reorganization of thought. Kohlberg's first four stages parallel Stages 1 to 4 in Selman's theory of social role-taking. In fact, studies indicate that children seem unable to attain a new stage of moral judgment without first entering the corresponding stage of role-taking (Rest, 1983; Walker, 1980). The first two stages in Kohlberg's theory form what is called the **premoral level,** because values simply reflect external pressures. The dominant motive at Stage 1 is to avoid punishment; at Stage 2, the motive is to serve one's own needs and interests. The next two stages form the **conventional level,** with value placed on maintaining the conventional social order and meeting the expectations of others. At Stage 3, the dominant motive is to be a good person in one's own (and others') eyes; at Stage 4, it is to avoid breakdowns in the social system. Our discussion is limited to these stages, because only highly educated adults test as high as Stage 5, which is at the **principled level** (where values reside in shared principles and standards), and because Stage 6 has been merged into Stage 5 by Kohlberg and his associates (Colby et al., 1983). As noted in Chapter 2, a person's level of moral reasoning is strongly affected by age, socioeconomic level, and education (see Figure 11.4).

Researchers have found that the speed with which children move through these stages is influenced by the nature of family interactions. Lawrence Walker and John Taylor (1991) rated children of various ages (grades 1, 4, 7, and 10) on Kohlberg's scale and then observed a family session in which the family discussed one of Kohlberg's dilemmas and an actual dilemma that the child had faced. (Most of the dilemmas reported by the children concerned friendships, theft, fighting, honesty, and cheating.) Two years later, the researchers again rated the children's level of moral development. They discovered that the parents' discussion style and level of moral reasoning predicted the children's moral reasoning. Children who had advanced had supportive parents who encouraged their participation, listened to them, praised them, asked clarifying questions, paraphrased statements, and checked to make certain the children understood what they had said. Children who showed little or no progress had parents who directly challenged their views and criticized their positions. Apparently the Socratic style of discussion used by supportive parents presented the cognitive conflict necessary for children to move to the next stage. The critical parents may have seemed hostile, putting their children on the defensive.

Figure 11.4   This figure shows the mean proportion of reasoning at each of Kohlberg's stages for each age group. As the boys matured, premoral reasoning (Stages 1 and 2) gradually disappeared, and advanced conventional reasoning (Stage 4) became more prevalent than early conventional reasoning (Stage 3). Principled reasoning (Stage 5) first appeared toward the end of adolescence but never accounted for more than 10 percent of moral thought. (*From Colby et al., 1983, p. 46*)

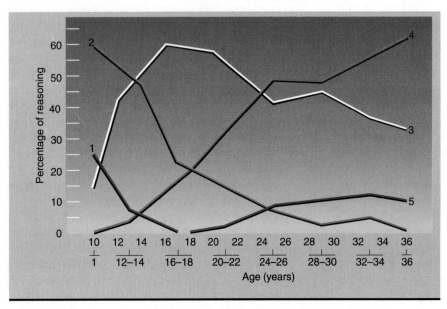

Is there any relation between people's level of reasoning on Kohlberg's scale and their moral behavior? There does appear to be some connection between the two, but the connection is not impressive. In an analysis of seventy-five studies, Augusto Blasi (1980) found that moral judgment and behavior were significantly related in 76 percent of the studies but that the connection was not strong. Moral judgment is only one player in a large cast, suggests James Rest (1983). People differ in the way they apply their thinking to a particular situation, in the degree to which religious or ideological doctrines influence their sense of fairness, in the way they interpret possible courses of action, in the way they integrate the various considerations that affect a situation, in the course of action they select, and in the way they execute their decision.

Piaget and Kohlberg both saw moral judgment as based on an ethic of justice, and as we saw in Chapter 2, some researchers have contended that an ethic of care, which focuses on responsibilities instead of rights, is equally tenable (Gilligan, 1982). Children may agree; asked how they would solve moral dilemmas, first- and third-graders generally felt that actions based on the ethic of care were better than actions based on the ethic of justice (Garrod, Beal, and Shin, 1990).

A broader approach to moral reasoning has been put forward by William Damon and Daniel Hart (1988), who separate the domain into four areas: (1) friendship, (2) justice and fairness, (3) obedience and authority, and (4) social rules and conventions. They argue that children develop separate moral concepts in each area, so their judgments would not be consistent in all situations. Preschoolers would think it naughtier to violate a moral code (stealing cookies) than to violate a social convention (talking during naptime) (Smetana, 1985). They judged violations in the moral area by their effect on others and violations in the conventional area by their tendency to create disorder.

In a study that explored the domain of justice and fairness, children as young as 5 were able to separate accidental damage not only from intentional damage but also from damage due to negligence (Shultz, Wright, and Schleifer, 1986). They assigned the most responsibility when damage (a smashed model airplane, a lost balloon, a ripped poster, a wrecked kite, a torn beach ball) was intentional, the least when it was accidental. Although 5-year-olds assigned more blame for accidental damage than older children did (see Figure 11.5), they considered negligence when they were assigning blame and weighed whether the culprit had made resti-

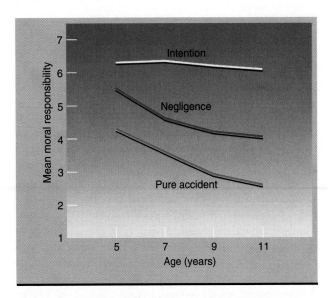

Figure 11.5 Children were asked to assign blame for similar types of damage, depending on whether the damage was caused by intent, negligence, or accident. Even 5-year-olds were able to make the distinction. (*From Shultz, Wright, and Schleifer, 1986, p. 182*)

tution when they were recommending punishment. The researchers contend that although these children cannot justify their moral judgments in terms that would place them very high on Kohlberg's scale, they use the same ideas as their elders do. But they are unable to reveal their understanding in the context of a typical moral-reasoning experiment.

Children's understanding of others and of their moral responsibilities develops slowly, hand in hand with their ability to apply their growing cognitive skills to the physical world. Research in social cognition has highlighted the tie between cognitive development and social development. It shows that children actively observe and think about the social interactions in their world and that the way they interpret their observations depends on their cognitive level. Thus, research in social cognition has opened new avenues for understanding social and personality development. Although young children are more capable than researchers once believed, their lack of experience and their inability to handle much information at one time make it difficult for them to show their abilities in most situations. In the next chapter, we watch children applying their developing ability to learn and reason in the context of the classroom.

AN INTELLECTUAL REVOLUTION

According to Piaget, the **preoperational thought** of the preschool child is intuitive, inflexible, and contradictory and is focused on individual events. Preschoolers are incapable of mental **operations.** As a result of the intellectual revolution that takes place between the ages of 4 and 10, children's thought changes in five ways: (1) Children acquire the concept of **identity** and understand that objects and people remain the same even if irrelevant properties are changed. (2) **Centration,** in which children's attention is so captured by a prominent feature of the stimulus that they **encode** only that aspect, gives way to decentered attention. (3) Thinking gains **reversibility,** so children can mentally reverse processes or changes in appearance. (4) Learning becomes self-regulated and strategic. (5) Language becomes instrumental for thinking. As children acquire strategies, they overcome **production deficiencies.**

CONCEPTUAL DEVELOPMENT

The schoolchild is capable of **concrete-operational thought** and can think flexibly and apply logic to concrete objects. A typical concrete operation is **conservation,** in which children understand that irrelevant changes in an object's external appearance do not affect its quantity. Children's ability to conserve depends on the changes of the intellectual revolution as well as on increased **cognitive capacity.** Before children grasp the reversible aspects of conservation, they conserve by applying the concept of identity.

According to Piaget, young children's understanding of causality is guided by **finalism, artificialism,** and **animism.** Preschool children are less animistic than Piaget believed; they ascribe thoughts, feelings, or life to inanimate objects primarily when they lack the knowledge required to make a correct judgment. They also know more about causality, but their knowledge is incomplete and continues to develop for many years.

Young children divide their experiences into fundamental categories and are aware that categories are related in a hierarchy, but they have problems with multiple attributes. They do best with **basic categories** but have trouble with **superordinate categories.** Piaget believed that young children could not understand **class inclusion** because they could not think about objects as simultaneously belonging to two different classes. Preoperational children apparently do not understand the logical basis of class-inclusion questions,

but they can solve them when the superordinate class is described as a collective noun instead of a class noun.

When shown up to three objects, children often rely on pattern differences instead of counting. Even 2-year-olds can count, although many can count only as far as two. Some studies indicate that preschoolers do not understand **cardinality,** perhaps because counting and cardinality are not as closely linked as has been supposed.

ADVANCES IN INFORMATION PROCESSING

Unlike older children, preschoolers do not scan systematically or exhaustively, and their attention is often caught by irrelevant information. The preschooler's inefficiency may be the result of an inability to exert conscious control over attention. The skills involved in the control of attention develop at different rates. Attentional set, which is detrimental to young children's information processing, can be used adaptively by older children.

Memory is the application of cognitive processes to the storage and retrieval of information. Children's memory improves with age because of their increased knowledge store, their grasp of **strategies,** and their understanding of **metamemory.** Storage strategies include **rehearsal** and **organization,** and children show production deficiencies in the development of each one. As metamemory develops and children understand the value of strategies, they begin developing and using them.

Children's success at problem solving depends on **task analysis,** the acquisition of mental rules, planning, the context of the problem, and collaboration. With age, mental rules become increasingly complex. The value of collaboration seems to depend on the child's skill relative to the problem and the partner's skill relative to the child.

Metacognition is knowledge about cognition and the ways in which people control cognitive activities. Metacognition consists of self-appraisal and self-management. Cognitive self-appraisal grows out of children's theories about mind, and it is closely tied to emotion and motivation. The major aspects of self-management are the evaluation of current knowledge and performance, the planning of actions that will allow the attainment of goals, and the self-regulation of performance.

Increases in the quality of self-management depend on experience, expertise, and social contexts as well as on age.

SOCIAL COGNITION

Understanding what another person can see is the least social and most cognitive aspect of social cognition. Children's skill at visual perspective taking apparently depends on the mental rules they use when encoding a scene. Preschoolers know that others' knowledge may differ from their own, but they lack the planning and monitoring skills required to identify the needed information or signal their own misunderstanding. School-children are developing these skills, and 8-year-olds can mislead others with an intentionally ambiguous message.

Preschoolers are aware of general behavioral tendencies in others but do not yet appreciate personality traits. By the age of 8, children begin to see others in terms of traits and abilities. Preschoolers are beginning to infer intentions, and 5-year-olds can distinguish between intentional and unintentional consequences of voluntary acts. Children's movement through the stages of role-taking is related to their increasing ability to understand differences between their own perspective and that of another.

According to Piaget, most young children are governed by the **morality of constraint.** They stress obedience to authority and believe in **imminent justice.** Older children are more likely to follow the **morality of cooperation,** which stresses fairness and justice. In Kohlberg's theory, moral reasoning goes through five stages, in a progressive series of developmental levels: the **premoral level,** the **conventional level,** and the **principled level.** There is a weak, but positive, connection between moral reasoning and moral behavior. Damon and Hart contend that moral judgment varies because children develop separate moral concepts in the realms of friendship, justice and fairness, obedience and authority, and social rules and conventions.

KEY TERMS

animism	encode	organization
artificialism	finalism	premoral level
basic category	identity	preoperational thought
cardinality	imminent justice	principled level
centration	memory	production deficiency
class inclusion	metacognition	rehearsal
cognitive capacity	metamemory	reversibility
concrete-operational thought	morality of constraint	strategy
conservation	morality of cooperation	superordinate category
conventional level	operations	task analysis

COGNITION: INTELLIGENCE AND SCHOOLING

• • • • • • • • • • • • • • •

Nine-year-old Karl Haglund has a serious learning problem. When he was in kindergarten, his teacher noted that he tried hard but was making little progress on his letters or numbers. Testing by the school psychologist uncovered a learning disability: Karl had problems processing auditory material, and so—despite his visual skills—he did not absorb information presented orally by the teacher. Without the early testing, Karl might still be struggling and failing, struggling and failing, in the regular classroom. After several years in a classroom for the learning disabled, however, Karl began to blossom. He is now back in the regular classroom for math, which he finds easy, perhaps because he can see how it relates to carpentry and model-building, two of his hobbies. But reading still comes slowly. Often he memorizes passages in assigned books so that it is difficult to detect the problem. Karl has other skills; he is good at soccer and video games and has a striking talent for drawing (Kotre and Hall, 1990). If Karl lived in a society that did not require reading, he would probably be among the most talented members of his peer group. In a society based on literacy, however, he may find it difficult to succeed in most professions. Yet many children whose school experience is disastrous have the cognitive capabilities to do well in the world.

● ● ● ● ● ●

In this chapter we investigate the nature of intelligence and its connection with the school. In an attempt to decide just what intelligence is, we look at various theories of intelligence and their implications for schooling. Then we examine the tests themselves, investigate their construction, discover the narrow nature of IQ scores, and explore alternative ways to measure cognitive skills. Our consideration of various influences on IQ scores demonstrates the profound effect of environmental factors on test scores. Next we take up the question of exceptional intellectual development in creative children, the academically gifted, and the retarded. With this background, we turn to schooling, which stresses the cognitive skills measured by IQ tests. We look at the development of skill in reading and arithmetic, and we close with an exploration of the connection between metacognitive skills and success in all academic areas.

What Is Intelligence?

The first problem is to define *intelligence*. When we say that someone is intelligent, what do we mean? If we looked at intelligence from an evolutionary standpoint, we would say that it consisted of mental skills that enhance the ability to function effectively in the environment. Without it, our species could not have survived long enough to leave any descendants. This description, although accurate, is not especially helpful when we try to analyze the concept of intelligence in terms of its specific components. Researchers have been trying to do this for decades but have not been able to reach any agreement.

Each of us has an implicit theory of intelligence that refers to our personal notion of intelligence. These theories are important, because we use them in evaluating ourselves and the people we encounter. The implicit views of most ordinary people are remarkably close to those of experts. Both groups agree that verbal intelligence, problem-solving ability, and social competence are important aspects of intelligence (Sternberg, 1990). The major difference seems to be that most experts emphasize the role played by motivation in determining academic intelligence whereas ordinary people emphasize social competence.

Like experts, most of us believe that intelligence is developmental in nature and that it reveals itself in different abilities at different ages. In one study, college students rated the characteristics of intelligence in order of importance (R. Siegler and Richards, 1982). They saw intelligence as becoming increasingly cognitive with age, emphasizing psychomotor skills in babies, language in 2-year-olds, reasoning and problem solving in older children and adults. Teachers' implicit theories

of intelligence can be important to schoolchildren, and research indicates that what teachers see as key aspects of intelligence change as a function of grade level (P. Fry, 1984). Elementary school teachers emphasize social competence, high school teachers emphasize verbal skills, and college teachers emphasize problem-solving skills.

Implicit theories of intelligence develop early in life. Researchers asked first-, third-, and sixth-graders what it meant to be smart (Yussen and Kane, 1985). First-graders regarded intelligence as a global quality, one that affects all aspects of life. They believed that intelligence is inborn and that social skills are important. They said that intelligent people can be spotted by what they say and do. Third- and sixth-graders disagreed; they believed that experience can increase intelligence or cause it to wither and that behavior is a poor guide to intelligence. These older children saw intelligence as something inside a person, primarily in the form of academic skills.

Researchers' implicit theories of intelligence are important, because they affect the hypotheses that direct research and the formulation of explicit theories. As we will see in the following section, Piaget focused on similarities across individuals, whereas many other theorists have been interested in individual differences and how to assess them.

Older children equate intelligence with academic skills and a vast store of information. They would expect the most intelligent child to win at Trivial Pursuit. *(Miro Vintoniv. The Picture Cube)*

Piaget's Theory of Intellectual Development

In Piaget's (1976) theory, intelligence is demonstrated by the way people adapt to the environment. Underlying intelligence are the cognitive structures of thought, which differ sharply at different ages and which Piaget described in his stages of cognitive development, as we saw in Chapter 2. Intelligence develops through interaction with the environment. This interaction involves maturation, experience with the physical environment, the influence of the social environment, and the child's own self-regulatory processes, which keep trying to establish an equilibrium.

Thus, Piaget explored intelligence by amassing evidence to show that widespread, consistent changes in the way children think emerged with predictable regularity. He was interested in the abstract rules, concepts, structures, and operations that underlie all cognition and how these change in a systematic fashion as children develop. For him, intelligence consisted of the organized and integrated system of thought that was shared by the human species. Quantitative aspects of intelligence did not interest him; he once said that his purpose was to "discover the actual operational mechanisms that govern such behavior and not simply to measure it" (Piaget, 1953).

Piaget's theory neglects cognitive change after adolescence and pays no attention to individual differences in performance that may be due to the characteristics of the task, the person's prior knowledge, and the method of instruction. Because of the general nature of his work, it is difficult to relate it to the academic performance of children. For these aspects of intelligence, we must turn to other theories.

Information-Processing Views

Researchers who take an information-processing view believe that intelligence derives from the processes used to represent and manipulate information. Differences in intelligence develop because people vary in the efficiency and speed with which they carry out these basic processes.

When analyzing the primary abilities that determine intelligence, Raymond Cattell (1971) and John Horn (1968) found that they could group most of them into two categories: fluid and crystallized intelligence. **Fluid intelligence** is based on the ability to perceive, encode, and reason about information. It includes abstract, nonverbal reasoning and problem-solving skills, and it reflects the ability to deal with novel information and novel situations. Fluid intelligence is developed through casual learning; its skills are neither taught in school nor pushed by the culture (Horn, 1984). **Crystallized intelligence** is based on the ability to understand relationships, make judgments, and solve problems that depend on schooling or cultural experience. It includes verbal skills and mechanical knowledge, and it reflects the ability to handle well-learned information in familiar situations. Crystallized intelligence develops as a person learns facts and absorbs information that is emphasized by the culture.

The **triarchic theory** of intelligence, proposed by Robert Sternberg (1985), is a broad view of intelligence that includes social, educational, and situational factors that affect the development and exercise of intelligence. As its name implies, the triarchic theory has three parts: (1) components, (2) experience, and (3) context. The *componential subtheory* breaks down the structures and mechanisms of intelligence into three types of components, each with its own function. *Metacomponents* are higher-order processes that correspond to the self-management aspects of metacognition (see Chapter 11). They plan, monitor, regulate, and evaluate performance on any task. *Performance components* are lower-order processes that execute the plans and decisions of the metacomponents. These processes encode information, combine or compare information, and respond. *Knowledge-acquisition components* are lower-order processes involved in learning new information. Knowledge-acquisition components also include encoding, combining, and comparing, but the processes operate selectively, sifting out important new information from what already is known and combining old ideas in creative ways.

The other two subtheories are concerned with how people use the components of intelligence to deal with the world. The *experiential subtheory* refers to attributes of tasks or situations that measure intelligence. It focuses on the way the individual deals with tasks and situations that are outside normal experience and how rapidly the individual becomes expert in these tasks so that processing becomes automatic. The *contextual subtheory* places intelligence in a sociocultural setting that draws on the practical and social aspects of intelligence. It focuses on the mental activity involved in adapting to the environment or in shaping the present environment to match a person's needs. This is the functional, practical aspect of intelligence and includes the ability to solve practical problems, verbal ability, and social competence. Sternberg's theory integrates the individual's inner world (components), experience, and the external world. It leads researchers to consider how people use their mental abilities to solve relevant problems in a variety of settings.

Multiple Intelligences

A second group of theories, known as **factor theories,** attempt to understand intelligence in terms of underlying abilities instead of processes. The task that faces proponents of factor theories is determining just what those abilities are and how many of them are involved. In their search for these abilities, most researchers use a technique called **factor analysis.** In factor analysis, the scores on a set of tests are correlated. Clusters of highly correlated scores indicate a factor that seems to underlie the differences among scores. This factor presumably reflects a common mental ability.

The first factor theory was put forth by Charles Spearman (1927), who proposed that intelligence was dominated by a single major factor, called g (general mental ability). Although other specific (s) factors existed, each of them was confined to a single ability. All intellectual activities relied on g, which involved seeing and manipulating the relations among bits of information.

Other theorists contended that intelligence was not as unified as Spearman had believed. Their research pointed to many more factors, although they could not agree on whether there were as few as 7 or as many as 150. Louis Thurstone (1947) identified seven primary intellectual abilities: verbal comprehension, word fluency, number, space, memory, perceptual speed, and reasoning. Yet after Thurstone had identified these factors and devised tests for each of them, he discovered that people's scores on the various tests were correlated. A person who made high scores on a vocabulary test (which measured verbal comprehension) also tended to make high scores on arithmetic tests (number) or tests that involved recalling lists of unrelated words (memory). It appeared that some general mental ability might affect performance on many tasks.

Intelligence became much more complicated in J. P. Guilford's (1982) theory. Guilford first proposed a complex set of 120 interconnecting factors, although later analysis pushed the total to 150. He arranged these factors according to whether they involved what the person was thinking about (contents of thought), the mental processes used to think about it (operations), or the results of thinking (products). Each factor resulted from the interaction of one type of content (language) with one of the operations (memory) and one kind of product (units). In this example (products × memory × units), the activity would result in remembering a list of words.

By dividing intelligence into domains instead of specific abilities, Howard Gardner (1983) produced a theory of **multiple intelligences.** Gardner proposed the existence of seven different kinds of intelligence: linguistic; musical; logical-mathematical; spatial; bodily-kinesthetic; and two forms of personal intelligence, intrapersonal (knowing and understanding oneself) and interpersonal (knowing and understanding others). Factor theories focus on some aspects of linguistic, logical-mathematical, and spatial skills but make no attempt to include any of the other intelligences. Each of these seven intelligences has its own core components, which interact and build upon one another. Musical intelligence, for example, is based on the processing of tones and rhythms. The interaction of heredity and experience determines the profile of each person's intellectual capacities, and various cultures value different intelligences. Spatial intelligence is valued among the Eskimo, for example, because they must be able to note slight cracks in the ice, perceive the angle and shape of snowdrifts, and detect coming changes in the weather from subtle cloud patterns.

To qualify as a separate intelligence, a domain must exhibit eight signs: (1) The intelligence can function or be damaged selectively, as when brain damage impairs speech but spares other intelligences. (2) Some individuals are gifted in the domain (art, music, or number) but severely retarded in other domains. (3) The domain is associated with one or more basic mental operations (such as sensitivity to pitch). (4) The domain shows a distinct developmental history of the skills involved. (5) The domain has an evolutionary history that is shared with other organisms. (6) Experimental evidence can show the domain's relative autonomy by isolating tasks involved. (7) Performance on tests that assess a domain are highly correlated. (8) The domain has its own symbol system (words, pictures, musical notes, numbers).

Researchers cannot agree on the number of domains or factors that are involved in intelligence. Because they begin their search for factors by using different tests, each of which presents a different range of problems and demands different kinds of answers, disagreement over the type and number of factors is almost guaranteed. One factor is probably not enough to describe intelligence adequately, but when the number of factors passes 100, it is impossible to chart the interrelation of the factors and distill the essential elements of intelligence. The issue is unresolved.

How Do We Measure Intelligence?

Ever since the nineteenth century, when researchers tried to rate intelligence on the basis of sensitivity to physical stimuli and reaction times, the problem has been to translate theories into objective measures. The search for practical, useful measures of intelligence became the **psychometric**, or mental-testing, approach to intelligence. The earliest attempts to measure intelligence were largely failures, but in 1904, the French Ministry of Education hired psychologists Alfred Binet and Theophile Simon to construct a test that would identify children who were failing in school but who might be able to learn in special classes. They devised a set of problems that emphasized judgment, comprehension, and reasoning—the qualities that the two psychologists considered the core of intelligence (Binet and Simon, 1916).

The problems were grouped by age level; for example, all tests passed by 90 percent of normal 5-year-olds were put at the 5-year level. Children's performance was rated in the same way. A 7-year-old who answered questions the way most 9-year-olds did was assigned a **mental age** of 9, as was a 12-year-old who answered the questions similarly. Binet and Simon were so successful and their test was so useful that psychologists around the world began translating the test into their own languages and using it to identify schoolchildren who had learning problems as well as those who were doing exceptionally well.

Modern Intelligence Tests

The Binet-Simon test came to the United States in 1916, when Lewis Terman and his associates at Stanford University adapted the Binet-Simon test for American children. Over the years, the test, now known as the Stanford-Binet test, has been revised several times in order to reflect changes in the culture and the educational system. The current version can be given to individuals of any age, from 2 years to adulthood. *Individuals* is the key word, because the Stanford-Binet is an individual intelligence test, administered to one child at a time by a highly skilled examiner.

The Stanford-Binet is made up of various subtests, grouped by age. Some of the tests assess verbal ability. For example, a child may be asked to tell what the pair of words *apple* and *peach* have in common or to answer questions about common activities. Other tests,

This child is working at items from the performance scale of the Stanford-Binet test. Such items as duplicating a block design depend less on cultural experience than do items on the verbal scale. *(Photos by John Oldenkamp with permission of the Houghton Mifflin Company from Terman and Merrill Stanford-Binet Intelligence Scale)*

known as **performance tests,** are nonverbal. They require the child to string beads, build blocks, match pictures, or add features to an incomplete drawing. The examiner begins by asking the child questions from a level for a slightly younger person; then the examiner gradually moves up the scale, asking more difficult questions, until the child can answer none of them. Should the child have difficulty with the first questions, the examiner drops back to items for a younger child. From the pattern of answers, the examiner computes the child's score.

Another set of popular tests was constructed by psychologist David Wechsler, who needed a test to use with adult patients at Bellevue Hospital in New York City. After devising the Wechsler Adult Intelligence Scale (WAIS), he added the Wechsler Intelligence Scale for Children (WISC) and the Wechsler Preschool and Primary Scale of Intelligence (WPPSI) for children from 4 to 6½ years old. Like the Stanford-Binet, the Wechsler tests are designed to be given individually. Unlike the Stanford-Binet, there are separate tests for different age groups. Also unlike the Stanford-Binet, Wechsler's tests

have separate verbal and performance scales, each with its own score (see Table 12.1). Tests on the verbal scale include general information questions ("How many nickels make a dime?"), general comprehension questions ("Why should people not waste fuel?"), arithmetic questions, similarity questions, ("In what way are a shoe and slipper alike?"), vocabulary items, and items testing digit span (repeating a series of numbers). Tests on the performance scale require children to complete pictures (a rabbit with a missing ear), to arrange pictures in chronological order, to reproduce block designs, to assemble small objects, to match symbols with numbers on the basis of an arbitrary code, and to trace routes through mazes.

As the variety of subtests indicate, test makers assume that different tests measure different aspects of intelligence. Some of the items in the tests depend on the child's experience. This is especially true of items on the verbal scale, except, perhaps, digit span. In Cattell and Horn's terms, these items test crystallized intelligence. Many of the items on the performance scale depend less on school experience; they may be tapping

TABLE 12.1   WECHSLER INTELLIGENCE SCALE FOR CHILDREN (WISC)*

Verbal Scale	Performance Scale
General information ("How many nickels make a dime?")	Picture completion (Child finds the missing part, e.g., rabbit with missing ear.)
Similarities ("In what way are a shoe and a slipper alike?")	Picture arrangement (Child arranges pictures in chronological order.)
Arithmetic (Child solves simple problems involving counting, mental computation, or reasoning.)	Block design (Child reproduces simple design made of colored blocks.)
Vocabulary (Child defines specific words.)	Object assembly (Child solves jigsaw puzzle depicting familiar object.)
General comprehension ("Why should people not waste fuel?")	Coding (Child matches symbols with letters, following code.)
Digit span (Child repeats a series of numbers.)	Mazes (Child traces route through maze.)

*Tests on the WISC verbal scale primarily test crystallized intelligence, whereas tests on the performance scale primarily test fluid intelligence. By providing verbal and performance IQs as well as general IQ scores, the WISC enables testers to diagnose children's strengths and weaknesses.

fluid intelligence. For example, a child should be able to assemble blocks in a design without having gone to school.

Scoring Intelligence Tests

Binet and Simon used a child's mental age as the score on their original tests. But unless educators knew the relation between a child's mental and chronological ages, they had no way of assessing how retarded or advanced that child was compared with other youngsters of the same age. A child with a mental age of 10 may be brilliant (if the chronological age is 7), a little slow (if the chronological age is 11), or mildly retarded (if the chronological age is 13). To solve the problem, German psychologist William Stern (1914) suggested using the ratio between the child's mental and chronological ages to represent the child's level of intelligence. He called this ratio the child's **intelligence quotient (IQ)**, or *IQ score*, which he produced by dividing the mental age by the chronological age and multiplying the result by 100 (to get rid of the decimals).

Although the tests are still called IQ tests, modern IQs no longer represent the ratio between a child's mental and chronological ages. Instead the IQ is actually a "deviation IQ." Test makers construct the tests so that a child whose score is the same as the average score of all children of that age who take the test will make the standard score of 100. Today's scores show how far a child's IQ deviates from the average scores of his or her own age group. About 68 percent of people fall within one standard deviation, or 15 points (on Stanford-Binet and WISC tests), of the average score of 100, and 95 percent fall within two standard deviations, or 30 points, of the average (see Figure 12.1). This means that an IQ score is not an absolute measure of mental capacity. It is simply a descriptive statistic relating a child's present performance to that of other children of the same chronological age.

Middle-class children generally do well on IQ tests, because they tend to be comfortable in the testing situation, motivated, and attentive. They have also been exposed to the knowledge on which they are tested. This bias toward middle-class culture is built into the test, because the schools represent that culture. IQ tests were designed to predict school performance, and so it is not surprising that the individual tests are the best single predictor of success in school for children of all socioeconomic levels. If researchers managed to eliminate this middle-class bias, the tests would lose their ability to predict success in school.

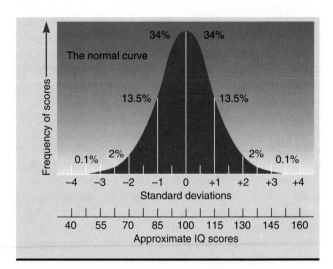

Figure 12.1 IQ scores follow the normal curve of distribution, with just over 68 percent of people making scores of 85 to 115. These scores are within one standard deviation of the average IQ of 100.

Alternative Measures of Intelligence

IQ tests measure what a child knows and is willing to say at the moment he or she sits down to take the test, but they do not always reveal what the child might be able to learn. Recently, some psychologists have been developing **dynamic assessment** tests, which evaluate what the child is prepared to learn, given a little assistance. Instead of measuring the child's current developmental level, these tests explore the child's zone of proximal development (see Chapter 2).

One of these dynamic assessment tests is Reuven Feuerstein's Learning Potential Assessment Device, a performance scale that Feuerstein devised to test the abilities of displaced Jewish children who had survived the Holocaust. The test does not draw on knowledge of reading or arithmetic or the child's store of general knowledge. The testing session is actually a tutorial, in which the examiner's goal is to find out what the child *can* learn. And so the examiner intervenes continually, asking for explanations and giving them, asking for repetitions, summing up the test experiences, warning the child about possible difficulties, and attempting to prod the child into reflective, insightful thinking. When children were tested in this way, it became apparent that many "mentally retarded" children could become competent thinkers.

From this work came Feuerstein's Instrumental Enrichment (FIE) Program, a two- or three-year program that teaches thinking skills (Feuerstein et al., 1980).

During the course of the FIE, children learn to identify basic principles of thinking and practice monitoring their use of these principles (see Figure 12.2). The teacher continually bridges back and forth between the principles and their application to various aspects of life.

In the United States, Joseph Campione and his associates (Campione et al., 1984; Ferrara, Brown, and Campione, 1986) also have used dynamic assessment techniques to evaluate children's ability to grasp the principles of inductive reasoning. In initial sessions, children learn to work series-completion problems and

Figure 12.2 These FIE exercises are meant to develop reflective, insightful thinking. In exercise 1, the student traces broken lines so that some of the squares appear to be on top of others. This exercise helps students learn to control impulsiveness, because darkening lines without thinking carefully leads to mistakes. In exercise 2, the student who explains how the water disappeared from the pot is learning to see objects and events in relation to one another. (*From Feuerstein et al., 1980*)

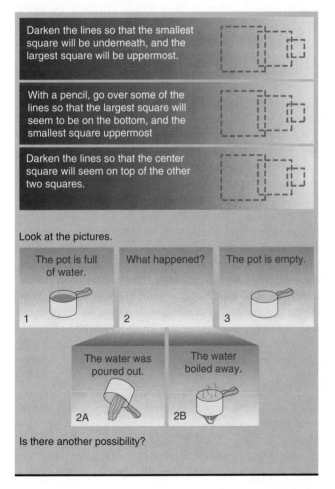

progressive matrices. When a child is unable to solve a problem, he or she is given a series of hints (as many as, but no more than, necessary). Before the session ends, the child learns the rules that govern the problem's solution. In later sessions, the child gets similar problems as well as problems that require him or her to combine old rules or figure out slightly different rules. The ease with which children can do this indicates their ability to transfer learning to new situations.

Such tests give educators a way to measure the width of the child's zone of proximal development; they show just how much instruction a child requires in order to learn. One advantage of such tests is that they can uncover hidden potential—children who are ready to move ahead but who would be denied the opportunity on the basis of traditional tests. They also can pinpoint a child's strengths and weaknesses. Some of the children in these studies learned quickly but had trouble transferring that learning to a new situation; others learned slowly but transferred the learning swiftly.

A third alternative way of measuring intelligence comes from the PASS model of intelligence, which assesses information-processing components of thought (Naglieri, 1989). PASS stands for *Planning, Attention, Simultaneous,* and *Successive* processing, and researchers have devised a battery of tasks that measure each of these four processes (Das and Naglieri, 1990). In the PASS model, cognitive processing involves three systems: (1) attention; (2) reception, processing, and storage of information, which may be simultaneous or successive; and (3) programming, regulation, and direction of mental activity. (The first two units encompass Sternberg's performance and knowledge-acquisition components, and the third unit is similar to Sternberg's metacomponents.) These systems respond to individual experiences, change during the course of development, and form an interrelated system.

PASS intelligence tests may help educators fit the curriculum to students. In one study (Naglieri, 1987), "normal" and reading-disabled students made similar scores on tasks measuring attention, simultaneous, and successive processing, but the reading-disabled group scored significantly lower on tasks that measured planning. As we will see, successful programs to improve reading skills teach skills associated with the planning system (Paris, Wasik, and Turner, 1990).

Another alternative measure of intelligence is the Adaptive Behavior Inventory for Children (ABIC), which attempts to overcome the middle-class bias of the traditional IQ test (J. Mercer, Gomez-Palacio, and Padilla, 1986). This test of "social-behavioral intelligence" assesses aspects of intelligence included in Sternberg's contextual subtheory, or what we might call practical intelligence or social competence. ABIC was developed when it became clear that the IQ net was screening out children whose backgrounds did not include material covered by the test but who would have been kept in normal classrooms if tested on their ability to function in the community. In one California school district, for example, 90 percent of the African-American children and 50 percent of the Hispanic children in the special-education class were socially competent (J. Mercer, 1973). These youngsters were "six-hour retarded children," living as retarded children during the school day but functioning on a normal level at home and in the community. Tests similar to the ABIC could be useful with children who do poorly at school but are highly competent at home.

Influences on IQ Scores

Although these alternative intelligence tests have demonstrated the narrowness of the traditional concept of IQ, American schools continue to rely on IQ tests, which were developed to assess children with learning problems. Stanford-Binet and Wechsler tests are used with only a few children, but most youngsters periodically take some sort of group test that assesses IQ. As we have seen, the scores of most children fall between 85 and 115, and all but a handful score between 70 and 130. What influences determine whether a child scores near the bottom of that range or near the top? In searching for the determinants of IQ, researchers try to explain the **variance** in IQ scores, which means that they try to account for the difference between the child's IQ and the average IQ of 100.

As with other aspects of development, genes and environment interact to determine the development of cognitive skills. In Chapter 3, we saw that each person's genetic makeup results in an individual reaction range of possible responses to environmental situations. Each person's reaction range for the skills tapped by IQ tests is fairly wide (at least 25 points), and aspects of the child's environment determine just where along that range IQ will develop.

As we will see in the following sections, many aspects of the child's environment are related to IQ: ethnic group, socioeconomic status, and a host of family characteristics. In a longitudinal study of intelligence that followed children from the prenatal period to age 13 (Sameroff et al., 1993), it was not which factors were present in the child's life, but the *number* of factors present that predicted IQ.

Family Characteristics and IQ Scores

The home environment is one important influence on cognitive development as measured by IQ tests. Aspects of the home environment that affect these cognitive skills include whether the parents encourage achievement, how responsive they are to the child's questions and interests, the presence of stimulating toys and books in the home, educational opportunities provided by the parents, the parents' teaching styles, whether the parents value intellectual achievement, and whether they provide models of such achievement. Although, as we saw in Chapter 3, adopted children's IQs correlate more strongly with the scores of their biological parents than with those of their adoptive parents, correlations refer to rank order, not to absolute scores. When we look at absolute scores, the IQs of adopted children are closer to the scores of their adoptive parents.

Factors in the home environment are at work long before children start school. Researchers have found, for example, that the availability of toys and reading material in the home when the child is 24 months old is a good predictor of IQ and achievement scores in the first grade (Bradley and Caldwell, 1984). The kind and amount of interaction between parent and child are also important, especially when the interaction involves language. Parents' use of reason instead of power-assertive discipline when children are 4 years old, combined with techniques that avoid direct commands and the insistence that preschoolers respond verbally during teaching tasks, is correlated with high achievement scores when the children are 12 (Hess and McDevitt, 1984). Other aspects of the home verbal environment that foster cognitive skills are asking information of children, permitting children to participate in mealtime conversations, spending time playing and talking with children, and reading aloud (Hess and Holloway, 1984).

Some researchers have speculated about the cognitive processes that are affected by these aspects of the home environment. An insistence on verbal responses from children, for example, may assist children in rehearsing information, thus enabling them to keep the information longer in short-term memory and perhaps encode it more efficiently (Price, 1984). The avoidance of authoritarian disciplinary tactics and the encouragement of autonomy may free the child's attention and

The physical and psychological environment of a home, including parents' teaching styles and the value they place on intellectual achievement, influence their children's cognitive development. *(Elizabeth Crews)*

encourage problem solving, thus convincing the child that he or she has the competence to solve problems and need not wait for a solution from an external source (Hess and McDevitt, 1984). Parents who consistently encourage their children's curiosity about the world about them, support their children's strivings for autonomy, and promote their children's interest in learning tend to have youngsters who are highly motivated to improve the quality of their intellectual skills and who have high standards for intellectual mastery. Such children are likely to have larger-than-average and more elaborately organized knowledge bases, an important aspect of crystallized intelligence and one of the cognitive differences that distinguish people who score high on IQ tests from those who receive low scores (Butterfield and Ferretti, 1987).

Another important family influence is the number of children in the home. As we saw in Chapter 9, children from large families tend to have lower IQ scores than children from small families. This relationship appears to have been consistent for at least the past century. Although IQ records were not available, researchers obtained scores from a vocabulary test (which corre-

lates highly with WAIS scores) for more than 12,000 people born between 1894 and 1964. When they examined the test scores, the researchers discovered that no matter which birth year they examined, the more brothers and sisters a person had, the lower his or her score (Van Court and Bean, 1985).

Racial Differences in IQ

By the time a child starts school, the average IQ of African-American children is about 15 points below that of white children (W. Kennedy, 1969). Such racial differences are still apparent among adults (Elliott, 1988; Reynolds et al., 1987). Most psychologists believe these differences can be traced primarily to environmental influences (Kamin, 1974). African-American mothers are less likely to have prenatal care, more likely to have premature births, and less likely to have continuing medical care for their children than are white mothers. Most of the environmental influences on IQ favor whites over African-Americans. Wide differences exist in the social, economic, cultural, motivational, nutritional, and medical situations of these groups. Finally, the tests require African-American youngsters to provide information that they have not encountered in their daily lives. All these environmental influences interact to weaken the performance of African-American children on IQ tests.

A number of studies have indicated that the conditions of life in lower social classes operate to depress IQ scores among whites as well as African-Americans (Hess, 1970; L. Hoffman, 1984). Because of the history of discrimination in the United States, however, African-Americans are disproportionately represented in the lower class, so what appear as racial differences in IQ are primarily class differences. Yet even controlling for social class does not adequately handle the problem, because African-Americans are often clustered in the most impoverished part of the lower class.

Racial differences in IQ almost as large as those between African-American and white children appear when test scores of white American children are compared with those of Japanese youngsters (R. Lynn, 1982). The average score of Japanese youngsters is 11 points higher than the average score of American children. Today, Japanese children's IQs average between 108 and 115—the highest national average IQ in the world.

Arguments have been made that racial differences in IQ, such as those between African-Americans and Caucasians and those between Caucasians and Japanese, result from genetic factors (Jensen, 1969). There is no empirical support for this view, and because of the widely differing environmental conditions among these different racial groups, it is impossible to test the genetic hypothesis (Scarr, 1981). Evidence for an environmental influence is, however, available. In the case of Caucasian-Japanese differences, for example, Japanese IQs have risen between 6 and 10 points over the past few decades, with the increase beginning among children born after World War II. The nutrition, prenatal care, and other factors that led to a postwar increase in birthweights, longevity, and adult height during the same period undoubtedly have had some effect on cognitive development. In addition, Japanese society puts a premium on intellectual skills that it expresses in educational attitudes and practices. Primary education in Japan is different from the education of American children in almost every aspect, as the accompanying box "Cultural Beliefs and School Achievement," indicates.

Community Influences on IQ

When examining the effect of the family environment on IQ, we looked primarily at processes within the family that foster cognitive development. But family processes may be influenced by aspects of the surrounding community. As we saw in Chapter 1, the simi-larity of IQ among reunited twins who had been separated at birth depended on the similarities of their communities during childhood (Bronfenbrenner, 1986). The scores of identical twins who grew up in radically different communities were no more alike than those of first cousins, who share only a quarter of their genes.

One aspect of the community that affects IQ is the amount of intellectual stimulation it provides. Studies in Switzerland, for example, showed that IQ and achievement test scores among 11-year-olds were higher in small towns than in the country and higher in cities than in small towns. Further investigation showed that these test differences were correlated with the richness and variety of children's cultural environment, especially such factors as the availability and use of libraries and learning opportunities outside the home (Bronfenbrenner, 1986).

Community beliefs about the nature of intelligence are another important factor. Among children in the Piedmont Carolinas, for example, community beliefs in the nature of intelligent behavior were related to school achievement (Heath, 1983). Children in Gateway, a middle-class community, did well in school. Their parents regarded language facility, understanding, and imagination as signs of competence. Parents encouraged early language use and imagination in their children,

Cultural attitudes toward schooling and the belief that effort, not ability, is the secret of academic success may be responsible for the fact that the average Japanese child scores 11 points higher than the average American child on IQ tests. *(Harriet Gans/The Image Works)*

CULTURAL BELIEFS AND SCHOOL ACHIEVEMENT

Most American parents seem satisfied with the education that their children are getting in elementary schools. Only about 10 percent of American mothers are "not satisfied" with their children's academic performance, compared with about 30 percent of Japanese mothers and 40 percent of Chinese mothers on Taiwan. But American children's knowledge of arithmetic falls far behind that of their Asian counterparts (Stevenson and Lee, 1990). Are Chinese and Japanese children brighter than American youngsters? Not at all. Harold Stevenson and his colleagues (1985) analyzed the cognitive skills of all three groups, looking at such tasks as perceptual speed, memory, vocabulary, and general information. They could find no major difference among fifth-graders in the level, variability, and structure of the skills.

Yet differences in math achievement among the three nationalities are striking, and the trend is disquieting. Small or nonexistent differences among kindergartners become wide gaps among fifth-graders, so much so that the average white American youngster in a Minnesota school would be a candidate for remedial help in a Japanese or Chinese school (see the accompanying graph). By fifth grade the average math score in the *best* American class is about the same as that in the *worst* Chinese class and below the score of the *worst* Japanese class. Although American children read better than Japanese children at all levels tested (kindergarten, first grade, and fifth grade), they do not read as well as Chinese at any age and Japanese fifth-graders are beginning to close the gap.

Why should American youngsters know so much less about math than their Asian counterparts? Several factors appear to contribute to the developmental lag. American schoolchildren spend less time in academic activities, do less homework, and get less encouragement at home (Stevenson, Lee, and Stigler, 1986). American youngsters spend less than half as much class time on academic work as Chinese children and just over half as much time as Japanese children. American youngsters spend more than 18 percent of their time outside the classroom during the school day, running errands for the teacher or going to the library. Chinese and Japanese children are almost never out of class. American teachers spend a smaller proportion of their time imparting information than teachers in Taiwan and Japan, but they spend a lot more time giving directions. American children also spend much less time on homework, perhaps because American teachers (and parents) rate it as less important than Chinese and Japanese teachers (and parents) do (Stevenson and Lee, 1990).

The heart of the matter is probably the difference in cultural beliefs about the essential ingredients of success and the value of academic achievement (Ste-

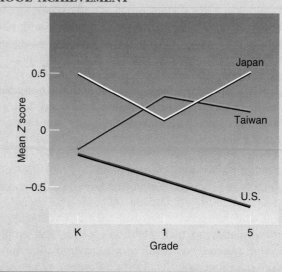

When compared with the performance of their counterparts in Taiwan and Japan, the math performance of American children falls further behind with each passing year. When these average scores were analyzed by classrooms, the highest-scoring American class ranked behind the lowest-scoring Japanese class and just above the lowest-scoring Chinese class. (*From Stevenson, Lee, and Stigler, 1986,* p. 694)

venson and Lee, 1990). Asian educational systems are built on the premise that, with enough effort and encouragement, every child can master the curriculum. Because parents of the Japanese and Chinese children in this study assumed that effort is the primary factor affecting school success, these parents did everything they could to assist their children and to provide an environment that fosters achievement. Parents of the American children in this study believed that ability is as important as effort, and mothers felt that it is better for children to be bright than to be good students. Instead of worrying about academic excellence, American mothers tried to provide experiences that foster general cognitive growth—and they thought schools should do the same. In addition, American parents tended to have low academic standards and to overestimate their children's abilities relative to peers, but Chinese and Japanese parents evaluated their children's relative academic, cognitive, and personality characteristics in a realistic manner. Thus, cultural views on the basis and importance of academic success may underlie differences in parental attitudes and in the nature of children's experiences in school.

continued to read to their school-age children, frequently read themselves, and answered their children's questions in a way that encouraged understanding. Children in Roadville, a nearby working-class community, found school more difficult. Their parents saw language facility, a good memory, and the absence of fantasy as signs of competence. They also encouraged early language use but suppressed imagination in their children; they demanded rote memorization and passive learning and did not encourage understanding. When their children started school, parents stopped reading aloud, and they rarely read themselves. Children in Trackton, a neighboring working-class community, had the most difficulty in school. Their parents saw the children's actions and ability to understand nonverbal signals as signs of competence. They did not talk to babies, paid little attention to their children's words, and emphasized nonverbal communication. Children were never asked questions, and they learned through watching actions that were unaccompanied by explanations. Few homes had books or magazines. Reading was a group affair, and children who read on their own were marked as being antisocial and as rejecting peer values. Given these differences, the relative school performance of children from the three communities is not surprising. Gateway children came from homes whose views matched the view of the school, but Roadville and Trackton children came from homes whose views of competence conflicted with the school's view. As Robert Sternberg (1990) has pointed out, how well a child functions in school and how competent he or she is perceived to be depends in good part on how well home and school views of intelligence match.

Exceptional Intellectual Development

The intelligence of most children and adults falls within a relatively narrow range. As we have seen, 95 percent of the people have IQs between 70 and 130. Although differences in that span have important implications in the classroom, they usually go undetected at a picnic, a party, a dance, or a ball game. Explaining the intellectual development of exceptional individuals—those whose intelligence falls on either side of that 60-point spread—has presented a challenge for psychologists.

Creativity and Talent

How do we explain the flowering of creative genius? Were the cognitive processes of Einstein, Darwin, Freud, Gandhi, King, Mozart, Shakespeare, and Renoir different from those of a banker, a pediatrician, a fire fighter, or an elementary school principal? Their creativity—and that of less gifted artists, writers, musicians, and scientists—apparently was not the result of exceptionally high IQs. There seems to be little correlation between IQ and creativity—although creative people generally have IQs at the higher end of the normal range (Wallach, 1985).

For years, psychologists searched for a cognitive skill that was responsible for creativity. This trait would not be tapped by IQ tests, and it would apply to all fields, much as Spearman's g applied to all intellectual endeavors. For a time, researchers supposed that creativity was the result of the ability to come up with many unusual ideas or associations, a skill they called **divergent thinking.** So they asked thousands of schoolchildren, musicians, artists, writers, and scientists to think of as many uses as possible for a brick, or of everything that was white and edible, or of all the possible occupations in which it would be appropriate to wear a bell on your clothes. Many of these tests for creativity turned out to correlate with IQ scores, and the few that did not could not account for creativity (Wallach, 1985). Some people who were good at divergent thinking were not at all creative.

Left without a general cognitive skill to explain creativity, researchers turned to personality. They found that most creative people shared a number of personality characteristics that were not related to IQ scores. Creative individuals showed independent judgment, intuition, flexibility, tolerance for ambiguity (they had no trouble with conflicting interpretations or outcomes), little concern for social norms, and a firm sense of themselves as creative (Janos and Robinson, 1985). This finding indicated that patterns of motivation and life styles might be more important in the encouragement of creativity than cognitive skills (Gallagher and Courtright, 1986).

Other psychologists decided that the notion of intelligence itself might be the problem. As long as we thought of intelligence as a unified characteristic, we were certain to have trouble with creativity, which just did not fit that construct. If we looked at intelligence in terms of Howard Gardner's (1983) multiple intelligences, however, creativity might be related to specific intelligences. A creative musician might have highly developed musical intelligence, but a person who is a creative musician is unlikely to be a creative politician (personal intelligence) or novelist (linguistic intelligence). Although each intelligence draws on some aspects of other domains, the fact that creative giftedness is usually limited to a single domain supports this view (Wallach, 1985).

No matter how large the potential, musical intelligence by itself cannot produce a Mozart; personal intelligence, a Gandhi; or linguistic intelligence, a Shakespeare. And if the talent is to flower during childhood, a particular set of environmental circumstances is necessary (see Table 12.2). Researchers have found that individuals who make significant creative strides consistently have a background of training, practice, and nurturance by others (Feldman, 1986). They seem caught up by dedication to their chosen field, and they apply themselves in a way that builds a rapid, extensive knowledge base. Their dedication often is the result of a "crystallizing experience," which is some kind of remarkable, memorable contact between the talented person and the field in which she or he will excel (Walters and Gardner, 1986). For violinist Yehudi Menuhin (1977), the crystallizing experience came when he was taken to a concert at the age of 3 to hear a noted violinist. Menuhin was entranced by the sound and asked for (and received) a violin for his fourth birthday. Finally, whenever the Mozarts or Shakespeares emerge, their talents appear at a time when historical and cultural forces allow their genius to flourish (Feldman, 1986). Had Einstein been born in Thailand and raised as a Buddhist, he probably never would have changed Western physics.

The Academically Gifted

Children considered academically gifted excel in what Howard Gardner (1983) called linguistic and logico-mathematical intelligence. They usually are identified on the basis of IQ scores, achievement tests, grades, or the recommendation of teachers. Researchers have found that young people selected by tests as gifted in one academic area often make only average scores in other areas (Colangelo and Kerr, 1990). Nor is academic giftedness always stable. Some youngsters who are identified early as gifted fail to live up to their early promise, either in school or in their occupational lives (DeLeon and VandenBos, 1985).

It took an extensive longitudinal study to convince the public that children with exceptionally high IQs were not eccentric, maladjusted creatures who became unhappy, friendless adults. In the 1920s, Lewis Terman (1959) collected data from more than 1500 California schoolchildren with IQs of at least 135 (their average IQ was 150). He followed these children through their school days and into their adult life, interviewing and testing them at regular intervals. The youngsters, who were affectionately known as "Termites," stayed two to four grades ahead of their same-age schoolmates. Most of them became happy, successful adults. Their average income was four times the national average; their rates of mental illness and suicide were lower than those in the general population. Many became national figures in their chosen profession, but none was a creative genius. In fact, as a whole, the group was low on artistic creativity (Goleman, 1980).

The latest data collection occurred in 1986, when the Termites were in their seventies. At that time, researchers examined the data that had been collected over the years to discover what aspects of childhood predicted later success and psychological adjustment among these academically gifted people (Tomlinson-Keasey and Little, 1990). The major predictor of personal adjustment during adulthood for Termites was harmony in their childhood families. Attachment to both parents, a lack of friction in the home, and a happy childhood seemed to have lasting effects. Childhood sociability had no relation to later personal adjustment. In other words, being popular, cheerful, and optimistic as children, having a sense of humor, and enjoying large groups left no mark on later emotional life. To the re-

TABLE 12.2 PRODUCING A CHILD PRODIGY: ENVIRONMENTAL INFLUENCES*

Culture that values particular talent
Particular domain at the appropriate level of development
Crystallizing experience that produces dedication to particular domain
Master teachers available
Family recognition of extreme talent
Family commitment to support talent

*Talent alone does not produce a child prodigy; prodigies appear only when the delicate balance of environmental influences that can foster the talent is present.

Source: Information from Feldman, 1986; Walters and Gardner, 1986.

searchers' surprise, Termites who were high in childhood sociability were less likely to maintain their intellectual skills and interests in later life. Perhaps an early lack of sociability directed gifted youngsters toward intellectual accomplishments or threw them into the company of adults who provided intellectual stimulations and direction.

About 70 percent of male Termites and 67 percent of female Termites graduated from college at a time when only 8 percent of young adults in California were completing college. The major predictor of college and of later graduate work was parents' levels of education. Apparently, having educated parents as models who held high expectations for their offspring was effective. To no one's surprise, educational attainment and intellectual skills together predicted occupational achievement in this group.

Among the women in the Terman study, less than half were employed full time in 1960. Those who were employed were concentrated in education and high-level clerical and accounting jobs. Although 10 percent of the men were lawyers or judges and 15 percent were scientists, engineers, or architects, less than 2 percent of the women had entered those five professions. The majority of these gifted women devoted their time and energy to their families, and those who focused on careers earned considerably less than their male counterparts (Sears and Barbee, 1977).

Most of the Termites were born about 1910, and so the women's reluctance to enter typical male careers undoubtedly was influenced by historical patterns of gender-role socialization. Many of them used their organizational abilities and leadership skills serving as unpaid volunteers. Among college students in a later generation of gifted women (born about 1940), 45 percent chose majors that were considered "masculine" at the time, such as mathematics, business, or chemistry (Schuster, 1990). Most of them went on to earn advanced degrees, and at midlife, 83 percent were employed in professional positions. Nearly half chose their careers before or during college and persisted in their fields. On measures of life satisfaction, perceptions of their own competence, and fulfillment of their potential, these gifted women equaled or surpassed women in earlier studies.

Despite the increase in the proportion of academically gifted women who pursue professional careers, girls are still less likely than boys to enter the fields of math or science, even if their talent lies in the domain of mathematics. Among the mathematically talented 12-year-olds identified by the Study of Mathematically

Gender-role socialization fosters interest in science and math among high-IQ boys but generally discourages such interest among girls with similarly high IQs. *(Elizabeth Crews)*

Precocious Youth, 60 percent of the boys and 50 percent of the girls planned to major in math or science (Benbow and Arjmand, 1990). But only 37 percent of the girls (and 59 percent of the boys) actually carried out their plans. Jacquelynne Eccles (1985b), who discovered that gifted girls often decline to enter gifted programs or to remain in them when they do enter, believes that gender-role socialization is responsible for the widening difference. When girls show interest in these areas, parents, educators, and peers tend to discourage it. Gifted girls are less likely than boys to consider careers in math and science, are less likely to perceive themselves as succeeding in them, and regard the cost of engaging in them as too high (giving up more attractive options, going against their gender schema, and so on).

Despite gifted girls' reluctance to enter accelerated programs, some psychologists and educators have concluded that radical acceleration might be the best way of meeting the gifted child's needs. Academically gifted children often become bored or frustrated in school, because they already have mastered most of the curriculum. Some schools try to combat this with an "enriched curriculum," but often the enrichment turns out to be simply more of the same work the other students are doing. (Instead of solving fifteen algebra problems each evening, the gifted child solves thirty.) According to Halbert Robinson (1983), most gifted children expend so little effort in elementary and high school that many never develop good study habits or learn to persevere in the face of difficulty. The demands of higher education may discourage them or even lead them to drop out of college or graduate school. In the program developed by Robinson at the University of Washington, academically precocious 5-year-olds are enrolled in a curriculum that allows them to enter college at the age of 14.

Some educators have been reluctant to place children in college at such a young age on the grounds that they will be socially isolated and emotionally maladjusted. But most gifted children seem to take such advancement in stride. More than 200 studies have searched for any negative effects from educational acceleration, and not a single one has found any sign of severe or permanent social or emotional harm (Daurio, 1979; Janos, 1987; Pollins, 1983; H. Robinson, 1983). When researchers studied young adults in their early twenties who had been identified as mathematically precocious at age 12, they found that acceleration had no effect on social or emotional development (T. Richardson and Benbow, 1990). Whether they had been accelerated or not, these gifted young adults reported high self-esteem and a sense of control over their lives. Among those who had been accelerated, only about 3 percent reported any negative effects on their emotional or social lives.

Mental Retardation

Low scores on an IQ test are not enough to classify children (or adults) as **mentally retarded;** the youngsters also must show impairment in their ability to adapt their behavior to the demands of the environment (American Association on Mental Deficiency, 1977). A child whose scores were more than two standard deviations below normal but who was able to dress herself, make friends, and meet the other demands of daily life would not be considered mentally retarded. More than 90 percent of mentally retarded people can lead productive lives and require little assistance from others. They are *mildly retarded* (IQ 55 to 69), and they can hold jobs, marry, and become successful parents. Their development is primarily characterized by slowness. Out on the playground, mildly retarded children often are indistinguishable from other youngsters.

Moderately retarded individuals (IQ 40 to 54) can hold simple jobs but are not totally independent. The majority can work, primarily in sheltered workshops, but few marry or have children. *Severely retarded* individuals (IQ 25 to 39) usually live in institutions, and they need considerable supervision. *Profoundly retarded* individuals (IQ below 25) usually have severe behavior problems or physical handicaps in addition to their cognitive problems. (See Table 12.3 for a summary of the four types of mental retardation.)

Genes, biology, and environment are all implicated in mental retardation. About 20 percent of retardation is

Like most mentally retarded individuals, this adolescent can look forward to a productive, self-sufficient life. *(Elizabeth Crews)*

TABLE 12.3   MENTAL RETARDATION

	IQ Range	Consequences
Mild retardation	55 to 69	Can lead normal lives. Individuals often marry and have children.
Moderate retardation	40 to 54	Can work at simple jobs. Few marry or have children.
Severe retardation	25 to 39	Usually institutionalized. Individuals require considerable supervision.
Profound retardation	<25	Institutionalized. Most have severe behavior problems and/or physical problems.

the result of genetic and biological factors (H. Robinson and Robinson, 1976). Down's syndrome, Klinefelter's syndrome, and PKU (which we explored in Chapter 3) are among the genetic disorders that lead to mental retardation. Biological causes of retardation include many of the teratogens discussed in Chapter 3, such as lead, alcohol, cocaine, and some prescription drugs. Severe anoxia during the birth process sometimes is followed by retardation, as is birth before a fetus is thirty-three weeks old.

Even biologically caused retardation is affected by the environment. As we saw in Chapter 3, babies with the conditions mentioned above who grow up in disadvantaged homes tend to show the most retardation. Children with Down's syndrome who grow up at home generally have IQs higher than those who grow up in institutions (Edgerton, 1979). The power of the environment in the development of retardation becomes especially clear when we recall the institutionalized toddlers in Chapter 8 who could not walk, talk, or feed themselves. Such extreme deprivation is rare, although cases do turn up from time to time.

The mildly retarded child's classroom problems may stem from poor strategies, a smaller store of organized knowledge, specific processing problems, poor metacognitive skills, or some combination of these factors. Some studies indicate that mildly retarded children often have trouble on memory tasks because they fail to use strategies that would help them master the material (Butterfield and Ferretti, 1987). Dynamic assessment tests have shown that mentally retarded children have

trouble transferring knowledge to new situations (Campione et al., 1985). When mentally retarded children with a mental age of 10 years were matched with normal 10 year olds, there was no difference between the groups during the learning period. But at the second session, differences appeared. The mentally retarded children required hints to solve the same kind of problems they had earlier solved with few errors. When the children had to transfer their learning to new kinds of problems, the differences widened sharply. Although they had learned to solve the original problems as well as the normal children, the mentally retarded children were unable to use their knowledge flexibly.

Schooling

The cognitive skills that are measured by IQ tests are applied most consistently in the classroom. Reading and arithmetic draw heavily on these skills, which is one reason that IQ scores are such good predictors of classroom performance. Yet there is more to school success than academic cognition. Children's motivations and beliefs may have powerful effects on their ability to learn, as well as on their IQ test performance.

Academic Cognition

Academic cognition differs from the cognition that children use in everyday life in three ways (A. Brown et al., 1983). First, academic cognition is *effortful.* Instead of the relatively effortless, undemanding thought that children bring to most daily activities, in their schoolwork they must make deliberate, often painful, attempts to learn. Second, academic cognition is *individual.* Instead of being measured by children's success in getting things done with others, progress through school is measured in terms of independent competence. Finally, academic cognition is *decontextualized knowledge.* When students learn facts stripped from their context, motivation and any practical use of information are ignored.

Reading

In today's schools, many kindergartners are learning to read. A generation ago, formal reading instruction was invariably postponed until first grade, but most American 5-year-olds have already been socialized to school—the traditional task of kindergarten (R. Anderson et al., 1985). At nursery schools or day-care centers, they learn to adapt to the group routines required to make classroom instruction possible. They learn to sit quietly and listen to instructions; they listen to stories, perhaps take field trips to the post office and fire station, and learn to participate in group activities.

The average child entering kindergarten today knows more about reading than children did a few decades ago. Their early awareness of the relation among graphic symbols, sounds, and meaning takes an enormous jump between the ages of 3 and 4 (Lomax and McGee, 1987). By the age of 4, many children understand that reading proceeds from left to right and top to bottom, that punctuation marks are different from words, and that the spaces between words indicate word boundaries (Clay, 1979). Exposure to print in signs, ads, and newspapers and on television teaches youngsters something about reading and writing, but children whose parents read to them have a great advantage over children whose parents rarely or never do. A major predictor of early reading ability is the amount of time parents devote to this activity, which teaches children initial concepts about print and reading (Mason and Allen, 1986).

Children who have not learned about the conventions of print and its connection to reading may be baffled by what seems a mysterious business. Some do not know that printed words can be turned into speech. They may believe that a story's meaning comes from the pictures, and thus they cannot tell the difference between reading a story or retelling it (Paris, Wasik, and Turner, 1990). Like the 5-year-old who memorized the story, closed his eyes, recited it, and proudly proclaimed, "Look, I can read with my eyes shut!" they may not realize that decoding skill is required. Even those whose emerging literacy is advanced have incomplete concepts about the nature of reading, print conventions and processes, and the varied purposes for reading.

In the primary grades, children work at phonological decoding and identifying words. They learn to discriminate speech sounds so that when the teacher asks them the first sound of the word "cup," they can separate it from the rest of the syllable. This may be more difficult than you might think. Although they had been talking and understanding others' speech for several years, few 5-year-olds were able to rap a desk twice when they heard the word "it" and three times when they heard "hit" (Liberman et al., 1974). Unless they can divide a word into its sounds, children will have trouble reversing the process, blending sounds into words when they try to read.

By the time they are 8 or 9 years old, most children have become skilled at phonological decoding and automatic word recognition. The child who reads fluently identifies words as adults do, using information from individual letters, the word as a whole, and the surrounding context. If the processes do not become automatic, the child may develop major reading problems (Bowey, Cain, and Ryan, 1992). When third-graders were asked to read an unfamiliar story aloud, good readers moved along at about 100 words per minute. But poor readers, whose identification skills had not become automatic, could manage only about 50 to 70 words per minute—a rate so slow that they often forgot the words they had decoded before they could grasp their meaning (Lesgold, Resnick, and Hammond, 1985). Such poor readers often rely primarily on the context of the surrounding sentence, as beginning readers do. Their pattern of errors reveals this technique. During their early months in the first grade, most youngsters' reading errors consist of substituting another word that makes sense in the situation but may not resemble the correct word. By the end of the year, as they gain reading skills, their substitution errors also resemble the visual form of the word.

Children's reading comprehension depends in good part on their metacognitive knowledge about reading (Paris, Wasik, and Turner, 1990). Good readers are those who are aware of the demands of various reading tasks and have figured out how to adapt their reading skills to the material at hand. They know that their goals are different when reading an adventure story and when reading their science textbook. They know when to

Beginning readers must learn to translate the visual patterns of letters into sounds.
(Lawrence Migdale/Photo Researchers)

skim, when to check back to see if they have understood the text, and when to summarize, ask themselves questions about the material, take notes, or underline important data.

Poor readers lack this knowledge. When researchers asked second- and sixth-graders what they did when they ran across words that they didn't know in a story, the good readers said that they either asked someone else or looked up the words in a dictionary (Myers and Paris, 1978). Poor readers couldn't say what they would do. Poor readers may be as competent intellectually as good readers but have low comprehension because of their failure to set reading goals and apply strategies efficiently and flexibly to meet them. They are passive, not active, readers, and as we will see, their passivity may be due to inappropriate motivation and attitudes (P. Johnston and Winograd, 1985).

Mathematics

Today's children enter school knowing more about mathematics than their parents did. Many preschoolers can already solve addition problems—as long as the sum is less than 10. Their parents were first-graders before they were as knowledgeable (R. Siegler, 1991). When formal instruction in arithmetic begins, children soon discover that they must learn their "number facts." Generations of schoolchildren have learned number facts, rattling off "seven" when the teacher flashes the card that says "3 + 4 = ?" and "three" when the card says "10 − 7 = ?" Generations of educators have assumed that children always memorize these facts by rote and associate the combinations without understanding them.

Researchers have concluded that educators have been partly mistaken. According to Arthur Baroody

(1985), children learn some facts by association, but they also rely on rules and strategies that they have worked out. Once they figure out that 0 stands for *nothing,* for example, they begin applying an informal rule: "When nothing is added to a number, the number does not change." When they are introduced to multiplication, they discover that simply adding a 0 multiplies by 10 or that multiplying by 5 produces an answer that always ends in a 5 or a 0. Instead of storing some 400 basic number combinations, children seem to develop internalized rules, procedures, and principles that interact with a network of specific number combinations. They memorize some number facts, use rules to generate others, and rely on counting to come up with others. Eventually they learn their number facts, providing themselves with automatic access to a knowledge base and freeing attention to be allocated to math processes (Goldman, Mertz, and Pellegrino, 1989). Their solutions become faster and more accurate.

While they are acquiring arithmetic skills, children use a wide variety of strategies, within problems as well as between them. In simple subtraction problems, for example, they may count down from the larger number, count up from the smaller, retrieve the number fact, decompose a problem so that they treat the tens and the ones separately, or simply guess (R. Siegler, 1989). With the accumulation of knowledge and experience, they use the single, most efficient strategy for each type of problem.

Teachers often discourage children from counting on their fingers to solve problems. However, this prohibition may slow their acquisition of number facts. Each time children retrieve an answer from memory, that answer is more strongly associated with the combination—whether the answer is right or wrong. Each association formed by an incorrect answer interferes with children's attempts to learn the right answer (Goldman, Mertz, and Pellegrino, 1989). Older children and brighter children do not have to use their fingers because they have either learned the combinations or figured out a rule that allows them to reconstruct the answer.

Often a gap develops between children's understanding of mathematical principles and the number problems they work in the classroom. The gap is so wide among first-graders that some believe that it is all right to come up with one answer when a problem is presented in numbers (3 + 4 = ?) and a different answer when the same problem is stated in words ("Andrea had three crayons and her teacher gave her four more cray-

ons"). It takes some time for children to learn that the symbols they manipulate mechanically on paper stand for something (+ means a joining together) or to connect Andrea's crayons with the formal symbolism of an arithmetic problem (Hiebert, 1984). Some never succeed.

A separation between symbols and the mathematical principles they stand for is more prevalent than many educators think. Most youngsters see mathematics as a puzzlelike system in which they apply arbitrary rules that they have learned. They know *how* to solve problems but not *why* the problems can be solved in that way, and they often are not certain *when* they should use the techniques (R. Siegler, 1991). Many who learn the rules without understanding the principles behind them get along all right in class, but they are unlikely to care much about the subject. Some who memorize rules apply them inappropriately. Others forget steps in the routines they have learned—or they never learn them. So they figure out a plausible routine and apply it. Because these routines usually violate basic math principles, they work in some situations but not in others—as when a problem in subtraction requires borrowing.

Most math classes emphasize the manipulation of symbols according to memorized rules, with children seeing little relation between the rules they learn to handle fractions, for example, and those they learn to handle decimals. Researchers have found that class time spent helping children to attach meaning to mathematical symbols increases their math competence and enables them to transfer processes to other tasks (Wearne and Hiebert, 1989).

Academic Motivation

Asked what he said to himself when he knew how to do his schoolwork, one youngster in a primarily African-American, inner-city middle school said, "I pat myself on the shoulder. Then I'll be very happy inside" (Rohrkemper and Bershon, 1984, p. 141). But another child in the same school had less pleasant experiences. When she didn't grasp a teacher's explanation, she kept silent: "You're afraid of people that would say, 'You can't do this easy stuff; you're stupid.' And that hurts me to be called names. I can't take it too well." Other students responded to classroom difficulties by just "putting down anything" to get the task over with or by castigating themselves: "I say, 'I'm so dumb'" (p. 135). As these examples suggest, children's attitudes toward school, the way they feel about themselves, and their beliefs about their ability to master the curriculum influence their academic achievement. The influence is so heavy that increasing numbers of cognitive psychologists have begun to look at the effects of motivation on children's learning and thinking.

Although studies indicate the importance of motivation, under certain circumstances, motivation may not be enough to ensure high achievement. When researchers looked at achievement and motivation in a representative sample of children in Chicago schools, they discovered that African-American and Hispanic children were more highly motivated than Anglo children and that their parents looked more favorably on homework, competency tests for promotion, and extension of the school day than did parents of Anglo children (Stevenson, Chen, and Uttal, 1990). Yet the minority children scored lower on achievement tests. Socioeconomic differences helped explain the disparity; Anglo families had incomes that were about twice as high as minority families. But even after researchers corrected for the mother's educational level and income, reading comprehension and vocabulary scores were still significantly lower among the minority children. The researchers suggest that the disparity remained in part because the material used in reading classes was based on experience and knowledge that neither the African-American nor the Hispanic children were likely to have encountered. In addition, Hispanic children were asked to read in a language that was not spoken in their homes. In math, where there was less disparity between content and children's experience, minority fifth-graders did as well as Anglos after correction for socioeconomic differences. In the case of these minority children, the expectations of others also may have undercut the effects of motivation. Noting that the minority children's evaluations of their reading and math skills bore no relation to their achievement scores, the researchers suggest that the unrealistic evaluations were the result of (1) low community norms for minority achievement, which made the children overestimate their achievement, and (2) low expectations on the part on teachers, which led the teachers to withhold the kind of feedback that would enable the children to improve. As we saw in Chapter 10, teachers' expectations may set up a self-fulfilling prophecy.

Attributions for Success or Failure

Kindergartners believe that effort and ability are the same: children who try hard are smarter than children who do not try; if you try harder, you will become smarter. They overestimate their own ability, but be-

cause they believe that with effort they can be smarter, these inflated estimates are not surprising (Harter, 1983). When they begin first grade, children say that they expect to do well in school. Whether they are bright, average, or somewhat slow, most believe that they are near the top of the class. Yet when asked about their classmates, they can tell you who is struggling and who is doing well (Stipek, 1981). This discrepancy may arise in part because to children on the threshold of formal education, success means finishing a task. Their optimistic outlook soon begins to change. From about the age of 7, children start to see intellectual competence as a stable personal characteristic, and their estimates of their own ability begin to match their teacher's estimate (Dweck and Elliott, 1983). They become less confident of success and increasingly vulnerable to failure. And they have become aware of their class standing; they are starting to use social comparison in assessing their own performance.

Succeeding or failing at an academic task can have widely different effects on the way children approach their schoolwork, depending on the way they interpret the outcome (B. Weiner, 1986). Children may interpret their successes or failures as due to causes inside them (ability, effort, mood) or causes in the outside world (difficulty, luck, the teacher not liking them), as Table 12.4 indicates. Some causes are stable (ability); others are transient (mood). Some causes are under the child's control (effort); others are not (ability). Whether they live in Berlin or Philadelphia, children begin to interpret their successes or failures in this manner about the time they reach the fifth grade (E. Skinner, 1990). At that time they begin to differentiate ability from effort. A child's past academic experiences also color his or her interpretation of the outcomes. Successful children and children who are struggling often interpret the same outcome in different ways. When researchers asked fifth-graders about the causes of success or failure in situations involving math and reading, good students tended to attribute their success to ability and effort and their failures to difficult assignments or luck (H. Marsh, 1986). Poor students were more likely than good students to attribute their failures to lack of ability.

A child who attributes a failure to transient internal causes and says, "I didn't do it careful enough," may try harder on the next lesson, but a child who attributes it to stable internal causes and says, "I'm just not very good at math," may put out just enough effort to get by—or even fail to finish the assignment. Researchers see the way children interpret their failures as inti-

TABLE 12.4   ATTRIBUTIONS FOR SUCCESS OR FAILURE ON SPECIFIC TASKS*

INTERNAL ATTRIBUTIONS†		EXTERNAL ATTRIBUTIONS‡	
Stable	Transient	Stable	Transient
Ability	Mood Effort Physical state	Difficulty	Luck Teacher bias

*How children explain their successes and failures affects their motivation and perhaps their perception
of their personal worth. Causes, whether internal or external, may be under their control (such as effort)
or outside their control (such as ability).
†Cause within the person.
‡Cause within the environment.

The way in which academic successes or failures influence a child's motivation depends on how the child interprets them. *(MacDonald Photography/The Picture Cube)*

mately bound up with their perceptions of their personal worth (Covington, 1984). If they attribute their failures to lack of effort, they may feel guilty for not trying harder, but they escape the humiliation of feeling incompetent. Effort is within their control, and if they apply themselves, they may succeed next time.

If they attribute their failures to lack of ability, they convict themselves of incompetence and their sense of self-worth is damaged. They are publicly humiliated, and their future is unpromising. Ability is beyond their control, and having failed today, they are likely to fail tomorrow. Some older children may be so afraid to discover that they lack ability that they simply quit trying. Those who adopt this strategy are probably not consciously aware that they have done so, but it keeps them from having to face the possibility that they are incompetent (Jagacinski and Nicholls, 1990). They can always say, "I should have tried harder." Other students give up because they have become convinced that they lack ability, and they are afraid to fail.

Beliefs and Self-Perceptions
Children who have given up are regarded as passive academic failures. They have developed learned helplessness and no longer see their efforts as having any bearing on the outcome of their school endeavors. As we saw in Chapter 10, the reactions of the teacher to the student's classroom efforts may be one factor in the development of passive failure. When teachers believe that a child is incapable of doing the work, their pity may encourage failure. Pity leads them to provide extra help, praise the student excessively for success at easy tasks, and refrain from criticism. Studies suggest that even 6-year-olds perceive a teacher's pity as a signal that they are incompetent (Graham, 1984). Unwarranted

praise and unsolicited offers of help also send children a similar message (Graham and Barker, 1990).

Appropriate praise, however, works against learned helplessness. No matter what a child's level of ability, praise from the teacher for schoolwork (but not for good behavior) affects the child's perception of his or her ability. Appropriate praise for good behavior tends to affect the child's perception of his or her effort. These influences were as strong among second-graders as among sixth-graders and among girls as among boys (Pintrich and Blumenfeld, 1985).

Among older children, boys are more likely than girls to believe that their grades depend on whether the teacher likes them. But whether girls or boys, children who see themselves as responsible for their own successes or failures do best in school (Connell, 1985). Studies indicate that unless children believe that their classroom efforts will bring success, they are unlikely to develop the metacognitive knowledge and strategies that are necessary if they are to become highly motivated, self-regulated learners (Borkowski et al., 1990).

Self-Regulated Learning

When schooling succeeds, the classroom is characterized by **self-regulated learning,** in which children plan, evaluate, and regulate their own learning skills and develop a lasting interest in learning (Paris and Byrnes, 1989). They are motivated to learn, possess the skills that enable them to learn, and adapt those skills to the learning situation. Self-regulated learners combine skill with will. Their self-efficacy is high: they expect to be successful in the future because they have been successful in the past (Zimmerman, 1989). In fact, studies indicate that a belief in their own capabilities and a conviction that school is interesting and important are strongly related to children's use of self-regulated learning strategies (Pintrich and De Groot, 1990).

Many good students become self-regulated learners more or less on their own. They learn to coordinate their knowledge, their learning strategies, and their motivation, and they feel competent in the classroom. Such children tend to come from homes in which parents promote autonomy, use inductive discipline, and provide a structured setting in terms of rules and expectations (Grolnick and Ryan, 1989). The average student,

however, uses self-regulating processes inconsistently, and the poor student has little grasp of them (Corno and Rohrkemper, 1985). Telling a student who lacks strategies and is afraid of failing to try harder is unlikely to induce self-regulation. When researchers compared children who were achievers with those who were underachievers, underachievers had lower self-esteem, negative attitudes toward reading, and lower levels of metacognitive knowledge, and they did not believe that their efforts could bring academic success (Carr, Borkowski, and Maxwell, 1991). Yet the IQ scores of the two groups were virtually identical (about 115). Underachievers are also less likely than other children to ask for help, as shown in the accompanying box, "Asking for Help."

Some researchers have concluded that more children could become self-regulated learners if they were taught some of the skills that good students already possess and knew *why* those skills lead to successful learning. In the hope of helping children become self-regulated learners, Scott Paris and his associates (Cross and Paris, 1989; Paris and Oka, 1986; Paris and Winograd, 1990) developed programs that help students use metacognitive strategies in reading. Third- to eighth-graders get direct knowledge about effective reading strategies (skimming, rereading, paraphrasing, making inferences, and checking) and opportunities to use them. Instruction is given two to three times per week for up to six months during the school year. Teachers demonstrate the strategies in structured group discussions and then gradually require the students to generate the strategies on their own. Students learn *how* to use the strategies, *when* to use them, and *why* they are likely to be helpful. Students share their experiences with the use of each strategy. At the close of the program, children at every reading level show increased comprehension and metacognitive knowledge about reading. The children also become convinced of the role of effort in school success, show pride and satisfaction at their own accomplishments, and tend to be more motivated to read (Paris and Winograd, 1990).

Children with these characteristics may become self-regulated learners. They have been given the essential tools, but their self-concepts, their achievement histories, and the way they evaluate their future successes or failures will determine the outcome.

ASKING FOR HELP: A GOOD WAY TO LEARN?

One way to increase competence is through the assistance of an adult or a more competent peer (Vygotsky, 1978). Children who ask for help are using a learning strategy that can help them acquire knowledge and skills. But many children are reluctant to ask for help, and unless a child asks, the teacher's unrequested assistance may convince a floundering child that he or she is incompetent (Graham and Barker, 1990). The problem is to get children who need help to ask for it.

Among sixth-graders, for example, students with low achievement scores were the most aware that they needed help but were the least likely to ask for it (R. Newman and Goldin, 1990). Low achievers said they were hesitant to ask for help because they believed they should already know the information that they needed and they were afraid that others would think they were dumb if they asked. Girls were more likely than boys to think that asking for help in math marked them as "dumb."

No matter what their achievement level, children who perceive themselves as incompetent (a stable cause) are reluctant to ask for help (R. Newman, 1990). Apparently, their low levels of efficacy and low self-esteem lead them to feel threatened by admissions of failure. In contrast, children with a firm sense of efficacy and high self-esteem interpret failure as caused by lack of information (a transient cause), and so they ask for assistance that will lead to future success. The pattern was weak among third- and fifth-graders, who were aware of the costs of help seeking yet asserted their intentions to ask for it. But among seventh-graders, who were conforming and highly sensitive to the opinion of their peers, the fear of displaying their incompetence was a powerful barrier to asking for help. At any age, however, children who are interested in learning new things and who strive for independent mastery usually ask for help when they need it.

These results, which came from a largely Anglo

Asking for help is an effective strategy for learning, but students who need help most are least likely to request it. *(Jeff Isaac Greenberg/Photo Researchers)*

(60 percent) and Hispanic (30 percent) group of California schoolchildren, were extended by a study with African-American students in Pittsburgh, all of whom were achieving on grade level (Nelson-Le Gall and Jones, 1990). Third- and fifth-graders who were interested in learning and who strove for mastery were most likely to ask for help when they needed it. Their mastery orientation also led them to prefer hints, which would allow them to solve the problems themselves, to direct answers. Perceived competence, intrinsic motivation, and mastery orientation are, of course, all related to self-regulated learning.

SUMMARY

WHAT IS INTELLIGENCE?

Theorists have never agreed on an explicit definition of intelligence. Piaget saw intelligence in terms of the cognitive structures that underlay adaptive action. In information-processing views, intelligence depends on the efficiency and speed with which individuals carry out basic processes used to represent and manipulate information. Intelligence seems to consists of **fluid intelligence,** which is neither taught by the schools nor pushed by the culture, and **crystallized intelligence,** which depends on schooling or cultural experience. In the **triarchic theory,** the development and use of intelligence depends on (1) the components of intelligence, (2) the attributes of tasks or situations, and (3) the sociocultural setting. **Factor theories** examine intelligence in terms of abilities instead of processes, and researchers search for basic abilities using the technique of **factor analysis.** The theory of **multiple intelligences** assumes the existence of seven different kinds of intelligences.

HOW DO WE MEASURE INTELLIGENCE?

The **psychometric,** or mental-testing, approach to intelligence was developed by Binet and Simon, who devised standardized tests to assess a child's **mental age. Performance tests** are nonverbal tests that are less influenced by schooling than are verbal tests. **Intelligence quotient (IQ)** represents the ratio between a child's mental and chronological ages. Modern tests, such as the Stanford-Binet or one of the Wechsler tests, assess intelligence in terms of deviation IQ. Some researchers are developing **dynamic assessment** tests, which evaluate what a child is prepared to learn with assistance.

INFLUENCES ON IQ SCORES

Researchers still disagree about explanations for the **variance** in IQ scores. Heredity and environment interact to produce intelligence, with genes setting the possible reaction range. Processes within the family, such as verbal interaction, type of discipline, and whether parents encourage autonomy, affect cognitive development. Environmental influences that are associated with socioeconomic differences are apparently responsible for racial differences in IQ. Factors in the community, including similarities between home and school views of intelligence, also affect IQ scores.

EXCEPTIONAL INTELLECTUAL DEVELOPMENT

Some psychologists have assumed that creativity was the result of **divergent thinking.** Others have supposed that personality traits are crucial. Great creative genius appears to require a delicate balance of environmental forces. Intellectually gifted children generally grow up to be successful, well-adjusted individuals, and it appears that they may do best in school if placed in an accelerated program. **Mentally retarded** children or adults have IQ scores more than two standard deviations (30 points) below normal and show an impaired ability to adapt to the demands of the environment. Retardation can be caused by genes, biology, or environment, and retarded children have specialized deficits in cognitive processes.

SCHOOLING

Children's early literacy rises sharply between the ages of 3 and 4, and the practice of reading to children in the home is the best predictor of early reading ability. In the primary grades, children learn phonological decoding and word identification, and by the age of 8 or 9, these processes have become automatic for most children. Children's reading comprehension depends on their metacognitive knowledge about reading. In mastering arithmetic, children memorize some number facts, develop rules to generate others, and rely on counting for the rest. When mathematical symbols and the principles they stand for are separated, children see math as a system with arbitrary rules and often try to solve problems with arbitrary rules of their own invention.

The way children interpret their school successes and failures determines what sorts of effects these will have on children's motivation and attitudes toward school. Children may assume that the causes are inside them or in the outside world, stable or transient, under their own control or outside it. Children who attribute their failures to lack of effort may try harder next time; those who attribute them to lack of ability often quit trying. Children who give up are passive academic failures, who suffer from learned helplessness. Children who are successful students engage in **self-regulated learning,** in which they plan, evaluate, and regulate their own learning skills. Such children are motivated to learn, skilled at learning, and expect to be successful.

KEY TERMS

crystallized intelligence	fluid intelligence	psychometrics
divergent thinking	intelligence quotient (IQ)	self-regulated learning
dynamic assessment	mentally retarded	triarchic theory
factor analysis	multiple intelligences	variance
factor theories	performance test	

ADOLESCENCE: BUILDING
AN IDENTITY

The physical changes of adolescence turn children into men and women. Sexual development obviously has wide psychological and social consequences, but the gradual transformation of dependent child into independent adult may be even more important. Moving out of the sheltered world of childhood into the unprotected terrain of adulthood brings new risks and new opportunities. As the prospect of striking out on one's own becomes real, the personality that developed in late childhood faces an inevitable test. Life's joys as well as its pains arise from this confrontation between the needs of a developing personality and the demands of society. Out of the inevitable conflict emerges an identity that reflects the adolescent's sense of self. These chapters show how girls and boys react to the transformations of adolescence, and how socioeconomic status, ethnicity, and cultural changes affect the ranges of choices that society presents to them.

ADOLESCENCE: BIOLOGICAL AND SOCIAL CHANGES

• • • • • • • • • • • • • •

BIOLOGICAL CHANGES
Sexual maturation in girls
Sexual maturation in boys
Reactions to physical changes

CHANGES IN THE SELF: IDENTITY
Identity formation
Gender differences in identity
   formation
Identity formation in minority groups
The individuated adolescent

THE ADOLESCENT WITHIN THE FAMILY
Parental style
Quest for autonomy
Changes in family relationships
Divorce and remarriage
Maternal employment

CHANGES IN FRIENDSHIP AND SOCIAL LIFE
Friendships
The peer group
Relations with the other sex

THE ADOLESCENT AS WORKER

SUMMARY

KEY TERMS

Twelve-year-old Candy Reed of Harmarville, Pennsylvania, attends a combined junior-senior high school. Each afternoon, when Candy comes home from school, her first task is to call her mother, a physical therapist's aide at a local hospital, to see if there's a special task to be done. Perhaps company is coming, and the living room needs cleaning. Or perhaps Candy is to start dinner. Then it's seventh-grade phone time—the daily check-in with friends from whom she has been separated for at least an hour. One of those calls is always the same, to a girl she "hangs around with a lot." The two share secrets and listen to each other's personal problems—problems in the family, at school, with boys. Candy's social life resembles that of many other young adolescents. She and her friends go to parties, dances, and movies in groups and then pair off with boys after they get there. Candy's special boyfriend is in the ninth grade, and he is a "real kind person," but Candy doesn't feel ready for sex. She knows about her mother's concerns:

> *I think she trusts me, but it's just the natural thing to worry about the big world that's out there, things like drugs and alcohol, and sex. And I'm starting to date, and she's kind of worried about what he's like—if he's cruel, if he's nice, if he's too old for me. (Kotre and Hall, 1990, p. 143)*

● ● ● ● ● ●

Candy has entered adolescence, a time of change in every aspect of a young person's life. Physically, cognitively, and socially, the 19-year-old is a different creature from the 11-year-old. Some changes are apparent to all—the rapid growth, the deepening voice, the development of body hair, breasts, or penis. These changes are so predictable that when they are late or do not occur at all, both child and family are alarmed. Psychosocial changes, which many observers feel are the most important changes of adolescence, are less obvious. In relation to others, especially the family, the child moves from dependency to increasing independence. The tempo of that movement and its conditions form a major theme of family life, with adolescent and parent preoccupied with what the adolescent can and cannot do, when she or he can do it, and how it will be done. Perhaps the most subtle change of all involves the adolescent's identity—the emerging sense of self that synthesizes so many elements of life. When these transitional years are complete, the girl or boy who embarked on adolescence as a child emerges as an adult.

In this chapter, we examine the biological and social changes of adolescence, beginning with its most obvious aspect, the biological changes that usher in this stage of life. After surveying sexual maturation and youngsters' reactions to changes in their bodies, we consider changes in the self. During adolescence, youngsters begin working at a major developmental task, the achievement of identity. The changes we consider affect the way the family system operates, and so we explore how puberty alters relations between parent and child, looking at one-parent as well as two-parent families. Then we turn to changes in the adolescent's social life, which alters dramatically as friends and peers take on a new importance and the adolescent embarks on a sexual life. The chapter closes with a look at the adolescent as worker.

Biological Changes

In the beginning, adolescence is a biological phenomenon. Early adolescence is characterized by **puberty,** the lengthy biological process that changes the immature child into a sexually mature person (Petersen, 1985). Since childhood, the endocrine system has been capable of initiating the change, but its functioning has been suppressed. Throughout childhood, both boys and girls produce low levels of **androgens** (male hormones) and **estrogens** (female hormones) in relatively equal amounts. Then, in response to some still-unexplained biological signal, the hypothalamus tells the pituitary gland to begin the hormonal production found in adult men and women. The pituitary gland stimulates other endocrine glands, primarily the thyroid, the adrenal glands, and the gonads (**ovaries** in girls and **testes** in boys). A surge in hormone production occurs, and the child enters puberty. The gonads and the adrenal glands secrete sex hormones directly into the bloodstream; they create a balance that includes more androgens in boys and more estrogens in girls. These new hormonal levels lead directly to the dramatic physical changes of puberty, and within about four years, the child's body is transformed into the body of an adult. She or he is now sexually mature, but hormone secretion continues to increase throughout adolescence and into young adulthood, peaking at about the age of 20.

Although we talk about puberty as if it were a smooth, single process, it is actually a series of correlated events that reflect a group of interrelated processes (Bogin, 1988; Brooks-Gunn and Warren, 1985). Youngsters progress through these events at different rates, with one girl reaching full breast development in two years, for example, while another takes five years to complete the same sequence of growth (see Figure 13.1). Nor do all events follow the same timetable;

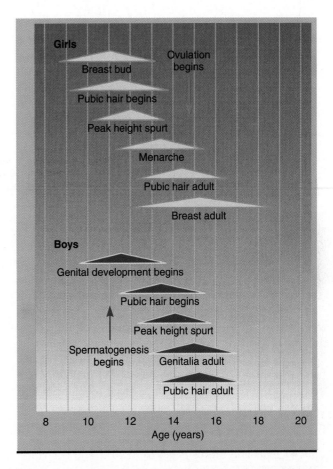

Figure 13.1 Sequence and approximate ages of major pubertal changes for boys and girls. Each triangle indicates the typical ages at which each event begins and ends. *(From Austin and Short, 1984, p. 138, as adapted from Marshall, 1970)*

breast development may be rapid in a girl whose pubic hair is developing more slowly than that of most girls. This lack of harmony produces a growth trend known as **asynchrony.** Because puberty is characterized by uneven growth, at any given time during maturation some body parts may be disproportionately large or small. Youngsters often complain that their hands and feet are too big. As growth progresses, body proportions usually become much more harmonious.

Because hormones are responsible for the physical changes of puberty, authorities once assumed that many of the behavioral changes of adolescence could be traced directly to hormonally caused increases in the sex drive. Yet no research has indicated that typical teenage behavior, such as interest in the other sex or increased conflict with parents, is directly related to hormone levels. Whatever contribution hormones make to adolescent behavior is heavily influenced by peer standards. Research indicates, for example, that a youngster's grade in school, not his or her pubertal status, is the best predictor of dating, preoccupation with the other sex, and wrangles with parents. Although early-maturing sixth-graders are the first to behave in this way, researchers discovered that once a majority of youngsters in a class are visibly pubertal, the entire class begins to act like "typical adolescents" (Petersen, 1985). When the class reaches "critical mass," many prepubertal youngsters begin dating—perhaps to keep from being dropped by their more sexually mature peer group.

Sexual Maturation in Girls

Although a girl's growth spurt can start at any time between the ages of 7 and 13 years, it typically begins at around age 10. Height increases rapidly, with growth peaking at the age of 12 and continuing until a girl is about 15 (see Figure 13.2). Her proportions change as her hips broaden more rapidly than her shoulders and she adds body fat. Sometime during the middle of her tenth year, breast buds appear as small mounds. As the breasts gradually enlarge, other changes occur. The areas around the nipples grow larger and more conical in form, and their color darkens. At the same time, a girl's vagina and uterus begin to mature, and her voice lowers. Pubic hair usually appears when a girl is about 11, underarm hair about two years later.

Parents and adolescents often regard **menarche**, or the first incidence of menstruation, as the true indicator of puberty, but this event occurs relatively late in the pubertal sequence. Several years before a girl begins to menstruate, her estrogen production anticipates the cyclic rhythm of the menstrual cycle. Menarche may come as early as 10 years or as late as 17. It is rare for a girl whose glands are functioning normally to begin menstruating before she is 9 or after she is 18.

For nearly a century, the average age of first menstruation has occurred earlier each decade. At the close of the nineteenth century, the average American girl began menstruating at age 14 or 15; today she reaches menarche a few months after her twelfth birthday (Bullough, 1981). The trend toward the earlier onset of puberty, which probably was the result of better nutrition, less disease, and reduced social stress, now seems to have stopped (Malina, 1979).

We do not yet understand the relation of menstruation to fertility. The notion that menarche signals the attainment of full reproductive functioning is a miscon-

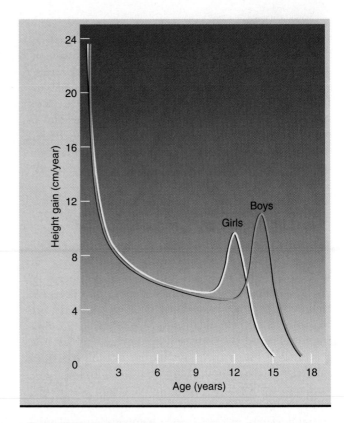

Figure 13.2 Typical height velocity curves for girls and boys from birth to maturity. After the relatively stable period of gain in height during later childhood, the adolescent growth spurt starts, with its onset and end occurring earlier for girls than for boys. *(From Tanner, 1978, p. 14)*

ception. Although some adolescent girls are able to conceive soon after menarche, about half of them remain infertile for a year or two. The period of infertility is briefer in well-nourished, inactive girls, perhaps because ovulation requires the deposit of adequate stores of fat (Lancaster, 1986). Better nutrition not only has led to earlier menstruation but may also have shortened the period of infertility that follows menarche.

Sexual Maturation in Boys

Boys generally begin their growth spurt about two years later than girls, and their growth peaks at the age of 14 (see Figure 13.2). Although most reach their adult height by the age of 16, some do not even begin to grow rapidly until that age. Their pattern of growth is different from that of girls: boys' shoulders broaden more than their hips, and much of the increase in body size comes from muscle, not fat. The increased proportion of muscle to fat in boys' bodies helps explain the increasing advantage in muscle strength that develops in boys (see Figure 13.3).

The penis and scrotum usually begin their accelerated growth when a boy is around 12 and reach mature size within three to four years. Although the external genitalia of girls change little, in boys the changes in penis, testes, and scrotum are substantial. The shaft of the penis lengthens, and its head enlarges; the scrotum and testes grow larger and become pendulous. About a year and a half after his penis begins to grow, a boy is able to ejaculate semen. But sperm production has been under way for some time. Shortly after the testes enlarge, usually by the age of 12 or 13, sperm can be detected in a boy's urine (D. Richardson and Short, 1978). Whether these early sperm are capable of fertilizing an ovum is not known, but boys may be capable of fathering children before their adolescent status becomes visible.

The growth of pubic hair accompanies the development of a boy's genitalia, with underarm and facial hair appearing about two years later (see Figure 13.1). As the boy's larynx enlarges and his vocal cords lengthen, his voice deepens. Chest hair is the last male characteristic to appear, and it may not develop fully until well into young adulthood.

Boys may enter puberty much earlier today than they did in earlier centuries. Records kept on members of the Leipzig church choir during the eighteenth century indicate that most boys' voices changed shortly after their seventeenth birthday—at least three years later than a boy's voice changes today (Kotre and Hall, 1990).

Reactions to Physical Change

Physical changes of the magnitude experienced by adolescents have a significant effect on how teenage boys and girls feel about themselves. Whether adolescents regard their adult bodies with pride, pleasure, embarrassment, or shame largely depends on the psychosocial context in which puberty occurs (Petersen,

Figure 13.3 Development of muscular strength in adolescent girls and boys, showing the widening disparity between genders. *(From Tanner, 1962)*

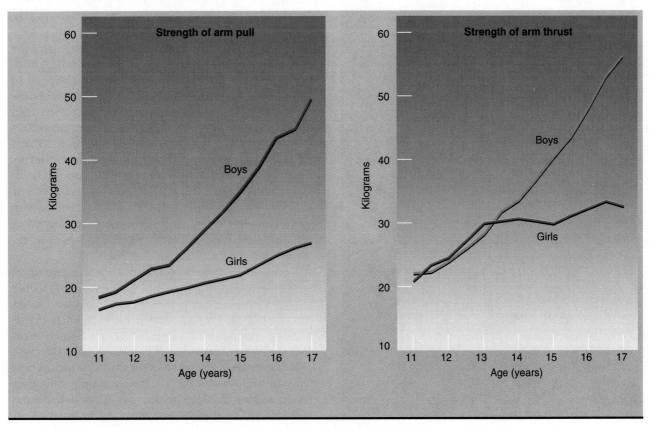

1985). Thus, adolescents' reactions to puberty depend in good part on their childhood patterns of thoughts and feelings about sexuality, the reaction of their parents and peers to their changed appearance, and the standards of the culture (both the local peer culture and the larger society).

Gender is another important influence on the youngster's reaction to physical changes. Each culture defines a particular body type as attractive and sexually appropriate for each sex. Young people learn the characteristics of this **body ideal** from peer and family expectations and from the images they see on television or in movies and magazines. The lesson may be particularly difficult for girls. In a large survey of adolescents, most of the boys but just over half of the girls were proud of

As their bodies change markedly, adolescents compare themselves with the culture's body ideal and worry over how they appear to the other sex. *(Tony Freeman/Photo Edit)*

their bodies (Offer, Ostrov, and Howard, 1981a). The rest said that they frequently felt ugly and unattractive. Adolescents who already feel unacceptable or who have low self-esteem may become anxious about their appearance, even though others find them as attractive as most of their peers (Petersen and Taylor, 1980).

A girl's reaction to menstruation seems to depend in good part on how well she has been prepared for the event. Girls who know what to expect generally have fewer menstrual symptoms, including pain, and their symptoms are less severe than those of girls who reach menarche without preparation (Ruble and Brooks-Gunn, 1982; Skandhan et al., 1988). Another important influence on a girl's attitude toward menstruation is its timing. Girls who begin to menstruate much earlier than their peers tend to have more negative feelings about the process than those who reach menarche late or "on time." However, a girl's belief about the timing of menarche has more influence on her feelings about the event than its actual timing does. In one study, girls who were "on time" but who believed that they had reached menarche early tended to have the same negative feelings as girls who actually matured ahead of schedule (Rierdan and Koff, 1985).

The timing of puberty affects boys' and girls' feelings about their bodies—but in different ways. Boys who mature earlier than their peers tend to be the most satisfied with their bodies, perhaps because they are taller and more muscular than other boys during early adolescence. Girls' reactions to puberty seem influenced by the cultural ideal of thinness. In a longitudinal study, girls who matured early generally felt worst about their weight, but as other girls matured, early maturers' feelings tended to fall into line (Blyth, Simmons, and Zakin, 1985). It was apparently the deposit of body fat and not the other visible aspects of puberty that bothered them. In general, maturational timing did not affect girls' self-esteem—except among girls who entered junior high school at about the time they reached menarche. When girls had to handle puberty and a new school at the same time, their self-esteem suffered.

Whether puberty comes early or late generally affects children's standing in the peer group. Early-maturing boys tend to be popular and active in school activities, and their greater strength and endurance may enhance their athletic prestige (Livson and Peskin, 1980). Perhaps because they tend to associate with older boys, they are more likely than late maturers to get into trouble with the authorities, whether the measure is school problems, truancy, or minor delinquency (Duncan et al., 1985). Late-maturing boys, who are often smaller and weaker than other boys, rarely become leaders, and they tend to be less popular (Livson and Peskin, 1980).

Among girls, peer-group status favors the late maturer. Late-maturing girls are generally popular and highly sociable, and they often tend to be leaders. By contrast, early-maturing girls tend to be less popular and self-assured than other girls (Livson and Peskin, 1980). Because they look older than the other girls, however, they may be sought out by older boys. Studies indicate that early-maturing girls of all races tend to date earlier than other girls and to have sexual intercourse at an earlier age (V. Phinney et al., 1990). Among all groups except African-Americans, early-maturing girls also tend to marry earlier.

If early sexual activity leads to marriage or pregnancy, it will have lasting effects on girls' lives. Indeed, among Swedish girls, earlier maturers were ready at an early age to marry and raise families (Magnusson, Stattin, and Allen, 1985). They sought out older friends and saw themselves as more mature than other girls their age. They were also less likely than other girls to go on to college. But early-maturing girls have some advantages over late maturers. By the time they are in their thirties, they seem more self-possessed, self-assured, and competent than late maturers (Livson and Peskin, 1980).

The timing of puberty may also have lasting effects on boys' lives. When they reach their late thirties, early maturers seem more confident, responsible, and cooperative than late maturers, but they also tend to be humorless, moralistic conformers. Late-maturing boys seem to profit from their extra years of childhood, when they were free to invent and learn without pressure. Although they still may seem impulsive and assertive, they may now be more perceptive and more adept at coping with new situations than are men who matured early (Livson and Peskin, 1980). Because the advent of puberty changes the nature of family interactions (Steinberg, 1988), as we will see, some effects associated with early or late puberty may be in part a result of a shift in the timing of these family changes.

Changes in the Self: Identity

During adolescence, youngsters face a variety of tasks whose outcome will affect the course of their future lives. They may be dealing with separation from their parents. They must make choices about schooling and vocation. Their emerging sexuality presents the possibility of intimacy with members of the other sex and the eventual formation of their own families. They are striving for autonomy and dealing with issues of principle, politics, and values. As they wrestle with these issues, they discover that their changed bodies evoke new expectations and behavior from friends, peers, and society.

Such changes occur in every aspect of their lives, including their emotions (see the accompanying box, "The Changing Moods of Adolescents"). It is no wonder, then, that adolescence is the time when boys and girls test their feelings about themselves. For some, it is a matter of consolidating their present self-concepts; for others, the process involves the development of new concepts of the self. Most adolescents handle these issues of the self with little difficulty and successfully resolve the conflict between their own needs and social demands. But a few, who still have unresolved conflicts from earlier stages of development, reexperience the earlier conflicts and may return to earlier ways of resolving them. Whether the issue that flares up concerns matters of trust, autonomy, initiative, or industry depends on the adolescent's history, individual strengths, and habitual ways of responding to stressful situations (Adelson and Doehrman, 1980). In Chapter 15, we will see how a minority of adolescents respond to the revival of old conflicts and other intolerable stress—perhaps by becoming pregnant, becoming addicted to drugs, or developing anorexia.

Identity Formation

One essential task of adolescence is the achievement of identity. **Identity** is a coherent sense of individuality formed out of the adolescent's traits and circumstances. But such a definition barely begins to explain a complicated concept. According to Erik Erikson (1980), the adolescent's identity develops silently, over time, as many bits and pieces of the self come together in an organized way. These elements may include inborn aspects of personality; developed aspects of personality, such as passivity, aggression, and sensuality; talents and abilities; identification with models, whether parent, peer, or culture figures; ways of handling conflicts and regulating conduct; and the adoption of consistent social, vocational, and gender roles. Identity formation is a lifelong task that has its roots in early childhood, but it becomes central around the time of adolescence. At that time, a youngster's physical development, cognitive skills, and social expectations mature enough to make the formation of a mature identity possible.

THE CHANGING MOODS OF ADOLESCENTS

Although adolescence has long been considered a time of moodiness and wide emotional swings, the vast majority of adolescents are happy, strong, and self-confident. They are hopeful about the future, look forward to adulthood, and believe that they can handle whatever challenges life has in store for them. This picture of the average adolescent emerged from the replies of more than 20,000 teenagers who were studied by Daniel Offer and his colleagues (Offer and Sabshin, 1984).

Even so, adolescents are moodier than adults. Research has consistently shown that adolescents are emotional creatures, whose moods are more intense and less stable than those of adults (Diener, Sandvik, and Larson, 1985; R. Larson, Csikszentmihalyi, and Graef, 1980). Looking for an onset to adolescent moodiness, Reed Larson and Claudia Lampman-Petraitis (1989) recently gave about 250 midwestern youngsters electronic pagers like those used by physicians. These 9- to 15-year-olds lived in four suburban neighborhoods of varying socioeconomic levels. For one week, the researchers beeped the youngsters at random intervals between early morning and bed-time. When signaled, the girls and boys rated their mood and alertness on a 7-point scale. The analysis of these reports suggests that the onset of adolescence does not make a great difference in a child's moods. Neither boys nor girls showed an increase in extreme states, and 15-year-olds reported more neutral moods than 9-year-olds. Life in general may, however, have seemed less sunny as children passed through adolescence. Among those monitored, 14- and 15-year-olds not only experienced fewer extremely happy occasions than 9- and 10-year-olds but also reported more mildly negative states, so their average mood was somewhat lower.

Adolescents' lives may change in ways that make their experiences less pleasant and carefree. But it is also possible that the way adolescents interpret their experiences has changed, producing a perception of a less pleasant existence (R. Larson and Lampman-Petraitis, 1989). In either case, adolescents less often felt as if they were on top of the world and more often felt slightly down than they did before they entered puberty.

Erikson saw adolescence as a moratorium, a time when definitive choices are postponed while the various elements of identity are coming together. During that period, young people can explore various fields, trying to find a match with their personal needs, interests, capacities, and values. Most know little about the choices they soon must make, about the pathways that alternative choices may lead to, or about the irreversibility of some choices. Yet all the choices adolescents make (which courses to take in school; whether to go to college; whom to date; whether to take drugs, have sex, work after school, join a church, or work in a political campaign) contribute to the forging of identity. Socioeconomic factors may widen or constrict the array of possible choices, and subcultural contexts, peer pressures, or family situations may push the adolescent in one direction or another.

Many youngsters, especially those who go on to college, go through such a lengthy moratorium that they enter young adulthood before the identity process is complete. Most college-bound students not only prolong their dependency on their parents but also postpone decisions concerning occupations, marital choice, and values. The college experience itself may have a considerable effect on their social and political views and on their choice of mates. The process of forging an identity is considerably different for those who step from high school into a full-time occupation. They may make many of the crucial decisions while they are in high school, and for a considerable number, the decisions will be accommodations to job availability or to unanticipated parenthood or marriage (to be discussed in Chapter 15). When the process of identity formation does not go well—as when a variety of conflicts make the choices difficult, or even impossible—the result is a confused identity, in which the young person makes no commitments.

Because Erikson's concept of identity is so complicated, assessing an adolescent's progress on this developmental task is extremely difficult. Researchers found a way to get around the problem. They began classifying an adolescent's progress toward identity formation in terms of her or his status on the tasks of selecting an occupation and forging religious or political beliefs—clearly major components of identity. Building on Erikson's theory, James Marcia (1980) proposed that adolescent identity took one of four forms: foreclosure, moratorium, diffusion, or achievement.

In **foreclosure,** the adolescent is pursuing occupational and ideological goals, but the goals have been chosen by others—either parents or peers. (Ideological goals may be religious or political—or both.) Foreclosed adolescents have never experienced an "identity crisis," because they have uncritically accepted the values and expectations of others. In **moratorium,** the final choices have been put off, and the adolescent is struggling with occupational or ideological issues. He or she is in an identity crisis. In **identity achievement,** the adolescent has completed the struggle, made his or her own choices, and is pursuing occupational or ideological goals. Finally, in **identity diffusion,** the adolescent may have attempted to deal with these issues (or may have ignored them) but has made no choices and is not particularly concerned about making such commitments. Because such youngsters feel no pressure to choose, they are *not* in an identity crisis.

Adolescents who go through a moratorium period (whether it lasts only through high school or until young adulthood) before they reach identity achievement seem to have taken the preferred path—at least in contemporary cultures. Such young people are generally more independent, self-confident, flexible, and intellectually creative than other youngsters. Those whose identities are foreclosed during adolescence tend to need the approval of others; they are conforming and respectful of authority, and they are more religious and behave in a more stereotypical fashion than other young people. In traditional societies, where young people automatically accept their parents' occupations and beliefs, most youngsters have foreclosed identities. Indeed, in such a society, an adolescent who made independent choices probably would be a misfit. Adolescents who have followed the identity diffusion pattern tend to be disturbed; they may lack a sense of direction, relate poorly to others, show a low level of moral reasoning, and use drugs heavily. Yet they can seem charming and carefree.

Among young people who go on to college, identity status is likely to be temporary. In longitudinal studies, the majority of college students shifted from one identity status to another (G. Adams and Fitch, 1982; Waterman and Goldman, 1976). Shifts from moratorium to identity achievement are, of course, expected. But at least half of the students with foreclosed identities and about a third of those who originally had been assessed as identity achievers also shifted into one of the other groups. Apparently, the college experience can reopen an identity status that once seemed resolved. Whether similar shifts frequently occur among young people who do not go on to college is uncertain.

Gender Differences in Identity Formation

Researchers have found that the process of identity formation may take somewhat different paths in boys and girls. When interviewed at the end of their junior or senior year in high school, boys who had achieved an occupational identity tended to be assertive, to prefer difficult, challenging tasks, and to have little concern about others' opinions of them (Grotevant and Thorbecke, 1982). Girls who had achieved an occupational identity were different: they believed that hard work was important, but they avoided competition.

Perhaps this difference is due in good part to the context in which boys and girls form their identities. Boys are urged to make career decisions, a pressure that tends to push them toward a moratorium and later identity achievement. But even in a world of changing gender roles, current research indicates that girls tend to define their identities in terms of their relations with others. Instead of being concerned with autonomous thinking and carving out careers for themselves, they are primarily concerned with relationships and responsibilities (Gilligan, 1982). Despite the fact that they are likely to spend most of their lives in the labor market, girls often feel less pressure to choose an occupation. During adolescence, some girls continue to view employment as a temporary way station between high school graduation and the birth of their first child. For them, marriage still plays a dominant role in identity formation.

Yet an increasing number of girls show a pattern of development in which achievement is as important as interpersonal success and traditionally feminine interests. This pattern was detected more than thirty years ago by Elizabeth Douvan and Joseph Adelson (1966) in the course of a classic study of adolescence. They found a group of girls with aspirations directed toward their own achievements rather than the status of their future husbands. These girls showed a greater interest in assuming adult roles and responsibilities than did traditionally feminine girls, and their perspective extended farther into the future. Girls in this group were feminine, but they dreamed of individual achievement. They tended to prefer risky jobs with opportunities for success, rather than secure, less rewarding jobs. Some researchers suggest that living in a single-parent household may foster such development, noting that adolescent girls in single-parent families are more likely than other girls to choose a traditionally male occupa-

An increasing number of adolescent girls have formed identities in which achievement and occupational success is as important as success in interpersonal relationships. *(Spencer Grant/The Picture Cube)*

tion and to want an identity separate from that of wife and mother (Barber and Eccles, 1992).

Girls who followed this pattern tended to have parents who encouraged them to "stand on their own two feet." Among a group of girls attending a private high school in Troy, New York, most showed this pattern. Virtually all agreed that young women need to be independent as well as responsible (Mendelsohn, 1990). Most did not want to marry until they had established a career or worked at a job for some time, and they tended to see their future work more clearly than they saw their future marriage and children. As one girl said:

It used to be what kind of person are you going to marry, and now we are talking about are we ever going to get married at all, and at this point, I don't think I can say "I don't think I will get married." I can't say that I am definitely going to get married because it all depends if I find

Identity Formation in Minority Groups

Most studies of identity formation have looked at middle-class high school and college students. Among minority adolescents (African-American, Native American, Hispanic, or Asian), the proportion of foreclosed identities is relatively large (M. Spencer and Markstrom-Adams, 1990). This difference in identity status may reflect socioeconomic differences, but it may also be the result of living in a group that encourages adherence to subcultural norms. When social and ideological roles have been clearly defined by the community, foreclosure may provide a sense of well-being.

For minority adolescents, the development of identity includes a sense of **ethnic identity,** in which young people reexamine their ethnic identification and internalize it, committing themselves to their ethnic identification and integrating it into their identity (J. Phinney and Tarver, 1988). In the process, the minority adolescent first rejects the majority culture's negative evaluation and then goes on to construct an identity that includes ethnicity as a positive and desired aspect of the self (J. Ward, 1990). Among African-American and Hispanic youths, those who have a strong ethnic identity tend to be higher in self-esteem than those who have not developed such a coherent identity (J. Phinney and Alipuria, 1990).

The Individuated Adolescent

Another aspect of identity formation is the process of individuation (Baumrind, 1991b). As adolescents deal with identity, they separate themselves emotionally from their parents and transfer some of their affection to their peers. Those who fail at this task and remain emotionally dependent on their parents generally have a foreclosed identity. Others may become emotionally detached from their parents but fail to become self-reliant or autonomous (Ryan and Lynch, 1989). Because they are not emotionally independent, they rely too much on their peers. When this happens, emotional distance may be accompanied by lowered school achievement, early sexual experience, and the use of drugs.

Ideally, the adolescent is neither enmeshed in the family nor totally detached; instead, he or she has struck

The inclusion of ethnicity as a valued aspect of the self is part of the identity formation process among adolescents in minority groups. *(Lawrence Migdale/Photo Researchers)*

a balance between the two positions and has become **individuated** (C. Cooper, Grotevant, and Condon, 1983). The individuated adolescent is still attached to parents but not dependent on them, responsive to parental needs and wishes but autonomous. As we will see, the process of individuation leads to changes in the family.

The Adolescent within the Family

The nature of family relations before puberty has a good deal to do with the way a child experiences adolescence. Communication between parent and child seems to be a key to a healthy adolescence. The better the communication between parent and child, the more positive an adolescent's self-image tends to be (Offer, Ostrov, and Howard, 1982). Good communication seems to reflect a smoothly functioning family system,

one in which parents are able to communicate their values, beliefs, and feelings to their children. Such families are usually characterized by particular styles of parenting.

Parental Style

In recent years, it has become increasingly clear that parental practices can either foster or hinder individuation, self-reliance, and academic achievement. In every aspect of psychosocial development, adolescents from authoritative homes, where parents are responsive and demanding, fare better than their counterparts whose parents use different parental styles. Among the children studied by Diana Baumrind (1986, 1991b), those from authoritative families were least likely to have emotional problems during adolescence or to use drugs (see Chapter 9). Their parents' nurturance, use of reason, and promotion of autonomy seemed to foster individuation. Children from permissive families, where parents are responsive but undemanding, were also individuated but were more likely to use drugs. Children from authoritarian families, where parents are unresponsive but demanding, were less individuated and more likely to have emotional difficulties. Although they used fewer drugs than adolescents from permissive homes, they tended to use more drugs than children from authoritative homes. Children with rejecting-neglecting parents (unresponsive and undemanding) were the least individuated, were the most likely to have emotional and behavioral problems, and had the highest drug use of any group.

Authoritative parenting also seems to promote academic success. Studies indicate that adolescents from authoritative families get higher grades than adolescents from either permissive or authoritarian families (Dornbusch et al., 1987). Authoritative parents accept their children, encourage their autonomy, and exert a high, but not arbitrary, degree of control over their behavior. All three aspects of this parenting style seem to facilitate academic success, primarily because they promote self-reliance, the formation of identity, and a positive work orientation (Steinberg, Elmen, and Mounts, 1989). Adolescents from authoritative families usually have good work skills, want to perform competently at whatever they do, and find pleasure in work.

Any parental practices that emphasize individuation seem to enhance children's academic success (Elmen, 1991). When the parent-child relationship encourages both autonomy and mature attachment, children tend to see themselves as competent in situations outside the family. As we saw in Chapter 10, self-efficacy leads to hard work and perseverance in all aspects of life.

Yet experiences within the peer group can either support or undermine the influence of the authoritative style on academic success (Steinberg, Dornbusch, and Brown, 1992). Anglo and Hispanic adolescents, whose peers support academic achievement, do best when their parents rely on authoritative methods. Parental style seems to have no effect on academic achievement among Asian-Americans, apparently because these students receive such strong social support from peers for academic achievement. Among African-American adolescents, the effects of authoritative parenting may be undermined by the peer group, which is unlikely to support academic achievement. Lawrence Steinberg and his colleagues (1992) found that most African-American adolescents who did well in school tended to affiliate with students from other ethnic groups.

The attitudes and values of the surrounding community may also mediate the effects of parental styles. Despite the success of authoritative parenting in white, middle-class families, it may not work nearly so well with troubled families in lower socioeconomic classes (McLoyd, Ceballo, and Mangelsdorf, 1993). Authoritarian parenting, which provides close supervision, may be more effective than authoritative parenting in preparing African-American adolescents to handle the hazards of life in the inner city (Baldwin, Baldwin, and Cole, 1990; Baumrind, 1991b). To ensure survival on the streets, inner-city parents may also encourage a high level of identification with peers.

Quest for Autonomy

During adolescence, autonomy becomes a prominent issue for the first time since toddlerhood. The adolescent's quest for autonomy is related to individuation and is thus part of the same processes that are involved in the development of identity.

One aspect of autonomy and identity is a distancing from parents. As young adolescents become emotionally detached from their parents, their resistance to peer pressure declines (Steinberg and Silverberg, 1986). Adolescents who are most detached and least dependent on their parents are most likely to succumb to peer pressure—whether the pressure is to leave shoelaces untied, drink Pepsi instead of Coke, smoke, or use drugs. This increased susceptibility to peer pressure may reflect temporary feelings of insecurity and a lack of parental acceptance by the emotionally detached adolescent (Ryan and Lynch, 1989). The result is that many children trade dependence on their parents for a period of dependence on their peers.

Such a shift in influence appeared among a group of more than 800 young adolescents (Krosnick and Judd, 1982). Whether sixth-graders smoked cigarettes was influenced more by their parents' attitudes than by the smoking habits of their peers. If parents thought their children "shouldn't smoke" or if they would be "really mad" if the youngsters smoked, few sixth-graders were likely to smoke. Among eighth-graders, peer influence had become stronger and the effect of parental attitudes weaker, so the example of peers was stronger than that of parents. As we saw in Chapter 10, researchers have found that conformity to peers peaks in the ninth grade, just at the point where this study ends. In Thomas Berndt's (1979) research, conformity to antisocial peer pressure declined during the high school years. Sixteen- and seventeen-year-olds no longer felt so compelled to conform to their peers' wishes. They had begun to accept conventional adult standards for their behavior.

In the quest for autonomy, adolescents tend to become detached from their parents and so become more vulnerable to peer pressure during early adolescence. *(Billy E. Barns/Southern Light)*

Despite conformity to peers on issues of fashion, music, leisure pursuits, and the like, most adolescents adhere to parental values on major issues. This has consistently been true, and researchers at the University of Michigan's Institute for Social Research have found that the attitudes of adolescents and parents seem to have moved even closer over the past fifteen years (see Table 13.1). Their views are closest on the value of education and farthest apart on how to spend money and acceptable dating behavior. Even in matters pertaining to sex, however, adolescents tend to follow their parents' views when they can see the long-term consequences of their actions. Parental beliefs have a heavy impact on whether adolescents use contraceptives, for example, but a smaller impact on their sexual behavior (Baker, Thalberg, and Morrison, 1988).

TABLE 13.1   **HIGH SCHOOL SENIORS' AGREEMENT WITH PARENTS' VIEWS**

Issue	SENIORS AGREEING (%)		
	1975	1985	1990*
What to do with your life	67	72	71
How to dress	63	66	62
How to spend money	48	44	41
What is permitted on a date	41	46	47
Value of an education	82	87	86
Roles for women	61	70	71
Environmental issues	58	53	55
Racial issues	56	63	64
Religion	65	69	68
Politics	49	52	48

*National sample consisted of more than 15,000 seniors.

Source: National Center for Education Statistics, 1988; additional data from Bachman, 1991.

Autonomy may follow a different course of development in girls and boys. Among a group of fifth- to ninth-graders, girls of any age who felt self-reliant found it easiest to resist peer pressure (Steinberg and Silverberg, 1986). But among boys, there was no relation between self-reliance and resistance to peer pressure. A strongly self-reliant boy was as likely to succumb to peer pressure as a boy with little self-reliance. To the researchers' surprise, at every age girls showed more autonomy in peer relationships than boys. They were better at resisting peer pressure (whether it involved cheating on an exam or choosing where to spend the afternoon) and were more self-reliant. Twice as many ninth-grade girls as boys were high in both autonomy and resistance to peer pressure.

Changes in Family Relationships

The adolescent's new body, changing social relationships, and new ability to engage in abstract thought affect the nature of family interactions. More or less compliant children, who saw their parents as wise and powerful dispensers of affection, discipline, and material goods, turn into "almost adults," whose quest for autonomy and lessened emotional dependence leads them to assert their rights, question family rules, and see their parents as imperfect human beings. Parents' responses to these changes in their children's bodies and intellects may reflect the parents' own ambivalence at the realization that their daughter or son is growing up (Hauser et al., 1991). Some tension is inevitable, as new and often unexpected problems and tensions erupt. But continual turmoil is rare. In three out of four families, a child's transition into adolescence, with its accompanying changes in family roles, causes only minor or sporadic conflict (J. Hill, 1985).

Yet puberty seems to be accompanied by a temporary disruption of relationships, characterized by increased conflict with mothers and ineffective attempts by parents to control and discipline children (Anderson, Hetherington, and Clingempeel, 1989). Parents find that their ability to monitor their children's behavior erodes, and they are less aware of their children's activities. Both boys and girls say that their relationships with parents become more distant, although parents often see much less disruption than do children. Children's reports of distance are highly correlated with pubertal maturation, and they may reflect the adolescent's new orientation toward peers as well as hormone-mediated changes in mood (Steinberg, 1988).

Conflicts frequently erupt between adolescent boys and their mothers. The result is often a shift of power within the family. When Laurence Steinberg (1981) followed thirty-one two-parent, middle-class families in which the oldest child was a boy on the brink of puberty, he found that the boy's sexual maturation ushered in mother-son conflict. The pair began interrupting each other in family discussions, and the son became increasingly less deferential to his mother. Eventually, the mother backed off and began to defer to her son. The father retained his dominance over the boy—in fact, the father's power seemed to increase.

In the case of girls, distance between mother and daughter is so highly correlated with pubertal development that some researchers have speculated that either emotional distance accelerates girls' development, that mother-daughter closeness slows it, or that menarche (which has social as well as hormonal influence) affects the relationship (Steinberg, 1988). Whatever explanation is correct, menarche ushers in a period of conflict between mother and daughter. Among the seventh-grade girls in one study, those who recently had begun menstruating saw their mothers as less accepting and the family as stricter and more controlling than did girls who had not yet reached menarche (J. Hill et al., 1985). The girls participated less in family activities, seemed less influenced by their families, and turned to them less often for guidance. Other studies have found that both parents become less effective at monitoring their adolescent daughter's behavior and that mothers—but not fathers—show their daughters less affection (E. Anderson, Hetherington, and Clingempeel, 1989).

However, parent-child conflict seems to peak in early adolescence, just before a youngster enters high school. Then disagreements wane, and relationships steadily become more harmonious. When adolescents report their moods while with family members, using the beeper technique described in the box "The Changing Moods of Adolescents," sixth- to eighth-graders report considerably less happiness than do fifth-graders. But by the ninth grade, time spent with the family becomes as pleasant as it was four years earlier (R. Larson and Richards, 1991). Among seventh- and eighth-graders in another study, issues of school performance, household rules and chores, and adolescent privileges and freedoms dominated family disagreements (R. Richardson et al., 1984). Most of these youngsters said, however, that their parents' disciplinary methods were fair.

Any family discord that accompanies the child's new status tends to occur within a context of general family harmony. The same seventh- and eighth-graders said that they were generally satisfied with family life and

Despite frequent conflicts with parents in early adolescence, most teenagers believe that their parents are patient, supportive, and proud of their offspring. *(Thomas Hopker/Woodfin Camp & Associates)*

enjoyed sharing activities. More than two-thirds of these adolescents felt comfortable discussing with their parents such issues as family relationships, their future goals and aspirations, and their relationships with same-sex peers. However, they drew the line at talking with parents about sexual issues or their relationships with adolescents of the other sex.

Divorce and Remarriage

The course of adolescent-parent relationships that prevails when children grow up with both parents present may not be typical of divorced, mother-headed families. Among middle-class families in one longitudinal study, relationships between divorced mothers and their sons showed no change when the boy entered puberty (Anderson, Hetherington, and Clingempeel, 1989). There was no rise in parent-child conflict and no increase in the boy's failure to comply with the mother's wishes. As the boys matured, the relationship between mother and son often improved. Apparently, the transformation that typifies mother-son relationships in two-parent families at adolescence takes place shortly after the divorce, and the process is not repeated. As we saw in Chapter 10, divorce is generally followed by mother-son conflict and a reduction in the mother's ability to monitor and control her son's behavior.

When the daughter of a divorced mother enters puberty, there may or may not be a resurgence of conflict, but, as is the case in two-parent families, mothers become less effective in monitoring their daughters' behavior (Hetherington et al., 1992). Whether the child is a son or daughter, however, mothers see themselves as more effective in controlling the child's behavior than does the child.

Divorced mothers tend to be permissive parents, granting their adolescent children autonomy much sooner than is the case when both parents are present (Dornbusch and Gray, 1988). Adolescents who live with divorced or single mothers, for example, are much more likely than other adolescents to make their own decisions concerning money, friends, clothes, and how late they can stay out. Autonomy comes early because of the heavy load of responsibility that single parents must bear. When another adult, whether grandparent, aunt, or mother's friend, is part of the household, decision making resembles that found in two-parent families.

When parents continue their conflict after the divorce, their adolescent children may suffer. As we saw in Chapter 10, parental conflict rather than divorce may play a major role in any behavioral problems that arise among children of divorced parents (Barber and Eccles, 1992). High levels of conflict between divorced parents seem to disrupt effective parenting, leading to lax control over adolescents, the tendency to use love withdrawal as a disciplinary technique, and the adolescent's perception that the mother has withdrawn her affection (Fauber et al., 1990). The most important predictor of difficulties is the perception of maternal rejection. Adolescents whose mothers use love withdrawal to control their behavior, making them feel anxiety, guilt, or shame, may internalize their problems, becoming anxious, withdrawn or depressed. Those whose mothers simply stop trying to monitor or supervise their behavior face other risks; they may become involved in aggressive or destructive behavior. The effect of continued parental conflict is particularly strong in boys (Forehand, Long, and Brody, 1988).

Adolescents in single-parent families generally do worse in school than children from two-parent families, and they are more likely to get into trouble with authorities. Much of the difference in school performance and delinquent behavior is probably the result of socioeconomic factors. As we saw in Chapter 10, divorce is usually followed by a sharp drop in a family's standard of living when the custodial parent is the mother—as most are. Yet, at every socioeconomic level, the lack of a second parent seems to increase the risk of trouble, apparently because of early autonomy. When researchers controlled for gender, parental education, income, and ethnicity, the early freedom to make decisions without consulting parents was still associated with low school grades and delinquent behavior—especially in boys (Dornbusch and Gray, 1988). Increases in delinquency may be explained by the fact that young adolescents in single-parent families are more susceptible to antisocial peer pressure than are young adolescents who live with both biological parents (Steinberg, 1987).

Remarriage may seem a way to solve behavior and school problems, but the presence of a stepfather does not seem to reduce the risk. Young adolescents who live with their mothers and stepfathers are about as susceptible to antisocial peer pressure and as likely to get low grades as those who live in single-parent families (Steinberg, 1987). Parenting styles change when mothers of adolescents remarry, but not always for the better. Remarried mothers tend to adopt authoritarian styles, and the stepfathers tend to be disengaged and to adopt the style of the sociable, polite stranger—undemanding but not warm. As a result, the adolescent lives in an ambiguous situation, which may foster emotional detachment (Sessa and Steinberg, 1991).

The effects of divorce or remarriage on adolescent development may differ depending on timing. When the change occurs just before puberty or during early adolescence, the ensuing changes in parent-child relationships may facilitate the development of autonomy (Sessa and Steinberg, 1991). Children realize that parents have other roles and responsibilities besides caring for children, and the youngsters grow up a little sooner than would otherwise have been the case. In any case, these mother-child relationships differ from those in families that have never experienced divorce.

When divorced mothers remarry *before* a boy reaches adolescence, the pattern at first follows that of one-parent families—the mother-son relationship does not change. Then, about a year after the boy enters puberty, the pattern shifts (Anderson, Hetherington, and Clingempeel, 1989). Relationships are disrupted, mother-son conflict erupts, and the boys become unresponsive to parental control. When the mother remarries *after* a boy enters puberty, the adolescent conflict often fails to appear, although boys may be less responsive to their mothers (Vuchinich et al., 1991). Adolescent boys also seem to get along relatively well with their stepfathers.

The pattern for girls in early adolescence is somewhat different. There is not a great deal of conflict, but the girls seem to have difficulty accepting their new stepfathers' overtures. Videotapes of interactions at family dinners indicate that girls tend to be sulky and resistant, to ignore their stepfathers, and to be highly critical (Vuchinich et al., 1991). Girls seem more likely than boys to treat a stepfather as an intruder. In addition, the closer the relationship between the mother and the stepfather, the more behavioral problems girls seem to have. Despite the apparent increase in adjustment problems among divorced and remarried families, some families escape these difficulties, reminding us that factors besides family status are also important (Hetherington et al., 1992).

Maternal Employment

Adolescents whose mothers are employed, and this includes the majority, generally do as well as those whose mothers stay at home. As youngsters spend increasing amounts of time away from the family, they might even find it an advantage to have their mothers in the workplace. Adolescents do not require continual parental supervision and contact; instead, the parental role calls for a relaxation of control and a demonstration of parental confidence and trust. Mothers who are at home all day may be inclined to set rules and offer advice in a way that precipitates family conflict (L. Hoffman, 1979).

Even among mothers in demanding jobs, work-related stress seems to have no effect on the nature of a mother's relationship with her adolescent children. Among young adolescents in a Canadian city, work-related stress in their mothers had no relation to an adolescent's adjustment, conflict between mother and child, or an adolescent's perception of maternal acceptance (Galambos and Maggs, 1990). The researchers speculate that the positive experiences connected with work, including having social contact with other adults, raising the family's standard of living, and feeling productive in a society that undervalues motherhood, contribute to maternal self-esteem and thus buffer the mother, and indirectly her children, from the negative effects of stress—whether from work or from family responsibilities.

Adolescents whose mothers are employed are likely to take responsibility for their own after-school care. Some studies suggest that the prevalence of self-care among young adolescents is a cause for concern. In one study, eighth-grade youngsters who were unsupervised after school were twice as likely as other eighth-graders to use tobacco, alcohol, or marijuana (J. Richardson et al., 1989). When researchers looked more closely at young adolescents in self-care, however, it became evident that adolescents who are required to go home to an empty house are no more likely to get into trouble than those whose mothers (or fathers) are home to greet them (Galambos and Maggs, 1991b).

Among youngsters who take care of themselves at a friend's house or who just "hang out," some children do seem to be at risk. These children may be susceptible to antisocial peer pressure and engage in a range of problem behavior, such as defying parents' orders, committing petty theft, or using drugs. When parents insist on knowing where and how their children spend their afternoons, the chances of trouble are slight. Thus, problem behavior is unlikely among adolescents with authoritative parents who require their children to check in by phone (Steinberg, 1986) (see Figure 13.4). Researchers differ as to whether both sexes are equally at risk or whether the effect is stronger among girls (Galambos and Maggs, 1991a; Steinberg, 1986). Those who believe that girls are at higher risk note that girls tend to date older boys; thus, girls who hang out may be introduced to the peer patterns of older adolescents or young adults.

Figure 13.4 Among latchkey adolescents who are at home or "hanging out" after school, susceptibility to peer pressure is related to the level of parental authoritativeness. Adolescents with highly authoritative parents, who listen to their child's opinions but retain the final say on his or her behavior, are significantly less susceptible to antisocial pressure from their friends than are adolescents whose parents are not authoritative. The effect is especially pronounced among girls. *(From Steinberg, 1986, p. 438)*

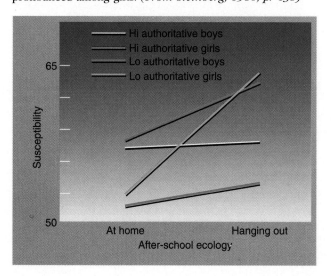

Changes in Friendship and Social Life

Throughout adolescence, friends and peers become increasingly important in a child's life. Their contribution to a youngster's social development may be especially important during early adolescence, when children are coming to terms with the physical and emotional changes in their lives (Crockett, Losoff, and Petersen, 1984). In most cases, this growing attachment to peers does not interfere with teenagers' relationships with their parents; rather, it complements those relationships.

When we consider how much time adolescents spend with their peers, the surprise is that peer influence is not more substantial than studies indicate. Several years ago researchers developed a fairly accurate picture of the company middle-class teenagers keep. In a study similar to the one described in the box "The Changing Moods of Adolescents," high school students reported whom they were with each time their electronic pager beeped (Csikszentmihalyi and Larson, 1984). When time with peers in the classroom (23 percent) and time with peers outside it (29 percent) were added together, it became apparent that the largest portion of most adolescents' waking hours is spent in the company of their contemporaries. Because teenagers are alone with parents for less than 5 percent of their time, with parents and siblings for about 8 percent, and with parents and friends together for another 2 percent, parents seem to have limited opportunities to influence their adolescent children. Girls are exposed to more adult socialization than boys, spending an additional 2½ hours each week talking to adults (usually their parents). Some youngsters spend more time with peers than others. Among the high school students in this study, too much time devoted to peers spelled trouble in other areas of the child's life. Teenagers who were with family more and peers less made better grades in school, were absent less often, and, according to their teachers, were "more intellectually involved" than other youngsters. (The correlation between how adolescents spend their time and whether they go on to college is examined in the accompanying box, "What Teenagers Do All Day.")

Friendships

The nature of friendship changes as the adolescent moves into an intimate relationship that is characterized by mutual sharing (Selman, 1981). Intimate friendships

WHAT TEENAGERS DO ALL DAY

How adolescents spend their spare time—whether they cruise in their cars, go out for sports, watch television, or read books—is related in important ways to the course of their future lives. Each year, researchers connected with Monitoring the Future, a project carried out by the Institute for Social Research at the University of Michigan, ask high school seniors in every part of the country about many aspects of their lives (Bachman, 1991). The accompanying table shows the proportion of high school seniors who engage in selected activities each day, but the important part of the story is how some of these activities correlate with their plans for the future.

About half of high school seniors, whether or not they are college-bound, go to movies at least once or twice a month, for example. But 47 percent of the college-bound, compared with 35 percent of those with no plans for college, go only a few times a year—or never. Similar differences appear in the popularity of cruising. Among seniors with college in their plans, 35 percent say that they never "just ride around" or that they do so no more than once or

twice a month. Among those who have no college plans, only 21 percent ride around less often than once a week.

Some activities are more likely to attract the college-bound than to attract other students. Seniors, especially boys, who have college in their plans are more likely (75 percent) to engage regularly in sports or exercise than seniors with no plans for college (59 percent). The disparity is even greater among those who go out for athletic teams: 55 percent of the college-bound compared with 29 percent of those who have no plans for further education. Seniors headed for college also participate more heavily in other school clubs and activities: 76 percent compared with 50 percent. Another striking difference has to do with time spent reading. Among seniors, 52 percent of the college-bound, but only 38 percent of those with no college plans, read books, magazines, or newspapers almost every day. Similarly, 48 percent of college-bound seniors spend time in creative writing at least once a month, whereas only 30 percent of those with no college plans do so.

LEISURE ACTIVITIES OF HIGH SCHOOL SENIORS*

Activity and Gender	SENIORS PARTICIPATING DAILY (%)		
	1980	1985	1990
Watch television	72	72	72
Males	72	74	74
Females	73	69	70
Read books, magazines, or newspapers	59	51	47
Males	59	50	50
Females	59	52	46
Get together with friends	51	47	49
Males	55	52	52
Females	47	43	45
Participate in sports or exercise	47	43	46
Males	57	53	56
Females	38	34	34
Spend at least 1 hr alone	42	42	41
Males	40	40	40
Females	44	45	42
Ride around for fun	33	35	34
Males	38	39	36
Females	28	31	32
Work around the house, yard, car	40	35	28
Males	39	28	22
Females	49	42	35

*Although participation in most daily activities has remained relatively steady over the past decade, the proportion of high school seniors who read or work around their homes or on their cars each day has dropped sharply.

Source: National Center for Education Statistics, 1988; additional data from Bachman, 1991.

The correlation of high school activities with college plans probably indicates a complex interaction, in which adolescents who intend to go on to college are more likely than others to be interested in certain activities and their participation in those activities is likely to deepen their interest in college. College plans, or the lack of them, are more closely related with such activities as attending movies, cruising, or reading than is gender or ethnicity.

increase sharply between the ages of 12 and 14, perhaps because by then adolescents are equipped for this type of deepening relationship. Their new cognitive powers allow them to take the friend's role, to see the friend's point of view, and to imagine how the friend understands them (see Chapter 14). As Carolyn Shantz (1983) describes the adolescent friendship, it is a mutual relationship in which the friends care for each other, share their thoughts and feelings, and comfort each other. By now the bonds that link friends are tough enough to endure some of the quarrels that rupture the friendships of 9- and 10-year-olds.

Most young adolescents have a close friend in whom they can confide. Among one group of eighth-graders, more than 80 percent said that they had a best friend, and the majority said that the friendship had lasted more than a year (Crockett, Losoff, and Petersen, 1984). Most children had one "best" friend and several "good" friends. They saw them every day at school, and about half visited each other's homes daily, with the rest exchanging visits at least weekly. Eighth-graders lived up to the popular stereotype of the adolescent as a creature with a telephone grafted to one ear while a rock tape blasts in the background. Besides seeing their friends at school and at each other's homes, half the boys and four-fifths of the girls phoned their friends every day. The girls spent more than an hour each day on the phone; about a third talked for at least ninety minutes. Boys were less talkative; they averaged just over thirty minutes a day, with about one in ten spending an hour or more on the phone.

During adolescence, friendships progress from the activity-centered pairs of childhood to interdependent, emotional relationships. At every age, adolescents say that intimacy is greatest with friends of the same sex (Asher and Parker, 1991). Among girls, the emotional deepening occurs more rapidly and is more intense. During middle adolescence, girls want someone to confide in, someone who can offer emotional support and understanding. At this age, a friend must be loyal and trustworthy and must be a reliable source of support in an emotional crisis (Douvan and Adelson, 1966; Steinberg, 1989).

For many mid-adolescent boys, friendships resemble the less intimate relationships of the 11- or 12-year-old girl. Yet boys seem to have as much intimate knowledge about their friends as girls do, and they are as ready to help a friend in trouble. Their method of assistance differs, however. When a boy's friend needs help, the boy is likely to jump in and aid him physically. When a girl's friend needs help, the girl tends to give verbal assistance, explaining what the friend might do (Zeldin, Small, and Savin-Williams, 1982). Given this preference for actions, perhaps boys share secrets about what they have done or plan to do, whereas girls tend to share their feelings as well. Girls' friendships are consistently higher than those of boys on *emotional* self-disclosure (Papini et al., 1990). If we rate the intimacy of a friendship by the level of emotional self-disclosure, boys' friendships are not as intimate as friendships between girls until late adolescence (Buhrmester and Furman, 1987).

Intimacy between friends is related to an adolescent girl's level of adjustment. Among girls in ethnically and racially diverse Los Angeles high schools, those who often shared secrets and private feelings with their friends felt more competent, more sociable, less hostile, and less anxious or depressed and had higher self-

Because girls are more likely than boys to share their feelings with a friend, girls' friendships tend to be more intimate. *(Jim Whitmer)*

esteem than did girls whose friendships lacked emotional self-disclosure (Buhrmester, 1990).

By the age of 17 or 18, girls feel more secure in their own identity and no longer need to identify with an emotional clone. They worry less about loyalty, security, and trust, and many have turned to boys for intimacy. As for older boys, many spend their social lives in cliques and gangs instead of in pairs. This gender difference makes the peer group loom especially large in the life of boys.

The Peer Group

During early adolescence, the structure of the peer group changes. For the first time, youngsters see the group as a community of like-minded people (Hartup, 1983). Now cliques begin to form, characterized by special activities and the firm exclusion of outsiders. The clique's importance increases during early and middle adolescence, apparently because the sense of belonging to a special group bolsters a child's sense of social security and eases the separation from family and the formation of identity (Gavin and Furman, 1989). Cliques may be based on popularity, sports, activities, academics, or wealth, but the most prevalent standard for clique membership is popularity. Thus, cliques are often made up of "average" or "unpopular" adolescents—who may resent the clique of popular youngsters.

What makes a young adolescent popular enough for the ruling clique? Athletic ability seems most important for boys, although by the eighth grade, appearance and personality have become nearly as important. For girls, appearance outweighs all other qualities by eighth grade, with personality running a poor second. Among young adolescents, academic achievement seems to play only a minor role in popularity, but boys see it as a more important aspect of popularity than girls do (Crockett, Losoff, and Petersen, 1984).

Adolescents often deny that their group has a hierarchical formation, but as we saw in Chapter 10, such hierarchies are apparent even among nursery school children. Boys are more willing than girls to admit the existence of dominant leaders, perhaps because their socialization has made them more comfortable with competition and dominance. By late adolescence, the hierarchical structure begins to weaken, and group membership becomes less important (Gavin and Furman, 1989). As we saw earlier, toward the end of high school, peer pressure becomes easier to resist, and conformity decreases.

As friends become increasingly important, older teenagers may find that having individual friendships—whether with their own or the other sex—is more important and gratifying than being one of the gang (Gavin and Furman, 1989). When this happens, older adolescents begin moving from one group to another, perhaps sticking with their clique for "good times" but sharing their personal feelings and problems with a friend or two and seeking out a different group, such as a church group, for serious conversations (Csikszentmihalyi and Larson, 1984). Although most portraits of adolescence lack any indication of young people's religious involvement, more than half of high school seniors say that religion is either "pretty important" or "very important" in their lives (Bachman, 1991) (see Figure 13.5).

Relations with the Other Sex

As they enter puberty, boys and girls already are interested in the other sex. When sixth-graders were asked what they thought about most, about half of the boys said "girls," and somewhat more girls said "boys" (Crockett, Losoff, and Petersen, 1984). By eighth-grade, 80 percent of the girls and about 65 percent of the boys were preoccupied with the other sex. Despite this fascination with the other sex, it is unclear how much early boy-girl interest and interaction is strictly sexual and how much is simply a variation of friendship.

Figure 13.5 After peaking in 1980, religious involvement among high school seniors has declined over the past decade. *(From National Center for Education Statistics, 1988; additional data from Bachman, 1991)*

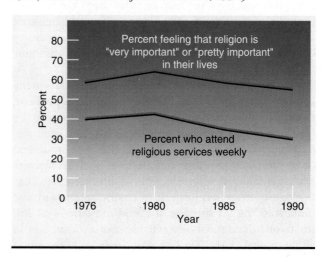

Dating

The age at which formal dating begins varies from one school to another. At first, girls and boys may attend dances and parties in groups. The pairing off, even if prearranged, occurs at the event. This allows young teenagers to avoid the responsibility of dating arrangements and helps reduce their initial anxieties about heterosexual relations. It also spares boys the expense of picking up the tab for admissions and spares both sexes the pain of having parents chauffeur them on a date.

Just how soon adolescents begin group dating seems determined more by the adolescent's peers than by the onset of puberty. As we have seen, early-maturing youngsters are the first to begin dating, but once the majority of their classmates are involved, even those who have not yet entered puberty join in (Petersen, 1985). Girls generally begin dating a year or so before boys, in part because they enter puberty earlier and in part because they often date boys a grade or two ahead of them.

Dating in pairs, also called "going out," generally begins in mid-adolescence. Away from the larger cities, the practice often hinges on the automobile. In a suburban area of Oregon, for example, pair dating takes over when one member of the pair (either the boy or the girl) acquires a driver's license and an available car. This "requirement" anchors the shift from groups to couples at the age of 16, the age at which Oregon adolescents may obtain a driver's license. The girl is almost as likely as the boy to ask for the date, but in most cases the boy still pays for the movies or Big Macs—at least in Oregon.

Long before they start dating, young adolescents believe that having a boyfriend or girlfriend is important. In a national sample, three-quarters said that having a boyfriend (or a girlfriend) was important to them (Offer, Ostrov, and Howard, 1981a). Yet only about a quarter of the young adolescents in another study were dating by the end of the seventh grade, with the proportion climbing to about half within the next year (Crockett, Losoff, and Petersen, 1984).

Sexuality

Girls' childhood and early adolescent socialization generally makes them more competent than boys in interpersonal relationships. So most girls incorporate sexual behavior into a social role and identity that already includes capacities for tenderness and sensitivity. Developmentalists generally assume that, because of their different socialization, boys are interested in sexuality first and only later does the capacity for concerned, tender, and loving sexual relationships develop. In fact, most research indicates that adolescent boys and girls approach sexual choices differently and that girls see the interpersonal relationship as much more important in sexual interactions than do boys (Bollerud, Christopherson, and Frank, 1990; Coles and Stokes, 1985). One high school girl's reflections on her own sexual dilemma exemplify this difference:

I was in love with this guy too, it wasn't a question of did I love him or not. I loved him. And I still didn't know if it was right or wrong. I can't make that decision because with guys my age, 'It's cool, it's great, you should do it definitely.' With my parents, 'No, don't do it.' And like with my friends, some say yes and some no. So I have no one to really look at and ask. . . . Yet, he loves me, but I am not his special love, you know. . . . I had the feeling right there, I thought maybe if I do, I will regret it, but I didn't know if I would. I couldn't—I didn't know what was right. (Bollerud, Christopherson, and Frank, 1990, p. 277)

When a relationship is in its early stages, boys are much more permissive than girls. They see a much wider range of sexual behavior as "proper" to the relationship than do girls, who generally reserve sexual intimacy for relationships in which they feel that they love their partners and are dating no one else. Four times as many boys as girls, for example, believe that sexual intercourse is proper when they feel affection, but not love, for their partners (J. Roche, 1986).

Despite these differences in attitude, the gender gap in sexual intercourse has been decreasing over the past few years. Although the rate of intercourse for boys has increased somewhat, the main source of the narrowing has been the enormous increase in the number of teenage girls who have had sexual intercourse. In 1970, 29 percent of girls between the ages of 15 and 19 had had premarital sexual intercourse. The figure climbed to 42 percent in 1980, and in 1988 the proportion reached 52 percent (Child Trends, 1992). The upswing is due primarily to increases in premarital intercourse among non-Hispanic white females, especially those with moderate or high family incomes (Forrest and Singh, 1990). Boys have traditionally begun having intercourse earlier than girls, and they still do. But by the end of adolescence, the gender gap has closed among whites although not among African-Americans (see Figure 13.6). By age 18, for example, 70 percent of white males have had intercourse, compared with only 56 percent of white females; by age 19, 76 percent of both sexes have had intercourse. Among African-American adolescents, sexual experience begins earlier, but the gender gap remains; at age 19, 79 percent of the females and 96 percent of the males have had intercourse (Child Trends, 1992).

A striking gender difference in the number of sexual partners probably reflects gender differences in attitudes and girls' emphasis on relationships. Among sexually experienced boys between the ages of 15 and 19, nearly as many (27 percent) reported having had six or more partners as reported having had only a single partner (28 percent) (Child Trends, 1990). Among sexually experienced girls, 42 percent have had only a single partner (Forrest and Singh, 1990).

Youngsters who begin sexual activity early tend to be early maturers, and some researchers believe that hormonal factors may be partly responsible. This is more likely to be true for boys, whose level of sexual activity is associated with testosterone levels, than for girls, whose level of sexual interest—but not of sexual activity—is also linked to testosterone levels (Udry, Tal-

bert, and Morris, 1986; Udry et al., 1985). Early-maturing girls tend to have older friends than other girls do, and their parents tend to grant them greater freedom. They also begin dating earlier. These social factors may be as important as hormone levels in the initiation of sexual activity.

When adolescents make their sexual decisions, they are influenced by parents, peers, the media, their religious attitudes and beliefs, their own needs, and their own standards. Parents have some effect on sexual behavior. When parents keep tabs on their children and supervise their children's activities, sexual activity tends to be delayed (Brooks-Gunn and Furstenberg, 1989). Communication between adolescents and parents also seems important, with poor communication associated with early sexual activity. The actual effect may, however, depend on the gender of parent and adolescent. In one study, sexual activity began relatively late among girls and boys who could talk freely with their mothers (Kahn, Smith, and Roberts, 1984). But boys who talked freely with their fathers tended to initiate sexual activity fairly early, perhaps because fathers may tend to condone sexual activity in their sons. Living with a single parent also seems to hasten the onset of sexual activity— but only among girls (Newcomer and Udry, 1987). It is

Figure 13.6 Adolescent sexual activity by gender and age. The proportion of adolescents who have premarital sexual intercourse before any given birthday has increased steadily over the past twenty-five years, with the traditional gender gap disappearing among white teenagers by the end of adolescence. Comparable data are not available for Hispanics. *(Data from Child Trends, 1992)*

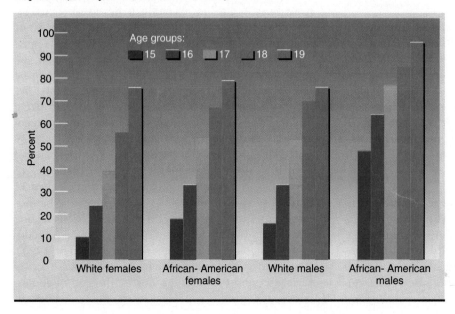

The sexual decisions of adolescents reflect the influence of parents, peers, media, religious beliefs, and the adolescents' own needs and standards. *(Frank Siteman/Stock, Boston)*

we tend to forget two things. First, teenagers may have a first intercourse at the age of 14 or 15 and then wait a year or two before they engage in sexual activity again (Brooks-Gunn and Furstenberg, 1989). Second, by the age of 18, a large minority of adolescents have never "gone all the way." Some are "technical virgins," who engage in extremely heavy petting and have avoided only one sexual experience—vaginal intercourse. Many of these youngsters see intercourse as sacred and powerful—an experience that should be reserved for a deeply committed relationship. Others see premarital intercourse as ill-advised, stupid, or immoral (Rosen and Hall, 1984).

Society has come to see some form of adolescent sexual experimentation as normal. The threat of AIDS has, however, led to rising concern over adolescents who have multiple partners. Reports from the Federal Centers for Disease Control indicate that 19 percent of all American high school students have had at least four sex partners, with the figure rising to 29 percent among high school seniors. Because AIDS can take up to ten years to develop, many of the cases that are diagnosed among young people in their twenties were contracted during the adolescent years. Yet fewer than half of sexually active adolescents are practicing "safe sex" ("Teenagers and AIDS," 1992). Such high-risk sexual behavior may be related in part to the adolescent's conviction that he or she is indestructible, a characteristic of adolescent thought that we will examine in Chapter 14. Apprehension over the spread of AIDS has led many parents and schools to swing from forbidding sexuality to preventing AIDS and pregnancy. In a survey of more than 1000 Americans, 83 percent urged teaching 12-year-olds about AIDS, and 84 percent said that school health clinics should make birth-control information available ("How the Public Feels," 1986). In Chapter 15, we examine the problem of teenage pregnancy.

uncertain whether early sexual activity among these girls results from the permissive discipline that more often characterizes single-parent families or stems from the single or divorced parent's likelihood to date and thus serve as a role model for a daughter's sexual activity.

Finally, an adolescent's academic achievement and educational plans also are linked to sexual activity. Poor grades and low educational aspirations are associated with early sexual activity, whereas academic success and college plans are associated with late sexual activity (Brooks-Gunn and Furstenberg, 1989).

Adolescents are not promiscuous. Most strongly reject casual, indiscriminate sexual activity in favor of committed, caring relationships. When looking at the number of teenagers who are having sexual intercourse,

Homosexual Activity

Some amount of homosexual activity is fairly common among young people before, during, and after the onset of puberty, although researchers are uncertain as to just how common the experience is (Savin-Williams, 1991). Pioneering studies by Alfred Kinsey and his associates (Kinsey, Pomeroy, and Martin, 1948; Kinsey et al., 1953) indicated that 27 percent of adolescent males and 5 percent of adolescent females had some homosexual contact by the age of 15, but there is no consensus concerning present levels of homosexual activity among adolescents. Kinsey concluded that many people's gender orientation could not be labeled. He discovered that sexual behavior fell along a broad continuum, with people at one end of the scale being exclusively heterosexual in both sexual fantasies and behavior and those at the other end being exclusively homosexual. The rest showed varying amounts of homosexual and heterosexual interest and activity.

The majority of adolescents who have homosexual experiences regard themselves as heterosexual and incorporate a heterosexual gender orientation into their identity. By early adolescence, however, some boys and girls already have developed a homosexual gender orientation. Although those who regard themselves as homosexual are more likely than other adolescents to engage in homosexual behavior, many gay and lesbian adolescents have no homosexual activity during adolescence. This difference is easier to understand if we separate homosexual behavior from homosexuality. Having a stimulating sexual experience with a person of one's own gender (sexual behavior) and developing an enduring homosexual gender orientation (preponderance of sexual feelings, erotic thoughts, fantasies and/or behavior directed toward members of one's own sex) may be unrelated (Savin-Williams, 1991).

The openness with which homosexuality is expressed and its choice as a life style is influenced by its social acceptance. Although many studies of adolescent homosexuality focus on feelings of isolation, alienation, and confusion that sometimes accompany it, the extent to which homosexuality is a source of disturbance depends on how society and the adolescent's immediate social group respond to it (Savin-Williams, 1991). Studies of gay and lesbian adolescents indicate that most are psychologically and socially healthy. In one study (Boxer, 1988), negative feelings about homosexual orientation were uncommon: 20 percent of the boys and 30 percent of the girls reported negative feelings when they realized they were attracted to members of their own sex; among those who had engaged in homosexual activity, 25 percent of the boys and only 15 percent of the girls reported similar feelings. For many, any conflict may be slight, and they tend to handle their awareness of homosexual feelings in a positive manner. A 17-year-old lesbian described her feelings:

I never went through a thing like, 'These feelings I have are gay feelings, so I better go talk to somebody like a shrink about them.' I always thought that it was natural. I just followed my feelings and went along with them, and everything was fine. (R. Bell, 1980, p. 114)

The Adolescent as Worker

Working at a job is a normal part of growing up in the United States. By the time they graduate from high school, most adolescents have had formal work experience. At any one time, more than 60 percent of boys and girls between the ages of 16 and 18 are employed (Mortimer et al., 1990), and among high school seniors in 1990, 77 percent had regular jobs (Bachman, 1991). Typical adolescent jobs do not, however, help most adolescents resolve an identity crisis, because these jobs rarely give the adolescent an opportunity to explore viable options. Peers usually predominate in the adolescent's working environment, so it may function simply as an extension of high school (Greenberger and Steinberg, 1986). Thus, although occupational decisions are a major part of a person's identity, only within the past few years have researchers begun studying the effects of adolescent employment on a young person's personality and future as a worker.

Young people begin working for pay outside their homes early. Among children in a national sample, about 50 percent of the 11-year-olds were earning at least part of their own money, with boys working, on the average, just under 6 hours per week and girls working 3½ hours (Yamoor and Mortimer, 1990). Most of the jobs were informal; 11-year-olds baby-sat, did yard work, and the like. In the early 1980s boys were more likely than girls to have some kind of formal employment, but among ninth-graders in St. Paul, Minnesota, girls now begin working earlier than boys (Mortimer et al., 1990). Recent studies have found few or no gender differences in employment rates among 16- to 18-year-olds (Bachman, 1991; Mortimer et al., 1990).

Gender differences in occupational plans are also disappearing. Girls used to see a future as full-time homemakers, but recent studies indicate that less than 25 percent of girls now see a life without paid employment (Ireson and Gill, 1988). Most girls, like boys, expect a combination of work, marriage, and parenthood, and today's adolescent girls have higher vocational aspirations than do boys. Part of the change may be the result of shifts in the portrayal of women on prime-time television. When fifth- and sixth-grade girls were asked about occupations they might encounter in life or on television, it became apparent that girls now saw such traditionally male occupations as police officer, lawyer, or private detective as open to women, and many expressed a high personal interest in entering these occupations (Wroblewski and Huston, 1987).

Although gender differences are narrowing, there are

still socioeconomic and ethnic differences in employment rates. Among high school seniors, 81 percent of whites and 63 percent of African-Americans work regularly (Bachman, 1991). This ethnic difference may arise in part from the fact that in the United States, teenage employment is concentrated in the middle class (Greenberger and Steinberg, 1986). Middle-class, white, native-born Americans believe that boys and girls should begin working at an early age (Mortimer et al., 1990). Middle-class parents are also likely to have contacts within the establishment that provide their children with an opportunity to work.

Although girls' and boys' first jobs are comparable in respect to their complexity, girls are more likely to work at informal jobs (such as baby-sitting), whereas boys are more likely to work as newspaper deliverers, as busboys in restaurants, or as laborers. There is also a marked gender difference in earnings: the average hourly rate paid to girls ($2.87) is only 60 percent of that paid to boys ($4.76). Girls, however, perceive their jobs more positively than do boys. Girls are more likely than boys to see their jobs as allowing innovative thinking, providing variety, and helping them to develop job skills that will benefit them in the future. In light of these perceptions, the work experience of young adolescent girls seems to be at least as likely to promote psychological well-being and vocational development as that of young adolescent boys (Mortimer et al., 1990).

Early studies showed that work experience enhanced the subsequent development of boys who were employed during the Great Depression of the 1930s (G. H. Elder, 1974). These boys were more responsible, more industrious, and showed greater social independence than boys who did not work. Later research supported the notion that working tends to increase youngsters' responsibility on the job, but these studies indicated that girls profited more from the experience (Steinberg et al., 1982). Girls, but not boys, became more self-reliant, more interested in jobs that allowed them to make decisions, and more likely to want additional education.

No matter how salutary its effect on personal development, however, too much work can interfere with an adolescent's commitment to school (Hamilton and Powers, 1990). Some researchers believe that among adolescents who work more than ten hours each week, employment may have more negative consequences than is generally supposed (Greenberger and Steinberg, 1986; Steinberg and Dornbusch, 1991). In a study of 4000 adolescents, those who worked longer hours had lower grades, used more drugs and alcohol, had higher

Adolescents who work long hours tend to get lower grades and use more drugs and alcohol than those who work only a few hours per week. *(Peter Glass/Monkmeyer)*

rates of delinquency, and were freer from parental supervision than those who did not work. As working hours increased, the negative effects grew stronger.

Among high school students in Orange County, California, working seemed to undermine adolescents' adherence to the work ethic, with employed adolescents tending to agree that "anyone who works harder than he or she has to is a little bit crazy" (Greenberger and Steinberg, 1986; Steinberg et al., 1982). Those who were from white-collar families also tended to accept unethical behavior on the job. There were, however, omissions in this research that may have affected the conclusions; students in school-sponsored work experiences and those who were working in a family business were excluded (Steinberg, 1984). Later research with seniors at a predominantly middle-class high school suggests that some concerns may be exaggerated (Green, 1990). When asked to relate their jobs or their decisions to the social context of employment, these older adolescents upheld the work ethic and interpreted their employment within the framework of middle-class values.

Among working-class senior girls in upstate New York, most saw their early work experience as beneficial (Hamilton and Powers, 1990). More than 60 percent said that they had gained a greater sense of responsibility, and almost 50 percent said that work had enhanced their social development. Working had, they said, made them more outgoing and less withdrawn; it had taught them how to tolerate, cooperate with, and deal more effectively with people of different backgrounds. Working had also given them the skills they needed to succeed in the workplace and had made them feel more like adults.

Today's teenagers earn substantial sums of money at their jobs. Among high school seniors, 32 percent work more than twenty hours each week, and the same proportion have a weekly income in excess of $75. Another 16 percent earn between $51 and $75 per week, and an additional 10 percent earn between $36 and $50. Most teenagers are conspicuous consumers who spend their earnings on themselves. Only half of seniors who work save any money at all for their future education or any long-range purpose other than buying a car, and less than 9 percent put aside at least half of their earnings for their education. Nor does much of their money go toward family living expenses (Bachman, 1991). Cars absorb much of their money, with 32 percent of the boys and 23 percent of the girls earmarking from half to all of their income for a car or its accompanying expenses. Jerald Bachman (1983) has suggested that this **premature affluence** on the part of high school students with large sums of spending money may not be a good thing. Students get used to spending for luxuries at a level that they will not be able to sustain when they begin to pay for their own food, rent, utilities, and other necessities.

Among high school seniors, African-Americans are more likely than whites to help out at home. Whereas about 63 percent of whites contribute nothing to family expenses, only 36 percent of African-Americans keep all their money for themselves. In fact, 20 percent of African-Americans but only 6 percent of whites contribute at least half of their earnings to their families (Bachman, 1991). This ethnic difference is consistent with other research indicating that African-Americans provide more economic support to their families than do whites (Stack, 1974). The ability to depend on offspring for financial assistance is reflected in survey replies of married couples and older adults, with African-Americans consistently more likely than whites to say that

children will help out in old age or in case of financial need (L. Hoffman and Manis, 1979; L. Hoffman, McManus, and Brackbill, 1987).

When times are hard, white adolescents also have come through for the family. Among boys who were adolescent workers during the Great Depression of the 1930s, sons of unemployed fathers gave most of their money to their families (G. H. Elder, 1974). A similar effect occurred among Iowa farm families during the depression of the 1980s, when employed adolescents also contributed their earnings to the family (Conger and Elder, in press). Although unemployment during a recession is usually transient, it may have lasting effects on adolescents (Flanagan, 1990). Adolescents whose parents were temporarily laid off during the 1980s tended to see their future options as limited. Many switched their aspirations from college to vocational training. Family financial pressures had an even stronger negative effect on girls' aspirations than on those of boys.

For adolescents who go on to college, the low-skill, low-paying jobs with little or no advancement that are characteristic of the youth market are merely a way to earn spending money. They anticipate a career after college. But adolescents who move directly into the full-time job market often find themselves continuing at the same job they worked at part time while in high school (Hamilton and Powers, 1990). Their hopes for a rewarding work life may vanish when they discover that after several months they have exhausted the possibilities of the jobs that are open to them. Although within a few years many find a more challenging occupation, as we will see in Chapter 16, whether a young person goes to college may be one of the primary determinants of later adult life.

More young people might overcome the barriers that keep them from high-quality jobs if U.S. society treated the workplace as a valuable learning environment, according to Stephen Hamilton (1990). On the basis of his research in Germany, Hamilton suggested that adapting elements of the apprenticeship system used there might overcome the barriers that stand between the 18-year-old high school graduate and improved job prospects. In Germany, experience-based career education, community service, and mentoring from older, experienced workers are incorporated in a system that fosters the transition from school to a satisfying occupation.

As we have seen, the biological changes of puberty usher in changes in every aspect of the adolescent's social and emotional life. In the next chapter, we will see that similar far-reaching changes are apparent in adolescent cognition.

BIOLOGICAL CHANGES

Puberty, the lengthy series of interrelated biological processes that change an immature child into a sexually mature person, begins when the hypothalamus signals the pituitary gland to start producing adult levels of hormones. In response, girls' **ovaries** begin to secrete **estrogens** and boys' **testes** to secret **androgens,** and the transformation begins. Because pubertal events do not all proceed at the same pace, puberty is characterized by **asynchrony** in growth rates.

Menarche is usually taken as an indication of sexual maturity, although about half of adolescent girls remain infertile for a year or two afterward. Sperm can be detected in a boy's urine by the age of 12 or 13. Youngsters' reaction to puberty depends on their feelings about sexuality, reactions of others to their changed appearance, and cultural standards. Adolescents quickly learn the characteristics of the culture's **body ideal,** and deviations from this ideal influence self-concept and self-esteem. Boys who mature early tend to be highly popular, but among girls, late maturers are popular leaders. The long-term psychological effects of pubertal timing may favor late maturers among the boys. Early maturers among the girls seem to profit, with one major exception—the early-maturing girl is less likely to go on to college.

CHANGES IN THE SELF: IDENTITY

Establishing an **identity** is a major developmental task of adolescence. A teenager's identity status may be one of **foreclosure,** of **moratorium,** of **identity achievement,** or of **identity diffusion.** Many contemporary Western cultures tend to favor the adolescent who goes through a moratorium period, which may last until young adulthood. Traditional gender differences in the process of identity formation may be narrowing as an increasing proportion of girls focus on achievement as well as on interpersonal relationships. Foreclosure is more common among minority adolescents than among white adolescents. Minority adolescents must also come to terms with their **ethnic identity. Individuated** adolescents are autonomous but still attached to their parents.

THE ADOLESCENT WITHIN THE FAMILY

Parental style affects adolescent development, with youngsters from authoritative families most likely to be individuated and least likely to have emotional or drug problems. Adolescents from rejecting-neglecting families are least likely to be individuated and most likely to have problems. Among families in lower socioeconomic classes and African-American families in the inner city, authoritarian parenting may be more successful than authoritative parenting, but this is not yet clear.

As adolescents develop autonomy, they tend to become emotionally detached from their parents and their resistance to peer pressure may decline. Most adolescents, however, hold to parental values on major issues. The nature of family life changes as adolescents move toward a more nearly peerlike relationship with their parents. Conflict between boys and their mothers may increase the adolescent boy's power in the family. Conflict between girls and their mothers may lead to emotional distance. In any case, parent-child conflict tends to peak in early adolescence.

The rise in mother-son conflict may be absent in divorced families, perhaps because boys' relationships with their mothers undergo a transformation after the divorce. Divorced mothers tend to be permissive, granting early autonomy. Early autonomy may be followed by declines in school grades and heightened risk of delinquent behavior. Remarriage does not seem to reduce the risks. Adolescents whose mothers are employed tend to take responsibility for their own after-school care, but as long as youngsters are required to go home or to check in with working parents, this latchkey status does not seem to heighten risks.

CHANGES IN FRIENDSHIP AND SOCIAL LIFE

During adolescence, friendships tend to become intimate, mutual relationships. Girls' friendships tend to be more intimate and higher on emotional self-disclosure than friendships between boys. Cliques become increasingly important during early adolescence; by late adolescence, group membership becomes less important.

There is a gender difference in the approach to sexuality, with girls seeing the interpersonal relationship as much more important than boys see it. In the early stages of a relationship, boys are more permissive than girls. Although boys tend to begin having intercourse at an earlier age than girls, the gender gap has shrunk dramatically over the past twenty years. Early maturers tend to be among the first to begin sexual activity, but parental supervision, communication within the family, and educational plans influence the teenager's sexual decisions. Many adolescents have homosexual experiences, but most develop a heterosexual gender identity. Important influences on the gay or lesbian adolescent's feelings about his or her sexual identity are the responses of society and of the adolescent's social group toward homosexuality.

THE ADOLESCENT AS WORKER

By high school graduation, most adolescents have formal work experience. Gender differences in occupational plans are disappearing, and girls tend to have higher vocational aspirations than boys. Most of today's working adolescents spend nearly all their money on themselves and are characterized by **premature affluence.** African-American adolescents, however, tend to contribute to family expenses. Work experience during hard times, when most adolescents contribute to family expenses, seems to enhance development. Employment may have negative effects on adolescents who work long hours. Adolescents who do not go on to college may find themselves stuck in low-skill, low-paying jobs after graduation.

KEY TERMS

androgens	identity	moratorium
asynchrony	identity achievement	ovaries
body ideal	identity diffusion	premature affluence
estrogens	individuated	puberty
ethnic identity	menarche	testes
foreclosure		

• • • • • • • • • • • • • •

ADOLESCENCE: COGNITIVE CHANGES

ADOLESCENCE: COGNITIVE CHANGES

● ● ● ● ● ● ● ● ● ● ● ● ●

Twelve-year-old Louis had been blind since he was 3. He was a student at a school for the blind in Paris, where he studied grammar, geography, history, arithmetic, and music in the mornings and learned a trade in the afternoons. But in 1820 the only way for blind people to read was by using their fingers to trace the shapes of 3-inch-high raised letters. It was a laborious process: the letters were easily confused and so large that only a few would fit on a page. Books made in this fashion were rare because they were so expensive to produce. Then Louis learned about a system of raised dots that was used by soldiers to send messages in the dark. To his sorrow, he discovered that the system was clumsy and crude, and it was so complicated that some words required almost a hundred dots. Nevertheless, Louis was determined. For three years he spent all his free time working on the system, using a sharp awl to punch raised dots on heavy paper. Nothing seemed to work. Then one day he had a sudden inspiration. He decided to switch from a system based on language sounds to one based on the alphabet.

Using a cell of six numbered dots, he devised a simple, logical pattern for representing all the letters. At the age of 15, Louis had solved a problem that had baffled people for centuries (Davidson, 1971). He had invented a method of writing that was easy for the blind to learn and that would make it possible to produce inexpensive books written in that system. The six-dot cells could also be used for numbers and musical notes. They could represent English or Spanish or Italian as easily as they represented French. The new system, called Braille, after its inventor, opened the world of written communication to the blind. The example of Louis Braille convincingly demonstrates that some adolescents have highly developed cognitive skills as well as the motivation required to make significant contributions to society.

● ● ● ● ● ●

In this chapter, we trace the developments in reasoning and thinking that distinguish adolescents from children, and we see how these cognitive changes affect various areas of life. We begin by briefly comparing the abstract thought of the adolescent with the concrete thought of the child. Then we examine Piaget's view of adolescent thought and the development of formal reasoning. Social cognition among adolescents, we find, changes in part because of new cognitive capacities and in part because of experiences. We then turn to practical intelligence, investigating changes in the way that adolescents solve problems, plan for the future, and make decisions. Next we investigate the possible bases for the changes in reasoning and problem solving: brain development, hormonal changes of puberty, and social and educational experiences. The chapter closes with a discussion of schooling, focusing on the effect of the transition to junior high school, changes in the adolescent's achievement motivation, and the role played by the expectations and beliefs of other people.

The Development of Abstract Reasoning

Adolescence ushers in a change in thinking that develops so unobtrusively that it may escape notice. This new way of thinking includes a number of separate skills that began to develop a few years earlier but at first could be used only in isolation (Neimark, 1982). Not until adolescence do the skills become coordinated so that the child can apply them generally. When this happens, for the first time children are able to deal with the realm of the possible, the hypothetical, the future, the remote. This new ability allows young people to see the world and the people in it, including themselves, in a different way. They speculate about what *might be* instead of accepting *what is*. Such changes affect their scientific reasoning, their grasp of society, and their understanding of other people (see Table 14.1).

Thinking about Possibilities

Although older children can see beyond minor changes in appearance and their thought no longer is captured by a single aspect of a problem, they are essentially limited to thinking about what *is*. Adolescents, in contrast, can think about possible outcomes before they happen or about situations they have never encountered. Because adolescents are not bound by the limits of their experience, they can imagine other ways of organizing the world and their own society. Adolescents can ask "What if?": What if I were as easy-going as Sandy? What if people lived forever? What if the world ran out of fossil fuels? What if the Confederacy had won the Civil War? They can then think about the implications of such possibilities in a systematic manner. Many children, of course, have vivid imaginations, but they approach problems the other way around. Instead of seeing reality as a portion of the much wider world of possibility, as adolescents do, they begin with their feet firmly grounded in reality. Only then can they move away, gingerly and in an inconsistent manner, from this safe, secure foundation to possibility (Flavell, 1985).

Thinking Abstractly

Until they are 11 or 12 years old, children think about their present situation and the concrete events in it. As they develop the ability to generate possibilities freely and systematically, adolescents begin to muse about the future and consider abstract concepts and ideas. They think about education, morality, religion,

TABLE 14.1   **THOUGHT IN CHILDHOOD AND ADOLESCENCE**

	Child	Adolescent
Possibilities	Is limited to what is	Considers possibilities
Abstractions	Is limited to present	Considers abstract concepts and ideas
Recursive thinking	May understand simple one-loop recursions	Understands complex recursions and applies this knowledge in formulating acts
Problem solving	Relies on haphazard testing or rigid approaches	Engages in planned testing of hypotheses
Perspective taking	Focuses on own view	Considers perspective of others

The ability to think in abstract terms leads some adolescents to participate in activities that advance their ideals. *(Jeff Isaac Greenberg/Photo Researchers)*

lescent thought in a dramatic fashion. In a classic experiment, researchers demonstrated this striking difference between the thought of children and that of adolescents (Osherson and Markman, 1975). Researchers picked up a poker chip, held it so that a youngster could see it, and said, "Either the chip in my hand is red *or* it is not red." When the chip was red, 10-year-olds invariably said "true"; however, when the chip was blue, they said "false." (If the chip was hidden from view, the 10-year-olds said, "I can't tell.") Adolescents, who know that the question has nothing to do with the color of the chips but everything to do with the logic of the statement, say "true" no matter what color chip they see in the researcher's hands. Similarly, if the researcher conceals a chip and says, "The chip in my hand is red *and* it is not red," the child responds to a perceived demand for the color of the concealed chip and says, "I can't tell." The adolescent responds to the logic of the statement and says "false."

justice, and truth—even about the nature of existence itself (R. Siegler, 1991). The contradictions and apparent hypocrisy they now detect in the world often lead them to argue for ideals and to enlist in causes. The clarification of values and attitudes that follows from abstract reasoning is part of the identity process discussed in Chapter 13.

Thinking through Hypotheses

Faced with a problem, children consider alternatives in a haphazard fashion, omitting some possible solutions and sticking rigidly to others that are clearly unproductive. They have to "try and see" if a solution will work. Adolescents can use logical reasoning to solve problems in a new way; they can pose hypotheses and test them in a systematic fashion. Because they are not tied to the specific situation before them, they can translate the problem into images, propositions, or some other mental representations (Bullinger and Chatillon, 1983). Using deduction and induction, they can then reason from premises to conclusions in a logical manner.

The ability to separate form from content frees ado-

Thinking about Thinking

Another important cognitive change is adolescents' ability to think about their own thoughts, an ability that reflects a sophisticated level of metacognition. Most adolescents understand the recursive nature of thought, as did the adolescent who remarked, "I found myself thinking about my future, and then I began to think about why I was thinking about my future." About half of 12-year-olds can understand one-loop recursions ("The boy is thinking that the girl is thinking of him"), but only a handful can understand two-loop recursions ("The boy is thinking that the girl is thinking of him thinking of her"). The ability to think recursively rises steadily across adolescence, so mentions of recursive thought occur frequently in 16-year-olds' conversations ("I didn't realize you thought I really meant it when I said that") (Flavell, 1985).

Once adolescents begin to think recursively, they become aware that other people may be thinking about the adolescent's intentions. This sort of recursive awareness enables adolescents to act deliberately in order to disguise their own intentions or to lead others to misinterpret their intentions (Shultz, 1980). Such actions demonstrate the ability to think about others' thoughts, an important aspect of social cognition and one that is related to the ability to take another person's point of view.

Considering the Perspective of Others

Adolescents' new command of thought allows them to explain another person's point of view. Since they were about 5 years old, they have understood that other people's interests, knowledge, and motivation are different from their own, as we saw in Chapter 11. In this sense, they are not egocentric. As yet, however, they do not understand how one person's perspective can affect the perspective of another. The important advance in adolescent thinking is the advance in the ability to explain and assume the psychological viewpoint of others. This allows adolescents to understand how others see them and also to understand that when other people reflect on the adolescent's actions and intentions, their views of the adolescent may change (Selman, 1976, 1980).

This expansion of cognitive powers may, however, enmesh adolescents in a different kind of egocentrism. According to David Elkind (1985), adolescents who can infer what other people are thinking tend to focus their inferences on what other people are thinking *about them.* This new egocentrism is a feature of early adolescence. By the time youngsters are 15 or 16, it is already on the wane. While it lasts, adolescents tend to think in terms of what Elkind calls the "imaginary audience" and to believe in the "personal fable."

The term **imaginary audience** refers to the adolescent's belief that other people share the adolescent's own preoccupation with himself or herself and hence are always noticing the young person's appearance, behavior, and actions. Continually onstage for the imaginary audience, the adolescent becomes highly self-conscious. The audience is one that the adolescent creates in his or her head—an accomplishment that is beyond the younger child. When combing his hair in front of a mirror, for example, the 14-year-old boy is more concerned with how his peers will admire him than with his own satisfaction in his appearance (Elkind, 1985).

The term **personal fable** refers to the adolescent's feeling that he or she is personally indestructible and unique. The teenager's feeling of indestructibility is reflected in the complaint by the exasperated mother of a 15-year-old:

As far as he is concerned, he can guzzle two six packs without getting drunk, he can drive a car without a lesson or a license, he can fly without wings. He probably feels that he could smoke, *snort, sniff, inhale, swallow, or inject any substance at all without overdosing, becoming an addict, or losing his grip. . . . His response to everything is: "I know. I know!"* (Karsh, 1987, p. 23)

The personal fable may play a role in adolescent pregnancies, for as we will see in Chapter 15, teenage girls are convinced that others may become pregnant but they never will.

The adolescent's uniqueness leads to the belief that his or her views and feelings are totally different from those of others. In fact, no one has ever experienced the world in the way that he or she is experiencing it (Harter, 1983). No one has ever loved as deeply, hurt as badly, or seen others' motivations with such clarity as the young adolescent. Most parents are familiar with their teenager's lament, "But you don't know how it feels."

Elkind believes that adolescent egocentrism is the result of the youngster's beginning grasp of abstract, scientific thought, but other researchers have questioned this explanation. Some studies have found that young adolescents who understand abstract thought are actually less preoccupied with the imaginary audience than those who do not (Gray and Hudson, 1984; Riley, Adams, and Nielsen, 1984), while others have found no consistent correlation between adolescent egocentrism and abstract, scientific thought among sixth- to twelfth-graders (Lapsley et al., 1986). Because this kind of egocentric thinking seems to decline about midway through adolescence, it may reflect the stage of mutual role-taking, which many children enter before they understand abstract, scientific thought (Lapsley and Murphy, 1985). In this view, as children pass into the most advanced stage of role-taking, which we will explore in our discussion of social cognition, the imaginary audience loses its power, and the personal fable crumbles.

Adolescent egocentrism may also reflect the adolescent's search for identity, as discussed in Chapter 13. In one study, there was no connection between abstract thought and egocentrism; instead, belief in the imaginary audience and in the personal fable was highest among adolescents who either (1) had achieved a personal identity and were pursuing occupational and ideological goals or (2) were in a state of moratorium and struggling with issues of identity (O'Connor and Nikolic, 1990). If identity is the crucial factor, then preoccupations with others' impressions and the invincibil-

Teenagers who engage in dangerous activities are demonstrating their belief in the personal fable of indestructibility. *(Richard Hutchings/Photo Researchers)*

ity of the self are aspects of social and personality development.

Piaget's Theory and the Period of Formal Operations

Piaget (1952) described the ability to deal with abstractions and logical possibilities as the stage of formal operations, and he regarded it as the culmination of cognitive development. Most of Piaget's explorations of **formal-operational thought** focused on scientific reasoning, in which children solved problems that required them to explain such concepts as force, inertia, and acceleration. When asked to account for some physical effect, a youngster who has acquired formal thought can isolate elements of the problem and systematically

explore all possible solutions. By contrast, a concrete-operational child is likely to forget to test some solutions and to keep testing other solutions that have failed. The differences between these problem-solving approaches become clear when we look at the pendulum experiment, which was conducted by Bärbel Inhelder and Piaget (1958).

The two investigators gave youngsters strings of different lengths and objects of different weights, which a child could attach to a rod so that they swung like pendulums (see Figure 14.1). Each of the pendulums swung through its arc at a different speed. The child's task was to determine the factor or factors that accounted for the speed of the pendulum's swing. The four possible causes are (1) the weight of the object, (2) the length of the string, (3) the height from which the object is released, and (4) the force of the initial push. Only the length of the string affects the speed of the pendulum. A child can discover this fact either by methodically try-

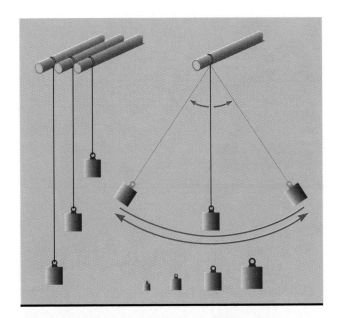

Figure 14.1 Piaget's pendulum problem. The child is given a set of weights *(bottom)* and a string that can be shortened or lengthened *(left)*. The task is to determine which factor or factors account for the speed with which a pendulum traverses its arc. *(After Inhelder and Piaget, 1958)*

ing all possible combinations of factors (varying a single factor on each trial) or by imagining trials of all possible combinations. Either method, believed Piaget, required formal operations.

Among the children tested by Inhelder and Piaget, only 14- and 15-year-olds were able to solve the problem by themselves. The youngest children, who were apparently at the preoperational stage, went about the problem unsystematically. They could not vary the factors separately, and none of their trials could convince them that their own initial push was unrelated to the pendulum's speed. The 8- to 13-year-olds, who were apparently in the concrete-operational stage, varied some of the factors but found it difficult to exclude any of them. They discovered that the length of the string had something to do with the solution but did not understand that it was the only factor involved. The 14- and 15-year-olds, who apparently were in the formal-operational period, anticipated all possible combinations, tested them experimentally, and deduced that the string's length affected the pendulum's speed *and* that all other factors were irrelevant.

The abstract, scientific thought of formal operations develops slowly during adolescence; in one study, only 32 percent of 15-year-olds and 34 percent of 18-year-

olds used formal operations to solve a problem (Blasi and Hoeffel, 1974). Most 13-year-olds, who are on the threshold of formal thought, can reason about a hypothetical situation only if it is one that allows them to use real-world knowledge to generate possibilities (Markovits and Vachon, 1990). They may be able to use formal thought in some situations but not in others. Gradually, adolescents become more at home with abstractions, but even when formal reasoning appears, its development is not complete before late adolescence.

There are wide individual differences in the speed with which formal operations develop, and their development can be generally fostered or hindered by the social environment (Piaget, 1972). Most studies indicate that the emergence of formal operations depends on experience in formal education. Yet some people in societies without formal schooling develop abstract thought. They can reason abstractly and systematically about familiar situations and events that have meaning in their cultures (Cole and Scribner, 1974). Nor is formal thought an all-or-nothing accomplishment. People often achieve formal thought in one domain and not another.

Once they have attained formal thought, adolescents (and adults) do not use it consistently. The sort of logical reasoning needed in daily life rarely requires formal thought. Even when they cease to use it, however, adolescents retain most of their capacity for formal thought. If they did not, they could not function adequately. By the age of 16, almost all adolescents can think about abstractions, and they have developed a sense of community, some idea of rights, some ability to recognize future consequences, and a sense of the multiple determinants of action. They may not apply these abilities uniformly, however, especially in unfamiliar or stressful situations.

Social Cognition

When adolescents apply their sophisticated cognitive skills to the social world, they see themselves and others in much less simplistic terms than do children. Adolescents describe themselves in terms of their ambitions, wants, expectations, fears, wishes, beliefs, attitudes, and values and by comparing themselves to others. Their understanding of others follows the same general course as their understanding of themselves, and so their grasp of human motivation improves markedly across adolescence, as does the understanding of political principles, their scope and limits.

Understanding Self and Others

When adolescents examine their self-concept, they see themselves as displaying different attributes, depending on whether they are with family, friends, classmates, romantic partners or whether they are acting as student, employee, or athlete. In a study tracing the development of self-understanding between the ages of 13 and 18 (Harter and Monsour, 1992), researchers found that young adolescents describe themselves in such terms as "caring" with family and "inconsiderate" with friends but cannot simultaneously compare the attributes and so are not distressed by their clash. During middle-adolescence, young people are aware of the clash and it distresses them. They may become confused as to which behavior represents the "true" self. By late adolescence, they have developed the cognitive skills required to integrate seeming contradictions within the self-concept. They realize that it is understandable, even desirable, to act differently in different social situations.

Adolescents' ability to analyze and interpret the behavior of others keeps pace with the ability to analyze and interpret their own behavior. By mid-adolescence, most young people have reached the stage of mutual role-taking, as indicated earlier. They know that both they and a friend can consider their own and each other's views at the same time. They also can understand how a third party might interpret their interaction with another person (Selman, 1980).

By the age of 16 or 17, some adolescents have progressed even further in their understanding of others. They have entered the final stage of role-taking and can consider society's point of view as well as that of individuals. At this point they grasp the fact that a person's thoughts and actions can be influenced by factors the person is not aware of and thus that others (as well as themselves) may not always understand their own motivations. In a specific situation, actions may be influenced as much by past experiences as by the situation and its context. Older adolescents also understand that people can be aware of each other's view and still disagree. In one study, 57 percent of 16-year-olds had reached this advanced stage (Byrne, 1973). As they move into young adulthood, virtually all adolescents will attain this final level of understanding (Selman, 1980).

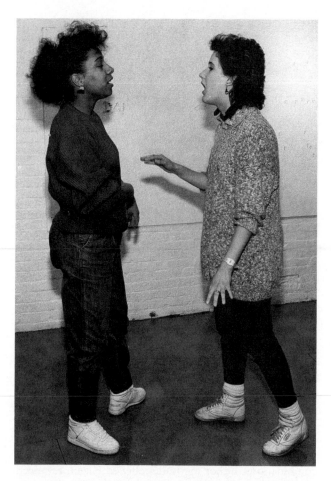

New ways of solving interpersonal conflicts may develop among older adolescents who understand that thought and action are influenced by factors outside awareness. *(Arlene Collins/Monkmeyer)*

Cultural and socioeconomic factors may affect the speed with which adolescents move through these stages. A longitudinal study indicated that socioeconomic status and gender determined how rapidly Icelandic youngsters progressed (Keller and Wood, 1989). By the age of 15, girls and boys in high socioeconomic families were most likely to have reached the stage of mutual role-taking, and they could see how a third person might interpret their interactions with a friend. Girls in low socioeconomic families progressed more slowly, and boys in low socioeconomic families progressed slowest. Many of these 15-year-olds were still in the stage of self-reflective role-taking and could not consider the roles of self and friend at the same time. According to the researchers, parents in low socioeconomic Icelandic families do not emphasize emotional and communicative processes during socialization, which presumably restricts children's role-taking opportunities.

Despite these changes in role-taking ability, adolescents may not apply their understanding to reasoning about family conflict (Smetana, 1989). They understand that their parents interpret family conflict in terms of its implication for parental goals of regulating the household, maintaining authority, and upholding conventional standards. Yet adolescents cast aside this understanding and reinterpret family conflict in terms of its implication for their own autonomy or as a matter of personal choice.

Understanding Social Institutions

Children's understanding of government and the law also changes from the concrete to the abstract as they move through adolescence. When Joseph Adelson (1983; Adelson and Hall, 1987) and his colleagues interviewed more than 300 youngsters between the ages of 10 and 18 in the United States, England, and Germany, and another group of 450 American adolescents, they discovered a remarkable consistency in the development of children's thought. The preadolescent cannot answer coherently questions about such topics as the purpose of government or law, cannot conceptualize "society" or "community," and can think of institutions only in personal terms. When asked "What is the purpose of government?" a typical 11-year-old said, "So everything won't go wrong in the country. They want to have a government because they respect him and they think he's a good man" (Adelson, 1983, p. 158). Like this youngster, preadolescents focus on the concrete; they speak of specific people, events, and objects. To them, *education* means *teacher*; *law* means *judge* or

As adolescents come to understand the rules and obligations that bind citizens together, they can evaluate actions in terms of communal needs. *(Bob Daemmrich/The Image Works)*

police. They do not seem to understand the relationship between the individual and the larger society. And so they evaluate all actions without respect for communal needs. As thought gradually becomes more abstract, adolescents begin to understand the invisible network of rules and obligations that bind citizens together. All 18-year-olds have some notion of the abstract, and nearly three-quarters are thinking at a high level of abstraction.

This dramatic shift in the way adolescents reorganize their perception of society also appears in their thinking about law, politics, and principles. Until children are about 15 years old, they see the law and other social institutions as primarily involved in suppressing wayward behavior. Children on the brink of adolescence tend to see government and law as purely restrictive. Gradually, their authoritarian, punitive attitude gives way to the notion that the purpose of law and government is to protect and benefit the citizen. By the time they are 18, adolescents tend to see laws as benevolent ("to protect people and help them out") and as an aid to community ("so that the country will be a better place to live").

The same shift from concrete to abstract thought allows adolescents to use moral and political principles in thinking about social issues. When asked to judge some social issue, 11-year-olds may glibly fall back on some phrase such as "freedom of religion" or "the majority rules," but probing reveals that they do not understand the principle. A 12-year-old who champions "freedom of speech," for example, may urge the imprisonment of unpopular speakers, or one who says "the majority rules" may follow up with the comment that the smartest person ought to make all the decisions. Within three years, most of these children will be able to grasp basic social principles and understand their application.

An understanding of such principles is, of course, necessary before an individual can begin to reason about moral issues at the principled level. Some evidence indicates that a high level of moral reasoning can develop only after the emergence of formal thought. In one study, a majority (60 percent) of people older than 16 showed advanced formal thought, but only a small proportion (10 percent) also reasoned on a principled level (Kohlberg and Gilligan, 1971). In fact, few people reach this stage of moral development before young adulthood. In Chapter 11, we saw that premoral reasoning on Kohlberg's scale declines steadily after the age of 10 and that adolescents tend to reason at the conventional level (Colby et al., 1983). Throughout adolescence, the boys in this original study increasingly

tended to define moral actions in terms of avoiding breakdowns in the social system and became less likely to justify actions in terms of seeming to be good people in their own or others' eyes.

Some researchers, as we saw in Chapter 2, believe that major theories of moral reasoning are biased against females (Gilligan, 1982). Theories that define moral development in terms of the acceptance of justice as an overriding principle and moral problems in terms of conflicting rights may favor traditional masculine socialization. In contrast, girls are traditionally socialized to focus on helping others and see moral problems in terms of conflicting responsibilities. Studies have, however, found few differences between the sexes in adolescent interpretations of moral problems. Among ninth-graders, for example, boys and girls both considered interpersonal relations as well as justice in deciding about situations involving lying, stealing, and breaking rules (Semtana, Killen, and Turiel, 1991). Their justifications depended on the situation, and there were no gender differences in the recognition of conflicts between justice and interpersonal relations. Similarly, high school girls in another study considered both the morality of justice and the morality of care when discussing their own moral conflicts (Lyons, 1990).

Understanding Work and Employment

If adolescents are to have successful careers as adults, they need to develop another aspect of social cognition: an understanding of the world of work. As we saw in Chapter 13, most U.S. adolescents have some kind of formal work experience, but their experience is usually in low-skill, low-paying jobs whose nature is often very different from their future occupations. Does this experience provide the knowledge and understanding of work they need, or is their understanding dependent on formal reasoning?

Studies indicate that young people's awareness and understanding of the details of adult work and employment increase steadily between the ages of 12 and 18 but that widening social experience rather than logical reasoning seems responsible for the development (Santili and Furth, 1987). Perceptions of the qualities required for successful employment changed in expected ways, with 12-year-olds focusing on occupational skills (work experience, training) and 18-year-olds focusing on personal traits (cooperative, trustworthy, friendly). Younger adolescents tended to give single, global—

often naive—explanations that indicated they had a general awareness of a specific skill or trait but did not understand the relation between that skill or trait and job performance. For example, asked to explain why he thought responsibility was important, a 15-year-old boy said that workers should be responsible about their work. Older adolescents tended to be specific and to give multiple explanations, as did the 17-year-old who said that self-confidence was important because "if a person doesn't believe in themself or their abilities then their work is not good, they won't care about the job" (Santili and Furth, 1987, p. 38). This age-related increase in advanced responses occurred whether or not adolescents showed skill in logical reasoning.

When asked about the general causes of unemployment, most adolescents (66 percent) focused on global economic problems, such as inflation, overseas competition, or increasing technology, instead of on individualistic causes such as laziness or lack of education or training (provided by 19 percent). Fifteen percent gave combined responses that placed equal stress on society and the individual. There were no age differences in *descriptions* of unemployment, but once again the explanations of younger adolescents tended to show awareness without the understanding displayed by older adolescents. A typical reply from a 15-year-old was that unemployment occurs "because there are no jobs," whereas a 17-year-old said, "Advances in technology [no longer] make jobs available. [People] are insufficiently trained for jobs" (Santili and Furth, 1987, p. 42). Explanations of the effects of unemployment showed a similar age trend, from a global awareness of its effects to an understanding of how unemployment changes people's material conditions and personal behavior. This time, however, logical reasoning was related to understanding. Adolescents who lacked logical reasoning showed little understanding, no matter what their age. But logical reasoning without experience was of little help; 12-year-olds who reasoned logically were unable to give explanations for their answers. Apparently, logical reasoning is necessary but not sufficient for the development of understanding.

Practical Intelligence

Another way of observing cognitive change in adolescence is through an examination of **practical intelligence,** which is the mental activity involved in solving problems that are encountered in daily life. Practical intelligence is related to the contextual aspect of triarchic intelligence (see Chapter 12), or the practical and social aspects of intelligence. It appears in a person's everyday interactions and involves adapting to the environment, shaping the immediate environment to match personal needs, or finding an environment that better matches those needs (Sternberg, 1985). As such, practical intelligence is quite different from the academic intelligence that is measured by IQ tests, which focus on the ability to manipulate facts that have been stripped from their context.

Practical intelligence emerges from experience in socially structured activities, in which children develop strategies for dealing with the demands of society and internalize these processes and practices. The development of practical intelligence is thus guided by the opportunities a culture provides to learn and practice various skills (Rogoff, Gauvain, and Ellis, 1984). Socially structured activity fosters the acquisition of new skills and knowledge, which are further transformed by later practical activity (Rizzo and Corsaro, 1988; Vygotsky, 1978). Our earlier discussion of social cognition examined some facets of practical intelligence. In this section, we explore some of its other aspects: the adolescent's ability to solve common problems, to plan for the future, and to make decisions.

Solving Common Problems

In their daily lives, adolescents encounter a wide variety of problems. These problems include negotiating changes in house rules with parents, caring for a pet, having unexpected company, making new friends, solving conflicts with friends, adjusting to a new school, and getting homework in on time. Adolescents who are high in practical intelligence are likely to have developed a set of effective strategies that they apply to such problems. They are good at generating solutions, considering the immediate and long-range consequences of various solutions, predicting obstacles they may encounter, and planning a series of actions that will enable them to carry out their solution (Spivack and Shure, 1982). If they do not have enough information, they will seek more before deciding on their course of action. What fosters the development of these problem-solving skills?

The knowledge of problem-solving strategies increases across childhood and adolescence, but studies indicate that experience with problem situations cannot account for this increase. There is no relation between the frequency with which young people encounter various problems and their knowledge of appropriate strategies for dealing with them (Berg, 1989). It is possible that adolescents who are good at solving problems learn quickly from their experiences how to avoid getting into problem situations. This sort of knowledge is not related to academic achievement scores, indicating that practical intelligence consists of different skills from those required on achievement tests.

The strategies adolescents use to cope with life's problems begin to develop during the preschool years. Among middle-class adolescents, the ability to delay gratification at the age of 4 was related to their ability to cope with frustration and stress at the age of 14 (Shoda, Mischel, and Peake, 1990). Preschoolers who successfully resisted the temptation of delicious treats on display (forgoing a single marshmallow now in order to get two marshmallows later) became adolescents who were high in self-regulation and good at coping with frustrating situations (see Chapter 11). Ten years after they had successfully resisted temptation, these adolescents were rated by their parents as attentive, intelligent, able to concentrate, able to resist temptation and wait for the things they wanted, unlikely to go to pieces under stress or to lose control when frustrated, and likely to think ahead. Preschoolers who had not been able to resist the delicious, chewy marshmallow in front of them became adolescents who were rated significantly lower by their parents on all these measures.

Although the ability to cope with frustration and stress is not part of academic intelligence, the self-regulation that is involved in delaying gratification may enhance adolescents' ability to apply themselves in the classroom. Among the same youngsters, the ability to delay gratification as a preschooler correlated 0.42 with their verbal scores on the Scholastic Aptitude Test (SAT) and 0.57 with their quantitative scores (Shoda, Mischel, and Peake, 1990).

Perhaps self-regulation in the face of temptation makes it easier for children to become self-regulated learners, who are highly motivated in the classroom, possess learning skills, and adapt those skills as the situation requires (see Chapter 12). Their self-regulation may foster the development of a range of strategies that help them control their attention, minimize their anxiety and emotion, and process information effectively (Paris and Newman, 1990). They have developed specific tactics as well as general tactics for making inferences and managing their own comprehension. They may have learned to tune out excessive noise, to take a few minutes' time out when studying, to control their emotions by positive inner speech (telling themselves, for example, "I cannot worry about this right now"),

and to control their environment, perhaps by moving to another room when noise or troublemakers make study impossible.

Planning for the Future

Making plans for a future that at times seems scary is a major concern among adolescents, and one that becomes imperative as high school graduation nears. Nuket Curran, who is 17, hopes to find a career as an artist, but her plans have yet to take definite shape:

The future's kind of foggy still. I have another year of high school. And I'm just gonna take it slow. I'm not in any rush. I mean, sure, I'd love to get out, get to college, and be independent. But the fact remains that I'm scared to death. What if I don't do well in college? What if I don't go? . . . I'd like to be successful, too. Get a good job and, like, graduate valedictorian. The goal is to try and get it all together. (Kotre and Hall, 1990, p. 182)

In all cultures that have been studied, adolescents' goals and interests focus on the future: their education, their occupation, their family, and the material aspects of their future lives (Nurmi, 1991). Most adolescents are consciously considering these goals and expect them to be attained toward the end of their teenage years or during their early twenties. Whether an adolescent is 13 or 17, the focus is the same, so young adolescents are actually thinking farther into the future than are older adolescents. Among Finnish adolescents, for example, young people hope to complete their education about the time they are 18, attain their occupational goals at about the age of 22, and attain their goals for family and property at about the age of 25 (Nurmi, 1989). Almost no adolescents think about remote goals that cannot be attained until after the age of 30.

Interest in the future increases with age, as does knowledge about possibilities, so older adolescents' plans are more realistic than those of young adolescents. Older adolescents are also more concerned about vocational opportunities and know more about various careers. Although relatively more intelligent adolescents plan more effectively than other adolescents (Osipow, 1983), there seems only a weak relation between an adolescent's level of cognitive skills and his or her future plans (Nurmi, 1991). Instead, interest in the future seems related to opportunities for planning presented by normative life events, such as entering high school, graduating, becoming romantically involved, and working.

Socioeconomic level affects future plans, with working-class youngsters focusing on occupational goals and middle-class youngsters focusing on education, career, and leisure activities. The plans of middle-class adolescents also tend to be more detailed and to extend farther into the future (Nurmi, 1991). Since the plans of middle-class adolescents generally include college and a postponed entry into the work force, this difference is not surprising.

As youngsters pass through adolescence, boys' plans for the future tend to become more optimistic, but girls' plans become more pessimistic. This difference may be due to a conflict experienced by girls between pressures for achievement in family and occupational spheres (Nurmi, 1991). Gender and culture interact to affect an adolescent's view of the future in other ways. The more highly urbanized a society is, the smaller the differences between genders concerning the importance of an occupation and adolescents' occupational hopes and fears. Thus, relatively large gender differences exist among adolescents in India and Swaziland, but gender differences among American, Austrian, English, Finnish, French, German, and Scottish adolescents are small or nonexistent (Bentley, 1983; Cartron-Guerin and Levy, 1982; Gillies, Elmwood, and Hawtin,

1985; Soltanaus, 1987; Sundberg, Poole, and Tyler, 1983; Trommsdorff et al., 1978).

Although there are no gender differences in adolescents' recognition of the importance of an occupation as a life goal, girls in Western cultures tend to focus on the importance of families and on making a contribution to society, while boys focus on the importance of wealth, status, and "showing others." And so it is not surprising that girls have a more structured picture of future family life whereas boys have a more structured picture of the material aspects of life. For girls and boys alike, culture affects the degree to which they make autonomous decisions about their future. In Western societies, the adolescents themselves tend to plan their future lives, but in traditional societies, the whole family tends to participate in the plans (Nurmi, 1991).

Decision Making

In order to realize their plans for the future, adolescents must make the decisions that will allow them to attain their goals. Many decisions made before they enter young adulthood have lifelong consequences: whether to drop out of school, go to college, have sex, try drugs, leave home, and so on. Decision making draws on the same skills as problem solving: adolescents must generate options, consider consequences, anticipate obstacles, and plan how to execute their decisions.

The ability to make competent decisions regarding the future, however, requires more than creative problem solving (Mann, Harmoni, and Power, 1989). First, adolescents need to be willing to make a decision; unless they believe that they have a degree of control over their lives, young people are likely to let matters slide. If they believe that they are powerless to make decisions or that important decisions should be made by adults, their lives will indeed be controlled by others. Second, adolescents need to be ready to accept compromises. Their ideal goals may not always be attainable, and they need the ability to understand the point of view of another person and to negotiate mutually acceptable courses of action. Third, they need to process information relating to the decision in a competent and logical manner so that their decisions will be as nearly correct as possible. Fourth, adolescents need the ability to assess the credibility of various sources of information in order to detect the vested interests of advice givers. Fifth, they need to establish some sort of consistent pattern in their decisions so that their major decisions are not subject to shifts of mood, enthusiasm, or social pressures. Finally, they need to follow through with their

Most adolescents are consciously considering their future education and occupation. *(Dennis MacDonald/Photo Edit)*

decisions. A decision to become a molecular biologist means little if the adolescent does not follow through by enrolling in the appropriate high school math and science courses.

Skill in decision making rises sharply during early adolescence, and many of the skills involved show a pattern of development similar to that of logical reasoning in academic and social cognition (D. Keating, in press). Although 12- and 13-year-olds are better at decision making than younger children, they still are relatively unskilled. They tend to be conformists and to rely on intuitive rather than rational strategies when making decisions. They tend to use strategies inflexibly and to make decisions without considering the risks and benefits of their choices. They seem unable to recognize possible vested interests, and they often fail to carry through on decisions they have made. By the age of 15, most adolescents have improved markedly, and on some aspects of decision making they are nearly as capable as adults. For example, they are using rational strategies in a flexible manner. Fifteen-year-olds still have a way to go, however. They tend to be conformists, and although they are beginning to consider risks and consequences, they are less competent than older adolescents in doing so. They are also unlikely to recognize

possible vested interests, and, like younger adolescents, they often fail to carry through on decisions they have made (Mann, Harmoni, and Power, 1989).

Over the past decade or so, certain legal rights, such as choice in custodial disputes and surgical procedures, have been extended to minors. Recognition has also grown concerning the critical nature of some decisions made by adolescents, such as whether to take drugs, quit school, or have sex. Studies generally indicate that younger adolescents are more capable than their performance would indicate and that with proper instruction they could make more competent decisions (Mann et al., 1988). As a result, researchers have devised courses to teach young people the theory and principles of sound decision making (see the accompanying box, "Teaching Adolescents to Make Competent Decisions").

Few high schools offer courses in decision making, and some court decisions have assumed that adolescents simply are not able to make sound judgments concerning many decisions, including their need for medical care or treatment (*Parham v. J.R.,* 1979). Despite this opinion, several state legislatures have passed laws that allow adolescents to decide for themselves concerning matters of contraception, abortion, psychological counseling, and mental hospitalization. It seems

TEACHING ADOLESCENTS TO MAKE COMPETENT DECISIONS

Adolescents might make more competent decisions if they understood the social, motivational, and emotional pressures that often interfere with the decision-making process as well as cognitive aspects of problem solving. In recent years, psychologists have begun to devise courses aimed at improving the quality of adolescents' decisions.

One such course, known as GOFER, has been developed by researchers in Australia (Mann et al., 1988) GOFER stands for five steps in decision making: *G*oals clarification, *O*ptions generation, *F*act-finding, consideration of *E*ffects, *R*eview and implementation. The aim behind GOFER is to help 12- to 16-year-olds become reasonably proficient at making competent decisions while under the stress that normally accompanies critical decisions. Thus, it covers such factors as how to avoid impulsive choice, passing the buck, and complacency.

GOFER requires fifty hours of classroom instruction, and the instruction is intended to be spread over at least one year. In order to personalize the course, a cartoon dog with human qualities (named

"Gofer") guides students through the various exercises. The first half of the course deals with the concept of decision making, describes the five GOFER steps, explains the relationship between self-esteem and decision making, and discusses techniques to assist the adolescent at each step of the process. Students learn how to recognize "goofers"—drifting, following the leader, copping out, and panicking—and what to do about them. In the second half of the course, students learn how these principles of decision making apply to their own lives: in groups, in friendships, in the choice of high school subjects, in money matters, and in various professions.

After 12-year-olds had taken the course, researchers found that, compared with young adolescents who had not taken the course, the students showed a better understanding of good decision making and felt more competent about their ability to make decisions (Mann et al., 1988). These 12-year-olds showed a decision-making skill comparable to that of 15-year-olds who had not taken the course.

likely that if adolescents have attained logical thought, they should be able to make competent decisions in matters where lengthy experience is not required.

When Lois Weithorn and Susan Campbell (1982) traced the development of decision making from age 9 to adulthood, they discovered that by the age of 14, adolescents made decisions concerning medical or psychological treatment that were virtually identical with the decisions of adults. The sample dilemmas described treatment alternatives for two medical problems (epilepsy and diabetes) and two psychological problems (depression and bed-wetting). The children were all middle-class youngsters with high IQs. In each case, researchers described the problem, alternative treatments, expected benefits and risks of each treatment, and probable consequences if no treatment was given. After describing the cases, they questioned the children to be certain the youngsters understood each problem, asking such things as (for the diabetes problem), "What happens if a person is taking insulin and misses one injection?" and (for the epilepsy problem) "What are the disadvantages [for 9 year olds, 'bad things'] about phenobarbital?" Additional questions required the youngsters to indicate that they appreciated possible consequences. In the epilepsy problem, for example, one question was "What might happen if Fred/Fran was in class and had a seizure?" (p. 1593). Even 9-year-olds seemed to comprehend the problems and expressed clear and sensible preferences for particular treatments. However, 9-year-olds failed to consider all the relevant factors, particularly the disadvantages of various treatments, and gave fewer reasons for their decisions. The competency of 14-year-olds was similar to that of adults on four criteria that are part of legal tests of competency: expression of preference; selection of a reasonable option; rational or logical reasons for the choice; and an understanding of the risks, benefits, and alternative treatments involved.

Yet competence and performance are often widely separated, as we saw in Chapter 11. Adolescents who show an adultlike competence to reason about critical decisions may feel that they lack the power to make such decisions. Because the role of adolescents in family and in society is restricted, many young people may feel that important decisions are not their responsibility (C. Lewis, 1987). As we have seen, one aspect of competent decision making is the readiness to make decisions and the feeling that one has the power to do so. In addition, when adolescents face critical decisions, the stress of time pressures or emotional involvement may lead them to rely on impulse and automatic responses instead of their newly developed cognitive powers (D. Keating, in press).

What Causes the Changes in Adolescent Reasoning and Problem Solving?

Adolescents reason more logically and solve problems more competently than do children. Their thought improves so radically that some theorists consider it different in kind as well as content. The enormous physiological changes that accompany puberty tempt us into assuming that the surge in adolescents' reasoning and problem-solving ability is the result of some biological difference. Is it due to spurts in brain growth and development? Is it due to the hormonal changes of puberty? Or is it due to accumulated educational and social experience? All of these factors may play a part in the change.

Brain Growth and Development

Nearly twenty years ago, a developmentalist proposed that advances in adolescent thought were caused by growth spurts in the brain, one occurring between the ages of 10 and 11 and a second between the ages of 14 and 15 (Epstein, 1974). He claimed that a child's head size increased at these times, just as it did at the age of 3 and again between the ages of 6 and 7. Since head size and brain mass were highly correlated, he conjectured, the advances in thought that characterized the stages in Piaget's theory of intellectual development had a physiological basis. Subsequent analysis, however, indicated that the original data on head circumference did not fit the theory (Marsh, 1985), and other researchers have not been able to establish any such link (D. Keating, in press).

Instead of looking at whole brain growth, other researchers focused on electrical activity in the cerebral hemispheres (Thatcher, Walker, Giudice, 1987). After correcting for head size and IQ, they found continuous changes in the power and coherence of brain waves, progressing at different rates in the two hemispheres, which they related to connections between neurons. They also found many sudden increases in the rate of growth: from birth to age 3, between ages 4 and 6, and between ages 8 and 10. During early adolescence (11 to 13 years) and mid-adolescence (16 years), they found consistent evidence of weak, but not always significant, growth spurts. Yet, as we saw in Chapter 5, any relation between brain growth and cognition is likely to be in the opposite direction: experience stimulates the development of new connections between neurons (Greenough, Black, and Wallace, 1987). Because adolescents are continually learning new things and having new experiences, we should expect increases in neuronal connections. Such increases do not necessarily indicate a restructuring in the brain.

Hormonal Changes of Puberty

Instead of looking at changes in the brain itself, other developmentalists suggested that the hormone-mediated growth of puberty might be responsible for cognitive advances. If this were true, then early maturers would have a cognitive advantage during the first few years of adolescence (Tanner, 1962). Reviews of research indicate that early maturers do have a slight cognitive advantage, but there is no sudden surge at puberty. The advantage, in the form of somewhat higher academic achievement and IQ scores, is present in childhood as well as in adolescence, and it persists into late adolescence and adulthood (Newcombe and Baenninger, 1989). The "puberty effect" on IQ may have a social basis, reflecting the response of parents, teachers, and peers to the physical appearance of children who will become early maturers, since they are likely to be taller and heavier than other children *before* puberty. Because they seem older, they may be treated that way, and so they are exposed to more sophisticated speech, more advanced games and toys, and demands to behave in a more mature fashion.

Another attempt to connect cognition with puberty was advanced by Deborah Waber (1977), who proposed that the effect of sex hormones on the brain at puberty accounted for the general male superiority on spatial tasks. As we saw in Chapter 9, boys tend to have superior spatial and mathematical skills, and girls tend to have superior verbal skills. Waber believed that the rise in hormones at puberty halted the process of brain lateralization (see Chapter 5) and resulted in less sharply defined specialization of skills in the brain's hemispheres. Boys generally attain sexual maturity later than girls, and Waber suggested that this two-year delay was responsible for their spatial superiority. She discovered that late maturers of both sexes were better at spatial tasks than were those who matured early. Later studies, however, indicated that gender differences in spatial skills are present before puberty and that although late maturers outperform early maturers in some studies, the later maturers do not show greater lateralization (Linn and Petersen, 1985). Besides, as we saw in Chapter 5, most research indicates that the hemispheres already are specialized at birth for different kinds of processing (Witelson, 1987).

Gender differences in spatial skills are relatively small, but they do appear consistently, although some girls perform better than the average boy and some boys perform worse than the average girl. Differences are most pronounced in the ability to mentally rotate an object in space, with much smaller differences in spatial perception (determining spatial relationships in reference to one's body) and with extremely small differences in spatial visualization (determining the effect on shapes of a series of manipulations) (Linn and Petersen, 1985). Researchers have not been able to determine the cause of these differences, with some suspecting *prenatal* hormonal influences, some suggesting a recessive

On the average, boys outperform girls on spatial tasks, but researchers have been unable to determine whether hormones, genes, gender-related strategies, or differences in experience are responsible. *(Richard Hutchings/Photo Researchers)*

spatial gene on the X chromosome, and others pointing to a propensity among girls to select and use less efficient strategies in the solution of spatial tasks (Linn and Petersen, 1985; Newcombe and Baenninger, 1989). One possibility is that boys and late maturers may use nonverbal strategies on spatial tasks, whereas girls and early maturers tend to favor verbal strategies (Newcombe and Baenninger, 1989). This view is strengthened by research indicating that girls' performance on spatial tasks correlates with their verbal IQ scores, whereas boys' performance shows no relationship (Ozer, 1987). Or perhaps the difference is the result of experience; boys tend to have more experience manipulating objects than girls do. As we saw in Chapter 9, sex-typed toys tend to foster mathematical and spatial skills in children. In one study of adolescents, late-maturing girls had superior spatial skills, but they also tended to favor typically masculine activities, such as building trains, model airplanes, and go-carts; doing mechanical drawing and carpentry; and using a compass (Newcombe and Bandura, 1983).

Although gender differences also exist in mathematical skills (with boys, on the average, outscoring girls) and verbal skills (with girls, on the average, outscoring boys), researchers have found no convincing evidence that hormones or brain lateralization are the cause.

Social and Educational Experiences

Since neither brain growth nor pubertal hormones can explain adolescent advances in reasoning and problem solving, perhaps social and educational experiences are responsible. With every passing year, adolescents learn more about the physical and social world. As their store of knowledge about the world grows, they find it easier to relate new information to old, and experience makes them skillful at processing information. They can recognize information, pull it out of memory, and compare it with other information faster than less-experienced younger children. Processes that are laborious for younger children become automatic for adolescents.

Because adolescents do not have to devote so much of their energy to basic processing, they are able to hold several complex ideas in mind at once. This dexterity promotes logical thinking, because it allows them to compare hypothesis with evidence—especially in situations where they are familiar with the content of the hypothesis or with the task involved (D. Keating, in press). Because knowledge and processing skills develop slowly, skill in logical reasoning improves gradually across adolescence.

Education plays a powerful role in this development. As we have seen, formal education may be necessary for the development of formal thought. Skill in reasoning and problem solving may in fact depend on developing expertise in a particular domain, and without practice, thinking skills may decline. Adults who have never been to college reason more logically than sixth-graders, but in some areas they do not reason as logically as ninth-graders (Kuhn, Amsel, and O'Loughlin, 1988). Apparently, once adults leave school, where logical reasoning is demanded, their skills decline.

Schooling

If formal education plays such an important role in developing and maintaining logical thought, we can see why developmentalists have become more interested in schooling over the past few years. Across history, culture and social class have determined whether adolescents have an opportunity to go to school, whether they choose science and math courses, and whether they follow career paths that lead to critical thinking. Among today's adolescents in technological societies, school is probably as central to their lives as occupation is to the life of an adult.

Transition and Adjustments to School

The shift from elementary school to a middle or junior high school is a pivotal event of early adolescence. Accustomed to spending the day with a single teacher in a single classroom, youngsters suddenly find themselves moving from one classroom to another and encountering a different teacher for each subject. The veteran student, one of the senior citizens of the elementary school, becomes a rookie who is looked down upon by other students. Candy Reed recalls her first day at a combined junior-senior high school:

> *A few seniors called us names. 'Oh, look at the little seventh-graders, those little twerps walking down the hall.' It was hard, being called a little seventh-grader. (Kotre and Hall, 1990, p. 141)*

Accompanying this disconcerting shift is the appearance of the competitive pressure of adolescence. Social popularity is now important. Although rigid academic sifting may be postponed until high school, it appears for many in junior high. Youngsters divide themselves (or are divided by the school) into college-bound and non-college-bound groups. With each passing year, students on these different academic tracks find themselves farther apart. The typical response to these changes is a temporary dip in self-esteem during the first part of the seventh grade, followed by a rebound in the latter part of the school year (Wigfield et al., 1991).

Some adolescents go on to thrive in this new environment. They become stars in athletic or academic domains or become immensely popular with their peers. Others may respond to these changes by withdrawing from competition. They find themselves unable to adapt to the changing requirements and the new academic demands. When they fail, they become discouraged, and their discouragement leads to further failure. Some who managed to get through elementary school without serious problems may develop learned helplessness. A young adolescent who is cut from the basketball team despite hours of practice or who studies hard but gets a failing grade in algebra may feel that effort is useless and may quit trying.

The nature of the transition affects adolescents' reaction to the school, with a transition into a traditional junior high school, especially one in an urban setting, having a more powerful impact on self-esteem, attitudes, and grades than does a transition from grade 8 (in a K–8 school) into a high school (Eccles et al., 1993). The more changes a student encounters, the poorer he or she is likely to do in school. In a longitudinal study of sixth- to eighth-graders, grades tended to decline during junior high school for most students, perhaps because of changes in academic content or perhaps because grading became tougher (Crockett et al., 1989; Schulenberg, Asp, and Petersen, 1984). But the decline was sharpest among those who transferred to a middle school and then switched again to a junior high school for seventh grade. The dual transition may have intensified the difficulty of their adjustment.

Researchers asked the junior high school students in this study whether they would rather be a star athlete, a straight-A student, or the most popular student. More boys and girls chose "straight-A student" than chose the other categories, although by eighth grade, girls were beginning to see popularity as more important than academic achievement. Nearly as many girls as boys said that they would like to be star athletes, but for both sexes the glamour of the athlete's life decreased between the sixth and eighth grades. For most students, however, athletics took precedence over music and student government as the preferred extracurricular activity.

Achievement Motivation

When adolescents enter junior high school, their achievement motivation declines, their intrinsic motivation is undermined, and they tend to become uncertain as to the reasons for their school successes or failures. Over the next two years, their attitudes toward the subjects they study and toward school itself tend to decline steadily (Eccles et al., 1993). More and more young teenagers, when asked why they go to school, reply, "Because I have to." For many young adolescents, academic achievement may seem less important as they become preoccupied with issues of autonomy, intimacy, or identity (Elmen, 1991). Yet this is a time when the consequences of academic achievement may affect critical decisions about the adolescent's future.

Adolescents' achievement motivation is affected by the value they attach to what they learn in school and to their own expectations of success in the classroom (Feather, 1988). Among seventh-graders in a small-town junior high school, expectations of success were a better predictor of math and English grades than was the value students placed on schooling (Berndt and Miller, 1990). Expectations and values were related, however, indicating that students who are confident about their academic success are more interested in school and value it more highly. On the downside, researchers were uncertain as to whether students who expect little success in school devalue it or whether the influence runs in the opposite direction; perhaps those who believe that school is not important don't try very hard and then lower their expectations. There was no difference between boys and girls in their perceptions of their own academic competence or in their tendency to attribute classroom success to ability, but girls were more involved in school and valued it more than did the boys.

When they make the transition into junior high school, adolescents' view of their general academic competence does not change, but their view of their competence in specific subjects tends to decline. Some researchers believe that the drop is the result of developmentally regressive changes in the educational environment (Eccles and Midgley, 1990). In their new schools, most students encounter (1) a competitive atmosphere that encourages social comparison and ability assessment at a time when adolescents are already focused on themselves, (2) decreased student autonomy and increased teacher control at a time when adolescents feel a need for greater autonomy, and (3) a disruption of their social networks at a time when adolescents are especially concerned with peer relationships. In addition, although their teachers use a higher standard for grading, classwork (especially in math classes) draws on lower-level cognitive skills than those demanded in their sixth-grade classes. Studies indicate that in a majority of junior high school classes, memorizing by rote, recognizing correct answers, and copying answers onto worksheets displace such processes as comprehending, applying principles, and finding consequences. Thus, the environment fails to match the developing needs of early adolescents. Students tend to respond by losing interest in learning math and become less confident of their own ability in math and English, although as time passes, many students regain their confidence in their English ability. The proportion of youngsters who prefer challenging to easy work also drops.

Among youngsters in twelve midwestern junior high schools, differences in students' conceptions of their own math ability tended to narrow: the confidence of high-ability seventh-graders dropped, while the confidence of low-ability seventh-graders increased (Wigfield et al., 1991). This seemed to be the result of moving from a heterogeneously grouped classroom, in which students of all abilities learn together, to the high school tracking system. Social-comparison groups changed, as high-ability students no longer found themselves outperforming the rest of the class and low-ability students found themselves competing on a more or less equal footing.

Over the next two years, expectations of success continue to be the major predictor of subsequent grades in math, with students' expectations predicting grades better than do their own grades from the previous year (Meece, Wigfield, and Eccles, 1990). By the ninth grade, perceptions of the value of studying math begin to predict students' intentions of enrolling in optional high school math courses.

One predictor of grades is time spent on homework. Although there is no relation between the time spent doing classwork and a student's grades, underachievers spend the least time on homework and overachievers spend the most (see Figure 14.2). Studies using electronic pagers (like those described in Chapter 13) indicate that the amount of time spent on homework decreases from grade 5 to grade 9—except for overachievers, who are also more likely than other groups to do some of their homework in the company of a parent or other family members (Leone and Richards, 1989). Overachievers do not seem to work harder because they enjoy it; they are as likely as other students to be unhappy, lethargic, and disinterested while doing their homework. Grades are also associated with a dedi-

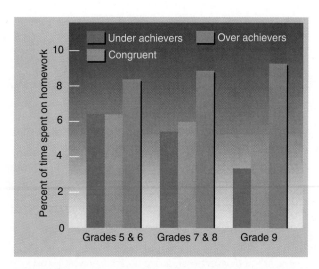

Figure 14.2 Homework and academic achievement. During early adolescence, the time adolescents spent on homework steadily decreased—except for overachievers, who worked as long and as hard as they ever did. *(From Leone and Richards, 1989, p. 538)*

cation to classroom norms, as indicated in the box, "Why High Grades Do Not Necessarily Predict High SAT Scores."

Expectations and Beliefs of Others

Adolescents' feelings about school, their goals, and the courses develop within a web of social relationships. No matter what their feelings about specific courses, adolescents' views about the value of education generally match those of their parents. In 1990, more than 86 percent of high school seniors said that they and their parents held similar views, and only about 16 percent said that their views differed (Bachman, 1991). The expectations of parents and others affect the educational choices adolescents make and their levels of achievement. Perhaps the popular, but unfounded, beliefs of others about girls' math and science abilities help explain why adolescent girls often avoid courses and careers in science or math.

The move to junior high school places adolescents in classrooms that are run in a more impersonal manner. It also places them with teachers whose views of students' characteristics are very different from those of elementary school teachers. Junior high school and high school math teachers are subject-matter specialists who work with many students for a much shorter period each day. This difference, combined with teachers' acceptance of cultural stereotypes, may be responsible for some of the changes in achievement motivation discussed earlier

Adolescence: Cognitive Changes

WHY HIGH GRADES DO NOT NECESSARILY PREDICT HIGH SAT SCORES

Adolescents who get straight A's in the classroom don't always do as well on the Scholastic Aptitude Test (SAT) as teachers and parents—and the adolescents themselves—expect. Perhaps it is a matter of motivation; that is, during high school, motivation that produces success in the classroom may differ from motivation that leads to success on a purely academic measure: SAT scores.

When Kathryn Wentzel (1989) studied students in San Francisco Bay Area High Schools, she found that motivation distinguished those with the highest grade point averages (GPAs) from those with the best scores on the SAT. Students with high GPAs had more goals than other students, and their goals involved social responsibility (getting things done on time, being dependable and responsible in the classroom), self-assertion (doing their very best), and academic mastery (being a successful student, understanding and learning new things). Only a minority (40 percent) of these students said that they always tried to have fun in their classes. They seemed to have discovered that social responsibility (a goal of 92 percent) was the way to a teacher's heart.

Students with the lowest GPAs, by contrast, tended to focus on goals connected with social interaction: they wanted to have fun in class and to make or keep friendships (74 percent). They were clearly not driven by social responsibility; only a minority were interested in being dependable and responsible (30 percent) or getting things done on time (22 percent). Wentzel notes that the least competent students made the least effort to conform to classroom norms.

But when Wentzel looked at SAT scores, she discovered that students who made the highest scores on this test were much less interested than the high-GPA students in trying to be dependable and responsible or to get things done on time. Instead, their two top goals were to be successful students and to understand things. Among the students with low SAT scores, the two most important goals were being on

Motivation that leads to success in the classroom is not identical with motivation that leads to high SAT scores. *(Kagan/Monkmeyer)*

time and being responsible and dependable—goals that characterized students with high GPAs. Understanding things and being a successful student seemed much less important to them. Wentzel concluded that students who make good grades pay attention to social as well as intellectual demands in the classroom and then pursue goals that meet both sets of expectations. Students who do well on SAT tests may be more motivated by broader cultural expectations for intellectual achievement.

(Eccles and Midgley, 1990). Junior high school teachers place more emphasis on classroom control and discipline than do teachers in earlier school grades. They also trust their students less. For example, they tend to believe that students will waste time if not given something to do and that students cannot be trusted to work together or to correct their own tests. They also tend to believe that students should not be permitted to contradict teachers, that students often misbehave in order to make the teacher look bad, and that some students are

just troublemakers. Despite their specialized background, junior high school math teachers feel much less confident than sixth-grade teachers about their ability to get through to difficult students, to help their students achieve at a high level, or to make a difference in their students' lives (Eccles et al., 1993).

Students' immediate response is to see their junior high school teachers as less supportive, less friendly, and less fair than their sixth-grade teachers. They also see math as less important than they did only a year before. But this devaluation of mathematics is not inevitable. In classrooms where math teachers feel more confident about their ability to get through to students and to help them achieve at a higher level than did the students' sixth-grade teachers, young adolescents see math as more important than they did the previous year (Eccles and Midgley, 1990).

At the same time that students begin to devalue the study of math, girls get further discouragement from the schools. Counselors and teachers urge boys to take math and stress its importance for their future, but they tend to discourage girls from enrolling in advanced math courses (Kavrell and Petersen, 1984). This discouragement is strengthened by the attitudes of parents, who tend to believe that math is a subject for boys.

Parents' beliefs about the general abilities of males and females tend to influence their beliefs of their children's ability and probable future success in various areas of endeavor, including English, sports, and math (Eccles, Jacobs, and Harold, in press). Thus, parents with stereotypical views of gender tend to believe that their daughters will be below average in math—or at least that the girls' success is due to hard work—and that their sons will do well in math and that the boys' success is due to ability. This is true even though girls do as well as boys in math classes and on standardized tests. These parental beliefs, which emerge when their children reach the sixth grade, have a direct effect on children's perceptions of their own math ability, on their interest in mastering math, on whether they have positive or negative feelings toward participating in activities that draw on math skills, and thus on the amount of time and effort children spend on math.

Parental beliefs may help explain why **math anxiety**, which is a dread of math and a nervousness or fear of math tests, is higher in girls than in boys (Meece, Wigfield, and Eccles, 1990). Moderate levels of math anxiety may lead adolescents to try harder, but high levels tend to disrupt attention and problem-solving skills. Math anxiety has only indirect effects on children's subsequent performance and their intentions to enroll in math classes, but it does have direct effects on their perceptions of their ability, which in turn affect performance.

Girls' dislike of math develops gradually. Among midwestern ninth-graders, girls liked math as well as boys did and perceived it as gender-neutral domain. Despite their equal liking of math, girls' concepts of their own ability in math were consistently lower than those of boys (Wigfield et al., 1991). As we saw in Chapter 12, as girls progress through high school, their liking for math

Some research suggests that parental beliefs concerning gender foster math anxiety among girls and a tendency for them to avoid courses in higher math. *(Joel Gordon)*

wanes and they become increasingly convinced that math is more useful for boys than for themselves (Eccles, 1985a). Although girls and boys get similar grades in math classes, girls expect to get lower grades and to have to work harder than boys do. It would seem that girls' low estimates of their ability and their belief that mathematics will not be especially helpful to them in their careers are responsible for their tendency to avoid advanced math courses.

Parents who have traditional views about gender roles may affect achievement orientation in other ways. As children enter adolescence, these parents tend to change the way they respond to their children's behavior and goals. They constrict a daughter's freedom and encourage her to be compliant, a practice that is generally incompatible with high achievement motivation. At the same time, they become increasingly tolerant about a son's independence, discourage his emotional displays, and may even encourage his sexual conquests, practices that may encourage his achievement (Elmen, 1991).

Do peers affect an adolescent's effort and interest in school? When adolescents are asked, they tend to say that their peers pressure them to get good grades (Brown, Clasen, and Eicher, 1986), but some studies indicate that the school-related attitudes of adolescent friends tend to become more similar over the school year (Kandel, 1978). A study with students in midwestern junior high schools indicated that friends do have some effect on adolescents' motivation and that the influence is not necessarily negative (Berndt, Laychak, and Park, 1990). Eighth-graders listened to a series of dilemmas that pertained to their academic values, such as whether they would go to a rock concert the night before a big exam or whether they would stay in a school sport or drop out to spend more time studying. Each student described his or her choices, then discussed the dilemmas with a friend. After the pair made joint decisions, each adolescent again responded to the dilemmas individually. The brief discussions indeed reduced differences between friends' earlier decisions, but only if the friend had presented new information about the dilemma. The final individual decisions, however, showed no pattern of change that suggested generally lowered academic motivation. Thus, fears about negative peer influence may be exaggerated.

Nevertheless, peers may play some role in the deci-sion to drop out of school. When researchers followed three seventh-grade classes across the years, they discovered that seventh-graders who dropped out of school before the twelfth grade tended to have friends who would themselves drop out of school (Cairns, Cairns, and Neckerman, 1989). Other factors proved more important, however. Highly aggressive seventh-graders with poor grades were the most likely to drop out before completing high school. The tendency to leave school was heightened by socioeconomic status (those from poorer homes were more likely to drop out), race (African-American males who failed a grade were *less* likely to drop out than white males who failed a grade), and the nature of the peer group. Thus, the most likely dropout was a highly aggressive white male from a poor family who had failed a grade and whose social group contained other potential dropouts. The students in this study were from rural and suburban schools in the South, and so the findings cannot be generalized to inner-city youths. Isolating the major causes that lead to school dropout is important, because nearly 27 percent of students in U.S. schools leave before completing high school (Noah, 1988).

Most adolescents do not drop out of school, and they cope capably with the enormous changes in their lives. In every culture, however, some are unable to handle the new demands faced by young people. In the next chapter, we explore the problems that arise when events overwhelm adolescents' resources.

SUMMARY

THE DEVELOPMENT OF ABSTRACT REASONING

Adolescents can think about possibilities, they can think about abstract concepts and ideas, they can systematically test hypotheses, they can think about their own thoughts and those of others, and they can consider the psychological viewpoints of others. Either their expanded cognitive powers or their concern with issues surrounding identity leads them into a new form of egocentrism, characterized by the **imaginary audience** and the **personal fable.**

PIAGET'S THEORY AND THE PERIOD OF FORMAL OPERATIONS

In Piaget's theory, the ability to deal with abstractions and logical possibilities was the result of an advance to a qualitatively different kind of thinking that he called **formal-operational thought.** Formal education may be required for the development of formal-operational thought, which may be acquired in one domain and not in another. People who attain formal thought may not use it consistently.

SOCIAL COGNITION

Adolescents take a far less simplistic view of others than they did as children. During adolescence, they move through the stage of mutual role-taking, and many enter the most advanced stage, in which they can consider the effect of society as well as the individual. Experience may affect the speed with which youngsters improve in their role-taking ability. Adolescents' understanding of social institutions moves from the concrete understanding of preadolescence to the abstract understanding of late adolescence. A grasp of abstract thought is necessary in order to reason about moral issues at the principled level, which is unlikely to develop before young adulthood. Although some theorists believe that most theories of moral development are biased against females, studies indicate that whether adolescents use the ethic of care or of justice depends on the context of the dilemma. Adolescents' understanding of work and employment increases steadily across adolescence, and it appears to depend on experience rather than on logical reasoning. Logical reasoning is necessary, however, to understand the causes and effects of unemployment.

PRACTICAL INTELLIGENCE

Practical intelligence emerges from experience in socially structured activities and is different from academic intelligence. Practical intelligence is related to solving problems in daily life, to making plans for the future, and to making competent decisions. Adolescents who are highest in self-regulation and good at handling the problems of daily life tend to be those who were best able to delay gratification as preschoolers. Adolescents in all cultures are involved in planning for the future, but their plans (which focus on education, occupation, family, and material aspects of life) go no farther than the midtwenties. Plans become more practical across adolescence, but there is only a weak relation between cognitive skills and planning. Gender differences in plans for the future are small in urbanized societies but widen in less developed societies. Competent decision making requires good problem-solving skills, together with a willingness to decide, an ability to accept compromise, logical thought, an ability to detect vested interests, and a consistent pattern in decisions. Younger adolescents are conformists who tend to make intuitive decisions, using inflexible strategies, and fail to consider risks and benefits. By mid-adolescence, young people are almost as capable as adults, but their performance may not match their competence. Their decision making may be flawed by a feeling of powerlessness, time pressures, or emotional involvement.

WHAT CAUSES THE CHANGES IN ADOLESCENT REASONING AND PROBLEM SOLVING?

Various theories have been advanced to explain changes in adolescent thought. Research has failed to support the notion that general brain growth is responsible, and the correlation between advances in thought and changes in the nature of brain waves does not indicate causation. Although early maturers seem to have a slight cognitive advantage throughout life, pubertal hormones do not seem to be responsible. Male superiority in spatial skills may be related to prenatal hormones, genetic influence, differential choices of strategies, or experience. Some theorists believe that more proficient information processing, a wider store of information, and education are responsible for observed changes in adolescent reasoning.

SCHOOLING

The nature of the transition to junior high school affects reactions to school, self-esteem, attitudes, and grades. The more changes a young adolescent goes through, the greater the impact of the transition. Achievement motivation tends to decline among junior high school students, and some researchers attribute this to developmentally regressive changes in the school environment. Adolescents' expectation of academic success is a better predictor of grades than is the value they attach to schooling. Junior high school teachers emphasize control more than do sixth-grader teachers. They also are less confident of their ability to reach children. The expectations, attitudes, and beliefs of teachers and parents may explain why **math anxiety** is higher in girls than in boys. Others' expectations and beliefs may also be responsible for girls' low estimates of their own math ability and the usefulness of math, two factors that probably explain why girls tend to avoid advanced math classes. Friends can influence an adolescent's achievement motivation, but only if the friend advances reasons for his or her attitudes. Highly aggressive behavior and low grades are the strongest predictors of school dropouts.

KEY TERMS

formal-operational thought   math anxiety   practical intelligence
imaginary audience   personal fable

CHAPTER

15

THE STRESSES OF ADOLESCENCE

• • • • • • • • • • • •

Fourteen-year-old Ray repeatedly told others that he intended to kill himself. "Life's a bitch," he said, and he often asked people about the best way to commit suicide. On three different occasions he tried to kill himself, but each time another person was present who managed to stop him. One day he asked his mother whether sticking the gun "in your mouth or your temple" was the most efficient way to commit suicide. The following afternoon, he took a fully loaded .357 Magnum from his mother's nightstand, put it to his temple, and pulled the trigger (Berman and Jobes, 1991).

● ● ● ● ● ●

Newspaper articles, weekly news magazines, and local TV news reports of such incidents throw parents into panic with their implication that any teenager is at high risk for suicide. Although the suicide rate among adolescents, which stands at 10.3 per 100,000, has indeed tripled since 1957, Ray's situation is highly unusual. He was not a "normal" boy, who simply decided to kill himself. If suicide is actually rare, is emotional upheaval or antisocial behavior a "normal" accompaniment of adolescence? The answer to this question is a resounding no. As we will see in this chapter, adolescence may be accompanied by a variety of stresses, but the overwhelming majority of young people take these social pressures in stride. For most teenagers, adolescence is *not* the stormy struggle portrayed in print and on videotape but a time of challenge and change.

In this chapter, after recalling the changes of adolescence, we explore the sort of stresses that may accompany them. Next we strip away the myths that have grown up about the perils of adolescence: the myth of adolescent turmoil, the myth of the self-limiting disturbance, the myth of conflict with parents, and the myth of the generation gap. For a minority of adolescents, the stresses become too great, and we explore six major ways in which adolescents express intolerable stress: substance abuse, crime, homelessness, suicide, pregnancy, and eating disorders. In closing, we explore the reasons for past increases in adolescent disorders and look at a theory that tries to predict their course.

Change and Stress

Adolescence is almost by definition a period of transition, the bridge between late childhood and young adulthood. Its major characteristic is *change,* change in every area of the teenager's life, as we saw in Chapters 13 and 14. As puberty propels them into adolescence, young people find that they have crossed into a period in which others treat them differently. Now, instead of being seen against the background of their earlier childish abilities, they are seen against the background of the adults they will become. With their new time perspective, adolescents begin thinking about the adult years that stretch before them.

One way of looking at adolescence is to see it as a preparation for departure (Douvan and Adelson, 1966). During the teenage years, young people prepare to sever their attachment to parents and home and get ready to establish themselves as independent beings. The rate at which youngsters make these preparations varies widely. Some become independent quickly, some slowly, some not at all. For the great majority, adolescence is the launching pad into self-sufficiency, a period when children learn and practice the academic, economic, and social skills that will turn them into well-functioning adults.

What does this extended preparation mean to young people? For some, the opportunities are wide, and the horizon is limited primarily by their imagination and capabilities. But the glittering promises require a series of choices. First, they must decide which courses to take, then which colleges to apply for and which one to accept, then which career to prepare for. At the same time, they are making other crucial decisions about dating, going steady, sexuality, and the like. For others, opportunities are few, and the horizon is so narrowed by hard socioeconomic truths that they may feel their choices are limited to the sexual area. Some adolescents may discover that college is out of the question, and others may find that their hopes of moving into steady jobs after high school are dim (Flanagan, 1990). Especially during times of widespread unemployment, some urban youths may see a jobless future stretching ahead of them, a situation that brings on the stresses of dissatisfaction, personal powerlessness, and low self-esteem (Bowman, 1990).

In some societies, all choices are determined by the adolescent's status or background. A young person is expected or required to take up a particular occupation or to marry a particular person—or at least a person from a specified group. Teenagers in technological societies have wider freedom of choice, but even those with unlimited horizons find that their freedoms come at some cost. They are accompanied by increased uncertainty and anxiety throughout the period of choosing.

All the elements—the lengthiness of adolescence, the myriad changes, the uncertainty about the future, the anxiety over choices—tend to make adolescence a stressful period. Every part of life is or seems to be shifting or unsettled. The adolescent's body and self as a whole are unstable. Hanging over everything else is an uncertainty about who or what the teenager will be. In this setting, the judgments made by others—other boys and girls, teachers, parents, even college entrance tests—seem to foreshadow the future. An adolescent who is shy and finds it difficult to make friends, one who does not seem to be sexually attractive to peers, or one who does poorly in school comes to believe that the present will continue into the future. Such an adolescent may decide that he or she is fated forever to remain unwanted, rejected, inadequate. Because they are seen as permanent, momentary disappointments and apprehensions are multiplied.

Stress also may develop within the family. There may

The prospect of a jobless future may produce dissatisfaction, low self-esteem, and sense of powerlessness among adolescents who live in areas of widespread unemployment. *(M. Richards/Photo Edit)*

be tension between teenager and parents over how much freedom he or she will be granted. Negotiations over rules and policies may lead the adolescent to test the limits of parental control. Such encounters have a great potential for generating conflict and bitterness on all sides. While struggling with these particularly adolescent issues, the young person is also encountering all the temptations and risks of adulthood—sex, drink, drugs. Choices that were previously unavailable present themselves to the young teenager.

Beset with all these factors, adolescents, it seems, must live through nearly a decade of turbulence. People are so convinced of this that most see adolescence as a time of trouble, turmoil, and stress. This view of adolescence has led to four myths that pervade most private beliefs and popular accounts in the media.

Myth 1 Adolescence is a period marked by emotional disturbance, which is often severe. The disturbance develops when the adolescent is overwhelmed by the changes, choices, and problems just discussed.

Myth 2 Any disturbances that appear in adolescence are limited and do not continue into adult life. Most of the emotional storms that buffet adolescents subside as soon as youngsters reach adulthood.

Myth 3 The normal outcome of young people's need to separate from their parents is a period of intensified conflict and open hostility.

Myth 4 There is invariably a generation gap between adolescents and their parents, which develops as adolescents challenge and then abandon the opinions and cherished values of their parents.

The problem with these myths is that they do not describe most adolescents.

Normal and Abnormal Adolescents

It is not surprising that most people think of adolescence as a tempest-tossed period and of most adolescents as emotionally upset youngsters who are camped on the far side of the generation gap. Most mental-health professionals have a similar view. A decade ago, Daniel Offer, Eric Ostrov, and Kenneth Howard (1981b) asked a group of psychiatrists, psychologists, and psychiatric social workers to pretend they were typical teenagers and to fill out a personality test designed for adolescents. Then Offer and his colleagues compared the answers with those given by normal adolescents, juvenile

delinquents, and seriously disturbed adolescents. In the eyes of these experts, the normal adolescent was worse off than actual delinquents or deeply disturbed youngsters in psychiatric hospitals. The professionals' "normal" answers portrayed mentally healthy adolescents as unhappy people with low self-esteem who found it difficult to deal with their moods, their families, and their friends and who were confused about their educational and vocational goals. The normal adolescents simply did not feel that way at all.

When mental-health professionals subscribe to most of the adolescent myths, it is no wonder that the press and the public have adopted them. Yet none of the pictures of adolescents that have emerged from systematic research supports any of these myths.

The Myth of Adolescent Turmoil

The major myth of adolescence—that it is a period marked by heightened emotional disturbance—falls apart with even a cursory look at the evidence. On the whole, the degree of disturbance among adolescents is about the same as it is among adults. In both populations, about 20 percent report feelings of distress that seem troubling enough to require professional attention. Every systematic study that has been carried out confirms the view that eight out of ten adolescents are neither rebellious nor emotionally troubled.

The first national survey of adolescents conducted by Elizabeth Douvan and Joseph Adelson (1966) showed that most adolescents had a realistic view of themselves, had no major conflicts with their parents over discipline or values, and held conventional, realistic ambitions concerning their future vocational and family aims. Subsequent studies turned up similar results, with the proportion of troubled youngsters hovering around 20 percent in each one (I. Weiner, 1982). Among a randomly chosen group of Chicago high school students, for example, Offer, Ostrov, and Howard (1984) found that 17 percent of the boys and 22 percent of the girls showed symptoms of emotional problems.

The Myth of the Self-Limiting Disturbance

The second myth of adolescence—that adolescent disturbances fade away as adulthood arrives—is seriously misleading. Adolescents who are troubled are not likely to get better without some assistance. Longitudinal studies of adolescents in distress indicate that their problems do not diminish or disappear with the mere passage of time. The teenager with emotional problems usually becomes a distressed adult, and the more severe the symptoms, the more likely it is that the adult disorder will be serious or disabling (Adelson, 1985). One reason that distress carries over into adulthood is that aspects of the family, community, and peer group that contribute to the disturbance are likely to continue influencing feelings and behavior as adolescents move on in life (Dishion et al., 1991). Another reason is that even when troubled behavior (drugs, risk taking, sex) is transitional, it can have long-lasting effects. Drugs can be addictive or lead to AIDS; sex can result in pregnancy or AIDS; risk-taking can result in accidental death or permanent injury.

A final reason is that more than half of troubled youngsters do not get the intervention that might help them overcome their problems. In the study of Chicago high school students, more than half of the disturbed teenagers had received no professional help (Offer, Ostrov, and Howard, 1984). The school authorities were unaware of their serious problems. Yet these teenagers' views of themselves were very similar to those of youths who had been hospitalized for emotional disturbance. There are 18 million high school students, and so there are probably 3.6 million (20 percent) troubled adolescents. If the Chicago students are typical, 1.8 million teenagers who need help are not getting it.

Boys were more likely than girls to have seen mental-health professionals. One-third of the disturbed boys but two-thirds of the disturbed girls had received no professional help. Why were adolescent boys more likely to get help than girls? Boys with emotional problems are more likely than girls to engage in obvious antisocial activity. About 65 percent of disturbed boys commit seriously delinquent acts or are picked up by the police, and so their problems are likely to come to the attention of authorities. But among girls, 62 percent suffer more or less in silence, never acting in a way that attracts notice.

The Myth of Conflict with Parents

The third myth of adolescence—that hostility and conflict between parent and child are almost inevitable—also crumbles in the face of the evidence. Most teenagers say that they have good relationships with their parents. They look up to them and seek their advice on important matters. Whether adolescents respond to questionnaires or take part in probing clinical interviews, the results of studies are similar. In the national Gallup Youth Survey, boys and girls between the ages of 13 and 18 told pollsters that they got along well with their parents (60 percent), that parental discipline was "about right" (82 percent), and that they would consult their parents instead of their friends if faced with a serious life decision (77 percent) (Adelson, 1985).

The Myth of the Generation Gap

The final myth—that parents and adolescents differ sharply on values and important issues—also has little basis in fact. There are few signs of significant differences between the generations on important matters, as we saw in Chapter 13. This not only is true today but was also true during the 1960s, when the activism of some students and the sensationalized counterculture that developed in the country's elite colleges and universities led to the perception of an exaggerated gap between parent and child (Feather, 1980).

Parental influences on adolescents remain stable and strong throughout the teenage years and into adulthood. Among high school seniors in 1990, 78 percent say that they adhere to their parents' values about important things in life (Bachman, 1991), and as we saw in Chapter 13, their views on such matters as the value of an education, what to do with their lives, roles for women, racial issues, and religion also tend to be similar to their parents' views. About half agree with their parents on politics. When researchers compare the responses to political questions of adolescents, their parents, and their friends, it becomes clear that parents have a more powerful influence on their children's political beliefs than do peers (Jennings and Niemi, 1981).

Where do parents and their adolescent children part company? The major differences appear on relatively unimportant questions having to do with style, music, leisure pursuits, and the like. Parent and child are most likely to disagree over such issues as the earring in a boy's earlobe, a punk hairstyle, or the sounds of a rap group. Even so, by the time they are seniors, 62 percent of adolescents are in general agreement with their parents about what clothes they should wear (Bachman, 1991). Disagreements also may arise over sex and drugs, but parents' and adolescents' values are rarely at opposite ends of the spectrum. Among adolescents, 53 percent say that their views on drinking are similar to their parents' views, 71 percent agree with parents on marijuana, and 77 percent agree with them on "other drugs" (Bachman, 1991).

On every count, adolescence fails to live up to its press image. Yet not all the news is good. Today's adolescents are more troubled than teenagers of the 1950s.

Punk hairstyles are one of the issues over which parents and their adolescent children are likely to clash. *(Ron Cooper/E.K.M.· Nepenthe)*

Over the past thirty years, there has been a clear and sometimes steep rise in some measures of adolescent disturbance.

Areas of Adolescent Stress

Newspaper headlines and newsweekly articles remind us that dealing with the tasks and stresses of adolescence is more than some young people can handle. Their inexperience may leave them unprepared to cope with the temptations and opportunities that come their way. When attractions are too strong, the potential price is obscured, or the stress becomes too great, teenagers may become involved in substance abuse or crime. Some develop eating disorders. Others may become pregnant. A few, overwhelmed by the world's demands, commit suicide.

Adolescent Drug Use

At midcentury, the use of illegal drugs was rare among adolescents. Alcohol was a temptation, but few adolescents had an opportunity to try marijuana—or even knew anyone who had. Cocaine and other drugs were virtually unknown in most parts of the country. As illegal drugs became widely available, young people faced a new source of stress—pressure from peers to use these drugs. Over the past few decades, children have been introduced to drugs at increasingly younger ages, and many begin using them while still in elementary school.

Patterns of Use

Tobacco and alcohol are still the most popular drugs: more than half of early adolescents have tried alcohol. The first drink typically occurs at about the age of 12 for boys and somewhat later for girls. By their senior year in high school, 90 percent have tried alcohol and 64 percent have tried cigarettes. Nearly one-fourth of young adolescents and about two-fifths of high school seniors have tried marijuana (Bachman, 1991; M. Newcomb and Bentler, 1989). Cocaine has been less popular; in 1990 it had been tried by 9 percent of high school seniors. Despite its wide availability, cheap freebased cocaine ("crack") has made few inroads among young people—only 3.5 percent of high school seniors have tried it (Bachman, 1991).

Alcohol used to be considered the "gateway" drug, because its use almost always preceded other drugs among adolescents. In the early 1980s, students rarely used marijuana and other illegal drugs unless they had used alcohol (Welte and Barnes, 1985). By the close of the decade, marijuana was also considered a gateway drug (M. Newcomb and Bentler, 1989). Adolescents who use alcohol or marijuana do not necessarily go on to try hard drugs, but unless they have already used alcohol or marijuana—or both—they are unlikely to move to other illegal drugs.

When more teenagers use drugs than abstain, some kind of drug use becomes a "normal" aspect of adolescence. Adolescents who have not experimented with cigarettes or alcohol or marijuana at least once by the end of high school are likely to be considered "deviant" by peers. The peer group plays a strong role in drug use. About a third of adolescents said that they used drugs because their friends used them. Alcohol and other drugs often serve a communal purpose. They strengthen social bonds, provide relaxation and ease, and initiate young people into adolescent rituals. Among nearly 500 Philadelphia high school students, the majority of users were not trying to escape reality, control their anger, or find a way to express their feelings, although about a third said that drugs made them feel "less tense or nervous" (Kovach and Glickman, 1986). But youngsters who begin experimenting with drugs very early in adolescence may be in need of help. Seventh-graders who use drugs tend to have low self-esteem, to be emotionally distressed, or to take risks (Bettes et al., 1990). At any age, heavy use of alcohol or drugs is not a normal

By their senior year in high school, nine out of ten adolescents have tried alcohol. *(Joseph Szabo/Photo Researchers)*

developmental phase. Heavy users are adolescents in trouble.

Excessive use of alcohol or drugs is associated with poor school performance, disrupted family life, and antisocial behavior. Among Philadelphia high school students, those who used drugs at least weekly were more likely than nonusers to have repeated a grade, to have been suspended from school, and to have conflicts with their teachers (Kovach and Glickman, 1986). They had more crises in their families and conflicts with their parents. They rarely participated in family activities or helped out in emergencies. They were also more likely to have had trouble with the law. Heavy substance use is also a warning of future trouble, usually of an antisocial or self-destructive nature. In fact, most varieties of adult alcoholism have their roots in problem drinking during adolescence (Zucker, 1987).

The Background of Substance Abuse
Drugs and alcohol are available to all adolescents, but some use them heavily, some never use them, and others use them only infrequently. In one study of California adolescents, those who used drugs or alcohol on an experimental or casual basis (one joint or no more than 2 ounces of alcohol less often than once a week) were as cognitively and socially competent as nonusers and were also more autonomous, with those who used marijuana being more gregarious than the others (Baumrind, 1991a). Those who used drugs or alcohol heavily (two joints or at least 3 ounces of alcohol at least several times a month) or became dependent on them were less competent in all areas.

Many factors have been associated with drug abuse, including socioeconomic status (drug usage is higher in disadvantaged groups); family background (drug usage is higher in disturbed families, families where adults use drugs, families without religious commitment); school performance (drug usage is higher among youngsters who do poorly in school); psychological factors (drug usage is higher among youngsters with poor self-esteem); attitudes (drug usage is higher among youngsters with nontraditional views); behavior (drug usage is higher among youngsters who violate the law in other respects); and factors related to emotional disorders (drug usage is higher among depressed or anxious youngsters and those whose life is filled with stressful events) (M. Newcomb and Bentler, 1989) (see Table 15.1).

Adolescents from different ethnic groups are at different risks for various drugs. Anglo youngsters, for example, are more likely to use alcohol than are African-

TABLE 15.1   FACTORS ASSOCIATED WITH ADOLESCENT DRUG ABUSE

Low socioeconomic status
Dysfunctional family
Rejecting-neglecting parents
Adult family member who uses drugs
Nonreligious family
Poor school performance
Low self-esteem
Nontraditional social attitudes
Delinquency
Depression or anxiety
Many stressful events

Source: Information from Baumrind, 1991a; M. Newcomb and Bentler, 1989.

Americans or Hispanics. But when Hispanic adolescents use alcohol, they are more likely than Anglos to develop dependency and other alcohol-related problems. Within the Hispanic group, adolescents from the Puerto Rican community are less likely to use alcohol than are adolescents from the Dominican community (Bettes et al., 1990). Puerto Rican teenagers, whose families often retain strong links to Puerto Rico and tend to visit back and forth, seem to have developed a strong ethnic identity. Dominican teenagers, whose parents generally are cut off from their Dominican contacts, seem less likely to have developed a strong ethnic identity. As we saw in Chapter 13, ethnic identity tends to boost self-esteem among minority young people and perhaps to protect them from drug use.

When psychologists compared youngsters' personalities during childhood with their use of drugs eight years later, they discovered that certain personality factors in childhood placed a child at risk for heavy drug usage in adolescence (Brook et al., 1986a). Youngsters who tended to get angry and lose their tempers, who were low achievers and often depressed, and who had eating problems were the most likely to abuse drugs as adolescents. But the progression was not inevitable. When youngsters at risk learned to control their tempers, became high achievers, and developed high educational aspirations, they seemed to be protected against substance abuse.

Family factors also seem important. Among middle-class white children in Diana Baumrind's (1991a) longitudinal study (see Chapters 10 and 13), those with authoritative parents, who are highly demanding and highly responsive, showed low levels of drug abuse.

They were unlikely to become dependent on drugs or alcohol or to become heavy users. Among the authoritarian families, children of parents who were demanding, restrictive, unresponsive, but *not* intrusive tended to have the lowest drug usage of any group. Children of authoritarian parents who were also intrusive and tended to subvert the child's independence had relatively high levels of alcohol use and about average levels of marijuana use. The highest levels of drug and alcohol use were among children of rejecting-neglecting parents.

In this study (Baumrind, 1991a), mothers of adolescents who became dependent on drugs or alcohol tended to be unconventional and unsupportive and asserted no control over their children. The majority of these mothers were divorced, and often both parents had abused alcohol. Mothers of adolescents who became heavy users of, but not dependent on, drugs or alcohol tended to be somewhat unconventional and exerted less control over their children than parents whose children were casual users or nonusers. Fathers seemed to lack self-awareness and self-confidence and had abused alcohol. Divorce rates in this group were average. Other researchers have found that when parents are poor role models, as manifested in alcoholism, antisocial behavior, or cynicism and mistrust, their adolescents may progress from problem drinking to alcoholism (Zucker, 1987).

National Trends in Drug Use

Social norms also affect drug usage. During the past decade, alcohol consumption has been declining among all age groups in the United States. During the 1980s, beer drinking dropped 7 percent, wine drinking fell 14 percent, and hard-liquor consumption was down 23 percent (T. Hall, 1989). Several factors probably contribute to the decline: (1) less tolerance of drunkenness and of alcohol in the workplace and on the highways, (2) new sensitivity to the dangers of alcohol, (3) the quest for physical fitness, and (4) the fact that cohorts moving into old age tend to be the heaviest consumers of whiskey. Adolescent drinking trends have followed those of the larger society. Over the past decade, the proportion of high school seniors who had used alcohol in the preceding month dropped from 72 percent in 1980 to 57 percent in 1990 (Bachman, 1991). Daily use dropped from about 7 percent in 1979 to less than 4 percent in 1990. One result has been a sharp drop in the proportion of teen motor vehicle deaths involving alcohol: from 62 percent in 1982 to 49 percent in 1987 (Zill, 1989).

Marijuana use has also declined. Since 1978, the proportion of high school seniors who had used marijuana in the preceding month dropped from 37 to 14 percent. In the same period, daily use of marijuana fell from nearly 11 percent to just over 2 percent (see Figure 15.1). Even cocaine use, which continued to rise until 1985, when nearly 7 percent of seniors had used it in the preceding month, has fallen to under 2 percent (including crack), with daily use declining from 0.4 percent to 0.1 percent (see Figure 15.2). The use of all drugs has declined (see Table 15.2). In 1979, 54 percent of high school seniors said they had taken some kind of illicit drug in the past year; in 1990, only 33 percent said they had taken an illicit drug during the past year (Bachman, 1991).

These encouraging statistics gloss over an important problem. They describe only those adolescents who remain in school. We have no accurate data on drug usage among high school dropouts, but these youngsters are likely to have had trouble in school and to belong to disadvantaged groups, thus being at higher risk for drug usage than the average teenager. Researchers have found a high concentration of adolescent crack users, for example, in public housing units in San Fran-

cisco's Bayview–Hunter's Point area (B. Bowser, Fullilove, and Fullilove, 1990). Many of these African-American teenagers were also selling crack to others. About 10 percent of adolescent crack users in this deteriorating area said they injected drugs, and many of them were sharing needles. Crack users told the researchers that they were hooked on the drug, that they often bartered sex for drugs, and that they rarely used condoms. Sexually transmitted diseases were high among these young people, and they were at great risk for AIDS.

Adolescent Crime

Age is the most important predictor of crime; 57 percent of all serious crimes are committed by people younger than 25. Those younger than 18, who account for 18 percent of the population, commit nearly one-half of the property crimes (robbery, theft, arson). Young people between the ages of 18 and 24, who account for 11 percent of the population, commit about one-third of all violent crimes (homicide, rape, assault) (U.S. Bureau of the Census, 1990). Rates remain relatively high during the rest of the twenties and then de-

Figure 15.1 Marijuana: Trends in perceived availability, perceived risk of regular use, and prevalence of use in past thirty days (high school seniors). Despite easy availability, as an increasing number of adolescents perceived marijuana as risky, its use declined. *(From L. Johnston, O'Malley, and Bachman, 1991)*

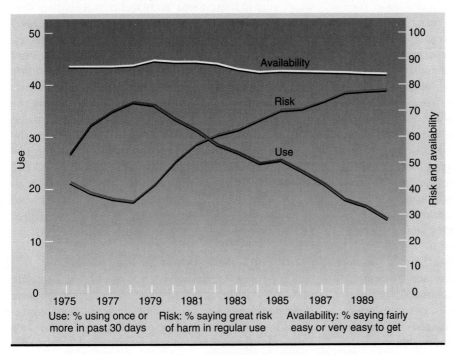

Use: % using once or more in past 30 days   Risk: % saying great risk of harm in regular use   Availability: % saying fairly easy or very easy to get

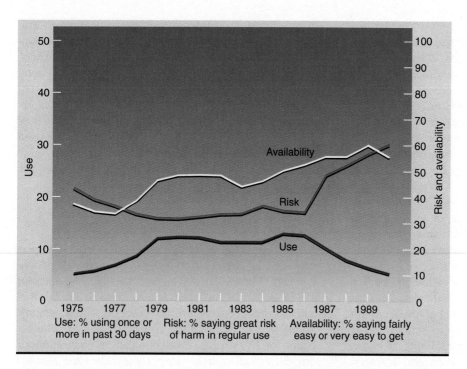

Figure 15.2 Cocaine: Trends in perceived availability, perceived risk of trying, and prevalence of use in past year (high school seniors). Like marijuana, cocaine use declined as adolescents came to perceive its use as dangerous, even though its availability did not decrease. This trend indicates that education may be more effective in preventing substance abuse than cutting off the source of supply. *(From L. Johnston, O'Malley, and Bachman, 1991)*

cline sharply throughout the rest of adulthood (see Table 15.3). Why should crime rates be so high among the young? No one is certain, but susceptibility to crime may be related to the nature of adolescence—a period when parental control is loosened but adult responsibilities have not yet begun to constrain behavior.

Crime is also an overwhelmingly masculine pursuit; at any age and in any country, males are more likely to become involved with the law than females. Among those arrested for serious crime in the United States, eight out of ten are males (U.S. Bureau of the Census, 1990). In a classic study, Marvin Wolfgang (1973) followed nearly 1000 boys in Philadelphia until they were 26 years old. Among these boys, born in 1945, 35 percent had been arrested by the time they were 18. These statistics are not unusual. In England, 20 percent of the boys in one major study were convicted of a serious offense by their seventeenth birthdays and 31 percent by their twenty-first birthdays (Farrington, 1979).

Victims of violent crime are also likely to be young. Adolescents between the ages of 16 and 19 are the prime targets of robbery, assault, and rape, but even 12-to 15-year-olds are more likely to become victims than are adults (Office of Educational Research and Improvement, 1988). Many of these young crime victims are homeless or runaway youths, as we will see in the next section (Whitbeck and Simons, 1990). Males are more likely to be victims of crime than females, and African-Americans more likely to be victims than whites of the same gender. For African-American males, the situation is deadly. Although motor vehicle accidents are the leading cause of death among all young people (34 deaths per 100,000 people between the ages of 15 and 24), the leading cause of death among African-American males is homicide (40 deaths per 100,000 African-American males between the ages of 15 and 24) (Office of Educational Research and Improvement, 1988).

What Do Arrest Figures Mean?

Neither arrest figures nor reports of crime are reliable indicators of the actual level of delinquency, because delinquent acts are both underreported and overreported. Underreporting has several causes. Many acts are never reported, and others are reported but the ado-

TABLE 15.2   ALCOHOL AND DRUG USE AMONG HIGH SCHOOL SENIORS

EVER USED DRUGS (% OF SENIORS)	1975	1980	1985	1990
Alcohol	90.4	93.1	92.2	89.5
Marijuana/hashish	47.3	60.3	54.2	40.5
Heroin	2.2	1.1	1.2	1.3
Cocaine (includes crack)	9.0	15.7	17.3	9.4
Hallucinogens (includes LSD & PCP)	16.3	15.6	12.1	9.7
Inhalants	NA	17.3	18.1	18.5
Stimulants (includes speed)	22.3	26.4	26.2	17.5
Sedatives ("downers")	18.2	14.9	11.8	5.3
USED DRUG IN LAST MONTH (% OF SENIORS)				
Alcohol	68.2	72.0	65.9	57.1
Marijuana/hashish	27.1	33.7	25.7	14.0
Heroin	0.4	0.2	0.3	0.2
Cocaine (includes crack)	1.9	5.2	6.7	1.9
Hallucinogens (includes LSD & PCP)	4.7	4.4	2.5	2.2
Inhalants	NA	2.7	3.0	2.9
Stimulants (includes speed)	8.5	12.1	6.8	3.7
Sedatives ("downers")	5.4	4.8	2.4	1.0

Source: L. Johnston, O'Malley, and Bachman, 1991.

lescents are not caught or—if caught—are not arrested. Whether an arrest is made depends heavily on the arresting officer's discretion. Some authorities believe that delinquency is higher among middle-class adolescents than statistics indicate, because the middle-class youth is more likely to be let off with a warning in situations in which the lower-class youth is booked. No one is certain just how large a discrepancy exists between offenses and arrests. One group of researchers estimates that only about one-third of crimes are ever reported to the police (Krisberg et al., 1986). And for some types of reported crimes, only a few arrests are made. There are probably seventy-five cases of aggravated assault by adolescent boys for every arrest and twenty-five cases of rape by adolescent boys for every arrest (Elliott, Huizinga, and Morse, 1985).

Overreporting occurs because many activities that can add a youngster to the delinquency records are not

TABLE 15.3 **CRIME RATES BY AGE, 1988 (PERCENT)***

Age Group (Years)	All Serious Crimes	Robbery	Burglary	Aggravated Assault	Larceny —Theft	Auto Theft	Homicide	Forcible Rape	Arson
< 15	11	6	13	4	13	10	1	5	28
< 18	28	22	34	13	30	40	11	15	43
18–24	29	37	34	28	27	32	35	29	21
25–44	37	39	31	51	36	26	46	50	31
> 45	6	3	3	8	7	2	9	7	6

*Males younger than 25 commit the majority of all serious crimes. Note that the figure for crimes committed by 25- to 44-year-olds brackets twenty years and includes the enormous baby-boom cohort. Even so, the smaller cohorts of individuals younger than 25 commit the majority of all crimes against property.

Source: Data from U.S. Bureau of the Census, 1990.

considered crimes if committed by adults. Acts in this category, called **status offenses,** include using alcohol, running away from home, cutting school, defying parental authority, and the like. As states have decriminalized many of these acts, an increasing number of youngsters who formerly would have gone to detention centers or reform schools are referred to some sort of therapy. Many youths who commit status offenses never come into contact with the law. In fact, if all status offenders were charged, few adolescents would escape the label "delinquent."

Paths to Delinquency

What sort of background characterizes the youth who commits a serious crime? Almost any negative factor you can think of is associated with delinquency, from poverty and divorce to physical discipline and child abuse. Like other outcomes, criminality is the result of many interacting variables, some within the child, some within the family, and some in the larger society.

For the most part, delinquents tend to have problems at school, and many have below-average IQs. Lacking self-control, they are impulsive, highly aggressive, risk takers who seek excitement. Most abuse alcohol and other drugs. Many of these characteristics are also linked to the quality of family life. Family life, of course, is affected by children as well as by parents. A child's temperament may help determine how he or she is treated by parents. Any genetic links that exist, however, are trivial compared with the influence of family and society.

Some developmentalists believe that a social-interactional model best explains adolescent delinquency. In this view, the first step toward delinquency is a pattern of parent-child interaction that models coercive behavior and either rewards it or punishes it erratically . The second step occurs when the child's antisocial behavior interferes with learning and school and leads to rejection by the peer group (see Chapter 10). In the third step, the disliked, antisocial child gravitates toward social settings that produce the most reinforcement—the company of other antisocial peers. Finally, the new peer group further reinforces antisocial behavior and encourages the development of new forms of problem behavior (Patterson, Reid, and Dishion, in press). Some research supports this social-interactional view. Among white boys in working-class homes, there was a strong link between parental practices at age 10 (coercive, power-assertive discipline and a lack of parental monitoring) and association with antisocial peers at age 12 (Dishion et al., 1991). Among adolescent boys in single-parent, mother-headed families, those who have been arrested for aggravated assault tend to have authoritarian mothers, low internalization of moral values, and high levels of association with antisocial peers (Blaske et al., 1989).

Children who grow up in quarrelsome, chaotic homes where parents are cold and discipline is erratic or lax tend to develop weak emotional bonds with their parents. The final, lifelong stage of attachment (see Chapter 8) goes awry. Bonding with parents is low, while bonding to deviant peers is high (Blaske et al., 1989). Such children have little wish to gain the approval of their parents and no certainty that their good behavior will earn them that approval. When they fail to develop self-control or to internalize their parents' standards, they are at high risk for delinquency.

Erratic, power-assertive discipline from cold parents,

The loosening of parental control combined with the lack of adult responsibilities may help explain the high adolescent crime rate. *(Paul Conklin/Photo Edit)*

attachment that delinquents felt for their families distinguished the two groups (Offer, Ostrov, and Howard, 1982). Whether middle- or working-class, the nondelinquents had positive feelings about their families, but delinquents endorsed such statements as "My parents are almost always on the side of someone else." (The effect of family relationships on problem behavior is explored further in the accompanying box, "Stopping the Cycle of Juvenile Crime.")

Social factors are involved, indirectly as well as directly. Studies have discovered an indirect effect in the influence of family economic problems on family life (Conger et al., 1992). Severe economic pressure (low income or unemployment) on the families of young adolescent boys is associated with rejecting-neglecting parental styles and parental hostility toward the adolescent and with aggressive, antisocial behavior on the part of the boy—a situation that other researchers (for example, Dishion et al., 1991) have linked with delinquency.

Unemployment is directly associated with property crimes: robbery, burglary, and auto theft (Schapiro and Ahlburg, 1986). Low income similarly increases the likelihood of delinquency. Adolescents who grow up watching the luxury-filled world portrayed on television but have no legal way of obtaining these goods may simply take them. Peer pressure can be an important force, as we have seen, although it is not a case of "pure" adolescents succumbing to the persuasions of "evil" company. Instead, adolescent gangs may set up delinquency as the norm for their members. Burglary, violence, and street-corner drug dealing are a part of young gang members' everyday world. In this context, the inability of the African-American adolescent who lives in the inner city to find a job may make drug dealing, pimping, or robbery seem like a sensible alternative (Ogbu, 1985).

Delinquency does not suddenly appear in adolescence. By the time future delinquents are 8 or 9 years old, they have had trouble in school or have turned up at a child-guidance clinic. At this age, the trouble is not always antisocial in nature but encompasses a wide variety of aggressive and disruptive behavior. In a longitudinal study, high levels of aggressiveness among first-grade boys were associated with delinquency and alcohol use at the age of 16 (Ensminger, 1990). As we saw in Chapter 10, impatient, impulsive kindergartners who were defiant in the classroom, disrupted the class, and broke classroom rules ran a high risk of trouble with the law during adolescence (Spivack, Marcus, and Swift, 1986).

as we saw in Chapter 9, also tends to produce highly aggressive youngsters, another characteristic of delinquents. In a study of African-American and Hispanic youth (Graham, Hudley, and Williams, 1992), researchers found continuation of a pattern described in Chapter 10. Highly aggressive boys and girls in junior high school who were disliked by their peers were more likely than nonaggressive, well-liked students to become angry at others' actions, to attribute hostile intentions to the actor, and to endorse immediate hostile responses. Such tendencies help explain the link between aggressiveness and delinquency.

By adolescence, delinquents no longer share the family-related values that characterize most young people. When researchers had delinquent and nondelinquent boys fill out a self-image questionnaire, the lack of

STOPPING THE CYCLE OF JUVENILE CRIME

A large proportion of juvenile crime is the work of repeat offenders. So many factors are implicated in juvenile delinquency that even when young offenders receive some kind of treatment, they frequently go on to criminal careers. A program that takes an extremely broad approach to treatment of inner-city adolescents shows signs of being more successful than most.

In Tennessee, Scott Henggeler and his colleagues (1986) have tested a program that uses a "multisystemic approach." This approach assumes that changing the interaction within and between the various settings in which a youngster lives is as important as changing the teenager's attitudes and feelings directly. Researchers worked with fifty-seven delinquent adolescents individually, with the parents, and with the entire family. At the close of the four-year program, the youngsters in the treatment group had fewer behavior problems than a matched control group of offenders. And while family relations in the control group had deteriorated, relations within the treatment group had noticeably improved.

With the adolescent, the researchers worked on social skills. In many cases, a therapist developed a close relationship with the young offender. When a youngster already had a close relationship with a responsible adult, the therapist helped the adult change the child's pattern of social interactions. Within the peer group and the school, the researchers encouraged the adolescent to become involved in group activities that would foster interpersonal skills. Within the families, the researchers encouraged authoritative parental styles, in which the parents set firm, consistent limits but allowed the youngster to take responsibility and earn privileges. They worked on marital conflicts and tried to improve the relationship between the youngster's parents. They showed families how to break the spiral of aggression, attack, and counterattack often found between aggressive boys and their parents (see Chapter 9).

Adolescents in the control group were assigned to existing programs. Many received individual counseling, family counseling was provided for some, and others were placed in alternative educational programs or vocational training.

By the close of the program, relations within the adolescents' families were warmer and more affectionate, whether the youngsters lived in two-parent families (38 percent) or in mother-headed, single-parent families (62 percent). In two-parent families, the husband-wife relationship improved. In all the families, the relationship between the teenager and his or her parent (or parents) improved. Before entering the program, most of these adolescents either had been emotionally disengaged from their families or had lived in open parent-child conflict. Afterward, the adolescents talked more in family discussions, took more responsibility, began to contribute to family decisions, and took part in family social activities. Parents of these youngsters reported that they had fewer behavior problems to deal with and that their sons or daughters acted more maturely and associated less with delinquent peers.

Among families in the control group, relations between the mother and father had grown more distant and cold over the four-year period, as had relations between father and adolescent. There was no change in relations between mother and adolescent. The researchers suggest that the additional coldness in families already marked by disengagement and discord probably pushed the adolescent into closer association with delinquent peers—a factor that is a strong predictor of delinquent activities.

Homeless Runaways

High delinquency rates and poor school experiences are typical of adolescents who run away from home. But those who *stay away* more than three months are usually fleeing dysfunctional families characterized by physical or sexual abuse, parental rejection, lack of any parental monitoring of the adolescents' activities, and the adolescents' perception that their parents favor one sibling over another (Whitbeck and Simons, 1990). Some homeless teenagers are not runaways but "throwaways": they have been encouraged to leave by their parents or forbidden to return home.

Runaways have proved difficult to study, because only those who come to shelters (fewer than half the runaways) are available to researchers. Studies have found that only about 20 percent left home because of short-term crises (divorce, sickness, death, or school problems), 44 percent left because of serious long-term crises (drug-abusing, alcoholic parents or crises in stepfamilies), and 36 percent left because of physical or sexual abuse. Among those who come to emergency shelters, however, approximately 70 percent have been beaten or sexually molested at home (Hersch, 1988) (see Table 15.4).

Once on the streets, runaways tend to congregate in urban areas, where they learn to look out for themselves. They may panhandle, look for food in dumpsters,

Adolescence: Building an Identity

408

TABLE 15.4   ABUSE HISTORY OF ADOLESCENT RUNAWAYS*

Type of Familial Abuse	RECIPIENTS OF ABUSE (%)		
	Total (n = 84)	Males (n = 44)	Females (n = 40)
Thrown something at you	61.8	57.2	66.7
Pushed, shoved, or grabbed you in anger	85.4	86.1	84.5
Slapped you	85.3	86.0	84.6
Spanked you	82.5	83.4	81.6
Hit you with an object	66.6	66.7	66.7
Beat you up	46.9	55.0	38.4
Threatened you with gun or knife	22.4	19.5	25.7
Assaulted you with gun or knife	11.3	9.7	12.8
Made a verbal request for sexual activity	27.1	19.1	35.9
Touched or attempted to touch you sexually	29.9	16.7	44.8
Forced you to engage in sexual activities	27.1	12.0	46.6

*Runaways in a midwestern city reported rates of violence and abuse in their homes that were many times higher than those predicted in national probability samples.

Source: Whitbeck and Simons, 1990, p. 117.

shoplift, deal drugs, or become prostitutes. Many begin taking drugs themselves, and those who survive by dispensing sexual favors are at high risk for AIDS. Runaways frequently find that the violence they ran away from is replaced by victimization on the city streets. Among the homeless youths in a midwestern city, 41 percent had been beaten up, 24 percent robbed, 26 percent sexually assaulted, 43 percent threatened with a weapon, and 30 percent assaulted with a weapon. Boys were more likely to have been assaulted with a weapon (51 percent) than girls, and girls more likely to have been sexually assaulted (43 percent) (Whitbeck and Simons, 1990).

Compared with other adolescents, runaways have high rates of depression, substance abuse, and other mental-health problems. They are also at risk for suicide. Among runaways in the St. Louis area, 30 percent had attempted suicide at least once (Stiffman, 1989). But the problem of suicide is not confined to runaways.

Adolescent Suicide

Once an uncommon cause of death among the young, suicide is now the second leading cause of death among adolescents—exceeded only by accidents. What leads a youth to see life as so hopeless that suicide is the

Runaways who have fled violence at home often find that they must panhandle, shoplift, deal drugs, or become prostitutes to survive. *(D. Greco/The Image Works)*

only solution? Is it a case of too many demands on to-day's youths? Unrealistic standards? As with other adolescent disorders, there is no simple answer to this troubling problem.

Race and gender heavily weight the chances that a young person will commit suicide. More whites kill themselves than African-Americans; more Native Americans kill themselves than whites; more boys kill themselves than girls. Girls apparently make as many attempts at suicide, but they usually fail. Boys and men generally are successful. What accounts for this difference? First, boys use more lethal means. The overwhelming majority shoot themselves; girls are seven times more likely than boys to use poison (Berman and Jobes, 1991). Second, girls usually want to be rescued; the suicide attempt is meant as a message. The typical girl attempter, for example, takes pills in front of her family after an argument. Boys are less willing to ask for help, even after they have made an unsuccessful attempt

to kill themselves. Third, girls have better social support systems than boys. As we saw in Chapter 13, girls tend to have more intimate friendships and to exchange emotional confidences, but boys tend to regard their friends as companions in fun. When adolescents talk about suicide, girls often see it as a solution to emotional problems; boys, as a response to job problems (Simons and Murphy, 1985).

Adolescents who are likely to make a suicide attempt tend to have similar family backgrounds. Usually, there have been changes—or threatened changes—in the family. Often their parents have divorced or separated; when the home is intact, it is filled with strife, or the youngster feels rejected by one or both parents. Nearly half of adolescents who try to kill themselves say that the attempt was the result of problems at home. Among white male adolescents, living in poverty is also associated with suicide (McCall, 1991), and among Native American adolescents, pervasive hardships appear to interact with the failure to develop a strong ethnic identity and with the loss of relationships (LaFromboise and Bigfoot, 1988).

A family history of suicide is especially ominous. In one study, one-third of the adolescents who killed themselves had a relative who had either committed suicide or attempted it (Holden, 1986). Among Native American adolescents, for example, suicides tend to cluster in families, with a male adolescent taking his life around the anniversary of a former death by suicide (LaFromboise and Bigfoot, 1988). A suicide attempt by a family member seems to make suicide a reasonable option for adolescents of all races. Why? The taboo against suicide is a powerful deterrent. When the family or the larger culture regards suicide as a horror, young people are unlikely to kill themselves. But a suicide attempt by a family member makes suicide an acceptable choice. This permission for suicide affects all age levels. Whenever a famous person commits suicide, the national suicide rate rises for the next few days (Berman and Jobes, 1991).

Sometimes a wave of suicides seems to sweep through the young people in a community. In Omaha, Nebraska, three adolescents committed suicide within five days, and another four made unsuccessful attempts. The dead youths knew one another only casually (Leo, 1986). Similarly, in Plano, a small Texas town north of Dallas, seven teenagers committed suicide within a year. In the sparsely populated countryside north of New York City, five boys killed themselves in one month. In such cases, the first suicide probably breaks the community taboo against such acts and makes it possible for other adolescents to consider suicide as a possible solution to their problems.

The adolescent who solves his or her problems with a gun, a rope, or an overdose of barbiturates is not a "normal" child who comes home one day and decides to commit suicide. Researchers have discovered that only a very small proportion of suicide victims (less than 10 percent) seem free of psychiatric symptoms before their deaths. Many boys who commit suicide have a history of depression, impulsivity, drug or alco-

When a cluster of teenage suicides appears, it is generally because an earlier suicide has broken the taboo against self-destruction and made suicide a "thinkable" option. (© 1987 by the New York Times Company. Reprinted by Permission. 3/12/87)

Youth Suicide: A Common Pattern

By JANE E. BRODY

The four suicides yesterday by teen-age friends in Bergenfield, N.J., are in one respect a rare phenomenon, but in others part of a pattern increasingly found in communities throughout the country.

According to Dr. David Shaffer, who has been conducting an in-depth study of 182 suicides among youths in the New York metropolitan area in the last two years, suicide pacts are extremely uncommon. However, in a high proportion of youth suicides, particularly among older teen-agers, drugs or alcohol are involved and school problems and antisocial behavior are commonplace.

Dr. Shaffer, a professor of child psychiatry at Columbia University, has also noted considerable "imitation" or "contagion" surrounding youth suicides.

Imitation Effect Feared

"The effect of highly publicized stories about teen-age suicides is a significant increase in successful suicides and suicide attempts among young people," he said in an interview yesterday. "The current situation, I'm afraid, is ripe for imitation and will no doubt cause a great deal of anxiety about still more such deaths occurring."

Dr. Shaffer said he believed there were far more suicide clusters among youngsters than came to public attention. "A very high proportion of the suicide victims in our study knew others who had committed suicide or attempted it," he said.

In learning about the suicide of another child, children come to see suicide as an easy solution to their problems and a kind of "instant martyrdom," the psychiatrist added.

The "contagious" aspect of suicide is a well-known phenomenon and is said to account for the periodic clusters of suicides among young people in a single community. In recent years, for example, there were five suicides among youngsters in Westchester County and seven in the boom town of Plano, Tex.

Feelings of Guilt

In the current case, the picture is complicated by the fact that one victim, Thomas Rizzo, was with his best friend, Joe Major, last September when the latter fell or jumped to his death from a cliff of the Palisades.

Charlotte Ross, executive director of the Youth Suicide National Center, said that sometimes a friend knew of another's intention to kill himself and was racked with guilt for failing to thwart it.

"The one who remained silent feels totally responsible and may not be able to handle the guilt," she said, prompting him to opt for the same solution used by his friend.

Yesterday's deaths are among more than 5,000 known suicides that occur each year among Americans between the ages of 15 and 24, making suicide the second leading cause of death in this age group, after accidents.

The actual number of successful teen-age suicides is believed to be much greater, but many are recorded as accidents. Four other recent deaths among teen-agers in Bergenfield, for example, were so recorded.

Certified deaths by suicide among teen-agers increased dramatically between 1960 and 1980, but the number has since begun to level off, possibly because of a decline in the use of mind-altering drugs and an increase in attention to children at risk of taking their own lives.

An estimated total of 400,000 teen-agers are said to attempt suicide each year, and most who succeed give one of more warnings of their suicidal intentions.

hol abuse, aggression, and antisocial behavior, or they may be rigid perfectionists who tended to isolate themselves from others (Berman and Jobes, 1991; Shafii et al., 1985). Although only 1 out of every 660 depressed youths becomes suicidal, suicide victims of both sexes often have a history of depression (Shaffer and Bacon, 1989). Depressed adolescents who kill themselves differ in several ways from depressed adolescents who do not consider suicide. Those who are suicidal tend to have disturbed family relationships, feel less control over their environment, and lack problem-solving skills, so they can generate fewer solutions to the problems that seem overwhelming (Berman and Jobes, 1991).

The particular events that trigger a suicide vary from one youth to the next. Often it is the breakup of a relationship. However, any experience that produces shame, guilt, and humiliation can precipitate a suicide attempt. Being arrested, beaten up, or raped often precedes suicide. The incident does not have to be violent. An adolescent boy may feel that life is not worth living when he is refused admittance to Harvard.

In a number of communities, alarmed parents, educators, and public officials have set up education programs to spread the word about the causes and effects of suicide to teenagers, their parents, educators, and the clergy. The typical school program attempts to heighten awareness about the problem of adolescent suicide, to present facts and debunk myths about suicide, to increase the recognition of youngsters at risk, to change attitudes about suicide, and to encourage troubled adolescents to seek help (Berman and Jobes, 1991). However, when researchers evaluated three such programs, they discovered that high-risk students may be turned off by them; on the positive side, many students felt that the programs boosted their confidence in their own ability to help other students in trouble (Shaffer, Garland, and Whittle, 1988). But researchers agree that teenagers who talk about suicide should be taken seriously. In one study of adolescent suicides, 85 percent of the youths had talked about their intent, and 40 percent had first made an unsuccessful try at killing themselves (Shafii et al., 1985).

Adolescent Pregnancy

Every year in this country, more than 500,000 babies are born to adolescent girls, and 67 percent of these girls are unmarried. Among white teenagers who give birth, 55 percent are not married; among Hispanics (who may be white or black), 54 percent are not married; and among African-American teenagers, 92 per-

cent are not married (Child Trends, 1992). Each year, 24 percent of sexually active adolescent girls become pregnant. Pregnancy adds to the crucial decisions that already face teenagers, for the decisions made by pregnant adolescents change the course of their lives.

Hazards of Teenage Pregnancy

The physical, economic, and social hazards that face young mothers and their babies have aroused the concern of many researchers. All sorts of complications increase sharply among adolescent mothers. When the mother is younger than 16, her risk of dying during pregnancy or childbirth is five times the national average (Bolton, 1980). Extremely young mothers face special risks because their pelvises are immature. The fetal head is often unable to pass safely through the immature pelvis, and so young teenagers are likely to have complicated deliveries and Caesarean sections (McCluskey, Killarney, and Papini, 1983).

Compared with other babies, more babies of adolescent mothers are born dead, and there are more cases of premature birth, low birthweight, respiratory distress syndrome, and neurological defects (Bolton, 1980). Most of the complications are unnecessary and not related to the mother's youth. They occur because many girls are reluctant to seek prenatal care and thus see a physician only late in pregnancy—or not at all. Because most adolescents know little about nutrition or prenatal development, the girls may not eat properly, or they may expose the fetus to such hazards as alcohol, tobacco, or drugs. Older adolescents who have good prenatal care from early in the first trimester and who have proper nutrition and avoid cigarettes, drugs, and alcohol have babies as healthy as those of women in their twenties.

Adolescents face further hazards if they breast-feed their babies. Because their bones are still growing, the simultaneous demands of milk production and new bone growth make it difficult for adolescent girls to take in enough calcium and phosphorus to supply their bodies' needs. Even those who take dietary supplements tend to lose large amounts of calcium and other minerals from their bones (Chan et al., 1982). This loss not only weakens their bones but may also put the girls at high risk for osteoporosis in later years.

These physical hazards probably do not exceed the social and economic risks run by adolescent mothers. As the public has come to accept unmarried mothers, fewer teenagers have given their babies up for adoption. Studies consistently find that 90 percent of adolescent mothers keep their babies (Unger and Wandersman,

1988). What happens to these young mothers? Their future seems to depend on the choices they make. Girls who stay at home with their parents and complete their education do best in the long run (Furstenberg, Brooks-Gunn, and Chase-Lansdale, 1989). Those who drop out are less likely to find stable, well-paying jobs and more likely to find themselves on the welfare rolls than those who at least complete high school. Dropouts lack the skills that enable them to get jobs, yet they are burdened with the emotional and economic responsibilities of caring for an infant. The care is usually more than they bargained for. The cuddly, sweet, smiling baby envisioned by pregnant girls turns into a colicky, wet crier, smelling of sour milk, who needs continual attention and keeps them awake at night. Some studies have found that, within two years, many adolescent mothers—even those who said they did not intend to have more children—are pregnant again, which only compounds their problem (Scott-Jones and Turner, 1990).

Girls who "solve" their problem by getting married may at first be financially ahead of the unmarried girl, but their advantage may not be permanent. They usually drop out of school, and many find themselves divorced and without job skills (K. Moore, 1985). Among a group of low-income mothers in rural South Carolina, about half were no longer involved with the baby's father by the time the baby was 8 months old (Unger and Wandersman, 1988). (The accompanying box, "When Teenagers Become Mothers" describes the problems faced by children of adolescent mothers.)

Some adolescent mothers eventually do well. Those who finish school, control their fertility, and later develop stable marriages are indistinguishable from women of the same socioeconomic level who postpone childbearing (Furstenberg, Brooks-Gunn, and Chase-Lansdale, 1989; Scott-Jones and Turner, 1990). The key to success appears to be social support, often from parents or other family members who provide economic assistance and help care for the child, thus permitting the girl to return to school. Among adolescents in one study, African-American mothers reported higher levels of support from their families than did Hispanic mothers (Wasserman et al., 1990). African-American mothers also had higher self-esteem. This social support buffers the effect of teenage pregnancy.

Why So Many Pregnancies?
Although sexual activity has increased among adolescents, this increase does not account for the tide of teenage pregnancy. In Sweden, a society that is more sexually permissive than the United States, the rate of adolescent pregnancy is only about one-third that of American teenagers. American adolescents get pregnant at a rate that is two times higher than the rate in Canada, Great Britain, or France; seven times higher than in the Netherlands; and eighteen times higher than in Japan (Leavitt, 1986).

Most adolescents who become pregnant do not do so intentionally. Instead, they seem to have no motivation to avoid pregnancy (K. Moore, 1985). In fact, lack of motivation in general characterizes girls who become pregnant. They tend to have little interest in academic matters, and most are doing poorly in school and going nowhere (Furstenberg, Brooks-Gunn, and Morgan, 1987). Some girls intentionally become pregnant. Among girls with no job and no prospects for college, pregnancy may become a status symbol that promotes them to adulthood (L. Hoffman and Manis, 1978).

Social trends play a part in teenage pregnancies and birth. As adolescent pregnancies have become more common and single-mother role models have appeared among celebrities and career women, the stigma that was once attached to out-of-wedlock pregnancies has nearly vanished. When, in 1986, Madonna recorded "Papa Don't Preach," officials of Planned Parenthood threw up their hands. "The message," said the executive director, "is that getting pregnant is cool and having the baby is the right thing and a good thing, and don't listen to your parents, the school, anybody who tells you otherwise" (Dullea, 1986). In his view, Madonna was offering teenagers a path to permanent poverty.

The Case of Contraceptives
The immediate reason for adolescent pregnancy is the incorrect use of contraceptives, their sporadic use, or the failure to use them at all. Most sexually active teenagers know that contraceptives exist, and the proportion of adolescents using them doubled between 1980 and 1988. By the close of the decade, two-thirds of adolescents used contraceptives during their first intercourse, usually a condom (Child Trends, 1990).

Many of these adolescents, however, play a risky game and use contraceptives on some occasions but not on others. Perhaps because of the power of the personal fable, most never seem to realize that pregnancy could happen to them. In one study of pregnant adolescents, no matter how much a girl knew about contraceptives and the risk of unprotected intercourse, she was surprised when she actually became pregnant (P. Smith et al., 1982). Another factor is feelings of guilt or ambivalence about sexual activity (Rosen and Hall, 1984). Girls who believe that premarital sex is improper tend

WHEN TEENAGERS BECOME MOTHERS

Because bearing a child clearly constricts the adolescent girl's future, researchers have worried about the future of her child as well. Does her offspring show any ill effects for having so young a mother? In most cases, children born to adolescent mothers pay a penalty in both cognitive and social development. The problem has been to separate the children's socioeconomic handicaps from the handicap of having a mother who is little more than a child herself.

Children of adolescent mothers tend to score lower on school achievement tests and on IQ tests than children of older mothers. They are more likely to be retarded than children born to older mothers. Those who are not retarded have lowered educational aspirations. Among preschoolers, the cognitive differences are small, but they widen steadily as children go through school. By the time they are in high school, children of teenage mothers are much more likely than other youngsters to have repeated a grade. Studies indicate that about 50 percent of the children of African-American teenage mothers fail at least one grade, whereas about 20 percent of the children of older African-American mothers fail a grade. Some children did well in school. In such cases, most mothers had moved off the welfare rolls, entered a stable marriage, and gone back to complete their own education (Brooks-Gunn and Furstenberg, 1986; Furstenberg, Brooks-Gunn, and Chase-Lansdale, 1989).

Socioeconomic factors account for most of the differences in the children's cognitive performance. Adolescent mothers generally are poor, are unmarried, and have not completed high school. The majority grow up in single-parent households. After allowing for all these socioeconomic factors, researchers found that having an adolescent mother added to the problem but that the effect was small (Brooks-Gunn and Furstenberg, 1986).

Socially, teenagers' children are also at a disadvantage. In elementary school, they tend to be more active, impulsive, easily frustrated, and hyperactive than children of older mothers. Boys seem especially affected; they tend to be more aggressive and willful than other boys. When they reach high school, children of adolescent mothers have trouble at school; often they are suspended, expelled, or subjected to other disciplinary action (Brooks-Gunn and Furstenberg, 1986). Again, socioeconomic conditions provide part of the explanation, but other factors are also important. In one study, half of the 15- and 16-year-old children of teenage African-American mothers had been expelled or suspended from school in the past five years compared to only a quarter of the children of older African-American mothers in comparable economic circumstances (Furstenberg, Brooks-Gunn, and Morgan, 1987). Finally, although most daughters of teenage mothers finish high school and do not become pregnant, about one-third of them repeat their mothers' history of adolescent pregnancy, keeping the adolescent childbearing cycle going.

Some of the differences that appear in these children may be in part the result of the mother's immaturity and inexperience when her child is small. Although adolescent mothers are just as warm as other mothers, they are less responsive to their infants, talk less to them, are less sensitive to their needs, and tend to punish them more than older mothers do (Elster, McAnarney, and Lamb, 1983). Most adolescent mothers know little about child development and have unrealistic expectations of their children. As Jeanne Brooks-Gunn and Frank Furstenberg (1986) put it, they expect "too little, too late" from their children in cognition and language but may expect too much, especially in physical development, from preterm babies. Such differences may explain the high level of insecure attachments found among babies of adolescent mothers (Lamb, Hopps, and Elster, 1987).

When teenage mothers have adequate social support, their children's problems generally are smaller. Social support can alleviate stress, provide practical assistance, inform the mother about children's capabilities, and enhance the mother's self-esteem (Elster, McAnarney, and Lamb, 1983). In one study, adolescent mothers who had good support from the fathers of their babies were less rejecting and tended to punish their babies less (Unger and Wandersman,1988). If there is another adult in the household, the youngster's cognitive and social development is enhanced (Brooks-Gunn and Furstenberg, 1986). The additional adult may act as a buffer against negative events, provide social and emotional support for the mother, and provide direct support to the child (Unger and Wandersman, 1988). Teenagers can be good mothers, but socioeconomic stress and a lack of social support often prevent them from giving their babies a good start in life.

---

to excuse their sexual activity if they are "swept away" by their emotions. Carrying contraceptives or taking birth-control pills indicates the intent to have sex and thus marks the girls as "bad" in their own eyes.

Some girls are simply misinformed. In one study of African-American adolescents age 15 to 19, many had only a hazy knowledge of reproduction, and at least half of the girls had become sexually active *before* they had sex education classes that provided information on contraception (Scott-Jones and Turner, 1990). Girls with such a vague knowledge may believe that if they take one of their mothers' birth-control pills before a date, they will be protected. Or they believe that intercourse in certain positions is "safe." Or that they must have an orgasm to conceive. Six out of ten adolescent girls are not sure just when during a menstrual cycle they are most likely to conceive (Hevesi, 1986). Some have exaggerated fears of the side effects of contraceptives. And some are afraid that if they go to a clinic, their parents will learn that they are sexually active.

Sporadic or inefficient users of contraceptives tend to differ in several ways from adolescents who use contraceptives effectively. Girls who use contraceptives irregularly tend to be from lower socioeconomic families, to belong to fundamentalist Protestant churches, to have low educational aspirations or achievement, to have poor communication with their parents, to have friends who are parents, to have intercourse infrequently, and to lack a steady partner (Brooks-Gunn and Furstenberg, 1989). Their personalities also differ. Their self-esteem is usually low, they are anxious and alienated, and they feel powerless. Among girls at a teen clinic, sporadic users also had trouble imagining themselves in the future. Either they had no goals or their goals were unrealistic and bore no relation to their activities. They rarely thought things through before acting (Spain, 1980). Girls who used contraceptives efficiently had thought about the future and realized that their present behavior had consequences for their future. Such girls felt in control of their own lives, tended to have their future planned, and could visualize their future career and family situations.

Reducing Adolescent Pregnancies

One in every five sexually active adolescent girls is not using any form of birth control. Among those who are poor, one in every four sexually active girls uses no birth control (Forrest and Singh, 1990). Over the past twenty years, the number of adolescent births has gone down, but recent statistics have reawakened concern. In 1970, while the baby-boom generation swelled the adolescent section of the population, teenagers gave birth to 644,700 infants. By 1986, the number had dropped to 472,081, only to rise over the next three years. In 1988, 517,989 babies were born to adolescent mothers (Child Trends, 1992). After dropping in the early 1980s, the birth *rate* has also increased 19 percent among younger (15- to 17-year-old) girls—from 30.6 births per 1000 girls in 1986 to 36.5 births per 1000 in 1989.

Researchers tend to believe that the rise is due to increased sexual activity, because the proportion of teenagers who have abortions has remained steady.

Efforts to prevent teenage pregnancies have taken three forms: (1) sex education courses that include information about contraception; (2) attempts to change adolescent attitudes toward early sexual activity; and (3) the provision of contraceptive and family-planning services (Furstenberg, Brooks-Gunn, and Chase-Lansdale, 1989). Evidence concerning the effect of sex education on sexual activity and contraceptive use is inconclusive, and efforts to postpone sexual activity are too recent to be evaluated. Most studies, however, indicate that contraceptive and family-planning services are the most likely to reduce the pregnancy rate—especially among African-American teenagers (Hofferth, 1987).

When high schools in St. Paul, Minnesota, began providing contraceptives as part of the general health-care services, births among high school girls declined from 59 per 1000 in 1977 to 37 per 1000 in 1985 (Leavitt, 1986). And when some high schools in Baltimore began providing birth-control services, the rate of pregnancies among students dropped 22.5 percent at a time when the pregnancy rate in other Baltimore high schools climbed 39.5 percent (Perlez, 1986). The presence of the clinics also seemed to slow the rate at which students became sexually active. After the clinics were installed, students in those high schools tended to postpone their first sexual activity by about six months. In most places, high school clinics have been controversial. In fact, students themselves tend to say that they would prefer going off the school grounds to clinics—primarily because they fear that clinic personnel will notify school officials about their visits.

No program can eliminate adolescent pregnancies, but those that are most successful in reducing the rate provide adolescents with the motivation to avoid pregnancy.

Adolescent Eating Disorders

Eating disorders recently have emerged as a common adolescent problem. As recently as twenty years ago, such terms as *anorexia* and *bulimia* were almost unknown except to clinical psychologists and psychiatrists, and most of them knew of these conditions only from descriptions in textbooks. Today, these disorders are so frequent that many colleges and universities offer counseling or therapy programs specifically designed for students who suffer from them. Eating disorders fall into three types: obesity, anorexia nervosa, and bulimia.

Although their provision of contraceptives has been controversial, many high schools that provide birth-control services have seen a drop in teenage pregnancies. *(Bernard Gotfryd/Woodfin Camp & Associates)*

among girls from high-income families. Although boys at all socioeconomic levels are unlikely to wish for a thinner body unless they are obese, the desire to be thin is correlated with socioeconomic level among girls (Dornbusch et al., 1984). Girls in low-income families tend to be dissatisfied only when they are fatter than the average girl, but girls in high-income families yearn to be thinner, no matter what their weight. Such a situation sets up these girls for eating disorders.

The results of a longitudinal study support this view. Among nonobese, upper-middle-class, adolescent girls in a private New York City middle school, the body fat that is a normal accompaniment of puberty seemed to provide the triggering event that established eating problems (Attie and Brooks-Gunn, 1989). These girls were neither bulimic nor anorectic, but their preoccupation with thinness, their almost pathological avoidance of fattening foods, their preoccupation with thoughts of food, and their tendency to binge at times were similar to those of girls with anorexia or bulimia. The more negative a girl felt about her body in early adolescence, the stronger the tendency to develop eating problems during the following two years. Thus, body image is a significant predictor of compulsive eating problems during adolescence.

Obesity

About 15 percent of American adolescents are obese; their body weight exceeds the ideal weight for their height by at least 20 percent (Maloney and Klykylo, 1983). Girls are much more disturbed about obesity than boys. Obese girls (and those who are not obese but believe they weigh more than they should) generally have low self-esteem and a distorted image of their bodies (they see themselves as fatter than they actually are) and feel helpless and frustrated when their dieting is unsuccessful. They are ashamed about their weight, and the shame extends to their appetite for food. Some girls are so upset by their weight and so dissatisfied with their bodies that they become depressed (Rodin, Silberstein, and Striegel-Moore, 1985).

There is no single cause of obesity. As we saw in Chapter 5, genes, metabolism, eating habits, inactivity, and a heightened responsiveness to environmental cues are all implicated in its development. There are some indications that girls' attempts to lose weight can make staving off obesity even more difficult. At puberty, increased estrogen and progesterone levels promote the development of fat cells and the storage of body fat. These normal fat deposits send many girls onto rigid diets. But research suggests that dieting during this pe-

Despite the distinctness of definition, they overlap somewhat in actuality: an adolescent with anorexia also may be bulimic, a once obese adolescent may become anorectic, and a youngster with bulimia also may be obese.

A common thread running through all the disorders is the culture's demand that women and adolescent girls be thin. The female body ideal is far thinner than the natural female figure, and that discrepancy has grown since the middle of the twentieth century. Between 1959 and 1979, the weight and body size of the *Playboy* magazine centerfold model and the contestants in the Miss America contest decreased significantly, and since 1970, the contest winners have been thinner than the other contestants (Garner et al., 1980). Because girls' self-concepts are strongly related to their perceived attractiveness, these cultural changes have increased the pressure on girls to stay slim—especially

riod, when hormonal production is being established, may disrupt the body's normal weight-regulation process (Rodin, Silberstein, and Striegel-Moore, 1985).

Obesity has negative effects on a girl's future but is less threatening to a boy's. In an early study, 52 percent of nonobese girls but only 32 percent of obese girls in a high school graduating class went on to college. Among the boys, 53 percent of the nonobese and 50 percent of the obese boys entered college (Canning and Mayer, 1966). Because college education is an important determinant of socioeconomic level, such patterns could have a permanent effect and may help explain why obese women—but not obese men—tend to wind up at a lower socioeconomic level than their parents. Part of this sex difference may be the result of discrimination by college admissions offices (Goldblatt, Moore, and Strunkard, 1965). In some girls, the struggle against obesity leads to more serious eating disorders.

Anorexia Nervosa

Anorexia nervosa is a pattern of self-starvation brought about by fanatical dieting. To be diagnosed as anorectic, a girl must have lost more than 25 percent of her original body weight and have no known medical or psychiatric illness (Sorosky, 1986). Girls sometimes accelerate the weight loss by using laxatives, diuretics, and appetite suppressants. Their initial aim may be to achieve a "perfect" body by taking off a few pounds, but when they reach that goal, they select a new target of an even lower weight. The pattern continues with the girl (up to 95 percent of anorectics are girls) becoming thinner and thinner. If the process is not interrupted, the girl eventually resembles a skeleton: her ribs protrude, her face takes on a skull-like appearance, and her hands resemble claws. In most cases, she seems to enjoy the loss of each additional pound and denies that she is skinny. Yet she is often so malnourished that she must be hospitalized and forced to eat. Left untreated, anorexia nervosa is an extremely dangerous disorder. The victim may starve herself to death or die from the medical complications of malnutrition.

Anorexia develops out of a fear that the anorectic shares with most adolescent girls: the fear of becoming fat. When researchers compared anorectic girls with healthy girls, they found that *both* groups were "always on a diet," continually used willpower to restrain their eating, and viewed their hunger as exaggerated and obscene (M. Thompson and Schwartz, 1982).

Anorexia is most common among affluent, well-educated girls in developed countries, where the pressure to be slim and willowy is intense. Yet there seems

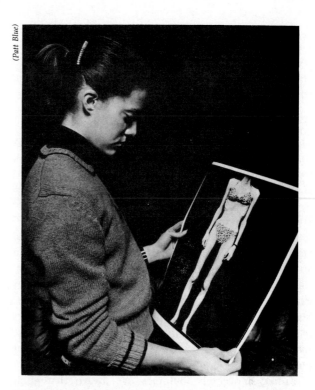

(Patt Blue)

After therapy for anorexia nervosa, this girl looks at an earlier picture of herself, taken at a time when her body image was so distorted that she regarded herself as "too fat." *(Patt Blue)*

to be something additional in the background of anorectic girls, or else most affluent girls would become anorectic. For one thing, most are high achievers. From her early years, the anorectic girl has strived for success, trying to be a straight-A student, a "perfect child." One such young woman, while in college, took twenty units of course work each semester, held a full-time job, was captain of an athletic team, tutored disadvantaged children, and exercised strenuously for at least two hours a day.

Some clinicians believe that fear of sexuality is a major factor in anorexia (Maloney and Klykylo, 1983). The severe weight loss stops menstruation and shrinks the girl's breasts and hips until she no longer is recognized as female. Anorexia eliminates any possibility of pregnancy. In effect, it restores the girl to her prepubertal status, in which she had no adult responsibilities.

Others believe that anorexia is the symptom of a deeply troubled, malfunctioning family, in which the girl's self-starvation maintains family stability. In this view, parents focus on protecting or blaming their child, a ploy that allows them to ignore their own conflicts and to see the girl as the primary family problem (Hsu, 1983).

If the girl otherwise feels powerless, self-starvation may give her a means of controlling an area of her life. Still others believe that there is a genetic component to anorexia and that the girl's hypothalamus (which regulates eating) malfunctions.

Bulimia

The anorectic girl exerts rigid control over her eating, to the point of starvation. By contrast, in **bulimia,** sometimes called the "binge-purge syndrome," a girl goes through repeated episodes in which her eating is out of control. During her periodic food binges, she consumes large quantities of high-calorie foods—several pounds of chocolate bars, perhaps, or several large pizzas—in the course of an hour or two. In an attempt to manage her weight, the girl may induce vomiting after each binge or train herself to throw up after each meal. Instead of vomiting, some bulimics use heavy doses of laxatives to control their weight. Others use diuretics or diet rigorously between binges. Those who purge themselves regularly run the risk of serious medical and dental problems.

Unlike anorectics, bulimics are aware that their binges are abnormal, are afraid that someday they will be unable to stop their eating, and feel ashamed and depressed after each episode. Although anorectics are by definition underweight, many bulimics are of average or above-average weight. But binge eating is not limited to adolescents with bulimia. Among a group of 1000 high school girls, nearly 17 percent of the "normal," nonbulimic girls went on food binges at least weekly, and 9 percent were vomiting at least once a month to control their weight (C. Johnson et al., 1984).

Girls who become bulimic differ in several ways from the "normal" adolescent who is preoccupied with her weight. Genetic, family, and personality factors seem to interact in the production of bulimia (DeAngelis, 1990). Like the anorectic, those suffering from bulimia have low self-esteem and may grow up in a dysfunctional family. Bulimics, however, often have difficulty regulating their own behavior. Many bulimics have symptoms of depression, and many of their relatives also have major affective disorders (such as depression) (J. Hudson et al., 1983).

Once her weight drops below a certain point, the anorectic's disorder cannot be hidden. But bulimics can binge or binge and purge secretly for years without being discovered. Treatment for anorexia and bulimia depends on the therapist. Both disorders have been treated by psychoanalysis, family therapy, behavior therapy, cognitive therapy, group therapy, and biochemical methods. Often a therapist combines two types of treatment, such as cognitive therapy and antidepressants. Each approach has achieved some success.

The Future of Adolescent Stress and Distress

Is the picture of adolescent disorders set forth in this chapter an enduring portrait of adolescence or simply a snapshot of the troubles that have beset adolescents over the past twenty-five years? A major change has taken place in the way developmentalists view the adolescent experience. Not so long ago, our knowledge of adolescents came from studies (primarily of boys) that made no attempt to fit the findings into a historical perspective (G.H. Elder, 1980). Today, researchers generally try to consider how social and historical influences affect the way that young people mature.

After nearly twenty years of a steady rise in adolescent disorders, the numbers turned around and in many cases began to decline. Drug use peaked in 1979. Youthful crime peaked in 1980. Suicide peaked in 1977. Out-of-wedlock births peaked in 1980. Then, after 1985, some of the numbers began to creep up again. Drug use is still declining—at least among adolescents who remain in school—but not all other disorders have continued their decline. The crime rate and out-of-wedlock birth rates have resumed their climb, as has the suicide rate, among 15- to 19-year-olds, while continuing to trend lower among young people in their early twenties (Berman and Jobes, 1991).

One intriguing theory explains the rise and subsequent fall between 1960 and 1985 as primarily an effect of the baby boom that produced a record crop of children between 1946 and 1964 (Easterlin, 1980). This **birth-cohort theory** holds that there is a strong relationship between the "crowdedness" of a generation and the amount of disturbance felt by its members. Those born during a baby boom are more likely to develop emotional problems than those born during a "baby bust," when there are few youngsters relative to the total population.

Children of a crowded generation find themselves competing with one another for limited resources. In each of life's races—for grades, admission to the best colleges, jobs, promotions—there are more runners to be edged out. Those who sense themselves falling behind or likely to fail tend to react with feelings of worth-

According to the birth-cohort theory, competition among members of the crowded baby-boom generation was responsible for much of the increase in adolescent crime and suicide. *(Jacques Chenet/Woodfin Camp & Associates)*

lessness and self-blame. Individuals who react with resentment tend to commit delinquent acts; those who react with feelings of worthlessness tend to become depressed or even commit suicide. As destructive or self-destructive acts accumulate, there is a sharp rise not only in the number of such acts but also in the rate. The practical effects can be dramatic. If the number of youngsters born in a given year doubles, and if the rate of a particular act triples, there is a 600 percent increase. This is exactly what happened between 1960 and 1980 in the case of suicides by young white males.

Early studies supported the birth-cohort theory. When cohorts from 1933 to 1976 were compared, suicide correlated 0.46 with the size of the cohort, and homicide correlated 0.52 with cohort size (Offer and Holinger, 1983). A similar pattern appeared in the case of all crimes, which began to rise when the first wave of baby-boomers hit adolescence and continued to rise until 1980, when members of this cohort moved into their thirties. The number of crimes rose because there was a larger share of people (young men between the ages of 15 and 29) who were likely to commit crimes.

Furthermore, the per capita crime rate rose: each 1000 young men committed more crimes than did 1000 young men in the 1960s. As job opportunities and income shrank for the baby-boomers, they found it increasingly difficult to equal their parents' economic position. Many could get only low-paying jobs or found no job at all. Psychological stress increased, and so did antisocial behavior. Young people who were at risk for delinquency (because of their family background and temperament) became more likely to turn to criminal acts (Schapiro and Ahlburg, 1986).

As birth-cohort theory predicted, the rates of adolescent problems began to decline around 1980. The decline continued for several years. Then something happened. Rates began to rise. The crime rate, for example, increased from 104.6 arrests per 1000 adolescents in 1984 to 118.6 arrests in 1985 (Office of Educational Research and Improvement, 1988). This trend did not continue: the proportion of crimes committed by adolescents has declined slightly—from 17 percent in 1985 to 16 percent in 1988 (U.S. Bureau of the Census, 1990). Clearly, the birth-cohort theory does not explain all changes. Economic fluctuations also seem to be involved. During the late 1980s, recession eroded the amount of resources available for teenagers. Economic stress and the transition to a service economy (which

eliminated many blue-collar jobs) have had a powerful impact on working-class youth, who can no longer expect to move from high school into a well-paying factory job. Between 1970 and 1985, the proportion of American families at lower socioeconomic levels grew from 21.9 to 23.5 percent (Koepp, 1986; McLoyd, 1989). A better way to explain fluctuations in the rate of adolescent problems might involve a combination of demographic shifts, which are the focus of birth-cohort theory, and economic fluctuations.

If we look at the future, the birth-cohort theory predicts a new wave of adolescent problems by the close of this decade. Today, the children of baby-boomers are entering puberty. Each year their numbers will increase until, by 1995, there will be nearly 2 million more 15- to 19-year-olds than there were in 1990; by 2000, the adolescent population will have grown by another 2 million and be larger than it was in 1980 (United Nations Population Division, 1976). Competition among peers and the consequent crowding out of the less attractive, the less able, or the less fortunate are likely to increase. Yet other factors may also be at work that could accelerate or dampen the stress felt by adolescents. Few social patterns have a single cause, and predictions about adolescents in the year 2000 remain uncertain.

SUMMARY

CHANGE AND STRESS

The adolescent years are spent in preparation for departure from the family. The lengthened period of adolescence in contemporary societies, together with young people's uncertainty about their future, and their anxiety over their choices can create stress.

NORMAL AND ABNORMAL ADOLESCENTS

Four myths have grown up about adolescence, but none has been supported by research. Adolescence is *not* a period of unusual emotional turmoil. When emotional disturbances arise during adolescence, they do *not* fade away as the young person enters adulthood. Hostility and conflict between adolescents and parents are *not* inevitable. A generation gap does *not* separate teenager and parents.

AREAS OF ADOLESCENT STRESS

A majority of adolescents use some drugs at some time, but those who use drugs heavily are troubled youngsters. Excessive use of drugs or alcohol is associated with poor school performance, disrupted family life, and antisocial behavior. Alcohol and marijuana are gateway drugs; teenagers almost always use one or the other before progressing to other drugs.

Across societies and historical eras, the crime rate is highest among the young and the male; in the United States, rates for violent crimes and crimes against property peak during adolescence. Adolescent crime rates are inflated by **status offenses,** because these offenses are not crimes when committed by adults. Delinquency is produced by interacting factors—some within the child, some within the family, and others within the larger society. Future delinquents generally are in trouble at school or have had severe enough home trouble to be taken to a child-guidance clinic by the time they are 8 or 9 years old.

Adolescents who run away from home are likely to be depressed, to have other emotional problems, and to abuse substances. A substantial proportion have been physically or sexually abused.

Suicide, which is the second leading cause of death among all adolescents except for African-American males, is concentrated among white and Native American males. Girls attempt suicide as often as boys, but boys use more lethal means, intend to kill instead of signal for help, and have poorer social support systems than girls. Most youngsters who commit suicide come from stress-ridden families; they either have severe behavior problems, are depressed, or are uptight, ambitious perfectionists.

Adolescents who become pregnant run increased risks of complications and death—both for themselves and their infants. Most of the risk is due to lack of prenatal care, but girls in early adolescence face additional risks because of their immature pelvises. Girls who keep their babies also face social and emotional problems; they are burdened with responsibility for a baby but lack job skills. The high rate of adolescent pregnancy seems due to a lack of motivation to avoid pregnancy and to social acceptance of out-of-wedlock births. Adolescents who do not use contraceptives generally believe that they will never become pregnant, feel guilty or ambivalent about premarital sex, are misinformed about the mechanics of conception, are afraid of contraceptives' side effects, or fear that their parents will discover their sexual activity.

Most adolescents with eating disorders are middle-class girls, and the disorders develop in good part because of the culture's unnaturally thin female body ideal. Obese teenagers tend to have low self-esteem, believe that they are much heavier than they actually are, and feel frustrated and helpless over their failures to lose weight. **Anorexia nervosa** is more prevalent among high achievers, whereas **bulimia** is associated with depression and lack of self-control.

THE FUTURE OF ADOLESCENT STRESS AND DISTRESS

Stress-related disorders among adolescents rose for twenty years, then declined for several years, only to increase again. According to the **birth-cohort theory,** this pattern is the result of the increased stress on members of the baby-boom generation. However, recent increases in most adolescent problem behavior suggest that economic fluctuations may also affect stress levels.

KEY TERMS

anorexia nervosa
birth-cohort theory

bulimia

status offense

YOUNG ADULTHOOD: SELECTING THE OPTIONS

SIX

• • • • • • • • • • • • • •

EARLY AND MIDDLE
ADULTHOOD

Our society has no rite or social ceremony to mark the passage from adolescence to adulthood. There is no single age at which a person becomes mature. So we will arbitrarily define early adulthood as the years from 18 until 40, using the end of high school as a convenient marker for entry into adulthood. A familiar saying has it that "life begins at 40," and that is where we begin middle adulthood. One popular marker for the close of middle adulthood is eligibility for full Social Security benefits. We accept that date and see middle adulthood as extending to age 65, because people in their early sixties have more in common with adults in their fifties than with their elders. These chapters begin with the story of young people struggling to establish intimacy and carving out occupational niches. They continue with the story of the "command generation"—middle-aged adults whose broadened responsibilities place them in charge of society.

YOUNG ADULTHOOD: SELECTING THE OPTIONS

• • • • • • • • • • • • • •

At 30, Patty Wilson works at two part-time jobs, as fire fighter and as crew dispatcher for a 911 emergency center, where she is responsible for sending ambulances, fire fighters, and police across a Pennsylvania county. Her husband Phil, 31, is a photographer for a local newspaper. The Wilsons have been married for nine years and have a 1-year-old daughter. When they met, neither had any plans for marriage. Phil had never given the subject much thought, and Patty saw a future as a high-powered reporter for the New York Times. *Within two years they were married; Patty was 21 and Phil was 22. For seven years, Patty worked as a reporter for the same paper that Phil worked for as a photographer. They saved money and bought a house. Then Patty became pregnant. She worked until a month before her baby was due. When Meredith was 5 months old, Patty went back to a full-time job as a reporter, working mornings and evenings. Meredith spent her mornings with Phil's mother, and during the evenings Phil took over as chief caregiver. When Meredith was about 9 months old, Patty decided that a 50-hour workweek was robbing her of an important relationship with Meredith. She switched from full- to part-time work—but she plans to go back to a full-time career within a few years.*

Parenthood has changed both partners in the Wilson marriage. When Patty tries to convey what Meredith has brought to her life, she becomes eloquent: "I feel like I found something that I had before but had no way to get to. Like a new room in your house. You pass the door so many times, but you never bother to open it. Well, I opened it. And it's the best room in the house" (Kotre and Hall, 1990, p. 83). Phil's view of his own life has also undergone a profound shift: "Now that I have a little girl, everything has changed. My expectations for the future are centered around what I can do for her. Not that I've become a selfless individual, but so far as I'm making plans, I'm really making them for her" (Seasons of Life, 1990).

● ● ● ● ● ●

For Patty and Phil, the decade of their twenties was not a period of exploration but a time when they got down to the business of life—of job, marriage, responsibilities, and children. For young adults who spend part of that decade in college, decisions concerning marriage and career still lie ahead. For a time, they are free from adult responsibilities and have merely reached the halfway point in their progress toward true adulthood.

In this chapter we will see how changes in society have altered young adulthood since the parents of Patty and Phil were 20 years old. The situations young people will face and the choices they must make as they live through the years from 18 to 39 will become clear as we trace the course of development in young adults. After looking at recent social changes, we briefly consider physical development during the young adult years. Next we examine various explanations of the changes that occur during the years between 18 and 40. With that background, we are ready to take up major aspects of the young adult's life, beginning with the way maturity and gender affect self-concept and self-esteem. Next we investigate work, a part of our lives that is so important that most of us would work even if we did not have to support ourselves. After considering the institution of marriage and its alternatives, we look at parenthood and its effects on us as couples and individuals, and we examine the twentieth-century addition to the cycle of many families—divorce and remarriage.

Social Change

Changes in society affect the attitudes and behavior of all its members. Women and men have "social clocks" in their heads to help them judge their own and other people's behavior as being early, late, or on time (Neugarten and Neugarten, 1986). The appropriate time for a particular developmental event may change from one generation to the next. In 1960, for example, nearly 90 percent of Chicago adults agreed that women should marry between the ages of 19 and 24; in 1980, only 40 percent believed that women should marry that early (Neugarten and Neugarten, 1986). Since 1980, the strength of social clocks has continued to weaken. Traditional norms and expectations have changed, and the appropriate time for such events as marriage, careers, and parenthood is becoming tied less closely to chronological age. It sometimes seems as if we are witnessing the development of what Bernice Neugarten (1979) has called an **age-irrelevant society,** in which there is no single appropriate age at which to take on the role of parent, student, worker, grandparent, and so forth. In an age-irrelevant society, developmental tasks remain the same, but adults do not feel that their social clocks are particularly early or late if they postpone or accelerate the social roles of adulthood.

An increasing number of young adults are postponing marriage. In 1956, half of all American men were married before the age of 23; in 1991, men were 26.3 years old before half of them were married. Women are also waiting longer to marry, with the median age at first marriage climbing from 20 in 1956 to 24.1 in 1991 (Barringer, 1992). The postponement is greatest among middle-class women, primarily because an increasing proportion are completing college, going on to graduate and professional schools, and then entering the professions. Families are changing as well. Women are waiting longer after they are married to start their families. The majority use some form of birth control, with the pill the most popular method among women who are postponing pregnancy (U.S. Bureau of the Census, 1990a).

Hand in hand with planned parenthood go smaller families. The majority of couples either have or want two children, and the proportion of women who say they expect to have only one child rose during the 1980s. High school graduates are more likely to say they intend to stop at one child than women with a college education, although married college graduates are more likely to say that they intend to remain childless (U.S. Bureau of the Census, 1990a). Yet the birth rate is higher than it was in 1976, when the national fertility rate was 1.74 births per woman; in 1990, the rate reached 2.1 births per woman—still down drastically from the 3.77 births per woman chalked up in the early 1960s at the height of the baby boom (Barringer, 1991). Most of the increase in births has come from women older than 30: in 1975, only 34 percent of women in their early thirties said that they expected to have a child (or another child) someday, but in 1988, 54 percent reported that they still hoped to have a child (Berke, 1989). Whether they actually have another child may depend on economic factors; during the first half of 1991, with the United States in a recession, birth rates dipped for the first time in a decade (Barringer, 1991).

Despite a rise in fertility, marriage is less popular than it has been for some years. Perhaps because more people are living together without marrying, the marriage rate has been declining, with the rate among eligible young women the lowest since this marker was established in 1940 (U.S. Bureau of the Census, 1990b).

After rising for two decades, the divorce rate leveled off in the 1980s, but among couples now entering their first marriage, more than half are expected eventually to divorce (Bumpass and Castro-Martin, 1989).

Another social change has taken place in the physical appearance of young Americans. Good nutrition, sanitation, and preventive medicine have combined to make women and men in the later portions of young adulthood look younger and more attractive than their parents and grandparents looked at the same age. The 35-year-old of the 1930s or 1940s seemed visibly older than the 35-year-old of the 1990s.

Physical Characteristics

During young adulthood, most people are at the peak of their physical agility, speed, and strength. Men tend to be proud of their bodies, women do not. When 300 college-age men and women were asked to rate their own bodies, women (no matter how slim) saw themselves as somewhat heavier than the male ideal and much heavier than their own ideal for the female body (Fallon and Rozin, 1985). Men (even those who were heavy) saw themselves as matching both the female and their own ideal body weights. Neither sex was on target in their notion of the other sex's standard for attractiveness. Men's ideal woman was heavier than women believed, and women's ideal man was lighter than men believed.

Although adults reach their physical peak in young adulthood, many of the hallmarks of aging begin in that same period of life. Around the age of 20, slow, continuing changes affect the workings of the human body (A. Spence, 1989). Muscle tone and strength, which generally peak between the ages of 20 and 30, decline after that. Visual acuity and hearing begin to decline in the twenties. The first tiny wrinkles begin to appear beside the eyes, and the skin is aging—especially among those who cultivate a suntan. The ultraviolet rays of the sun interfere with the production of DNA and protein synthesis in the skin. In response, skin cells regenerate more slowly, and the skin thins and becomes wrinkled (Perlmutter and Hall, 1992).

Changes also occur deep within the body. Even if weight remains constant, by the close of young adulthood the proportion of fatty tissue to muscle begins to increase. In addition, the amount of air that can be drawn into the lungs in a single breath begins to decline

in the twenties, decreasing about 1 percent per year, as does the rate at which the kidneys filter blood (Vestal and Dawson, 1985). The arteries also begin to age, with hard, yellow, fatty plaques appearing on the arterial walls of individuals who are susceptible to atherosclerosis. Poor diet and lack of exercise have begun to contribute to the development of chronic diseases that will not become apparent until middle or late adulthood.

Few young adults are concerned about these changes, although some 30-year-olds may be carefully plucking an occasional gray hair. Perhaps the lack of concern comes in part from a sense of peak physical fitness and performance. Reaction times generally are at their peak until about the age of 26, and so young adults excel in sports that demand quick reactions, strength, and speed, such as basketball, boxing, tennis, skiing, and baseball (Schulz and Curnow, 1988). The slowing of reaction time is one reason that most professional athletes begin to "feel their age" when they enter their thirties.

As reaction time slows and small declines in strength appear, professional athletes in their thirties find it increasingly difficult to maintain their careers. *(Nancy Ploeger/Monkmeyer Press)*

Theories and Issues of Young Adulthood

As people move through adulthood, they focus their energies and motivations on different developmental tasks. Among the major tasks faced by young adults are completing their education, entering the work force, marrying, and becoming parents. Everyone faces these tasks, for even the decision *not* to marry or have children is a way of handling this aspect of development. The various theories of adult development seek to explain general patterns of growth and change and to identify dominant themes that characterize adult lives. Some theorists believe that the course of development they have charted applies to people in any society; others are more cautious and regard their theories as applying primarily to adults in a Western technological society. When theories clash, the disagreements point up important issues in adult development that have not been resolved by research.

Erikson's Psychosocial Theory

Erik Erikson's (1982) view of adult development derives from his eight-stage theory of the life cycle. As we saw in Chapter 2, Erikson proposed that development consists of the progressive resolution of inevitable conflicts between needs and social demands. At each of the eight stages, a person must at least partially resolve the major developmental conflict of that stage before he or she can begin to work effectively on the problems of the next.

The major task facing young adults is the development of intimacy, an advance that presupposes the earlier development of identity in adolescence (see Chapter 13). The alternative to intimacy is isolation. When adults resolve the conflict successfully, they are able to commit themselves to a relationship that demands sacrifice and compromise. They are able to love another person more or less unselfishly. If isolation dominates intimacy, their emotional relationships are cold and unspontaneous, and there is no real emotional exchange. A person may establish sexual relationships without developing intimacy, especially if he or she fears the emotional fusion involved in a committed relationship. When this pattern of noncaring sexual relationships characterizes a person's life, he or she may feel isolated (Erikson and Hall, 1987).

Erikson's psychosocial theory is meant to be a uni-versal theory, applying to both genders and all societies, but Erikson assumes that cultural differences influence the way the developmental tasks of each stage are met. Researchers who have conducted longitudinal studies of adult development believe, however, that Erikson's picture of healthy personality development applies only in cultures in which individualism is held in high esteem and individuals' roles are not tightly controlled by society (Vaillant and Milofsky, 1980).

Carol Gilligan (1982) believes that the developmental tasks are also very different for men and women because of differing socialization practices. Throughout childhood, women meet developmental tasks within a context of relationships, so achieving intimacy does not present a great departure from their earlier development. Many women are working on identity and intimacy simultaneously. This is not true for men, Gilligan maintains, because during their earlier development relationships were not stressed. Intimacy requires men to change their adolescent identity.

Levinson's Seasons

Another stage theory of adult development has been formulated by Daniel Levinson (Levinson et al., 1978), who has said that it portrays "the seasons of a man's life." He regards his theory as building on Erikson's psychosocial theory. Levinson's theory describes male development from about the age of 17 through the middle years, noting an orderly sequence that alternates between stable and transitional phases. During the stable phases, men pursue their goals more or less tranquilly, because the pertinent developmental tasks have been solved. The transitional phases can lead to major changes in a man's life structure, because at these times men are questioning the pattern of their lives and exploring new possibilities. Levinson based his theory on a series of in-depth interviews with forty men (African-American as well as white; working class as well as middle class).

Levinson sees the years from 17 to 22 as a time of transition to early adulthood. In a development similar to Erikson's identity achievement, men work at becoming psychologically independent from their parents. At about 22, they become autonomous and move into a stable phase as they try to establish themselves in the adult world. At the same time, they are learning to relate to women and establishing a home and family—developing intimacy, in Erikson's terms. Within six years, when they are about 28, they go into another transitional phase. This time they see flaws in the pattern of their lives and make new choices. Then, at about 33, they are ready to settle down. Career consolidation becomes a major goal, and men concentrate on developing their skills and deepening the bases of experience. They also work at reaching the major goals that they have set for themselves, whether that entails becoming a corporate executive or owning a truck. But along with this urge to get their lives in order and to achieve their goals comes an urge to be free and unattached.

Attempts to apply Levinson's theory to young women have found some similarities. Several studies indicate that women pass through the same stages as men during early adulthood, at about the same time—but with some differences (Kogan, 1990). Women's age-30 transition takes the form of a reappraisal, as they tend to switch focus from occupation to family (or vice versa). Instead of "settling down," women spend their thirties trying to integrate new commitments into their life structure (P. Roberts and Newton, 1987).

Gould's Transformations

Roger L. Gould's (1975, 1978) theory of adult development applies to both sexes, but all 524 men and women whose experiences form the basis of his theory were middle-class whites. From their responses to an exhaustive questionnaire, Gould concluded that adult development progresses through a series of transformations. In each transformation, people reformulate self-concepts, face childish illusions, and resolve conflicts.

In Gould's theory, young adults move through four phases. In the first phase, which begins in late adolescence and lasts until the age of 22, people are forging an identity and moving away from their parents' world. With autonomy established, they move into the second phase, during which they apply themselves to attaining their goals. Between the ages of 28 and 34, they pass through a transitional stage, in which they question some of their early goals and reevaluate their marriages. At about the age of 35, their discontent deepens, and the awareness of approaching middle age becomes acute. Life may seem painful, difficult, and uncertain. During this unstable period, which lasts until they are about 43, some may tear apart the fabric of their lives and put it together in a new way. A bachelor may marry; a married person may get a divorce; a mother may go back to school or work; a childless couple may decide to start a family. Gould's theory parallels Levinson's life seasons but places equal emphasis on women. Both theories were developed about the same time—in the 1970s—with Levinson studying men in the northeastern United States and Gould studying men and women in California.

Gutmann's Parental Imperative

In recent years, several developmentalists have offered theories of adult development based on a connection between evolutionary biology and human patterns of courtship and parenting (Buss et al., 1990). Most of this work focuses on the idea that because the survival of the species depends on its members' reproducing and rearing offspring to a reproductive age, human development should reflect this imperative. In the theory developed by David Gutmann (1987), adult personality development revolves around the **parental imperative.** He believes that the species has evolved to produce men and women with characteristics that ensure the emotional and physical safety of infants and children. In early human societies, a father's aggression, autonomy, competence, and control protected his child from predators and sent the father out to hunt for large game. Nurturance, sympathy, gentleness, and understanding kept the mother near her child and provided emotional security.

According to Gutmann, evolution provides only the *potential* for these gender roles. Through years of socialization men and women become comfortable with the prescribed traits and enjoy exercising them. When they become parents, fathers become more traditionally masculine: their concern is the security (physical and economical) of their family. Because being a passive, dependent, sympathetic father might interfere with the ability to bring home the necessary resources or to defend his child, men suppress any urges to be dependent or sympathetic. New mothers become more traditionally feminine: their concern is for the care and nurturance of the child. Because an aggressive, insensitive mother might harm her baby or drive off her mate, women suppress any urges to be assertive, masterful, or aggressive. Not until the last child leaves home is each sex free to express those aspects of the self that have been muffled by parental responsibilities.

Although Gutmann's theory is meant to apply to all societies in all historical periods, sharply restricted parental roles may not be so important to a modern technological society. When mothers and fathers share in providing their children's material support, care, and emotional security, parenthood may demand less in-

When young adults move to another city, they may enter a transition in their life cycle, when they restructure their life and goals. *(The Photo Works)*

tense changes in role and personality than Gutmann's theory suggests.

Issues in the Young Adult Years

Some theories of adult development place great importance on transitions in the life cycle. **Transitions** are changes in which we restructure our lives or reorder our goals in response to changing experiences. Getting married, taking a new job, having children, being fired, buying a home, moving to another city are the sort of events that stimulate developmental transitions.

The Nature of Transitions

How stressful are these changes? Researchers disagree about whether life transitions are times of physical and psychological distress. Levinson (Levinson et al., 1978) maintains that transitions are highly stressful. Among his forty men, twenty-five (62 percent) went through either a moderate or a severe crisis during the "Age-30 transition." Only seven men (18 percent) said that the period was unruffled by psychological stress. Neugarten (1979) disagrees; she has found that transitions are highly stressful only when unexpected. When an event is anticipated and seen as part of the normal course of life, it causes little stress. But if the event is not part of the normal life course, if an expected event fails to

occur, or if the event conflicts with a person's social clock, coming too early or too late, it can cause great stress and precipitate an emotional crisis. A three-year study of white, lower- and middle-class women supported Neugarten's view (Baruch, Barnett, and Rivers, 1983). When asked about crises in their lives, these women rarely mentioned anticipated developmental events (such as marriage or childbirth). Instead, they reported events that upset the course of their lives (divorce, an automobile accident, a job transfer) or events that conflicted with their social clocks (the early death of a parent).

The conflict between Levinson and Neugarten may arise from differing views of a transition's source. Neugarten sees the social or physical event as the cause of the transition. Levinson would agree that the event (such as a divorce) may trigger a transition, but he would argue that the process had been building within the person as old developmental tasks lost their relevance and new tasks appeared. In his view, the divorce is the result of the inner process and not the cause. The debate continues, and in Chapter 18 we will meet it again when considering the transitions of middle adulthood.

The Timing of Adulthood

Another issue that has no simple answer is the timing of adulthood. When does a person become mature? Chronological age is not much help here, because one person seems mature at 20 and another still seems hopelessly immature at 40. Some elements of maturity are common to all theories of adult development. All theorists regard the ability to be intimate, to give and accept love, and to be affectionate and sexually responsive as necessary to the attainment of maturity. All stress the ability to be sociable, to have friends, to be devoted to others, and to nurture them. All agree that mature individuals have a sense of their abilities and goals, an interest in productive work, and the ability to do it.

One way to look at maturity is to think of it in terms of an ability to cope successfully with events and decisions that most people face at characteristic times in their lives. In terms of Erikson's theory, maturity in early adulthood would include a successful resolution of the developmental tasks of childhood and adolescence, the ability to commit the self to a close relationship with another (intimacy), and some concern with guiding the next generation and with productive work (generativity) (Whitbourne and Waterman, 1979).

Another way to look at maturity is in terms of people's self-perceptions. What makes a person feel grown up? Researchers asked more than 2000 married men and women which event in their lives was most important in making them feel that they were really an adult (L. Hoffman and Manis, 1979). Becoming a parent and supporting oneself were the most consistent markers of maturity, but as Table 16.1 indicates, gender and ethnic group affected people's perceptions.

No matter how we define adulthood, it is cumulative and changing. Maturity involves a continual adjustment to constantly changing expectations and responsibilities. Although people can be mature without marrying, having children, or working hard at a career, mature adults know who they are and where they want to go, and they work toward their goals. The phrase "getting it all together" accurately sums up the young adult's struggle toward maturity.

Self-Concept and Self-Esteem

As people move from adolescence to adulthood, they rarely experience a sharp discontinuity between their adolescent and adult selves. Yet we would expect some sort of change in **self-concept,** which is the organized, coherent, and integrated pattern of perceptions related to the self. Self-concept goes beyond a person's current view of the self to encompass a variety of possible selves—desired or feared concepts of a self one might become. Among young adults in college, 65 percent say that they think about their future selves a great deal of the time, and they are much more likely to focus on desirable future selves (sexy, confident, powerful) than on undesirable selves (depressed, destitute, unimpor-

TABLE 16.1   WHAT MADE YOU FEEL LIKE AN ADULT?

| | WOMEN (%) | | | | | MEN (%) | | |
| | PARENTS | | | NONPARENTS | | PARENTS | | NONPARENTS |
Life Event	White	African-American	Hispanic	White	African-American	White	African-American	White
Becoming a parent	40.2	34.8	33.3	11.1	14.3	31.6	11.5	5.3
Getting married	19.8	21.7	21.2	19.9	35.7	15.0	3.8	13.7
Supporting yourself	13.9	14.1	15.2	34.8	21.4	24.7	46.2	47.4
Getting a job	8.1	3.3	6.1	9.1	14.3	9.1	7.7	6.3
Finishing school	5.8	8.7	18.2	7.3	0.0	5.6	3.8	5.3
Moving out of parental home	5.1	10.9	3.0	9.8	7.1	7.8	23.1	7.4
Other	7.1	6.5	3.0	8.0	7.1	6.2	3.8	14.8
N	1113	92	33	287	14	320	26	95

*When asked which event was (or might be) most important in making them feel like an adult, most mothers and white fathers chose parenthood. For nonparents, "supporting yourself" was the most common reply by white men and women; most African-American women regarded marriage as the crucial event.

Source: L. Hoffman and Manis, 1979, p. 589.

tant) (Markus and Nurius, 1986) (see Table 16.2). Possible selves are important because they affect motivation and guide present behavior, influencing a person to avoid or to take specific actions.

Physical appearance, social roles, and abilities are closely related to self-concept, and all of them change during young adulthood. Longitudinal studies indicate both continuity and change in personality during young adulthood, with some researchers finding pronounced shifts in personality as people leave adolescence and enter young adulthood (Haan, Millsap, and Hartka, 1986). Once they leave adolescence, both sexes show less self-centered impulsiveness and an increased ability to cope with problems (Block, 1971). When they rate their own personalities, young women and men have similar levels of self-esteem and they value themselves more highly than they did as adolescents (Frieze et al., 1978). Some developmentalists believe that personality is best understood in terms of contextual theory, which assumes that various roles (worker, spouse, student, parent) interact with general historical influences (depression, war) to affect self-concept and personality (Kogan, 1990).

Any examination of self-concept that does not look at men and women separately may be misleading. Men and women measure their lives against such radically different standards that different factors probably influence their self-concepts (Hagestad and Neugarten, 1985). The concepts men and women have about themselves reflect the impact of gender-role stereotypes and their own gender schema. As we have seen, girls are traditionally socialized to be dependent, passive, emotionally expressive, and warm, whereas boys learn to be assertive and independent. Brought up in this way, young women are less likely than men to have a sense of control over their lives, successes, and failures. Young men tend to believe in their power to control their fates, but women are more likely to believe that outside powers are in control.

Men and Self-Esteem

Self-esteem in young men generally rises after they leave high school, but there is no sharp shift as they move from high school to college or the world of work. Among 1600 young men who were followed for five years after high school, the gradual rise seemed to reflect the increase in status, opportunities, and privileges that comes with increasing maturity (Bachman, O'Malley, and Johnston, 1978). When these men were adolescents, their family background, their own intellectual

TABLE 16.2   POSSIBLE-SELVES SURVEY OF COLLEGE STUDENTS*

Item	QUESTION (% OF "YES" REPLIES)	
	Does this describe you now?	Have you ever considered this a possible self?
Personality:		
Happy	88.0	100.0
Confident	83.8	100.0
Depressed	40.2	49.6
Lazy	36.2	48.3
Life style:		
Travel widely	43.6	94.0
Have lots of friends	74.6	91.2
Be destitute	4.5	19.6
Have nervous breakdown	11.1	42.7
Physical:		
Sexy	51.7	73.5
In good shape	66.7	96.5
Wrinkled	12.0	41.0
Paralyzed	2.6	44.8
General abilities:		
Speak well publicly	59.0	80.3
Make own decisions	93.2	99.1
Manipulate people	53.5	56.6
Cheat on taxes	9.4	17.9
Others' feelings toward you:		
Powerful	33.3	75.2
Trusted	95.7	99.1
Unimportant	12.8	24.8
Offensive	24.8	32.5
Occupation:		
Media personality	2.2	56.1
Owner of a business	1.4	80.3
Janitor	2.6	6.8
Prison guard	0.0	4.3

*Sample items from questionnaire describing 150 possible selves (⅓ positive, ⅓ neutral, ⅓ negative). The ratio of positive to negative selves ever considered by college students was almost four to one.

Source: Markus and Nurius, 1986, p. 959.

ability, and their academic achievement contributed heavily to their self-esteem. When the men became engaged in their careers, these factors faded in importance, and job status became more important. Higher-status jobs led to higher self-esteem. Lengthy unemployment was associated with declines in self-esteem, and the self-esteem of unemployed high school dropouts declined most.

Among a group of men who attended college, overall self-concept remained stable over fourteen years, but elements of their self-perceptions showed some change (Mortimer, Finch, and Kumka, 1982). Feelings of competence declined during college, only to rebound on graduation, whereas perceptions of the self as unconventional declined as the men became established in the business world. Once again, self-esteem suffered during periods of unemployment or among men forced to take jobs beneath their abilities and skills.

Women and Self-Esteem

Men generally express their needs for self-control and mastery in their jobs, but women with a high need for achievement may not always express that need directly. Some do, pursuing a career or becoming involved in politics or community work. Others meet their need for achievement indirectly and derive satisfaction from the successes of their husbands and children.

Toward the close of young adulthood, self-esteem sometimes slips in high-achieving women who devote themselves to their families. Judith Birnbaum (1975) compared highly intelligent full-time homemakers (all were honor graduates from college) with married professional women (all were mothers) and single professional women. She found that homemakers had the lowest self-esteem and the lowest sense of personal competence—even in the areas of social skills and child care. They tended to feel lonely and missed a sense of challenge and creative involvement. Apparently, as their children started school and no longer required extensive care, these women found the role of wife and mother inadequate for expressing their need to achieve.

Gender Roles and Self-Esteem

Perhaps as a result of the Women's Movement over the past twenty-five years, young men's and women's concepts of masculinity and femininity are changing. Among many young adults, gender-role stereotypes are breaking down, and those whose personalities do not fit

the traditional stereotype for either gender show the highest self-esteem and most advanced psychosocial development (Hyde, Krajnik, and Skuldt-Niederberger, 1991). These women and men are **androgynous;** they are high both in personality traits considered masculine (they are self-reliant, independent, and assertive) and in traits considered feminine (they are affectionate, sympathetic, and understanding). Among college students studied by Janet Spence (1979) more than a decade ago, those who were *low* in both masculine and feminine traits also had low self-esteem. Male students who fit the traditional gender-role stereotype (high in their own gender's traits and low in traits ascribed to the other gender) tended to be higher in self-esteem than women who fit their traditional gender-role stereotype. It seems that women who are not independent, self-reliant, and assertive have low self-esteem. This aspect of the traditional gender role may explain why many women see themselves as less competent than men. Recent studies have found an increase in the proportion of androgynous students, with women now being twice as likely as men to have androgynous personalities (Hyde, Krajnik, and Skuldt-Niederberger, 1991).

Most young men and women seem comfortable with androgyny. Among one group of young adults, men felt easy about expressing their "feminine" qualities, as women did about expressing their "masculine" side (Reedy, 1977). Both genders wanted to see themselves as self-confident, intelligent, independent, loving, and

Young women who are androgynous are more likely than traditionally feminine women to enter male-dominated occupations. *(Bob Daemmrich/Stock, Boston)*

understanding. This way of thinking about masculinity and femininity widens the possibilities for both sexes.

Work

Work occupies a considerable portion of the adult life span, and its influence touches almost every part of life. It defines our position in society, and if we are fortunate, it gives meaning to our lives and provides satisfying activity, an outlet for creativity, and a source of social stimulation (Perlmutter and Hall, 1992). Self-concept is so bound up with work that most people define themselves in terms of what they do. "I'm with IBM," they say, or "I'm a teacher," or "I'm just a housewife"—a self-disparaging response that has become common now that a majority of women are in the labor force. When introducing a friend to a new person, we usually include the person's occupation: "I want you to meet Jerry. He runs the shoe store on Chestnut Drive." At some level, we apparently realize the importance of work, as Freud did when he summed up the requirements for a healthy life as *lieben und arbeiten* (to love and work). Culture, social class, and gender have far-reaching effects on this vital part of our existence; they influence the kind of work we do, where we do it, and when we do it. In technological societies, for example, the proportion of women in the work force has grown rapidly since 1970 (U.S. Bureau of Labor Statistics, 1991). Yet in Italy, only 30 percent of the women work outside the home (see Figure 16.1).

Importance of Work

Work affects personality, family life, social relations, and attitudes. To say that work affects personality may sound odd, but when we consider that the work environment is a stimulus that is present over a long period of time, we can see that prolonged exposure could have a cumulative effect on personality (Garfinkel, 1982). When workers were followed for ten years, the major influence seemed to come from the complexity of the work (Kohn and Schooler, 1983). The degree to which a person's job required thought and independence affected many aspects of personality. Job complexity seemed to lead to increased flexibility, which in turn affected values, self-concept, and attitudes toward society. In another study, workers in a manufacturing plant who participated in solving problems and making work-related decisions showed an increase in interpersonal

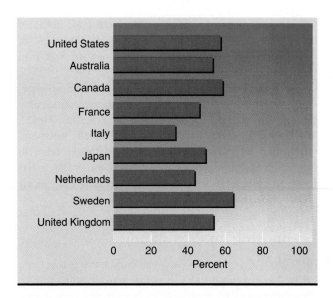

Figure 16.1 In 1990, U.S. women had a higher rate of work participation than women in other industrialized countries, except Sweden and Canada. Women in Italy had the lowest rate of participation among women in all nine industrialized countries for which data were available. Data for the Netherlands are for 1988, the latest available. *(From U.S. Bureau of Labor Statistics, 1991)*

skills, communication skills, and the ability to listen to others (Crouter, 1984).

The emotional tone of the work situation also carries over into a worker's daily life. Research indicates, for example, that stress on the job affects the tone of interaction between mates and between parents and children (Repetti, 1989, 1991). Employees' social relations at work are also related to self-esteem, levels of anxiety, and tendencies toward depression (Repetti, 1985).

Work can be a source of stress, especially when a person becomes overinvolved in a job and devotes long hours to it (L. Hoffman, 1986). Many aspects of work can produce stress: unemployment, too little money, low status, unpleasant job-related tasks, conflict between job values and personal values, lack of control and autonomy, and the job's intrusion into other areas of a person's life. Overinvolvement can lead to intolerable stress, even when a worker is highly successful.

Work-related stress can lead to depression, but this is most likely to occur in people who have few social roles. Rena Repetti and Faye Crosby (1984) studied more than 400 women and men whose jobs ranged from waitress and truck driver to physician and lawyer. They discovered that single people (whose major social role is worker) were most likely to be depressed by their jobs, and parents (whose major social roles include worker, spouse, and parent) were least likely to be depressed. Within each group, those in low-prestige occupations showed more depression than those in high-prestige occupations.

Work can be a source of enormous satisfaction, especially when it gives the worker a sense of creating, producing, or achieving something (Garfinkel, 1982). Workers at all levels find employment highly satisfying when their jobs are challenging and financially rewarding, when they are given whatever resources they need to do the job well, and when their working conditions are comfortable (Seashore and Barnowe, 1972).

Choosing an Occupation

Personality, interests, and values are often the basis for occupational choice, but many people wander into their life's work by accident. Such apparently irrelevant factors as decisions in some other area of life, the location of their homes, luck, and gender may determine the career or job that awaits them.

Some of the decisions that determine which ticket a person draws in the great occupational lottery are made in high school, as we saw in Chapters 13 and 14. Among other important influences is place of residence, which helps decide occupational choice in two ways. First, the nature of local industries determines what sort of job is available, especially for working-class adults. Second, adults in the community provide the role models that turn the young person's thoughts to various jobs and careers.

People enter occupations they know about; for example, most of those who work on commercial fishing boats have grown up near the sea. *(Therese Frare/The Picture Cube)*

Personality differences are central to John L. Holland's (1985) theory of job and career choice, in which six basic personality themes correlate with appropriate occupational choices. People who exhibit the basic themes (realistic, investigative, artistic, social, conventional, and enterprising) are drawn to occupations that are compatible with these themes. A farmer, for example, is both realistic (strong and practical) and conventional (prefers structured activities). When occupation and personality match, a person tends to be satisfied, remain with a job, and advance up the career ladder.

As the structure of the economy has changed, the occupational future of most young adults without college or specialized vocational training is less promising than it was twenty years ago. Whether they aim for blue-collar or semiskilled white-collar work, young adults are likely to find that they are unable to establish themselves in occupations that allow them to strike out on their own, buy a car and a house, and take an occasional vacation trip, as their parents did. Studies by the Economic Policy Institute indicate that during the 1980s, the income of households headed by adults younger than 25 fell 19 percent in real terms (see Figure 16.2). Incomes of households headed by adults between the ages of 25 and 34 fell by 5 percent (Kilborn, 1990). By 1991, the average hourly wage for blue-collar workers bought 6.8 percent less in goods and services than it did ten years earlier (Kilborn, 1991).

Especially troubling is the situation of many African-American young adults. These young people tend to enter the labor market earlier than their white counterparts, are more likely to be hampered by inadequate education, go through longer periods of joblessness, and experience greater frustrations in their search for jobs (Bowman, 1990). In a study of young African-American men and women who were living in three-generational families, 41 percent were unemployed, and the majority (regardless of gender) had been looking for work for more than two months. About one-third had been out of work for more than six months. Phillip Bowman (1990), who conducted the study, suggests that long-term joblessness and discouragement in the job search may undermine the ability of young African-Americans to handle the developmental tasks of the life cycle, including identity, intimacy, and generativity. The strong bonds of the African-American extended family, ethnic coping patterns, and religion will enable some to cope effectively, but many may develop confused identities or fail at the tasks of forming intimate bonds with a mate and becoming family providers.

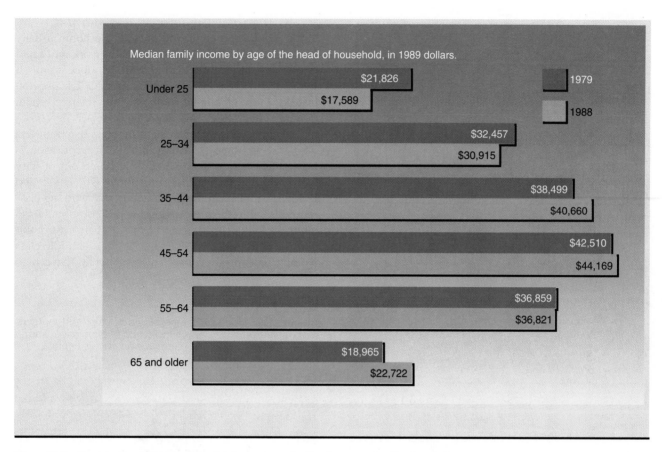

Median family income by age of the head of household, in 1989 dollars.

	1979	1988
Under 25	$21,826	$17,589
25–34	$32,457	$30,915
35–44	$38,499	$40,660
45–54	$42,510	$44,169
55–64	$36,859	$36,821
65 and older	$18,965	$22,722

Figure 16.2 During the 1980s, median family income declined among families headed by adults younger than 35. During the same period, real income among middle-age and older workers either stabilized or rose. *(From Kilborn, 1990, B10; based on data from Economic Policy Institute)*

Gender Differences in the Work Force

Gender is an accident of birth that has far-reaching effects on the availability of jobs and careers, on individual work patterns, and on the way occupational choices are made. As women's roles have changed, however, the pattern of their participation in the labor force has come to resemble that of men (see Figure 16.3).

Gender Differences in Work Patterns

The early working years are fairly similar for men and women, but at about the time the young working man shifts from casual to committed work and the young middle-class man's career is beginning to stabilize, the paths of men and most women separate. Many men and women who remain single tend to have orderly occupational lives, although longitudinal surveys indicate that most men change occupations (not just jobs) at least

once during their working lives (J. Jacobs, 1983). When men and single women leave college, they take entry-level positions. After some shifting in a search for the right position, they settle down in their chosen field. During the years from their midtwenties to their mid-thirties, they are becoming established in their fields. At about the age of 35, when they have become experienced and knowledgeable, they devote themselves so intently to consolidating their careers that some researchers believe that a stage of career consolidation should be inserted between Erikson's periods of intimacy and generativity (Vaillant and Milofsky, 1980).

Until the 1980s, married women generally followed a different path. Most left the labor market to start families at just the time when men and single women were establishing themselves. Whether they went back to work when their last child was 3, 6, or 18 years old, the interruption nearly always was detrimental to their ca-

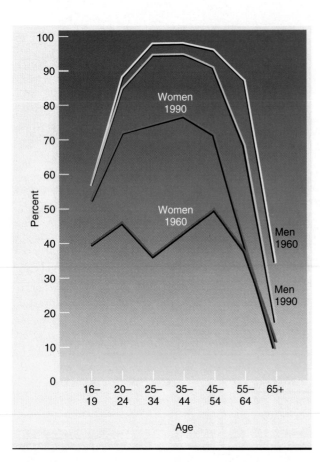

Figure 16.3 In 1960, women's participation in the labor force was strongly affected by marriage and motherhood, with a sharp drop for women between the ages of 25 and 34 and, as the nest emptied, a peak for women between the ages of 45 and 54. As women's roles have changed, their participation in the work force has come to resemble that of men. *(From U.S. Bureau of Labor Statistics, 1991)*

reers (L. Hoffman and Nye, 1974). Many women today have either eliminated or shortened this break in their work pattern. Less than 40 percent of women who had their first child during the 1960s were back at work within five years, but during the early 1980s, 40 percent were back at work within five *months*, and more than 50 percent were back within a year (O'Connell, 1989). Interruptions in employment take women off their occupational track and are partly responsible for the fact that women who work full time earn only $700 for every $1000 earned by men (A. Cowen, 1989). Another factor that contributes to the income gap is married women's willingness to accept low-paying jobs that mesh comfortably with other aspects of their lives. Even today, however, gender differences in pay often reflect discriminatory practices.

Maternal Employment and Morale

Mothers who are employed outside the home usually bear the major responsibility for housework and child care. Does this double load of work produce so much stress that it damages a mother's morale? Usually not; instead, most employed mothers have relatively high morale. They show less depression, fewer psychosomatic symptoms, and fewer signs of stress than mothers who stay at home (L. Hoffman, 1989). Depression is highest among mothers who stay at home out of duty when they would rather be employed (Hock and DeMeis, 1990). Employment builds the working-class mother's self-esteem by giving her a sense of achievement, a challenge, stimulation, and a chance for adult companionship (L. Hoffman, 1984). Middle-class women with professional careers generally have high

Despite their added role responsibilities, employed mothers have higher morale, a lower incidence of depression, and report less stress than do mothers who stay at home. *(Robert Brenner/Photo Edit)*

self-esteem, rarely feel lonely, and see themselves as personally competent.

Despite the benefits of employment, many employed mothers worry about "not having enough time," about possibly harming their children by working, and about finding adequate child care. Yet among women who complained of experiencing role conflict and having too many demands placed on them, only those who did not work outside the home showed symptoms of anxiety (Barnett and Baruch, 1987). Employed mothers are most likely to show stress when they have no social support, when a child is handicapped or chronically ill, or when they have several preschool children (L. Hoffman, 1989). In some cases, switching to part-time employment can reduce the stress of these mothers.

How does a woman's employment affect the quality of her marriage? Researchers have found no clear effect of maternal employment on the marital relationship (L. Hoffman, 1989). Some marriages seem to improve, especially in cases where the mother wants to work, the father does not oppose her employment, or the family is middle-class. Some marriages deteriorate, especially in cases where the mother would rather be at home, the father opposes her employment, or the couple is working-class. Although the divorce rate is higher among families with employed mothers, most researchers feel that a mother's employment does not lead to divorce. Instead, by making it possible to fund a divorce, employment provides an escape hatch from a failed marriage.

Marriage

Most people marry, at least once in their lives, although today they tend to be older, if not wiser, when they make the legal commitment than they were twenty-five years ago. In 1960, about 72 percent of women and 47 percent of men between the ages of 20 and 24 were married. Today, only 34.6 percent of women and 21.4 percent of men between those ages are married (U.S. Bureau of the Census, 1990b). These figures indicate that we are returning to marriage patterns of the last century, when women married at about the same age as they now do. This tendency to postpone marriage varies in its strength among different ethnic groups (see Figure 16.4).

The trend toward delayed marriage is in part a reflection of increased college enrollment. People who go to college often postpone marriage until they have finished their education, and young women who are establishing careers postpone marriage longer than any other group. The delay is heightened by other changes in society: a widening acceptance of couples who live together without marriage, a new acceptance of the single state as an appropriate way of life, and perhaps a hesitation to marry fostered by high divorce rates. In line with their earlier assumption of other adult responsibilities, working-class couples are more likely than middle-class couples to follow the early marriage pattern of the 1960s. One reason that working-class couples seem reluctant to delay marriage is its role in making them inde-

Figure 16.4 Among young men and women between the ages of 20 and 24, Hispanics are most likely to be married and African-Americans least likely. *(Data from U.S. Bureau of the Census, 1990a)*

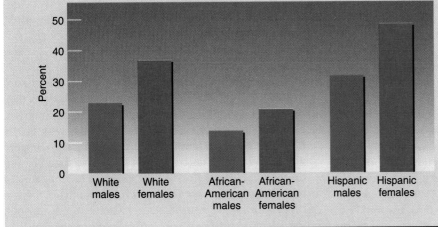

pendent. Middle-class adults usually leave home to go to college; working-class adults usually leave home to marry.

Choosing a Mate

Selecting a mate is not simply a matter of the heart. Some of the same social factors that determine friendship also influence the choice of a spouse. Before a couple can marry, they must meet, and so where a person lives and where he or she goes to school limit the pool of possible mates. Because people who live in the same area and have the same educational experiences tend to be of similar religion, race, ethnic background, and socioeconomic status, married couples also are similar in these respects. Even so, marriage across racial, ethnic, and religious groups occurs more often than it once did (Murstein, 1985). Even couples who fall in love at their first meeting are unlikely to develop a lasting intimate relationship unless they also have common interests, backgrounds, and goals (Wong, 1981).

A first meeting rarely leads to the immediate conviction that the pairing will be permanent. Instead, there is a series of meetings—either dates or informal contacts that result from common friends, common classes in school, or common interests. External influences often affect the readiness to marry. Sometimes a working-class adult may be more interested in getting away from a conflict-ridden home than in building a life with a marital partner. Class or ethnic standards concerning the "right" age for marriage, income, job security, and the person's own inclinations toward the married state may combine either to keep a person from thinking about marriage or to lead the person to perceive most members of the other sex as possible marital partners (Ankarloo, 1978). When a person is in the latter state, the choice of a mate is probably close at hand, and relationships may be initiated in a more deliberate and less playful fashion.

Once partners develop a committed relationship, sexual intimacy often follows. Among unmarried women in their early twenties, about 75 percent have had sexual intercourse (Forrest and Singh, 1990). Casual sexual relationships appear to be on the decline in this country, although they certainly have not disappeared. Fear of AIDS is changing the way people view casual sex. Originally concentrated among gay men or transmitted during transfusions or drug injections by contaminated blood or needles, AIDS has moved into the heterosexual population through drug use and sexual intercourse. Singles bars have become less popular, and many people have become wary about having sex without a committed relationship. As one woman put it, "It may not be the person you know. It may be the person that person knows" (M. Clark, Gosnell, and Hagar, 1986). In national surveys, 52 percent of single adults between the ages of 18 and 44 have said that the fear of AIDS has changed their sexual behavior, causing them either to use condoms or to limit their partners (Kagay, 1991). The change is probably spurred by the fact that 21 percent of American adults know someone who either has AIDS or has died of the disease—up from 2 percent in 1985.

Once couples reach the stage of commitment, their friends and families begin to see them as a unit. One is not invited to a party without the other. Gradually, the two begin to think of themselves as "us" and become aware that they depend on each other. If they have openly declared their intention to marry, one—or both—may go through a period of anxiety, wondering if he or she has made the right decision.

Making Marriage Work

Marriage establishes the family as a social system, and each partner has to adjust to the social roles connected with the institution of marriage. Before the first year of marriage is over, couples develop a way of handling the division of power. This division is central to the establishment of marital roles, and traditionally the man has dominated the relationship. After studying more than 3500 married couples in three cities, researchers concluded that several factors affect the power balance in marriage: (1) the income of each partner, with women's power tending to parallel their earnings; (2) the degree to which partners adhere to the traditional view that the male is the provider, with men clearly dominating when both partners hold the traditional view; and (3) the degree to which one partner "loves less" than the other, because the partner who loves more will work and suffer more to preserve the marriage (Blumstein and Schwartz, 1983).

As couples build their marriages and deal with issues of power, authority, and control, most marriages pass through three predictable phases: blending, nesting, and maintaining (Kurdek and Schmitt, 1986). During the blending phase, which generally extends through the first year, the man and woman learn to live together and to think of themselves as an interdependent pair, in which the actions of one have consequences for the other. During the nesting phase, which extends through the second and third years, they explore the limits of their compatibility. The resulting conflicts may cause both partners to feel simultaneously attracted by the marriage and repelled by it. During the maintaining phase, which usually begins in the fourth year, family traditions are established and each partner's individuality reappears. The conflicts of the nesting period are generally resolved, and the quality of most relationships improves.

Young couples vary widely in the satisfaction that they derive from their marriages. Among white and African-American couples in new marriages, the major influence on marital satisfaction was the communication of emotions (Veroff, Douvan, and Hatchett, in press). Each partner in a happy marriage felt that the other made the partner's life interesting and exciting, cared deeply for the partner, and supported the partner's individuality. Much of this communication came indirectly, through the ways that couples resolved conflicts or experienced their sexual lives. Working against marital satisfaction were frequency of conflicts and an unwillingness to include the partner in interactions, as when a partner found it easier to talk to a third party about personal problems. In addition, some researchers have proposed that individual differences in personality, attitudes, and values act as filters, through which partners process all information about the relationship (Bradbury and Fincham, 1988). Thus, situations that one person finds satisfying may be neutral or evoke dissatisfaction in another.

Gender roles certainly govern marital interactions,

Newly married couples who can communicate their emotions, even if the communication is indirect, tend to be satisfied with their marriages. *(Leslye Borden/Photo Edit)*

but they seem to affect marital quality only when partners differ in their views (Went, 1990). When the wife is less traditional than the husband, the marriage tends to be unhappy, but when the husband is less traditional than the wife, the marriage is especially happy. Social contexts also affect marital satisfaction, with strong support from family and friends leading to happiness (Veroff, Douvan, and Hatchett, in press). Factors that predict unhappiness include low levels of education and the failure to pool finances at the time of marriage (Kurdek, 1991b). Low education may be related to unrealistically high expectations for marriage and poorly developed conflict-resolution skills, whereas the failure to pool finances may be related to a lack of trust in the partner. The accompanying box, "Social Context and Marriage," shows how social contexts foster ethnic differences in marital interaction.

Cohabitation

Nearly five times as many unmarried men and women live together today as did so in 1970; the number of unmarried couples of all ages has increased from 523 million to 2588 million (U.S. Bureau of the Census, 1990a). Living together, or **cohabitation,** became popular on college campuses toward the close of the 1960s. By 1988, more than one-third of American women between the ages of 15 and 44 had lived with a boyfriend or partner without being married to him (London, 1991). As *Three's Company* reminded us, cohabiting does not necessarily involve sex (or even friendship), but it often does.

The commitment to the relationship ranges from slight (in which the partners see the arrangement as a temporary convenience and feel free to have intimate relationships with other people) to intense (in which the partners regard it as either a way station to marriage or a permanent substitute for it) (E. Macklin, 1988). Most cohabitants either marry or break up within a year or so, so the arrangement seems to be a new step in the courtship process. Cohabitation may be a way of testing the waters to see if the relationship might be strong enough for marriage.

Cohabitants who eventually marry tend to pool their finances when they move in together, to hold relatively traditional gender views, and to spend most of their time together (Blumstein and Schwartz, 1983). Once they are married, they are difficult to distinguish from couples who never cohabited before marriage. They are, however, more likely to divorce than couples who never cohabited.

SOCIAL CONTEXT AND MARRIAGE

The social context within which a marriage unfolds may have important influences on the happiness and stability of the relationship. For this reason, marriage in various ethnic groups may differ in specific ways. African-American couples, for example, marry in the face of unavoidable structural problems: they are more likely than white couples to have low incomes and insecure jobs. Joseph Veroff, Elizabeth Douvan, and Shirley Hatchett (in press) believe that these structural problems may be responsible for some of the ethnic differences in marital interaction that appeared in their four-year study of recently married couples.

Perhaps because African-American men are so often confronted with financial and job insecurity, they seem especially sensitive to their power status within the family. This sensitivity leads African-American couples to work hard at maintaining a perception of male dominance; in fact, whether men are satisfied with their marriages and whether they stay committed to the relationship may depend on their perception of the power status. The importance of

power may be one reason that African-American couples try harder than white couples to avoid conflict and why they are more upset when a conflict does arise. Other reasons may be the realization that structurally based problems are difficult to resolve in discussion and the conviction, which is deeper than among white couples, that unresolved conflicts can destroy a marriage.

Perhaps because of these convictions, African-American couples report fewer conflicts than do white couples. Yet the convictions may also explain why African-American partners are more likely than white partners to handle their problems by consulting someone other than their spouse. As noted in the text, the tendency to talk to a third party in preference to the spouse is a major contributor to marital dissatisfaction among couples in general. Veroff and his associates suggest that the tendency may contribute to the fact that, after four years of marriage, 21 percent of the African-American couples in their study but only 9 percent of the white couples were either separated or divorced.

The official definition of cohabitation limits it to male-female couples, but many homosexuals live together in a similar fashion. In fact, both cohabiting and homosexual couples (whether gay men or lesbians) pass through the same blending, nesting, and maintaining phases in their relationships as married couples do (Kurdek and Schmitt, 1986).

Most studies of male homosexuals have been rendered outdated by recent events. An early comprehensive study, now more than fifteen years old, showed that only 10 percent of gay men lived in close-coupled relationships that resembled traditional marriages and another 18 percent lived in stable sexual relationships that resembled open marriages, in which partners were free to have sexual relationships with others (A. Bell and Weinberg, 1978). The rest either resembled swinging singles, had no partners, or could not be classified.

After AIDS began sweeping through the gay community in the early 1980s, many gay men either entered a close-coupled relationship, confined their sexual partners to members of a small group, or practiced "safe sex," especially in urban areas (Stall, Coates, and Hoff, 1988). As a result, among large groups of gays that have been followed for a number of years, the proportion who have contracted the AIDS virus each year (but not yet developed the disease) has dropped from 7.5 per-

cent to 1 or 2 percent (Cowley, 1990). Although fear of AIDS accelerated the prevalence of committed relationships among gay men, earlier studies indicated that marriagelike relationships were on the rise before the AIDS epidemic began (E. Macklin, 1980).

Lesbians seem more likely than gay men to live in a stable, committed relationship. In the same study that showed only 10 percent of gay men in close-coupled relationships, 28 percent of lesbians were close-coupled, and another 17 percent lived in committed relationships but were free to have sexual relationships with others (A. Bell and Weinberg, 1978). In later studies, gay couples were twice as likely as lesbian couples to permit sexual relationships with others (Kurdek, 1991a). The difference between lesbian and gay relationships has been attributed to different patterns of childhood socialization. In a relationship between gay men, both partners have been socialized to be independent; in a lesbian relationship, both partners have been socialized to be nurturant and to have a strong interest in love and affection. Lesbians, as well as gays, may find unanticipated conflicts in their relationships, because they cannot use gender roles as a guideline for roles and decisions (Blumstein and Schwartz, 1983). Because they cannot legally marry, and thus encounter no institutional barriers to leaving an unsatisfactory relationship, gay and lesbian couples are more likely than heterosexuals to separate when they find desirable alternatives to the relationship (Kurdek, 1991a).

Staying Single

Singlehood is on the rise in the United States, in part because adults are postponing marriage (see Table 16.3). So many people are marrying so late that demographers cannot agree on the ultimate size of the single population. Not all single adults live by themselves; some cohabit, some move in with a friend or relative, and others never leave home.

At one time, people who stayed single faced public disapproval. In 1975, 80 percent of Americans believed that women who chose to remain unmarried must be "sick," "neurotic," or "immoral" (Yankelovich, 1981). The same charge was not made about single men, although early colonists looked on them with disfavor. In an attempt to steer them into marriage, colonial governments taxed bachelors and collected the money every week (Scanzoni and Scanzoni, 1981). By 1980, society had come to accept the single state, and 75 percent of Americans described single women as healthy people who had decided to follow a different way of life (Yankelovich, 1981).

Microwaves, frozen foods, clothes that do not need ironing, improved transportation, and other services that cater to unmarried adults have made it easier to be single today than it was thirty years ago. Television makes the single life less lonely. Yet, perhaps because of economic stresses, an increasing number of single men are not leaving home. Among 25- to 34-year-olds, 32 percent of single men live with their parents (Gross, 1991). Among single women of the same age, 20 percent are still at home. At one time, women married for security. Today many are financially independent; they

can marry for companionship. Economic freedom has made them more selective in their search for a mate.

People who prefer the single life say that it has many advantages: personal freedom, career opportunities, sexual availability and diversity, and a chance for self-improvement. In one study, single individuals were as physically and emotionally healthy as those who married (C. Rubinstein, Shaver, and Peplau, 1979). In some ways, single women are better off than single men. Women who have never married have more education, higher incomes, and better mental health than single men (E. Macklin, 1980).

Having Children

Americans are having fewer children and having them later in life, but most eventually become parents. Much about parenthood remains the same today as it always was, but changes in society have altered the experience in ways that have radical effects on parents' lives. Cheap, effective contraceptives have wrought some of the changes. They have led to a decline in family size, which means that men and women spend fewer years actively engaged in child rearing. In our great-grandparents' day, it was not uncommon for a woman to give birth again at about the same time that her eldest daughter became a mother. Contraceptives also have made it easy to postpone the first birth, allowing women to establish careers and couples to establish some financial security before they embark on parenthood. This control over the timing of parenthood makes children more welcome.

Because of technological changes, parenthood is less onerous today. All the innovations that make single life easier, along with such devices as disposable diapers, ease the drudgery of parenthood. They make it possible

TABLE 16.3	AMERICANS WHO HAVE NEVER MARRIED (PERCENT)										
	AGE (YEARS)										
	18–19	20–24	25–29	30–34	35–39	40–44	45–54	55–64	65–74	75–84	>84
Men	97.2	77.4	45.9	25.8	15.2	8.3	6.7	5.6	4.9	4.6	3.2
Women	90.5	62.5	29.4	16.9	9.9	6.3	5.4	4.4	4.5	5.8	5.6

Source: Data from U.S. Bureau of the Census, 1990a.

Changes in society over the last few decades have made the single life more convenient and more pleasant than it once was. *(Rameshwar Das/Monkmeyer)*

for mothers to enter (or stay in) the labor market. But high divorce rates and increases in the number of unwed mothers mean that more adults experience at least part of their parenthood without the support of a partner.

Pregnancy

Parenthood actually begins with pregnancy. As soon as partners are aware that they are to have a child, their relationship begins to change. For some couples, pregnancy is a highly stressful time; for others, it is a time of personal growth. The emotional course of the pregnancy may stabilize the marriage or disrupt it (Osofsky and Osofsky, 1984). Some of a woman's feelings about her pregnancy are positive: she may feel special, fertile, and womanly, excited and impatient. Other feelings are negative: she may be fearful, exhausted, worried about her unborn child, and concerned about her ability to cope with motherhood (Grossman, Eichler, and Winickoff, 1980). Because she feels vulnerable, the reactions of her partner have an important influence on the way she feels about her pregnancy. As one pregnant woman wrote, "I am not the self-sufficient woman he knows and

loves. After work I need somebody to mother me" (Kates, 1986).

Men generally feel excited and proud at the prospect of becoming a parent, but negative feelings are also common. A husband may worry about how the baby's birth will change the marital relationship, be envious of his wife's ability to carry a child, be jealous of the coming baby, experience an overwhelming sense of responsibility, or feel shut out from the mystery and intimacy of the childbearing process (Osofsky and Osofsky, 1984).

The quality of the marital relationship affects the course of the pregnancy. Among 100 traditional middle-class couples who were expecting their first or second child, women whose marital satisfaction was high and who shared in decision making experienced few physical and emotional problems (Grossman, Eichler, and Winickoff, 1980). And when the baby had been wanted at the time of conception, stress and complications during pregnancy decreased—findings that have been supported by later studies (Heim, 1992).

Most couples embark on a first pregnancy with little idea of what becoming a parent entails. The more that expectant parents know, however, the better they seem to adjust to their changed lives. In a longitudinal study of young working- and middle-class couples expecting their first child, couples who knew what to expect during pregnancy, childbirth, and the child's first year coped better with all aspects of the process (Entwisle and Doering, 1981). And among couples from a wide range of socioeconomic and ethnic backgrounds (Anglo, African-American, Asian-American, and Hispanic), those who participated in a couples group that met weekly throughout the pregnancy also handled the transition to parenthood more smoothly than couples who did not (P. Cowan and Cowan, 1988).

Adjusting to Parenthood

The birth of the first child causes a major upheaval in a couple's life. It changes a person's social roles, friendship patterns, family relationships, personality, values, and community involvement. Many women claim that the greatest change in their lives came about not as a result of their marriage but with the birth of the first child. Earlier, we saw that people view becoming a parent as a major mark of adulthood. It introduces a new form of responsibility for both parents. Now they must protect and nurture another life, a being who comes into the world virtually helpless.

During the first week or so after the baby is born, many women go through a brief period of "baby blues," when they are tearful, have crying spells, and sometimes are confused. Up to 20 percent may develop postpartum depression (see Chapter 5), which includes nightmares, feelings of hopelessness or sadness, and fears or worries about the baby. But only 8 percent have a depression that is severe enough to require psychiatric treatment (Fedele et al., 1988).

The experience of being a parent affects personality, but the nature of the change depends on the characteristics of the person, the infant, the marital relationship, and the level of available social support. Self-concepts are modified as people see themselves as parents as well as partners and lovers. In most cases, self-esteem either remains stable or rises, parents tend to feel more valuable, and their self-confidence often increases (Antonucci and Mikus, 1988). As indicated in the accompanying box, "Does Parenthood Intensify Gender Roles?" becoming a parent tends to heighten traditional gender roles in many adults.

The quality of the marital relationship affects the way parents approach their new baby. Among white, middle-class couples, mothers in close, confiding relationships were especially warm and sensitive toward their babies,

perhaps because such marriages met the mothers' emotional needs (Cox et al., 1989). (Fathers in these marriages tended to have positive attitudes toward their babies and toward the paternal role.) As we saw in Chapter 8, a mother's sensitivity and warmth is associated with the security of her baby's attachment.

The demands and responsibilities of parenthood may also alter the marriage relationship. Most studies report small, but significant, declines in marital satisfaction after the first baby is born. Nevertheless, some new parents report that their marriages become more satisfying after the baby arrives (P. Cowan and Cowan, 1988). Whether marital satisfaction increases or declines, couples tend to remain in the same order when ranked as to satisfaction, with correlations ranging from 0.52 to 0.79 between early pregnancy and nine months after the baby's birth (Belsky, Spanier, and Rovine, 1983). The continuity that consistently appears in studies indicates that babies neither create distress where none existed nor bring together couples whose marriages are in trouble (P. Cowan and Cowan, 1988). Nevertheless, wives'

Although small declines in marital satisfaction appear after the birth of the first child, babies do not create distress where none existed. *(Elizabeth Crews)*

DOES PARENTHOOD INTENSIFY GENDER ROLES?

According to several developmental theories, gender roles become more pronounced when people become parents. Some research has supported this view. In one typical study, young fathers rated themselves as more masculine and young mothers as more feminine than did other men and women of their age (Abrahams, Feldman, and Nash, 1978). This was true whether the parents were compared with cohabiting couples, childless married couples, or married couples expecting their first child. But such studies are cross-sectional, and they do not show us whether the experience of parenthood actually intensifies gender roles.

Only longitudinal studies that trace changes across pregnancy and early parenthood can reveal the changes as they occur. In one such study that focused on middle-class, well-educated couples, the notion of strengthened gender roles was partially supported. Women indeed felt more feminine after their babies were born, showing increased nurturance, warmth, sensitivity, responsiveness to babies, and tolerance for others' shortcomings (Feldman and Aschenbrenner, 1983). But so did men. On each of these aspects of femininity, the men's scores increased. The fathers' increased femininity did not lower their masculine rating. They were just as independent, decisive, and self-reliant as they had been before their babies were born.

Although both parents had changed similarly, their perceptions of the change differed. Women saw a greater difference between masculine and feminine roles than they had while they were pregnant, but men saw the difference diminishing. How can we explain these changes? Feldman and Aschenbrenner believe that fatherhood has a much stronger impact on men's gender typing than psychologists had suspected. Even though parenthood may increase the divergence in gender roles, as the women noted, men may respond to the new nurturant qualities they observe in themselves. These couples were not traditional: a third of the women had already returned to work, and more than a third of the men shared equally in household responsibilities. Perhaps recent changes in gender roles, which are concentrated in the middle class, are leading to changes in the way men experience fatherhood.

The importance of gender-role changes lies in the way they affect family functioning. Other researchers have pointed out that in the adaptive families they have studied, partners' roles are not rigidly fixed (Fedele et al., 1988). If the parent who usually handles a particular role cannot handle it or wishes not to do so, the other parent steps in. Although the marked division in traditional families seems to work well while infants are small, unless partners have a flexible, reciprocal attitude toward gender roles, they will not be able to adapt to new situations as the child grows.

positive feelings toward their husbands generally decline after the baby is born (see Figure 16.5). Their feelings bottom out when the baby is about 3 months old, only to rise again; by the time the baby is 16 months old, they feel as warmly toward their husbands as they ever did (Fleming et al., 1990).

Many couples find that they communicate less after the birth of their first baby; they find the spontaneity that characterized their social and sexual lives greatly reduced. They report more tensions and anxieties, more disagreements, and less mutual understanding during the early years of parenthood than at any other time. All of this stress may not be due to parenthood; childless couples show similar stress and conflict during the second and third years of their marriages—about the time that most couples have their first child (Kurdek and Schmitt, 1986).

When couples feel pushed apart by children, the estrangement seems to grow out of the diminished time they have together, disagreements over child rearing, or the husband's feeling that the wife is so absorbed in the children that she forgets him (L. Hoffman and Manis, 1978). It seems that parenthood intensifies pleasures and dissatisfactions, and the situation of the particular marriage determines which way the scales are tipped.

With the birth of the first child, no matter how egalitarian a couple's arrangement has been, the partners shift toward a more traditional division of household tasks (P. Cowan and Cowan, 1988). How the tasks are divided does not affect marital satisfaction, but the partners' satisfaction with the division has a pronounced effect on the marriage. After the baby is 6 months old, most men help out less with household tasks but spend more time on child care than they did during the early months. Whether parents agree on the way children should be reared is also important. In one study, differences in parents' attitudes about rearing their 3-year-old predicted divorce by the time the child was 11 (G. Roberts, Block, and Block, 1984).

Despite its stress, parenthood appears to be a rewarding experience. When researchers asked parents of 18-month-old babies, "What has been the best part of be-

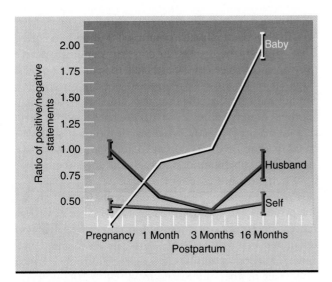

Figure 16.5 When young mothers were followed from pregnancy until their babies were 16 months old, the proportion of positive statements about their babies steadily increased. The proportion of positive statements about their husbands dropped steadily until the baby was 3 months old; then they rebounded. *(From Fleming et al., 1990, p. 140)*

coming a family for each of you?" almost every woman and man said it was their child (P. Cowan and Cowan, 1988). They spoke of the thrill of watching a child develop, of rediscovering the world from a child's perspective, of learning to solve problems more efficiently, of more positive connections with their own parents, of a renewed sense of purpose in their work and involvement in the community, of feelings of pride and closeness. These feelings are apparently enduring. Among parents of preschoolers in a large national sample, from 95 to 98 percent of mothers and fathers—no matter what their level of education—said that they derived a great deal of satisfaction from being parents (L. Hoffman and Manis, 1978).

Timing of Parenthood

The latest baby boom has been concentrated among women in their thirties, and the experience of becoming a parent for the first time at age 35 is clearly different from the same experience at the age of 25 (W. Goldberg, 1988). Material as well as psychological factors affect the nature of parenthood.

When members of a couple are in their early twenties, the birth of a child may be especially stressful. One or both may find their education interrupted. Neither is established in an occupation. Few couples at this age

own a home, and most are paying for furniture and cars. In most cases, they have no savings and are stretching to make two salaries cover all expenses. Such young couples are still getting used to the idea of marriage.

Often both parents still have a lot of growing up to do and may not be psychologically ready for parenthood (W. Goldberg, 1988). Among the couples in one study that examined the timing of parenthood, women who gave birth in their late teens or early twenties found themselves having to mother both their babies and their husbands (Daniels and Weingarten, 1982). Yet there are advantages to becoming a parent while still so young. Young parents have enough energy to keep up with their children's seemingly incessant activities. And twenty or twenty-five years later, when the children strike out on their own, the parents are still relatively young themselves. Their free time comes during middle age, when parents who waited to start their families are still struggling with adolescent children.

When couples postpone childbearing until their thirties or forties, their physical energy may be diminished, but they feel less pressure and the marital relationship undergoes less strain. By this time, the parents generally have assets and may even own their own home. With one or both established in an occupation, their income is higher, and they can afford a few luxuries. Both are also likely to be more mature. They are more likely to have the self-confidence and self-knowledge that goes with age and accomplishment (W. Goldberg, 1988). In the study of parenthood timing, fathers in such families tended to be nurturant and aware of the mothers' emotional needs (Daniels and Weingarten, 1982). Unlike most younger fathers, they tended to assume part of the household duties and to become involved in child care. When mothers of first babies are observed in the laboratory, older mothers seem more sensitive to their babies' needs than younger mothers, and the emotional tone of the mother-infant relationship is more positive (Ragozin et al., 1982). However, regardless of the age at which they give birth, most new mothers are satisfied with the timing (R. Mercer, 1986).

Childless or Child-Free?

Compared with the rate in the 1960s, the rate of childless couples today is high. Yet we cannot say that voluntary childlessness is becoming a social trend (L. Hoffman, 1982). Because birth rates are climbing among women in their thirties, what seems to be an increase in childlessness is primarily a postponement of births.

Although many people pity those who are childless by choice, the decision not to have children does not condemn a couple to unhappiness, misery, and loneliness. Couples without children appear to be no different from couples with children in their self-esteem, life satisfaction, or maturity (Silka and Kiesler, 1977). Many young childless couples, especially the husbands, report greater satisfaction with their lives than do couples with young children. Without the responsibility of children, couples are not tied down, they have money for luxury items and timesaving devices, and the partners have more time for each other.

Will people who have decided to remain child-free one day regret their decision? In Erikson's theory of adult development, human beings have a need for generativity (Erikson and Hall, 1987), and Gutmann's (1987) parental imperative centers around the protection and nurturance of children. But Erikson points out that what he calls "the procreative urge" can be effectively expressed through creativity and productivity, as well as by caring for the children of others—whether as teachers, medical personnel, or day-care workers. And in Gutmann's theory, the imperative does not begin to operate until it is triggered by the birth of a child.

Single Mothers

A 33-year-old unmarried junior high school teacher is artificially inseminated and gives birth to a daughter. A 38-year-old unmarried computer executive adopts a baby from Mexico. A 35-year-old unmarried school psychologist asks a friend from college to father her child (Kantrowitz, 1985). Across the country, an increasing number of children are being born to single women in their twenties and thirties who have good jobs and financially secure futures. Either they have postponed marriage and feel that biology will not allow them to wait any longer, or they are women who know that they want children but do not want husbands. These highly publicized cases among the middle class obscure the situation of most unmarried women who are having children. The vast majority of unmarried mothers do not have the financial prospects of the "new single mother." These women have less education, have fewer financial resources, get less prenatal care, and are more likely to bear a low-birthweight baby than their married counterparts (Ventura, 1985). Many of these mothers deal daily with severe economic hardship (McLoyd, Ceballo, and Mangelsdorf, 1993).

Although the proportion of births to unmarried women has risen in many countries, as shown in Figure 16.6, such births do not automatically indicate that a woman is rearing a child by herself. In many countries, a large share of these births are to cohabiting couples. Studies indicate that 45 percent of unmarried Australian mothers of new babies live with the baby's father, as do a large majority of unmarried Swedish mothers (Burns, 1992). Some of these couples later marry, but as we have seen, cohabitation is a fragile arrangement.

When cohabiting couples separate, the split produces lone parents; other lone parents have acquired the position as the consequence of divorce or death. An increasing number of parents find themselves bringing up children by themselves. Between 1970 and 1989, the proportion of families in which children lived with only their mothers increased from 9.9 to 20.2 percent, and the proportion in which children lived with only their fathers increased from 1.2 to 3.3 percent (U.S. Bureau of the Census, 1991). Many of these single-parent families contain more than one child. Although most of the information we have about single-parent families comes from studies of mother-headed households, information from father-headed households indicates that many of the problems are similar, no matter which gender is in charge.

The major problem, as we saw in Chapter 9, is that one person is saddled with the responsibilities carried by two people in intact families. Compared with married mothers at the same socioeconomic level, single mothers of preschoolers are under greater stress, work longer hours, and receive substantially less support from their social network (Weinraub and Wolf, 1986). Most single parents say that this role overload is the most stressful aspect of their situation.

Despite the strain, many single parents feel proud and happy about their accomplishments. They find themselves developing new aspects of their personalities. Women, functioning on their own, become more self-reliant; men, forced to assume a maternal role, become more nurturant (Weiss, 1979a).

The role of single parent also affects the way a man or woman performs on the job. Fathers say that child care limits their job mobility, cuts into their working hours and earnings, changes their work priorities, and hampers transfers (Keshet and Rosenthal, 1978a). It also limits their behavior on the job and restricts the kind of work they do, their promotions, and their relations with coworkers and supervisors. Employed mothers face similar restrictions.

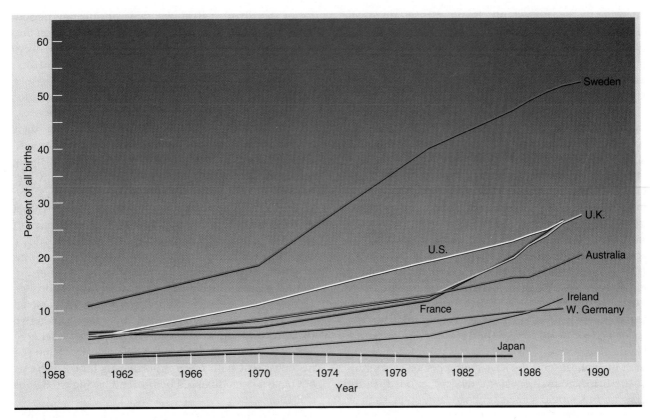

Figure 16.6 Since 1970, the proportion of births to unmarried women has increased in most developed countries. *(From Burns, 1992, p. 10)*

Divorce

Married couples have become less likely to persist in a dismal relationship. In the United States, about one in two new marriages now ends in divorce (Bumpass and Castro-Martin, 1989), and other couples separate but do not divorce. Among women in a national survey, 8 percent of white women but 33 percent of African-American women whose marriages had dissolved were separated but not divorced (London, 1991).

Social changes may be responsible for the high rate of marriage dissolution. The same developments that have led to a rise in singlehood have made people less likely to cling to an unsatisfactory marriage. Women no longer must rely on men for economic security. Technological changes have made the one-adult (or one-adult-plus-children) household manageable. Society has removed the social stigma that once accompanied the divorced state.

Along with the removal of these barriers to divorce

came the demand that marriage reach a level of happiness that it had never before been expected to provide, creating a burden perhaps too heavy for the institution to bear. At one time, our definition of a happy marriage was one in which the partners drifted along comfortably from day to day, feeling that things were "okay." Only a highly unpleasant situation drove them to sever the marital bond. Today we expect marriage to provide romantic love, personal growth, and self-fulfillment for both partners. If it does not, we may be quick to end it.

Some relationships seem to last in spite of it all; others quickly break apart. Most divorces among young adults take place within the first four years of marriage, and nearly 40 percent of all divorces occur among couples in which the woman is younger than 30 (National Center for Health Statistics, 1990). What places a marriage at high risk? Several factors contribute to divorce: marrying when the first child has already been conceived; being younger than 20 at the time of the marriage; being older than 30; attending religious services infrequently or not at all; being African-American. (Being Hispanic reduces the chances of divorce.) Being poor or failing to complete school heightens the risk; however, a woman's advanced education and successful career, which make her independent, also increase the chances of divorce (Glenn and Supanic, 1984).

When divorced couples are asked why their marriages failed, women blame communication problems, basic unhappiness, incompatibility, emotional abuse, and financial problems (Cleek and Pearson, 1985). Other, less frequently given reasons are a husband's alcoholism, infidelity, or physical abuse. Men blame communication problems, basic unhappiness, incompatibility, sexual problems, and financial problems, with a few saying that their wives' infidelity or their own alcohol abuse was responsible.

In attempting to explain why seemingly satisfactory marriages break up, Graham Spanier and Robert Lewis (1980) suggest that outside forces may play an important role. They see marital stability as determined by the balance of costs and rewards perceived by each partner. Satisfaction with a life style, the rewards of interacting with the spouse, and the social and personal resources of the marriage may equal the dissatisfactions that are present. But should some alternative attraction, such as another possible mate or a crucial career decision, upset the balance, the marriage may founder.

Once the process of divorce begins, it takes a long time to complete. Divorces appear to pass through three stages: separation, adjustment to divorce, and reconstruction (Golan, 1981). The first phase begins when partners are unable to resolve a basic conflict and emotional bonds begin to fray. Unpleasant feelings—anger, guilt, bitterness, inadequacy, loneliness—accompany their interactions. Finally, they separate. But long after they have ceased to love each other, their attachment endures. Away from the partner, each suffers an emotional stress much like the separation anxiety that develops in infants and toddlers (see Chapter 8). Although still angry at the former partner and distrustful, each is also preoccupied by him or her and often jealous (Hetherington and Camara, 1984). Each is eager for news of the absent partner. Is she seeing someone else? Did he go to the Johnsons' party? Not all divorcing people go through this anxiety, but even those who have asked for the divorce in order to marry someone else often go through periods of deep pain. Once it becomes clear that reconciliation is out of the question, each partner may be pervaded with loneliness.

Once the divorce has been granted, people move into the second phase, in which they adjust to the real-ity of the divorce. It is generally an unhappy period. They may relish their new freedom, but some soon find that their expectations about life after divorce were unrealistic. They may feel cast adrift, rootless, and anxious. They have lost a primary social role (wife, husband) and have assumed a new role (divorced adult) for which society has developed no standards and few expectations. Most find themselves shut out of their former social activities, which were centered around married couples. Many, primarily women, find themselves in serious financial straits. Some become depressed.

Yet some people come through divorce with a heightened feeling of well-being and show evidence of personal growth (Wallerstein and Blakeslee, 1989). Among working-class women who were in the process of getting a divorce, those with less traditional attitudes toward gender roles tended to fare the best (P. Brown, 1976). Other characteristics that predicted personal growth from the experience included having an active social life, making new friends, having little social contact with the former husband, reaching a separation status consistent with one's goals, having a high income, not having been divorced before, and having a religious affiliation.

Toward the end of the second year, most divorced adults have begun to move into the third phase, in which they reconstruct their lives. Their financial situation has improved, their new households are established, their new social lives are under way. Those who were unduly attached to their former spouses may have broken those bonds by means of a new intimate relationship (Hetherington and Camara, 1984). With their rebuilding under way, many are ready to remarry, and hope for success on the next try.

Remarriage

About 40 percent of all marriages involve people who have been married before. Most remarriages take place about three years after the divorce, and young adults are the most likely to remarry (Glick and Lin, 1986). Among young adult women in a national survey who had either divorced or been widowed, 53 percent of white women, 25 percent of African-American women, and 30 percent of Hispanic women remarried within five years (London, 1991). Second marriages appear to be less stable than first marriages, with about 60 percent eventually failing (Kantrowitz and Wingert, 1990). Some researchers have suggested that this greater readiness to divorce may not be due to the fact that remarriages are necessarily unsatisfactory. Remarried individuals have already proved willing to end a difficult marital relationship, and their earlier experience has provided them with knowledge about how to do it (Glick, 1980).

Remarriages differ in several ways from first marriages, according to Frank Furstenberg (1982). First, remarried people may consciously develop a new style of interaction with the second spouse. They judge the new marriage against the first and recall what went wrong the first time around; then they alter their behavior to avoid the same pitfalls. Second, contact with the previous spouse often affects the marriage, especially if the first marriage produced children. Relationships become complicated, and financial ties from the first marriage (support payments, property, insurance policies, wills) may affect the economic situation of the new marriage.

Third, people who remarry are older, are more experienced, and perhaps have moved up in social status since they entered the first marriage relationship. A 32-year-old who is established in an occupation does not approach marriage in the same way as a 23-year-old, perhaps just out of school. The age spread between the partners is also greater in second marriages. In remarriages, the man is usually six years older than the woman; in first marriages, the age gap is only two or three years. A divorced man generally marries someone younger than his first wife, and a divorced woman generally marries someone older than her first husband (Glick, 1980). Finally, social patterns may have changed since the first marriage. Shifts in cultural standards can alter expectations and responsibilities in such areas as contraceptive use, gender roles, economic expectations, women's employment, and child care.

In other ways, second marriages are similar to first marriages. Once the honeymoon period is over, the levels of marital satisfaction and spousal conflict, as well as the partners' interactional styles, seem to be about the same as those among couples who are still in their first marriage. Remarried couples in a longitudinal study were as positive, communicated as well with their partners, and displayed no more coercive behavior than did nondivorced couples in first marriages (Hetherington et al., 1992). The less romantic aura of the second marriage may help explain why remarried people say that their marital problems have changed. Instead of worrying about their spouses' immaturity, sexual problems,

When adults remarry, their relationship may be influenced by the presence of children from their former marriages, as well as by the children they have together. *(Spencer Grant/ The Picture Cube)*

and their own unreadiness for marriage, remarried people worry about money and children (Messenger, 1976). When children are involved, the major difference between first and second marriages may be that in second marriages, at least during the early years, the marital relationship is not as strong as the mother-child bond that was developed in the original family and strengthened during the interval of the single-parent family (Hetherington et al., 1992).

As our survey of young adulthood indicates, U.S. society is made up of a diversity of life styles. Socioeconomic level, education, gender, and ethnic group affect every aspect of development, as does the nature of society. In the next chapter, we will see that many of these same factors also affect cognitive development during the years from 20 to 65.

SOCIAL CHANGE

The appropriate times for such events as marriage, careers, and parenthood are becoming less tied to age, especially in the middle class, making the United States an **age-irrelevant society.** Young adults are marrying later, postponing the births of their children, and having smaller families.

PHYSICAL CHARACTERISTICS

During young adulthood, men and women are at the peak of physical agility, strength, and speed. Within the body, however, organs are aging; by the thirties, reflexes have slowed.

THEORIES AND ISSUES OF YOUNG ADULTHOOD

In Erikson's psychosocial stage theory, young adults face the task of developing intimacy. This universal task differs for women and men because of their earlier socialization. In Levinson's stage theory, men go through an orderly sequence that alternates between tranquil, stable phases and transitional phases during which men question the pattern of their lives and explore new possibilities. During young adulthood, they develop autonomy and intimacy and consolidate their careers. In Gould's theory, young adults go through four phases; during each phase they reformulate their self-concepts, face illusions, and resolve conflicts. In Gutmann's theory, personality development is heavily influenced by the **parental imperative.**

One issue concerning adult development is the nature of **transitions.** Some researchers maintain that transitions are highly stressful; others believe that they create stress only when they are unexpected and not part of the normal life course. A second issue is the timing of adulthood: When does a person become mature?

SELF-CONCEPT AND SELF-ESTEEM

Self-concept shows both continuity and change during young adulthood. Self-esteem seems to rise in men throughout young adulthood, although it generally declines among the unemployed. Although women tend to feel less control over their lives than men do, their self-esteem generally is high. When high-achieving women become full-time homemakers, their self-esteem may suffer. An increasing number of young adults are **androgynous.**

WORK

Work affects personality, family life, social relations, attitudes, and values. Job complexity appears to be a major influence on personality. Work can be a source of stress or satisfaction, and its potential for affecting morale may be greatest for those with few social roles. Most men and single women tend to have orderly occupational histories, but other women may move in and out of the labor market. Employed mothers seem to have higher morale and show fewer symptoms of stress than mothers who stay home.

MARRIAGE

Adults are marrying later in life than they did several decades ago. Couples are likely to be similar in religion, race, ethnic background, and socioeconomic stress. Marriage establishes the family as a social system, with marital roles affected by the way power is divided. The power balance is affected by the income of each partner, their views of the male as provider, and the degree to which one partner loves less than the other. Marital satisfaction seems to depend primarily on how successfully partners can convey positive emotions, with other factors important as they affect this process.

Cohabitation varies in commitment from slight to intense, and it may have become a new step in the courtship process. Cohabiting couples and married couples seem to be much alike and derive the same satisfaction from their relationships. Cohabiting gay and lesbian couples are very similar to cohabiting or married heterosexual couples and go through the same processes in establishing a relationship. An increasing number of men and women are remaining single, in part because the single life is easier than it once was and in part because women no longer are economically dependent on men.

HAVING CHILDREN

Parenthood begins with pregnancy, and the quality of the marital relationship affects the course of the pregnancy. When a person becomes a parent, social roles, friendship patterns, family relationships, personality, and community involvements all change. Shortly after the child is born, a minority of women may develop postpartum depression. Although studies show a decline in marital satisfaction, satisfaction before childbirth correlates highly with satisfaction afterward. Couples who decide not to have children are similar to

Some have pointed to quick-wittedness—the rapidity with which a person responds to a problem or situation. Some have relied on academic skills and educational achievement. Some have used test scores. And others believe that the ability to reason in practical, everyday situations is the hallmark of intelligence. None of these alternatives is entirely satisfactory, for each view captures a different aspect of intelligence. When studying the development of intelligence across the life span, most researchers tend to use either a psychometric or a practical approach.

Psychometric Intelligence

Researchers who use the psychometric approach trace changes in intelligence across the life span by measuring adults' performance on standardized tests. In Chapter 12, we saw how such tests, based on factor theories of intelligence, were devised to assess children's abilities on tasks required for success in school. By using different tasks to test large groups of adults of various ages, researchers hope to show age-related changes in various aspects of intelligence.

Not all researchers are comfortable with the psychometric approach to adult intelligence. They believe that several factors make IQ tests poor measures of adult intelligence. Most of the tests have been standardized on young adults and may not be relevant to the functioning of intelligence in middle-aged and older individuals. Items on mental tests require the sort of reasoning that is valued in the classroom. Each task is clearly defined, includes all the information needed for its solution, and has only one correct answer, and usually there is only one method of reaching that answer (Wagner and Sternberg, 1986). To produce such items, test makers must abstract the tasks from life. To solve them, a person must ignore influences that the test maker has eliminated, even though they would affect the problem if encountered in daily life. Adults often find the premises of such stripped problems oversimplified. Presented with such a problem, a 55- or 60-year-old may rebel against having to "stick to the facts," because his or her experience indicates that the solution called for is impractical (Labouvie-Vief, 1985).

The results of IQ tests are strongly related to success in school and are good predictors of competence in entry-level positions for such professions as engineering, piloting, and computer programming (Willis and Schaie, 1986). This makes the tests a useful tool with some young adults. But test results are only modestly related to success on most jobs, with a correlation of

Although IQ tests are good predictors of success at the entry level in a few occupations, the scores have only a modest correlation with success on most jobs. *(Bob Daemmrich/Stock, Boston)*

about +0.20 (Wagner and Sternberg, 1986). Apparently, IQ taps only a portion of the intellectual competencies that are important in the adult world—a finding that is not surprising, given our discussion of intelligence in Chapter 12. Dissatisfied with an approach that limits intelligence to academic skills, an increasing number of developmentalists have focused on practical approaches to the study of intelligence.

Practical Intelligence

Underlying practical approaches to intelligence is the view that development is an active, lifelong process of adaptation to the environment (Dixon and Baltes, 1986). Because human development takes place in a social context, intelligence is best studied within the context in which it is used, as indicated in the box, "When Picking the Ponies, Don't Rely on IQ." Thus, the appropriate measure of adult intelligence is people's

WHEN PICKING THE PONIES, DON'T RELY ON IQ

Handicapping horses involves assigning the odds for or against a horse's chance of winning a particular race. An expert handicapper takes into account seven aspects of the horse's record: best lifetime speed, the speed at its last race, the horse's past speed during the first and last quarter-miles, the horse's maneuvers during a race, the quality of the horses it has run against in the past, the jockey, and the track conditions. Considering the way these variables interact and deciding a horse's chance of winning is a complex cognitive task. If psychometric tests measure a person's general intelligence, then expert handicappers must have high IQs. But if there is no relation between such expertise and IQ, then some important aspects of intelligence are not being measured by IQ tests.

Determined to find out, Stephen Ceci and Jeffrey Liker (1986) spent three years studying middle-aged and older men who attended harness races almost every day during the racing season. All the men in their study had an extensive factual knowledge of harness racing. All bought and read the "early form," a racing form published the day before the races that gives full statistics on the horses but no odds. On the basis of their ability to handicap ten regular races, the men were separated into "expert handicappers" and "nonexperts." (When their picks were compared with the post-time odds of the paid track handicappers, those who did as well as the professionals were considered experts.) Each man also took a standard IQ test.

There was no relation between IQ and track ex-

pertise. One expert, a construction worker with an IQ of 85, picked the top horse in all ten races and picked the top three horses in the correct order in five of the races. He had been coming to the track for sixteen years. One nonexpert, a lawyer with an IQ of 118, picked the top horse in only three races and the top three horses only once. He had been coming to the track for fifteen years. Overall, the experts' IQs ranged from 81 to 128; nonexperts' from 83 to 130. Experience clearly was important, but it was not the sole factor in the development of handicapping expertise. The nonexperts had from seven to twenty-three years' experience in following the races.

Ceci and Liker asked each man to handicap fifty pairs of unnamed horses, based on the statistics given them by the experimenters. In response to questions, the men explained their reasoning in assessing the odds. The experts consistently used a complex interaction of the seven variables to handicap the horses. The nonexperts used this complex form of reasoning only occasionally; most of the time they considered the variables separately. When experts and nonexperts were matched on experience and factual knowledge about racing, the expert with an IQ of 81 reasoned in a more complex manner than the nonexpert with an IQ of 130. Ceci and Liker (1987) concluded that the challenges we meet in daily life, such as handicapping horses, force us to develop practical intelligence—specific styles and modes of thought that are unrelated to successful performance on academic tasks.

---

ability to solve the demanding tasks they encounter in their daily lives. In this contextual view of intelligence, researchers assume that accumulated general knowledge, experience, and individual expertise in various domains affect the way that people think about and meet these tasks. Adults should do well on tasks that draw on skills they use frequently in their occupational or daily lives and do less well on tasks that draw on skills they rarely use—or have not used since they left school. Given the great diversity of adult experience and expertise, differences are bound to appear among individuals in the nature of their thought and the developmental pattern of cognitive skills.

The closeness of practical intelligence to everyday functioning makes it a more valuable way of looking at intelligence with each decade that passes in an adult's life. When we assess middle-aged and older adults solely in terms of psychometric intelligence, we are likely to

underestimate their intellectual readiness to take on various tasks, their ability to adapt to various situations, and their handling of situations in daily life (Dixon and Baltes, 1986). When middle-aged and older adults are asked to solve problems involving landlords, social relationships, work, and financial matters, for example, they provide more effective solutions than do young adults (Cornelius and Caspi, 1987).

The Dual-Process Model of Intelligence

Even if psychometric tests are not the best measure of intelligence across adulthood, they give us a comparative measure of performance on basic intellectual skills when taken out of context (Schaie, 1990a). Yet practical intelligence may be more important in successful living. Researchers have discovered, for example, that

Comparing the size and cost of articles in the supermarket requires people to relate their knowledge, expertise, and basic cognitive skills to a practical problem. *(Charles Gupton/Stock, Boston)*

by disease or poor health (Perlmutter, 1988). The mechanics of intelligence are measured by performance scales on IQ tests or other tests of fluid intelligence (see Chapter 12). The **pragmatics of intelligence** include all the procedures that relate stored knowledge, expertise, and basic cognitive skills (mechanics) to daily life. The pragmatics of intelligence encompass two parts of the triarchic theory (see Chapter 12): the metacomponents of the componential subtheory and the experiential subtheory. These functions and abilities continue to develop during adulthood, as knowledge is elaborated, maintained, and transformed. Verbal scales on IQ tests or tests of crystallized intelligence measure some, but not all, aspects of pragmatics. The pragmatics of intelligence adds to crystallized intelligence metacognition, expertise, and the sort of interpretive knowledge we call *wisdom,* which we will explore in Chapter 20.

Stages of Intellectual Development

During childhood, intelligence changes rapidly. As children acquire experience, facts, and thinking skills, their understanding of the world and its ways widens and becomes more sophisticated. The changes are so predictable and so characteristic that we can discern a lot about a 10-year-old if we know that she thinks like most 8-year-olds or most 12-year-olds. This developmental pace makes cognitive development in children relatively easy to study. Cognitive changes in adults develop slowly and are less predictable than in children. We have not learned much about the intelligence of a-40-year-old man if we are told that he thinks like most 35-year-olds. The different pace has made it difficult for researchers to study adults' intellectual development.

Extending Piagetian Theory

For decades, there was almost no research into cognitive development after adolescence. As we saw in Chapter 13, Piaget regarded the formal operations of adolescence as the peak of intelligence. Because many adolescents were slow to develop formal operations (at least the sort of deductive reasoning from hypotheses that Piaget studied), there seemed little reason to look for further advances in the way adults thought.

With the emergence of interest in development across the life span, the situation changed. Once psychologists discovered that life was not simply a downhill course after adolescence, they began to look for

there is no relation between a person's ability to make intelligent choices (comparing size and cost of similar items in a supermarket) and his or her scores on formal tests of the arithmetic operations involved (Scribner, 1986). The key may be to look at intelligence as consisting of two general processes, as Paul Baltes and his associates have suggested (Baltes, 1987).

In this **dual-process model,** intellectual functioning consists of mechanics and pragmatics. The **mechanics of intelligence** include the basic operations of thought used in processing information and solving problems. These functions and abilities are roughly similar to the componential subtheory in the triarchic view of intelligence (see Chapter 12). They probably reach full development by the end of adolescence, and from that time they remain relatively stable unless damaged

signs of cognitive development among adults. Formal thought is conscious, logical, and abstract, and it is supposed to show few, if any, traces of emotion, intuition, or imagination. According to Gisela Labouvie-Vief (1989), formal thought leads to rigidity and an inability to handle change and novelty. She believes that during middle age a more complex stage of thought, known as **postformal thought,** begins to emerge. Life experiences and an increasingly complex social environment lead adults to integrate objective, analytic thought with subjective, symbolic thought. This integrative style of thought is less literal and more interpretative than formal thought. If formal thought involves the application of operations to the elements of a system, then postformal thought involves the application of operations to different systems and their interrelationships (Rybash, Hoyer, and Roodin, 1986).

Postformal thought has three basic characteristics: relativism, contradiction, and synthesis (Kramer, 1983). The postformal reasoner realizes that knowledge is relative. Absolute truth is out of reach because people's assumptions and ways of thinking influence the knowledge that they glean from the world. The postformal reasoner realizes that contradiction is a basic aspect of reality. People (and objects) have contradictory features. A person can be loving and cold, generous and greedy, strong and weak at the same time. The postformal reasoner goes on to synthesize contradictory thoughts, emotions, and experiences into a larger framework. A choice between alternatives no longer is necessary, because adults in the postformal stage can integrate them.

Because postformal thought is stimulated by the questions, doubts, and contradictions that arise as people interact with society and because it involves the synthesis of contradictions, some cultural-contextual theorists refer to the stage of postformal thought as the stage of **dialectical operations** (Basseches, 1984). At this stage, thought involves a continuing dialectic, in which each idea interacts with its opposite to form a synthesis on a new, higher level. As the dialectic continues, thought reaches a new level of functioning.

Some research indicates that middle-aged adults are more adept than younger people at integrating conflicting information (Labouvie-Vief, 1985). When they encounter a person whose words contradict his or her facial expressions or gestures, middle-aged adults tend to take both sources of information into account. In the same situation, young adults tend to accept the words and ignore the other evidence.

When reasoning about the messy dilemmas of life, middle-aged men and women show more advanced reasoning than do adolescents or young adults. Psychologist Fredda Blanchard-Fields (1986) asked adolescents, young adults, and middle-aged adults to resolve several dilemmas, such as a conflict between a man and a woman over whether to abort an unplanned pregnancy. Most of the subjects showed some grasp of formal operations, but such understanding bore no relation to the level of reasoning they displayed when resolving the dilemmas. Adolescents tended to take one side or the other, and adults in their twenties, while aware of discrepancies, tended to say that a neutral observer could reach the "truth." Adults in their thirties or forties, however, tried to reconcile the differences, separating the facts from the interpretations of the people involved. These experienced adults tended to see each perspective as valid and unique.

Some theorists believe that postformal thought is not a separate stage that requires a reorganization of thought but is instead a *style* of thinking that emerges in adulthood (Rybash, Hoyer, and Roodin, 1986). The evidence is mixed. Researchers who matched young, middle-aged, and older adults on educational level found that relativistic and dialectical thinking became more common with age, as proponents of postformal thought predicted (Kramer and Woodruff, in press). Also as predicted, all adults who had developed formal operations showed relativistic thought, and most reasoned dialectically. But many adults who had *not* developed formal thought showed relativistic thought, indicating that relativistic thinking is not part of a separate stage. If postformal thought does indicate a new stage of development, it is not a tightly defined stage as are those in Piaget's theory.

Stages of Adult Cognition

Proponents of postformal thought build their view of cognitive development on Piaget's system. Warner Schaie (1977–1978), however, has developed a stage approach to adult intelligence that relates cognition to developmental tasks. His view of intelligence is compatible with Erikson's system (see Chapters 16 and 18), and because of the large variability in adult cognition, his stages are not tightly defined. In Schaie's theory (see Figure 17.1), cognitive changes *before* adulthood reflect increasingly efficient ways of acquiring new information; changes *during* adulthood reflect different ways of using information. For that reason, he places childhood and adolescence together in a single stage: the **acquisitive stage.** Throughout this period, young

Older adults may make better jurors than young adults because experience makes people better at coordinating conflicting information and drawing on several sources for a conclusion. *(Southern Light)*

people are engaged in learning new skills and in amassing a store of knowledge, but the knowledge is primarily acquired for future use. It is a time of learning for learning's sake, of acquiring knowledge without knowing whether it ever will be useful. The motivating question is, "What should I know?" Indeed, by demanding that young people spend most of their day in school, society insists that they devote themselves to the acquisition of knowledge.

During the three stages Schaie proposed for young and middle adulthood, the question is, "How should I use what I know?" Young adulthood is the time of Schaie's second stage, the **achieving stage.** The time has arrived to apply the knowledge that has been accumulating for years. Young adults already on the job immediately begin applying their knowledge toward their occupational goals. Those in college continue to acquire knowledge, but this time the acquisition has

Figure 17.1 Stages of adult cognitive development. Warner Schaie's theory relates cognition to developmental tasks. The first stage (childhood and adolescence) is devoted to acquiring knowledge; adult stages reflect different ways of using knowledge. *(From Schaie, 1977—1978)*

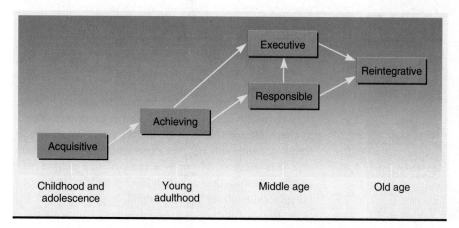

immediate application to vocational interests. During the achieving stage, young people also apply their knowledge in their personal lives, as many marry and begin families. They also may apply their knowledge in the pursuit of their hobbies, whether they hang-glide, ski, paint, or restore classic cars. During this stage, the consequences of problem solving may be enormous, especially when the problem involves such decisions as whether (or whom) to marry, whether (or when) to have children, or which occupation to enter.

The achieving stage prepares young adults for the cognitive stages of middle adulthood: the **responsible stage** and the **executive stage.** These stages require them to apply their intelligence in a socially responsible manner. The responsible stage begins first. During this stage, people apply themselves to practical problems of living and to their obligations to family members and coworkers. Many people go on to the executive stage, in which the responsibility moves from a person's im-

During the responsible stage of middle adulthood, people apply their intelligence to practical problems involving their fellow employees. *(Charles Harbutt)*

mediate family and coworkers to society. Now adults are concerned with managing organizations—a department at work, a factory team, a service club. Their interest also turns to complex community or national issues—town zoning, school boards, taxes, or foreign policy.

Schaie sees later adulthood as spent in the **reintegrative stage.** It is a time when the demand to acquire knowledge has slackened and the consequences of decisions are limited. The motivating question becomes, "Why should I know?" Instead of stretching themselves over occupational concerns, family matters, and community or national issues, older adults may focus on a single area. Perhaps retirement leaves them free to become active in politics, church affairs, or community betterment. Perhaps they devote their skills to their relations with their spouses and grandchildren. Some may continue to follow a profession but cut back on their involvement in other areas of life.

Passage from one of these stages to another is determined not by age but by developmental tasks. During the acquisitive stage, people must remain flexible. They do not know what the shape of their lives will be or in what sort of context they will exercise their skills. They excel at the sort of context-free thought demanded by schools. As they move into adulthood, they begin making commitments—to occupations, to a spouse, to child rearing. Situations arise and are resolved within the context of home or work. Problems no longer are sharply defined, and answers are no longer clear. Instead of being concerned with "the facts" and the "correct" solution, adults are involved with handling ambiguous situations and understanding the implications for themselves and others (Labouvie-Vief, 1985).

Each major approach to cognitive development in adulthood has identified major aspects of intelligence. But no matter what theory researchers use, they agree that a central issue in the study of adult intelligence is whether cognitive skills change as people age.

Does Intelligence Change with Age?

The body is physically programmed to age, so it seems only natural to assume that cognitive functions decline in the same inevitable way. Scores on IQ tests consistently decline with age, yet experience seems to contradict this picture. There is a pool of old people who continue to function at a high level long after their mental processes should have slowed. Supreme Court justices, public officials, writers, painters, sculptors, musicians, philosophers, psychologists, architects, and actors in their seventies, eighties, and even nineties continue to make important contributions to society. Although the quantity of their productive activity tends to decline during these later decades, its quality seems to remain stable (Perlmutter, 1988; Simonton, 1990).

Analyzing the Decline

Yet scores on psychometric measures continue to decline with age. Why are declines in test scores so consistent while the performance of many adults remains high? A look at test performance indicates that a single IQ score is probably not a useful measure of adult intelligence, because it tells us little about changes in the way people think. If various aspects of intelligence change in different ways, the same IQ score may mean different things at different ages. The picture that emerges from test performance indicates that decline may be limited to specific skills and that it is less debilitating than scores would indicate.

Cross-Sectional Studies

Cross-sectional studies consistently show a peaking of most abilities in early midlife, then a plateau that lasts until the late fifties or early sixties, followed by a gradual decline that accelerates after the late seventies (Schaie, 1989a). When we look at the scores more closely, it becomes apparent that not all aspects of intelligence age in the same way. Scores on the verbal scale, which measures crystallized intelligence, continue to increase until the midsixties. The decline seems to be concentrated on the performance scale, which measures fluid intelligence, where scores generally remain stable during middle adulthood and then decline across the rest of the life span. This pattern, known as the **classic aging pattern,** seems universal. It is found in men and women, in whites and African-Americans, in middle-class and working-class individuals, in institutionalized adults and adults who live in the community (Schaie, 1989a).

Studies of fluid and crystallized intelligence show the patterns followed by various components of IQ. On tests of fluid intelligence, adults do worse with each passing decade on abstract, nonverbal reasoning and problem solving and on tasks that require them to deal with novel information. What accounts for the decline? According to John Horn (1982), with each passing decade adults find it more difficult to organize information when they first encounter a problem. They find it more difficult to keep their attention focused on the matter at

hand, and they find it more difficult to form expectations about a task.

This decline in fluid intelligence is unlikely to trouble middle-aged adults, because its loss is matched by a rise in crystallized intelligence (see Figure 17.2). Until they are about 65 years old, adults keep getting better at solving problems that depend on manipulating well-learned information in familiar situations. As for specific skills, adults in their early sixties do better than those in their twenties, thirties, or forties on vocabulary tests, tests that require them to understand analogies, and tests of divergent thinking. (As we saw in Chapter 12, tests of divergent thinking assess original thought.) Horn (1982) believes that crystallized intelligence improves in part because more information accumulates

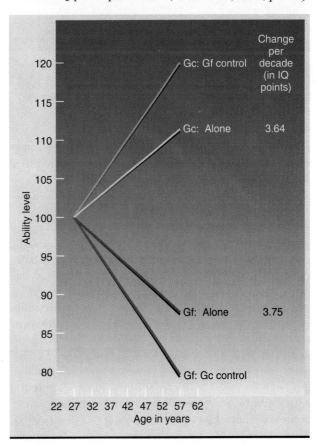

Figure 17.2 Aging of fluid and crystallized intelligence. Throughout middle adulthood, crystallized intelligence (Gc) rises with age, but fluid intelligence (Gf) declines. When fluid intelligence is controlled, the rise in crystallized intelligence becomes sharper; when crystallized intelligence is controlled, the drop in fluid intelligence becomes sharper. The figures to the right indicate the rise or fall in IQ points per decade. *(From Horn, 1982, p. 267)*

Throughout middle adulthood, people get better at manipulating well-learned information in familiar situations. This woman is probably much better at solving crossword puzzles than she was at age 25. *(Michael Weisbrot & Family)*

with each passing decade. Older adults have more information to draw on and seem to have it organized in a more efficient and flexible manner.

Longitudinal Studies

Longitudinal studies allow us to examine changes within individuals and to untangle any distortion due to cohort effects (see Chapter 1). Cohort effects usually cited as responsible for differences in IQ reflect improved health and education in succeeding cohorts, as well as an increasingly stronger focus on cognitive skills in most occupations (P. Baltes, 1987). Over this century, the health of each succeeding generation has profited from improved nutrition and the conquest of childhood diseases, and people's store of world knowledge has been enlarged by increased education, experience with sophisticated technology, and a childhood spent in homes pervaded by radio or television (Schaie, 1990b). There is evidence for such cohort effects on intelli-

gence. When IQ tests were given in 1916, scores peaked at age 16 and began to drop among people in their twenties. In 1939, IQ peaked in the late twenties; by the 1950s, IQ was still rising in the early thirties.

Among subjects followed since birth or early childhood in the California Intergenerational Studies, most middle-aged adults (36 to 48 years) showed a small increase in IQ scores over their scores as 18-year-olds (Eichorn, Hunt, and Honzik, 1981). Yet some individuals showed large gains or drops in IQ. Most of those whose IQs rose sharply during the period had either traveled extensively outside the United States, married a spouse whose IQ was at least 10 points higher than their own, or both. Most of those whose IQs declined drank heavily and had serious health problems. When retested a dozen years later (at 48 to 61 years), scores for the group as a whole continued to improve to age 54, reflecting their increased knowledge and experience. After that time scores continued to improve on verbal tests but declined on performance tests that depended on speed (Sands, Terry, and Meredith, 1989). The effect of social and cultural factors on tests was clear: scores improved on items that adults encountered frequently, either in daily life or in the media, but declined on items that were not part of their lives.

The parents of these participants, all members of the Berkeley Older Generation Study, have been tested regularly for 50 years, and their IQ scores also show the classic aging pattern (D. Field, Schaie, and Leino, 1988). Among the "young" group (age 74 to 84), 62 percent showed no decline on verbal tests (and some showed gains), and 44 percent of the "old" group (age 85 to 93) showed no decline. Decline on performance tests was, however, pervasive, with only 15 percent of the 74- to 84-year-olds and 6 percent of the 85- to 93-year-olds showing no decline.

The most important longitudinal study, conducted by Warner Schaie (1989a, 1990a, 1990b), is sequential in design (see Chapter 1). It has followed adults since 1956, measuring their IQ every seven years, and adding a new group of subjects at each measurement. Birthdates ranged from 1889 to 1959, so the study covered all periods of adulthood. At the last testing, the oldest adults were 81 years old. Statistically reliable declines appeared in all cohorts during their fifties, but the declines were too small to affect intellectual performance in a noticeable manner. Between the ages of 46 and 60, the decline amounted to only 3 IQ points. Few individuals showed declines in all subtests, which included verbal meaning, spatial orientation, inductive reasoning, number, and word fluency (see Figure 17.3). At age 60,

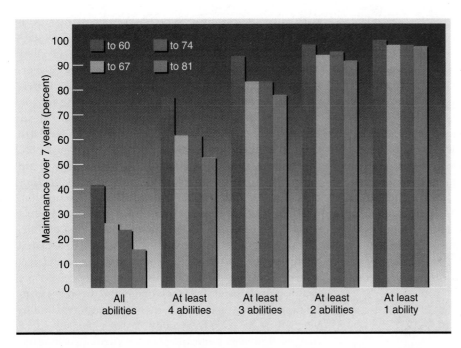

Figure 17.3 Stable levels of performance on multiple cognitive abilities. In a major sequential study, adults were assessed over a seven-year period on five measures of cognitive ability: verbal meaning, spatial orientation, inductive reasoning, number, and word fluency. Although, on the average, cognitive abilities declined with age, few adults declined on all abilities, and a minority continued into their eighties with no decline in either crystallized or fluid intelligence skills. *(From Schaie, 1990a, p. 297)*

75 percent of adults showed no decline on at least four of the five IQ subtests, and at 81 more than 50 percent still showed no decline on at least four subtests (Schaie, 1990b). Such results remind us that even if the average IQ declines during later life, many people show no drop in IQ until they are well into their seventies, and a few are in their early eighties before the first measurable decline appears.

Cohort differences were also apparent among the adults in this study. On tests of inductive reasoning (problem-solving skill), verbal meaning (word knowledge), and spatial ability, younger cohorts (born later) had the highest scores. But on word fluency, older cohorts performed better than the young, and the two youngest cohorts (born in 1952 and 1959) had the lowest scores on number skills. Schaie's analysis indicates that during the 1990s age differences in the scores of young adults and of the young-old will shrink noticeably and that 60-year-olds should be able to compete on equal terms with the young. However, as they enter old-old age, poor health and other age-related changes will again magnify age differences.

Some theorists believe that society itself may play a substantial role in age-related cognitive decline

(Schooler, 1990). Each culture has its own expectations about the activities and power that are appropriate for various age groups. In this culture, older adults are expected to be powerless and to think in a plodding, if not childish, fashion (Heise, 1987). Through early retirement, nonchallenging work, and internalized personal expectations, social pressure may force older adults into powerless roles that encourage them to give up potent thought.

Terminal Drop

Some researchers have suggested that the connection between health and IQ is reflected in **terminal drop,** a critical decline in IQ scores that appears shortly before death. The drop is not related to age (time since birth); instead, it is related to mortality (distance from death). It is apparently the result of physical deterioration or damage. In some longitudinal studies, these sharp declines appear as long as five years before death; in others, the declines are limited to the last ten months of life.

Some researchers have found the clearest terminal drop in verbal information skills; some have found it in performance skills; others have found it in both. In

Schaie's sequential study, discussed earlier, terminal drop appeared in four subtests: verbal meaning, word fluency, number, and spatial orientation (Cooney, Schaie, and Willis, 1988). Recent studies suggest that, although the decline may be pervasive, it is easier to detect in verbal skills (White and Cunningham, 1988). Terminal drop may be most apparent in verbal skills because crystallized abilities are not generally affected by normal aging. Any decline is easily recognized. But fluid intelligence normally declines with age, and so "normal" declines obscure any evidence of terminal drop (Cooney, Schaie, and Willis, 1988). Thus, in a study of more than 1000 older adults, only vocabulary skills were related to a person's distance from death (White and Cunningham, 1988). Among these adults, the drop appeared approximately two years before death, but it was *not* apparent among adults older than 70.

Accounting for Continued High Performance

Although performance IQ scores decline with age, performance in everyday life seems unimpaired. Individuals in late middle age and older adulthood hold some of the most responsible and demanding jobs in government and corporation life, yet most adults in these age groups have IQ test scores that are significantly lower than scores of younger adults (Schludermann et al., 1983). According to Timothy Salthouse (1990), there are four possible reasons for this discrepancy (see Table 17.1). First, IQ tests and the activities involved in occupations and daily life may depend on *different types of cognition*. Second, highly successful middle-aged and older adults *may not be representative* of their age groups. It may be that only older adults

with superior cognitive functioning retain their positions, whereas those whose cognitive powers have deteriorated have retired, changed occupations, or died. Another possible explanation is that cognitive impairment is selective; that is, cognitive deterioration is present, but the skills required for successful functioning in the adults' professions have escaped decline. Third, competence in adult life depends on lower levels of cognitive functioning than does competence measured by IQ tests, so *different standards of evaluation* are used. Fourth, successful older adults have *high levels of expertise,* which makes them highly competent, whereas IQ tests measure performance in novel situations that are removed from the context of daily life.

As we saw in the discussion of IQ scores, age-related declines appear to be concentrated in fluid intelligence, which relies on the mechanics of intelligence. People draw on processing skills included in the mechanics (attention, perceptual speed, memory, and reasoning) when they are faced with new tasks, especially those that at first seem meaningless to them (Perlmutter, 1988). As they master various skills or domains, they draw more heavily on the pragmatics of intelligence, which include crystallized intelligence, expertise, and knowledge about skills required for intelligent action. These aspects of intelligence do not appear to decline with age.

After reviewing more than a dozen studies, researchers concluded that most workers, especially those in the professions, tend to become more efficient on the job as they age (Waldman and Avolio, 1983). They are as accurate as younger adults and tend to work more steadily. They have fewer accidents and are absent less often (Stagner, 1985). Older employees are also highly motivated. They tend to be more involved in their work and more committed to their organization than younger

TABLE 17.1   **EXPLAINING CONTINUED COGNITIVE COMPETENCE**

Factors in the IQ tests	Activities demanded by occupation of high-scoring individuals depend on types of cognition not measured by test.
	Competence in life and that on IQ tests are evaluated by different standards.
Factors in the individual	High-scoring individuals are unrepresentative of their age groups.
	High-scoring individuals have developed high levels of expertise.

Researchers have suggested four factors that may account for the discrepancy between age-related declines in IQ scores and the obvious competence of many late middle-aged and older adults.

Source: After Salthouse, 1990.

As professionals pass through middle age, they become increasingly effective as a result of their accumulated knowledge, practice in job-related skills, and deeper commitment to their work. *(Bob Daemmrich/Stock, Boston)*

the material they are copying than younger typists do (Salthouse, 1984). When researchers arrange the material so that typists cannot see ahead, the speed of older typists drops, but the younger typists are as fast as ever.

Some theorists, however, have suggested that we should not be so quick to assume that losses and gains are causally connected (Uttal and Perlmutter, 1989). Perhaps typing expertise involves looking ahead, and the older typists' extended preview developed independently from their loss of basic skills (reaction time and keystroke speed). In that case, the gains and losses that appear simultaneously are each the result of different, unrelated causes.

Aspects of Intellectual Change

Our picture of intelligence across adulthood is not a simple one. The pattern of intellectual change seems almost as complex as thinking processes themselves. In general, intellectual development across adulthood seems to follow three principles: (1) The basic mechanics decline with age, but well-practiced functions and skills stabilize or even improve. (2) The performance of older adults improves when they are interested, try hard, or are highly motivated, indicating that they have a reserve capacity that they often fail to apply. (3) Because of selective optimization, drops in performance tend to be localized and much smaller than test measures would lead us to expect (Dixon and Baltes, 1986). In short, intellectual functioning in adulthood appears to depend on three principles: practice, motivation, and expertise.

Some theorists (for example, Willis, 1987) explain observed age-related declines in basic mechanics as resulting from the failure to use various cognitive skills, but recent research by Timothy Salthouse (1991; Salthouse et al., 1990) suggests that other factors besides practice are involved in at least one aspect of fluid intelligence. Salthouse studied spatial visualization in architects (age 21 to 71) and in engineers (age 21 to 80), and in both instances, he found that as age increased, scores on tests of spatial ability declined. Such tests measure the ability to infer three-dimensional shapes from two-dimensional drawings, to see how objects change as they move in space, and to detect the perspective of objects in relation to one another. Older architects performed considerably better than older nonarchitects, but the difference was as wide between younger groups as between older groups. As Salthouse notes (Salthouse et al., 1990), this does not mean that older architects are less professionally competent than

employees. In addition, skills related to an activity that has been thoroughly mastered, whether related to an occupation or a hobby, often continue to improve (Perlmutter, 1988). Such improvement reflects an efficiently organized knowledge base as well as strategic, job-related skills.

Another factor that affects intelligence among older adults may be what Paul Baltes (1987) calls **selective optimization** with compensation. He sees intellectual development during the last half of life as a joint expression of gain (growth) and loss (decline). As biologically based losses appear, adults refocus their efforts and abilities on fewer areas, strengthening important old skills and developing new, compensating skills that prevent deterioration in performance. For example, reaction time is a component of typing skill. When their reaction time is tested, older typists are slower than younger typists. Yet they type just as fast as the young. Studies have shown that older typists appear to compensate for their slowed reactions by looking farther ahead in

younger architects. The tests, which remove the forms from any context, focus on basic cognitive processes that minimize the contribution of knowledge and experience. We will return to this question in Chapter 19, where we examine specific changes in information processing among older adults.

A helpful way to look at adult intelligence is in terms of four conceptions suggested by Roger Dixon and Paul Baltes (1986). They propose that adult intelligence is composed of many separate mental abilities; thus, intelligence is *multidimensional.* Each of these abilities may have its own distinct structure, function, and possibility for change. Each may also follow its own pattern of development, some abilities increasing, some remaining stable, and others declining; thus, intelligence is *multidirectional.* The pattern of the developmental process differs from one individual to the next; thus, intelligence is characterized by *interindividual variability.* Finally, throughout life, people are adaptable and are able to acquire new information, develop new strategies, and perfect old ones; thus, intelligence is also characterized by *intraindividual plasticity.*

How Health and Life Style Affect Cognition

When well into his eighties, British philosopher Bertrand Russell had a long discussion of technical mathematics with three mathematicians. Afterward, one of them said, "It was not merely that his brain was beautifully clear for somebody of 87; it was beautifully clear for anybody at any age" (R. Clark, 1975, p. 549). The example of exceptional older people has led some developmentalists to conclude that cognitive decline is not an inevitable accompaniment of age. In Schaie's (1990a) longitudinal study, many individuals showed no decline with advancing age, although less than 20 percent of those in their eighties showed no decline in *any* of the tested cognitive abilities (see Figure 17.3). Because of such findings, researchers have looked for factors that affect cognition during adulthood. Earlier we noted that education seems to be one such factor. Personality, life style, and chronic disease appear to be other important factors.

How does personality affect the way we think? Research indicates that personality patterns may affect cognitive functioning in highly stressful situations. Some people are highly competitive, become hostile when

thwarted, and behave as if they were always racing the clock. Others are relaxed and give no indication that they feel the pressure of time. In most situations, the clock racers (known as *Type A's*) are highly productive and outperform the relaxed *Type B's.* But in highly stressful situations, Type A people seem to have a strong need to maintain control, and this can get them into trouble. In one study, Type A's and Type B's solved a group of problems, thinking out loud as they worked at the solutions (Brunson and Matthews, 1981). After they had completed the problems, they began work on a second set. But this time the problems were unsolvable. As they struggled with one unsolvable problem after another, the Type A's became increasingly frustrated and annoyed. They said that the test was too hard and that they lacked the ability to handle it. Instead of trying new attacks, they gave up and kept producing the same incorrect answer even though the researchers said it was wrong. The Type B's responded in a completely different manner. They seemed unhappy and bored, but they were not angry. Instead, they kept trying to find a solution and seemed to think they would eventually succeed.

Life styles also have an important influence on adult cognition. They can predict the course of IQ in later adulthood. Schaie (1984) has found that middle-aged people whose lives are high in environmental stimulation, especially those who continue to pursue educational interests, generally retain their intellectual abilities during later adulthood. Apparently, the complexity of a person's environment is related to the absence of cognitive decline. Supporting evidence appeared when researchers studied the way young adults (age 20 to 40) and older adults (age 60 to 80) spent their time during one month (Perlmutter, Nyquist, and Adams-Price, 1989). Older adults' (but not younger adults') performance on tests of fluid intelligence correlated with the amount of time they generally devoted to mental activity, especially to creative activity.

Some researchers have suggested that intelligence may begin to decline when adults retire and withdraw from full participation in the economic and social life of the society (Labouvie-Vief, 1985). Among members of the Berkeley Older Generation Study, older adults who had been caring for a sick spouse at an earlier testing showed increases in fluid intelligence fourteen years later, after the spouse had died and they were free to pursue new activities and interests (D. Field, Schaie, and Leino, 1988). In Schaie's study, large declines in IQ were associated with being poor, socially isolated, widowed, or divorced and with having stopped working

(Gribbin, Schaie, and Parham, 1980). The sharpest drops were among women living in relatively inaccessible environments who withdrew from social activities after being widowed. Adults who retained a highly active life style, full of social and intellectual activity, performed best on IQ tests.

Exercise also seems to foster mental fitness, even among the young. The reaction time of young adults who are out of shape resembles that of older adults. Among women in middle adulthood, those who regularly ran at least thirty minutes a day reacted more quickly than working women who did not exercise (Baylor and Spirduso, 1988). In this case, the test was relevant to daily life. In response to a warning signal, each runner removed his or her foot more quickly from a car accelerator, which could help avoid auto accidents. The advantage continues into older adulthood. Women in their late sixties who followed a vigorous exercise program for at least ten years reacted as rapidly

Adults who embark on a regular exercise program generally find that it improves their reaction time, attention span, and memory. *(Herve Donnezan/Rapho/Photo Researchers)*

as college students (Rikli and Busch, 1986). Some researchers have found that three hours of exercise each week—enough to improve respiratory fitness—seems to have no effect on cognitive performance (Madden et al., 1989). But other researchers have found that adults between the ages of 55 and 88 who spend at least five hours each week in strenuous exercise have faster reaction times, better working memory, and reason more accurately than those who are sedentary (Clarkson-Smith and Hartley, 1989).

Regular exercise seems to relieve anxiety and tension. It also reduces blood pressure and improves the condition of the circulatory system. Exercise reduces cholesterol levels, causes an increase in the number of red blood cells, and improves the condition of blood vessels around the heart.

The effect of exercise on blood pressure and the circulatory system is especially important, because some studies have uncovered a connection between these factors and IQ decline. When researchers followed 300 adults (age 20 to 75) for ten years, they discovered that elevated diastolic blood pressure (the lower of the two numbers, which indicates pressure between the heart's contractions) predicted cognitive losses when they controlled for age, gender, and education (Elias et al., 1990). These researchers are convinced that high blood pressure, which is a symptom of cardiovascular disease, may account for a good part of the age-related decline on cognitive tests.

Other researchers have connected cardiovascular disease with cognitive decline. In one study, blood pressure, adjusted for age and education, correlated negatively with scores on tests of fluid intelligence (Robbins, Elias, and Pechinski, 1989); in another, with scores on the WAIS test (Elias, Robbins, and Schultz, 1987); and in an eleven-year longitudinal study, with scores on tests involving attention and memory (Sands and Meredith, 1992). Cardiovascular disease also has been linked with declines in the ability to solve problems that require formal reasoning (La Rue and Jarvik, 1982; Robbins, Elias, and Pechinski, 1989). Middle-aged and older adults tried to solve several Piagetian tests of formal reasoning (see Chapter 14). Age had no effect on scores, but health did.

When researchers use self-reported health as a measure of mental fitness, results are mixed. Among adults between the ages of 20 and 79, self-reported health (rated on a 5-point scale) was unrelated to cognitive performance, but age was (Salthouse, Kausler, and Saults, 1990). Yet among another group of adults between the ages of 20 and 90, self-reported health (rated on an 11-point scale and combined with a self-administered checklist of symptoms) was clearly related to fluid intelligence, especially among older adults (Perlmutter and Nyquist, 1990). Self-ratings of health accounted for a considerable portion—but not all—of the age differences among these adults. In the Berkeley Older Generation Study, self-reported health was related only weakly to intelligence scores among individuals younger than 85, except among individuals who showed extreme changes (either increases or declines) in IQ scores (D. Field, Schaie, and Leino, 1988). The researchers noted, however, that when observers' reports of health were also taken into account, the relation became stronger in both groups and that among the very old the relation to performance scores was clear.

Education and a highly active life style appear to be the best defense against declining intelligence. Perhaps the current popularity of physical fitness programs and rising enrollments in adult education will increase the proportion of older adults whose IQs remain stable.

Adult Education

Anyone who doubts the popularity of adult education need only drop by a community college or public high school on a weekday evening. Courses are offered in

The majority of students in adult-education courses are young or middle-aged adults with higher than average incomes and education. *(Beringer/Dratch/The Image Works)*

everything from gourmet cooking, yoga, and obedience training for dogs to psychology, computer science, and economics. As a society, the United States seems to have switched from viewing education as a vaccine (with a large dose during childhood and adolescence providing immunity against the need for further learning) to viewing education as a lifelong learning process (Birren and Woodruff, 1973). Participation in formal adult-education classes provides a potent stimulus for personal intellectual growth.

Who enrolls in adult education? Women and men of every age can be found in these classes, but the majority are young and middle-aged adults with higher-than-average income and education. According to government figures, 17 percent of middle-aged adults (35 to 54 years) and nearly 6 percent of those older than 54 have returned to school (U.S. Bureau of the Census, 1990). Because completion of high school seems to be the marker of further interest in education, experts are predicting that enrollments among older adults will increase as soon as more highly educated cohorts pass through late middle age (Birren and Woodruff, 1973). (One innovative program designed specifically for older adults is discussed in the accompanying box, "Learning the Elderhostel Way.")

The Adult Student's Objectives

Adults have many reasons for returning to school, and their goals shift slightly with age. In a study of community college students, younger adults emphasized their desire to get a job, a general education, and more money (Daniel, Templin, and Shearon, 1977). Older adults who were enrolled in courses for credit saw contributing to society as their primary goal, followed closely by becoming a more cultured person and earning more money. Older adults in noncredit courses were intent on learning interesting things, meeting interesting people, and contributing to society. In most cases, students had more than one reason for coming back to school.

Few studies of the middle-aged adult's educational goals exist, but Sherry Willis (1985) has suggested four broad objectives that are related to occupational and personal development. First, many adults are preparing themselves for second careers. Some are individuals in their forties or fifties who have worked in occupations that provide early retirement; they have been armed forces personnel, police officers, fire fighters, or airline pilots. Some, especially nurses and mental-health counselors, are victims of "burnout." They have lost all interest in their present occupations, often because the jobs require an intense emotional involvement or the daily grappling with overwhelming problems. Some are women who are entering the labor market after spending fifteen or twenty years rearing children. Finally, some are workers displaced by basic changes in the American economy. Former steelworkers, oil-field employees, farmers, and middle managers enroll in courses that train them for new jobs.

A second educational objective is combating technological or sociocultural obsolescence. Physicians or other professionals return to school in order to keep abreast of changes that affect their work. Some workers have training provided or subsidized by their employers. Business and industry provide education for more adults than do colleges and universities. Workers whose factories have been automated learn to handle robot-dominated assembly lines. Office workers learn to operate information-processing equipment. Some corpora-

tions subsidize university classes. Harvard, Stanford, and MIT, for example, each provide a three-month course in advanced management for bankers and other midlevel executives in their forties. The course, which is paid for by employers, prepares these men and women to climb the corporate ladder. In 1986, seventy-three universities provided some sort of management education for executives, and about 15,000 middle-aged American executives were enrolled in the courses (Wayne, 1986).

A third educational objective is the generation of satisfactory retirement roles. In this instance, the goal is personal satisfaction instead of economic gain. Adults enroll in courses that help them to develop leisure pursuits after retirement. Some are acquiring skills and information that help them to serve as semiprofessional volunteers in the human services. Others are developing hobbies and various leisure interests.

Finally, understanding the biological and psychological changes of adulthood may become an important ob-

LEARNING THE ELDERHOSTEL WAY

Sometimes adults past the age of 60 wish to return to school but are not interested in preparing for a second career or pursuing a degree. For them, colleges and universities around the world have developed a series of inexpensive, short-term courses meant to challenge the older adult and expose him or her to new ideas. The concept is called **Elderhostel,** because it is a combination of adult education and hosteling. Students often live in college dorms and eat in college dining halls, although some Elderhostelers are housed in camps, conference centers, science field stations, hotels, or on ships. Regular faculty members teach the courses, which run from one to three weeks. The first Elderhostel program was offered by five New Hampshire colleges in 1975; 220 adults enrolled. By 1991, there were nearly 250,000 students in all fifty states and at sites in forty-five countries ("Welcome to Elderhostel," 1991).

Elderhostel programs have been popular because they offer adults change, a chance to travel, and the opportunity to develop new interests and catch up on old ones. The majority of Elderhostelers have advanced degrees or some postgraduate training (53 percent), another 15 percent have completed college, and an additional 20 percent have at least two years of college (Portrait of an Elderhosteler, 1990). The majority are in their late sixties and have an income that is above the average for retired individuals; only 67 percent are fully retired. About 60 percent are women, and most enrollees have attended

previous Elderhostels. Not all Elderhostelers have reached the minimum age of 60. Spouses of any age are welcome, and companions of Elderhostelers may be as young as 50.

Programs are available year-round, and the offerings span virtually every possibility. Elderhostelers can study politics, architecture, literature, religion, history, civil rights, languages, computer science, or the arts. They can snorkel, ski, or canoe, join an archeological dig, train in simulated spacecraft, or research their family trees.

Upper-middle-class students dominate Elderhostel classes, which are likely to have even greater appeal as educational levels rise among older adults. They also dominate the "Learning in Retirement" study groups, in which adults pay universities an annual fee and often design their own courses (Beck, 1991). A popular program among those whose profile matches today's typical older adult is the Senior Center Humanities Program, which relies on local discussion groups in neighborhood settings (Moody, 1986). Using anthologies of literature, philosophy, autobiography, folklore, and the arts that have been adapted to local interests, the groups discuss such topics as local history.

No matter which program they choose, older adults who attend these courses have probably increased their chances of remaining mentally fit and avoiding intellectual decline.

*Intellectual Development
in Early and Middle Adulthood*

jective of many older adults. Throughout human history, adults have taken the aging process for granted, accepting the physical and cognitive changes that they assumed were inevitable. As we shall see in Chapter 19, researchers have developed ways of teaching cognitive strategies that may stave off or reverse declines in learning, memory, or problem solving.

The Problem of Adult Illiteracy

Not everything in the field of adult education is coming up roses. In recent years, concern has mounted about the rate of adult illiteracy in the United States. Among the 158 countries that belong to the United Nations, the United States ranks forty-ninth in literacy rate. This figure is likely to get larger, because the high school dropout rate is increasing.

How bad is the situation? Estimates vary. On the basis of studies conducted in the 1970s, Jonathan Kozol (1985) charged that one-third of the population was illiterate. A decade later, the U.S. Census Bureau reported that 18.7 million adults, or approximately 13 percent of the population, were illiterate (A. Newman and Beverstock, 1990). No one is certain just how many illiterate adults actually live in the United States, and guesses depend on whether we look at completely illiterate people, who cannot read or write at all, or at **functional illiterates,** people who lack the basic reading and writing skills needed for productive performance in American society. In his statement, Kozol referred to functional illiterates.

Functional literacy has had almost as many definitions as people who have written about the subject. One social definition is the ability to accomplish transactions involving reading and writing that an individual wishes—or is compelled—to carry out (Kintgen, Kroll, and Ross, 1988). Because there is little agreement about the minimum skill required for literacy, national assessments of reading ability have deemphasized literacy and begun to describe levels of literacy. After testing a representative national sample of young adults (age 20 to 25), researchers concluded that nearly 100 percent could handle tasks at the simplest level (Kirsch and Jungblut, 1986). They could match single known items with requests for information. At this level, people handle such simple tasks as signing their names in the appropriate place on various forms. The overwhelming majority (84 percent) functioned at the second level of

literacy. They could choose correct information from several possible answers, find a location on a map, and use a table to calculate eligibility for benefits. Only 20 percent functioned at the third level of literacy, which required the ability to answer questions that required them to match multiple features, to infer information stated in different terms from those used in test questions, and to deal with distracters. Many school dropouts can operate at the second level of literacy, but only those with advanced schooling are likely to perform at the highest level.

A major problem is that functional illiteracy is strongly related to ethnicity in the United States (A. Newman and Beverstock, 1990). Since the economically and educationally disadvantaged are concentrated among ethnic minorities, African-Americans and Hispanics often find that their level of literacy has shut the door to further progress. Among adults who enroll in literacy programs, 16 percent are African-Americans, 30 percent are Hispanic, 3 percent are Native Americans, and 13 percent are Asian-Americans (A. Newman and Beverstock, 1990). Most are low-income: 70 percent have family incomes of less than $10,000.

Most adult school dropouts cannot read at all or, at best, can manage to puzzle out the program listings in *TV Guide.* At least a third of illiterates are more than 60 years old and may have grown up in states that had no compulsory education laws (Deigh, 1986). Many of the rest come from poverty areas, such as the inner cities or Appalachia. But some are working-class adults who struggled with school for a while and then dropped out. There was Hal, a Yonkers plumber with three children, who refused to go into a store unless a family member accompanied him. He couldn't read the labels on merchandise, couldn't write a check, couldn't even draw money out of his bank account. Hal quit school at the end of junior high school because the other youngsters teased him for his inability to read. He hid his illiteracy on the job by asking other people to read the blueprints with him. He refused to answer a telephone at work because he might have had to write down a message. At last Hal entered a literacy program for adults with normal IQs, where he learned to read (Spear, 1985). There was also Laura, a part-time college student whose reading skills were limited to her recognition of about fifty words by sight (A. Newman and Beverstock, 1990). Despite individual instruction, Laura did not learn to read until her instructor began using a whole-language approach, in which Laura began independent writing with invented spelling.

Using elaborate strategies to hide his inability to read or write, middle-class businessman John Corcoran "lived like a fugitive" for forty years. Overcoming his fear and frustration, he sought out an adult learning program, where he learned to read with the aid of a tutor. *(Tony Korody/SYGMA)*

An approach to literacy that works with one adult who cannot read will not be equally effective with another. Some authorities suggest that adult literacy programs be viewed as a process of mutual discussion and that instructors must understand that becoming literate is a personal and social process that depends on culture and context (A. Newman and Beverstock, 1990).

After surveying the research on intelligence in adulthood, what can we expect of our cognitive powers as we move through middle age and approach later adulthood? What seems clear is that we have some control over what happens to us. If we can stay healthy, keep active, and continue to use our minds, we are unlikely to experience major cognitive declines. Werner Schaie and Sherry Willis (1986a) summed up the typical pat-

tern of cognition across adulthood by saying, "Those who live *by* their wits die *with* their wits."

In this chapter we have focused on intelligence, which has been studied primarily with psychometric or Piagetian methods. Such research takes a developmental approach and focuses on progressive shifts in general thinking. In Chapter 19, we examine cognition in late adulthood, which has been studied primarily with the methods of experimental gerontology. Such research focuses on information-processing tasks and attempts to identify specific aspects of information processing that might change during old age. As we look at information processing in the later years, we will see how changes in physiology and life style may affect older adults' ability to learn, think, and remember.

INTELLIGENCE

Most research on adult intellectual development explores either psychometric intelligence or practical intelligence. Psychometric studies trace intelligence across adulthood through performance on IQ tests, using simple tasks that draw on memory, calculation, comprehension, and problem solving. Practical-intelligence studies grow out of the view that adapting to the environment is an active, lifelong process. They take a contextual view of intelligence, in which intelligence is demonstrated by the application of knowledge, expertise, and experience to problems of daily life. The **dual-process model** of intelligence draws on both these traditions. In this model, the **mechanics of intelligence** can be measured through psychometric tests of fluid abilities, but only some aspects of the **pragmatics of intelligence** can be measured through psychometric tests of crystallized abilities.

STAGES OF INTELLECTUAL DEVELOPMENT

Adult cognitive development may include a stage of **postformal thought,** or **dialectical operations,** which goes beyond formal operations and is based on relativism, contradiction, and synthesis. In another view, adult cognitive development is related to developmental tasks, with the **acquisitive stage** covering the years through adolescence; the **achieving stage** covering young adulthood; the **responsible stage** and the **executive stage** covering middle adulthood; and the **reintegrative stage** covering late adulthood.

DOES INTELLIGENCE CHANGE WITH AGE?

Cross-sectional studies reflect the **classic aging pattern** of declines in fluid intelligence during middle adulthood but a continued rise in crystallized intelligence until later adulthood. Longitudinal studies indicate cohort differences in patterns of IQ scores as well as wide interindividual differences, with some people failing to show declines until they reach their eighties. Test scores of some older adults may be affected by **terminal drop,** a decline in IQ scores—especially verbal scores—that appears before death.

Intelligence among older adults may be affected by **selective optimization** with compensation, in which adults develop new, compensating skills that circumvent the effects of biologically based loss. Adult intellectual development appears to follow three principles: (1) a decline in basic mechanisms that can be partially offset by practice, (2) an improvement in performance with motivation, and (3) selective optimization, which minimizes drops in performance.

HOW HEALTH AND LIFE STYLE AFFECT COGNITION

Personality may affect intellectual functioning in stressful situations, with highly competitive, clock-racing individuals becoming so frustrated and annoyed that they quit trying. Life style affects intellectual functioning; adults who live in a stimulating environment and pursue intellectual interests tend to retain a high level of functioning, whereas those who withdraw from life tend to show declines. Exercise seems to affect intellectual functioning; adults in peak condition tend to have faster reaction times, have better working memory, and reason more accurately than sedentary adults. Cardiovascular disease is connected with intellectual decline. The connection between self-reported health and cognitive performance is not clear.

ADULT EDUCATION

The majority of students in adult-education classes are young and middle-aged adults with above-average incomes and education. The adult who returns to school is usually working toward at least one of four goals: (1) preparing for a second career, (2) combating technological or sociocultural obsolescence, (3) establishing satisfactory retirement roles, or (4) understanding biological and psychological changes of adulthood. **Elderhostels** are a popular form of adult education among older adults. Approximately 13 percent of the population may be illiterate, but a much larger proportion of people may be **functional illiterates.** Because of economic and educational disadvantages, the rate of functional illiteracy is highest among ethnic minorities.

KEY TERMS

achieving stage
acquisitive stage
classic aging pattern
dialectical operations
dual-process model

Elderhostel
executive stage
functional illiterate
mechanics of intelligence
postformal thought

pragmatics of intelligence
reintegrative stage
responsible stage
selective optimization
terminal drop

MIDDLE ADULTHOOD: MAKING THE MOST OF IT

• • • • • • • • • • • • • •

At 48, Harry Biolsi has found that the American dream is out of his grasp. Biolsi, a truck driver who lives in the Astoria region of New York City's borough of Queens, earns $30,000 a year at his job. But $30,000 no longer provides the good life for a traditional American family: Biolsi, his wife Arlene, and their four children. Nicole, the oldest child, is 10; Harry, Jr., is 8; and the twins, Natalie and Emily, are 2 years old. Harry works a twelve-hour day delivering office furniture, and he adds to his income by doing minor repairs and home improvements on his friends' houses. The Biolsis are unable to buy their own home in Astoria, because even modest houses in this area of pleasant streets, convenient public transportation, and good shopping sell for $275,000—nearly three times the $100,000 that they could afford. And so the Biolsis live with Harry's mother in her house, paying her rent. Since the economy turned sour and a single salary no longer stretches as far as it did, says Harry, an increasing number of his mother's friends have found themselves in the same situation, with children who once left the nest moving back home. If Arlene were in the labor market, as are the majority of women in her situation, the Biolsis might be able to buy a home, but neither partner wants Arlene to go back to work until the twins are in school (Chira, 1989).

● ● ● ● ● ●

For the Biolsis, as for many adults in middle adulthood, this period of life is not as secure as it once was. Stagnant wages, coupled with inflated housing costs in many areas of the country, have meant that steady jobs do not automatically translate into the good life these adults grew up expecting to have. In this chapter, we examine the developmental tasks that adults encounter during the years that stretch from 40 to 65. Despite the instability that many feel when they compare themselves with their parents' generation, the midlife years, from 40 to 65, may be the most satisfying part of the life span. The majority of middle-aged Americans are healthy, and their financial situation is relatively secure. Living through their period of maximum productivity and maximum rewards, they are part of the "command generation," the group that controls American society. We begin with recent social changes that have affected the experience of middle age in American society; then we examine the changes in appearance, body function, and sexuality that accompany middle adulthood. Returning to the theories discussed in Chapter 16, we see what sort of picture they paint of middle age. After exploring self-concept and self-esteem in midlife, we discover how men's and women's occupational lives differ at this period. The rest of the chapter is devoted to the family. In the section on marriage, we focus on changes in marital satisfaction and the sexual relationship and then examine midlife trends in divorce and remarriage. Parenthood at midlife, we find, can take three paths: the birth of the first baby, the nurturance of adolescents, and the adjustment to the empty nest. Next we look at the middle-aged adult's relationship with his or her own parents, and we close with an exploration of what it means to become a grandparent.

Social Change

As we near the end of the twentieth century, the nature of middle age is changing in this country. Fifty years ago, people in their forties and fifties looked "middle-aged." Gray hair, a "middle-aged spread," a sedate life style, and "mature" clothes set most of them apart from younger adults. Today, many seem young. They are healthier, more physically active, and more attractive than their parents and grandparents were at the same age. When journalist Gloria Steinem reached 50, an interviewer said that she didn't "look 50." Steinem, who was born in 1934, replied, "This is what 50 looks like today."

At midlife, most of today's couples are at an earlier stage of family development than their parents and grandparents were. Delayed marriage and childbearing postpone the time when children leave home, especially among the middle class. Middle-class parents tend to be older when their first-born leaves the nest, yet younger when the last-born departs. Because couples are having fewer children, the period of life devoted to child rearing has been curtailed for today's adults. When the nest begins to empty, it does so rapidly, perhaps in the space of two or three years, and parents get less time to adjust to the change. Working-class couples who have limited the size of their families but have not postponed parenthood may be in their midforties when the last child departs—at a similar age, the grandparents or great-grandparents might have been anticipating the birth of their last child. Because most people spend a greater proportion of the life span as a couple, the marital relationship takes on new importance and is subject to new stresses. In fact, Erik Erikson (Erikson and Hall, 1987) has suggested that the prospect of sixty years of married life may have played an important role in the growing tendency to divorce and remarry.

Fewer people die in middle adulthood, and the consequent rise in the proportion of older Americans means that today's middle-aged parents are likely to have living parents. This is the first time in history that the average middle-aged couple has had more living parents than children (Gatz, Bengston, and Blum,

1990). Unlike their mothers, few women today are widowed during middle age, although they are more likely than their mothers to be single, divorced, divorcing, or cohabiting. The rate of remarriage among middle-aged women has dropped since their mothers' day. The divorced or widowed male, however, is more likely than his female counterpart to remarry during middle age—and to marry someone younger. As a result, while the nest is emptying for most men and women, some men are starting new families.

The world outside the home also has changed for people in middle adulthood. They are better educated. In 1970, 52 percent of adults older than 25 had completed high school; by 1988, the figure had risen to 63 percent. Among the middle-aged, 73 percent had finished high school, and 37 percent had spent at least one year at college (U.S. Bureau of the Census, 1990). When today's young adults move into middle adulthood, educational levels will increase further. As we saw in Chapter 17, many adults are going back to school to prepare

Men who are divorced or widowed during middle age are more likely than their female counterparts to remarry. *(Charles Feil/Stock, Boston)*

themselves either for occupational changes or, in the case of many women, for entry into the labor market. Most middle-aged women are employed, either because they have always worked or because they are returning to the labor market as their children reach school age. Many farmers, factory workers, and miners whose occupations are evaporating have enrolled in vocational courses geared to high-technology jobs.

The prosperity of people in middle adulthood depends on general economic conditions as well as on their own education. The first wave of the post-World War II baby boom entered middle adulthood in 1986, and these adults are not doing as well as those who are in their late fifties and early sixties. Many of those in their forties have discovered that they will not live better than their parents and may not do nearly so well. Their parents and grandparents saw their real incomes increase sharply after the age of 30, but many of today's workers have seen their real incomes fall. Production workers in Peoria, Illinois, for example, have seen their wages go up 157 percent since 1973, but the consumer price index has risen 203 percent in the same period (Uchitelle, 1991). Today, fewer men and women in their early forties feel that they have freedom to do what they wish with their lives, although many still face the future with confidence. And despite the fact that they have begun to age, they still feel young.

Physical Changes

During midlife, people begin to notice obvious changes in the way their bodies look and work. All the little changes that began in early adulthood progress steadily, and they force adults to realize that they are no longer young. The realization is unsettling, and it leads most to look backward, wishing that they could recapture their youthful appearance and vigor. The face that looks back at them from the mirror clearly has a few wrinkles, the skin no longer stretches so tightly over the body, the hair may thin and begin to gray.

In a culture that emphasizes youth, we might expect middle-aged women and men to be less happy about themselves and their physical appearance than younger adults are. Yet body image appears to be stable. People older than 45 report just as much overall satisfaction with their bodies as do people younger than 45 (Berscheid, Walster, and Bohrnstedt, 1973). Women tend to be concerned with their faces, perhaps because the earlier atrophy of oil-producing glands beneath the skin allows time's traces to show about ten years before they become apparent in men. Men's oil-producing glands continue to function, postponing wrinkles, and their daily shave scrapes away old cells and hastens the growth of new cells (A. Spence, 1989). Women regard facial signs of aging as affecting their general attractiveness. Men are less concerned about their general attractiveness, and with good reason: both women and men say that age enhances a man's attractiveness (Nowak, 1977).

Functional Changes

Even if middle-aged adults can deny the visible traces of age, they cannot escape other signs. Their muscles do not work as strongly, as quickly, or as long as they used to, in part because muscle mass begins to shrink after people reach the age of 40. At least part of this shrinkage is the result of a less active life; regular exercise in midlife can increase lean body mass (Buskirk, 1985). Muscle shrinkage is accompanied by an increase in fat that can lead to "middle-aged spread."

Yet these early declines in muscle strength and reaction speed have only marginal significance in most people's everyday lives. Midlife adults are not likely to be bothered much by these losses, because they are slight—only about 10 percent—and because people have learned to compensate for them (A. Spence, 1989). Daily life is not affected, because by paying attention to the features of various tasks, people discover how they can maintain or even improve their performance in the face of changing activity—another instance of selective optimization with compensation (see Chapter 17). At work, middle-aged adults may avoid jobs that depend on speed, for example, and instead look for jobs in which they can work at their own pace. When they first find it difficult to read small print, middle-aged adults hold the page farther from their eyes. Before they are 50, however, most adults require reading glasses.

During middle age, many people, especially men, become concerned about their health. This worry has some basis, because the incidence of chronic and life-threatening illness rises during the middle years. The most common major disorders in otherwise healthy, middle-aged Americans are overweight, hypertension, and arthritis (Weg, 1983a). Midlife also marks the appearance of "maturity-onset diabetes," a form of diabetes in which the body produces normal levels of insulin but the individual's tissues have become insensitive to it. During middle adulthood, the death rate begins to increase, and it accelerates as people approach the age of 60. The most common cause of death until the age of 54 is cancer; beyond that age, heart disease is the leading killer. Causes of death, however, vary by gender and race (U.S. Bureau of the Census, 1991) (see Table 18.1).

Yet more than three-quarters of middle-aged Americans have no chronic health problems and no limitations on their daily activities (U.S. Bureau of the Census, 1990). Despite their weakened immune systems, people between the ages of 45 and 64 retain their resistance to diseases that they already have encountered. This, together with changes in life style, means that middle-aged adults have fewer bouts of acute illness (infections, respiratory and digestive diseases) than young adults.

Not all the physical changes that we connect with middle age are necessary or due to the normal processes of aging. Some are due to disease. Some are due to abuse: smoking, alcohol, drugs, poor nutrition, and stress can cause bodily deterioration. Some are due to disuse: regular exercise can maintain muscular strength and endurance, increase joint mobility, increase fitness in the cardiovascular and respiratory systems, reduce obesity, and slow or prevent the bone loss of osteoporosis (de Vries, 1983). Most women, for example, show a drop in activity levels after the age of 40; five years later, they show a corresponding drop in cardiorespiratory fitness and bone mass (Dan et al., 1990). Among Harvard alumni, those who burned at least 3000 calories each week in *moderate* activity had 35 percent fewer heart attacks than alumni who lived sedentary lives (Paf-fenbarger et al., 1986). But alumni who burned at least 3000 calories in *strenuous* exercise had 50 percent fewer heart attacks. Other large-scale studies have shown that death rates are closely tied to heart and respiratory fitness; as fitness rises, death rates fall (Blair et al., 1989). By establishing good health habits, people can decrease their susceptibility to the physical changes that are generally considered an inevitable part of middle age. Good nutrition, exercise, a decrease in alcohol consumption, the elimination of cigarettes, and the avoidance of direct sunlight can retard many of the expected changes in health and appearance.

Sex and Sexuality in the Middle Years

Changes in the reproductive system provide women with the medical marker of middle age: **menopause,** or the cessation of menstruation. Before menstrual cycles cease, periods may become irregular and farther apart. When women are about 50, menstruation stops altogether. Ovulation and reproductive capacity have ended. Because menopause signals the end of reproductive capacity and youth, popular wisdom says that menopause must be a psychological crisis. A menopausal woman, in the popular mind, is irritable, nervous, and depressed. She has headaches or backaches and is always tired. Psychology and physiology are so intertwined that women who believe the myths about menopause may have a difficult time. Yet the notion that

TABLE 18.1 LEADING CAUSES OF DEATH IN MIDDLE ADULTHOOD (BY RACE & GENDER)

Age (Years)	All Men	All Women	All Whites	All African-Americans
35–44	Cancer Accident Heart disease	Cancer Heart disease Accident	Cancer Accident Heart disease	Heart disease Cancer Accident
45–54	Heart disease Cancer Accident	Cancer Heart disease Stroke	Cancer Heart disease Accident	Heart disease Cancer Stroke
55–64	Heart disease Cancer Stroke	Cancer Heart disease Stroke	Cancer Heart disease Chronic pulmonary disease (e.g., emphysema)	Heart disease Cancer Stroke

Data from U.S. Bureau of the Census, 1991.

menopause is a developmental crisis is clearly wrong. Menopause no longer signifies the "change of life" that once accompanied it. At 50, women view their childbearing years as far behind them, and so there is no major discontinuity in their lives. In a five-year study of 2500 Massachusetts women, age 45 to 55, only 3 percent viewed menopause negatively; 75 percent either were relieved or had neutral feelings about it (Seligmann, 1990).

Nearly 75 percent of menopausal women in the United States report some sort of distress during this transition, but their expectations may lead them to attribute any symptom or mood change that occurs to the approach of menopause (Brim, 1992; Leiblum, 1990). The most common physiological symptom is the "hot flash," which refers to a sudden sensation of heat, often accompanied by profuse sweating. Researchers believe that hot flashes, which may persist from one to five years, reflect pulses of hormone release by the pituitary gland (Harman and Talbert, 1985). When the release occurs during sleep, the woman awakes covered with perspiration, a condition commonly called a "night sweat." Because night sweats disturb sleep, some researchers believe such sleep disturbances account for reports of tiredness and irritability among some menopausal women (J. Brody, 1992). Other physical symptoms may be either triggered or exaggerated by poor nutrition, lack of exercise, or a history of alcohol, drug, or tobacco abuse (Leiblum, 1990).

Most symptoms connected with menopause in the United States are not found among all women or in all societies, apparently because the way women experience this change depends on cultural attitudes, socioeconomic realities, work opportunities, sexual beliefs, and health status (Flint, 1989). Because fat cells release stored estrogen, which protects against the loss of calcium, the quest for thinness may lead to an exaggeration of symptoms among many women, who have no estrogen reserves to draw upon (Tavris, 1992). In some cultures, no connection exists between menopause and unpleasant physical or psychological manifestations. Mayan women, who spend their premenopausal lives bearing children, look forward to menopause and seem baffled at the notion of hot flashes. Peasant women on the Greek island of Evia, who have about the same number of children as American women, have hot flashes but, perhaps because their culture does not stress youth, report few negative feelings about menopause (see Beck, 1992). Among high-caste women in India, few women experience any symptoms at all (Flint, 1982). Apparently, the anticipation of freedom from menstrual taboos that keep them veiled and segregated, along with the retention of meaningful work roles and the wisdom attributed to their new status, makes menopause something that socially advantaged Indian women look forward to.

Women who dread menopause often discover the discomfort is minor. But even those who find the phase uncomfortable emerge to a new freedom. Studies indicate that postmenopausal women typically feel better, more confident, and freer than before they entered menopause (Neugarten et al., 1963).

At menopause, the body's production of female sex hormones (estrogen and progesterone) drops off to a negligible level. Afterward, a woman's risk of heart disease increases, and her bones may lose calcium, leading to osteoporosis. Estrogen replacement therapy, when started at the onset of menopause, retards bone loss, reduces the risk of heart disease by 60 percent, and eliminates hot flashes in most women (see Table 18.2). For a time, physicians were reluctant to prescribe estrogen therapy, in the belief that it increased the likelihood of breast and uterine cancer. Recent studies, however, indicate that low-dose estrogen therapy, supplemented with progesterone, actually reduces the chances of uterine cancer below the level found in untreated women, but some risk of developing breast cancer remains, especially among women with a family history of breast cancer (J. Brody, 1992; Gambrell, 1989). Lack of exercise is a major factor in the development of osteoporosis, and studies indicate that regular exercise slows or prevents its development (Buskirk, 1985).

Unlike women, most men do not lose their reproductive ability at midlife. During the forties, sperm production declines in some men, but healthy men of proven fertility show no change in sperm count. Among all men, 69 percent of those in their fifties have live sperm in their semen (Harman and Talbert, 1985).

How do these physiological changes affect sexual response? Many women find that vaginal lubrication is slower and less intense and that the vagina is less elastic, leading to discomfort during intercourse. Estrogen therapy alleviates this condition, as does an artificial lubricant. Regular sexual activity also seems to slow vaginal atrophy, perhaps because it is associated with higher estrogen levels in postmenopausal women. Women's subjective sensation of arousal remains the same and orgasmic ability is not significantly impaired with age, although the intensity and duration of the physical response is reduced (Leiblum, 1990). Many women, however, report slackened sexual desire, perhaps because blood levels of testosterone decline with menopause

TABLE 18.2

HORMONE REPLACEMENT THERAPY

Benefits	Risks	Comments
Prevents osteoporosis and fractured bones	Cancer of the uterine lining	Exercise can slow or prevent the development of osteoporosis.
Reduces risk of heart attack and stroke	Breast cancer	Inclusion of progesterone may eliminate danger of uterine cancer.
Eliminates hot flashes and night sweats	Hypertension	
	Blood clots	
Prevents vaginal atrophy and dryness, which cause discomfort during intercourse	Gallstones	Family history of breast cancer increases risk of developing breast cancer.
	Vaginal bleeding	
Prevents laxity of pelvic muscles, which causes urinary stress incontinence	Symptoms similar to premenstrual syndrome (PMS)	Artificial lubricants can alleviate dryness during intercourse.

Source: Information from J. Brody, 1992.

(Bancroft, 1989). Researchers generally consider testosterone responsible for sexual desire, and some gynecologists give the hormone to menopausal women who complain that their sexual interest has waned (Leiblum, 1990).

The major change in men's sexual response is in its speed. Men are slower to be aroused and slower to climax, and they do not necessarily feel the urge to climax at every sexual encounter. Slowed physical arousal characterized the middle-aged men in one study, in which penile responsiveness was measured while they watched erotic movies (Solnick and Birren, 1977). Among 50-year-olds, penile diameter increased about six times more slowly than among men in their twenties. However, older men have more control over ejaculation than younger men do, a change that their partners

Sexuality is still an important part of marriage for the majority of middle-aged couples.
(Chuck Fishman/Woodfin Camp & Associates)

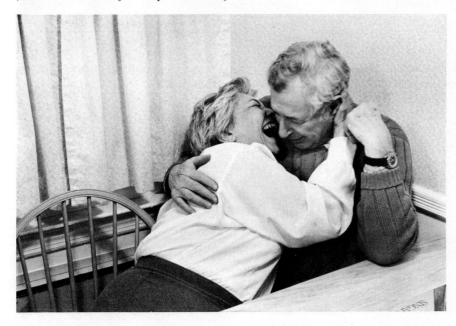

may welcome. Middle-aged men find that they need more direct stimulation to become aroused and that, after a climax, they require more time before they can be aroused again. These changes in sexual response affect the nature of the sexual experience but do not decrease its pleasure.

In the absence of major health problems (such as diabetes), loss of sexual responsiveness is likely to be due to psychological factors, not physiological ones. Men are more susceptible than women to such losses, and their incidence of sexual inadequacy rises sharply after the age of 50. An important factor in reduced sexual responsiveness among middle-aged men appears to be the monotony of a repetitious sexual relationship (W. Masters and Johnson, 1974). Other factors may reduce a man's sexual interest or responsiveness. He may be so preoccupied with work that he has no physical or mental energy for sex. Overindulgence in food or alcohol can also leave him "too tired" for sex. Finally, a man may avoid sex because he fears impotence. If he finds himself unable to respond on one occasion, he may start avoiding sex because he is afraid of another failure.

The majority of middle-aged adults continue to be both interested in sex and sexually active. Among those between the ages of 46 and 50, 90 percent of the men and 70 percent of the women express moderate to strong sexual interest (Pfeiffer and Davis, 1972). In general, the richer and more regular an individual's sex life has been, the more likely it is that sexual activity and interest will be maintained throughout the middle years.

Theories and Issues of Middle Adulthood

Being middle-aged means being part of the age group that runs society, the group that is in command and responsible. The middle years are characterized by a concern with expanding and asserting one's adulthood and sometimes with developing a new way of life. As people enter middle adulthood, most find their energies focused on different issues. Yet some changes are re-

As the baby-boomers reached middle age, they began to take positions of power, a transfer that was officially marked by the success of two baby-boomers in the 1992 presidential election. *(Dennis Brack/Black Star)*

lated more closely to life circumstances than to chronological age, and so many middle-aged adults, such as those with young children, still are absorbed with the tasks of early adulthood. Other issues of middle adulthood, such as the acceptance of physical limitations and the prospect of mortality, are common to all adults. As they deal with the realization that life will end, individuals develop an increasing sense of not having enough time to do most of the things that they want to do.

There is often personal turmoil in the middle years. Yet when life changes are expected and occur on time, these years are fairly stable in terms of an individual's identity, coping capacities, influence, and productivity. Once people resolve their uncertainties about their past and future, life often becomes mellow. By returning to the theories we explored in Chapter 16, we can trace the way motivations tend to change as adults deal with their new developmental tasks.

Erikson's Psychosocial Theory

When people move into middle adulthood, said Erikson (1982), they face a struggle between generativity and the forces of self-absorption and stagnation. As we saw in Chapter 2, **generativity** involves a concern for future generations. Many people express this concern directly, by nurturing their own children and guiding them into adulthood. Some express it by working with other people's children, as teachers, physicians, or nurses, or by serving as mentors to younger workers in their professions. But Erikson saw generativity as being much wider than direct involvement with the young. He proposed that it can be expressed through creativity or productivity as well. The writer, the artist, and the musician satisfy the need for generativity through their creative output, and the carpenter does so by building houses for future generations. Anyone can express generativity by helping to maintain or improve society (Erikson and Hall, 1987). According to Erikson, generativity is the driving power in human organizations. Women and men who express generativity in any of these ways develop *care,* the strength of middle adulthood, which includes the capacity for empathy as well as the willingness to accept responsibility for others.

The person who shows no concern for future generations or for society may find his or her life stagnating. Such people become preoccupied with themselves. They may become bored, find their lives frustrating, and feel a vague sense of loss, even though they do not understand its source.

Little research has been done on later stages of Erikson's theory, but some longitudinal studies have supported its broad outlines. Among men who were followed into middle adulthood, only those who developed generativity seemed mature and skilled at coping with the world (Vaillant and Milofsky, 1980). Whether white or African-American, Harvard graduates or men from the inner city, generative men also had mastered the developmental tasks of earlier stages. They had successful marriages and stable occupations, and they enjoyed their children. Regardless of income, they were more altruistic than other men and usually active in some kind of public service. Men who had not developed generativity tended to have insecure identities and had trouble developing intimate relationships.

Levinson's Seasons

Among the men studied by Daniel Levinson and his associates (Levinson et al., 1978), the years between 40 and 45 served as a transition to middle adulthood. Men tended to reevaluate their lives at this time and to conclude that their youthful dreams were out of reach. Levinson saw this period as a time of turmoil, when men whose illusions were gone reassessed their goals and tried to restructure their lives. A central issue at this time was discovering "what I really want." Some men in his study went so far as to change occupations, divorce their wives, or move to distant cities. As wrinkles, gray hairs, and minor declines in strength forced them to come to terms with their mortality, many began to act as mentors to younger adults.

Once through the transition period, men began building their lives on the basis of their new choices. Those who were successful found life productive and more satisfying than it had ever been. Those who had not been able to solve the tasks of the midlife transition spent the rest of their forties in a period of stagnation and decline. When they began the transition into their fifties, men who had escaped major changes during the midlife transition often found that turmoil had caught up with them. It was now their turn to struggle with the mismatch between their goals and the paths their lives were taking. By the midfifties, men were in the period Levinson calls the culmination of middle adulthood. They settled into their lives, and many found the rest of the decade a time of great fulfillment. At 60, the transition into late adulthood began, another five-year period of reappraisal, when men's choices would define the shape of their remaining years.

Gould's Transformations

The transformations of middle adulthood described by Roger L. Gould (1975, 1978) are similar to the seasons of Levinson's men. But Gould found the midlife transition beginning earlier, at about the age of 35, and lasting until women and men were about 43 years old. Gould also found turmoil, questioning, and radical life changes during this period. After weathering the storms of this transformation, women and men found the rest of their forties a time of stability and satisfaction. Many became more realistic about their goals and tended increasingly to agree that "I try to be satisfied with what I have and not to think so much about the things I probably won't be able to get." Friends, family, and marriage became their central concerns, and money seemed less important.

As they entered their fifties, women and men became increasingly aware of their mortality and sensed the running out of time. The personal relationships that were of concern in the forties took on increased importance. Marriage became more satisfying, children became a potential source of warmth and satisfaction, and parents were no longer seen as the cause of personal problems. People showed increased self-acceptance, and many expressed their generativity by becoming actively involved in their communities. Both Levinson and Gould collected their data during the 1970s, when the U.S. economy was expanding. How accurately their findings describe cohorts in the socioeconomic conditions of the 1990s is uncertain.

Jung's Concept of Middle Adulthood

Like Erikson, Carl Jung (1969) based his theory of adulthood on a psychoanalytic view of human development. Jung saw adult development as a process characterized by growth and change, in which people are guided by their aims for the future as well as by their past experiences. He believed that healthy development involves striving to reach one's full potential. Such self-actualization requires people to develop all parts of their personalities and then unite the parts into a balanced, integrated self.

As people approach middle age, said Jung, they may feel that they have their lives all worked out, from the course of their careers and families to their ideals and the principles that guide their behavior. But soon aspects of the personality that have been lying "in the lumber room among dusty memories" begin to assert themselves. In some people, there are gradual changes in personality; in others, new inclinations and interests develop. Not everyone changes in this way; some people seem to feel threatened by impending change and respond by becoming rigid and intolerant. According to Jung, each person has both masculine and feminine aspects, and among the unexpressed sides of personality that become apparent at midlife are men's femininity and women's masculinity. Once women's years of active mothering are finished and men no longer are absorbed in "making it," the other side of gender becomes apparent. Women become more tough-minded and may go into business or develop an interest in broader social concerns; men become tender-hearted and less assertive. Those who stifle such inclinations may find themselves in emotional trouble, because the suppressed masculinity or femininity is likely to assert itself in some indirect, irrational way.

Jung saw midlife changes in personality, goals, and interests as natural: "We cannot live the afternoon according to the programme of life's morning," he wrote, "for what was great in the morning will be little in the evening, and what in the morning was true will at evening have become a lie" (1969, p. 399). As people pass through middle adulthood, they must set new goals instead of living with diminished forms of old ones. A great ballerina should not keep performing as her precision and grace decline; instead, she should become an equally great choreographer or teacher of ballet.

Gutmann's Parental Imperative

David Gutmann's (1987) parental imperative picks up Jung's idea of unexpressed gender potentials that reassert themselves in middle adulthood. In his view, once the "chronic emergency" of active parenting has passed, women become more aggressive, less affiliative, and more managerial or political. Men become less interested in their occupations and more interested in companionship and sensual enjoyment—good food, pleasant sights and sounds. Men become more dependent on their wives, but women become less dependent on their husbands. Gutmann sees this change as developmental, predictable, and a positive sign of growth.

Gutmann and Jung both see adults becoming more androgynous as they enter the second half of life. Research has supported some aspects of this claim. Studies generally find that men and women are most different during late adolescence and early adulthood and become more similar during late middle age (Huyck, 1990). Other studies have confirmed increased androgyny in men after the age of 40 (Hyde, Krajnik, and Skult-

Niederberger, 1991). Gutmann's (1987) own research in the United States, Central America, and the Middle East has shown increasing androgyny in each society he studied. Similar results emerged from an Israeli study (Friedman, 1987), but researchers who assessed white and African-American women in the United States and black women in Kenya found that socioeconomic status was more important than age in women's shift toward increased power (Todd, Friedman, and Kariuki, 1990). The progression was clear among white American women and middle-class Kenyan women, but it did not appear among African-American women or lower-class Kenyan women. Before women can feel powerful, they may require either economic security or secure social status. Virtually all of these studies are cross-sectional, and so no one can be certain whether the trend toward androgyny will appear in middle-aged Americans of the twenty-first century. If today's young adults are free to express both sides of their gender potential, the tendency toward a reversal of sex roles in middle adulthood may diminish.

Issues in Theories of Middle Adulthood

Two controversies dominate discussions of personality in middle adulthood. Researchers cannot agree on whether personality remains stable over adulthood, and they cannot decide whether the "midlife crisis" is an inevitable part of human development.

Continuity vs. Change

When we reach middle adulthood, most of us seem to think our personalities have changed a good deal since adolescence—and mostly for the better. A group of women and men who had taken a personality test at the age of 20 retook the same test when they were 45. Then they took the test yet again, this time answering as they believed they had answered in their youth. Most indicated that they had been much less competent and less well adjusted as 20-year-olds than they were in midlife. But when researchers compared the results, they discovered that the adults had responded to the tests similarly at 20 and at 45 (Woodruff and Birren, 1972). The discrepancy was in people's midlife view of their youthful selves. Although their personalities had remained relatively stable for 25 years, the adults perceived themselves as having changed.

What actually happens as we live through adulthood? Do we change, or does personality remain stable? The question is not whether change is possible; researchers agree that it is. The controversy centers around how much change is probable and whether predictable developmental experiences change people in predictable ways. As we have seen, some theorists of adult development propose regular, age-related changes in personality, such as an increase in assertiveness among midlife women, that appear when people encounter various developmental tasks.

Yet in both cross-sectional and longitudinal studies, major dimensions of personality generally remain stable across adulthood (Costa and McCrae, 1989). Impulsive teenagers become impulsive adults, assertive teenagers still are assertive in old age, and shy teenagers still are shy even after they retire. Because longitudinal studies allow investigators to separate generational differences from maturational changes, their results may tell us more about personality development than do results of cross-sectional studies. In a longitudinal study of Californians, researchers found an orderly progression in the development of many aspects of personality (Haan, Millsap, and Hartka, 1986). From adolescence to their midfifties, cheerful, confident people tended to become more cheerful and confident, fearful people became more fearful and distrusting, and so on. Personality seemed least stable during the transition into young adulthood, when people were taking on occupational roles and getting married. Once that transition was complete, personality tended to regain its consistency. Some people did show personality changes, but these shifts generally were associated with some unusual, unexpected experience (the early death of a spouse, an unexpected inheritance).

It seems that personality remains relatively stable as long as a person's life situation does not change in some radical fashion (Bengston, Reedy, and Gordon, 1985). Personality develops as a person, with all of his or her predispositions, interacts with environmental events. These events may be either common tasks (achieving economic independence) or individual events (an automobile accident). The relative stability of a person's personality may primarily reflect that person's psychosocial situation rather than the inevitable course of development.

The Midlife Crisis

Closely related to the question of stability in personality is the issue of the midlife crisis. According to Levinson (Levinson et al., 1978) and Gould (1978), the transition into middle age is almost invariably accompanied by a **midlife crisis**—a state of physical and psychological distress that arises when developmental tasks threaten to overwhelm a person's internal resources and system of social support (Cytrynbaum et al., 1980). Among Levinson's men, for example, 80 percent went through such an upheaval in their early forties. The notion of a midlife crisis has grabbed our imagination, perhaps because of its popularization by journalist Gail Sheehy (1976), whose book about changes in the lives of midlife men and women became a national best-seller. The idea so permeated popular writing on middle age that most people probably accept such a crisis as an inevitable part of life.

Yet most longitudinal studies have not uncovered a general crisis in midlife. Whether researchers looked at male Harvard graduates (Vaillant, 1977), middle-aged women (Baruch, Barnett, and Rivers, 1983), Californians of both sexes (Clausen, 1981), or a national sample of more than 10,000 Americans (Costa et al., 1986), they were unable to find a predictable emotional upheaval in early midlife—or at any other age period they examined (see Figure 18.1). Certainly, some people have life crises during their forties, but at no greater rate than people in their twenties, thirties, fifties, or sixties. One researcher notes that midlife often is the most satisfying and rewarding period of life (Clausen, 1981), and another believes that the midlife crisis is a "useful fiction" that provides an anchorpoint on which to hang whatever changes occur during the forties and early fifties (Brim, 1992).

Developmental events such as marriage, childbirth, job promotion, menopause, or retirement may be followed by changes in self-concept and identity. But when such events are "on time," arriving at whatever point in life our social clock has led us to expect them, most of us cope without caving in (Neugarten and Neugarten, 1986). The serenity of our lives may be ruffled, but no crisis develops. Two factors seem responsible for our ability to handle expected events. First, because we anticipate them, we work through them ahead of time, rehearsing them mentally until we can cope with their actual occurrence. Second, because most of our peers are going through the same transitions, we get social support from them and a sense that we are all "in the same boat." It is the unexpected event (the divorce, the automobile accident) or the expected event that arrives at the wrong time (the early death of a parent or spouse) that is likely to precipitate a crisis (Sanders, 1988). Yet unexpected change in midlife is not always bad; it may even lead to positive growth. A young widow whose roles suddenly shift may discover dormant talents and abilities and find herself expressing new aspects of her personality.

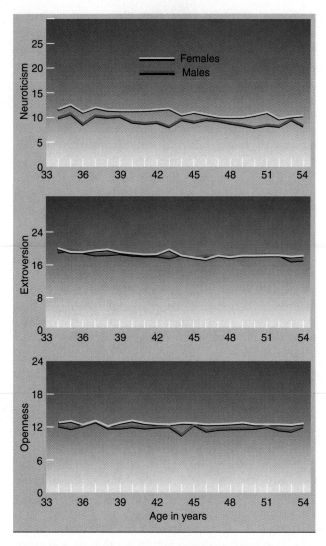

Figure 18.1 Personality ratings from a large national sample provide no evidence of a midlife crisis. Mean levels of neuroticism, extroversion, and openness to experience show remarkable stability between the ages of 33 and 54. *(From Costa et al., 1986, p. 148)*

Self-Concept and Self-Esteem

The way we respond to life's challenges and changes affects the way we feel about ourselves. Stress may be an inevitable part of changes in middle adulthood, but as Richard Lazarus (1985) argues, the stress itself does not lower self-esteem, erode self-concept, or destroy the sense of self-efficacy. The sense of self remains firm when people under stress can alleviate or tolerate the distress, maintain a sense of personal worth in the face of defeat, maintain good relationships with friends and family members, and meet any stress-related challenge.

Once they reach late middle age, most adults feel better about themselves than they did during early adulthood. When researchers surveyed adults in thirteen nations, they discovered that young adults were the most dissatisfied with their lives, whereas adults older than 50 were the most satisfied (Butt and Beiser, 1987). This increase in satisfaction may be in part the result of increases in the sense of self-control and confidence that continue during the forties. As men pass through middle age, they tend to use more mature strategies in coping with personal problems and to assume greater responsibility for them than they did as adolescents and young adults (Vaillant, 1977). They also show a more realistic sense of their strengths and weaknesses, and when they encounter a problem, they try to solve it, either with some constructive action, with the aid of social support, or through direct confrontation of the problem (Folkman et al., 1987). Women change in similar ways, becoming more decisive, self-confident, and responsible (Helson and Wink, 1992). Thus, it is not surprising that the sense of self-esteem tends to increase during middle adulthood.

To some extent, mental health at midlife depends on the match between what a person has and what he or she expects. In one study, unmarried women felt good about themselves because life had turned out much better than they had expected (Birnbaum, 1975). They discovered that satisfaction did not depend on being married and having children. People who had extremely high expectations of success, joy, or passion or who had been convinced that their children would be perfect may become depressed after they take stock at midlife.

Among African-Americans, however, those who are at midlife today are the generation least likely to see their expectations fulfilled. For the majority, socioeconomic status is not only lower than that of their middle-aged white counterparts but also lower than that of younger African-Americans. Middle-aged African-Americans feel more stress, have more personal and emotional problems, and are more likely to die from stress-related diseases than are African-Americans who have entered late adulthood (R. Gibson, 1986). Midlife may be smoother for their children, who have faced fewer barriers to occupational advancement.

Work

When Studs Terkel (1974) interviewed Larry Ross, the middle-aged ex-president of a conglomerate, Ross told

him why he was now a management consultant instead of a corporation executive:

I've always wanted to be a teacher. I wanted to give back the knowledge I gained in corporate life. . . . In every sales group, you always have two or three young men with stars in their eyes. They always sat at the edge of the chair. I knew they were comers. I always felt I could take 'em, develop 'em, and build 'em. . . . I'd like to get involved with the young people and give my knowledge to them before it's buried with me. (p. 540)

As it has for Larry Ross, the place of work in most people's lives undergoes a decided shift during middle adulthood. Occupation continues to be important, but attitudes toward work are likely to change, sometimes drastically.

Men's Work

For most men, work is no longer the all-absorbing interest it was during their thirties. Work is still vitally important, but men have climbed about as far as they can expect to go. At least for those who have reached their goals, the drive to get ahead subsides and work seems more satisfying (Bray and Howard, 1983; Clausen, 1981). Many become mentors to younger workers; they provide their juniors with guidance and smooth the young workers' way to advancement.

The change becomes apparent at around the age of 45, when most men tend to cut back on their working time. Among men in a longitudinal study of Californians, this curtailment appeared in both working- and middle-class men, except for top executives and professionals (Clausen, 1981). The highly successful men increased the time they devoted to their occupations by about three hours each week. When such a pattern develops, men may devote so much time and energy to their careers that the quality of family life is diminished, the marital relationship erodes, and relationships with their children suffer (L. Hoffman, 1986).

For some men, the problem is too little work. When they are dispossessed by structural changes in the economy, working-class men with limited training go through a grieving process in which they question their self-esteem and wonder if they can ever qualify for another position. Matt Nort, a 52-year-old Pittsburgh steelworker with two children, has been making do with near-minimum-wage jobs for two years. Nort knows he has become obsolete. "The dream is gone—probably forever," he says, and he admits that for a time he even thought of suicide (Kotre and Hall, 1990, p. 290).

As the drive to get ahead subsides, middle-aged men who have reached their goals become mentors to younger men, providing guidance and opening career doors. *(W. Will/The Image Works)*

Occupation is so intertwined with the sense of self that, among men in their fifties, several personality attributes can be ranked by occupational level. Men in the California study who had made it to the top scored lowest in anxiety, fearfulness, and punitiveness (Clausen, 1981). Middle-class men who had managed to move up from the working class tended to be warmer and more sympathetic than other men, to have developed intellectual skills and interests, and to hold conventional views. Job loss or demotion, by contrast, can result in severe depression.

Women's Work

The majority of single women follow an occupational path similar to that of men (N. Keating and Jeffrey, 1983). But the way the careers of married women develop during midlife depends in good part on the nature of family finances, marital support, and strains within the family (R. Ackerman, 1990). Married women, especially those with children, relate to work in a different manner than do men or single women. At a time when many men are becoming less involved with their occupations, many women are either becoming more involved or making their first foray into the world of work. The freshness of their involvement may explain why many midlife women seem more excited about their work than men or women who have been working continuously. Coming from the relative isolation of the homemaker's world, these new workers may find satisfaction primarily in the social aspects of the job. Most men and single women place more importance on work's financial rewards or its challenging aspects (Kessler and McRae, 1981).

When asked about the satisfactions that they derive from employment, women speak about the chance to work on their own, a sense of competence and accomplishment, and the joy of having a job that fits their interests and skills (Baruch and Barnett, 1986). These satisfactions far outweigh any distresses they encounter, and their major complaints center around overload: having too much to do and having to juggle conflicting tasks.

Women who have been holding back on their commitment to their occupations and those who have just joined the labor force may benefit from employment during the time when children leave the nest. The new commitment fills a gap left by departing children and adds zest to the women's lives. Women who have been committed to a career throughout the child-rearing period miss out on this source of exhilaration. Consequently, they may either feel the loss of their children keenly or simply welcome the removal of a source of restraint in their lives.

Marriage at Midlife

Delays in marriage and parenthood may be changing the experience of the marriage relationship at midlife. Earlier research on midlife marriage focused on how the marital partners related to adolescent children and how they adjusted to an empty nest after the children left home. As the family life cycle entered a new phase, both partners had to adjust to new roles and develop new ways of seeing themselves in the context of changing relationships. Today's middle-aged couple may have infants or young children at home, so in many ways their

During middle adulthood, women derive occupational satisfaction from a sense of competence, the chance to work on their own, and a job that fits their interests and skills. *(Jose Carrillo/Photo Edit)*

marriage may resemble the marriage of early adulthood. Most couples, however, especially those in the working class, continue to encounter the traditional marital adjustments of midlife.

Marital Satisfaction

Cross-sectional studies generally show that marital satisfaction starts to decline as soon as children are born and drops to its lowest point when they reach adolescence. As soon as the children leave, satisfaction rises and remains high throughout middle adulthood (Perlmutter and Hall, 1992). It is reasonable to assume that once the strains of active parenting have passed and demands on income are reduced, couples enter a new era of freedom: freedom from financial responsibilities, freedom to be mobile, freedom from household responsibilities and chores connected with children, and freedom to be the people they want to be.

Some couples do feel this way. The partners report that after the children have left, they laugh more together, have more discussions, and work together more often on projects. (The accompanying box, "Mixing Marriage and a Second Career," looks at some of these

couples.) Women especially are likely to feel more satisfied with their marriages once the children have left home, primarily because the possibilities of companionship increase. Wife and husband again can enjoy each other's company.

The problem with this portrait is that cross-sectional studies are not following the developmental course of marriages but giving us simultaneous snapshots of marriage in different cohorts. Margaret Huyck (1982) suggests that marital statistics may show high satisfaction in the last part of middle adulthood because most unhappy couples have divorced by then. Hints that this may be true appear in national surveys. Between 1957 and 1976, the level of marital satisfaction rose substantially in the United States and paralleled the rise in the divorce rate (Veroff, Douvan, and Kulka, 1981).

In one longitudinal study, neither the length of the marriage nor the stage of the family cycle had any effect on marital satisfaction (Skolnick, 1981). Couples were just as satisfied with adolescent children at home as they had been sixteen to eighteen years earlier, when they had had no parenting problems to contend with. Happily married partners in this study said that their marriage had improved with time and that they liked,

Marital satisfaction rises across middle adulthood, in part because the departure of children opens the marriage to new freedom and companionship and in part because many unhappy marriages have ended in divorce. *(Joel Gordon)*

admired, and respected each other. Such marriages, known as **companionate marriages,** are not typical. Researchers estimate that only about 20 percent of American marriages center around the close personal relationships that characterized these marriages.

Most American marriages tend to be **institutional marriages,** in which couples have established a utilitarian living arrangement that both partners find satisfactory. In these marriages, there are no strong emotional bonds between the partners. Instead, satisfaction comes from material possessions and from the children.

When researchers studied middle-aged married couples in Michigan, they discovered the highest levels of satisfaction among partners who had strong dual identities: as individuals and as part of a couple (Laurence, 1982). The spouses were deeply committed to their relationship and realized that marriage required hard

work. Among these couples, there was no relation between marital satisfaction and sexual activity, communication skills, division of power, or problem-solving ability. In fact, studies generally indicate that the primary factors in marital stability are commitment to the spouse and to the institution of marriage, followed by valued personal characteristics in the spouse (Bengston, Rosenthal, and Burton, 1990).

The Sexual Relationship

For some couples, marital sex improves in midlife. The man requires longer to climax, which increases pleasure for both partners, and the woman no longer fears pregnancy. Yet many couples report sexual problems in midlife, ranging from impotence, to lack of interest, to extramarital affairs.

Sometimes middle-aged couples, who have watched the culture's rules for sexuality change since they reached young adulthood, feel that they have missed out on some of life's excitement. If a partner decides that he or she has been cheated, the disgruntled person may grasp what seems a last chance for adventure and embark on an extramarital relationship. Successful middle-class men often find that they are more attractive to women than they were in their youth. The teenage boy with acne is now a corporate executive who looks much better, relative to his age group, than he did thirty-five years ago. Women executives in midlife may also find themselves more attractive to men as they begin to move in the corridors of power. Among midlife couples in 1980, men were more likely than women to have an affair, with more than half of men but only about a quarter of women reporting at least one extramarital relationship during middle age (R. E. Gould, 1980). This disparity may disappear as the young adults of the 1980s enter middle age. The first extramarital relationship now comes earlier in the marriage, and middle-class, educated wives in their twenties or thirties are about as likely to have an affair as their husbands are (Blumstein and Schwartz, 1983; E. Macklin, 1980).

A last grab at youth is not the only reason for an extramarital relationship. Some people become involved in an affair because they are dissatisfied with their marriages, because they are under pressure at home, or because they are seeking status, asserting their independence, or trying to punish a spouse. Men who find themselves impotent at home may try to reaffirm their waning sexual powers by seeking out a younger woman (R. E. Gould, 1980). Some men and women even find the guilt that frequently accompanies an ex-

MIXING MARRIAGE AND A SECOND CAREER

Many people follow the same general occupation throughout their working lives, but during midlife some individuals strike out in an entirely new direction. Either they become dissatisfied with their earlier line of work or they retire early. Some occupations (the military, law enforcement) provide for early retirement; sometimes a person no longer can meet the physical requirements of the job; sometimes he or she has accumulated enough assets to retire but takes up a new career to keep busy.

Curious about the way second careers are incorporated into the marriage relationship, Leslie and Leonard Lieberman (1986) studied a group of men and women who had begun new careers in the field of art. Some of the men had been professionals; others had had business or blue-collar jobs. Some of the women had never been employed outside the home; others had held white-collar or professional jobs. Their new careers combined art and travel: after creating their work, they traveled to art and craft shows across the United States, where they showed and sold their handiwork.

Among the sixty-eight artists interviewed by the Liebermans, several patterns appeared. Some wives and husbands had separate artistic careers; some worked jointly in the same medium; sometimes only one partner was an artist, but the other assisted in either producing the work (stretching canvas, framing), setting up the display, or handling sales. A few of the artists (six men, three women) received no support from their spouses. This pattern usually ap-

peared when the spouse was busy with his or her primary career.

How did the second career affect the marriage? One couple who worked as a team creating dried flower arrangements found their marriage more satisfying. According to the wife, "We have a lot of fun at this; he does some of the things that I do just because he likes being with me." The husband was even more enthusiastic, saying, "Oh, my God—never in our entire life have we had a better time" (Lieberman and Lieberman, 1986, p. 222). A painter reported that helping with her second career had changed her husband; he no longer felt that gender roles should follow traditional standards.

In fact, for many of these couples, the income from the new career was secondary to other benefits. Starting a new—and often radically different—career provided them with challenging opportunities. But it was the context of the career that was especially satisfying. It allowed the partners to work together in ways that increased communication between them, enhanced their respect for one another, and provided companionship. As one man said:

We will work until one a.m.; neither wants to quit. In general my wife and I are able to enjoy our total life together. After the sales are done we talk for two or three hours—in the past we never had that. (Lieberman and Lieberman, 1986, p. 223)

---

tramarital relationship pleasurable and exciting. Men often remain detached from the relationship, separating "love" and "sex," as many did during adolescence. But women are more likely to become involved, with the attempt to confirm a romantic self-image often turning into a full-blown love affair (Blumstein and Schwartz, 1983; R. E. Gould, 1980).

If the transgression is discovered, no matter what the reason for the affair, marital trust and intimacy often are destroyed. Participants may overendow extramarital relationships with emotion and see the affair as "true love" or live under a heavy burden of guilt, while their spouses frequently are filled with hurt and anger. Affairs threaten American marriages, because they conflict with the socialization experience of the culture. In fact, when people are asked why they are *not* having an affair, they usually talk about the consequences to their marriages instead of referring to their love for their

spouses or the fact that such a relationship would violate ethical or religious precepts (M. Hunt, 1974).

Divorce and Remarriage

When couples realize that their children soon will be leaving, their marriages may come under increased strain. As wife and husband begin thinking about life after children, they may size each other up and wonder how they will get along without the buffer of the children between them. Either or both may have changed so much over the past twenty years or so that the prospect of undiluted companionship seems unattractive. Like many other middle-aged couples, they may decide to get a divorce.

Although midlife marriages are less likely to end in

divorce than marriages of young adults, the divorce rate is still considerable, especially during the years just after the children leave home. The divorce rate for people past 45 has doubled since 1960, and today 19 percent of divorcing husbands and 13 percent of divorcing wives are older than 45 (National Center for Health Statistics, 1990). About 12 percent of 40-year-old women who are still married to their first husbands eventually will divorce, as will a larger proportion of those in second or third marriages. Although divorce rates stabilized in 1980 among younger adults, they continued to rise among midlife women until 1986.

Some midlife marriages that end have been held together "for the sake of the children." Others end when some other major life event disrupts a marital relationship that had been satisfactory to both partners (N. Turner, 1980). Serious illness, an emotional disorder, a religious conversion, a radical career change, or a deeply disappointing experience with a child may sour a marriage. The husband may lose his job, and the wife may take on the breadwinner's responsibilities. As the couple adjusts to such an event, their unspoken agreements about the balance of power, their respective duties, or other aspects of the marriage may be broken. The changes in marital roles may not be acceptable to one of the partners.

Yet some couples remain deeply dissatisfied with their marriages for years before they decide to divorce. In a study of California divorces, 36 percent of the men and 42 percent of the women said their marriages had been conflict-ridden from the beginning, and 15 percent were unhappy for at least twelve years before the divorce (Kelly, 1982). Among most middle-aged couples, the woman is the first to realize that the marriage is heading for disaster (Hagestad and Smyer, 1983). Middle-aged men may drift on complacently for another seven or eight years before realizing that the marriage is on shaky ground.

No matter which partner first realizes the seriousness of the problems, in the majority of cases, the woman decides to seek the divorce (Kelly, 1982). (The woman is twice as likely as the man to file suit for divorce, whether she or the man has decided to end the marriage [National Center for Health Statistics, 1990].) The decision usually is precipitated by some single event: infidelity, a critical outside event that throws the relationship into a new focus (moving, getting a new job), or some sort of "last straw" (a second suicide attempt, an alcoholic binge). The partner who makes the decision may feel guilty, sad, or apprehensive, but he or she escapes the feelings of humiliation or rejection felt by the other partner. By having gone through the grieving process earlier, the partner who seeks the divorce also may recover his or her self-esteem earlier and start to put life back together.

In some ways, divorce is more difficult for people in midlife than it is for young adults. Neither party may have had recent practice in developing new intimate relationships with the other sex, and the process is likely to take longer and be more stressful than it is for younger people. A middle-aged woman in a traditional marriage who has depended on her husband's position for her own identity and her financial security may find divorce particularly distressing. Cathy Knapp of Houston, divorced at 41, said, "When I walked out of that courtroom, my feelings were, 'How am I going to survive?' I only had a high school education; I had not worked in years" (Diegmueller, 1986, p. 10). Knapp found a job and went back to college to work toward a paralegal degree as the first step in her occupational training. Knapp's experience is typical for today's midlife divorced woman; divorced women past the age of 40 have fewer economic resources and are less likely to own their own homes than are widows (Uhlenberg, Cooney, and Boyd, 1990). As today's young adults enter midlife with established occupations, the divorced woman who loses both identity and income will become increasingly rare.

Although many people who divorce in midlife find new mates, the remarriage rate for divorced women has declined sharply since 1965 (Uhlenberg, Cooney, and Boyd, 1990). Middle-aged men are much more likely than women to remarry. Several factors contribute to this situation. First, death rates increase for men in midlife, reducing the pool of possible mates for women. Second, as noted in Chapter 16, women tend to marry older men, and men marry younger women. This further reduces the pool of possible mates. Third, men are willing to marry someone with less education than they have, but most women want a mate with a similar educational background. This requirement again reduces their possibilities. Finally, an increasing number of employed women whose divorce brought them financial and sexual independence have no interest in remarrying (Gross, 1992).

Parenthood at Midlife

Until recently, midlife parents were thought of as parenting adolescents and young adults. Today middle-aged couples have children of all ages. Some mothers with new babies are in their forties; in other cases, the new mother is in her twenties or thirties, but the new father is in his forties, his fifties, or even his sixties. These latter situations usually come in second marriages, and the father often has adolescent children by a former marriage. Other couples who have postponed parenthood or whose children have left the nest decide to adopt children.

Delayed Parenthood

Women who delay childbearing until their forties may find it difficult to conceive. Fertility declines only slightly until the age of 35 but drops sharply after that time (Menken, Trussell, and Larsen, 1986). Among women in their early forties, 60 percent may be sterile. Even those who are still fertile may take more than a year to conceive, a nerve-wracking delay when the biological clock is ticking away. Most men in midlife can father children; among men in their early fifties, the fertility rate is about 73 percent of what it was during their early twenties.

Once a couple conceives, concern does not end. The likelihood of certain birth disorders, such as Down's syndrome or spinal cord defects, rises with age. The 40-year-old mother has 1 chance in 100 of producing a child with Down's syndrome, but at the age of 45, the chance rises to 1 in 45 (Omenn, 1983). When middle-aged women do conceive, many have amniocentesis to make certain that the fetus is normal (see Chapter 3). Historically, older women have had more miscarriages, more complications during pregnancy, and more difficult deliveries and have run a greater risk of dying in

When her first baby is delayed until midlife, a woman tends to enjoy her infant and find great satisfaction in motherhood. *(Eastcott/Momatiuk/The Image Works)*

childbirth than women in their twenties (Vider, 1986). But advances in obstetrical techniques have greatly reduced these hazards, so most healthy older mothers have normal pregnancies and healthy babies.

Middle-class couples who have midlife babies often become "professional parents," centering their lives around the young child. Many study prenatal development and child psychology is if they were cramming for an examination. Once the baby arrives, most seem absorbed by the infant and find parenthood enormously rewarding. They seem settled, relaxed, and calmer than younger parents do. The high levels of satisfaction among midlife parents seem in good part due to their lack of economic worries. Fifty-six-year-old Dick Lord, the president of a Manhattan advertising agency and the father of a toddler, summed it up:

> *It all boils down to the economic thing. When the first kids were little, I was always scrambling. I couldn't turn off my work life, even on weekends. Now I feel secure. And I can have fun with the kids. (Wolfe, 1982, p. 30)*

Among these affluent, middle-class families, fathers tend to be absorbed with their children and emotionally available to both children and spouse. When children arrive during young adulthood, fathers are absorbed in their careers and so seem much less committed to child rearing and family life. No one knows how this difference in a youngster's early life will affect the socialization process.

Parenting Teenagers

Some family conflict is inevitable when children reach adolescence, because each generation is at a different point in its developmental agenda and faces different developmental tasks. Middle-aged parents and their almost-grown children often argue over one another's changing roles and various responsibilities, the children's strivings for autonomy, and what the parents may see as the disintegration of family ties. Yet as we saw in Chapter 15, in the majority of families, conflict is sporadic and mostly about minor matters.

Limit testing is part of the adolescent's search for identity and independence. It is a developmental issue not only for the teenager but for his or her middle-aged parents as well. Parents may have to pull back at exactly the moment when they want to hang onto or even increase control (L. Hoffman, 1985). As the child copes with identity, autonomy, and sexuality, parents worry about all the disasters they read about in the paper or see on the evening newscast. Each report of an automobile accident, a teenage pregnancy, or a teenage suicide stirs new apprehension. The stakes and dangers seem much greater than they were in the preteen years, but the opportunities for surveillance have shrunk.

The age at which a child enters adolescence and whether the child is a boy or a girl appears to affect the way parents approach these issues. When a daughter matures early, parents are most likely to report high levels of conflict over her behavior (Savin-Williams and Small, 1986). Parents may feel that their daughter's early sexual maturation places her in situations that she is not equipped to handle.

Changes in society may be altering the way midlife mothers and their adolescent daughters handle the daughter's individuation. Mothers who grew up with traditional gender-role expectations but are going back to school or entering the labor market find themselves caught up in a process of separation and self-definition that resembles their daughters' developmental tasks. The relationship may develop into a seesaw between the pair's intimate involvement and their attempts at separation (La Sorsa and Fodor, 1990).

No matter when boys mature, their arrival at puberty shifts the family balance of power, as we saw in Chapter 13. After a period of increased conflict between mother and son, the mother seems to back off and become deferential (Steinberg, 1981). The son apparently takes over much of the mother's authority and power in family decisions. Although this power shift puts the mother at a disadvantage when she tries to exert control over her son, the tensions may be eased for the employed mother, who is likely to encourage independence in her adolescent offspring (L. Hoffman, 1985).

The Empty Nest

Whether parenting adolescent children has been a joy or a trial, eventually the children leave home. Usually, the parents are in their midfifties before the last child departs. At one time, psychiatrists and psychologists assumed that this period was extremely difficult for parents and especially for women. Faced with the loss of their children, the loss of their youth, and the ordeal of menopause, women were supposed to be prone to depression. But when researchers began to separate theory from fact, the picture became quite different. The rate of depression among women turned out to be about the same whether women were younger than 45, between 45 and 55, or older than 55 (Weiss-

man, 1979). That did not rule out the possibility of the **empty-nest syndrome,** an emotional crisis following the children's departure that threatened a woman's defenses even if it did not plunge her into a depression.

Other researchers looked directly at the empty-nest phenomenon. Studies consistently found that midlife women whose children were gone were happier and more satisfied than those whose children were still at home (Neugarten, 1970; B. Turner, 1982). When Lillian Rubin (1979) interviewed midlife women, most said that they were relieved when their last child left home. A typical response came from a 50-year-old, middle-class homemaker:

When the youngest one was ready to move out of the house, I was right there helping him pack. We love having the children live in the area, and we love seeing them and the grandchildren, but I don't need for any of them to live in this house ever again. I've had as much as I ever need or want of being tied down with children. (L. Rubin, 1979, p. 16)

When children leave home "on time," parents have prepared for the event. But the empty nest may well foster an emotional crisis when the children leave home too early, as when a 15-year-old runs away. The nest that doesn't empty on time may also be a source of serious discomfort. Parents live under continual strain and have a sense of personal failure. One midlife father exploded in angry bewilderment:

Last night we had a confrontation. . . . A disgust on my part for a 20-year-old not in school, not working, not putting anything into the house. . . . It's all taking . . . food, car, clothing. (Hagestad, 1984, p. 151)

Equally distressing may be the refilling of the nest when grown children return home. Some of these "boomerang kids" return after divorce or separation, some because of problems with drugs or alcohol, but many, like the Biolsi family whose story begins this chapter, are back home because of the high costs associated with housing (Perlmutter and Hall, 1992).

When children leave home on time, several factors affect their parents' reactions to the departure, including the speed at which the nest empties, the parents' own relationship, the woman's relationship to her children, and her own occupational situation. First, parents may feel the pangs more sharply when the nest empties rapidly, over the period of a year or two, than when they have children leaving over a five- to ten-year span. Second, parents who care deeply for one another may respond to the children's departure with relief and delight. They have time for each other, can travel when they like, and can return to the spontaneous intimacy and sexuality they enjoyed before their first child was born. Couples with a satisfactory institutional marriage may also respond positively, for each partner is free to pursue his or her own interests while both live comfortably together. Couples with a conflict-ridden, unhappy marriage may divorce.

A third important factor is the mother-child relationship (Baruch, Barnett, and Rivers, 1983). Women who are *autonomous mothers* see their children as individuals. They enjoy doing things with their children, encourage their children's strivings for maturity, and like the kind of people the children have become. These women are usually high in self-esteem and feel in control of their lives. They are likely to find the empty nest a pleasant place. Other women are *coupled mothers,* who see their children as extensions of themselves. Children give meaning to the lives of coupled mothers; they make the women feel needed. Compared with autonomous mothers, coupled mothers are low in self-esteem and feel less in control of their lives. They are more likely to complain of anxiety or depression. Such mothers may find the empty nest a bleak and desolate place.

Finally, midlife women who are in the labor market may be too busy to be devastated by the departure of their offspring. When the notion of the empty-nest syndrome was popular, only about a third of midlife women were employed outside the home. Today, the majority of women between the ages of 45 and 64 have jobs that take them out of the house and provide a broad base for their identities (U.S. Bureau of the Census, 1990).

Relating to Aging Parents

Most middle-aged adults have living parents, and an increasing number can expect their parents to be alive when the adults themselves reach old age (Gatz, Bengston, and Blum, 1990). The nature of the parent-child bond changes as people age, but it generally remains firm over their half-century or more of shared time. Some researchers believe that relationships between adult children and their parents are closer today than they have ever been. According to Andrew Cherlin (1983), such relationships were cold and distant in colonial America, apparently because the older father retained control of the land and ruled the family in an authoritarian manner. Cherlin proposes that adult children and their parents are likely to be closest and most affectionate when neither generation has to depend on the economic support of the other.

Although most adult children and parents are not dependent on one another, gifts and services flow up and down the generational tree (Gatz, Bengston, and Blum, 1990). Middle-aged adult children assist their parents in a number of ways. They may provide economic support or personal care, help with transportation, share outings and holidays, prepare food, or help with home chores. Aging parents are appreciative, but they value their children's affection and respect more than they prize material assistance (Treas, 1983). As Table 18.3 indicates, as long as parents remain healthy and independent, they return similar gifts and services to their grown children (L. Hoffman, McManus, and Brackbill, 1987).

Sometimes midlife adults must assume most of the responsibility for an aging parent. Although they still have adolescent children at home or are supporting young adults through college, they are faced with the burden of providing for their own parents. This simultaneous push from an older and a younger generation is known as **life-cycle squeeze.** It is especially stressful when the midlife parents also have adult children whose own development is "off time" (Hagestad, 1984). One such midlife woman who complained of role overload had a jobless son in his late twenties; another had a daughter who had left her husband and moved back home. The amount of stress felt by the caregiver caught in the life-cycle squeeze depends on the demands involved, the caregiver's perception of the situation, and the caregiver's resources and coping skills (Gatz, Bengston, and Blum, 1990).

Women are usually under greater stress than men, in part because sons are less likely than daughters to provide routine, daily assistance. Sons tend to help with shopping, financial management, and heavy chores, whereas daughters do such tasks and also provide hands-on care and emotional support (Stoller, 1990). Yet women feel the squeeze more strongly than men, even when the two are providing the same level of care. Researchers believe that this increased stress may have two sources: the intimate relationship between mothers and daughters and the responsibilities (household management, child rearing, emotional support) that most

Middle-aged children provide frequent services and gifts for their older parents, and most parents reciprocate. *(Rae Russel)*

TABLE 18.3   **FINANCIAL AID BETWEEN THE GENERATIONS**

		OLDER ADULTS (%)					
	All Older Adults	**GENDER**		**RACE**		**AGE**	
		Women	**Men**	**African-American**	**White**	**<75**	**>75**
Receive aid from children	11.3	11.9	10.2	18.2	8.6	8.9	14.3
Need aid from children	18.6	22.1	13.0	42.1	9.8	21.3	15.0
Give aid to children	47.2	42.6	53.3	52.8	44.3	54.8	36.4

*Among 160 older adults, more were providing financial assistance to their children than were getting it, and many of those who needed help were not getting it.

Source: L. Hoffman, McManus, and Brackbill, 1987.

Early and Middle Adulthood

women assume, even when they are employed outside the home (Brody, 1981). The level of stress is even higher among single, divorced, or widowed women, who lack the social support provided by a spouse (Brody et al., 1992).

In the future, midlife adults may face serious problems when an aging parent needs hands-on care. First, the proportion of middle-aged women who are committed to an occupation is likely to increase when today's young adults reach their forties and fifties. This shift means that when an aging parent requires care, the daughter will have three options: she can quit her job, she can hire someone else to care for her parent, or she can place the parent in a nursing home. No matter which course she chooses, she is likely to feel guilty or resentful.

Second, the trend toward smaller families means that there will be fewer daughters to provide the daily care that traditionally has been expected from daughters. When today's youngsters are middle-aged, most will have only a single sibling with whom to share parental care. Only children will have to assume the entire burden themselves. This not only increases the squeeze on the child but also affects the quality of the relationship. Studies already indicate that only children have poorer relationships with their mothers (age 60 to 79) than do children with siblings, after correcting for mother's health, marital status, race, educational level, and age (Uhlenberg and Cooney, 1990).

Finally, because so many women are delaying childbirth, there is a rising possibility that they will still have children at home when an aging parent requires assistance. The family network in the twenty-first century may be overburdened by cross-generational demands.

Becoming Grandparents

As life expectancy has increased, the number of multigenerational families has risen rapidly. At the same time, decreases in fertility have produced **beanpole families,** which have more living generations but fewer members in each generation (Bengston, Rosenthal, and Burton, 1990). Many middle-aged adults become grandparents while their own parents are still living. About half of older adults have great-grandchildren, and among women who live past their eightieth birthdays, one-fifth are great-great-grandmothers (Hagestad, 1986, 1988). In such four- and five-generation families, the middle-aged grandparents are not the family elders but an intermediate generation. Each parent-child linkage in that family is part of a chain, in which each person except the oldest and the youngest simultaneously occupies the roles of parent and child (Hagestad, 1984). The particular link a person occupies probably affects the experience of being a grandparent in some way.

New grandparents come in a wide variety of ages, from the grandmother in her late thirties whose adolescent daughter has just given birth, to the grandmother in her late sixties whose career-committed daughter has had her long-postponed baby. New grandfathers may be even older. The wide span of possible ages guarantees that no "typical" grandparent exists, because the cohorts involved grew up under widely different influences and are dealing with different life tasks.

In the United States, becoming a grandparent has been a task of middle adulthood throughout this century. In 1900, however, first-time grandparents generally were busy with their own children (Cherlin and Furstenberg, 1986). Although today's grandparents can devote attention, energy, and money to grandchildren that would once have gone to their own children, most are still involved in their careers. Grandmother is too busy to baby-sit, because she goes to the office each day.

Most grandparents enjoy the experience. They derive comfort, satisfaction, and pleasure from relating to the child of their child, as indicated in the accompanying box, "What Does It Mean to Be a Grandparent?" Yet not all grandparents find the experience a delight. Adults who are most likely to be ill at ease in the role tend to fall at the extremes of the age span. In a study of African-American women, 83 percent of those who had become grandmothers "too soon"—between the ages of 25 and 38—rejected the role (Burton and Bengston, 1985). They still felt like young women but were suddenly saddled with a role they perceived as "old." Those who are 80 or older when the first grandchild arrives may have neither the energy nor the patience to deal with boisterous children.

Grandparents tend to follow one of three styles when relating to their grandchildren: companionate, remote, or involved (Cherlin and Furstenberg, 1986). About 55 percent are **companionate grandparents,** who have an informal, affectionate style and see their grandchildren at least every few months. Another 29 percent are **remote grandparents,** who have a formal, reserved style and see their grandchildren infrequently. The remaining 16 percent are **involved grandparents,** who are immersed in an exchange of services with their

Four-generational families have become common, which means that many of today's grandparents are no longer the family elders. *(Paul Conklin)*

WHAT DOES IT MEAN TO BE A GRANDPARENT?

Being a grandparent may mean day-to-day delight and an enriched life or disappointment and bitterness, depending on the expectations of the grandparents and the quality of the relationships with their grandchildren. When Helen Kivnick (1982) decided to find out just what it meant to most grandparents, she interviewed nearly 300 men and women about the experience.

The grandparents' replies clustered around five major dimensions. All grandparents experienced all the dimensions, but their emphasis varied—from grandparent to grandparent, from one grandchild to another, and from time to time with the same grandchild. Being a grandparent, they said, gave *meaning to life.* When this dimension was emphasized, activities with the grandchild became important to both child and grandparent, and grandparents incorporated the role into their identity. A second dimension focused around the grandparent's role as a *valued older adviser* and resource person. When this dimension was emphasized, grandparents were concerned about the ways in which their grandchildren would remember them. A third dimension focused on the grandparents' *sense of personal immortality* through his or her descendants. A fourth dimension centered on the grandparent's *reinvolvement with the past.* When this dimension was emphasized, grandparents referred to the stories they told their grandchildren about their own grandparents and to the way they relived experiences from their early

lives with their grandchildren. Finally, grandparents emphasized the classic grandparental role, in which they *spoiled their grandchildren* by indulging them and refusing to hold them to strict rules.

Grandparents did not mention other aspects of the grandparental role directly, but the chance to cuddle and hug a young grandchild may be an important benefit in a culture that allows few expressions of intimacy. Playing children's games and acting in a carefree manner also gives grandparents the opportunity to break the norms of middle-aged adult behavior. For the staid, respectable adult, playing a grandparent provides a holiday from propriety.

In this study, the grandparents' own experience as a grandchild affected the way they saw their relationships with their grandchildren. Grandmothers who had positive memories of being a grandchild and who had a favorite grandparent were most likely to relive their own past in the relationship, to see their role as grandparent as central in their identity, and to see themselves as a valued elder. Grandfathers who had positive memories of their own grandparents were most likely to emphasize the joys of spoiling and indulging a grandchild.

From the interviews, Kivnick concluded that the experiences that go along with being a grandparent and grandchild help individuals resolve the psychosocial conflicts connected with stages of the life cycle and can enhance psychological well-being.

Middle-aged grandparents often say that the relationship with their grandchild gives meaning to their lives. *(Courtesy of James Kilroy)*

grandchildren and who provide advice and sometimes discipline. They see their grandchildren at least every couple of months. Major influences affecting a grandparent's style are age and distance. Older grandparents and those who live great distances from their grandchildren tend to adopt the remote style.

African-American adults are more likely (27 percent) to be involved grandparents than are white adults (15 percent), but they are less likely (78 percent) than whites (92 percent) to kid or joke with grandchildren (Cherlin and Furstenberg, 1986). One reason for the greater involvement of African-American grandparents is the emphasis their ethnic tradition places on relationships among members of the extended family. Another reason is the greater prevalence of three-generation households, which occur at a higher rate among African-Americans at every socioeconomic level (Taylor, 1988). Three-generation families are even more common among African-Americans than are blended families with stepparents among whites (R. Hunter and Ensminger, in press).

Studies of two- and three-generation African-American families indicate that the resident grandmother serves a stabilizing and organizing function (Tolson and Wilson, 1990). She enables the family to serve its caregiving and nurturing function in a more relaxed fashion, so family members perceive the atmosphere as less rigidly structured and are able to handle unexpected events without disruption. In another study of African-American families with resident grandmothers, the grandmother tended to be the household member who put the child to bed, even when both parents lived in the home (Pearson et al., 1990). Although grandmothers played the most active and involved role when the family included no other adult but the child's mother, a grandmother's own employment did not affect her behavior with her grandchild.

Grandchildren seem to enjoy their grandparents as

much as grandparents enjoy them. Unless the grandparents are functioning as parents, the relationship has little of the tension that often exists between parent and child. When grandparents are not responsible for rearing the child, they can enjoy the youngster without worrying about the consequences.

Grandparents influence their grandchildren in many ways. Their direct influence as caregivers and playmates is fairly obvious. Grandchildren also see their grandparents as historians who tell them about their ethnic heritage and family history and traditions (Kornhaber and Woodward, 1981). They see grandparents as mentors, who guide and advise them, as role models for aging, and as models of possible occupations. Finally, they also see their grandparents as buffers between themselves and their parents, comforters who often step in to smooth waters and reduce tensions. Other researchers have noted that grandparents also influence their grandchildren indirectly, by way of the children's parents (Tinsley and Parke, 1984). Grandparents model childrearing skills, and they provide emotional and financial support, advice, and information.

Second marriages create stepgrandchildren for many middle-aged adults. In a study of more than 500 grandparents, researchers found that one-third had at least one stepgrandchild (Cherlin and Furstenberg, 1986). Of these grandparents, about two-thirds said that the bond was similar to that between the grandparent and his or her biological grandchild. Important to the establishment of an attachment were the age of the child on entering the family and the child's residence. A close relationship was most likely when the child was younger than 5 at the time of remarriage and when the child lived with the grandparent's daughter or son.

During middle adulthood, most people develop a greater sense of command over their lives even as they begin to come to terms with physical limitations. As they become less concerned with "making it," their concern for the generations that will follow them is strengthened. Many now find that their suppressed psychological traits are free to flower, opening new possibilities. They are ready to begin the passage to later adulthood.

SUMMARY

SOCIAL CHANGE
Most adults between the ages of 40 and 65 look and feel younger and healthier today than their parents and grandparents did at the same age. Many are at an earlier stage of family development, they are more likely to have living parents, and fewer women are widowed. Middle-aged adults also are better educated, and the women are more likely to be employed.

PHYSICAL CHANGES
Muscle strength and reaction time decline in midlife, and chronic disorders (especially obesity, hypertension, arthritis, and diabetes) begin to appear. Many of the physical changes associated with early aging are not necessary, they develop when bodies are abused, contract some chronic disease, or are simply not used. **Menopause** ends women's reproductive capacity but creates only minor discomfort for most. Healthy midlife men do not lose their reproductive capacity, although their sexual response is slowed. In healthy adults, the loss of sexual responsiveness is probably the result of psychological factors.

THEORIES AND ISSUES OF MIDDLE ADULTHOOD
According to Erikson, midlife brings on a struggle between **generativity** and stagnation. Generativity may be expressed through creativity and productivity as well as by having children or caring for them. Jung saw midlife personality changes as the emergence of unexpressed aspects of the self. Both Jung and Gutmann see unexpressed gender potentials reasserting themselves at midlife. In Levinson's and Gould's theories, most men and women face a **midlife crisis,** but most studies have not supported this conjecture. Personality seems fairly stable across midlife, although personality may change when people encounter unexpected events that lead to radical change in their lives.

SELF-CONCEPT AND SELF-ESTEEM
The stresses of midlife are unlikely to affect the sense of self unless a person sees the situation as uncontrollable and the result of personal deficiencies that affect many aspects of life. Self-control and self-confidence generally

increase across middle adulthood, and mental health appears to depend on how well people's situations match their expectations.

WORK

Work becomes less absorbing to men, and many cut back on their working time. Many midlife women become more absorbed in their work, especially those who have just entered the job market or those whose children have just left home.

MARRIAGE AT MIDLIFE

Although cross-sectional studies show a decline in marital satisfaction that lasts until children leave the nest, longitudinal studies show no changes in satisfaction related to age of children or length of marriage. Most marriages are **institutional marriages,** with only about 20 percent considered **companionate marriages.** Those who find marriage most satisfying tend to have strong individual identities as well as an identity as part of a couple. Extramarital affairs are relatively common during midlife; they may develop when one of the partners makes a last try at youth, becomes dissatisfied at home, feels pressure at home, seeks status, asserts his or her independence, or tries to punish a spouse.

DIVORCE AND REMARRIAGE

Some divorces among midlife adults are due to changes in marital roles that one partner considers unacceptable; others develop when some outside event leads an already dissatisfied partner to end the marriage. Midlife women are less likely to remarry than men because men's higher death rates, the tendency for women to marry men older than themselves, and women's insistence on a mate with a similar educational background combine to produce a small pool of potential mates.

PARENTHOOD AT MIDLIFE

The nature of parenthood depends on the couple's stage in the family life cycle. Older parents of young children are likely to be middle-class and to be absorbed in the child. Parents of adolescents generally face sporadic family conflict as children test limits, with the age and gender of the adolescent affecting the nature of the parents' reaction. The **empty-nest syndrome** seems confined to mothers whose children leave home extremely early or who are overinvolved with their children and see them as an extension of themselves. Most women welcome the empty nest, which often ushers in a period of freedom and fosters a new intimacy in their marriages.

RELATING TO AGING PARENTS

Gifts and services flow both ways between generations. The need to care for two generations at once may place many midlife adults, especially women, in a **life-cycle squeeze.** The needs of aging parents may place future middle-aged adults in a serious squeeze because more women are committed to occupations, an increasing proportion of middle-aged adults will have no siblings to help in the care, and postponed parenthood will keep children in the nest until later in their parents' life span.

BECOMING GRANDPARENTS

A declining birthrate has produced the **beanpole family.** Adults tend to relate to a grandchild as either **companionate grandparents, remote grandparents,** or **involved grandparents.** Age and distance, not social class or race, tend to determine which style a person adopts. Grandparents influence their grandchildren as caregivers, playmates, family historians, mentors, and role models and as buffers between grandchildren and their parents.

KEY TERMS

beanpole family	generativity	menopause
companionate marriage	institutional marriage	midlife crisis
companionate grandparent	involved grandparent	remote grandparent
empty-nest syndrome	life-cycle squeeze	

SEVEN

● ● ● ● ● ● ● ● ● ● ● ● ● ●

LATER ADULTHOOD

The years after age 65 place their own unique demands on the individual to grow, develop, and change. Equipped with more memories and a longer history, older individuals retain the human capacity and desire to control the environment and the human need to love and be loved. How they meet the developmental tasks of old age depends in good part on how they have met the tasks of previous life stages. Although most older adults are ready to relinquish their responsibility for society, many remain active and involved with younger generations. In fact, the growing pool of "young-old" adults, who are healthy and vigorous, is extending the phase of generativity far into old age. This means that for many people, life's final task—coping with death—comes later in the life span than it did for their parents and grandparents. ■

CHAPTER

19

THOUGHT AND FUNCTION
IN LATER ADULTHOOD

• • • • • • • • • • • • • • •

"When I have time—and I mean something on the order of half an hour—I can almost always recall a name if I have already recalled the occasion for using it," said B. F. Skinner (1983) at the age of 79.

"It's embarrassing when you have trouble finding the word you want, particularly when you are lecturing to an undergraduate class and must ask them to tell you the word you can't remember," said neuropsychologist Donald Hebb (1978) at the age of 74.

These eminent psychologists agreed that faulty recall was one of the problems of growing old. Both had figured out ways to keep a sluggish memory from interfering with their professional work. Hebb, who kept a card in his wallet listing terms he had trouble remembering, began writing out his lectures instead of speaking from notes. Skinner said that his problem was not how to have ideas but how to have them when he could use them. He found that a pocket notebook, a pad and pencil on his bedside table, and a tape recorder made his ideas accessible when he needed them. His techniques were successful. Only two weeks before he died in 1990 at the age of 86, he delivered the keynote address at the American Psychological Association's annual meeting.

To remember names, Skinner used such techniques as going through the alphabet, testing for the name's initial letter. Although Skinner was unruffled at such memory lapses, many older women and men become anxious when words or names begin to elude them. But forgotten words are not gone, just temporarily inaccessible during tension. Hebb noted that, despite his forgetfulness during a lecture, he could still work the difficult crossword puzzles in the *London Observer*. Many older individuals become so afraid they will forget that their very fear makes a memory lapse inevitable. Skinner's solution was to reduce the unpleasant consequences of failure, thereby reducing anxiety and increasing the chances that the names would be recalled. Explain your failure gracefully, he said:

Appeal to your age. Flatter your listener by saying that you have noticed that the more im-portant the person, the easier it is to forget the name. Recall the amusing story about forgetting your own name when you were asked for it by a clerk. If you are skillful at that sort of thing, forgetting may even be a pleasure. (Skinner, 1983, p. 240)

Although names may be temporarily forgotten and objects misplaced, most older adults are unlikely to have serious memory problems. As our investigation will show, cognitive losses among healthy adults are not nearly so large as people believe. After discussing myths and misconceptions about mental decline, we look at the biological changes of later adulthood that have implications for cognitive functioning. Next we investigate learning and problem solving in later life. We then return to the topic of memory and discover why recall sometimes becomes a problem. After looking at changes in encoding and retrieval, we examine strategies that reduce memory failure. The chapter closes with a look at plasticity and the possibility of reversing cognitive decline.

Myths about Aging

What do you think it is like to grow old? Myths and misconceptions about aging are even more widespread than myths about adolescence. The chances are that your expectations are nothing like the experience of most women and men in this society. To find out, take the following abbreviated quiz, which taps knowledge about aging. It was devised by medical sociologist Erdman Palmore (1988), who coordinated the longitudinal studies of aging at Duke University that have helped explode myths about growing old. Decide whether each of the following statements is true or false; then check your scores to see how many misconceptions you need to shed.

_____ 1. The majority of old people (age 65 and older) are senile (have defective memory, are disoriented, or demented).

_____ 2. The five senses (sight, hearing, taste, touch, and smell) all tend to weaken in old age.

_____ 3. The majority of old people have no interest in, nor capacity for, sexual relations.

_____ 4. Lung vital capacity tends to decline in old age.

_____ 5. The majority of old people feel miserable most of the time.

_____ 6. Physical strength tends to decline in old age.

_____ 7. At least one-tenth of the aged are living in long-stay institutions (such as nursing homes, mental hospitals, and homes for the aged).

_____ 8. Aged drivers have fewer accidents per driver than those under age 65.

_____ 9. Older workers usually cannot work as effectively as younger workers.

_____ 10. Over three-fourths of the aged are healthy enough to carry out their normal activities.

_____ 11. The majority of old people are unable to adapt to change.

_____ 12. Old people usually take longer to learn something new.

_____ 13. It is almost impossible for the average old person to learn something new.

_____ 14. Older people tend to react slower than younger people.

_____ 15. In general, old people tend to be pretty much alike.

_____ 16. The majority of old people say they are seldom bored.

_____ 17. The majority of old people are socially isolated.

_____ 18. Older workers have fewer accidents than younger workers.

All odd-numbered statements in this quiz are false; all even-numbered statements are true. Few people answer all items correctly; even college professors tend to miss about three. No matter what their age, sex, or race, most college students miss about six, and high school graduates do no better than chance—they miss about nine (Palmore, 1992).

Palmore's quiz addresses only a few of the misconceptions about cognition among the elderly. Most people believe that older men and women, even if they are not senile, have lost the capacity to change and grow. According to stereotypes, older adults forget where

they had lunch yesterday but remember the distant past with clarity. They are inactive, idle, and have no desire to learn anything new. Another stereotype portrays old age as a time of second childhood, in which old people are childish and require paternalistic treatment, a view that diminishes the individual responsibility of the old and reduces their social status (Arluke and Levin, 1984). Such erroneous beliefs have led to **ageism,** which is prejudice against old people. The view that old people are incompetent at best and perhaps even senile is partly responsible for society's tendency to discriminate against them, ignore them, or fail to take them seriously. As the accompanying box, "The Subtle Effects of Ageism," indicates, ageism affects the sort of behavior that is expected from the old. Yet most old people are capable of handling the tasks of daily life, and some are among the most capable and intelligent members of society. Perhaps a look at the biological changes of old age that relate to cognition will give us a more accurate picture of thought processes after the age of 65.

Biological Changes

People who answer "true" to the first statement in Palmore's quiz are probably afraid to grow old. Yet the assumption that old age means confused thought, disorientation, and the inability to handle the problems of living is wrong. When the condition commonly called "senility" develops, it is never the result of aging itself. Aging is associated with changes in the brain and nervous system, but in healthy individuals the practical consequences are relatively minor.

Sensory Capacities and Processing Speed

Stimulation from the environment reaches the brain through the sensory system. As people age, all five senses become less acute, which makes access to knowledge about the world more difficult to obtain. Most people also take longer to process information. It takes them longer than it once would have to figure out how to operate a microwave oven or to record a TV program on a VCR.

What is the practical effect of less acute sensory systems? Suppose that you smeared Vaseline over the lenses of your glasses, put cotton plugs in your ears, and then pulled on a pair of rubber gloves. With much of your sensory information cut off, your movements

THE SUBTLE EFFECTS OF AGEISM

As the picture of aging presented in the various media becomes less stereotypical, an increasing proportion of the population is aware that many older women and men are alert, active, and able to contribute to society. Even so, stereotypes about the aging mind may be embedded so deeply that they affect the way we perceive older adults. Ageism has produced a pervasive double standard that affects not only the young but older adults as well.

The double standard showed clearly when young and old adults rated the seriousness of single instances of memory failures in a series of situations involving either a young (23- to 32-year-old) or an old (63- to 74-year-old) woman (Erber, Szuchman, and Rothberg, 1990). In eight vignettes, a woman hid money in her house and forgot where she placed it, forgot to buy an item on her shopping list, recognized someone but could not recall where she had seen the person before, failed to recognize a familiar face in a new context, forgot what her friend had said and what she had planned to say in a conversation, went upstairs to get a stamp and forgot why she had gone up, was introduced to someone and forgot the person's name, and began to dial a phone number but

forgot it and had to look it up once more. The adults who judged the failures were told that each vignette involved a different person.

Old as well as young adults consistently judged the older women as displaying more serious mental difficulty than the younger women in identical instances of memory failure. Younger women who forgot something were generally seen as forgetting because other things were on their minds or other events were going on around them. But older women were seen as having mental difficulty and perhaps being in need of evaluation for physical or psychological problems. Older adults were, however, less harsh in their judgments than younger adults. They tended to see the memory lapses as less serious and less in need of professional attention than did the young—no matter what the forgetful woman's age. Society's double standard for memory failures indicates that we expect older adults to be forgetful and less competent than the young. Such expectations can affect the way we treat older people; they can also affect the self-image and behavior of older adults.

would probably slow, and you would become extremely cautious. This situation may resemble the world of many older individuals, leading psychologist Diane Woodruff (1983) to suggest that older men and women are in a state of sensory deprivation. Yet there

are ways to compensate for some—but not all—of these sensory losses. Such losses are not uniform, and many older individuals are not isolated from the world around them. As with aging in other bodily systems, wide interindividual differences appear in the degree of

Slowed information processing may delay older adults' mastery of their home computer, but most eventually become proficient operators. *(Grapes/Michaud/Photo Researchers)*

sensory deterioration that develops. Some 80-year-olds can read small print without glasses, hear as well as the average 25-year-old, play the piano with skill, or detect subtle changes in a cook's use of spices.

Vision

Most older people have no severe visual impairment, but the visual changes that began in middle adulthood continue to progress. By the time they reach later adulthood, people are more bothered by glare, see less well in the dark, require more light to see clearly, and have more trouble distinguishing details than they once did (A. Spence, 1989). Their eyes also adjust more slowly to sudden changes in illumination, so it takes them longer to regain their vision when moving from light to dark or back again. The visual field constricts, so some peripheral vision is lost. Glasses, appropriately placed lights, and heightened environmental contrasts (such as horizontal stair treads covered with different material from that used on risers) can solve many of the visual problems of aging (Sekuler and Blake, 1987).

If objects are not clear, older adults may compensate for lessened acuity by relying on context. When sentences were flashed on a screen with the last word degraded by the presence of asterisks between each of the letters, older adults recognized and read off the word much more quickly when the sentence provided a meaningful clue ("The accountant balanced the B*O*O*K*S") than when it did not ("They said it was the B*O*O*K*S") (Madden, 1988). Although older adults were slower than young adults in all conditions, the presence of usable context narrowed age differences.

The effect of visual changes on many older individuals may be most noticeable when they try to drive at night. They have trouble reading highway signs under night-driving conditions (which gives them less time than younger drivers to react). They also take longer to recover from the glare of oncoming headlights or changes in illumination as they pass from lighted intersections to darkened stretches of road. It is not surprising that many older drivers will not get behind the wheel after dark. Some older individuals, however, are no more sensitive to glare or shifts of illumination than is the average young driver (Sterns, Barrett, and Alexander, 1985).

Hearing

The ability to hear high-frequency tones begins to decline after the age of 45 and becomes marked among people in their late seventies. By this time, about 75 percent have noticeable hearing problems, with hearing loss generally more severe in men than in women. Although people who live in less noisy environments show smaller hearing losses than people who live amid noise, some hearing loss appears with age in every cross-cultural study (Olsho, Harkins, and Lenhardt, 1985).

Older adults have the most difficulty when straining to follow a conversation against background noise, when words overlap or are interrupted, or when speech is especially rapid. When hearing loss is great, they may miss so many of the words that they either guess at the course of the conversation (which may lead to embarrassment when the guess is wrong) or withdraw and stop listening. The difficulty can be partially overcome when other people pitch their voices lower, speak slowly and distinctly, and look directly at the older person's face, providing visual cues. Additional cues can be provided by emphasizing stress and intonation patterns (Wingfield, Wayland and Stine, 1992). Indeed, older adults are much better at understanding conversation than their ability to hear pure tones would indicate. Many older adults compensate for hearing loss by using the linguistic context of a sentence to determine meaning. When sentences were spoken against background noise, healthy adults between the ages of 60 and 75 understood such sentences as "The bird of peace is the dove" about as well as young adults (Hutchinson, 1989). But when context gave no clue to the words, as in "I will now say the word cards," wide age differences appeared.

Processing Speed

As people age, it takes them longer to dial a telephone, zip up a jacket, or balance their checkbooks. This slowness seems to affect every kind of behavior. Psychologists have not been able to determine exactly what sort of biological change is responsible for the slowed execution of actions. According to the **peripheral slowing hypothesis,** aging in the **peripheral nervous system** is responsible (Salthouse, 1989). This network of nerves and sensory receptors transmits sensations from the outside world to the central nervous system and motor commands to the muscles. Pointing to the sensory changes that accompany aging, researchers have proposed that as people age, the quality of this transmission declines. It takes longer for stimulation from the environment to reach the brain and for commands from the brain to reach and activate the muscles involved.

Other researchers explain the slowdown in terms of the **generalized slowing hypothesis.** In this view, processing slows throughout the brain as well as in the peripheral nervous system (Cerella, 1990). If slowing were confined to the peripheral nervous system, the differences in speed between young and old would remain the same on simple and complex tasks. On both tasks, transmitting sensory information and motor commands would take the same amount of time; the complexity is in the processing of information within the brain. But as tasks become more complex, age differences increase, suggesting that activity in the central nervous system (brain and spinal cord) also slows with age.

A recent study indicates, however, that peripheral slowing may account for a large proportion of age-related changes in cross-sectional cognitive tests (Hertzog, 1989). When scores on a battery of psychometric tests were corrected for perceptual speed and speed in working with answer sheets, age differences among adults between the ages of 43 and 89 shrank dramatically. People in their eighties did better than those in their forties on tests of verbal comprehension (which includes verbal meaning and vocabulary) and numerical skills. Declines on tests of induction (reasoning ability), spatial relations, spatial visualization, and flexibility of closure (finding hidden patterns and figures) were sharply reduced. Among adults in Schaie's (1989b) sequential study of intelligence (discussed in Chapters 2 and 17), correction for perceptual speed also markedly reduced age differences, and once again the effect was stronger on tests of crystallized skills than on tests of fluid skills. Such results suggest that typical age changes may not indicate a loss in thinking capacity but a slowing in the rate of intelligent thought (Hertzog, 1989). Even so, performance on tasks that require quick response, such as piloting an aircraft, may deteriorate during old age.

Brain and Nervous System

If the centralized slowing hypothesis is correct, biological changes in the brain are responsible for slowed processing speed. As breaks occur in systems of neurons, the basic mechanisms slow at each stage of processing, either because signals must take detours through other neurons or because some information is lost at each break (Cerella, 1990). Yet researchers have been unable to determine the effects of normal aging on the brain and spinal cord. Most of the information that we have about biological changes comes from the examination of brain tissue taken after death. At that time, it is difficult to separate the effects of normal aging from the effects of cardiovascular disease, respiratory func-

tion, brain disease, damage from drugs and alcohol, and other destructive forces (Bondareff, 1985).

The brain may shrink with age. As tissue shrinks, the spaces deep within the brain (called *ventricles*) expand. A technique known as **computerized axial tomography** (CT) enables researchers to reconstruct cross sections of the living brain at any depth or at any angle. In a study using this technique, researchers discovered that the brain begins to shrink slightly when people are in their thirties (Takeda and Matsuzawa, 1985). Whether the shrinkage, which increases each decade, is part of the normal course of aging is not certain. Although the researchers eliminated people with nervous system damage, they included adults with diabetes and with cardiovascular, kidney, and respiratory disorders. No significant shrinkage appears in studies of mentally normal adults who have been carefully screened for all diseases (Duara, London, and Rapaport, 1985).

A factor that may contribute to cognitive decline is a reduced concentration of chemicals that transmit signals in the brain. Neurons may stop manufacturing one of the essential transmitters. Without the transmitter, connections between neurons are lost, neuronal circuits are disrupted, and the connecting fibers may disappear. Long before the neurons themselves die, functions may fail (Bondareff, 1985). Yet throughout life, neuronal fibers are lost and new fibers grow. Environmental stimulation promotes the growth of new connections in older adults, just as it does among the young (Cotman, 1990). In fact, new fibers become more prevalent with age, and their sprouting may prevent a progressive decline in functioning during late old age (Bondareff, 1985).

Recordings of brain waves provide another measure of central nervous system activity. Whether the healthy adult brain shows predictable changes in electrical activity is uncertain, because observed age differences often reflect the inclusion of adults with chronic disease. Existing studies indicate that when older adults are relaxed, there is a decrease in the frequency and proportion of alpha waves, which generally appear when people are not actively processing information. Slow wave activity, which normally accompanies sleep, increases. But when older adults are actively engaged in thought, they show more very fast beta waves, which accompany concentration, and fewer slow waves than do younger adults. Some researchers have explained these findings as indicating a lack of arousal in older adults due to impaired nighttime sleep (Prinz, Dustman, and Emmerson, 1990). Because the quality of sleep tends to decline with age, older adults, when not challenged mentally, may be less aroused and perhaps drowsier than young adults. The researchers also suggest that an increase in strenuous physical activities among older adults might minimize such changes, producing healthier functioning in the central nervous system.

Such suggestions are supported by the beliefs of many developmentalists that cognitive declines traceable to disrupted neuronal circuits or the loss of neurons primarily affect older adults who are in poor health. Until recently, most studies of cognitive changes in older adults were conducted in nursing homes, where few of the residents are in good health.

Disease

Most declines in cognitive functioning are more closely related to health than to age (Perlmutter and Hall, 1992; I. Siegler and Costa, 1985). As we saw in Chapter 17, hypertension and cardiovascular disease are associated with IQ test declines during middle age. Older adults show the same connection; those with cardiovascular problems do worse on memory tasks than those who are healthy, and researchers speculate that much of the age-related decline that appears in experimental studies is caused by undiagnosed cardiovascular disease (Barrett and Watkins, 1986).

A small group of older adults show various forms of serious mental deterioration, known as *organic brain disorders* (see Table 19.1). Researchers estimate that about 5 percent of U.S. elderly have moderate to severe organic brain disorders and that another 10 percent have mild disorders (La Rue, Dessonville, and Jarvik, 1985). The rate of organic brain disorders may be similar across cultures; screening tests indicated that the rate of cognitive impairment is nearly identical in

Shanghai, China and New Haven, Connecticut (Yu et al., 1989).

Organic brain disorders have different causes but produce similar changes in cognitive processes and behavior. The signs of organic brain disorders include (1) a severe loss of intellectual ability that interferes with social or occupational functioning, (2) impaired memory, and (3) impaired judgment or impaired thought processes (American Psychiatric Association, 1980). Organic brain disorders produce the deterioration of thought and personality commonly called "senility."

Multiinfarct Dementia

Up to 20 percent of adults with organic brain disorders have **multiinfarct dementia,** a condition caused by vascular disease. It develops when blockages in small arteries repeatedly cut off the blood supply to various parts of the brain. The blockages, which are actually a series of tiny "strokes," may go unnoticed; the first symptoms may be headaches or dizziness. Sometimes, however, spotty memory loss or an attack of confusion is the first sign of trouble (R. Butler and Lewis, 1982). A major difference between multiinfarct dementia and other organic brain disorders is the existence of periods during which the person seems lucid and memories return. Diagnosis is important, because medical treatment of hypertension and the underlying vascular disease can markedly slow the course of this disorder.

Alzheimer's Disease

The commonest form of organic brain disorder is **Alzheimer's disease,** which accounts for about half of all cases. Another 12 percent have both Alzheimer's disease *and* multiinfarct dementia (R. Butler and Lewis, 1982). Alzheimer's disease usually is diagnosed by eliminating other possible disorders, but a certain diagnosis is not possible until after the patient dies. The brains of Alzheimer's victims usually show four characteristics. First, they are infested with twisted clumps of nerve fibers, called *neurofibrillary tangles.* A few of these tangles appear in most aging brains, but only in Alzheimer's victims do they spread throughout the cortex and the hippocampus. Second, similar concentrations of *plaques,* which consist of degenerating nerve fibers wrapped around a component of nerve cells called amyloid protein, appear outside the neurons. Third, the fibers that bring impulses into the nerve cells have atrophied. Fourth, the brain has shrunk markedly, and its surface shows fewer folds (see Figure 19.1).

Alzheimer's disease may be a disorder with many

TABLE 19.1 MAJOR ORGANIC BRAIN DISORDERS

Disorder	Course
Multiinfarct dementia	Irreversible, but treatment can markedly slow its progression
Alzheimer's disease	Irreversible
Delirium	Reversible

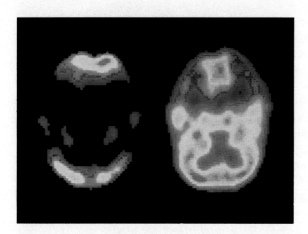

Figure 19.1 The difference between the normal brain of a 72-year-old adult (*right*) and the brain of a 73-year-old with Alzheimer's disease (*left*) shows clearly in this PET scan. PET scans are made by injecting radioactive glucose into the body and tracing the brain's uptake of the substance. More active brain sites take up more glucose, and the presence of the decaying radioactive ions shows brain function. (*NIH/Science Source-Photo Researchers*)

possible causes. Cases that appear during middle adulthood seem to be the result of a genetic defect. One group of researchers has discovered a segment of chromosome 19 that is responsible for some cases of inherited Alzheimer's disease (Marx, 1991). Other researchers have turned up two different defects on chromosome 21 (the chromosome responsible for Down's syndrome) that appeared in all members of a family (over several generations) who developed early Alzheimer's disease and in none of the family members who escaped it (Marx, 1991; Murrell et al., 1991). Both defects involve mutations of the gene responsible for a normal brain chemical, *amyloid precursor protein (APP)*, which produces amyloid protein. The mutation causes the protein to break, creating fragments that accumulate in the brain and serve as the basis of plaques. Other cases of Alzheimer's disease may be caused by different genes, some slow-acting virus, or some unknown environmental toxin. Researchers still are not certain why no genetic involvement can be found in many cases, especially among those who develop the disease after the age of 70.

The progression of Alzheimer's disease within the brain is always the same (Coyle, Price, and DeLong, 1983). Either because of protein fragmentation or because the mutated gene alters the function of the amyloid precursor protein, brain cells begin to die. When neurons that are responsible for producing a critical enzyme die, the brain's supply of acetylcholine is drastically reduced. Starved of acetylcholine, neurons in other areas of the brain also die, especially those in the hippocampus, a brain structure that is involved in memory (Hyman et al., 1984). Because signals cannot get in or out of the hippocampus, memory is destroyed.

Alzheimer's disease develops very slowly, and memory loss frequently is the first sign. Although the chance of an older adult's developing Alzheimer's disease is relatively small, extensive media coverage of the disorder may needlessly frighten older people who experience minor memory lapses. The loss in Alzheimer's disease becomes severe and soon bears little relation to the memory failures of normal aging. A person who is aging normally misplaces the car keys; a person with Alzheimer's disease forgets that he or she ever owned a car. The ability to write checks or to make change disappears. The same book can be read over and over, because the person cannot remember having read it. The ability to read remains intact long after the ability to understand what a person has read deteriorates.

Researchers have discovered that recall is the first cognitive process to decline (Vitaliano et al., 1986). When patients with mild Alzheimer's disease were compared with normal individuals, scores on recall tests distinguished between the groups, but scores on tests of attention and recognition were similar in both groups. As the disease progresses, attention and recognition memory begin to fail. Patients with mild or moderate Alzheimer's disease made equally poor scores on recall tests, but only among those with moderate cases had attention and recognition deteriorated. Two years later, the disease had progressed among patients with formerly mild cases; they also had developed problems with attention and recognition memory.

As the disease develops, people may dress for a snowstorm in midsummer, forget the names of their children, fail to recognize a spouse, or, while sitting in their own living room, ask when they will be going home. They cannot feed or dress themselves. In the disease's final stages, people cannot speak or walk. Eventually, they die, often from pneumonia, urinary tract infections, or other complications that develop in bedridden patients.

There is no cure for Alzheimer's disease. Trials with drugs that increase the brain's supply of acetylcholine were stopped when patients showed liver damage (Marx, 1987). Some researchers have suggested that brain implants or injections of nerve growth factor (NGF) might promote the survival of acetylcholine-producing neurons and thus halt the disease's progress.

But since amyloid protein already spurs the growth of abnormal fibers, which contribute to plaque formation, NGF may not be the answer (Marx, 1990).

Although the progress of Alzheimer's disease cannot be halted, behavioral techniques can increase the period during which patients can function independently. Simple aids, such as notes around the house ("Your lunch is in the refrigerator" on the refrigerator door; "Turn off the burner" above the stove; "Write down the name and number" beside the telephone; "Don't go out; I will be home at 3:30" on the front door) allow patients to substitute recognition for recall. In one study (Quayhagen and Quayhagen, 1989), deliberate stimulation and challenge of patients' memory, problem-solving, and communication skills for six hours each week kept cognitive skills stable over an eight-month period when patients in a control group showed a steady decline.

When objects in the environment are labeled, adults with Alzheimer's disease can rely on recognition instead of recall and thus extend the period of independent functioning. *(Freda Leinwand/Monkmeyer)*

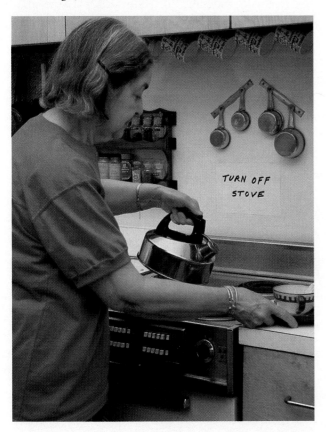

Delirium

As many as 20 percent of people with organic brain disorders have a reversible condition that responds to treatment. This acute disorder, known as **delirium,** is the result of disturbed metabolism throughout the brain. Patients with delirium show the symptoms of organic brain disorder but also may hallucinate, show paranoia, and display such physiological symptoms as fever, muscular tremors, rapid heartbeat, sweating, dilated pupils, and elevated blood pressure.

Delirium has many causes: acute alcohol intoxication, brain tumors, liver disease, cardiovascular disease, strokes, fever, emphysema, malnutrition, or any drug that affects the central nervous system. Often more than one of these factors is involved (Kolata, 1987). Frequently, delirium develops in older people with cardiovascular disease who mistakenly take multiple doses of some prescribed medication. When the underlying cause is treated, the delirium passes and the patient may recover completely. But if the cause of delirium is not detected, which may happen when physicians assume that the patient has a chronic brain disorder like multiinfarct dementia, the patient may indeed develop a chronic disorder—or even die.

Learning and Thinking

A look at people functioning in the world provides a convincing demonstration that thought processes need not deteriorate and that the ability to learn remains robust in old age. In 1983, Frederick F. Bloch received his Ph.D. in history at New York University ("A Sense of History," 1983). The topic of his dissertation was the common soldier in the Victorian British Army. This news would be unremarkable except for Bloch's age. He was 81 years old. It took him fifteen years to earn his doctorate, a program he embarked on after he sold his paper-export business and retired. Bloch's plans included a little teaching at NYU and writing a book on minorities in nineteenth-century Britain.

Few older adults engage in enterprises that produce such tangible evidence of their successful learning. Because we cannot see learning, but can only infer it from people's behavior, the process is as difficult to study in older people as it is in the young. Adults may learn many things but have no occasion to use the knowledge they have acquired. Suppose that older adults are placed in a situation that calls for such knowledge but they fail

When they have an incentive and are given plenty of time, older people are efficient learners. This woman, who was never taught to read or write, is now on the road to literacy. *(Mark Mittelman)*

to use it. Did they fail to learn? There is no way to be certain. Perhaps they are simply too tired to use the knowledge or lack the motivation or opportunity to use it.

Older adults probably cannot learn as swiftly or as competently as they once did. Studies consistently show that younger adults outperform them on most aspects of learning. Yet because studies of learning are nearly always cross-sectional, it has been impossible to say exactly when an individual's skills begin to decline or how rapid the decline is likely to be. Researchers find it difficult to eliminate cohort effects or the effects of poor health, such as silent cardiovascular disease or early, undiagnosed Alzheimer's disease. At least one study has found that older adults who follow a regular, vigorous exercise program react faster, have more efficient short-term memories, and reason more accurately than older adults who lead sedentary lives (Clarkson-Smith and Hartley, 1989). Perhaps by looking at age-associated changes in attention and problem solving, we can sort out the research findings.

Attention

Aging in the central nervous system makes it difficult for older adults to concentrate attention on a task, according to some researchers. Whether this hypothesis is true depends on what aspect of attention is examined (see Table 19.2). Attention is a complicated procedure that involves alertness, arousal, attention span, whether the task requires automatic or effortful processing, whether the person is prepared for the event, and what

TABLE 19.2   **AGE DIFFERENCES IN ATTENTION**

Type of Attention	Differences
Selective (Selecting specific stimuli from an assortment of stimuli)	No age differences on simple tasks; age differences appear when irrelevant material must also be processed.
Sustained (Monitoring a single task for long periods)	No age differences on simple, unpressured tasks; age differences appear on speeded or high-pressure tasks.
Divided (Performing two tasks at once)	No age differences on simple tasks; age differences appear on complex tasks.
Switching (Monitoring first one task, then another)	No age differences.

signals are selected for processing. As we have seen, studies of brain waves indicate that many older adults may be less alert and aroused because of sleep disturbances.

Unless older adults can screen out irrelevant information and focus on relevant information, they will have difficulty learning. Whether age differences appear in *selective attention* depends on the situation. When the task is simple, older adults do as well as the young; they are somewhat slower but at least as accurate. When additional, irrelevant information must also be processed, however, the speed of older adults drops sharply, and age differences are clear (McDowd and Birren, 1990).

Learning also requires people to keep their attention focused on a task for relatively long periods of time. In simple tests of *sustained attention,* older adults were as accurate as younger adults, and in a longitudinal study, accuracy did not decline over eighteen years (Giambra and Quilter, 1988). As attention is focused on a task for long periods, accuracy declines in everyone, and no age differences appear in the rate of decline. When given high-pressure tests, in which events come rapidly (forty times per minute), age differences appear: older adults are less accurate than the young, even with extensive practice (Parasuraman and Giambra, 1991). Neither sluggish arousal nor slowed processing explained the results. High rates of speed (which should increase arousal) magnified age differences, and no age differences appeared in preliminary practice sessions, indicating that slowed processing was not involved.

When adults are required to divide their attention between two tasks, older adults are as accurate as the young when the task is simple, as when they must note only whether particular stimuli are present (McDowd and Birren, 1990). As soon as the task becomes complex, age differences appear in *divided attention.* Researchers asked adults to monitor two tasks (simulated driving and counting dots in a video display) on a second-by-second basis (Ponds, Brouwer, and Wolffelaar, 1988). Older adults were as accurate as the young on each task, but when the tasks were presented at the same time, the performance of older adults deteriorated significantly more than that of young and middle-aged adults. Yet when a task involves *switching attention* (shifting attention back and forth between two sources), older adults are as fast and as accurate as younger adults (McDowd and Birren, 1990).

Some researchers suggest that older adults' attention is not defective but simply inefficient. Although they still have the ability to learn, they either fail to attend to all aspects of a task or simply do not make the effort required. In this view, older adults have a limited supply of mental energy. Because learning requires a deliberate application of attention that drains mental energy, older adults are unlikely to make a conscious effort to learn.

When people apply their attention to a learning task, they reorganize the information, elaborate it, make inferences about it, and relate it to other knowledge. Left to their own devices, older adults supposedly do not carry out this deep processing, but when the situation makes such processing easy or accessible, they generally do so (Craik and Byrd, 1982).

Problem Solving

Older adults' lives are filled with problems of all shapes and sizes, just as are the lives of the young and middle-aged. Some problems are as trivial as opening a "child-proof" medicine bottle or deciding which brands and sizes of supermarket products to buy. Some are worrisome but can usually be solved: what to do when the refrigerator stops making ice or how to get into a locked apartment when the key has been left inside. The solutions to others are more specific to older adults, and some can have serious consequences. Is the protection of Medicare sufficient, or is a supplementary Medigap policy a wise idea? If so, which kind? Is it best to sell a Nebraska home and move to the sunny Southwest, buy a condominium in a town where a child lives, or simply stay put?

Faced with a problem, an adult may use any of a variety of strategies to solve it. The aggravation of the child-proof cap may be solved by carefully following instructions on the cap, by destroying the plastic bottle and placing the tablets in another container, or by asking the pharmacist to use a different kind of cap. Adults may meet problems by applying old strategies rigidly, by adjusting their strategies to meet the new situation, by ignoring the problem, or by manipulating the environment so that the problem changes (as when older adults refuse to buy medication in a child-proof container) (Reese and Rodeheaver, 1985).

When older adults are asked to solve laboratory tasks that require deductive reasoning, they generally do worse than young adults. In fact, on traditional laboratory reasoning problems, performance generally declines after young adulthood (Reese and Rodeheaver, 1985). Whether older adults also are less competent at solving practical problems is uncertain. In one study, middle-aged adults provided the most competent solutions to problems that elderly adults might encounter,

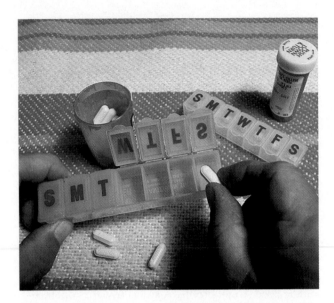

When the problem is to remember to take medication each day, some older adults solve it by using labeled pill boxes while others devise a different strategy. *(Tony Freeman/Photo Edit)*

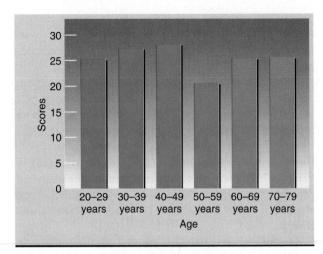

Figure 19.2A Adults become more adept at solving some kinds of practical problems during middle adulthood; then problem-solving ability declines. Despite the decline, older adults continue to solve practical problems as efficiently as young adults. (*Data from Denny and Pearce, 1989*)

with both young and older adults apparently less able to handle the problems by themselves (Denney and Pearce, 1989) (see Figure 19.2A). Adults had to decide, for example, how an elderly woman could get groceries and other necessities in winter when bad weather made it impossible to drive her car. In another study, however, older adults were the most efficient at solving such practical problems as how to get some expensive repairs made after the landlord has refused to do them (Cornelius and Caspi, 1987) (see Figure 19.2B).

How can we resolve these conflicting results? Many factors, such as differences in the task, differences in the people studied, and a method that is insensitive to differences in learning styles and problem-solving strategies may be responsible. Another possible factor is the demand placed on intellectual resources. In the first study, which showed declining performance after middle age, investigators required adults to generate the solutions themselves. In the second study, which showed improved performance after middle age, adults had only to choose which solution they would adopt from a list of possible responses. This method, which required less information processing, may place smaller demands on the intellectual resources of older adults.

It is risky, however, to generalize from such findings. The best solution for such situations would differ from person to person, depending on the individual's experience in related situations and his or her physical condi-

tion. Some older adults solve abstract problems as well as younger men and women. They play cognitive games efficiently, apply deductive logic, organize elements of the problem, and devise (and follow) systematic strategies. In fact, when older and younger adults are matched on tests of fluid intelligence, there is little or

Figure 19.2B When asked to solve everyday problems, performance increased with age, as it did on the verbal-meaning test of crystallized intelligence. But traditional age differences appeared on the letter-series test, a measure of fluid intelligence. (*From Cornelius and Caspi, 1987*)

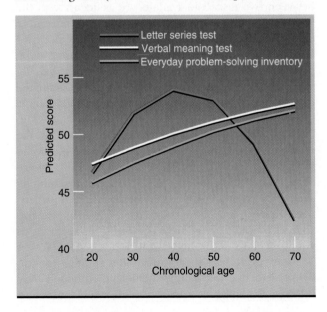

no age-related decline in problem solving (Rabbitt, 1988).

When researchers tested teams of managers on their ability to deal with the computer-generated problems of a mythical country, there was little difference between the performance of young (age 28 to 35) and middle-aged (age 45 to 55) managers (Streufert et al., 1990). Older managers (age 65 to 75) performed at considerably lower levels, engaging in lengthy discussions, making fewer decisions, and coming up with fewer problem-solving strategies than the two younger groups. When faced with sudden emergencies, however, the older managers responded as quickly, efficiently, and decisively as did the young and middle-aged. The researchers suspect that the exhaustive searches for information carried out by the younger groups left them in a state of information overload during the emergencies but that the older managers' tendency to absorb information selectively acted as protection against overload and allowed them to perform at maximum effectiveness. Whether the differences in performance were the result of age is not certain. Some of the older managers were retired and without recent experience in management. Some may have had cardiovascular or other degenerative diseases. Although educational backgrounds were similar, cohort-related factors such as changing leadership expectations and style also may have affected the outcome.

Some researchers believe that consistent use of problem-solving skills may prevent declines in these skills. This belief was supported by a study of adults between the ages of 55 and 77 (Clarkson-Smith and Hartley, 1990). Those who played bridge frequently failed to show the decline with age on standard reasoning tests that was apparent among non–bridge players. Because problem solving and learning both depend on the ability to acquire, retain, recall, and manipulate knowledge in consciousness, memory declines may be responsible for much of whatever cognitive decline appears in later adulthood. In fact, older bridge players perform much more efficiently on tests of short-term memory than do older adults who never play bridge (Clarkson-Smith and Hartley, 1990).

Wisdom

When developmentalists were primarily interested in the early part of the life span, wisdom was rarely, if ever, mentioned in discussions of intelligence. Wisdom grows out of experience and is different from knowledge, because it requires more than the possession of

facts. Researchers have found that adults of all ages generally agree on the personal attributes that constitute wisdom (Holliday and Chandler, 1986). The major factors appear to be exceptional understanding, judgment and communication skills, general intellectual competence, interpersonal skills, and social unobtrusiveness (see Table 19.3). Adults of all ages also agree that wisdom is one of the few desirable characteristics that increase with age, and most believe that it begins to develop at about the age of 55 (P. Baltes et al., 1991). Not everyone becomes wise with age, and whether a particular person becomes wise depends on specific life experiences, motivation, and personal resources.

Some researchers see wisdom as primarily cognitive in nature. According to Paul Baltes and his associates (P. Baltes et al., 1991; J. Smith and Baltes, 1990), wisdom is expert knowledge about fundamental life matters. The wise person has (1) a rich store of factual knowledge about life, (2) a rich store of knowledge about ways of dealing with life's problems, (3) an understanding that life is embedded in a series of interrelated contexts, (4) an awareness that all judgments are relative to a particular culture and value system, and

TABLE 19.3 WHAT MAKES A PERSON WISE?

Major Factors	Characteristic Examples
Exceptional understanding	Sees things in a larger context Uses common sense Has learned from experience
Judgment and communication skills	Understands life Weighs consequences Is a source of good advice
Generally competent	Curious Intelligent Creative
Interpersonal skills	Fair Even-tempered Kind
Social unobtrusiveness	Discreet Nonjudgmental Quiet

Source: Holliday and Chandler, 1986.

(5) an awareness that life is unpredictable and uncertain. This definition is, in effect, an application of postformal thought by an expert in the fundamental pragmatics of life (see Chapter 17).

In a test of this definition, adults of various ages tried to solve developmental problems that involved planning for the future by thinking out loud about the various options (J. Smith and Baltes, 1990). All five criteria were highly correlated, and only about 5 percent of adults displayed what judges considered wisdom. Although older adults produced some of the wisest answers, there were as many wise answers from middle-aged and young adults. Because some of the developmental problems involved gender-role reversal and the possibility of combined career-family roles for women, the researchers suggested that cohort differences may have affected the results.

Looking for wisdom in purely cognitive terms may allow it to elude researchers. As we have seen, the general public agrees that wisdom requires certain interpersonal skills (fairness, sensitivity, sociability, kindness, and an even temper) and social unobtrusiveness (discretion, quietness, and a nonjudgmental attitude) (Holliday and Chandler, 1986). Lucinda Orwoll and Marion Perlmutter (1990) believe that wisdom is as dependent on personality as it is on cognition. With exceptional growth in personality as well as in cognition, the wise person experiences emotions in a way that fosters self-awareness, and the sense of self expands beyond personal identity and immediate context to embrace all humanity. A developmental spiral occurs, in which self-transcendence promotes information processing and enables a person to perceive situations more clearly. As wisdom-related cognition is enhanced, the person develops a more mature insight into motives and emotions, which leads to further cognitive growth.

Because older adults are assumed to be wise, they may be expected to solve conflicts, provide advice, know the society's history and rituals, and instruct the young with stories, myths, and legends. *(Marc & E. Bernheim/Woodfin Camp & Associates)*

This view of wisdom is compatible with Erik Erikson's theory of successful personality development in old age, as we will see in Chapter 20. The problem for developmentalists is to discover how cognitive and personality processes interact to produce wisdom. Even wise people may, however, find that they have to make allowances for changes in the memory system.

Memory in Later Life

At the beginning of the chapter, we met two eminent psychologists who complained about memory lapses. Skinner (1983) recommended memory cues as an aid to daily activities. He found that he could remember to take an umbrella on a day that threatened rain by hanging the umbrella over the doorknob as soon as the thought crossed his mind. Hebb (1978) was not quite as optimistic, saying that such a strategy worked best for him when the object was big enough to trip him as he went out the door.

Memory research rarely focuses on such everyday tasks as remembering to carry an umbrella or take prescribed medication. Instead, most studies try to determine how aging affects various aspects of the information-processing system that are involved in the storage and retrieval of information (see Figure 2.1 on page 44). Information from the environment enters the sensory register as a fleeting sense impression; there it is stored briefly—for less than a second. If the information catches our attention, it moves into the phase of short-term memory, which is a temporary holding system for information that is being consciously processed. During this phase, we apply strategies, organize material, and encode it for later retrieval. As information fades from consciousness, it is either lost or stored in long-term memory. When we need information, it is retrieved from long-term memory and returned to short-term memory, where we are aware of it. Problems with memory may arise during any of these processes.

As people age, not all parts of the memory system change in the same manner. Sensory memory, either for sights or for sounds, appears to be relatively unaffected by aging (Poon, 1985). Aging also does not affect the contents of memory; the knowledge stored in long-term memory is stable and may increase with age (Perlmutter, 1986). Such information may become momentarily unavailable, but is it unlikely to be lost. Once information has been placed in long-term memory, 80-year-olds retain it as efficiently as do 20-year-olds. The problem

for older adults is to find the cue that will enable them to retrieve the information.

Studies of memory generally do not assess the contents of long-term storage. Instead, when searching for the reason that older adults consistently do worse than young or middle-aged adults on various memory tasks, researchers test the efficiency of the processes used to place material in storage or to retrieve it (Perlmutter et al., 1987). Most studies indicate that aging affects the efficiency of these processes.

Processing and Encoding

The *structural capacity* of short-term memory seems relatively unaffected by age (Dobbs and Rule, 1989; Salthouse and Mitchell, 1989). There are few age differences in digit- or word-span tests, in which people passively repeat a string of digits or words that they have just heard. Yet when people must manipulate or reorganize information in some way, age differences become obvious: the *operational capacity* of short-term memory apparently shrinks with age. Thus, if asked to repeat the string of digits or words backward, older people can handle fewer items. Adults also draw on operational capacity when asked to hold an excess of items in short-term memory. Depending on the person, short-term memory apparently holds from five to seven items; anything over that amount must be retrieved from long-term memory. When researchers asked adults to retain and then dial phone numbers, there were no age differences in the retention of area codes (three digits) (West and Crook, 1990). By the age of 70, small age differences appeared with local numbers (seven digits), and when the adults were required to retain long-distance numbers (ten digits), age differences were apparent from the age of 60.

Researchers have been trying to discover the source of age differences in operational capacity, which they often refer to as **working memory.** One possibility is that centralized processing becomes less efficient with age. Some researchers have indeed found that when they vary the complexity of tasks, age differences widen as processing demands increase (Wingfield et al., 1988), but others have found that the age differences remain relatively constant (Babcock and Salthouse, 1990).

Perhaps age differences in capacity are at least as important as decreased processing efficiency; that is, older adults may find it difficult to hold information in working memory while simultaneously processing the same—or other—information (Salthouse, Mitchell, and Palmon, 1989). This conclusion was supported by a study in which adults solved three addition problems mentally but held the answers in mind until all three problems were solved (Foos, 1989). The pattern of results indicated that older adults process information efficiently but that when they direct their resources to processing, they no longer have enough resources to keep information in working memory.

In an intricate study, Timothy Salthouse and Renee Babcock (1991) examined digit span, word span, computation, sentence comprehension, and the ability to solve visually presented arithmetic problems while simultaneously answering questions concerning spoken sentences. For example, while hearing the sentence "The boy ran with the dog" and telling "who" ran, adults had to solve problems like "9 − 2 = ?" The researchers found that the effects of storage capacity on working memory were largely due to diminished processing efficiency. When measures of processing efficiency were controlled, age differences shrank dramatically. The researchers also discovered that the major influence on processing efficiency was perceptual

speed, measured by how rapidly adults could compare two letters or patterns and indicate that they were "same" or "different." Salthouse and Babcock propose that it is not the number or complexity of operations that causes age-related declines in working memory; instead, it is the speed with which elementary operations can be successfully executed (see Figure 19.3). Slowed activation of information would decrease the flexibility of processing, so older adults would find it more difficult to shift from one process to another (Dobbs and Rule, 1989).

If older adults are at a disadvantage when they must manipulate or reorganize information in some way, is their ability to store new knowledge impaired? Reorganization is an important aid when information is to be encoded for permanent storage; it is one sort of encoding strategy. When encoding material, older adults may not be using such strategies. Some researchers believe that the failure to use efficient encoding strategies indicates that older adults' processing abilities have deteriorated, making it impossible for them to use strategies

Figure 19.3 This path analysis model of relations among age and hypothesized components of working memory indicates that age has a large direct effect on perceptual speed (simple comparison speed), which in turn has both direct and indirect effects on working memory. The indirect effects, which are the major influence, operate through the effect of perceptual speed on processing efficiency. Processing efficiency affects working memory directly and indirectly, through its influence on storage capacity. (*From Salthouse and Babcock, 1991, p. 773*)

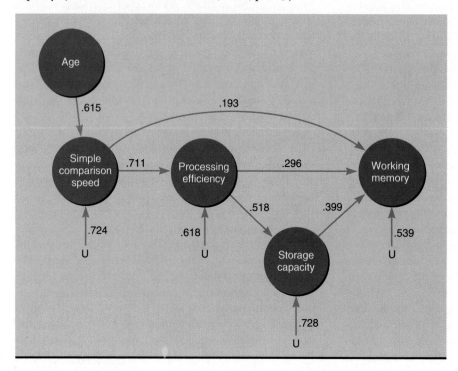

that they once employed. Other researchers are convinced that the problem is less a processing deficiency than a production deficiency. That is, older adults are capable of encoding information efficiently, but they do not make spontaneous use of helpful memory strategies. This view was supported by a study in which older adults had to organize a word list by category, a procedure that forced them to think about the meaning of each word (Mitchell and Perlmutter, 1986). On an unexpected test of recall, the age differences disappeared. Older adults recalled about as many words as young adults did.

Retrieval

Although encoding problems apparently are responsible for a major part of the age difference on memory tasks, the retrieval process may add to the problem. Sometimes the material may be stored but may elude the older person's search. This conjecture is supported by older adults' ability to recognize material that they have previously encountered. When adults recognize a word list that they have not been able to recall, for example, the deficiency is in the search process. Seeing the original list seems to act as a cue, which makes it easier for them to retrieve the information.

The results of recognition experiments presumably test the efficiency of the encoding process, because recognition involves little retrieval effort. The results of recall experiments test the retrieval process, because recall requires recollection that either occurs spontaneously or arises in response to some cue (Perlmutter et al., 1987). Age differences appear in both recognition and recall memory, but experiments indicate a much smaller decline in recognition. This finding should not be surprising, for we saw in Chapter 11 that recognition is a simple skill that shows little developmental change after the age of 4 or 5 years. Thus, in some conditions older adults' recognition memory is as good as that of young adults. When shown a series of photographs and line drawings, for example, adults in their late sixties later recognized the pictures as accurately as college students did (Park, Puglisi, and Smith, 1986). Yet after a lapse of four weeks, college students' recognition was more accurate, and older adults turned in many more "false alarms" (claiming to recognize pictures that were not part of the original set).

In some situations, the characteristics of the people studied determine whether age differences appear on tests of recognition. Adults in their seventies with high verbal IQs recognized words as efficiently as did college students with similar IQs (Bowles and Poon, 1982). But among adults with low verbal IQs, those in their seventies did much worse than young adults with similar IQs. Apparently, a large store of knowledge can compensate for processing declines related to recognition.

Age differences in recall are generally larger when people expect to be tested. In such studies, people memorize a word list and then try to repeat the words spontaneously (a procedure known as *free recall*). Age differences in free recall first appear when people reach their thirties, and the gap between 20-year-olds and their elders gets wider with each passing decade. The gap widens further when young and old are given as much study time as they wish and encouraged to use any aid to memorization they find helpful. These results indicate that the young profit more than the old from such conditions (Rabinowitz, 1989). However, age differences shrink when experimenters present a retrieval cue (such as the name of a category) at the time of testing; this demonstrates that older people often learn more than tests indicate (Poon, 1985).

Memory for Meaningful Information

Most assessments of memory depend on adults' ability to recall isolated words. Such tasks are rarely encountered in daily life. More important is the ability to read and recall meaningful information or to remember whether one has performed specific activities.

In the case of memory for spoken or written information, the goal is to recall the gist of the text, not its literal wording. Does older adults' ability to recall what they have read in newspapers, magazines, or books show a decline with age? Whether age differences appear in the comprehension of articles depends on such factors as individual differences (in skills or prior knowledge), the nature of the task (recall or recognition), the type of material to be remembered (written or spoken, clearly organized or discursive), and the type of instructions given (Hultsch and Dixon, 1990). Older adults with high verbal ability, for example, are as competent as younger adults in recalling the important ideas from a written article, but consistent age differences appear among adults with low verbal ability (Hultsch, Hertzog, and Dixon, 1984). In a group of adults between the ages of 19 and 90, vocabulary was the major determinant of scores on a multiple-choice test covering the content of a television newscast (West, Crook, and Barron, 1992). Older adults may also recall stories in a different manner than the young. Consistent with the development of postformal thought, discussed in

Older adults of high verbal ability can recall the gist of newspaper articles they have read just as competently as a younger person. *(Barbara Rios/Photo Researchers)*

Chapter 17, older adults tend to recall stories in a more integrative and interpretive style than do younger adults, whose recall tends to be detailed and based on the text (C. Adams et al., 1990).

People rarely carry out activities with the conscious intent of remembering them, so their recollections are examples of incidental, automatic memory (Hultsch and Dixon, 1990). Older adults remember such actions as effectively as young adults in some situations but not in others. When researchers asked adults to perform a short list of simple actions ("Lift the spoon," "Look into the mirror," "Smell the flower"), no age differences appeared in the accuracy of adults' recollections as to whether they had performed them (Knopf and Neidhardt, 1989). But when the list of actions they performed was lengthy, typical age differences appeared in the accuracy of recall.

Older adults also tend to be less accurate than the young when recalling the source of events they have watched or read about. After they had viewed a short film in which a middle-aged man is abducted by four youths, older and young adults read either an accurate

version of the film or a version that incorporated false accounts of two critical incidents (G. Cohen and Faulkner, 1989). Afterward they answered eighteen multiple-choice questions about the film. Among those who had read the correct version of the film, older adults remembered events from the film as accurately as did the young. But among those who read the false version, older adults were more likely than the young to claim that the misrepresented incidents in the text had been in the film. The older adults' tendency to confuse the source of remembered information may be due to encoding problems. Some studies indicate that older adults encode less contextual information, and so they lack contextual cues that would help them identify the source of their recollections (Burke and Light, 1981).

Metamemory

Why do older adults fail to use strategies on memory tasks? This failure is not the result of ignorance about basic memory processes. Most studies indicate that older adults know as much about how memory works, the factors that make remembering easier or more difficult, and the usefulness of various memory skills as do younger adults (Hultsch, Hertzog, and Dixon, 1987; Loewen, Shaw, and Craik, 1990). Yet younger adults are much more likely to use encoding strategies when trying to commit something to memory. Even more puzzling is the consistent finding that older adults are at least as good as the young in predicting when they will be able to recognize factual answers that they cannot recall (a skill that is tested with multiple choice questions) and as good in monitoring and evaluating their performance in recall (Brigham and Pressley, 1988).

These findings led researchers to determine whether older adults also monitored the effectiveness of memory strategies on their own recall performance (Brigham and Pressley, 1988). The study involved the use of two different strategies in learning new words. One strategy, which is moderately effective, required older adults to make up a sentence using the new word in a meaningful context. The other strategy, which is highly effective, required them to note a familiar word related to the new word and then make up a sentence using both the familiar word and the new word. Younger adults realized which strategy was more effective and switched to it when learning additional words. But most older adults seemed unaware of the power of the highly effective strategy, although they recalled more words when using it. What is more, older adults who realized the effectiveness of the second strategy did not continue to use it.

Perhaps older adults are less concerned than the young with the effectiveness of strategies. In contrast to younger adults, who said they switched strategies in order to increase their recall, older adults tended to say that they used a strategy because it was simpler or easier to employ.

The observed age-related decline in the use of mental encoding strategies is accompanied by an increase in the use of external aids to bolster memory; older adults are more likely than college students to use calendars, diaries, shopping lists, and notes. Some researchers have speculated that the use of such external aids is another example of compensation for failing cognitive abilities (Dixon and Hultsch, 1983). But a recent study indicates that the switch from mental to external strategies may be as much a consequence of life style as it is of cognitive change. When researchers compared the strategy-use practices of college students, noncollege adults in their twenties, and older adults, they found that the noncollege adults resembled older adults in their use of strategies (Loewen, Shaw, and Craik, 1990). These employed young adults used mental encoding strategies no more often than did older adults, and their use of external aids fell between the patterns of the other two groups. The researchers suggest that adults with varied lives and many obligations tend to rely on external memory aids, whereas students, whose lives are dominated by the need to recall information they have learned, have a greater need for internal encoding strategies. Indeed, the use of external aids seems to peak in middle age, when life's obligations produce the most pressure, and then decline somewhat among older adults (Hultsch, Hertzog, and Dixon, 1987).

Self-Efficacy and a Sense of Control

Strategies are not the only aspects of metamemory that determine recall. Older adults' self-efficacy and sense of control over their intellectual capacities may also influence performance on memory tasks. As we saw in Chapter 11, self-efficacy affects children's performance in the classroom, apparently because it affects motivation. People who are high in self-efficacy tend to set higher goals for themselves, expend more effort on various tasks, and work longer at them. No matter how much older adults know about memory processes, if they believe that their own ability to remember in a particular situation is poor, they may perform below their capacity (Hertzog, Hultsch, and Dixon, 1989).

Memory self-efficacy encompasses how highly adults evaluate their own memory capacity (for example, be-

lieving that they are good at remembering names) and how much they believe their memory has changed with age (for example, believing that they find it more difficult to remember things than they used to). Self-efficacy levels generally predict memory performance in adults of any age (Berry, West, and Dennehey, 1989). Indeed, beliefs concerning self-efficacy may be more powerful than actual performance in regard to the way older adults approach situations involving memory. In one study, training in a new memory strategy improved the *performance* of older adults but did not increase their *self-efficacy* (Rebok and Balcerak, 1989). Thus, few of the older adults used the strategy on a new task. When younger adults were taught the same strategy, their confidence in their memory increased along with their performance, and most adopted the strategy on a new task.

Closely related to self-efficacy is the perception of personal control over the ability to remember. Research indicates that young adults perform at a higher level when they have control over the content of the task to be performed (Kausler, 1990). Whether the effect of perceived cognitive control over task content or cognitive processes changes with age is not certain. In one study, older adults' belief that exerting effort would enable them to remember affected their ability to recall the gist of prose passages they had read (Dixon and Hultsch, 1983). Among adults in their seventies who had been followed for five years, there was no significant change in either intelligence or the average feeling of control over cognitive processes—except among those whose fluid-intelligence scores had declined (Lachman and Leff, 1989). Even among highly educated adults whose intelligence, self-efficacy, and cognitive control remained stable, there was, however, an increase in the belief that they had to rely on other people to solve cognitive problems. The researchers suggest that older adults may accept cultural stereotypes about the inevitability of cognitive decline despite their own elevated performance. Their extra-sensitivity to predicted changes may lead them to protect their self-image by relinquishing some control, having others carry out such tasks as filling out tax forms.

The impact of metamemory, self-efficacy, and control on memory performance of older adults is similar to the impact on children. In children, the reasons for the impact may be due to naiveté and level of cognitive development, whereas in older adults the impact is probably due to erroneous beliefs, lack of experience, and worry. Expectations, attributions, and beliefs may affect the memory of older adults in a complicated fashion, depending on the way each individual evaluates his or her

ANXIETY, DEPRESSION, AND MEMORY

Seemingly healthy older adults frequently complain about memory failures, and approximately 20 percent worry about their ability to remember (Cavanaugh and Morton, 1988). This anxiety about memory lapses may even increase memory failure.

Long ago, studies with college students showed that worry, which is the cognitive aspect of anxiety, is responsible for most of the negative effects of test anxiety on performance (Doctor and Altman, 1969). It is not a student's pounding heart, queasy stomach, and sweaty palms that produce low test scores but cognitive concern over failure. Worry, which is apparently a consequence of low self-efficacy, leads people to focus on themselves instead of on the task, and so their attention is pulled away from the task at hand (Perlmutter et al., 1987). Because worry is incompatible with relaxation, researchers have found that if older adults have relaxation training before they embark on a memory training program, they do much better at the final testing (Yesavage and Jacob, 1984).

Anxiety is not the only emotion that has been connected with memory. Seriously depressed people of all ages find it difficult to learn, to recall new information, to use appropriate memory strategies, or to pay attention (see, for example, R. Cohen et al., 1982), but mild depression seems to have little effect on memory. Several studies have found a strong connection between older adults' complaints of forgetfulness and measures of depression but no connection between these complaints and scores on objective tests of memory (O'Hara et al., 1986). Compared with older adults who are not depressed, mildly depressed adults complain more about forgetting names, faces, words, phone numbers, and where they put things. They rate their memory as poorer than that of most other adults of their own age, and they are more likely to say that their memory is not nearly as good as it was in young adulthood. When given a free-recall test, however, they remember as many words as nondepressed adults do. In other words, the older adult who complains most bitterly about memory lapses tends to perform just as well on tests of memory as the adult who has no particular complaints.

Why should mildly depressed adults believe that their memory is so poor? Perhaps their depression leads them to focus on the unpleasant aspects of their lives. They complain about their appetite, their loss of interest in activities, their fatigue, their inability to make decisions—and their memory lapses. Aware of the myths about aging, they may be especially sensitive to each sign of a failing memory and exaggerate its importance (Zarit, 1980).

Older adults who believe such myths may become so worried about the consequences of a deteriorating memory that their general efficiency and psychological well-being suffer (Hulicka, 1982). Yet the slight memory impairment that accompanies aging does not interfere with daily life among adults who are free from organic brain disorders.

---

own past and future development (Brandtstädter, 1989). Cognitive and emotional appraisals may be equally powerful (as the accompanying box, "Anxiety, Depression, and Memory," suggests), so how the older adult interprets events may be as important as the event itself. The perception of control and self-efficacy may be vital to the retention of an optimistic outlook.

Cognitive Plasticity and Training

Age-related cognitive decline among adults with no organic brain disorders consistently appears in experimental research, but the magnitude of change is relatively small and has little effect on daily life. If deterioration in the nervous system is the cause of this cognitive decline, then nothing can be done about it. Once the decline begins, it cannot be reversed. But according to contextual theories, development is heavily affected by the individual's cognitive, social, and physical environment. Because these influences are so powerful, older minds may still be plastic and open to change.

More than a decade of research has supported this view (Lerner, 1990). Through various training programs, older adults have improved the quality of problem-solving ability, the functioning of working memory, and scores on tests of fluid intelligence. This research indicates that disuse and lack of cognitive stimulation are responsible for at least part of the declines that consistently appear in experimental studies.

No matter what technique is used to improve learning and problem-solving skills, the training is usually effective. Presented with the same sort of problem they solved during training, older adults tend to use the new strategies. The question is whether adults who use them effectively on specific problems will transfer the strategies to problems that are not obviously similar. As a general rule, transfer tends to be limited to similar situations.

In an intervention program that used video games to speed information processing in older adults, transfer was apparent (Clark, Lanphear, and Riddick, 1987). Video games demand controlled attention and rapid information processing. Seven weeks of daily play at Pac Man and Donkey Kong resulted in an enormous increase in older adults' scores on the games, as we might expect. But the adults' skills transferred into more efficient responses in other situations. They became faster and more accurate in a key-pressing test of reaction time.

Memory training programs in which adults learn new encoding strategies have been successful in improving memory skills. In one study (Kliegl and Baltes, 1987), healthy adults in their sixties and seventies learned some of the strategies that memory experts use to memorize lists of words and digits. After intensive training, these older adults with above-average IQs gave impressive performances. Using a strategy that involved recoding digits into a list of well-known historical dates, the most proficient adult, a woman of 69, could recall a string of 120 digits presented at the rate of one digit every eight seconds. She could remember more digits correctly than young adults with average IQs who learned the same technique. Clearly, most older adults have untapped cognitive reserves.

Yet some age differences remain. When forced to recall digits at a rapid rate, the woman—and all the older adults in the study—performed much worse than younger adults. Young adults also have untapped reserve capacities, and they can process material more rapidly. In another memory study (Kliegl, Smith, and Baltes, 1990), the use of a new memory strategy dramatically improved performance, but it also magnified age differences. Young adults improved more than did older adults, suggesting that reserve capacity diminishes with age. And once again, older adults were proficient only when words were presented slowly.

When taught a technique for mentally squaring two-digit numbers, older adults learned at about the same rate as young adults but required twice as long to come up with the answers (J. Campbell and Charness, 1990). Adults of all ages learned to calculate the squares twice as fast and with half as many errors as during the learning phase, but age differences remained. By the end of the study, there were no age differences in calculation errors, but older adults continued to make more working-memory errors (such as omitting a subgoal or selecting a wrong figure from an earlier stage).

Training programs for fluid-intelligence skills have also shown impressive gains by older adults. One such study used Raven's Progressive Matrices, a test that requires a person to select which of several alternatives would complete a design that is missing a section (Denney and Heidrich, 1990). Performance on this test generally decreases with age. After a single, brief session, men and women of all ages performed significantly better on the test than did those in a control group. The training effect was the same for all ages, so age differences did not diminish.

Working with adults between the ages of 64 and 95, researchers have succeeded in reversing long-term declines on two tests of fluid intelligence: inductive reasoning and spatial orientation (Schaie and Willis, 1986b). The adults were members of a longitudinal study of IQ and had been tested several times over a fourteen-year period. Nearly half had shown no decline in either skill, about one-third had declined in one skill but not the other, and nearly one-fourth had declined in both skills. After a five-hour training course, 40 percent of the adults who had declined completely reversed the drop; their scores were as high as they had been fourteen years earlier (see Figure 19.4). Another 20 percent showed improvement, although their scores had not

Figure 19.4 A five-hour training course was sufficient to return many older adults' scores on IQ subtests to their previous levels. (*From Schaie and Willis, 1986b, p. 231*)

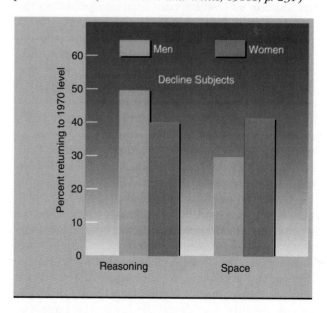

returned all the way to the earliest level. Among adults whose scores had been stable for fourteen years, more than 50 percent showed significant gains in inductive reasoning and 40 percent showed significant gains in spatial orientation. Neither age nor education nor income level affected this pattern.

Other older adults who had received training in figural relations, another fluid-intelligence skill, retained a major portion of the benefits over seven years, as they moved deeper into old age (Willis and Nesselroade, 1990). The adults received five training sessions at each of three phases (1979, 1981, 1986). At the final testing, these adults in their late seventies and early eighties were still performing significantly better than they had before the first training session, indicating that considerable cognitive plasticity remains into late old age.

Elaborate sessions with trainers are not required for the sort of gains made in these studies. Healthy older adults between the ages of 63 and 90 who worked by themselves on a practice booklet made gains in figural relations that were as impressive as those made by adults who had specific instruction and training (P. Baltes, Sowarka, and Kliegl, 1989). Apparently, older adults can activate their cognitive reserves on their own.

Training studies give short-term training and then send adults back to their typical environment. If the intervention lasted considerably longer, cognitive functioning might be enhanced far more than these studies indicate (Lerner, 1990). Perhaps much of the typical age-related deterioration in cognitive function might be prevented if the environment of older adults provided adequate cognitive stimulation. In the next chapter, as we consider the context of older adults' lives, keep this possibility in mind.

SUMMARY

MYTHS ABOUT AGING

Most people have many misconceptions about growing old. These misconceptions are partly responsible for the development of **ageism** and for our expectations concerning behavior of the old.

BIOLOGICAL CHANGES

Some sensory loss occurs with age, but the losses are not uniform and vary greatly from one person to the next. Motor actions, decisions, and problem solving take longer than they once did. According to the **peripheral slowing hypothesis,** this slowed execution is the result of aging in the **peripheral nervous system.** According to the **generalized slowing hypothesis,** processing is slowed in the brain as well.

By using **computerized axial tomography (CT),** researchers have found some shrinkage of the brain with age, except among older adults who have been carefully scanned for all diseases. Neural death following a depletion of neurotransmitters may be responsible for slowed processing, although the growth of new fibers may compensate for such loss. Some researchers suggest that drowsiness due to lack of arousal may magnify the effects of cognitive aging.

Health, not age, is the primary predictor of cognitive decline, and severe cognitive impairment is usually a sign of organic brain disorder. Irreversible disorders include **multiinfarct dementia** (caused by cardiovascular disease) and **Alzheimer's disease** (apparently caused by defective genes or a combination of genetic and environmental circumstances). **Delirium,** which reflects disturbed metabolism throughout the brain, has many causes and often can be reversed.

LEARNING AND THINKING

Older adults seem to have more trouble than younger adults in learning new material. Whether researchers look at selective attention, sustained attention, or divided attention, older adults seem to do well on simple tasks, but their performance suffers when the task is speeded or complex. On tasks that require switching attention, older adults are as fast and accurate as the young. Some researchers explain age differences in attention and problem solving as the result of limited supplies of mental energy among the old. Others believe that consistent age-related declines in problem solving may be the result of a failure to use these skills on a regular basis.

Whether older adults become wise with age depends on their experiences, motivation, and personal resources. Some researchers see wisdom as the application of postformal thought by an expert in the fundamental pragmatics of life, but others believe that wisdom depends as much on exceptional personality development as it does on highly developed cognition.

MEMORY IN LATER LIFE

Sensory memory does not appear to decline with age, nor is there any deterioration in the structural capacity of short-term memory or in the retention of information in long-term memory. But the operational capacity of short-term memory, or **working memory,** becomes less efficient. When older adults must manipulate or reorganize information, age differences are apparent. The failure of adults to use efficient encoding strategies may be primarily a production deficiency. Age differences in recognition are small, but the decline in recall is much larger, especially when no clues are available.

Memory for meaningful information shows little decline among adults with high verbal ability, but the decline is clear among those with low verbal ability. Older adults may have trouble recalling the source of stored information because they encode less contextual information. Even when older adults are aware of the effectiveness of sophisticated encoding strategies, they are less likely to use them, preferring external strategies that are simple or easy to use. This change may be the result of life style, because it also appears among employed young adults. Among adults of all ages, self-efficacy level is an important predictor of memory performance.

COGNITIVE PLASTICITY AND TRAINING

Older minds retain a degree of plasticity. Training programs have speeded information processing, minimized differences in recall, and reversed declines in fluid intelligence skills.

KEY TERMS

ageism	delirium	peripheral nervous system
Alzheimer's disease	generalized slowing hypothesis	peripheral slowing hypothesis
computerized axial tomography (CT)	multiinfarct dementia	working memory

CHAPTER

20

SELF AND SOCIETY: LIVING SUCCESSFULLY

• • • • • • • • • • • • • •

Vivian and Tom Russell are on the threshold of late adulthood. Like many Americans in this generation, they have chosen early retirement. Vivian, 60, left her job as a drug-abuse counselor when Tom, 64, retired from a supervisory position with the U.S. postal service. Through their own efforts, this African-American couple has risen from poverty to the middle class. Tom grew up in a poor sharecropper's family in the segregated South. He credits his escape to the G.I. bill, which gave veterans of World War II an opportunity to go to college. Vivian, whose father was a janitor in Arkansas, dropped out of high school during World War II to work in a defense plant. After the war, when she found herself cleaning houses for a living, she finished high school, took night courses, and became a licensed practical nurse. While their three daughters were small, Vivian worked the night shift so that she could be home during the day. Today, Vivian and Tom have a house in the Detroit suburbs, but their retirement is more than gardening and grandchildren. They are giving something of themselves back to society, with Vivian volunteering at a local hospice, where she nurses terminal patients, and Tom participating in a Christian ministry program at a federal prison. As they talk about their activities, their generativity is apparent. "Playing golf is good," says Tom, "but golf only satisfies the person that's doing it. . . . I want to do something where it will be a benefit to a person that's less fortunate than I am." Vivian agrees. "I need to feel useful," she says. "You aren't just on earth to take up space. It's important to make some kind of contribution" (Kotre and Hall, 1990, pp. 346–348).

● ● ● ● ● ●

The last stage of life promises to be fulfilling for Vivian and Tom Russell. In this chapter we see that while many adults find later adulthood satisfying, others find it a disappointing conclusion to their lives. Once more we begin with a look at the influences of social change on development. After considering the physical changes that typify the last decades of life, we return to the theories discussed earlier and see how they apply to late adulthood. In tracing the final development of self-

concept, we take up the stress of old age and the importance of social support and control. Because few older adults work past the age of 65, our exploration of the occupational sphere of life focuses on retirement. Our examination of family life explores the effects of retirement on the marital relationship, divorce and remarriage, the adjustment to widowhood, and the way relationships with children and grandchildren may change. Next we look at the living arrangements of older adults and find that they are generally determined by health. We also examine the process of preparing for death and the process of dying. The chapter closes with a brief overview of various forms of immortality and notes the relationship between believing in immortality and perceiving the meaning of life.

Social Change

Different cohorts age in different ways, and changes in life patterns are the result of historical events during the cohort's lifetime (Hagestad and Neugarten, 1985). Today's older adults are finding that old age has changed dramatically since their grandparents reached the age of 65, in part because of changes in the age structure of the population. In 1900, when 40 percent of the population was younger than 17, only 4 percent of the population (3 million people) had reached the age of 65, and 50 percent of the babies born in that year would be dead within forty-nine years. In 1990, only about 11 percent of the population was younger than 17, and 12.7 percent of the population (nearly 32 million people) was at least 65 years old. Fifty percent of the babies born in 1990 will still be alive after seventy-five years (U.S. Bureau of the Census, 1990). The rise in the proportion of the over-65 crowd obscures the even more dramatic rise in the oldest group of all—Americans past the age of 85, whose ranks expanded from 0.2 percent of the population at the beginning of the century (123,000 people) to 1.3 percent (3,313,000 people) in 1990.

What is the quality of these extra years of life? Much better for some, and worse for others. Older Americans who do not develop a debilitating disease are healthier and more vigorous than their counterparts of several generations ago. They look, feel, and act younger than their parents and grandparents did at the same age. These young-old (and many have passed their eightieth birthdays) consistently tell researchers, "I am much younger than my mother—or my father—was at my age" (Neugarten and Hall, 1987). For most people, significant health-related problems do not arise until at least the age of 75. Among those between the ages of 65 and 74, for example, about 80 percent have no problems with any of the activities involved in home management—including heavy housework (Dawson, Hendershot, and Fulton, 1987).

Since 1900, the living arrangements of older adults have changed past all recognition. When the twentieth century began, few older adults had their own house-

holds. Whether it was a house, an apartment, or a room in a boarding house, only 29 percent of married older adults and 11 percent of single older adults had independent living arrangements. By 1986, the situation had reversed itself, as Figure 20.1 indicates (Brock, Guralnik, and Brody, 1990). Two factors have fostered this trend. One is affluence. The typical older adult has more assets than he or she did at the turn of the century. Fewer older adults are forced by circumstance to live with a child or other kin (usually a sibling). The second factor is the low birth rate during the Great Depression. By 1975, older Americans had few living children to depend on when they entered old age. In fact, 20 percent had no children at all (Thornton and Freedman, 1983).

Parents of the baby-boom generation, who are now entering retirement, will also be an affluent cohort, because they were born during the Great Depression and entered the labor market in a time of economic expansion, when their relatively few numbers gave them wide economic opportunities. Although they will have more living children to depend on (Himes, 1992), most are less likely than previous generations to need them. When the baby-boomers themselves retire, they may be less affluent than their parents and, because of their low birth rate, will probably have fewer living children.

In the future, an increasing number of couples will enter older adulthood at discrepant stages of the life span. As an ever larger proportion of middle-aged women are employed outside the home, more men are going to find that, although they are ready to retire, their wives are still deeply absorbed in their own occupations. Because most women are younger than their husbands, this trend will be magnified—and the greater the age discrepancy, the more acute the problem will become. Another enormous change has fostered this problem. In 1870, there were no problems with retirement. Most men died at the age of 61, when they were still hard at work, and those who lived beyond that age could not retire because there were no pensions and no Social Security (Miernyk, 1975). Today's older Americans have years of leisure that were unknown to previous generations.

Physical Changes

Some people have long, active, healthy lives and seem to sail through their later years. Others seem to age

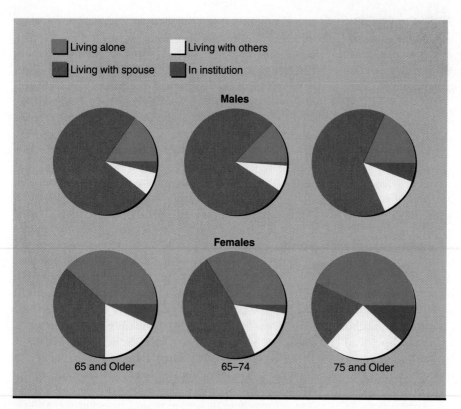

Figure 20.1 Living arrangements of older persons by age and sex, 1985–1986. Data from U.S. Bureau of the Census; unpublished data from the Current Population Survey, National Center for Health Statistics; and unpublished data from the 1985 National Nursing Home Survey. *(From Brock, Guralnik, and Brody, 1990, p. 8)*

quickly, spend most of their time in physicians' offices and in hospitals, and die at a relatively early age. Genes, gender, ethnicity, environment, diet, and activity appear to affect a person's chances of living a long life. Life expectancy also varies from one culture to another, and the variations reflect a society's socioeconomic standards. In Japan, for example, women's life expectancy from birth is 82.5 years; in the United States, it is 79.2 years. Japanese men born today can expect to live for 76.5 years; American men can expect 72.7 years. In Sao Tome and Principe, an island republic off the west coast of Africa that is one of the world's least developed countries, life expectancy is only 63.1 years for women and 60.7 years for men (United Nations, 1991).

In the United States, a person's ethnic background also affects the length of life. Socioeconomically based differences in nutrition, sanitation, and medical care are primarily responsible, because socioeconomic disadvantages tend to result in early death for less hardy members of an ethnic group. Some of the difference, however, may be the result of specific gene-linked dis-

eases that are overrepresented in certain ethnic groups, such as high blood pressure among African-Americans (J. Jackson, Antonucci, and Gibson, 1990; Wing et al., 1985). The life expectancy of an African-American baby at birth is six years less than that of a white baby, but by the age of 65, the difference in life expectancy has narrowed to just over a year (National Center for Health Statistics, 1986). Among adults in their eighties, African-Americans have a longer life expectancy than do whites, presumably because surviving African-Americans are robust and hardy. Studies indicate that the cross-over takes place at the age of 73 for men and at 85 for women (Wing et al., 1985). A similar cross-over occurs for Hispanic Americans, but it takes place in early adulthood, whereas Asian-Americans have a longer life expectancy from birth (J. Jackson, Antonucci, and Gibson, 1990).

No matter what one's culture, ethnic group, or socioeconomic level, however, aging and death are inevitable. Researchers have advanced several different ideas as to why some people seem to age faster and die sooner than others.

Theories of Aging

Aging refers to the increasing inability of a person's body to maintain itself and perform its operations as it once did. The result is that with the passing of time, the probability of impending death increases. Although this definition describes the biological process, it does not explain why people age. Theories of aging refer to the process of **primary aging,** which encompasses the inevitable, gradual, age-related changes that appear in all members of a species. This kind of aging is normal and occurs despite a healthy, active life style and freedom from disease.

Researchers have not been able to agree on a single theory of primary aging or even on the major focus for their theories. Eight theories are under consideration. The first three theories assume that aging is under some kind of genetic control.

The *genetic program theory* assumes that regulatory genes turn off and on during development. At the approach of middle age, either youthful genes turn off or aging genes turn on (Lockshin and Zakeri, 1990).

The *pacemaker theory* assumes that a biological clock within the hypothalamus is set to reduce signals to the pituitary. When the clock goes off, the body's hormone balance is upset and aging begins.

The *immunological theory* assumes that the aging program works through the immune system. When aging starts, the immune system begins to attack the body and also has trouble recognizing foreign substances and abnormal cells, which it normally destroys.

The last five theories focus on accumulated damage to the human body, especially individual cells. They assume that the wear and tear of living damages biological systems.

The *DNA-repair theory* assumes that the body's ability to repair DNA cannot keep up with the damage that occurs during metabolism or from contact with pollution or radiation. Aging occurs as the store of damaged DNA accumulates. In recent years, this theory has become less popular because no one yet has been able to support it in the laboratory (Tice and Setlow, 1985).

The *error catastrophe theory* assumes that increased biological damage is the result of errors built up during the synthesis of protein within the cells. During the repeated copying of the genetic message, errors accumulate until they reach catastrophic proportions and cells cannot function normally. This theory also has lost many adherents, because there is no supporting evidence (Reff, 1985).

The *cross-linkage theory* is based on the fact that changes during metabolism permanently alter the nature of protein molecules within body cells. The molecules form stable bonds and thus become rigid, so they cannot function properly or be repaired. Cross-linkage may be responsible for stiffened joints, hardened arteries, and some loss of skin elasticity, but most researchers believe that it makes only a minor contribution to aging (Perlmutter and Hall, 1992).

The *free-radical theory* is based on the fact that normal cell processes produce unstable molecules whose free electrons damage chromosomes and cell membranes and also combine to form compounds that initiate cross-linkages. Free radicals are self-propagating; each time they react with a molecule, they produce more free radicals (A. Spence, 1989).

The *cellular garbage theory* sees free radicals as one factor in aging, but it also assumes that other damaging substances build up within the cells and interfere with their function (A. Spence, 1989).

Each of these theories assumes that human beings have a natural life span, that is, a maximum number of years that a person can expect to live under the best conditions. Researchers estimate the human life span at around 110 years. The longest verified human life span is 120 years, set by Shigechijo Izumi, who died on February 21, 1986 ("Transition," 1986).

Typical Signs of Aging

If our natural life span is more than 100 years, we still have quite a way to go before the average person can expect to live that long (see Table 20.1). There are wide individual differences in the rate of aging, but eventually the typical changes catch up with us. The hair turns white and becomes sparse. The skin loses its natural moisture and elasticity, and wrinkles trace their patterns on the face. As the skeletal structure changes, people tend to get shorter, due to changes in posture, a thinning of cartilage in disks between the vertebra, and a loss of water in these disks (Perlmutter and Hall, 1992). Lack of exercise may accelerate muscle shrinkage, and joints may stiffen, impairing strength and movement. As calcium is lost, bones become spongy and fragile, so they break more easily. Fractures still knit, but it takes much longer for bones to repair themselves than it once did (A. Spence, 1989).

Within the older adult's body, other changes take

TABLE 20.1   PROJECTED LIFE EXPECTANCY AT AGE 65 (IN YEARS), 1900–2050

Base Year	Both Sexes	Males	Females
1900	11.9	11.5	12.2
1950	13.9	12.8	15.0
1960	14.3	12.8	15.8
1970	15.2	13.1	17.0
1980	16.4	14.1	18.3
1985	16.8	14.6	18.6
1990	17.2	15.0	19.5
2000	NA	15.7	20.5
2050	NA	17.4	23.1

The number of years one can expect to live after reaching the age of 65 have increased steadily since 1900, and researchers predict a continued increase.

Source: National Center for Health Statistics, 1986; G. Spencer, 1984; U.S. Bureau of the Census, 1992.

place. These invisible changes have a profound effect on a person's ability to adapt to stress and change. In healthy, active people, the heart works as well as it ever did when they are resting. But when they are exposed to the stress of exercise or emotional upset, the heart does not react as fast or as well as it did in earlier years (Lakatta, 1990). Afterward, the older heart takes longer to return to a normal heartbeat. Even during mild exertion, the circulatory system no longer carries the blood as well as it once did. As arterial walls stiffen and become less elastic, circulation slows and blood pressure may rise. Less air can be drawn into the lungs with each breath, a condition that leads to shortness of breath and discomfort after exercise.

Changes in sexual response that were apparent during middle age continue in the later years of life, with orgasmic contractions becoming fewer and less intense but remaining just as pleasurable (Weg, 1983b). Despite the promise of continued pleasure, a majority of men report impotence by the age of 75 (Harman and Talbert,

1985). Although psychological factors are responsible for some cases, physiological factors become more prevalent with each passing year. Any disease or disorder that·affects nerve pathways or blood supply to the penis can lead to impotence. Among the major factors associated with impotence in men and reduced sexual responsiveness in women are chronic disease, drugs, malnutrition, and fatigue (Weg, 1983b). As we will see, however, many older adults continue to enjoy sexual relations long into later adulthood.

About a third of older people complain that they sleep badly, but most spend seven to eight hours out of every twenty-four in sleep, just as younger adults do. The perception of poor sleep may arise because of changed sleep patterns and a decrease in the quality of sleep. Older adults spend less time in the deepest sleep stage and tend to wake during the night. They may make up for this deprivation with naps during the day, but, as we saw in Chapter 19, their fragmented sleep often produces periods of drowsiness during the day (G. Richardson, 1990). Among a group of middle-class adults between the ages of 65 and 95, the average adult slept eight hours and eighteen minutes when sleep was recorded in the home (Ancoli-Israel et al., 1985).

Insomnia is not a normal accompaniment of aging, but it may be caused by depression, too much caffeine or alcohol, or the use of sleeping pills. The pills interfere with sleep because (1) a person builds up a tolerance for the drug, becoming dependent on it, and (2) the drug seems to increase the incidence of apnea (in which breathing stops for at least ten seconds) and irregular heartbeat. Older adults who have trouble sleeping may find that they sleep more deeply and wake less frequently if they spend less time in bed, avoid daytime naps, and stop using sleeping pills (Woodruff, 1985).

How Much Physical Decline Is Inevitable?

When researchers report that older adults tend to have fragile bones, or high blood pressure, or little stamina, we generally assume that these results are the inevitable accompaniments of age. Yet most of these studies include many adults who suffer from some degenerative disease. But as noted earlier, some of the early studies that cast a pall over the prospect of aging were done in institutions, where nearly *all* the subjects were frail or ill.

As we saw in Chapter 18, hidden disease, disuse, and abuse probably are responsible for a majority of the changes that we assume are a natural part of aging.

These environmentally induced changes are known as **secondary aging,** and because they correlate with age, they make it difficult to establish the normal course of aging. The aged, weathered, wrinkled skin that we take for granted is primarily the result of exposure to sun and wind. Osteoporosis was once believed to be inevitable, but a diet deficient in calcium and a lack of exercise may be critical to its development. Women between the ages of 69 and 95 who participated in regular exercise sessions over a three-year period had a 4.2 percent *increase* in bone density (Buskirk, 1985). Women who did not exercise lost 2.5 percent of their bone density in the same period. Emphysema was once thought to be part of normal aging. Today researchers know that, like lung cancer, it is caused by smoking and other types of environmental damage.

Researchers have discovered that many of the physiological changes once assumed to be part of primary aging, such as increases in blood pressure, body weight, and serum cholesterol level, accompany aging in prosperous industrial countries but not in traditional herding or agricultural societies (Rowe and Kahn, 1987). A diet that is high in fiber and low in saturated fat (typical of most traditional societies) has been connected with lowered rates of heart disease, hypertension, cancer, and diabetes (Hallfrisch et al., 1988; Monmaney, 1988; Schafer et al., 1989). In fact, the "carbohydrate intolerance" responsible for age-related increases in diabetes does not appear among physically trained older adults of normal weight (Rowe and Kahn, 1987). Regular exercise prevents muscle atrophy, improves joint mobility, increases respiratory endurance, improves circulation, and reduces the risk of heart disease. Yet many of today's older adults do not understand the value of exercise and believe that it is dangerous for the old to be active. Actually, "take it easy" probably is the worst advice an old person can get.

During later adulthood, the chronic conditions of secondary aging become more prevalent. More than 80 percent of adults older than 65 have at least one chronic condition, and many have two or more (U.S. Senate Special Committee on Aging, 1987–1988). The most prevalent ailments are arthritis, hypertension, impaired hearing, and heart conditions. Women are more likely than men to suffer from arthritis, but men are more likely to develop heart conditions. Despite the prevalence of chronic, preventable conditions, most older adults lead a normal, active life. Some are remarkably productive even in their eighties and nineties (see the accompanying box, "Getting Older or Getting Better").

Older adults tend to think they should take it easy, but those who continue to exercise are likely to have a healthier—and longer—old age. *(Ulrike Welsch/Photo Researchers)*

GETTING OLDER OR GETTING BETTER?

Among the oldest Americans, those past the age of 80, is a group who seem twenty to thirty years younger than their age—at least as far as productivity is concerned. A look at their achievements provides ample proof that disengagement does not characterize all old people. It also assures us that life can be exciting, productive, creative, and full of meaning until the very end.

George Abbot At 92, this playwright-director wrote a book *(Try-Out)*; at 100, he directed a revival of a Broadway musical and completed writing a new play.

George Burns At 80, he won the Academy Award for best supporting actor; at 88, he starred in the film *Oh God! You Devil.* At 96, he was still performing and announced that he was booked to play The Palladium in London when he was 100.

Erik Erikson At 80, this psychoanalyst and influential theorist published a book that summed up his thoughts concerning development and proposed changes in Freud's psychosexual theory. At 84, he collaborated with his wife and a psychologist on a study of old age.

Ruth Gordon At 83, she won an Emmy Award; at 84, she appeared in the movie *Any Which Way You Can.* When she was 85, her book, *Shady Lady,* was published.

Alberta Hunter At 88, this talented jazz singer was not only giving occasional concerts but also drawing capacity crowds to her regular weekend performances at a Manhattan jazz club.

Harry Lieberman At 80, he began painting and kept it up until his death at the age of 106. His watercolors and oil paintings have been exhibited in museums and galleries across the country.

Odilon Long At 81, this former telephone company worker was the oldest Peace Corps volunteer in service. He taught vocational skills, such as welding and carpentry, in a remote area of southwest Haiti that had neither plumbing nor electricity.

Scott O'Dell At the age of 90, he finished the manuscript of his twenty-sixth book for children and the next day began work on his twenty-seventh. Although he did not begin writing for children until he was 61, he won national and international literary awards for his work.

Georgia O'Keeffe At the age of 90, this artist was still busy painting and sculpting. At the same age, she received the Presidential Medal of Honor. At 95, she had a solo exhibition of her work.

Pablo Picasso At 91, this painter was still at work, concentrating on drawings and prints. He continued to work in oils until he was 90. At the age of 79, he married for the last time.

Scott O'Dell *(Jim Kalett)*

Alberta Hunter *(AP/Wide World Photos)*

Theories and Issues of Later Adulthood

The early part of life is spent gathering experiences and increasing strength. During middle adulthood, the experience and strength are put to productive social use. The developmental tasks of the later years are personal. Older people's major task is to understand and accept their lives and to use their long experience to deal with personal changes or loss. During later adulthood, people face three separate issues. They must (1) adjust to decreasing physical strength and health, (2) adjust to retirement, and (3) come to terms with their own mortality.

Some older adults react to decreasing physical strength and health by becoming preoccupied with their physical condition; they focus on every ache and pain. Others seem to accept what cannot be changed and find enjoyment in their relationships with other people and in activities that do not require strength or stamina.

When they retire, people whose identity is based on their occupations face the problem of redefining themselves. Some may become demoralized. Some cultivate their other roles—spouse, grandparent—or find new ones.

Eventually, older adults must come to terms with their own mortality. Some face death with fear, some with anger and resentment, some with resignation. Others use the confrontation to find meaning in their lives, either from the way their influence will live on through their children or their contributions to society, from their part in a meaningful biological cycle, or from their religious convictions. When contemplating death, Florida Scott-Maxwell (1979), then in her eighties, wrote:

> *I feel the solemnity of death, and the possibility of some form of continuity. Death feels a friend because it will release us from the deterioration of which we cannot see the end. (p. 138)*

As people deal with these issues, their motivations may change in characteristic ways. Various aspects of the process have drawn the attention of theorists.

Erikson's Psychosocial Theory

When adults enter the final stage of life, said Erikson (1982), their task is to see their lives as whole and coherent. They need to accept their own life as they lived it, see meaning in it, and believe that they did the best they could have done under the circumstances. If they succeed at this task, they will have developed **ego integrity.** Ego integrity can be gained only after a struggle with despair. When despair dominates, the person fears death and, although he or she may express disdain for life, continues to yearn for a chance to live life over again. When integrity dominates, the person possesses the strength of old age, which is wisdom. With wisdom, the adult is able to accept limitations. The wise adult knows when to accept change and when to oppose it, when to sit quietly and when to fight.

The passage into later adulthood does not end a person's generativity. As the ranks of older adults grow larger, Erikson predicts that older people will remain involved in matters of the world much longer (Erikson and Hall, 1987). He sees later adulthood as a more productive and creative period than it has been in the past— one in which the 80-year-old artist, writer, or musician will no longer seem exceptional.

Jung's Concept of Later Adulthood

Jung saw older adults as still striving to develop the self, for he believed that the search for an integrated personality rarely was completed. Within each person, he saw conflicting forces and tendencies that needed to be recognized and reconciled. Part of this recognition is reflected in the tendency for each gender to express traits usually associated with the other. As we saw in Chapter 18, Jung proposed that this tendency first appeared in midlife, and he saw the expression of hidden gender potential as increasing during late adulthood.

During later adulthood, men's expression of femininity and women's expression of masculinity are accompanied by another attempt to reconcile conflicting tendencies. Jung proposed that within each person were an orientation toward the external world, which he called **extraversion,** and an orientation toward the inner, subjective world, which he called **introversion.** During young adulthood and most of middle adulthood, people express their extraversion. Once the family is grown and the career is over, women and men are free to cultivate their own concerns, reflect on their values, and explore their inner world. "For a young person," wrote Jung (1969), "it is almost a sin, or at least a danger, to be too preoccupied with himself; but for the aging person it is a duty and a necessity to devote serious attention to himself" (p. 399). This change of orientation leads to a steadily developing trend toward introversion among older adults.

Disengagement Theory

During the 1960s, many researchers assumed that the typical pattern of adjustment to old age could best be described as disengagement. According to **disengagement theory,** as people's capacities changed, so did their preferences. By choice they gradually withdrew from social roles and decreased their involvements with others. As Jung had proposed, they became highly introverted, not in order to reconcile the conflicting aspects of personality but in order to prepare for incapacity and death. At the same time, society gradually withdrew from the old and handed over to the young the roles and responsibilities once held by the old. Disengagement supposedly was a universal, biologically based process, welcomed by the old and highly satisfactory to both older adults and society. This theory, proposed by Elaine Cumming and William Henry (1961), came out of a longitudinal study of older adults in Kansas City. Cumming and Henry believed that older adults who disengaged would be more satisfied with life than those who remained engaged and active.

The trouble with this view was that although older adults lose some social roles as they age, most do not become disengaged. Anthropological research showed that in some cultures, older adults remained highly involved with both society and other people (Featherman, 1981). Several longitudinal studies showed no evidence of general disengagement and no sign that disengagement made later life more satisfying. In a study at Duke University, it was the highly active adults, not the disengaged, who were most satisfied with life (Palmore, 1970). Such findings led other researchers to propose that **activity theory** described the preferred adjustment to old age and that life satisfaction hinged on social integration and high involvement.

Today's view is that each theory is right—for some people (Maddox and Campbell, 1985). Although socially involved older adults are more likely than others to say that they are satisfied, some disengaged adults are just as content. It seems that there are many ways to adapt to aging and that each is a continuation of a person's way of adapting in young and middle adulthood. Disengaged older adults were disengaged midlife adults and disengaged young adults.

Issues in Later Adulthood

Just as it is easy to confuse the effects of primary aging with the effects of environmentally induced secondary aging, so it is tempting to fall back on aging as the explanation for any behavior that seems prevalent among older adults. As we saw in Chapter 1, however, each cohort is influenced by historical events and the social norms and practices of its time. Events that affect the whole society (depression, war, assassinations, prosperity), politics, and technological advances influence the way people feel about many issues. Because all the members of a cohort feel the impact of general circumstances at the same point in development, the shared experience and perspective tend to affect their attitudes similarly.

Cohort effects on attitudes are especially plain in the area of politics. People are supposed to start out liberal, filled with ideas of changing society. As they grow older, they become conservative, either more content with society the way it is or convinced that efforts to change it are fruitless. Polls consistently show, for example, that older adults are more likely than the young to oppose abortion, changes in women's roles, birth control, pornography, and homosexuality and to stand with conservatives on such issues as capital punishment, gun control, and protection of the rights of the accused (R. Hudson and Strate, 1985).

This trend toward conservatism is supposedly responsible for the tendency of older adults to support Republican rather than Democratic candidates and policies. Indeed, political polls indicated that during the late 1940s and 1950s, the proportion of Republicans among various age groups (from 21 to 65 years old) steadily increased with age. But when researchers analyzed these same polls by cohort, they discovered that there was no drift toward the Republican party with age (Cutler, 1983). The proportion of Republicans in each cohort fluctuated, presumably in response to historical events, and the preponderance of Republicans among older voters seemed to be the results of their earlier socialization.

People in later adulthood during the 1950s were socialized before the Great Depression of the 1930s, when the Republican party dominated the political process. As a result of their shared experience, they saw conservatism as sound fiscal policy, limited spending, and a balanced budget. To them, liberalism meant big government and socialism. By contrast, midlife adults were socialized during the Great Depression and World War II. Their shared experience led them to see conservatism in terms of free enterprise, limited government, and a resistance to change and new ideas. To them, liberalism meant an acceptance of change, new ideas, and progressive policy (R. Hudson and Strate, 1985).

Socialization continues to affect political outlooks. As

more liberal cohorts have moved into later adulthood, Republican strength among older adults has waned. As the country swung toward conservatism in the 1980s, younger adults became more likely than older adults to consider themselves Republicans (B. Jacobs, 1990).

Because each cohort responds to general trends in society, when the country as a whole shifts to conservatism, even those socialized in a time of liberalism may show some shift in this direction. And age itself may affect political attitudes toward specific issues. When the issue affects the cohort's self-interest, cohort members are likely to change more or less than average, depending on the way the issue affects them. We can see this effect in older adults' strong support for Social Security and young adults' support for day care.

Personality, Self-Concept, and Control

Instead of becoming more conservative and cranky with age, older adults in one longitudinal study became more open-minded, frank, and cheerful over a period of fourteen years (D. Field and Millsap, 1991). As they moved into late old age, more than half showed no change in self-esteem or satisfaction with life, and about one-third showed significant increases. Cross-sectional studies consistently show that self-esteem of older people is at least as high as the self-esteem of younger people, with about half the studies showing higher levels of self-esteem among older adults (Bengston, Reedy, and Gordon, 1985).

Although political events may affect all cohorts similarly, the change will be heightened or diminished depending on each cohort's self-interest; for example, a major goal of the Gray Panthers is the establishment of a national health service. *(Paul Conklin/Photo Edit)*

Such findings at first may seem puzzling. For most older adults, the fading of youthful beauty, the withdrawal of productive work roles, and the ageism they may encounter apparently does not damage their self-esteem, self-concept, well-being, or happiness. How can we explain this paradox? Some developmentalists believe that age has little effect because old people do not feel "old." Studies indicate that most older adults think of themselves as younger than their actual age (R. Goldsmith and Heiens, 1992), with about two-thirds identifying themselves as "middle-aged" or "young" (R. Ward, 1984b) (see Table 20.2). As long as older adults refuse to see themselves as old, they do not have to accept the negative status that is often associated with age. Social comparison may protect older adults from the stigma associated with age. In their daily involvement with their friends, they do not stand out as "older"; in fact, they may even seem young or middle-aged in comparison to slightly older friends or those in poor health. Older adults who still have a living parent—and an increasing proportion of those in their sixties and seventies do—are protected against the feeling that they are part of the "oldest" generation.

The key to continued satisfaction and well-being in later adulthood may be a complex self-concept, consisting of many social roles (such as spouse or grandparent), self-conceptions (such as gardener or bridge player), and aspects of personality (such as independent or competent) (Markus and Herzog, in press). Adults who are most satisfied may be those whose self-concept

still includes desired possible selves, which, as we saw in Chapter 16, affect motivation and behavior. These desired changes represent goals, and researchers have found that, among 70-year-olds, those with life goals were usually healthy and had a sense of well-being (Holahan, 1988).

A final factor that may bolster the satisfaction of older adults is their view of development across the life span. Among middle-class men and women in Germany, for example, adults of all ages expected gains in various positive attributes, such as wisdom and dignity, to continue until about the age of 85 (Heckhausen, Dixon, and Baltes, 1989). In addition, older adults expected increases in more attributes as the years passed than did the young.

Culture, ethnic group, and social status may have a direct impact on these views. Most older adults in the United States, for example, fear becoming dependent on their children, and those who see themselves in this situation may tend to become less satisfied with their lives. In India, however, where dependence on children is considered a prime means of successful aging, such a development may seem much less important (L. Thomas and Chambers, 1989). Yet the determination to be independent may work to the older person's advantage. When researchers compared the ways young adults in the United States and India viewed the old, they discovered that Americans had a more positive view of old people than did Indians (Williams et al., 1987). Young adults in the United States not only liked

TABLE 20.2   HOW OLDER AMERICANS SEE THEMSELVES

	SUBJECTIVE AGE (% OF RESPONDENTS)			
Actual Age (Years)	I feel at least 10 years younger than I am.	I look at least 10 years younger than I am.	I do things as if I were at least 10 years younger than I am.	My interests are those of people at least 10 years younger than I am.
60–69	77	73	89	82
70–79	72	83	86	78
80–89	86	100	100	100

Middle-class whites and African-Americans consistently rated their subjective feeling, appearance, actions, and interests as comparable to those of people younger than themselves.

Source: Data from R. Goldsmith and Heiens, 1992.

older adults more than did young adults in India but also saw older people as more nurturing and less critical and demanding.

Gender Differences in Aging

Theories of adult development predict that traditional gender differences in self-concept narrow as people move into later adulthood. Most studies support this view, indicating that men and women are least alike during late adolescence and early adulthood and become similar, even androgynous, in later years (L. Cohn, 1991). Many older men (regardless of social class) see themselves as fairly cooperative and nurturant and as less dominant than they once did. Many older women see themselves as more assertive, less dependent, more capable of solving problems, and more authoritative at home than when they were younger (Bengston, Reedy, and Gordon, 1985). As we saw in Chapter 16, Gutmann (1987) attributes this shift to the ending of the parental imperative. Another factor may be just as important. As men retire, they abruptly lose power and influence in the public sphere. They may indeed feel less dominant. Older women, whose lives traditionally have been spent cultivating family relationships, are freed from the restrictions of child care but retain their emotional power over their grown children (C. Fry, 1985). In one study, retirement indeed led to greater androgyny and greater egalitarianism among married couples (Calasanti, 1988).

When self-concept and self-esteem suffer, older men and women tend to respond in different ways. Men are more likely than women to abuse alcohol, whereas older women, at least those younger than 80, are more likely than men to become depressed (NIH Consensus Development Conference, 1991). The rate of major depression among nursing home residents is especially high—up to 25 percent, compared with 3 percent among older adults living in the community. Depression is less common among older African-Americans than among older whites, and African-American men seem less vulnerable than African-American women. In a study conducted in Nashville, medical problems and low self-esteem were associated with depression in both genders (Husaini et al., 1991). Older African-American women, however, also became depressed as their social support networks constricted, but men did not. The researchers suggest that traditional socialization practices, which emphasize social relationships for women and self-reliance for men, may be responsible for this differ-

ence. Yet some researchers have found that once people reach their eighties, both mild and severe episodes of depression become more common among men than among women (Gurland et al., 1980).

Depressed people are sometimes suicidal, and this shift may help explain why suicide rates are highest among the oldest white men but drop steadily across old age among white women. Once white men pass the age of 84, they kill themselves at the rate of 66.3 per 100,000—thirteen times as often as the oldest white women and nearly four times as often as the oldest African-American men (U.S. Bureau of the Census, 1990). Some researchers have noted a correlation between the tendency to resort to prayer and low suicide rates (R. Gibson, 1986). White men are the least likely to respond to worrisome events with prayer, and African-American women are the most likely to pray in time of trouble. Whether or not prayer actually can be a shield against suicide, in recent years the suicide rate among men in both racial groups has increased sharply, but there has been little change in women's suicide rates (see Table 20.3). In addition to being depressed, most men who have suicidal thoughts are unmarried, have few friends, and do not believe in an afterlife (Kastenbaum, 1985). As we will see, having friends or some other kind of social support makes it much easier for older adults to cope with stress.

Coping with Stress

Unrelieved stress or stress that is beyond an adult's coping ability can erode self-esteem. It also can be responsible for the deterioration of physical and mental health. Because gender, marital status, ethnic background, socioeconomic level, and education can affect the way an event is perceived and how a person will react, blanket predictions about the effects of various stressful events are impossible. In addition, as we saw in Chapter 18, it is the way a person responds to stress and not the stress itself that affects the body, self-concept, and self-esteem.

Older adults actually encounter fewer stressful events than the young. But many of the stresses of younger adults' lives, such as leaving home, getting married, and buying a house, bring challenge and reward. Many of the stresses faced by older adults are primarily negative: poor health, reduced income, death of a spouse. In addition, an aging immune system makes older adults more vulnerable to the effects of stress and thus more likely to respond by developing a disease

TABLE 20.3 **SUICIDE RATES (PER 100,000 INDIVIDUALS), 1970–1989**

Age (Years)	WHITE			AFRICAN-AMERICAN		
	1970	1980	1989	1970	1980	1989
MEN						
20–24	19.3	27.8	26.8	18.7	20.0	23.7
25–34	19.9	25.6	24.9	19.2	21.8	22.0
35–44	23.3	23.5	23.8	12.6	15.6	18.1
45–54	29.5	24.2	24.2	13.8	12.0	10.9
55–64	35.0	25.8	26.6	10.6	11.7	10.4
65–74	38.7	32.5	35.1	8.7	11.1	15.7
75–84	45.5	45.5	55.3	8.9	10.5	15.4
>84	45.8	52.8	71.9	8.7	18.9	**
WOMEN						
20–24	5.7	5.9	4.3	4.9	3.1	3.4
25–34	9.0	7.5	5.9	5.7	4.1	3.7
35–44	13.0	9.1	7.1	3.7	4.6	3.9
45–54	13.5	10.2	8.0	3.7	2.8	3.0
55–64	12.3	9.1	7.9	2.0	2.3	2.5
65–74	9.6	7.0	6.4	2.9	1.7	**
75–84	7.2	5.7	6.3	1.7	1.4	**
>84	5.8	5.8	6.2	2.8	*	*

*Represents or rounds to zero.
**Base figure too small to provide reliable statistic.

Source: U.S. Bureau of the Census, 1992.

(Rodin, 1986). The strain is magnified if they already suffer from some degenerative disease, such as heart trouble or diabetes.

If events mount and if older adults' sense of control has been seriously eroded, stress can become especially destructive. According to Judith Rodin (1986), as people age, the relation between a sense of control and the quality of their health increases. A sense of control can reduce the destructive effects of stress in three ways. First, when people believe that they are not helpless but have some control, the power of unpleasant events over their lives is diminished. Second, a sense of control decreases the physiological responses to stress, lowers blood pressure and heart rate, reduces gastric ulceration, and lowers the level of factors in the blood that promote the formation of plaques in the arteries. Animal studies indicate that uncontrollable stress reduces the immune system's ability to fight cancer (Laudenslager et al., 1983). Finally, people who feel that they have some control over their environments are more likely to take actions that improve or maintain their health. They are more likely to seek health-related information, care for themselves, adhere to medical routines, and interact actively with health-care providers. In one study, adults who felt in control were more likely to have used problem-solving strategies during the most stressful episode of the past month than were adults who felt that they lacked control (Aldwin, 1991).

Although a sense of control is extremely valuable, there are situations in which it can be detrimental. When people are given control but lack the skills or information needed to handle a situation, the sense of control can itself cause stress (Bandura, 1986). Control can also produce stress and affect health adversely when people are made to feel guilty about the development of health-related problems (Rodin, 1986). These factors cause some older people to become anxiety-ridden when given responsibility for themselves and their health.

Although, as we have seen, older adults report fewer stressful events than do the young, their perceptions may be the result of their coping strategies. In one study, young adults responded to stress with a greater proportion of active techniques, focusing on the problem itself; they looked for ways to solve it, either by themselves or with outside help. Older adults, however, used a greater proportion of passive techniques, distancing themselves from the situation, accepting responsibility for it, or reappraising the problem in a positive fashion ("I found new faith") (Folkman et al., 1987). The methods favored by older adults serve to redefine the situation and may short-circuit the stress process.

Social support is another factor that helps to reduce stress. Networks of family, friends, and acquaintances not only help older adults maintain their social identity but also provide emotional support, material aid, information, and services (Antonucci, 1985). There are ethnic differences in these networks. The support system of white adults tend to focus on close family members,

but the morale of older African-Americans is bolstered by a far-reaching informal system that includes distant relatives as well as friends who have been redefined as kin and who function in that capacity (Gibson, 1986; C. Johnson and Barer, 1990).

Older adults without families often find support among others like themselves. When researchers followed the older residents of New York City's single-room-occupancy hotels over a three-year period, they found that social support helped hotel residents cope with the stresses of deteriorating neighborhoods, family illness, muggings, personal injury due to crime, and financial problems (C. Cohen, Teresi, and Holmes, 1985). The support both cushioned the impact of stressful events on the older adults and had a direct effect on their health.

In another study, Neil Krause (1986) traced the way in which social support eased stress among older adults in the Galveston, Texas, area. Caring relationships, material aid, and the provision of information enabled adults to avoid depression in a variety of situations. Such social support was ineffective only in the case of financial problems. Later, Krause (1991) found that stress in the form of chronic financial strain and fear of crime tended to promote isolation among a national sample of older adults. Financial problems and fear of crime seemed to foster a general distrust of others, which in turn eroded personal relationships and eventually left some older adults without anyone to call on for advice or assistance.

Social isolation is highly detrimental; older adults who feel lonely, unappreciated, and friendless tend to be dissatisfied with their lives (Steinkamp and Kelly, 1987). But as we saw in Chapter 10, support networks do not have to be large to be effective. Among elderly condominium owners in a high-crime area of Miami Beach who were relocated to make way for a redevelopment project, the presence of a single close personal relationship bolstered emotional well-being during the disruption of their lives and affected the degree of satisfaction they felt afterward (Levitt et al., 1987). A sense of control also affected well-being and satisfaction among these adults, indicating that control and social support are equally important.

Work and Retirement

The transition from work to retirement is a major change, and one that we would expect to be stressful. It

Friends play an important part in social networks and increase the well-being and satisfaction of older adults. *(Paul Conklin/Monkmeyer)*

may involve the loss of income, occupational identity, social status, associates, and the daily structure of time and activities (P. Robinson, Coberly, and Paul, 1985). But among the men in a longitudinal study of adulthood, 70 percent of those who retired during the year found the transition "not at all" or "only a little" stressful (Bosse et al., 1991). The general level of stress among men who were still at work (which included middle-aged as well as older adults) was higher than that among men who retired.

In the United States, most people seem eager to retire. The proportion of older men in the work force has been dropping steadily ever since Social Security and private pensions were established. At the turn of the century, about 68 percent of men and 9 percent of women older than 65 were still employed. Fifty years later, when Social Security covered a large part of the labor force, about 50 percent of men and 10 percent of women were still working after 65. Today's older workers have virtually abandoned the labor market: only about 16 percent of the men and 8 percent of the women are still working (U.S. Bureau of the Census, 1991).

A large proportion of today's retirees left the labor force before they were 65. Among men, early retirement has been on the increase. At a time when more women between the ages of 55 and 64 are in the labor force than ever before, the proportion of male workers has declined rapidly.

The Decision to Retire

Why do some people retire early, others retire "on time" at 65, and a small group keep working as long as they are physically able? Many factors go into the decision to retire, and not all are within the worker's control.

Early Retirement

A major factor in the surge toward early retirement is the availability of Social Security payments at the age of 62 and even earlier payments from private pension funds. In 1978, 68 percent of all eligible older workers retired early (R. Ward, 1984a), even though they knew that their Social Security payments would be substantially reduced. When workers choose to retire before the age of 65, their health, their money, and the availability of employment are major factors in the decision. The largest group of early retirees are in poor health. Social Security makes it possible for them to leave the labor force, and work has become so burdensome that they are willing to accept reduced, often inadequate, benefits. Another group of early retirees enjoy good health, have no financial worries, and have positive attitudes toward retirement (P. Robinson, Coberly, and Paul, 1985). Pat Christy, a New York State junior high school teacher who retired at the age of 56, is a member of this group. After three years, she was still enthusiastic about her decision and said that she was "born to retire" (G. Collins, 1986).

A third group of early retirees have left the labor market reluctantly. Although they prefer to work, they have lost their jobs and are unable to find others (P. Robinson, Coberly, and Paul, 1985). When unemployment checks stop, they become discouraged and apply for Social Security benefits.

On-Time Retirement

Although health heavily influences the decision to retire early, it does not seem to play a major role in the retirement plans of people who work until they are 65. Although retired workers queried in *cross-sectional* studies often report that health was a major factor in their decision to retire on time, these workers may retrospectively exaggerate the influence of their health when recalling the decision. Poor health is a socially acceptable reason for retiring, and it denies the notion that a worker has been rejected by his or her employer. The lack of connection between health and on-time retirement became clear when *longitudinal* studies revealed no connection between health and retirement at the time workers left the labor force (Palmore, George, and Fillenbaum, 1982).

Late Retirement

The majority of workers who stay on the job after the age of 65 are either middle-class professionals or people who own small businesses (Quinn and Burkhauser, 1990). The rest keep working because they cannot afford to retire. In one survey of people past 65 who were still employed, 46 percent of the women and 39 percent of the men said that the need for money kept them on the job (G. Collins, 1986). Among the older men and women in the Social Security Administration's Retirement History Study, 25 percent took a new job (either part or full time) after they retired from their major occupations (Quinn, Burkhauser, and Myers, 1990).

Those most likely to embark on new jobs tended to come from both ends of the economic spectrum: they were either poor or wealthy.

Among African-Americans, the concept of retirement may have a different meaning from the one held by most white adults. A considerable proportion of older African-Americans are not working, but they do not consider themselves retired. Either they have never held a full-time job or they still work sporadically (R. Gibson, 1991). Because their work history lacks continuity, the line between work and nonwork has become blurred for them. African-Americans who do not report themselves as "retired" may be excluded from studies of retirement, perhaps producing distorted pictures of retirement. These "nonretired" adults are more likely than other African-Americans to have physical disabilities and less likely to have retirement incomes or to feel financially secure. The concept of retirement may be as difficult to apply to older Hispanic Americans, who also have sporadic work histories and little retirement income (Zsembik and Singer, 1990).

The Nature of Retirement

After studying retired workers, researchers have concluded that retirement is not an isolated event but a process that progresses through a series of predictable, but not rigid, phases (Atchley, 1976). Some people skip some of the phases and repeat others (see Table 20.4). First is the *preretirement phase,* in which people begin to separate themselves emotionally from their jobs and may fantasize about the nature of retired life. Second is the *honeymoon phase,* which begins when workers leave their jobs and try to live out their preretirement fantasies: a life of leisure that is one long vacation. Although for some the honeymoon lasts for years, among 2000 men in a longitudinal study, it seemed sweetest during the first six months (Ekerdt, Bosse, and Levkoff, 1985).

Eventually, the honeymoon is over. Those whose fantasies were unrealistic now move into the *disenchantment phase.* They feel empty and let down, and they may even become depressed. Gardening every day is less fun than gardening on weekends, just as spending the entire day with a spouse may be less gratifying than having a relationship that is confined to evenings and weekends. Among retirees in the longitudinal study, life satisfaction and levels of physical activity were lowest at the end of the first year (Ekerdt, Bosse, and Levkoff, 1985). As disenchanted retirees give up their fantasies and search for realistic choices that offer moderate lev-

TABLE 20.4   PHASES OF RETIREMENT

Preretirement	Emotional preparation for retirement
Honeymoon	Actualization of pre-retirement fantasies
Disenchantment	Lessened satisfaction
Reorientation	Search for realistic choices
Stability	Successful adaptation to retirement
Termination	Return to work or assumption of sick and disabled role

Source: After Atchley, 1976.

els of satisfaction, they move into the *reorientation phase.* This seemed to occur toward the end of the second retirement year among men in the longitudinal study (Ekerdt, Bosse, and Levkoff, 1985).

When individuals find a predictable, satisfying life style, they have entered the *stability phase.* They are self-sufficient adults who have mastered the retirement role, adapting to retirement in a way that suits them. Workers who retire with realistic expectations of retirement may move directly into this phase from the honeymoon phase.

Finally comes the *termination phase,* in which people move out of the retirement role. Some go back to work. For most, however, the role ends when they become frail and ill; no longer able to care for themselves, they must assume the sick and disabled role.

Once into the stability phase, most people enjoy their retirement. In a longitudinal study of 5000 men, 80 percent of retirees said that retirement fulfilled or exceeded their expectations, and 75 percent said that were they given the chance to do it over again, they would retire at the same age—or perhaps even earlier (Parnes, 1981). Only about 13 percent of whites and 17 percent of African-Americans said they had retired too soon. Few studies have focused on women, but an analysis of Social Security data indicates that a substantial minority of retired unmarried women (17 percent) live on incomes that are near or below the official poverty

line (Logue, 1991). These women had worked steadily, and all had spent at least ten years in the same job. Financial burdens were distributed unequally; those who were African-American, less-educated, or suffered activity limitations were most likely to find themselves living in poverty. As most research has indicated, people who are healthy and have enough money to meet their needs find retirement the most satisfying.

A key to the effects of retirement on life satisfaction is whether the experience adds some new element to life. Those who retire *to* a new life are likely to find retirement more satisfying than those who retire *from* a job.

Marriage in Later Adulthood

The most significant event in many marriages between older adults is the man's retirement. A man suddenly finds himself without his occupation and shorn of his daily contacts with coworkers. Yet most husbands look forward to their retirement more than their wives do. Wives who do not work outside the home must adjust to having their husbands home all day. Among 400 couples, 42 percent of the husbands (all retired teachers) discovered that retirement had created problems in their marriages (N. Keating and Cole, 1980). The wives took a dimmer view: 78 percent reported marital problems, which included decreased personal freedom, too much togetherness, and too many demands on their time.

Most studies of retirement have looked at couples in which the woman has not worked steadily. When working wives retire, they face the same loss of income and social contacts as husbands do, but they lose independence as well. The thought of losing that independence may make them more reluctant to give up an occupation, especially if they began their careers in midlife and are still absorbed in their work. As occupationally absorbed wives indicate their reluctance to tie their retirement to their husbands' age, male retirement may involve additional stress for many couples. Some older couples may adjust to the changes in marital roles when their marriages enter the stage of "husband retirement" (M. Riley and Riley, 1986). For example, when her husband retired, 58-year-old Peggy Zeitler kept working as a secretary at Long Island Community College. This led to a role reversal in the Zeitler family. Her husband, a former bank vice president, said, "She's just not ready to retire. But it works out well for both of us. It's the first time in 40 years that I can stay in bed and wave goodbye to my wife" (G. Collins, 1986, C1).

Regardless of whether one or both spouses have occupations, retirement brings new demands: worries over money, disagreements about moving into a smaller house or an apartment, or health problems (Stinnett, Carter, and Montgomery, 1972). Yet most married couples who reach later adulthood together probably have lived through enough stress to weather this period. Their major conflicts—over divisions of responsibility and power, sex, money, children, and in-laws—have been settled. Most couples who were unable to work out solutions to such problems divorced earlier.

Many couples continue to enjoy sexual activity well into their later years. Among older adults in a national sample, 53 percent of married persons past the age of

Contrary to popular belief, sexual interest and activity can continue as long as life itself; all that's required is an interested—and interesting—partner. *(Wayne Miller/ Magnum)*

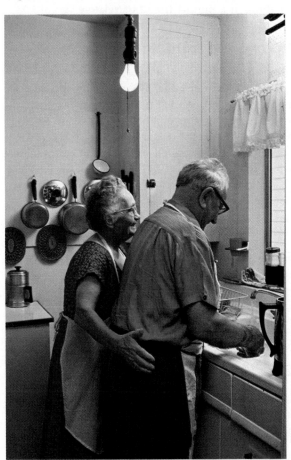

60 reported sexual relations at least once during the past month, as did 24 percent of those older than 75 (Marsiglio and Donnelly, 1991). Among those who reported having sex during the preceding month, the majority did so slightly more often than four times. Factors that tended to predict sexual activity were good health, self-esteem, feelings of competence, and shared activities. Ethnicity had no effect on the presence or frequency of sexual activity. Among couples in the Duke Longitudinal Study, the husband's declining health and lack of interest were the primary reasons given for reducing or stopping sexual activity (Pfeiffer, Verwoerdt, and Davis, 1972). In only a quarter of the cases did the wife's lack of interest play a major part in the decision.

Older people often tend to find gentler, caring lovemaking more important than a focus on orgasm. Sexual activity becomes less a matter of compelling passion and more an expression of person-oriented intimacy (Weg, 1983b). Erik Erikson describes it as a "generalized sexuality, which has something to do with play and the importance of the moment" (Erikson and Hall, 1987, p. 132). One 70-year-old woman described sexuality as "not so much how powerful the orgasm is or how many orgasms you have. It's just touching and being together and loving" (Kotre and Hall, 1990, p. 331).

Because society does not see older people as sexy, interested in sex, or sexually active, some healthy adults give up sexual activity during their later years. For these people, the sexless older years are the result of a self-fulfilling prophecy; they lose their desire for sex because they are "supposed to." In some cases, adults who have thought of sex as a duty, or as unpleasant, use their age as an acceptable excuse for ending sexual relations.

Whether or not they continue regular sexual activity, most older couples describe their marriages as "happy" or "very happy." Only newlyweds find their marriages as satisfying as older adults do. Most adults in their seventies and eighties describe their marriages as if they had been blissful from the beginning. But a study that has followed adults for more than half a century indicates that people tend to "rewrite" their memories of the early years. When researchers looked back over years of interviews with adults who were now between the ages of 75 and 95, they discovered that couples who consistently spoke of lifelong affection, supportiveness, and understanding frequently had gone through periods of bitter strife and some had even considered divorce (Erikson, Erikson, and Kivnick, 1986). The researchers suggest that the present satisfaction these adults received from their marriages had colored their memories so that they recalled only the good aspects of bygone years.

Divorce and Remarriage

When partners who have been married for forty years divorce, they are likely to show much more psychological stress than younger people in a similar situation. Over the years, they have become firmly entrenched in the established social order as a married couple (Burrus-Bammel and Bammel, 1985). The loss of marital roles as well as occupational roles can disrupt their sense of identity.

The number of older adults who divorce is rising. The government keeps no statistics on over-65 divorces, but 2 percent of all divorces involve women older than 60 (Uhlenberg, Cooney, and Boyd, 1990). Why should an older couple sever deep-seated bonds after forty years of marriage? Among a group of older divorcees in Michigan, women who had initiated the divorce said that their husbands were either chronic alcoholics who refused to get help, tyrants, or womanizers (Cain, 1982). But in most cases, the men had initiated the divorce in order to marry another woman. These men had been deeply involved in the aggressive pursuit of their careers, and their decision to leave the marriage usually coincided with their retirement.

The women in this study, socialized to see marriage as their lifetime occupation, had based their primary identity on their marriage role. When their marriages failed, some felt that their entire lives were failures. After reacting with shock, dismay, and denial, most set about building a new life structure. But as one 65-year-old woman said, "Divorce after 60 is a double whammy. You're too old to start all over, and you're too young to toss it all in" (Cain, 1982, p. 90). Women who adapted best generally had a confidante with whom they could share their problems and fears. When married children lived nearby, the reminder of the women's maternal and grandmaternal roles also helped.

Unless divorced men and women remarry, their prospects for satisfactory lives diminish, and their levels of psychological stress rise (Burrus-Bammel and Bammel, 1985). Divorced older men generally stay single for only a short time. As we have seen, the intention to take a new partner is the deciding factor in many late adult divorces. But divorced older women rarely reenter the ranks of the married. Only a small proportion of women past 65 find new partners. Because there are 3.6 divorced, widowed, or single women for every man in this age group, there simply are not enough men to go around (U.S. Bureau of the Census, 1990).

Widowhood

Although most older men are married, the story of marriage in later adulthood has little relevance for the majority of older women. Because of men's shorter life span and because husbands are generally older than their wives, the ranks of husbands are depleted so rapidly that widowhood seems to be the "normal" situation of older women (see Figure 20.2). There are 8.3 million older widows in the United States, but only 1.7 million older widowers (U.S. Bureau of the Census, 1990). About 20 percent of older widowers remarry, but only 2 percent of older widows find a new partner (Bengston, Rosenthal, and Burton, 1990). When they do remarry, the new husband or wife is generally someone they knew before the first spouse died or someone they meet through a mutual friend or relative.

Recovering from Bereavement

The loss of a husband or wife is a source of intense emotional stress at any age. The surviving spouse goes through a lengthy period of **bereavement,** which typically moves through several phases (Weiss, 1988) (see Table 20.5). The initial response is usually *shock.* During this phase, the bereaved spouse experiences numbness and refuses to believe in the reality of the loss. The grief that characterizes the next phase, the first stage of actual bereavement, is one of *protest:* the grieving spouse is agitated, fearful, oppressed by intense pain,

TABLE 20.5   PHASES OF BEREAVEMENT

Initial response: Shock	Numbness, disbelief
Stage 1: Protest	Agitation, anxiety
Stage 2: Despair	Lethargy, depression
Stage 3: Recovery	Cognitive and emotional acceptance, identity change

After Weiss, 1988.

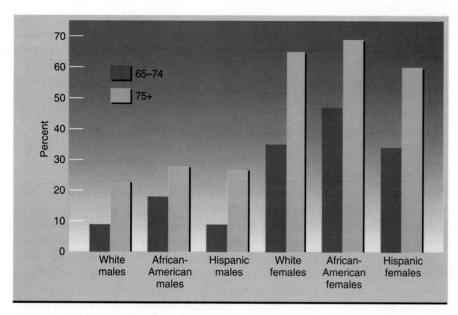

Figure 20.2 In all ethnic groups, women are far more likely than men to be widowed, with widowhood becoming the norm for women after the age of 75. *(Source: Data from U.S. Bureau of the Census, 1990b.)*

and subject to bouts of anxiety that border on panic. These feelings seem to be the result of compulsive urges to search for the dead spouse, accompanied by the recognition that the search is futile. With the strengthening of the conviction that the search is hopeless, the grieving spouse enters the phase of *despair,* a lethargic depression that endures until recovery begins. Even so, grief is not constant; it comes in surges and, after the phases of intense grief, may be triggered by anniversaries or reminders of the loss (Rosenblatt, 1988).

The final phase, *recovery,* involves three processes: cognitive acceptance, emotional acceptance, and identity change (Weiss, 1988). The bereaved person (1) develops a satisfactory account of the reasons for the death, (2) manages to neutralize memories and associations so that their recall no longer paralyzes functioning, and (3) develops a new self-image, in which attachment to the dead spouse is seen as part of a past self. This new identity permits the person to make commitments to new relationships.

In some circumstances, recovery is impeded and grief may become chronic (Weiss, 1988). If the loss makes no sense or if the surviving spouse feels primarily responsible for the death (as sometimes happens to widows and widowers of a suicide), the process of cognitive acceptance is short-circuited. If the surviving spouse had ambivalent feelings toward the deceased, as

when the death represented freedom from a conflict-ridden marriage, these confused feelings may prevent the process of emotional acceptance from moving forward. If the surviving spouse not only suffers from low self-esteem but was also highly dependent on the deceased partner, the development of a new self-image may not be possible. Finally, a surviving spouse who has deep feelings of responsibility to the dead partner and maintains an emotional commitment to his or her "well-being" may feel that recovery would be disloyal. In such cases, the pledge never to forget the spouse may become a pledge never to recover.

Earlier we saw that an eroded sense of control amplified the effects of stress. Among widowers and widows whose spouses die unexpectedly, those with a weak sense of personal control tend to suffer the most and recover the least (Stroebe, Stroebe, and Domittner, 1988). A prospective study indicates that social support is also an important factor in recovery from bereavement. After several years, researchers recontacted more than 1000 older women who had been interviewed concerning their socioeconomic status, physical health, social support, and psychological status (Goldberg, Comstock, and Harlow, 1988). Among women who had been widowed about six months earlier, the only factors that predicted the development of emotional problems were a lack of closeness to children and the absence of friends.

Adjusting to the Role of Widowed Spouse

Women seem to adapt to the solitary life of a widow much better than men adjust to life as a widower. Compared with widows, widowers have poorer health, greater emotional isolation, and weaker emotional ties to the family, and they are less likely to have a confidant. Some researchers believe that these findings may not actually indicate a gender difference in adaptive abilities but simply reflect the fact that women tend to be widowed at a younger age than men (Bengston, Rosenthal, and Burton, 1990). They point out that among the oldest widows and widowers, whose health has begun to fail, differences in social support, mental health, and general well-being narrow sharply.

During the first year of bereavement, older widows and widowers reported higher levels of depression, anxiety, and phobic reactions than did controls who had not lost a spouse (L. Thompson et al., 1991). By thirty months after the spouse's death, there was no difference between the widowed and the controls on these measures. The widowed, however, continued to report feelings of grief. In another study that recontacted older adults (age 65 to 74) ten years after the death of a spouse, psychosocial functioning had returned to normal (McCrae and Costa, 1988). Survival rates among the widowed were identical to those among married adults and were predicted by age, gender, and educational levels, but not by marital status. In addition, widowhood seemed to have no long-term effects on self-ratings of health or well-being.

Among older Americans in 1986, the highest rates of poverty were found among widows (Smeeding, 1990). Whether this will continue to be the case is uncertain. Most of tomorrow's older widows will have a relatively high level of education as well as an occupation and will see themselves as workers as well as wives and mothers. They will be used to handling money and getting things done by themselves. The change may already have begun. Among older women in a midwestern metropolitan area who had been widowed for eighteen months, 68 percent said they were "comfortably fixed" and 12 percent said they were "fairly well off" (O'Bryant and Morgan, 1989). Most of these women had considerable financial experience; a large majority had handled household accounts during their marriages, and about one-third had credit in their own name, a personal bank account, or their own investments at some time during marriage. Women who were at the greatest financial risk were those who had no experience in managing money

and had not discussed economic plans for widowhood with their late husbands. As other studies indicate (O'Bryant and Morgan, 1990), many of today's widows are relatively self-sufficient. The degree to which they rely on their children depends more on their financial situation than on their age or their health.

Family Relations in Later Adulthood

The household unit established by marriage generally shrinks to husband and wife in later adulthood and finally ends when one partner dies. But the larger family goes on, and the connections among older parents and the family systems initiated by their children and their children's children remain firm, relatively close, and usually frequent. When distance makes face-to-face visits impossible, telephone calls and letters act as substitutes. Older parents and their children prefer the freedom and independence of separate households, but the bonds between them are so strong that researchers refer to Americans as living in **modified extended families,** a term describing generations that live in separate dwellings but are linked by mutual aid and affection (Litwack, 1960).

Relationships with siblings may become increasingly important among older adults (Goetting, 1986). Contacts with siblings provide an opportunity to reminisce at a time when many adults undertake the process of life review. This sharing of experiences may become a major source of comfort and pride, and it may also validate the older adult's perceptions of self and reality. Although children and grandchildren provide the major sources of support during later adulthood, siblings frequently help out if an older adult's main sources of support break down. Thus, their existence provides older adults with an additional sense of security (Bengston, Rosenthal, and Burton, 1990). A sibling's gender is important. Older adults with a close bond to a sister are less likely than other older adults to develop depression, but whether an older adult is close to a brother seems to have no measurable effect on well-being (Cicirelli, 1989).

In comparing relationships among African-American and white siblings, researchers discovered that older African-Americans reported warmer relationships with their siblings than did whites and that they were more interested than older whites in providing siblings with assistance (D. Gold, 1990). Among older white dyads, 22 percent of the relationships were characterized by

Sharing experiences with a sibling not only provides an opportunity to reminisce but also may validate an older adult's perception of self and reality. *(David M. Grossman)*

envy or resentment (usually between brothers), but only 5 percent of African-American dyads displayed envy or resentment (invariably between sisters). This difference may reflect the nature of the African-based family, which, as we saw in Chapter 9, was organized around siblings of the same gender.

Children

The family relationships that have received the most attention are those with children and grandchildren. Gifts, services, influence, and affection travel up and down the generational tree, as we saw in Chapter 18. Both sides generally see their relations as close, but older adults may perceive the relationship as being closer than their children do. The tendency for older parents to see deeper trust, respect, understanding, and affection may reflect each party's **developmental stake** in the relationship (Bengston et al., 1985). Aging

parents have a stake in a close relationship; it indicates that their children are perpetuating the parents' ideals. But children have a stake in a more distant relationship; it indicates their own autonomy and distinctness from their parents. These stakes lead older adults to deny differences between the generations and their children to magnify them.

The strength of the bond between aging parents and their children shows in the frequency of their contacts. Daughters visit or call their parents more often than sons do, and they tend to contact mothers somewhat more often than fathers (L. Hoffman, McManus, and Brackbill, 1987). Three out of four older parents live within half an hour's drive of at least one child and see that child often, but whether the older parents live in the country or the city has no effect on the frequency of contact (Krout, 1988). In a national sample of nearly 4000 older adults, distance determined contact (Moss, Moss, and Moles, 1985). More than half of those who lived in the same neighborhood saw their children daily, but those who lived more than 500 miles from their children saw them only about once a year. Letters were exchanged monthly, however, and about one-third spoke by phone on a monthly basis.

Although close relationships with children are important, they have less influence on the well-being and satisfaction of older adults than do relationships with friends (R. Adams and Blieszner, 1989; Antonucci, 1990). Two factors may help to explain such findings. First, being with friends is more stimulating than being with family. When researchers asked retired adults to wear electronic pagers and write down what they were doing when the pager beeped, it became apparent that family time involved humdrum activities whereas time with friends involved active socializing and intellectually stimulating conversation (Larson, Mannell, and Zuzanek, 1986). Second, at least for a large minority of older widows, there is often a power reversal in the parent-child relationship, which can be a source of stress (Talbott, 1990). Some older widows felt unappreciated, some were emotionally dependent on their children, and others tried to maintain close relationships by providing goods and services they really could not afford to give.

The importance of friends may explain why childless adults (age 50 and older) in one national survey were just as happy as adults with grown children (Glenn and McLanahan, 1981). In a sample of older Canadians, childless adults (average age, 72) were wealthier, happier, and more satisfied with their health than were older parents (Rempel, 1985). But they also were more likely to be lonely. Those with children tended to have more friends, were better integrated into the community, and were more satisfied with life than the childless.

Among a group of childless, never-married older women, most had developed other key relationships that provided satisfaction and social support (R. Rubinstein et al., 1991). Some cultivated sibling relationships; some developed quasi-parental relationships with nieces or nephews; some were "adopted" by a nonkin family; some developed a quasi-parental tie to an unrelated young person who was "like a son" or "like a daughter"; and some cultivated companionate relationships with a friend. These enhanced friendships often stretched back into their youth.

At the close of life, however, health declines and roles dwindle. When this happens, even childless adults who have developed many nonfamily roles (volunteer work, church activities, clubs, community organizations, paid employment) may find their social isolation

increasing (Bachrach, 1980). The isolating effects of childlessness may be felt most keenly by old-old adults who are ill and frail.

Grandchildren and Great-Grandchildren

Grandparents in their late sixties and seventies are likely to adopt a remote style of relating to their grandchildren (see Chapter 18). Ethnic differences continue to appear in the grandparental relationship as adults move into old age. In a study of older white and African-American grandfathers in rural North Carolina, the grandparent role was more central to the lives of African-American grandfathers (Kivett, 1991). Among the grandfathers, all of whom had been either farmers or farm laborers, there was no ethnic difference in the importance they assigned to the grandfather role, and both groups saw their role as primarily affectionate. However, African-American grandfathers had more association with their grandchildren, stronger beliefs that their grandchildren shared their views, greater feelings of closeness, and greater expectations of help should they need it. Some researchers believe that this difference emerges from ethnic differences in time orientation (Willie, 1988). Older whites tend to emphasize the past and see themselves as role models, whereas older African-Americans tend to emphasize the future and so do not press their customs and ways of doing things on the young.

Most young adult grandchildren feel closer to their grandmothers than to their grandfathers and closer to their maternal grandmother than to their paternal grandmother (G. Kennedy, 1990). A study with college students indicates that the nature of the relationship between the young adult's parents and grandparents is also crucial (Matthews and Sprey, 1985). Unless at least one parent had a close relationship with a grandmother, the adult grandchild did not feel close. However, even those with distant relationships believed that they were obliged to help their grandparents whenever help was needed. Among another group of young adult grandchildren, most felt close to at least one grandparent (G. Kennedy, 1990). They also expected grandparents to advise them, to understand them, to serve as a role model, and to function as a liaison between them and their parents.

When great-grandchildren arrive, older adults are unlikely to be as involved with the new generation as they were with their grandchildren. By this time, most older women have less time and energy than they once

The role of great-grandparent, once a rarity, has become increasingly common as life expectancy has grown.
(Amanda Merulle/Stock, Boston)

did, and they pass most grandmaternal responsibilities on to their own children (Wentowski, 1985). In one study of great-grandparents, only one-third had a close relationship with a great-grandchild, and the relationships developed only when the great-grandchild lived within 25 miles (Doka and Mertz, 1988).

Living Arrangements of Older Adults

When someone mentions the living arrangements of older adults, retirement communities and nursing homes spring to mind. Actually, these two situations are home to only a small minority of adults past the age of 65. Only 5 percent live in nursing homes, and another 5 percent live in planned retirement communities (Kane

and Kane, 1990). Fewer than 5 percent live in three-generation families, but another 16 percent live in two-generation families, usually with a child who is either unmarried or childless (Coward, Cutler, and Schmidt, 1989). Wherever older adults live, the choice reflects a balance struck between the conflicting goals of autonomy and security, and private homes within the community provide the maximum amount of both (P. Parmelee and Lawton, 1990). Thus, it is not surprising that the overwhelming majority of older adults live in ordinary homes in ordinary communities, either by themselves, with relatives, or with nonrelatives.

How the Young-Old Live

The young-old are nearly always independent. Only 1 percent of adults between the ages of 65 and 74 live in nursing homes, with the figure climbing to 6 percent among those age 75 to 84 (U.S. Senate Special Committee on Aging, 1987–1988). Most live alone or with a spouse. The tendency is to "age in place," to stay in the houses where they reared their children and which many own. This arrangement has much in favor of it. The house is full of memories, its familiarity gives the older person a feeling of competence, and home ownership conveys status to the older person (Lawton, 1985).

Older adults are much less likely than the young to move, but when they do, their moves follow a developmental pattern (Longino, 1990). Among those younger than 74 who move each year, most make **amenity migrations.** They change their residences in order to maintain a network of friends or to improve their life style. Older adults who make such moves tend to be relatively healthy couples with enough income to give them a choice of locations. Those who cross state lines tend to be more affluent than those who do not move, whereas those who make local moves tend to be worse off, primarily because they are often tenants who move involuntarily (Kendig, 1990).

The affluent young-old who make amenity migrations into retirement communities tend to be extremely satisfied, and most live highly active lives (Lawton, 1985). Morale is high, crime is low, and residents are spared the annoyance of noisy children. The presence of peers with common problems encourages friendships, the development of support networks, and social activities.

As health declines and old-old age approaches, some sort of adjustment often must be made. Such moves generally take the form of **kinship migration,** in which the move is to areas inhabited by children or other close relatives (Longino, 1990). The move is usually to an independent house or apartment with access to services by children. People tend to make kinship migrations when one or both spouses develop a chronic condition or when one spouse dies. Sometimes simple alterations, such as grab bars in the bathroom, higher toilet seats, handrails, remote controls for appliances, phone amplifiers, nightlights, and knob turners for arthritic fingers can prolong older adults' independence for several years.

How the Old-Old Live

As life expectancy increases, the group of Americans who are older than 85 is expanding rapidly. Eventually, many will be unable to live independent lives, and they will make the final kind of move, **assistance migration** (Longino, 1990). They generally either move in with children or enter a nursing home or other care facility.

Most older adults who live with their children are either past 85 or the victims of some chronic degenerative disease. Researchers predict that more than one-third of Americans will live with an adult child at some time during their lives (Gatz, Bengston, and Blum, 1990). Earlier (see Chapter 18) we considered the stress that such situations place on the caregiving child. Being dependent on a child, which reverses the original parent-child relationship, also may place older adults under considerable stress. In a study of ninety older adults who were receiving care from family members, many reported that the prospect of continued dependence loomed so large in their minds that they found it difficult to think of anything else (Rakowski and Clark, 1985).

Sometimes home care—whether by family or friends—is impossible, and the old-old adult must enter some form of protective care. Disabled but otherwise healthy adults may enter a **residential care home,** where nonmedical personal care but no professional nursing care is provided. Some are family-run homes and have quarters for three or four adults; others are run by corporations and have quarters for twenty or more. The quality of these facilities varies widely, with some providing a familylike atmosphere and others marked by abuse or neglect (Namazi et al., 1989). Stays in a residential care home are usually temporary, with adults who deteriorate moving to nursing homes and those who improve returning to their own homes or to the home of a relative. Nonwhites are more likely than whites to return to the home of a family member (Bear, 1990).

Old-old adults who require extensive care enter nursing homes, which today care for 22 percent of adults older than 85 (Kane and Kane, 1990). Most residents are single or widowed white women who either are childless or have only one living child. Some adults begin to fail after moving into a nursing home, and the nature of institutional life may play a major part in this deterioration (Langer, 1985). Nursing homes provide total security but at the expense of autonomy. The rules, regulations, and arbitrary schedules, together with the unstimulating environment, initiate a process of psychological deterioration. Staff members encourage dependency, and their actions are likely to erode the older adult's sense of control. Studies by Margaret Baltes and her associates (Baltes et al., 1987) showed that attendants provided attention and approval when residents asked for help in dressing, using the toilet, or eating. But when residents acted in a competent, independent manner, staff members ignored them and moved on to other residents. Older adults who live under such conditions may become psychologically and physically dependent on the staff and, as time passes, begin functioning in a "mindless," automatic fashion (Piper and Langer, 1986). As indicated in the accompanying box, "Restoring Control in Nursing Homes," researchers have experimented with ways of developing feelings of mastery and control in residents of nursing homes.

No single solution meets the needs of all older people. The individual's health and personal characteristics, family situations, and the quality and structure of the nursing home interact to determine whether an older adult would be more satisfied living independently, with children, or in an institution. From a social standpoint, the more alternatives that are available, the more likely it is that individual needs will be met.

Death as a Developmental Issue

As adults cross the border into old-old age, physical decline and the loss of capacities bring death into focus. Just when a frail adult begins preparations for death depends on his or her social, physical, and mental situation (Marshall, 1980). These preparations may occur several years before the person dies or may be postponed until the death trajectory has begun.

RESTORING CONTROL IN NURSING HOMES

More than a decade ago, researchers discovered that making simple changes in nursing home routines improved the activity, health, and satisfaction of residents. In a classic experiment, Ellen Langer and Judith Rodin (1976) introduced a series of simple choices into the lives of residents that gave them a degree of control over day-to-day events. Each of the residents in the experimental group was allowed to choose a potted plant and was expected to care for it. Group members were also allowed to choose which night they preferred to watch a movie. Residents in a control group also got plants, but they did not get to choose them and were told that staff members would care for their plants. They also saw a movie each week, but they had no choice as to which night they would attend.

Three weeks later, the residents who had been given small amounts of control over their lives seemed more alert. Other residents and the nurses rated them as more sociable, happy, and active than members of the control group. Eighteen months later, when the researchers returned to the nursing home, they discovered that the intervention appeared to have lasting effects (Rodin and Langer, 1977). Physicians' records indicated that the health of residents who had been given a degree of responsibility showed a significant improvement compared with members of the group that had been given no choices. Death rates also seemed to be affected. Among residents who had been given control, 15 percent had died; among residents who had been encouraged in their dependency, 30 percent had died. The normal death rate in this nursing home was 25 percent.

Although the changes seemed trivial, Rodin notes that against a background of no choice at all, having any choice is dramatic (Rodin and Hall, 1987). She suggests that when the residents felt they had the power to alter their environment, their sense of efficacy increased. This change led them to respond to others differently, and that enabled their families and the nursing staff to respond to them in a more positive fashion. The process reverberated in all areas of their lives.

The results of these studies led Rodin and her associates to provide control before entry into nursing homes. They worked with two major hospitals, studying adults older than 62 who entered as patients. From those who were scheduled to enter a nursing home, they selected a group at random. Half of these patients were allowed to participate in the decision to enter the nursing home; the other half were given no choice. The level of health in both groups was similar. A year later, members of the group that had control over the decision were more likely to be living at home than members of the group that had no control. They were also healthier, and fewer had died (Rodin and Hall, 1987). Even those who chose to *enter* a nursing home were more likely to be back at home within a year than those who were given no choice.

This research also showed that in order to reap the benefits of control, it is not necessary to exercise that control. If people believe that they can cause an intended event to occur or that the environment will be responsive to their attempts at control, they may feel freedom when they decide *not* to exercise an option (Rodin, 1986).

Preparing for Death

As part of their preparation for death, old people may turn inward. They withdraw from activities and may try to make sense of their lives by a process known as **life review.** According to Robert Butler (1975), the awareness of death leads people to reflect on their past, looking back over the events of their lives in an attempt to adjust to their eventual deaths. They take up old conflicts, review old relationships, and try to come to terms with their past actions in light of their present situation. As older adults probe past conflicts, they may feel anxiety, guilt, depression, or despair. But when the conflicts can be resolved, adults may overcome despair and emerge with integrity, having discovered meaning in their lives.

Research suggests that life review may foster the development of integrity. In a study of older adults who were disabled and could not leave their homes, those who undertook a structured life review under the guidance of a researcher were more satisfied with their lives and scored higher on measures of psychological well-being than were those who simply received a friendly visit from the researcher (Haight, 1992). The beneficial effects of the life review were still present one year later.

Butler saw life review as a universal developmental process that was part of Erikson's (1982) struggle between integrity and despair. He believed that the task involved problem solving and was a sign of maturity. When successful, it led to serenity; when unsuccessful, the person was left in turmoil. Yet studies indicate that not all older people review their past lives (Kastenbaum, 1985) and that those who do are not always restructuring the past in a way that promotes integrity. Morton Lieberman and Sheldon Tobin (1983) believe that when life review occurs, its purpose may not be to resolve past conflicts or to accept one's present life as inevitable but to rework that life and create a personal myth. Instead of promoting integrity, such a review becomes a defensive reaffirmation of one's current self-concept.

Life review may be a developmental task that is limited to societies in which people expect to live into old age. When death is common, unpredictable, and uncontrollable—as likely to come at the age of 15 or 25 as at 75 or 80—people may not fear it (Aries, 1981). In such societies, there may be no reason to reflect on past conflicts and come to terms with death. Victor Marshall (1980) proposes that instead of regarding life review as a universal process, we consider it a twentieth-century response to predictable death in old age.

The Dying Trajectory

Unless death comes suddenly, perhaps from accident or a massive heart attack, people go through a **dying trajectory,** which is the interval between the time a person realizes that death is imminent and the moment of death itself (Glaser and Strauss, 1968). This trajectory may last for weeks or months, or it may be over in a few days. For some, it takes the shape of a slow, downhill process, as when death comes from emphysema. For others, it may be a kind of staircase, as when periods of remission occur during the course of cancer.

After working with more than 200 dying persons, Elisabeth Kubler-Ross (1969) proposed that individuals approaching death pass through five separate stages. At first the dying person denies the possibility of his or her death. In the second stage, the person becomes filled with rage because his or her life is being cut short. In the third stage, the dying person attempts to bargain for life, trying to buy time from God, the physician or nurse, or loved ones. The fourth stage is one of depression. The patient is depressed over losing family, friends, home, possessions. The final stage is acceptance. The patient quietly expects death but feels peace instead of anxiety.

Although Kubler-Ross's stages of death sound plausible, they apparently do not reflect the experiences of most dying people (Kastenbaum, 1985; Marshall and Levy, 1990; Shneidman, 1980). Her research was primarily with young and middle-aged adults, who saw their deaths as untimely and who exhibited a fear of death that studies do not find among older adults in this and other societies. Researchers have also found that dying people may experience only some of the stages described by Kubler-Ross. Or they may experience them in a different order. Or they may move back and forth among the stages in a period of hours, or even minutes. Another problem with these stages is their failure to allow for individual differences, both in the kind of death that a person faces and in the way that he or she meets it. A patient's gender, cultural background, personality, developmental level, and surroundings (whether at home, in an intensive-care unit, or in a nursing home) interact with the nature of the terminal illness so as to make each death different.

An Appropriate Death

All societies have conceptions concerning proper and improper ways to die (Marshall and Levy, 1990). The "good death" among the Kaliai of the South Pacific requires that kin gather round the dying person, possessions be dispersed, and any obligations be taken care of. A similar concept of a good death in American society envisions the dying person surrounded by family and friends, a minimum of technological interference, and the control of pain and discomfort. Life-extending technology has taken this good death out of the reach of many people. The process of dying is prolonged days, weeks, or months, as people exist in a comatose condition, connected to respirators, feeding tubes, and monitoring equipment. Such a death deprives a person of control and dignity, especially when medical personnel keep trying to "heal" a person who is far along in the dying trajectory.

Increasingly, people have asked that their dying not be prolonged and that they be allowed to die an **appropriate death,** protected from demeaning medical procedures but kept free from pain and allowed to participate in medical decisions (Weisman, 1972). An appropriate death is possible only when patients are kept informed, but many physicians find it difficult to tell patients that they are dying. Families often collaborate in this pretense.

Why do physicians and family so often withhold such news? Many physicians believe that people do not want to know that they are dying. Hearing the truth about their condition would confuse patients, cause them mental anguish, and destroy their hopes. But this deceit deprives people of the opportunity to complete unfinished business, make important decisions about the way they will spend their last days, restore harmony to social relations, and say farewell to loved ones (Kalish, 1985).

During the past twenty-five years, two related efforts have been made to widen the availability of an appropriate death. One has been the establishment of **hospices,** where people can die gracefully. In hospices, no extraordinary measures are used to prolong life. There are no blood transfusions, feeding tubes, or respirators. The aim of the hospice is to provide a humane, dignified environment for the dying. Home and hospice care are coordinated, with hospice personnel supervising home care as long as is feasible. Patients who go to a hospice generally stay at home at least two weeks longer than patients who are transferred to a regular hospital, and some never have to go to the hospice at all (Schulz, 1978). Whether at home or in the hospice, the dying patient retains some control and gets medication that relieves pain without reducing alertness. Friends and family may visit at any hour. Hospices offer dying people a warm, homelike atmosphere in which they can face death without placing the burden of care on their families.

The second effort to keep deaths appropriate has been the development of the **living will,** which gives a person the opportunity to decide how he or she will die. The person is able to set forth the desired circum-stances in this document at a time when he or she can make reasonable decisions. The standard living will specifies that when recovery from extreme physical or mental disability is impossible, physicians are not to use medication, artificial means, or "heroic measures" to keep the person alive. It often requests painkilling medication, even when the medication is likely to hasten the person's death. Living wills are not legally binding in all states, but some states have legalized **health proxies,** which are durable powers of attorney that set forth the conditions for medical care and name a person to make necessary decisions. Living wills and health proxies provide guidance at the time when medical decisions can affect the quality of a person's death.

The Life Span Ends

Eventually, the longest life must end. In the face of inevitable biological death, societies generally provide their members with some type of immortality concept. In most preindustrial cultures, immortality takes the form of an afterlife, during which relationships between the deceased and the living continue. Among the Swazi in Africa, for example, rites safeguard the living from attacks by inhabitants of the spirit world. The Native

In a hospice, terminally ill patients can die in a supportive, homelike atmosphere, confident that their existence will not be prolonged by technology. (*John Moss/Photo Researchers*)

American Washo of California burned the dead person's home to make certain that he or she would not return to harm the living (Leming and Dickinson, 1985). When relationships are seen as beneficial, rituals preserve the bonds. The Japanese custom of building an altar within the home, where the dead person's photograph and ashes are placed, is meant to maintain the relationship. Among the Mangan of New Guinea, survivors maintain exchange relationships with the dead (Marshall and Levy, 1990).

In postindustrial societies, interactions with elders end with biological death. Instead, the dead move on to another existence. The religious promise of immortality helps people make sense out of the cycle of life and death, with everlasting life compensating for giving up time on earth (Kastenbaum, 1985). Some people see death as the end of existence and seek immortality in different ways (Lifton, 1971). They may see themselves as living on through their descendents or through future generations of society. Or they may see themselves as living on through their creative works (literature, paintings, music, buildings, institutions) or through their human influences (the lives they touch that go on to touch other lives). Others may see themselves as surviving through nature itself. Their bodies decay, become part of the earth, and survive through the natural cycle of life. No matter which view of immortality people take, the conviction helps them to find meaning in life and thus to leave with a sense of integrity.

SUMMARY

SOCIAL CHANGE
Americans are living longer, with nearly 13 percent of the population over 65 years old, and the quality of later adulthood has changed. Most older adults are healthier and more vigorous than old people were at the beginning of the century, and they are more likely to have their own households, to live above the poverty line, and to have few adult children.

PHYSICAL CHANGES
Culture and ethnic background both affect life expectancy. Theories of **primary aging** assume that aging either is under genetic control or is the result of wear and tear. Changes in the circulatory and respiratory systems reduce the ability of the aging adult to adapt to stress and change. Most of the physical changes that we associate with old age are the result of **secondary aging.**

THEORIES AND ISSUES OF LATER ADULTHOOD
The major developmental tasks of later adulthood are adjusting to decreasing physical strength and health, adjusting to retirement, and coming to terms with death. Erikson's theory focuses on coming to terms with mortality and developing **ego integrity.** Jung stressed a change in orientation, as people shifted from **extraversion** to **introversion.** This view was echoed in **disengagement theory,** which saw withdrawal from the world as the most satisfactory adjustment to aging. **Activity theory** took the opposite approach, emphasizing continued involvement in society. Either course may lead to a satisfactory old age. Cohort effects may sometimes be mistaken for the effects of aging.

PERSONALITY, SELF-CONCEPT, AND CONTROL
Self-esteem remains high in later adulthood, in part because most older adults retain a younger self-concept and are protected by social comparison. When self-concept is damaged, men are more likely to abuse alcohol, whereas women are more likely to become depressed. Stress is especially damaging if a sense of control has been eroded or if adults lack social support.

WORK AND RETIREMENT
Although poor health is a major factor in the decision to take early retirement, it is not connected with retirement decisions among people who work until they are 65. Retirement is a process that progresses through the phases of preretirement, honeymoon, disenchantment, reorientation, stability, and termination. Most people enjoy retirement.

MARRIAGE IN LATER ADULTHOOD
Retirement may create problems in traditional marriages, and in marriages in which the wife works, the husband may encounter additional stress when he retires. The majority of married couples continue sexual activity into later adulthood, with the man's declining health or lack of interest the primary reasons for its end-

ing. Most older couples say their marriages have always been extremely happy, but this may reflect a reworking of memories to coincide with current levels of marital satisfaction.

DIVORCE AND REMARRIAGE

Divorce in later adulthood may be highly stressful and disrupt the divorcing adult's sense of identity. After a divorce those who fail to remarry tend to remain under stress and to find diminished satisfaction in life. Men generally remarry, but women do not, primarily because of a scarcity of partners.

WIDOWHOOD

When a marital partner dies, the surviving spouse goes through a lengthy period of **bereavement,** which usually passes through the phases of shock, protest, despair, and recovery. The recovery process involves developing a satisfactory account of why the person died, neutralizing memories and associations, and developing a new self-image. During the first year of bereavement, the surviving spouse may be depressed and anxious and may display phobic reactions. Even after recovery is in place, grief continues.

FAMILY RELATIONS IN LATER ADULTHOOD

The American family is a **modified extended family,** in which the generations may live apart but are linked by aid and affection. Parents and their adult children each have a **developmental stake** in their relationship. Relationships with friends seem to have a stronger influence on older adults' well-being than do relationships with children. Most young adults feel closer to their grandmothers than to grandfathers and closest to their maternal grandmother.

LIVING ARRANGEMENTS OF OLDER ADULTS

Older adults' choice of living arrangements reflects a balance between the goals of autonomy and security. Most young-old adults live independently, and many prefer to age in place, but some make an **amenity migration.** After the death of a spouse or a significant decline in health, older adults may make a **kinship migration.** When old-old age arrives, those who are unable to live independently make **assistance migrations,** often entering a **residential care home** or a nursing home. The nature of institutional life may erode the sense of control and lead to declines in health.

DEATH AS A DEVELOPMENTAL ISSUE

As people prepare for death, they may begin the process of **life review.** When death becomes imminent, people enter a **dying trajectory,** whose length varies widely. Medical technology has made an **appropriate death** increasingly difficult to obtain; in order to allow people to die in a dignified manner, **hospices** have been established and many people have either made **living wills** or enacted **health proxies.**

THE LIFE SPAN ENDS

Societies generally provide their members with some type of immortality concept that gives life meaning. In preindustrial societies, immortality usually takes the form of an afterlife. In postindustrial societies, many religions provide an afterlife. Those who reject the religious afterlife may seek immortality in other ways: through descendents, creative works, human influences, or incorporation into the natural cycle of life.

KEY TERMS

activity theory	dying trajectory	life review
amenity migration	ego integrity	living will
appropriate death	extraversion	modified extended family
assistance migration	health proxy	primary aging
bereavement	hospice	residential care home
developmental stake	introversion	secondary aging
disengagement theory	kinship migration	

GLOSSARY

accommodation Piaget's term for the modification of schemes to incorporate new knowledge that does not fit them.

achieving stage In Schaie's theory of adult cognition, the stage of young adulthood during which knowledge is applied toward vocational and family goals.

acquired immune deficiency syndrome (AIDS) Disease that attacks the immune system, so the individual has no protection against infection. It can be passed through the placenta from mother to fetus.

acquisitive stage In Schaie's theory of adult cognition, the period of childhood and adolescence during which knowledge is acquired in increasingly efficient ways.

active learner Student who has an independent, exploring attitude, is willing to challenge authority, and insists on explanations.

activity theory Proposal that life satisfaction in old age depends on being highly involved with others and integrated into society.

acuity Ability to see objects clearly and to resolve detail.

adolescence Period from puberty until the assumption of adult economic and social roles.

adulthood Period from the assumption of adult economic and social roles until death.

afterbirth Placenta, its membranes, and the remainder of the umbilical cord, all expelled during the final stage of labor.

age-irrelevant society Society in which major life events, such as marriage, schooling, and retirement, are not closely tied to chronological age.

ageism Prejudice against old people, in which they are seen as incompetent. It leads to discrimination against older adults.

allele Alternative form of a gene found at a given site on a chromosome.

Alzheimer's disease Debilitating, irreversible organic brain disorder characterized by increasingly serious memory loss and deterioration of attention, judgment, and personality.

amenity migration Change of residence for the purpose of improving life style or maintaining friendships.

amniocentesis Procedure that detects fetal abnormalities, in which chromosomal analyses are performed on a sample of amniotic fluid.

amnion Inner membrane of the sac that forms during the germinal period and surrounds the developing organism.

androgens Male hormones.

androgyny Self-concept that incorporates both masculine and feminine characteristics.

animism Belief that inanimate objects have thoughts, feelings, and life.

anorexia nervosa Eating disorder characterized by self-starvation brought about by fanatical dieting; found primarily among affluent, well-educated girls in developed countries.

anoxia Absence of oxygen; birth complication that may occur in a breech or transverse delivery.

Apgar score Common scoring system, developed in 1962 by Virginia Apgar, by which the newborn's physiological condition is assessed.

appropriate death Dignified death, in which the person is protected from demeaning medical procedures, kept as free from pain as possible, and allowed to participate in medical decisions.

artificial insemination Procedure in which a donor's sperm is injected into a woman's cervix.

artificialism Belief, caused by inability to separate physical from psychological causes, that either God or humans have built or made everything in the world.

assimilation Piaget's term for the incorporation of new knowledge into existing schemes.

assistance migration Move to an institution when life at home is no longer possible.

asynchrony Maturation of different body parts at different rates; a growth characteristic typical of adolescence.

attachment Primary social bond that develops between infant and caregiver and that provides the baby with emotional security.

authoritarian parents Parents who demand that the child meet high standards but are relatively cold and unresponsive to the youngster.

authoritative parents Parents who demand that the child meet high standards and are warm and responsive to the youngster.

autonomy Feeling of self-control and self-determination.

avoidant attachment Insecure form of attachment in which the infant pays little attention to the caregiver and seems almost too independent.

basic category Category formed at the level at which members are most like one another, with similar shapes and parts, and most different from members of other categories (e.g., bird or flower).

beanpole family Multigenerational family with many generations but few members in each generation.

bereavement Grief following the death of a loved one.

birth cohort theory Theory proposing that the twenty-year rise, peak, and subsequent decline of stress-related disorders among adolescents is due to increased economic and social stress on members of a crowded birth group.

blended family Family formed by the remarriage of the custodial parent.

body ideal Particular body type defined by each culture as attractive and sexually appropriate for each sex.

bulimia Eating disorder characterized by periodic eating binges, often followed by purging; found primarily among affluent, well-educated girls in developed countries.

canalization Process in which growth is channeled along a predictable path when genes are expressed within a normally occurring human environment. Such growth is therefore difficult to deflect from its course.

cardinality Absolute numerical size, as opposed to order or rank.

catch-up growth Rapid growth that occurs after the elimination of a condition that was retarding growth.

centration Concentration of attention on a prominent feature of a stimulus, to the exclusion of all other aspects of the situation.

cephalocaudal development Progression of growth from head to foot. The head develops and grows before the torso, arms, and legs.

cervix Pinhead-size opening that separates the vagina from the uterus.

child abuse Physical injury of a child because of intentional acts or failures to act on the part of the caregiver.

childhood Period from age 2 until puberty.

chorion Outer membrane of the sac that forms during the germinal period and surrounds the developing organism.

chorionic villi sampling Procedure that detects fetal abnormalities through inspection of chromosomes in cells from the chorion.

chromosomes Beadlike strings of genes present in every cell of the body. Except in the gametes, they occur in pairs.

classic aging pattern Typical pattern of age-related changes in IQ scores, in which crystallized abilities remain steady or increase while fluid abilities begin to decline in middle age.

classical conditioning Simple form of learning in which one stimulus is associated with another so that the first evokes the response that normally follows the second stimulus.

class inclusion Aspect of deductive reasoning based on the knowledge that a superordinate class is always larger than any of its basic classes.

codominant (genes) Alleles for genetic traits that are not determined by a simple dominant-recessive arrangement. The allele's expression may depend on environmental conditions.

cognition Psychological ability that accounts for mental life, encompassing all the processes used to gain knowledge of the world.

cognitive capacity Number of symbols that the conscious mind can include at one time.

cognitive social-learning theory Bandura's restated version of social-learning theory, in which thoughts, expectations, beliefs, goals, and other internal processes interact with environmental influences to determine behavior.

cohabitation Arrangement in which unmarried couples live together.

cohort Group of people of the same age; members of a particular age group.

companionate grandparent Grandparent who has an informal, affectionate relationship with the grandchild.

companionate marriage Marriage characterized by strong emotional bonds. The partners like, admire, and respect each other, and they enjoy each other's company.

computerized axial tomography (CT) X-ray technique that enables researchers to reconstruct cross sections of the living brain at any depth or angle.

concrete-operational thought Flexible, logical thought in regard to concrete objects and situations. According to Piaget, it develops when children are about 6 or 7.

conditioned reflex Involuntary response that, through conditioning, follows a formerly neutral stimulus.

conditioning theories Learning theories that interpret developmental changes in terms of learning to associate one event with another.

confluence theory Theory that family size and spacing between siblings affect cognitive development through their effect on the level of the family's intellectual environment. The larger the family and the closer the spacing, the smaller the child's IQ.

conservation Ability to understand that irrelevant changes in the physical appearance of objects do not affect their quantity, mass, weight, or volume; one of Piaget's concrete operations.

constructive play Play that consists of manipulating objects to construct or create something.

constructivist Piaget's term for the child's understanding of reality. Knowledge comes from the child's actions on objects; from this knowledge, the child constructs an understanding of the world.

contingency awareness Ability to understand that, under certain conditions, specific actions have predictable consequences.

control group Group that has the same characteristics as the experimental group in a study but that does not undergo the experimental treatment.

conventional level Middle level in Kohlberg's theory of moral reasoning. Value is placed on maintaining the conventional social order and on meeting the expectations of others.

convergence Mechanism by which the slightly different images seen by each eye come together to form a single image.

cooing Uttering sounds of joy. Babies coo from about the third month of age.

correlation Numerical expression of how closely two sets of measures correspond. Correlations range from +1.00 (perfect positive correlation) to −1.00 (perfect negative correlation).

correlational study Study that investigates the relationship between variables to determine whether they occur together at a rate that is higher than chance.

cortex Mantle of neural cells that covers the cerebral hemispheres. It is heavily involved in sensation, speech, learning, memory, and voluntary movements.

cross-modal perception Integration of information picked up by the various senses.

cross-sectional design Experimental design that compares the performance of different age groups on a single occasion.

crystallized intelligence Intelligence that includes verbal skills and mechanical knowledge and reflects the ability to handle well-learned information in familiar situations. Its skills are taught in schools and emphasized by the culture.

defense mechanism Technique used by the ego to reduce anxiety, either by distorting the source of anxiety or by excluding it from consciousness.

deferred imitation Behavior in which mimicking of a person or re-creating of an action occurs some time after the original was witnessed.

delirium Reversible organic brain disorder that reflects disturbed metabolism throughout the brain.

deoxyribonucleic acid (DNA) Complex chemical containing the genetic code that guides development.

dependent variable Factor in a study that changes as the result of the introduction of an independent variable.

development Any age-related change in body or behavior from conception to death.

developmental stake Individual's personal interest in the relationship between generations, which affects his or her perceptions of that relationship.

dialectical operations See **postformal thought.**

disengagement theory Proposal that life satisfaction in old age depends on a gradual withdrawal from society and a decreasing involvement with other people.

disorganized attachment Form of attachment in which the infant seems dazed or disorganized during reunions.

divergent thinking Ability to come up with many unusual ideas or associations.

dominance hierarchy Social ranking of group members in terms of dominance and submission; usually based on aggression.

dominant (gene) Allele whose corresponding trait appears in an individual when the allele is paired with a different allele for the same trait.

Down's syndrome Condition that results when an extra chromosome 21 is present in the zygote or when extra material from chromosome 21 becomes attached to another chromosome. It produces various physical abnormalities and varying degrees of mental retardation.

dual-process model View that intellectual functioning consists of basic cognitive skills (mechanics of intelligence) and of procedures that relate these skills, knowledge, and expertise to daily life (pragmatics of intelligence).

dying trajectory Interval between the time a person realizes that death is imminent and the moment of death.

dynamic assessment Evaluation of what a child is prepared to learn with assistance; measure of the child's zone of proximal development.

ecological theory Bronfenbrenner's theory of development, in which the process is a joint function of the person and all levels of the environment.

ego Conscious self, which in psychodynamic theories guides behavior and mediates the conflict between id and superego.

egocentrism Among babies, the inability to distinguish between the self and the external world; among young children, the belief that everyone sees the world and responds to it as the child does.

ego integrity In Erikson's theory, ego strength of old age, in which the adult perceives a sense of coherence and wholeness to his or her life.

Elderhostel Brief, residential program of courses for older adults that is given under auspices of colleges and universities.

embryo Developing organism from the second to the eighth week of development within the uterus.

embryonic period Period from second to eighth week of prenatal development, during which organ systems form.

empathy Understanding of another person's emotional state.

empty-nest syndrome Emotional crisis produced by departure of children from the home; occurs primarily when children leave at an extremely young age or when the mother sees the children primarily as an extension of herself.

encode To register information in memory.

equilibration Piaget's developmental principle, which states that the organism always tends toward biological and psychological balance.

estrogens Female hormones.

ethnic group Any group that is distinguished by race, religion, or national identity and that has its own attitudes, traditions, values, and beliefs.

ethnic identity Identity formed by internalizing ethnicity and integrating it as a desired aspect of the self.

ethological theories Theories that view development in terms of evolutionary concepts.

event-related potential (ERP) Characteristic electrical response in the brain that is evoked by a new stimulus, such as a sight or a sound.

executive stage In Schaie's theory of adult cognition, the period in middle adulthood during which knowledge is applied to managing organizations.

exosystem Bronfenbrenner's term for the structure that links a person's context with other settings that may influence the person.

experiment Study in which researchers control the arrangement and manipulation of conditions, in order to systematically observe particular phenomena.

experimental group Group of research subjects that undergoes the experimental treatment.

expressive jargon Babbling in older infants that has the intonation and pitch of speech.

externalized conscience Conscience that dictates adherence to morally accepted behavior solely to avoid punishment.

extinction Elimination of a response that is not reinforced.

extraversion In Jung's theory, a major personality orientation, in which the person's primary interest is directed toward the external world.

factor analysis Technique in which scores on a series of tests are correlated in the hope of finding clusters of highly correlated items that reflect a common ability.

factor theories Theories of intelligence based on abilities uncovered through factor analysis.

Fallopian tube Passage leading from either ovary to the uterus.

fetal alcohol syndrome Condition that afflicts many babies born to alcoholic mothers. The infants may be small for gestational age, have abnormal head and facial features, and be mentally retarded.

fetal period Period from approximately eight weeks after conception until birth, during which the structure of organs is organized and their function established.

fetus Developing organism from eighth week after conception until birth.

field study Study in which the investigator introduces some factor into the natural situation that changes it.

finalism Belief that nothing happens by accident.

fixated In Freudian theory, stalled emotionally at an immature level of personality development.

fluid intelligence Intelligence that includes abstract, nonverbal reasoning and problem-solving skills and reflects the ability to deal with novel information in novel situations. Its skills are neither taught in school nor emphasized by the culture.

foreclosure Identity status in which the adolescent is committed to an occupation or ideology that has been chosen by others, generally parents.

formal-operational thought Logical, abstract thought that can be applied to hypothetical situations. According to Piaget, it develops during adolescence.

fraternal twins Twins that develop from two ova, each fertilized by a different sperm.

functional illiterate Person who has a rudimentary ability to read and write but lacks the literacy skills required for productive performance in society.

functional play Play that consists of simple, repetitive movements.

gametes Mature reproductive cells; spermatozoa and ova.

gender constancy Concept that gender will never change—that boys always become men and girls always become women.

gender identity Inner experience of gender; unchanging sense of self as male or female.

gender role Socially prescribed pattern of behavior and attitudes considered characteristic of a specific gender.

gender-role stereotype Simplified, exaggerated conception about the behavior and traits typical of a specific gender.

gender schema Self-constructed theory made up of sex-related associations for each gender, which organize a person's perceptions of the world and determine the way that new information is organized.

generalized slowing hypothesis Theory that age-related declines in cognition are the result of slowed processing throughout the brain.

generational cycle of abuse View that child abuse is perpetuated by adults who were themselves abused or neglected as children.

generativity Ego strength of middle age in Erikson's theory; made up of procreativity, productivity, and creativity.

genes Microscopic particles of DNA that contain instructions for development; located at specific sites on chromosomes.

genetic epistemology Piaget's basic approach to development, focusing on the development of intelligence.

genotype Specific combination of alleles that makes up each individual's genetic inheritance.

germinal period Period of the first two weeks after conception, during which the zygote is primarily engaged in cell division.

gestational age Age of the fetus as calculated from the date of conception.

gestation period Period of prenatal development, which may be calculated from fertilization (thirty-eight weeks) or from the date of the last menstruation (forty weeks).

goodness of fit Degree to which the baby's temperament and the parent's style mesh.

grammatical frames Word patterns used by children to produce sentences that are different from the sentences they hear.

grasping reflex Newborn's unlearned tendency to clutch any small object placed in the hand. It is strongest in the first month and disappears at about 3 or 4 months.

growth hormone (GH) Hormone that promotes growth throughout the body, stimulating muscle cells to divide and long bones to grow.

habituation Reduction in the response to a stimulus after repeated or continuous encounters with it. The simplest form of learning, it is analogous to boredom with the stimulus.

haptic perception Perception based on the sense of touch.

health proxy Durable power of attorney that names a person to make specified decisions concerning medical care.

heterozygous Condition in which the alleles at a given chromosome site are different. In such cases, the dominant gene generally determines the appearance of the affected trait.

holophrase One-word sentence of the toddler that depends on context to communicate meaning.

homozygous Condition in which the alleles at a given chromosome site are identical.

hospice Institution where people can die with dignity. Patients are kept pain-free, but no life-prolonging measures are used.

hydrocephaly Condition in which fluid accumulates within the skull and presses on the brain; often appears in individuals with spina bifida.

hypothesis Prediction, based on theory, that can be tested by the gathering of appropriate information.

id In psychodynamic theories, aspect of the personality that contains unconscious impulses or drives.

identical twins Twins that develop from a single ovum that splits after fertilization but before implantation into the uterine wall.

identification Internalization of another person's values and standards in an attempt to become like that person.

identity In Piaget's theory, the understanding that objects and people remain the same, even if irrelevant properties are changed. In Erikson's theory, a complex sense of self that develops during adolescence, when various life roles and aspects of the personality coalesce.

identity achievement Identity status in which the adolescent is committed to self-chosen occupational or ideological goals.

identity diffusion Identity status in which the adolescent has no occupational or ideological goals but is not particularly concerned about the situation.

imaginary audience Aspect of adolescent egocentrism in which the adolescent assumes that others share the adolescent's own concern with himself or herself and thus are close observers of the adolescent's appearance and actions.

imitation Process of copying or reproducing observed behavior.

imminent justice Punishment perceived as an inevitable consequence of breaking rules; characteristic of Piaget's morality of constraint.

independent variable Factor in a study that is selected or changed in some way by the investigator.

individuated Term applied to an adolescent who has developed autonomy but remains attached to the family.

inductive discipline Disciplinary technique whose power lies in appeals to pride or to concern for others. It relies heavily on reason and attempts to induce empathy or role-taking.

infancy Period in development from birth to a child's second birthday.

infertile Not fertile; unable to conceive.

information-processing theory Theory of cognition that sees individuals as processing information much as a computer does; thought and behavior are believed to be built on a small set of primitive processes.

institutional marriage Utilitarian marriage held together by satisfaction in possessions and children.

intelligence quotient (IQ) Ratio between a person's mental and chronological ages.

interaction Spiraling developmental process in which hereditary characteristics influence the environment, which in turn affects further development, and vice versa.

interview study Study in which the investigator asks questions of the subjects and then analyzes the replies.

introversion In Jung's theory, a major personality orientation, in which the person's primary interest is directed toward the self.

in-vitro fertilization Conception in which sperm and ovum are mingled in a glass dish.

involved grandparent Grandparent whose relationship with the grandchild resembles that of a parent.

kinship migration Change of residence to an area near relatives in order to obtain services from family.

Klinefelter's syndrome Condition resulting from the presence in boys of an extra female sex chromosome (XXY). The boys are sterile, have rounded bodies, and may be somewhat retarded.

kwashiorkor Serious, often fatal, disease that develops in children who may get enough calories but whose diets are severely deficient in protein.

labor Three-stage process in which the fetus emerges through the birth canal and is born.

language acquisition device (LAD) Innate human capacity that ensures the acquisition of language by any child who is exposed to speech.

latchkey children Youngsters who come home from school to an empty house and take responsibility for their own care; so called for the house key that the child carries.

lateralization Establishment of various information-processing functions in one hemisphere of the brain or the other.

learned helplessness Condition in which repeated

failure in situations over which a person has no control leads to apathy and refusal to try.

libido Freud's term for the life instinct, the "psychic energy" that fuels all human motivation.

life-cycle squeeze Economic or emotional stress caused by overlapping responsibilities for younger and older generations.

life review Process of reflecting on the past in an attempt to resolve old conflicts and come to terms with death.

living will Document that specifies desired medical care when recovery is impossible and the person can no longer make reasonable decisions; usually asks that life-prolonging measures no longer be used.

longitudinal design Experimental design that follows the same subjects over time and compares their behavior at different ages.

love withdrawal Disciplinary technique whose power lies in the fear of losing emotional support, affection, or approval. It includes withdrawing physically, refusing to speak or listen to a person, telling the person that one dislikes him or her, and threatening to leave the person.

macrosystem Bronfenbrenner's term for a culture or subculture, which influences development through values, belief systems, and life styles.

math anxiety Dread of math or intense fear or nervousness at the prospect of taking a math test.

maturational theories Theories of development that see the process as self-regulating and unfolding according to a maturational timetable.

mechanics of intelligence Basic cognitive skills (similar to abilities of fluid intelligence) used to process information and solve problems; see also **dual-process model.**

meiosis Form of cell division followed in gametes; produces four cells, each containing twenty-three single chromosomes.

memory Application of cognitive processes (involved in perceiving, thinking, and learning) to the storage and retrieval of information.

menarche First incidence of menstruation.

menopause Cessation of menstruation. The medical marker of middle age in women, it appears at about the age of 50.

menstrual age Age of the fetus as calculated from the beginning of the mother's last menstrual period.

menstrual cycle Hormonal cycle characterized by the periodic discharge of blood and tissue from the uterus. Cycles occur monthly from puberty to menopause, except during pregnancy and lactation.

mentally retarded Classification applied to persons who score at least two standard deviations (30 points) below normal on IQ tests and who also show an impaired ability to adapt to the demands of the environment.

mesosystem Bronfenbrenner's term for the interrelations among the various microsystems in which a person develops.

metacognition Knowledge about cognition and an understanding of the ways in which a person can control his or her own cognitive activity.

metamemory Understanding of the workings of memory; one aspect of metacognition.

microsystem Bronfenbrenner's term for a person's immediate surroundings.

midlife crisis State of physical and psychological distress that arises when the developmental tasks of midlife threaten to overwhelm a person's internal resources and social support.

minority As used by many researchers, term applied to any group that suffers discrimination or subordination because of its physical or cultural characteristics.

modified extended family Family structure in which each unit has its own separate dwelling but family members are held together by bonds of aid and affection.

modifier genes Genes that do not carry the basic instructions for a trait but affect the way the trait is expressed.

morality of constraint According to Piaget, the first stage of morality, in which virtuous conduct is based on obedience to authority; sometimes called *moral realism.*

morality of cooperation According to Piaget, the second stage of morality, in which virtuous conduct is based on what is expected, fair, or just; sometimes called *morality of reciprocity.*

moratorium Identity status in which the adolescent is struggling with occupational or ideological issues and may be in an identity crisis.

Moro reflex Newborn's unlearned response in which the neonate thrusts out the arms and curls the hands when support for the neck and head is removed; disappears by 5 or 6 months.

motherese Altered, simplified speech used by adults with infants; also called *baby talk, infant-directed speech,* or *child-directed speech.*

multiinfarct dementia Irreversible organic brain disorder that results from cardiovascular disease.

multiple intelligences Theory that intelligence consists of seven different domains: linguistic, musical, logical-mathematical, spatial, bodily-kinesthetic, intrapersonal, and interpersonal.

mutation Change in the chemical structure of a single gene.

naturalistic study Study in which a researcher observes and records behavior without interfering with it in any way.

neglected children Children who are not chosen as friends by their classmates. They are not disliked but are simply ignored.

neonate Technical term for the infant during the first month of life outside the uterus.

norms Typical patterns of growth or performance that describe the approximate ages at which important attributes and skills appear.

obesity Condition in which body weight is at least 20 percent more than the norm for height and in which there is an excessive proportion of fat to muscle.

object concept Mental representation of objects as remaining the same although they may move from place to place (object identity) and as continuing to exist when out of sight (object permanence).

observational learning Learning that occurs by watching others and observing their behavior and its consequences.

observational study Study in which a researcher observes people as they go about daily activities and carefully records their behavior. See also **naturalistic study** and **field study.**

operant conditioning Form of learning in which a response is strengthened or changed as a result of reinforcement.

operations Flexible and rigorous cognitive processes that first appear during the concrete-operational stage.

ordinal position Child's position in the family birth order.

organization Memory strategy that consists of grouping items that are to be remembered around some common element (e.g., all the animals).

ovaries Female reproductive glands, which mature and release ova.

overextension Process in which the child extends a word's meaning to cover objects or events that resemble the original labeled item in some way.

overregularization Temporary error in language acquisition in which the child applies a rule rigidly and makes the language more regular than it actually is.

ovum Female reproductive cell; the largest cell in the body.

parental imperative View that parenthood exerts a controlling influence over adult personality; based on the proposal that basic gender differences in personality have evolved in order to protect and nurture children.

performance test Nonverbal test of intelligence.

peripheral nervous system Division of the nervous system that connects the central nervous system (brain and spinal cord) with all parts of the body, sending sensory information to the brain and transmitting commands to various muscles and organs.

peripheral slowing hypothesis Theory that age-related declines in cognition are the result of slowed processing in the peripheral nervous system.

permissive parents Parents who place few demands on the child but are warm and responsive to the youngster.

personal fable Aspect of adolescent egocentrism in which the adolescent believes that he or she is unique and indestructible.

phenotype Nature of physical or behavioral traits as they appear in the individual, reflecting the influence of genes and environmental influences.

phenylketonuria (PKU) Inherited inability to metabolize phenylalanine, a component of milk and other foods.

placenta Pliable structure of tissue and blood vessels that transmits nourishment and wastes between mother and fetus.

placing reflex Newborn's unlearned ability to lift up a foot and place it on top of a surface; generally disappears between the third and fourth months.

polygenic Term referring to traits produced by a combination of several genes. All the genes may have an equal and cumulative effect in producing the trait, or some may have more influence than others.

positron emission tomography (PET) Method of studying brain function in which injections of radioactive glucose produce maps of brain activity.

postformal thought Level of cognition that is more advanced than Piaget's formal operations. Thinking is relativistic and dialectical, and the individual realizes that contradiction is a basic aspect of reality.

postpartum depression Emotional letdown that often follows the birth of a child; frequently called *baby blues.*

power-assertive discipline Disciplinary technique whose force resides in power. It includes using blows, threats, and commands, removing the person bodily, and withdrawing privileges.

practical intelligence Intelligence that includes the cognitive skills required to solve the problems of daily life.

pragmatics Social uses of language, in which words are used to accomplish the speaker's or writer's purpose.

pragmatics of intelligence Procedures that relate stored knowledge, expertise, and basic cognitive skills to everyday life; see also **dual-process model.**

premature affluence Situation in which a working adolescent has large sums of spending money but no financial responsibility for basic self-support.

premoral level Most primitive level in Kohlberg's theory of moral reasoning. Value is placed on physical acts and needs, not on people or social standards.

prenatal period First stage of development; the period from conception to birth.

preoperational thought Intuitive, inflexible, contradictory thought that is focused on individual events. According to Piaget, it emerges at about 18 months to 2 years.

preparedness Genetic predisposition to respond in ways that increase the chances of survival and to learn certain events easily.

pretend play Play that involves fantasy or role-taking.

primary aging Lifelong, universal, and inevitable aging process that cannot be prevented by diet, life style, or medical care.

primary circular reaction Repetition of behavior (such as sucking or kicking) for the stimulation it provides; characteristic of Substage 2 of Piaget's sensorimotor period.

principled level Third, and highest, level in Kohlberg's theory of moral reasoning. Value is placed on self-chosen principles and standards that have a universal logical validity and therefore can be shared.

production deficiency Person's failure to use a skill or capability that he or she possesses.

prosocial behavior Any action that promotes or benefits another person.

proximodistal development Progression of growth and development from the center of the body to its periphery.

psychometrics Mental testing; branch of psychology that has developed intelligence tests.

psychosexual theory Freud's psychodynamic theory of personality development, which focuses on the changing seat of sensual pleasures in the individual.

psychosocial theory Erikson's psychodynamic theory of personality development, which focuses on the individual's interactions with society.

puberty Biological process that turns a child into a sexually mature individual.

punishment Any unpleasant outcome of an action that makes it less likely that the action will be repeated.

pupil Student who is obedient, respects authority, shares materials and time, and controls any impulses or wishes for immediate gratification.

reaction range Range of possible responses within which a genetic trait can express itself.

reactivity Typical level of response to stimulation; regarded as an aspect of temperament.

recall Ability to remember information in the absence of the object or information to be remembered.

receptive learner Student who is task-oriented, is responsible, and maintains an acceptable level of academic achievement.

recessive (gene) Subordinate member of a pair of alleles. Unless matched by another recessive gene, its corresponding trait fails to appear in an individual who carries it.

recognition Perception of an object as familiar.

reflex Unlearned response to a specific stimulus that is not affected by motivation and that is common to all members of a species.

rehearsal Memory strategy in which a person facilitates encoding by repeating information that is to be remembered.

reinforcement Any consequence following an action (response) that makes it likely that a person will repeat the action.

reinstatement Reestablishment of a memory following a brief encounter with the original stimulus.

reintegrative stage In Schaie's theory of adult cognition, the period of later adulthood during which knowledge is applied to personal interests.

rejected children Children who are actively disliked by their classmates.

rejecting-neglecting parents Parents who place few demands on the child and are relatively cold and unresponsive to the youngster.

releasing stimulus Event that regularly evokes certain behavior in members of a species and helps explain regularities in typical behavior.

remote grandparent Grandparent whose relationship with the grandchild is reserved and formal.

replicate To repeat a scientific study, thereby supporting the accuracy of its findings.

residential care home Institution that provides personal care but no professional nursing services.

resistant attachment Least secure form of attachment bond, in which the infant becomes extremely upset when the caregiver leaves but is not comforted by the caregiver's return.

resource theory Theory that family size and spacing between siblings affect cognitive development through their effect on the amount of time and material parents can provide. The larger the family and the closer the spacing, the smaller the child's IQ.

respiratory distress syndrome Lung condition in which the preterm infant cannot maintain necessary surfactin levels.

responsible stage In Schaie's theory of adult cognition, the period in middle adulthood during which knowledge is used to fulfill family and vocational obligations.

reversibility Ability to understand that irrelevant changes in appearance can be reversed and that such changes tend to compensate one another; one of Piaget's concrete operations.

rooting reflex Newborn's unlearned tendency to turn the head and mouth in the direction of any object that gently stimulates the mouth area; disappears by 3 or 4 months.

rough-and-tumble play Play that involves chasing, scuffling, wrestling, and laughing, accompanied by signals indicating its lack of hostility.

scheme Piaget's term for patterns of action (banging, sucking) or mental structures (classification of objects) that are involved in the acquiring and structuring of knowledge.

secondary aging Environmentally induced deterioration of cognition and body; often difficult to distinguish from primary aging.

secondary circular reaction Repetition of learned behavior (such as shaking a rattle) because the event is interesting; characteristic of Substage 3 of Piaget's sensorimotor period.

secure attachment Form of attachment in which the infant actively seeks the caregiver on separation and is comforted by contact with the caregiver.

selective optimization Process of strengthening important skills and developing compensating skills to make up for biologically based losses that accompany aging.

self-concept Organized and integrated pattern of perceptions related to the self, including self-esteem and self-image.

self-efficacy Individual's judgment of personal competence in a specific situation. It influences the person's participation, motivation, and persistence in that situation.

self-fulfilling prophecy Expectation about behavior that evokes a situation in which the expectation is confirmed.

self-regulated learning Learning in which children are motivated, possess the required skills, plan and regulate these skills, and adapt them to the situation.

self-regulation Ability to control one's behavior so as to fulfill an intention.

semantics Aspect of language having to do with the meaning attached to language forms.

sensorimotor stage First stage in Piaget's theory, during which knowledge develops from the infant's sensations and physical actions.

separation distress Distress at being parted from an attachment figure.

sequential design Experimental design that combines elements from cross-sectional and longitudinal designs in a single study.

sleeper effect Any influence of teratogens that is not apparent at birth but appears later in development.

small for gestational age (SGA) Condition in which a baby is underweight for his or her gestational age.

social cognition Understanding of thoughts, emotions, and behavior, whether one's own or those of another person.

social comparison Process by which an individual assesses his or her own performance or ability by comparing it with that of other people in a reference group.

socialization Process by which an individual acquires the behavior, attitudes, values, and roles that society expects of its members.

social-learning theory Version of learning theory that views development as the result of conditioning, observation, and imitation.

socio-historical theory Theory that development proceeds through interaction between the individual and society, with social context channeling development.

somatomedins Growth hormones that promote cell division in muscles and in cartilage cells at the ends of bones.

sonogram Picture produced by bouncing sound waves off an object; used to guide tests for birth defects and to detect the presence of twins and other visible complications of pregnancy.

species-specific influences Genetic characteristics

that are shared by all members of a species and that produce similarities among the members.

speech act Utterance used for communication and intended to help the speaker achieve some goal.

spermatozoon Male reproductive cell—a sperm.

spina bifida Protrusion of spinal cord nerves through an opening in the back; caused by the failure of the neural tube to close during prenatal development.

stage Particular pattern of abilities, motives, or behavior that is predicted by a specific theory of development.

state Level of arousal along the continuum from deep sleep to crying that reflects response to inner and outer environment.

status offense Any delinquent act committed by adolescents that would not be illegal if committed by adults (e.g., drinking, cutting school, running away from home).

stepping reflex Newborn's unlearned tendency to straighten out the legs at the hip and knee as if to stand, when held with feet touching a surface; usually disappears by 3 or 4 months.

stranger wariness Natural reaction of babies to strangers that helps infants avoid potentially dangerous situations. The feeling is heightened when the attachment figure is absent.

Strange Situation Experimental design used to assess an infant's attachment bond.

strategy Technique used to encode or retrieve information, such as scanning, rehearsal, or organization.

sudden infant death syndrome (SIDS) Unexpected death, during sleep, of an apparently healthy infant; also known as *crib death.*

superego In psychodynamic theories, the conscience, which Freud saw as developing in early childhood when a child internalizes parental values and standards.

superordinate category Category determined primarily by function (e.g., vehicle, furniture); the most abstract level of categorization.

surfactin Liquid that coats the air sacs of the lungs and enables infants to transmit oxygen from the air to the blood.

symbolic representation Mental model or symbol that allows an object to be thought about in its absence.

syntax Body of structural principles that determine the form of sentences.

task analysis Process of defining a problem, understanding its particular demands, and choosing an appropriate goal.

telegraphic speech Speech in which utterances have been stripped to basic content words; typical of children in the two-word stage.

temperament Early, observable differences in the intensity and duration of babies' arousal and emotionality.

teratogen Agent that can disrupt fetal growth or cause malformation in the developing fetus.

term Gestational age of 266 days from conception.

terminal drop Noticeable drop in IQ scores that appears shortly before death and apparently is the result of physical deterioration or damage.

tertiary circular reaction Intelligent, systematic adaptation to a specific situation, characteristic of Substage 5 of Piaget's sensorimotor period.

testes Male reproductive glands, which manufacture and release sperm.

theory Set of logically related statements that generates testable hypotheses and explains some aspect of experience.

transition Change that involves the reordering of one's life or restructuring of one's goals in response to changing experiences, often in relation to a developmental task.

transitional object Specific object that provides emotional comfort to a distressed toddler.

triarchic theory Theory of intelligence that includes social, educational, and situational factors in addition to cognitive components of the information-processing system.

Turner's syndrome Condition resulting from the absence in girls of one female sex chromosome (XO). The girls generally are short, lack secondary sex characteristics, and have retarded spatial skills but normal verbal skills.

ultrasound Technique that produces sonograms.

umbilical cord Flexible cord, containing two arteries and one vein, that connects the developing organism to the placenta.

unconditioned reflex Response to a stimulus that occurs naturally and without any learning.

unconscious In psychodynamic theories, the part of the mind that contains forgotten or repressed memories and impulses.

variable Factor that can vary in size or strength and that may affect the results of a study.

variance Statistic that describes the distribution of individual scores.

very low birthweight Birthweight of less than 1250

grams (about 2 pounds 12 ounces), which places a baby in a high-risk category.

visual accommodation   Ability to alternate focus in order to see objects at different distances clearly.

working memory   Operational capacity of short-term memory.

zone of proximal development   Vygotsky's term for the area in which children, with the help of adults or more competent peers, can solve problems they are unable to solve by themselves.

zygote   Fertilized ovum; refers to developing organism during the first two weeks of development, when it is primarily engaged in cell division.

BIBLIOGRAPHY

Aboud, F. E. (1981). Egocentrism, conformity, and agreeing to disagree. *Developmental Psychology, 17,* 791–799. (Chap 10)

Abrahams, B., Feldman, S. S., & Nash, S. C. (1978). Sex role self-concept and sex role attitudes. *Developmental Psychology, 14,* 393–400. (Chap 16)

Abramovitch, R., Corter, C., Pepler, D. J., & Stanhope, L. (1986). Sibling and peer interaction. *Child Development, 57,* 217–229. (Chap 9)

Abramson, P. (1985, November 25). Genentech's drug problem. *Newsweek,* p. 70. (Chap 5)

Abravanel, E., & Gingold, H. (1985). Learning via observation during the second year of life. *Developmental Psychology, 21,* 614–623. (Chap 6)

Abravanel, E., & Sigafoos, A. A. (1984). Exploring the presence of imitation during early infancy. *Child Development, 55,* 381–392. (Chap 6)

Acheson, R. M. (1960). Effects of nutrition and disease on human growth. In J. M. Tanner (Ed.), *Human growth.* New York: Pergamon. (Chap 5)

Ackerman, B. P. (1988). Search set access problems in retrieving episodic information from memory in children and adults. *Journal of Experimental Child Psychology, 45,* 234–261. (Chap 11)

Ackerman, R. J. (1990). Career developments and transitions of middle-aged women. *Psychology of Women Quarterly, 14,* 513–530. (Chap 18)

Acredolo, K. (1982). Conservation-nonconservation. In C. J. Brainerd (Ed.), *Children's logical and mathematical cognition.* New York: Springer-Verlag. (Chap 11)

Acredolo, L. P. (1979). Laboratory vs. home. *Developmental Psychology, 15,* 666–667. (Chap 6)

Acredolo, L. P., & Evans, D. (1980). Developmental changes in the effects of landmarks on infant spatial behavior. *Developmental Psychology, 16,* 312–318. (Chap 6)

Adams, C., Labouvie-Vief, G., Hobart, C. J., & Dorosz, M. (1990). Adult age group differences in story recall style. *Journal of Gerontology: Psychological Sciences, 45,* P17–27. (Chap 19)

Adams, G., & Fitch, S. (1982). Ego stage and identity status development: A cross-sequential analysis. *Journal of Personality and Social Psychology, 43,* 574–583. (Chap 13)

Adams, R. G., & Blieszner, R. (1989). *Perspectives on later life friendships.* Beverly Hills, CA: Sage. (Chap 20)

Adamson, L. B., & Bakeman, R. (1985). Affection and attention. *Child Development, 56,* 582–593. (Chap 1)

Adelson, J. (1983, Summer). The growth of thought in adolescence. *Educational Horizons,* pp. 156–162. (Chap 14)

Adelson, J. (1985). Adolescence for clinicians. In G. Stricker & R. Keisner (Eds.), *From research to clinical practice.* New York: Plenum. (Chap 15)

Adelson, J., & Doehrman, M. J. (1980). The psychodynamic approach to adolescence. In J. Adelson (Ed.), *Handbook of adolescent psychology.* New York: Wiley. (Chap 13)

Adelson, J., & Hall, E. (1987). Children and other political naifs. In E. Hall, *Growing and changing.* New York: Random House. (Chap 14)

Ainsworth, M. D. S. (1967). *Infancy in Uganda.* Baltimore: Johns Hopkins University Press. (Chap 8)

Ainsworth, M. D. S., Blehar, M. C., Waters, E., & Wall, S. (1978). *Patterns of attachment.* Hillsdale, NJ: Erlbaum. (Chap 8)

Aldwin, C. M. (1991). Does age affect the stress and coping process? Implications of age differences in perceived control. *Journal of Gerontology: Psychological Sciences, 46,* P174–180. (Chap 20)

Allen, T. (1982). *Oral-oral and oral-visual object discrimination.* Paper presented at the meeting of the International Conference on Infant Studies, Austin, TX. (Chap 6)

Allen, V. L., & Newtson, D.

(1972). Development of conformity and independence. *Journal of Personality and Social Psychology, 22,* 18–30. (Chap 10)

American Association on Mental Deficiency. (1977). *Manual on terminology and classification of mental retardation* (rev. ed.). Washington, DC: Author. (Chap 12)

American Psychiatric Association. (1980). *Diagnostic and statistical manual of mental disorders* (3rd ed.). Washington, DC: Author. (Chap 19)

Ancoli-Israel, S., Kripke, D. F., Mason, W., & Kaplan, O. J. (1985). Sleep apnea and periodic movements in an aging sample. *Journal of Gerontology, 40,* 419–425. (Chap 20)

Anderson, E. R., Hetherington, E. M., & Clingempeel, W. G. (1989). Transformation in family relations at puberty: Effects of family context. *Journal of Early Adolescence, 9,* 310–334. (Chap 13)

Anderson, G. C., Burroughs, A. K., & Measel, C. P. (1983). Nonnutritive sucking opportunities. In T. Field & A. Sostek (Eds.), *Infants born at risk.* New York: Grune & Stratton. (Chap 4)

Anderson, R. C., Hiebert, E. H., Scott, J. A., & Wilkinson, I. A. G. (1985). *Becoming a nation of readers.* Washington, DC: National Institute of Education. (Chap 12)

Anisfeld, M. (1991). Neonatal imitation. *Developmental Review, 11,* 60–97. (Chap 6)

Ankarloo, B. (1978). Marriage and family formation. In T. K. Hareven (Ed.), *Transitions.* New York: Academic Press. (Chap 16)

Antell, S. E., & Keating, D. P. (1983). Perception of numerical invariance in neonates. *Child Development, 54,* 695–701. (Chaps 6, 11)

Antonucci, T. C. (1985). Personal characteristics, social supports, and social behavior. In R. H. Binstock & E. Shanas (Eds.), *Handbook of aging and the social sciences* (2nd ed.). New York: Van Nostrand Reinhold. (Chap 20)

Antonucci, T. C. (1990). Social supports and social relationships. In R. H. Binstock & L. K. George (Eds.), *Handbook of aging and the social sciences* (3rd ed.). San Diego, CA: Academic Press. (Chap 20)

Antonucci, T. C., & Mikus, K. (1988). The power of parenthood: Personality and attitudinal changes during the transition to parenthood. In G. Y. Michaels & W. A. Goldberg (Eds.), *The transition to parenthood.* New York: Cambridge University Press. (Chap 16)

Apgar, V., Holaday, D. A., James, L. S., Weisbrot, I. M., & Berrien, C. (1958). Evaluation of the newborn infant—second report. *Journal of the American Medical Association, 168,* 1985–1988. (Chap 4)

Aries, P. A. (1962). *Centuries of childhood.* New York: Vintage. (Chap 1)

Aries, P. A. (1981). *The hour of our death.* New York: Knopf. (Chap 20)

Arling, G. L., & Harlow, H. F. (1967). Effects of social deprivation on maternal behavior of rhesus monkeys. *Journal of Comparative and Psychological Psychology, 64,* 371–377. (Chap 8)

Arluke, A., & Levin, J. (1984, August). Another stereotype: Old age as a second childhood. *Aging,* pp. 7–11. (Chap 19)

Arterberry, M., Yonas, A., & Bensen, A. S. (1989). Self-produced locomotion and the development of responsiveness to linear perspective and texture gradients. *Developmental Psychology, 25,* 976–982. (Chap 6)

Asher, S. R. (1990). Recent advances in the study of peer rejection. In S. R. Asher & J. D. Coie (Eds.), *Peer rejection in childhood.* New York: Cambridge University Press. (Chap 10)

Asher, S. R., & Parker, J. G. (1991). Significance of peer relationship problems in childhood. In B. H. Schneider, G. Attili, J. Nadel, & R. P. Weissberg (Eds.), *Social competence in developmental perspective.* Amsterdam: Kluwer Academic Publishing. (Chaps 10, 13)

Asher, S. R., Singleton, L. C., & Taylor, A. R. (1982). *Acceptance vs. friendship.* Paper presented at the meeting of the American Research Association, New York. (Chap 10)

Ashmead, D. H., & Perlmutter, M. (1980). Infant memory in everyday life. In M. Perlmutter (Ed.), *New directions for child development*

(No. 10). San Francisco: Jossey-Bass. (Chap 6)

Aslin, R. N., Pisoni, D. B., & Jusczyk, P. W. (1983). Auditory development and speech perception in infancy. In P. H. Mussen (Ed.), *Handbook of child psychology* (Vol. 2, 4th ed.). New York: Wiley. (Chaps 4, 7)

Atchley, R. C. (1976). *The sociology of retirement.* New York: Halstead Press. (Chap 20)

Attie, I., & Brooks-Gunn, J. (1989). Development of eating problems in adolescent girls: A longitudinal study. *Developmental Psychology, 25,* 70–79. (Chap 15)

Au, T. K.-F., & Glusman, M. (1990). The principle of mutual exclusivity in word learning: To honor or not to honor. *Child Development, 61,* 1474–1490. (Chap 7)

Austin, C. R., & Short, R. V. (1984). *Reproduction in mammals.* Vol. 3: *Hormond control of reproduction* (2nd ed.). (Chap 13)

Azmitia, M., & Perlmutter, M. (1989). Social influences on children's cognition: State of the art and future directions. In H. W. Reese (Ed.), *Advances in child development and behavior* (Vol. 22). San Diego, CA: Academic Press. (Chap 11)

Babcock, R. L., & Salthouse, T. A. (1990). Effect of increased processing demands on age differences in working memory. *Psychology and Aging, 5,* 421–428. (Chap 19)

Babson, S. G., Pernoll, M. L., Benda, G. I., & Simpson, K. (1980). *Diagnosis and management of the fetus and neonate at risk* (4th ed.). St. Louis: Mosby. (Chap 3)

Bachman, J. G. (1983, Summer). Premature influence: Do high school students earn too much? *Economic Outlook USA,* pp. 64–67. (Chap 13)

Bachman, J. G. (1991). High school senior class of 1990. Unpublished data, Institute for Social Research, University of Michigan, Ann Arbor. (Chaps 13, 14, 15)

Bachman, J. G., O'Malley, P. M., & Johnston, J. (1978). *Youth in transition* (Vol. 6). Ann Arbor, MI: Institute for Social Research. (Chap 16)

Bachrach, C. A. (1980). Childlessness and social isolation among the elderly. *Journal of Marriage and the Family, 42,* 627–637. (Chap 20)

Bakeman, R., Adamson, L. B., Konner, M., & Barr, R. G. (1990). !Kung Infancy: The social context of object exploration. *Child Development, 61,* 794–809. (Chap 8)

Baker, S. A., Thalberg, S. P., & Morrison, D. M. (1988). Parents' behavioral norms as predictors of adolescent sexual activity and contraceptive use. *Adolescence, 23,* 265–282. (Chap 13)

Baldwin, A. L., Baldwin, C., & Cole, R. E. (1990). Stress resistant families and stress resistant children. In J. Rolf, A. S. Masten, D. Cicchetti, K. Neuchterlein, & S. Weintraub (Eds.), *Risk and protective factors in the development of psychopathology.* Cambridge, England: Cambridge University Press. (Chaps 9, 13, 16)

Baltes, M. M., Kindermann, T., Reisenzein, R., & Schmid, U. (1987). Further observational data on the behavioral and social world of institutions for the aged. *Psychology and Aging, 2,* 390–403. (Chap 20)

Baltes, P. B. (1987). Theoretical propositions of life-span developmental psychology: On the dynamics between growth and decline. *Developmental Psychology, 23,* 611–626. (Chap 17)

Baltes, P. B., Reese, H. W., & Nesselroade, J. R. (1977). *Life-span developmental psychology.* Monterey, CA: Brooks/Cole. (Chap 1)

Baltes, P. B., Smith, J., Staudinger, U. M., & Sowarka, D. (1991). Wisdom: One facet of successful aging? In M. Perlmutter (Ed.), *Late life potential.* Washington, DC: Gerontological Society of America. (Chap 19)

Baltes, P. B., Sowarka, D., & Kliegl, R. (1989). Cognitive training research on fluid intelligence in old age: What can older adults achieve by themselves? *Psychology and Aging, 44,* 217–221. (Chap 19)

Bancroft, J. (1989). *Human sexuality and its problems.* London: Churchill Livingstone. (Chap 18)

Bandura, A. (1977). *Social learning theory.* Englewood Cliffs, NJ: Prentice-Hall. (Chap 7)

Bandura, A. (1982). The psychology of chance encounters and life

paths. *American Psychologist, 37,* 747–755. (Chap 1)

Bandura, A. (1986). *Social foundations of thought and action.* Englewood Cliffs, NJ: Prentice-Hall. (Chaps 2, 7, 9, 10, 20)

Bandura, A. (1989a). Regulation of cognitive processes through perceived self-efficacy. *Developmental Psychology, 25,* 729–735. (Chap 11)

Bandura, A. (1989b). Social cognitive theory. *Annals of Child Development, 6,* 1–60. (Chaps 2, 9)

Bandura, A., Ross, D., & Ross, S. A. (1966). Imitation of film-mediated aggressive models. *Journal of Abnormal and Social Psychology, 66,* 3–11. (Chap 10)

Bandura, A., & Walters, R. H. (1963). *Social learning and personality development.* New York: Holt, Rinehart and Winston. (Chap 2)

Banks, M. S., & Salapatek, P. (1983). Infant visual perception. In P. H. Mussen (Ed.), *Handbook of child psychology* (Vol. 2, 4th ed.). New York: Wiley. (Chaps 4, 6)

Barber, B. L., & Eccles, J. S. (1992). Long-term influence of divorce and single parenting on adolescent family- and work-related values, behaviors, and aspirations. *Psychological Bulletin, 111,* 108–126. (Chap 12)

Barglow, P., Vaughn, B. E., & Molitor, N. (1987). Effects of maternal absence due to employment on the quality of infant-mother attachment in a low risk sample. *Child Development, 58,* 945–954. (Chap 8)

Barnett, R. C., & Baruch, G. K. (1987). Social roles, gender, and psychological distress. In R. C. Barnett, L. Biener, & G. K. Baruch (Eds.), *Gender & stress.* New York: Free Press. (Chap 16)

Baroody, A. J. (1985). Mastery of basic number combinations. *Journal for Research in Mathematics Education, 16,* 83–98. (Chap 12)

Barr, H. M., Streissguth, A. P., Darby, B. L., & Sampson, P. D. (1990). Prenatal exposure to alcohol, caffeine, tobacco, and aspirin: Effects on fine and gross motor performance in 4-year-old children. *Developmental Psychology, 26,* 339–348. (Chap 3)

Barrett, T. R., & Watkins, S. K. (1986). Word familiarity and cardiovascular health as determinants of

age-related recall differences. *Journal of Gerontology, 41,* 222–224. (Chap 19)

Barringer, F. (1991, November 3). Drop in births reported, and recession is blamed. *New York Times,* pp. A1, A28. (Chap 16)

Barringer, F. (1992, July 17). Rate of marriage continues to decline. *New York Times,* p. A20. (Chap 16)

Bartsch, K., & Wellman, H. M. (1989). Young children's attribution of action to beliefs and desires. *Child Development, 60,* 946–964. (Chap 11)

Bartz, K. W., & Levine, E. S. (1978, November). Child rearing by black parents: A description and comparison to Anglo and Chicano parents. *Journal of Marriage and the Family,* pp. 709–719. (Chap 8)

Baruch, G. K. (1972). Maternal influences upon college women's attitudes toward women and work. *Developmental Psychology, 6,* 32–37. (Chap 9)

Baruch, G. K., & Barnett, R. (1986). Role quality in multiple role involvement and psychological well-being in midlife women (Working Paper No. 149). Wellesley, MA: Center for Research on Women, Wellesley College. (Chap 18)

Baruch, G. K., Barnett, R. C., & Rivers, C. (1983). *Life prints.* New York: McGraw-Hill. (Chaps 16, 18)

Basseches, M. (1984). Dialectical thinking as metasystematic form of cognitive organization. In M. L. Commons, F. A. Richards, & C. Armon (Eds.), *Beyond formal operations: Late adolescent and adult cognitive development.* New York: Praeger. (Chap 17)

Bates, E. (1979). *The emergence of symbols.* New York: Academic Press. (Chap 7)

Bates, E., Bretherton, I., Beeghly-Smith, M., & McNew, S. (1982). Social bases of language development. In H. W. Reese & L. P. Lipsitt (Eds.), *Advances in child development and behavior* (Vol. 16). New York: Academic Press. (Chap 7)

Bates, E., Thal, D., Whitesell, K., Fenson, L., & Oakes, L. (1989). Integrating language and gesture in infancy. *Developmental Psychology, 25,* 1004–1019. (Chap 7)

Bauer, P. J., & Mandler, J. M. (1989). One thing follows another:

Effects of temporal structure on 1- to 2-year-olds' recall of events. *Developmental Psychology, 25,* 197–206. (Chaps 6, 11)

Baumrind, D. (1967). Childcare practices anteceding 3 patterns of preschool behavior. *Genetic Psychology Monograph, 4* (1, Pt. 2). (Chap 9)

Baumrind, D. (1986). *Familial antecedents of social competence in middle childhood.* Unpublished monograph, Institute of Human Development, University of California, Berkeley. (Chaps 9, 13)

Baumrind, D. (1991a). The influence of parenting style on adolescent competence and substance use. *Journal of Early Adolescence, 11,* 56–95. (Chap 15)

Baumrind, D. (1991b). Parenting styles and adolescent development. In J. Brooks-Gunn, R. Lerner, & A. C. Petersen (Eds.), *The encyclopedia on adolescence.* New York: Garland Press. (Chap 13)

Bayley, N. (1956). Individual patterns of development. *Child Development, 27,* 45–74. (Chap 5)

Bayley, N. (1969). *Manual for the Bayley scale of infant development.* New York: Psychological Corporation. (Chap 7)

Baylor, A. M., & Spirduso, W. W. (1988). Systematic aerobic exercise and components of reaction time in women. *Journal of Gerontology: Psychological Sciences, 43,* P121–126. (Chap 17)

Beal, C. R. (1985). Development of knowledge about the use of cues to aid prospective retrieval. *Child Development, 56,* 631–642. (Chap 11)

Beal, C. R., & Belgrad, S. L. (1990). The development of message evaluation skills in young children. *Child Development, 61,* 705–712. (Chap 11)

Bear, M. (1990). Social networks and health: Impact on returning home after entry into residential care homes. *Gerontologist, 30,* 30–34. (Chap 20)

Beck, M. (1991, November 11). School days for seniors. *Newsweek,* pp. 60–65. (Chap 17)

Beck, M. (1992, May 25). Menopause. *Newsweek,* pp. 71–79. (Chap 18)

Becker, J. (1989). Preschoolers' use of number words to denote one-to-one correspondence. *Child Development, 60,* 1147–1157. (Chap 11)

Becker, J. M. (1977). A learning analysis of the development of peer-oriented behavior in 9-month-old infants. *Developmental Psychology, 13,* 481–491. (Chap 8)

Becker, W. C. (1964). Consequences of different kinds of parental discipline. In M. L. Hoffman & L. W. Hoffman (Eds.), *Review of child development research* (Vol. 1). New York: Russell Sage Foundation. (Chap 9)

Begley, S. (1986). The troubling question of "fetal rights." *Newsweek.* (Chap 3)

Bell, A. P., & Weinberg, M. S. (1978). *Homosexualities.* New York: Simon & Schuster. (Chap 16)

Bell, R. (1980). *Changing bodies, changing lives.* New York: Random House. (Chap 13)

Bell, R. Q., & Harper, L. V. (1977). *Child effects on adults.* Hillsdale, NJ: Erlbaum. (Chap 9)

Bell, S. M. (1970). The development of the concept of object as related to infant-mother attachment. *Child Development, 41,* 291–311. (Chap 8)

Bellinger, D., Leviton, A., Waternaux, C., Needleman, H., & Rabinowitz, M. (1987). Longitudinal analysis of prenatal and postnatal lead exposure and early cognitive development. *New England Journal of Medicine, 316,* 1037–1043. (Chap 3)

Belsky, J., Spanier, G. M., & Rovine, M. (1983). Stability and change in marriage across the transition to parenthood. *Journal of Marriage and the Family, 45,* 567–577. (Chap 16)

Bem, S. L. (1983). Gender schema theory and its implications for child development. *Signs, '8,* 598–616. (Chap 9)

Bem, S. L. (1989). Genital knowledge and gender constancy in preschool children. *Child Development, 60,* 649–662. (Chap 9)

Benbow, C. P., & Arjmand, O. (1990). Predictors of high academic achievement in mathematics and science by mathematically talented students: A longitudinal study. *Journal of Educational Psychology, 82,* 430–441. (Chap 12)

Bengston, V. L., Cutler, N. E., Mangen, D. J., & Marshall, V. W. (1985). Generations, cohorts, and relations between age groups. In R. H. Binstock & E. Shanas (Eds.), *Handbook of aging and the social sciences* (2nd ed.). New York: Van Nostrand Reinhold. (Chap 20)

Bengston, V. L., Reedy, M. N., & Gordon, C. (1985). Aging and self-conceptions: Personality processes and social contexts. In J. E. Birren & K. W. Schaie (Eds.), *Handbook of the psychology of aging.* (2nd ed.). New York: Van Nostrand Reinhold. (Chaps 18, 20)

Bengston, V. L., Rosenthal, C., & Burton, L. (1990). Families and aging: Diversity and heterogeneity. In R. H. Binstock & L. K. George (Eds.), *Handbook of aging and the social sciences* (3rd ed.). San Diego, CA: Academic Press. (Chaps 18, 20)

Bentley, A. M. (1983). Personal and global futurity in Scottish and Swazi students. *Journal of Social Psychology, 12,* 223–229. (Chap 14)

Berg, C. A. (1989). Knowledge of strategies for dealing with everyday problems from childhood through adolescence. *Developmental Psychology, 25,* 607–618. (Chap 14)

Berg, W. K., & Berg, K. M. (1979). Psychophysiological development in infancy. In J. D. Osofsky (Ed.), *Handbook of infant development.* New York: Wiley. (Chap 4)

Berke, R. L. (1989, June 22). Late childbirth is found on the rise. *New York Times,* p. A16. (Chap 16)

Berkowitz, G. S., Skovron, M. S., Lapinski, R. H., & Berkowitz, R. L. (1990). Delayed childbearing and the outcome of pregnancy. *New England Journal of Medicine, 332,* 659–664. (Chap 3)

Berman, A. L., & Jobes, D. A. (1991). *Adolescent suicide: Assessment and intervention.* Washington, DC: American Psychological Association. (Chap 15)

Berndt, T. J. (1979). Developmental changes in conformity to peers and parents. *Developmental Psychology, 15,* 608–616. (Chaps 10, 13)

Berndt, T. J. (1986). Children's comments about their friends. In M. Perlmutter (Ed.), *Minnesota symposia on child psychology* (Vol. 18). Hillsdale, NJ: Erlbaum. (Chap 10)

Berndt, T. J., & Hoyle, S. G. (1985). Stability and change in childhood and adolescent friendships. *Developmental Psychology, 21,* 1007–1015. (Chap 10)

Berndt, T. J., Laychak, A. E., & Park, K. (1990). Friends' influence on adolescents' academic achievement motivation: An experimental study. *Journal of Educational Psychology, 82,* 664–670. (Chap 14)

Berndt, T. J., & Miller, K. E. (1990). Expectancies, values, and achievement in junior high school. *Journal of Educational Psychology, 82,* 319–326. (Chap 14)

Berry, J. M., West, R. L., & Dennehey, D. M. (1989). Reliability and validity of the Memory Self-Efficacy questionnaire. *Developmental Psychology, 25,* 701–713. (Chap 19)

Berscheid, E., Walster, E., & Bohrnstedt, G. (1973, November). Body image. *Psychology Today,* pp. 119–131. (Chap 18)

Bertenthal, B. I., & Fischer, K. W. (1983). The development of representation in search. *Child Development, 54,* 846–857. (Chaps 6, 8)

Bettes, B. A., Dusenbury, L., Kerner, J., James-Ortiz, S., & Botvin, G. J. (1990). Ethnicity and psychosocial factors in alcohol and tobacco use in adolescence. *Child Development, 61,* 557–565. (Chap 15)

Bielicki, T., & Welon, Z. (1982). Growth data as indicators of social inequalities: The case of Poland. *Yearbook of Physical Anthropology, 25,* 153–167. (Chap 5)

Bijou, S. W., & Baer, D. M. (1965). *Child development* (Vol. 2). New York: Appleton-Century-Crofts. (Chap 7)

Biller, H. D. (1981). Father absence, divorce, and personality development. In M. E. Lamb (Ed.), *The role of the father in child development* (2nd ed.). New York: Wiley. (Chap 9)

Binet, A., & Simon, T. (1916). *The development of intelligence in children.* Baltimore: Williams & Wilkins. (Chap 12)

Birnbaum, J. A. (1975). Life patterns and self-esteem in gifted family-oriented and career-committed women. In M. T. S. Mednick, S. S. Tangi, & L. W. Hoffman (Eds.), *Women and achievement.* New York: Halstead Press. (Chaps 16, 18)

Birnholz, J. C., & Benacerraf, B. R. (1983). The development of human fetal hearing. *Science, 222,* 516–518. (Chaps 3, 4)

Biron, O., Mongeau, J.-G., & Bertrand, D. (1977). Familial resemblance of bodyweight and weight/height in 374 homes with adopted children. *Journal of Pediatrics, 91,* 555–558. (Chap 5)

Birren, J. E., & Birren, B. A. (1990). The concepts, models, and history of the psychology of aging. In J. E. Birren & K. W. Schaie (Eds.), *Handbook of the psychology of aging* (3rd ed.). San Diego. CA: Academic Press. (Chap 1)

Birren, J. E., & Woodruff, D. S. (1973). Human development over the life span through education. In P. B. Baltes & K. W. Schaie (Eds.), *Life-span developmental psychology: Personality and socialization.* New York: Academic Press. (Chap 17)

Bisping, R., Steingrueber, H. J., Oltmann, M., & Wenk, C. (1990). Adults' tolerance of cries: An experimental investigation of acoustic features. *Child Development, 61,* 1218–1229. (Chap 4)

Bjorklund, D. F. (1987). A note on neonatal imitation. *Developmental Review, 7,* 86–92. (Chap 6)

Blair, S. N., Kohl, H. W., Paffenbarger, R. S., Clark, D. G., Cooper, K. H., & Gibbons, L. W. (1989). Physical fitness and all-cause mortality. *New England Journal of Medicine, 262,* 2395–2401. (Chap 18)

Blanchard-Fields, F. (1986). Reasoning on social dilemmas varying in emotional saliency. *Psychology and Aging, 1,* 325–333. (Chap 17)

Blasi, A. (1980). Bridging moral cognition and moral action. *Psychological Bulletin, 88,* 593–637. (Chap 11)

Blasi, A., & Hoeffel, E. C. (1974). Adolescence and formal operations. *Human Development, 17,* 344–363. (Chap 14)

Blaske, D. M., Borduin, C. M., Henggeler, S. W., & Mann, B. J. (1989). Individual, family, and peer characteristics of adolescent sex offenders and assaultive offenders. *Developmental Psychology, 25,* 846–855. (Chap 15)

Blass, E. M. (1990). Suckling: Determinants, changes, mechanisms, and lasting impressions. *Developmental Psychology, 26,* 520–533. (Chap 4)

Blass, E. M., & Smith, B. A. (1992). Differential effects of sucrose, fructose, glucose, and lactose on crying in 1- to 3-day-old human infants: Qualitative and quantitative considerations. *Developmental Psychology, 28,* 804–810. (Chap 4)

Block, J. (1971). *Lives through time.* Berkeley, CA: Bancroft Books. (Chap 16)

Block, J. H., Block, J., & Gjerde, P. F. (1986). The personality of children prior to divorce. *Child Development, 57,* 827–840. (Chap 9)

Bloom, L. M. (1970). *Language development.* Cambridge, MA: MIT Press. (Chap 7)

Bloom, L. M., & Capatides, J. B. (1987). Expression of affect and the emergence of language. *Child Development, 58,* 1513–1522. (Chap 7)

Blumstein, P., & Schwartz, P. (1983). *American couples.* New York: Morrow. (Chaps 16, 18)

Blurton-Jones, N. (1976). Rough-and-tumble play among nursery school children. In J. Bruner, A. Jolly, & K. Sylva (Eds.), *Play.* New York: Basic Books. (Chap 5)

Blyth, D. A., Simmons, R. G., & Zakin, D. F. (1985). Satisfaction with body image for early adolescent females. *Journal of Youth and Adolescence, 14,* 207–226. (Chap 13)

Boccia, M., & Campos, J. (1983). *Maternal emotional signaling.* Paper presented at the meeting of the Society for Research in Child Development, Detroit. (Chap 8)

Bogin, B. (1988). *Patterns of human growth.* New York: Cambridge University Press. (Chaps 5, 13)

Bohannon, J. H., III, & Warren-Leubecker, A. (1985). Theoretical approaches in language acquisition. In J. B. Gleason (Ed.), *The development of language.* Columbus, OH: Charles E. Merrill. (Chap 7)

Bohlin, G., Hagekull, B., Germer, M., Andersson, K., & Lindberg, L. (1989). Avoidant and resistant reunion behaviors as predicted by maternal interactive behavior and infant temperament. *Infant Behavior and Development, 12,* 105–117. (Chap 8)

Boldizar, J. P., Perry, D. G., & Perry, L. C. (1989). Outcome values and aggression. *Child Development, 60,* 571–579. (Chap 9)

Boller, K., Rovee-Collier, C. K., Borovsky, D., O'Connor, J., & Shyi, G. (1990). Developmental changes in the time-dependent nature of memory retrieval. *Developmental Psychology, 26,* 770–779. (Chap 6)

Bollerud, K. H., Christopherson, S. B., & Frank, E. S. (1990). Girls' sexual choices: Looking for what is right. In C. Gilligan, N. P. Lyons, & T. J. Hammer (Eds.), *Making connections.* Cambridge, MA: Harvard University Press. (Chap 13)

Bolton, F. G., Jr. (1980). *The pregnant adolescent.* Beverly Hills, CA: Sage. (Chap 15)

Bondareff, W. (1985). The neural basis of aging. In J. E. Birren & K. W. Schaie (Eds.), *Handbook of the psychology of aging* (2nd ed.). New York: Van Nostrand Reinhold. (Chap 19)

Boom, J., & Molenaar, P. C. M. (1989). A developmental model of hierarchical stage structure in objective moral judgements. *Developmental Review, 9,* 133–145. (Chap 1)

Bootzin, R. R., Loftus, E. F., Zajonc, R. B., & Hall, E. (1982). *Psychology today: An introduction* (5th ed.). New York: Random House. (Chap 10)

Borkowski, J. G., Carr, M., Rellinger, E., & Pressley, M. (1990). Self-regulated cognition: Interdependence of metacognition, attributions, and self-esteem. In B. Jones & L. Idol (Eds.), *Dimensions of thinking.* Hillsdale, NJ: Erlbaum. (Chap 12)

Bornstein, M. H. (1985). Habituation of attention as a measure of visual processing in human infants. In G. Gottlieb & N. A. Krasnego (Eds.), *Development of audition and vision during the first year of postnatal life.* Norwood, NJ: Ablex. (Chap 6)

Bornstein, M. H. (1988). Perceptual development. In M. H. Bornstein & M. E. Lamb (Eds.), *Developmental psychology* (2nd ed.). Hillsdale, NJ: Erlbaum. (Chap 4)

Bornstein, M. H. (1989). Cross-cultural developmental comparisons: The case of Japanese-American infant and mother activities and interac-

tions. What we know, what we need to know, and why we need to know. *Developmental Review, 9,* 171–204. (Chap 1)

Bornstein, M. H., & Benasich, A. A. (1986). Infant habituation. *Child Development, 57,* 87–99. (Chap 6)

Bornstein, M. H., Gaughran, J., & Homel, P. (1986). Temperament. In C. E. Izard & P. B. Read (Eds.), *Measurement of emotion in infants and children* (Vol. 2). New York: Cambridge University Press. (Chap 4)

Bornstein, M. H., & Ruddy, M. G. (1984). Infant attention and maternal stimulation. In H. Bouma & D. G. Bouwhuis (Eds.), *Attention and performance* (Vol. 10). London: Erlbaum. (Chap 7)

Bornstein, M. H., & Sigman, M. (1986). Continuity in mental development from infancy. *Child Development, 57,* 251–274. (Chap 6)

Bornstein, M. H., Tal, J., Rahn, C., Galperin, C. Z., Pecheux, M.-G., Lamour, M., Toda, S., Azuma, H., Ogino, M., & Tamis-LeMonda, C. S. (1992). Functional analysis of the contents of maternal speech to infants of 5 and 13 months in four cultures: Argentina, France, Japan, and the United States. *Developmental Psychology, 28,* 593–603. (Chap 8)

Bosse, R., Aldwin, C. M., Levenson, M. R., & Workman-Daniels, K. (1991). How stressful is retirement? Findings from the Normative Aging Study. *Journal of Gerontology: Psychological Sciences, 46,* P9–14. (Chap 20)

Bouchard, T. J., & McGue, M. (1981). Familial studies of intelligence: A review. *Science, 29,* 1055–1059. (Chap 1)

Bower, T. G. R., & Wishart, J. (1972). The effects of motor skill on object permanence. *Cognition, 1,* 165–172. (Chap 6)

Bowey, J. A., Cain, M. T., & Ryan, S. M. (1992). A reading-level design study of phonological skills underlying fourth-grade children's word reading difficulties. *Child Development, 63,* 999–1011. (Chap 12)

Bowlby, J. (1951). *Maternal care and mental health.* Geneva: World Health Organization. (Chap 9)

Bowlby, J. (1969). *Attachment and loss.* Vol. 1: *Attachment.* New York: Basic Books. (Chaps 2, 8)

Bowlby, J. (1973). *Attachment and loss.* Vol. 2: *Separation.* New York: Basic Books. (Chap 8)

Bowlby, J. (1980). *Attachment and loss.* Vol. 3: *Loss.* New York: Basic Books. (Chap 8)

Bowles, N. L., & Poon, L. W. (1982). An analysis of the effect of aging on recognition memory. *Journal of Gerontology, 37,* 212–219. (Chap 19)

Bowman, P. J. (1990). The adolescent-to-adult transition: Discouragement among jobless black youth. In V. C. McLoyd & C. A. Flanagan (Eds.), *New directions for child development* (No. 46). San Francisco: Jossey-Bass. (Chaps 15, 16)

Bowser, B. P., Fullilove, M. T., & Fullilove, R. E. (1990). African-American youth and AIDS high-risk behavior: The social context and barriers to prevention. *Youth & Society, 22,* 54–66. (Chap 15)

Boxer, A. M. (1988). Betwixt and between: Developmental discontinuities of gay and lesbian youth. Paper presented at the biennial meeting of the Society for Research on Adolescence, Alexandria, VA. (Chap 13)

Bradbury, T. N., & Fincham, F. D. (1988). Individual difference variables in close relationships: A contextual model of marriage as an integrative framework. *Journal of Personality and Social Psychology, 54,* 713–721. (Chap 16)

Bradley, R. H., & Caldwell, B. M. (1984). The relation of infants' home environments to achievement test performance at fifty-four months: A follow-up study. *Child Development, 55,* 803–809. (Chap 12)

Branch, C. W., & Newcombe, N. (1986). Racial attitude development among young black children as a function of parental attitude. *Child Development, 57,* 712–721. (Chap 10)

Brandtstadter, J. (1989). Personal self-regulation of development: Cross-sequential analyses of development-related control beliefs and emotions. *Developmental Psychology, 25,* 96–108. (Chap 19)

Bray, D. W., & Howard, A. (1983). The AT&T longitudinal study of managers. In K. W. Schaie

(Ed.), *Longitudinal studies of adult psychological development.* New York: Guilford Press. (Chap 18)

Brazelton, T. B. (1973). *The Neonatal Behavioral Assessment Scale.* Philadelphia: Lippincott. (Chap 4)

Brazelton, T. B. (1990). Saving the bathwater. *Child Development, 61,* 1661–1671. (Chap 4)

Brigham, M. C., & Pressley, M. (1988). Cognitive monitoring and strategy choice in younger and older adults. *Psychology and Aging, 3,* 249–257. (Chap 19)

Brim, G. (1992). *Ambition: How we manage success and failure throughout our lives.* New York: Basic Books. (Chap 18)

Brock, D. B., Guralnik, J. M., & Brody, J. A. (1990). Demography and epidemiology of aging in the United States. In E. L. Schneider & J. W. Rowe (Eds.), *Handbook of the psychology of aging* (3rd ed.). San Diego, CA: Academic Press. (Chap 20)

Brody, E. M. (1981). Women in the middle and family help to older people. *Gerontologist, 21,* 471–480. (Chap 18)

Brody, E. M., Litvin, S. J., Hoffman, C., & Kleban, M. H. (1992). Differential effects of daughters' marital status on their parent care experiences. *Gerontologist, 32,* 58–67. (Chap 18)

Brody, G. H., & Shaffer, D. R. (1982). Contributions of parents and peers to children's moral socialization. *Developmental Review, 2,* 31–75. (Chap 9)

Brody, J. E. (1992, May 19). Can drugs "treat" menopause? Amid doubt, women must decide. *New York Times,* pp. C1, C8. (Chap 18)

Bronfenbrenner, U. (1970). *Two worlds of childhood.* New York: Russell Sage Foundation. (Chaps 8, 10)

Bronfenbrenner, U. (1979). *The ecology of human development.* Cambridge, MA: Harvard University Press. (Chap 2)

Bronfenbrenner, U. (1986). Ecology of the family as a context for human development: Research perspectives. *Developmental Psychology, 22,* 723–742. (Chaps 1, 3, 12)

Bronfenbrenner, U. (1989a, April). The developing ecology of human development: Paradigm lost or paradigm regained. Paper presented at the biennial meeting of the Society for Research in Child Development, Kansas City, MO. (Chaps 2, 10)

Bronfenbrenner, U. (1989b). Ecological systems theory. In R. Vasta (Ed.), *Six theories of child development.* Greenwich, CT: JAI Press. (Chap 2)

Bronfenbrenner, U., Moen, P., & Garbarino, J. (1984). Child, family, and community. In R. D. Parke (Ed.), *Review of child development research* (Vol. 7). Chicago: University of Chicago Press. (Chap 5)

Brook, J., Whiteman, M., Gordon, A., & Cohen, P. (1986). Dynamics of childhood and adolescent personality traits and adolescent drug use. *Developmental Psychology, 22,* 1032–1043. (Chap 15)

Brooks-Gunn, J., & Furstenberg, F. F., Jr. (1986). The children of adolescent mothers. *Developmental Review, 6,* 224–251. (Chap 15)

Brooks-Gunn, J., & Furstenberg, F. F., Jr. (1989). Adolescent sexual behavior. *American Psychologist, 44,* 249–257. (Chaps 13, 15)

Brooks-Gunn, J., & Warren, M. P. (1985). Measuring physical status and timing in early adolescence. *Journal of Youth and Adolescence, 14,* 163–190. (Chap 13)

Brophy, J. E. (1983). Research on the self-fulfilling prophecy and teacher expectations. *Journal of Educational Psychology, 75,* 631–661. (Chap 10)

Brown, A. L., Bransford, J. D., Ferrara, R. A., & Campione, J. C. (1983). Learning, remembering, and understanding. In P. H. Mussen (Ed.), *Handbook of child psychology* (Vol. 3, 4th ed.). New York: Wiley. (Chaps 6, 11, 12)

Brown, B., Clasen, D., & Eicher, S. (1986). Perceptions of peer pressure, peer conformity dispositions, and self-reported behavior among adolescents. *Developmental Psychology, 22,* 521–530. (Chap 14)

Brown, P. (1976). Psychological distress and personal growth among women coping with marital dissolution. Unpublished doctoral dissertation, University of Michigan. (Chap 16)

Brown, R. (1970). *Psycholinguistics.* New York: Free Press. (Chap 7)

Brown, R. (1973). *A first language.* Cambridge, MA: Harvard University Press. (Chap 7)

Brozan, N. (1985, March 9). Fetal health. *New York Times,* p. 15. (Chap 3)

Bruner, J. S. (1970). The growth and structure of skill. In K. J. Connelly (Ed.), *Motor skills in infancy.* New York: Academic Press. (Chap 5)

Bruner, J. S. (1976). From communication to language. *Cognition, 3,* 255–287. (Chap 7)

Bruner, J. S. (1981). Intention in the structure of action and interaction. In L. P. Lipsitt & C. K. Rovee-Collier (Eds.), *Advances in infancy* (Vol. 1). Norwood, NJ: Ablex. (Chap 7)

Bruner, J. S. (1983). *Child's talk.* New York: Norton. (Chap 7)

Bruner, J. S. (1985). Vygotsky: A historical and conceptual perspective. In J. V. Wertsch (Ed.), *Culture, communication, and cognition: Vygotskyian perspectives.* New York: Cambridge University Press. (Chap 2)

Brunson, B. L., & Matthews, K. A. (1981). The Type A coronary-prone behavior pattern and reactions to uncontrollable stress. *Journal of Personality and Social Psychology, 40,* 906–918. (Chap 17)

Bryant, P. (1974). *Perception and understanding in young children.* New York: Basic Books. (Chap 6)

Buhrmester, D. (1990). Intimacy of friendship, interpersonal competence, and adjustment during preadolescence and adolescence. *Child Development, 61,* 1101–1111. (Chap 13)

Buhrmester, D., & Furman, W. (1987). The development of companionship and intimacy. *Child Development, 58,* 1101–1113. (Chap 13)

Buhrmester, D., & Furman, W. (1990). Perceptions of sibling relationships during middle childhood and adolescence. *Child Development, 61,* 1387–1398. (Chap 9)

Bullinger, A., & Chatillon, J.-F. (1983). Recent theory and research of the Genevan school. In P. H. Mussen (Ed.), *Handbook of child psychology* (Vol. 3, 4th ed.). New York: Wiley. (Chaps 11, 14)

Bullock, M. (1985). Animism in childhood thinking: A new look at an old question. *Developmental Psychology, 21,* 217–225. (Chap 11)

Bullock, M., & Gelman, R. (1979). Preschool children's assumptions about cause and effect. *Child Development, 50,* 89–96. (Chap 11)

Bullough, V. L. (1981). Age at menarche. *Science, 213,* 365–366. (Chap 13)

Bumpass, L., & Castro-Martin, T. (1989). Recent trends in marital disruption. *Demography, 26,* 37–51. (Chap 16)

Burke, D. B., & Light, L. L. (1981). Memory and aging: The role of retrieval processes. *Psychological Bulletin, 90,* 513–546. (Chap 19)

Burns, A. (1992). Mother-headed families: An international perspective and the case of Australia. *Social Policy Report, 6,* 1. (Chap 16)

Burns, B., & Lipsitt, L. P. (1991). Behavioral factors in crib death: Toward an understanding of the sudden infant death syndrome. *Journal of Applied Developmental Psychology, 12,* 159–184. (Chap 5)

Burrus-Bammel, L. L., & Bammel, G. (1985). Leisure and recreation. In J. E. Birren & K. W. Schaie (Eds.), *Handbook of the psychology of aging* (2nd ed.). New York: Van Nostrand Reinhold. (Chap 20)

Burton, L. M., & Bengston, V. L. (1985). Black grandmothers: Issues of timing and continuity of roles. In V. L. Benston & J. F. Robertson (Eds.), *Grandparenthood.* Beverly Hills, CA: Sage. (Chap 18)

Bushnell, E. W. (1985). The decline of visually guided reaching during infancy. *Infant Behavior and Development, 8,* 139–156. (Chap 5)

Buskirk, E. R. (1985). Health maintenance and longevity. In C. E. Finch & E. L. Schneider (Eds.), *Handbook of the biology of aging* (2nd ed.). New York: Van Nostrand Reinhold. (Chaps 18, 20)

Buss, D., Abbott, M., Angleitner, A., & Asherian, A. (1990). International preferences in selecting mates, a study of 37 cultures. *Journal of Cross Cultural Psychology, 21,* 5–47. (Chap 16)

Butler, J. A., Starfield, B., & Stenmark, S. (1984). Child health policy. In H. W. Stevenson & A. W. Siegel (Eds.), *Child development research and social policy.* Chicago: University of Chicago Press. (Chap 5)

Butler, R. (1990). The effects of mastery and competitive conditions on self-assessment at different ages. *Child Development, 61,* 201–210. (Chap 10)

Butler, R. N. (1975). *Why survive?* New York: Harper & Row. (Chap 20)

Butler, R. N., & Lewis, M. I. (1982). *Aging and mental health* (3rd ed.). St. Louis: Mosby. (Chap 19)

Butt, D. S., & Beiser, M. (1987). Successful aging: A theme for international psychology. *Psychology and Aging, 2,* 87–94. (Chap 18)

Butterfield, E. C., & Ferretti, R. P. (1987). Toward a theoretical integration of cognitive hypotheses about intellectual differences among children. In J. G. Borkowski & J. D. Day (Eds.), *Cognition in special children.* Norwood, NJ: Ablex. (Chap 12)

Byrne, D. (1973). The development of role-taking in adolescence. Unpublished doctoral dissertation, Graduate School of Education, Harvard University. (Chap 14)

Cain, B. S. (1982, December 19). Plight of the gray divorcee. *New York Times Magazine,* pp. 89–93. (Chap 20)

Cairns, R. B. (1983). The emergence of developmental psychology. In W. Kessen (Ed.), *Handbook of child psychology* (Vol. 1, 4th ed.). New York: Wiley. (Chap 1)

Cairns, R. B., Cairns, B. D., & Neckerman, H. J. (1989). Early school dropouts: Configurations and determinants. *Child Development, 60,* 1437–1452. (Chap 14)

Calasanti, T. H. (1988, November). Gender differences and family roles in retirement. Paper presented at the 41st Annual Scientific Meeting of the Gerontological Society of America, San Francisco. (Chap 20)

Callanan, M. A. (1989). Development of object categories and inclusion relations: Preschoolers' hypotheses about word meanings. *Developmental Psychology, 25,* 207–216. (Chap 11)

Campbell, J. I. D., & Charness, N. (1990). Age-related declines in working-memory skills: Evidence from a complex calculation task. *Developmental Psychology, 26,* 879–888. (Chap 19)

Campbell, R. T., & O'Rand, A. M. (1988). Settings and sequences: The heuristics of aging research. In J. E. Birren & V. L. Bengston (Eds.), *Emergent theories of aging.* New York: Springer. (Chap 2)

Campione, J. C., Brown, A. L., Ferrara, R. A., & Bryant, N. H. (1984). The zone of proximal development. In B. Rogoff and J. V. Wertsch (Eds.), *New directions for child development* (No. 23). San Francisco: Jossey-Bass. (Chap 12)

Campione, J. C., Brown, A. L., Ferrara, R. A., Jones, R. S., & Steinberg, E. (1985). Breakdowns in the flexible use of information. *Intelligence, 9,* 297–315. (Chap 12)

Campos, J. J. (1976). Heart rates. In L. P. Lipsitt (Ed.), *Developmental psychobiology.* Hillsdale, NJ: Erlbaum. (Chap 6)

Campos, J. J., Barrett, K. C., Lamb, M. E., Goldsmith, H. H., & Stenberg, C. (1983). Socioemotional development. In P. H. Mussen (Ed.), *Handbook of child psychology* (Vol. 2, 4th ed.). New York: Wiley. (Chap 4)

Campos, J. J., Campos, R. G., & Barrett, K. C. (1989). Emergent themes in the study of emotional development and emotion regulation. *Developmental Psychology, 25,* 394–402. (Chap 4)

Campos, J. J., Hiatt, S., Ramsay, D., Henderson, C., & Svejda, M. (1978). The emergence of fear on the visual cliff. In M. Lewis & L. Rosenblum (Eds.), *The origins of affect.* New York: Plenum. (Chap 6)

Campos, R. G. (1989). Soothing pain-elicited distress in infants with swaddling and pacifiers. *Child Development, 60,* 781–792. (Chap 4)

Canning, H., & Mayer, J. (1966). Obesity—Its possible effect on college acceptance. *New England Journal of Medicine, 275,* 1172–1174. (Chap 15)

Carey, S. (1982). Semantic development. In E. Wanner & L. R. Gleitman (Eds.), *Language acquisition*. Cambridge, England: Cambridge University Press. (Chap 7)

Carpenter, C. J., Huston, A. C., & Spera, L. (1991). Children's use of time in their everyday activities during middle childhood. In M. Bloch & A. Pellegrini (Eds.), *The ecological context of children's play*. Norwood, NJ: Ablex. (Chap 10)

Carr, M., Borkowski, J. G., & Maxwell, S. E. (1991). Motivational components of underachievement. *Developmental Psychology, 27,* 108–118. (Chap 12)

Carraher, T., Carraher, D., & Schliemann, A. (1985). Mathematics in the streets and schools. *British Journal of Developmental Psychology, 3,* 21–29. (Chaps 2, 11)

Carter, B. (1991, May 1). Children's TV, where boys are king. *New York Times,* pp. A1, C18. (Chap 10)

Cartron-Guerin, A., & Levy, P. (1982). Achievement and future time perspective among preadolescents: Range, nature, and optimism of future plans. *Psychological Abstracts, 67,* 1020. (Chap 14)

Case, R. (1985). *Intellectual development: Birth to adulthood*. New York: Academic Press. (Chaps 2, 11)

Cattell, P. (1940). *The measurement of intelligence of infants and young children*. New York: Psychological Corporation. (Chap 5)

Cattell, R. B. (1971). *Abilities*. Boston: Houghton Mifflin. (Chap 12)

Caudill, W. A., & Weinstein, H. (1969). Maternal care and infant behavior in Japan and America. *Psychiatry, 32,* 12–43. (Chap 1)

Cavanaugh, J. C., & Morton, K. R. (1988). Older adults' attributions about everyday memory. In M. M. Gruenberg, P. E. Morris, & R. N. Sykes (Eds.), *Practical aspects of memory: Current research and issues* (Vol. 1). New York: Wiley. (Chap 19)

Ceci, S. J., & Liker, J. K. (1986). A day at the races. *Journal of Experimental Psychology: General, 115,* 255–266. (Chap 17)

Ceci, S. J., & Liker, J. K. (1987). Academic and nonacademic intelligence. In R. J. Sternberg & R. K. Wagner (Eds.), *Practical intelligence*. New York: Cambridge University Press. (Chap 17)

Cerella, J. (1990). Aging and information-processing rate. In J. E. Birren & K. W. Schaie (Eds.), *Handbook of the psychology of aging* (3rd ed.). San Diego, CA: Academic Press. (Chap 19)

Cernoch, J. M., & Porter, R. H. (1985). Recognition of maternal axillary odors by infants. *Child Development, 56,* 1593–1598. (Chap 4)

Chabon, I. (1966). *Awake and aware*. New York: Delacorte. (Chap 3)

Chan, G. M., Ronald, N., Slater, P., Hollis, J., & Thomas, M. R. (1982). Decreased bone mineral status in lactating adolescent mothers. *Journal of Pediatrics, 101,* 767–770. (Chap 15)

Chapman, M., Skinner, E. A., & Baltes, P. B. (1990). Interpreting correlations between children's perceived control and cognitive performance: Control, agency, or means-ends beliefs? *Developmental Psychology, 26,* 246–253. (Chap 11)

Chase-Lansdale, P. L., & Owen, M. T. (1987). Maternal employment in a family context: Effects on infant-mother and infant-father attachments. *Child Development, 58,* 1505–1512. (Chap 8)

Cherfas, J. (1990). Embryology gets down—to the molecular level. *Science, 250,* 33–34. (Chap 3)

Cherlin, A. (1983). A sense of history. In M. W. Riley, B. B. Hess, & K. Bond (Eds.), *Aging in society*. Hillsdale, NJ: Erlbaum. (Chap 18)

Cherlin, A., & Furstenberg, F. F Jr. (1986). *The new American grandparent*. New York: Basic Books. (Chap 18)

Chi, M. T. H. (1978). Knowledge structure and memory development. In R. S. Siegler (Ed.), *Children's thinking: What develops?* Hillsdale, NJ: Erlbaum. (Chap 11)

Chi, M. T. H., & Klahr, D. (1975). Span and rate of apprehension in children and adults. *Journal of Experimental Child Psychology, 19,* 434–439. (Chap 11)

Chi, M. T. H., & Koeske, D. R. (1983). Network representation of a child's dinosaur knowledge. *Developmental Psychology, 19,* 29–39. (Chaps 2, 11)

Child Trends, Inc. (1990, November). *Facts at a Glance*. (Chaps 13, 15)

Child Trends, Inc. (1992, January). *Facts at a Glance*. (Chaps 13, 15)

Chira, S. (1989, October 3). Working-class families losing middle-class dreams. *New York Times,* pp. B1, B6. (Chap 18)

Chomsky, N. (1975). *Reflections on language*. New York: Pantheon. (Chap 7)

Chomsky, N. (1979). *Language and responsibility*. New York: Pantheon. (Chap 7)

Chugani, H. T., & Phelps, M. E. (1986). Maturational changes in cerebral function in infants determined by [18]FDG positron emission tomography. *Science, 231,* 840–843. (Chap 5)

Cicchetti, D., & Carlson, V. (Eds.). (1989). *Child maltreatment*. New York: Cambridge University Press. (Chap 9)

Cicirelli, V. G. (1989). Feelings of attachment to siblings and well-being in later life. *Psychology and Aging, 4,* 211–216. (Chap 20)

Claridge, G., & Mangan, G. (1983). Genetics of human nervous system functioning. In J. L. Fuller & E. C. Simmel (Eds.), *Behavior genetics*. Hillsdale, NJ: Erlbaum. (Chap 3)

Clark, E. V. (1983). Meanings and concepts. In P. H. Mussen (Ed.), *Handbook of child psychology* (Vol. 3, 4th ed.). New York: Wiley. (Chap 7)

Clark, J. E., Lanphear, A. K., & Riddick, C. C. (1987). The effect of videogame playing on the response selection processing of elderly adults. *Journal of Gerontology, 42,* 82–85. (Chap 19)

Clark, J. E., Phillips, S. J., & Petersen, R. (1989). Developmental stability in jumping. *Developmental Psychology, 25,* 929–935. (Chap 5)

Clark, M., Gosnell, M., & Hager, M. (1986, July 14). Women and AIDS. *Newsweek,* pp. 60–61. (Chap 16)

Clark, R. W. (1975). *The life of Bertrand Russell*. New York: Knopf. (Chap 17)

Clarke, A. M., & Clarke, A. D. B. (1977). *Early experience*. New York: Free Press. (Chap 8)

Clarke-Stewart, K. A. (1989). Infant day care: Maligned or malignant? *American Psychologist, 44,* 266–273. (Chap 8)

Clarke-Stewart, K. A., & Fein, G. (1983). Early childhood programs. In P. H. Mussen (Ed.), *Handbook of child psychology.* (Vol. 2., 4th ed.). New York: Wiley. (Chap 8)

Clarkson-Smith, L., & Hartley, A. A. (1989). Relationships between physical exercise and cognitive abilities in older adults. *Psychology and Aging, 4,* 183–189. (Chaps 17, 19)

Clarkson-Smith, L., & Hartley, A. A. (1990). The game of bridge as an exercise in working memory and reasoning. *Journal of Gerontology: Psychological Sciences, 45,* P233–238. (Chap 19)

Claudy, J. G., Farrell, W. S., & Dayton, C. W. (1979). *The consequences of being an only child.* Palo Alto, CA: American Institute for Research. (Chap 9)

Clausen, J. A. (1981). Men's occupational careers in the middle years. In D. H. Eichorn, J. A. Clausen, N. Haan, M. P. Honzik, & P. Mussen (Eds.), *Present and past in middle life.* New York: Academic Press. (Chap 18)

Clay, M. M. (1979). *The early detection of reading difficulties.* Auckland, New Zealand: Heinemann. (Chap 12)

Cleek, M. B., & Pearson, T. A. (1985). Perceived causes of divorce: An analysis of interrelationships. *Journal of Marriage and the Family, 47,* 179–191. (Chap 16)

Clingempeel, W. G. (1981). Quasi-kin relationships and marital quality in stepfather families. *Journal of Personality and Social Psychology, 41,* 890–901. (Chap 9)

Clingempeel, W. G., Brand, E., & Ievoli, R. (1984). Stepparent-stepchild relationships in stepmother and stepfather families. *Child Development, 33,* 465–573. (Chap 9)

Clingempeel, W. G., & Segal, S. (1986). Stepparent-stepchild relationships and the psychological adjustment of children in stepmother and stepfather families. *Child Development, 57,* 474–484. (Chap 9)

Cohen, C., Teresi, J., & Holmes, D. (1985). Social networks, stress, and physical health. *Journal of Gerontology, 40,* 478–486. (Chap 20)

Cohen, G., & Faulkner, D. (1989). Age differences in source forgetting: Effects on reality monitoring and on eyewitness testimony. *Psychology and Aging, 4,* 10–17. (Chap 19)

Cohen, L. B. (1972). Attention-getting and attention-holding processes in infant visual perception. *Child Development, 43,* 869–879. (Chap 6)

Cohen, R. M., Weingartner, H., Smallberg, S. A., Pickar, D., & Murphy, D. L. (1982). Effort and cognition in depression. *Archives of General Psychiatry, 39,* 593–597. (Chap 19)

Cohn, J. F., Campbell, S. B., Matias, R., & Hopkins, J. (1990). Face-to-face interactions of postpartum depressed and nondepressed mother-infant pairs at 2 months. *Developmental Psychology, 26,* 15–23. (Chap 4)

Cohn, L. D. (1991). Sex differences in the course of personality development: A meta-analysis. *Psychological Bulletin, 109,* 252–266. (Chap 20)

Coie, J. D., Dodge, K. A., & Kupersmidt, J. B. (1990). Peer group behavior and social status. In S. R. Asher & J. D. Coie (Eds.), *Peer rejection in childhood.* New York: Cambridge University Press. (Chap 10)

Colangelo, N., & Kerr, B. A. (1990). Extreme academic talent: Profile of perfect scorers. *Journal of Educational Psychology, 82,* 404–409. (Chap 12)

Colby, A., Gibbs, J., Kohlberg, L., Speicher-Dubin, B., Power, C., & Candee, D. (1980). *Standard form scoring manual.* Cambridge, MA: Center for Moral Education, Harvard University. (Chap 2)

Colby, A., Kohlberg, L., Gibbs, J., & Lieberman, M. (1983). A longitudinal study of moral development. *Monographs of the Society for Research in Child Development, 48* (1–2, Serial No. 200). (Chaps 2, 11, 14)

Cole, M. (1985). The zone of proximal development: Where culture and cognition create each other. In J. V. Wertsch (Ed.), *Culture, communication, and cognition: Vygotskyian perspectives.* New York: Cambridge University Press. (Chap 2)

Cole, M., & Scribner, S. (1974). *Culture & thought.* New York: Wiley. (Chap 14)

Cole, M., & Scribner, S. (1978). Introduction. In L. S. Vygotsky, *Mind in society.* Cambridge, MA: Harvard University Press. (Chap 2)

Coles, R., & Stokes, G. (1985). *Sex and the American teenager.* New York: Harper & Row. (Chap 13)

Collins, G. (1986, April 3). As more men retire early, more women work longer. *New York Times,* pp. C1ff. (Chap 20)

Collins, W. A., Berndt, T. J., & Hess, V. I. (1974). Observational learning of motives and consequences for television aggression. *Child Development, 45,* 799–802. (Chap 10)

Colombo, J., Mitchell, D. W., O'Brien, M., & Horowitz, F. D. (1987). The stability of visual habituation during the first year of life. *Child Development, 58,* 474–487. (Chap 6)

Colombo, J., Moss, M., & Horowitz, F. D. (1989). Neonatal state profiles: Reliability and short-term prediction of neurobehavioral status. *Child Development, 60,* 1102–1110. (Chap 4)

Condry, J. C., & Condry, S. (1976). Sex differences. *Child Development, 47,* 812–819. (Chap 9)

Condry, J. C., & Ross, D. F. (1985). Sex and aggression. *Child Development, 56,* 225–233. (Chap 9)

Conel, J. L. (1939–1959). *The postnatal development of the human cerebral cortex* (6 vols.). Cambridge, MA: Harvard University Press. (Chap 5)

Conger, R. D., Conger, K. J., Elder, G. H., Jr., Lorenz, F. O., Simons, R. L., & Whitbeck, L. B. (1992). A family process model of economic hardship and adjustment of early adolescent boys. *Child Development, 63,* 526–541. (Chaps 10, 15)

Conger, R. D., & Elder, G. H., Jr. (in press). *Families in a changing society.* Hawthorne, NY: Aldine de Gruyter. (Chap 13)

Connell, J. P. (1985). A new multidimensional measure of children's perceptions of control. *Child Development, 56,* 787–809. (Chap 12)

Connolly, K., & Dalgleish, M. (1989). The emergence of a tool-using skill in infancy. *Developmental*

Psychology, 25, 894–912. (Chap 5)
Conroy, M., Hess, R. D., Azuma, H., & Kashiwagi, K. (1980). Maternal strategies for regulating child behavior. *Journal of Cross-Cultural Psychology, 11,* 153–172. (Chap 10)
Cooney, T. M., Schaie, K. W., & Willis, S. L. (1988). The relationship between prior functioning on cognitive and personality dimensions and subject attrition in longitudinal research. *Journal of Gerontology: Psychological Sciences, 43,* P12–17. (Chap 17)
Cooper, C. R., Grotevant, H. D., & Condon, S. M. (1983). Individuality and connectedness in the family as a context for adolescent identity formation and role-taking skill. In H. D. Grotevant & C. R. Cooper (Eds.), *New directions for child development.* No. 22: *Adolescent development in the family.* San Francisco: Jossey-Bass. (Chap 13)
Cooper, H. M. (1979). Pygmalion grows up. *Review of Educational Research, 49,* 389–410. (Chap 10)
Cooper, R. P., & Aslin, R. N. (1990). Preference for infant-directed speech in the first month after birth. *Child Development, 61,* 1584–1595. (Chaps 4, 7)
Cornelius, S. W., & Caspi, A. (1987). Everyday problem solving in adulthood and old age. *Psychology and Aging, 2,* 144–153. (Chaps 17, 19)
Corno, L., & Rohrkemper, M. M. (1985). The intrinsic motivation to learn in classrooms. In C. Ames & R. Ames (Eds.), *Research on motivation and education.* Orlando, FL: Academic Press. (Chap 12)
Corsale, K., & Ornstein, P. A. (1980). Developmental changes in children's use of semantic information in recall. *Journal of Experimental Child Psychology, 30,* 231–245. (Chap 11)
Cortissoz, M. (1991, January 24). Abortion foes using fetal-rights strategy in court, ACLU tells White Plains audience. *Reporter Dispatch,* p. 12. (Chap 3)
Costa, P. T., Jr., & McCrae, R. R. (1989). Personality continuity and the changes of adult life. In M. Storandt & G. R. VandenBos (Eds.), *The adult years: Continuity and change.* Washington, DC: American Psychological Association. (Chap 18)

Costa, P. T., Jr., McCrae, R. R., Zonderman, A. B., Barbano, H. E., Lebowitz, B., & Larson, D. M. (1986). Cross-sectional studies of personality in a national sample: 2. Stability in neuroticism, extraversion, and openness. *Psychology and Aging, 1,* 144–149. (Chap 18)
Coster, W. J., Gersten, M. S., Beeghly, M., & Cicchetti, D. (1989). Communicative functioning in maltreated toddlers. *Developmental Psychology, 25,* 1020–1029. (Chap 7)
Cotman, C. W. (1990). Synaptic plasticity, neurotrophic factors, and transplantation in the aged brain. In E. L. Schneider & J. W. Rowe (Eds.), *Handbook of the biology of aging* (3rd ed.). San Diego, CA: Academic Press. (Chap 19)
Covington, M. V. (1984). The self-worth theory of achievement motivation. *Elementary School Journal, 85,* 5–20. (Chap 12)
Cowan, A. L. (1989, August, 21). Women's gains on the job: Not without a heavy toll. *New York Times,* pp. A1, A14. (Chap 16)
Cowan, P. A., & Cowan, C. P. (1988). Changes in marriage during the transition to parenthood: Must we blame the baby? In G. Y. Michaels & W. A. Goldberg (Eds.), *The transition to parenthood.* New York: Cambridge University Press. (Chap 16)
Coward, R. T., Cutler, S. J., & Schmidt, F. E. (1989). Differences in household composition of elders by age, gender, and area of residence. *Gerontologist, 29,* 814–821. (Chap 20)
Cowley, G. (1990, June 25). AIDS: The next ten years. *Newsweek,* pp. 20–27. (Chap 16)
Cox, M. J., Owen, M. T., Lewis, J. M., & Henderson, V. K. (1989). Marriage, adult adjustment, and early parenting. *Child Development, 60,* 1015–1024. (Chap 16)
Coyle, J. T., Price, D. L., & DeLong, M. R. (1983). Alzheimer's disease. *Science, 219,* 1184–1190. (Chap 19)
Craik, F. I. M., & Byrd, M. (1982). Aging and cognitive deficits. In F. I. M. Craik and S. Trehub (Eds.), *Aging and cognitive processes.* New York: Plenum. (Chap 19)
Cravioto, J., & Delicardie, E. (1970). Mental performance in school age children. *American Jour-*

nal of Diseases of Children, 120, 404. (Chap 5)
Crockett, L., Losoff, M., & Petersen, A. (1984). Perceptions of the peer group and friendship in early adolescence. *Journal of Early Adolescence, 4,* 155–181. (Chap 13)
Crockett, L. J., Petersen, A. C., Graber, J. A., Schulenberg, J. E., & Ebata, A. (1989). School transitions and adjustment during early adolescence. *Journal of Early Adolescence, 9,* 181–210. (Chap 14)
Crook, C. K. (1979). The organization and control of infant sucking. In H. W. Reese & L. P. Lipsitt (Eds.), *Advances in child development and behavior* (Vol. 14). New York: Academic Press. (Chap 4)
Crook, C. K., & Lipsitt, L. P. (1976). Neonatal nutritive sucking. *Child Development, 47,* 518–522. (Chap 4)
Cross, D. R., & Paris, S. G. (1988). Developmental and instructional analyses of children's metacognition and reading comprehension. *Journal of Educational Psychology, 80,* 131–142. (Chaps 11, 12)
Crouter, A. C. (1984). Participative work as an influence on human development. *Journal of Applied Developmental Psychology, 5,* 71–90. (Chap 16)
Csikszentmihalyi, M., & Larson, R. (1984). *Being adolescent.* New York: Basic Books. (Chap 13)
Cumming, E., & Henry, W. E. (1961). *Growing old: The process of disengagement.* New York: Basic Books. (Chap 20)
Cummings, E. M., Iannotti, R. J., & Zahn-Waxler, C. (1985). Influence of conflict between adults on the emotions and aggression of young children. *Developmental Psychology, 21,* 1274–1282. (Chap 8)
Cummings, E. M., Zahn-Waxler, C., & Radke-Yarrow, M. (1981). Young children's responses to expressions of anger and affection by others in the family. *Child Development, 52,* 1273–1282. (Chap 8)
Curtiss, S. R. (1977). *Genie.* New York: Academic Press. (Chap 7)
Cutler, N. E. (1983). Age and political behavior. In D. S. Woodruff & J. E. Birren (Eds.), *Aging* (2nd ed.). Monterey, CA: Brooks/Cole. (Chap 20)
Cytrynbaum, S., Blum, L., Patrick, R., Steein, J., Wadner, D., &

Wilk, C. (1980). Midlife development. In L. W. Poon (Ed.), *Aging in the 1980s.* Washington, DC: American Psychological Association. (Chap 18)

Daehler, M. W., & Greco, C. (1985). Memory in very young children. In M. Pressley & C. J. Brainerd (Eds.), *Cognitive learning and memory in children.* New York: Springer-Verlag. (Chap 6)

Damon, W., & Hart, D. (1988). *Self-understanding in childhood and adolescence.* New York: Cambridge University Press. (Chap 11)

Dan, A. J., Wilbur, J., Hedricks, C., O'Connor, E., & Holm, K. (1990). Lifelong physical activity in midlife and older women. *Psychology of Women Quarterly, 14,* 531–542. (Chap 18)

Daniel, D. E., Templin, R. G., & Shearon, R. W. (1977). The value orientation of older adults toward education. *Educational Gerontology, 2,* 33–42. (Chap 17)

Daniels, P., & Weingarten, K. (1982). *Sooner or later.* New York: Norton. (Chap 16)

Dannefer, D., & Perlmutter, M. (1990). Development as a multidimensional process: Individual and social constituents. *Human Development, 33,* 108–137. (Chap 6)

Dannemiller, J. L., & Stephens, B. R. (1988). A critical test of infant pattern preference models. *Child Development, 59,* 210–216. (Chap 6)

Darwin, C. (1955). *The expressions of the emotions in man and animal.* New York: Philosophical Library. (Original work published 1872.) (Chap 2)

Das, J. P., & Naglieri, J. A. (1990). *Das-Naglieri: Cognitive assessment system.* New York: Psychological Corporation. (Chap 12)

Dasen, P. R. (1973). Piagetian research in central Australia. In G. E. Kearney, P. R. deLacy, & G. R. Davidson (Eds.), *The psychology of aboriginal Australians.* Sydney, Australia: Wiley. (Chap 11)

Das Gupta, P., & Bryant, P. E. (1989). Young children's causal inferences. *Child Development, 60,* 1138–1147. (Chap 11)

Daurio, S. P. (1979). Educational enrichment versus acceleration. In W. C. George, S. J. Cohn, & J. C. Stanley (Eds.), *Educating the gifted.* Baltimore: Johns Hopkins University Press. (Chap 12)

Davidson, M. (1971). *Louis Braille: The boy who invented books for the blind.* New York: Scholastic. (Chap 14)

Davies, D. P. (1985). Cot death in Hong Kong: A rare problem? *Lancet, 2,* 1346–1349. (Chap 5)

Davis, J. M., & Rovee-Collier, C. K. (1983). Alleviated forgetting of a learned contingency in 8-week-old infants. *Developmental Psychology, 19,* 353–365. (Chap 6)

Dawson, D., Hendershot, G., & Fulton, J. (1987, June 10). Aging in the eighties: Functional limitations of individuals age 65 years and over. *Advance data* (No. 1331). Hyattsville, MD: National Center for Health Statistics. (Chap 20)

Day, M. C. (1975). Developmental trends in visual scanning. In H. W. Reese (Ed.), *Advances in child development and behavior* (Vol. 10). New York: Academic Press. (Chap 11)

DeAngelis, T. (1990, December). Who is susceptible to bulimia, and why? *APA Monitor,* p. 8. (Chap 15)

DeCasper, A. J., & Fifer, W. P. (1980). Of human bonding. *Science, 208,* 1174–1176. (Chaps 4, 7)

DeCasper, A. J., & Spence, M. J. (1986). Prenatal maternal speech influences newborns' perception of speech sounds. *Infant Behavior and Development, 9,* 133–150. (Chaps 3, 4)

Deci, E. L., Neziek, J., & Sheinman, L. (1981). Characteristics of the rewarder and intrinsic motivation of the rewardee. *Journal of Personality and Social Psychology, 40,* 1–10. (Chap 10)

Deigh, R. (1986, September 29). Curse it, count it, cure it. *Insight,* pp. 10–14. (Chap 17)

DeLeon, P. H., & VandenBos, G. R. (1985). Public policy and advocacy on behalf of the gifted and talented. In F. D. Horowitz and M. O'Brien (Eds.), *The gifted and talented.* Washington, DC: American Psychological Association. (Chap 12)

DeLoache, J. S. (1980). Naturalistic studies of memory for object location in very young children. In M. Perlmutter (Ed.), *New directions for child development* (No. 10). San Francisco: Jossey-Bass. (Chap 6)

DeLoache, J. S. (1989). The development of representation in young children. In H. W. Reese (Ed.), *Advances in child development and behavior* (Vol. 22). San Diego, CA: Academic Press. (Chap 6)

DeLoache, J. S., & Brown, A. L. (1984). Where do I go next? *Developmental Psychology, 20,* 37–44. (Chap 6)

DeLoache, J. S., Cassidy, D. J., & Brown, A. L. (1985). Precursors of mnemonic strategies in very young children's memory. *Child Development, 56,* 125–137. (Chap 6)

Demos, V. (1986). Crying in early infancy: An illustration of the motivational function of affect. In T. B. Brazelton & M. W. Yogman (Eds.), *Affective development in infancy.* Norwood, NJ: Ablex. (Chap 8)

Denham, S. A., McKinley, M., Couchoud, E. A., & Holt, R. (1990). Emotional and behavioral predictors of preschool peer ratings. *Child Development, 61,* 1145–1152. (Chap 8)

Denney, N. W., & Heidrich, S. M. (1990). Training effects on Raven's Progressive Matrices in young, middle-aged, and elderly adults. *Psychology and Aging, 5,* 144–145. (Chap 19)

Denney, N. W., & Pearce, K. A. (1989). A developmental study of practical problem solving in adults. *Psychology and Aging, 4,* 438–442. (Chap 19)

Dennis, W. (1960). Causes of retardation among institutional children. *Journal of Genetic Psychology, 96,* 47–59. (Chap 5)

Dennis, W., & Najarian, P. (1957). Infant development under environmental handicap. *Psychological Monographs, 71,* 436. (Chap 5)

Dennis, W., & Sayegh, Y. (1965). The effect of supplementary experiences upon the behavioral development of infants in institutions. *Child Development, 36,* 81–90. (Chap 5)

Desai, S., Chase-Lansdale, P. L., & Michael, R. T. (1989). Mother or market? Effects of maternal employment on the intellectual ability of four-year-old children. *Demography, 26,* 545–561. (Chap 9)

de Villiers, J. G., & de Villiers, P. A. (1978). *Language acquisition.* Cambridge, MA: Harvard University Press. (Chap 7) de Villiers, J. G., & de Villiers, P. A. (1979). *Early language.* Cambridge, MA: Harvard University Press. (Chap 7)

de Vries, H. A. (1983). Physiology of exercise and aging. In D. S. Woodruff & J. E. Birren (Eds.), *Aging* (2nd ed.). Monterey, CA: Brooks/Cole. (Chap 18)

deVries, M., & Sameroff, A. J. (1984). Culture and temperament. *American Journal of Orthopsychiatry, 54,* 83–96. (Chap 4)

DeVries, R. (1969). Constancy of generic identity in the years 3 to 6. *Monographs of the Society for Research in Child Development, 34* (3, Serial No. 127). (Chap 11)

Diamond, A. (1985). Development of the ability to use recall to guide action, as indicated by infants' performance on AB. *Child Development, 56,* 868–883. (Chap 6)

Dick-Read, G. (1944). *Childbirth without fear.* New York: Harper & Brothers. (Chap 3)

Diegmueller, K. (1986, October 13). Divorce. *Insight,* pp. 8–13. (Chap 18)

Diener, E., Sandvik, E., & Larson, R. (1985). Age and sex effects for emotional intensity. *Developmental Psychology, 21,* 542–546. (Chap 13)

Dietz, W. H., & Gortmaker, S. L. (1985). Do we fatten our children at the television set? Obesity and television viewing in children and adolescents. *Pediatrics, 75,* 807–812. (Chap 5)

DiPietro, J. A. (1981). Rough and tumble play. *Developmental Psychology, 17,* 50–58. (Chap 5)

Dishion, T. J., Patterson, G. R., Stoolmiller, M., & Skinner, M. L. (1991). Family, school, and behavioral antecedents to early adolescent involvement with antisocial peers. *Developmental Psychology, 27,* 172–180. (Chap 15)

Dixon, R. A., & Baltes, P. B. (1986). Toward life-span research on the function of pragmatics of intelligence. In R. J. Sternberg & R. K. Wagner (Eds.), *Practical intelligence.* New York: Cambridge University Press. (Chap 17)

Dixon, R. A., & Hultsch, D. F. (1983). Structure and development of metamemory in adulthood. *Journal of Gerontology, 38,* 682–688. (Chap 19)

Dobbs, A. R., & Rule, B. G. (1989). Adult age differences in working memory. *Psychology and Aging, 4,* 500–503. (Chap 19)

Doctor, R. M., & Altman, F. (1969). Worry and emotionality as components of test anxiety: Replication and further data. *Psychological Reports, 24,* 563–568. (Chap 19)

Dodge, K. A. (1983). Behavioral antecedents of peer social status. *Child Development, 54,* 1386–1399. (Chap 10)

Dodge, K. A., Pettit, G. S., McCloskey, C. L., & Brown, M. M. (1986). Social competence in children. *Monographs of the Society for Research in Child Development, 51* (2, Serial No. 213). (Chaps 2, 10)

Dodge, K. A., & Somberg, D. R. (1987). Hostile attributional biases among aggressive boys are exacerbated under conditions of threat to the self. *Child Development, 58,* 213–224. (Chap 10)

Doe, J. (1991, May 11). The recession hits home. *New York Times,* p. 23. (Chap 10)

Doka, K. J., & Mertz, M. E. (1988). The meaning and significance of great-grandparenthood. *Gerontologist, 28,* 192–197. (Chap 20)

Dollard, J., & Miller, N. E. (1950). *Personality and psychotherapy.* New York: McGraw-Hill. (Chap 2)

Donaldson, M. (1979). *Children's minds.* New York: Norton. (Chap 11)

Dontas, C., Maratos, O., Fafoutis, M., & Karangelis, K. (1985). Early social development in institutionally reared Greek infants. *Monographs of the Society for Child Development, 50* (1–2, Serial No. 209). (Chap 8)

Dornbusch, S. M., Carlsmith, J. M., Duncan, P. D., Gross, R. T., Martin, J. A., Ritter, P. L., & Siegel-Gorelick, B. (1984). Sexual maturation, social class, and the desire to be thin among adolescent females. *Developmental and Behavioral Pediatrics, 5,* 308–314. (Chap 15)

Dornbusch, S. M., & Gray, K. D. (1988). Single-parent families. In S. M. Dornbusch & M. H. Strober (Eds.), *Feminism, children, and the new families.* New York: Guilford Press. *(Chaps 9, 13)*

Dornbusch, S. M., Ritter, P. L., Leiderman, P. H., Roberts, D. F., & Fraleigh, M. J. (1987). The relation of parenting style to adolescent school performance. *Child Development, 58,* 1244–1257. (Chaps 9, 13)

Dorr, A. (1979, March). *Children's reports of what they learn from daily viewing.* Paper presented at the biennial meeting of the Society for Research in Child Development, San Francisco. (Chap 10)

Douvan, E., & Adelson, J. (1966). *The adolescent experience.* New York: Wiley. (Chaps 13, 15)

Drabman, R. S., Cordua, C. D., Hammer, D., Jarvie, G. J., & Horton, W. (1979). Developmental trends in eating rates of normal and overweight children. *Child Development, 50,* 211–216. (Chap 5)

Drabman, R. S., & Thomas, M. H. (1976). Does watching violence on television cause apathy? *Pediatrics, 57,* 329–331. (Chap 10)

Duara, R., London, E. D., & Rapaport, S. I. (1985). Changes in structure and energy metabolism of the aging brain. In C. E. Finch & E. L. Schneider (Eds.), *Handbook of the biology of aging* (2nd ed.). New York: Van Nostrand Reinhold. (Chap 19)

DuBois, D. L., & Hirsch, B. J. (1990). School and neighborhood friendship patterns of blacks and whites in early adolescence. *Child Development, 61,* 524–536. (Chap 10)

Dubowitz, L. M. S., Dubowitz, V., & Goldberg, C. (1970). Clinical assessment of gestational age in the newborn infant. *Journal of Pediatrics, 77,* 1. (Chap 4)

Duffy, F. H., Als, H., & McAnulty, G. B. (1990). Behavioral and electrophysiological evidence for gestational age effects in healthy preterm and fullterm infants studied two weeks after expected due date. *Child Development, 61,* 1271–1286. (Chap 4)

Dullea, G. (1986, September 18). Madonna's new beat is a hit, but song's message rankles. *New York Times,* pp. B1ff. (Chap 15)

Duncan, P., Ritter, P., Dornbusch, S., Gross, R., & Carlsmith, J. (1985). The effects of pubertal timing on body image, school behavior, and deviance. *Journal of Youth and Adolescence, 14,* 227–236. (Chap 13)

Dunn, J. (1977). *Distress and comfort.* Cambridge, MA: Harvard University Press. (Chap 8)

Dunn, J. (1983). Sibling relationships in early childhood. *Child Development, 54,* 787–811. (Chaps 8, 9)

Dunn, J., & Kendrick, C. (1982). *Siblings.* Cambridge, MA: Harvard University Press. (Chap 8)

Dunn, J., & Munn, P. (1985). Becoming a family member. *Child Development, 56,* 480–492. (Chap 8)

Dunn, J. F., & Plomin, R. (1990). *Separate lives: Why children are so different.* New York: Basic Books. (Chap 1)

Dunn, J. F., Plomin, R., & Daniels, D. (1986). Consistency and change in mothers' behavior toward young siblings. *Child Development, 57,* 348–356. (Chap 1)

Dunn, J. F., Plomin, R., & Nettles, M. (1985). Consistency of mothers' behavior toward infant siblings. *Developmental Psychology, 21,* 1188–1195. (Chap 1)

Durant, W., & Durant, A. (1963). *The story of civilization.* Vol. 8: *The age of Louis XIV.* New York: Simon & Schuster. (Chap 3)

Durrett, M. E., O'Bryant, S., & Pennebaker, J. W. (1975). Child-rearing report of white, black, and Mexican-American families. *Developmental Psychology, 2,* 871. (Chap 8)

Dweck, C. S., Davidson, W., Nelson, S., & Enna, B. (1978). Sex differences in learned helplessness. *Developmental Psychology, 14,* 268–276. (Chap 10)

Dweck, C. S., & Elliot, E. S. (1983). Achievement motivation. In P. H. Mussen (Ed.), *Handbook of child psychology.* (Vol. 4, 4th ed.). New York: Wiley. (Chaps 6, 10, 12)

Easterbrooks, M. A., & Goldberg, W. A. (1984). Toddler development in the family. *Child Development, 55,* 740–752. (Chap 8)

Easterbrooks, M. A., & Goldberg, W. A. (1985). Effects of early maternal employment on mothers, toddlers, and fathers. *Developmental Psychology, 21,* 774–783. (Chap 8)

Easterlin, R. (1980). *Birth and fortune.* New York: Basic Books. (Chap 15)

Eccles, J. S. (1985a). Sex differences in achievement patterns. In T. Sonderegger (Ed.), *Nebraska symposium on motivation.* Lincoln: University of Nebraska Press. (Chaps 10, 13)

Eccles, J. S. (1985b). Why doesn't Jane run? In F. D. Horowitz and M. O'Brien (Eds.), *The gifted and talented.* Washington, DC: American Psychological Association. (Chap 12)

Eccles, J. S., Amberton, A., Buchanan, C. M., Jacobs, J., Flanagan, C., Harold, R., MacIver, D., Midgley, C., Reuman, D., and Wigfield, A. (1993). School and family effects on the ontogeny of children's interests, self-perceptions, and activity choice. In J. Jacobs (Ed.), *Nebraska symposium on motivation, 1992.* Lincoln: University of Nebraska Press. (Chaps 9, 10, 14)

Eccles, J. S., & Hoffman, L. W. (1984). Sex roles, socialization, and occupational behavior. In H. W. Stevenson & A. E. Siegel (Eds.), *Child development research and social policy.* Chicago: University of Chicago Press. (Chaps 9, 10)

Eccles, J. S., Jacobs, J. E., & Harold, R. D. (1990). Gender-role stereotypes, expectancy effects, and parents' role in the socialization of gender differences in self-perceptions and skill acquisition. *Journal of Social Issues, 46,* 182–201. (Chap 14)

Eccles, J. S., & Midgley, C. (1990). Changes in academic motivation and self-perception during early adolescence. In R. Montemayor, G. R. Adams, & T. G. Gullota (Eds.), *From childhood to adolescence: A transitional period.* Newbury Park, CA: Sage. (Chap 14)

Eckerman, C. O., Davis, C. C., & Didow, S. M. (1989). Toddlers' emerging ways of achieving social coordinations with a peer. *Child Development, 60,* 440–453. (Chap 8)

Edelman, M. S., & Omark, D. R. (1973). Dominance hierarchies in young children. *Social Science Information, 12,* 103–110. (Chap 10)

Eder, R. A. (1989). The emergent personologist: The structure and content of 3½-, 5½-, and 7½-year-olds' concept of themselves and other persons. *Child Development, 60,* 1218–1228. (Chap 11)

Edgerton, R. B. (1979). *Mental retardation.* Cambridge, MA: Harvard University Press. (Chap 12)

Egeland, B., & Farber, E. A. (1984). Infant-mother attachment. *Child Development, 55,* 753–771. (Chap 8)

Ehrman, L., & Probber, J. (1983). Fundamentals of genetics and evolutionary theory. In J. L. Fuller & E. C. Simmel (Eds.), *Behavior genetics.* Hillsdale, NJ: Erlbaum. (Chap 3)

Eichorn, D. H., Clausen, J. A., Haan, N., Honzik, M. P., & Mussen, P. H. (Eds.). (1981). *Present and past in middle life.* New York: Academic Press. (Chap 1)

Eichorn, D. H., Hunt, J. V., & Honzik, M. P. (1981). Experience, personality, and IQ. In D. H. Eichorn, J. A. Clausen, N. Hann, M. P. Honzik, & P. H. Mussen (Eds.), *Present and past in middle life.* New York: Academic Press. (Chap 17)

Eisenberg, N., Fabes, R. A., Schaller, M., & Miller, P. A. (1989). Sympathy and personal distress: Development, gender differences, and interrelation of indexes. In N. Eisenberg (Ed.), *New directions for child development.* No. 44: *Empathy and related emotional responses.* San Francisco: Jossey-Bass. (Chap 8)

Ekerdt, D. J., Bosse, R., & Levkoff, S. (1985). An empirical test for phases of retirement. *Journal of Gerontology, 40,* 95–101. (Chap 20)

Elder, G. H., Jr. (1974). *Children of the Great Depression.* Chicago: University of Chicago Press. (Chaps 1, 13)

Elder, G. H., Jr. (1980). Adolescence in historical perspective. In J. Adelson (Ed.), *Handbook of adolescent psychology.* New York: Wiley. (Chap 15)

Elder, G. H., Jr. (1986). Military times and turning points in men's lives. *Developmental Psychology, 22,* 244–245. (Chap 1)

Elder, G. H., Jr., Caspi, A., & Nguyen, T. (1986). Resourceful and vulnerable children: Family influence in hard times. In R. K. Silvereisen, K. Eyferth, & G. Rudinger (Eds.), *Development as action in context.* New York: Springer-Verlag. (Chap 10)

Elder, G. H., Jr., Liker, J., & Cross, C. (1984). Parent-child behavior in the Great Depression: Life course and intergenerational influences. In P. Baltes & O. Brim (Eds.), *Life span development and behavior* (Vol. 6). Orlando, FL: Academic Press. (Chap 10)

Elder, J. L., & Pederson, D. R. (1978). Preschool children's use of objects in symbolic play. *Child Development, 49,* 500–504. (Chap 6)

Elias, M. F., Robbins, M. A., & Schultz, N. R., Jr. (1987). Influence of hypertension on intellectual performance: Causation or speculation? In J. W. Elias and P. H. Marshall (Eds.), *Cardiovascular disease and behavior.* Washington, DC: Hemisphere. (Chap 17)

Elkind, D. (1985). Egocentrism redux. *Developmental Review, 5,* 218–226. (Chap 14)

Elliott, D. S., Huizinga, D., & Morse, B. J. (1985). *The dynamics of deviant behavior: A national survey progress report.* Boulder, CO: Behavioral Research Institute. (Chap 15)

Elliott, R. (1988). Test, abilities, race, and conflict. *Intelligence, 12,* 333–350. (Chap 12)

Elmen, J. D. (1991). Achievement orientation in early adolescence: Developmental patterns and social correlates. *Journal of Early Adolescence, 11,* 125–151. (Chaps 13, 14)

Elster, A. B., McAnarney, E. R., & Lamb, M. E. (1983). Parental behavior of adolescent mothers. *Pediatrics, 71,* 494–503. (Chap 15)

Emde, R., Johnson, W., & Easterbrooks, M. (1987). The do's and don'ts of early moral development: Psychoanalytic tradition and current research. In J. Kagan & S. Lamb (Eds.), *The emergence of morality in young children.* Chicago: University of Chicago Press. (Chap 8)

Emde, R. N., Swedberg, J., & Suzuki, B. (1975). Human wakefulness and biological rhythms after birth. *Archives of General Psychiatry, 32,* 780–783. (Chap 4)

Enns, J. T., & Akhtar, N. (1989). A developmental study of filtering in visual attention. *Child Development, 60,* 1188–1199. (Chap 11)

Ensminger, M. E. (1990). Sexual activity and problem behavior among black, urban adolescents. *Child Development, 61,* 2032–2046. (Chap 15)

Entwisle, D. R., & Doering, S. G. (1981). *The first birth.* Baltimore: Johns Hopkins University Press. (Chap 16)

Epstein, H. T. (1974). Phrenoblysis: Special brain and mind growth periods. *Developmental Psychobiology, 7,* 207–216. (Chap 14)

Erber, J. T., Szuchman, L. T., & Rothberg, S. T. (1990). Everyday memory failure: Age differences in appraisal and attribution. *Psychology and Aging, 5,* 236–241. (Chap 19)

Erikson, E. H. (1963). *Childhood and society* (2nd ed.). New York: Norton. (Chaps 5, 8, 9)

Erikson, E. H. (1980). *Identity and the life cycle.* New York: Norton. (Chap 13)

Erikson, E. H. (1982). *The life cycle completed.* New York: Norton. (Chaps 2, 16, 18, 20)

Erikson, E. H., Erikson, J. M., & Kivnick, H. Q. (1986). *Vital involvement in old age.* New York: Norton. (Chap 20)

Erikson, E. H., interviewed by E. Hall. (1987). The father of the identity crisis. In E. Hall, *Growing and changing.* New York: Random House. (Chaps 2, 16, 18, 20)

Eron, L. D., Huesmann, L. R., Dubow, E., Romanoff, R., & Yarmel, P. W. (1987). Aggression and its correlates over 22 years. In D. Crowell, I. M. Evans, & C. R. O'Donnell (Eds.), *Childhood aggression and violence.* New York: Plenum. (Chap 10)

Eron, L. D., Huesmann, L. R., Lefkowitz, M. M., & Walder, L. O. (1972). Does television cause aggression? *American Psychologist, 27,* 253–263. (Chap 10)

Eyler, F. D., Delgado-Hachey, M., Woods, N. S., & Carter, R. L. (1991). Quantification of the Dubowitz Neurological Assessment of preterm infants: Developmental outcome. *Infant Behavior and Development, 14,* 451–469. (Chap 4)

Fabricius, W. V., & Cavalier, L. (1989). The role of causal theories about memory in young children's memory strategy choice. *Child Development, 60,* 298–308. (Chap 11)

Fagan, J. F., III. (1979). The origins of face perception. In M. H. Bornstein and W. Kessen (Eds.), *Psychological development from infancy.* Hillsdale, NJ: Erlbaum. (Chap 6)

Fagot, B. I. (1978). The influence of sex of child on parental reactions to toddler children. *Child Development, 49,* 459–465. (Chap 8)

Fagot, B. I. (1982). Adults as socializing agents. In T. M. Field, A. Huston, H. C. Quay, L. Troll, & G. E. Finley (Eds.), *Review of human development.* New York: Wiley. (Chap 9)

Fagot, B. I. (1985). Changes in thinking about early sex role development. *Developmental Review, 5,* 83–98. (Chap 8)

Fagot, B. I., & Leinbach, M. D. (1989). The young child's gender schemas: Environmental input, internal organization. *Child Development, 60,* 663–672. (Chap 9)

Fagot, B. I. Leinbach, M. D., & O'Boyle, C. (1992). Gender labeling, gender stereotyping, and parenting behaviors. *Developmental Psychology, 28,* 225–230. (Chap 8)

Fajardo, B., Browning, M., Fisher, D., & Paton, J. (1990). Effect of nursery environment on state regulation in very-low-birth-weight premature infants. *Infant Behavior and Development, 13,* 287–303. (Chap 4)

Fajardo, B. F., & Freedman, D. G. (1981). Maternal rhythmicity in three American cultures. In T. M. Field, A. M. Sostek, P. Vietze, & P. H. Liederman (Eds.), *Culture and early interactions.* Hillsdale, NJ: Erlbaum. (Chap 8)

Falbo, T. (1984). Only children. In T. Falbo (Ed.), *The single-child family.* New York: Wiley. (Chap 9)

Falbo, T. (1988, Fall). In search of the little emperor. *Division 34 News, 14,* 7–8, 26. (Chap 9)

Fallon, A., & Rozin, P. (1985). Sex differences and perception of desirable body shapes. *Journal of Abnormal Psychology, 94,* 102–105. (Chap 16)

Fantz, R. L. (1961, May). The origin of form perception. *Scientific American,* pp. 66–72. (Chap 6)

Fantz, R. L., Fagan, J. F., III, & Miranda, S. B. (1975). Early visual selectivity. In L. B. Cohen &

P. Salapatek (Eds.), *Infant perception* (Vol. 1). New York: Academic Press. (Chap 6)

Fantz, R. L., & Miranda, S. B. (1975). Newborn infant attraction to form of contour. *Child Development, 46,* 224–228. (Chap 6)

Farrington, D. P. (1979). Longitudinal research on crime and delinquency. In N. Morris & M. Tonry (Eds.), *Crime and justice* (Vol. 1). Chicago: University of Chicago Press. (Chap 15)

Fauber, R., Forehand, R., Thomas, A. M., & Wierson, M. (1990). A mediational model of the impact of marital conflict on adolescent adjustment in intact and divorced families: The role of disrupted parenting. *Child Development, 61,* 1112–1123. (Chap 13)

Fausto-Sterling, A. (1985). *Myths of gender.* New York: Basic Books. (Chap 9)

Feather, N. T. (1980). Values in adolescence. In J. Adelson (Ed.), *Handbook of adolescent psychology.* New York: Wiley. (Chap 15)

Feather, N. T. (1988). Values, valences, and course enrollment: Testing the role of personal values within an expectancy-valence framework. *Journal of Educational Psychology, 80,* 381–391. (Chap 14)

Featherman, D. L. (1981). The life-span perspective in social science research. Paper prepared for the Social Science Research Council, University of Wisconsin. (Chap 20)

Fedele, N. M., Golding, E. R., Grossman, F. K., & Pollack, W. S. (1988). Psychological issues in the adjustment to first parenthood. In G. Y. Michaels & W. A. Goldberg (Eds.), *The transition to parenthood.* New York: Cambridge University Press. (Chap 16)

Feldman, D. H. (1986). *Nature's gambit.* New York: Basic Books. (Chap 12)

Feldman, S. S., & Aschenbrenner, B. (1983). Impact of parenthood on various aspects of masculinity and femininity. *Developmental Psychology, 19,* 278–289. (Chap 16)

Ferguson, C. A. (1977). Baby talk as a simplified register. In C. E. Snow & C. A. Ferguson (Eds.), *Talking to children.* New York: Cambridge University Press. (Chap 7)

Fernald, A., & Mazzie, C. (1991).

Prosody and focus in speech to infants and adults. *Developmental Psychology, 27,* 209–221. (Chap 7)

Fernald, A., & Simon, T. (1984). Expanded intonational contours in mothers' speech to newborns. *Developmental Psychology, 20,* 104–113. (Chap 4)

Ferrara, R. A., Brown, A. L., & Campione, J. C. (1986). Children's learning and transfer of inductive reasoning rules. *Child Development, 57,* 1087–1099. (Chap 12)

Feshbach, N. D. (1969). Student teacher preferences for elementary school pupils varying in personality characteristics. *Journal of Educational Psychology, 60,* 126–132. (Chap 10)

Feshbach, S. (1972). Reality and fantasy in filmed violence. In J. P. Murray, E. A. Rubenstein, & G. A. Comstock (Eds.), *Television and social behavior* (Vol. 2). Washington, DC: U.S. Government Printing Office. (Chap 10)

Feschbach, S. (1980). Child abuse and the dynamics of human aggression. In G. Gerbner, C. J. Ross, & E. Zigler (Eds.), *Child abuse.* New York: Oxford University Press. (Chap 9)

Feuerstein, R., Rand, Y., Hoffman, M. B., & Miller, R. (1980). *Instrumental enrichment.* Baltimore: University Park Press. (Chap 12)

Field, D. (1981). Can preschool children really learn to conserve? *Child Development, 48,* 326–334. (Chap 11)

Field, D., & Millsap, R. E. (1991). Personality in advanced old age: Continuity or change? *Journal of Gerontology: Psychological Sciences, 46,* P299–308. (Chap 20)

Field, D., Schaie, K. W., & Leino, E. V. (1988). Continuity in intellectual functioning: The role of self-reported health. *Psychology and Aging, 3,* 345–392. (Chap 17)

Field, T. M. (1981). Infant arousal, attention, and affect during early interaction. In L. P. Lipsitt (Ed.), *Advances in infancy* (Vol. 1). Norwood, NJ: Ablex. (Chaps 4, 6)

Field, T. M. (1983). Early interaction and interaction coaching of high-risk infants and parents. In M. Perlmutter (Ed.), *Minnesota symposium on child psychology*

(Vol. 16). Hillsdale, NJ: Erlbaum. (Chap 1)

Field, T. M., Healy, B., Goldstein, S., & Guthertz, M. (1990). Behavior-state matching and synchrony in mother-infant interactions of nondepressed versus depressed dyads. *Developmental Psychology, 26,* 7–14. (Chap 4)

Field, T. M., Sandberg, D., Garcia, R., Vega-Lahr, N., Goldstein, S., & Guy, L. (1985). Pregnancy problems, postpartum depression, and early mother-infant interactions. *Developmental Psychology, 21,* 1152–1156. (Chap 4)

Field, T. M., & Widmayer, S. M. (1981). Mother-infant interaction among lower SES black, Cuban, Puerto Rican, and South American immigrants. In T. M. Field, A. M. Sostek, P. Vietze, & P. H. Leiderman (Eds.), *Culture and early interactions.* Hillsdale, NJ: Erlbaum. (Chap 8)

Fincham, F. D., Hokoda, A., & Sanders, R., Jr. (1989). Learned helplessness, test anxiety, and academic achievement. *Child Development, 60,* 138–145. (Chap 10)

Flanagan, C. A. (1990). Families and schools in hard times. In V. C. McLoyd & C. A. Flanagan (Eds.), *New directions for child development* (No. 46). San Francisco: Jossey-Bass. (Chaps 10, 13, 15)

Flavell, J. H. (1985). *Cognitive development* (2nd ed.). Englewood Cliffs, NJ: Prentice-Hall. (Chaps 1, 2, 6, 11, 14)

Flavell, J. H. (1992). Cognitive development: Past, present, and future. *Developmental Psychology, 28,* 998–1005. (Chap 11)

Flavell, J. H., Beach, D. R., & Chinsky, J. M. (1966). Spontaneous verbal rehearsal on a memory task as a function of age. *Child Development, 37,* 283–299. (Chap 11)

Flavell, J. H., Botkin, P. T., Fry, C. L., Jr., Wright, J. W., & Jarvis, P. E. (1975). *The development of role-taking and communication skills in children.* Huntington, NY: Krieger. (Original work published 1968.) (Chap 11)

Flavell, J. H., Friedrichs, A. G., & Hoyt, J. D. (1970). Developmental changes in memorization processes. *Cognitive Psychology, 1,* 324–340. (Chap 11)

Flavell, J. H., Green, F. L., & Flavell, E. R. (1986). Development of knowledge about appearance-reality distinction. *Monographs of the Society for Research in Child Development, 51* (1, Serial No. 212). (Chap 11)

Flavell, J. H., Green, F. L., & Flavell, E. R. (1989). Young children's ability to differentiate appearance-reality and Level 2 perspectives in the tactile modality. *Child Development, 60*, 201–213. (Chap 11)

Flavell, J. H., Shipstead, S. G., & Croft, K. (1978). Young children's knowledge about visual perception. *Child Development, 49*, 1208–1211. (Chap 6)

Fleming, A. S., Ruble, D. N., Flett, G. L., & Van Wagner, V. (1990). Adjustment in first-time mothers: Changes in mood and mood content during the early postpartum months. *Developmental Psychology, 26*, 137–143. (Chap 16)

Flint, M. (1982). Male and female menopause: A cultural put on. In A. Voda, M. Dinnerstein, & S. O'Donnell (Eds.), *Changing perspectives on menopause.* Austin: University of Texas Press. (Chap 18)

Flint, M. (1989). Cultural and subcultural meanings to the menopause. *Menopause Management, 2*(3), 11. (Chap 18)

Fogel, A., & Thelen, E. (1987). Development of early expressive and communicative action: Reinterpreting the evidence from a dynamic systems perspective. *Developmental Psychology, 23*, 747–761. (Chap 4)

Folkman, S., Lazarus, R., Pimley, S., & Novacek, J. (1987). Age differences in stress and coping procedures. *Psychology and Aging, 2*, 171–184. (Chaps 18, 20)

Foos, P. W. (1989). Adult age differences in working memory. *Psychology and Aging, 4*, 269–275. (Chap 19)

Forehand, R., Long, N., & Brody, G. (1988). Divorce and marital conflict. In E. M. Hetherington & J. D. Arasteh (Eds.), *Impact of divorce, single parenting, and stepparenting on children.* Hillsdale, NJ: Erlbaum. (Chaps 9, 13)

Forrest, J. D., & Singh, S. (1990). The sexual and reproductive behavior of American women, 1982–1988. *Family Planning Perspectives, 22*, 206–214. (Chaps 13, 15, 16)

Forssberg, H. (1985). Ontogeny of human locomotor control. *Experimental Brain Research, 57*, 480–493. (Chap 5)

Fox, N. A. (1989). Psychophysiological correlates of emotional reactivity during the first year of life. *Developmental Psychology, 25*, 364–372. (Chap 4)

Fox, N. A., Kimmerly, N. L., & Schafer, W. D. (1991). Attachment to mother/attachment to father: A meta-analysis. *Child Development, 62*, 210–225. (Chap 8)

Fox, R., Aslin, R. N., Shea, S. L., & Dumais, S. G. (1980). Stereopsis in human infants. *Science, 207*, 323–324. (Chap 6)

Frankenburg, W. K. (1978). *Denver developmental screening test.* Denver: University of Colorado Medical Center. (Chap 5)

Freedman, D. G. (1979, January). Ethnic differences in babies. *Human Nature*, pp. 36–43. (Chap 1)

Freedman, J. L. (1984). Effect of television violence on aggression. *Psychological Bulletin, 96*, 227–246. (Chap 10)

Freud, S. (1955). Three essays on the theory of sexuality. In *The standard edition of the complete psychological works of Sigmund Freud* (Vol. 7). London: Hogarth Press. (Original work published 1905.) (Chap 2)

Fried, P. A., & Watkinson, B. (1990). 36- and 48-month neurobehavioral follow-up of children prenatally exposed to marijuana, cigarettes, and alcohol. *Developmental and Behavioral Pediatrics, 11*, 49–58. (Chap 3)

Friedman, A. (1987). Getting powerful with age: Changes in women over the life cycle. *Israel Social Science Research, 5*, 76–86. (Chap 18)

Frieze, I. H., Parsons, J. E., Johnson, P. B., Ruble, D. N., & Zellman, G. I. (1978). *Women and sex roles.* New York: Norton. (Chap 16)

Frisch, H. L. (1977). Sex stereotypes in adult-infant play. *Child Development, 48*, 1671–1675. (Chap 8)

Frodi, A. M., Lamb, M. E., Leavitt, L. A., & Donovan, W. L. (1978). Fathers' and mothers' responses in infant smiles and cries. *Infant Behavior and Development, 1*, 187–198. (Chap 4)

Fry, C. L. (1985). Culture, behavior, and aging in the comparative perspective. In J. E. Birren & K. W. Schaie (Eds.), *Handbook of the psychology of aging* (2nd ed.). New York: Van Nostrand Reinhold. (Chap 20)

Fry, P. S. (1984). Teachers' conceptions of students' intelligence and intelligent functioning: A cross-sectional study of elementary, secondary, and tertiary level teachers. In P. S. Fry (Ed.), *Changing conceptions of intelligence and intellectual functioning.* New York: North-Holland. (Chap 12)

Frye, D., Braisby, N., Lowe, J., Maroudas, C., & Nicholls, J. (1989). Young children's understanding of counting and cardinality. *Child Development, 60*, 1158–1171. (Chap 11)

Furman, W., & Buhrmester, D. (1985). Children's perceptions of the qualities of sibling relationships. *Child Development, 56*, 448–461. (Chap 9)

Furstenberg, F. F., Jr. (1982). Conjugal succession: Reentering marriage after divorce. In P. B. Baltes & O. G. Brim, Jr. (Eds.), *Life-span development and behavior* (Vol. 4). New York: Academic Press. (Chap 16)

Furstenberg, F. F., Jr., Brooks-Gunn, J., & Chase-Lansdale, L. (1989). Teenaged pregnancy and childbearing. *American Psychologist, 44*, 313–320. (Chap 15)

Furstenberg, F. F., Jr., Brooks-Gunn, J., & Morgan, S. P. (1987). *Adolescent mothers in later life.* New York: Cambridge University Press. (Chap 15)

Fuson, K. C. (1988). *Children's counting and concept of number.* New York: Springer-Verlag. (Chap 11)

Gaensbauer, T. J. (1982). Regulation of emotional expression in infants from 2 contrasting caretaker environments. *Journal of the American Academy of Child Psychiatry, 21*. (Chap 9)

Galambos, N. L., & Maggs, J. L. (1990). Putting mothers' work-related stress in perspective: Mothers and adolescents in dual-earner families. *Journal of Early Adolescence, 10,* 313–328. (Chap 13)

Galambos, N. L., & Maggs, J. L. (1991a). Children in self-care: Figures, facts, and fiction. In J. V. Lerner & N. L. Galambos (Eds.), *The employment of mothers during the childbearing years.* New York: Garland Press. (Chaps 9, 13)

Galambos, N. L., & Maggs, J. L. (1991b). Out-of-school care of young adolescents and self-reported behavior. *Developmental Psychology, 27,* 644–645. (Chap 13)

Galambos, N. L., & Silbereisen, R. K. (1987). Influences of income change and parental acceptance on adolescent transgression proneness and peer relations. *European Journal of Psychology of Education, 1,* 17–28. (Chap 10)

Gallagher, J. J., & Courtright, R. D. (1986). The educational definition of giftedness and its policy implications. In R. J. Sternberg & J. E. Davidson (Eds.), *Conceptions of giftedness.* New York: Cambridge University Press. (Chap 12)

Gambrell, R. D. (1989). Endometrial cancer from ERT: An unfounded fear. *Menopause management, 11*(2), 13–15. (Chap 18)

Ganchrow, J. R., Steiner, J. E., & Daher, M. (1983). Neonatal facial expressions in response to different qualities and intensities of gustatory stimuli. *Infant Behavior and Development, 6,* 473–484. (Chap 4)

Garbarino, J., & Crouter, A. (1978). Defining the community context for parent-child relations. *Child Development, 49,* 606–616. (Chap 9)

Garcia-Coll, C. T. (1990). Developmental outcome of minority infants: A process-oriented look into our beginnings. *Child Development, 61,* 270–289. (Chaps 8, 10)

Gardner, H. (1983). *Frames of mind.* New York: Basic Books. (Chap 12)

Gardner, W., & Rogoff, B. (1990). Children's deliberateness of planning according to task circumstances. *Developmental Psychology, 26,* 480–487. (Chap 11)

Garfinkel, R. (1982). By the sweat of your brow. In T. M. Field, A. Huston, H. C. Quay, L. Troll, & G. E. Finley (Eds.), *Review of human development.* New York: Wiley. (Chap 16)

Garner, D. M., Garfinkel, P. E., Schwartz, D., & Thompson, M. (1980). Cultural expectations of thinness in women. *Psychological Reports, 47,* 483–491. (Chap 15)

Garrod, A., Beal, C., & Shin, P. (1990). The development of moral orientation in elementary school children. *Sex Roles, 22,* 13–27. (Chap 11)

Gatz, M., Bengston, V. L., & Blum, M. J. (1990). Caregiving families. In J. E. Birren & K. W. Schaie (Eds.), *Handbook of the psychology of aging* (3rd ed.). San Diego, CA: Academic Press. (Chaps 18, 20)

Gauvain, M., & Rogoff, B. (1986). Influence of the goal on children's exploration and memory of large-scale space. *Developmental Psychology, 22,* 72–76. (Chap 11)

Gauvain, M., & Rogoff, B. (1989). Collaborative problem solving and children's planning skills. *Developmental Psychology, 25,* 139–151. (Chap 11)

Gavin, L. A., & Furman, W. (1989). Age differences in adolescents' perceptions of their peer groups. *Developmental Psychology, 25,* 827–834. (Chap 13)

Geary, D. C., & Wiley, J. G. (1991). Cognitive addition: Strategy choice and speed-of-processing differences in young and elderly adults. *Psychology and Aging, 6,* 474–483. (Chap 19)

Gelman, D. (1985, July 15). Playing both mother and father. *Newsweek,* pp. 42–50. (Chap 9)

Gelman, R. (1982a). Accessing one-to-one correspondence. *British Journal of Psychology, 73,* 209–220. (Chap 11)

Gelman, R. (1982b). Basic numerical abilities. In R. J. Sternberg (Ed.), *Advances in the psychology of human intelligence* (Vol. 1). Hillsdale, NJ: Erlbaum. (Chap 6)

Gelman, R., & Baillargeon, R. (1983). A review of some Piagetian concepts. In P. H. Mussen (Ed.), *Handbook of child psychology* (Vol. 3, 4th ed.). New York: Wiley. (Chap 11)

Gelman, R., & Gallistel, C. R. (1978). *The child's understanding of number.* Cambridge, MA: Harvard University Press. (Chap 11)

Gelman, S. A., & Coley, J. D. (1990). The importance of knowing a dodo is a bird: Categories and inferences in 2-year-old children. *Developmental Psychology, 26,* 796–804. (Chap 11)

Gelman, S. A., & Kremer, K. E. (1991). Understanding natural cause: Children's explanations of how objects and their properties originate. *Child Development, 62,* 396–414. (Chap 11)

Gelman, S. A., & Markman, E. M. (1985). Implicit contrast in adjectives vs. nouns. *Journal of Child Language, 12,* 124–143. (Chap 7)

Gelman, S. A., & Markman, E. M. (1986). Categories and induction in young children. *Cognition, 23,* 183–209. (Chap 11)

Gelman, S. A., & Markman, E. M. (1987). Young children's inductions from natural kinds: The roles of categories and appearances. *Child Development, 58,* 1532–1541. (Chap 11)

Gentile, A. M., et al. (1975). The structure of motor tasks. *Movement, 7,* 11–28. (Chap 5)

George, C., & Main, M. (1979). Social interactions of young abused children. *Child Development, 50,* 306–318. (Chap 9)

Gesell, A. L. (1925). *The mental growth of the preschool child.* New York: Macmillan. (Chap 5)

Gesell, A. L. (1956). *Youth.* New York: Harper & Row. (Chap 2)

Gesell, A. L., & Ilg, F. L. (1946). *The child from five to ten.* New York: Harper & Row. (Chap 2)

Gesell, A. L., Ilg, F. L., & Ames, L. B. (1940). *First five years of life.* New York: Harper. (Chap 2)

Getchell, N., & Roberton, M. A. (1989). Whole body stiffness as a function of developmental level in children's hopping. *Developmental Psychology, 25,* 920–928. (Chap 5)

Giambra, L. M., & Quilter, R. (1988). Sustained attention in adulthood: A unique, large-sample, longitudinal and multicohort analysis using the Mackworth Clock-Test. *Psychology and Aging, 3,* 75–83. (Chap 19)

Gibson, E. J. (1974). Trends in perceptual development. In A. D. Pick (Ed.), *Minnesota symposia on child psychology* (Vol. 8). Minneapolis: University of Minnesota Press. (Chap 11)

Gibson, E. J., & Walk, R. D. (1960, April). The visual cliff. *Scientific American*, pp. 67–71. (Chap 6)

Gibson, R. C. (1986, Winter). Blacks in an aging society. *Daedalus, 115,* 349–371. (Chaps 18, 20)

Gibson, R. C. (1991). The subjective retirement of black Americans. *Journal of Gerontology: Social Sciences, 46,* S204–209. (Chap 20)

Gillies, P., Elmwood, J. M., & Hawtin, P. (1985). Anxieties in adolescents about employment and war. *British Medical Journal, 291,* 383. (Chap 14)

Gilligan, C. (1982). *In a different voice.* Cambridge: Harvard University Press. (Chaps 2, 11, 13, 14, 16)

Glaser, B. G., & Strauss, A. L. (1968). *Time for dying.* Chicago: Aldine. (Chap 20)

Gleason, J. B. (1967). Do children imitate? *Proceedings of the International Conference on Oral Education of the Deaf, 2,* 1441–1148. (Chap 7)

Gleason, J. B., & Weintraub, S. (1978). Input language and the acquisition of communicative competence. In K. Nelson (Ed.), *Children's language* (Vol. 1). New York: Gardner Press. (Chap 7)

Gleitman, L. R., & Wanner, E. (1982). Language acquisition. In E. Wanner & L. R. Gleitman (Eds.), *Language acquisition.* Cambridge, England: Cambridge University Press. (Chap 7)

Glenn, N. D., & McLanahan, S. (1981). The effect of offspring on the psychological well-being of older adults. *Journal of Marriage and the Family, 43,* 409–421. (Chap 20)

Glenn, N. D., & Supanic, M. (1984). The social and demographic correlates of divorce and separation in the United States: An update and reconsideration. *Journal of Marriage and the Family, 37,* 105–110. (Chap 16)

Glick, P. C. (1980). Remarriage. *Journal of Family Issues, 1,* 455–478. (Chap 16)

Glick, P. C. (1984). Marriage, divorce, and living arrangements: Prospective changes. *Journal of Family Issues, 5,* 7–26. (Chap 9)

Glick, P. C., & Lin, S.-L. (1986). Recent changes in divorce and remarriage. *Journal of Marriage and the Family, 48,* 737–748. (Chap 16)

Goetting, A. (1986). The developmental tasks of siblingship over the life cycle. *Journal of Marriage and the Family, 48,* 703–714. (Chap 20)

Golan, N. (1981). *Passing through transitions.* New York: Free Press. (Chap 16)

Gold, D., & Andres, D. (1978). Developmental comparisons between 10-year-old boy children with employed and nonemployed mothers. *Child Development, 49,* 74–84. (Chap 9)

Gold, D. T. (1990). Late-life sibling relationships: Does race affect typological distribution? *Gerontologist, 30,* 741–748. (Chap 20)

Gold, M. (1981, January–February). Pregnant pauses. *Science 81, 3,* 34–39. (Chap 3)

Goldberg, E. L., Comstock, G. W., & Harlow, S. D. (1988). Emotional problems and widowhood. *Journal of Gerontology: Social Sciences, 43,* S206–208. (Chap 20)

Goldberg, W. A. (1988). Introduction: Perspectives on the transition to parenthood. In G. Y. Michaels & W. A. Goldberg (Eds.), *The transition to parenthood.* New York: Cambridge University Press. (Chap 16)

Goldblatt, P. M., Moore, M. E., & Stunkard, A. D. (1965). Social factors in obesity. *Journal of the American Medical Association, 192,* 1039–1044. (Chap 15)

Goldfield, E. C. (1989). Transition from rocking to crawling: Postural constraints on infant movement. *Developmental Psychology, 25,* 913–919. (Chap 5)

Goldin-Meadow, S. (1991, April 7). Deaf children are able to create their own sign language. *New York Times,* p. E18. (Chap 7)

Goldin-Meadow, S., & Morford, M. (1985). Gesture in early child language: Studies of deaf and hearing children. *Merrill-Palmer Quarterly, 31,* 145–176. (Chap 7)

Goldman, S. R., Mertz, D. L., & Pellegrino, J. W. (1989). Individual differences in extended practice functions and solution strategies for basic addition facts. *Journal of Educational Psychology, 81,* 481–496. (Chap 12)

Goldman-Rakic, P. S. (1987). Development of cortical circuitry and cognitive function. *Child Development, 58,* 601–622. (Chaps 5, 7)

Goldman-Rakic, P. S., Isseroff, A., Schwartz, M. L., & Bugbee, N. M. (1983). The neurobiology of cognitive development. In P. H. Mussen (Ed.), *Handbook of child psychology* (Vol. 2, 4th ed.). New York: Wiley. (Chap 5)

Goldsmith, H. H., & Alansky, J. A. (1987). Maternal and infant temperamental predictors of attachment: A meta-analytic review. *Journal of Consulting and Clinical Psychology, 55,* 805–816. (Chap 8)

Goldsmith, R. E., & Heiens, R. A. (1992). Subjective age: A test of five hypotheses. *Gerontologist, 32,* 312–317. (Chap 20)

Goleman, D. (1980, February). 1,528 little geniuses and how they grew. *Psychology Today,* pp. 28–53. (Chap 12)

Goodall, M. M. (1980). Left-handedness as an educational handicap. In R. S. Laura (Ed.), *Problems of handicap.* Melbourne, Australia: Macmillan. (Chap 5)

Goodnow, J. J. (1962). A test of milieu differences with some of Piaget's tasks. *Psychological Monographs, 76* (Serial No. 555). (Chap 11)

Gopnik, A., & Meltzoff, A. (1987). The development of categorization in the second year and its relation to other cognitive and linguistic developments. *Child Development, 58,* 1523–1531. (Chap 7)

Gorman, K. S., and Pollitt, E. (1992). Relationship between weight and body proportionality at birth, growth during the first year of life, and cognitive development at 36, 48, and 60 months. *Infant Behavior and Development, 15,* 279–296. (Chap 5)

Gottesman, I. (1974). Developmental genetics and ontogenetic psychology. In A. D. Pick (Ed.), *Minnesota symposia on child psychology* (Vol. 8). Minneapolis: University of Minnesota Press. (Chap 3)

Gottfried, A. W., & Bathurst, K.

(1983). Hand preference across time is related to intelligence in young girls, not boys. *Science, 221,* 1074–1076. (Chap 5)

Gottlieb, G. (1983). The psychobiological approach to developmental issues. In P. H. Mussen (Ed.), *Handbook of child psychology* (Vol. 2, 4th ed.). New York: Wiley. (Chap 4)

Gottlieb, G. (1991). Experimental canalization of behavioral development: Theory. *Developmental Psychology, 27,* 4–13. (Chap 5)

Gottman, J. M., & Katz, L. F. (1989). Effects of marital discord on young children's peer interaction and health. *Developmental Psychology, 25,* 373–381. (Chap 9)

Gould, R. E. (1980). Sexual problems. In W. H. Normal & T. J. Scaramella (Eds.), *Midlife.* New York: Brunner-Mazel. (Chap 18)

Gould, R. L. (1975, February). Adult life stages. *Psychology Today,* pp. 74–78. (Chaps 16, 18)

Gould, R. L. (1978). *Transformations.* Simon & Schuster. (Chaps 16, 18)

Graham, S. (1984). Teacher feelings and student thoughts. *Elementary School Journal, 85,* 91–104. (Chap 12)

Graham, S., & Barker, G. P. (1990). The down side of help: An attributional-developmental analysis of helping behavior as a low-ability cue. *Journal of Educational Psychology, 82,* 7–14. (Chap 12)

Graham, S., Hudley, C., & Williams, E. (1992). Attributional and emotional determinants of aggression among African-American and Latino young adolescents. *Developmental Psychology, 28,* 731–740. (Chap 15)

Gray, W., & Hudson, L. (1984). Formal operations and the imaginary audience. *Developmental Psychology, 20,* 619–627. (Chap 14)

Greco, C., Rovee-Collier, C., Hayne, H., Griesler, P., & Early, L. (1986). Ontogeny of early event memory: I. Forgetting and retrieval by 2- and 3-month-olds. *Infant Behavior and Development, 9,* 441–461. (Chap 6)

Green, D. L. (1990). High school student employment in social context: Adolescents' perception of the role of part-time work. *Adolescence, 25,* 425–434. (Chap 13)

Greenberg, B. S. (1982). Television and role socialization. In D. Pearl, L. Bouthilet, & J. Lazer (Eds.), *Television and behavior.* Washington, DC: National Institute of Mental Health. (Chap 10)

Greenberger, E., & Steinberg, L. (1986). *When teenagers work: The psychological and social costs of adolescent employment.* New York: Basic Books. (Chap 13)

Greenough, W. T., Black, J. E., & Wallace, C. S. (1987). Experience and brain development. *Child Development, 58,* 539–559. (Chaps 5, 14)

Greer, L. D. (1980). Children's comprehension of formal features with masculine and feminine connotations. Master's thesis, University of Kansas. (Cited in Huston, 1983.) (Chap 10)

Gribbin, K., Schaie, K. W., & Parham, I. A. (1980). Complexity of lifestyle and maintenance of intellectual abilities. *Journal of Social Issues, 36,* 47–61. (Chap 17)

Griffiths, R. (1954). *The abilities of babies.* New York: McGraw-Hill. (Chap 5)

Grobstein, C. (1988). *Science and the unborn.* New York: Basic Books. (Chap 3)

Grolnick, W. S., & Ryan, R. M. (1989). Parent styles associated with children's self-regulation and competence in school. *Journal of Educational Psychology, 81,* 143–154. (Chap 12)

Gross, J. (1991, June 16). More young single men hang onto apron strings. *New York Times,* pp. A1, A18. (Chap 16)

Gross, J. (1992, December 7). Divorced, middle-aged and happy: Women, especially, adjust to the 90s. *New York Times,* p. A14. (Chap 18)

Grossman, F. K., Eichler, L. S., & Winickoff, S. A. (1980). *Pregnancy, birth, and parenthood.* San Francisco: Jossey-Bass. (Chaps 3, 16)

Grossmann, K., Grossmann, K. E., Spangler, G., Suess, G., & Unzner, L. (1985). Maternal sensitivity and newborns' orientation responses as related to quality of attachment in Northern Germany, *Monographs of the Society for Research in Child Development, 50*

(1–2, Serial No. 209). (Chap 8)

Grotevant, H. D., & Thorbecke, W. L. (1982). Sex differences in styles of occupational identity formation in late adolescence. *Developmental Psychology, 18,* 396–405. (Chap 13)

Gruendel, J. M. (1977). Referential overextension in language development. *Child Development, 48,* 1567–1576. (Chap 7)

Guidubaldi, J., Perry, J. D., & Cleminshaw, H. K. (1983, Summer). The legacy of parental divorce. *School Psychology Review.* (Chap 9)

Guilford, J. P. (1982). Cognitive psychology's ambiguities. *Psychological Review, 89,* 48–59. (Chap 12)

Gunderson, V., & Sackett, G. P. (1982). Parental effects on reproductive outcome and developmental risk. In M. E. Lamb & A. L. Brown (Eds.), *Advances in developmental psychology* (Vol. 2). Hillsdale, NJ: Erlbaum. (Chap 3)

Gurland, B. J., Dean, L., Cross, P. S., & Golden, R. (1980). The epidemiology of depression and dementia in the elderly. In J. O. Cole & J. E. Barrett (Eds.), *Psychopathology in the aged.* New York: Raven Press. (Chap 20)

Gustafson, G. E., & Green, J. A. (1991). Developmental coordination of cry sounds with visual regard and gestures. *Infant Behavior and Development, 14,* 51–58. (Chap 7)

Gustafson, G. E., & Harris, K. L. (1990). Women's responses to young infant cries. *Developmental Psychology, 26,* 144–152. (Chap 4)

Gutmann, D. (1987). *Reclaimed powers.* New York: Basic Books. (Chaps 16, 18, 20)

Haan, N., Millsap, R., & Hartka, E. (1986). As time goes by: Change and stability in personality over fifty years. *Psychology and Aging, 1,* 220–232. (Chaps 16, 18)

Habel, L., Kaye, K., & Lee, J. (1990). Trends in reporting of maternal drug abuse and infant mortality among drug-exposed infants in New York City. *Women and Health, 16,* 41–58. (Chap 3)

Hagestad, G. O. (1984). The continuous bond. In M. Perlmutter (Ed.), *Minnesota symposia on child de-*

velopment (Vol. 17). Hillsdale, NJ: Erlbaum. (Chap 18)

Hagestad, G. O. (1986, Winter). The aging society and family life. *Daedalus, 115,* 119–139. (Chap 18)

Hagestad, G. O. (1988). Demographic changes and the life course: Some emerging trends in the family realm. *Family Relations, 37,* 405–410. (Chap 18)

Hagestad, G. O., & Neugarten, B. L. (1985). Age and the life course. In R. H. Binstock & E. Shanas (Eds.), *Handbook of aging and the social sciences* (2nd ed.). New York: Van Nostrand Reinhold. (Chaps 16, 20)

Hagestad, G. O., & Smyer, M. (1983). Divorce at middle-age. In S. Weissman, R. Cohen, & B. Cohler (Eds.), *Dissolving personal relationships.* New York: Academic Press. (Chap 18)

Hahn, S. R., & Paige, K. E. (1980). American birth practices. In J. E. Parsons (Ed.), *The psychobiology of sex differences.* New York: McGraw-Hill. (Chap 3)

Haight, B. K. (1992). Long-term effects of a structured life review process. *Journal of Gerontology: Psychological Sciences, 47,* P312–315. (Chap 20)

Hainline, L. (1978). Developmental changes in the scanning of faces and nonface patterns in infants. *Journal of Experimental Psychology, 25,* 90–115. (Chap 6)

Hainline, L., & Feig, E. (1978). The correlates of father absence in college-aged women. *Child Development, 49,* 37–42. (Chap 9)

Haith, M. M. (1980). *Rules that babies look by.* Hillsdale, NJ: Erlbaum. (Chap 4)

Haith, M. M., Bergman, T., & Moore, M. J. (1977). Eye contact and face scanning in early infancy. *Science, 198,* 853–855. (Chap 6)

Haith, M. M., & McCarty, M. E. (1990). Stability of visual expectations at 3.0 months of age. *Developmental Psychology, 26,* 68–74. (Chap 6)

Hall, J. W., Murphy, J., Humphreys, M. S., & Wilson, K. P. (1979). Children's cued recall. *Journal of Experimental Child Psychology, 27,* 501–511. (Chap 11)

Hall, T. (1989, March 15). A new temperance is taking root in America.

New York Times, pp. A1, C6. (Chap 15)

Hallfrisch, J., Tobin, J. D. Muller, D. C., & Andres, R. (1988). Fiber intake, age, and other coronary risk factors in men of the Baltimore Longitudinal Study (1959–1975). *Journal of Gerontology: Medical Sciences, 43,* M64–68. (Chap 20)

Hamilton, S. F. (1990). *Apprenticeship for adulthood: Preparing youth for the future.* New York: Free Press. (Chap 13)

Hamilton, S. F., & Powers, J. L. (1990). Failed expectations: Working-class girls' transition from school to work. *Youth & Society, 22,* 241–262. (Chap 13)

Hareven, T. Historical changes in the family and the life course implications for child development. In A. B. Smuts & J. W. Hagen (Eds.), History and research in child development. *Monographs of the Society for Research in Child Development, 50* (4–5, Serial No. 211). (Chap 1)

Harlow, H. F., & Harlow, M. K. (1966). Learning to love. *American Scientist, 54,* 244–272. (Chap 8)

Harlow, H. F., & Harlow, M. K. (1969). Effects of various mother-infant relationships on rhesus-monkey behaviors. In B. M. Foss (Ed.), *Determinants of infant behaviour* (Vol. 4). London: Methuen. (Chap 8)

Harman, S. M., & Talbert, G. B. (1985). Reproductive aging. In C. E. Finch & E. L. Schneider (Eds.), *Handbook of the biology of aging* (2nd ed.). New York: Van Nostrand Reinhold. (Chaps 18, 20)

Harris, M. B., & Vorhees, S. D. (1981). Sex-role stereotypes and televised models of emotion. *Psychological Reports, 48,* 826. (Chap 10)

Harris, P. L. (1983). Infant cognition. In P. H. Mussen (Ed.), *Handbook of child psychology* (Vol. 2, 4th ed.). New York: Wiley. (Chaps 2, 6)

Harris, P. L. (1987). Bringing order to the A-not-B error: Commentary. *Monographs of the Society for Research in Child Development, 51* (3, Serial No. 214). (Chap 6)

Harrison, A. O., Wilson, M. N., Pine, C. J., Chan, S. Q., & Buriel, R. (1990). Family ecologies of ethnic minority children. *Child Development, 61,* 347–362. (Chap 10)

Hart, C. H., Ladd, G. W., & Burleson, B. R. (1990). Children's expectations of the outcomes of social strategies: Relations with sociometric status and maternal disciplinary styles. *Child Development, 61,* 127–137. (Chap 9)

Hart, D., & Damon, W. (1986). Developmental trends in self-understanding. *Social Cognition, 4,* 388–407. (Chap 11)

Harter, S. (1983). Developmental perspectives on the self-system. In P. H. Mussen (Ed.), *Handbook of child psychology* (Vol. 4, 4th ed.). New York: Wiley. (Chaps 8, 12, 14)

Harter, S., & Monsour, A. (1992). Developmental analysis of conflict caused by opposing attributes in the adolescent. *Developmental Psychology, 28,* 251–260. (Chap 14)

Hartup, W. W. (1983). Peer relations. In P. H. Mussen (Ed.), *Handbook of child psychology* (Vol. 4, 4th ed.). New York: Wiley. (Chaps 8, 10, 13)

Hartup, W. W. (1989). Social relationships and their developmental significance. *American Psychologist, 44,* 120–126. (Chap 10)

Harwood, R. L. (1992). The influence of culturally derived values on Anglo and Puerto Rican mothers' perceptions of attachment behavior. *Child Development, 63,* 822–839. (Chap 8)

Hatano, G., & Osawa, K. (1983). Digit memory of grand experts in abacus-derived mental calculation. *Cognition, 15,* 95–110. (Chap 11)

Hauser, S. T., Borman, E. H., Jacobson, A. M., Powers, S. I., & Noam, G. C. (1991). Understanding family contexts of adolescent coping. *Journal of Early Adolescence, 11,* 96–124. (Chap 13)

Hay, D. F. (1980). Multiple functions of proximity seeking in infancy. *Child Development, 51,* 636–645. (Chap 8)

Hay, D. F., Nash, A., & Pedersen, J. (1983). Interaction between 6-month-old peers. *Child Development, 54,* 557–562. (Chap 8)

Hay, D. F., & Ross, H. S. (1982). The social nature of early conflict. *Child Development, 53,* 105–113. (Chap 8)

Heath, S. B. (1983). *Ways with*

words. New York: Cambridge University Press. (Chap 12)

Hebb, D. O. (1978, November). On watching myself grow old. *Psychology Today,* pp. 15–23. (Chap 19)

Heckhausen, J., Dixon, R. A., & Baltes, P. B. (1989). Gains and losses in development throughout adulthood as perceived by different adult age groups. *Developmental Psychology, 25,* 109–121. (Chap 20)

Heer, D. M. (1985). Effect of sibling number on child outcome. *American Review of Sociology, 11,* 27–47. (Chap 9)

Heim, L. (1992). Associations among maternal characteristics and resources during pregnancy and subsequent mother-infant interactions at 3-months postpartum. Doctoral dissertation, University of Michigan. Available on microfilm. (Chap 16)

Heimann, M., Nelson, K. E., & Schaller, J. (1989). Neonatal imitation of tongue protrusion and mouth opening: Methodological aspects and evidence of early individual differences. *Scandinavian Journal of Psychology, 30,* 90–101. (Chap 6)

Heise, D. (1987). Sociocultural determination of mental aging. In C. Schooler & K. W. Schaie (Eds.), *Cognitive functioning and social structure over the life course.* Norwood, NJ: Ablex. (Chap 17)

Helson, R., & Wink, P. (1992). Personality change in women from the early 40s to the early 50s. *Psychology and Aging, 7,* 46–55. (Chap 18).

Henggeler, S. W., Rodick, J. D., Borduin, C. M., Hanson, C. L., Watson, S. M., & Urey, J. R. (1986). Multisystemic treatment of juvenile offenders: Effects on adolescent behavior and family interaction. *Developmental Psychology, 22,* 132–141. (Chap 15)

Hernandez, D. J. (1988). Demographic trends and the living arrangements of children. In E. M. Hetherington & J. D. Arasteh (Eds.), *Impact of divorce, single parenting, and stepparenting on children.* Hillsdale, NJ: Erlbaum. (Chap 9)

Hersch, S. (1988, January). Coming of age on the city streets. *Psychology Today,* pp. 28–37. (Chap 15)

Hertzberger, S. (1983). Social cognition and the transmission of abuse. In D. Finkelhor, R. Gelles, G. Hotaling, & M. Straus (Eds.), *The darkside of families: Current family violence research.* Beverly Hills, CA: Sage. (Chap 9)

Hertzog, C. (1989). Influences of cognitive slowing on age differences in intelligence. *Developmental Psychology, 25,* 636–651. (Chap 19)

Hertzog, C., Hultsch, D. F., & Dixon, R. A. (1989). Evidence for the convergent validity of two self-report metamemory questionnaires. *Developmental Psychology, 25,* 687–700. (Chap 19)

Hess, R. D. (1970). Social class and ethnic influences on socialization. In P. H. Mussen (Ed.), *Handbook of child psychology* (Vol. 2, 3rd ed.). New York: Wiley. (Chap 12)

Hess, R. D., & Holloway, S. D. (1984). Family and school as educational institutions. In R. D. Parke (Ed.), *Review of child development research* (Vol. 7). Chicago: University of Chicago Press. (Chaps 10, 12)

Hess, R. D., & McDevitt, T. M. (1984). Some cognitive consequences of maternal intervention techniques: A longitudinal study. *Child Development, 55,* 2017–2030. (Chap 12)

Hess, R. D., & Shipman, V. C. (1968). Early experience and the socialization of cognitive modes in children. *Child Development, 34,* 869–886. (Chap 10)

Hess, R. D., Shipman, V. C., Brophy, J., & Baer, D. (1968). *The cognitive environment of urban preschool children.* Chicago: University of Chicago Press. (Chap 10)

Hetherington, E. M. (1972). Effects of father absence on personality development in adolescent daughters. *Developmental Psychology, 7,* 313–326. (Chap 9)

Hetherington, E. M., & Camara, K. A. (1984). Families in transition. In R D. Parke (Ed.), *Review of child development research* (Vol. 7). Chicago: University of Chicago Press. (Chaps 9, 16)

Hetherington, E. M., Clingempeel, W. G., Anderson, E. R., Deal, J. E., Hagan, M. S., Hollier, E. A., & Lindner, M. S. (1992). Coping with marital transitions. *Monographs of the Society for Research in Child Development, 57* (2–3, Serial No. 227). (Chaps 13, 16)

Hetherington, E. M., Cox, M., & Cox, R. (1982). Effects of divorce on parents and children. In M. E. Lamb (Ed.), *Nontraditional families.* Hillsdale, NJ: Erlbaum. (Chap 9)

Hevesi, D. (1986, December 17). Harris poll reports teenagers favor contraceptives at clinics. *New York Times,* p. B12. (Chap 15)

Hiebert, J. (1984). Children's mathematics learning. *Elementary School Journal, 84,* 497–513. (Chap 12)

Hill, J. P. (1985). Family relations in adolescence. *Genetic, Social, and General Psychology, 111,* 244–248. (Chap 13)

Hill, J. P., Holmbeck, G. N., Marlow, L., Green, T. M., & Lynch, M. E. (1985). Menarcheal status and parent-child relations in families of 7th-grade girls. *Journal of Youth and Adolescence, 14,* 301–316. (Chap 13)

Hill, K. T., & Eaton, W. O. (1977). The interaction of test anxiety and success-failure experiences in determining children's arithmetic performance. *Developmental Psychology, 13,* 205–211. (Chap 10)

Hill, R., & Mattessich, P. (1979). Family development theory and life-span development. In P. B. Baltes & O. G. Brim (Eds.), *Life-span development and behavior* (Vol. 2). New York: Academic Press. (Chap 9)

Hilts, P. J. (1991, April 6). U.S. reports drop in infant deaths. *New York Times,* pp. 1, 8. (Chap 3)

Himes, C. L. (1992). Future caregivers: Projected family structures of older persons. *Journal of Gerontology: Social Sciences, 47,* S17–26. (Chap 20)

Hinde, R. A. (1983). Ethology and child development. In P. H. Mussen (Ed.), *Handbook of child psychology* (Vol. 2, 4th ed.). New York: Wiley. (Chaps 2, 10)

Hochschild, A. (1989). *The second shift: Working parents and the revolution at home.* New York: Viking. (Chap 9)

Hock, E., & DeMeis, D. K. (1990). Depression in mothers of infants: The role of maternal employment. *Developmental Psychology,*

26, 285–291. (Chap 16)

Hofferth, S. L. (1987). The effects of programs and policies on adolescent pregnancy and childbearing. In S. L. Hofferth & C. D. Hayes (Eds.), *Risking the future: Adolescent sexuality, pregnancy, and childbearing* (Vol. 2). Washington, DC: National Academy Press. (Chap 15)

Hoff-Ginsberg, E. (1986). Function and structure in maternal speech. *Child Development, 22,* 155–163. (Chap 7)

Hoffman, J. (1990, August 19). Pregnant, addicted—and guilty? *New York Times Magazine,* pp. 33–35, 44, 53–57. (Chap 3)

Hoffman, L. W. (1977). Changes in family roles, socialization, and sex differences. *American Psychologist, 32,* 644–657. (Chap 9)

Hoffman, L. W. (1979). Maternal employment. *American Psychologist, 24,* 859–865. (Chaps 9, 13)

Hoffman, L. W. (1980). The effects of maternal employment on the academic attitudes and performance of school-aged children. *School Psychology Review, 9,* 319–336. (Chap 9)

Hoffman, L. W. (1982). Social change and its effect on parents and children. In P. Berman & E. Ramey (Eds.), *Women: A developmental perspective.* Washington, DC: U.S. Government Printing Office. (Chap 16)

Hoffman, L. W. (1983, July). *Population psychology.* Paper presented at the Inter-American Congress of Psychology, Quito, Ecuador. (Chap 9)

Hoffman, L. W. (1984). Work, family, and the socialization of the child. In R. D. Parke (Ed.), *Review of child development research* (Vol. 7). Chicago: University of Chicago Press. (Chaps 8, 9, 10, 12, 16)

Hoffman, L. W. (1985, March). *Social change and the effects of maternal employment on the child.* Paper presented at the International Seminar on the Educational Role of the Family, Hiki-Gun, Saitama, Japan. (Chap 18)

Hoffman, L. W. (1986). Work, family, and the children. In M. S. Pallak & R. O. Perloff (Eds.), *Work, family, and the children.* Washington, DC: American Psychological Association. (Chaps 9, 16, 18)

Hoffman, L. W. (1988). Cross-cultural differences in childrearing goals. In R. A. LeVine, P. M. Miller, & M. M. West (Eds.), *New directions for child development.* No. 40: *Parental behavior in diverse societies.* San Francisco: Jossey-Bass. (Chap 10)

Hoffman, L. W. (1989). Effects of maternal employment in the two-parent family. *American Psychologist, 44,* 283–292. (Chaps 8, 9, 16)

Hoffman, L. W. (1991). The influence of the family environment on personality: Accounting for sibling differences. *Psychological Bulletin, 110,* 187–203. (Chaps 1, 3, 9)

Hoffman, L. W., & Manis, J. D. (1978). Influences of children on marital interaction and parental satisfaction and dissatisfactions. In R. Lerner & G. Spanier (Eds.), *Child influences on marital and family interaction.* New York: Academic Press. (Chaps 15, 16)

Hoffman, L. W., & Manis, J. D. (1979). The value of children in the United States: A new approach to the study of fertility. *Journal of Marriage and the Family, 41,* 583–596. (Chaps 13, 16)

Hoffman, L. W., McManus, K. A., & Brackbill, Y. (1987). The value of children to young and elderly parents. *International Journal of Aging and Human Development, 25,* 309–312. (Chaps 13, 18, 20)

Hoffman, L. W., & Nye, F. I. (1974). *Working mothers.* San Francisco: Jossey-Bass. (Chaps 9, 16)

Hoffman, M. L. (1983). Affective and cognitive processes in moral internalization. In E. T. Higgins, D. N. Ruble, & W. Hartup (Eds.), *Social cognition and social development.* New York: Cambridge University Press. (Chap 9)

Hoffman, M. L. (1988). Moral development (2nd ed.). In M. H. Bornstein & M. E. Lamb (Eds.), *Developmental psychology.* Hillsdale, NJ: Erlbaum. (Chaps 1, 8, 9, 11)

Hoffman, M. L., & Saltzstein, H. D. (1967). Parent discipline and the child's moral development. *Journal of Personality and Social Psychology, 5,* 45–57. (Chap 9)

Hofsten, C. von. (1982). Eye-hand coordination in the newborn. *Developmental Psychology, 18,* 450–461. (Chap 5)

Hofsten, C. von. (1983). Catching skills in infancy. *Journal of Experimental Psychology: Human Perception and Performance, 9,* 75–85. (Chap 5)

Hofsten, C. von. (1984). Development changes in the organization of prereaching movements. *Developmental Psychology, 20,* 378–388. (Chap 5)

Holahan, C. K. (1988). Relation of life goals at age 70 to activity participation and health and psychological well-being among Terman's gifted men and women. *Psychology and Aging, 3,* 286–291. (Chap 20)

Holden, C. (1986). Youth suicide. *Science, 233,* 839–841. (Chap 15)

Holland, J. L. (1985). *Making vocational choices.* Englewood Cliffs, NJ: Prentice-Hall. (Chap 16)

Holliday, S. G., & Chandler, M. J. (1986). *Wisdom: Exploration in adult competence. Contributions to human development* (Vol. 17). Basel: Karger. (Chap 19)

Hopkins, B., & Westra, T. (1990). Motor development, maternal expectations, and the role of handling. *Infant Behavior and Development, 13,* 117–122. (Chap 5)

Horn, J. L. (1968). Organization of abilities and the development of intelligence. *Psychological Review, 75,* 242–259. (Chap 12)

Horn, J. L. (1982). The theory of fluid and crystallized intelligence in relation to concepts of cognitive psychology and aging in adulthood. In F. I. M. Craik & S. Trehub (Eds.), *Aging and cognitive processes.* New York: Plenum. (Chap 17)

Horn, J. L. (1984). Remodeling old models of intelligence. In B. B. Wolman (Ed.), *Handbook of intelligence.* Englewood Cliffs, NJ: Prentice-Hall. (Chap 12)

Howe, N., & Ross, H. S. (1990). Socialization, perspective-taking, and the sibling relationship. *Developmental Psychology, 26,* 160–165. (Chap 8)

Howes, C. (1988). Peer interaction of young children. *Monographs of the Society for Research in Child Development, 53* (1, Serial No. 217). (Chap 8)

Howes, C., & Matheson, C. C. (1992). Sequences in the development of competent play with peers: Social and pretend play. *Developmental Psychology, 28,* 961–974. (Chap 7)

Howes, C., & Wu, F. (1990). Peer interactions and friendships in an ethnically diverse school setting. *Child Development, 61,* 537–541. (Chap 10)

How the public feels. (1986, November 24). *Time,* pp. 58–59. (Chap 13)

Hsu, L. K. G. (1983). The aetiology of anorexia nervosa. *Psychological Medicine, 13,* 231–237. (Chap 15)

Hudson, J., & Nelson, K. (1984). Play with language. *Journal of Child Language, 11,* 337–346. (Chap 7)

Hudson, J. I., Pope, H. G., Jr., Jonas, J. M., & Urgelun-Todd, D. (1983). Family history studies of anorexia nervosa and bulimia. *British Journal of Psychiatry, 142,* 133–138. (Chap 15)

Hudson, R. B., & Strate, J. (1985). Aging and political systems. In R. H. Binstock & E. Shanas (Eds.), *Handbook of aging and the social sciences* (2nd ed.). New York: Van Nostrand Reinhold. (Chap 20)

Huesmann, L. R., Lagerspetz, K., & Eron, L. D. (1984). Intervening variables in the TV violence-aggression relation. *Developmental Psychology, 20,* 746–775. (Chap 10)

Hulicka, I. M. (1982). Memory functioning in late adulthood. In F. I. M. Craik & S. Trehub (Eds.), *Aging and cognitive processes.* New York: Plenum. (Chap 19)

Hultsch, D. F., & Dixon, R. A. (1990). Learning and memory in aging. In J. E. Birren & K. W. Schaie (Eds.), *Handbook of the psychology of aging* (3rd ed.). San Diego, CA: Academic Press. (Chap 19)

Hultsch, D. F., Hertzog, C., & Dixon, R. A. (1984). Text recall in adulthood: The role of intellectual abilities. *Developmental Psychology, 20,* 1193–1211. (Chap 19)

Hultsch, D. F., Hertzog, C., & Dixon, R. A. (1987). Age differences in metamemory: Resolving the inconsistencies. *Canadian Journal of Psychology, 41,* 193–208. (Chap 19)

Humphreys, A. P., & Smith, P. K. (1987). Rough and tumble, friendship, and dominance in schoolchildren. *Child Development, 58,* 201–212. (Chap 10)

Hunt, C. E. (1991). Sudden infant death syndrome: The neurobehavioral perspective. *Journal of Applied Developmental Psychology, 12,* 185–188. (Chap 5)

Hunt, M. (1974). *Sexual behavior in the 1970s.* New York: Dell. (Chap 18)

Hunter, A. G., & Ensminger, M. E. (in press). Diversity and fluidity in children's living arrangements: Life course and family transitions in an urban Afro-American community. *Journal of Marriage and the Family.* (Chap 18)

Hunter, M. A., Ames, E. W., & Koopman, R. (1983). Effect of stimulus complexity and familiarization time on infant preferences for novel and familiar stimuli. *Developmental Psychology, 19,* 338–352. (Chap 6)

Husaini, B. A., Moore, S. T., Castor, R. S., Neser, W., Whittenstovall, R., Linn, J. G., & Griffin, D. (1991). Social density, stressors, and depression: Gender differences among the black elderly. *Journal of Gerontology: Psychological Sciences, 46,* P236–242. (Chap 20)

Huston, A. C. (1983). Sex-typing. In P. H. Mussen (Ed.), *Handbook of child psychology.* (Vol. 4, 4th ed.). New York: Wiley. (Chaps 8, 9)

Huston, A. C. (1985). The development of sex typing. *Developmental Review, 5,* 1–17. (Chap 9)

Huston, A. C., Watkins, B. A., & Kunkel, D. (1989). Public policy and children's television. *American Psychologist, 44,* 424–433. (Chap 10)

Huttenlocher, J., Haight, W., Bryk, A., Seltzer, M., & Lyons, T. (1991). Early vocabulary growth: Relation to language input and gender. *Developmental Psychology, 27,* 236–248. (Chap 7)

Huyck, M. H. (1982). From gregariousness to intimacy: Marriage and friendship over the adult years. In T. M. Field, A. Huston, H. C. Quay, L. Troll, & G. E. Finley (Eds.), *Review of human development.* New York: Wiley. (Chap 18)

Huyck, M. H. (1990). Gender differences in aging. In J. E. Birren & K. W. Schaie (Eds.), *Handbook of the psychology of aging* (3rd ed.). San Diego, CA: Academic Press. (Chap 18)

Hyde, J., Krajnik, M., & Skuldt-Nierderberger, K. (1991). Androgyny across the life span: A replication and longitudinal follow-up. *Developmental Psychology, 27,* 516–519. (Chaps 16, 18)

Hyman, B. T., Van Hoesen, G. N., Damasio, A. R., & Barnes, C. L. (1984). Alzheimer's disease. *Science, 225,* 1168–1170. (Chap 19)

Hymel, S. (1986). Interpretations of peer behavior. *Child Development, 57,* 431–445. (Chap 10)

Inhelder, B., & Piaget, J. (1958). *Growth of logical thinking from childhood to adolescence.* New York: Basic Books. (Chap 14)

Inhelder, B., & Piaget, J. (1964). *The early growth of logic in the child.* London: Routledge. (Chap 11)

Interprofessional Task Force on Health Care of Women and Children. (1978). *The development of family-centered maternity/newborn care in hospitals.* Chicago: Author. (Chap 3)

Ireson, C., & Gill, S. (1988). Girls' socialization for work. In A. H. Stromberg & S. Harkness (Eds.), *Women working* (2nd ed.). Mountain View, CA: Mayfield. (Chap 13)

Istvan, J. (1986). Stress, anxiety, and birth outcomes. *Psychological Bulletin, 100,* 331–348. (Chap 3)

Jackson, C. M. (1929). Some aspects of form and growth. In W. J. Robbins, S. Brody, A. F. Hogan, C. M. Jackson, & C. W. Green (Eds.), *Growth.* New Haven, CT: Yale University Press. (Chap 5)

Jackson, J. S., Antonucci, T. C., & Gibson, R. G. (1990). Cultural, racial, and ethnic minority influences on aging. In J. E. Birren & K. W. Schaie (Eds.), *Handbook of the psychology of aging* (3rd ed.). San Diego, CA: Academic Press. (Chap 20)

Jacobs, B. (1990). Aging and politics. In R. H. Binstock & L. K. George (Eds.), *Handbook of aging and the social sciences* (3rd. ed.). San Diego, CA: Academic Press. (Chap 20)

Jacobs, J. (1983). Industrial sector and career mobility reconsidered. *American Sociological Review, 48,* 415–420. (Chap 16)

Jacobson, J. L., Boersma, D. C., Fields, R. B., & Olson, K. L. (1983). Paralinguistic features of adult speech to infants and small children. *Child Development, 54,* 436–442. (Chap 7)

Jacobson, J. L., Jacobson, S. W., Padgett, R. J., Brumitt, G. A., & Billings, R. L. (1992). Effects of prenatal PCB exposure on cognitive processing and sustained attention. *Developmental Psychology, 28,* 297–306. (Chap 3)

Jacobson, S. W. (1979). Matching behavior in the young infant. *Child Development, 50,* 436–442. (Chap 6)

Jacobson, S. W., Fein, G. G., Jacobson, J. L., Schwartz, P. M., & Dowler, J. K. (1984). Neonatal correlates of prenatal exposure to smoking, caffeine, and alcohol. *Infant Behavior and Development, 7,* 253–265. (Chap 3)

Jacobson, S. W., Fein, G. G., Jacobson, J. L., Schwartz, P. M., & Dowler, J. K. (1985). The effect of intrauterine PCB exposure on visual recognition memory. *Child Development, 56,* 853–860. (Chap 3)

Jagacinski, C. M., & Nicholls, J. G. (1990). Reducing effort to protect perceived ability: "They'd do it but I wouldn't." *Journal of Education Psychology, 82,* 15–21. (Chap 12)

James, W. (1950). *The principles of psychology* (Vol. 1). New York: Dover. (Original work published 1890.) (Chap 4)

Janos, P. M. (1987). A fifty year follow-up of Terman's youngest college students and IQ-matched agemates. *Gifted Child Quarterly, 31,* 55–58. (Chap 12)

Janos, P. M., & Robinson, N. M. (1985). Psychosocial development in intellectually gifted children. In F. D. Horowitz & M. O'Brien (Eds.), *The gifted and talented.* Washington, DC: American Psychological Association. (Chap 12)

Jelliffe, D. B., & Jelliffe, E. F. P. (1979). *Human milk in the modern world.* New York: Oxford University Press. (Chap 5)

Jennings, M., & Niemi, R. G. (1981). *Generations and politics.* Princeton, NJ: Princeton University Press. (Chap 15)

Jensen, A. R. (1969). How much can we boost IQ and scholastic achievement? *Harvard Educational Review, 39,* 1–123. (Chap 12)

Jiao, S., Ji, G., & Jing, Q. (C. C. Ching). (1986). Comparative study of behavioral qualities of only children and sibling children. *Child Development, 57,* 357–361. (Chap 9)

Joachim, C. L., & Selkoe, D. J. (1989). Minireview: Amyloid protein in Alzheimer's disease. *Journal of Gerontology: Biological Sciences, 44,* B77–82. (Chap 3)

Johnson, C., Lewis, C., Love, S., Lewis, L., & Stuckey, M. (1984). Incidence and correlates of bulimic behavior in a female high school population. *Journal of Youth and Adolescence, 13,* 15. (Chap 15)

Johnson, C. L. (1983). Interdependence and aging in Italian families. In J. Sokolovsky (Ed.), *Growing old in different societies.* Belmont, CA: Wadsworth. (Chap 10)

Johnson, C. L., & Barer, B. M. (1990). Families and networks among older inner-city blacks. *Gerontologist, 30,* 726–733. (Chap 20)

Johnson, E. M., & Kochlar, D. M. (Eds.). (1983). *Teratogenesis and reproductive toxicology.* New York: Springer. (Chap 3)

Johnson, K. (1992, August 19). Hard logic on drugs before birth. *New York Times,* p. B5. (Chap 3)

Johnston, L. D., O'Malley, P. M., & Bachman, J. G. (1991). *Drug use among American high school seniors, college students and young adults, 1975–1990.* Vol. 1: *High school seniors.* Washington, DC: National Institute on Drug Abuse. (Chap 15)

Johnston, P. H., & Winograd, P. N. (1985). Passive failure in reading. *Journal of Reading Behavior, 17,* 279–301. (Chap 12)

Jung, C. G. (1969). *The structure and dynamics of the psyche.* Princeton, NJ: Princeton University Press. (Chaps 18, 20)

Jusczyk, P. W. (1977). Perception of syllable–final stop consonant by 2-month-old infants. *Perception and Psychophysics, 21,* 450–454. (Chap 7)

Kagan, J. (1958). The concept of identification. *Psychological Review, 65,* 296–305. (Chap 2)

Kagan, J. (1984). *The nature of the child.* New York: Basic Books. (Chap 8)

Kagan, J., & Tulkin, S. R. (1971). Social class differences in child-rearing during the first year. In H. R. Schaffer (Ed.), *The origins of human social relations.* New York: Academic Press. (Chap 8)

Kagay, M. R. (1991, June 18). Poll finds AIDS causes single people to alter behavior. *New York Times,* p. C3. (Chap 16)

Kahn, J., Smith, K., & Roberts, E. (1984). *Familial communication and adolescent sexual behavior.* (Final report to the Office of Adolescent Pregnancy Programs.) Cambridge, MA: American Institutes for Research. (Chap 13)

Kail, R. (1990). *The development of memory in children* (3rd ed.). New York: Freeman. (Chaps 6, 11)

Kalish, R. (1985). *Death, grief, and caring relationships* (2nd ed.). Monterey, CA: Brooks/Cole. (Chap 20)

Kalnins, I. V., & Bruner, J. S. (1973). The coordination of visual observation and instrumental behavior in early infancy. *Perception, 2,* 307–314. (Chap 6)

Kamin, L. J. (1974). *The science and politics of IQ.* Potomac, MD: Erlbaum. (Chap 12)

Kandel, D. (1978). Homophily, selection, and socialization in adolescent friendships. *American Journal of Sociology, 84,* 427–436. (Chap 14)

Kane, R. L., & Kane, R. A. (1990). Health care for older people: Organizational and policy issues. In R. H. Binstock & L. K. George (Eds.), *Handbook of aging and the social sciences* (3rd ed.). San Diego, CA: Academic Press. (Chap 20)

Kantrowitz, B. (1985, December 23). Mothers on their own. *Newsweek,* pp. 66–67. (Chap 16)

Kantrowitz, B., & Joseph, N. (1986, May 26). Building baby biceps. *Newsweek,* p. 79. (Chap 5)

Kantrowitz, B., & Wingert, P. (1990). Step by step. *Newsweek,* [Special edition: The 21st century family], pp. 24–34. (Chap 16)

Kaplan, H., & Dove, H. (1987). Infant development among the Ache of eastern Paraguay. *Developmental Psychology, 23,* 190–198. (Chap 5)

Karsh, E. (1987, January 3). A teen-ager is a ton of worry. *New York Times,* p. 23. (Chap 14)

Kastenbaum, R. (1985). Dying and death. In J. E. Birren & K. W. Schaie (Eds.), *Handbook of the psychology of aging* (2nd ed.). New York: Van Nostrand Reinhold. (Chap 20)

Kates, J. (1986, September 18).

Hers. *New York Times*, p. C2. (Chap 16)

Kaufman, J., & Cicchetti, D. (1989). Effects of maltreatment on school-age children's socioemotional development: Assessments in a day-camp setting. *Developmental Psychology, 25,* 516–524. (Chap 9)

Kaufman, J., & Zigler, E. (1989). The intergenerational transmission of child abuse. In D. Cicchetti & V. Carlson (Eds.), *Child maltreatment.* New York: Cambridge University Press. (Chap 9)

Kausler, D. H. (1990). Motivation, aging, and cognitive performance. In J. E. Birren & K. W. Schaie (Eds.), *Handbook of the psychology of aging* (3rd ed.). San Diego, CA: Academic Press. (Chap 19)

Kavrell, A., & Petersen, A. (1984). Patterns of achievement in early adolescence. *Advances in Motivation and Achievement, 2,* 1–35. (Chap 14)

Kaye, K. (1982). *The mental and social life of babies.* Chicago: University of Chicago Press. (Chap 4)

Keating, D. P. (in press). Adolescent thinking. In S. Feldman & G. Elliott (Eds.), *At the threshold: The developing adolescent.* Cambridge, MA: Harvard University Press. (Chap 14)

Keating, N. C., & Cole, P. (1980). What do I do with him 24 hours a day? *Gerontologist, 20,* 84–89. (Chap 20)

Keating, N. C., & Jeffrey, B. (1983). Work careers of ever married and never married retired women. *Gerontologist, 23,* 416–421. (Chap 18)

Kedar-Voivodas, G. (1983). The impact of elementary children's roles and sex roles on teacher attitudes. *Review of Educational Research, 53,* 414–437. (Chap 10)

Kee, D. W., Gottfried, A. W., Bathurst, K., & Brown, K. (1987). Left-hemisphere language specialization: Consistency in hand preference and sex differences. *Child Development, 58,* 718–724. (Chap 5)

Keeney, T. J., Cannizzo, S. R., & Flavell, J. H. (1967). Spontaneous and induced verbal rehearsal in a recall task. *Child Development, 38,* 953–966. (Chap 11)

Keil, F. C. (1981). Constraints on knowledge and cognitive development. *Psychological Review, 88,* 197–227. (Chap 6)

Keil, F. C. (1989). *Concepts, kinds, and cognitive development.* Cambridge, MA: MIT Press. (Chap 11)

Keller, M., & Wood, P. (1989). Development of friendship reasoning: A study of interindividual differences in intraindividual change. *Developmental Psychology, 25,* 820–826. (Chap 14)

Kelley, M. L., Power, T. G., & Wimbush, D. D. (1992). Determinants of disciplinary practices in low-income black mothers. *Child Development, 63,* 573–582. (Chap 10)

Kelly, J. B. (1982). Divorce. In B. B. Wolman (Ed.), *Handbook of developmental psychology.* Englewood Cliffs, NJ: Prentice-Hall. (Chap 18)

Kemler-Nelson, D. G., Hirsh-Pasek, K., Jusczyk, P. W., & Cassidy, K. W. (1989). How the prosodic cues in motherese might assist language learning. *Journal of Child Language, 16,* 55–68. (Chap 7)

Kempe, R. S., & Kempe, H. C. (1978). *Child abuse.* Cambridge, MA: Harvard University Press. (Chap 9)

Kendig, H. L. (1990). Housing, aging, and social structure. In R. H. Binstock & L. K. George (Eds.), *Handbook of aging and the social sciences* (3rd ed.). San Diego, CA: Academic Press. (Chap 20)

Kennedy, G. E. (1990). College students' expectations of grandparent and grandchild role behavior. *Gerontologist, 30,* 43–48. (Chap 20)

Kennedy, W. A. (1969). A follow-up normative study of Negro intelligence and achievement. *Monographs of the Society for Research in Child Development, 34* (Serial No. 126). (Chap 12)

Keshet, H. F., & Rosenthal, K. M. (1978a). Fathering after marital separation. *Social Work, 23,* 11–18. (Chap 16)

Keshet, H. F., & Rosenthal, K. M. (1978b). Single parent fathers: A new study. *Children Today, 7*(3), 13–17. (Chap 9)

Kessen, W. (1965). *The child.* New York: Wiley. (Chap 1)

Kessler, R. C., & McRae, J. A., Jr. (1981). Trends in the relationship between sex and psychological distress. *American Sociological Review, 46,* 443–453. (Chap 18)

Kilborn, P. T. (1990, November 27). Youths lacking special skills find jobs leading nowhere. *New York Times,* pp. A1, B10. (Chap 16)

Kilborn, P. T. (1991, September 2). Unions at a loss to reverse falling fortunes of workers. *New York Times,* pp. 1, 10. (Chap 16)

Kimura, K. (1984). Studies on growth and development in Japan. *Yearbook of Physical Anthropology, 27,* 179–214. (Chap 5)

Kinsbourne, M., & Hiscock, M. (1983). The normal and deviant development of functional lateralization of the brain. In P. H. Mussen (Ed.), *Handbook of child psychology* (Vol. 2, 4th ed.). New York: Wiley. (Chap 5)

Kinsey, A. C., Pomeroy, W. B., & Martin, C. E. (1948). *Sexual behavior in the human male.* Philadephia: Saunders. (Chap 13)

Kinsey, A. C., Pomeroy, W. B., Martin, C. E., & Gebhard, P. H. (1953). *Sexual behavior in the human female.* Philadelphia: Saunders. (Chap 13)

Kintgen, E. R., Kroll, B. M., & Ross, M. (Eds.). (1988). *Perspectives on literacy.* Carbondale: Southern Illinois University Press. (Chap 17)

Kirsch, I. S., & Jungblut, A. (1986). *Literacy: Profiles of America's young adults* (NAEP Report No. 16-PL-02). Princeton, NJ: National Assessment of Educational Progress. (Chap 17)

Kitchen, W., Ford, G., Orgill, A., Rickards, A., Astbury, J., Lissenden, J., Bajuk, B., Yu, V., Drew, J., & Campbell, N. (1987). Outcome in infants of birth weight 500-to-900 g: A continuing regional study of 5-year-old survivors. *Journal of Pediatrics, 111,* 761–766. (Chap 3)

Kivett, V. R. (1991). Centrality of the grandfather role among older rural black and white men. *Journal of Gerontology: Social Sciences, 46,* S250–258. (Chap 20)

Kivnick, H. Q. (1982). Grandparenthood: An overview of meaning and moral health. *Gerontologist, 22,* 59–66. (Chap 18)

Kleiner, K. A. (1987). Amplitude and phase spectra as indices of infant's pattern preferences. *Infant Behavior and Development, 10,* 54–55. (Chap 6)

Kleiner, K. A. (1990). Models of neonates' preferences for facelike patterns: A response to Morton, Johnson, and Maurer. *Infant Behavior and Development, 13,* 105–108. (Chap 6)

Kliegl, R., & Baltes, P. B. (1987). Theory-guided analysis of mechanisms of development and aging through testing-the-limits and research on expertise. In C. Schooler & K. W. Schaie (Eds.), *Cognitive functioning and social structure over the life course.* Norwood, NJ: Ablex. (Chap 19)

Kliegl, R., Smith, J., & Baltes, P. B. (1990). On the locus and process of magnification of age differences during mnemonic training. *Developmental Psychology, 26,* 894–904. (Chap 19)

Kline, M., Tschann, J. M., Johnston, J. R., & Wallerstein, J. S. (1989). Children's adjustment in joint and sole physical custody families. *Developmental Psychology, 25,* 430–438. (Chap 9)

Knopf, M., & Neidhardt, E. (1989). Aging and memory for action events: The role of familiarity. *Developmental Psychology, 5,* 780–786. (Chap 19)

Kobasigawa, A. (1977). Retrieval strategies in the development of memory. In R. V. Kail & J. W. Hagen (Eds.), *Perspectives on the development of memory and cognition.* Hillsdale, NJ: Erlbaum. (Chap 11)

Koepp, S. (1986, November 3). Is the middle class shrinking? *Newsweek,* pp. 54–56. (Chap 15)

Kogan, N. (1990). Personality and aging. In J. E. Birren & K. W. Schaie (Eds.), *Handbook of the psychology of aging* (3rd ed.). San Diego, CA: Academic Press. (Chap 16)

Kohlberg, L. (1969). Stage and sequence. In D. A. Goslin (Ed.), *Handbook of socialization theory and research.* Chicago: Rand-McNally. (Chap. 2, 11)

Kohlberg, L., & Gilligan, C. (1971). The adolescent as a philosopher. *Daedalus, 100,* 1051–1086. (Chap 14)

Kohn, M. (1979). The effects of social class on parental values and practices. In D. Reiss & H. A. Hoffman (Eds.), *The American family.* New York: Plenum. (Chap 10)

Kohn, M. L., & Schooler, C. (1983). *Work and personality.* Norwood, NJ: Ablex. (Chap 16)

Kolata, G. B. (1986). Obese children. *Science, 232,* 20–21. (Chap 5)

Kolata, G. B. (1987). Panel urges dementia be diagnosed with care. *Science, 237,* 725. (Chap 19)

Kolata, G. B. (1991, January 1). Temperance: An old cycle repeats itself. *New York Times,* pp. 35, 40. (Chap 1)

Konner, M. (1977). Infancy among the Kalahari Desert San. In P. H. Leiderman, S. R. Tulkin, & A. Rosenfeld (Eds.), *Culture and infancy.* New York: Academic Press. (Chap 8)

Konner, M., & Worthman, C. (1980). Nursing frequency, gonadal function, and birth spacing among !Kung hunter-gatherers. *Science, 207,* 788–791. (Chap 4)

Kopp, C. B. (1979). Perspectives on infant motor system development. In M. H. Bornstein & W. Kessen (Eds.), *Psychological development from infancy.* Hillsdale, NJ: Erlbaum. (Chap 5)

Kopp, C. B. (1989). Regulation of distress and negative emotions: A developmental view. *Developmental Psychology, 25,* 343–354. (Chap 8)

Kopp, C. B., & Kaler, S. R. (1989). Risk in infancy: Origins and implications. *American Psychologist, 44,* 224–230. (Chap 3)

Korner, A. F., Hutchinson, C. A., Koperski, J. A., Kraemer, H. C., & Schneider, P. A. (1981). Stability of individual differences of neonatal motor and crying patterns. *Child Development, 52,* 83–90. (Chap 4)

Kornhaber, A., & Woodward, K. L. (1981). *Grandparent/grandchild.* Garden City, NY: Anchor Press. (Chap 18)

Kotre, J., & Hall, E. (1990). *Seasons of life.* Boston: Little, Brown. (Chaps 12, 13, 14, 16, 18, 20)

Kovach, J. A., & Glickman, N. W. (1986). Levels and psychosocial correlates of adolescent drug usage. *Journal of Youth and Adolescence, 15,* 61–78. (Chap 15)

Kozol, J. (1985). *Illiterate America.* Garden City, NY: Anchor Press. (Chap 17)

Kramer, D. A. (1983). Post-formal operations? A need for further conceptualization. *Human Development, 26,* 91–105. (Chap 17)

Kramer, D. A., & Woodruff, D. S. (1986). Relativistic and dialectical thought in three age groups. *Human Development, 29,* 280–290. (Chap 17)

Krause, N. (1986). Social support, stress, and well-being among older adults. *Journal of Gerontology, 41,* 512–519. (Chap 20)

Krause, N. (1991). Stress and isolation from close ties in later life. *Journal of Gerontology: Social Sciences, 46,* S183–194. (Chap 20)

Kremenitzer, J. P., Vaughan, H. G., Jr., Kurtzberg, D., & Dowling, K. (1979). Smooth-pursuit eye movements in the newborn infant. *Child Development, 50,* 442–448. (Chap 6)

Kreutzer, M. A., Leonard, C., & Flavell, J. H. (1975). An interview study of children's knowledge about memory. *Monographs of the Society for Research in Child Development, 40* (1, Serial No. 159). (Chap 11)

Krisberg, B., Schwartz, I., Fishman, G., Eisikovits, Z., & Guttman, E. (1986). *The incarceration of minority youth.* Minneapolis: Hubert H. Humphrey Institute of Public Affairs, National Council on Crime and Delinquency. (Chap 15)

Krosnick, J. A., & Judd, C. M. (1982). Transition in social influence at adolescence. *Developmental Psychology, 18,* 359–368. (Chap 13)

Krout, J. A. (1988). Rural versus urban differences in elderly parents' contact with their children. *Gerontologist, 28,* 198–203. (Chap 20)

Kubler-Ross, E. (1969). *On death and dying.* New York: Macmillan. (Chap 20)

Kuczaj, S. A., II. (1978). Children's judgments of grammatical and ungrammatical irregular past-tense verbs. *Child Development, 49,* 319–326. (Chap 7)

Kuczaj, S. A., II, & Brannick, N. (1979). Children's use of "wh-" question modal auxiliary placement rule. *Journal of Experimental Child Psychology, 28,* 43–67. (Chap 7)

Kuczynski, L. (1983). Reasoning, prohibitions, and motivations for compliance. *Developmental Psychology, 19,* 126–134. (Chap 9)

Kuczynski, L., Zahn-Waxler, C., &

Radke-Yarrow, M. (1987). Development and content of imitation in the second and third years of life: A socialization perspective. *Developmental Psychology, 23,* 276–282. (Chap 6)

Kuhn, D. (1988). Cognitive development. In M. Bornstein & M. E. Lamb (Eds.), *Developmental psychology* (2nd ed.). Hillsdale, NJ: Erlbaum. (Chap 2)

Kuhn, D., Amsel, E., & O'Loughlin, M. (1988). *The development of scientific thinking skills.* San Diego, CA: Academic Press. (Chap 14)

Kurdek, L. A. (1991a). Correlates of relationship satisfaction in cohabiting gay and lesbian couples: Integration of contextual, investment, and problem-solving models. *Journal of Personality and Social Psychology, 61,* 910–922. (Chap 16)

Kurdek, L. A. (1991b). Predictors of increases in marital distress in newlywed couples: A 3-year prospective longitudinal study. *Developmental Psychology, 27,* 627–636. (Chap 16)

Kurdek, L. A., & Schmitt, J. P. (1986). Early development of relationship quality in heterosexual married, heterosexual cohabiting, gay, and lesbian couples. *Developmental Psychology, 22,* 305–309. (Chap 16)

Laboratory of Comparative Human Cognition. (1983). Culture and cognitive development. In P. H. Mussen (Ed.), *Handbook of child psychology* (Vol. 1, 4th ed.). New York: Wiley. (Chaps 2, 11)

Labouvie-Vief, G. (1985). Intelligence and cognition. In J. E. Birren & K. W. Schaie (Eds.), *Handbook of the psychology of aging* (2nd ed.). New York: Van Nostrand Reinhold. (Chap 17)

Labouvie-Vief, G. (1989). Modes of knowledge and the organization of development. In M. L. Commons, C. Armon, F. A. Richards, & J. Sinnott (Eds.), *Beyond formal operations: 2. The development of adolescent and adult thinking and perception.* New York: Praeger. (Chap 17)

Lachman, M. E., & Leff, R. (1989). Perceived control and intellectual functioning in the elderly: A five-year longitudinal study. *Developmental Psychology, 25,* 722–728. (Chap 19)

Ladd, G. W. (1990). Having friends, keeping friends, making friends, and being liked by peers in the classroom: Predictors of children's early school adjustment? *Child Development, 61,* 1081–1100. (Chap 10)

Lafromboise, T. D., & Bigfoot, D. S. (1988). Cultural and cognitive considerations in the prevention of American Indian adolescent suicide. *Journal of Adolescence, 11,* 139–153. (Chap 15)

Lahey, B. B., Hammer, D., Crumrine, P. L., & Forehand, R. L. (1980). Birth order × sex interactions in child behavior problems. *Developmental Psychology, 16,* 608–615. (Chap 9)

Lakatta, E. G. (1990). Heart and circulation. In E. L. Schneider & J. W. Rowe (Eds.), *Handbook of the biology of aging* (3rd ed.). San Diego, CA: Academic Press. (Chap 20)

Lamb, M. E. (1978). Interactions between 18-month-olds and their preschool-aged friends. *Child Development, 49,* 51–59. (Chap 8)

Lamb, M. E. (1981). The development of father-infant relationships. In M. E. Lamb (Ed.), *The role of the father in child development* (2nd ed.). New York: Wiley. (Chap 8)

Lamb, M. E. (1988). Social and emotional development in infancy. In M. H. Bornstein & M. E. Lamb (Eds.), *Developmental psychology* (2nd ed.). Hillsdale, NJ: Erlbaum. (Chap 9)

Lamb, M. E., & Bornstein, M. H. (1986). *Development in infancy* (2nd ed.). New York: Random House. (Chap 4)

Lamb, M. E., & Bronson, S. K. (1980). Fathers in the context of family relations. *School Psychology Review, 51,* 336–353. (Chap 9)

Lamb, M. E., Easterbrooks, M. A., & Holden, G. W. forcement and punishment among preschoolers. *Child Development, 51,* 1230–1236. (Chap 10)

Lamb, M. E., Hopps, K., & Elster, A. B. (1987). Strange situation behavior of infants with adolescent mothers. *Infant Behavior and Development, 10,* 39–48. (Chap 15)

Lamb, M. E., Pleck, J. H., & Levine, J. (1986). The role of the father in child development. In A. Kazdin (Ed.), *Advances in clinical child psychology* (Vol. 8). New York: Plenum. (Chap 9)

Lamb, M. E., Thompson, R. A., Gardner, W. P., & Charnov, E. L. (1985). *Infant-mother attachment.* Hillsdale, NJ: Erlbaum. (Chap 8)

Lancaster, J. B. (1986). Human adolescence and reproduction: An evolutionary perspective. In J. B. Lancaster & B. A. Hamburg (Eds.), *School-age pregnancy and parenthood.* New York: Aldine. (Chap 13)

Lancioni, G. E. (1980). Infant operant conditioning and its implications for early intervention. *Psychological Bulletin, 88,* 516–534. (Chap 6)

Langer, E. J. (1985). Playing the middle against both ends: The usefulness of older adult cognitive activity as a model for cognitive activity in childhood and old age. In S. Yussen (Ed.), *The growth of reflection in children.* New York: Academic Press. (Chap 20)

Langer, E. J., & Rodin, J. (1976). The efforts of choice and enhanced personal responsibility for the aged: A field experiment in an institutional setting. *Journal of Personality and Social Psychology, 34,* 191–198. (Chap 20)

Langlois, J. H. (1986). From the eye of the beholder to behavioral reality: Development of social behaviors and social relations as a function of physical attractiveness. In C. P. Herman, M. P. Zanna, & E. T. Higgins (Eds.), *Physical appearance, stigma, and social behavior.* Hillsdale, NJ: Erlbaum. (Chap 1)

Langlois, J. H., & Downs, A. C. (1980). Mothers, fathers, and peers as socialization agents of sex-typed play behaviors in young children. *Child Development, 51,* 1237–1247. (Chap 9)

Langlois, J. H., Ritter, J. M., Roggman, L. A., & Vaughn, L. S. (1991). Facial diversity and infant preferences for attractive faces. *Developmental Psychology, 27,* 79–84. (Chap 6)

Langlois, J. H., Roggman, L. A., Casey, R. J., Ritter, J. M., Rieser-Danner, L. A., & Jenkins, V. Y. (1987). Infant preferences for attractive faces: Rudiments of a stereotype? *Developmental Psychology, 23,* 363–369. (Chap 6)

Langlois, J. H., Roggman, L.A., & Rieser-Danner, L. A. (1990). Infants' differential social responses to attractive and unattractive faces. *De-*

velopmental Psychology, 26, 153–159. (Chap 6)

Langlois, J. H., & Stephan, C. F. (1977). The effects of physical attractiveness and ethnicity on children's behavioral attributions and peer preference. *Child Development, 48,* 1694–1698. (Chap 10)

Laosa, L. M. (1980). Maternal teaching strategies in Chicano and Anglo-American families: The influence of culture and education on maternal behavior. *Child Development, 51,* 759–765. (Chap 8)

Laosa, L. M. (1988). Ethnicity and single parenting in the United States. In E. M. Hetherington & J. D. Arasteh (Eds.), *Impact of divorce, single parenting, and stepparenting on children.* Hillsdale, NJ: Erlbaum. (Chap 9)

Lapsley, D. K., Milstead, M., Quinitana, S. M., Flannery, D., & Buss, R. R. (1986). Adolescent egocentrism and formal operations: Tests of a theoretical assumption. *Developmental Psychology, 22,* 800–807. (Chap 14)

Lapsley, D. K., & Murphy, M. N. (1985). Another look at the theoretical assumptions of adolescent egocentrism. *Developmental Review, 5,* 201–217. (Chap 14)

Larson, E. (1987, November/December). Trends in neonatal infections. *Journal of Obstetrical, Gynecological, and Neonatal Nursing,* pp. 404–409. (Chap 3)

Larson, R., Csikszentmihalyi, M., & Graef, R. (1980). Mood variability and the psychosocial adjustment of adolescents. *Journal of Youth and Adolescence, 9,* 469–490. (Chap 13)

Larson, R., & Lampman-Petraitis, C. (1989). Daily emotional states as reported by children and adolescents. *Child Development, 60,* 1250–1260. (Chap 13)

Larson, R., Mannell, R., & Zuzanek, J. (1986). Daily well-being of older adults with friends and families. *Psychology and Aging, 1,* 117–126. (Chap 20)

Larson, R., & Richards, M. H. (1991). Daily companionship in late childhood and early adolescence: Changing developmental contexts. *Child Development, 62,* 284–300. (Chap 13)

La Rue, A., Dessonville, C., & Jarvik, L. F. (1985). Aging and mental disorders. In J. E. Birrin & K. W. Schaie (Eds.), *Handbook of the psychology of aging* (2nd ed.). New York: Van Nostrand Reinhold. (Chap 19)

La Rue, A., & Jarvik, L. F. (1982). Old age and biobehavioral change. In B. B. Wolman (Ed.), *Handbook of developmental psychology.* Englewood Cliffs, NJ: Prentice-Hall. (Chap 17)

Lasko, J. K. (1954). Parent behavior toward first and second children. *Genetic Psychology Monographs, 49,* 97–137. (Chaps 1, 9)

Lasky, R. E., Klein, R. E., Yarbrough, C., Engle, P. L., Lechtig, A., & Martorell, R. (1981). The relationship between physical growth and infant behavioral development in rural Guatemala. *Child Development, 52,* 219–226. (Chap 5)

La Sorsa, V. A., & Fodor, I. G. (1990). Adolescent daughter/midlife mother dyad: A new look at separation and self-definition. *Psychology of Women Quarterly, 14* 593–606. (Chap 18)

Laudenslager, M. L., Ryan, S. M., Drugan, R. C., Hudson, R. L., & Maier, S. F. (1983). Coping and immunosuppression: Inescapable but not escapable shock suppresses lymphocyte production. *Science, 221,* 568–570. (Chap 20)

Laurence, L. T. (1982). *Couple constancy.* Ann Arbor, MI: UMI Research Press. (Chap 18)

Lave, J. (1990). The culture of acquisition and the practice of understanding. In J. W. Stigler, R. A. Shweder, & G. Herdt (Eds.), *Cultural psychology: Essays on comparative human development.* New York: Cambridge University Press. (Chap 2)

Lawton, M. P. (1985). Housing and living environments of older people. In R. H. Binstock & E. Shanas (Eds.), *Handbook of aging and the social sciences* (2nd ed.). New York: Van Nostrand Reinhold. (Chap 20)

Lazarus, R. (1985). Stress and adaptational concerns. *American Psychologist, 40,* 770–780. (Chap 18)

Leavitt, H. (1986, December 22). School clinics vs. teen pregnancies. *Insight,* p. 26. (Chap 15)

Lee, C. L., & Bates, J. E. (1985). Mother-child interaction at age 2 years and perceived difficult temperament. *Child Development, 56,* 1314–1325. (Chap 4)

Leiblum, S. R. (1990). Sexuality and the midlife woman. *Psychology of Women Quarterly, 14,* 495–508. (Chap 18)

Leming, M. R., & Dickinson, G. E. (1985). *Understanding dying, death, and bereavement.* New York: Holt, Rinehart and Winston. (Chap 20)

Lenneberg, E. H. (1967). *Biological foundations of language.* New York: Wiley. (Chap 7)

Lenneberg, E. H. (1973). Biological aspects of language. In G. A. Miller (Ed.), *Communication, language, and meaning.* New York: Basic Books. (Chap 7)

Leo, J. (1986, February 24). Could suicide be contagious? *Time,* p. 59. (Chap 15)

Leonard, C. O. (1981). Serum AFP screening for neural tube defects. *Clinical Obstetrics and Gynecology, 24,* 1121–1132. (Chap 3)

Leone, C. M., & Richards, M. H. (1989). Classwork and homework in early adolescence: The ecology of achievement. *Journal of Youth and Adolescence, 18,* 531–548. (Chap 14)

Leopold, W. F. (1949). *Grammar and general problems in the first two years, Speech development of a bilingual child: A linguist's record* (Vol. 3). Evanston, Ill.: Northwestern University Press. (Chap. 7)

Lepper, M. R. (1983). Social control processes, attributions of motivation, and the internalization of social values. In E. T. Higgins, D. N. Ruble, & W. W. Hartup (Eds.), *Social cognition and social behavior.* New York: Cambridge University Press. (Chap 6)

Lepper, M. R., Greene, D., & Nisbett, R. E. (1973). Undermining children's intrinsic interest with extrinsic rewards. *Journal of Personality and Social Psychology, 18,* 129–137. (Chap 6)

Lerner, R. M. (1990). Plasticity, person-context relations, and cognitive training in the aged years: A developmental contextual perspective. *Developmental Psychology, 26,* 911–915. (Chap 19)

Lerner, R. M. (1991). Changing

organism-context relations as the basic process of development: A developmental contextual perspective. *Developmental Psychology, 27,* 27–32. (Chap 5)

Lesgold, A., Resnick, L. B., & Hammond, K. (1985). Learning to read. In T. G. Waller & G. E. MacKinnon (Eds.), *Reading research* (Vol. 4). New York: Academic Press. (Chap 12)

Lester, B. M. (1983). A biosocial model of infant crying. In L. P. Lipsitt & C. Rovee-Collier (Eds.), *Advances in infancy research* (Vol. 3). Norwood, NJ: Ablex. (Chap 4)

Lester, B. M. (1990, August). *Neurobehavioral syndromes in cocaine-exposed newborn infants.* Paper presented at the annual meeting of the American Psychological Association, Boston. (Chap 3)

Lester, B. M., & Dreher, M. (1989). Effects of marijuana use during pregnancy on newborn cry. *Child Development, 60,* 765–771. (Chap 4)

Lester, B. M., Kotelchuck, K., Spelke, E., Sellers, M. J., & Klein, R. E. (1974). Separation protest in Guatemalan infants. *Developmental Psychology, 10,* 79–85. (Chap 8)

LeVay, S., Wiesel, T. N., & Hubel, D. H. (1980). The development of ocular dominance columns in normal and visually deprived monkeys. *Journal of Comparative Neurology, 191,* 1–51. (Chap 5)

Levinson, D. J., Darrow, C. N., Klein, E. B., Levinson, M. H., & McKee, B. (1978). *The seasons of a man's life.* New York: Knopf. (Chaps 1, 16, 18)

Levitt, M. J., Antonucci, T. G., & Clark, M. C. (1984). Object-person permanence and attachment. *Merrill-Palmer Quarterly, 30,* 1–10. (Chap 8)

Levitt, M. J., Clark, M. C., Rotton, J., & Finley, G. E. (1987). Social support, perceived control, and well-being: A study of an environmentally stressed population. *International Journal of Aging and Human Development, 25,* 247–258. (Chap 20)

Lewin, T. (1991, April 20). Appeals court in Florida backs guilt for drug delivery by umbilical cord. *New York Times,* p. 6. (Chap 3)

Lewis, C. C. (1987). Minors' competence to consent to abortion. *American Psychologist, 42,* 84–88. (Chap 14)

Lewis, M. (1971). Social interaction in the first days of life. In H. R. Schaffer (Ed.), *The origins of human social relations.* New York: Academic Press. (Chap 8)

Lewis, M., & Brooks-Gunn, J. (1979). *Social cognition and the acquisition of self.* New York: Plenum. (Chap 8)

Lewis, M., Brooks-Gunn, J., & Jaskir, J. (1985). Individual differences in self-recognition as a function of the mother-infant attachment relationship. *Developmental Psychology, 21,* 1181–1187. (Chap 8)

Liberman, I. Y., Shankweiler, D., Fischer, F. W., & Carter, B. (1974). Explicit syllable and phoneme segmentation in the young child. *Journal of Experimental Child Psychology, 18,* 201–212. (Chap 12)

Licht, B. G., & Dweck, C. S. (1984). Determinants of academic achievement. *Developmental Psychology, 20,* 628–638. (Chap 10)

Lieberman, L., & Lieberman, L. (1986). Husband-wife interaction in second careers. *Journal of Family Issues, 7,* 215–229. (Chap 18)

Lieberman, M. A., & Tobin, S. (1983). *The experience of old age.* New York: Basic Books. (Chap 20)

Lifton, R. J. (1971). *History and human survival.* New York: Vintage. (Chap 20)

Lin, C.-Y. C., & Fu, V. R. (1990). A comparison of child-rearing practices among Chinese, immigrant Chinese, and Caucasian-American parents. *Child Development, 61* 429–433. (Chap 10)

Lin, P.-J., Schwanenflugel, P. J., & Wisenbaker, J. M. (1990). Category typicality, cultural familiarity, and the development of category knowledge. *Developmental Psychology, 26,* 805–813. (Chap 11)

Linde, E. V., Morrongiello, B. A., & Rovee-Collier, C. K. (1985). Determinants of retention in 8-week-old infants. *Developmental Psychology, 21,* 602–613. (Chap 6)

Linn, M. C., & Petersen, A. C. (1985). Emergence and characterization of sex differences in spatial ability: A meta-analysis. *Child Development, 56,* 1479–1498. (Chap 14)

Lipton, E. L., Steinschneider, A., & Richmond, J. B. (1965). Swaddling, a child care practice: Historical, cultural, and experimental observations. *Pediatrics, 34,* 521–567. (Chap 4)

Litwack, E. (1960). Reference group theory, bureaucratic career and neighborhood primary group cohesion. *Sociometry, 23,* 72–84. (Chap 20)

Livson, N., & Peskin, H. (1980). Perspectives on adolescence from longitudinal research. In J. Adelson (Ed.), *Handbook of adolescent psychology.* New York: Wiley. (Chap 13)

Lockshin, R. A., & Zakeri, Z. F. (1990). Programmed cell death: New thoughts and relevance to aging. *Journal of Gerontology: Biological Sciences, 45,* B135–140. (Chap 20)

Loehlin, J. C., Willerman, L., & Horn, J. M. (1988). Human behavior genetics. *Annual Review of Psychology, 39,* 101–133. (Chap 4)

Loewen, E. R., Shaw, R. J., & Craik, F. I. M. (1990). Age differences in components of metamemory. *Experimental Aging Research, 16,* 43–48. (Chap 19)

Logue, B. J. (1991). Women at risk: Predictors of financial stress for retired women workers. *Gerontologist, 31,* 657–665. (Chap 20)

Lomax, R. G., & McGee, L. M. (1987). Young children's concepts about print and reading: Toward a model of word reading acquisition. *Reading Research Quarterly, 22,* 237–256. (Chap 12)

London, K. A. (1991). Cohabitation, marriage, marital dissolution, and remarriage: United States, 1988. *Advance data from vital and health statistics* (No. 194). Hyattsville, MD: National Center for Health Statistics. (Chap 16)

Longino, C. F., Jr. (1990). Geographical distribution and migration. In R. H. Binstock & L. K. George (Eds.), *Handbook of aging and the social sciences* (3rd ed.). San Diego, CA: Academic Press. (Chap 20)

Lorenz, K. (1942–1943). Die Angeborenen former moglicher Ehfahrung. *Zeitschrift fur Tierpsychologies, 5,* 239–409. (Chap 2)

Lounsbury, M. L., & Bates, J. E. (1982). The cries of infants of differing levels of perceived temperamental qualities. *Child Development, 53,*

677–686. (Chap 4)

Lucas, A., Morley, R., Cole, T. J., Lister, G., & Leeson-Payne, C. (1992). Breast milk and subsequent intelligence quotient in children born preterm. *Lancet, 339,* 261–264. (Chap 5)

Lutkenhaus, P., Grossmann, K. E., & Grossmann, K. (1985). Infant-mother attachment at 12 months and style of interaction with a stranger at the age of 3 years. *Child Development, 56,* 1538–1542. (Chap 8)

Lynn, R. (1982). IQ in Japan and the United States shows a growing disparity. *Nature, 297,* 222–223. (Chap 12)

Lyons, N. P. (1990). Listening to voices we have not heard. In C. Gilligan, N. P. Lyons, & T. J. Hanmer (Eds.), *Making connections.* Cambridge, MA: Harvard University Press. (Chap 14)

Maccoby, E. E. (1988). Gender as a social category. *Developmental Psychology, 24,* 755–765. (Chap 10)

Maccoby, E. E., & Martin, J. A. (1983). Socialization in the context of the family. In P. H. Mussen (Ed.), *Handbook of child psychology* (Vol. 4, 4th ed.). New York: Wiley. (Chap 9)

MacDonald, K. (1985). Early experience, relative plasticity, and social development. *Developmental Review, 5,* 99–121. (Chap 8)

MacKinnon, C. E., Brody, G. H., & Stoneman, Z. (1982). The effects of divorce and maternal employment on the home environments of preschool children. *Child Development, 53,* 1392–1399. (Chap 9)

Macklin, E. D. (1980). Nontraditional family forms. *Journal of Marriage and the Family, 42,* 905–922. (Chaps 16, 18)

Macklin, E. D. (1988). Heterosexual couples who cohabit nonmaritally. In C. S. Chilman, E. W. Nunnally, & F. M. Cox (Eds.), *Variant family forms.* Newbury Park, CA: Sage. (Chap 16)

Macklin, M. C., & Kolbe, R. H. (1984). Sex role stereotyping in children's advertising: Current and past trends. *Journal of Advertising, 13,* 34–42. (Chap 10)

Macnamara, J. (1972). Cognitive basis of language learning in infants.

Psychological Review, 79, 1–13. (Chap 7)

Madden, D. J. (1988). Adult age differences in the effects of sentence context and stimulus degradation during visual word recognition. *Psychology and Aging, 3,* 167–172. (Chap 19)

Madden, D. J., Blumenthal, J. A., Allen, P. A., & Emery, C. F. (1989). Improving aerobic capacity in healthy older adults does not necessarily lead to improved cognitive performance. *Psychology and Aging, 4,* 307–320. (Chap 17)

Maddox, G. L., & Campbell, R. T. (1985). Scope, concepts, and methods in the study of aging. In R. H. Binstock & E. Shanas (Eds.), *Handbook of aging and the social sciences* (2nd ed.). New York: Van Nostrand Reinhold. (Chap 20)

Magnusson, D., Stattin, H., & Allen, V. L. (1985). Biological maturation and social development. *Journal of Youth and Adolescence, 14,* 267–284. (Chap 13)

Main, M., & George, C. (1985). Responses of abused and disadvantaged toddlers to distress in agemates. *Developmental Psychology, 21,* 407–412. (Chaps 1, 9)

Main, M., Kaplan, N., & Cassidy, J. (1985). Security in infancy, childhood, and adulthood: A move to the level of representation. *Monographs of the Society for Research in Child Development, 50* (1–2, Serial No. 209). (Chap 8)

Main, M., & Weston, D. R. (1981). The quality of the toddler's relationship to mother and to father. *Child Development, 52,* 932–940. (Chap 8)

Makin, J. W., & Porter, R. H. (1989). Attractiveness of lactating females' breast odors to neonates. *Child Development, 60,* 803–810. (Chap 4)

Malatesta, C. Z., Culver, C., Tesman, J. R., & Shepard, B. (1989). The development of emotion expression during the first two years of life. *Monographs of the Society for Research in Child Development, 54* (1–2, Serial No. 219). (Chap 8)

Malina, R. M. (1979). Secular changes in size and maturity. *Monographs of the Society for Research in Child Development, 44* (3–4, Serial No. 179). (Chap 13)

Maloney, M. J., & Klykylo, W. M. (1983). An overview of anorexia nervosa, bulimia, and obesity in children and adolescents. *Journal of the American Academy of Child Psychiatry, 22,* 99–197. (Chap 15)

Mamay, P. D., & Simpson, R. L. (1981). Three female roles in commercials. *Sex Roles, 7,* 1223–1232. (Chap 10)

Mangelsdorf, S., Gunnar, M., Kestenbaum, R., Lang, S., & Andreas, D. (1990). Infant proneness-to-distress temperament, maternal personality, and mother-infant attachment: Associations and goodness of fit. *Child Development, 61,* 820–831. (Chap 8)

Mann, L., Harmoni, R., & Power, C. (1989). Adolescent decision-making: The development of competence. *Journal of Adolescence, 12,* 265–278. (Chap 14)

Mann, L., Harmoni, R., Power, C, Beswick, G., & Ormond, C. (1988). Effectiveness of the GOFER course in decision making for high school students. *Journal of Behavioral Decision Making, 1,* 159–168. (Chap 14)

Maratsos, M. P. (1983). Some current issues in the study of the acquisition of grammar. In P. H. Mussen (Ed.), *Handbook of child psychology* (Vol. 3, 4th ed.). New York: Wiley. (Chap 7)

Maratsos, M. P. (1989). Innateness and plasticity in language acquisition. In M. L. Rice & R. L. Schiefelbusch (Eds.), *The teachability of language.* Baltimore: Brooks/Cole. (Chap 7)

Marcia, J. E. (1980). Identity in adolescence. In J. Adelson (Ed.), *Handbook of adolescent psychology.* New York: Wiley. (Chap 13)

Marcus, G. F., Pinker, S., Ullman, M., Hollander, M., Rosen, T. J., & Xu, F. (1992). Overregularization in language acquisition. *Monographs of the Society for Research in Child Development, 57* (4, Serial No. 228). (Chap 7)

Marcus, T. L., & Corsini, D. A. (1978). Parental expectations of preschool children as related to child gender and socioeconomic status. *Child Development, 49,* 245–246. (Chap 10)

Markides, K. S., Liang, J., & Jackson, J. S. (1990). Race, ethnicity, and aging: Conceptual and methodological issues. In R. H. Binstock & L. K. George (Eds.), *Handbook of aging and the social sciences* (3rd ed.). San Diego, CA: Academic Press. (Chaps 9, 10)

Markman, E. M. (1981). Two different principles of conceptual organization. In M. E. Lamb & A. L. Brown (Eds.), *Advances in developmental psychology* (Vol. 1). Hillsdale, NJ: Erlbaum. (Chap 11)

Markman, E. M. (1989). *Categorization and naming in children: Problems of induction.* Cambridge: MA: MIT Press. (Chap 7)

Markovits, H., & Vachon, R. (1990). Conditional reasoning, representation, and level of abstraction. *Developmental Psychology, 26,* 942–951. (Chap 14)

Markus, H. R., & Herzog, A. E. (in press). The role of self-concept in aging. *Annual Review of Gerontology and Geriatrics.* (Chap 20)

Markus, H. R., & Nurius, P. (1986). Possible selves. *American Psychologist, 41,* 954–969. (Chaps 9, 16).

Marsh, H. W. (1986). Self-serving effect (bias?) in academic attributions. *Journal of Educational Psychology, 78,* 190–200. (Chap 12)

Marsh, R. W. (1985). Phrenoblysis: Real or chimera? *Child Development, 56,* 1059–1061. (Chap 14)

Marshall, V. W. (1980). *Last chapters.* Monterey, CA: Brooks/Cole. (Chap 20)

Marshall, V. M., & Levy, J. A. (1990). Aging and dying. In R. A. Binstock & L. K. George (Eds.), *Handbook of aging and the social sciences* (3rd ed.). San Diego, CA: Academic Press. (Chap 20)

Marshall, W. A. (1970). *Journal of Biosocial Science,* (Suppl. 2), 31–41. (Chap 13)

Marsiglio, W., & Donnelly, D. (1991). Sexual relations in later life: A national study of married persons. *Journal of Gerontology: Social Sciences, 46,* S338–344. (Chap 20)

Marx, J. L. (1987). Alzheimer's drug trial put on hold. *Science, 238,* 1041–1042. (Chap 19)

Marx, J. L. (1990). NGF and Alzheimer's: Hopes and fears. *Science, 247,* 408–410. (Chap 19)

Marx, J. L. (1991). Mutation identified as a possible cause of Alzheimer's disease. *Science, 251,* 867–877. (Chap 19)

Mason, J., & Allen, J. (1986). A review of emergent literacy with implications for research and practice in reading. In E. Rothkopf (Ed.), *Review of research in education in America* (Vol. 13). Washington, DC: American Educational Research Association. (Chap 12)

Masters, J. C., & Furman, W. (1981). Popularity, individual friendship, and specific peer interaction among children. *Developmental Psychology, 17,* 344–350. (Chap 10)

Masters, W. H., & Johnson, V. E. (1974). Emotional poverty. In American Medical Association, *The quality of life.* Acton, MA: Publishing Sciences Group. (Chap 18)

Masur, E. F., McIntyre, C. W., & Flavell, J. H. (1973). Developmental changes in apportionment of study time among items in a multitrial free recall task. *Journal of Experimental Child Psychology, 15,* 237–246. (Chap 11)

Matas, L., Arend, R., & Sroufe, L. A. (1978). Continuity of adaptation in the second year. *Child Development, 49,* 547–556. (Chap 8)

Mathew, A., & Cook, M. (1990). The control of reaching movements by young infants. *Child Development, 61,* 1238–1257. (Chap 5)

Matthews, S. H., & Sprey, J. (1985). Adolescents' relationships with grandparents. *Journal of Gerontology, 40,* 621–626. (Chap 20)

Maurer, D., & Salapatek, P. (1976). Developmental changes in the scanning of faces by infants. *Child Development, 47,* 523–527. (Chap 6)

McCall, P. L. (1991). Adolescent and elderly white male suicide trends: Evidence of changing well-being? *Journal of Gerontology: Social Sciences, 46,* S43–51. (Chap 15)

McCall, R. B. (1979). *Infants.* Cambridge, MA: Harvard University Press. (Chap 4)

McCarthy, D. (1954). Language development in children. In L. Carmichael (Ed.), *Manual of child psychology* (2nd ed.). New York: Wiley. (Chap 7)

McCluskey, K. A., Killarney, J., & Papini, D. R. (1983). Adolescent pregnancy and parenthood. In E. J. Callahan & K. A. McCluskey (Eds.),

Life-span developmental psychology: Nonnormative events. New York: Academic Press. (Chap 15)

McCrae, R. R., & Costa, P. T., Jr. (1988). Psychological resilience among widowed men and women: A 10-year follow-up of a national sample. *Journal of Social Issues, 44*(3), 129–142. (Chap 20)

McDowd, J. M., & Birren, J. E. (1990). Aging and attentional processes. In J. E. Birren & K. W. Schaie (Eds.), *Handbook of the psychology of aging* (3rd ed.). San Diego, CA: Academic Press. (Chap 19)

McGuinness, D. (1985). *When children don't learn.* New York: Basic Books. (Chap 9)

McGuire, K. D., & Weisz, J. R. (1982). Social cognition and behavior correlates of preadolescent chumship. *Child Development, 53,* 1478–1484. (Chap 10)

McKenna, J. J. (1983, April). *Sudden infant death syndrome in an anthropological context.* Paper presented at the World Congress of Infant Psychiatry, Cannes, France. (Chap 5)

McLoyd, V. C. (1989). Socialization and development in a changing economy: The effects of paternal job and income loss on children. *American Psychologist, 44,* 293–302. (Chaps 10, 15)

McLoyd, V. C., Ceballo, R., & Mangelsdorf, S. (1993). The effects of poverty on children's socioemotional development. In J. Noshpitz et al. (Eds.), *Handbook of child and adolescent psychiatry.* New York: Basic Books. (Chaps 8, 9, 10, 13)

McNeill, D. (1970). *The acquisition of language: The study of developmental psycholinguistics.* New York: Harper & Row. (Chap 7)

Mead, M. (1968). *Coming of age in Samoa.* New York: Dell. (Original work published 1928.) (Chap 1)

Mead, M., & Newton, N. (1967). Cultural patterning of perinatal behavior. In S. A. Richardson & A. F. Guttmacher (Eds.), *Childbearing.* Baltimore: Williams & Wilkins. (Chap 3)

Meadow, K. P. (1978). The "natural history" of a research project as illustration of methodological issues in research with deaf children. In L. S. Liben (Ed.), *Deaf children.* New York: Academic Press. (Chap 4)

Mebert, C. J. (1989). Stability and change in parents' perceptions of infant temperament: Early pregnancy to 13.5 months postpartum. *Infant Behavior and Development, 12,* 237–244. (Chap 4)

Medrich, E. A., Roizen, J., & Rubin, V. (1982). *The serious business of growing up.* Berkeley: University of California Press. (Chap 9)

Meece, J. L., Wigfield, A., & Eccles, J. S. (1990). Predictors of math anxiety and its influences on young adolescents' course enrollment. *Journal of Educational Psychology, 82,* 60–70. (Chap 14)

Mehler, J., Jusczyk, P. W., Lambertz, G., Halsted, N., Bertoncini, J., & Amiel-Tison, C. (1988). A precursor of language acquisition in young infants. *Cognition, 29,* 143–178. (Chap 4)

Meisels, S. J., & Plunkett, J. W. (1988). Developmental consequences of preterm birth: Are there long-term deficits? In P. B. Baltes, D. L. Featherman, & R. M. Lerner (Eds.), *Life-span development and behavior* (Vol. 9). Hillsdale, NJ: Erlbaum. (Chaps 3, 4)

Meltzoff, A. N., & Moore, M. K. (1977). Imitation of facial and manual gestures by human neonates. *Science, 198,* 75–78. (Chap 6)

Meltzoff, A. N., & Moore, M. K. (1983). Newborn infants imitate adult facial gestures. *Child Development, 54,* 702–709. (Chap 6)

Meltzoff, A. N., & Moore, M. K. (1989). Imitation in newborn infants: Exploring the range of gestures imitated and the underlying mechanism. *Developmental Psychology, 25,* 954–962. (Chap 6)

Mendelsohn, J. (1990). The view from step number 16. In C. Gilligan, N. P. Lyons, & T. J. Hanmer (Eds.), *Making connections.* Cambridge, MA: Harvard University Press. (Chap 13)

Menken, J., Trussell, J., & Larsen, U. (1986). Age and infertility. *Science, 233,* 1389–1394. (Chap 18)

Menuhin, Y. (1977). *Unfinished journey.* New York: Knopf. (Chap 12)

Menyuk, P. (1971). *The acquisition and development of language.* Englewood Cliffs, NJ: Prentice-Hall. (Chap 7)

Menyuk, P., & Bernholtz, N. (1969). Prosodic features and children's language production. *MIT Research Laboratory of Electronics Quarterly Progress Reports, 93,* 216–219. (Chap 7)

Mercer, J. R. (1973). *Labeling the mentally retarded.* Berkeley: University of California Press. (Chap 12)

Mercer, J. R., Gomez-Palacio, M., & Padilla, E. (1986). The development of practical intelligence in cross-cultural perspective. In R. J. Sternberg & R. K. Wagner (Eds.), *Practical intelligence.* New York: Cambridge University Press. (Chap 12)

Mercer, R. T. (1986). *First-time motherhood: Experiences from teens to forties.* New York: Springer-Verlag. (Chap 16)

Meredith, H. V. (1984). Body size of infants and children around the world in relation to socioeconomic status. In H. W. Reese (Ed.), *Advances in child development and behavior* (Vol. 18). Orlando, FL: Academic Press. (Chap 5)

Merriman, W. E., & Bowman, L. L. (1989). The mutual exclusivity bias in children's word learning. *Monographs of the Society for Research in Child Development, 54* (3–4, Serial No. 220). (Chap 7)

Mervis, C. B., & Johnson, K. E. (1991). Acquisition of the plural morpheme: A case study. *Developmental Psychology, 27,* 222–235. (Chap 7)

Messenger, L. (1976). Remarriage between divorced people with children from previous marriages. *Journal of Marriage and the Family, 2,* 193–200. (Chap 16)

Meyer, B. (1980). The development of girls' sex-role attitudes. *Child Development, 52,* 508–514. (Chap 9)

Michel, G. F. (1981). Right-handedness. *Science, 212,* 685–687. (Chap 5)

Michel, G. F., Harkins, D. A., & Ovrut, M. R. (1986, April). *Assessing infant (6–13 months old) handedness status.* Paper presented at 5th International Conference on Infant Studies, Los Angeles. (Chap 5)

Miernyk, W. H. (1975). The changing life cycle of work. In N. Datan & L. H. Ginsberg (Eds.), *Life-span developmental psychology:*

Normative life crises. New York: Academic Press. (Chap 20)

Miller, N., & Maruyama, G. (1976). Ordinal position and peer popularity. *Journal of Personality and Social Psychology, 33,* 123–131. (Chap 9)

Miller, N. E., & Dollard, J. (1941). *Social learning and imitation.* New Haven, CT: Yale University Press. (Chap 2)

Miller, P. H., & Bigi, L. (1979). The development of children's understanding of attention. *Merrill-Palmer Quarterly, 2,* 235–250. (Chap 11)

Miller, S. A. (1986). Certainty and necessity in the understanding of Piagetian concepts. *Developmental Psychology, 22,* 3–18. (Chap 11)

Miller, W., & Newman, L. (1978). *The first child and family formation.* Chapel Hill: University of North Carolina Press. (Chap 9)

Minuchin, P. (1985). Families and individual development. *Child Development, 56,* 289–302. (Chap 9)

Minuchin, P., & Shapiro, E. K. (1983). The school as a context for development. In P. H. Mussen (Ed.), *Handbook of child psychology* (Vol. 4, 4th ed.). New York: Wiley. (Chap 10)

Mischel, H. N., & Mischel, W. (1983). The development of children's knowledge of self-control strategies. *Child Development, 54,* 603–619. (Chap 11)

Miscione, J. L., Marvin, R. S., O'Brien, R. G., & Greenberg, M. T. (1978). A developmental study of preschool children's understanding of the words "know" and "guess." *Child Development, 49,* 1107–1113. (Chap 7)

Mitchell, D. B., & Perlmutter, M. (1986). Semantic activation and episodic memory. *Developmental Psychology, 22,* 86–94. (Chap 19)

Miyake, K., Chen, S., & Campos, J. J. (1985). Infant temperament, mother's mode of interaction, and attachment in Japan: An interim report. *Monographs of the Society for Research in Child Development, 50* (1–2, Serial No. 209). (Chap 8)

Moely, B. E., Hart, S. S., Leal, L., Santulli, K. A., Rao, N., Johnson, T., & Hamilton, L. B. (1992). The teacher's role in facilitating memory and study strategy development in the elementary classroom. *Child Development, 63,* 653–672. (Chap 11)

Moerk, E. L. (1989). The LAD was a lady and the tasks were ill-defined. *Developmental Review, 9,* 21–57. (Chap 7)

Mohseni, N. (1966). La comparaison des réactions aux épreuves d'intelligence en Iran et en Europe. Master's thesis, University of Paris. (Chap 11)

Money, J., & Ehrhardt, A. A. (1972). *Man & woman; boy & girl.* Baltimore: Johns Hopkins University Press. (Chap 9)

Monmaney, T. (1988, February 8). The cholesterol connection. *Newsweek,* pp. 56–58. (Chap 20)

Moody, H. R. (1986, Winter). Education in an aging society. *Daedalus, 115,* 191–210. (Chap 17)

Moore, K. A. (1985, Summer). Teenage pregnancy. *New Perspectives,* pp. 11–15. (Chap 15)

Moore, K. L. (1974). *Before we are born* (2nd ed.). Philadelphia: Saunders. (Chap 3)

Moore, T. W. (1975). Exclusive early mothering and its alternatives. *Scandinavian Journal of Psychology, 16,* 256–272. (Chap 9)

Moorehouse, M. J., & Sanders, P. E. (in press). Children's feelings of school competence and perception of parents' work. *Social Development.* (Chap 9)

Morin, N. C., Wirth, F. H., Johnson, D. H., Frank, L. M., Presburg, H. J., Van de Water, V. L., Chee, E. M., & Mills, J. L. (1989). Congenital malformations and psychosocial development in children conceived by in vitro fertilization. *Journal of Pediatrics, 115,* 222–227. (Chap 3)

Mortimer, J. T., Finch, M. D., & Kumka, D. (1982). Persistence and change in development. In P. B. Baltes & O. G. Brim, Jr. (Eds.), *Life-span development and behavior* (Vol. 4). New York: Academic Press. (Chap 16)

Mortimer, J. T., Finch, M. E., Owens, T. J., & Shanahan, M. (1990). Gender and work in adolescence. *Youth & Society, 22,* 201–224. (Chap 13)

Morton, J., Johnson, M. J., & Maurer, D. (1990). On the reasons for newborns' responses to faces. *Infant Behavior and Development, 13,* 99–103. (Chap 6)

Moss, M. S., Moss, S. Z., & Moles, E. L. (1985). The quality of relationships between elderly parents and their out-of-town children. *Gerontologist, 25,* 134–140. (Chap 20)

Mother cleared of passing drugs to baby while she was pregnant. (1991, February 5). *New York Times,* p. B6. (Chap 3)

Muir, D., & Field, J. (1979). Newborn infants orient to sounds. *Child Development, 50,* 431–436. (Chap 4)

Mukherjee, A. M., & Hodgen, G. D. (1982). Maternal ethanol exposure induces transient impairment of umbilical circulation and fetal hypoxia in monkeys. *Science, 218,* 700–702. (Chap 3)

Murrell, J., Farlow, M., Ghetti, B., & Benson, M. D. (1991). A mutation in the amyloid precursor protein associated with hereditary Alzheimer's disease. *Science, 254,* 97–99. (Chap 19)

Murstein, B. I. (1985). *Paths to marriage.* Beverly Hills, CA: Sage. (Chap 16)

Myers, M., & Paris, S. G. (1978). Children's metacognitive knowledge about reading. *Journal of Educational Psychology, 70,* 680–690. (Chaps 11, 12)

Naglieri, J. A. (1987, August). *Evidence for the planning, attention, simultaneous and successive cognitive processing theory.* Paper presented at the annual convention of the American Psychological Association, New York. (Chap 12)

Naglieri, J. A. (1989). A cognitive processing theory for the measurement of intelligence. *Educational Psychologist, 24,* 185–206. (Chap 12)

Nakamura, C. Y., & Finck, D. N. (1980). Relative effectiveness of socially oriented and task-oriented children and predictability of their behaviors. *Monographs of the Society for Research in Child Development, 45* (Serial No. 185). (Chap 10)

Namazi, K. H., Eckert, J. K., Kahana, E., & Lyon, S. M. (1989). Psychological well-being of elderly board and care home residents. *Gerontologist, 29,* 511–516. (Chap 20)

National Center for Education Statistics. (1988). *Youth Indicators.* Washington, DC: U.S. Government Printing Office. (Chap 13)

National Center for Health Statistics. (1986, December). *Health, United States, 1986* (DHHS Publication No. PHS 87-1232). Washington, DC: Department of Health and Human Services. (Chap 20)

National Center for Health Statistics. (1990, May 15). Advance report of final divorce statistics, 1987. *Monthly Vital Statistics Report, 38* (Suppl. 2), 12. (Chaps 16, 18)

Neill, S. (1976). Aggressive and non-aggressive fighting in twelve-to-thirteen-year-old pre-adolescent boys. *Journal of Child Psychology and Psychiatry, 17,* 213–220. (Chap 10)

Neimark, E. D. (1982). Adolescent thought. In B. B. Wolman (Ed.), *Handbook of developmental psychology.* Englewood Cliffs, NJ: Prentice-Hall. (Chap 14)

Nelson, C. A., & Collins, P. F. (1991). Event-related potential and looking-time analysis of infants' responses to familiar and novel events: Implications for visual recognition memory. *Developmental Psychology, 27,* 50–58. (Chap 6)

Nelson, J., & Aboud, F. E. (1985). The resolution of social conflict between friends. *Child Development, 56,* 1009–1017. (Chap 10)

Nelson, K. E., & Kosslyn, S. M. (1976). Recognition of previously labeled or unlabeled pictures by 5-year-olds and adults. *Journal of Experimental Child Psychology, 21,* 40–45. (Chap 6)

Nelson-Le Gall, S., & Jones, E. (1990). Cognitive-motivational influences on the task-related help-seeking behavior of black children. *Child Development, 61,* 581–589. (Chap 12)

Neugarten, B. L. (1970). Adaptation and the life cycle. *Journal of Geriatric Psychiatry, 4,* 222–228. (Chap 18)

Neugarten, B. L. (1979). Time, age, and the life cycle. *American Journal of Psychiatry, 136,* 887–894. (Chap 16)

Neugarten, B. L., interviewed by E. Hall. (1987). Acting one's age.

In E. Hall, *Growing and changing.* New York: Random House. (Chaps 1, 20)

Neugarten, B. L., & Neugarten, D. A. (1986, Winter). Age in the aging society. *Daedalus, 115,* 31–49. (Chaps 1, 16, 18)

Neugarten, B. L., Wood, V., Kraines, R. J., & Loomis, B. (1963). Women's attitudes toward the menopause. *Vita Humana, 6,* 140–151. (Chap 18)

Newcomb, A. F., & Bukowski, W. M. (1984). A longitudinal study of the utility of social preference and social impact of sociometric classification schemes. *Child Development, 55,* 1434–1447. (Chap 10)

Newcomb, M. D., & Bentler, P. M. (1989). Substance use and abuse among children and teenagers. *American Psychologist, 44,* 242–248. (Chap 15)

Newcombe, N. (1989). The development of spatial perspective taking. In H. W. Reese (Ed.), *Advances in child development and behavior* (Vol. 22). San Diego: Academic Press. (Chap 11)

Newcombe, N. S., & Baenninger, M. (1989). Biological change and cognitive ability in adolescence. In G. R. Adams, R. Montemayor, & T. P. Gullotta (Eds.), *Biology of adolescent behavior and development.* Newbury Park, CA: Sage. (Chap 14)

Newcombe, N. S., & Bandura, M. M. (1983). Effect of age of puberty on spatial ability in girls: A question of mechanism. *Developmental Psychology, 19,* 215–224. (Chap 14)

Newcomer, S., & Udry, J. R. (1987). Parental marital status effects on adolescent sexual behavior. *Journal of Marriage and the Family, 49,* 235–240. (Chap 13)

Newman, A. P., & Beverstock, C. (1990). *Adult literacy: Contexts and challenges.* Newark, DE: International Reading Association. (Chap 17)

Newman, L. F. (1981). Social and sensory environment of low birth weight infants in a special care nursery: An anthropological investigation. *Journal of Nervous and Mental Disease, 169,* 448–455. (Chap 3)

Newman, R. S. (1990). Children's help-seeking in the classroom: The role of motivational factors and attitudes. *Journal of Educational Psychology, 82,* 81–91. (Chap 12)

Newman, R. S., & Goldin, L. (1990). Children's reluctance to seek help with schoolwork. *Journal of Educational Psychology, 82,* 92–100. (Chap 12)

NIH Consensus Development Conference. (1991, November). Diagnosis and treatment of depression in late life. *Consensus Statement, 9,* 3. (Chap 20)

Ninio, A. (1983). Joint book reading as a multiple vocabulary acquisition device. *Developmental Psychology, 19,* 445–451. (Chap 6)

Noah, T. (1988, May 2). Saving one high school. *Newsweek,* pp. 56–65. (Chap 14)

Nowak, C. A. (1977). Does youthfulness equal attractiveness? In L. E. Troll, J. Israel, & K. Israel (Eds.), *Looking ahead.* Englewood Cliffs, NJ: Prentice-Hall. (Chap 18)

Nurmi, J.-E. (1989). Development of orientation to the future during early adolescence: A four-year longitudinal study and two cross-sectional comparisons. *International Journal of Psychology, 24,* 195–214. (Chap 14)

Nurmi, J.-E. (1991). How do adolescents see their future? A review of the development of future orientation and planning. *Developmental Review, 11,* 1–59. (Chap 14)

Nyhan, W. L. (1990). Structural abnormalities. *Clinical Symposia, 42,* 2. (Chap 3)

O'Brien, D. H., Schneider, A. R., & Traviesas, H. (1980). Portraying abuse. In G. Gerbner, C. J. Ross, & E. Zigler (Eds.), *Child abuse.* New York: Oxford University Press. (Chap 9)

O'Bryant, S. L., & Morgan, L. A. (1989). Financial experience and well-being among mature widowed women. *Gerontologist, 29,* 245–251. (Chap 20)

O'Bryant, S. L., & Morgan, L. A. (1990). Recent widows' kin support and orientations to self-sufficiency. *Gerontologist, 30,* 391–398. (Chap 20)

Ochs, E. (1979). Introduction. In E. Ochs & B. B. Schieffelin (Eds.), *Developmental pragmatics.* New York: Academic Press. (Chap 7)

O'Connell, M. (1989, May/June). Management women: Debating the facts of life [Letters]. *Harvard Business Review, 67,* 214. (Chap 8)

O'Connor, B. P., & Nikolic, J. (1990). Identity development and formal operations as sources of adolescent egocentrism. *Journal of Youth and Adolescence, 19,* 149–158. (Chap 14)

O'Discoll, P., & Neuman, J. (1983, December 12). Federal hunger report due. *USA Today,* pp. 1–2. (Chap 5)

Offer, D., & Holinger, P. C. (1983, May). *Toward the prediction of violent deaths among the young.* Paper presented at the meeting of the American Association for the Advancement of Science, Detroit. (Chap 15)

Offer, D., Ostrov, E., & Howard, K. I. (1981a). *The adolescent.* New York: Basic Books. (Chaps 13, 15)

Offer, D., Ostrov, E., & Howard, K. I. (1981b). The mental health professional's concept of the normal adolescent. *Archives of General Psychiatry, 38,* 149. (Chap 15)

Offer, D., Ostrov, E., & Howard, K. I. (1982). Values and self-conceptions held by normal and delinquent males. *Journal of Psychiatric Treatment and Evaluation, 4,* 503–509. (Chaps 13, 15)

Offer, D., Ostrov, E., & Howard, K. I. (1984). Epidemiology of mental health and mental illness among adolescents. In J. Call (Ed.), *Significant advances in child psychiatry.* New York: Basic Books. (Chap 15)

Offer, D., & Sabshin, M. (1984). *Normality and the life cycle.* New York: Basic Books. (Chap 13)

Office of Educational Research and Improvement. (1988). *Youth indicators, 1988.* Washington, DC: U.S. Department of Education. (Chap 15)

Ogbu, J. U. (1981). Origins of human competence: A cultural-ecological perspective. *Child Development, 52,* 413–429. (Chap 8)

Ogbu, J. U. (1985). A cultural ecology of competence among inner-city blacks. In M. B. Spencer, G. K. Brookins, & W. R. Allen (Eds.), *Beginnings: The social and affective development of black children.* Hillsdale, NJ: Erlbaum. (Chaps 10, 15)

Ogbu, J. U. (1987). Variability in minority school performance: A problem in search of an explanation. *Anthropology and Education Quarterly, 18,* 312–334. (Chap 10)

O'Hara, M. W., Hinrichs, J. V., Kohout, F. J., Wallace, R. B., & Lemke, J. H. (1986). Memory complaint and memory performance in the depressed elderly. *Psychology and Aging, 1,* 208–214. (Chap 19)

Olsho, L. W., Harkins, S. W., & Lenhardt, M. L. (1985). Aging and the auditory system. In J. E. Birren & K. W. Schaie (Eds.), *Handbook of the psychology of aging* (2nd ed.). New York: Van Nostrand Reinhold. (Chap 19)

Olson, G. M., & Sherman, T. (1983). Attention, learning, and memory in infants. In P. H. Mussen (Ed.), *Handbook of child psychology* (Vol. 2, 4th ed.). New York: Wiley. (Chaps 4, 6)

Omenn, G. S. (1983). Medical genetics, genetic counseling, and behavior genetics. In J. L. Fuller & E. C. Simmel (Eds.), *Behavior genetics.* Hillsdale, NJ: Erlbaum. (Chaps 3, 18)

Ornstein, P. A., Medina, R. G., Stone, B. P., & Naus, M. J. (1985). Retrieving for rehearsal. *Developmental Psychology, 21,* 633–641. (Chap 1)

Ornstein, P. A., & Naus, M. J. (1978). Rehearsal processes in children's memory. In P. A. Ornstein (Ed.), *Memory development in children.* Hillsdale, NJ: Erlbaum. (Chap 11)

Ornstein, R. E., Herron, J., Johnstone, J., & Swencionis, C. (1979). Differential right hemisphere involvement in two reading tasks. *Psychophysiology, 16,* 398–401. (Chap 5)

Orwoll, L., & Perlmutter, M. (1990). The study of wise persons: Integrating a personality perspective. In R. Sternberg (Ed.), *Wisdom: Its nature, origins, and development.* New York: Cambridge University Press. (Chap 19)

Osherson, D. N., & Markman, E. M. (1975). Language and the ability to evaluate contradictions and tautologies. *Cognition, 3,* 213–226. (Chap 14)

Osipow, S. H. (1983). *Theories of career development.* Englewood Cliffs, NJ: Prentice-Hall. (Chap 14)

Oski, F. A., Honig, A. S., Helu, B., & Howanitz, P. (1983). Effect of iron therapy on the behavior performance in nonanemic, iron deficient children. *Journal of Pediatrics, 71,* 877–880. (Chap 5)

Osofsky, J. D., & Connors, K. (1979). Mother-infant interaction: An integrative view of a complex system. In J. D. Osofsky (Ed.), *Handbook of infant development.* New York: Wiley. (Chap 4)

Osofsky, J. D., & Osofsky, H. J. (1984). Psychological and developmental perspectives on expectant and new parenthood. In R. D. Parke (Ed.), *Review of child development research* (Vol. 7). Chicago: University of Chicago Press. (Chap 16)

Otaki, M., Durrett, M. E., Richards, P., Nyguist, L., & Pennebaker, J. W. (1986). Maternal and infant behavior in Japan and America: A partial replication. *Journal of Cross-Cultural Psychology, 17,* 251–268. (Chap 1)

Ozer, D. J. (1987). Personality, intelligence, and spatial visualization: Correlates of mental rotations test performance. *Journal of Personality and Social Psychology, 53,* 129–134. (Chap 14)

Paffenbarger, R. S., Hyde, R. T., Wing, A. L., & Hsieh, C. C. (1986). Physical activity, all-cause mortality, and longevity of college alumni. *New England Journal of Medicine, 314,* 605–613. (Chap 18)

Palmer, C. F. (1989). The discriminating nature of infants' exploratory behavior. *Developmental Psychology, 25,* 885–893. (Chap 5)

Palmore, E. B. (1970). The effects of aging on activity and attitudes. In E. B. Palmore (Ed.), *Normal aging.* Durham, NC: Duke University Press. (Chap 20)

Palmore, E. B. (1988). *The facts on aging quiz.* New York: Springer. (Chap 19)

Palmore, E. B. (1992). Knowledge about aging: What we know and need to know. *Gerontologist, 32,* 149–150. (Chap 19)

Palmore, E. B., George, L. K., & Fillenbaum, G. G. (1982). Predictors of retirement. *Journal of Gerontology, 37,* 733–742. (Chap 20)

Panneton, R. K. (1985). *Prenatal experience with melodies: Effect on postnatal auditory preference in human newborns.* Unpublished doctoral dissertation, University of North Carolina, Greensboro. (Chap 4)

Papini, D. R., Farmer, F. F., Clark, S. M., Micka, J. C., & Barrett, J. K. (1990). Early adolescent age and gender differences in patterns of emotional self-disclosure to parents and friends. *Adolescence, 25,* 959–976. (Chap 13)

Papousek, H., & Papousek, M. (1984). Learning and cognition in the everyday life of human infants. In *Advances in the study of behavior* (Vol. 14). New York: Academic Press. (Chap 4)

Papousek, M., Bornstein, M., Nuzzo, C., Papousek, H., & Symmes, D. (1990). Infant responses to prototypical melodic contours in parental speech. *Infant Behavior and Development, 13,* 539–545. (Chap 7)

Papousek, M., Papousek, H., & Bornstein, M. (1985). The naturalistic vocal environment of young infants. In T. M. Field & N. Fox (Eds.), *Social perception in infants.* Norwood, NJ: Ablex. (Chap 7)

Papousek, M., Papousek, H., & Symmes, D. (1991). The meanings of melodies in motherese in tone and stress languages. *Infant Behavior and Development, 14,* 415–440. (Chap 7)

Parasuraman, R., & Giambra, L. M. (1991). Skill development in vigilance: Effects of event rate and age. *Psychology and Aging, 6,* 155–169. (Chap 19)

Parham v. J.R. (1979). 99 S. Ct. 2493. (Chap 14)

Paris, S. G., & Byrnes, J. P. (1989). The constructivist approach to self-regulation and learning in the classroom. In B. J. Zimmerman & D. H. Schunk (Eds.), *Self-regulated learning and academic achievement.* New York: Springer-Verlag. (Chap 12)

Paris, S. G., & Cross, D. R. (1983). Ordinary learning. In J. Bisanz, G. Bisanz, & R. Kail (Eds.), *Learning in children.* New York: Springer-Verlag. (Chap 11)

Paris, S. G., & Cross, D. R. (1988). The zone of proximal development: Virtues and pitfalls of a metaphorical representation of children's learning. *Genetic Epistemologist, 26,* 27–37. (Chap 2)

Paris, S. G., & Lindauer, B. K. (1977). Constructive processes in children's comprehension and memory. In R. V. Kail & J. W. Hagen (Eds.), *Perspectives on the development of memory and cognition.* Hillsdale, NJ: Erlbaum. (Chap 11)

Paris, S. G., & Lindauer, B. K. (1982). The development of cognitive skills during childhood. In B. W. Wolman (Ed.), *Handbook of developmental psychology.* Englewood Cliffs, NJ: Prentice-Hall. (Chaps 2, 11)

Paris, S. G., & Newman, R. S. (1990). Developmental aspects of self-regulated learning. *Educational Psychologist, 25,* 87–102. (Chap 14)

Paris, S. G., Newman, R. S., & Jacobs, J. E. (1985). Social contexts and functions of children's remembering. In M. Pressley & C. J. Brainerd (Eds.), *Cognitive learning and memory in children.* New York: Springer-Verlag. (Chap 6)

Paris, S. G., Newman, R. S., & McVey, K. A. (1982). Learning the functional significance of mnemonic actions. *Journal of Experimental Child Psychology, 34,* 490–509. (Chap 11)

Paris, S. G., & Oka, E. R. (1986). Children's reading strategies. *Developmental Review, 6,* 25–56. (Chap 12)

Paris, S. G., Wasik, B. A., & Turner, J. C. (1990). The development of strategic readers. In P. D. Pearson (Ed.), *Handbook of reading research* (2nd ed.). New York: Longman. (Chap 12)

Paris, S. G., & Winograd, P. (1990). How metacognition can promote academic learning and instruction. In B. J. Jones & L. Idol (Eds.), *Dimensions of thinking and cognitive instruction.* Hillsdale, NJ: Erlbaum. (Chaps 11, 12)

Park, D. C., Puglisi, J. T., & Smith, A. D. (1986). Memory for pictures. *Psychology and Aging, 1,* 11–17. (Chap 19)

Parke, R. D. (1981). *Fathers.* Cambridge, MA: Harvard University Press. (Chap 8)

Parke, R. D., & Collmer, C. W. (1975). Child abuse. In E. M. Hetherington (Ed.), *Review of child development research* (Vol. 5). Chi-

cago: University of Chicago Press. (Chap 9)

Parke, R. D., Grossmann, K., & Tinsley, B. R. (1981). Father-mother-infant interaction in the newborn period. In T. H. Field, A. M. Sostor, P. Vietze, & P. H. Leiderman (Eds.), *Culture and early interaction.* Hillsdale, NJ: Erlbaum. (Chap 10)

Parke, R. D., & Sawin, D. B. (1975, April). *Infant characteristics and behavior as elicitors of maternal and paternal responsivity in the newborn period.* Paper presented at the meeting of the Society for Research in Child Development, Denver. (Chaps 1, 9)

Parke, R. D., & Slaby, R. G. (1983). The development of aggression. In P. H. Mussen (Ed.), *Handbook of child psychology* (Vol. 4, 4th ed.). New York: Wiley. (Chap 10)

Parke, R. D., & Tinsley, B. J. (1988). Family interaction in infancy. In J. D. Osofsky (Ed.), *Handbook of infant development* (2nd ed.). New York: Wiley. (Chap 8)

Parker, J. G., & Asher, S. R. (1987). Peer relations and later personal adjustment: Are low-accepted children at risk? *Psychological Bulletin, 102,* 357–389. (Chap 10)

Parmelee, A. H., Jr., & Sigman, M. D. (1983). Perinatal brain development and behavior. In P. H. Mussen (Ed.), *Handbook of child psychology* (Vol. 2, 4th ed.). New York: Wiley. (Chaps 4, 5)

Parmelee, P. A., & Lawton, M. P. (1990). The design of special environments for the aged. In J. E. Birren & K. W. Schaie (Eds.), *Handbook of the psychology of aging* (3rd ed.). San Diego, CA: Academic Press. (Chap 20)

Parnes, H. (1981). *Work and retirement.* Cambridge, MA: MIT Press. (Chap 20)

Patterson, G. R., Reid, J. B., & Dishion, T. J. (in press). *Antisocial boys.* Eugene, OR: Castalia. (Chap 15)

Pavlov, I. P. (1927). *Conditioned reflexes.* London: Oxford University Press. (Chap 2)

Pearson, J. L., Hunter, A. G., Ensminger, M. E., & Kellam, S. G. (1990). Black grandmothers in multigenerational households: Diversity in family structure and parenting in-

volvement in the Woodlawn community. *Child Development, 61,* 434–442. (Chap 18)

Pederson, D. R., Moran, G., Sitko, C., Campbell, K., Ghesquire, K., & Acton, H. (1990). Maternal sensitivity and the security of infant-mother attachment. *Child Development, 61,* 1974–1983. (Chap 8)

Pederson, F. (1975, September). *Mother, father, and infant as interactive system.* Paper presented at the annual meeting of the American Psychological Association, Denver. (Chap 9)

Pellegrini, A. D. (1988). Elementary-school children's rough-and-tumble play and social competence. *Developmental Psychology, 24,* 802–806. (Chap 10)

Perlez, J. (1986, October 6). Nine New York high schools dispense contraceptives to their students. *New York Times,* pp. A1ff. (Chap 15)

Perlmutter, M. (1980). Development of memory in the preschool years. In R. Greene & T. D. Yawkey (Eds.), *Childhood development.* Westport, CT: Technemic. (Chap 6)

Perlmutter, M. (1984). Continuities and discontinuities in early human memory paradigms, processes, and performances. In R. V. Kail, Jr., & N. E. Spear (Eds.), *Comparative perspectives on the development of memory.* Hillsdale, NJ: Erlbaum. (Chap 6)

Perlmutter, M. (1986). A life-span view of memory. In P. B. Baltes & D. Featherman (Eds.), *Life-span development and behavior* (Vol. 7). San Diego, CA: Academic Press. (Chap 19)

Perlmutter, M. (1988). Cognitive potential throughout life. In J. E. Birren & V. L. Bengston (Eds.), *Emergent theories of aging.* New York: Springer. (Chap 17)

Perlmutter, M., Adams, C., Berry, J., Kaplan, M., Person, D., & Verdonik, F. (1987). Aging and memory. *Annual Review of Gerontology and Geriatrics, 7,* 57–92. (Chap 19)

Perlmutter, M., Behrend, S. D., Kuo, F., & Muller, A. (1989). Social influences on children's problem solving. *Developmental Psychology, 25,* 744–754. (Chap 11)

Perlmutter, M., & Hall, E. (1992). *Adult development and*

aging (2nd ed.). New York: Wiley. (Chaps 10, 16, 18, 19, 20)

Perlmutter, M., & Nyquist, L. (1990). Relationships between self-reported physical and mental health and intelligence performance across adulthood. *Journal of Gerontology: Psychological Sciences, 45,* P145–155. (Chap 17)

Perlmutter, M., Nyquist, L., & Adams-Price, C. (1989). *Activity and cognitive performance across adulthood.* Unpublished paper, University of Michigan. (Chap 17)

Perrucci, C., & Targ, D. (in press). Effects of a plant closing on marriage and family life. In P. Voydanoff & L. Majka (Eds.), *Families and economic distress.* Beverly Hills, CA: Sage. (Chap 10)

Perry, D. G. (1989, April). *Social learning theory.* Paper presented at the biennial meeting of the Society for Research in Child Development, Kansas City. (Chap 2)

Peters, M. F. (1981). Parenting in black families with young children. In H. P. McAdoo (Ed.), *Black families.* Beverly Hills, CA: Sage. (Chap 10)

Petersen, A. C. (1985). Pubertal development as a cause of disturbance. *Genetic, Social, and General Psychology Monographs, 111,* 205–232. (Chap 13)

Petersen, A. C., & Taylor, B. (1980). The biological approach to adolescence. In J. Adelson (Ed.), *Handbook of adolescent psychology.* New York: Wiley. (Chap 13)

Pettit, G. S., Bakshi, A., Dodge, K. A., & Coie, J. D. (1990). The emergence of social dominance in young boys' play groups: Developmental differences and behavioral correlates. *Developmental Psychology, 26,* 1017–1025. (Chap 10)

Pettit, G. S., Dodge, K. A., & Brown, M. M. (1988). Early family experience, social problem solving patterns, and children's social competence. *Child Development, 59,* 107–120. (Chap 10)

Pfeiffer, E., & Davis, G. C. (1972). Determinants of sexual behavior in middle and old age. *Journal of the American Geriatrics Society, 20,* 151–158. (Chap 18)

Pfeiffer, E., Verwoerdt, A., & Davis, G. C. (1972). Sexual behavior in middle life. *American Journal of Psychiatry, 128,* 1261–1267. (Chap 20)

Phinney, J. S., & Alipuria, L. L. (1990). Ethnic identity in college students from four minority groups. *Journal of Adolescence, 13,* 171–183. (Chap 13)

Phinney, J. S., & Tarver, S. (1988). Ethnic identity search and commitment in black and white eighth-graders. *Journal of Early Adolescence, 8,* 265–277. (Chap 13)

Phinney, V. G., Jensen, L. C., Olsen, J. A., & Cundick, B. (1990). The relationship between early development and psychosexual behaviors in adolescent females. *Adolescence, 25,* 322–332. (Chap 13)

Piaget, J. (1951). *Play, dreams, and imitation in childhood.* New York: Norton. (Chaps 6, 11)

Piaget, J. (1952). *The origins of intelligence in children.* New York: International Universities Press. (Chaps 6, 14)

Piaget, J. (1953). *Logic and psychology.* Manchester, England: Manchester University Press. (Chap 12)

Piaget, J. (1954). *The construction of reality in the child.* New York: Basic Books. (Chap 6)

Piaget, J. (1965). *The moral judgment of the child.* New York: Free Press. (Original work published 1932.) (Chap 11)

Piaget, J. (1968a). *On the development of memory and identity.* Barre, MA: Clark University Press. (Chap 6)

Piaget, J. (1968b). *Six psychological studies.* New York: Vintage Press. (Chap. 11)

Piaget, J. (1972). Intellectual evolution from adolescence to adulthood. *Human Development, 15,* 1–12. (Chap 2, 14)

Piaget, J. (1976). *The psychology of intelligence.* Totowa, NJ: Littlefield, Adams. (Chap 12)

Piaget, J. (1978). *Success and understanding.* Cambridge, MA: Harvard University Press. (Chap 1)

Piaget, J., & Inhelder, B. (1941). *Le développement des quantités chez l'enfant.* Neuchâtel, Switzerland: Delachaux et Niestle. (Chap 11)

Piaget, J., & Inhelder, B. (1969). *The psychology of the child.* New York: Basic Books. (Chap 11)

Pick, A. D., & Frankel, G. W. (1973). A study of strategies of visual attention in children. *Developmental Psychology, 4,* 348–357. (Chap 11)

Pintrich, P. R., & Blumenfeld, P. C. (1985). Classroom experience and children's self-perceptions of ability, effort, and conduct. *Journal of Educational Psychology, 77,* 646–657. (Chap 12)

Pintrich, P. R., & De Groot, E. V. (1990). Motivational and self-regulated learning components of classroom academic performance. *Journal of Educational Psychology, 82,* 33–40. (Chap 12)

Piper, A. I., & Langer, E. J. (1986). Aging and mindful control. In M. M. Baltes & P. B. Baltes (Eds.), *The psychology of control and aging.* Hillsdale, NJ: Erlbaum. (Chap 20)

Plomin, R. (1990). The role of inheritance in behavior. *Science, 248,* 183–188. (Chap 3)

Plomin, R., & Defries, J. C. (1985). *Origins of individual difference in infancy: The Colorado Adoption Project.* Orlando, FL: Academic Press. (Chap 4)

Pollins, L. D. (1983). The effects of acceleration on the social and emotional development of gifted students. In C. P. Benbow & J. C. Stanley (Eds.), *Academic precocity.* Baltimore: Johns Hopkins University Press. (Chap 12)

Pollit, D. F. (1982). *Effects of family size.* Washington, DC: American Institute for Research. (Chap 9)

Pollitt, E., Garza, C., & Leibel, R. L. (1984). Nutrition and public policy. In H. W. Stevenson & A. E. Siegel (Eds.), *Child development research and social policy.* Chicago: University of Chicago Press. (Chap 5)

Ponds, R. W. H. M., Brouwer, W. H., & van Wolffelaar, P. C. (1988). Age differences in divided attention in a simulated driving task. *Journal of Gerontology: Psychological Sciences, 43,* P151–156. (Chap 19)

Poon, L. W. (1985). Differences in human memory with aging: Nature, causes, and clinical implications. In J. E. Birren & K. W. Schaie (Eds.), *Handbook of the psychology of aging* (2nd ed.). New York: Van Nostrand Reinhold. (Chap 19)

Portrait of an Elderhosteler. (1990, September). *Elderhostel: United States and Canada catalog,* p. 5. (Chap 17)

Poulson, C. L., Nunes, L. R. P., & Warren, S. F. (1989). Imitation in infancy: A critical review. In H. W. Reese (Ed.), *Advances in child development and behavior* (Vol. 22). San Diego, CA: Academic Press. (Chap 6)

Prader, A., Tanner, J. M., & Von Harnack, G. A. (1963). Catch-up growth following illness or starvation: An example of developmental canalization in man. *Journal of Pediatrics, 62.* (Chap 5)

Prechtl, H. F. R. (1982). Regressions and transformations during neurological development. In T. G. Bever (Ed.), *Regressions in mental development.* Hillsdale, NJ: Erlbaum. (Chap 4)

Price, G. G. (1984). Mnemonic support and curriculum selection in teaching by mothers. *Child Development, 55,* 659–668. (Chaps 6, 12)

Prinz, P. N., Dustman, R. E., & Emmerson, R. (1990). Electrophysiology and aging. In J. E. Birren & K. W. Schaie (Eds.), *Handbook of the psychology of aging* (3rd ed.). San Diego, CA: Academic Press. (Chap 19)

Puttalaz, M., & Wasserman, A. (1990). Children's entry behavior. In S. R. Asher & J. D. Coie (Eds.), *Peer rejection in childhood.* New York: Cambridge University Press. (Chap 10)

Quayhagen, M. P., & Quayhagen, M. (1989). Differential effects of family-based strategies on Alzheimer's disease. *Gerontologist, 29,* 150–155. (Chap 19)

Quinn, J. F., & Burkhauser, R. V. (1990). Work and retirement. In R. H. Binstock & L. K. George (Eds.), *Handbook of aging and the social sciences* (3rd ed.). San Diego, CA: Academic Press. (Chap 20)

Quinn, J. F., Burkhauser, R. V., & Myers, D. C. (1990). *Passing the torch: The influences of economic incentives on work and retirement.* Kalamazoo, MI: Upjohn Institute for Employment. (Chap 20)

Rabbitt, P. M. A. (1988). How old people prepare themselves for events which they expect. In H. Bouma & D. G. Bouwhuis (Eds.), *Attention and performance X.* Hillsdale, NJ: Erlbaum. (Chap 19)

Rabinowitz, J. C. (1989). Age deficits in recall under optimal study conditions. *Psychology and Aging, 4,* 378–380. (Chap 19)

Radin, N. (1981). The role of the father in cognitive, academic, and intellectual development. In M. E. Lamb (Ed.), *The role of the father in child development* (2nd ed.). New York: Wiley. (Chap 9)

Radin, N. (1986). The influence of fathers on their sons and daughters. *Social Work in Education, 8,* 77–91. (Chap 8)

Radke-Yarrow, M., Zahn-Waxler, C., & Chapman, M. (1983). Children's prosocial dispositions and behavior. In P. Mussen (Ed.), *Handbook of child psychology* (Vol. 4, 4th ed.). New York: Wiley. (Chap 10)

Ragozin, A., Basham, R. B., Crnic, K. A., Greenberg, M. T., & Robinson, N. M. (1982). Effects of maternal age on parenting role. *Developmental Psychology, 18,* 627–634. (Chap 16)

Rajecki, D. W., & Flanery, R. C. (1981). Social conflict and dominance in children. In M. E. Lamb & A. L. Brown (Eds.), *Advances in developmental psychology* (Vol. 1). Hillsdale, NJ: Erlbaum. (Chaps 2, 10)

Rakowski, W., & Clark, N. M. (1985). Future outlook, caregiving, and care receiving in the family context. *Gerontologist, 25,* 618–623. (Chap 20)

Rathbun, C., McLaughlin, H., Bennett, O., & Garland, J. A. (1965). Later adjustment of children following radical separation from family and culture. *American Journal of Orthopsychiatry, 35,* 604–609. (Chap 8)

Rebok, G. W., & Balcerak, L. J. (1989). Memory self-efficacy and performance differences in young and old adults: The effect of mnemonic training. *Developmental Psychology, 25,* 714–721. (Chap 19)

Reedy, M. N. (1977). *Age and sex differences in personal needs and the nature of love.* Unpublished doctoral dissertation, University of Southern California. (Chap 16)

Reese, H. W., & Rodeheaver, D. (1985). Problem solving and complex decision making. In J. E. Birren & K. W. Schaie (Eds.), *Handbook of the psychology of aging* (2nd ed.). New York: Van Nostrand Reinhold. (Chap 19)

Reff, M. E. (1985). RNA and protein metabolism. In C. E. Finch & E. L. Schneider (Eds.), *Handbook of the biology of aging* (2nd ed.). New York: Van Nostrand Reinhold. (Chap 20)

Reinisch, J. M. (1981). Prenatal exposure to synthetic progestins increases potential for aggression in humans. *Science, 211,* 1171–1173. (Chap 9)

Remington, J. S., & Kleine, J. O. (1990). *Infectious diseases of the fetus and newborn infant* (3rd ed.). Philadelphia: W. B. Saunders.

Rempel, J. (1985). Childless elderly. *Journal of Marriage and the Family, 47,* 343–348. (Chap 20)

Repetti, R. L. (1985). *The social environment at work and psychological well-being.* Unpublished doctoral dissertation, Yale University. (Chap 16)

Repetti, R. L. (1989). Effects of daily work load on subsequent behavior during marital interaction: The roles of social withdrawal and spouse support. *Journal of Personality and Social Psychology, 57,* 651–659. (Chap 16)

Repetti, R. L. (1991, April). *The short-term effects of job stress on parent-child interaction.* Paper presented at the biennial meeting of the Society for Research in Child Development, Seattle, WA. (Chap 16)

Repetti, R. L., & Crosby, F. (1984). Gender and depression. *Journal of Social and Clinical Psychology, 2,* 57–70. (Chap 16)

Rest, J. R. (1983). Morality. In P. H. Mussen (Ed.), *Handbook of child psychology* (Vol. 3, 4th ed.). New York: Wiley. (Chaps 2, 11)

Reynolds, C. R., Chastain, R. L., Kaufman, A. S., & McLean, J. E. (1987). Demographic characteristics and IQ among adults: Analysis of the WAIS-R standardization sample as a function of the stratification variables. *Journal of School Psychology, 25,* 323–342. (Chap 12)

Rheingold, H. L., & Eckerman, C. O. (1970). The infant separates himself from his mother. *Science, 168,* 78–83. (Chap 8)

Ricco, R. B. (1989). Operational thought and the acquisition of taxonomic relations involving figurative dissimilarity. *Developmental Psychology, 25*, 996–1003. (Chap 11)

Rice, M. L., Huston, A. C., Truglio, R., & Wright, J. (1990). Words from "Sesame Street": Learning vocabulary while viewing. *Developmental Psychology, 26*, 421–428. (Chap 10)

Richardson, D. W., & Short, R. V. (1978). Time of onset of sperm production in boys. *Journal of Biosocial Science, 5* (Suppl.), 15–25. (Chap 13)

Richardson, G. S. (1990). Circadian rhythms and aging. In E. L. Schneider & J. W. Rowe (Eds.), *Handbook of the biology of aging* (3rd ed.). San Diego, CA: Academic Press. (Chap 20)

Richardson, J. L., Dwyer, K., McGuigan, K., Hansen, W. B., Dent, C., Johnson, C. A., Sussman, S. Y., Brannon, B., & Flay, B. (1989). Substance use among eighth-grade students who take care of themselves after school. *Pediatrics, 84*, 556–566. (Chap 13)

Richardson, R. A., Galambos, N. L., Schulenberg, J. E., & Petersen, A. C. (1984). Young adolescents' perceptions of their family environment. *Journal of Early Adolescence, 4*, 131–154. (Chap 13)

Richardson, T. M., & Benbow, C. P. (1990). Long-term effects of acceleration on the social-emotional adjustment of mathematically precocious youths. *Journal of Educational Psychology, 82*, 464–470. (Chap 12)

Richman, A. L., LeVine, R. A., New, R. S., Howrigan, G. A., Welles-Nystrom, B., & LeVine, S. E. (1988). Maternal behavior to infants in five cultures. In R. A. LeVine, P. M. Miller, & M. M. West (Eds.), *New directions for child development. Parental behavior in diverse societies.* (No. 40) San Francisco: Jossey-Bass. (Chap 8)

Richman, A. L., Miller, P. M., & LeVine, R. A. (1992). Cultural and educational variations in maternal responsiveness. *Developmental Psychology, 28*, 614–621. (Chap 8)

Richman, C. L., Nida, S., & Pittman, L. (1976). Effects of meaningfulness on child free-recall learning. *Developmental Psychology, 12*, 460–465. (Chap 11)

Ridley, C. A., Avery, A. W., Harrell, J. E., Haynes-Clements, L. A., & McCunney, N. (1981). Mutual problem-solving skills training for premarital couples. *Journal of Applied Developmental Psychology, 2*, 89–116. (Chap 1)

Rierdan, J., & Koff, E. (1985). Timing of menarche and initial menstrual experience. *Journal of Youth and Adolescence, 14*, 237–244. (Chap 13)

Riese, M. L. (1987). Temperamental stability between the neonatal period and 24 months. *Developmental Psychology, 23*, 216–222. (Chap 4)

Riese, M. L. (1990). Neonatal temperament in monozygotic and dizygotic twin pairs. *Child Development, 61*, 1230–1237. (Chap 4)

Rikli, R., & Busch, S. (1986). Motor performance of women as a function of age and physical activity level. *Journal of Gerontology, 41*, 645–649. (Chap 17)

Riley, M. W., & Riley, J. W., Jr. (1986, Winter). Longevity and social structure: The added years. *Daedalus, 115*, 51–75. (Chap 20)

Rizzo, T. A., & Corsaro, W. A. (1988). Toward a better understanding of Vygotsky's process of internalization: Its role in the development of the concept of friendship. *Developmental Review, 8*, 219–237. (Chap 14)

Robbins, M. A., Elias, M. F., & Pechinski, J. M. (1989, June). *Circulo-respiratory fitness as a predictor of fluid intelligence.* Paper presented at the Maine Biological and Medical Sciences Symposium, Portland. (Chap 17)

Roberts, G., Block, J. H., & Block, J. (1984). Continuity and change in parents' child-rearing practices. *Child Development 55*, 586–597. (Chap 16)

Roberts, P., & Newton, P. M. (1987). Levinsonian studies of women's adult development. *Psychology and Aging, 2*, 154–163. (Chap 16)

Roberts, R. J., Jr., & Patterson, C. J. (1983). Perspective taking and referential communication. *Child Development, 54*, 1016–1021. (Chap 11)

Robertson, S. S. (1982). Intrinsic temporal patterning in the spontaneous movement of awake neonates. *Child Development, 53*, 1016–1021. (Chap 4)

Robertson, S. S., Dierker, L. J., Sorokin, Y., & Rosen, M. G. (1982). Human fetal movement. *Science, 218*, 1327–1330. (Chap 3)

Robinson, H. B. (1983). The case for radical acceleration. In C. P. Benbow & J. C. Stanley (Eds.), *Academic precocity.* Baltimore: Johns Hopkins University Press. (Chap 12)

Robinson, H. B., & Robinson, N. M. (1976). *The mentally retarded child: A psychological approach* (2nd ed.). New York: McGraw-Hill. (Chap 12)

Robinson, P. K., Coberly, S., & Paul, C. E. (1985). Work and retirement. In R. H. Binstock & E. Shanas (Eds.), *Handbook of aging and the social sciences* (2nd ed.). New York: Van Nostrand Reinhold. (Chap 20)

Roche, A. F. (1981). The adipocyte-number hypothesis. *Child Development, 52*, 31–43. (Chap 5)

Roche, J. P. (1986). Premarital sex: Attitudes and behavior at the dating stage. *Adolescence, 21*, 107–121. (Chap 13)

Rockwell, R., & Elder, G. (1982). Economic deprivation and problem behavior: Childhood and adolescence in the Great Depression. *Human Development, 25*, 57–64. (Chap 10)

Rodin, J. (1983, August). *Insulin levels, hunger, and food intake.* Presidential address, Division 38, American Psychological Association, Anaheim, CA. (Chap 5)

Rodin, J. (1986). Aging and health: The effects of the sense of control. *Science, 233*, 1271–1276. (Chap 20)

Rodin, J., interviewed by E. Hall (1987). A sense of control. In E. Hall, *Growing and changing.* New York: Random House. (Chaps 1, 5, 20)

Rodin, J., & Langer, E. J. (1977). Long-term effects of a control-relevant intervention with the institutionalized aged. *Journal of Personality and Social Psychology, 35*, 897–902. (Chap 20)

Rodin, J., Silberstein, L., & Striegel-Moore, R. (1985). Women and weight. In T. B. Sonderegger (Ed.), *Nebraska symposium on motivation*. Lincoln: University of Nebraska Press. (Chap 15)

Rodman, H., Pratto, D. J., & Nelson, R. S. (1985). Child care arrangements and children's functioning. *Developmental Psychology, 21*, 413–418. (Chap 9)

Rogoff, B., Gauvain, M., & Ellis, S. (1984). Development viewed in its cultural context. In M. H. Bornstein & M. E. Lamb (Eds.), *Developmental psychology*. Hillsdale, NJ: Erlbaum. (Chaps 1, 2, 14)

Rogosch, F. A., & Newcomb, A. F. (1989). Children's perceptions of peer reputations and their social reputation among peers. *Child Development, 60*, 597–610. (Chap 10)

Rohrkemper, M. M., & Bershon, B. L. (1984). Elementary school students' report of the causes and effects of problem difficulty in mathematics. *Elementary School Journal, 85*, 127–147. (Chap 12)

Roland, E. H., & Volpe, J. J. (1989). Effect of maternal cocaine use on the fetus and newborn: Review of the literature. *Pediatric Neuroscience, 15*, 88–94. (Chap 3)

Rose, S. A. (1983). Behavioral and psychophysiological sequelae of preterm birth. In T. Field & A. Sostek (Eds.), *Infants born at risk*. New York: Grune & Stratton. (Chap 4)

Rose, S. A., Feldman, J. F., & Wallace, I. F. (1992). Infant information processing in relation to six-year cognitive outcomes. *Child Development, 63*, 1126–1141. (Chap 6)

Rose, S. A., Gottfried, A. W., & Bridger, W. H. (1978). Crossmodal transfer in infants: Relation to prematurity and socioeconomic background. *Developmental Psychology, 14*, 643–552. (Chap 6)

Rosen, R., & Hall, E. (1984). *Sexuality*. New York: Random House. (Chaps 13, 15)

Rosenberg, B. G., & Falk, F. (1989, April). *The only child: Sibling presence-absence or single parent effects?* Paper presented at the biennial meeting of the Society for Research on Child Development, Kansas City, MO. (Chap 9)

Rosenblatt, P. C. (1988). Grief: The social context of private feelings. *Journal of Social Issues, 44*(3), 67–78. (Chap 20)

Rosenfeld, D., Sheehan, D. S., Marcus, M. M., & Stephan, W. G. (1981). Classroom structure and prejudice in desegregated schools. *Journal of Educational Psychology, 73*, 17–26. (Chap 10)

Rosenthal, R. (1966). *Experimenter effects in behavioral research*. New York: Appleton-Century-Crofts. (Chap 10)

Rosenthal, R., & Jacobson, L. (1968). *Pygmalion in the classroom*. New York: Holt, Rinehart and Winston. (Chap 10)

Rosenwasser, S. M., Lingenfelter, M., & Harrington, A. F. (1989). Nontraditional gender role portrayals on television and children's gender role perceptions. *Journal of Applied Developmental Psychology, 10*, 97–105. (Chap 10)

Ross, H., Tesla, C., Kenyon, B., & Lollis, S. (1990). Maternal intervention in toddler peer conflict: The socialization of principles of justice. *Developmental Psychology, 26*, 994–1003. (Chap 8)

Rotheram-Borus, M. J., & Phinney, J. S. (1990). Patterns of social expectations among black and Mexican-American children. *Child Development, 61*, 542–556. (Chap 10)

Rovee-Collier, C. K. (1984). The ontogeny of learning and memory in human infancy. In R. Kail & N. E. Spear (Eds.), *Comparative perspectives on the development of memory*. Hillsdale, NJ: Erlbaum. (Chap 6)

Rovee-Collier, C. K., & Gekoski, M. J. (1979). The economics of infancy. In H. W. Reese (Ed.), *Advances in child development and behavior* (Vol. 13). New York: Academic Press. (Chap 4)

Rovet, J., & Netley, C. (1982). Processing deficits in Turner's syndrome. *Developmental Psychology, 18*, 77–94. (Chap 3)

Rowe, D. C., & Plomin, R. (1978). The Burt controversy: A comparison of Burt's data on IQ with data from other studies. *Behavior Genetics, 8*, 81–84. (Chap 3)

Rowe, J. W., & Kahn, R. L. (1987). Human aging: Usual and successful. *Science, 237*, 143–149. (Chap 20)

Rubin, K. H., Fein, G., & Vandenberg, B. (1983). Play. In P. H. Mussen (Ed.), *Handbook of child psychology* (Vol. 4, 4th ed.). New York: Wiley. (Chaps 5, 7)

Rubin, K. H., & Krasnor, L. R. (1986). Social cognitive and social-behavioral perspectives on problem solving. In M. Perlmutter (Ed.), *Minnesota symposia on child psychology* (Vol. 18). Hillsdale, NJ: Erlbaum. (Chap 10)

Rubin, K. H., & Maioni, T. (1975). Play preference and its relation to egocentrism, popularity, and classification skills in preschoolers. *Merrill-Palmer Quarterly, 21*, 171–179. (Chap 5)

Rubin, L. (1979). *Women of a certain age*. New York: Harper & Row. (Chap 18)

Rubin, R. T., Reinisch, J. M., & Haskett, R. F. (1981). Postnatal gonadal steroid effects on human behavior. *Science, 211*, 1318–1324. (Chap 3)

Rubinstein, C., Shaver, P., & Peplau, L. A. (1979, February). Loneliness. *Human Nature*, pp. 58–65. (Chap 16)

Rubinstein, R. L., Alexander, B. B., Goodman, M., & Luborsky, M. (1991). Key relationships of never married, childless older women: A cultural analysis. *Journal of Gerontology: Social Sciences, 46*, S270–277. (Chap 20)

Ruble, D. N. (1988). Sex-role development. In M. H. Bornstein & M. Lamb (Eds.), *Developmental psychology* (2nd ed.). Hillsdale, NJ: Earlbaum. (Chap 9)

Ruble, D. N., Boggiano, A. K., Feldman, N. S., & Loebl, J. H. (1980). Developmental analysis of the role of social comparison in self-evaluation. *Developmental Psychology, 16*, 105–115. (Chap 10)

Ruble, D. N., & Brooks-Gunn, J. (1982). The experience of menarche. *Child Development, 53*, 1557–1566. (Chap 13)

Ruble, D. N., Parsons, J. E., & Ross, J. (1976). Self-evaluative responses of children in an achievement setting. *Child Development, 47*, 990–997. (Chap 10)

Ruff, H. A. (1984). Infants' manipulative exploration of objects. *Developmental Psychology, 20*, 9–20. (Chap 6)

Ruff, H. A., Saltarelli, L. M., Capozzoli, M., & Dubiner, K. (1992). The differentiation of activity in infants' exploration of objects. *Developmental Psychology, 28*, 851–861. (Chap 6)

Rutter, M. (1979). Maternal deprivation, 1972–1978. *Child Development, 50*, 283–305. (Chap 8)

Rutter, M. (1990). Commentary: Some focus and process considerations regarding effects of parental depression on children. *Developmental Psychology, 26*, 60–67. (Chap 3)

Ryan, R. M., & Lynch, J. H. (1989). Emotional autonomy versus detachment: Revisiting the vicissitudes of adolescence and young adulthood. *Child Development, 60*, 340–356. (Chap 13)

Rybash, J. M., Hoyer, W. J., & Roodin, P. A. (1986). *Adult cognition and aging.* New York: Pergamon. (Chap 17)

Sachs, J. (1985). Prelinguistic development. In J. B. Gleason (Ed.), *The development of language.* Columbus, OH: Merrill. (Chap 7)

Saegert, S., & Hart, R. (1976). The development of sex differences in the environmental competence of children. In P. Burnett (Ed.), *Women in society.* Chicago: Maaroufa Press. (Chap 9)

Sagi, A., Lamb, M. E., Lewkowicz, K. S., Shohan, R., Dvir, R., & Estes, D. (1985). Security of infant-mother, -father, and -metapelet attachments among kibbutzim-raised Israeli children. *Monographs of the Society for Research in Child Development, 50* (1–2, Serial No. 209). (Chap 8)

St. Peters, M., Fitch, M., Huston, A. C., Wright, J. C., & Eakins, D. J. (1991). Television and families: What do young children watch with their parents. *Child Development, 62*, 1409–1423. (Chap 10)

Salapatek, P. (1975). Pattern perception in early infancy. In L. B. Cohen & P. Salapatek (Eds.), *Infant perception* (Vol. 1). New York: Academic Press. (Chap 6)

Salkind, N. J. (1985). *Theories of human development* (2nd ed.). New York: Wiley. (Chap 2)

Salthouse, T. A. (1984). Effects of age and skill in typing. *Journal of Experimental Psychology: General, 113*, 345–371. (Chap 17)

Salthouse, T. A. (1989). Age-related changes in basic cognitive processes. In APA Master Lectures, *The adult years: Continuity and change.* Washington, DC: American Psychological Association. (Chap 19)

Salthouse, T. A. (1990). Cognitive competence and expertise in aging. In J. E. Birren & K. W. Schaie (Eds.), *Handbook of the psychology of aging* (3rd ed.). San Diego, CA: Academic Press. (Chap 17)

Salthouse, T. A. (1991). Age and experience effects on the interpretation of orthographic drawings of three-dimensional objects. *Psychology and Aging, 6*, 426–433. (Chap 17)

Salthouse, T. A., & Babcock, R. L. (1991). Decomposing adult age differences in working memory. *Developmental Psychology, 27*, 763–776. (Chap 19)

Salthouse, T. A., Babcock, R. L., Skovronek, E., Mitchell, D. R. D., & Palmon, R. (1990). Age and experience effects in spatial visualization. *Developmental Psychology, 26*, 128–136. (Chap 17)

Salthouse, T. A., Kausler, D. H., & Saults, J. S. (1990). Age, self-assessed health status, and cognition. *Journal of Gerontology: Psychological Sciences, 45*, P156–160. (Chap 17)

Salthouse, T. A., & Mitchell, D. R. D. (1989). Structural and operational capacities in integrative spatial ability. *Psychology and Aging, 4*, 18–25. (Chap 19)

Salthouse, T. A., Mitchell, D. R. D., & Palmon, R. (1989). Memory and age differences in spatial manipulation. *Psychology and Aging, 4*, 480–486. (Chap 19)

Saltzstein, H. D. (1983). Critical issues in Kohlberg's theory of moral reasoning. *Monographs of the Society for Research in Child Development, 48* (1–2, Serial No. 200). (Chap 2)

Sameroff, A. J. (1968). The components of sucking in the human newborn. *Journal of Experimental Child Psychology, 6*, 607–623. (Chap 6)

Sameroff, A. J., Seifer, R., Baldwin, A., & Baldwin, B. (1993). Stability of intelligence from preschool to adolescence: The influence of social and family risk factors. *Child Development, 64*, 80–97. (Chap 12)

Sandberg, E. C., Riffle, N. L., Higdon, J. V., & Getman, C. E. (1981). Pregnancy outcome in women exposed to diethylstilbestrol in utero. *American Journal of Obstetrics and Gynecology, 140*, 194–205. (Chap 3)

Sands, L. P., & Meredith, W. (1992). Blood pressure and functioning in late midlife. *Journal of Gerontology: Psychological Sciences, 47*, P81–84. (Chap 17)

Sands, L. P., Terry, H., & Meredith, W. (1989). Change and stability in adult intellectual functioning assessed by Wechsler item responses. *Psychology and Aging, 4*, 79–87. (Chap 17)

Santili, N. R., & Furth, H. G. (1987). Adolescent work perception: A developmental approach. In J. H. Lewko (Ed.), *New directions for child development* (No. 35). San Francisco: Jossey-Bass. (Chap 14)

Santrock, J. W., Warshak, R. A., & Elliott, G. L. (1982). Social development and parent-child interaction in father-custody and stepmother families. In M. E. Lamb (Ed.), *Nontraditional families.* Hillsdale, NJ: Erlbaum. (Chap 9)

Savin-Williams, R. C. (1991). *Gay and lesbian youth: Expressions of identity.* Washington, DC: Hemisphere. (Chap 13)

Savin-Williams, R. C., & Small, S. A. (1986). The timing of puberty and its relationship to adolescent and parent perception of family interactions. *Developmental Psychology, 22*, 342–347. (Chap 18)

Saxe, G. B., Guberman, S. R., & Gearhart, M. (1987). Social processes in early number development. *Monographs of the Society for Research in Child Development, 52* (2, Serial No. 216). (Chap 11)

Scafidi, F. A., Field, T. M., Schanberg, S. M., Bauer, C. R., Tucci, K., Roberts, J., Morrow, C., & Kuhn, C. M. (1990). Massage stimulates growth in preterm infants: A replication. *Infant Behavior and Development, 13*, 167–188. (Chap 4)

Scanzoni, J., & Scanzoni, J. (1981). *Men, women, and change* (2nd ed.). New York: McGraw-Hill. (Chap 16)

Scarr, S. (1981). *Race, social class, and individual differences in IQ.* Hillsdale, NJ: Erlbaum. (Chaps 3, 12)

Scarr, S. (1982). On quantifying the intended effects of intervention.

In L. A. Bond & J. M. Joffe (Eds.), *Facilitating infant and early childhood development*. Hanover, VT: University Press of New England. (Chap 3)

Scarr, S. (1983). An evolutionary perspective on human intelligence. In M. Lewis (Ed.), *Origins of intelligence* (2nd ed.). New York: Plenum. (Chap 1)

Scarr, S., & Kidd, K. E. (1983). Developmental behavioral genetics. In P. H. Mussen (Ed.), *Handbook of child psychology* (Vol. 2, 4th ed.). New York: Wiley. (Chap 3)

Scarr, S., & McCartney, K. (1983). How people make their own environments. *Child Development, 54*, 425–435. (Chap 3)

Scarr, S., & Salapatek, P. (1970). Patterns of fear development in infancy. *Merrill-Palmer Quarterly, 16*, 53–90. (Chap 6)

Scarr, S., & Weinberg, R. A. (1983). The Minnesota adoption studies. *Child Development, 54*, 260–267. (Chap 3)

Schaefer, C., Harrison, H. R., Boyce, W. T., & Lewis, M. (1985). Illnesses in infants born to women with *Chlamydia trachomatis* infection. *American Journal of Diseases of Children, 139*, 127–133. (Chap 3)

Schafer, W. R., Kim, R., Sterne, R., Thorner, J., Kim, S.-H., & Rine, J. (1989). Genetic and pharmacological suppression of oncogenic mutations in RAS genes of yeast and humans. *Science, 245*, 379–385. (Chap 20)

Schaffer, H. R., & Emerson, P. E. (1964). The development of social attachments in infancy. *Monographs of the Society for Research in Child Development, 29* (Serial No. 94). (Chap 8)

Schaie, K. W. (1977–1978). Toward a stage theory of adult development. *International Journal of Aging and Human Development, 8*, 129–138. (Chap 17)

Schaie, K. W. (1983). The Seattle Longitudinal Study. In K. W. Schaie (Ed.), *Longitudinal studies of adult psychological development*. New York: Guilford Press. (Chap 1)

Schaie, K. W. (1984). Midlife influences upon intellectual function in old age. *International Journal of Behavioral Development, 7*, 463–478. (Chap 17)

Schaie, K. W. (1989a). Individual differences in rate of cognitive change in adulthood. In V. L. Bengston & K. W. Schaie (Eds.), *The course of later life: Research and reflections*. New York: Springer. (Chap 17)

Schaie, K. W. (1989b). Perceptual speed in adulthood: Cross-sectional and longitudinal studies. *Psychology and Aging, 4*, 443–453. (Chap 19)

Schaie, K. W. (1990a). Intellectual development in adulthood. In J. E. Birren & K. W. Schaie (Eds.), *Handbook of the psychology of aging* (3rd ed.). San Diego, CA: Academic Press. (Chap 17)

Schaie, K. W. (1990b). Late life potential and cohort differences in mental abilities. In M. Perlmutter (Ed.), *Late life potential*. Washington, DC: Gerontological Society of America. (Chaps 1, 17)

Schaie, K. W., & Hertzog, C. (1982). Longitudinal methods. In B. B. Wolman (Ed.), *Handbook of developmental psychology*. Englewood Cliffs, NJ: Prentice-Hall. (Chap 1)

Schaie, K. W., & Hertzog, C. (1985). Measurement in the psychology of adulthood and aging. In J. E. Birren & K. W. Schaie (Eds.), *Handbook of the psychology of aging* (2nd ed.). New York: Van Nostrand Reinhold. (Chap 1)

Schaie, K. W., & Willis, S. L. (1986a). *Adult development and aging* (2nd ed.). Boston: Little, Brown. (Chap 17)

Schaie, K. W., & Willis, S. L. (1986b). Can declines in adult intellectual functioning be reversed? *Developmental Psychology, 22*, 224–232. (Chap 19)

Schapiro, M. G., & Ahlburg, D. A. (1986). Why crime is down. *American Demographics*. (Chap 15)

Schludermann, E. H., Schludermann, S. M., Merryman, P. W., & Brown, B. W. (1983). Halstead's studies in the neuropsychology of aging. *Archives of Gerontology and Geriatrics, 2*, 49–172. (Chap 17)

Schnabel, H., & Schnabel, R. (1990). An organ-specific differentiation gene, *pha-1*, from *Caenorhabditis elegans*. *Science, 250*, 686–688. (Chap 3)

Schneider, W., & Sodian, B. (1988). Metamemory-memory behavior relationships in young children: Evidence from a memory-for-location task. *Journal of Experimental Child Psychology, 45*, 209–233. (Chap 11)

Schneider-Rosen, K., Braunwald, K. G., Carlson, V., & Cicchetti, D. (1985). Current perspectives in attachment theory. *Monographs of the Society for Research in Child Development, 50* (1–2, Serial No. 209). (Chap 8)

Schooler, C. (1990). Psychosocial factors and effective cognitive functioning in adulthood. In J. W. Birren & K. W. Schaie (Eds.), *Handbook of the psychology of aging* (3rd ed.). San Diego, CA: Academic Press. (Chap 17)

Schulenberg, J. E., Asp, C. E., & Petersen, A. C. (1984). School from the young adolescent's perspective. *Journal of Early Adolescence, 4*, 107–130. (Chap 14)

Schulz, R. (1978). *The psychology of death, dying, and bereavement*. Reading, MA: Addison-Wesley. (Chap 20)

Schulz, R., & Curnow, C. (1988). Peak performance and age among superathletes: Track and field, swimming, baseball, tennis, and golf. *Journal of Gerontology, 43*, P113–120. (Chap 16)

Schuster, D. T. (1990). Fulfillment of potential, life satisfaction, and competence: Comparing four cohorts. *Journal of Educational Psychology, 82*, 471–478. (Chap 12)

Schwartz, G. M., Izard, C. E., & Ansul, S. E. (1985). The 5-month-old's ability to discriminate facial expressions of emotion. *Infant Behavior and Development, 8*, 65–77. (Chap 6)

Scollan, R. (1979). A real early stage. In E. Ochs & B. B. Schieffelin (Eds.), *Developmental pragmatics*. New York: Academic Press. (Chap 7)

Scott, J. P. (1962). Genetics and the development of social behavior in mammals. *American Journal of Orthopsychiatry, 32*, 878–893. (Chap 8)

Scott-Jones, D., & Turner, S. L. (1990). The impact of adolescent childbearing on educational attainment and income of black females. *Youth & Society, 22*, 35–53. (Chap 15)

Scott-Maxwell, F. (1979). *The measure of my days*. New York: Penguin. (Chap 20)

Scribner, S. (1986). Thinking in action: Some characteristics of practical thought. In R. J. Sternberg & R. K. Wagner (Eds.), *Practical intelligence.* New York: Cambridge University Press. (Chap 17)

Sears, P. S., & Barbee, A. H. (1977). Career and life satisfaction among Terman's gifted women. In J. Stanley, W. George, & C. Solano (Eds.), *The gifted and creative: Fifty-year perspective.* Baltimore: Johns Hopkins University Press. (Chap 12)

Seashore, S. E., & Barnowe, J. T. (1972, August). Collar color doesn't count. *Psychology Today,* pp. 119–128. (Chap 16)

Seasons of life [PBS television series on human development]. Pittsburgh: WQED & University of Michigan. (Chap 16)

Seginer, R. (1983). Parents' educational expectations and children's academic achievement. *Merrill-Palmer Quarterly, 29,* 1–23. (Chap 10)

Sekuler, R., & Blake, R. (1987, December). Sensory underload. *Psychology Today,* pp. 48–51. (Chap 19)

Self, P. A., & Horowitz, F. D. (1979). The behavioral assessment of the neonate. In J. D. Osofsky (Ed.), *Handbook of infant development.* New York: Wiley-Interscience. (Chap 4)

Seligman, M. E. P. (1975). *Helplessness.* San Francisco: Freeman. (Chap 10)

Seligmann, J. (1990, August 6). Not past their prime. *Newsweek,* pp. 66–68. (Chap 18)

Selman, R. L. (1976). Social-cognitive understanding. In T. Lickona (Ed.), *Moral development and behavior.* New York: Holt, Rinehart and Winston. (Chaps 11, 14)

Selman, R. L. (1980). *The growth of interpersonal understanding.* New York: Academic Press. (Chaps 11, 14)

Selman, R. L. (1981). The child as a friendship philosopher. In S. R. Asher & J. M. Gottman (Eds.), *The development of friendship.* New York: Cambridge University Press. (Chaps 10, 13)

A sense of history. (1983, June 9). *New York Times,* p. B1. (Chap 19)

Sessa, F. M., & Steinberg, L. (1991). Family structure and the development of autonomy during

adolescence. *Journal of Early Adolescence, 11,* 38–55. (Chap 13)

Shaffer, D., & Bacon, K. (1989). A critical review of preventive efforts in suicide, with particular reference to youth suicide. In *Report of the Secretary's Task Force on Youth Suicide. Vol. 3: Prevention and intervention in youth suicide.* (DHHS Publication No. ADM 89-1623). Washington, DC: U.S. Government Printing Office. (Chap 15)

Shaffer, D., Garland, A., & Whittle, B. (1998, March). An evaluation of youth suicide prevention programs. *New Jersey adolescent suicide prevention program.* (Final project report.) Trenton, NJ: Division of Mental Health and Hospitals. (Chap 15)

Shafii, M., Carrigan, S., Whittinghill, J. R., & Derrick, A. (1985). Psychological autopsy of completed suicide in children and adolescents. *American Journal of Psychiatry, 142,* 1061–1064. (Chap 15)

Shanghai Preschool Education Study Group. (1980). Family education of only children. *Chinese Women, 5,* 16–17. (Chap 9)

Shantz, C. U. (1983). Social cognition. In P. H. Mussen (Ed.), *Handbook of child psychology* (Vol. 3, 4th ed.). New York: Wiley. (Chaps 11, 13)

Shatz, M. (1983). Communication. In P. H. Mussen (Ed.), *Handbook of child psychology* (Vol. 3, 4th ed.). New York: Wiley. (Chap 7)

Shatz, M. (1984). Contributions of mothers and mind to the development of communicative competence. In M. Perlmutter (Ed.), *Minnesota symposia on child psychology* (Vol. 17). Hillsdale, NJ: Erlbaum. (Chap 7)

Shatz, M., Wellman, H. M., & Silber, S. (1983). The acquisition of mental verbs. *Cognition, 14,* 301–321. (Chap 7)

Sheehy, G. (1976). *Passages.* New York: Dutton. (Chap 18)

Sherif, M., Harvey, O. J., White, B. J., Hood, W. R., & Sherif, C. W. (1961). *Intergroup conflict and cooperation.* Norman, OK: Institute of Group Relations. (Chap 10)

Sherif, M., & Sherif, C. W. (1953). *Groups in harmony and tension.* New York: Harper & Row. (Chap 10)

Shneidman, E. S. (1980). *Death: Current perspectives* (2nd ed.). Palo Alto, CA: Mayfield. (Chap 20)

Shoda, Y., Mischel, W., & Peake, P. K. (1990). Predicting adolescent cognitive and self-regulatory competencies from preschool delay of gratification: Identifying diagnostic conditions. *Developmental Psychology, 26,* 978–986. (Chap 14)

Shouval, R. H., Venaki, S. K., Bronfenbrenner, U., Devereux, E., & Kiely, E. (1975). Anomalous reactions to social pressure of Israeli and Soviet children raised in family vs. collective settings. *Journal of Personality and Social Psychology, 32,* 477–489. (Chap 10)

Shreve, A. (1984, September 9). The working mother as role model. *New York Times Magazine,* pp. 39–43ff. (Chap 8)

Shultz, T. R. (1980). Development of the concept of intention. In W. A. Collins (Ed.), *Minnesota symposia on child psychology* (Vol. 13). Hillsdale, NJ: Erlbaum. (Chaps 11, 14)

Shultz, T. R., Wright, K., & Schleifer, M. (1986). Assignment of moral responsibility and punishment. *Child Development, 57,* 177–184. (Chap 11)

Siegal, M., & Share, D. L. (1990). Contamination sensitivity in young children. *Developmental Psychology, 26,* 455–458. (Chap 11)

Siegal, M., & Storey, R. M. (1985). Day care and children's conceptions of moral and social rules. *Child Development, 56,* 1001–1008. (Chap 8)

Siegler, I. C., & Costa, P. T., Jr. (1985). Health behavior relationships. In J. E. Birren & K. W. Schaie (Eds.), *Handbook of the psychology of aging* (2nd ed.). New York: Van Nostrand Reinhold. (Chap 19)

Siegler, R. S. (1981). Developmental sequences within and between concepts. *Monographs of the Society for Research in Child Development, 46* (2, Serial No. 189). (Chap 11)

Siegler, R. S. (1989). Hazards of mental chronometry: An example from children's subtraction. *Journal of Educational Psychology, 81,* 497–506. (Chap 12)

Siegler, R. S. (1991). *Children's thinking* (2nd ed.). Englewood Cliffs, NJ: Prentice-Hall. (Chaps 2, 6, 7, 11, 12, 14)

Siegler, R. S., & Richards, D. D. (1982). The development of intelligence. In R. J. Sternberg (Ed.), *Handbook of human intelligence.* New York: Cambridge University Press. (Chap 12)

Sigman, M., Neumann, C., Jansen, A. A. J., & Bwibo, N. (1989). Cognitive abilities of Kenyan children in relation to nutrition, family characteristics, and education. *Child Development, 60,* 1463–1474. (Chap 5)

Silka, L., & Kiesler, S. (1977). Couples who choose to remain childless. *Family Planning Perspectives, 9,* 16–35. (Chap 16)

Simons, R. L., & Murphy, P. I. (1985). Sex differences in the causes of adolescent suicide ideation. *Journal of Youth and Adolescence, 14,* 423–434. (Chap 15)

Simons, R. L., Whitback, L. B., Conger, R. D., & Chyi-In, W. (1991). Intergenerational transmission of harsh parenting. *Developmental Psychology, 27,* 159–171. (Chap 9)

Simonton, D. K. (1990). Does creativity decline in the later years? Definition, data, and theory. In M. Perlmutter (Ed.), *Late life potential.* Washington, DC: Gerontological Society of America. (Chap 17)

Simpson, E. L. (1974). Moral development research. *Human Development, 17,* 81–106. (Chap 2)

Singer, J. L., & Singer, D. G. (1979). The values of the imagination. In B. Sutton-Smith (Ed.), *Play and learning.* New York: Gardner Press. (Chap 5)

Singer, L. M., Brodzinsky, D. M., Ramsay, D., Stein, M., & Waters, E. (1985). Mother-infant attachment in adoptive families. *Child Development, 56,* 1543–1551. (Chap 8)

Singleton, L. C., & Asher, S. R. (1979). Racial integration and children's peer preferences. *Child Development, 50,* 936–941. (Chap 10)

Skandhan, K. P., Pandy, A. K., Skandhan, S., & Mehta, Y. B. (1988). Menarche: Prior knowledge and experience. *Adolescence, 23,* 149–154. (Chap 13)

Skinner, B. F. (1938). *The behavior of organisms.* New York: Appleton-Century-Crofts. (Chap 2)

Skinner, B. F. (1957). *Verbal behavior.* New York: Appleton-Century-Crofts. (Chap 7)

Skinner, B. F. (1983). Intellectual self-management in old age. *American Psychologist, 38,* 239–244. (Chap 19)

Skinner, E. A. (1990). Age differences in the dimensions of perceived control during middle childhood: Implications for developmental conceptualizations and research. *Child Development, 61,* 1882–1890. (Chap 12)

Skolnick, A. (1981). Married lives. In D. H. Eichorn, J. A. Clausen, N. Haan, M. P. Honzik, & P. H. Mussen (Eds.), *Present and past in middle life.* New York: Academic Press. (Chap 18)

Slobin, D. I. (1986). Crosslinguistic evidence for the language-making capacity. In D. I. Slobin (Ed.), *The crosslinguistic study of language acquisition.* Hillsdale, NJ: Erlbaum. (Chap 7)

Smeeding, T. M. (1990). Economic status of the elderly. In R. H. Binstock & L. K. George (Eds.), *Handbook of aging and the social sciences* (3rd ed.). San Diego, CA: Academic Press. (Chap 20)

Smetana, J. G. (1985). Preschool children's conception of transgressions. *Developmental Psychology, 21,* 18–29. (Chap 11)

Smetana, J. G. (1989). Adolescents' and parents' reasoning about actual family conflict. *Child Development, 60,* 1052–1067. (Chap 14)

Smetana, J. G., Killen, M., & Turiel, E. (1991). Children's reasoning about interpersonal and moral conflicts. *Child Development, 62,* 629–644. (Chap 14)

Smith, B. A., Fillion, T. J., & Blass, E. M. (1990). Orally mediated sources of calming in 1- to 3-day-old human infants. *Developmental Psychology, 26,* 731–737. (Chap 4)

Smith, C., & Lloyd, B. (1978). Maternal behavior and perceived sex of infant. *Child Development, 49,* 1263–1265. (Chap 8)

Smith, J., & Baltes, P. B. (1990). Wisdom-related knowledge: Age/cohort differences in response to life-planning problems. *Developmental Psychology, 26,* 494–505. (Chap 19)

Smith, M. C. (1978). Cognizing the behavior stream. *Child Development, 48,* 736–743. (Chap 11)

Smith, P. B., Nenney, S. W., Weinman, M. L., & Mumford, D. M. (1982). Factors affecting perception of pregnancy risk in the adolescent. *Journal of Youth and Adolescence, 22,* 207. (Chap 15)

Smith, P. K. (1977). Social and fantasy play in young children. In B. Tizard & D. Harvey (Eds.), *Biology of play.* Philadelphia: Lippincott. (Chap 5)

Smith, S. B. (1985, January 13). Why TV won't let up on violence. *New York Times,* pp. B2ff. (Chap 10)

Smuts, A. B. (1985). The National Research Council Committee on Child Development and the founding of the Society for Research in Child Development, 1925–1933. In *Monographs of the Society for Research in Child Development, 50* (4–5, Serial No. 211). (Chap 1)

Sodian, B. (1989, April). *Understanding the effects of cognitive strategies: Evidence from young children's interactions with a competitor.* Paper presented at the annual meeting of the American Educational Research Association, San Francisco. (Chap 11)

Solnick, R. L., & Birren, J. E. (1977). Age and male erectile responsiveness. *Archives of Sexual Behavior, 6,* 1–9. (Chap 18)

Solomons, H. (1978). The malleability of infant motor development. *Clinical Pediatrics, 17,* 836–839. (Chap 5)

Soltanaus, T. (1987). Hopes and worries of young people in three European countries. *Health Promotion, 2,* 19–27. (Chap 14)

Somerville, S. C., Wellman, H. M., & Cultice, J. C. (1983). Young children's deliberate reminding. *Journal of Genetic Psychology, 143,* 87–96. (Chap 6)

Sophian, C. (1988). Early developments in children's understanding of number: Inferences about numerosity and one-to-one correspondence. *Child Development, 59,* 1397–1414. (Chap 11)

Sophian, C., & Wellman, H. M. (1983). Selective information use and perseveration in the search behavior of infants and young children. *Journal of Experimental Child Psychology, 35,* 369–390. (Chap 6)

Sorosky, A. D. (1986). Introduction: An overview of eating disorders.

Adolescent Psychiatry, 13, 221–229. (Chap 15)

Spain, J. (1980). Psychological aspects of contraceptive use in teenage girls. In B. L. Blum (Ed.), *Psychological aspects of pregnancy, birthing, and bonding.* New York: Human Sciences Press. (Chap 15)

Spanier, G. B., & Lewis, R. A. (1980). Marital quality. *Journal of Marriage and the Family, 42,* 825–839. (Chap 16)

Spear, L. (1985, December 1). Literacy program focuses on severely disabled adults. *New York Times,* pp. WC6–7. (Chap 17)

Spearman, C. (1927). *The abilities of man.* New York: Macmillan. (Chap 12)

Spence, A. P. (1989). *Biology of human aging.* Englewood Cliffs, NJ: Prentice-Hall. (Chaps 16, 18, 19, 20)

Spence, J. T. (1979). Traits, roles, and the concept of androgyny. In J. F. Gullahorn (Ed.), *Psychology and women in transition.* New York: Wiley. (Chap 16)

Spencer, G. (1984, May). Projections of the population of the United States by age, sex, and race: 1983 to 2080. *Current population reports* (Series P-25, No. 952). (Chap 20)

Spencer, M. B., & Markstrom-Adams, C. (1990). Identity processes among racial and ethnic minority children in America. *Child Development, 61,* 290–310. (Chaps 10, 13)

Spitz, R. A. (1949). The role of ecological factors in emotional development. *Child Development, 20,* 145–155. (Chap 8)

Spivack, G., Marcus, J., & Swift, M. (1986). Early classroom behavior and later misconduct. *Developmental Psychology, 22,* 124–131. (Chaps 10, 15)

Spivack, G., & Shure, M. B. (1982). The cognition of social adjustment: Interpersonal cognitive problem-solving thinking. In B. Lahey & A. E. Kazdin (Eds.), *Advances in clinical child psychology* (Vol. 5). New York: Plenum. (Chaps 10, 14)

Sroufe, L. A., Fox, N. E., & Pancake, V. R. (1983). Attachment and dependency in developmental perspective. *Child Development, 54,* 1615–1627. (Chap 8)

Sroufe, L. A., & Jacobvitz, D. (1989). Diverging pathways, developmental transformations, multiple etiologies, and the problem of continuity in development. *Human Development, 32,* 196–203. (Chap 8)

Sroufe, L. A., Waters, E., & Matas, L. (1974). Contextual determinants of infant affective response. In M. Lewis & L. Rosenblum (Eds.), *The origins of fear.* New York: Wiley. (Chap 8)

Stack, C. (1974). *All my kin.* New York: Harper & Row. (Chap 13)

Stagner, R. (1985). Aging in industry. In J. E. Birren & K. W. Schaie (Eds.), *Handbook of the psychology of aging* (2nd ed.). New York: Van Nostrand Reinhold. (Chap 17)

Stall, R. D., Coates, T. J., & Hoff, C. (1988). Behavioral risk reduction for HIV infection among gay and bisexual men: A review of results from the United States. *American Psychologist, 43,* 878–885. (Chap 16)

Stark, R. E. (1986). Prespeech segmental feature development. In P. Fletcher & M. Garman (Eds.), *Language acquisition* (2nd ed.). New York: Cambridge University Press. (Chap 7)

Starkey, P., & Cooper, R. G., Jr. (1980). Perception of numbers by human infants. *Science, 210,* 1033–1035. (Chap 6)

Starkey, P., Spelke, E., & Gelman, R. (1980, April). *Number competence in infants.* Paper presented at the meeting of the International Conference on Infant Studies, New Haven, CT. (Chap 6)

Stechler, G., & Halton, A. (1982). Prenatal influences on human development. In B. B. Wolman (Ed.), *Handbook of developmental psychology.* Englewood Cliffs, NJ: Prentice-Hall. (Chap 3)

Stein, A. H., & Friedrich, L. K. (1975). The effects of television content on young children. In A. D. Pick (Ed.), *Minnesota symposia on child psychology* (Vol. 9). Minneapolis: University of Minnesota Press. (Chap 10)

Steinberg, L. D. (1981). Transformation in family relations at puberty. *Developmental Psychology, 17,* 833–840. (Chaps 13, 18)

Steinberg, L. D. (1984). The varieties and effects of work during adolescence. In M. Lamb, A. Brown, & B. Rogoff (Eds.), *Advances in developmental psychology* (Vol. 3). Hillsdale, NJ: Erlbaum. (Chap 13)

Steinberg, L. D. (1986). Latchkey children and susceptibility to peer pressure: An ecological analysis. *Developmental Psychology, 22,* 433–439. (Chaps 9, 13)

Steinberg, L. D. (1987). Single parents, stepparents, and the susceptibility of adolescents to antisocial peer pressure. *Child Development, 58,* 269–275. (Chap 13)

Steinberg, L. D. (1988). Reciprocal relation between parent-child distance and pubertal maturation. *Developmental Psychology, 24,* 122–128. (Chap 13)

Steinberg, L. D. (1989). *Adolescence* (2nd ed.). New York: McGraw-Hill. (Chap 13)

Steinberg, L. D., & Dornbusch, S. M. (1991). Negative correlates of part-time employment during adolescence: Replication and elaboration. *Developmental Psychology, 27,* 304–313. (Chap 13)

Steinberg, L. D., Dornbusch, S. M., & Brown, B. B. (1992). Ethnic differences in adolescent achievement: An ecological perspective. *American Psychologist, 47,* 723–729. (Chap 13)

Steinberg, L. D., Elman, J. D., & Mounts, N. S. (1989). Authoritative parenting, psychosocial maturity, and academic success among adolescents. *Child Development, 60,* 1424–1436. (Chap 13)

Steinberg, L. D., Greenberger, E., Garduque, L., Ruggiero, M., & Vaux, A. (1982). Effects of working on adolescent development. *Developmental Psychology, 17,* 833–840. (Chap 13)

Steinberg, L. D., & Silverberg, S. B. (1986). The vicissitudes of autonomy in early adolescence. *Child Development, 57,* 841–851. (Chap 13)

Steiner, J. E. (1979). Facial expressions in response to taste and smell stimulation. In H. W. Reese & L. P. Lipsitt (Eds.), *Advances in child development and behavior* (Vol. 13). New York: Academic Press. (Chap 4)

Steinkamp, M. W., & Kelly, J. R. (1987). Social integration, leisure activity, and life satisfaction in older adults: Activity theory revisited. *International Journal of Aging and*

Human Development, 25, 293–307. (Chap 20)

Stephan, C., & Langlois, J. H. (1984). Baby beautiful: Adult attributions of infant competence as a function of infant attractiveness. *Child Development, 55*, 576–585. (Chap 1)

Stern, P. N. (1978). Stepfather families. *Issues in Mental Health Nursing, 1*, 50–56. (Chap 9)

Stern, W. (1914). *The psychological methods of testing intelligence.* Baltimore: Warwick & York. (Chap 12)

Sternberg, R. J. (1985). *Beyond IQ: A triarchic theory of human intelligence.* New York: Cambridge University Press. (Chaps 12, 14)

Sternberg, R. J. (1990). Prototypes of competence and incompetence. In R. J. Sternberg & J. Kolligian, Jr. (Eds.), *Competence considered.* New Haven, CT: Yale University Press. (Chap 12)

Sterns, H. L., Barrett, G. V., & Alexander, R. A. (1985). Accidents and the aging individual. In J. E. Birren & K. W. Schaie (Eds.), *Handbook of the psychology of aging* (2nd ed.). New York: Van Nostrand Reinhold. (Chap 19)

Stevenson, H. W., Chen, C., & Uttal, D. H. (1990). Beliefs and achievement: A study of black, white, and Hispanic children. *Child Development, 61*, 508–523. (Chap 12)

Stevenson, H. W., & Lee, S.-Y. (1990). Contexts of achievement. *Mongraphs of the Society for Research in Child Development, 55* (1–2, Serial No. 221). (Chap 12)

Stevenson, H. W., Lee, S.-Y., & Stigler, J. W. (1986). Mathematics achievement of Chinese, Japanese, and American children. *Science, 231*, 693–699. (Chap 12)

Stevenson, H. W., Stigler, J. W., Lee, S.-Y., Lucker, G. W., Kitamura, S., & Hsu, C.-C. (1985). Cognitive performance and academic achievement of Japanese, Chinese, and American children. *Child Development, 56*, 718–734. (Chap 12)

Stiffman, A. R. (1989). Suicide attempts in runaway youth. *Suicide and Life-Threatening Behavior, 11*, 86–92. (Chap 15)

Stifter, C., & Fox, N. A. (1990). Infant reactivity: Physiological correlates of newborn and 5-month temperament. *Developmental Psychology, 26*, 582–588. (Chap 4)

Stigler, J. W. (1984). Mental abacus. *Cognitive Psychology, 16*, 145–176. (Chap 11)

Stinnett, N., Carter, L., & Montgomery, J. (1972). Older persons' perceptions of their marriages. *Journal of Marriage and the Family, 34*, 665–670. (Chap 20)

Stipek, D. J. Children's perceptions of their own and their classmates' ability. *Journal of Educational Psychology, 73*, 404–410. (Chap 12)

Stipek, D. J., Gralinski, J. H., & Kopp, C. B. (1990). Self concept development in the toddler years. *Developmental Psychology, 26*, 972–977. (Chap 8)

Stoel-Gammon, C., & Cooper, J. A. (1984). Patterns of early lexical and phonological development. *Journal of Child Language, 11*, 247–271. (Chap 7)

Stoller, E. P. (1990). Males as helpers: The role of sons, relatives, and friends. *Gerontologist, 30*, 228–235. (Chap 18)

Straus, M. A., Gelles, R. J., & Steinmetz, S. K. (1980). *Behind closed doors.* Garden City, NY: Doubleday. (Chap 9)

Strauss, M. S., & Cohen, L. B. (1980, April). *Infant immediate and delayed memory for perceptual dimensions.* Paper presented at the International Conference on Infant Studies, New Haven, CT. (Chap 6)

Strayer, F. F. (1984). Biological approaches to the study of the family. In R. D. Parke (Ed.), *Review of child development research* (Vol. 7). Chicago: University of Chicago Press. (Chap 10)

Strayer, F. F., Chapeski, T. R., & Strayer, J. (1978). The perception of preschool social dominance. *Aggressive Behavior, 4*, 183–192. (Chap 10)

Streissguth, A. P., Barr, H. M., Sampson, P. D., Darby, B. L., & Martin, D. C. (1989). IQ at age 4 in relation to maternal alcohol use and smoking during pregnancy. *Developmental Psychology, 25*, 3–11. (Chap 3)

Streufert, S., Pogash, R., Piasecki, M., & Post, G. M. (1990). Age and management team performance. *Psy-*

chology and Aging, 5, 551–559. (Chap 19)

Stroebe, W., Stroebe, M. S., & Domittner, G. (1988). Individual and situational differences in recovery from bereavement: A risk group. *Journal of Social Issues, 44*(3), 143–158. (Chap 20)

Sudarkasa, N. (1981). Interpreting the African heritage in Afro-American family organization. In H. McAdoo (Ed.), *Black families.* Beverly Hills, CA: Sage. (Chap 9)

Sulik, K. K., Johnston, M. C., & Webb, M. A. (1981). Fetal alcohol syndrome. *Science, 214*, 936–938. (Chap 3)

Sun, M. (1988). Anti-acne drug poses dilemma for FDA. *Science, 240*, 714–715. (Chap 3)

Sundberg, N. D., Poole, M. E., & Tyler, L. E. (1983). Adolescents' expectations of future events—A cross-cultural study of Australians, Americans, and Indians. *International Journal of Psychology, 18*, 415–427. (Chap 14)

Suomi, S. J. (1977). Development of attachment and other social behaviors in rhesus monkeys. In T. Alloway, P. Pliner, & L. Kranes (Eds.), *Attachment behavior* (Vol. 3). New York: Plenum. (Chap 5)

Suomi, S. J., & Harlow, H. F. (1975). The role and reason of peer relationships in rhesus monkeys. In M. Lewis & L. A. Rosenblum (Eds.), *Friendship and peer relations.* New York: Wiley. (Chap 8)

Suomi, S. J., & Harlow, H. F. (1978). Early experience and social development in rhesus monkeys. In M. E. Lamb (Ed.), *Social and personality development.* New York: Holt, Rinehart and Winston. (Chap 10)

Suomi, S. J., & Ripp, C. (1983). A history of motherless mother monkey mothering at the University of Wisconsin Primate Laboratory. In *Child abuse.* New York: Alan R. Liss. (Chap 9)

Super, C. M. (1976). Environmental effects on motor development. *Developmental Medicine and Child Neurology, 18*, 561–567. (Chap 5)

Super, C. M., & Harkness, S. (Eds.). (1982). *New directions for child development.* No. 8: *Anthropological perspectives on child development.* San Francisco: Jossey-Bass. (Chap 10)

Super, C. M., Herrera, M. G., & Mora, J. O. (1990). Long-term effects of food supplementation and psychosocial intervention on the physical growth of Colombian infants at risk of malnutrition. *Child Development, 61*, 29–49. (Chap 5)

Swanson, L. (1990). Influence of metacognitive knowledge and aptitude on problem solving. *Journal of Educational Psychology, 82*, 306–319. (Chap 11)

Tabor, A., Philip, J., Madsen, M., Bang, J., Obel, E., & Norgaard-Petersen, B. (1986, June 7). Randomised controlled trial of genetic amniocentesis in 4606 low-risk women. *Lancet*, pp. 1287–1292. (Chap 3)

Takahashi, K. (1990). Are the key assumptions of the "strange situation" procedure universal? A view from Japanese research. *Human Development, 33*, 23–30. (Chap 8)

Takeda, S., & Matsuzawa, T. (1985). Age-related brain atrophy. *Journal of Gerontology, 40*, 159–163. (Chap 19)

Takeuchi, T. (1972). Biological reactions and pathological changes in human beings and animals caused by organic mercury contamination. In R. Hartung & B. D. Dinman (Eds.), *Environmental mercury contamination.* Ann Arbor, MI: Ann Arbor Science. (Chap 3)

Talbott, M. M. (1990). The negative side of the relationship between older widows and their adult children: The mothers' perspective. *Gerontologist, 30*, 595–603. (Chap 20)

Tamis-LeMonda, C. S., & Bornstein, M. H. (1989). Habituation and maternal encouragement of attention in infancy as predictors of toddler language, play, and representational competence. *Child Development, 60*, 738–751. (Chap 6)

Tan, L. E. (1985). Laterality and motor skills in 4-year-olds. *Child Development, 56*, 119–124. (Chap 5)

Tanner, J. M. (1962). *Growth at adolescence.* Oxford, England: Basil Blackwell. (Chap 13)

Tanner, J. M. (1978). *Fetus into man: Physical growth from conception to maturity.* Cambridge, MA: Harvard University Press. (Chaps 5, 13)

Tao, K., & Chiu, J. (1985). A one-child-per-family policy: A psychological perspective. In W. S. Tseng & D. Y. H. Wu (Eds.), *Chinese culture and mental health.* Orlando, FL: Academic Press. (Chap 9)

Tavris, C. (1992). *The mismeasure of woman.* New York: Simon & Schuster. (Chap 18)

Taylor, R. J. (1988). Aging and supportive relationships among Black Americans. In J. S. Jackson (Ed.), *The Black American elderly.* New York: Springer. (Chap 18)

Teenagers and AIDS: The risk worsens. (1992, April 14). *New York Times*, p. C3. (Chap 13)

Templin, M. C. (1957). *Certain language skills in children: Their development and interrelationships.* Minneapolis: University of Minnesota Press. (Chap 7)

Terkel, S. (1974). *Working.* New York: Pantheon. (Chap 18)

Terman, L. M. (Ed.). 1959. *Genetic studies of genius* (Vol. 5). Stanford, CA: Stanford University Press. (Chap 12)

Thatcher, R. W., Walker, R. A., & Giudice, S. (1987). Human cerebral hemispheres develop at different rates and ages. *Science, 236*, 1110–1113. (Chap 14)

Thelen, E. (1979). Rhythmical stereotypes in normal human infants. *Animal Behavior, 27*, 699–715. (Chap 4)

Thelen, E. (1981). Rhythmical behavior in infancy. *Developmental Psychology, 17*, 237–257. (Chap 6)

Thelen, E. (1985). Developmental origin of motor coordination. *Developmental Psychology, 18*, 1–22. (Chap 5)

Thelen, E. (1989). The (re)discovery of motor development: Learning new things from an old field. *Developmental Psychology, 25*, 946–949. (Chap 5)

Thelen, E., & Adolphe, K. E. (1992). Arnold L. Gesell: The paradox of nature and nurture. *Developmental Psychology, 28*, 368–380. (Chap 2)

Thelen, E., Fisher, D. M., & Ridley-Johnson, R. (1984). The relationship between physical growth and a newborn reflex. *Infant Behavior and Development, 7*, 479–493. (Chaps 4, 5)

Thelen, E., Kelso, J. A. S., & Fogel, A. (1987). Self-organizing systems and infant motor development. *Developmental Review, 7*, 39–65. (Chap 5)

Thoman, E. B., Acebo, C., & Becker, P. T. (1983). Infant crying and stability in the mother-infant relationship. *Child Development, 54*, 653–659. (Chap 4)

Thoman, E. B., & Graham, S. E. (1987). Self-regulation of stimulation by premature infants. *Pediatrics, 78*, 855–860. (Chap 5)

Thoman, E. B., Korner, A. F., & Beason-Williams, L. (1977). Modification of responsiveness to maternal vocalization in the neonate. *Child Development, 48*, 563–569. (Chap 5)

Thoman, E. B., & Whitney, M. P. (1989). Sleep states of infants monitored in the home: Individual differences, developmental trends, and origins of diurnal cyclicity. *Infant Behavior and Development, 12*, 59–75. (Chap 4)

Thomas, A., & Chess, S. (1977). *Temperament and development.* New York: Brunner-Mazel. (Chap 4)

Thomas, L. E., & Chambers, K. O. (1989). Phenomenology of life satisfaction among elderly men: Quantitative and qualitative views. *Psychology and Aging, 4*, 284–289. (Chap 20)

Thomas, M. H., Horton, R. W., Lippincott, E. C., & Drabman, R. S. (1977). Desensitization to portrayals of real-life aggression as a function of exposure to television violence. *Journal of Personality and Social Psychology, 35*, 450–458. (Chap 10)

Thomas, R. M. (1979). *Comparing theories of child development.* Belmont CA: Wadsworth. (Chap 2)

Thompson, L. W., Gallagher-Thompson, D., Futterman, A., Gilewski, M. J., & Peterson, J. (1991). The effects of late-life spousal bereavement over a 30-month interval. *Psychology and Aging, 6*, 434–441. (Chap 20)

Thompson, M. G., & Schwartz, M. (1982). Life adjustment of women with anorexia and anorexic-like behavior. *International Journal of Eating Disorders, 1*, 47–60. (Chap 15)

Thompson, R. A. (1986). Temperament, emotionality, and infant social cognition. In J. V. Lerner &

R. M. Lerner (Eds.), *New directions in child development.* No. 31: *Temperament and social interaction during infancy.* San Francisco: Jossey-Bass. (Chap 8)

Thorne, B. (1986). Girls and boys together . . . but mostly apart: Gender arrangements in elementary schools. In W. Hartup & Rubin (Eds.), *Relationships and development.* Hillsdale, NJ: Erlbaum. (Chap 10)

Thornton, A., & Freedman, D. (1983, October). The changing American family. *Population Bulletin, 38*(4). (Chap 20)

Thornton, M. C., Chatters, L. M., Taylor, R. J., & Allen, W. R. (1990). Sociodemographic and environmental correlates of racial socialization by black parents. *Child Development, 61,* 401–409. (Chap 10)

Thurstone, L. L. (1947). *Multiple factor analysis.* Chicago: University of Chicago Press. (Chap 12)

Tice, R. R., & Setlow, R. B. (1985). DNA repair and replication in aging organisms and cells. In C. E. Finch & E. L. Schneider (Eds.), *Handbook of the biology of aging* (2nd ed.). New York: Van Nostrand Reinhold. (Chap 20)

Tinsley, B. R., & Parke, R. D. (1984). Grandparents as support and socialization agents. In M. Lewis (Ed.), *Beyond the dyad.* New York: Plenum. (Chap 18)

Tizard, B., & Hodges, J. (1978). The effect of early institutional rearing in the development of 8-year-old children. *Journal of Child Psychology and Psychiatry, 19,* 99–118. (Chap 8)

Todd, J., Friedman, A., & Kariuki, P. W. (1990). Women growing stronger with age. *Psychology of Women Quarterly, 14,* 567–577. (Chap 18)

Tolson, T. F. J., & Wilson, M. N. (1990). The impact of two- and three-generational black family structure on perceived family climate. *Child Development, 61,* 416–428. (Chaps 9, 18)

Tomasello, M., & Farrar, M. J. (1984). Cognitive bases of lexical development. *Journal of Child Language, 11,* 477–493. (Chap 7)

Tomlinson-Keasey, C., & Little, T. D. (1990). Predicting educational attainment, occupational achievement, intellectual skill, and personal adjustment among gifted men and women. *Journal of Educational Psychology, 82,* 442–455. (Chap 12)

Tracy, R. E., Lamb, M. E., & Ainsworth, M. D. S. (1976). Infant approach behavior as related to attachment. *Child Development, 47,* 571–578. (Chap 8)

Transition. (1986, March 3). *Newsweek,* p. 71.

Trause, M. A. (1977). Stranger responses. *Child Development, 48,* 1657–1661. (Chap 8)

Treas, J. (1983). Aging and the family. In D. S. Woodruff & J. E. Birren (Eds.), *Aging* (2nd ed.). Monterey, CA: Brooks/Cole. (Chap 18)

Trehub, S. E., Schneider, B. A., Thorpe, L. A., & Judge, P. (1991). Observational measures of auditory sensitivity in early infancy. *Developmental Psychology, 27,* 40–49. (Chap 4)

Trickett, P. K., & Kuczynski, L. (1986). Children's misbehaviors and parental discipline strategies in abusive and nonabusive families. *Developmental Psychology, 22,* 113–123. (Chap 9)

Trommsdorff, G., Burger, C., Fuchsle, T., & Lamm, H. (1978). *Erziehung für die Zukunft.* Dusseldorf, Germany: Padagogischer Verlag Schwann. (Chap 14)

Tronick, E. Z. (1992). Introduction: Cross-cultural studies of development. *Developmental Psychology, 28,* 566–567. (Chap 1)

Tronick, E. Z., Morelli, G. A., & Ivey, P. K. (1992). The Efe forager infant and toddler's pattern of social relationships: Multiple and simultaneous. *Developmental Psychology, 28,* 568–577. (Chap 8)

Tseng, W.-S., Kuotai, T., Hsu, J., Jinghua, C., Lian, Y., & Kameoka, V. (1988). Family planning and child mental health in China: The Nanjing survey. *American Journal of Psychiatry, 145,* 1396–1403. (Chap 9)

Tudge, J., & Rogoff, B. (1989). Peer influences on cognitive development: Piagetian and Vygotskian perspectives. In M. Bronstein & J. Bruner (Eds.), *Interaction in human development.* Hillsdale, NJ: Erlbaum. (Chap 11)

Turkewitz, G., & Kenny, P. A. (1982). Limitations on input as a basis for neural organization and perceptual development. *Developmental Psychobiology, 15,* 357–368. (Chap 4)

Turkle, S. (1984). *The second self.* New York: Simon & Schuster. (Chap 11)

Turner, B. F. (1982). Sex-related differences in aging. In B. B. Wolman (Ed.), *Handbook of developmental psychology.* Englewood Cliffs, NJ: Prentice-Hall. (Chap 18)

Turner, N. W. (1980). Divorce in mid-life. In W. H. Norman & T. J. Scaramella (Eds.), *Midlife.* New York: Brunner-Mazel. (Chap 18)

Tversky, B. (1989). Parts, partonomies, and taxonomies. *Developmental Psychology, 25,* 983–995. (Chap 11)

Twain, M. (1936). *The adventures of Tom Sawyer.* New York: Heritage Press. (Original work published 1876.) (Chap 6)

Uchitelle, L. (1991, November 17). Trapped in the impoverished middle class. *New York Times,* Business sec., pp. 1, 10. (Chap 18)

Udry, J. R., Billy, J. O. G., Morris, N. M., Groff, T. R., & Raj, M. H. (1985). Serum androgenic hormones motivate sexual behavior in boys. *Fertility and Sterility, 43,* 90–94. (Chap 13)

Udry, J. R., Talbert, L., & Morris, N. M. (1986). Biosocial foundations for adolescent female sexuality. *Demography, 23,* 217–230. (Chap 13)

Uhlenberg, P., & Cooney, T. M. (1990). Family size and mother-child relations in later life. *Gerontologist, 30,* 618–625. (Chap 18)

Uhlenberg, P., Cooney, T. M., & Boyd, R. (1990). Divorce for women after midlife. *Journal of Gerontology: Social Sciences, 45,* S3–11. (Chaps 18, 20)

Unger, D. G., & Wandersman, L. P. (1988). The relation of family and partner support to the adjustment of adolescent mothers. *Child Development, 59,* 1056–1060. (Chap 15)

Ungerer, J. A., & Sigman, M. (1984). The relation of play and sensorimotor behavior to language in the 2nd year. *Child Development, 55,* 1448–1455. (Chap 7)

United Nations. (1991). *Statistical yearbook.* New York: United Nations. (Chap 20)

United Nations Population Division. (1976). *Population by sex and age for regions and countries, 1950–2000, as assessed in 1973: Medium variant.* New York: United Nations, Department of Economic and Social Affairs. (Chap 15)

U.S. Bureau of Labor Statistics. (1990, November). Marital and family characteristics of the labor force from the March 1990 current population survey. Washington, DC: U.S. Department of Labor. (Chap 9)

U.S. Bureau of Labor Statistics. (1991). *Working women: A chartbook.* Washington, DC: U.S. Department of Labor. (Chap 16)

U.S. Bureau of the Census. (1982). *Statistical abstract of the United States* (102nd ed.). Washington, DC: U.S. Government Printing Office. (Chap 9)

U.S. Bureau of the Census. (1990a). *Statistical abstract of the United States* (110th ed.). Washington, DC: U.S. Government Printing Office. (Chaps 9, 15, 16, 17, 18, 20)

U.S. Bureau of the Census. (1990b, June). Marital status and living arrangements: March 1989. *Current population reports: Population characteristics* (Series P-20, No. 445). (Chap 16)

U.S. Bureau of the Census. (**1991**). *Statistical abstract of the United States* (111th ed.). Washington, DC: U.S. Government Printing Office. (Chaps 16, 18, 20)

U.S. Bureau of the Census. (1992). *Statistical abstract of the United States* (112th ed.). Washington, DC: U.S. Government Printing Office. (Chap 20)

U.S. Senate Special Committee on Aging. (1987–1988). *Aging in America: Trends and projections.* Washington, DC: U.S. Department of Health and Human Services. (Chap 20)

Uttal, D. H., & Perlmutter, M. (1989). Toward a broader conceptualization of development: The role of gains and losses across the life span. *Developmental Review, 9,* 101–132. (Chap 17)

Uzgiris, I. C. (1964). Situational

generality of conservation. *Child Development, 35,* 831–841. (Chap 11)

Vaillant, G. E. (1977). *Adaptation to life.* Boston: Little, Brown. (Chap 18)

Vaillant, G. E., & Milofsky, E. (1980). Natural history of male psychological health: IX. Empirical evidence for Erikson's model of the life cycle. *American Journal of Psychiatry, 137,* 1348–1359. (Chaps 2, 16, 18)

Valsiner, J. (1989). *Human development and culture.* Lexington, MA: Lexington Books. (Chap 5)

Van Court, M., & Bean, F. D. (1985). Intelligence and fertility in the United States. *Intelligence, 9,* 23–32. (Chap 12)

Vandell, D. L., & Corasanati, M. A. (1988). The relation between third graders' after-school care and social, academic, and emotional functioning. *Child Development, 59,* 868–875. (Chap 9)

Vandell, D. L., & Ramanan, J. (1992). Effects of early and recent maternal employment on children from low-income families. *Child Development, 63,* 938–949. (Chap 9)

van Loosbroek, E., & Smitsman, A. W. (1990). Visual perception of numerosity in infancy. *Developmental Psychology, 26,* 916–922. (Chap 6)

Vaughn, B. E., Bradley, C. F., Joffe, L. S., Seifer, R., & Barglow, P. (1987). Maternal characteristics measured prenatally are predictive of ratings of temperamental "difficulty" on the Carey Infant Questionnaire. *Developmental Psychology, 23,* 152–161. (Chap 4)

Vaughn, B. E., Deane, K. E., & Waters, E. (1985). The impact of out-of-home care on child-mother attachment quality: Another look at some enduring questions. *Monographs of the Society for Research in Child Development, 50* (1–2, Serial No. 209). (Chap 8)

Ventura, S. J. (1985, April). *Recent trends and variations in births to unmarried women.* Paper presented at the biennial meeting of the Society for Research in Child Development, Toronto. (Chap 16)

Veroff, J., Douvan, E., & Hatch-

ett, S. (in press). Marital interaction and marital quality in the first year of marriage. In W. Jones & D. Perlman (Eds.), *Advances in personal relationships.* London: Kingsley Publishers. (Chap 16)

Veroff, J., Douvan, E., & Kulka, R. (1981). *The inner American.* New York: Basic Books. (Chap 18)

Vestal, R. E., & Dawson, G. W. (1985). Pharmacology and aging. In C. E. Finch & E. L. Schneider (Eds.), *Handbook of the biology of aging* (2nd ed.). New York: Van Nostrand Reinhold. (Chap 16)

Vider, E. (1986). Late motherhood. In H. E. Fitzgerald & M. G. Walraven (Eds.), *Human development 86/87.* Guilford, CT: Dushkin. (Chap 18)

Vintner, A. (1986). The role of movement in eliciting early imitation. *Child Development, 57,* 66–71. (Chap 6)

Vitaliano, P. P., Russo, J., Bren, A. R., Vitiello, M. V., & Prinz, P. N. (1986). Functional decline in the early stages of Alzheimer's disease. *Psychology and Aging, 1,* 41–46. (Chap 19)

Vogel, S. R., Broverman, I. K., Broverman, D. M., Clarkson, F., & Rosenkrantz, P. (1970). Maternal employment and perception of sex roles among college students. *Developmental Psychology, 3,* 384–391. (Chap 9)

Volling, B. L., & Belsky, J. (1992). The contribution of mother-child and father-child relationships to the quality of sibling interaction: A longitudinal study. *Child Development, 63,* 1209–1222. (Chap 9)

Vuchinich, S., Hetherington, E. M., Vuchinich, R. A., & Clingempeel, W. G. (1991). Parent-child interaction and gender differences in early adolescents' adaptation to stepfamilies. *Developmental Psychology, 27,* 618–626. (Chap 13)

Vurpillot, E., & Ball, W. A. (1979). The concept of identity and children's selective attention. In G. A. Hale & M. Lewis (Eds.), *Attention and cognitive development.* New York: Plenum. (Chap 11)

Vygotsky, L. S. (1962). *Thought and language.* Cambridge, MA: MIT Press. (Chap 2)

Vygotsky, L. S. (1978). *Mind in society.* Cambridge, MA: Harvard

University Press. (Chaps 2, 7, 11, 12, 14)

Waber, D. P. (1977). Sex differences in mental abilities, hemispheric lateralization, and rate of physical growth in adolescence. *Developmental Psychology, 13,* 29–38. (Chap 14)

Wagner, R. K., & Sternberg, R. J. (1986). Tacit knowledge and intelligence in the everyday world. In R. J. Sternberg & R. K. Wagner (Eds.), *Practical intelligence.* New York: Cambridge University Press. (Chap 17)

Waldman, D. A., & Avolio, B. S. (1983). *Enjoy old age.* New York: Norton. (Chap 17)

Walker, H. A. (1988). Black-white differences in marriage and family patterns. In S. M. Dornbusch & M. H. Strube (Eds.), *Feminism, children and the new families.* New York: Guilford Press. (Chap 9)

Walker, L. J. (1980). Cognitive and perspective-taking prerequisites for moral development. *Child Development, 51,* 131–139. (Chap 11)

Walker, L. J., & Taylor, J. H. (1991). Family interactions and the development of moral reasoning. *Child Development, 62,* 264–283. (Chap 11)

Wallach, M. A. (1985). Creativity testing and giftedness. In F. D. Horowitz & M. O'Brien (Eds.), *The gifted and the talented.* Washington, DC: American Psychological Association. (Chap 12)

Wallerstein, J. S., & Blakeslee, S. (1989). *Second chances.* New York: Ticknor & Fields. (Chaps 2, 9, 16)

Walters, J., & Gardner, H. (1986). The crystallizing experience: Discovering an intellectual gift. In R. J. Sternberg & J. E. Davidson (Eds.), *Conceptions of giftedness.* New York: Cambridge University Press. (Chap 12)

Ward, J. V. (1990). Racial identity formation and transformation. In C. Gilligan, N. P. Lyons, & T. J. Hanmer (Eds.), *Making connections.* Cambridge, MA: Harvard University Press. (Chap 13)

Ward, R. A. (1984a). *The aging experience.* New York: Harper & Row. (Chap 20)

Ward, R. A. (1984b). The marginality and salience of being old: When

is age relevant? *Gerontologist, 24,* 227–232. (Chap 20)

Wasserman, G. A., Rauh, V. A., Brunelli, S. A., Garcia-Castro, M., & Necos, B. (1990). Psychosocial attributes and life experiences of disadvantaged minority mothers: Age and ethnic variations. *Child Development, 61,* 566–580. (Chap 15)

Waterlow, J. C. (1973). Note on the assessment and classification of protein-energy malnutrition in children. *Lancet, 2,* 87–89. (Chap 5)

Waterman, A., & Goldman, J. (1976). A longitudinal study of ego identity development at a liberal arts college. *Journal of Youth and Adolescence, 5,* 361–369. (Chap 13)

Watson, J. B. (1970). *Behaviorism.* New York: Norton. (Original work published 1924.) (Chap 1)

Watson, J. S., & Ramey, C. T. (1972). Reactions to response-contingent stimulation in early infancy. *Merrill-Palmer Quarterly, 18,* 219–228. (Chap 6)

Waxman, S. R., & Kosowski, T. D. (1990). Nouns mark category relations: Toddlers' and preschoolers' word-learning rules. *Child Development, 61,* 1461–1473. (Chap 7)

Wayne, L. (1986, January 4). Attaché-case education is enriching everybody. *New York Times Education Life,* pp. 72–76. (Chap 17)

Wearne, D., & Hiebert, J. (1989). Cognitive changes during conceptually based instruction on decimal fractions. *Journal of Educational Psychology, 81,* 507–513. (Chap 12)

Weed, K., Ryan, E. B., & Day, J. (1990). Metamemory and attributions as mediators of strategy use and recall. *Journal of Educational Psychology, 82,* 849–855. (Chap 11)

Weg, R. B. (1983a). Changing physiology of aging. In D. S. Woodruff & J. E. Birren (Eds.), *Aging* (2nd ed.). Monterey, CA: Brooks/Cole. (Chap 18)

Weg, R. B. (1983b). The physiological perspective. In R. B. Weg (Ed.), *Sexuality in the later years.* New York: Academic Press. (Chap 20)

Weiner, B. (1986). *An attributional theory of motivation and emotion.* New York: Springer-Verlag. (Chap 12)

Weiner, I. B. (1982). *Child and adolescent psychopathology.* New York: Wiley. (Chap 15)

Weinraub, M., & Wolf, B. M. (1987). Stressful life events, social supports, and parent-child interaction: Similarities and differences in single-parent and two-parent families. In Z. Boukydis (Ed.), *Research on support for parents and infants in the postnatal period.* Norwood, NJ: Ablex. (Chaps 9, 16)

Weinstein, R. S., Marshall, H. H., Sharp, L., & Botkin, M. (1987). Pygmalion and the student: Age and classroom differences in children's awareness of teacher expectations. *Child Development, 58,* 1079–1093. (Chap 10)

Weisman, A. D. (1972). *On dying and denying.* New York: Behavioral Publications. (Chap 20)

Weiss, R. S. (1979a). *Going it alone.* New York: Basic Books. (Chap 16)

Weiss, R. S. (1979b). Growing up a little faster. *Journal of Social Issues, 35,* 97–111. (Chap 9)

Weiss, R. S. (1988). Loss and recovery. *Journal of Social Issues, 44*(3), 37–52. (Chap 20)

Weissberg, J. A., & Paris, S. G. (1986). Young children's remembering in different context. *Child Development, 57,* 1123–1129. (Chap 6)

Weissman, M. M. (1979). The myth of involutional melancholia. *Journal of the American Medical Association, 242,* 742–744. (Chap 18)

Weithorn, L. A., & Campbell, S. B. (1982). The competency of children and adolescents to make informed treatment decisions. *Child Development, 53,* 1589–1598. (Chap 14)

Welcome to Elderhostel. (1991, September). *Elderhostel United States and Canada catalog,* p. 2. (Chap 17)

Wellman, H. M. (1990). *Children's theories of mind.* Cambridge, MA: MIT Press. (Chap 11)

Wellman, H. M., Cross, D., & Bartsch, K. (1987). Infant search and object permanence: A meta-analysis of the A-not-B error. *Monographs of the Society for Research in Child Development, 51* (3, Serial No. 214). (Chap 6)

Wellman, H. M., & Johnson, C. N. (1979). Understanding of mental processes. *Child Development, 50,* 79–88. (Chap 11)

Wellman, H. M., & Somerville, S. C. (1980). Quasi-naturalistic tasks in the study of cognition. In M. Perlmutter (Ed.), *New directions for child development* (No. 10). San Francisco: Jossey-Bass. (Chap 6)

Wellman, H. M., & Somerville, S. C. (1982). The development of human search ability. In M. E. Lamb & A. L. Brown (Eds.), *Advances in developmental psychology* (Vol. 2). Hillsdale, NJ: Erlbaum. (Chap 6)

Wellman, H. M., Somerville, S. C., Revelle, G. L. Haake, R. J., & Sophian, C. (1984). The development of comprehensive search skills. *Child Development, 55,* 472–481. (Chap 6)

Welte, J. W., & Barnes, G. M. (1985). Alcohol. *Journal of Youth and Adolescence, 14,* 487. (Chap 15)

Went, D. (1990). *Sex role traditionalism: Its relationship to marital well-being.* Unpublished paper, University of Michigan. (Cited in Veroff, Douvan, & Hatchett, in press.) (Chap 16)

Wentowski, G.-J. (1985). Older women's perception of great-grand-motherhood. *Gerontologist, 25,* 593–596. (Chap 20)

Wentzel, K. R. (1989). Adolescent classroom goals: Standards for performance and academic achievement: An interactionist perspective. *Journal of Educational Psychology, 81,* 131–142. (Chap 14)

Werker, J. F., & Tees, R. C. (1984). Cross-language speech perception. *Infant Behavior and Development, 7,* 49–63. (Chap 7)

Werner, J. S., & Perlmutter, M. (1979). Development of visual memory in infants. In H. W. Reese & L. P. Lipsitt (Eds.), *Advances in child development and behavior* (Vol. 14). New York: Academic Press. (Chap 6)

Werner, L. A., & Gillenwater, J. M. (1990). Pure-tone sensitivity of 2- to 5-week-old infants. *Infant Behavior and Development, 13,* 355–376. (Chap 4)

Wertsch, J. V., & Tulviste, P. (1992). L. S. Vygotsky and contemporary developmental psychology. *Developmental Psychology, 28,* 548–557. (Chap 2)

West, R. L., & Crook, T. H. (1990). Age differences in everyday memory: Laboratory analogues of telephone number recall. *Psychology and Aging, 5,* 520–529. (Chap 19)

West, R. L., Crook, T. H., & Bar-ron, K. L. (1992). Everyday memory performance across the life span: Effects of age and noncognitive individual differences. *Psychology and Aging, 7,* 72–82. (Chap 19)

Whitbeck, L. B., & Simons, R. L. (1990). Life on the streets: The victimization of runaway and homeless adolescents. *Youth & Society, 22,* 108–125. (Chap 15)

Whitebourne, S. K., & Waterman, A. S. (1979). Psychosocial development during the adult years. *Developmental Psychology, 15,* 373–378. (Chap 16)

White, N., & Cunningham, W. R. (1988). Is terminal drop pervasive or specific? *Journal of Gerontology: Psychological Sciences, 43,* P141–144. (Chap 17)

White, S. H. (1992). G. Stanley Hall: From philosophy to developmental psychology. *Child Development, 28,* 25–34. (Chap 1)

Whitehurst, G. J. (1982). Language development. In B. B. Wolman (Ed.), *Handbook of developmental psychology.* Englewood Cliffs, NJ: Prentice-Hall. (Chap 7)

Whitehurst, G. J., & Vasta, R. (1975). Is language acquired through imitation? *Journal of Psycholinguistic Research, 4,* 37–59. (Chap 7)

Wicks-Nelson, R., & Israel, A. C. (1984). *Behavior disorders of childhood.* Englewood Cliffs, NJ: Prentice-Hall. (Chap 5)

Wiesenfeld, A. R., & Malatesta, C. Z. (1982). Infant distress. In L. W. Hoffman, R. J. Gandelman, & H. R. Schiffman (Eds.), *Parenting.* Hillsdale, NJ: Erlbaum. (Chap 4)

Wigfield, A., Eccles, J. S., Mac Iver, D., Reuman, D. A., & Midgley, C. (1991). Transitions during early adolescence: Changes in children's domain-specific self-perceptions and general self-esteem across the transition to junior high school. *Developmental Psychology, 27,* 552–565. (Chap 14)

Wilkerson, I. (1989, May 27). Jury in Illinois refuses to charge mother in drug death of newborn. *New York Times.* (Chap 3)

Willer, B., Hofferth, S. L., Kisker, E. E., Divine-Hawkins, P., Farquhar, E., & Glantz, F. B. (1991). *The demand and supply of child care in 1990.* Washington, DC: National Association for the Education of Young Children. (Chap 8)

Willerman, L. (1979). Effects of families on intellectual development. *American Psychologist, 34,* 923–929. (Chap 3)

Williams, J. E., Pandey, J., Best, D. L., Morton, K. R., & Pande, N. (1987). Young adults' views of old adults in India and the United States. In C. Kagitcibasi (Ed.), *Growth and progress in cross-cultural psychology.* Berwyn, IL: Swets North America. (Chap 20)

Willie, C. V. (1988). *A new look at black families* (3rd ed.). Dix Hills, NY: General Hall. (Chap 20)

Willis, S. L. (1985). Educational psychology of the older adult learner. In J. E. Birren & K. W. Schaie (Eds.), *Handbook of the psychology of aging* (2nd ed.). New York: Van Nostrand Reinhold. (Chap 17)

Willis, S. L. (1987). Cognitive training and everyday competence. In K. W. Schaie (Ed.), *Annual review of gerontology and geriatrics* (Vol. 7). New York: Springer. (Chap 17)

Willis, S. L., & Nesselroade, C. S. (1990). Long-term effects of fluid ability training in old-old age. *Developmental Psychology, 26,* 905–910. (Chap 19)

Willis, S. L., & Schaie, K. W. (1986). Practical intelligence in later adulthood. In R. J. Sternberg & R. K. Wagner (Eds.), *Practical intelligence.* New York: Cambridge University Press. (Chap 17)

Wilson, M. N. (1986). The black extended family: An analytical consideration. *Developmental Psychology, 22,* 246–258. (Chap 9)

Wilson, M. N. (1989). Child development in the context of the black extended family. *American Psychologist, 44,* 380–385. (Chap 9)

Wing, S., Manton, K. G., Stallard, E., Hames, C. G., & Tryoler, H. A. (1985). The black/white mortality crossover. *Journal of Gerontology, 40,* 78–84. (Chap 20)

Wingfield, A., Stine, E. L., Lahar, C. J., & Aberdeen, J. S. (1988). Does the capacity of working memory change with age? *Experimental Aging Research, 14,* 103–107. (Chap 19)

Wingfield, A., Wayland, S. C., & Stine, E. A. L. (1992). Adult age differences in the use of prosody for syntactic parsing and recall of spoken sentences. *Journal of Gerontology:*

Psychological Sciences, 47, P350–356. (Chap 19)

Witelson, S. F. (1987). Neurobiological aspects of language in children. *Child Development, 58,* 653–688. (Chaps 5, 14)

Wolfe, L. (1982, April). Mommy's 39, daddy's 57—and baby was just born. *New York,* pp. 28–33. (Chap 18)

Wolfenstein, M. (1955). Fun mortality. In M. Mead & M. Wolfenstein (Eds.), *Childhood in contemporary culture.* Chicago: University of Chicago Press. (Chap 2)

Wolff, G. (1935). Increased bodily growth of school children since the war. *Lancet, 228,* 1006–1011. (Chap 5)

Wolfgang, M. (1973). Crime in a birth cohort. *Proceedings of the American Philosophical Society, 117,* 404–411. (Chap 15)

Wong, H. (1981). Typologies of intimacies. *Psychology of Women Quarterly, 5,* 435–443. (Chap 16)

Woodruff, D. S. (1983). Physiology and behavior relationships in aging. In D. S. Woodruff & J. E. Birren (Eds.), *Aging* (2nd ed.). Monterey, CA: Brooks/Cole. (Chap 19)

Woodruff, D. S. (1985). Arousal, sleep, and aging. In J. E. Birren & K. W. Schaie (Eds.), *Handbook of the psychology of aging* (2nd ed.). New York: Van Nostrand Reinhold. (Chap 20)

Woodruff, D. S., & Birren, J. E. (1972). Age changes and cohort differences in personality. *Developmental Psychology, 6,* 252–259. (Chap 18)

Woodson, R. H. (1983). Newborn behavior and the transition to extrauterine life. *Infant Behavior and Development, 6,* 139–144. (Chap 4)

Woolley, J. D., & Wellman, H. M. (1990). Young children's understanding of realities, nonrealities, and appearances. *Child Development, 61,* 946–961. (Chap 11)

Worobey, J., & Bajda, V. M. (1989). Temperament ratings at 2 weeks, 2 months, and 1 year: Differential stability of activity and emotionality. *Developmental Psychology, 25,* 257–263. (Chap 4)

Wright, J. C., & Vliestra, A. G. (1975). The development of selective attention. In H. W. Reese (Ed.), *Advances in child development and behavior* (Vol. 10). New York: Academic Press. (Chap 11)

Wroblewski, R., & Huston, A. C. (1987). Televised occupational stereotypes and their effects on early adolescents: Are they changing? *Journal of Early Adolescence, 7,* 283–298. (Chaps 10, 13)

Yamoor, C. M., & Mortimer, J. T. (1990). Age and gender differences in the effects of employment on adolescent achievement and well-being. *Youth & Society, 22,* 225–240. (Chap 13)

Yaniv, I., & Shatz, M. (1990). Heuristics of reasoning and analogy in children's visual perspective taking. *Child Development, 61,* 1491–1501. (Chap 11)

Yankelovich, D. (1981). *New rules.* New York: Random House. (Chap 16)

Yeates, K. O., & Selman, R. L. (1989). Social competence in the schools: Toward an integrative developmental model for intervention. *Developmental Review, 9,* 64–100. (Chap 2)

Yesavage, J. A., & Jacob, R. (1984). Effects of relaxation and mnemonics on memory, attention, and anxiety in the elderly. *Experimental Aging Research, 10,* 211–214. (Chap 19)

Yogman, M. W. (1982). Development of the father-infant relationship. In H. E. Fitzgerald, B. M. Lester, & M. W. Yogman (Eds.), *Theory and research in behavioral pediatrics* (Vol. 1). New York: Plenum. (Chap 8)

Young, K. T. (1990). American concepts of infant development from 1955 to 1984: What the experts are telling parents. *Child Development, 61,* 17–28. (Chap 2)

Younger, B. A. (1990). Infants' detections of correlations among feature categories. *Child Development, 61,* 614–620. (Chap 7)

Younger, B. A., & Cohen, L. B. (1983). Infant perception of correlations among attributes. *Child Development, 54,* 858–867. (Chap 7)

Yu, E. S. H., Liu, W. T., Levy, P., Zhang, M.-Y., Katzman, R., Lung, C.-T., Wong, S.-C., Wang, Z.-Y., & Qu, G.-Y. (1989). Cognitive impairment among elderly adults in Shanghai, China. *Journal of Gerontology: Social Sciences, 44,* S97–106. (Chap 19)

Yussen, S. R., & Kane, P. T. (1985). Children's concept of intelligence. In S. R. Yussen (Ed.), *The growth of reflection in children.* New York: Academic Press. (Chap 12)

Zahn-Waxler, C., Radke-Yarrow, M., Wagner, E., & Chapman, M. (1992). Development of concern for others. *Developmental Psychology, 28,* 126–136. (Chap 8)

Zahn-Waxler, C., Robinson, J., & Emde, R. (1991, April). *The development and heritability of empathy.* Poster presented at the meeting of the Society for Research in Child Development, Seattle, WA. (Chap 8)

Zajonc, R. B. (1983). Validating the confluence model. *Psychological Bulletin, 93,* 457–480. (Chap 9)

Zarit, S. H. (1980). *Aging and mental disorders.* New York: Free Press. (Chap 19)

Zeanah, C., & Anders, T. (1987). Subjectivity in parent-infant relationships: A discussion of internal working models. *Infant Mental Health Journal, 8,* 237–250. (Chap 4)

Zelazo, P. R. (1983). The development of walking. *Journal of Motor Behavior, 15,* 99–137. (Chaps 4, 5)

Zeldin, R., Small, S., & Savin-Williams, R. (1982). Prosocial interaction in two mixed-sex adolescent groups. *Child Development, 53,* 1492–1498. (Chap 13)

Zigler, E. (1980). Controlling child abuse: Do we have the knowledge and/or the will? In G. Gerbner, C. J. Ross, & E. Zigler (Eds.), *Child abuse: An agenda for action.* New York: Oxford University Press. (Chap 9)

Zigler, E., & Hall, N. W. (1989). Physical child abuse in America: Past, present, and future. In D. Cicchetti & V. Carlson (Eds.), *Child maltreatment.* New York: Cambridge University Press. (Chap 9)

Zill, N. (1989, Winter). U.S. children and their families: Current condition and recent trends, 1989. *SRCD Newsletter,* pp. 1–3. (Chap 15)

Zimiles, H., & Lee, V. (1991). Adolescent family structure and educational progress. *Developmental Psychology, 27,* 314–320. (Chap 9)

Zimmerman, B. J. (1989). A social cognitive view of self-regulated academic learning. *Journal of Educational Psychology, 81*, 329–339. (Chap 12)

Zsembik, B. A., & Singer, A. (1990). The problem of defining retirement among minorities: The Mexican Americans. *Gerontologist, 30*, 749–757. (Chap 20)

Zucker, R. A. (1987). The four alcoholisms. In *Nebraska symposium on motivation* (Vol. 14). Lincoln: University of Nebraska Press. (Chap 15)

Zuckerman, D. M., & Zuckerman, B. S. (1985). Television's impact on children. *Pediatrics, 75*, 233–240. (Chap 10)

PERMISSIONS ACKNOWLEDGMENTS

Figure 1.2 From M. Main and G. George, "Responses of Abused and Disadvantaged Toddlers to Distress in Agemates: A Study in the Day Care Setting," *Developmental Psychology,* 21 (1985), p. 410. Copyright 1985 by the American Psychological Association. Reprinted by permission of the author.

Figure 3.3 From I. Gottesman, *Minnesota Symposia on Child Psychology,* vol. 8, edited by Anne D. Pick, University of Minnesota Press. Copyright © 1974 by the University of Minnesota.

Table 3.1 From D. C. Rowe and R. Plomin, "The Burt Controversy: A Comparison of Burt's Data on IQ with Data from Other Studies," *Behavior Genetics,* 8, 1978. Reprinted by permission of Plenum Publishing Corporation.

Table 3.2 From L. Willerman, "Effects of Families on Intellectual Development," *American Psychologist,* 34 (1979), pp. 923–929. Copyright 1979 by the American Psychological Association. Reprinted with permission of the author.

Table 3.3 From J. C. Birnholz and B. R. Benacerraf, "The Development of Human Fetal Hearing," *Science,* 222 (1983), pp. 516–518. Copyright 1983 by the American Association for the Advancement of Science. Reprinted with permission of Drs. J. C. Birnholz and B. R. Benacerraf.

Figure 3.5 Adapted from "The 'Stress' of Being Born," by Hugo Lagercrantz and Theodore A. Slokin, *Scientific American,* April 1986. Copyright © 1986 by Scientific American, Inc. All rights reserved.

Figure 3.6 From K. L. Moore, *Before We Are Born,* 1989. Philadelphia, W. B. Saunders Co. Reprinted by permission.

Figure 4.1 From R. G. Campos, "Soothing Pain-elicited Distress in Infants with Swaddling and Pacifiers," *Child Development,* 60 (1989), p. 788. © The Society for Research in Child Development, Inc.

Figure, p. 99 From J. E. Steiner, "Facial Expressions in Response to Taste and Smell Stimulation," in H. W. Reese and L. P. Lipsett, (eds.), *Advances in Child Development and Behavior,* vol. 13, 1979. Reprinted by permission of Academic Press.

Figure 4.2 From T. M. Field, B. Healy, S. Goldstein, and M. Guthertz, "Behavior-state Matching and Synchrony in Mother-infant Interactions of Nondepressed Versus Depressed Dyads," *Developmental Psychology,* 26 (1990), p. 10. Copyright 1990 by the American Psychological Association. Reprinted by permission.

Figure 5.1 From C. M. Jackson, "Some Aspects of Form and Growth," in W. J. Robbins, S. Brody, A. F. Hogan, C. M. Jackson, and C. W. Green, (eds.), *Growth.* Copyright 1929. Reprinted by permission of Yale University Press.

Figure 5.3 Adapted from A. Prader, J. M. Tanner, and G. A. Von Harneck, "Catch-up Growth Following Illness or Starvation: An Example of Developmental Canalization in Man," *Journal of Pediatrics,* 26 (1963). Reprinted by permission of C. V. Mosby Co.

Figure, p. 117 From H. T. Chugani and M. E. Phelps, "Maturational Changes in Cerebral Function in Infants Determined by [18]FDG Positron Emission Tomography," *Science,* 231 (1986), p. 841. Copyright 1986 by the American Association for the Advancement of Science.

Figure 5.4 From J. L. Conel, *The Postnatal Development of the Human Cerebral Cortex,* vols. 1–6, 1939–1959. Reprinted by permission of Harvard University Press.

Figure 5.8 From K. Connolly and M. Dalgleish, "The Emergence of a Tool-using Skill in Infancy," *Developmental Psychology,* 25 (1989), p. 898. Copyright 1990 by the American Psychological Association. Reprinted by permission.

Figure 6.1 From R. L. Fantz, "The Origins of Form Perception," *Scientific American,* May 1961. Copyright © 1961 by Scientific American, Inc. All rights reserved.

Figure 6.2 From D. Maurer and P. Salapatek, "Developmental Changes in the Scanning of Faces by Infants," *Child Development,* 47 (1976), pp. 523–527. © The Society for Research in Child Development, Inc.

Figure 6.3 From J. Morton, M. J. Johnson, and D. Maurer, "On the Reasons for Newborns' Responses to Faces," *Infant Behavior and Development,* 13 (1990), pp. 99–103. Stimuli from K. A. Kleiner, "Amplitude and Phase Spectra as Indices of Infant's Pattern Preferences," *Infant Behavior and Development,* 10 (1987), pp. 49–59. Reprinted with permission from Ablex Publishing Corporation.

Figure 6.5 From I. V. Kalnins and J. S. Bruner, "The Coordination of Visual Observation and Instrumental Behavior in Early Infancy," *Perception,* 2 (1973), pp. 307–314.

Figure 6.6 Adapted from M. R. Lepper, D. Greene, and R. E. Nisbett, "Undermining Children's Intrinsic Interest with Extrinsic Rewards: A Test of the 'Overjustification' Hypothesis," *Journal of Personality and Social Psychology,* 18 (1973), pp. 129–137. Copyright 1973 by the American Psychological Association. Adapted by permission of the author.

Figure, p. 147 From A. N. Meltzoff and M. K. Moore, "Imitation of Facial and Manual Gestures by Human Neonates," *Science,* 198 (1977), pp. 75–78. Copyright 1977 by The American Association for the Advancement of Science.

Figure 6.7 From E. V. Linde, B. A. Morrongiello, and C. K. Rovee-Collier, "Determinants of Retention in 8-week-old Infants," *Developmental Psychology,* 21 (1985), p. 609. Copyright 1985 by the American Psychological Association. Reprinted by permission of the author.

Figure 6.8 Adapted from J. H. Flavell, S. G. Shipstead, and K. Croft, "Young Children's Knowledge about Visual Perception: Hiding Objects from Others," *Child Development,* 49 (1978), p. 1209. © by the Society for Research in Child Development, Inc.

Quote, Ch. 6 Excerpt from J. Piaget, *The Origins of Intelligence in Children,* International Universities Press, 1952.

Figure 7.1 From B. Younger, "Infants' Detection of Correlations Among Feature Categories," *Child Development,* 61, (1990), p. 616. © The Society for Research in Child Development, Inc.

Table 7.2 Adapted from *The Acquisition of Language: The Study of Developmental Psycholinguistics* by David McNeill. Copyright © 1970 by David McNeill. Reprinted by permission of HarperCollins Publishers.

Figure 7.2 From P. Menyuk, *The Acquisition and Development of Language,* © 1971, p. 62. Adapted by permission of Prentice-Hall, Inc., Englewood Cliffs, New Jersey.

Figure 8.1 Adapted from H. R. Schaffer and P. E. Emerson, "The Development of Social Attachment in Infancy," *Monographs of the Society for Research in Child Development,* 29 (1964). © The Society for Research in Child Development, Inc.

Table 8.2 Adapted from M. D. S. Ainsworth, M. C. Blehar, E. Waters, and S. Wall, *Patterns of Attachment.* Copyright 1978. Reprinted by permission of Lawrence Erlbaum Associates, Inc.

Figure 9.1 From J. M. Reinisch, "Prenatal Exposure to Synthetic Progestins Increases Potential for Aggression in Humans," *Science,* 211 (1981), p. 1172. Copyright 1981 by the American Association for the Advancement of Science.

Table 9.5 Adapted from J. Kaufman and E. Zigler, "The Intergenerational Transmission of Child Abuse," in D. Cicchetti and V. Carlson, *Child Maltreatment,* 1989, p. 139. Reprinted by permission of Cambridge University Press.

Figure 10.1 From K. A. Dodge and D. R. Somberg, "Hostile Attributional Biases among Aggressive Boys are Exacerbated under Conditions of Threats to the Self," *Child Development,* 58 (1987), p. 218. © The Society for Research in Child Development, Inc.

Figure 10.2 From T. J. Berndt, "Developmental Changes in Conformity to Peers and Parents," *Developmental Psychology,* 15 (1979), pp. 608–615. Copyright 1979 by the American Psychological Association. Reprinted by permission.

Table 10.1 From B. G. Licht and C. S. Dweck, "Determinants of Academic Achievement: The Interaction of Children's Achievement Orientation with Skill Area," *Developmental Psychology,* 20 (1984), pp. 628–636. Copyright 1984 by the American Psychological Association. Reprinted by permission of the author.

Figure 10.4 Adapted from L. D. Eron, L. R. Huesman, M. M. Lefkowitz, and L. O. Walder, "Does Television Cause Aggression?" *American Psychologist,* 27 (1972), pp. 253–263. Copyright 1972 by the American Psychological Association. Adapted by permission of the author.

Table 10.3 From A. L. Harrison, M. N. Wilson, C. J. Pine, S. Q. Chan, and R. Buriel, "Family Ecologies of Ethnic Minority Children," *Child Development,* 61 (1990), p. 350. © The Society for Research in Child Development, Inc.

Table 11.2 Adapted from M. Bullock, "Animism in Childhood Thinking: A New Look at an Old Question," *Developmental Psychol-*

ogy, 21 (1985), p. 222. Copyright 1985 by the American Psychological Association. Adapted by permission of the author.

Figure 11.2 From W. V. Fabricius and L. Cavalier, "The Role of Causal Theories about Memory in Young Children's Memory Strategy Choice," *Child Development,* 60 (1989), pp. 298–308. © The Society for Research in Child Development, Inc.

Figure 11.3 From M. Gauvain and B. Rogoff, "Influence of the Goal on Children's Exploration and Memory of Large-Scale Space," *Developmental Psychology,* 22 (1986), pp. 72–76. Copyright 1986 by the American Psychological Association. Reprinted by permission of the author.

Figure, p. 301 From J. W. Stigler, "'Mental Abacus': The Effect of Abacus Training on Chinese Children's Mental Calculation," *Cognitive Psychology,* 16 (1984), pp. 145–176. Reprinted by permission of Academic Press.

Table 11.3 From T. Lickona, *Moral Development and Behavior.* © 1976. Reprinted by permission of T. Lickona.

Figure 11.4 From A. Colby, L. Kohlbert, J. Gibbs, and M. Leiberman, "A Longitudinal Study of Moral Judgment," *Monographs of the Society for Research in Child Development,* 48 (1983), entire serial no. 200. © The Society for Research in Child Development, Inc.

Figure 11.5 From T. R. Shultz, K. Wright, and M. Schleifer, "Assignment of Moral Responsibility and Punishment," *Child Development,* 57 (1986), pp. 177–184. © The Society for Research in Child Development, Inc.

Figure 12.2 From R. Feuerstein, Y. Rand, M. B. Hoffman, and R. Miller, *Instrumental Enrichment,* 1980. Published by University Park Press.

Figure, p. 325 From H. W. Stevenson, S–Y. Lee, and J. W. Stigler, "Mathematics Achievement of Chinese, Japanese, and American Children," *Science,* 231 (1986), pp. 693–699. Copyright 1986 by the American Association for the Advancement of Science.

Figure 13.1 Adapted from C. R. Austin and R. V. Short, *Reproduction in Mammals, Vol. 3: Hormonal Control of Reproduction,* 2nd Edition, 1984, p. 138. Reprinted by permission of Cambridge University Press.

Figure 13.1 From W. A. Marshall, *Journal of Biosocial Science,* Supplement 2, 1970, pp. 31–41. Reprinted by permission.

Figure 13.2 Reprinted by permission of the publishers from *Fetus into Man* by J. M. Tanner, Cambridge, Mass.: Harvard University Press, Copyright © 1978 by J. M. Tanner.

Figure 13.3 From J. M. Tanner, *Growth at Adolescence,* 2nd Edition, 1962. Reprinted by permission of Blackwell Scientific Publications Ltd.

Figure 13.4 From L. D. Steinberg, "Latchkey Children and Susceptibility to Peer Pressure: An Ecological Analysis," *Developmental Psychology,* 22 (1986), p. 438. Copyright 1986 by the American Psychological Association. Reprinted by permission.

Figure 14.1 After B. Inhelder and J. Piaget, *The Growth of Logical Thinking from Childhood to Adolescence.* © 1958 by Basic Books, Inc. Reprinted by permission of the publisher.

Figure 14.2 From C. M. Leone and M. H. Richards, "Classwork and Homework in Early Adolescence: The Ecology of Achievement," *Journal of Youth and Adolescence,* 18 (1989), p. 538. Reprinted by permission of Plenum Publishing Corporation.

Table 15.4 From L. B. Whitbeck and R. L. Simons, "Life on the Streets: The Victimization of Runaway and Homeless Adolescents," *Youth and Society,* 22 (1990), pp. 108–125, Table 3. Reprinted by permission of Sage Publications, Inc.

Figure, p. 411 From Jane E. Brody, "Youth Suicide: A Common Patter," *The New York Times,* March 12, 1987. Copyright © 1987 by The New York Times Company. Reprinted by permission.

Table 16.1 From L. W. Hoffman and J. D. Mains, "The Value of Children in the United States: A New Approach to the Study of Fertility," *Journal of Marriage and the Family,* 43 (1979), p. 589. Copyrighted 1979 by the National Council on Family Relations, 3989 Central Ave., NE., Suite 550, Minneapolis, MN 55421. Reprinted by permission.

Table 16.2 From H. Markus and P. Nurius, "Possible Selves," *American Psychologist,* 41 (1986), p. 959. Copyright 1986 by the American Psychological Association. Reprinted by permission.

Figure 16.2 From "Young Workers Fall Behind," *The New York Times,* November 27, 1990. Copyright © 1990 by The New York Times Company. Reprinted by permission.

Figure 16.5 From A. S. Fleming, D. N. Ruble, G. L. Flett, and V. Van Wagner, "Adjustment in First-time Mothers: Changes in Mood and Mood Content During the Early Postpartum Months," *Developmental Psychology,* 26 (1990), p. 140. Copyright 1990 by the American Psychological Association. Reprinted by permission.

Figure 16.6 From A. Burns, "Mother-headed Families: An International Perspective and the Case of Australia," *Social Policy Report,* 6 (1992), p. 10. Reprinted by permission of the author.

Figure 17.1 From K. W. Schaie, "Toward a Stage Theory of Adult Cognitive Development," *Journal of Aging and Human Development,* 8 (1977), pp. 129–138. Copyright 1977 by Baywood Publishing Co., Inc.

Figure 17.2 From J. L. Horn, "The Theory of Fluid and Crystallized Intelligence in Relation to Concepts of Cognitive Psychology and Aging in Adulthood," in F. I. M. Craik and S. Trehub (eds.), *Aging and Cognitive Processes,* 1982, p. 267. Reprinted by permission of Plenum Publishing Corporation.

Figure 17.3 From K. W. Schaie, "Intellectual Development in Adulthood," in J. E. Birren and K. W. Schaie, (eds.), *Handbook of the Psychology of Aging,* 3rd Edition, 1990, p. 297. Reprinted by permission of Academic Press.

Figure 18.1 From P. T. Costa, Jr., R. R. McCrae, A. B. Zonderman, H. E. Barbano, B. Lebowitz, and D. M. Larson, "Cross-Sectional Studies of Personality in a National Sample: 2. Stability in Neuroticism, Extraversion, and Openness," *Psychology and Aging.* 1 (1986), p. 148. Copyright 1986 by the American Psychological Association. Reprinted by permission of the author.

Table 18.3 From L. W. Hoffman, K. A. McManus, and Y. Brackbill, "The Value of Children to the Elderly," *International Journal of Aging and Human Development,* 25 (1987), pp. 309–321. Copyright © 1987. Reprinted by permission of the Baywood Publishing Co., Inc.

Figure 19.2b From S. W. Cornelius and A. Caspi, "Everyday Problem Solving in Adulthood and Old Age," *Psychology and Aging,* 2 (1987), pp. 144–153. Copyright 1987 by the American Psychological Association. Reprinted by permission.

Figure 19.3 From T. A. Salthouse and R. L. Babcock, "Decomposing Adult Age Differences in Working Memory," *Developmental Psychology,* 27 (1991), p. 773. Copyright 1991 by the American Psychological Association. Reprinted by permission.

Figure 19.4 From K. W. Schaie and S. L. Willis, "Can Decline in Adult Intellectual Functioning be Reversed?" *Developmental Psychology,* 22 (1986), p. 231. Copyright 1986 by the American Psychological Association. Reprinted by permission.

Figure 20.1 From D. B. Brock, J. M. Gurallnik, and J. A. Brody, "Demography and Epidemiology of Aging in the United States," in E. L. Schneider and J. W. Rowe, (eds.), *Handbook of the Biology of Aging,* 3rd Edition, 1990, p. 8. Reprinted by permission of Academic Press.

Table 20.6 Adapted from S. H. Matthews and J. Sprey, "Adolescents' Relationships with Grandparents: An Empirical Contribution to Conceptual Clarification," *Journal of Gerontology,* 40, (1985), pp. 621–626. Copyright © 1985 The Gerontological Society of America.

Chapter 20 Excerpts from E. B. Palmore, *The Facts on Aging Quiz,* pp. 3–4. Copyright © 1988. Used by permission of Springer Publishing Company, Inc., New York, NY 10012.

Excerpts From *Seasons of Life* by J. Kotre and E. Hall, pp. 83, 141, 143, 182, 290, 331, 346–348. Copyright © 1990 by The Regents of the University of Michigan. By permission of Little, Brown and Company.

NAME INDEX

Index note: *f* after a page number refers to a figure; *t.* to a table.

Cortissoz, M., 69
Costa, P. T., Jr., 487, 488, 513, 552
Coster, W. J., 185
Cotman, C. W., 512
Couchoud, E. A., 208
Courtright, R. D., 326
Covington, M. V., 335
Cowan, C. P., 445–447
Cowan, P. A., 445–447
Coward, R. T., 555
Cowley, G., 442
Cox, M. J., 445
Cox, Martha, 236, 237, 241
Cox, Roger, 236, 237, 241
Coyle, J. T., 517
Craik, F. I. M., 517, 524, 525
Cravioto, J., 125
Crnic, K. A., 447
Crockett, L., 357, 359–361
Crockett, L. J., 388
Croft, K., 158, 159
Crook, Charles K., 94, 99
Crook, T. H., 521, 523
Crosby, Faye F., 435
Cross, C., 271
Cross, D., 158
Cross, D. R., 47, 303
Cross, P. S., 543
Crouter, A., 244
Crouter, A. C., 435
Crumrine, P. L., 232
Csikszentmihalyi, Mihaly, 348, 357, 360
Cultice, J. C., 156
Culver, C., 209
Cumming, Elaine, 540
Cummings, E. Mark, 210
Cundick, B., 347
Cunningham, W. R., 466
Curnow, C., 428
Curran, Nuket, 382
Curtiss, S. R., 184
Cutler, N. E., 540, 553
Cutler, S. J., 555
Cytrynbaum, S., 488

Daehler, M. W., 159
Daher, M., 98
Dalgleish, M., 112, 119, 121
Damasio, A. R., 514
Damon, William, 305, 309, 311
Dan, A. J., 481
Daniel, D. E., 471
Daniels, D., 14
Daniels, P., 447
Dannefer, D., 143
Dannemiller, J. L., 139
Darby, B. L., 78–80
Darrow, C. N., 16, 429–431, 452, 485–488, 502
Darwin, Charles, 21, 30, 39
Das, J. P., 321
Dasen, P. R., 286
Das Gupta, P., 290
Daurio, S. P., 329
Davidson, M., 372
Davidson, W., 265
Davies, D. P., 128
Davis, C. C., 212

Davis, G. C., 484, 549
Davis, Janet M., 154
Dawson, D., 533
Dawson, G. W., 428
Day, J., 297
Day, M. C., 293, 294
Dayton, C. W., 233
Deal, J. E., 355, 356, 451
Dean, L., 543
Deane, K. E., 205
DeAngelis, T., 418
DeCasper, Anthony J., 69, 100, 165
Deci, E. L., 263
Defries, J. C., 102
De Groot, E. V., 336
Deigh, R., 473
DeLeon, P. H., 327
Delgado-Hachey, M., 88
Delicardie, E., 125
DeLoache, Judy S., 159, 160
DeLong, M. R., 514
DeMeis, D. K., 438
Demos, V., 209
Denham, S. A., 208
Dennehey, D. M., 525
Denney, Nancy W., 518, 527
Dennis, Wayne, 129
Dent, C., 356, 357
Derrick, A., 412
Desai, S., 235
Dessonville, C., 513
Devereux, E., 277
de Villiers, J. G., 173, 179
de Villiers, P. A., 173, 179
de Vries, H. A., 481
deVries, M., 102
DeVries, Rheta, 283
Diamond, Adele, 158
Dickinson, G. E., 560
Dick-Read, Grantly, 73
Didow, S. M., 212
Diegmueller, K., 494
Diener, E., 348
Dierker, L. J., 68
Dietz, William H., 126
DiPietro, Janet A., 124
Dishion, T. J., 399, 406, 407
Divine-Hawkins, P., 205
Dixon, Roger A., 457, 458, 467, 468, 523–525, 542
Dobbs, A. R., 521, 522
Doctor, R. M., 526
Dodge, Kenneth A., 45, 253–256, 258
Doe, J., 272
Doehrman, M. J., 347
Doering, S. G., 445
Doka, K. J., 555
Dollard, John, 38
Domittner, G., 551
Donaldson, Margaret, 287
Donnelly, D., 549
Donovan, W. L., 106
Dontas, C., 200
Dornbusch, S., 346
Dornbusch, S. M., 225, 238–240, 352, 355, 356, 365, 416
Dorosz, M., 524
Dorr, Aimee, 268

Douvan, Elizabeth, 349, 359, 396, 398, 441, 442, 491
Dove, H., 130
Dowler, J. K., 77, 80
Dowling, K., 137
Downs, A. Chris, 229
Drabman, R. S., 126, 267
Drake, Samantha, 218
Dreher, M., 92
Drew, J., 82
Drugan, R. C., 545
Duara, R., 512
Dubiner, K., 141
DuBois, D. L., 261
Dubow, E., 268
Dubowitz, L. M. S., 88
Dubowitz, V., 88
Duffy, F. H., 89
Dullea, G., 413
Dumais, S. G., 140
Duncan, P., 346
Duncan, P. D., 352, 416
Dunn, J., 199, 212, 213, 232
Dunn, Judy F., 14
Durant, A., 61
Durant, W., 61
Durrett, M. E., 11, 202
Dusenbury, L., 401, 402
Dustman, R. E., 512
Dvir, R., 204
Dweck, Carole S., 146, 264, 265, 334
Dwyer, K., 356–357

Eakins, D. J., 266
Early, L., 154
Easterbrooks, M. A., 198, 205, 208, 251
Easterlin, R., 418
Eaton, W. O., 264
Ebata, A., 388
Eccles, Jacquelynne S., 228, 229, 263, 265, 328, 350, 355, 388–391
Eckerman, Carol O., 193, 212
Eckert, J. K., 556
Edelman, M. S., 257
Eder, R. A., 305
Edgerton, R. B., 330
Egeland, B., 195, 196
Ehrhardt, A. A., 226
Ehrman, L., 60
Eicher, S., 392
Eichler, L. S., 70, 444
Eichorn, D. H., 20, 464
Eisenberg, N., 208
Eiskovits, Z., 405
Ekerdt, D. J., 547, 548
Elder, G., 272
Elder, G. H., Jr., 10, 20, 271, 272, 365, 366, 407, 418
Elder, J. L., 160
Elias, M. F., 469
Elkind, David, 375
Elliot, E. S., 334
Elliott, D. S., 405
Elliott, Elaine S., 146, 264
Elliott, G. L., 238, 239, 241
Elliott, R., 323
Ellis, S., 11, 46, 381
Elman, J. D., 352

Elmen, J. D., 352, 388, 392
Elmwood, J. M., 383
Elster, A. B., 414
Emde, R., 208
Emde, Robert N., 92
Emerson, P. E., 192f., 202
Emery, C. F., 469
Emmerson, R., 512
Engle, P. L., 125
Enna, B., 265
Enns, J. T., 294
Ensminger, M. E., 407, 501
Entwisle, D. R., 445
Epstein, H. T., 385
Erber, J. T., 510
Erikson, Erik H., 33–36, 50, 123, 207, 215,
    219, 347, 348, 429, 431, 437, 448, 452,
    460, 479, 485, 486, 502, 521, 538, 539,
    549, 557, 560
Erikson, J. M., 549
Eron, L. D., 268
Estes, D., 204
Evans, D., 158
Eyler, F. D., 88

Fabes, R. A., 208
Fabricius, W. V., 297, 298f.
Fafoutis, M., 200
Fagan, J. F. III, 138, 139
Fagot, Beverly I., 210, 227, 229
Fajardo, B., 90
Fajardo, B. F., 202
Falbo, T., 233, 234
Falk, F., 233
Fallon, A., 428
Fantz, Robert L., 137, 138
Farber, E. A., 195, 196
Farlow, M., 514
Farmer, F. F., 359
Farquhar, E., 205
Farrar, M. J., 169
Farrell, W. S., 233
Farrington, D. P., 404
Fauber, R., 355
Faulkner, D., 524
Fausto-Sterling, Anne, 230
Feather, N. T., 388, 399
Featherman, D. L., 540
Fedele, N. M., 445, 446
Feig, E., 239
Fein, Greta G., 77, 80, 123, 124, 203
Feldman, D. H., 327
Feldman, J. F., 143
Feldman, N. S., 252
Feldman, Shirley S., 446, 574
Fenson, L., 172
Ferguson, C. A., 168
Fernald, A., 100, 168
Ferrara, R. A., 154, 285, 295, 302, 321, 330,
    331
Ferretti, R. P., 323, 330
Feshbach, N. D., 262
Feshbach, Seymour, 243, 267
Feuerstein, Reuven, 320, 321
Field, Dorothy, 288, 464, 468, 470, 541
Field, J., 100
Field, Tiffany M., 23, 90, 104, 105, 145, 202
Fields, R. B., 168

Fifer, W. P., 100, 165
Fillenbaum, G. G., 547
Fillion, T. J., 94
Finch, M. D., 434
Finch, M. E., 364, 365
Fincham, F. D., 264, 441
Finck, D. N., 254
Fischer, Anna, 206f.
Fischer, F. W., 331
Fischer, Kurt W., 158, 208
Fisher, D., 90
Fisher, D. M., 98, 122
Fishman, G., 405
Fitch, M., 266
Fitch, S., 574
Flanagan, C., 229, 263, 388, 390
Flanagan, C. A., 271, 272, 366, 397
Flanery, R. C., 30, 257
Flannery, D., 375
Flavell, John H., 4, 8, 44, 149, 158, 159, 283,
    285, 286, 287, 294–297, 303–305, 373,
    374
Flay, B. 356, 357
Fleming, A. S., 446, 447f.
Flett, G. L., 446, 447f.
Flint, M., 482
Fodor, I. G., 496
Fogel, A., 107, 117, 121
Folkman, S., 489, 545
Foos, P. W., 522
Ford, G., 82
Forehand, R., 232, 237, 355
Forrest, J. D., 361, 362, 415, 440
Forssberg, H., 123
Fox, N. A., 103
Fox, N. E., 197
Fox, R., 140
Fraleigh, M. J., 225
Frank, E. S., 361
Frank, L. M., 57
Frankel, G. W., 294
Frankenburg, W. K., 114, 115f.
Freedman, D., 533
Freedman, D. G., 11, 202, 266, 267
Freud, Sigmund, 8, 31–34, 38, 50, 435
Fried, P. A., 79, 80
Friedman, A., 487
Friedman, S., 143f.
Friedrich, Lynette K., 268
Friedrichs, A. G., 303
Frieze, I. H., 433
Frisch, Hannah L., 210
Frisch, Karl von, 30
Frodi, Ann M., 106
Fry, C. L., 543
Fry, C. L., Jr., 305
Fry, P. S., 315
Frye, D., 292
Fu, V. R., 274
Fuchsle, T., 383
Fullilove, M. T., 403
Fullilove, R. F., 403
Fulton, J., 533
Furman, Wyndol, 230, 231, 251, 359, 360
Furson, K. C., 292
Furstenberg, F. F., 499, 501, 502
Furstenberg, Frank, 362, 363, 414, 415
Furstenberg, Frank F., Jr., 413–415, 451

Furth, H. G., 380, 381
Futterman, A., 552

Gaensbauer, T. J., 243
Galambos, N. L., 236, 272, 354, 356, 357
Gallagher, J. J., 326
Gallagher-Thompson, D., 552
Gallistel, C. Randy, 292
Galperin, C. Z., 201
Gambrell, R. D., 482
Ganchrow, J. R., 98
Garbarino, J., 127, 244
Garcia, R., 104
Garcia-Coll, C. T., 201, 202, 273
Garcia-Coll, M., 413
Gardner, Howard, 317, 326, 327
Gardner, W., 299
Gardner, W. P., 193, 195
Garduque, L., 365
Garfinkel, P. E., 416
Garfinkel, R., 435, 436
Garland, A., 412
Garland, J. A., 201
Garner, D. M., 416
Garrod, A., 309
Garza, C., 124–126
Gatz, M., 479, 497, 556
Gaughran, J., 102, 103
Gauvain, Mary, 11, 46, 298–300, 381
Gavin, L. A., 360
Gearhart, M., 293
Gebhard, P. H., 363
Gekoski, M. J., 91
Gelles, R. J., 243
Gelman, D., 218, 238
Gelman, Rochel, 149, 284, 288, 290, 292
Gelman, Susan A., 176, 289, 291
Genie, 184
Gentile, A. M., 113
George, Carol, 13, 243
George, L. K., 547
Germer, M., 195
Gersten, M. S., 185
Gesell, Arnold L., 29, 30, 50, 114
Getchell, N., 123
Getman, C. E., 79
Ghesquire, K., 195
Ghetti, B., 514
Giambra, L. M., 517
Gibbons, L. W., 481
Gibbs, J., 43t., 308, 380
Gibson, Eleanor J., 140, 146, 293
Gibson, R. C., 489, 543, 545, 547
Gibson, R. G., 534
Gilewski, M. J., 552
Gill, S., 364
Gillenwater, J. M., 100
Gillies, P., 383
Gilligan, Carol, 43, 309, 349, 380, 429
Gingold, H., 148
Giudice, S., 385
Gjerde, P. F., 237
Glantz, F. B., 205
Glaser, Barney G., 558
Gleason, Jean Berko, 180, 185
Gleitman, L. R., 169
Glenn, N. D., 450, 554
Glick, P. C., 450, 451

Glickman, N. W., 401
Glusman, M., 176
Goetting, A., 552
Golan, N., 450
Gold, D., 235
Gold, D. T., 552
Gold, Michael, 75
Goldberg, C., 88
Goldberg, E. L., 551
Goldberg, W. A., 198, 205, 447
Goldblatt, P. M., 417
Golden, R., 543
Goldfield, E. C., 121, 122
Goldin, L., 337
Golding, E. R., 445, 446
Goldin-Meadow, S., 177
Goldman, J., 349
Goldman, S. R., 333
Goldman-Rakic, P. S., 116, 117, 165
Goldsmith, H. H., 103, 196
Goldsmith, R. E., 542
Goldstein, S., 104, 105
Goleman, D., 327
Gomez-Palacio, M., 321
Goodall, M. M., 121
Goodman, M., 554
Gopnik, A., 170
Gordon, A., 402
Gordon, C., 487, 541, 543
Gordon, Ruth, 538
Gorman, K. S., 125
Gortmaker, S. L., 126
Gosnell, M., 440
Gottesman, I., 61*f.*
Gottfried, A. W., 121, 141
Gottlieb, G., 98, 112, 117
Gottman, J. M., 237
Gould, R. E., 492, 493
Gould, Roger L., 430, 452, 486, 487, 502
Graber, J. A., 388
Graef, R., 348
Graham, S., 335–337, 407
Graham, S. E., 128
Gralinski, J. H., 207, 208
Gray, K. D., 225, 238–240, 355, 356
Gray, W., 375
Greco, C., 154, 159
Green, D. L., 365
Green, F. L., 283
Green, J. A., 167
Green, Melanie, 69
Green, T. M., 354
Greenberg, B. S., 269
Greenberg, M. T., 182, 447
Greenberger, E., 364, 365
Greene, D., 145
Greenough, W. T., 117, 118, 386
Greer, L. D., 269
Gribbon, K., 469
Griesler, P., 154
Griffin, D., 543
Griffiths, R., 114
Grobstein, C., 64, 66, 68
Grolnick, W. S., 336
Gross, J., 494
Gross, R., 346
Gross, R. T., 352, 416

Grossman, F. K., 70, 444–446
Grossmann, K., 196, 197, 276
Grossmann, K. E., 196, 197
Grotevant, H. D., 349, 351
Gruendel, J. M., 175
Guberman, S. R., 293
Guidubaldi, J., 239
Guilford, J. P., 317
Gunderson, V., 76
Gunnar, S., 196
Guralnik, J. M., 533, 534*f.*
Gurland, B. J., 543
Gustafson, G. E., 106, 107, 167
Guthertz, M., 104, 105
Gutmann, David L., 430, 431, 448, 452, 486, 487, 502, 543
Guttman, E., 405
Guy, L., 104

Haake, R. J., 160
Haan, N., 20, 433, 487
Habel, L., 79
Hagan, M. S., 355, 356, 451
Hagekull, B., 195
Hager, M., 440
Hagestad, Gunhild O., 433, 494, 496, 497, 499, 533
Haglund, Karl, 574
Hahn, S. R., 71
Haight, B. K., 557
Hainline, L., 138, 239
Haith, Marshall M., 101, 137, 138
Hall, David, 136
Hall, E., 6, 7, 24, 33, 34*t.*, 126, 263*f.*, 273, 314, 342, 345, 363, 379, 382, 387, 413, 426, 428, 429, 435, 448, 479, 485, 489, 491, 496, 513, 532, 533, 535, 539, 549, 557
Hall, Elizabeth, 136
Hall, G. Stanley, 21, 30
Hall, J. W., 296
Hall, N. W., 242, 244
Hall, T., 402
Hallfrisch, J., 537
Halsted, N., 100
Halton, A., 80, 81
Hames, C. G., 534
Hamilton, Stephen F., 365, 366
Hammer, D., 126, 232
Hammond, K., 331
Hansen, W. B., 356, 357
Hanson, C. L., 408
Hardy, Kimberly, 69
Hareven, T., 22
Harkins, D. A., 121
Harkins, S. W., 511
Harkness, S., 276
Harlow, Harry F., 191, 200, 254
Harlow, Margaret K., 191
Harlow, S. D., 551
Harmon, S. M., 482, 536
Harmoni, R., 383, 384
Harold, R., 229, 263, 388, 390
Harold, R. D., 391
Harper, L. V., 244
Harrell, J. E., 23
Harrington, A. F., 269
Harris, K. L., 106, 107
Harris, Paul L., 42, 158

Harrison, A. O., 273–275
Harrison, H. R., 77
Hart, C. H., 223
Hart, D., 305
Hart, Daniel, 309, 311
Hart, R., 228
Harter, S., 207, 334, 375, 378
Hartka, E., 433, 487
Hartley, Alan A., 469, 516, 519
Hartup, Willard W., 212, 251, 252, 256–258, 261, 360
Harvey, O. J., 259
Harwood, R. L., 202
Haskett, R. F., 76
Hatano, G., 301
Hatchett, Shirley, 441, 442
Hauser, S. T., 354
Hawtin, P., 383
Hay, Dale F., 193, 212
Hayne, H., 154
Haynes-Clements, L. A., 23
Healy, B., 104, 105
Heath, S. B., 324
Hebb, Donald O., 508, 521
Heckhausen, J., 542
Hedricks, C., 481
Heer, D. M., 232
Heidrich, S. M., 527
Heiens, R. A., 542
Heim, L., 444
Heimann, M., 147
Heise, D., 465
Helson, R., 489
Helu, B., 125
Hendershot, G., 533
Henderson, V. K., 445
Henggeler, Scott W., 406, 408
Henry, William E., 540
Hernandez, D. J., 236
Herrera, M. G., 126, 127
Herron, J., 118
Hersch, S., 408
Hertzbereger, S., 243
Hertzog, C., 18, 21, 512, 523–525
Herzog, A. E., 542
Hess, Robert D., 262, 270, 271, 276, 322, 323
Hess, V. I., 268
Hetherington, E. Mavis, 236, 237, 239, 241, 354–356, 450, 451
Hevesi, D., 415
Hiebert, E. H., 331
Hiebert, J., 333
Higdon, J. V., 79
Hill, J. P., 354
Hill, K. T., 264
Hill, R., 244
Himes, C. L., 533
Hinde, R. A., 30, 258
Hinrichs, J. V., 526
Hirsch, B. J., 261
Hirsh-Pasek, K., 168
Hiscock, M., 118
Hobart, C. J., 524
Hochschild, A., 229
Hock, E., 438
Hodgen, G. D., 79
Hodges, J., 200
Hoeffel, E. C., 377

Hoff, C., 442
Hofferth, S. L., 205, 415
Hoff-Ginsberg, E., 169
Hoffman, C., 499
Hoffman, J., 69
Hoffman, Lois Wladis, 11, 14, 62, 190, 201, 205, 206, 219, 227, 229, 231–234, 237, 244, 265, 270, 271, 275, 323, 356, 366, 413, 432, 435, 438, 439, 446, 447, 489, 495–498, 553
Hoffman, M. B., 320–321
Hoffman, Martin L., 4, 208, 220–223, 305
Hofsten, Claes von, 120, 121
Hokoda, A., 264
Holaday, D. A., 88, , 89t.
Holahan, C. K., 542
Holden, C., 411
Holden, G. W., 251
Holinger, P. C., 419
Holland, John L., 436
Hollander, M., 180
Holliday, S. G., 519, 520
Hollier, E. A., 355, 356, 451
Hollis, J., 412
Holloway, Susan D., 262, 271, 322
Holm, K., 481
Holmes, D., 545
Holmes, Oliver Wendell, 69
Holt, R., 208
Homel, P., 102, 103
Honig, A. S., 125
Honzik, M. P., 20, 464
Hood, W. R., 258
Hopkins, B., 114, 131
Hopkins, J., 104, 105
Hopps, K., 414
Horn, J. M., 102
Horn, John L., 316, 463
Horowitz, F. D., 88, 91, 142
Horton, R. W., 267
Horton, W., 126
Howanitz, P., 125
Howard, A., 489
Howard, Kenneth I., 346, 351, 361, 398, 399, 407
Howe, N., 213
Howes, Carollee, 172, 212, 262
Howrigan, G. A., 204
Hoyer, W. J., 460
Hoyle, Sally G., 260
Hoyt, J. D., 303
Hsieh, C. C., 481
Hsu, C.-C., 325
Hsu, J., 234
Hsu, L. K. G., 417
Hubel, D. H., 118
Hudley, C., 407
Hudson, J., 177
Hudson, J. I., 418
Hudson, R. B., 540
Hudson, R. L., 545
Huesmann, L. R., 268
Huizinga, D., 405
Hulicka, Irene M., 526
Hultsch, David F., 523–525
Humphreys, Anne P., 254
Humphreys, M. S., 296
Hunt, C. E., 128

Hunt, J. V., 464
Hunt, M., 493
Hunter, A. G., 501
Hunter, Alberta, 538
Hunter, M. A., 138
Husaini, B. A., 543
Huston, A. C., 211, 227–229, 239, 260, 265, 266, 269, 270, 364
Hutchinson, C. A., 102, 103
Huyck, Margaret H., 486, 491
Hyde, J., 434, 486–487
Hyde, R. T., 481
Hyman, B. T., 514
Hymel, S., 252

Iannotti, Ronald J., 210
Ievoli, R., 241
Inhelder, Bärbel, 286, 291, 376, 377f.
Ireson, C., 364
Israel, A. C., 126
Isseroff, A., 116, 117
Istvan, J., 80
Ivey, P. K., 204
Izard, C. E., 138
Izumi, Shingechijo, 535

Jackson, C. M., 113f.
Jackson, J. S., 240, 273, 534
Jacob, R., 526
Jacobs, B., 541
Jacobs, J., 229, 263, 388, 390, 437
Jacobs, J. E., 155, 391
Jacobson, A. M., 354
Jacobson, J. L., 77, 80, 168
Jacobson, Lenore, 262
Jacobson, Sandra W., 77, 80, 147
Jacobvitz, D., 197
Jagacinski, C. M., 335
James, L. S., 88, 89t.
James, William, 88
James-Ortiz, S., 401, 402
Janos, P. M., 326, 329
Jansen, A. A. J., 125
Jarvie, G. J., 126
Jarvik, L. F., 469, 513
Jarvis, P. E., 305
Jaskir, J., 208
Jeffrey, B., 490
Jelliffe, D. B., 125
Jelliffe, E. F. P., 125
Jenkins, V. Y., 139
Jennings, M., 399
Jensen, Arthur R., 324
Jensen, L. C., 347
Ji, Guiping, 234
Jiao, Shulan, 234
Jing, Quicheng, 234
Jinghua, C., 234
Joachim, C. L., 76
Jobes, D. A., 396, 410–412, 418
Joffe, L. S., 102
Johnson, C., 418
Johnson, C. A., 356, 357
Johnson, C. L., 273, 545
Johnson, C. N., 297
Johnson, D. H., 57
Johnson, E. M., 77
Johnson, Jennifer, 69

Johnson, K., 69
Johnson, K. E., 176, 181
Johnson, M. J., 139
Johnson, P. B., 433
Johnson, V. E., 484
Johnson, W., 208
Johnston, J., 433
Johnston, L. D., 403–405f.
Johnston, M. C., 79
Johnston, P. H., 332
Johnstone, J., 118
Johnstone, J. R., 240
Jonas, J. M., 418
Jones, E., 337
Jones, R. S., 330
Joseph, N., 131
Judd, C. M., 352
Judge, P., 100
Jung, Carl G., 486, 502, 539, 540, 560
Jungblut, A., 472
Jusczyk, P. W., 99, 100, 165, 168

Kagan, Jerome, 38, 193, 201
Kagay, M. R., 440
Kahana, E., 556
Kahn, J., 362
Kahn, R. L., 537
Kail, R., 153, 294, 295, 297
Kaler, S. R., 76, 79
Kalish, Richard, 59
Kalnins, Ilze V., 143, 144f.
Kameoka, V., 234
Kamin, L. J., 323
Kandel, D., 392
Kane, R. A., 555, 556
Kane, R. L., 555, 556
Kantrowitz, B., 131, 448, 451
Kaplan, H., 130
Kaplan, M., 521, 523, 526
Kaplan, N., 194
Kaplan, O. J., 536
Karangelis, K., 200
Kariuki, P. W., 487
Karsh, E., 375
Kashiwagi, K., 276
Kastenbaum, R., 543, 558, 560
Kates, J., 444
Katz, L. F., 237
Katzman, R., 513
Kaufman, A. S., 323
Kaufman, J., 242t., 243, 245
Kausler, Donald H., 469, 525
Kavrell, A., 391
Kaye, K., 79, 105
Keating, D. P., 149, 292, 384, 385, 387
Keating, Norah C., 490, 548
Kedar-Voivodas, G., 262
Kee, D. W., 121
Keeney, T. J., 285
Keil, F. C., 149, 290
Kellam, S. G., 501
Keller, M., 378
Kelley, M. L., 274
Kelly, J. B., 494
Kelly, J. R., 545
Kelso, J. A. S., 117, 121
Kemler-Nelson, D. G., 168
Kempe, Henry C., 243

Lin, S.-L., 450
Lindauer, B. K., 44, 295–297, 303
Lindberg, L., 195
Linde, Eleanor Vander, 146, 154, 155f.
Lindner, M. S., 355, 356, 451
Lingenfelter, M., 269
Linn, J. G., 543
Linn, M. C., 386, 387
Lippincott, E. C., 267
Lipsitt, Lewis P., 99, 128
Lipton, E. L., 94
Lissenden, J., 82
Lister, G., 125
Little, T. D., 327
Litvin, S. J., 499
Litwak, E., 552
Liu, W. T., 513
Livson, N., 346, 347
Lloyd, Barbara, 210
Lockshin, R. A., 535
Loebl, J. H., 252
Loehlin, J. C., 102
Loewen, E. R., 524, 525
Loftus, E. F., 263f.
Logue, B. J., 548
Lollis, S., 211
Lomax, R. G., 331
London, E. D., 512
London, K. A., 441, 449, 450
Long, N., 237, 355
Long, Odilon, 538
Longino, C. F., Jr., 555, 556
Loomis, B., 482
Lord, Dick, 495
Lorenz, F. O., 271, 407
Lorenz, Konrad, 30
Losoff, M., 357, 359–361
Lounsbury, M. L., 107
Love, S., 418
Lowe, J., 292
Luborsky, M., 554
Lucas, A., 125
Lucker, G. W., 325
Lung, C.-T., 513
Lutkenhaus, P., 197
Lynch, J. H., 350, 352
Lynch, M. E., 354
Lynn, R., 323
Lyon, S. M., 556
Lyons, N. P., 380

McAnarney, E. R., 414
McAnulty, G. B., 89
McCall, P. L., 410
McCall, Robert B., 92
McCartney, K., 60
McCarthy, D., 178f.
McCarty, M. E., 137
McCloskey, C. L., 45, 253
McCluskey, K. A., 412
Maccoby, E. E., 221, 224, 225, 258
McCrae, R. R., 487, 488, 552
McCunney, N., 23
McDevitt, T. M., 322, 323
MacDonald, K., 200, 201
McDowd, J. M., 517
McGee, L. M., 331
McGue, M., 9

McGuigan, K., 356, 357
McGuinness, Diane, 229
McGuire, K. D., 260
McIntyre, C. W., 303
MacIver, D., 229, 263, 388–391
McKee, B., 16, 429–431, 452, 485–488, 502
McKenna, James J., 128
McKinley, M., 208
MacKinnon, C. E., 238
Macklin, E. D., 441–443, 492
Macklin, M. C., 269
McLanahan, S., 554
McLaughlin, H., 201
McLean, J. E., 323
McLoyd, V. C., 201, 244, 271, 272, 352, 420, 448
McManus, K. A., 366, 497, 498t., 553
Macnamara, J., 169
McNeill, David, 174t.
McNew, S., 172
McRae, J. A., Jr., 490
McVey, Kelly A., 297
Madden, D. J., 469, 511
Maddox, G. L., 550
Madonna, 413
Madsen, M., 74
Maggs, J. L., 236, 356, 357
Magnusson, D., 347
Maier, S. F., 545
Main, Mary, 13, 194, 198, 243
Maioni, T., 124
Makin, Jennifer W., 99
Malatesta, C. Z., 106, 209
Malina, R. M., 344
Maloney, M. J., 416, 417
Mamay, P. D., 269
Mandler, J. M., 155, 290
Mangan, G., 61
Mangelsdorf, S., 196, 201, 244, 271, 352, 448
Mangen, D. J., 553
Manis, J. D., 366, 413, 432, 446
Mann, B. J., 406
Mann, L., 383, 384
Mannell, R., 554
Manton, K. G., 534
Maratos, Michael P., 177, 179, 184, 185
Maratos, O., 200
Marcia, James E., 348
Marcus, Gary F., 180
Marcus, J., 407
Marcus, Janet, 257
Marcus, M. M., 261
Marcus, T. L., 271
Markides, K. S., 240, 273
Markman, Ellen M., 176, 291, 292, 374
Markovits, H., 377
Markstrom-Adams, C., 274, 350
Markus, H. R., 227, 433, 542
Marlow, L., 354
Maroudas, C., 292
Marsh, H. W., 334
Marsh, R. W., 385
Marshall, H. H., 263
Marshall, Victor W., 553, 556, 558, 560
Marshall, W. A., 343f.
Marsiglio, W., 549
Martin, C. E., 363
Martin, D. C., 79, 80

Martin, J. A., 221, 224, 225, 352, 416
Martorell, R., 125
Maruyama, G., 232
Marvin, R. S., 182
Marx, J. L., 514, 515
Mason, J., 331
Mason, W., 536
Masters, J. C., 251
Masters, W. H., 484
Masur, E. F., 303
Matas, Leah, 193, 196, 197
Matheson, C. C., 172
Matias, R., 104, 105
Matsuzawa, T., 512
Mattessich, P., 244
Matthew, A., 121
Matthews, K. A., 468
Matthews, S. H., 554
Maurer, D., 138, 139
Maxwell, S. E., 336
Mayer, J., 417
Mazzie, C., 168
Mead, M., 6, 71
Meadow, K. P., 98
Measel, C. P., 90
Mebert, C. J., 102
Medina, R. G., 17
Medrich, E. A., 233, 238
Meece, J. L., 389, 391
Mehler, J., 100
Mehta, Y. B., 346
Meisels, S. J., 67, 81, 82, 89
Meltzoff, Andrew N., 146, 147f., 170
Mendelsohn, J., 350
Menken, J., 495
Menuhin, Yehudi, 327
Menyuk, P., 174, 175f.
Mercer, J. R., 321, 322
Mercer, R. T., 447
Meredith, H. V., 127
Meredith, W., 464
Merriman, W. E., 176
Merryman, P. W., 446
Mertz, D. L., 333
Mertz, M. F., 555
Mervis, C. B., 176, 181
Messenger, L., 451
Meyer, B., 229
Michael, R. T., 235
Michel, G. F., 121
Micka, J. C., 359
Midgley, C., 229, 263, 388–391
Miernyk, W. H., 533
Mikus, K., 445
Miller, George, 183
Miller, K. E., 388
Miller, N., 232
Miller, Neal E., 38
Miller, P. A., 208
Miller, P. H., 302
Miller, P. M., 201
Miller, R., 320, 321
Miller, S. A., 286
Miller, W., 231
Mills, J. L., 57
Millsap, R., 433, 487
Millsap, R. E., 541
Milofsky, E., 36, 429, 437, 485

Parke, Ross D., 12, 197, 198, 231, 242, 254, 268, 276, 502
Parker, J. G., 250, 251, 256, 260, 359
Parmelee, Arthur H., Jr., 92, 116, 117, 125
Parmelee, P. A., 555
Parnes, H., 548
Parsons, J. E., 252, 433
Paton, J., 90
Patrick, R., 488
Patterson, Charlotte J., 305
Patterson, G. R., 399, 406, 407
Paul, C. E., 546, 547
Pavlov, Ivan P., 37
Peake, P. K., 382
Pearce, K. A., 518
Pearson, J. L., 501
Pearson, T. A., 450
Pecheux, M.-G., 201
Pechinski, J. M., 469
Pedersen, F., 245
Pedersen, J., 212
Pederson, D. R., 160, 195
Pellegrini, A. D., 254
Pellegrino, J. W., 333
Pennebaker, J. W., 11, 202
Peplau, L. A., 443
Pepler, D. J., 231
Perlez, J., 415
Perlmutter, Marion, 143, 154–156, 273, 299, 300, 302, 415, 428, 435, 459, 463, 466–468, 470, 491, 496, 513, 520, 521, 523, 526, 535
Pernoll, M. L., 78
Perrucci, C., 272
Perry, D. G., 38, 229
Perry, J. D., 238
Perry, L. C., 229
Person, D., 521, 523, 526
Peskin, H., 346, 347
Peters, M. F., 274
Petersen, A., 357, 359–361, 391
Petersen, A. C., 343–346, 354, 361, 386–388
Petersen, R., 123
Peterson, J., 552
Pettit, G. S., 45, 253, 256, 258
Pfeiffer, E., 484, 549
Phelps, Michael E., 117
Philip, J., 74
Phillips, S. J., 123
Phinney, J. S., 274, 350
Phinney, V. G., 347
Piaget, Jacqueline, 149, 153
Piaget, Jean, 8, 16, 39–42, 44, 46, 50, 148–153, 157, 158, 161, 282, 286–292, 299, 304, 306–307, 310, 311, 315, 316, 372, 376, 377, 392, 459, 460, 469, 473
Piaget, Laurent, 149, 151–153
Piaget, Lucienne, 149, 151, 152, 289
Piasecki, M., 519
Picasso, Pablo, 538
Pick, A. D., 294
Pickar, D., 526
Pimley, S., 489, 545
Pine, C. J., 273–275
Pinker, S., 180
Pintrich, P. R., 336
Piper, A. I., 556
Pisoni, D. B., 99, 100, 165

Pittman, L., 295
Pleck, J. H., 240
Plomin, R., 14, 60–62, 102
Plunkett, J. W., 67, 81, 82, 89
Pogash, R., 519
Pollack, W. S., 445, 446
Pollins, L. D., 329
Pollit, D. F., 233
Pollitt, Ernesto, 124–126
Pomeroy, W. B., 363
Ponds, R. W. M., 517
Poole, M. E., 383
Poon, L. W., 521, 523
Pope, H. G., Jr., 418
Porter, Richard H., 99
Post, G. M., 519
Poulson, C. L., 146
Power, C., 43t., 383, 384
Power, T. G., 274
Powers, J. L., 365, 366
Powers, S. I., 354
Prader, A., 116f.
Pratto, D. J., 236
Prechtl, H. F. R., 96
Presburg, H. J., 57
Pressley, M., 336, 524
Price, D. L., 514
Price, G. G., 156, 322
Prinz, P. N., 512, 514
Probber, J., 60
Puglisi, J. T., 523
Puttalaz, M., 253

Qu, G.-Y., 513
Quayhagen, M., 515
Quayhagen, M. P., 515
Quilter, R., 517
Quinitana, S. M., 375
Quinn, J. F., 547

Rabbitt, P. M. A., 518, 519
Rabinowitz, J. C., 523
Rabinowitz, M., 80
Radin, N., 198, 238
Radke-Yarrow, Marian, 148, 208, 210, 269
Ragozin, A., 447
Rahn, C., 201
Raj, M. H., 362
Rajecki, D. W., 30, 257
Rakowski, W., 556
Ramanan, J., 234
Ramey, Craig T., 146
Ramsay, D., 200
Rand, Y., 320, 321
Rapaport, S. I., 512
Rathbun, C., 201
Rauh, V. A., 413
Rebok, G. W., 525
Reed, Candy, 342, 387
Reedy, M. N., 434, 487, 541, 543
Reese, H. W., 21, 517
Reff, M. E., 535
Reid, J. B., 406
Reinisch, J. M., 76, 230, 231f.
Reisenzein, R., 556
Rellinger, E., 336
Rempel, J., 554
Repetti, Rena L., 435

Resnik, Lauren B., 331
Rest, James R., 43, 308, 309
Reuman, D., 229, 263, 388, 390
Reuman, D. A., 388, 389, 391
Revelle, G. L., 160
Reynolds, C. R., 323
Rheingold, Harriet L., 193
Ricco, R. B., 291
Rice, M. L., 266
Richards, D. D., 315
Richards, M. H., 389
Richards, P., 11
Richardson, D. W., 345
Richardson, G. S., 536
Richardson, J. L., 356, 357
Richardson, R. A., 354
Richardson, T. M., 329
Richman, Amy L., 201, 204
Richman, C. L., 295
Richmond, J. B., 94
Rickards, A., 82
Riddick, C. C., 527
Ridley, C. A., 23
Ridley-Johnson, R., 98, 122
Rierdan, J., 346
Riese, M. L., 102
Rieser-Danner, L. A., 139
Riffle, N. L., 79
Rikli, Roberta, 469
Riley, J. W., Jr., 548
Riley, M. W., 548
Rine, J., 537
Ripp, C., 243
Ritter, J. M., 139
Ritter, P., 346
Ritter, P. L., 225, 352, 416
Rivers, C., 431, 488, 497
Rizzo, T. A., 381
Robbins, M. A., 469
Roberton, M. A., 123
Roberts, D. F., 225
Roberts, E., 362
Roberts, G., 446
Roberts, J., 90
Roberts, P., 430
Roberts, Ralph J., Jr., 305
Robertson, Steven S., 68, 89
Robinson, Halbert B., 329, 330
Robinson, J., 208
Robinson, N. M., 326, 329, 330, 447
Robinson, P. K., 546, 547
Roche, Alex F., 126
Roche, J. P., 361
Rockwell, R., 272
Rodeheaver, D., 517
Rodick, J. D., 408
Rodin, Judith, 24, 126, 416, 417, 543–545, 557
Rodman, H., 236
Roggman, L. A., 139
Rogoff, Barbara, 11, 45, 298–300, 381
Rogosch, F. A., 255, 256
Rohrkemper, M. M., 333, 336
Roizen, J., 233, 238
Roland, E. H., 79
Romanoff, R., 268
Ronald, N., 412
Roodin, P. A., 460

SUBJECT INDEX

Index note: *f* after a page number refers to a figure; *t*. to a table.

Health proxies, 559
Hearing:
   in later adulthood, 511
   in neonates, 71t., 99–100
Hemophilia, 60
Heterozygous offspring, 59
Holistic development, 5
Holophrases, 174
Homeless runaways, 408–410
Homosexuality, 363–364
Homozygous offspring, 58–59
Honeymoon phase, 547, 548t.
Hospices, 559
"How the Public Feels," 363
Hydrocephaly, 75
Hypothesis, 11
   adolescent thinking and, 374

Id, 31
Identical twins, 9
Identification, 219
Identity achievement, 349
Identity diffusion, 349
Identity formation, 283, 347–349
   cultural factors, 350, 351f.
   individuated, 350–351
Identity stage, 34, 35
Illiteracy, 472–473, 516f.
Imaginary audience, 375
Imitation, 38, 146–148, 151, 170–171, 227f.
Imminent justice, 306
Immunological theory, 535
Impulsive stage, 42
Independent variables, 17
Indiscriminate attachment, 192f.
Individuated, 350–351
Inductive discipline, 222–223
Industry stage, 34–35, 215
Infancy, 7
Infant mortality rate, 81
Infertility, 57
Information processing, 293–303
Information-processing theories, 43–45, 49t., 316–317
Initiative stage, 34
Innate survival response, 147
Institute for Social Research (University of Michigan), 353
Institutional marriages, 492
Instrumental conditioning, 37, 149
Intellectual development in early and middle adulthood:
   adult education, 470–473
   health and life style and, 468–470
   intelligence, 456–457
      changes in, 462–468
      dual-process model, 458–459
      practical, 457–459, 462f.
      psychometric, 457
   stages of, 459–462
Intelligence, 314–315
   exceptional development, 326–330
   gender role and, 328
   in later adulthood, 22f.
   measuring, 318–322
   multiple, 317–318
   Piaget's theory of, 316
Intelligence quotient (see IQ)

Intention in language development, 172–173
Interaction, 117–118
Interaction between heredity and environment, 4, 8–12, 60–63
Interindividual variability intelligence, 468
Interprofessional Task Force on Health Care of Women and Children, 74
Interview studies, 13t., 16
Intimacy stage, 34t., 35
Intraindividual plasticity intelligence, 468
Introversion, 539
Invented expressions, 176–177
In-vitro fertilization, 57
Involved grandparents, 499, 501
IQ (intelligence quotient), 320
   adoption studies, 62–63
   in adulthood, 466
   betting and, 458
   birth order and, 232, 233
   genetic similarity, 61–62
   influences on scores, 322–326
   memory training and, 527
   nutrition and, 125
   work and, 457f.
Irritability of neonates, 102
Isolated child, 255–256

Jurors, 461f.

Kibbutzim, childrearing in, 204
Kinship migration, 555–556
Kitwalse, 130–131
Klinefelter's syndrome, 76
Knowledge, 295
Knowledge-acquisition components, 316
Kwashiokor, 125

Labeling, 298f., 515f., 518f.
Labor, 69–72
Laboratory of Comparative Human Cognition, 45, 299
LAD (language acquisition device), 184
Lamaze method, 73
Language:
   acquisition theories, 182–185
   cognition and, 285
   complex constructions, 181–182
   correlated features and, 170f., 176
   development highlights, 178f.
   early utterances, 173–177
   intonation patterns, 175f.
   nonverbal communication, 172f.
   prelinguistic development, 164–173
   simple constructions, 177–182
   (See also Speech)
Language acquisition device (LAD), 184
Latchkey children, 236, 357f.
Late retirement, 547
Latency period, 31–33
Later adulthood, 505
   aging myths, 508–509
   aging theories, 535
   biological changes during, 509–515
      brain and nervous system, 512–513
      sensory capacities, 509–512
   death and, 556–559
   divorce during, 550
   family and, 552–555

Later adulthood (Cont.)
   gender differences, 543
   intelligence in, 22f.
   issues of, 540–541
   learning and thinking during, 515–521
   living arrangements, 524f., 555–556
   marriage during, 548–550
   memory during, 508, 521–528
   physical changes during, 533–537
   remarriage during, 550
   self-concept during, 541–545
   self-view of, 542t.
   sex and coffee-drinking correlation, 18
   social change during, 533
   theories of, 539–540
   widowhood, 550–552
   work and retirement during, 545–548
Lateralization, 118–119
Laughter, speech and, 166–167
Lead pollution, 80
Learned helplessness, 146, 264–265
Learning Potential Assessment Device, 320
Learning process, 142–148
   children's attributions and mastery of new material, 264t.
   information processing, 293–363
   in later adulthood, 515–521
   new words, 175–177
   peers and, 302
   self-regulated and strategies, 284–285
Learning theories, 29, 36–38
Libido, 31
Life-cycle squeeze, 497
Life expectancy at age 65, 536t.
Life review, 557–558
Life span, 6, 7f.
Limb manipulation, 113–114, 119–121
Linguistic development (see Language)
Living will, 559
Locomotion, 113, 114f., 121–123, 130–131
LOGO, 302
Longitudinal designs, 19–21
   of intellectual decline, 464–465
   of retirement, 547
Looking time, 140
Love withdrawal, 222

Macrosystem, 47–48
Malnutrition, 125–126
Marijuana, 403
Marriage:
   in later adulthood, 548–550
   in middle adulthood, 490–493
   parenthood and, 445f., 447f.
   societal factors, 442
   in young adulthood, 439–443
   (See also Divorce; Remarriage)
Maternal employment (see Working mothers)
Math anxiety, 391
Mathematics:
   cultural factors, 301, 325
   infants and counting, 149
   number knowledge and skill, 292–293
   school and, 332–333
Maturational theories, 29
Mechanics of intelligence, 459
Median family income, 437f.
Meiosis, 57, 58f., 70